P9-AFB-938

DATE DUE

AP 17 '95			
AP 2 8 '95			
OC 30 '96			
MR 2 6 '97			
MY 2 8 '97			
JY 2 '97			
JY 3 0 '98			
JY 3 0 '98			
AP 21 '99			
DE 1 '99			
NO 1 4 '00			
MY 9 '01			
JE 8 '01			
JE 4 '02			
NO 28 '05			
DE 1 8 '08			

DEMCO 38-296

AN INTRODUCTION TO SPECIAL EDUCATION

Third Edition

A. Edward Blackhurst and William H. Berdine, Editors

University of Kentucky, Lexington

HarperCollinsCollegePublishers

Riverside Community College
Library
4800 Magnolia Avenue
AUG '94   Riverside, California 92506

Executive Editor: Christopher Jennison
Development Editor: Anita Portugal
Project Coordination and Text Design Adaptation: Lachina Publishing Services
Cover Design: Kay Petronio
Photo Researcher: Rosemary Hunter
Production Manager: Michael Weinstein
Production/Manufacturing: Linda Murray/Paula Keller
Compositor: Omegatype Typography, Inc.
Printer and Binder: R. R. Donnelley & Sons Company
Insert Printer: New England Book Components, Inc.
Cover Printer: The Lehigh Press, Inc.

For permission to use copyrighted material, grateful acknowledgment is made to the copyright holders on p. 600, which is hereby made part of this copyright page.

An Introduction to Special Education / Third Edition

Copyright © 1993 by HarperCollins College Publishers

All rights reserved. Printed in the United States of America. No part of this book may be used or reproduced in any manner whatsoever without written permission, except in the case of brief quotations embodied in critical articles and reviews. For information address HarperCollins Publishers Inc., 10 East 53rd Street, New York, NY 10022.

Library of Congress Cataloging-in-Publication Data

An Introduction to special education / A. Edward Blackhurst and
   William H. Berdine, editors.
      p.   cm.
   Includes bibliographical references and index.
   ISBN 0-673-52197-4
   1. Handicapped children—Education.   2. Handicapped children—
Education—United States.   3. Special education—Computer-assisted
instruction.   I. Blackhurst, A. Edward.   II. Berdine, William H.
   LC4019.I57   1992
   371.91—dc20   92-33803
                                                             CIP

93 94 95 96 9 8 7 6 5 4 3 2 1

Riverside Community College
Library
4800 Magnolia Avenue
Riverside, California 92506

Brief Contents

Contents

Preface

This text is an introduction to, and a comprehensive survey of, the field of special education. Special education is that branch of education responsible for meeting the needs of exceptional children—those who are gifted or who have disabilities that affect intellectual, physical, emotional, or sensory abilities. We will examine the body of contemporary literature for each of the traditional areas of special education and strive to develop an understanding of the developmental and learning characteristics of people with exceptionalities. Also, for each area of exceptionality we will describe the types of educational services that have been found to be effective in helping persons with special education needs to reach their potential. Although this book is not a methods of teaching or a curriculum text, we will describe some specific teaching techniques and curricular approaches that are becoming common to special education.

Whether you are a student entering a special education teacher training program, or planning to pursue a career in any of the number of professional areas that have an impact on exceptional persons, or simply interested in broadening your knowledge of individuals with exceptionalities, you will find the information in this text to be current and useful. After completing the reading of the text, you should be able to accomplish the following:

- define the terms that are commonly used in special education
- understand the major issues and trends in special education and explain how they relate to general education and other related fields
- define the various traditional categories of exceptionality and explain reasons for de-emphasizing categorical labels
- describe the developmental and learning characteristics of children with exceptionalities
- describe the various educational services available to children with exceptionalities
- describe the various types of supportive services needed by persons with exceptionalities and their families

Organization

The sixteen chapters making up this book are divided into three parts. Part I, the first seven chapters, contains information that provides a foundation critical to understanding all areas of special education. We define major terms and basic concepts and trace the growth of the field. We also analyze the critical issues confronting both teachers and special education students in today's society. These issues focus primarily on student identification, normalization, individualized instruction, and cultural diversity. A new chapter describes the role of modern technology, including the growing use of assistive and adaptive devices, in learning settings for individuals with exceptionalities.

We then explore the basic principles of child development within the context of early childhood special education. It is our contention that knowledge of normal child development is a prerequisite to understanding disabilities. Increasing concerns have emerged about the special problems that accompany the transition of students from school to community. We examine these concerns and alternative approaches to meeting the challenges associated with such transition. We then turn our attention to the significant role that families of people with exceptionalities play in helping them to achieve their fullest potentials. Finally, we address the critical role of professional development in providing quality services to special education students. We present a model that can be used to guide the design of continuing professional development programs and make suggestions for their implementation.

Building upon the broad foundation created in Part I, we go on to examine communication and sensorimotor disabilities. Because communication skills lie at the base of much of what we do in special education, we begin Part II with a chapter on communication problems. We then discuss the significant impact that hearing losses have on learning and development, and we study visual impairments and the ways teachers can help students with visual impairments attain maximum benefit from school and society. This part closes with a chapter on the broad array of physical and health-related disabilities that may be encountered by special education teachers and related services personnel.

In Part III we examine individual differences in learning and behavior. Chapters on mental retardation, learning disabilities, behavioral disabilities, severe developmental disabilities, and unique gifts and talents are included. Although we believe that the kind of educational services created should not be determined solely by the type of exceptionality being addressed, we have examined the various categories of exceptionality in separate chapters. This approach not only helps facilitate your understanding of the different developmental characteristics and varying needs of children with exceptionalities, but it also enables us to present information in an organized manner.

Format

This book has a number of distinctive features that will help readers master the content.

COMPETENCY STATEMENTS. In each chapter we identify key principles that we believe students should learn in an introductory course in special education. These competency statements, which are printed in color, are followed by the presentation of content that is related to them. The competency statements will help focus your attention as you read through each chapter.

PAGE MARGIN QUESTIONS. In the page margins throughout the text you will find questions pertaining to key content. The questions help call attention to important facts, concepts, and principles and will facilitate your mastery of the content.

PROBES. Lists of questions, called probes, appear at various points within the chapters. There is one probe or set of questions for each competency statement. The probes will enable you to check whether you have learned the material that has been presented. We encourage you to answer each probe as you come to it. This will enhance your learning and retention of the material and, along with the competency statements and marginal questions, will become an invaluable tool for reviewing chapters. Answers to the probes are provided at the end of the book.

FUNCTIONAL MODEL. In the first chapter, a model based on principles of human development and functioning is presented and its elements are described. Understanding the functional model and its implications has significant potential for reducing the tendency that many have to dwell on a person's disability. Such a tendency is reflected by such things as categorizing individuals into groups according to disability label.

The functional model provides a vehicle for focusing on the variables that affect the ability of people to function, and how those variables interact to enable a person to make a functional response to environmental demands. Illustrations of various applications of the model are provided in each chapter. They are set off from the text in boxes titled "A Functional Approach to Exceptionality."

TECHNOLOGY IN ACTION. Each chapter features a brief vignette describing how modern technology is playing an active role in the respective areas of special education. The vignettes are intended to provide interesting and educationally relevant information.

HUMAN INTEREST FEATURES. Examples, anecdotes, photo essays, and excerpts from popular literature have been incorporated into the text. They will give you insight into some of the unique problems that exceptional people face in their everyday lives. We hope that these human interest features will help you develop positive attitudes toward people with disabilities and those who have unique gifts and talents.

GLOSSARY. Because we encounter a rather vast array of terminology in special education, we have included an extensive glossary at the end of the book. The first time a glossary term appears in the text, it is highlighted in boldface to alert you to the fact that the term is defined in the glossary.

WRITING STYLE. The diversity of special education dictates that a great deal of content be covered, and we have attempted to deal with the breadth and depth of knowledge without overwhelming you with a tedious, encyclopedia style of writing. We have written this text in a relatively informal style that we hope will make your reading of it an enjoyable, as well as educational, experience.

Changes in the Third Edition

Most of the concepts presented in this book are based upon information that has been presented in the professional literature relating to special education and related areas, as attested to by the lengthy reference list that is included. For the Third Edition, we have updated many of the references, deleted outdated ones, and added many new ones. In addition, several other significant modifications have been made:

- Coverage has been expanded on current issues, such as student assessment, labeling, normalization, least restrictive environment, educational service options, technology, collaborative consultation, the Regular Education Initiative, early education, transition, cultural diversity, and students who are at risk.
- Terminology has been revised to reflect the current practice of focusing on the individual, as opposed to diagnostic labels. The terminology changes have been brought into line with definitions recently promulgated by professional groups and federal legislation.

- The functional model, as described earlier, has been added.
- Content has been provided on recent federal legislation and initiatives that affect services to people with disabilities. These include the Individuals with Disabilities Education Act, the Americans with Disabilities Act, the Technology-Related Assistance for People with Disabilities Act, and the America 2000 initiative.
- A new chapter has been added on applications of technology in special education.
- A new chapter has been added on continuing professional development.
- Several new authors have been added, resulting in major chapter revisions. Brief biographical sketches are provided about each author near the end of the book.

Acknowledgments

This text, covering an enormous amount of information, is the product of a concerted team effort. We, the editors, would like to thank our contributing authors for their cooperation and willingness to make this book successful.

We also wish to thank professors who adopted the First and Second Editions of this text and who answered our questions and provided valuable insights into what needed to be changed for this Third Edition. In addition to users' comments we also benefited from the advice and ideas of our colleagues who read selected chapters or all of the Third Edition manuscript. We wish to thank our colleagues whose reviews were instrumental in developing the Third Edition: Sandra Alper, University of Missouri–Columbia; Robert Gable, Old Dominion University; Doug Guess, University of Kansas; James Delisle, Kent State University; Katherine G. Butler, Syracuse University; Martha Parnell, University of Missouri–Columbia; James Crowner, Southern Illinois University–Carbondale; John F. Vokurka, Western Kentucky University; James Van Tassel, Ball State University; Gaylen Kapperman, Northern Illinois University; Robert K. Rittenhouse, University of Arkansas at Little Rock; Deborah C. Simmons, Vanderbilt University; Thomas G. Roberts, Arizona State University; John Maag; Helen McRae, Trenton State College; and Richard Rodriguez, Western New Mexico University. Their careful reviews of various drafts were extremely helpful. Of particular value were the efforts of James Van Tassel and Katherine Butler, who responded to the entire manuscript. Many of their excellent suggestions have been incorporated into the text.

Anita Portugal, Development Editor, provided invaluable services in helping us with our initial planning, coordinated the reviews of manuscripts, synthesized the reviewers' comments, and attended to the many details associated with the generation and revision of various drafts of the manuscript. She also helped to keep us on schedule.

We wish to extend our gratitude to Marcia Bowling, who typed the several versions of the manuscript, and Debra Bauder, who compiled the references, set up the chapter probe answer keys, and revised the glossary of terms.

The Executive Editor at HarperCollins, Christopher Jennison, carefully coordinated the many steps in producing the book from manuscript. Shadla Grooms ably assisted with details associated with these tasks. Linda Murray, Production Coordinator, also provided valuable help. Copy editor Beverly Cory was a joy to work with. Her valuable insights and experience brought the original manuscripts into readable final form. Last, but certainly not least, we are extremely grateful for the careful attention to detail of Ed Huddleston and the capable staff at Lachina Publishing Services, who coordinated final production of the book.

AEB

WHB

AN INTRODUCTION TO SPECIAL EDUCATION

Foundations of Special Education

Over the past decade it has become clear that the similarities between regular education and special education are greater than their differences. Gone is the suspicion that the techniques, materials, and technology of special education cannot be used in other areas of education. Regular classroom teachers can no longer disregard the role and contributions of their colleagues in special education. Similarly, special educators can no longer isolate themselves from the mainstream of educational thinking. We now accept the premise that the same principles and procedures, with some modifications, can be used in the instruction of all children.

Special education grew from the proposition that all children can reach higher levels of their potential given the opportunity, effective teaching, and proper resources. Because of this belief in the power of education, special education has indeed become an integral part of contemporary education.

The first seven chapters of this book contain information designed to provide a foundation for understanding the field of special education. Concepts presented in these chapters have relevance for all aspects of special education. Thus, we begin our study by looking at the development of the field, the issues and forces that are shaping it, the impact that technology is having, the importance of early childhood special education, concepts related to the transition from school to adulthood, the role of families of exceptional children, and ways that persons who are employed in various special education roles can continue their own professional development.

THE DEVELOPMENT OF SPECIAL EDUCATION

In Chapter 1 we discuss the terminology, origins, and development of special education. A model is introduced that describes a functional approach to exceptionality, explaining the interaction of the many factors that come into play when exceptional children are faced with demands placed on them from their environment. The model is based on research and theory in human development, and we believe that it provides a valuable way to approach many of the issues, decisions, and practices facing special educators and related service personnel. Examples of applications of the model are provided throughout the text. We also describe the federal legislation and litigation that has had an effect on shaping the field as we know it today.

ISSUES IN SPECIAL EDUCATION

The special issues that helped to create the field need to be understood by all educators. In Chapter 2 we describe the process of identifying children who can benefit from special education, and we analyze issues related to assessment. A vital element in special education is the normalization concept, and we look at it in relation to deinstitutionalization, mainstreaming, and the least restrictive environment. In addition, we examine the major notions involved in individualizing instruction, accounting for cultural differences, and dealing with children who are at risk.

TECHNOLOGY IN SPECIAL EDUCATION

Technology is playing an increasingly important role in special education. In Chapter 3, we explain concepts related to the technology of teaching. We then describe how technology can be used to facilitate the instruction of students in special education programs. Finally, we address the ways that assistive technology can be used to help those with disabilities to function more independently in the environment and improve their quality of life.

EARLY CHILDHOOD SPECIAL EDUCATION

The field of early childhood special education has become a generally accepted and mandated function in education. Research has clearly shown that early educational experiences benefit all children and are of critical importance for exceptional children. In Chapter 4 we examine the rationale for providing special education services to young children with disabilities and describe related issues and historical precedents. Methods of identifying young children with disabilities are also presented, along with a description of the different methods of delivering special education services to preschool children.

TRANSITION TO ADULTHOOD

An important aspect of today's special education is the preparation of the student for living and working in the community. In Chapter 5, we examine the circumstances that have led to the development of transition programs. Models for providing transition services are described. We also look at several instructional approaches, methods, and activities that are particularly useful in preparing students for adulthood. In addition, a description of vocational rehabilitation services is provided. We conclude with a discussion about issues and future directions of transition services.

FAMILIES OF EXCEPTIONAL CHILDREN

The role of the family is critical in the planning and delivery of special education services. This role has long been recognized, and since the passage of PL 94-142 in 1975, parental involvement has been mandated. In Chapter 6, we examine the role of not only the parent but also the child in shaping parental involvement. Emphasis is placed on incorporating all family members into the process of education and development. We also describe some of the major supporting services and agencies that are available to families of exceptional children.

CONTINUING PROFESSIONAL DEVELOPMENT

One of the challenges facing special educators and related service personnel is to keep up with the many new developments that are occurring in the field. Chapter 7 describes a seven-step process that can be used to design and implement a professional development program. We offer suggestions for how to develop a philosophy of special education and build upon it to improve your professional competencies. The role of professional organizations is described, and the chapter closes with a discussion of ethical standards that should guide special education practices.

BILL OF RIGHTS FOR PEOPLE WITH DISABILITIES

1. The right to prevention, early diagnosis, and proper care.

2. The right to a barrier-free environment and accessible transportation.

3. The right to an appropriate public education.

4. The right to necessary assistance, given in a way that promotes independence.

5. The right to a choice of lifestyles and residential alternatives.

6. The right to an income for a lifestyle comparable to that of the able-bodied.

7. The right to training and employment as qualified.

8. The right to petition social institutions for just and humane treatment.

9. The right to self-esteem.

1

The Development of Special Education

A. Edward Blackhurst

Society's awareness of the needs and rights of people who have disabilities is evident in a number of tangible ways. For example, curb cut-outs, ramps, and buses with wheelchair lifts facilitate travel for people with physical disabilities. Elevators and room numbers in public buildings are frequently labeled in braille to assist those who have visual impairments. Sign language and printed captions are superimposed on the screen during many television programs so that people with hearing losses can enjoy the programs. Activities such as the Special Olympics provide opportunities for people with mental retardation to engage in athletic competition.

Society is also responding to people with disabilities in many less tangible ways. Although less readily observed, they are probably more important than the visible accommodations mentioned above. For example, public schools are required to provide a free and appropriate education to all children who have been diagnosed as having a disability. Colleges and universities must admit people with disabilities and make the programs in which they are enrolled accessible to them. Furthermore, it is now illegal to deny employment to a qualified person because that person has a disability.

We wish we could state that society has always been responsive to the needs of people with disabilities. Sadly, such has not been the case. Most of the accommodations described above are the result of hard-won battles in courtrooms and legislatures. During the 1970s people with disabilities and those who served as advocates for them became extremely active in seeking legal remedies to the injustice and discrimination that existed at the time.

The "Bill of Rights for People with Disabilities" that appears at the beginning of this chapter reflects the results of these campaigns. These rights were codified by the United Cerebral Palsy Association and represent a mixture of moral, ethical, and legal responsibilities that society should assume in responding to the needs of people with disabilities. Special educators and other professionals who provide related services need to be aware of these rights and know how to respond to them. Chapter 1 will provide a basis for understanding the meaning of these rights. The impact of historical events, litigation, and legislation on the growth and development of special education services will also be explained.

DEFINITIONS AND RELATED CONCEPTS

> **You should be able to define terminology related to special education and explain the functional approach to providing special education services.**

If you asked a teacher or school administrator how schools should serve children, the response would probably include the comment that school programs should respond to the children's individual differences. Almost everyone thinks this is a desirable goal for a school system.

It is easy to state a goal. Achieving it can be another matter. If you think back to your elementary and secondary school career, you will undoubtedly recall many examples of individual differences. Some of your classmates were better than you in some subjects, while you were better in others. These differences *between* students are called **interindividual differences.** Similarly, you were probably better in some subjects than in others and

---

AMERICA'S EDUCATION GOALS

The following six goals were developed in conjunction with the nation's governors and were announced by President George Bush on April 18, 1991. They were accompanied by a list of objectives and strategies for attaining the goals. The America 2000 program is intended to provide a blueprint for national initiatives to improve education as we move into the twenty-first century. Special educators will be faced with the challenge of responding to these goals within the context of numerous legal mandates, alternative educational provisions, and parental concerns that will be described in detail throughout this book.

By the year 2000:

1. All children in America will start school ready to learn.
2. The high school graduation rate will increase to at least 90 percent.
3. American students will leave grades four, eight, and twelve having demonstrated competency in challenging subject matter including English, mathematics, science, history, and geography; and every school in America will ensure that all students learn to use their minds well, so they may be prepared for responsible citizenship, further learning, and productive employment in our modern economy.
4. U.S. students will be first in the world in science and mathematics achievement.
5. Every adult American will be literate and will possess the knowledge and skills necessary to compete in a global economy and exercise the rights and responsibilities of citizenship.
6. Every school in America will be free of drugs and violence and will offer a disciplined environment conducive to learning.

Source: America 2000: An Educational Strategy (1991, p. 19).

enjoyed some more than others. These differences *within* students are called **intraindividual differences.**

How do schools
respond to
individual
differences?

Your school probably responded to these differences by assigning children to groups in elementary school and by providing different electives and tracks in secondary school. In fourth grade, for example, you may have been a member of the Eagles reading group or the Buzzards math group. In high school you may have taken an academic rather than a vocational curriculum, and you may have taken several courses in subjects that were of particular interest to you. Such arrangements are adequate to respond to the interindividual and intraindividual differences of most students.

For other students, however, these arrangements are not enough. Students who take longer to learn, who have severe difficulty in learning, who exhibit disruptive behavior, who have severe physical problems that interfere with learning, who are exceptionally intelligent or talented—all have needs that are not met by the general education program. They need programs designed to meet their needs individually. Special education exists to provide such programs.

Special education, then, is *instruction designed to respond to the unique characteristics of children who have needs that cannot be met by the standard school curriculum.* Such needs are met by developing an individualized education program, unique to each child, that typically requires a modification of the standard school curriculum. The individualized program may call for changes in content, methods of instruction, instructional materials, and expected rate of progress. It may also call for supportive services from speech pathologists, audiologists, physical and occupational therapists, psychologists, physicians, counselors, and others. Such services are commonly referred to as **related services.**

Special education and related services can be delivered in a variety of settings, depending on the needs of a particular child. Some special education students can be enrolled in regular classes where the teacher and the child receive help from specialists. Some receive instruction for part of the day in resource rooms. Some require placement in a full-time special education class. Others need to be placed in homebound, hospital, or residential school programs. These options will be discussed in more detail in Chapter 2.

Terminology

The term most often associated with special education is **exceptional children.** Many people believe this term refers only to very intelligent children, whereas others believe it refers only to those with disabilities or handicaps. Both beliefs are misconceptions; the term encompasses both groups.

What differences
surround the terms
*exceptional
children,
impairment,
disability,* and
handicap?

Exceptional children are children who have physical, mental, behavioral, or sensory characteristics that differ from the majority of children so that they require special education and related services to develop to their maximum capacity. The category includes children with communication problems, hearing losses, physical disabilities, visual impairments, mental retardation, learning disabilities, behavior disorders, multiple handicaps, high intelligence, and unique talents. More precise definitions of these categories will be presented in the chapters that follow.

Several other terms are also used to refer to children who receive special education services. Although the use of varying terminology is quite common in special education, there are technical differences in meaning among a number of terms. In one of the earliest attempts to develop a system for classification of special education concepts, Stevens (1962) differentiated the following terms, which are still useful today:

Impairment refers to diseased or defective tissue. For example, a lack of oxygen at birth may cause brain damage or neurological impairment that will result in cerebral palsy. Similarly, a birthmark or scar could be considered an impairment because it is different from the tissues that surround it.

Disability refers to the reduction of function, or the absence, of a particular body part or organ. A person who has an arm or leg missing has a physical disability. Similarly, someone who cannot control the muscles required for speech has a disability in communication. The terms *disorder* and *dysfunction* are frequently used as synonyms for disability.

Handicap refers to the problems that people with impairments or disabilities have when interacting with their environment. A Vietnam War veteran who must use a wheelchair put it this way: "Sure I have a disability; but I'm not handicapped—until I try to get into a building that has a flight of steps and revolving door as its only entrance."

It should be noted that many people treat these terms as synonyms. It is common practice to refer to children with impairments or disabilities as children with handicaps. This practice came about largely because early federal legislation directed our public schools to provide special education to all "handicapped children" (Public Law 94-142). However, the trend is to avoid the use of the term *handicapped*.

Governmental officials have recognized the inappropriateness of using such terminology by changing the name of the major federal legislation that affects special education programs, amending the title of the Education of the Handicapped Act (PL 94-142) to the Individuals with Disabilities Education Act (PL 101-476).

In addition, the Americans with Disabilities Act (PL 101-336) broadens the definition of *disability* as it describes who is covered by the provisions of the act:

> (1) a person with a physical or mental impairment that substantially limits that person in some major life activity (such as walking, talking, breathing, or working); (2) a person with a record of such a physical or mental impairment (such as a person with a history of mental illness or heart disease who no longer has the disease, but who is discriminated against because of [his/her] record of an impairment); or (3) a person who is regarded as having such an impairment (such as a person who has a significant burn on his/her face which does not limit him/her in any major life activity but who is discriminated against). (*Americans with Disabilities Act of 1990: What Should You Know?* 1990, p. 1)

What is the most acceptable way to refer to someone with a disability?

If at all possible, you should avoid the use of the terms *handicapped child, handicapped person,* or *the handicapped* when referring to someone with a disability. Those who have disabilities view such terminology as demeaning. They assert that this usage sets up negative expectations. If it is necessary to refer to someone with a disability, it is preferable to use the terminology *child with a disability* or *student with mental retardation* as opposed to *disabled child* or *mentally retarded student*. It also is inappropriate to refer to classes of individuals, such as *the blind, the mentally retarded,* or *the physically disabled*. The emphasis should be on the person first and only secondarily on the existence of a disability. For an interesting perspective on how a person with cerebral palsy reacts to the use of such terminology, see the report in Stephens, Blackhurst, and Magliocca (1988, pp. 35–36).

Although they may appear to be subtle, there are distinct differences between the terms *impairment, disability,* and *handicap*. A person can be handicapped in one situation and not in another. A boy with a birthmark on his face may have an impairment, but he does not have a disability. He may, however, be handicapped in getting dates. A musician, such as Stevie Wonder, may have a visual disability but not be handicapped when it comes to producing music. Consider the case of Kitty O'Neil, described in the box on the facing page. *Does Kitty have an impairment?* Probably. Her various childhood diseases probably damaged her auditory nerve or central nervous system. *Does she have a disability?* Yes. She cannot hear. *Is she handicapped?*

IMPAIRMENT, DISABILITY, OR HANDICAP?

If Kitty O'Neil merely parked cars for a living instead of driving them at 600 mph and faster, she would still be a very unusual person. At one time or another, she has held 22 speed records. As a teenager, she was an Olympic class diving champion. She plays the cello and piano. And she's one of Hollywood's top stuntwomen.

She also is totally deaf.

Parade caught up with the 33-year-old Kitty at her home in Glendale, Calif. Communicating with her is easy. Her mother spent years teaching her to read lips and to speak. She does not know sign language and she doesn't need it.

Kitty was raised in Wichita Falls, Tex., born to a part Cherokee Indian mother and an Irish father. At 4 months, she almost died from the simultaneous onslaught of chicken pox, measles and mumps—illnesses that robbed her of her hearing.

At the age of 12, she began competitive swimming and diving, becoming an AAU Junior Olympic diving champion and earning a wall full of medals. Obsessed with speed and motion— "I love to go fast and I love danger"—Kitty began racing in any vehicle she could climb onto or into: production sports cars, motorcycles, drag racers, speedboats, dune buggies and snowmobiles. She tried skydiving, scuba diving and hang gliding. At one time Kitty held the world's record for women's water skiing, zipping across the water at better than 104 mph. She tackled anything to prove that a deaf, 95-pound, 5-foot-3 slip of a woman could do as well as anyone, male or female. Eventually, she turned inward and began competing against herself. Her vehicle: the rocket car.

At 38 feet long and developing 48,000 horsepower, the rocket car she drove was little more than an earthbound guided missile made principally of aluminum and fiberglass. After testing on the Bonneville Salt Flats in Utah, Kitty and her crew went to the Alvord Dry Lake in Oregon to try and beat the women's land speed record of 308 mph.

On Dec. 6, 1976, she was strapped into the cockpit of the rocket car and attained an average speed of 512.7 mph. Later that day she made another run and hit an incredible 618.3 mph—just 4 miles an hour under the world record held by Gary Gabelich.

Kitty supports herself these days as a movie stuntwoman.

Source: M. Satchell, "Ladies, Start Your Engines," *Parade*, May 6, 1979. Reprinted by permission.

Certainly not when she is racing or working as a stuntwoman. Yet she would be handicapped if she attempted to use a conventional telephone.

Even though a person has an impairment or disability, that person will not necessarily be handicapped in all situations. Similarly, the severity of the disability may have little relationship to the severity of the ensuing handicap. The physical environment and psychological situation of those with impairments or disabilities are crucial in dealing with these people. As Gearheart put it:

> The degree of the disability does not necessarily determine the degree of the handicap. Most children with special needs are more normal than abnormal and will likely spend most of their lives in a basically nonhandicapped world. They, therefore, must have programming that will help them to adjust to their social and physical environment and minimize the handicapping effect of their disability. [1974, pp. 22–23]

Terms have also been developed to refer to different areas of special education. Thus, children with speech and language problems are said to have *communication disorders;* those with visual problems have *visual impairments;* children in wheelchairs have *physical disabilities;* and those who are seriously mentally retarded with other physical problems are referred to as having *severe* [or *profound*] *developmental disabilities.*. The commonly used terminology is reflected in the chapter titles in this text.

A Functional Approach to Special Education

When decisions are being made about the provision of special education services, it is important to base them on factors related to human function rather than on the child's diagnosis as being mentally retarded, physically disabled, or emotionally disturbed.[1] The real issue is the problem the child has in functioning within his or her environment. For example, a small child with cerebral palsy may lack the fine muscle control that will permit her to fasten buttons so that she can get dressed independently. A boy with a visual impairment may be unable to use printed material that is being used for instruction in an English class. Another student, due to an unknown cause, may be unable to solve math problems. Similarly, a child who has been in an automobile accident may have had a severe head injury that has impaired her ability to speak clearly.

In each of these cases, the environment has placed a demand to perform some function that the child finds difficult to execute because of a set of unique circumstances or some restriction in his or her functional capability caused by the lack of personal resources. For example, the children described above lack, respectively, the physical or mental capability to button, to read, to calculate, and to speak.

All of us face situations daily in which environmental demands are placed on us. Our goal is to understand these processes and relate them to the lives of exceptional children who face more complex and restrictive situations. We need to recognize many things, such as the nature of the demands that the environment places on the child and how those demands create the requirements to perform different human functions, such as learning, walking, talking, seeing, and hearing. It is important to know how such requirements are—or are not—being met by the child and how factors such as the child's perceptions and the availability of personal resources such as intelligence, sight, and mobility may affect the responses the child can make. In addition, it is important to understand how the availability of external supports, such as special education, different types of therapy, and technology, can affect the child's ability to produce functional responses to the environmental demands.

Although each exceptional child is unique, the common challenge is to identify and apply the best possible array of special education and related services that will provide support, adjustment, or compensation for the child's functional needs or deficits. A variety of responses may be appropriate. For example, Velcro fasteners may be used to replace buttons on garments for the child having difficulty with buttoning. Braille or audio materials may be provided for the child who cannot read conventional print. The student who has difficulty calculating may require specialized, intense, direct math instruction, while a computerized device that produces speech may enable the child who cannot talk to communicate.

Why is an understanding of categories of human function important?

The term *function* has been used several times in the preceding paragraphs. **Function** can be defined as *an action that a person takes in response to a demand to meet some need*. Human functions can be grouped into several categories. Following is one way to categorize functions, accompanied by examples of how special education and related services may be provided to facilitate the functions associated with each category.

[1]The functional model described in this section evolved from approximately 25 years of research and development activities by Joseph F. Melichar. The content for this section is adapted from training materials developed by Melichar and Blackhurst (1992).

EXISTENCE. Functions associated with the category of existence are those needed to sustain daily life. These include feeding, elimination, bathing, dressing, grooming, and sleeping. Special education services, particularly those for preschool children and those with severe disabilities, may focus on teaching children to perform such functions. Special devices such as buttonhooks, weighted eating utensils, and combs with long handles may be provided to help children. Assistance in using such devices may be provided by occupational therapists.

COMMUNICATION. The reception, internalization, and expression of information are functions included in the category of communication. Communication aids, speech synthesizers, telephone amplifiers, hearing aids, and the services of speech-language pathologists and audiologists might be appropriate to support communication functions.

BODY SUPPORT, ALIGNMENT, AND POSITIONING. Some children need assistance to maintain a stable position or to support portions of their body. Braces, support harnesses, slings, and body protectors are useful devices in this functional category; also useful are the services of a physical therapist. Other medical personnel may also provide supporting services.

TRAVEL AND MOBILITY. Functions in this category include the ability to move horizontally, vertically, or laterally. Wheelchairs, special lifts, canes, walkers, specially adapted tricycles, and crutches can be used to support these functions. Specialists, such as those who provide mobility training for children who are blind, may be called upon to provide services associated with this category.

ENVIRONMENTAL ADAPTATION. The environment can be adapted or the person can adapt to the environment. This category includes functions associated with these adaptations as seen in the performance of many of the activities of daily living, both indoors and outdoors.

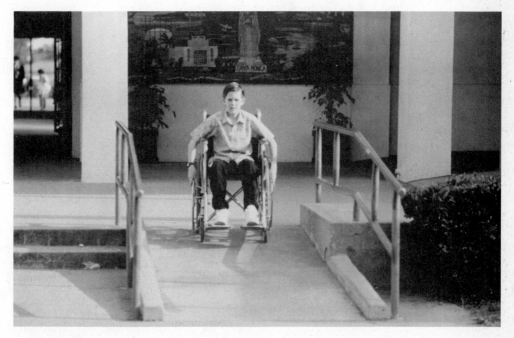

Modifications such as ramps can make school buildings accessible to children who need to use wheelchairs.

Examples include driving, food preparation, operation of appliances, and alteration of the living space.

To accommodate functions in this category, it may be necessary to make a number of modifications to school facilities, such as enlarged doorknobs, special switches for controlling computers, grabbers to reach items on high shelves, chalkboards and desks that can be raised so that a student in a wheelchair can use them, and ramps to accommodate wheelchairs. Often, assistive technology specialists are called upon to provide help with environmental adaptations.

LEARNING, EDUCATION, AND REHABILITATION. Functions in this category include those associated with school activities and various types of therapies and rehabilitation processes. Special education teachers and regular class teachers, speech-language therapists, rehabilitation counselors, psychologists, and others may be involved in providing direct services to students. In addition, numerous technologies may be used within the context of schools. Included may be computer-assisted instruction, instructional audiotapes, print magnifiers, book holders, and other materials and equipment that can facilitate education.

SPORTS, LEISURE, AND RECREATION. Functions associated with group and individual sports and productive use of leisure time are included in this category. The services of a person trained in adapted physical education may provide a valuable resource. In addition, a wide array of equipment and devices can facilitate functions in this category, including balls that emit audible beeps so that children with visual impairments can hear them, specially designed skis for one-legged skiers, braille playing cards, and wheelchairs for basketball players who are unable to use their legs.

Many more examples of services and devices could be provided, but these should be sufficient to illustrate the importance of attending to human functions when planning and implementing special education and related services. The important thing to remember is that it is more relevant to focus on the functions that a student can perform and those with which the student has difficulty than to focus on a diagnostic label when planning special education services. A functional orientation enables teachers and those providing related services to more directly address a child's needs.

How can a functional model be used to guide the delivery of special education services?

Melichar has developed a model that illustrates the interrelationships among the different elements of life associated with a functional approach to special education (Melichar & Blackhurst, 1992). The model is illustrated in Figure 1-1. When studying this model, note that the items in each box are meant to be illustrative and not all-inclusive.

To illustrate the elements of the model, their interrelationships, and how the model can apply to special education, let's assume that we have a 6-year-old student, named Ann, who has cerebral palsy. Although she appears to have average intellectual abilities, her speech is almost impossible to understand. Ann's teacher often uses instructional games in class to teach various concepts, such as Simon Says to help children learn how to follow directions. Clearly, one of Ann's primary *functional needs* is to be able to communicate.

Let's begin with the box at the bottom of the model, labeled *environment and context*. The environment we are dealing with is Ann's first grade classroom. The context is that several games are played each week and that the teacher wants Ann to be an active participant.

The environment and context place *demands* on all of us. The environmental demand placed on Ann is to participate in the classroom games, either as a member of the group or as the leader of the group, such as playing the part of Simon in Simon Says.

In preparing to make responses to environmental demands, people formulate a *response strategy*. Their response strategy may involve exploring a series of options that are available to them, including using strategies for coping with the environmental demand, or making adaptations that will enable them to respond to the demand in a constructive fashion.

FIGURE 1-1 Unifying Functional Model

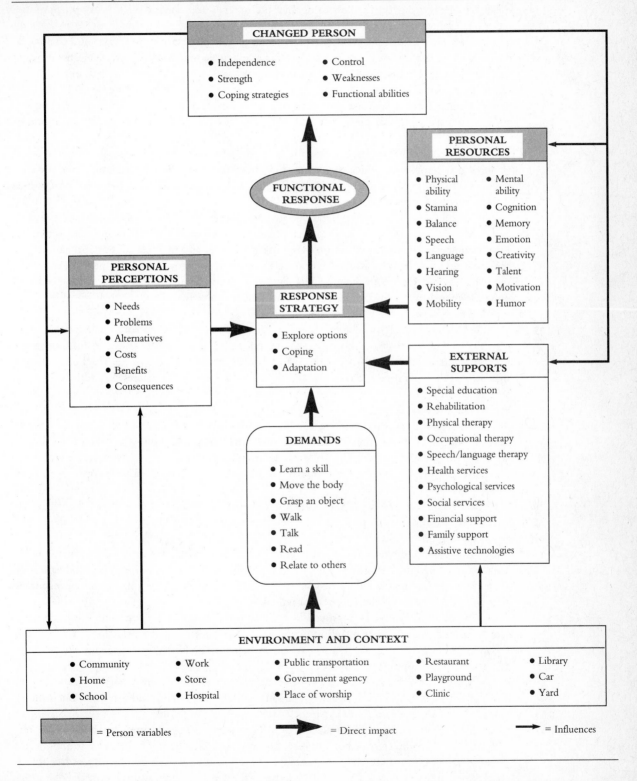

In Ann's case, she and the teacher might explore options such as letting other students speak for her during the games, using her picture communication board, or using a tape recorder with the appropriate prerecorded tapes for each game.

One's *personal perceptions* play a big part in exploring response strategies and making a decision about which to accept. For example, some people may not perceive that a need exists or that they have a problem. Such would be the case when a person with a hearing loss refuses to wear a hearing aid, even though it might help in hearing, because the person perceives that it draws negative attention or is a sign of old age. People also have perceptions about the psychological, physical, and monetary costs of different alternatives and their consequences.

A second factor in making decisions about response strategies involves the *personal resources* that people have available to them. These relate to their abilities in areas such as physical functioning, cognitive ability, intelligence, motivation, and other personal dimensions that can be used in producing actions.

A third factor influencing decisions involves the *external supports* a person has available. Supports are resources available to assist individuals in responding to environmental demands. For example, family members can provide both emotional and physical support. Social service agencies can provide supportive services, such as instruction about ways to cope with environmental pressures. Health insurance agencies can sometimes provide financial support for the purchase of assistive and adaptive devices. Special education is another major form of external support.

Let's see how all these areas relate to Ann. In the area of personal perceptions, Ann realizes that she has a problem in making herself understood, yet she wants to find a way to participate in the games. In surveying her personal resources, Ann and her teacher conclude that she has the cognitive and physical abilities to participate in the games. In addition, she has a fierce desire to do things for herself. This makes the possibility of another student speaking for her an undesirable option.

In further exploring options, she decides against her picture communication board because the 20 other students in the classroom would have a difficult time seeing the board while playing the game. In the area of external supports, she and the teacher elect to try a tape recorder. The teacher volunteers to locate a tape and have it recorded with input from Ann about the content.

The *functional response* is the result of the decision making that was just described. In Ann's case, it is the use of a prerecorded audiocassette tape that will enable her to be the leader when playing Simon Says.

As a result of the functional response to the environmental demand, the *person is changed*. Changes may be either positive or negative, dramatic or subtle, depending upon the nature of the environmental demand, the decision making that was done, and the nature of the resources that were expended and the supports provided.

Our student, Ann, has improved her ability to function in her environment by using a tape recorder to participate in educational games. Furthermore, the availability of the tape recorder has led her and her teacher to think of other activities in which use of the tape recorder may be appropriate.

There are a few more things to notice about the model. The heavy arrows indicate that some variables have a direct impact on various model components and activities. Such direct impacts should have been quite apparent in the example with Ann.

The lighter arrows indicate that there is an influence on the component, but perhaps not a strong one or a direct one. For instance, because Ann changed her ability to function, her perceptions have probably changed somewhat. It is possible that her perceptions of her ability to communicate are enhanced through the use of the tape recorder, and she now may be more confident in her ability to interact with her classmates. There may be an improvement in her personal resources. For example, things she learns as a result of participating in the games will be available to her in the future. Her language skills may improve. (You will learn the difference between speech and language in the chapter on communication problems.) Her stamina may improve because she does not have to expend as much physical energy in attempting to make herself understood. External supports may also be modified, perhaps in more subtle ways. For example, her speech therapist may decide to explore other forms of communication aids because Ann has demonstrated that she understands how to use devices such as the tape recorder and is able to successfully integrate them into her classroom environment. Members of her family may be encouraged by the improvement in her ability to communicate and may incorporate the use of the tape recorder in the home, thus improving the quality of life for all concerned.

With both types of arrows, it is important to realize that they not only represent an area of influence, but also reflect time. The changes that occur do so over time. The impact may be sudden or it may take a while.

We should not overlook the fact that the model, as presented in this two-dimensional format, represents a "snapshot" of a person's situation at a single moment in time. As such, it does not reflect that changes are constantly occurring in each component and that these changes have the potential for influencing the other components and subsequently the functional responses made by the child.

The final feature to note in the model is the shaded areas, which represent personal variables. As we just noted, in this presentation the model is two-dimensional. However, the central focus is the individual child and the decisions that are involved in helping that child respond to environmental demands. That process is certainly complex and more than two-dimensional.

IMPLICATIONS OF THE FUNCTIONAL MODEL. The functional model has a number of implications for those who are involved in providing special education and related services. It helps us understand how a person functions, what factors are important in making decisions, and how the decisions that are made can affect the child. It also identifies many of the factors that should be taken into consideration when making decisions about the nature of special education services that are provided to a given child.

It illustrates the interrelationships among component factors and their potential for influencing each other. Although the model does not define cause-and-effect relationships, it does help people realize that many factors are involved and that they interact in complex ways.

The model provides direction for those making referrals of children for special education services. All who make referrals should be aware of the model and its components. Furthermore, they should be encouraged to obtain as much information as possible about the various factors and provide data about them as part of the referral process.

Finally, it can guide assessment and instructional planning activities. By attending to the factors in the model, and others that may be identified, those performing assessments of children who have been referred for special education services can use the model to identify variables that should be evaluated for their potential impact on a child. Assessments of those variables should generate data that can aid in making decisions about the types of special education and related services that could help children respond successfully to environmental demands. Such decisions should result in the development of individualized education programs (IEPs) for children enrolled in special education programs. (Further information will be provided about IEPs later in this chapter. An example of an IEP will be provided in Chapter 2.)

PROBE 1-1   Definitions and Related Concepts

1. What is your definition of special education?
2. T F The term *exceptional children* refers primarily to children who are gifted and talented.
3. Differentiate between *disability* and *handicap*.
4. Choose the most appropriate terminology and explain your answer.
   handicapped individual   child with a disability   the disabled
5. Instead of focusing on diagnostic labels, we should focus primarily on a person's ability to _____ .
6. Describe three functional categories and explain some of the special education and related services that are appropriate for each.
7. Match the functions on the right with the categories in which they belong.

Category	*Function*
_____ Environment and context	a. Coping
_____ Demands	b. Independence
_____ Personal perceptions	c. Special education
_____ Personal resources	d. Needs
_____ External supports	e. Physical ability
_____ Response strategy	f. Learning a skill
_____ Changed person	g. School

8. What is the value of the functional approach to special education?

PREVALENCE

You should be able to determine the number of students needing special education services and explain why it is difficult to specify an exact number.

To plan for the provision of special education services, it is important to know how many exceptional children there are at present and how many can be expected at a given point in the future. Accurate estimates can be used to get funds for programs and to determine how many teachers and other professionals will be needed to staff them.

Why is it difficult to determine the exact number of children who need special education services?

The exact number of children who need special education services is difficult to determine for several reasons. First, there are many different definitions of the categories used to group children—especially those with learning problems. A child placed in one category by one authority might be placed in another by a different authority. For example, a child who has severe problems with academic subjects and who is very disruptive in class because of an inability to do academic work may be classified as learning disabled by one diagnostician and emotionally disturbed by another. Second, categories often overlap. Children with more than one problem may be arbitrarily placed in one category or another. A child who has cerebral palsy, who must use a wheelchair, and who has difficulty reading may be classified in one school district as having a physical disability, in another as having a learning disability, and in a third as being multiply handicapped. Third, school officials simply have not identified all of the children who require special services.

Estimates of the proportion of school-age children needing special education services have ranged from 10 to 15 percent. In 1976, as part of planning for the implementation of Public Law 94-142, the prevalence of children with handicaps in the United States was estimated by the Bureau of Education for the Handicapped in the United States Office of Education. By surveying various special education organizations, the bureau was able to estimate the percentage of the population that had different types of handicaps. The estimate was that nearly 8 million children under the age of 19 were in need of special education services.

Since that time, an annual count is made of children who actually receive special education services. Because of the time it takes to collect all this information, the annual counts are usually about two years behind. In 1991, the United States Department of Education determined how many children ages 6 to 21 were actually being served in special education programs. Although reported in 1991, conclusions were based on data collected on students served during the 1988–89 school year, which represented the latest information when this book went to press. The figures are displayed in Table 1-1.

Information presented in the same report from which the figures in Table 1-1 were obtained also indicated that 494,954 infants and toddlers (birth through age 2) and 388,625 preschoolers (ages 3 through 5) also received special education services during this period of time. Data for those populations are not reported by disability category.

It has been estimated that approximately 2.5 million gifted children are in need of special education services (Clark, 1988). It has been reported that approximately 1.5 million gifted and talented children received special services during 1986 and 1987 (*State of the States: Gifted and Talented Educated,* 1988).

Adding the figures for preschoolers and gifted students to those in Table 1-1, it is estimated that approximately 6,645,250 students were receiving special education services during the time the data were collected. Thus, it seems safe to assume that annually somewhere between 6.6 million and 9.5 million children need special education services.

You will note that the more recent figures indicate that only about 4.2 million students are receiving special education services. Does this mean that the original estimate of 8 million needing services was grossly in error? Not necessarily. The original estimate was indeed probably too high, but the more recent figures represent only those who are actually receiving

TABLE 1-1   Number of Children Ages 6–21 Receiving Special Education Services During the 1989–90 School Year

Category	Percentage of School Enrollment	Number
Specific learning disabilities	4.79	2,064,892
Speech or language impairments	2.39	976,186
Mental retardation	1.17	566,150
Serious emotional disturbances	0.89	382,570
Multiple disabilities	0.18	87,956
Hearing impairments	0.13	58,164
Other health impairments	0.12	53,165
Orthopedic impairments	0.11	47,999
Visual impairments	0.05	22,960
Deaf-blindness	0.01	1,634
Total	9.84	4,261,676

Source: Thirteenth Annual Report to Congress on the Implementation of The Individuals with Disabilities Education Act. Washington, DC: U.S. Department of Education, 1991.

services. The newer figures do not include those who need special education but have not yet been identified. The true prevalence figure probably lies somewhere between the 8 million estimate of 1976 and the 4.2 million being served in 1990. But because of difficulties in identifying these children, we may never know the actual number who need services.

A word of caution is in order about the percentages listed in Table 1-1. Those percentages apply to the population as a whole. The actual prevalence for a particular population may vary according to the gender of the children being studied, the population's ethnic makeup and geographical region, and many other factors. For example, frequently more males than females are identified as having behavioral disabilities, perhaps because males may be more active, or because there may be a lower tolerance for deviant behavior in males. Often, more children need special education services in remote rural areas or inner cities where impoverished living conditions exist. Conversely, fewer special education students are found in upper-middle class and upper class communities where better health care is available, where parents may place a premium upon education for their children, or families may be able to afford to purchase support services such as private tutoring for children who are encountering difficulty in school. Litigation and more restrictive criteria for diagnosing conditions, such as mental retardation, may also influence the number of students served. In addition, many children raised in non-English-speaking homes are placed (often inappropriately) in special education programs. Reasons for such variations will be explained in greater detail later in this book.

Because variations such as these exist, prevalence figures should be used primarily for the early stages of planning. To project service needs accurately, the exceptional children in the area to be served must actually be identified. Estimated projections of prevalence often differ considerably from the number of people who actually need services.

What are the prevalence trends?   It also is important to note that prevalence trends change over the years. The 1991 annual report cited earlier reported the following trends:

- Since 1976, the inception of Public Law 94-142, the total number of children served in special education programs has increased by 26.4 percent.
- The percentage of children identified with disabilities grew from 8.2 percent in 1976–77 to 9.9 percent in 1989–90.
- Early identification of children with disabilities may result in treatment programs that will remediate some of those disabilities before the children reach school age.
- Increased drug and alcohol abuse among pregnant women may increase the number of children born with disabilities.
- The number of students served in programs for children with learning disabilities has increased while the number served in programs for children with mental retardation has decreased.
- Prevalence of children needing speech and language therapy is highest in the elementary years.
- Prevalence of students needing programs for severe emotional disturbance is highest during the teen years.

Trends like these have important implications for the provision of special education services. They affect teacher preparation practices, planning for special education services, teacher supply and demand, public education programs, provision of preventive programs, and facility planning. It is important to accurately identify children in need of special education services and the numbers actually served in order to make intelligent decisions about the provision of a wide variety of special education practices and related services.

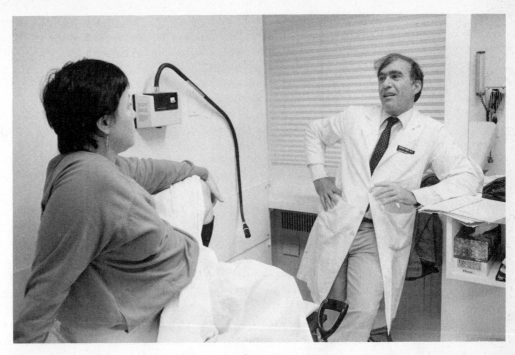

Good prenatal care can often prevent disabilities. The prevalence of disabilities is higher among groups that cannot afford to obtain prenatal care.

PROBE 1-2   Prevalence

1. Between _____ million and _____ million children are in need of special education services.
2. What factors make it difficult to obtain accurate information about the number of students needing special education services?
3. Explain some of the environmental factors that affect the prevalence of children needing special education services.
4. T F School officials should be wary of using national prevalence figures for estimating special education needs in their school districts.
5. Describe three trends in the number of students receiving special education services and speculate about the cause and effect of those trends.
6. Why is an accurate census of special education students being served important?

HISTORICAL DEVELOPMENTS

You should be able to describe the effects of historical forces on special education.

A knowledge of history helps us understand present practices and plan improvements. When we examine the historical forces that have influenced special education, we realize that the programs, practices, and facilities established at any given time reflect the prevailing social climate. People's attitudes have been particularly important; as attitudes have changed, so have the services that have been provided. For example, when many believed that people with mental retardation were a genetic threat to the future of the human race, there was a dramatic increase in the practice of sterilizing those with mental retardation. Similarly, when the prevailing attitude was that it was wrong to deny people with physical disabilities access to buildings, legislation to require the removal of architectural barriers was developed. Efforts to foster positive attitudes toward exceptional people are crucial in improving the services provided them. The history of these attitudes and the related developments can be divided into distinct periods.[2]

Early Practices: 1552 B.C.–1740 A.D.

We know little about how early cultures dealt with people with disabilities. The significance of the few reports that are available has been exaggerated. Saint Nicholas Thaumaturgos, for example, has been described as a champion of those with mental retardation. Kanner (1964) pointed out, however, that although "he may well have put in a good word for them now and then . . . he is also regarded as the patron saint of *all* children, of sailors, and of pawn brokers; the fact that at a much later date he was made to serve as the prototype of 'Santa Claus' certainly does not qualify him to figure in the chronicles of mental deficiency" (p. 3).

How has society treated people with disabilities across the centuries?

An Egyptian papyrus dated 1552 B.C. (known as the *Therapeutic Papyrus of Thebes)* contains the first-known written reference to those with disabilities. Other references entreating people to care for those with disabilities and handicaps are found in the Bible, the Talmud, and the Koran, but at the time those works were written, many such individuals were forced to beg for food and shelter.

Treatment did not improve in classical times. The ancient Greeks and some of the Romans thought that those with disabilities were cursed, and sometimes drowned them in efforts to preserve the strength of their races. At other times those who could not care for themselves were simply allowed to perish. Some Romans did employ them in high positions— as "fools" who performed for the elite.

During the Middle Ages, people with disabilities were viewed with a mixture of fear and reverence, because they were thought to be somehow connected with the unknown. Some were wandering beggars; others were jesters in royal courts.

The Renaissance and the Reformation brought a change for the worse. Exorcism and demonology flourished, along with the persecution of those with disabilities. Martin Luther and John Calvin, for example, accused people who were mentally retarded of being "filled with Satan," and many were put in chains and thrown into dungeons.

By the early 1600s, there were indications that attitudes were beginning to change. A hospital in Paris began to provide treatment for those who were emotionally disturbed. The first manual alphabet for people who were deaf was developed. John Locke became the first person to differentiate between people who were mentally retarded and those who were emotionally disturbed.

Change occurred slowly, however. In colonial America people with mental disorders that made them violent were treated as criminals. Those who were harmless were generally treated as paupers. Those who were mentally retarded, for example, were subjected to one of three

---

[2]Many of the events examined in this section were drawn from the following authorities: Doll, 1962; Kanner, 1964; Nazzaro, 1977; Payne, Kauffman, Patton, Brown, and DeMott, 1979.

treatments. They were either (1) kept at home and given partial public support, (2) put in poorhouses, or (3) auctioned off to the bidder who would support them at the lowest cost to the community in return for whatever work the bidder could extract from them. The last practice was eventually halted by public outrage. People with mental retardation were then put in poorhouses, where they faced conditions often worse than those provided by the people who had won the bid for their services.

The Movement for Training: 1798–1890

Who were the special education pioneers and what were their contributions?

One of the first to investigate methods of educating exceptional children was the French physician Jean Marc Itard. Itard's initial contribution was the result of his effort to alter the wildly uncivilized behavior of Victor, a boy who had been found living naked and alone in the woods near Aveyron, France, in 1799 (Itard, 1932; Lane, 1976). Although Itard did not consider his efforts with Victor completely successful, the techniques he documented and promoted gave the initial impetus to the movement to provide education for children with mental retardation.

Itard's investigations exerted a strong influence on special educators working in the United States in the early 1800s. Two of the most important were Thomas Hopkins Gallaudet and Samuel Gridley Howe. In 1817 Gallaudet founded the first school for children who were deaf in Hartford, Connecticut. Howe, a physician turned political and social reformer, was instrumental in founding the Perkins School for the Blind in Watertown, Massachusetts, in 1829.

During the middle of the 1800s major contributions were made by two special educators, Jacob Guggenbuhl and Edward Seguin. In the 1840s Guggenbuhl opened, in Switzerland, a facility for people with mental retardation caused by a thyroid condition (cretinism). His facility was to become world-famous, and although he was later discredited and drummed out of business, he is acknowledged as the originator of institutional care for those with mental retardation.

Jean Marc Gaspard Itard

Thomas Hopkins Gallaudet

Edward Seguin

Seguin was a student of Itard's who emigrated to the United States in 1848. After completing his medical training in 1861 he worked with Howe, Gallaudet, and other American educators and continued to develop Itard's scientific techniques. Seguin's text, *Idiocy and Its Treatment by the Physiological Method,* was published in 1866.

By the 1870s the movement to establish residential institutions had begun. An organization that urged the establishment of institutions was formed in 1876, with Seguin as its president. This organization, originally called the Association of Medical Officers of American Institutions for Idiotic and Feeble-minded Persons, later became the American Association on Mental Deficiency and is now known as the American Association on Mental Retardation.

Although they were designed to be used for education, institutions during this period came to be used primarily for custodial care. By 1890 it was generally accepted that the states had the responsibility for providing institutional services for those with disabilities and handicaps.

Measurement and Social Control: 1890–1919

The first standardized test of intelligence was published in 1908 by Alfred Binet in Paris, France. The test was developed to identify children with mental retardation. It was then standardized on American populations by Henry Goddard and published in the United States in 1910. The intelligence quotient (IQ) was introduced by Lewis M. Terman in a 1916 revision of the test. IQ tests have been used ever since to identify persons with retarded or advanced intellectual development.

What was the impact of the IQ test?

Unfortunately, IQ tests have been subject to much abuse. Many people have ignored Binet's warning that the results of IQ tests are not to be trusted without taking into account other information about a child's performance. Abuses have led to federal legislation that prohibits the placement of exceptional children in special education programs solely on the basis of an intelligence test score.

Maria Montessori's work also began in the early 1900s. An Italian physician concerned with early childhood education, Montessori further developed Seguin's elaboration of Itard's techniques. Her text on methods of instruction, published in 1912, detailed a sequence of instructional procedures for working with children with mental retardation. The so-called Montessori methods are still an important part of the curriculums of many regular and special preschool education programs.

In 1912 the famous psychologist Goddard published a study about the Kallikak family, which traced five generations of the offspring of a man who had fathered both a legitimate and an illegitimate child. A large percentage of the descendants of the illegitimate child had mental retardation, whereas the descendants of the legitimate child were reported to have average or superior intelligence. Goddard's report led to the belief that mental retardation was an inherited trait and therefore a threat to the human race. The so-called Eugenic Scare that followed prompted many states to enact laws authorizing the sterilization of criminals and people with mental retardation. (Goddard's work was later questioned because it did not take into account the impact of environmental conditions on the two groups of offspring.)

Other trends were more encouraging. At the same time that many people with mental retardation were being institutionalized and sterilized, the number of special education programs in the public schools was gradually being increased. The first college programs for the preparation of special education teachers were established in 1906 at New York University (Morsink, 1984).

Expansion of Services: 1920–1949

There were a number of new developments in the United States during the 1920s, 1930s, and 1940s. Many of them were good. Halfway houses were established to bridge the gap between institution and community; follow-up studies were performed to examine the relative effectiveness of various programs; outpatient clinics were established in hospitals; the use of social workers and other support personnel was increased; new diagnostic instruments were developed; and comprehensive statewide programs were initiated.

The periods of progress proved to be of short duration in some areas, however. The number of special education programs begun in public schools increased fairly rapidly until 1930 and then began to fall. The impetus of the 1920s toward humane, effective treatment for people with disabilities died out in the 1930s and 1940s. These decades were a period of stagnation, characterized by large-scale institutionalization and the segregation of children with disabilities from the rest of society. The economic depression of the 1930s was one cause. Another was the widespread dissatisfaction with poorly planned programs staffed by inadequately trained teachers.

During this period, attitudes were influenced by the "Progressive Education Movement." One by-product of this movement was the attitude that any "good" teacher could teach handicapped children and that special education teacher preparation programs were unnecessary. This idea proved to be wrong. As a result, many special education programs were poorly designed because school administrators were uninformed. The situation was further confounded because many teachers employed for these programs were not adequately prepared to teach children who had needs that could not be met by the standard school curriculum.

How did wars affect special education services?

Even while the number and quality of services were being cut back, however, important changes in attitude and awareness were occurring. Cruickshank and Johnson (1975) point out that the massive screening of young men and women for service in World War II made it clear how many people had physical, mental, or behavioral disabilities or handicaps. Few had expected to find that such a large segment of the population had significant disabilities. The return from World War II and from the wars in Korea and Vietnam of soldiers with injuries that had resulted in physical disabilities made the public more sensitive to the problem, and the acceptance offered them was extended to others with disabilities in the population. The Veterans Administration also developed a number of services for returning veterans with disabilities.

Advocacy and Litigation: 1950–1974

Of all the factors that were significant in the rapid growth and expansion of special education during the period between 1950 and 1974, three stand out: (1) parent activism, (2) increased research and development activities, and (3) changes in teacher education practices. The advocacy of parent activists and the effects of the litigation they instigated will be discussed in this section. More will be said about the other two topics later in the text.

What is NARC?

Most activities related to advocacy and litigation were initiated by parent groups and have been nurtured and supported by professional organizations. In 1950 the National Association for Retarded Children (NARC) was formed. This agency (later renamed the National Association for Retarded Citizens) pressured public schools to initiate programs for those with moderate mental retardation and to expand other special education services. The next 25 years saw a rapid growth in services.

Residential institutions also were subjected to pressures, partly as a result of Burton Blatt's *Christmas in Purgatory* (Blatt & Kaplan, 1966). In this exposé of the squalid conditions in many American institutions for those with disabilities and handicaps, Blatt presented photographs of some of the most deplorable conditions imaginable and then contrasted them with photos of an institution in which humane treatment was provided. More than a decade later, Blatt and his colleagues reported a follow-up to the original study in *The Family Papers: A Return to Purgatory* (Blatt, Ozolins, & McNally, 1979). Unfortunately, many of the injustices that he found earlier still existed. (We recommend these works for a perspective on conditions and practices that recently existed in many large residential institutions.)

How has litigation changed special education practices?

A different tactic was used by a parents' group to fight for public support of services for children with severe mental retardation. In January 1971 the Pennsylvania Association for Retarded Children filed a class action suit against the Commonwealth of Pennsylvania for failing to provide free and appropriate public education for all citizens with mental retardation residing in the state (*Pennsylvania Association for Retarded Children v. Commonwealth of Pennsylvania,* 1972). The plaintiffs in this suit, which came to be known as the PARC case, were thirteen school-age children with mental retardation and all other school-age children of their class in Pennsylvania. The plaintiffs contended that the state had not give them due process before denying them "life, liberty and property" (Fifth Amendment). It also was argued that they were not afforded equal protection under the law (Fourteenth Amendment). To support their position, the plaintiffs provided expert testimony regarding the educability of all children with mental retardation, regardless of its severity.

Conceding defeat, the Commonwealth of Pennsylvania entered into a court-approved consent agreement with the plaintiffs. This agreement defined the Commonwealth's obligation to provide a publicly supported, appropriate education to all children with mental retardation between the ages of 6 and 21, effective September 1972. Included in the agreement were procedures for reevaluation, placement, and due process. Ages of attendance were established, as were regulations calling for homebound and preschool instruction.

The case of *Mills v. Board of Education of the District of Columbia* (1972) reinforced and extended the rights accorded exceptional children as a result of the PARC case. The Mills lawsuit, brought on behalf of seven children with handicaps of varying types and degrees, established the right to equal educational opportunities for all children with disabilities, not just those with mental retardation. In this landmark decision, United States District Court Judge Joseph Waddy ruled (1) that all children, regardless of their disability, have the right to a publicly supported education, and (2) that the defendant's policies, which excluded children from educational services, denied the rights of the plaintiffs and their class to due process and equal protection under the law (Weintraub & Abeson, 1976). The Board of Education claimed that it did not have enough money to pay for the services demanded in the lawsuit. In his ruling on the case, Judge Waddy stated that lack of money was no excuse for not providing services. He said:

> The District of Columbia's interest in educating children must clearly outweigh its interest in preserving its financial resources. If sufficient funds are not available to finance all services and programs that are needed and desirable in the system, then the available funds must be expended equitably in such a manner that no child is entirely excluded from a publicly supported education consistent with [his or her] needs and ability to benefit therefrom. [Weintraub & Abeson, 1976, p. 9]

The PARC and Mills lawsuits served as an impetus for subsequent litigation designed to confirm the educational rights of all handicapped children. These suits included *The Kentucky Association for Retarded Children et al. v. Kentucky State Board of Education et al.* (1973) and *Maryland Association for Retarded Children v. State of Maryland* (1974). In the six-year period from

1969 through 1974, the following court decisions had a dramatic impact on special education programs and practices:

- Children with moderate retardation were not receiving a suitable education (*Wolf v. Legislature of Utah*, 1969).
- Mexican American children were being inappropriately placed in classes for children with mental retardation (*Diana v. State Board of Education in California*, 1970).
- The constitutional rights of hospitalized patients with mental illness are being violated if they receive inadequate treatment or rehabilitation (*Wyatt v. Anderholt*, 1970).
- Adequate treatment is the right of patients with mental illness in state hospitals. This determination resulted in the setting of standards for treatment (*Wyatt v. Stickney*, 1971).
- Children with severe and profound mental retardation are entitled to a public school education (*Pennsylvania Association for Retarded Children v. Commonwealth of Pennsylvania*, 1972).

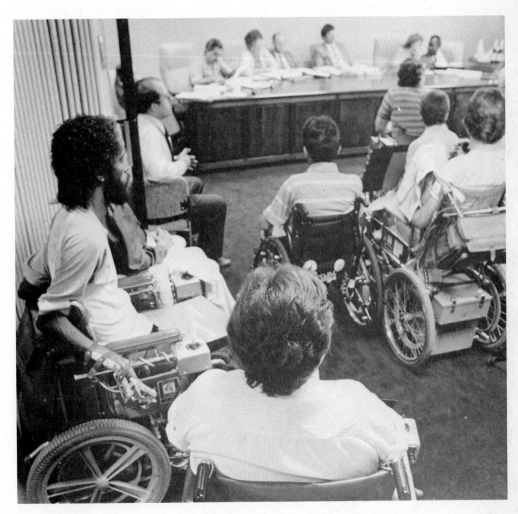

Litigation has provided a significant impetus for the improvement of services to people with disabilities.

- No African American student may be placed in a class for children with mild mental retardation solely on the basis of an IQ test (*Larry P. v. Riles, 1972*).
- Unjust transfers from one institution to another are prohibited (*Kessalbrenner v. Anonymous, 1973*).
- Non-English-speaking students are entitled to bilingual special education (*Lau v. Nichols, 1974*).

In addition, 36 right-to-education lawsuits had been filed in 25 states by 1974.

In the late 1970s and early 1980s, several court decisions appeared to provide a setback for some of the earlier gains. For example, in 1979 the Supreme Court ruled in the Davis case (*Southeastern Community College v. Davis, 1979*) that a student who was deaf could be excluded from a program to prepare registered nurses. The ruling in *PASE v. Hannon* (1980) was that IQ tests are not necessarily biased against particular groups. In 1982 the appeal of a girl who was deaf and seeking the services of an interpreter during the school day was denied by the Supreme Court in *Hendrick Hudson Board of Education v. Rowley* (Morsink, 1984). Each of these cases had features that were unique to the situation under question, however. Care should be taken not to generalize the decisions to all cases involving admission to higher education programs, use of IQ tests, or provision of interpreters.

These and other cases are reviewed in authoritative works on issues related to the right-to-education movement by Kindred, Cohen, Penrod, and Shaffer (1975); Weintraub, Abeson, Ballard, and LaVor (1976); and Turnbull and Turnbull (1978). One of the most thorough references on the early litigation related to special education is the work edited by Burgdorf (1980). That book contains many of the actual texts of court decisions and judicial opinions about cases related to the legal rights of people with handicaps. The work was updated in a supplement by Burgdorf and Spicer (1983). Rothstein (1990) and Turnbull (1990) provide excellent contemporary discussions of how major legislation and case law affect special education practices. These resources are recommended for those who are interested in obtaining a more comprehensive account of how people with disabilities and their advocates have fought for legal rights.

Which historical concepts are reflected in current special education practices?

The litigation mentioned in the last section, coupled with the passage of Public Law 94-142 (to be discussed later in this chapter), has been most important in providing appropriate special education services. The concepts underlying the methods employed in providing these services, however, have their roots in the work of persons such as Itard, Seguin, and Montessori. These fundamental concepts include the following:

- Education should be provided for all exceptional children in order to maximize whatever potential for learning they may have.
- Since children with disabilities and handicaps do have the potential to learn, they should be *educated,* not just cared for in residential institutions.
- Exceptional children should be identified as early as possible, and their education should begin before they reach school age.
- Special education programs should be individualized and should be based on the behavior each child exhibits.
- Educational tasks should be stimulating and should progress from the easy to the difficult. The instructional environment should be carefully structured to increase the probability of success.
- When children produce correct responses and exhibit appropriate behavior, they should receive positive reinforcement, which will increase the likelihood of the recurrence of the behavior.
- A major emphasis of special education should be preparation for gainful employment and social adjustment in the community.

Over a century has passed since Itard published his first text, and nearly that long since Montessori first described her methods; the seven concepts listed above are now widely recognized as fundamental. The challenge continuing to face special education is to ensure that these concepts, and other more contemporary ones, are being applied in educational programs for exceptional children.

PROBE 1-3   Historical Developments

1. Match the contribution on the left with the appropriate name.

Contribution	*Name*
____ First school for children who were deaf	a. Itard
____ Preschool educational methods	b. Howe
____ Worked with a "wild boy"	c. Gallaudet
____ First school for children who were blind	d. Seguin
____ Brought special education to the United States	e. Montessori
____ First intelligence test	f. Guggenbuhl
____ Introduced the IQ	g. Terman
	h. Binet

2. List four concepts developed by early contributors to special education that are relevant today.
3. T   F   There has been a steady, even growth in special education services since the early 1900s.
4. T   F   Institutions were originally set up for custodial purposes.
5. The name of the parent organization that fought for more public school services is the

   _____.
6. Contrast the PARC and Mills right-to-education cases.

LEGISLATIVE IMPLICATIONS

You should be able to describe the impact of legislation on special education practices.

The delivery of special education services in public schools is governed primarily by state laws. These vary from state to state. For example, some states mandate special education services for very young preschool children; others do not. Funding patterns for special education programs also differ considerably across the country.

What is the difference between laws, regulations, and policies?

Once laws are passed, regulations follow. Regulations describe the procedures necessary to comply with the laws, and like laws, they are not uniform among states. For example, all states have laws requiring that teachers who are employed to teach special education students in public schools be certified by a state agency as being qualified to do so, but the regulations that specify the requirements for such certification are not the same from state to state. This situation results from different philosophies about what is needed to be a special education teacher.

At the local level, boards of education are responsible for the direct delivery of special education services, and their policies reflect the state laws and regulations. Each board's policies are also a product of local attitudes and biases.

If you plan to become a special education teacher, you should be familiar with the laws, regulations, and policies that affect special education in your school district. You can obtain information from your state Department of Education or Department of Public Instruction, which typically includes a unit that administers programs for exceptional children. Regardless of where you work, you should also be aware of federal laws that concern special education practices. Table 1-2 describes some of this legislation.

Of the legislation mentioned in Table 1-2, four acts have been of outstanding importance: Section 504 of the Vocational Rehabilitation Act of 1973; PL 94-142, the Education for All Handicapped Children Act (now called the Individuals with Disabilities Education Act) and its amendments; PL 100-407, the Technology-Related Assistance for Individuals with Disabilities Act; and PL 101-336, the Americans with Disabilities Act.

Section 504 of the Vocational Rehabilitation Act of 1973

> No otherwise qualified handicapped individual in the United States . . . shall, solely by reason of his handicap, be excluded from the participation in, be denied the benefits of, or be subjected to discrimination under any program or activity receiving Federal financial assistance.

This rather awkward sentence, Section 504 of the Rehabilitation Act of 1973, is perhaps the most important ever written regarding the rights of people with disabilities and handicaps. The language is almost identical to that of the Civil Rights Act of 1964, which applied to racial discrimination, and that of Title IX of the Education Amendments of 1972, which dealt with discrimination in education on the basis of gender. The enactment of Section 504 reflects the realization that those with disabilities, too, had been subjected to discrimination for many years.

Ending discrimination is an extremely difficult task; it took nearly four years to develop the federal regulations to implement this law. When he issued the regulations in 1977, Secretary of Health, Education, and Welfare Joseph Califano stated:

> The 504 Regulation attacks the discrimination, the demeaning practices and the injustices that have afflicted the nation's handicapped citizens. It reflects the recognition of the Congress that most handicapped persons can lead proud and productive lives, despite their disabilities. It will usher in a new era of equality for handicapped individuals in which unfair barriers to self-sufficiency and decent treatment will begin to fall before the force of law.

How has Section 504 influenced American life?

As a result of these regulations (Nondiscrimination on Basis of Handicap, 1977), the following changes have occurred:

- Employers are required to provide equal recruitment, employment compensation, job assignments, and fringe benefits for those with disabilities.
- All new public facilities are required to be accessible to people with disabilities.
- School-age children with disabilities are entitled to a free and appropriate public education.
- Discrimination in admission to institutions of higher education is prohibited.
- Discrimination is forbidden in providing health, welfare, and other social service programs.

As you can see, Section 504 opened up a whole spectrum of new opportunities for those with disabilities and handicaps. The provisions of Section 504, as originally passed, applied only in those cases in which federal funding was involved; this limitation has since been removed by the Americans with Disabilities Act. The next important step in ending discrimination was the enactment of PL 94-142, which provided for the education of all children with disabilities or handicaps.

TABLE 1-2   Major Milestones in Federal Legislation for People with Disabilities

1879	Funds to produce braille materials are granted to the American Printing House for the Blind (PL 45-186)
1920	Vocational rehabilitation services previously authorized for World War I veterans are extended to civilians (PL 66-236)
1936	Blind persons are authorized to operate vending stands in federal buildings (PL 74-732)
1962	Provisions are made for production and distribution of captioned films for the deaf (PL 87-715)
1963	Funds are provided to train teachers for all disabilities; research and demonstration projects are established to study education of exceptional children (PL 88-164)
1965	Support is provided to aid handicapped children in state institutions (PL 89-313); National Technical Institute for the Deaf is established (PL 89-36)
1966	Authorization is provided for establishing the Bureau of Education for the Handicapped and a National Advisory Committee on the Handicapped (PL 89-750); talking book services for those with visual impairments are expanded to include those with physical disabilities who are unable to handle printed material (PL 89-522)
1968	Experimental demonstration centers for preschoolers with handicaps are established (PL 90-538); provisions are made for deaf-blind centers, resource centers, and expansion of media services for those with disabilities (PL 90-247)
1970	Facilities constructed with federal funds are required to be accessible to those with physical disabilities (PL 91-205)
1972	Ten percent of the enrollment opportunities in Head Start must be available to handicapped children (PL 92-424)
1973	Rights of handicapped individuals in employment and educational institutions receiving federal funds are guaranteed through Section 504 of the Rehabilitation Amendments (PL 93-112)
1974	Due process procedures in placement, nondiscriminatory testing, and confidentiality of school records are guaranteed; programs for gifted and talented children are authorized (PL 93-380)
1975	Free appropriate public education and other procedural guarantees are mandated for all handicapped children (PL 94-142)
1983	PL 94-142 is amended to provide added emphasis on parent education and preschool, secondary, and postsecondary programs for handicapped children and youth (PL 98-199)
1986	PL 94-142 is amended to extend its provisions to infants and toddlers from birth through age 2 (PL 99-457)
1988	Authorization is provided for the establishment of statewide assistive technology services (PL 100-407)
1990	Discrimination against people with disabilities in employment in the private sector is banned; new and renovated public buildings, transportation, and communication systems must be made accessible (PL 101-336); PL 94-142 is amended to provide additional services and is renamed the Individuals with Disabilities Education Act (PL 101-476)

Note: The PL stands for *Public Law.* The first two or three digits represent the number of the congressional session in which the law was passed. Thus, PL 94-142 was the 142nd law that was passed by the Ninety-fourth Congress.

PL 94-142: The Education for All Handicapped Children Act

At about the time Section 504 was being enacted, Congress was investigating other aspects of the lives of children with disabilities and handicaps. Such investigations were conducted partly in reaction to permissive and mandatory legislation previously passed by some of the states (e.g., Massachusetts). Congress determined that state and local educational agencies have a responsibility to provide education for all such children, even though present financial resources are inadequate. It also concluded that the national interest is served by the federal government's assisting state and local efforts to provide special education programs, thereby assuring children with disabilities of equal protection under the law (PL 94-142, 89 Stat. 774–775).

What responsibility does society have for educating children with disabilities and handicaps?

As a result of the congressional studies and pressures by advocacy groups, PL 94-142 was passed and signed into law by President Gerald Ford on November 29, 1975. This law, commonly referred to as the Education for All Handicapped Children Act, establishes the right of all children with disabilities or handicaps to an education. (The title of this legislation has since been amended. It is now called the Individuals with Disabilities Education Act and is referred to by the acronym IDEA.) This act explains the procedures for distributing federal resources to state and local agencies for the development and operation of special education programs. It is the most important federal mandate of services for children with special education needs. The act is intended to do the following:

- Ensure that a free, appropriate education be made available to all children with disabilities or handicaps.
- Assist state and local education agencies in providing this education.
- Assess the effectiveness of these educational efforts.
- Provide children with disabilities or handicaps and their parents with the assurances of due process.

The effect of PL 94-142 and its amendments on both state and federal policy for special education service delivery was reviewed by Abeson and Ballard (1976). A summary of the provisions of the law, now known as IDEA, follows.

What guarantees does IDEA provide?

DUE PROCESS. Children with disabilities or handicaps and their parents are guaranteed procedural safeguards in all matters related to identification, evaluation, and educational placement. This means that parents must be notified when their children are to be tested, and they must give permission for the test to be given. Parents must also be actively involved in any decision about the educational placement of their children who have disabilities or handicaps.

LEAST RESTRICTIVE ENVIRONMENT. When appropriate, children with disabilities or handicaps are to be educated with children who have no disabilities. This provision has resulted in major changes in the organization of school programs. Many self-contained special education classes have been eliminated in favor of integrating children with mild learning or behavioral disabilities into regular classes for much of the school day, with part-time instruction provided in resource rooms. (The various educational options will be explained in Chapter 2.)

NONDISCRIMINATORY ASSESSMENT. When children are tested to determine whether they are eligible for special education services, the tests and testing procedures must not be culturally or racially biased. Under this provision, all testing must be done in the native language of the child. In addition, no educational decisions can be made solely on the basis of a single test score. The use of a variety of assessment techniques is required.

INDIVIDUALIZATION. An individualized education program (IEP) must be developed for each child who is enrolled in a special education program. The plan is to be developed in consultation with the child's parents and based on the information obtained from assessment. The IEP must be reviewed at least once a year and revised as necessary.

CONFIDENTIALITY AND RECORD KEEPING. The confidentiality provision reiterates the provisions of the Family Educational Rights and Privacy Act (PL 93-380), also known as the Buckley Amendment, which guarantees parental control of school records. No one may have access to the records of children in special education programs without specific written parental permission. In addition, the Buckley Amendment guarantees parents the right to examine all the school records of their children.

PARENT SURROGATE. If the parents or guardians of children who have disabilities or handicaps are either unknown or unavailable, someone else can be appointed to work on behalf of the child. This person, known as a **parent surrogate,** is responsible for approving the testing and placement of the child. This person also serves on the committee that develops the individualized education program. The parent surrogate is, in effect, an advocate for the child.

CATEGORICAL PRIORITIES. The law determines priorities in the provision of services. The first priority is for children with disabilities or handicaps who are currently receiving no services. Second are those with the most severe disabilities and who are receiving inadequate services. This means that schools must identify and serve children with disabilities both in school and not in school. They must also identify those who are in an inappropriate educational program.

AGE LEVELS. The law requires that all children with disabilities or handicaps who are between birth and 21 years of age be served.

PRIVATE SETTINGS. Any child placed in, or referred to, a private school or institution by the state or local education agency must receive special education services at no cost to the parents. The agency receiving the child must meet state and local education standards. In addition, the children served by these private agencies must be accorded the same educational rights they would have if they were being served by the public agency directly. Thus, all the conditions we are discussing in this section must be adhered to by private agencies that provide services under contract to local school districts.

FINANCES. The law establishes a formula according to which the federal government substantially increases its monetary contribution to state and local education agencies for their compliance with the provisions of IDEA. Funds received by local districts must be used only for the extra costs of educating children who are served. That is, a district must spend as much of its own revenue for educating a child with disabilities or handicaps as it does for educating a child without disabilities if it is to be eligible for IDEA funds.

PLANNING. Each state Department of Education must submit to the United States Commissioner of Education a plan describing in detail how it proposes to provide a free and appropriate education to all its children with disabilities and handicaps. A similar plan must be submitted by local school districts to the state educational agency. These plans must be examined and revised annually. The plans are subject to public review and comment prior to their submission.

MAJOR PL 94-142 AMENDMENTS. In 1983, the Education for All Handicapped Children Act was amended by PL 89-199, resulting in several significant changes. Additional financial assistance was made available to develop early childhood projects as models to aid children with disabilities and extend service levels from age 3 down to birth. New programs were authorized in the area of secondary special education, with services that would aid the transition of special education students from school to the world of work or to postsecondary education. Increased support for information dissemination and training for parents of children with disabilities was also provided. Greater emphasis on planning, evaluation, and accountability was also provided to further strengthen the provisions of PL 94-142.

In 1986, PL 94-142 was again amended to strengthen provisions for very young children with disabilities or those who are at risk for substantial developmental delay. PL 99-457 mandated that states develop a system of services for infants and toddlers with disabilities, birth through age 2. States must now provide multidisciplinary assessments of the children and provide written individualized family service plans (IFSP), which are analogous to the IEPs required for school-age children. Statewide Interagency Coordinating Councils have been established in each state for the purpose of bringing together the resources of various agencies that serve this population of children and their families. The delivery of services specified in the IFSP should help to enhance the development of these young children and help to prevent more serious handicaps in later years.

PL 94-142 was once again amended in 1990. In addition to the new title (IDEA), the list of disabilities covered by the act was expanded to include autism and traumatic brain injury. The amended law requires that transition services be included in the individualized education plans for students by age 16. Definitions of assistive technologies and the schools' responsibilities for providing them were added. Refinements were made in regulations regarding services for deaf-blind children, preschool children, those with severe disabilities, and those with severe emotional disturbance. Refinements also were made in funding authorization for personnel preparation and research projects. Undoubtedly, IDEA will be subject to additional amendments as time passes and more information becomes available about the most effective ways to provide special education services.

PL 100-407: The Technology-Related Assistance for Individuals with Disabilities Act

Many people with disabilities can benefit from the use of assistive and adaptive devices that are designed to reduce barriers in the environment, enhance their ability to communicate, and otherwise improve their independence. Such devices might include things such as computers that produce speech, hearing aids, remote-control switches that operate appliances, automobiles with hand-operated controls, or special lifts that enable people to get in and out of the bathtub. These devices, and the services that accompany them, have come to be known as *assistive technology*. (More information is provided about assistive technology in Chapter 3.)

What assistive technology activities are supported under PL 100-407?

Congress recognized the importance of assistive technology when it passed PL 100-407 in 1988. Funding provided by this law is helping states to develop statewide networks of people and agencies that provide assistive technology services. Under the provisions of this law, statewide surveys, concerned with people of all ages with disabilities, are being conducted to identify needs that might be met through assistive technology and resources that are available to provide or support such services.

States funded under the "Tech Act," as it has come to be known, are helping to provide services such as assistive technology assessment, assistance in the selection of appropriate devices, training in their use, fabrication of devices that are not available commercially, and evaluation of the effectiveness of devices. The states are also helping people locate sources of funds to purchase devices. Some are providing short-term loan of devices so that people can try them out while making their purchasing decisions.

Many states are developing networks connected to databases that can be accessed by people who are searching for information about assistive technologies. Newsletters and public service announcements in newspapers and on radio and television are being provided in an effort to educate the general public about the potential of assistive technology. Collaborative efforts between the public and private sectors are also being supported under the auspices of this law. Efforts such as those supported by PL 100-407 will do much to make assistive technologies more readily available to children and adults with disabilities who can benefit from them.

PL 101-336: The Americans with Disabilities Act

President George Bush signed into law the Americans with Disabilities Act (ADA) on July 26, 1990. ADA broadens the definition of disabilities beyond those that traditionally come to mind. For example, people who are recovering alcoholics or drug addicts fall under the provisions of ADA. Likewise, it includes individuals with acquired immunodeficiency syndrome (AIDS) or those who might have an impairment (such as a facial scar) that does not limit ability but might result in discrimination. Congress estimated that approximately 43 million Americans of all ages will be affected by this legislation (PL 100-336, 104 Stat. 328). This is nearly one-fifth of the population of the United States.

How will ADA affect society?

ADA requires that, within four years of its passage, the Section 504 protections against discrimination in employment of people with disabilities be extended to all businesses that employ 15 or more people. In addition, employers must make reasonable modifications in job requirements or structure to enable a person with a disability to perform that job, as long as such modifications do not impose an undue hardship on the employer. For example, an employer could provide an adjustable desk that would enable someone in a wheelchair to perform tasks that require desk work.

A second major requirement of ADA is that public transportation be made accessible. This applies to all new vehicles, such as buses, purchased by public transit authorities. One car per train must be accessible, and all new and existing bus and rail stations must be barrier-free. Transit services, such as specially equipped vans, must be made available for those who cannot use the mainline transportation systems.

A third major provision is that all newly constructed public facilities, such as restaurants, hotels, theaters, stores, schools, professional offices, and recreation facilities, must be accessible to people with disabilities. To the extend possible, owners of existing public facilities must attempt to remove barriers that make their facilities inaccessible. (See Chapter 11 for examples of modifications that are required to make buildings accessible.)

Finally, ADA mandates that all telephone companies offering service to the general public must provide relay services for those who are deaf or who have communication problems that preclude them from using the conventional telephone system. This will require the use of special telecommunication devices, called *telecommunication devices for the deaf* (TDDs). Such services must be provided on a round-the-clock basis.

The provisions of these laws have brought and will continue to bring tremendous changes in the American society. They put great pressure on schools to change their special education service systems. Employers and those who provide services to the general public are likewise being affected.

As might be expected, some provisions of the laws are controversial. Critics argue that the federal government should not meddle in what are essentially local concerns. In response, advocates for people with disabilities point out that local school districts, employers, and public service providers have neglected the needs of people with disabilities for years. Without federal legislation, they argue, most of the changes that have revolutionized life for a significant portion of our society would not have occurred.

PROBE 1-4   Legislative Implications

1. What is the difference between a law and a regulation?
2. Identify, by number, the law that relates to each of the following provisions.

   504   94-142   100-407   101-336

   a. ____ Guarantees civil rights for people with disabilities
   b. ____ Requires an IEP for all children with disabilities
   c. ____ Provides for statewide assistive technology networks
   d. ____ Mandates accessible transportation systems
   e. ____ Ensures due process safeguards
   f. ____ Mandates building accessibility
   g. ____ First to require a free, appropriate education for children with handicaps
   h. ____ Provides help in locating communication aids
   i. ____ Makes TDD services available to people with hearing losses
   j. ____ Provides for a parent surrogate
   k. ____ Prohibits discrimination in higher education
   l. ____ Mandates fair employment practices in the private sector
   m. ____ Ensures nondiscriminatory assessment

3. T F All states must provide services to children with disabilities under the age of 2.
4. Which of the following items established the right of privacy of educational records?
   a. Section 504
   b. The Buckley Amendment
   c. PL 94-142
   d. PL 101-336

SUMMARY

1. Special education is individually planned instruction designed to respond to the unique characteristics of children who have needs that cannot be met by the standard school curriculum.
2. In addition to children who are gifted or talented, the category of exceptional children includes those with communication disorders, hearing disorders, visual impairments, physical disabilities, mental retardation, learning disabilities, behavior disorders, and multiple handicaps.
3. Handicaps are the result of a person's interaction with the environment. A child with an impairment or disability may be handicapped in some situations but not in others.
4. It is estimated that between 10 and 15 percent of the children under the age of 21 need special education services. Thus, there are about 1.5 million gifted children and between 6.6 and 9.5 million children with disabilities in the United States.
5. In the past people with disabilities have sometimes been cared for and sometimes abused and persecuted. The development of genuinely beneficial programs began in 1950 with the founding of the National Association for Retarded Children.
6. Litigation has resulted in court determinations that affirm the right of all children with disabilities to a publicly supported education.

7. Section 504 of the Rehabilitation Act of 1973 is civil rights legislation that prohibits discrimination against people with disabilities in employment, access to facilities, education, and other social services.
8. Public Law 94-142 and its amendments, now referred to as the Individuals with Disabilities Education Act, guarantee a free and appropriate public education to all children with disabilities.
9. The Americans with Disabilities Act requires employers to provide facilities to accommodate those with disabilities and insists on accessible public facilities, transportation, and telecommunication systems.

TASK SHEET 1   Simulation of Disability

Select one of the following simulations of disabilities and perform the required tasks for a minimum of three hours. *Do not* spend the majority of this time resting or studying, or you will defeat the purpose of the simulation. Be sure to do the follow-up report.

Hearing Loss

Wear a pair of foam rubber earplugs. During this simulation you should attempt to communicate with someone. Also try to watch part of a TV show with the sound turned off. Spend a portion of your time outdoors.

Blindness

Blindfold yourself so that you can see no light. Try to perform several routine tasks, including grooming, dressing, and eating. Make a brief venture outdoors, but take a companion with you to protect you from injury.

Physical Disability

Do one of the following:

1. Wrap your hands so that you cannot use your fingers.
2. Use a pair of crutches.
3. Spend several hours in a wheelchair.
4. Restrain your dominant arm by tying your wrist to your belt or waist.

During the above simulations, attempt tasks that you perform every day, such as preparing food, eating, dressing, grooming, performing your job, studying, and so on.

Follow-Up Report

Following your experience, write a brief report. Refer to the functional model in Figure 1-1. Describe your reaction to each of the elements in the model by responding to each of the following:

1. Describe the disability you selected.
2. What environment(s) and context did you experience?
3. What environmental demands were placed on you? What problems did you encounter?
4. What were your personal perceptions and feelings?
5. What options did you consider? What things could you do without difficulty?
6. What personal resources did you bring to bear on the problem?
7. What external supports did you use?
8. What coping strategies and adaptations did you employ?
9. What functional responses did you make?
10. How was your personal situation changed as a result of the functional responses you selected? What effect did this simulation have on you?

Freddy had difficulty with reading from the time he started first grade. When he entered second grade, he was reading at the beginning first grade level. School officials told his parents that he was just a "late bloomer" and not to worry. They said that he would catch up as he matured. At the end of second grade, Freddy's father, who was in the Marines, was transferred.

At his new school, Freddy's reading problem was diagnosed as a "learning disability," and it was recommended that he receive part-time reading instruction from a special education teacher in a resource room. Following another transfer two years later, the psychologist in his new school diagnosed Freddy as being "educable mentally retarded" and suggested full-time placement in a special education class.

As he entered sixth grade, Freddy was still behind in reading. By that time, his inability to read was having adverse effects on his performance in other subjects. In an effort to draw attention away from his academic problems, he began to create disturbances in the classroom. He became known as the "class clown." His behavior also became more aggressive, and he began to get into fights with other students. After his father's next transfer, Freddy's unacceptable behavior led to further testing, which resulted in his being labeled "emotionally disturbed."

As a seventh grader, Freddy was referred to a special school in which he received intensive reading instruction in a highly structured environment. This enabled him to bring his behavior under control. After six months at that school, he was transferred back to public school, where he entered a work-study program designed to develop prevocational skills.

By the time Freddy was ready to enter high school, he had a 2-inch-thick set of records. He had been tested and retested by educational diagnosticians, psychologists, and psychiatrists, who had applied at least three different diagnostic labels. He could read at about the fifth grade level. At age sixteen, Freddy dropped out of school and obtained a job driving a cement truck for a local construction company.

2

Issues in Special Education

A. Edward Blackhurst and William H. Berdine

Unfortunately, Freddy's educational career is not an isolated case. Too many "Freddys" have met a similar fate in our nation's school systems. Why is this so? Did Freddy have some innate characteristics that caused him to fail at reading? Did school officials misdiagnose the nature and cause of his problems? How many of Freddy's problems were caused by his parents' frequent moves? Was Freddy placed in inappropriate school programs? Were his educational needs ignored by school personnel? Did he get incompetent instruction? Could his problems have been prevented by earlier identification and treatment? What was the quality of the special education services he received? Did they help him or did they further aggravate his problems?

We will never know the answers to these questions. Perhaps only one of these factors was the primary cause of Freddy's educational problems. In all likelihood, however, several of the factors interacted to contribute to his problems and make them worse.

One thing is fairly certain about the Freddys of the world, however, and that is that school personnel can do very little about the characteristics that students bring to school. Teachers cannot control the environmental factors that influence a student outside of school. They typically have little impact on child-rearing practices and what happens to the child in the home and community.

While Freddy's tale is a depressing one, it is happily not a reflection of the typical practices in special education. Effective teachers and related personnel can perform accurate diagnoses of children with disabilities. They can design instructional programs to meet student needs, and they can implement and evaluate instructional programs that will enable students with characteristics similar to Freddy's to succeed in school and become contributing members of society. Fortunately, cases such as Freddy are the exception rather than the rule.

The primary way that school personnel can help students like Freddy is to manipulate the variables under their control to give these students the highest-quality education possible. These variables involve assessing the nature and severity of any educational difficulties that may exist, selecting an appropriate educational placement, providing individualized instruction that is specifically targeted to improve performance, being sensitive to the influence of cultural diversity, treating students humanely, and manipulating the environment to ensure that students are integrated into the mainstream of society.

A number of issues involved in providing special education and other services in these areas will be discussed in this chapter. We begin each section by posing a number of questions associated with the topic. As you will see in the discussions that follow, we do not have definitive answers for all of our questions. Some of the conclusions we draw must be considered to be the best professional judgment available at the time this book was written. One of the biggest challenges facing special educators today is to develop research projects that will yield empirical data that can be used to make more informed decisions about the issues we discuss here and elsewhere in this book.

STUDENT IDENTIFICATION

You should be able to describe how students are identified as being in need of special education services.

Public Law 94-142 mandates that school officials develop specific procedures to locate students who should receive special education services. Sometimes, students with disabilities are held out of school by their parents. On other occasions, students have been misdiagnosed, while some may be in school but are not receiving services. Activities surrounding the search for special education students are referred to as **Child Find** activities and are mandated by PL 94-142. The following paragraphs describe how students are identified for special education services.

Many students who receive special education services are identified before they enter school. This is particularly true of those who have severe problems such as blindness, deafness, severe mental retardation, or physical disabilities. Other students are placed in special education programs as a result of an accident or disease that occurs after they enter school. Still others are identified through the formal screening programs conducted in the schools on a regularly scheduled basis. Problems exhibited by children who fall into the above categories are usually significant enough that they are readily apparent to personnel who are engaged in Child Find activities.

The great majority of special education students, however, have mild to moderate disabilities that go unnoticed until they are in school programs. These are students who, like Freddy, have trouble learning or adjusting to school situations. Most frequently, these students are first identified by regular classroom teachers.

These teachers usually notice that a student is having difficulty mastering a particular academic task or is seemingly unable to engage in appropriate behavior for the classroom. After trying to remedy the problem, the teacher may refer the student to the appropriate school officials, who start the process of conducting a thorough assessment to determine the child's particular difficulty. These procedures must follow the due process guidelines set out by the rules and regulations of the Individuals with Disabilities Education Act, as described in Chapter 1.

How are students labeled?

If assessment indicates that the child has a significant problem that could be solved through special education services, the child is assigned a diagnostic **label.** The child may be labeled as *educable mentally retarded, learning disabled, speech impaired, physically handicapped,* or be placed in one of a number of other diagnostic categories. This label is required to document the delivery of special education services in the schools. Assignment of children to diagnostic categories is also used as the basis for obtaining funds for special education teachers, program facilities, and related services, such as physical and occupational therapy and speech-language pathology.

Many questions can be raised about the assessment and labeling process. Among the most important are these:

- How reliable and valid are the tests used in the assessment?
- Do the tests discriminate against children from culturally diverse backgrounds?
- Are test results used appropriately?
- How does labeling affect the children labeled?
- How does labeling affect the people who work with labeled children?
- Are there any alternatives to labeling?

Issues associated with these questions will be explored in the following pages.

Assessment

The many methods of assessing the educational performance of exceptional children can be divided into two categories, informal and formal.

What is the difference between informal and formal assessment?

Informal assessment relies on (1) observations of children's varying skills in different areas, which may be recorded in what are called anecdotal records; (2) teacher-constructed tests designed to determine whether a child has learned what is being taught; and (3) interviews with students and others who have interacted with them, such as parents and other teachers. Most activities associated with informal assessments are conducted in the context of the child's classroom.

Formal assessment implies the administration of single tests (or a battery of tests) that have been developed to assess specific attributes and skills and are available commercially. These may include achievement tests to measure academic attainment, intelligence tests to estimate level of ability, and parent interviews to obtain information about social skills. Language, personality, creativity, physical ability, vocational interest, and other tests may also be used. Specialists such as psychologists, speech-language pathologists, physicians, and other related personnel are usually involved in formal assessments.

Most of the assessment materials available from commercial publishers are **standardized tests.** This means the test has been given to a large number of people under identical conditions: All people received the same instructions and had the same amount of time to complete the test. In addition, all the tests have been scored the same way. According to test publishers, the test must be administered and scored precisely as the directions indicate for the results to be valid and reliable.

How do norm-referenced and criterion-referenced tests differ?

Some tests are **norm-referenced,** whereas others are **criterion-referenced.** Norm-referenced tests are those that compare a particular student's performance to that of the norm group, the group of people on whom the test was standardized. For example, a score at the 2.0 level in reading on an achievement test indicates that the child reads about as well as most children at the beginning of the second grade. Most of the achievement tests you took in school are norm-referenced tests.

A criterion-referenced test, on the other hand, does not compare one child's performance with that of other children. Instead, the child's performance is compared to a set of clearly defined objectives, tasks, behaviors, or competencies. For example, a teacher giving a multiplication test on the sevens table is interested only in whether a child can correctly multiply the numbers 0 through 10 by 7. The criterion (sometimes called the domain of content) of this test would be multiplication of the sevens table.

The performance standard or "cutoff score" for measuring the student's proficiency would be 100 percent accuracy (or perhaps 80 percent or 90 percent, depending on the teacher's goal and the child's ability). The teacher would conclude that children who scored at the standard that was established had mastered the sevens multiplication task, whereas those children who scored less than the preestablished standard need more practice to master the skill.

Criterion-referenced tests are also referred to as domain-referenced tests, mastery tests, basic skills tests, competency tests, or proficiency tests. They are similar to the curriculum-based assessment (described later in this chapter) used by many special educators and are useful in determining whether or not a child can perform a particular task, not how well his or her performance compares to other children's.[1]

All tests have a certain degree of **validity** and **reliability.** A test is valid when it actually measures what its authors say it will measure. If a test designed to assess reading ability accurately measures a child's ability to read material written at different grade levels, the test has a high degree of validity. Reliability is the consistency with which a test measures a particular trait. If we administered the same test to a student twice within a short period of time and got the same results, the test would be considered reliable.

Standardization alone does not ensure validity or reliability. Furthermore, the normative population upon which the standardization was developed may not be appropriate for your purposes. If the types of children you are testing were not represented in the norm group, interpreting test results according to the standardized instructions may be inappropriate.

Many tests with poor reliability and validity and inappropriate norms have been used to make educational decisions about exceptional children. For example, Thurlow and Ysseldyke (1979) found that out of 30 tests widely used in programs for children with learning disabilities, only 5 had appropriate norms, 10 had adequate reliability, and 9 had sufficient validity. Clearly there is much potential for abusing test results. Those who test or use test results should use great caution to ensure that appropriate tests are administered and that appropriate decisions are made on the basis of their results. The test administration manual for publisher-made tests usually includes information about test norms, reliability, and validity. Additional information about assessment of exceptional children can be found in the very informative texts by McLoughlin and Lewis (1990), Salvia and Ysseldyke (1991), and Berdine and Meyer (1987).

The assessment of most exceptional children requires the use of formal and informal techniques, standardized and teacher-made tests, and norm- and criterion-referenced tests. Children are assessed for three primary purposes: (1) for identification, to determine who needs special education services; (2) for teaching, to determine what and how a child should be taught; and (3) for program evaluation, to determine the effectiveness of the special education and related services that have been provided.

ASSESSMENT FOR IDENTIFICATION. For most children in school, assessment for identification begins with the regular classroom teacher. If the teacher notices a child is doing very poorly or especially well in a particular area, the child may be referred to a specialist for in-depth assessment. The specialists are selected on the basis of the child's suspected special needs and may include educational diagnosticians, psychologists, physicians, speech-language pathologists, or others.

---

[1]The authors appreciate the suggestions of Craig Jurgensen for this interpretation.

What is screening?

Many schools and health agencies prefer not to rely exclusively on teachers to discover exceptional children; there is always a chance that someone will be missed. As a result, systematic procedures to **screen** children have been developed. The vision screening program most schools conduct is a good example. In this program children are given a quick, easy eye examination every two years or so. When the results show that a child may have a problem, the child is referred to a vision specialist. The best identification programs rely on a combination of teacher observation and screening.

Whereas a child's visual acuity, hearing, physical ability, speech, and language can be measured fairly accurately, traits such as intelligence, personality, emotional stability, academic achievement, social adjustment, and creativity are very difficult to assess. One reason is that many of the tests used to identify them are imprecise. Tests are sometimes used inappropriately as well. For example, the administration of an English IQ test to a child whose primary language is Spanish may produce a very low IQ score, one that does not accurately reflect the child's ability to perform academic tasks. The use of inappropriate tests and testing practices has resulted in laws forbidding the identification and placement of children on the basis of a single test score. Ideally, assessment for identification should be based on the results of a number of tests, in combination with the anecdotal records of teachers, the observations of parents, and the findings of physicians and other professionals who come in contact with the child.

What kinds of tests are most useful to teachers?

ASSESSMENT FOR TEACHING. The purpose of assessment for teaching is to provide information useful in planning *what* to teach (content) and *how* to teach it (methods). In this kind of assessment, teacher-made tests and observations are generally more helpful than the more sophisticated standardized tests. Teachers are more likely to use a teacher-made or commercial criterion-referenced test than a standardized, norm-referenced test. This may surprise you, but which would help you *teach* a child best: an hour-long IQ test or a five-minute session in which the child was asked to identify the initial consonants of words presented on flash cards? The IQ score would indicate the child's intellectual ability relative to that of a group of children of the same chronological age. The flash card test, on the other hand, would indicate which consonants the child could pronounce and which needed to be taught. What's more, by paying careful attention to the types of errors the child makes, the teacher should get some insight into how the unknown consonants should be taught.

What is curriculum-based assessment?

Effective teachers generally assess children regularly, not just at fixed times of the year—such as at the beginning and end of the grading period. A systematic procedure that teachers can use to obtain data that is useful in making instructional decisions is known as **curriculum-based assessment** (Fuchs, Deno, & Mirkin, 1984).

> Curriculum-based assessment includes (1) direct observation and analysis of the learning environment, (2) analysis of the processes used by students in approaching tasks, (3) examination of pupil products, and (4) control and arrangement of tasks for students. Focus is on assessment of a student's ongoing performance in the existing curriculum. (Salvia & Ysseldyke, 1991, pp. 26–27)

In this form of assessment, teachers carefully analyze the content of the curriculum that has been designed for their students. The skills required for mastering the content are identified and translated into objectives. Short tests are then developed to assess whether the objectives have been met. Teachers administer these pretests prior to teaching in order to determine whether students have mastered the skills or concepts associated with the objective. Such pretesting also determines whether students have the prerequisite skills necessary for beginning instruction on that task. Instructional decisions are made on the basis of the pretesting. Tests are again administered after instruction to see if students have mastered the content.

ASSESSMENT FOR PROGRAM EVALUATION. Both formal and informal tests are used to determine whether students are meeting objectives that have been specified for them and whether the special education and related services they have been receiving are having an impact. Although many schools require annual formal assessment programs, teachers typically find that the informal assessment procedures they use, particularly those associated with the curriculum-based assessment approach, provide the most useful information for making instructional decisions.

The *test-teach-test* principle enables the teacher to immediately determine whether concepts and skills have been learned. If the tests indicate that learning has occurred, the teacher can move on. If not, the concept is taught again—perhaps using different methods after the teacher has developed some hypotheses about why the child did not learn during the first instructional sequence.

Additional assessments are administered at different times during the school year to determine whether students remember the skills and concepts mastered earlier. More detailed information about curriculum-based assessment is available in a special issue of the journal *Exceptional Children* (vol. 52, no. 3, 1985) and in the texts by Berdine and Meyer (1987), Howell and Moorehead (1987), and Salvia and Hughes (1990).

This teacher is using flash cards to test the student's comprehension of vocabulary. By noting the student's responses and error patterns, she can determine whether her instruction was effective and gain insight about what should be taught next and any consistent errors the student may be making that will deserve special attention.

Labeling

Consider the image you see when you visualize the following terms:

idiot   *spastic*
nerd   *epileptic fit*
cripple   *crazy*
deaf and dumb   *vegetable*

If you are like most people, each of these terms conjures up an image of a person who has a certain physical appearance or who is behaving in a certain way. Generally, the images are negative and stereotypical. We learn them from television, literature, and other media. For example, a person who does something unusual is called "crazy"; a bright child is often portrayed as a frail individual who wears glasses; stories sometimes have a "village idiot" as a character; an umpire may be referred to as "blind." The stereotypes that result are reinforced by daily conversations and the attitudes of the people we grew up with.

Labels of a different sort have been used by authorities for many years to categorize children with disabilities or handicaps. Children have been identified, diagnosed, and labeled as emotionally disturbed, learning disabled, and educable mentally retarded, for example. It was argued that placing children in categories helped in the effective delivery of instruction. Further, labeling was helpful in obtaining funds.

Today the trend is to reduce diagnostic labeling, particularly of children with mild disabilities. In addition to the obvious humanitarian reasons, there are some very pragmatic ones. Years ago, for example, Gillung and Rucker (1977) found that regular educators and some special education teachers had lower expectations for children who were labeled than for children with identical behaviors who were not labeled. A label can thus become a self-fulfilling prophecy. Even if the label were incorrectly assigned, children might eventually behave as the label said they would, simply because people expected them to. Although research on the effect of labeling on children has yielded mixed results, this at least seems clear: Most people tend to view a labeled person differently than a nonlabeled one.

What are the arguments for and against labeling?

Controversy about labeling reached such proportions in the early 1970s that an eminent psychologist, Nicholas Hobbs, was commissioned to begin a study called the Project on Classification of Exceptional Children. In his summary report, Hobbs (1975) described some problems with diagnostic categories. His conclusion included the following points: (1) labels are applied imprecisely; (2) labeled children are stigmatized; (3) labels yield too little information for planning; (4) the classification of children with multiple problems in terms of a dominant set of attributes leads to the neglect of other conditions; (5) classification tends to be deviance-oriented; (6) classification systems are insensitive to the rapid changes that take place in children; (7) classification of a child can result in the disregard of important etiological (causative) factors.

In favor of labeling, one could argue that administrators need to be able to categorize children in order to qualify for state and federal financial support. Labels can also help focus public attention and legislation on a particular problem. One could argue further that if one set of labels were eliminated it would soon be replaced by another, and that labels are useful in discussing children with similar characteristics.

As much as we might like to do away with labels, their use is almost inevitable. Labels and categories are used whenever something is being organized. For example, we organized the information in the last nine chapters of this text into categorical areas to present it in the most efficient manner. In addition, labels are applied to children for their benefit—to make them eligible for special education services.

For an interesting discussion of some of the pros and cons of labeling, you may like to review the article by Braaten, Kauffman, Braaten, Polsgrove, and Nelson (1988), who argue that although labels can stigmatize, we should be cautious in discarding them because that may lead to reduction in services. On the other hand, Reynolds, Wang, and Walberg (1987) argue that labels are meaningless because, in part, the criteria for assignment to diagnostic categories continue to change. Indeed, Wolman, Thurlow, and Bruininks (1989) found that labels have shown to be unreliable in allocating special education services to children and that a number of children were assigned different labels at different times in their lives. (Freddy's case at the beginning of this chapter may not be as unusual as you may think.)

Regardless of the pros and cons, the important thing to remember is that labeling can have bad effects if used incorrectly. Labels should be used only when necessary. The focus of attention should always be on the individual, not a group or class. For special educators the crucial question is, *How should this particular child's strengths and weaknesses influence the teaching strategy I've devised?* and not, *What type of child is this—mentally retarded? emotionally disturbed? learning disabled?*

PROBE 2-1   Student Identification

1. T   F   Standardized tests always have good reliability and validity.
2. T   F   Most exceptional children are identified prior to entering school.
3. Give an example of an informal and a formal assessment technique.
4. _____ is the extent to which a test measures what it purports to measure.
5. _____ is the consistency with which a test measures what it is attempting to measure.
6. Differentiate between norm-referenced and criterion-referenced tests.
7. The three major types of assessment are assessment for _____, assessment for _____, and assessment for _____.
8. How can curriculum-based assessment be used in special education?
9. Give three reasons why labels should be de-emphasized.
10. Give one of the arguments in favor of labeling.

NORMALIZATION

You should be able to discuss the principle of normalization and its effect on exceptional children and adults.

Normalization can be defined as the philosophy that all people with disabilities or handicaps should have the opportunity to live lives as close to the normal as possible; patterns and conditions of everyday life as close as possible to the norms and patterns of the mainstream of society should be made available to them. This philosophy evolved in the late 1960s (Nirje, 1969) and early 1970s (Wolfensberger, 1972) as a result of parental dissatisfaction with the placement of their children with disabilities. Many were being placed in isolated residential institutions or in programs in public schools that were segregated from children enrolled in regular education classes.

Normalization has resulted in the greater integration of people with disabilities into business and social activities. Its greatest influence on special education, however, has been the promotion of two practices, deinstitutionalization and education in the least restrictive environment.

A number of questions have been raised about the normalization principle. Chief among them are these:

- Should all large residential institutions for people with disabilities be closed?
- What effect will group homes have on the communities in which they are located?
- Should we do away with self-contained special education classes?
- How is normalization related to mainstreaming?
- Who should be mainstreamed?

These questions and others will be addressed in the following pages.

Deinstitutionalization

Deinstitutionalization refers to the movement to eliminate large residential institutions, particularly those for people with mental retardation. Wolfensberger (1972), an early advocate of normalization, proposed that long-term, total-life-care institutions be replaced by small, community-based group homes that would permit residents to participate in local activities and be closer to their families. The establishment of group homes and other alternative living arrangements is being encouraged by many parents and special education professionals.

Deinstitutionalization has its problems, however. It is often difficult to find qualified staff for group homes. States that have invested large sums to build or renovate institutions are reluctant to support moves to other facilities. What is more, the establishment of some group homes is opposed by the communities in which they hope to locate.

What appears to be happening to large residential institutions?

Some authorities, such as Blatt, Ozolins, and McNally (1979), were early advocates for the closing of all residential institutions and moving toward smaller, community-based facilities. The fact that large investments of money have been made in the physical plants of large institutions makes this unlikely, however. It is more likely that smaller facilities will be built as the larger ones become obsolete. These facilities will probably have slightly different missions than strict residential care, however. For example, in 1982 the Kentucky Association for Retarded Citizens went to court to prevent the rebuilding of an obsolete residential facility. The judge ruled that the institution could be rebuilt, but its size was drastically reduced. In addition, however, he ruled that the facility should provide space for emergency temporary care of people with mental retardation in cases where it would be impossible for their parents or legal guardians to travel or pursue business if they had to maintain responsibility for the people in their charge.

COMMUNITY-BASED RESIDENTIAL SERVICES—AN EVOLVING MODEL. One of the more critical tests of the 1990s will be whether the public will continue to pay for the expanded array of community-based services. This test will be especially critical in the area of services for adults with severe disabilities, such as severe mental retardation, for whom the public has historically placed greater emphasis on institutional or life-care residential service provisions. The 1970s saw an evolving array of services for adults with mental retardation that closely resembled those available for their peers without retardation. While the principle of normalization has enjoyed popular appeal among both professional and lay persons as indicated by the definitive expansion of services, continuation of the expansion, and perhaps even its maintenance, is not guaranteed.

What is the continuum of residential services?

Residential services can be viewed on a continuum, which is illustrated in Figure 2-1. Such services represent an evolving service array that will continue to change as economic and community attitudes shift. These services are described in the following pages.

FIGURE 2-1   Continuum of Residential Services

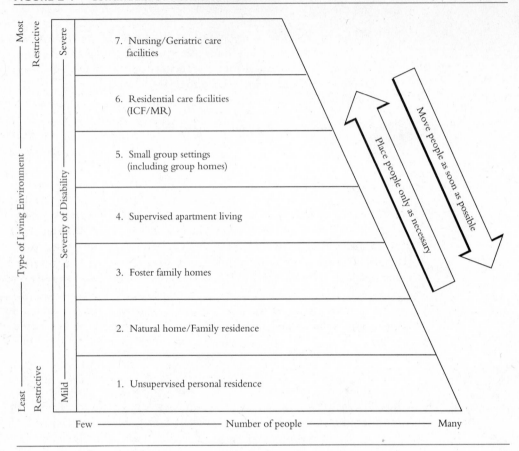

Unsupervised Personal Residence. Living in one's own home or apartment has tradition-ally been a goal of young adults. This least restrictive residential living environment offers at once the greatest degree of personal freedom, expression of individuality, and personal and social responsibility. Historically, persons with disabilities often have not been permitted this expression of freedom. Professionals generally agree that anyone exhibiting responsible behav-ior commensurate with that of age peers ought to have equal access to the benefits of responsible behavior. If a person with disabilities can cope with the demands of making a life independent from family, state, or community agency supervision, then that person ought to be permitted to exercise a free choice in selecting a residential lifestyle.

The economic benefits of adding contributing members to a community far outweigh the alleged additional expense of providing community-based services. The institutional service model is both more expensive and less effective in providing habilitative and rehabili-tative services (Conley, 1979; Center on Human Policy, 1979; McCormick, Balla, & Zigler, 1975). However, this does not warrant a wholesale abandonment of all institutional services for persons with severe disabilities, such as mental retardation.

Natural Home/Family Residence. For many families with young adults with disabilities, living at home with parents or members of one's extended family has for a long time been the only alternative to residential institutions. Traditionally, the problem with this form of residen-tial service has been the lack of community-based supportive services such as vocational or

What problems are encountered with traditional family residences for people with disabilities?

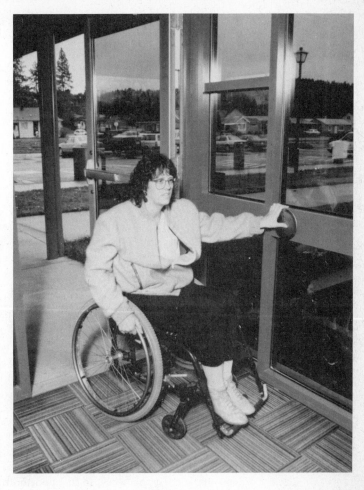

This person lives independently in her own apartment and commutes to work using accessible public transportation. She relies on the services of a personal attendant to provide assistance with some activities of daily living. Technology also plays an important role, as illustrated in her use of a remote-controlled automatic door opener.

prevocational training, recreation, or even respite care. Increased availability of such services is now making the natural home a more attractive and feasible alternative than placement in residential facilities outside the home. (Other issues related to families of people with disabilities will be described in greater detail in Chapter 6.)

What are ALUs?   **Alternative living units** (ALUs) are generally defined as any form of residential setting other than a person's natural family setting. A variety of ALUs are illustrated by settings 3 through 7 in Figure 2-1. Those will be described below.

Foster Family Homes. To develop adaptive behavior skills, it is extremely important that the child and adolescent with disabilities grow up in a family. Most foster family arrangements are regulated by state and municipal licensing boards. In most cases, foster parents receive fees, but they do not usually receive training. Supervision of foster care homes is usually less rigorous than it is for group homes or other alternative living units. One effective model for foster family planning was developed by the Eastern Nebraska Community Office of Retardation (ENCOR) program. ENCOR's concept of a "developmental home" plan is similar to the foster home plan used nationwide today. This program places considerable emphasis on training the participating parents to work with persons classified as mentally retarded, and planned, systematic supervision of their care is provided.

Supervised Apartment Living. Apartment living arrangements are less common than group homes, but they are expected to grow more popular as the ALU arrangement becomes more familiar to the public. In some programs the apartment ALU begins with the supervisor living in an apartment with the person being supervised; or the individual being supervised may live in a cluster of apartments in a separate part of the same building as the supervisor. As individuals acquire the skills necessary to live independently, they are encouraged to move into an apartment of their own or to share an apartment with an acquaintance, with supervisors dropping by at regular intervals. In most ALU programs, clients with disabilities attend a training program that helps them develop vocational and independent living skills. The individuals being provided services should have their recreation and work independent from agency staff but remain part of life-care and counseling programs.

What is the role of the Core Home?

Small Group Settings. Singleton (1981) and Skarnulis (1980) described a community-based services delivery strategy called *Core Home* and *cluster of services.* Since its inception in the late 1970s, the community-based model embodied in the Core Home concept has been expanded upon with a wide variety of similar endeavors nationwide under numerous labels (e.g., community residential facility or CRF, group home, transition apartment or home).

The Core Home serves as a focal point for the coordination of community-based services, with responsibility for the following:

1. Management, to provide support and supervision for the cluster of services in the community.
2. Intake procedures, for all new individuals, to assess their needs.
3. Training, for new clients and service delivery staff.
4. Respite care, for families with children exhibiting disabilities, crisis support for homes in the cluster and for other clients who need such services.
5. Community advocacy, providing a focal point for local services.

Core Homes can also ease the adjustment of people moving from institutional settings to other alternative living units. During the short-term stay in the Core Home, the individual in transition is assisted in exploring the community's cluster of services, adapting to its demands, and gaining access to its opportunities.

Group Homes. Typically, in group homes, from 3 to 5 people live together, share household responsibilities, work, and recreate in the immediate community. Both males and females may live in the group home, but cohabitation is generally not permitted. The group home is usually staffed full-time by live-in personnel who rotate shifts.

In many cases the group home is the first living arrangement for the person with disabilities after leaving a residential institution. It is also a good first step outside the immediate family for adults leaving home for the first time. Whether moving from home or from an institution, individuals with disabilities should be moved on from the group home to a different living arrangement, such as an apartment, as soon as they demonstrate the ability to function more independently.

What is an ICF/MR?

Residential Care Facilities. When federal funding became available for residential construction, many private corporations were formed to sponsor construction of residential facilities designed to house 50 to 100 persons. These facilities, known as Intermediate Care Facilities for the Mentally Retarded (ICF/MR), are regulated by the federal government. Most ICF/MRs are designed to provide total care throughout their lives for clients labeled as mentally retarded.

It is sometimes difficult to operate a profit-making corporation and at the same time provide a normalized service delivery system to persons with mental retardation. There has been some litigation by advocates claiming that services are sacrificed for the sake of profit. Just as there were major court cases during the 1970s and 1980s involving large institutions for persons with mental retardation, it seems likely that there will be cases during the 1990s involving claims that the civil rights of persons with mental retardation in ICF/MRs are being violated.

What types of living arrangements are appropriate for older persons with disabilities?

Nursing or Geriatric Care Facilities. Attention has only recently been focused on providing care for elderly individuals with disabilities. With today's emphasis on community-based facilities, services for the elderly are becoming a major issue. This is particularly the case with those who have one of the dementias, such as Alzheimer's disease. Schapiro and Eigerdorf (1975) described nine types of arrangements that are appropriate for the elderly person with disabilities:

1. Older adult apartments: any apartment complex built or modified to serve the elderly.
2. Alternative living units: two- or three-bedroom apartments with supervision within the apartment.
3. Rural living arrangements: provisions for rural housing for the elderly provided under HUD's (now HEW's) Housing Rural Development Act.
4. Mobile home living: resembling any other mobile home park, but providing supervision and assistance to the elderly.
5. Congregate housing: supervised existing public housing.
6. Nursing homes: public or private; the elderly patients with disabilities should be integrated.
7. Institutions: may include hospitals with units designed to provide long-term life care.
8. Extramural care: care provided in the home.
9. Sheltered housing: a situation in which assistance in managing daily activities is provided in the client's own home; not a nursing home or apartment setting.

Living arrangements available to the elderly person with disabilities ought to resemble in quality of living those typically made available in the community for their peers without disabilities. The ultimate goal is to provide an array of services that assures the elderly person with disabilities the same quality of healthcare programs throughout life that we would want for ourselves.

The Least Restrictive Environment

The second aspect of normalization that relates to special education is a reflection of a provision of PL 94-142. The provision stipulates that children with disabilities be educated in "the **least restrictive environment.**" This means that children with disabilities or handicaps are to be educated with their peers who do not have disabilities whenever possible, in as nearly normal an environment as possible.

What is the difference between mainstreaming and the least restrictive environment concept?

The term **mainstreaming** (which does not appear in PL 94-142) was originally coined to describe the process of educating special education students in the least restrictive environment. Through common usage, however, mainstreaming now refers to the practice of integrating such children into regular classes for all or part of the school day (Stevens, Blackhurst, & Magliocca, 1989). The least restrictive environment, on the other hand, refers to the educational placement of students in a setting as close to the regular classroom as possible. For some children, the least restrictive environment might be placement in a regular class. For others, it might mean placement in a self-contained special education class or homebound instruction. The type of placement is dictated by the child's specific instructional needs.

Placement decisions are made at the time that the individualized education program is planned and should be based upon the child's unique needs. The options are illustrated in Figure 2-2. These options are frequently referred to as the "continuum of special education services" or the "cascade of services" (Deno, 1973). You will note that there are ten educational settings listed. The least restrictive setting is at the bottom, and the most restrictive is at the top. The arrows on the right illustrate that children should be placed in a more restrictive setting only if it is to their educational advantage; they should be moved to a less restrictive setting as soon as they are capable of being educated in that environment. In general, the more restrictive environment will have fewer children, and these will have more severe disabilities. (You may find it interesting to note the similarities between Figure 2-1, which describes a continuum of alternative living provisions, and Figure 2-2, which describes a continuum of alternative educational provisions. You should be able to see how both of these relate to the normalization concept.)

FIGURE 2-2   Continuum of Special Education Services

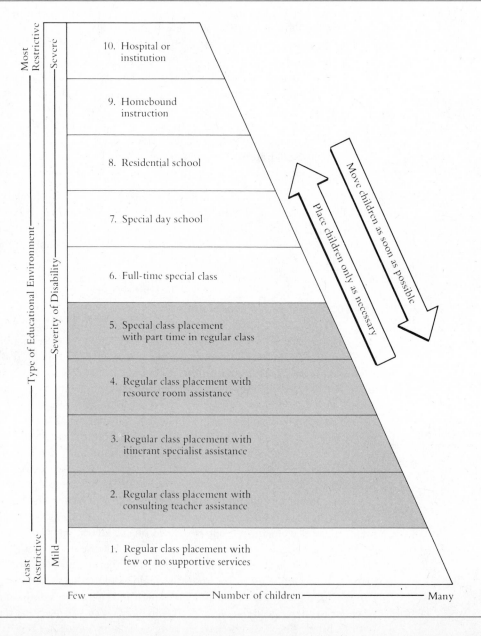

Educational environments 1 through 4 are all variations of the regular class. Environment 1 is a class that resembles the one that most children attend. In environment 2, specialists provide consulting services to the regular class teacher but do not work directly with children. In environment 3, direct assistance is provided by itinerant specialists such as speech-language pathologists and mobility instructors to children who are blind. In environment 4, children leave the regular classroom for part of the day to obtain direct instruction individually or in small groups from a resource teacher.

Educational Service Options

When considering educational options for children with disabilities, it is important to keep in mind that (1) educational placement should be based on the child's needs; (2) the child should be placed in the most facilitative (or least restrictive) environment; and (3) placement should be flexible enough so that a child could be moved to a different setting if the situation warrants it. The following pages provide additional information about each of the educational settings described in Figure 2-2.

What is prereferral intervention?

THE REGULAR CLASSROOM. Every attempt should be made to place children with disabilities, regardless of classification level, in their home school and in an age-appropriate classroom with their peers without disabilities. Any deviation from placement, regardless of type, should be based on the results of a thorough **prereferral intervention** process. The process of prereferral intervention refers to a systematic set of activities in which students believed to be at risk for school failure are evaluated with regard to their learning and educational needs as well as their abilities. The process does not determine eligibility for special education, but rather identifies what the regular education curriculum can do (or can be adapted to do) to maintain an effective learning environment for the student.

Only after prereferral intervention activities have been documented as not being effective, and in the best interest of the student's continued education, should eligibility for special education services be considered. Services that may be involved in the prereferral process include the traditional educational support services such as speech therapy, academic tutoring, behavioral counseling, physical therapy, and mobility training for those with visual impairments.

Frequently, too little attention is paid to prereferral activities and the entire referral process. Teachers often refer a child for special education because they are bothered by the child's academic performance or behavior. Insufficient attention is paid to relevant details related to the child's performance, resulting in follow-up assessment activities that are inappropriate or incomplete. Teachers who have been working with an individual child can provide information that is invaluable to specialists who may be involved in assessment activities that are performed as a result of the referral process.

The functional model that was described in Chapter 1 is a good resource for identifying variables that teachers should consider when planning prereferral activities and also when making decisions about referring students as potential candidates for special education programs. Some of the factors that teachers should include in a referral request are illustrated in Figure 2-3. You will note that the items to be provided relate to the elements in the functional model.

If you are ever in a position to make such a referral, assessment specialists will appreciate a report that contains information on the topics that are listed in Figure 2-3. The more information they have about a student, the more effectively and efficiently they will be able to conduct their assessments. (You may want to refer back to Figure 1-1 and its accompanying

FIGURE 2-3 **A Functional Approach to Exceptionality: Referral**

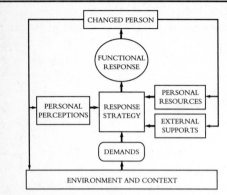

Provide this information on referral:

Demographic Information
- List name, address, age, gender, ethnicity.

Problem Statement
- Explain the reason for the referral.

Environment and Context
- Describe the classroom environment and the context that prompted the referral.

Demands
- Describe primary and secondary demands that were placed on the student.

Response Strategies
- Describe strategies you observed the student attempt in response to the demands. Make particular note of coping and adaptation skills.

Personal Resources
- Provide estimate or data on student's personal resources, such as:

Intellectual abilities	Physical abilities	Adaptive abilities
Hearing	Speech and language	Vision
Motivation	Social adjustment	Mobility
Creativity	Academic skills	Memory

External Supports
- List any external supports that were provided to assist the student in responding to the demands. Include information such as:

| Assistive technology | Physical therapy | Family support |
| Speech-language therapy | Special education methods or materials | |

Personal Perceptions
- Provide your observations of behavior or statements made by the student that might reflect his or her perceptions of needs, problems, deficits, or consequences.

Functional Response
- Describe specific behavior that the student exhibited in response to the demand.

Changed Person
- Explain how the person changed in behavior, attitudes, or functional abilities.

discussion in Chapter 1 for additional information about the model and its interpretation. It is important that you have a good understanding of the model, because information based on it will be presented in each chapter in this book.)

Before leaving the topic, we should note that some people disagree with the term *prereferral intervention*. For example, Graden (1989) dislikes the term because it implies that placement in a special education program is imminent. In fact, one of the purposes of prereferral intervention is to determine whether instructional strategies can be put in place that will enable the student to stay in his or her current educational setting without being referred for special education services. Graden proposes the use of the term **intervention assistance** as being more descriptive of the purpose and procedures associated with the intervention that is done prior to referring a student for special education. Pugach and Johnson (1989) concur with this conceptualization. They believe that activities such as prereferral intervention (or intervention assistance) should be a regular part of the classroom teacher's instructional strategies to meet the diverse needs of a variety of children who are not receiving special education services.

Contemporary support services such as collaborative consultation (to be described later in greater detail) can also be provided by specialists working with the regular class teacher to provide instruction in the regular classroom where social or behavioral problems are not responding to routine intervention procedures. The consulting teacher provides collaborative consultation to the teacher but typically does not provide direct intervention with the students. Additional itinerant or part-time support in the form of a learning disabilities specialist may be needed where specific problems in academic areas are pervasive, such as reading or mathematics.

To conclude, unless serious social or behavioral problems are present and not responsive to the regular class teacher's intervention, the position taken by most contemporary authorities is that the student classified as having disabilities will profit best from educational placement in a heterogeneous setting such as that provided by the regular class in the student's home or neighborhood school. Individualized instruction may still be needed, with appropriate related services as prescribed, but that instruction should be delivered within the first five levels of the continuum illustrated in Figure 2-2.

Many students with sensory or physical disabilities can function satisfactorily in regular classes with only minimal classroom modifications and supporting services. For example, many students who must use wheelchairs may require only a few modifications, such as adjustable desks and chalkboards that can be raised to accommodate a wheelchair. Many students with visual impairments can function very well with the addition of low-vision aids, audio instructional materials, braille textbooks, and the services of resource teachers to assist in the administration of tests and to provide instruction in mobility and how to cope with barriers imposed by the school environment. Children with hearing losses may also be able to function very well in the regular classroom if they have appropriate hearing aids and are provided with instruction in lipreading.

Among children with learning and behavior disorders, those who fall within the upper, or mild, range are most likely to be successful in the regular classroom. Those with lower intellectual and adaptive behavior levels most likely will require more special services that cannot be provided in the context of the regular classroom.

Students with severe and profound intellectual disabilities will probably not flourish in most regular class academic settings. For those students, if effective instruction in the regular classroom is not feasible, placement within one of the four variations of the regular class may be recommended (see levels 2 through 5 on the continuum of services in Figure 2-2).

Placement in any setting other than the regular classroom should rarely be on a full-time basis. All persons with disabilities should be provided with the opportunity to experience their home school's heterogeneous social environment as found in the traditional homeroom, assemblies, cafeteria, after-school events, and off-campus activities such as field trips. Academic and skill development instruction outside the regular classroom should be only a partial component of the student's total school experience.

Scheduling of instruction outside the regular classroom should run parallel to that provided for students without significant learning problems and not be segregated or completely set aside from the events of the school day. When separate instructional settings are needed, they should be viewed as partial programming, with the student returning to the regular setting whenever age-appropriate learning and skill development are possible.

THE SPECIAL CLASS. When the conditions described earlier for prereferral intervention are met, there are traditionally two special class options in the continuum of educational services: *part-time placement* and *full-time placement*. Only those whose academic and adaptive behavior problems preclude placement in the regular classroom should be placed in the special class. In any case, as noted earlier, referral from a student's regular class program should never occur without a thorough and well-documented prereferral intervention period.

It may be both academically and socially more effective for students who demonstrate significant academic problems, but exhibit adaptive behavior similar to that of their normal peers, to remain in the special class for academic work and join their regular classmates for physical education, art, music, vocational education, home economics, field trips, and other curricular support or nonacademic classes.

Full-time academic and skill-building instruction in a special class may be warranted *only* for those children who need intensive instruction in academic areas, adaptive behavior, or social or behavioral programming. Some children who have relatively age- or grade-appropriate academic skills but poor adaptive behavior often are placed full-time in a special

Which "type" of child with disabilities would be most successful in the regular class?

When should a special class placement be made?

This teacher is working with a small group of children in a resource room. One is receiving direct instruction from the teacher while the others are doing independent work that has been specifically designed for them. All are working on the development of skills that will help them be successful when they return to their regular classroom later in the day.

class. When this is the case, every effort should be made to improve the child's adaptive behavior so that he or she can be moved as soon as possible to a less restrictive environment.

Presently, most children classified in the moderate, severe, or profound range of intellectual disability are educated in full-time, self-contained special classes with partial participation with regular class age-mates in subject areas or classes where their prior academic or cognitive skills are not of primary importance (e.g., music, physical education). The instructional emphasis in such classrooms is primarily on self-help skills, basic communication skills, and vocational skill development that will eventually permit the child to be employed in a supervised or sheltered job site.

Although most individuals with moderate to severe intellectual disabilities require some form of supervision throughout their lives, it is not unusual for such individuals to acquire in school all the life-care skills needed to work independently or live in an alternative living arrangement such as a group home or supervised apartment.

In those instances where full-time pupils in a special class are in educational settings in which they are segregated from their peers without disabilities, it is important that they be allowed maximal opportunities to participate in the chronologically age-appropriate social and nonacademic life of their schoolmates (Snell & Renzaglia, 1986). Such children will typically benefit from social and leisure time interaction with children not exhibiting disabilities or handicapping conditions. This should not be surprising, considering that it parallels interactions that occur out of school and in the community.

For the most part, all children with disabilities or handicapping conditions interact most frequently with children not exhibiting either disabilities or handicaps when they are not in school. School personnel should try to foster such interactions and should attempt to provide pupils with disabilities the skills that will permit them to interact successfully. The inclusion of recreation, social and leisure time activities with nondisabled age-mates is rapidly becoming an important feature of many school-based programs. You may want to examine the work of Perske (1988) for more information on this topic.

THE SPECIAL DAY SCHOOL. The service day school is rapidly disappearing as a service delivery option in public schools. Such facilities still exist, but they are generally quite specialized and are appropriate only for children who have a documented history of not benefiting educationally, behaviorally, or socially from either partial participation or full-time special class placement in their community's public schools. Quite often these schools were established to provide services for children with disabilities prior to enactment of PL 94-142 in 1975, when public school services were typically not available to this population. With the passage of PL 94-142 and it subsequent amendments, special day schools have become less common and exist today most often as private alternative schools for families wishing to select this legal option.

When are placements in special day schools appropriate?

Special day schools are generally found only in high-population-density urban areas or large metropolitan areas where the population of individuals with similar disabilities (usually moderate to severe) is large enough to justify the operation of a separate educational facility. The use of special day schools as an alternative to inclusion, even on a partial participation basis, for any classification of school-age special education students is acceptable only if it is the personal preference of family or parents. Few public school systems still maintain such facilities, responding to legal pressure brought to bear by litigation, federal and state regulations, and the popular movement in the United States toward a full inclusion of all school-age persons in the regular public school setting.

Who usually receives homebound instruction?

HOMEBOUND INSTRUCTION. Homebound instruction for people with disabilities is relatively uncommon, again because of the passage of PL 94-142. When it is used, this type of instruction is generally provided only to those who cannot attend school because of a medical or physical problem, such as a child who requires complete bed care. Most homebound instruction is short-term and provided only while the student is recuperating from a temporary illness, disorder, or hospitalization. The continuum-of-services model requires that the student be moved back into the appropriate least restrictive environment as soon as feasible.

When are children placed in residential institutions?

RESIDENTIAL INSTITUTIONS. Individuals, regardless of age, should be placed in facilities such as residential institutions only when they have medical or severe behavioral problems that preclude their safe care and treatment within a group setting within their community. Unless they have severe or dangerous behavioral problems, individuals with disabilities should typically not be considered for placement in such settings.

Although children with severe disabilities are found more frequently in these settings, they should be placed there only after other nonresidential small, community-based options have been thoroughly explored and found ineffective. As a result of PL 94-142, children and young adults with disabilities are being served more frequently in public schools.

Collaborative Consultation

You will note that levels 2 through 5 in Figure 2-2 are shaded. Those levels all involve placement of special education students for at least part of the school day in regular classrooms. When such placements occur, it is usually necessary to provide additional support services to help the regular class teacher who must teach the students assigned to that class. Several alternatives are used in providing such assistance. In some cases specialists, such as speech-language pathologists, provide suggestions that the teacher can follow in a particular subject matter area. In other cases, the special education resource teacher can provide help with topics, such as classroom management. In still other cases, teams of individuals, sometimes called *support teams* or *school assistance teams,* work together to provide assistance.

What is collaborative consultation?

Collaborative consultation is a concept that has emerged to describe the type of assistance that is very beneficial to the regular class teacher. Basic to this concept is the idea that regular class teachers and the various specialists and resource people who are available to support them should work together in collaborative ways to solve the problems of mainstreamed students. In the past, provision of support services carried the implication that the resource teacher or specialist was the "expert" who provided advice for the regular class teacher to implement. Such a conceptualization implies that regular class teachers lack insight or ideas for solutions to problems that they may encounter.

Collaborative consultation provides a more positive and constructive approach to support services. In this approach, the regular class teacher and the resource teacher (or other specialists) engage in mutual problem-solving activities. Problems that are encountered are viewed as shared problems, and all parties involved are viewed as having valuable information toward the solution of the problems.

Not only are collaborative consultation models useful for implementing instructional programs after a student has been assigned to a special education program, they also have been effective in prereferral interventions (Pugach & Johnson, 1989). In this type of application, special assistance teams (of which the regular class teacher is a collaborating member) are used to investigate solutions to difficulties students may be having that, if left unattended, may result in referral for special education placement. In some cases, such approaches can lead to remediation of educational difficulties before they get severe enough to warrant special education placement.

Additional information about collaborative consultation can be obtained from works by Conoly (1989), Friend (1984), Friend and Cook (1992), Idol, Paolucci-Whitcomb, and Nevin (1986), and Pugach and Johnson (1988).

The Regular Education Initiative (REI)

Although mainstreaming and placement in the least restrictive environment result in more appropriate education for most children, these concepts can cause problems. Unfortunately, some school administrators have interpreted the least restrictive environment provisions of PL 94-142 to mean that special education students can be placed in regular classes without being provided the support services they or their teachers need. Others have terminated self-contained classes and have attempted to integrate all special education students into regular classes—often with disastrous results.

What are the pros and cons of the REI?

One of the major issues facing regular and special education is what has become known as the **Regular Education Initiative,** or REI. The REI is an effort to reform educational practices by placing greater emphasis on educating children with disabilities in regular classrooms. Advocates for the REI (e.g., Bickel & Bickel, 1986; Gartner & Lipsky, 1987; Lilly, 1988; O'Neil, 1988; Wang, Reynolds & Walburg, 1986; Will, 1986) claim that special education practices in which students are removed from regular classes for instruction (pull-out programs) have not proved to be beneficial.

Advocates also claim that pull-out special education programs create barriers to the full integration of children with disabilities into society, contribute to lowered academic and social expectations for the children, have eligibility requirements that exclude many children who could benefit from educational services commonly offered to special education students, focus on failure as opposed to prevention, and lead to problems with parents. They also claim that research has shown that special education students in regular classes perform better academically than those in pull-out programs.

On the surface these are attractive arguments, and the REI appears to be a worthwhile goal. However, a number of authorities (e.g., Braaten, Kauffman, Braaten, Polsgrove, & Nelson, 1988; Bryan, Bay, & Donahue, 1988; Hallahan, Keller, McKinney, Lloyd, & Bryan, 1988; Heller & Schilit, 1987; Kauffman, Gerber, & Semmel, 1988; Sachs, 1988; Safran & Safran, 1987; Bergason & Anderegg, 1988) have expressed caution about its wholesale implementation. These individuals take the position that regular class teachers are not adequately prepared to assume greater responsibility for the education of special education students who have been integrated into their classes, and that many regular class teachers are not willing or able to devote the extra time that would be involved in providing such services. They also claim that school administrators often attempt to implement integration without providing the necessary support services to teachers. In addition, they assert that the curriculum in many regular classes is not appropriate for some special education students, who often need intense, individualized instruction that can best be provided in settings outside the regular classroom. Finally, they claim that much of the research cited by advocates of the REI is flawed, or, as Deno, Maruyama, Espin, and Cohen (1990) found, subject to varying interpretations.

While there are compelling arguments on both sides of the REI issue, we believe that there is probably a middle ground between the extremes. On the one hand, it is probable that many students in pull-out special education programs could benefit from more time in regular classes. On the other hand, many students with disabilities require intensive individual instruction that is either difficult or impossible to provide in regular class settings.

It is our position that the continuum of services, as represented in Figure 2-2, provides the best model to accommodate the needs of all children. We think the phrase *most facilitative environment* more clearly embodies the spirit of PL 94-142 than the term *least restrictive environment*. The former conceptualization is more positive and clearly places the focus on the best interests of the child. We should ask, What educational setting will be best for meeting the objectives that have been specified for the child? In some cases, it will be full-time placement in a regular class with support services. In other (fewer) cases, it may be full-time placement in a self-contained class. For those with mild learning and behavior disabilities it will, in all likelihood, be a combination of regular class and resource room placements.

Considerations for Mainstreaming

Who should be mainstreamed?

When considering educational options, one of the most difficult tasks is to determine which students to place in regular classes for what subjects and for what amounts of time. Firm guidelines are not yet available to aid in these difficult decisions; but Schubert and Glick (1981) made seven suggestions following a study of successful mainstreaming practices common to a number of schools. According to those authors, the following should be true if students are to be mainstreamed:

- Students should be capable of doing some work at grade level.
- Students should be capable of doing some work without requiring special materials, adaptive equipment, or extensive assistance from the regular class teacher.
- Students should be capable of "staying on task" in the regular classroom without as much help and attention as they would receive in the special classroom or resource room.
- Students should be capable of fitting into the routine of the regular classroom.

- Students should be able to function socially in the regular classroom and profit from the modeling of appropriate behavior by their classmates.
- The physical setting of the classroom should not interfere with the students' functioning (or it should be adapted to their needs).
- It should be possible to work out scheduling to accommodate the students' various classes, and the schedules should be kept flexible and be easy to change as students progress.

Students who cannot meet these criteria should probably not be placed in regular classes. They should instead be educated in one of the other types of educational arrangements, such as a resource room or self-contained special education class. A major goal for many of these students, however, should be to develop the skills needed to function in the regular class. In addition, as their skills develop, efforts should be made to integrate them into the regular class for short periods. This will give them opportunities to practice skills so they may eventually spend longer periods in the more normalized environment as they learn and mature.

Mainstreaming will not be effective if teachers and administrators reject the concept and believe that it will not work. One of the leading authorities on mainstreaming conducted a series of interviews with school personnel and identified six attitudes that appeared to be most conducive to successful mainstreaming (Birch, 1974, p. 94):

- Belief in the right to education for all children.
- Readiness of special education and regular class teachers to cooperate with each other.
- Willingness to share competencies as a team in behalf of pupils.
- Openness to include parents as well as other professional colleagues in planning for and working with children.
- Flexibility with respect to class size and teaching assignments.
- Recognition that social and personal development can be taught, and that they are equally as important as academic achievement.

If these attitudes are prevalent among school personnel, mainstreaming seems likely to be successful. Of course, something more than good attitudes is needed. Classroom teachers also need to have specific competencies related to mainstreaming. These are described in considerable detail in the mainstreaming text by Stephens, Blackhurst, and Magliocca (1988). Additional information about mainstreaming can be found in books by Gloeckler and Simpson (1988), Lewis and Doorlag (1983), McCoy and Prehm (1987), and Morsink (1984).

PROBE 2-2   Normalization

1. Two concepts associated with normalization are _____ and _____.
2. List four different types of ALUs.
3. T F Finding staff is one of the major problems in establishing more group homes.
4. Number the following settings, with 1 being the least restrictive and 10 being the most restrictive:
   ____ Special day school
   ____ Regular class with consulting teacher help
   ____ Hospital or institution
   ____ Regular class with no support services
   ____ Residential school
   ____ Regular class with resource room help
   ____ Full-time special class
   ____ Regular class with itinerant help
   ____ Homebound instruction
   ____ Special class with part-time regular class placement

5. Define *mainstreaming* as the term is commonly used.
6. T   F   Students with mild disabilities should always be educated entirely in regular classes.
7. What is the potential impact of prereferral intervention?
8. What role do special day schools play in the continuum of services?
9. How can collaborative consultation assist a teacher?
10. Describe the pros and cons of the Regular Education Initiative. What is your position on the REI?

INDIVIDUALIZED INSTRUCTION

You should be able to describe the components of the individualized education program that is legally required for all students enrolled in special education programs.

You should recall from Chapter 1 that an individualized education program (IEP) is required for all students who have been admitted to a special education program. Several questions have been raised about the IEP and the process for developing it:

- How should the IEP be developed and what should its format be?
- Who should be involved in the development of the IEP?
- How can the myriad details associated with the IEP process be managed efficiently?

The IEP is the foundation on which the special education student's education is built. The IEP requirements generally do not apply to gifted students unless they also have a disability. However, West Virginia and some other states have regulations that require the development of IEPs for gifted children as well as those who have disabilities.

The development of the IEP is one part of the due process requirements of PL 94-142. Many people believe that it is the most important part, because it specifies in detail the nature of the special education and related services that will be delivered to a particular student. It is a written document developed by a committee of school personnel and at least one of the child's parents. Parent surrogates can be appointed to represent the child when necessary. In addition, the law provides that the student shall participate in the IEP deliberations if he or she is willing and able.

Who attends IEP meetings?

The school principal (or a designate) generally chairs the meeting at which the IEP is developed. The child's parents or guardian must always be included, but the composition of the rest of the IEP committee will vary considerably, depending on the nature of the child's disabilities. The psychologist or diagnostician who performed the assessment is often present. The teacher who referred the child and the teacher in whose program the child may be placed are often present as well. A variety of other professionals may attend, including a teacher consultant, speech-language pathologist, audiologist, physical therapist, occupational therapist, social worker, guidance counselor, and medical personnel.

IEP Requirements

What should be included in the IEP?

At the IEP meeting, discussions center around the nature of the child's educational needs and the best type of program to meet these needs. PL 94-142 requires that at least eight pieces of information be included in the IEP:

1. *The student's present levels of performance.* Typically, this information is presented in a statement of educational strengths and weaknesses based on the results of the assessment.
2. *Annual goals for the student's program.* These are broad, general statements that help to focus on the general areas in which individualized services will be provided.
3. *Short-term objectives associated with each goal.* These focus on the specific things that the student will learn during the time the IEP is in effect.
4. *The special education and related services* to be provided to the student. The services are described and the names of the people responsible for providing them are included.
5. *The extent of child's participation in regular education.* This requirement helps the IEP committee address the normalization and REI concepts described earlier.
6. *The projected date for initiating services.* This is given so that all parties will know when to begin implementing the IEP.
7. *The anticipated duration of services specified by the IEP team.*
8. *Objective evaluation procedures.* These provide specific criteria for determining when the objectives have been reached. The procedures to be used in the evaluation and the schedules for conducting the evaluation are included. The IEP must be reviewed at least annually and redone every three years.

To document that due process procedures have been followed, a number of other items typically appear on the IEP. These include the meeting date, the people who attended, the date that consent for testing was provided, the native language of the parent, the child's primary language, the rationale for the least restrictive environment placement recommendation, the annual review date, the birth date and ethnicity of the child, and the parent's signature indicating approval of the IEP.

An excerpt from an IEP is illustrated in Figure 2-4. The IEP is for Barbara, a 16-year-old girl with a mild learning disability who is enrolled in a work-study program in her high school. To conserve space, excerpts from only a few pages have been included. These excerpts illustrate demographic data, student strengths and weaknesses, goals and objectives, educational services to be provided, the evaluation process to be used for the goals and objectives that are specified, and the parent and school verification components. The complete IEP from which Figure 2-4 was derived also had goals and objectives in business education, home economics, physical education, social competence, and reading. If you take the time to examine Figure 2-4 closely, you will be able to pick out the eight required components described above and most of the supplementary items that were described in the previous paragraph.

From the teacher's perspective, the most important part of the IEP is the list of goals and objectives because they provide direction for what should be taught. Tymitz (1980) studied objectives written by teachers for inclusion in a hypothetical IEP and discovered many weaknesses. In some cases, the objectives were nothing more than restatements of the goals, or they were descriptions of activities. In others, the objectives were incomplete.

To be most useful, objectives should include (1) a description of the performance required of the child, (2) the conditions under which such performance should be demonstrated, and (3) the criterion to be used to determine whether the objective has been met (Mager, 1962). (See if you can identify these three components in the IEP objectives listed in Figure 2-4.) The usefulness of IEPs is significantly reduced when they include objectives that do not have these three features.

Being able to write good instructional objectives is a major skill required of special education teachers. A checklist for determining the adequacy of IEP goals and objectives can be found in the work of Tymitz-Wolf (1982).

FIGURE 2-4   An Excerpt from an Individualized Education Program

INDIVIDUALIZED EDUCATION PROGRAM

A. Student Information

Name: Barbara T.
Chronological age: 16-0
Language spoken in home: English
School: Blanton Senior High
Current placement: Regular Business Education class

Date: September 26, 1992
Gender: Female
Ethnicity: Caucasian
Grade 11

B. Present Level of Functioning

Math Strengths
Barbara is able to recite all of the number facts. She can perform addition and subtraction problems with regrouping. She can successfully compute two- and three-digit multiplication and division problems. She can apply these skills when given practical problems that require their application.

Math Weaknesses
Barbara does not know how to budget money. She has only a superficial understanding of the purpose and operation of banks. She cannot use a checkbook.

C. Annual Goals

Math

1. Barbara will learn how to develop a budget.
2. Barbara will learn the purpose of banks, the services they provide, and how to use them.
3. Barbara will learn how to write checks and balance a checkbook.

D. Short-Term Objectives

MATH GOAL 3: Writing checks and balancing a checkbook

1. Given 10 completed checks, Barbara will state their date, monetary value, the signator, recipient, and the bank name with 100% accuracy.
2. Given 20 sets of dates, monetary values, and recipients, Barbara will correctly complete blank checks.
3. Given an initial balance of $750 and 20 checks of various denominations totaling $670, Barbara will be able to compute correctly a running balance in her checkbook.
4. Given a check register with 20 entries and a bank statement with 5 outstanding checks and a service charge. Barbara will be able to reconcile her check register correctly.

E. Educational Services

MATH GOAL 3: Writing checks and balancing a checkbook

Barbara will receive the services of a resource teacher for math instruction one hour each day. These services will commence on October 15 and continue until the objectives have been met. Ms. Ima Whizz will provide the resource room instruction. Barbara will spend one period per week in an elective physical education course and the remaining four school periods in the regular Business Education program pursuing the secretarial science curriculum. Given her current levels of achievement, her career aspirations, and these goals and objectives, this placement is in Barbara's best interests.

continued

FIGURE 2-4   (continued)

F. Evaluation Procedures

MATH GOAL 3: Writing checks and balancing a checkbook
Each of the four math objectives will be evaluated by a teacher-constructed simulation that will present Barbara with a hypothetical income, a list of expenditures that must be paid by check, blank checks, and a bank statement that she must reconcile. The evaluation will be performed four weeks after instruction on the use of a checkbook is initiated.

This Individualized Education Program will be reviewed in September 1993.

G. Approvals

This Individualized Education Program was discussed in a meeting held at Blanton High School on September 26, 1992, with the following people in attendance:

Mary Ann Sunshine, Principal (and Committee Chair)
Justin Inkblot, School Psychologist
Ima Whizz, Resource Teacher
B. Z. Fingers, Business Education Coordinator
Mr. T., Barbara's father

I have had the opportunity to participate in the development of my daughter's Individualized Education Program and agree with its provisions.

_____
Parent's Signature

It is important to note that the parents should be active participants in the development of the IEP. Although school officials typically make a presentation to explain their findings and recommendations, parents are encouraged to make recommendations based upon their knowledge of the child and their perceptions of what would be in the child's best interest.

On occasion, parents disagree with the plan that is suggested and an impasse results. Parents may signify their disapproval by refusing to sign the IEP. When this happens, the due process procedures described in PL 94-142 are set in motion. Although negotiations about the IEP are preferred, parents do have the right to a due process hearing conducted by an impartial third party. If this course is taken, a recommendation is made by the hearing officer, which is subject to still further appeals by both the parents and school officials if disagreements remain. In the event that appeals and hearings are conducted, the child has the right to remain in his or her current educational placement. The implementation of special education services cannot commence until the issues related to the IEP are resolved.

IEP Management

It should not be a surprise that the development of the IEP is a complicated and time-consuming process. In addition to the time required for assessment, considerable staff time and paperwork are needed to develop a draft of the IEP, participate in the meeting, finalize the IEP, maintain the necessary records, and conduct annual reviews.

The cost of developing an IEP will vary with the complexity of the case and the number of professionals involved. A California study by Enell and Barrick (1983) found that the cost of professional time involved in the preparation of IEPs using conventional manual methods ranged from $35 to $720 per case. This did not include clerical time or other costs such as transportation for parents, supplies, parent time, or interpreter service. Costs for annual IEP reviews ranged from $76 to $156. Since that study was performed in 1983, costs obviously will be higher today. It is no wonder that school districts are interested in finding more efficient ways to manage the entire IEP process.

The Technology in Action box (below) describes one particular computerized IEP system. In 1983, Enell and Barrick listed information about 30 different computer-based IEP systems that were available. Many of those systems were used with large mainframe computers, some of which contained data banks of more than 10,000 objectives. Since that time, numerous IEP systems have been developed that operate on microcomputers (e.g., IEPs Unlimited, PennStar, Talley Special Education Management System). Some of these programs provide a complete IEP management system that can be used to generate letters to parents, send notices of time for review of the IEP, prepare lesson plans based upon IEP objectives, and generate correspondence and mailing labels to facilitate mailing.

Are computerized IEP systems effective?

Enell and Barrick (1983) went on to conduct a study of five California school districts that used computers in the IEP process. These researchers were interested in determining whether districts using computers had different costs than those that did not. A more important goal, however, was to find out whether there were differences between the acceptability and usefulness of the resulting IEPs. They interviewed school officials and parents to obtain their information. The list at the top of the next page summarizes some of their findings.

TECHNOLOGY IN ACTION

Hesperia School District serves 234 special education students. It is using an IEP computer program . . . that produces a proposed IEP . . . that is divided into three major sections. These sections are (1) student data, (2) the assessment data, and (3) the goals and objectives. The computer program records the student data and then preselects a range of goals and objectives using the assessment data. The IEP team selects the goals and objectives from this range.

The student section has three subsections. The first is the school system information—school system name and school address. The second section is student identification—name, birth date, grade, student number, dominant language, etc. The third subsection is information for the Individual Education Plan—the type of meeting, meeting date, implementation date, etc.

The assessment section lists the scores on 17 different tests of academic, motor, intellectual, speech, and other functioning. The scores entered are the age equivalent or grade equivalent scores. Judgments are recorded for adaptive behavior, mobility, vision and hearing, and other areas. A graphic profile of present functioning is presented using the scores and judgments. . . .

[The computer determines whether there are discrepancies between the student's actual and expected scores.] When discrepancies are found, goals and objectives may be preprinted by the computer in any of the following areas: written expression, reading recognition, reading comprehension, math computation, math reasoning, social/emotional, fine motor/gross motor, listening comprehension, visual discrimination, oral/expressive language, and spelling.

Paperwork flows to the district psychologist. A secretary enters the student data and test scores into the microcomputer and a Proposed Individual Education Plan is printed. Since the district serves 234 special education students, the number of IEPs entered each day is few. Estimated time for data entry and printing for one student is 45 minutes.

Source: Reprinted from a report by Enell and Barrick (1983, pp. 34–35).

- When computers were used, nearly 30 minutes were saved at each annual review meeting, and varying amounts of time were saved during initial placement meetings. Compared to those who used manual methods, those who used computers saved 18 percent of the costs for personnel.
- Parents and teachers found the computerized IEPs more legible and easier to understand. Parents believed that assessment information and the IEP meeting were helpful, and they found the IEP a useful reference. They felt involved in the process, even though objectives were preselected. Most people believed that the computer-generated objectives were better written.
- Teachers were able to adapt to the computerized systems without difficulty. They did not object to its use and reported that the IEP systems had many advantages and few disadvantages.

The above findings seem to be consistent with those reported by Jenkins (1987), Krivacska (1987), Lillie (1983), and Ryan and Rucker (1986). It appears that the use of information processing systems has considerable merit for managing the IEP process.

Two caveats should be noted, however. First, it is imperative that users of such systems learn how to write objectives and become knowledgeable about IEP development *before* they use an automated system. Such knowledge is needed in order to evaluate critically the IEP that is generated. One should always view the computer output in light of what is known about the child and what is known about sequencing of instruction. We have seen several computer-generated IEPs that listed objectives that were either inappropriate for the age of the child, poorly stated, or recommended in sequences that were not educationally sound.

Second, whether generated manually or by computer, the initial IEP should be viewed only as a draft to be used in the IEP meeting. The IEP should not be made final until the child's parents have a chance to react and propose modifications.

PROBE 2-3   Individualized Instruction

1. T F Parents are required by law to participate in the development of their child's IEP.
2. List the eight required components of an IEP.
3. T F Parents have a right to disagree with school officials about their child's IEP and proposed special education placement.
4. T F Teachers find the use of computerized IEP systems offensive and are opposed to their use.
5. T F Parents find computerized IEPs easier to read and understand than those that have been prepared manually.

CULTURAL DIVERSITY

You should be able to describe the implications of children's diverse cultural backgrounds for special education practices.

In 1954, racially segregated systems of public education were declared unconstitutional by the United States Supreme Court in the landmark case of *Brown v. Topeka Board of Education* (347 U.S. 483, 1954). Since that time, schools have made progress toward integrating students of various cultural and ethnic backgrounds. Unfortunately, we continue to find a disproportionately large number of children from minority groups in special education programs.

How many minority
children are in
special education
programs?

The results of a 1986 study conducted by the Office of Civil Rights (OCR) of nearly 24 million students are reported in Table 2-1. The data in the table indicate that African American, Hispanic, and Native American children were overrepresented in classes for children with mental retardation and underrepresented in classes for gifted and talented children, when compared with their representation in the total sample of students who were studied. African American students also appear to be overrepresented in classes for children with learning disabilities and those who were seriously emotionally disturbed. It is interesting to compare these findings with the data for white students in the last column of the table.

The data reported here are relatively consistent with four prior studies conducted by the OCR (Chinn & Hughes, 1987). All of these studies were designed to be representative of the United States as a whole.

The rest of this chapter will address issues related to these findings. Questions that can be raised include the following:

- Are minority children more frequently handicapped than other children?
- Why do we find statistics like the ones just cited?
- What can be done to rectify inequities in placement and improve education for children from culturally diverse backgrounds?

Baca and Chinn (1982), Baca and Cervantes (1989), and Gollnick and Chinn (1990) have addressed these questions and a number of other issues related to cultural diversity in special education programs. The information presented below is organized around the major issues that these authorities raise and draws heavily from their work.

Identification, Assessment, and Placement

One of the major reasons we find more minority children in special education programs is improper assessment techniques. It was mentioned earlier, for example, that many students were placed in special education programs because they did not perform well on standardized tests administered in a language they did not fully understand. This is one of the reasons federal legislation requires that tests for special education placement be given in the child's native language. It was also the reason that California banned the use of IQ tests for placing African American students in classes for children diagnosed as being educable mentally retarded (*Larry P. v. Riles,* 1972).

What problems are
encountered when
testing culturally
diverse children?

There is considerable potential for bias when attempting to assess children from culturally diverse backgrounds. Oakland (1980) described problems with inappropriate norms, reliability, and validity in tests used for diagnostic purposes. Problems during the assessment

TABLE 2-1   Percentage of Students in Special Education Classes

Placement	African American	Hispanic	Asian	Native American	White
Educable mentally retarded	44.2	6.3	0.9	1.3	57.8
Trainable mentally retarded	31.4	10.7	2.1	1.2	54.8
Speech impaired	21.4	9.4	2.1	1.2	65.9
Emotionally disturbed	26.6	6.2	0.6	1.0	65.6
Learning disabled	22.0	11.9	1.4	1.5	63.3
Gifted	11.5	6.5	6.7	0.5	74.8
Percentage of total sample	**21.1**	**12.5**	**3.6**	**1.1**	**61.8**

Note: Based on a sample of 22,386,677 students surveyed (Office of Civil Rights, 1986).

process were also identified. These included factors such as language differences, test wiseness, motivation, anxiety, cultural differences with the examiner, and bias in examiner attitudes, among others.

There are two major problems when testing children who are linguistically different (e.g., those whose primary language is not English). First, there are few valid and reliable tests that can be used to assess the aptitude and achievement of the children. Second, tests that are used often provide little information that is useful for instructional programming. The result is that many such children are placed in remedial programs that do not adequately meet their needs (Duran, 1989).

Some efforts have been devoted to the development of assessment techniques that consider the child's ethnic and environmental background as well as the more traditional factors such as intellectual performance. Examples of this approach are the System of Multicultural Pluralistic Assessment, commonly referred to as SOMPA (Mercer, 1979), and the Kaufman Assessment Battery for Children (Kaufman & Kaufman, 1983). SOMPA norms were developed for white, African American, Mexican American, and Navajo children, ages 5 to 11. Even so, some authorities have raised questions about the usefulness of the norms that have been developed (e.g., Figueroa, 1989). Other procedures, such as peer nomination, are being used to identify gifted culturally different children (Blackshear, Sullivan, Ewell, & Rogers, 1980).

What is dynamic assessment?

Because of the problem of obtaining valid and reliable information from traditional, standardized tests, a procedure called **dynamic assessment** has been recommended for culturally different children (as well as for others). Dynamic assessment combines the assessment of a student's readiness to learn with immediate instruction about the learning task. The amount of assistance required for instruction is also defined through identification of hints and cues that are required to facilitate learning.

Duran (1989) describes two different approaches to dynamic assessment. One of these requires that a student's readiness to master new skills be probed using procedures such as Feuerstein's (1979) Learning Potential Assessment Device. Those using this approach make clinical judgments about the readiness of the student and the hints and cues that can be used to promote learning. In the second approach, teaching cues and hints are developed to match different skill area hierarchies. Student performance is then matched against these hierarchies and the predefined hints and cues are used with the student.

Dynamic assessment is another variation of the test-teach-test model that was described earlier in this chapter. See the text by Lidz (1987) for more information about the topic.

Activities such as the above may be steps in the right direction, but much remains to be done. Extra care is especially important in interpreting test data on children not represented in the group on which the test was standardized. For example, if there were no Hispanic children in the norm group of a reading test you are using, you should view with caution the test scores of any Hispanic children in your class. Even if there were Hispanic children, it is important to know their cultural background and the cultural backgrounds of those in the norm group. For example, a Hispanic child from inner-city New York will differ considerably from a Hispanic child who travels with migrant workers in the southwestern United States. If you use criterion-referenced tests, you should be certain your assessment is not biased by conflicts between the criterion and the culture of the child being tested.

Attitudes of Students and Teachers

Unfortunately, many minority students also come from families that are living at poverty levels. Thus, some special education students are in triple jeopardy: They have disabilities, belong to a minority, and are poor.

Most authorities agree that people from such backgrounds have different attitudes toward education than those in the middle and upper socioeconomic classes. For example, families from the middle and upper classes traditionally place a high value on education. This may not be the case in impoverished minority cultures. In fact, some minority parents have become disillusioned by education. This attitude can carry over into the attitudes of their children, which makes teaching them very difficult.

How do cultural assimilation and cultural pluralism differ?

Teachers have widely differing attitudes about the education of minority students. Some are proponents of *cultural assimilation,* the view that America is a melting pot and that the job of the schools is to foster the development of similar cultural patterns and lifestyles, regardless of the cultural background of the students. Cultural-assimilation extremists would actually deny the importance of cultural diversity and fail to recognize its worth. Most members of minority groups find such positions offensive.

The more widely accepted view is called *cultural pluralism.* Those who endorse this concept acknowledge that there is no single "model American" and recognize the unique contributions that different cultural groups make to enrich our society. As Baca and Chinn (1982, p. 38) point out, "The teacher who supports the concept of cultural pluralism is more prone to recognize individual needs and differences among culturally diverse children and more likely to work toward providing for their needs appropriately."

Teaching Practices

What competencies should special education teachers have to teach culturally different students?

The topic of multicultural education is so important that the National Council for Accreditation of Teacher Education (NCATE) adopted a standard in 1979 requiring a multicultural component in all teacher education programs. Bessant-Byrd (1981, pp. 94–103) proposed that people preparing to teach minority students in special education programs should be able to do the following:

- Demonstrate knowledge of the role of a value system and evaluate its influence on behavior.
- Demonstrate knowledge of the philosophy of various cultures and exhibit an interest in expanding that knowledge.
- Use relevant information and materials characteristic of both traditional and contemporary lifestyles of various cultures.
- Understand different patterns of human growth and development within and between cultures.
- Recognize potential cultural and linguistic biases in the composition, administration, and interpretation of existing assessment instruments.
- Demonstrate the ability to provide a flexible learning environment that meets the individual needs of learners from various culture groups.

Language Differences

How should teachers deal with language differences in students?

Perhaps the most serious consequences occur when students and school personnel from different cultural backgrounds have language differences. When exceptional students speak a foreign language, it may be necessary to provide bilingual special education programs. In other cases, students' language patterns may differ from the standard middle-class language used in schools. When this happens, there is considerable potential for difficulties to arise. Taylor (1973) suggested some questions a teacher should consider when dealing with the language of some African American students:

- Is language used to make inaccurate statements about cultures and to miseducate children?
- What is the mismatch between the language accepted by schools and the language that a substantial portion of African American children bring to schools?
- What is the impact of language diversity on the performance of African American children on standardized tests?
- How does language diversity affect the attitudes of teachers?
- Is an awareness of language diversity reflected in educational materials?
- [To what extent are] inaccurate diagnoses . . . related to an ignorance of the unique linguistic features of large numbers of African Americans?

In summary, it is important to realize that when a child's cultural orientation differs from that of the school's personnel, the potential for a cultural conflict exists. When such conflicts occur, the child is usually the loser.

You may want to review the work of Omark and Erickson (1983), the special issue of *Exceptional Children* (vol. 56, no. 2, 1989), and the work of Baca and Almanza (1991) for additional information about bilingual special education programs. Further discussion of children with limited English proficiency is provided in the final section of this chapter, which deals with at-risk students.

PROBE 2-4   Cultural Diversity

1. T F   Minority children are overrepresented in programs for children with disabilities.
2. A procedure that has promise for testing children from diverse cultures is known as
   _____ _____ .
3. What is the triple jeopardy that minority students with disabilities frequently find themselves in?
4. Select the preferred attitude toward cultural differences:
   a. Cultural assimilation   b. Cultural pluralism
5. T F   The National Council for Accreditation of Teacher Education requires that all teacher education programs provide multicultural education.
6. The most serious consequences for culturally different students occur when their _____ differs from that used in the schools.

STUDENTS AT RISK

You should be able to explain factors associated with students who have been identified as being at risk and the implications that such children have for special education practices.

The following quotation was taken from the foreword to the Council for Exceptional Children (CEC) *Mini-Library on Exceptional Children at Risk* (1991):

> Many of today's pressing social problems, such as poverty, homelessness, drug abuse, and child abuse, are factors that place children and youth at risk in a variety of ways. There is a growing need for special educators to understand the risk factors that students must

face and, in particular, the risks confronting children and youth who have been identified as exceptional. A child may be at risk *due to* a number of quite different phenomena,
such as poverty or abuse. Therefore, the child may be at risk *for* a variety of problems,
such as developmental delays; debilitating physical illnesses or psychological disorders;
failing or dropping out of school; being incarcerated; or generally having an unreward-
ing, unproductive adulthood. Compounding the difficulties that both the child and the
educator face in dealing with these risk factors is the unhappy truth that a child may
have more than one risk factor, thereby multiplying his or her risk and need.

Many questions can be raised about students who are at risk, including the following:

- What factors might cause students to be at risk?
- How many students are at risk?
- What are the responsibilities of special educators to at-risk students?

This section will provide a brief review of information related to these questions. As with many
of the other issues raised in this chapter, however, it is often not possible to provide definitive
answers because of our lack of knowledge and the absence of research evidence on the topics
under question.

Abuse and Neglect

Child abuse or neglect is harm that is done to children by the willful behavior of their parents,
guardians, or caregivers (Garbarino, 1987). Such harm can include physical and mental injury,
sexual abuse or exploitation, and negligent treatment or maltreatment.

How widespread is the problem of child abuse and neglect?

It is estimated that approximately 1 million children are the victims of abuse or neglect
each year (National Center on Child Abuse and Neglect, 1988). Such estimates may be low,
however, with many cases going unreported. In addition, prevalence figures may vary according to factors such as misinterpretation of injuries by medical personnel, reluctance of
professionals to report abuse, interpretation of reporting laws and regulations, and parents not
taking their abused children for medical treatment. Psychological maltreatment is rarely
reported.

Little reliable information is available about the prevalence of children with disabilities
who have been the victims of child abuse and neglect. Warger, Tewey, and Megivern (1991)
summarized the literature on the topic and reported that there were disproportionate percentages of children with disabilities in groups of children who were identified as being abused.
For example, in groups that were studied, they reported that between 8 percent and 43 percent
had mental retardation, 29 percent had abnormal social behavior, and 25 percent had physical
disabilities.

Although children with disabilities do not appear to be at higher risk for abuse (West,
Leconte, & Cahn, 1988), some factors may serve to place such children at risk for abuse. Warger
et al. (1991) cite factors such as being less able to physically defend themselves, being less able
to articulate incidents of abuse, being reluctant to report abusive incidents for fear of losing
needed care or support, and lacking the ability to differentiate between appropriate and
inappropriate physical or sexual contacts. Some forms of violent abuse can also cause disabilities, such as brain damage, mental retardation, impaired growth, and blindness.

Child abusers come from all socioeconomic levels and all racial, ethnic, and religious
groups (Mullins, 1986). Although little is known about the factors that cause child abuse, it
does appear that child abusers tend to have been abused themselves by their parents (Zirpoli,
1990).

What are the legal
responsibilities of
teachers who
suspect abuse or
neglect?

Educators have a legal responsibility in all states to report suspected cases of child abuse or neglect to appropriate authorities. Additional information about legal responsibilities and how to report abuse and neglect are provided by Warger et al. (1991) and in Chapter 11 of this text, which deals in greater detail with physical and health-related disabilities.

Substance Abuse

It has been reported that, of the industrialized nations, the United States has the highest rate of substance (i.e., drug and alcohol) abuse among high school students and young adults (Johnston, O'Malley, & Bachman, 1988). It is difficult to establish a causal relationship between substance abuse and being at risk. One could speculate that substance abuse puts individuals at risk, while others could claim that other factors (e.g., poverty, peer pressure, emotional instability) cause a person to be a substance abuser and also to be at risk. At this time, it appears that the most defensible conclusion is that there are correlates between substance abuse and being at risk.

In reviewing the literature on the topic, Leone (1991) reported that a number of studies have found strong associations among alcohol and drug abuse, school failure, low commitment to school, absenteeism, accelerated school dropout, juvenile delinquency, family conflict, and personal problems. Such variables are related to the personal competence and abilities of the substance abuser. Leone (1991) went on to claim that the context in which the substance abuser functioned was also important. He cited factors such as peer use, family use, age at initial use, socioeconomic status, gender, and attachment to social institutions such as schools and churches as also being related to substance abuse and the danger of being at risk.

A similar relationship seems to exist among substance abusers in the special education population. Such a conclusion was drawn by Brown, Ridgely, Pepper, Levine, and Ryglewicz (1989), who concluded that there was a relationship (but not necessarily a causal one) between young adults with behavior or emotional disturbance and substance abusers. Similar findings have been reported among students with learning disabilities (Fox & Forbing, 1991), traumatic brain injury (Jones, 1989), and those with spinal cord injuries (Heinemann, Doll, & Schnoll, 1989).

What can school
personnel do about
substance abuse?

School personnel who come into contact with special education students must recognize at least four issues. The first is that some special education students use alcohol and other drugs, just as their counterparts in regular education do (Moore & Polsgrove, 1991). A second is that some disabilities can obscure the use and abuse of controlled substances (Fox & Forbing, 1991). A third is that professionals may contribute to the problem by not dealing head-on with suspected substance abuse (Johnson, 1988). And, finally, professionals need to realize that substance abuse treatment services for students with disabilities are not well developed.

Leone (1991) recommends that persons who provide services to special education students be concerned with prevention, referral, and reentry. He further recommends that such individuals educate themselves about the drug culture in their community, learn when and how to discuss problems with parents or guardians, and refer students to treatment programs, as necessary.

What effect can
substance abuse
have during
pregnancy?

Before leaving the topic, it is important to note that babies born to mothers who were substance abusers are also included in the at-risk category. Vincent, Poulsen, Cole, Woodruff, and Griffith (1991) reviewed the research on this population and concluded that the effect of maternal substance abuse on their children is unclear. As with children and young adults who are substance abusers, in most cases it is unclear whether the substance abuse caused a problem with the child or whether external factors, such as poor prenatal care or poor nutrition, placed the child at risk for developmental delays.

There appear to be some exceptions, however. It seems clear that alcohol abuse by the mother can contribute to fetal alcohol syndrome and fetal alcohol effects. (More information about these conditions will be provided in Chapter 12.) In fact, it has been estimated that 5 percent of all birth defects are associated with prenatal exposure to alcohol, and that alcohol abuse is the leading cause of mental retardation in the United States (Streissguth, Sampson, & Barr, 1989). Similarly, between 2 and 17 percent of children born to mothers who used cocaine during pregnancy will display congenital malformations at birth (Burkett, Yasin, & Palow, 1990).

Although the research appears to be somewhat inconclusive, there does appear to be enough evidence to prompt the conclusion that women should avoid the use of all nonprescription drugs and any amount of alcohol during pregnancy. Obviously, it is incumbent upon special educators to educate their students of child-bearing age about the dangers of substance abuse.

Students with Limited English Proficiency

Students with limited English proficiency (LEP) will continue to make up a greater proportion of our school-age children. Often, such students underachieve in regular classes and are misdiagnosed as having learning disabilities (Carrasquillo, 1991). In addition, even when an appropriate diagnosis is made for those with disabilities, they often do not receive appropriate educational services, which should include bilingual, multicultural, or English as a second language (ESL) instruction (Baca, 1990).

How many students with LEP are there?

It is estimated that there are approximately 1 million students in the United States with LEP who could qualify for special education services (Baca & Cervantes, 1989). Such children are often referred to as *culturally and linguistically different exceptional* (CLDE) students (Baca, 1990; Carrasquillo & Baecher, 1991).

Baca and Almanza (1991) have surveyed the literature on CLDE students and have made a number of suggestions for meeting their needs. They recommend prereferral intervention (described earlier in this chapter) in an attempt to devise instructional strategies that can be implemented within the context of the regular classroom environment. Second, they call for psychological, language, and educational assessment procedures that are more realistically attuned to the needs and characteristics of the children. Third, they propose the use of instructional strategies that, among other things, take into account the cultural and language backgrounds of the students. These authorities note that greater use of bilingual teachers is critical for success with these students.

Readers interested in this topic should examine the work of Baca and Almanza (1991), who provide additional useful suggestions for working with this population.

Rural and Remote Areas

While the dropout rate for children in American schools is around 20 percent, it has been estimated that the average dropout rate for rural schools may be between 40 and 50 percent (Phelps & Prock, 1991). Helge (1990) conducted a national survey on at-risk students and concluded that rural children fared worse than nonrural children on 34 of 39 comparisons that she made. In addition, students with disabilities who were at risk fared worse than those without disabilities.

It appears that rural and remote areas with low-density populations have disproportionate percentages of children from poor families. Such communities often have large numbers of non-English-speaking migrant workers, and many are composed of minorities, such as might be found in predominantly black communities in the South or on Native American reservations (Helge, 1991).

There are also significant problems in delivering high-quality educational services in rural and remote areas. The great distances, sparse and scattered populations, unwillingness of highly trained personnel to live in remote areas, lack of good medical services, and poor financial bases all can combine to raise the number of at-risk children. Cultural factors, such as rugged individualism and negative attitudes about the value of education, also can serve as barriers to the delivery of services.

What factors can influence the delivery of services in rural areas?

In attempting to deliver educational services, it is important to remember that no single model is appropriate for all rural and remote areas. Service delivery systems must be designed specifically for a particular area. Helge (1991) identified factors that must be considered, including population density, geographic barriers, climatic barriers, language spoken, cultural diversity, economy, available personnel, and nature of the children to be served.

Communication satellites have been used successfully to beam instructional television programs to schools in rural and remote areas. Such programs have been used to provide direct instruction, such as advanced placement physics, to gifted students and in-service training for special education teachers.

In the actual delivery of services, Helge (1991) cited a variety of approaches that have been successful. These include using noneducation personnel, such as mail carriers and county extension agents, to assist in facilitating planning; establishing a rapport with community leaders prior to attempting to develop and implement programs; and using technology such as citizens band radio, videotapes, satellite transmission, and teleconferencing. It is clear that many logistical problems exist in the delivery of educational services to rural and remote areas. Considerable creativity is required in meeting the needs of at-risk children in such locations.

Other Factors Placing Children at Risk

There are other circumstances under which children and youth with disabilities can be considered to be at risk. However, space limitations preclude further discussion of those. Interested readers may want to explore information about aggressive and violent children (Simpson, Miles, Walker, Ormsbee, & Downing, 1991), those who are depressed or suicidal (Guetzloe, 1991), dropouts from special education programs (MacMillan, 1991), children who are homeless (Heflin & Rudy, 1991), pregnant teens and children of parents with disabilities (Muccigrosso, Scavarda, Simpson-Brown, & Thalacker, 1991), and those in juvenile correction facilities (Nelson, Rutherford, & Wolford, 1987).

PROBE 2-5   Students at Risk

1. T   F   Child abusers come primarily from lower socioeconomic classes.
2. Approximately how many children are abused or neglected each year?
3. What is the special education teacher's legal responsibility when she or he suspects a case of child abuse or neglect?
4. T   F   There is little direct evidence that the use of alcohol during pregnancy can lead to birth defects, including mental retardation.
5. List four things special education teachers should do when dealing with substance abuse among their students.
6. The acronym CLDE stands for _____.
7. Describe two approaches that appear to be particularly useful for providing services to rural and remote areas.

SUMMARY

1. Most students assigned to special education services are not identified until after they start to attend school.
2. Both norm-referenced and criterion-referenced tests are used to assess children for purposes of identification and instruction.
3. Poor educational decisions are often made about children on the basis of assessment information from tests with poor reliability and validity and inappropriate norms.
4. In addition to test results, teachers should use other techniques, such as direct observation and samples of children's work, in making instructional decisions.
5. Assigning labels to exceptional children can lead to improper practices and should be avoided whenever possible.

6. Deinstitutionalization and mainstreaming are efforts to provide opportunities and environments similar to those that are normal for people without disabilities.

7. Exceptional children are educated in a variety of environments, including regular classrooms, resource rooms, special schools, residential facilities, homes, and hospitals. It is best to place the child in the least restrictive educational environment that meets the child's needs.

8. When placing a special education student in a regular class for a portion of the school day, it is important that the student be able to work at the same level as some of the other students in the class, work without much extra effort on the part of the teacher, handle the routine of the regular class, stay on task, and adapt socially.

9. Appropriate attitudes among teachers and principals toward mainstreaming are as important as the actual teaching competencies needed for successful mainstreaming.

10. An individualized education program must be developed for every child enrolled in a publicly supported special education setting.

11. Computers can be used effectively to assist in the development of IEPs.

12. Special educators should be particularly sensitive to the unique characteristics and needs of exceptional children from diverse cultures.

13. Among the students who may be considered at risk are those who are abused or neglected, are substance abusers, have limited English proficiency, or are from rural and remote areas.

TASK SHEET 2   Issues in Special Education

Select one of the following and perform the assigned tasks.

Assessment Observation

Get in touch with a school psychologist or the director of a special education diagnostic facility in your community and ask if you can observe the administration of a psychological or educational test. (You may have some difficulty with this because of right-to-privacy regulations. Some agencies have observation facilities that permit unobtrusive observation. Agency policies may preclude such activities, however.) Record your observations and prepare a three-page report that describes what you observed and your reactions to the visit.

Professional Interview

Arrange to visit a school principal, special education teacher, director of special education, diagnostician, or school psychologist. Inquire about the topics that were discussed in this chapter. In a three-page report, answer the following questions:

1. With whom did you talk and what did you ask the person?
2. What were the person's reactions to the issues you raised?
3. What problems did the person encounter in implementing special education programs?
4. What did you learn from this experience?

Interview with a Parent

If possible, visit with a parent who has gone through the IEP process. Ask the parent to describe his or her experience and reactions. Find out if the parent felt that he or she was permitted sufficient input in the development of the IEP. In a three-page paper, describe your interview and your personal reactions.

Library Study

Locate three articles in the library related to the issues raised in this chapter. Write a one-page abstract of each, concluding with a paragraph about your reactions to the article. Here are the names of some journals in which you can find articles about these topics:

Exceptional Children
Exceptionality
Journal of Special Education
Journal of Special Education Technology
Remedial and Special Education
Teacher Education and Special Education
Teaching Exceptional Children

Design Your Own Field Experience

If you know of a unique experience you can have that is related to the topics covered in this chapter, or if you do not want to do any of the listed options, discuss your alternatives with your instructor and complete the task that you both agree on.

Tim is enrolled in a resource room for students with learning disabilities. He uses a computer as part of his spelling instruction. His teacher has selected a group of five words for him to learn. Using a speech synthesizer, the computer pronounces the word for Tim to spell. If he doesn't know how to spell the word, he waits five seconds and the computer spells it for him. He then practices the correct spelling by typing the word on the keyboard. Gradually, Tim memorizes the spelling of the word and is able to spell it without having to wait for the correct answer. The computer keeps track of his responses. After he has spelled it correctly on three consecutive days, the computer only presents the word for review. The computer program permits Tim to learn his spelling words while making a minimum number of errors.

Claire was injured in an automobile accident and was paralyzed from the neck down. She also lost her ability to speak. Claire uses a special device to help her communicate with others: a small, pen-shaped device that emits an infrared light beam and is attached to the temple on her eyeglasses. By moving her head, she can aim the light beam at different sensors on a traylike device that is attached to the arms of her wheelchair. The sensors select words and phrases that have been stored in the device, which then "speaks" them.

Melissa is 11 years old and was born with multiple physical impairments. A mechanical ventilator is required to help her breathe. She is fed through a gastrostomy tube inserted into her stomach and a saline solution is injected into her lungs through a tracheostomy tube in her neck. Mucus is suctioned from her lungs to facilitate her breathing. A healthcare professional tends to her physical needs and monitors her vital signs. Melissa is very bright and is mastering all subjects typically taught to students of her age.

José is in a class for children with severe developmental disabilities. His teacher, Ms. Demeaner, is teaching him to wash his hands. She says, "Wash your hands," and waits five seconds. José picks up the toothbrush. She says, "No. Wash your hands. Turn the water on," and waits five seconds. José turns the water on and receives praise for doing so. She says, "Wash your hands," and waits five seconds. José doesn't respond. Ms. D. says, "Wash your hands," and then models the correct response by washing her hands and waits five seconds. José touches the faucet. Ms. D. says, "No, wash your hands," and physically prompts José's response by grasping his hands and guiding him through the motion of washing them. She then praises him. This sequence is repeated several times over a period of several sessions. Gradually, José washes his hands earlier in the sequence of instructions. Eventually, he learns to respond correctly to the teacher's first request to wash his hands.

3

Technology in Special Education

A. Edward Blackhurst and Donald P. Cross

The field of special education has benefited greatly over the years from advances in technology. For example, the development of the audiometer permitted a more accurate evaluation of hearing; the Perkins brailler enabled quick transcription of braille symbols for people who are blind; programmed instruction enhanced the learning of students experiencing difficulty with academic subjects; machines that can produce speech sounds have helped facilitate communication with children who cannot talk; systematic approaches to classroom management have reduced problems encountered by students with behavior disorders; and specially designed keyboards have enabled people with physical disabilities to use the typewriter. These are only a few of the many benefits of technology.

In recent years, advances in knowledge and electronics—particularly computers—have had a significant impact on meeting the needs of children and adults with disabilities. These advances are being applied in many different ways, several of which are reflected in the vignettes at the beginning of this chapter. Tim's story illustrates the use of technology to facilitate education. Applications such as Tim's are referred to as **instructional technology.** Claire is using technology to enable her to communicate with others. Her application falls into the category of **assistive technology.** Melissa requires technology to keep her alive. Children such as Melissa are sometimes referred to as being **technology dependent.** After reading the vignette about José, you may have wondered why it was included in a chapter about technology. José's story reflects that fact that very precise, systematic approaches to teaching represent a *technology of teaching.*

Although there have been many technological advances, the potential that technology has for improving special education services and the quality of life of exceptional people has yet to be fully realized. It is becoming increasingly evident that special educators and related professional personnel need to be aware of and know how to use various technologies if they are to be maximally effective in helping exceptional children. This chapter will provide a foundation for the understanding of technology and its ramifications for special education programs. Concepts related to the technology of teaching, instructional technology, and

What is
instructional
technology?

assistive technology will be presented. Additional information about the use of technology to facilitate health care will be provided in Chapter 11.

There is considerable confusion about the terms *technology, instructional technology,* and *educational technology* (Gentry, 1991). Many people equate the term *technology* with hardware, such as audiovisual equipment, teaching machines, and computers. However, the Commission on Instructional Technology (1970) pointed out in its report to the president and Congress that technology is much broader than the use of hardware and software:

> Instructional technology is a systematic way of designing, carrying out, and evaluating the total process of learning and teaching in terms of specific objectives, based on research in human learning and communication, and employing a combination of human and nonhuman resources to bring about more effective instruction. (p. 199)

At about the time the Commission released its findings, Haring (1970) reviewed the application of instructional technology to special education design. He concluded:

> In the natural setting, educational technology is being applied in two ways: (1) through automated and nonautomated media for display and measurement as part of the task of instruction, and (2) as a set of procedures which systematizes instruction. (p. 25)

Gentry (1991) concluded that debate over the various terms will probably continue for a long time. In the absence of clear-cut definitions, we will take a very operational approach to technology terms and concepts in this chapter. We will first discuss systematic methods of instruction, which we will refer to as the *technology of teaching.* We will then focus on *instructional technology,* which will describe the applications of computers and related equipment in the curriculum (keeping in mind that these are not used in isolation from instructional methods). Next we will address *assistive technologies,* which deal with the use of assistive and adaptive devices that can help people with special needs improve their ability to function within their environment. (The differentiation between instructional technology and assistive technology that is presented here parallels the one evolving in federal legislation and funding of technology applications in special education at the time this book was written.) Finally, we will provide information about the knowledge and skills special education teachers should have to use technology.

THE TECHNOLOGY OF TEACHING

You should be able to describe how systematic approaches to instruction can enhance the education of exceptional children.

Three major types of systematic instruction will be summarized in this section: (1) direct instruction, (2) applied behavior analysis, and (3) competency-based instruction. These approaches are illustrative of what we call the technology of teaching. Although computers and related equipment can be used within the approaches described here, the focus is primarily upon the methodologies of instruction.

Direct Instruction

What are the
features of direct
instruction?

Direct instruction is a teaching method that uses a model-lead-test format in the presentation of material. The process is interactive and very systematic, with the teacher demonstrating new information (modeling), providing controlled student practice in using the information (leading), and then evaluating student mastery levels (testing).

In addition to modeling, leading, and testing, teachers apply a number of principles to guide their teaching behavior. A high degree of teacher activity in the instructional process is required. Teachers actively define instructional goals and make frequent presentations to the students. High levels of student involvement with academic learning tasks are required, so the teacher applies classroom management skills that will increase student involvement with academic tasks and decrease off-task behaviors. Material is presented in small units, and teachers use a number of cues and signals to help focus students' attention on what is to be learned. Students are given many opportunities to respond, and they receive considerable feedback about the correctness of their responses. Instruction is designed to provide a high level of student success. The DISTAR reading materials provide a good example of the application of the principles of direct instruction (Englemann & Stearns, 1973).

Direct instruction is a very systematic way of teaching, but it should not be used for teaching all subjects. It is particularly effective in teaching basic skills in reading and math, but it would be inappropriate for teaching such topics as art, social studies, or inquiry skills. According to Peterson (1979), direct instruction is particularly appropriate for students who have difficulty learning. More information about direct instruction can be found in the work of Becker (1986), Becker and Carnine (1981), Carnine, Silbert, and Kameenui (1990), and Engelmann and Carnine (1982).

This teacher is using direct instruction with her student. She is using a signal to direct and hold the student's attention while she provides instruction.

Applied Behavior Analysis

How do teachers use applied behavior analysis?

One of the most promising instructional technologies to evolve during the 1970s and 1980s was **applied behavior analysis.** This is a structured, systematic approach to teaching and behavior management that employs direct observation and charting of student behavior. Teachers who use applied behavior analysis precisely analyze the tasks they want their students to learn, break these tasks down into small units of instruction, carefully sequence their teaching, use systematic reinforcement procedures, and continuously monitor student performance.

In teaching a student how to tell time, for example, the teacher studies the different tasks that a student must learn, such as identifying the numbers from 1 to 12, differentiating between the hour and minute hands, counting by fives to 60, and so on. Those tasks that the student can perform are determined and recorded. Instruction then follows the sequence selected by the teacher, with care being taken to reward correct responses. Progress is recorded on the student's record in order to evaluate the effectiveness of instruction. This also provides feedback to the teacher about whether a change in instructional procedures is necessary in the event that those being used are ineffective.

Applied behavior analysis is a very powerful instructional tool in the hands of a well-trained educator. It can be used to improve academic skills in direct instruction, to develop appropriate social behavior, and to reduce inappropriate behavior in students. Additional information about this topic is provided in Chapters 12, 13, 14, and 15 of this text, which deal with individual differences in learning and behavior. Those interested in reading more about applied behavior analysis should review the work of Alberto and Troutman (1990) and Wolery, Bailey, and Sugai (1988).

Competency-Based Instruction

In the early 1970s, a movement was initiated to design instruction that was focused on student outcomes. The idea was to define the specific knowledge, skills, and attitudes that students should emerge with upon completion of instruction. Once those competencies were identified, very specific instructional programs focusing on their attainment were designed and implemented. This movement was called the competency-based instruction (CBI) movement. Although CBI has relevance for all learners in a variety of instructional settings, perhaps its strongest advocates have appeared among those who are involved in the preparation of teachers.

Competency-based teacher education (CBTE) is a technology of teaching that is based on several principles: (1) competencies that are required for any professional preparation program should be publicly stated; (2) specific objectives for the various educational experiences in a teacher education program should be explained and the criteria for evaluating when these objectives have been met should be made clear to students; (3) when possible, alternative learning activities should be made available to students, and time for completing instructional activities should be variable while level of achievement is kept constant; and (4) both instructors and students should share accountability for performance. More detailed information about CBTE can be found in an earlier work by one of the authors of this chapter (Blackhurst, 1977).

What has been the impact of CBTE?

CBTE is one of the most significant forces to affect the preparation of special education teachers in many years. A number of colleges and universities have completely redesigned their teacher preparation programs as a result of studying the competencies needed by special education teachers and the curriculum that is required to develop those competencies.

You will notice that this textbook incorporates a number of the principles associated with CBTE technology. At the beginning of each major section, we have listed a competency we want our readers to develop. We have also placed questions in the margins of the text to emphasize some of the more important objectives associated with each competency. Probes are provided to test whether the objectives and competencies are being met, and criteria, in the form of correct answers to the probes, appear at the end of the text. In addition, we have listed some alternative activities to facilitate learning in the task sheets at the end of each chapter. Additional examples include the competency list later in this chapter (Figure 3-8) and the procedures that are described for designing a professional development program in Chapter 7.

The procedures described in this section represent only a few of the systematic approaches to instruction that could be included in a discussion of the technology of teaching. For example, procedures such as concept teaching through the use of examples and non-examples and adjusting instruction through error analysis (Kameenui & Simmons, 1990) could be included. Teaching students how to use learning strategies (Deshler & Schumaker, 1986) represents another very important systematic approach to instruction. Response-prompting procedures are particularly useful when teaching students with moderate to severe disabilities. The vignette about José at the beginning of this chapter illustrates one of these, called the "system of least prompts" (Wolery, Ault, & Doyle, 1992). Response-prompting procedures are now being applied to the instruction of students with mild disabilities (e.g., Stevens & Schuster, 1991). Unfortunately, space limitations preclude a full explanation of these and other methodologies. However, if you are planning to major in special education, you will receive additional information about them in courses on instructional methods for teaching exceptional children.

PROBE 3-1   The Technology of Teaching

1. T   F   It is important to include hardware and software when you use direct instruction.
2. The three steps in using direct instruction are _____, _____, and _____.
3. T   F   Applied behavior analysis can be used to teach both academic and social skills.
4. Teachers who use applied behavior analysis systematically provide _____ when their students make correct responses.
5. CBTE stands for _____.
6. List three characteristics of a competency-based instruction program.

INSTRUCTIONAL TECHNOLOGY

You should be able to describe how technology can be integrated into the educational programs of students enrolled in special education programs.

The procedures described in the previous section are primarily methodological in nature. Although computers and related equipment can be used in conjunction with those methods, they are not really necessary. This section of the chapter provides information about the integration of computers and related equipment into instructional programs for students. Keep in mind, however, that the application of hardware and software is never done in isolation. Rather, it is done within the context of the curriculum that has been designed to meet the individual needs of the students. In this context, technology is viewed as a tool to facilitate instruction.

Designing Instructional Technology Applications

How is the IEP related to technology?

In one bold move, the implementation of PL 94-142 placed instructional technology at center stage. The major operational component of PL 94-142 is the individualized education program (IEP), which was described in Chapter 2. While the term *program* can be used in a variety of ways in education, the definition used in PL 94-142 resembles the concept of program developed in instructional technology in the late 1960s (Corey, 1967). In fact, the process for designing IEPs was developed in accordance with the principles of instructional technology.

Where does technology fit into the curriculum?

Figure 3-1 illustrates where technology applications fit into the instructional program for any given student. The activities in Figure 3-1 are organized in a flow chart that illustrates the instructional process, which evolves from the IEP. Note that the first step is to identify the characteristics of the child. This is done through formal and informal assessment, as described in Chapter 2. Goals and objectives for instruction are then specified. Next, the teacher decides on the instructional strategies and management procedures that are most appropriate for meeting the goals and objectives. Not until after this activity has occurred are decisions made about the instructional media, materials, and technologies that should be used. The entire program is then implemented, evaluated, and revised if it is not effective. (Take a moment to trace the *yes* and *no* arrows to see how this model can guide the teacher in making decisions about what to change if evaluation shows that teaching is not being effective. This is another example of the systematic approach to instruction that was described in the first section of this chapter.)

The way that we are viewing instructional technology in this section of the chapter is similar to the way that educational media are conceptualized: namely, as the nonhuman resources that can be used for instructional purposes. Such a conceptualization has three components: hardware (the equipment), software (the materials, such as computer programs, that are used with the hardware), and content (the messages transmitted by the software and hardware).

Most people are familiar with the use of devices such as film projectors, tape recorders, slide projectors, and television in education, so these will not be reviewed here. Several other technologies, however, have significant implications for special education, which will be highlighted.

Computer-Assisted Instruction (CAI)

No technological innovation has more potential for improving the quality of life and education for exceptional people than the microcomputer. Microcomputers, and the programs and equipment that can be used with them, have already been applied in many different ways in special education, and new applications are continually being developed. We will describe some of the ways they are being used in both general and special education.

DRILL AND PRACTICE. New concepts are usually not presented to students when the computer is used for drill and practice. Such programs generally permit practice and reinforcement of concepts that are already learned or are in the process of being learned.

What is the major criticism of computers in education?

Perhaps the greatest single criticism of microcomputers in education is that their use is too frequently restricted to routine drill and practice. Unfortunately, this criticism is often justified. On the other hand, *meaningful* drill and practice used *appropriately* are an important part of the educational process with many children, and they can be delivered very effectively by computer.

FIGURE 3-1   **Decision Model for Diagnostic Teaching**

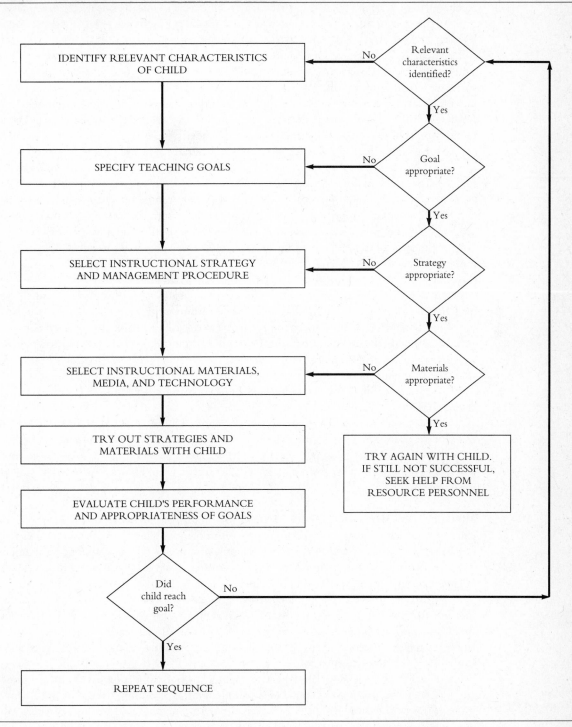

Source: Adapted from G.P. Cartwright and C.A. Cartwright (1972). Gilding the Lily: Comments on the Training-based Model. *Exceptional Children, 39*(3), 231–234.

One assumption about teaching children who have learning difficulties is that repetition facilitates their learning. A major challenge facing special education teachers who must use drill and practice with their students is to provide meaningful activities that contribute to learning and yet are varied enough to keep their students motivated.

Microcomputers have some unique qualities that make them particularly well suited for drill and practice. Taking an anthropomorphic view, we could say that computers have infinite patience, provide opportunities for intense on-task engagement, offer varied and novel tasks, provide feedback and correction, and do not get frustrated with incorrect responses. In fact, for many drill and practice applications, it is quite likely that they can perform better than teachers or traditional drill activities such as worksheets.

Some highly motivating drill and practice programs in arcade game formats are being developed. Students seem to enjoy playing these games, which require them to work math problems or perform language arts activities. Some of these are especially useful for those students who have limited physical abilities because they can be operated by pressing a single key on the computer keyboard. The teacher must be careful in selecting drill and practice programs for use with special education students, however. Programs with fancy sound and graphics may be distracting to some students. Some research indicates that "plain vanilla" programs may be more effective than those that have fancy sound and graphics (Gerber, 1990).

Why is the computer's ability to branch so important?

TUTORIAL. When the computer is used for tutorial purposes, new concepts are taught. Some drill and practice exercises might be included in a tutorial program, but the focus is on the initial teaching of concepts. One of the computer's real strengths, the ability to branch, can be used to advantage in tutorial programs. Branching is the process by which, on the basis of a student's response, the computer moves the student to the appropriate part of a program. For example, it might repeat a certain section or teach in a different way for concepts that have not been learned. Similarly, branching can be used to bypass portions of a program that a student has already mastered.

Many tutorial programs are being used in public schools. Care must be taken, however, to select programs carefully. Although the quality of tutorial software is improving considerably, a number of poorly designed programs are still on the market. LeBlanc, Hoko, Aangeenbrug, and Etzel (1985) provide an excellent list of criteria that should be considered when selecting software.

SIMULATION AND PROBLEM SOLVING. In simulation, the computer is used to model experiments or real-world events. Simulation or problem-solving programs sometimes resemble laboratory assignments. For example, a program might allow a student to manipulate variables in a theoretical science experiment and then observe the different results. Students are often given information and then required to use it to solve a particular problem.

For which children are computer simulations particularly beneficial?

Although simulation and problem-solving programs can benefit many types of students, they are especially valuable to gifted students. A number of interesting and very sophisticated simulation programs are beginning to appear in the educational market. These include simulations of nuclear disasters, election politics, strategic planning, science experiments, and the free enterprise system, to mention just a few.

When should the different types of software be used?

Selection of the appropriate type of computer software should be based on each student's **stage of learning** for the content under consideration. For example, students just beginning to learn the fives multiplication table are in the *acquisition* stage of learning. Teachers should use tutorial software for those students. When they master the fives table, they move into the *proficiency* stage of learning (sometimes called the *fluency* stage). At this point, the teacher should switch to drill and practice software to teach the students to respond quickly and accurately as the multiplication facts are presented.

These students are engaged in a collaborative learning activity in which a simulation program on the computer is being used.

It is important for students to be able to use information that they have learned in other contexts. This is called the *generalization* stage of learning. In this stage, the teacher would select a software program other than the one being used, but of the same general type, in order to determine whether the students can transfer the information learned in one program to another. (The teacher also would provide activities away from the computer to determine whether the students can transfer their learnings to different contexts.)

It is important for students to remember the things they have been taught. This is referred to as the *maintenance* stage of learning. A period of time after the students have mastered the multiplication tables, the teacher would again use drill and practice software to determine whether the students have remembered their math facts. If not, tutorial software again may be used as a remedial tool.

The final stage of learning is the *application* stage. In this stage the teacher might use simulation or problem-solving software to determine whether the students can apply their mastery of the fives table to other situations, such as word problems. Tutorial software programs may be used to actually teach the students how to apply the facts that they have mastered.

Knowledge of stages of learning and the different types of educational software appropriate for each is important for special education teachers. Without such knowledge, it is easy to make one of the most frequent errors in instructional applications of computers: namely, inappropriate selection of computer software. Too often, students are assigned the use of a software program that is not suitable for their stage of learning (e.g., using drill and practice instead of tutorial software during the acquisition stage).

Using Computers for Reinforcement

How can computers be used for reinforcement?

As noted earlier, a major area of interest to special educators is applied behavior analysis. Much research has been conducted on the use of reinforcement in learning. We know that positive reinforcement of desired responses will increase the likelihood of the recurrence of that response. Special education teachers must design ways to collect data about student performance to be used in making instructional decisions, develop ways to increase the frequency of positive reinforcement, and locate effective reinforcers.

Teachers can offer permission to use microcomputers and computer games as reinforcers for desired academic or social behavior. Polsgrove and Reith (1985) report that this is a useful application for some special education students. Care must be taken, however, to avoid using computers simply to keep students busy. Their use should be for some direct instructional purpose or as a reinforcer for some desired behavior.

Using Computers for Planning and Information Management

The implementation of PL 94-142 has placed many demands on public schools. Highly specific due process procedures must be followed in locating, testing, and placing students in special education programs. In addition, individualized education programs (IEPs) must be developed for each child who receives special education services. Detailed reports must be prepared to verify compliance with the federal law.

Several microcomputer programs (e.g., PennStar, 1987) can help school administrators manage such information, and others are being developed. A number of similar programs are also being developed to help maintain student records. Many school systems are designing their own data management systems, using data management programs that are available for general use.

Other programs, such as AimStar, developed by Hasselbring and Hamlett (1984), can be useful in the management of student information. AimStar accepts data about a child's performance and provides graphs that help the teacher decide when to change the instructional methods and materials being used with the child.

Expert systems are relatively new software programs that can also be valuable for decision-making purposes. Information, in the form of rules, is stored in expert system programs. For example, expert systems have been developed to assist people in making decisions about placing students in special education classes (Hofmeister & Ferrera, 1986).

Multimedia and Hypermedia

When teachers use a combination of equipment that presents information through text, graphics, sound, animation, or video, they are using multimedia with their students. For example, a program that uses slides and audiotapes would be considered a multimedia presentation, as would a videotape program that is controlled by a computer.

What is the potential of videodisc and CD-ROM technology?

Two relatively recent technologies that will have tremendous impact on education are videodiscs and CD-ROM disks. Videodisc systems present a dramatic change in storage capacity and flexibility over systems such as videotape and videocassette because they can store single images in addition to the typical moving pictures that we see on our television screens. It is possible to quickly find and play back a single image or a segment of a program recorded on the disc.

It is possible to store 54,000 single images, such as slides or photos of pages, on one side of a videodisc and be able to gain quick access to each of them. One side of a disc can store 30 minutes of video programming. A disc's visual images also can be stored with more than one audio track, which would greatly facilitate education for bilingual children. Several promising applications of videodisc technology with special education students have been explored (e.g., Browning, 1988; Hasselbring, 1990; Thorkildsen, Bickel, & Williams, 1979).

CD-ROM (Compact Disc, Read Only Memory) technology can store vast amounts of text, graphics, sound, data, or related information that can be retrieved when the CD-ROM drive is connected to a computer. CD-ROM discs are similar in size to audio CDs. Libraries are now providing access to large files of articles and other references that are stored on CD-ROM discs. A single, inexpensive CD-ROM can store the entire contents of a complete set of encyclopedias using only a small percentage of its available capacity.

Educational programs for teaching such diverse concepts as anatomy, foreign language vocabulary, American history, music appreciation, and literature have been developed (e.g., Apple Computer, 1988a; 1988b). In addition, exploratory adventure games can be useful either for recreational purposes or as a stimulus for creative writing exercises (e.g., The Manhole, 1988; Cosmic Osmo, 1989). We will see increasing use of videodisc and CD-ROM technologies in special education programs in future years.

What is hypermedia?

The term *hypermedia* refers to systems whereby people can use computers to control access to text, graphics, sound, and animated images. For example, during an American history unit, students may be able to use a computer to access information stored on a CD-ROM disc. The students might select items from a menu that would allow them to see an animated view of the route that Lewis and Clark took during their expedition, select samples of music that was being played at that time, view sketches of various personalities of a particular period, watch a narrated presentation about the gold rush, examine historical timelines, or read relevant historical documents. In addition, the students may elect to have the information presented from the perspective of different types of people who were involved in the activities. Thus, the students could select "guides," such as pioneer women, Native Americans, slaves, merchants, or miners. The information presented to the students would then reflect historical events that had particular impact on that group of individuals (Visual Almanac, 1988).

The important concept in hypermedia programs is that they are under the control of the user. Students can select the information they want to retrieve, and they can navigate through the information in a variety of ways. This is most often done by using a computer's mouse device to click on different menus, buttons, or other navigational aids that appear on the computer screen.

Hypermedia applications are beginning to be used in special education. Hasselbring (1990), for example, developed a story that paralleled one of the Indiana Jones adventure movies which had been transferred to a videodisc. If students reading the story encountered a word they did not understand, they could click on it. The word would be pronounced by the computer and a definition (which also could be read aloud by the computer) was displayed. In addition, a brief excerpt from the videodisc could be played to illustrate concepts associated with the word. The future will bring many more hypermedia applications in special education and teacher preparation programs.

Telecommunication Systems

How effective is instruction transmitted by telephone?

The most readily available telecommunications system is, of course, the nation's telephone system. This can be used to transmit lectures and data, conduct interviews and audio teleconferences, and perform many other functions. Telephone systems have been very useful in providing instruction to homebound students. Parker (1977) concluded that classroom instruction conducted by telephone is at least as effective as face-to-face instruction.

Inservice training has been effectively conducted by telephone (Hershey, 1977). Tawney (1977) demonstrated that telephones could be used to link various instructional devices located in the homes of infants with severe disabilities to a central computer control station. Computer-assisted instruction has also been transmitted over telephone lines.

Other telecommunications systems that have been used for educational purposes include open-circuit audio and video broadcast systems such as educational television and public radio. For special education, the best use of these media is the broadcast of programs that educate the public about exceptional people. The use of TV courses can also enhance teacher education. Donaldson and Martinson (1977) showed that video and audio programming also can influence adults' attitudes toward people with disabilities.

Although expensive to use, communications satellites have considerable potential for specialized communications. For example, the Council for Exceptional Children relayed portions of the First World Congress on Special Education from Scotland to the United States, enabling people who could not afford to attend the conference to participate in its activities from remote sites. One of the authors of this chapter directed a project in which a NASA satellite was used in conducting a conference among special educators separated by approximately 2500 miles. Other applications, such as remote diagnosis of physical problems by medical specialists and teleconferences on assistive technologies, have demonstrated that satellites can be used to eliminate the need for travel and to solve communications problems in unique ways.

What is SpecialNet?

GTE Educational Services maintains a very useful system for the dissemination and exchange of information. This service, called "SpecialNet," provides electronic bulletin boards for displaying information about a variety of topics and a system for contacting any individual subscriber or the entire membership of the network. What is unique about SpecialNet is that all of this is done electronically, using a computer connected to a telephone line. A number of states have developed their own telecommunications networks using SpecialNet. There have also been applications in which special education students in remote areas, such as Hawaii, have communicated with students in other parts of the world through SpecialNet. See the Technology in Action box for an example of how a teacher, Ms. Holmes, uses SpecialNet.

On some of her "electronic visits," Ms. Holmes enters information; on others she is primarily a recipient. Some days bring no information. The important thing to Ms. Holmes, however, is that SpecialNet enables her to exchange information easily with other teachers of deaf-blind children throughout the country. Through the bulletin board system, she also learns many things that improve her professional skills.

What trends are emerging in the use of instructional technology?

Although various types of technology, such as films and audiotapes, have been used in schools for many years, the use of computers is a relatively recent phenomenon and is growing dramatically. Those interested in applications of instructional technology, however, are just beginning to learn about the best ways to approach the use of computers for instruction. The earlier discussion about the use of different types of software according to the various stages of learning identifies a trend that is emerging; namely, applications of technology will be based more and more frequently on theories about what learning is and how it occurs.

A second trend is that instructional technology applications will have an empirical basis. That is, they will be based on the results of research studies that have generated data to support different instructional approaches. The vignette about Tim at the beginning of this chapter is a good illustration. The CAI program Tim is using to learn spelling is based on a particular theory of how students learn through application of an instructional procedure known as *constant time delay response prompt fading,* which research has shown to be effective in teaching spelling words (e.g., Stevens, Blackhurst, & Bott, 1991). We should expect to see many exciting new instructional technology hardware and software applications emerge as we move closer to the twenty-first century.

TECHNOLOGY IN ACTION

Libby Holmes teaches children who are both deaf and blind in a medium-sized school district in Indiana. Unlike many other teachers, she does not have colleagues to turn to for advice about different instructional approaches for her students or for support when she encounters difficulties. Thanks to SpecialNet, however, the frustration of her situation has been considerably reduced.

The principal of the school where she works has had a computer installed in the teachers' lounge. It is connected to a telephone line with a device called a modem. Twice a week, Ms. Holmes uses the computer to interact with SpecialNet. She simply loads a telecommunications computer program into the computer. It has been configured to automatically dial a telephone number that gives her access to the TELENET communications system. The computer uses a local telephone to avoid the long distance charges that normally would be involved in hooking into the SpecialNet computer, which is located in Virginia.

The software program also automatically logs her onto the SpecialNet system by providing her user name and a password that protects the confidentiality of any messages that might have been sent to her by others using the telecommunication network.

This message then appears: WELCOME TO TELEMAIL! YOUR LAST ACCESS WAS TUESDAY, FEBRUARY 24, AT 4:12 P.M. The computer informs her that there is a message for her from Lee McNulty, a teacher of deaf-blind children in San Francisco, who has been corresponding with her electronically since shortly after the school year began. Each had placed a message requesting information about instructional materials for deaf-blind children on one of the electronic bulletin boards that are available on SpecialNet. After seeing her request, Mr. McNulty left a message for Ms. Holmes, and they began corresponding about mutual problems and concerns. Several other teachers of deaf-blind children periodically communicate through this system, as well.

McNulty's message contains information about a new instructional game he has been using with his students. He includes the reference of a book that has a description of the game. Ms. Holmes presses a key on the keyboard and the reference is stored on disk so she can print it after she finishes her telecommunication session. She types a note to McNulty, expressing her appreciation for the information; also, she promises to send him some information on a new diagnostic test she is using after she has finished evaluating it.

Next, she types CHECK DEAFBLIND, which is the name of one of more than a dozen electronic message boards that deal with different special education topics. She has not checked this board for a week, so she types, SCAN SINCE FEB 17. Four items are listed as having been posted since that date. Each has its own number, the date posted, the name of the sender, a one-line description of the contents of the message, and the number of lines in the message.

Three of the messages don't appear to be relevant to her current interests, but message number 3 is labeled NEW PRODUCT ANNOUNCEMENT. She types READ 3 and the message appears. It lists ten new products for children with multiple disabilities, several of which potentially have some merit for her children. She stores the message on her computer disk. She then checks bulletin boards on Deafness, Multihandicapped, Assistive-Device, and Vision. Nothing else appears to be relevant, so she types BYE and the computer disconnects the telephone.

After hanging up, she commands the computer to print the information she had stored so she will have a paper copy of the message and the new product information. She was on-line a total of 13 minutes and found some very useful information.

PROBE 3-2   Instructional Technology

1. T F The next consideration after specifying goals for a student is to select the instructional technology that will be used.
2. In considering technology, hardware = _____; software = _____; and content = _____ .
3. T F Drill and practice software should not be used in special education programs.
4. During the acquisition phase of learning, _____ software should be used.
5. T F Plain software programs are often more effective than those that are rich in graphics.
6. Simulations can be particularly effective with _____ children.

7. Describe the stages of learning and explain what is happening in each.
8. Differentiate between multimedia and hypermedia.
9. _____ is a telecommunication system that has useful information for special educators.
10. Describe two trends that are emerging in the use of instructional technology.

ASSISTIVE TECHNOLOGY

You should be able to explain how assistive technologies can be used to facilitate the functioning of people with disabilities.

People with disabilities often experience difficulties coping with the demands that the environment places on them. For example, people with severe visual impairments may encounter problems in traveling from place to place. Those with hearing losses may have difficulty understanding information presented on television. Children with severe speech impairments may have difficulty communicating with others in school. Others with physical disabilities may be unable to control common appliances in their environment. Adults with severe learning disabilities may not be able to read printed materials required for them to perform their jobs.

Assistive and Adaptive Devices

It is possible to use a variety of devices and services to respond to needs such as the ones just described. Some devices help people with disabilities perform a given task. These are often called *assistive* devices. For example, a board with pictures on it may assist people who cannot talk, increasing their ability to communicate. Other devices change the environment or help the person to modify the environment. These are called *adaptive* devices. A switch that would allow control of different appliances from a wheelchair is an example of an adaptive device. Another is a ramp that could be used in place of steps for someone in a wheelchair.

What is assistive technology?

The two terms are frequently used as a single phrase when discussing the general topic (*assistive and adaptive devices*). In reality, many people use them interchangeably. The evolving trend is to use the term *assistive technology* to encompass both types of devices, plus the services associated with their use. We will use that terminology in this book.

As noted in Chapter 1, the potential of assistive technology was recognized through the enactment of PL 100-407, the Technology-Related Assistance for Individuals with Disabilities Act. The definition of assistive technology included in PL 100-407 was modified slightly in the federal regulations for the Individuals with Disabilities Education Act (PL 101-476) to make the definition more applicable to children with disabilities:

> Assistive technology means any item, piece of equipment or product system, whether acquired commercially off the shelf, modified, or customized, that is used to increase, maintain, or improve the functional capabilities of children with disabilities. (*Federal Register,* August 19, 1991, p. 41272)

The federal regulations go on to state that an array of services is included when considering applications of assistive technology. Such services include activities such as evaluation of a person's needs for assistive technology devices, purchasing or leasing assistive technology devices for people, designing and fabricating devices, coordinating services offered by those who provide assistive technology services, and providing training or technical assistance to a person who uses assistive technology, as well as to those who work with people who use assistive technology devices, such as teachers or employers.

To elaborate further on the definition: Assistive technologies include mechanical, electronic, and microprocessor-based equipment, nonmechanical and nonelectronic aids, specialized instructional materials, services, and strategies that people with disabilities can use either to (1) assist them in learning, (2) make the environment more accessible, (3) enable them to compete in the workplace, (4) enhance their independence, or (5) otherwise improve their quality of life. These may include commercially available or homemade devices that are specially designed to meet the idiosyncratic needs of a particular individual (Melichar & Blackhurst, 1992).

You may recall that the functional model presented in Chapter 1 listed a number of areas of human function in which people need to be able to perform in order to respond successfully to demands placed on them by the environment. Assistive technology devices and services can be used to enhance those functions. (Note how the functional model relates to the definition of assistive technology provided in the federal regulations cited above, which explicitly mention the improvement of "functional capabilities.") For your review, Figure 3-2 lists the functional areas associated with the model.

What is the assistive technology continuum?

Just as in the case of instructional technology, when many people think of assistive technology, they think primarily about computers or sophisticated electronic devices. However, it is important to realize that assistive technology applications can be viewed as a continuum that ranges from high-tech to "no-tech." Generally speaking, high-tech devices incorporate sophisticated electronics or computers. Medium-tech devices are relatively complicated mechanical devices, such as wheelchairs. Low-tech items are less sophisticated and can include adapted spoon handles, nontipping drinking cups, and Velcro fasteners. No-tech solutions are those that make use of procedures, services, and existing conditions in the

FIGURE 3-2   A Functional Approach to Exceptionality: Assistive Technology Applications

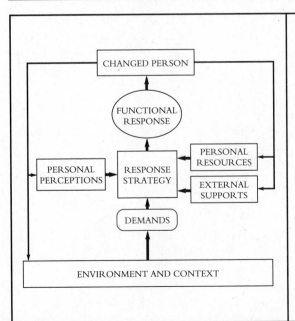

FUNCTIONS AIDED BY ASSISTIVE TECHNOLOGY

Assistive technology devices and services fall into the category of *External Supports.* They can be used to improve the person's ability to function in the following areas:

- *Existence*: Activities needed to support life.

- *Communication*: Reception, internalization, and expression of information.

- *Body Support and Positioning*: Procedures to stabilize, align, and support the position of the body.

- *Travel*: Moving horizontally, vertically, or laterally.

- *Environmental Adaptation*: Modifications required to make facilities accessible.

- *Learning, Education, and Rehabilitation:* Activities associated with school, preparing for work, and various therapies.

- *Sports, Leisure, and Recreation*: Activities associated with individual and group sports and the productive use of leisure time.

environment without the use of devices or equipment. These might include services such as physical or occupational therapy. They also might include the application of procedures that do not require special equipment, such as teaching a person with one arm to wedge a bowl into a kitchen drawer and hold it with the hip to facilitate mixing dough for cookies.

Many different devices are available to people with a wide array of disabilities to enhance their ability to function. Brief descriptions of just a few of these devices are provided here to give an idea about the scope of available products.

What devices are available to facilitate functioning?

EXISTENCE. Special devices such as modified eating utensils, dressing aids, and specially designed personal hygiene aids may be required for those who have difficulty with the motor movements necessary for such tasks. An example is the dorsal feeding splint that is illustrated in Figure 3-3. It provides assistance with independent feeding to the person who lacks wrist extension and flexion and who is unable to grasp. The dorsal feeding splint is structured to support the palm, wrist, and forearm. An 8-inch band of lightweight metal or rubber with soft underpadding extends lengthwise on the dorsal side of the individual's forearm; three adjustable leather or Velcro straps are attached to the band, winding around the user's palm, wrist, and mid-forearm. An adaptable utensil holder is usually inserted or otherwise attached to the palmar strap.

COMMUNICATION. Communication aids include closed-circuit television systems that magnify print for people who have difficulty seeing, television programs with special captions for people who are deaf, communication boards that use symbols to aid people who cannot talk, and speech synthesizers that electronically generate vocal speech. The vignette about Claire at the beginning of this chapter represents another form of communication aid. Devices such as these open new worlds for their users.

Numerous devices have been developed to aid those with visual impairments. A hand-held battery-powered calculator that speaks the name of each key as it is pressed is inexpensive and widely available. The Optacon converts printed materials into tactile images that can be read with the fingers, while the Kurzweil reader can convert print into spoken language. An

FIGURE 3-3   Dorsal Feeding Splint

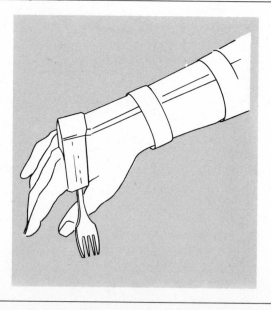

electronic "paperless braille" machine uses audiocassettes to store braille information, which is then converted into tactile images. A special tape recorder can compress speech so that people who are blind can listen to recorded materials at a faster-than-normal rate. These and other devices will be explained in greater detail in the chapter on visual impairments.

The automatic page turner illustrated in Figure 3-4 is an interesting and useful device that enables the person with impaired upper extremity function to turn magazine or book pages automatically. The device operates to turn pages with a slight momentary touch or movement of a sensitive switch mechanism by any part of the body.

BODY SUPPORT, ALIGNMENT, AND POSITIONING. Adapted seating, standing tables, seat belts, cushions and wedges to maintain posture, and devices to prompt trunk alignment may be needed by people who have difficulty sitting and standing or who have to maintain a particular position in order to operate different assistive devices. Also included are support harnesses, stabilizers, slings, and body protectors.

The institutional relaxation chair illustrated in Figure 3-5 allows the person with no sitting balance and a severely involved trunk area to sit comfortably. The chair may be adjusted to a 30-degree angle; the seat tilts to a full jackknifed position; the padded headrest is contoured; and the platform is on casters. These chairs are used in therapy units to accommodate patients whose disabilities are too severe to allow them to use a conventional chair or wheelchair.

TRAVEL AND MOBILITY. A wide array of items is included in this category, including hoists, wheelchairs, scooters, cycles, ambulators, walkers, crutches, and canes.

The standard rear-wheel-drive wheelchair, illustrated in Figure 3-6, provides mobility to the nonambulatory person who functions best in a seated position. Users may propel themselves independently by hand or be pushed by another person. The standard wheelchair is constructed of two light tubular side frames stiffened by cross bracing. Most models are collapsible. Large-diameter driving wheels on a fixed axle placed in the rear make negotiating curbs and curves an easier task. Small swivel wheels attached to the front uprights permit easy

FIGURE 3-4   Automatic Page Turner

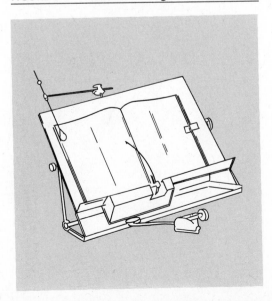

FIGURE 3-5   Institutional Relaxation Chair

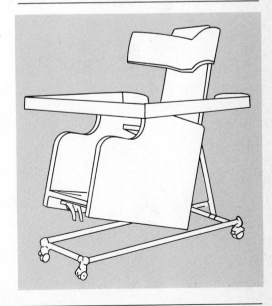

steering. The large wheels resemble bicycle wheels with narrow rims, spokes, and solid rubber tires. Hand rims for self-propulsion are slightly smaller in diameter and attach on the outside of the large wheels. The back and seat are made of smooth, foldable materials. The chair arms may be part of the side frame and may be equipped with clothing guards as well as armrests. An adjustable leg rest and hinged footrest assembly may be attached to the front uprights. Motorized wheelchairs are becoming increasingly available. Their use is often dependent upon the ability of the person with physical disabilities to access and accurately manipulate the power controls of the wheelchair.

ENVIRONMENTAL ADAPTATION. Computers are being used in conjunction with a variety of other devices to assist people with physical disabilities in adapting to their environment. Some of these devices facilitate physical functioning, while others provide control over the environment. For example, people confined to their beds can operate equipment such as television sets, telephones, and word processors through environmental controls. Driving aids are included in this category, as well as special fixtures, kitchen utensils, and appliances.

The drive control unit illustrated in Figure 3-7 consists of a hand lever, positioned on the left side and directly behind the steering wheel, that has been connected by long rods to the brake and accelerator. There are various types of mounting; some are attached to the steering column, others to the lower portion of the dashboard. Also located on the hand control is a headlight dimmer switch.

The hand control is operated by pushing it downward, toward the floor, and pulling it back toward the driver's lap to accelerate. In some models it is possible to brake and accelerate simultaneously, as would be necessary in starting on a hill.

Many devices are available to help people overcome physical disabilities. Special keyboards for typewriters and computers that permit operation with fewer keystrokes have been developed. Those who have poor hand and finger movement can use switches manipulated by other parts of their bodies to control devices. Switches have been designed to be controlled

FIGURE 3-6 **Standard Wheelchair**	FIGURE 3-7 **Drive Control Unit**

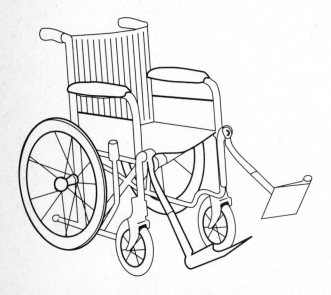

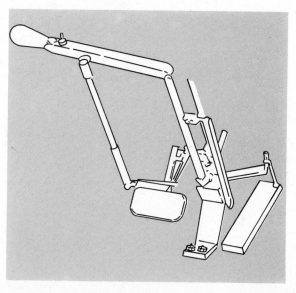

by strawlike devices that the person sips or puffs. There are even switches that can be controlled by eyebrow movements. Systems to activate computers by voice commands are now available, as well.

LEARNING, EDUCATION, AND REHABILITATION. Many of the other devices already described, such as computers with adaptive switches and keyboards for those who have physical disabilities that interfere with normal keyboard use or conventional handwriting, audiotape players for students with visual impairments, adapted book and pencil holders for academic tasks, and page turners, have implications for learning and education. Other devices, such as special exercise equipment, would be useful for rehabilitation purposes.

SPORTS, LEISURE, AND RECREATION. Various devices have been developed to enable people with disabilities to participate in sports and recreation activities. For example, balls and ring-toss games equipped with beepers can enable children with visual impairments to play games with other children. Special computer chips can be installed to slow down fast-paced computer games so that children with slow reaction time can respond. Specially designed artificial feet and limbs can enable those who need them to run and engage in a variety of other sports.

It should be emphasized that the above examples are illustrative and are not meant to be all-inclusive. They do indicate the potential range of assistive technologies that might be available to individuals with different functional needs.

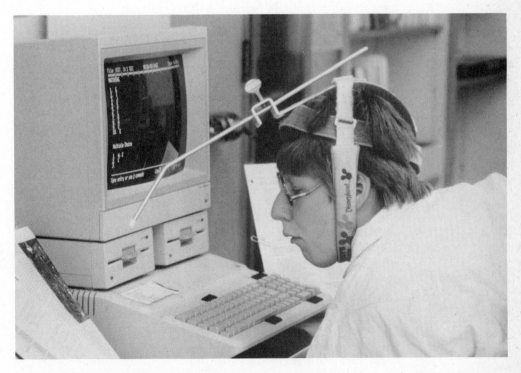

This person, whose paralysis prohibits him from using his hands, is using a head wand to operate the keyboard on this computer.

How can people
locate information
about assistive
technologies?

Literally thousands of assistive and adaptive devices are currently on the market. One of the problems faced by people who are interested in the topic is to locate the specific devices that will meet an individual's specific needs. There are several excellent printed manuals and directories available (e.g., *Assistive Technology Sourcebook,* 1990; *Apple Computer Resources in Special Education and Rehabilitation,* 1990; Bergin, Presperin, & Tallman, 1990; Church & Glennen, 1992; *Closing the Gap Resource Directory,* 1992; *The Trace Resource Book: Assistive Technologies for Communication, Control and Computer Access,* 1990).

Several specialized microcomputer programs that permit the fast retrieval of information about assistive technologies are also available. The largest and most comprehensive one is HyperABLEDATA (1989), which contains information about more than 17,000 different items. SOLUTIONS (1992) provides information about hardware, software, and information sources that can be used primarily with Apple computers. Efficient use of these two programs, however, requires knowledge about device names, vendors, or functions that various devices perform.

Perhaps the most unique computerized system for locating assistive technologies is the Adaptive Device Locator System (1989), which is referred to as ADLS. Users can access the information in ADLS without knowing the names of devices or the vendors that manufacture or distribute them. The reason they can search in this way is that ADLS is based on the functional model described in Chapter 1. Users of ADLS who are interested in locating an assistive or adaptive device identify the functions that the person is required to perform in a given area (such as those described in Figure 3-2). They then interact with the computer by making selections from options that are presented by the ADLS program. The Technology in Action box illustrates how a typical search would be conducted.

Regardless of whether a person uses a program such as ADLS or a printed directory such as those described earlier to locate assistive technologies, it is important to consult with appropriate professionals before acquiring and using a device for a particular person. For example, there may be reasons why a certain communication aid may be inappropriate for a particular child. Consequently, a speech-language pathologist should be consulted. Similarly, the services of a physical therapist may be required to provide advice about positioning when certain types of devices are being considered for children with physical disabilities.

Promising Developments

Technological advances are occurring at such a rapid rate that it is difficult to make projections about future assistive technology applications. We cannot predict the technological break-throughs that might occur, nor the speed at which new developments might be implemented. Following are a few areas, however, in which current research and development efforts may eventually produce significant products to enhance the quality of life for people with disabilities.

When considering promising developments, it is important to recognize that assistive technologies are not limited to those who have physical or sensory impairments. For example, special computer-assisted instruction programs (e.g., Stevens & Blackhurst, 1992) are being developed for children who have learning disabilities. Small, portable electronic databases also are available for those who have difficulty remembering important information. The following examples, then, may have implications for a wide variety of exceptional children.

What might the
future hold for
assistive
technology?

Voice recognition has great potential for those who are unable to use conventional or adapted keyboards to interact with the computer. In this technology, a computer is pro-grammed to respond to voice commands of the person using it. Such an application would also be very useful for controlling different devices and appliances in a person's home.

TECHNOLOGY IN ACTION

Anita is a third grader with a degenerative muscle disease. She has some use of her legs and uses canes to help her walk. When she goes to the playground with her classmates, however, she often stands or sits by herself because she cannot engage in the active games with the other children. Her parents would like to see her have as normal a school experience as possible and are concerned with her isolation on the playground. Her medical team does not want her to use a wheelchair because they think she may develop a premature dependency on it.

Mr. Alvarez, the school's special education resource teacher, schedules a meeting with the school district's itinerant physical therapist, Ms. Dickinson, to explore possible solutions to this problem. They decide to use a computer software program, the Adaptive Device Locator System, to see if they can find a piece of equipment that Anita could use to travel around on the playground.

They sit at the computer and engage in a dialogue with the software. The dialogue is in the form of options that are presented in response to choices they make. The computer asks them to select the functional category of interest from a list, such as *Existence, Communication, Travel,* or *Environmental adaptation.* Since they are looking for a device to help Anita travel, they select the travel category.

The computer then asks about the type of travel: *Vertical* or *Horizontal.* Information, in the form of Decision Aids, is provided on screen to help them make decisions in the event they aren't sure about what a particular category means. They select the horizontal category because Anita needs to move around on the playground, which is flat.

The computer responds by asking whether the person will be *Standing, Sitting,* or *Prone.* Since Anita would more than likely be seated, they select the appropriate category. The computer then asks whether the device will be *Self-propelled* or *Attendant-propelled.* Since

they want Anita to be independent, they select the self-propelled category. The computer then asks whether the person operating the device can use the *Upper extremities, Lower extremities,* or *All four extremities.* Since Anita does have some functional use of her legs, they select the last option.

At this point, the computer reaches a conclusion and recommends two types of devices that might work for Anita. The first is a hand-operated tricycle and the second is a device called an Irish Mail. The Irish Mail is a scooter that is operated with hand controls that are pumped back and forth. It is steered with slight movements of the legs. A graphic image of both devices is presented so they can get an idea of what they look like, and a generic description of each device is displayed on the screen.

Ms. Dickinson recommends the Irish Mail because it will allow Anita to continue to exercise her legs. In addition, it is equipped with a seat belt for added safety. Once the selection has been made, the computer provides a list of companies that manufacture or sell various versions of the Irish Mail. The computer then permits them to enter names and addresses and will print mailing labels and letters to each of the companies, requesting a catalog and information about the Irish Mail. They will receive the catalogs and be able to do comparative shopping for the features and prices of the products produced by different manufacturers. (ADLS can generate mailing labels for all of the more than 700 companies contained in its database. Some schools use these to send for catalogs which are then kept in a file cabinet so the ADLS users will not have to wait for the mail.)

In a matter of a few minutes, Mr. Alvarez and Ms. Dickinson were able to conduct a search and locate a device that could potentially meet Anita's functional needs. The search strategy employed by the ADLS program enabled them to find the device without advance knowledge of its name or manufacturer.

Robotics also may hold significant implications. Behrmann (1987) and Howell (1988) have conducted initial studies on the use of this intriguing technology with people who have disabilities. Kurzweil (1990) provides a fascinating overview of the potential of robotics in his work called *The Age of the Intelligent Machine.*

The work of Jerrold Petrofsky has attracted considerable attention in the area of *computer-controlled prostheses* (see Chapter 11). He has been experimenting with computer-controlled electronic stimulation of the leg muscles of paralyzed people to elicit movement of the paralyzed limbs. One of his subjects, a college student paralyzed in an automobile accident, walked ten steps to receive her diploma at graduation. This landmark research suggests that someday we may be able to implant in the body devices resembling heart pacemakers that will enable people with paralysis to walk.

Developments in the area of *virtual reality* may provide some exciting possibilities for people with disabilities. Virtual reality technology enables people to experience activities through the senses without physically participating in them. For example, by donning a special helmet and glove, people can "visit" a place where they have never been before. Visitors are able to change their orientation by movements of the head and hand. They can "look" to the left or right and "move" forward and backward in their simulated space. The potential for those who are restricted in mobility is exciting.

One of the implications of assistive technology is that it is opening a new field of professional endeavor. PL 100-407 is doing much to increase awareness about the need for assistive technology services. Various states are developing networks of assistive technology information, training, and related services under the auspices of PL 100-407. School personnel are becoming more and more aware of the potential of assistive technology for many of their students.

As a result of this heightened awareness, school personnel will be needed to provide the following services associated with the selection and use of assistive technologies:

- Assess the child's capabilities and needs.
- Make a determination of the assistive technologies that are required to meet the child's needs.
- Provide the assistive technologies necessary for the attainment of the IEP objectives.
- Design strategies for the use of the technologies selected, including adaptations and customization that may be required for their successful use.
- Implement the planned strategies, including the provision of the support systems for training personnel and maintaining the technologies.
- Evaluate the effectiveness of the assistive technologies and the strategies for using them.
- Revise plans, based on evaluation and continued assessment of the child's needs.

In addition to the provision of direct services, specialists will be required to head teams of professionals who will be involved in assistive technology assessments and decision making. If you are interested in career opportunities in this area, you may want to contact professional organizations such as the Council for Exceptional Children or the American Speech-Hearing-Language Association for information about programs that provide personnel preparation on the topic.

What are the assistive technology employment opportunities?

PROBE 3-3   Assistive Technology

1. What is assistive technology?
2. T   F   Services are included in the definition of assistive technology.
3. Describe four functions that can be enhanced through the use of assistive technology.
4. What are the four parts to the assistive technology continuum?
5. In which functional category would you expect to find slings and splints?
6. Why are driving aids not in the travel category?
7. Why is ADLS unique?
8. _____ is the most comprehensive computer database for locating assistive technologies.
9. Why is it important to consult professionals from different disciplines when selecting assistive technologies?
10. List three promising developments in the field of assistive technology.
11. T   F   Employment opportunities in the field of assistive technology appear to be promising.

TECHNOLOGY COMPETENCIES

You should be able to identify the knowledge, skills, and attitudes that special education teachers should have in order to use technology effectively.

Although the potential is enormous, the full impact of technology remains largely untapped because many colleges and universities do not provide sufficient training on the topic to students who are preparing for various roles in special education (Blackhurst, MacArthur, & Byrom, 1988). Thus, special education graduates are often not well equipped to use technology when they start to work. One reason for this is that the special education teacher preparation curriculum at many universities is too overcrowded to include much instruction on technology. Another factor is the lack of hardware and software resources at many institutions of higher education. In addition, research has found that a large number of special education professors do not have sufficient knowledge or skills to provide instruction on technology applications in special education (Blackhurst & MacArthur, 1986).

Because technology training at the preservice level (i.e., prior to graduation) has not been adequate for many special educators, it is incumbent on them to develop their own programs of professional development. (Chapter 7 describes how such a program can be planned and implemented.) Figure 3-8 provides a checklist that you can use to perform a self-assessment of the competencies you have that are related to the use of technology. The general functions that need to be performed are in boldface type. These subsume the competency statements. You can use this checklist to monitor the development of your technology competencies and to help you set priorities for seeking out formal and informal opportunities to further enhance your technology knowledge and skills.

Professional Organizations

What is TAM?

If you are interested in becoming involved in the fascinating topic of technology in special education, you may consider joining one of the professional organizations devoted to the study of the topic. The Technology and Media (TAM) Division of the Council for Exceptional Children was established to stimulate the development of new technologies for special education, to provide information about technology, and to foster cooperation among special educators and educational technologists. This group publishes the *Journal of Special Education Technology* as a vehicle for disseminating information about technology. It also sponsors an annual conference on the topic. Interested readers can write to the Council for Exceptional Children, 1920 Association Drive, Reston VA 22091, to obtain information about TAM.

By affiliating with groups such as TAM, you will be kept apprised of the latest developments in special education technology. You will also learn about the availability of interesting jobs that involve applying technology to special education problems. Such jobs can provide excellent career options for those who are interested in this topic.

Because technology's impact on special education is so pervasive, each chapter—beginning with Chapter 2—includes one or more vignettes titled "Technology in Action," which illustrate how technology is being applied to the topic of that chapter. Space limitations do not permit a more thorough exploration of technology, but the vignettes should give some indication of its great potential. As you read these brief accounts, you will note that examples of the technology of teaching, instructional technology, and assistive technology have been included. If you are interested in more information about technology applications, you may want to consult one of the textbooks on the subject (e.g., Behrmann, 1985; Bennett, 1987; Lindsey, 1987; Male, 1989).

FIGURE 3-8   Technology Competency Checklist

Technology Competencies for Special Education Teachers
Self-Assessment

DIRECTIONS: Provide an assessment of how well you can perform each of these tasks.
Use the following key.

> **X** = I don't know what this means.
> **N** = I have no competencies in this area.
> **A** = I have an awareness of information in this area.
> **S** = I have some skills in this area.
> **C** = I am already competent in this area.

In order to use technology effectively in special education programs, teachers should be able
to do the following:

**Acquire a body of knowledge about the use of microcomputers and related
technology in special education.**

1. Explain historical developments and trends in the application of microcomputers and
   related technology in special education.   X N A S C
2. Define terms, concepts, and issues related to technology applications in special education.   X N A S C
3. Identify ways that microcomputers and related technology, such as interactive video, robotics,
   and adaptive devices, can be incorporated into the special education curriculum to meet
   the instructional goals and objectives of students.   X N A S C
4. Read, evaluate, and apply information about technology research and applications in special
   education that appear in the professional literature and trade magazines.   X N A S C
5. Maintain a professional development program to ensure the acquisition of knowledge and
   skills about new developments in technology as they become available.   X N A S C

**Evaluate microcomputer software and related materials for their potential application
in special education programs.**

6. Identify the purpose of instructional software programs, their objectives, their validity, and
   the adequacy of the program documentation.   X N A S C
7. Determine the characteristics of learners for whom a program is appropriate.   X N A S C
8. Identify the commands required to use the materials and the academic and physical demands
   placed on the student.   X N A S C
9. Identify the options that exist to enable the teacher to modify features of the program.   X N A S C

Develop a plan for technology use in a special education program.

10. Articulate goals and a philosophy for using technology in special education.   X N A S C
11. Identify elements of the special education curriculum for which technology applications
    are appropriate and ways they can be implemented.   X N A S C
12. Ensure that special education students have equitable access to technology in any plans that
    are developed.   X N A S C
13. Prepare guidelines and rules for technology use in the special education classroom.   X N A S C
14. Write proposals to obtain funds for technology hardware and software.   X N A S C

continued

FIGURE 3-8 *(continued)*

Use technology in special education assessment and planning.

15. Identify and use programs for assessing exceptional children and planning their educational programs. X N A S C
16. Use computer software programs to analyze, summarize, and report student performance data to aid instructional decision making. X N A S C
17. Use microcomputers to generate assessment reports. X N A S C
18. Explain the pros and cons of computerized programs that generate IEPs. X N A S C

Use technology to facilitate instruction in special education programs.

19. Use technology to support effective instructional practices. X N A S C
20. Teach special education students to operate equipment and run microcomputer software. X N A S C
21. Use tutorial, drill and practice, simulation, and problem-solving software programs appropriately. X N A S C
22. Arrange and manage the classroom environment to facilitate the use of technology. X N A S C
23. Evaluate the effectiveness of technology applications in the special education classroom. X N A S C
24. Adhere to ethical standards when applying technology in special education. X N A S C
25. Maintain a resource file of information about technology in special education. X N A S C

Use technology to compensate for learning barriers that are due to communication disorders, physical disabilities, or visual impairments.

26. Determine the adaptive switches, software, and related equipment needed for students with communication disorders, physical disabilities, or visual impairments. X N A S C
27. Connect and use alternate keyboards, other adaptive input and output devices, and construct materials for their use. X N A S C
28. Use technology to enable students to control other devices in their environment. X N A S C
29. Work with assistive technology specialists and related personnel to use technology with students who need assistive and adaptive devices. X N A S C

Use a microcomputer to generate teaching aids for the special education classroom.

30. Use software programs to produce worksheets, tests, signs, transparency masters, and other visual aids. X N A S C
31. Use instructional shell programs and authoring systems to develop computer-assisted instruction lessons. X N A S C

Use a microcomputer as an aid to personal productivity.

32. Use a word processor to prepare lesson plans, class notes, correspondence, and other written documents. X N A S C
33. Use database programs to maintain student records and resource files. X N A S C
34. Use an electronic spreadsheet program to store and report student grades. X N A S C
35. Use telecommunication systems and electronic message services (e.g., SpecialNet). X N A S C
36. Access information from electronic data bases to support professional activities (e.g., ERIC). X N A S C

Assemble, operate, and maintain the components of technology systems in a special education environment.

37. Connect and operate audio and video equipment and input and output devices such as disk drives, printers, monitors, speech synthesizers, graphics tablets, video systems, and modems. X N A S C
38. Configure software to ensure that all of its features will work properly with the equipment being used. X N A S C
39. Demonstrate the proper care of technology systems and related software. X N A S C
40. Use simple diagnostics to determine problems that arise and perform routine maintenance. X N A S C
41. Use the operating system software and utility software programs that accompany the computer being used to initialize disks, load, run, save, and copy programs. X N A S C

PROBE 3-4   Technology Competencies

1. List four technology functions that special education teachers should be able to perform.
2. _____ is the abbreviation of an organization for special educators who are interested in technology.

SUMMARY

1. The technology of teaching employs systematic procedures in the education of exceptional children.
2. Direct instruction, applied behavior analysis, and competency-based instruction are systematic approaches to instruction.
3. There are many similarities between the characteristics of IEPs and instructional technology applications.
4. Microcomputers are being used to provide drill and practice, tutorial programming, simulations, reinforcement, information management, and communications in special education programs.
5. Software selections should be based on the student's stages of learning.
6. Multimedia and hypermedia applications have great potential for instructing students in special education programs.
7. Telecommunication systems, such as SpecialNet, are a valuable service for special educators.
8. Assistive technologies are used to enhance the person's ability to function in the environment.
9. Assistive technology services are being provided on a national basis under the auspices of PL 100-407.
10. Computer software programs, such as the Adaptive Device Locator System and HyperABLEDATA, provide a useful way to search for assistive technologies.
11. Voice recognition, robotics, computer-controlled prostheses, and virtual reality hold promise for future special education applications.
12. The Technology and Media Division of the Council for Exceptional Children is an organization for special educators interested in applications of technology to the education of exceptional children.

TASK SHEET 3   Technology in Special Education

Competency Self-Assessment

Complete the technology self-assessment that is included in Figure 3-8. Keep a copy of it to use as a guide as you progress through the remainder of your educational program.

Technology Observation

Arrange to visit a program in which either instructional technology or assistive technology applications are being conducted. Inquire about the topics that were discussed in this chapter. In a three-page report, answer the following questions:

1. What did you observe?
2. Did you observe any problems in the technology application?

3. What is your impression about the effectiveness of the application you observed?
4. What did you learn from this experience?

Functional Analysis

Select an assistive technology application and perform a functional analysis of its potential impact. Use the functional model that appears in Chapter 1. Write a three-page paper on your study.

Library Study

Locate three articles in the library related to instructional technology or assistive technology. Write a one-page abstract of each, concluding with a paragraph about your reactions to the article. Here are the names of some journals in which you can find articles about these topics:

Assistive Technology
Computers in Education
Educational Technology
Exceptional Children
Journal for Computer Users in Speech and Hearing
Journal of Special Education Technology
Teaching Exceptional Children

Design Your Own Field Experience

If you know of a unique experience you can have that is related to the topics covered in this chapter, or if you do not want to do any of the listed options, discuss your alternatives with your instructor and complete the task that you both agree on.

Hoi was born several weeks premature and experienced a difficult birth. Soon after birth he suffered a severe cerebral hemorrhage that left him with many developmental needs. Over the months he spent in the neonatal intensive care unit (NICU) at a local hospital, the staff of the NICU and people working with a local program assisted his family in understanding his condition, put them in contact with other families in similar situations, and helped them develop a transition plan to a local early intervention program. The transition plan includes regular physical therapy and regular contact with a special educator trained in early childhood special education.

Dawn is 18 months old and has Down syndrome. Although she currently appears to be developing within normal limits, it is likely that she and her family will need considerable assistance over the next several years. Since birth, her family has had contact with a home-based intervention program. Staff members from the program visit the family each week. They have assisted the family in finding a day care program for Dawn and will help the day care staff include Dawn in the regular activities of the program. They have also provided her family with information on how to interact with her to promote play and communication skills, and have helped her parents define their goals for Dawn.

Michael is 4 years old, has been diagnosed as having a communication disorder, and attends preschool in a four-day-per-week Head Start program. Although his parents knew he was slow in talking, he was not diagnosed until after being screened in his Head Start program. His mother volunteers in the program one morning every other week. The speech-language pathologist at the program works with Michael and his peers twice a week in the classroom. She also provides information to his teachers on how to promote his communication development. An early childhood special educator from Michael's local school district meets with his teachers regularly to provide consultation and monitor his progress.

Lashanda is 5 years old, has a mild hearing loss, and has cerebral palsy, which requires her to be in a wheelchair. Although she obviously has disabilities, her cognitive development is within normal limits. She attends kindergarten at her local public school and receives physical therapy from the district's physical therapist. Her teacher also receives consultation from an educator of children with hearing losses and from a special education teacher. Lashanda spends her entire day in kindergarten, appears to be making friends, and likes school.

4

Early Childhood Special Education

Mark Wolery

Few areas of education, including special education, are as new as early childhood special education—also called *early intervention*. Although a few communities have had isolated programs for many years, amazing growth in the number and variety of programs has occurred in the past 20 to 25 years. Today, early childhood special education is a vital and important component of public education. This chapter provides a definition of early childhood special education, identifies the societal forces that have influenced its current status, and reviews the goals and rationale for early intervention services. It also includes a discussion of the effectiveness of early intervention and its current legal status. The major portion of the chapter presents current practices in early intervention and the challenges faced by professionals involved in early intervention programs.

INTRODUCTION TO EARLY CHILDHOOD SPECIAL EDUCATION

You should be able to define early intervention, list societal influences, describe the rationale for doing early intervention, and list its goals.

Definition of Early Childhood Special Education

As the name implies, early childhood special education focuses on providing services to young children with special needs. A broad definition of the field is as follows: **Early childhood special education** *(early intervention) is the provision of services by the "helping professions" to promote the development of infants, toddlers, and preschoolers under the age of 6 who are at risk for* *or have developmental delays and disabilities, and to promote the well-being of families with such infants or children.* An analysis of this definition identifies some key dimensions of early intervention programs; some of these are described in the following paragraphs and are shown in Table 4-1.

What type of infants and children are served by early childhood special education programs?

  This definition does not stipulate the type of disability infants or children must have to be eligible for services. Early intervention programs serve children such as those described at the beginning of this chapter, with almost any disability at any level of severity. This practice is known as cross-categorical programming. Three broad categories of children are included: (1) those who are at risk for developmental delays and disabling conditions, (2) those who have developmental delays, and (3) those with identified disabilities (Graham & Scott, 1988). Children may be at risk for developmental delays and disabilities because of environmental factors such as poor economic conditions, child abuse and neglect, inadequate social environments, and lack of adequate nutrition. Others are at risk for developmental delays because of biological factors such as low birth weight, birth trauma, seizure activity, prenatal exposure to drugs and alcohol, and genetic or physiological conditions (Scott & Carran, 1989). The environmental and biological factors act together to cause an increased likelihood of developmental delays.

  The second group of children, those with developmental delays, already exhibit developmental levels that are not within normal limits. **Developmental delay** means that the child's development is not progressing as expected in the cognitive, communication, social, physical, and self-care areas. These children, for whatever reason or combination of reasons, are not progressing within normal limits. Their delays may be in one or two areas or in all areas, and the delays may range from mild to severe.

TABLE 4-1   **Dimensions of the Definition of Early Childhood Special Education**

Dimension
 Description

Who is served?
 Infants, toddlers, and preschoolers.
 Families of infants, toddlers, and preschoolers.

What categories of children are included?
 Children who are at risk for developmental delays and disabilities.
 Children who have developmental delays.
 Children who have identified disabilities.

Who provides early intervention services?
 Members of the helping professions, including early educators, early childhood special
  educators, physicians, nurses, speech-language pathologists, physical therapists,
  occupational therapists, social workers, and others.

What services are provided?
 Services are individualized to the needs of the infant or child *and* the family, based on an
  assessment of what each needs.
 Services may include those designed to promote the development of infants and children,
  promote the well-being of families, and/or promote positive interactions between the
  infants or children and other family members.

Where are services provided?
 Family homes, specialized child development centers, public schools, regular child care
  programs, clinics, hospitals, neonatal intensive care nurseries, and others.

The third group of children, those with disabilities, may display a broad range of conditions including mental retardation, physical disabilities, autism, visual or hearing impairments, communication disorders, and social and behavioral disorders. Further, these disabilities may range from mild to severe. A single program may include one child with severe cerebral palsy, another with a moderate hearing loss, a child with congenital blindness, a child with severe mental retardation, another with moderate mental retardation, several with communication disorders, some children with behavior disorders, and a few with developmental delays.

The definition states that early intervention services are provided to children below the age of 6. There is no universally accepted age that defines the upper limit of early childhood. The National Association for the Education of Young Children uses 8 years because of the belief that children under the age of 8 learn differently from older children, and thus should be provided with different educational experiences. The definition of early childhood special education in this chapter uses the age of 6 for two practical reasons. First, the federal laws and regulations governing the provision of services for children under age 6 differ from those related to older children. Second, the manner and nature of programs for children above the age of 6 are frequently quite different from those for young children, although some schools are reorganizing their services for 6-, 7-, and 8-year-old children so that those programs are similar to early intervention efforts. Of importance, however, is the fact that the age range birth through 5 years is very broad. Newborns are different from infants, who in turn are quite different from toddlers, who also are very different from 4- and 5-year-old children. Thus, unlike professionals in other areas of special education, the early childhood special educator must be prepared to work with children who have almost any disability expressed in varying levels of severity and who represent a broad age range (newborns to preschoolers).

What are the major focuses of early intervention services?

The definition does not state what services are provided—only that they are implemented to promote the development of infants, toddlers, and preschoolers and the well-being of families with children who have special needs. The services are not restricted to traditional educational services. Many of the programs described in this text for school-age children focus primarily on students with disabilities. In early intervention, the family as well as the child is the focus of services (Dunst, Trivette, & Deal, 1988). Some programs focus primarily on supporting the family (Seitz & Provence, 1990; Simeonsson & Bailey, 1990), others on teaching the infant or child (Bailey & Wolery, 1989, 1992; Bricker & Veltman, 1990), and still others on helping the family and child interact with one another (Barnard & Kelly, 1990; Mahoney & Powell, 1988).

The definition does not prescribe the place or manner in which the services are provided. Early intervention services occur in many different contexts and agencies. Some programs exist in hospitals, clinics, the homes of families, public school preschool programs, and other child-care centers. Although the services may involve direct teaching of the infant or child, they may also include helping family members interact with their child, helping families find social support and other resources, providing information to families, and many others.

Who provides early intervention services?

The definition also implies that multiple disciplines are involved. It is clear that no single profession is capable of providing all of the services needed by families of infants and children with disabilities. Disciplines such as special education, regular early childhood education, physical therapy, occupational therapy, speech-language pathology, social work, medicine, nursing, and psychology are frequently involved in early intervention services (McCollum & Hughes, 1988; Thorp & McCollum, 1988).

Thus, early childhood special education programs tend to be cross-categorical (have children of different disabilities) and serve a broad age range (newborns to kindergarten-age children). Further, the programs are situated in many different settings, employ members of many disciplines, and provide a wide array of services. Taken together, these characteristics mean that early childhood special educators must be highly skilled and capable of doing many different things well. They must also stay abreast of new developments in the field.

Societal Forces Influencing Early Intervention Services

Early childhood special education has its roots in the broad changes that have recently occurred in American society. Three of these changes are particularly noteworthy.

What broad social changes have influenced the current status of early intervention services?

CHANGES IN ATTENTION TO THE NEEDS OF MINORITY GROUPS. In the 1960s, American society began to recognize the needs and interests of minority groups. This was expressed in civil rights legislation and litigation. Racial minority groups were the initial focus of this change; however, other minority or underrepresented groups also benefited. These groups included women, the elderly, and individuals with disabilities. The Education of All Handicapped Children Act (PL 94-142) and its subsequent amendments (currently titled the Individuals with Disabilities Education Act, or IDEA) were a direct result of this attention and interest in the needs of previously neglected children and youth with disabilities.

CHANGES IN PERCEPTIONS ABOUT DEVELOPMENT. A second major change that promoted the growth of early intervention was a shift in how children were perceived. In the first half of this century, it was believed that biological forces caused children to develop and learn (Gesell, Halverson, Thompson, Ilg, Castner, Ames, & Amatruda, 1940). However, the work of several theorists with different orientations changed this view. Piaget's (1952) work in Switzerland showed that children play an active role in their own development. Bijou and Baer (1961, 1965, 1978) documented the effect of the environment on children's development. In 1961, Hunt provided convincing evidence that environmental forces exert powerful influence on cognitive development. Further, these theorists suggested that the early years were particularly formative and important. The perception that the environment, and thus education, could produce changes in young children and the fact that many children were failing in school prompted action on the government's part. Specifically, the Head Start program was initiated in 1965 for preschool children from economically disadvantaged homes. The goal of Head Start was to reduce school failure in the elementary grades by providing stimulating preschool experiences, involving parents in those experiences, and providing medical and health screenings and services. Although the success of Head Start in meeting its goal has been hotly debated (cf. Cicirelli et al., 1969; Smith & Bissell, 1970), the current consensus is that such programs can produce immediate and enduring positive effects on children if they participate in *high-quality* preschool programs (Haskins, 1989).

CHANGES IN FAMILIES AND IN THE PERCEPTION OF FAMILIES. A third major change in society that influenced early intervention services occurred in the American family and the way it was perceived. In the past, families were viewed as unchanging, independent, and easily defined units (Foster, Berger, & McLean, 1981). Current perspectives on families, however, are different. Families are viewed as changing dramatically with the passage of time, as subsystems within broader societal (ecological) systems, and as highly varied and thus difficult to define (Bailey & Simeonsson, 1988a). This change in perspective, the larger number of children in single-parent families (about a 48 percent increase in the 1980s), and the increased number of mothers in the work force (about an 80 percent increase since 1970) led to a recognition of the need for quality child care outside the home (Edelman, 1989). Similarly, there was an increased realization of the importance of early relationships between children and their parents (Shonkoff & Meisels, 1990). These changes were coupled with considerable political rhetoric about "family values" and the need to support the family. Simultaneously, many social programs were seen as fostering dependency rather than independence. Thus, assisting families in building positive relationships with their infants and children and in using their own resources and supports is a major part of many early intervention programs (Dunst et al., 1988).

Rationale for Providing Early Intervention Services

What are the reasons for providing early intervention services?

At least five rationales exist for providing early intervention services. First, these services may result in the identification of secondary disabilities that would have been ignored without intervention. For example, children with Down syndrome frequently have developmental delays and/or mental retardation; a smaller but significant proportion also have hearing losses. If a child did not get intervention, her failure to talk might be attributed to mental retardation rather than to hearing impairment. However, children who are enrolled in high-quality intervention programs should be in contact with professionals who would suspect, identify, and treat the hearing loss.

Second, provision of early intervention services may result in the prevention of secondary disabilities. For example, children with communication disorders may develop behavior problems because of their difficulties in communication. With intervention, the communication disorders can be treated and the behavior problems prevented or their impact minimized (Dunlap, Johnson, & Robbins, 1990).

Third, it is clear that maintaining children in their community with their parents is less expensive than providing round-the-clock care in a residential institution (Bailey & Wolery, 1984). When early intervention programs allow families to keep their children at home, the cost of those children to society is reduced. With some children, particularly at-risk children and those with mild disabilities (e.g., mild communication disorders, mild developmental delays, and mild mental and physical conditions), the early intervention services may eliminate or diminish the need for later special education services, and may reduce the likelihood that they will be retained in grade. Both of these outcomes result in considerable savings to society. However, some children will need extensive special education services from birth until they have completed their eligibility for services at age 21. Thereafter, they will need vocational and rehabilitation services.

Fourth, early intervention services are useful to the family. The programs may reduce stress, provide information, offer support, instill a feeling of control over the situation, and impart hope for the future. The programs may allow parents to interact with and manage their infants or children more easily and with greater skill. Parents may also meet other families who have children with disabilities, thereby reducing their sense of being alone. Thus, even if the program did not cause changes for the children, the benefits to the family might be well worth the effort and cost.

Fifth, provision of early intervention services may result in children becoming more developmentally advanced and more independent. Many well-controlled studies have demonstrated that particular intervention strategies can promote positive changes in children's skills and behavior (see Bailey & Wolery, 1992; Odom & Karnes, 1988). As will be described later, less well controlled research indicates that broad changes in children's development occur as a result of early intervention programs.

Goals of Early Intervention Services

What are the goals of early intervention for infants and children, their families, and society?

The goals of early intervention programs vary depending upon the purpose of individual programs; however, broad goals can be stated and are important in understanding the field. General goals for three different groups (infants and children, families, and society) are listed in Table 4-2.

For infants and children, the major efforts of early intervention programs are focused on two goals: promoting development and fostering independence. Programs attempt to help children to develop more rapidly and to acquire skills that will make them more competent in specific situations. Frequently, this means the same thing; for example, if children are taught to walk, they learn an important developmental skill and increase their independence. At other times, particularly with children who have severe disabilities or with any child who is changing programs or placements, professionals should focus on making the children more competent in specific situations. This may occur at the expense of developmental programming, but may allow them to lead more normalized lives and be less dependent upon others. The relative emphasis placed on these two goals depends upon the intervention team, which, of course, includes family members.

The remaining two goals for children should always receive some attention, but they are rarely the primary focus of intervention. Programs may sometimes attempt to make children more easily controlled and thus more manageable (goal 3), or they may work on improving the child's environment so that it is more comfortable or stimulating (goal 4).

The intent of family goals is to preserve the autonomy of the family, help them make decisions about their child's program and life, and minimize the disruptions caused by the birth of a child with disabilities. An important function of early intervention programs is to help

---

TABLE 4-2   General Goals of Early Childhood Special Education

Goals for Infants, Toddlers, and Preschoolers

1. To accelerate the rate at which infants and children achieve a broad range of developmental skills.
2. To maximize the independence (competence) of infants and children in specific settings and situations, including future placements and the communities in which they live.
3. To increase the manageability with which care can be provided to infants and children.
4. To increase the quality of life experienced by infants and children.

Goals for Families

1. To provide information, training, and support to families so that they are able to make informed decisions about their infant or child.
2. To provide information, training, and support to families so that they can interact with their infant or child in a manner that is mutually satisfying and beneficial to the family and the infant or child.
3. To provide information, training, and support to families so that they can promote the development of their infant or child.
4. To provide assistance and support to families so that they are able to function as normally as possible within their communities.

Goals for Society

1. To promote a general awareness, understanding, and acceptance of infants and children with disabilities, their families, and the programs that support them.
2. To promote support and advocacy for infants and children with disabilities, their families, and the programs that serve them.

Learning functional skills, such as independent use of eating utensils, is often an objective in a preschooler's individualized education plan.

families become independent decision makers. Families must live with the results of any decisions, and therefore are the persons who should have primary control over those decisions. Professionals are responsible for providing them with the relevant information and support to help them make informed decisions.

Family goals 2 and 3 are designed to assist the family in interacting with and promoting the development of their child. The intent is not to convert parents into teachers, but to help them interact with their child in pleasing ways and to provide the child with experiences that will promote developmental progress and competence (Rosenberg & Robinson, 1988; Barber, Turnbull, Behr, & Kerns, 1988). Clearly, family members can choose to participate in program activities at many different levels (Simeonsson & Bailey, 1990). Family goal 4 is designed to minimize the negative impact that an infant or child with disabilities has on the family. The birth or diagnosis of a child with disabilities can cause increased stress and dysfunction within families (Gallagher & Bristol, 1989). However, with proper support, many families adjust to the situation and lead productive and happy lives.

The goals for society recognize that the services currently provided are a result of hard-won battles in courts and legislatures. The current support for early intervention programs would not be possible if community leaders and legislators were not aware of the importance of these programs. To ensure that adequate services become a reality for infants and young children with special needs, professionals must educate the public and get assistance in advocating for needed services.

In summary, early intervention programs should be provided because they hold benefits for infants and children, their families, and society at large. Similarly, the goals for early intervention are focused on these three groups. Actually, early intervention services are provided in many localities because of the state's policies. The next section provides a brief overview of the effectiveness of early intervention and a description of current governmental policy on early intervention services.

PROBE 4-1   Introduction to Early Childhood Special Education

1. T   F   Early intervention programs serve only infants and children with disabilities under the age of 6.
2. T   F   Some early intervention programs provide services to infants and children and to their families.
3. What societal force caused the government to establish the Head Start program?
4. List one goal of early intervention for infants and children, one goal for families, and one for society at large.
5. What reasons could you give to a legislator who asked you why funds should be provided for early intervention services?

EFFECTIVENESS OF AND CURRENT POLICY ON EARLY INTERVENTION

You should be able to describe the effects of providing early intervention services and identify the provisions of PL 99-457.

Effects of Early Intervention

In the past ten years, considerable debate occurred over the effectiveness of early intervention with children who have identified disabilities (cf. Casto & Mastropieri, 1986a, 1986b, 1986c; Dunst & Snyder, 1986; Strain & Smith, 1986). It is too simplistic to ask, Is early intervention effective? The question cannot be answered without raising additional questions: What is early intervention? Effective in doing what? Effective for whom? Effective in which situations?

How effective are early intervention services?

Many factors make it difficult to conduct research on the effectiveness of early intervention. Three of these will illustrate the complexity of the issue (Casto, 1988). First, it is difficult to randomly assign infants and children to early intervention and to control groups. Many families would object to being placed in the control group. One solution might be to assign infants and children to different interventions, but this strategy really asks, Is one intervention better than another? rather than, Is early intervention effective?

Second, early intervention services must be individualized and are very different across infants and children and across families. For example, what may be appropriate and effective for an infant with severe physical and cognitive disabilities would be quite different from what would be appropriate and effective for a 5-year-old child with a mild speech disorder. Thus, the question of what intervention is being evaluated becomes important.

Third, it is difficult to select appropriate measures when evaluating the effectiveness of early intervention. Common measures include changes in IQ and changes in developmental performance. However, these measures do not capture many of the positive changes that may occur as a result of early intervention, such as the control of seizures, increased peer interactions, placement in the general education program, increased family cohesiveness, better family functioning, more appropriate parent-child relationships, and many others.

Despite these difficulties, a lot of effort has been devoted to studying the question. In a recent review of more than 100 reports, Dunst, Snyder, and Mankinen (1989) make several summary statements about the adequacy of the research base and of the findings that come from it. Their findings are presented in Table 4-3. They acknowledge that studying effectiveness is a complex endeavor, but they identify situations in which particular types of intervention appear to make a difference with children and families. As with early intervention for economically disadvantaged children, it is likely that high-quality programs that attend to individual needs of infants or children and their families will produce more immediate and lasting effects than programs that are less well organized, have poorly trained staff members, and do not have a clear philosophy (Dunst et al., 1989).

Current Policy Related to Early Intervention

What historical initiatives have influenced the current policy on early intervention?

HISTORICAL PRECEDENTS TO CURRENT POLICY. Current policy on early intervention must be viewed in light of the events over the past 20 to 30 years (Garwood & Sheehan, 1989; Smith, 1988). As noted earlier, Head Start was initiated in 1965 as the first nationwide intervention program for preschool children. Later, in 1972 to 1974, the Head Start legislation was amended to require that 10 percent of the enrollment be children with disabilities. In 1967, through the Medicaid program, the federal government established the Early and Periodic Screening, Diagnosis, and Treatment (EPSDT) program to identify and treat low-income children with developmental and medical problems. This program has never quite lived up to its promise, but it continues to provide some services (Margolis & Meisels, 1987).

In 1968, the Handicapped Children's Early Education Program (currently called the Early Education Program for Children with Disabilities) was initiated through the Handicapped Children's Early Education Assistance Act. The program provided federal grants to develop, evaluate, and disseminate model services for young children with disabilities. This program continues today, funding demonstration and research projects for young children; it has enjoyed a rich history of developing programs, securing local support for early intervention, and helping many families and children. As described in Chapter 1, the government

TABLE 4-3   Summary of Research on the Effectiveness of Early Intervention

Findings

1. Most children in early intervention programs make developmental progress and acquire new behaviors, but it is difficult to know whether it is due to the program.
2. The research with environmentally at-risk children is more convincing that early intervention is effective than is the research with biologically at-risk infants and children. More research with the latter group is needed.
3. Cognitively and behaviorally oriented programs appear to result in the greatest effects, but these programs tend to be implemented for longer periods of time.
4. Little evidence exists supporting the use of physical and occupational therapy, but this statement comes primarily from short-term studies.
5. Several variables, such as how old the child is when intervention starts, how long it lasts each day, and how many months/years the child is enrolled, seem to influence how effective the program is, and seem to be more important in center- rather than home-based programs.
6. Support from within and outside the program has strong positive influences on parent functioning and to a lesser degree on child behavior.
7. Rate of progress is similar across handicapping conditions, but the more severely handicapped the child is, the slower the rate of progress.
8. Children who are high-functioning at program entry tend to make the most progress.
9. Child characteristics, such as behavior problems and level of motivation, tend to influence the amount of progress.
10. Certain family characteristics appear to make early intervention programs more effective.
11. With biologically at-risk infants, researchers have relied too much on child progress data rather than on broader measures of child and family functioning.

Source: Adapted from C. J. Dunst, S. W. Snyder, and M. Mankinen (1989). Efficacy of early intervention. In M. C. Wang, M. C. Reynolds, and H. J. Walberg (Eds.), *Handbook of special education: Research and practice,* vol. 3, *Low incident conditions.* New York: Pergamon.

established PL 94-142 in 1974 as Part B of the Education of the Handicapped Act (now called IDEA). While PL 94-142 provided some funds for children from 3 to 5 years of age, this part of the program was primarily voluntary for states. With few exceptions, most states did not provide a free appropriate public education to infants and preschoolers with disabilities. Two amendments to this act, however, added significant provisions for preschoolers. PL 98-199 (1983) provided funds to help states plan comprehensive services for young children with disabilities. PL 99-457 (1986) included many amendments and two major initiatives for early intervention: the birth through age 2 program, and the ages 3 through 5 program, as described in the following sections.

What are some basic provisions of PL 99-457 for infants and toddlers?

BIRTH THROUGH AGE 2 PROGRAM OF PL 99-457. The birth through age 2 program (Part H of IDEA) is voluntary for states; however, if they choose to participate, they must make progress to ensure that services are available to all infants and toddlers with disabilities. At present, all states are making such progress. Three groups of infants are eligible under this program: those with developmental delays; those with physical and mental conditions that may result in developmental delays; and, at the state's option, those who are at risk for delays. This law calls for the establishment of a statewide comprehensive service system. Currently, states are developing this system and attempting to ensure that they have adequate funding, personnel, and programs in place to address the needs of infants and toddlers and their families.

Although much has been written about this legislation (e.g., Garwood & Sheehan, 1989; Gallagher, Trohanis, & Clifford, 1989; Smith, 1988), a few points are noteworthy. First, this program requires agencies to interact with one another in developing and implementing the statewide system. Rather than creating a new system, interagency collaboration is mandated. Second, the legislation attempts to correct some of the flaws in PL 94-142, such as the responsibility of private insurance companies, the role of agencies other than education, and others. Third, the legislation makes individuals who are at risk for disabilities eligible for services. This gives states financial assistance to begin programs focusing on prevention as well as treatment.

Fourth, a transition plan must be developed for each eligible infant and toddler so that services will not be disrupted when the child reaches 3 years of age. Fifth, the legislation requires the development of an individualized family service plan (IFSP). Rather than an IEP, which would have goals and objectives for the infant only, the legislation recognizes the important role of parents and requires that, with their permission and assistance, goals and objectives be developed to help them promote the child's development. The plan must be based on a multidisciplinary assessment and must be written by the multidisciplinary team, including the family. The components of the IFSP are shown in Table 4-4. This change means that early interventionists must acquire skills in assisting families as well as children.

What are some basic provisions of PL 99-457 for preschoolers?

AGES 3 THROUGH 5 PORTION OF PL 99-457. This portion of PL 99-457 amends Part B of IDEA to give financial assistance to states that agree to provide a free appropriate public education to preschoolers with disabilities between the ages of 3 and 5 years. This ensures that preschoolers with disabilities and their families will have the rights that have been enjoyed by school-age children under PL 94-142. The state educational agency is responsible for ensuring that those services are provided.

Two components of this legislation are noteworthy. First, the states are not required to report by disability the number of children served. Thus, some of the states are using "developmental delay" as a category that makes children eligible for services. Second, the IEP may include goals and objectives for the family as well as the child, if desired.

SUMMARY OF EARLY INTERVENTION POLICY. Despite the difficulties in studying the effectiveness of early intervention, some forms of early intervention produce positive outcomes for infants and children with disabilities and their families. Further, most individuals believe

TABLE 4-4   Components of the Individualized Family Service Plan

1. A statement of the infant's or toddler's present levels of physical development, cognitive development, communication development, social and emotional development, and adaptive skills, based on acceptable objective criteria.
2. A statement of the family's resources, priorities, and concerns relating to enhancing the development of the family's handicapped infant or toddler.
3. A statement of the major outcomes expected to be achieved for the infant and toddler and the family, and the criteria, procedures, and timelines used to determine the degree to which progress toward achieving the outcomes are being made and whether modifications or revisions of the outcomes or services are necessary.
4. A statement of specific early intervention services necessary to meet the unique needs of the infant or toddler and the family, including the frequency, the intensity, and the method of delivering services.
5. The projected dates for initiation of services and the anticipated duration of such services.
6. The name of the case manager from the profession most immediately relevant to the infant's and toddler's or family's needs who will be responsible for the implementation of the plan and coordination with other agencies and persons.
7. The steps to be taken supporting the transition of the handicapped toddler to services provided under part B to the extent such services are considered appropriate.
8. A statement of the extent to which services will be provided in the natural environments.

Source: Federal Register, 41[252], p. 5692.

that early intervention services should be provided. Thus, over the past 20 to 30 years, the federal government has taken a larger role in ensuring that such services are a reality. As of the 1992–93 school year, all states in the nation provide free appropriate public education to all preschool children with disabilities.

PROBE 4-2   Effectiveness of and Current Policy on Early Intervention

1. T   F   Children make progress in early intervention programs, but it is difficult to determine if that progress is caused by those programs.
2. Which types of programs seem to be more effective?
3. T   F   All early intervention programs appear to be effective.
4. What was the first nationwide intervention program to include preschoolers with disabilities?
5. How are the provisions for infants and toddlers in PL 99-457 different from the provisions for 3-, 4-, and 5-year-old children?

PRACTICES IN EARLY INTERVENTION

You should be able to describe the foundational assumptions of early intervention practice.

Like most educational programs, early childhood special education has certain foundational assumptions that govern its practice. This section lists ten foundational assumptions and their implications and describes the components of early intervention practice.

Foundational Assumptions

Because early intervention frequently involves the family as well as the child, the ten foundational assumptions of early intervention address issues relating both to infants and children with disabilities and to their families.

Are there differences in the ways infants and children with disabilities and their families are treated?

1. The needs of infants and children with disabilities and the needs of their families differ from one case to another; thus, professionals must develop individualized intervention plans.

Because of the wide age range served (infants through preschool years) and the number of different disabilities, interventions must be individualized. Similarly, families differ on many dimensions, including educational level, amount of social support from their family and friends, financial resources, the nature of their goals and aspirations for their children, and the number of other demands on their time and energy. Thus, a single family-involvement program will not adequately address the needs of all families. To identify the needs of infants and children and their families, professionals conduct assessments. With infants and children, they use direct testing, interviews with the adults who know them, and direct observation in their natural environment (Bailey & Wolery, 1989; Wachs & Sheehan, 1988). With families, they use checklists, rating scales, interviews with the family members, and observation (Bailey & Simeonsson, 1988a; Dunst et al., 1988).

Why must family environment be considered when planning interventions?

2. Infants and children are influenced by and influence their environments; thus, professionals must recognize those influences when planning interventions.

We often view education as a matter of influencing students; however, another factor comes into play in early childhood special education. As most teachers and parents know, infants and young children have a major influence on the adults around them. When planning interventions, professionals must recognize the effects of the child on his or her family. These may range from producing great joy and happiness to creating high levels of dissatisfaction and stress. Professionals must be alert to such effects when conducting assessments and providing intervention. Frequently, families need respite care (Salisbury & Intagliata, 1986), contact with other parents, skills in teaching and managing the child, and other similar help in adapting to the influences of their infant or child (Fewell & Vadasy, 1986; Seligman & Darling, 1989).

3. Most infants and children with disabilities interact with and act upon their physical and social environment; thus, interventions should take advantage of their skills, attention, and motivation.

As parents know, young children (including those with disabilities) tend to move, observe, and act on their social and physical surroundings. Such interactions are usually purposeful; they are not just random responses to unrelated events. Young children appear to be trying to figure out and master their environment (Dunst, 1981). Professionals must recognize the child's propensity to interact and make it a part of the intervention plan. To this end, early childhood education should be structured differently from school-age programs. It should include toys, stimulating materials, frequent opportunities for infants and children to make choices about how they spend their time, and activities that occur on the floor. Much of the intervention must be done in the context of play and regularly occurring routines such as bathing and mealtimes. The environment should be designed so that children's actions result in responses (Hanson & Lynch, 1989). Often it is useful to follow the child's focus of attention rather than attempting to direct attention to a particular object or toy in order to teach from it (Dunst et al., 1987; Warren & Kaiser, 1988). Because of a child's propensity to act, the home and other environments in which infants and young children spend their time must be designed for safety. Interventionists should help families make environments "childproof" and safe.

4. Most infants and children with disabilities do not learn from their environments efficiently; thus, interventions must be designed to teach needed skills purposefully and systematically.

Most infants and children in early intervention programs are there because they are having problems in learning and development. To ensure that they learn important skills, interventions must be planned and implemented carefully. This does not necessarily require a separate, specialized program for children with disabilities. Many young children with disabilities can be served in quality early childhood education programs designed for young normally developing children, although such programs may require some modification (Safford, 1989; Wolery, Strain, & Bailey, in press). Researchers in early childhood special education have designed many effective intervention strategies and curricula; these must be implemented systematically if infants and children are to learn the skills that have been identified as important (Bailey & Wolery, 1992; Hanson & Lynch, 1989).

What area besides developmental skills should be assessed?

5. Most infants and children with disabilities have developmental delays across areas; thus, intervention programs should address all developmental domains and all the settings in which the children spend time.

The content of the early childhood special education curriculum comes from two sources: normal child development and the demands of the environments in which children live (Wolery & Gast, 1984). Researchers have identified five types of development: (1) cognitive, perceptual, and intellectual development; (2) speech, language, and communication development; (3) gross and fine motor development; (4) play, interaction, and social development; and (5) feeding, toileting, dressing, and self-care development (Bailey & Wolery, 1989). Professionals must assess infants and children in each of these areas to identify their needs and develop suitable intervention plans. In addition, they must assess the environments in which the children live and in which they will soon be expected to function (Salisbury & Vincent, 1990). After identifying the skills children will need in those environments, they assess the children on those skills and develop plans for teaching the skills as needed.

How do family and societal systems affect the intervention program?

6. Families are systems that exist within broader societal systems; thus, to plan an effective intervention, professionals must recognize the relationships between the different systems.

Each family is a system composed of different members. These members and the relationships between them constitute the family's structure. The interactions of family members are influenced by their beliefs, cultural influences, the roles and functions each member assumes, the subsystems within the family, and the communication between family members. The family, like its individual members, has a life cycle or a series of stages through which it passes (Seligman & Darling, 1989). Further, the family exists within a broader set of systems known as its *social ecology* (Bronfenbrenner, 1979). These broader systems are characterized as comprising three levels (Seligman & Darling, 1989).

The first level includes the individuals and agencies with whom the family interacts, such as friends, extended family, individuals with whom they work, personnel from the intervention program, healthcare providers, church and other social groups, and the general community. The interactions with these individuals and groups influence both positively and negatively the family's adaptation to living with an infant or child with disabilities. The second level includes agencies with which the family does not have direct interaction, but which can influence how they adapt (Seligman & Darling, 1989); these include the mass media and governmental agencies whose policies and practices relate to education, health, and social services. The third level is society at large, characterized by its prevailing beliefs and its institutions.

The birth of an infant with disabilities can cause considerable disruption to the interaction patterns within a family and to the family's life cycle. Professionals must recognize how the family functions as a unit and how that unit interacts with its social ecology. Part of the intervention plan may be to help families deal with the agencies and individuals with whom they interact, for example, in explaining the child's condition to the extended family (e.g., grandparents, aunts, and uncles), in securing health and social services, and in finding respite care from members of their church or synagogue. Such assistance may result in the child receiving more services and the family learning how to use the resources available to them, with reduction in stress and negative interaction patterns.

7. Families have different needs, resources, and goals; thus, interventions should be designed to address their priorities using existing resources, supports, and social networks.

As noted in the first assumption, a given family may have needs that are quite different from those of other families. Similarly, each family will have different resources and may have different goals. Some families live near their extended family and can rely on them for social, financial, and other support. Other families do not, and need to secure that support from other sources. Since the resources of early intervention programs are limited, programs should help families identify and use resources that are already available to them. This practice not only conserves resources but can help families become more independent in securing help from their social ecologies (Dunst et al., 1988).

Why should
progress in
intervention be
monitored
over time?

8. The needs of infants and children with disabilities and the needs of their families change over time; thus, professionals must monitor progress and adjust the intervention accordingly.

As infants and children change over time, the intervention program must be adjusted accordingly. Similarly, adjustments must be made as the needs of families and the resources available to them change. In quality intervention programs, the professionals are constantly monitoring the progress and needs of the participating infants or children and their families (Wolery & Bailey, 1984). Although six-month and yearly reviews of intervention plans are required, the monitoring must occur even more frequently to be effective. In fact, each contact with the infant or child and the family should be an intervention *and* monitoring occasion.

9. Infants and children with disabilities and their families present diverse and complex needs; thus, programs must include members of different disciplines.

As noted in the definition of early childhood special education, the cooperation of several helping professions is required to meet the needs of infants and children with disabilities and the needs of their families. The professionals that unite to serve a family are called the intervention team. Frequently, such teams have two types of members: core members and consultant members. The core members are those who have direct and frequent contact with the families. Although only one member, called a *facilitator,* may work with a given family, the core team members are available to help the facilitator and may meet with the family on a periodic basis. The professions of the core members will vary, but teams frequently include an early childhood special educator, a speech-language pathologist, a physical therapist, an occupational therapist, and a social worker. The disciplines of the consultant members may include pediatrics, nursing, audiology, and psychology, among others. Consultant members may work with selected families, may provide selective service to all families, or may consult only with core team members (McCollum & Hughes, 1988; Thorp & McCollum, 1988).

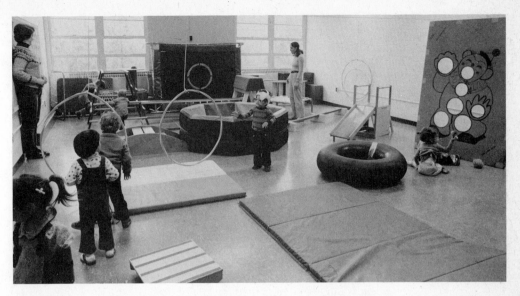

Many children with disabilities can be successfully integrated into regular preschool programs. The child in the center of the picture has difficulty maintaining his balance and is wearing headgear to protect him in the event of a fall.

10. Infants and children with disabilities are similar in many ways to typically developing infants and children; thus, interventions should be normalized.

Although infants and children with disabilities have unique needs, they also have needs that are shared by all other children; for example, they need to be accepted, well fed, nurtured, and safe. Also, there is considerable evidence that they can be adequately served in programs designed for young typically developing children (Guralnick, 1990; Peck, Odom, & Bricker, in press). Thus, intervention services are probably best provided in high-quality, regular early education programs (cf. Bredekamp, 1987; Wolery, Strain, & Bailey, in press). To the extent possible, normalized interventions should be used (Bailey & McWilliam, 1990). To serve children adequately in mainstreamed placements, teams must identify the children's needs, establish a schedule of activities for meeting those needs, provide training and consultation to the staff of the program, monitor the implementation and effects of the plan, and adjust it as needed (Bricker & Cripe, 1992; Salisbury, 1991; Wolery & Fleming, in press).

PROBE 4-3   Practices in Early Intervention

1. T   F   A single family-involvement program is likely to meet the needs of all families in an early intervention program.
2. T   F   Infants and young children with disabilities influence the reactions of their families.
3. If infants and children with disabilities do not necessarily learn efficiently from their environments, what implication does this hold for their teachers?
4. Who are some of the individuals in the first level of the family social ecology, and of what importance are they?
5. T   F   Although infants and children with disabilities may be quite different from one another, their families are very similar.
6. If infants' and children's needs change over time, what implications does this hold for their teachers?
7. What disciplines are likely to be represented on the core intervention team?

COMPONENTS OF EARLY INTERVENTION PRACTICE

> You should be able to describe the various components of the three
> major phases of early intervention practice.

Early intervention programs have at least three major phases: (1) identification of children who need services (Child Find) and program entry, (2) program planning and implementation, and (3) program exit (Bricker & Veltman, 1990). For each phase, professionals engage in different practices; these are described in the following section.

Child Find and Program Entry

METHODS OF CHILD FIND. In school-age programs the identification of children with special needs often starts when teachers in regular education programs, suspecting that a student is in need of special education services, initiate the referral process. Infants and young children, however, may not be in any sort of program and thus may have little contact with professionals. To counter this problem, early intervention programs frequently engage in Child Find activities. Public schools are required by law to find and identify young children with disabilities.

What are the two methods of Child Find?

Child Find is accomplished through two primary methods. In one method, children are identified as a result of their performance on a screening instrument (Wolery, 1989a). Developmental screening instruments are frequently norm-referenced tests, which can be given quickly and provide estimates of children's developmental functioning across different areas. Examples of commonly used screening tests are the *Denver Developmental Screening Test* (Frankenburg, Dodds, & Fandal, 1975), *Developmental Profile II* (Alpern, Boll, & Shearer, 1980), *Minnesota Child Development Inventory* (Ireton & Thwing, 1974), *The Early Screening Inventory* (Meisels & Wiske, 1983), and the *Developmental Indicators for the Assessment of Learning—Revised* (Mardell-Czudnowski & Goldenberg, 1983). Frequently, vision and hearing tests and a physical examination are also included. The purpose of all such screening is to determine whether children should be referred for a diagnostic or program-eligibility assessment.

A second method of Child Find is to seek referrals from professionals and others in contact with young children. Professionals who have regular contact with infants and children are informed of the program, the type of children served, and the procedures for referring them (Bourland & Harbin, 1987). Professionals in neonatal intensive care nurseries, physicians, public health nurses, and parents frequently make direct referrals. When a diagnosis has not already been made, the children are screened and a decision is made about sending them for a diagnostic evaluation.

DIAGNOSTIC/ELIGIBILITY ASSESSMENT. After being identified through screening or referral, infants and children suspected of needing special services receive a diagnostic evaluation. The methods and content of this evaluation vary, depending on the suspected disability. For example, if a child is suspected of having a hearing loss, an audiologist would use the most appropriate method to assess that possibility. In general, the definitions and criteria described in other chapters of this book for each disability are used for diagnosis. Although labeling children is viewed as undesirable, it is frequently necessary to secure eligibility for early intervention services.

How is a
developmental
delay determined?

Infants and toddlers are eligible for services under PL 99-457 if they have a developmental delay or a condition that is likely to result in such a delay. In some states, if infants and toddlers are at risk for developmental delays, they are eligible for services. Each state, however, must define *at risk* and develop a method for measuring it. For preschoolers (ages 3 through 5), states use the diagnostic categories specified by PL 94-142, although some states simply use the category *developmental delay*. Again, the states must define and select measurement procedures. Usually when a developmental delay is suspected, a psychologist or special educator administers a developmental scale; this often is a thorough, norm-referenced test that assesses the extent to which infants or children are developing within normal limits. Examples include the *Bayley Scales of Infant Development* (Bayley, 1969), *McCarthy Scales of Children's Abilities* (McCarthy, 1972), and *The Battelle Developmental Inventory* (Newborg, Stock, Wnek, Guidubaldi, & Svinicki, 1984). After it has been determined that an infant or child is eligible for services, the child is referred for enrollment in an intervention program.

Program Planning and Implementation

Program planning and implementation progresses through four steps: (1) assessment of the infant or child and the family for program planning; (2) development of the IFSP or the IEP; (3) implementation and monitoring of the intervention; and (4) review and evaluation of the program (Bricker & Veltman, 1990). The following section describes each of these steps in some detail.

ASSESSMENT OF INFANTS AND CHILDREN. Screening and diagnostic evaluations have limited value in planning intervention programs. For program planning, both the infant or child and the family should be assessed. For the infant or child, this assessment takes several forms, including direct testing with criterion- and curriculum-referenced measures, informal evaluations with interventionist-devised assessments, direct observation, and interviews with the family and other adults who know the infant or child. Usually, the team observes the infant or child in his or her natural environment (e.g., home, day care setting) and notes the activities and routines that occur in those settings. If a skill deficit is noted, it is then assessed and becomes a potential focus of instruction.

The team also uses criterion- and curriculum-referenced measures that cover all areas of development. These may be supplemented with measures that address single areas of development (e.g., cognitive skills). Some commonly used measures that assess multiple developmental areas are listed in Table 4-5. The purpose of this assessment is fourfold: (1) to identify the skills the infant or child has (i.e., those that do not need to be taught); (2) to identify the skills the infant or child does with assistance; (3) to identify the skills the infant or child does not have but needs to learn; and (4) to identify the intervention strategies that will be effective (Bailey & Wolery, 1989). This assessment should be conducted over several days or a few weeks in familiar settings with familiar adults. The program planning assessment should address all areas of development and should be conducted by members of different professions. The areas of development, the subareas, and some sample skills are detailed in the following paragraphs.

What
developmental
areas should be
assessed?

Cognitive skills and development include at least three subareas: sensorimotor skills, concept development, and preacademic skills. *Sensorimotor skills* are motor movements that infants make in interacting with their environment. As described by Piaget, these motor movements progress through a series of stages that culminate in a primitive ability to think or symbolize (Dunst,

---

TABLE 4-5   Commonly Used Criterion- and Curriculum-Referenced Measures That Assess Multiple Developmental Areas

---

Adaptive Performance Instrument (Consortium on Adaptive Performance, 1980)

Battelle Developmental Inventory (Newborg, Stock, Wnek, Guidubaldi, & Svinicki, 1984)

Brigance Inventory of Early Development (Brigance, 1978)

Carolina Curriculum for Handicapped Infants and Infants at Risk (Johnson-Martin, Jens, & Attermeier, 1986)

Carolina Curriculum for Preschoolers with Special Needs (Johnson-Martin, Attermeier, & Hacker, 1990)

Developmental Programming for Infants and Young Children (Brown & Donovan, 1985)

Early Learning Accomplishment Profile (Glover, Preminger, & Sanford, 1978)

Evaluation and Programming System for Infants and Young Children (Bricker, Bailey, Gummerlock, Buhl, & Slentz, 1986)

Learning Accomplishment Profile—Diagnostic (LeMay, Griffin, & Sanford, 1978)

Hawaii Early Learning Profile (Furono, O'Reily, Hoska, Instauka, Allman, & Zeisloft, 1985)

HICOMP Preschool Curriculum (Willoughby-Herb & Neisworth, 1980)

Uniform Performance Assessment System (Haring, White, Edgar, Affleck, Hayden, Munson, & Bendersky, 1981)

1981; Langley, 1989). Examples include imitation—copying the behavior of others; purposeful problem solving (means-ends)—using tools and objects to achieve goals (e.g., a toddler pushing a chair to the table and climbing up on it to get a cookie on the table); object permanence—the awareness that things continue to exist even when they are not present; spatial relationships—understanding the position of objects in relation to one another; causality—understanding what makes things work; and play—learning to manipulate objects in play.

Concept development refers to understanding the notions of the world. Examples of concepts that are acquired during the preschool years are object properties (e.g., heat, mass, shape, color); object relationships in space (e.g., order, size, location, number); events in time and space (e.g., movement, changes in energy, changes in group composition); and relationships among events in time and space (e.g., cause and effect) (Becker, Englemann, & Thomas, 1975).

Preacademic skills include those behaviors that are necessary for beginning first grade instruction. These include prereading skills (e.g., language system, print awareness, visual discrimination); prewriting skills (e.g., grasping markers, combining strokes); and premath skills (e.g., rote counting, rational counting, matching sets) (Wolery & Brookfield-Norman, 1988; Wolery & Wolery, 1992).

Communication skills and development include at least five subareas: semantic functions and relationships, pragmatic functions, syntactical development, lexical development, and phonological development. *Semantic functions and relationships* refer to the meaning of language, such as the meaning of objects, events, relationships; meaning progresses from nonverbal to verbal expressions. Examples of semantic functions are expressing that an object exists, that the speaker wants something to stop, that someone owns something, or that someone did something. Semantic relationships are combinations of these and other functions, such as noting that someone did a particular thing to an object, or that some object is in a particular place (McLean & Snyder-McLean, 1978; Roberts & Crais, 1989).

Pragmatic functions refer to the intentions or purposes for communicating and the skills required to carry on a conversation. Examples of these skills include requesting assistance, protesting or communicating displeasure, commenting on objects and actions, greeting others, and answering questions. Skills such as knowing at what point in a conversation it is your turn to speak, or when the listener needs additional information, are also pragmatic skills (Coggins & Sandall, 1983; Roberts & Crais, 1989).

Syntactical and morphological development refers to the rules used to combine words in sentences and the combination of word parts to change the meaning. Examples include using a verb phrase; using inflections (e.g., use of *-ing* plurals, possessive *-s*); using interrogative sentences (e.g., yes/no questions, *wh-* words such as *why* and *where*); and using negative sentences (Coggins & Carpenter, 1979).

Lexical development refers to behavior related to the type and number of words children use. Examples include nominals (names of specific objects), general nominals (classes of objects), action words, and modifier words (Coggins & Carpenter, 1979).

Phonological development refers to children's use of speech sounds and their processing of those sounds. This includes imitation of sounds, spontaneous production of sounds, and putting sounds together to form words. In many cases, speech is used as the mode of communication. In other instances, manual sign language, electronic communication systems, or communication boards are used (Miller & Allaire, 1987).

Social skills and development include at least four subareas: parent-infant or parent-child interactions and relationships, child-child interactions and social play, toy play, and social skills. Parent-infant or parent-child interactions and relationships include such things as attachment, initiating social interactions, responding to social initiations, and taking turns. Behaviors used in these skills include such things as eye contact, movements of the arms and legs, and vocalizations, among others (Comfort, 1988; Mahoney & Powell, 1986). Child-child interactions and social play include such things as attending to others' interactions, initiating social interactions, responding to others' social initiations, sustaining interactions, and engaging in cooperative play and associative play (Musslewhite, 1986; Odom & McConnell, 1989). Toy play involves manipulating objects in functional ways. These include exploratory behaviors, movements of objects (e.g., shaking, pounding, squeezing), manipulating movable parts of toys, separating parts of toys, and using toys in pretend routines (Musslewhite, 1986; Wolery & Bailey, 1989). Social skills involve such things as sharing, using play organizers (e.g., saying "Come play with me"), showing affection, and giving help to those who need it (Strain, 1985).

Facilitating the development of social interactions, play, and other social skills is a primary focus of many intervention programs. Play skills are seen as a major means by which children can acquire and practice other skills (e.g., language and cognitive skills), and as a precursor to later leisure skills. Further, the development of adequate social skills is important in ensuring that children can be educated in integrated settings and will live productive lives in society.

Self-care skills and development involve at least three subareas: eating and feeding, dressing and undressing, and toileting (Snell, 1987). Eating and feeding include such skills as chewing, sucking, finger feeding, and using utensils such as cups, spoons, and forks (Morris & Klein, 1987). Dressing and undressing refer to skills such as taking off and putting on garments and fastening buttons, zippers, and snaps. Toileting includes urinating and defecating in the toilet, knowing when to go to the toilet, and washing hands after using the toilet (Bailey & Wolery, 1992).

Motor skills and development include at least two broad subareas: gross motor skills and fine motor skills. *Gross motor* refers to the movements of large body muscles; examples include rolling over, crawling, walking, running, and jumping (Smith, 1989). *Fine motor* skills include movements of the small muscles of the body; examples include movement of the hands in different grasp patterns to manipulate objects, movement of the tongue and lips to speak or chew food, and movement of the eyes to follow a moving target (Smith, 1989). With children who have motor disabilities, occupational and physical therapists often provide therapy to normalize children's movements, promote normalized tension in the muscles, and ensure adequate balance both while stationary and while moving (Campbell, 1987a, 1987b; Orelove & Sobsey, 1987).

What aspects of family functioning should be assessed?

ASSESSMENT OF FAMILIES. Program planning assessment for families involves the use of interviews, rating scales, checklists, and observations to identify the family needs, strengths, resources, and critical events (Bailey & Simeonsson, 1988a; Dunst et al., 1988). Family needs commonly include the needs for information, support, help in explaining the child's condition to others, securing community services, finding financial aid, and family functioning (Bailey, 1988a). Strengths include such things as the amount of commitment, appreciation, purpose, communication, coping strategies, and problem-solving abilities displayed by families (Dunst et al., 1988). Resources include the amount and type of social support, financial resources, and material resources available to the family (Dunst et al., 1988). Critical events are changes that occur in a family's development that may result in increased stress and disruption (Bailey, 1988b). Examples include transitions such as changing jobs, learning that a child has a disability, a child's entering school, a child's leaving home, medical crises, and the death of a close relative.

Conducting assessments of families requires unique skills. Ideally, a rapport and relationship between the professional and family should be established prior to dealing with sensitive issues. The assessment activities should have a clear purpose (i.e., to identify needs and resources) and should be conducted with sensitivity to the family's culture, language, and perceptions. The assessment should result in the identification of goals that the family values and the identification of procedures for meeting those goals that are acceptable to the family. The professional must treat the information with respect and confidentiality (McGonigel, Kaufmann, & Johnson, 1991).

DEVELOPMENT OF THE IFSP OR THE IEP. After the assessment of the infant or child and the family are completed, the individualized family service plan (IFSP) or individualized education plan (IEP) is developed. The IFSP, as described in Table 4-4 (p. 115), must include goals based on the assessment of both the infant or toddler and family. An excerpt from an IFSP is shown in Figure 4-1 (pp. 126–128). The IEP for children ages 3, 4, and 5 must include goals for the children and may include goals for families. These documents are to be the plans from which the intervention program operates. They are developed *with* the family. Thus, after the assessment is completed and the results are analyzed, the professionals and parents should meet to draft and finalize the plan. These meetings are designed to identify the most important objectives and to plan interventions. Too often, plans are developed for parents without their participation; when parents are involved in their children's assessments, they provide more input into the plan (Brinckerhoff & Vincent, 1986).

IMPLEMENTING AND MONITORING INTERVENTION. Once the goals are identified and high-priority objectives specified, an intervention plan is developed to ensure that the objectives are accomplished. Because of the diversity in age and disabling conditions of infants and children and because of the diversity of families and their needs and goals, no single intervention plan will work in all situations. Further, the nature of the intervention program will influence how the intervention plan is designed. If the intervention program is home-based or clinic-based, with professionals seeing the family once or twice a week for a short visit, the intervention plan must be different from programs in which children are taught in centers or classrooms.

What are the basic types of home-based programs?

Home-based and clinic-based programs require that the parent be the primary interventionist (Bailey & Simeonsson, 1988b). There are two types of such programs. In the first, the parents receive training and information on how to teach their infant or child (Hanson, 1987; Shearer & Shearer, 1976). The early childhood special educator goes to the home, assesses the child, and develops an intervention plan with the family. The interventionist usually uses a four-step process to teach families how to implement the intervention. This process includes (1) telling the family how to implement the intervention strategies and activities; (2) showing the family how to implement them; (3) watching the family implement the intervention; and (4) giving feedback to the family on their attempts. At each visit, the professional checks the child's progress and reviews the intervention plan with the family. This type of parent-implemented program has been very successful but requires considerable work on the part of family members.

A variation of this type of program is the Seattle Inventory of Early Learning software (Schlater, 1987). The program is used with the *Seattle Inventory of Early Learning Test* (Fewell & Sandall, 1987). It allows home intervention programs to be designed by personal computer and can be used for families who live a long distance from the program. The computer will generate home programs that are developed around daily routines such as eating, bathing, playing independently, and diapering and dressing (Bagnato, Neisworth, & Munson, 1989). The computer program will also track progress and summarize program data.

In the second type of home-based or clinic-based program, the parents receive information and training on how to interact with their child and develop a positive relationship. The Transactional Intervention Program is an example of such a program (Mahoney & Powell, 1986). It has a hierarchy of interactive objectives that include, among many others, playing frequently together, balancing the turn taking, increasing parents' responsiveness to the child, increasing the length of turn taking, and matching the interaction to the child's developmental levels (Mahoney & Powell, 1986).

One of the disadvantages of home- and clinic-based programs is that parents must do much of the work; some families cannot do this. Also, unless there are a large number of siblings or other children in the neighborhood, infants and children have few opportunities for learning important child–child interaction and social play objectives. Another disadvantage of home-based programs is that the interventionist must travel from home to home, which can waste valuable professional time. Sometimes all the team members do not observe the infant or child regularly; this disadvantage occurs more often in home-based than in clinic-based programs. However, there are advantages to these programs. For one thing, the professional and the family in many cases develop a strong supportive relationship. Further, the need to transport the infant or child is reduced, and the infant or child has the opportunity to learn in his or her natural environment.

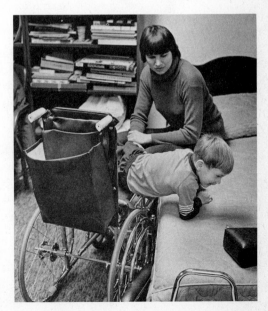

As part of a home-based preschool program, this boy's mother was taught ways to instruct him in how to climb from his wheelchair onto his bed.

FIGURE 4-1   Excerpt from an Individualized Family Service Plan (IFSP)

Individualized Family Service Plan*
(IFSP)

Child's Name: Benjamin Griffin
Date: 6/7/90

Family Name: Griffin

Address: 127 Aspen Lane

Mountain

Child's Name: Benjamin Griffin

Birthdate: 1/5/90

Phone: 729-0631

Referral Date: 6/1/90

By Whom: NICU

Coordinator: Pat White, MD

Assessment: 5/90 and 6/90

IFSP Team and Signatures:

Leslie Griffin 6/7/90   *Michael Griffin* 6-7-90

Parent or Guardian   Date   Parent or Guardian   Date

Pat White, MD   *Neal Salos, MD*

Kylie Talbot, LPT   *Adrienne Wales, OTR*

Amanda Grey, M.S.   *Timothy John, RL*

Family Members/Social Supports: **Relationship**

Leslie   mother
Michael   father
Caroline   sister
Heather   neighbor

Child's Present Levels of Development:

Ben is alert and responds preferentially to his mother. He is becoming more able to tolerate being touched and to comfort himself. (For more information, see Assessment Report).

Domain	Age Level	Age Range
Cognitive	2–3 months	0–3 months
Fine Motor	2–3 months	0–3 months
Gross Motor	2–3 months	0–4 months
Language	1–2 months	0–3 months
Self-Help	0–1 month	0–1 month
Social/Emotional	0–2 months	1–2 months
Vision	within normal limits	
Hearing	within normal limits	

Early Intervention Services (Frequency and Intensity)

Family Information and Support—with each visit to the NICU, as specified in the activities.

PT and OT Evaluation and Monitoring—twice weekly during Ben's hospitalization.

After Discharge:

Physical therapy once a week;
Occupational therapy once a week;
Once a week home visits from the early intervention specialist.

Other Services

None

Transition Plan Attached: _____ Yes   X   Not Applicable

Child's Health Status:

Ben's health is stabilizing. He is responding well to a reduction of his oxygen levels, and plans are being made to discharge Ben in about a month if his good progress continues.

Other Agencies Involved:

Agency	Contact Person	Phone
Mountain Early Intervention Program	Kathleen Sanford	891-7026
Pulmonary Clinic	Dale Peavy	787-9576
Mountain Medical Supply, Inc.	Alice Strickland	891-2514

What intervention strategies are commonly used in center-based programs?

Center-based programs do not require the parents to be the primary interventionists. However, such programs do often try to involve families, and the methods just described for home-based programs are useful in supplementing the intervention activities that occur in the center. In center-based programs all team members are usually readily available without extensive travel. This allows the team to interact and develop appropriate plans for children who are particularly challenging. Over the past 20 years, a number of useful curricula and intervention strategies have been developed for center-based programs. Early childhood special educators should be skilled in designing the center-based environment and implementing four different types of interventions: child-directed learning activities, naturalistic teaching strategies, peer-mediated interventions, and direct teaching strategies. Each of these may be used with the same child within a given day; they are not mutually exclusive strategies.

Figure 4-2 (p. 129) illustrates some of the targets that special educators use in early intervention programs. These and others described elsewhere in this chapter help to focus on the content of an early intervention program (*what* to teach). The following descriptions of instructional strategies illustrate methodologies for teaching (*how* to teach).

CHILD-DIRECTED STRATEGIES. Child-directed learning activities are common in early childhood programs for nonhandicapped children (Bredekamp, 1987). These activities require the teacher to arrange and equip the classroom in interesting ways. The role of the teacher is to establish a daily routine, to provide materials, to assist children in planning what they will do for the day or for some segment of the day, and to monitor the children and use verbal

FIGURE 4-1   *(continued)*

Child's Name: Benjamin Griffin

Date: 6/7/90

Child's Name: Benjamin Griffin

Date: 6/7/90

Outcome # 1:

Leslie wants to be more secure in her ability to care for Ben at home.

Identified By: Leslie

Family Concerns, Priorities, and Resources for This Outcome:

Although I have formal training in child development and an older child, I worry that I don't know enough about Ben's needs to take care of him at home. I am sure that Michael and I can read professional literature to learn by ourselves, and we can learn from the medical team at the hospital and from the experiences of the other parents. We have many friends who have volunteered to help us in any way they can, but I'm not sure what to ask them for. What I really need is to be confident that when Ben comes home, I'll know what to do. (Leslie)

Service/Action	Dates and Evaluations		
	Begin	Review	End
1. Leslie will spend some time during each visit to the nursery holding and feeding Ben.	6/9/90	7/8/90	#7 7/8/90
2. Ben's neonatologist and his primary nurse will help Leslie recognize and read Ben's cues and find ways to soothe and comfort him.	6/9/90	7/8/90	#7 7/8/90
3. Ben's primary nurse and the other unit nurses will help Leslie assume as much of Ben's care as she wants to while he is in the nursery.	6/9/90	7/8/90	#7 7/8/90
4. Leslie and Michael are attending the NICU parent-to-parent support group and will continue after Ben is discharged, as long as they want to go. They plan to bring up their fears about taking Ben home at the next meeting. The Griffins will ask the other families about ways these families have used their friends for support and assistance.	Already Begun	Continuing	#7

Service/Action	Dates and Evaluations		
	Begin	Review	End
5. The medical team and the hospital infant development specialist will give the Griffins resource materials about the needs and behaviors of preemies.	6/9/90	7/8/90	7/8/90

Criteria/Timeline

These activities will begin immediately and continue throughout Ben's hospitalization. Leslie will determine whether or not her need has been met, in consultation with Dr. White.

Source: Reproduced with permission of the Association for the Care of Children's Health, 7910 Woodmont Ave., Suite 300, Bethesda, MD 20814.

prompts to stimulate their reflection and thinking about the activity. When this model is used, emphasis is placed on play and active engagement—that is, attending to and interacting with objects, activities, or others (McWilliam, 1991). Teachers employ several strategies for promoting play and engagement, including using interesting materials, ensuring that children have roles in the activities, reinforcing engagement, and switching tasks frequently (McWilliam & Bailey, 1992). However, as stated earlier, infants and children with developmental delays and disabilities frequently do not learn efficiently from their environments. Therefore, if this type of instruction is used exclusively, some children's needs may not be met. For example, children with disabilities are more likely to engage in interactions with peers when the play activities are structured rather than unstructured (DeKlyen & Odom, 1989). Nonetheless, child-directed learning activities may be useful from a couple of perspectives. First, they can help prepare children for their next educational placement, which may well be designed in this manner. Second, child-directed learning activities provide children with opportunities to practice and use the skills learned in other situations. Thus, most programs for children with disabilities and developmental delays should include this type of instruction. It should be supplemented, however, with the other strategies to be described in this section.

What are naturalistic teaching strategies?

NATURALISTIC TEACHING STRATEGIES. Naturalistic teaching strategies are those that occur throughout the day when the infant or child is engaged in daily activities or frequently occurring routines (Kaiser, Yoder, & Keetz, 1992). Naturalistic teaching strategies for promoting language development are incidental teaching, the mand-model procedure, and naturalistic

FIGURE 4-1   *(continued)*

Child's Name: Benjamin Griffin

Date: 6/7/90

DATE	NOTES/COMMENTS
6/7/90	The Griffin's IFSP is being developed by an interagency team consisting of the Griffins, their hospital team, the infant specialist from their local early intervention program, and their pediatrician, who will serve as their care coordinator.
	Benjamin has been making steady progress, and tentative plans are being made to discharge him home in four weeks. The IFSP is being written as his discharge plan.
10/9/90	Leslie and Michael are unhappy with some aspects of their IFSP, and Dr. White has asked the other members of the IFSP team to meet with the Griffins and her to make some revisions. Outcomes 3–4, which relate to OT and PT for Benjamin, have been very problematic for Leslie. Having two separate appointments each week on different days means four hours of commuting to the hospital. Leslie is beginning to hate the drive and dislikes leaving Caroline with her neighbor so often. The team discussed options to eliminate this problem. Kylie and Adrienne have agreed to work together in the future, thereby requiring only one visit a week. To meet hospital review board requirements, OT and PT outcomes will be written separately, but therapy will be provided jointly.
	Initially, Adrienne and Kylie will see Ben together. After they have had a chance to learn each other's activities with Ben, they will alternate, each seeing Ben every other week. Leslie also feels swamped by the demands of carrying out Ben's therapy at home, given all the time she must spend caring for him. She would like some time to spend with Caroline or spend alone and has asked that Amanda come to the house twice a week rather than once a week. Amanda will take over Ben's home therapy during that extra day.
	Leslie has decided that she now wants to be co-care coordinator with Pat White.

Source: M. J. McGonigel, R. K. Kaufmann, and B. H. Johnson (1991). *Guidelines and recommended practices for the individualized family service plan* (2nd ed.). Bethesda, MD: Association for the Care of Children's Health.

---

time delay (Kaiser et al., 1992; Warren & Kaiser, 1988). These strategies are characterized as (1) building upon the child's focus of attention, (2) being brief teaching interactions that allow children to learn or practice a needed skill, and (3) being positive in nature.

With the incidental teaching procedure, the teaching episode begins when the child request an object, action, assistance, or permission. The teacher then asks the child for a more elaborate or complex language request and waits for a few seconds. If the child responds correctly, the teacher presents the object of the request. If the child does not respond, the teacher provides a model of the more complex language skill; if the child then imitates the model, the teacher grants the request.

What is the mand-model procedure?

The mand-model procedure is similar, but is not initiated by the child's request. Instead the teacher observes the child and notes the focus of his or her attention. At that point the teacher approaches the child, states a question about the focus of attention, and waits a short interval for the child to respond. If the child responds correctly, the teacher praises the child and the interaction is stopped; if the child does not respond, the teacher provides a model and gives reinforcement when the child imitates.

The strategy termed naturalistic time delay is used during a routine in which the teacher typically provides the child with help. At the point in the routine when help has usually been given, it is withheld for a few seconds. If the child speaks, the routine is continued and the

FIGURE 4-2   A Functional Approach to Exceptionality: Early Intervention

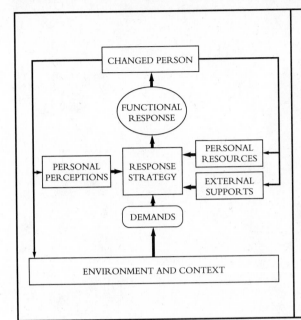

TARGETS FOR EARLY INTERVENTION

Personal Resources are the skills, knowledge, attitudes, and personality characteristics that young children call upon to meet demands that are placed on them by their environment. Those who are involved in providing early intervention are concerned with developing these personal resources to the maximum extent possible. Following are some of the targets for such intervention:

- Speech, language, and communication skills.

- Self-help skills, such as eating, dressing, and toileting.

- Motor skills, such as walking and object manipulation.

- Understanding of cause-and-effect relationships.

- Recognition of concepts, such as size, shape, and color.

- Development of decision-making abilities to help them cope with demands.

- How to play with other children.

help is provided, if necessary. If the child does not speak, a model is provided (Halle, Baer, & Spradlin, 1981).

Each of these procedures has been highly effective in teaching preschoolers a number of different and important language skills (Kaiser et al., 1992; Warren & Gazdag, 1990). Further, these procedures tend to teach children to use the skills when they are needed. Although these strategies have been used primarily for teaching language skills, they have also been used for teaching social skills such as giving affection (Charlop & Walsh, 1986).

PEER-MEDIATED STRATEGIES. Peer-mediated interventions have been used extensively to teach preschoolers who are socially withdrawn and have limited social skills to engage in social interactions (Kohler & Strain, 1990). These strategies involve the use of nonhandicapped peers to teach the child with disabilities to engage in play and social interactions. The training involves directly teaching a nonhandicapped peer to initiate social interactions with the child who has disabilities, perhaps by offering a toy or asking the child to play (Strain & Odom, 1986). The teacher observes and praises the peer confederate for implementing the intervention. Peer confederates can also be taught to praise and give other children feedback on their social interactions. These strategies have been successful in getting a wide range of children with disabilities to engage in more frequent social interactions (Odom, Hoyson, Jamieson, & Strain, 1985) and have not produced negative effects in the peer confederate (Strain & Odom, 1986). Using group rewards and praise when a small group of children meet a criterion of social interactions is also effective in increasing the social behavior of children with disabilities (Lefebvre & Strain, 1989).

Another commonly used strategy is known as affection training (McEvoy et al., 1988). In affection training, children meet in a group to play common preschool games. The games are adapted to cause frequent displays of affection, frequent physical contact between children,

A major value of center-based preschool programs is the opportunity for children to develop socialization skills through cooperative play.

and discussions of friends and their importance. This strategy has been successful in teaching children to interact outside of the affection training activity (McEvoy et al., 1988; McEvoy, Twardosz, & Bishop, 1990).

DIRECT INSTRUCTIONAL STRATEGIES. Direct teaching strategies have a long history of effectiveness with children who have disabilities (Wolery, Bailey, & Sugai, 1988). These strategies include the system of least prompts (increasing assistance), most–to–least prompts, and time delay. All involve the teacher providing the child with help and then systematically removing that help. With the system of least prompts, a hierarchy of more helpful prompts is used (Doyle, Wolery, Ault, & Gast, 1988). The child is first given an opportunity to perform the skill without assistance. If the child is not successful, the teacher provides the least amount of help and gives the child another opportunity to perform. If this is not successful, the teacher provides a more helpful prompt. This continues until the child performs correctly; then reinforcement is given.

With the most-to-least prompts procedure, the child is given a level of help that will ensure a correct response. After several opportunities at this level, the help is systematically decreased. Again, after several opportunities, the assistance is decreased further. This continues until the child performs correctly without assistance.

With time delay, the child is presented with the amount of assistance necessary to perform correctly. After a few opportunities with the necessary assistance, the prompt is delayed in time. Thus, the child has a short interval (a few seconds) to attempt the skill alone, but help is available if needed.

These procedures have been effective in teaching children to perform language, pre-academic, self-care, motor, and social skills (Wolery, Ault, & Doyle, 1992). When using direct teaching procedures with most preschool children who have disabilities, it is best to teach in small groups (Alig-Cybriwsky, Wolery, & Gast, 1990; Hoyson, Jamieson, & Strain, 1984).

The combination of child-directed learning activities, naturalistic teaching strategies, peer-mediated interventions, and direct teaching procedures constitutes the state of the art in intervention procedures with preschoolers who have disabilities. However, when these strategies are used, children's performance should be monitored frequently. Such monitoring allows the teacher to adjust the intervention to ensure that it is working.

REVIEW AND EVALUATION OF THE PROGRAM. The IFSPs for infants and toddlers must be reviewed each six months and revised once per year. The IEPs for children ages 3 to 5 should be reviewed and revised yearly. As just noted, intervention teams should continually monitor the implementation and effects of intervention programs; it is also necessary to review the progress with the family periodically. These formal reviews are for the purpose of making major adjustments in the intervention plan by readministering the assessment protocols, setting new objectives, and developing new intervention plans.

Program Exit

Where do children go when they exit a program?

Infants and children exit from programs for two primary reasons: They are no longer in need of intervention, or they are moving on to other programs. One purpose of the annual review of progress is to determine whether the infants or children continue to need the intervention program. When they do not, the parents should be prepared to monitor their performance to ensure that the children continue to develop without problems. More commonly, infants and children move from one program to another. There are four types of moves from program to program: (1) from the hospital or neonatal intensive care nursery to a community-based intervention program; (2) from an infant-toddler intervention program to a preschool intervention program; (3) from a preschool intervention program to a school-age program; and (4) from any of the above programs to a program designed only for children without disabilities (Wolery, 1989b). These transitions to different programs are not simple moves. Thorough preparation of the child for the next placement (Sainato & Lyon, 1989), preparation of the family (Fowler, Schwartz, & Atwater, 1991), and preparation of the receiving site (Wolery, 1989b) are necessary.

Summary of Early Intervention Practice

The three major phases of early childhood special education programs are Child Find and program entry, program development and implementation, and planning for termination of program services (Bricker & Veltman, 1990). In the Child Find and program entry phase, children are identified through mass screening programs or by referrals from professionals or parents. A diagnostic assessment is conducted to determine whether the infant or child is eligible for services. If eligible, then assessment of the child's skills across domains and of the family's needs, strengths, and resources must occur. An IFSP or IEP is developed on the basis of that assessment, and intervention plans are devised. The interventions vary depending on whether the program is home-based or center-based. Finally, from regular reviews of the program, transition plans are developed to move the child to other programs.

PROBE 4-4   Components of Early Intervention Practice

1. What are the two methods by which infants and children are identified for early intervention programs?
2. List two subareas for each of the following developmental areas: cognitive, communication, social, self-care, and motor.
3. When assessing families, what areas are assessed other than their needs?
4. What is the parents' role in planning the IFSP or the IEP?
5. What are the two types of emphasis in home- and clinic-based programs?
6. If a teacher has set out an interesting activity, is helping children plan their day, and is asking questions to help them think about the activity, what center-based intervention strategy is the teacher using?
7. List and describe two naturalistic teaching strategies and two direct teaching strategies.
8. What are some types of transitions that infants and young children may encounter?

CHALLENGES FACED BY EARLY INTERVENTION PROGRAMS

You should be able to list some of the challenges faced by early intervention programs.

The field of early childhood special education faces many intriguing challenges. Three of these are described briefly in this section: implementing mainstreaming, designing intervention programs for diverse families, and preparing personnel. Many other challenges exist: ensuring that adequate funding is provided to operate quality programs, developing interventions for infants who were exposed to cocaine and alcohol prior to birth, designing interventions for infants with AIDS, ensuring smooth transitions from preschool to school-age programs, promoting interactions between agencies that benefit families, identifying children who are at risk for delays, and increasing the efficiency of our interventions, to name just a few (Meisels & Shonkoff, 1990; Widerstrom, Mowder, & Sandall, 1991; Bailey & Wolery, 1992).

Implementing Mainstreaming

Is mainstreaming widely practiced in the nation's preschool programs?

Mainstreaming refers to the practice of enrolling children with disabilities in programs for children without disabilities and attending to the needs of all the children in the program. Early childhood researchers have been studying mainstreaming for about 20 years. The following quotations describe the current status of mainstreaming:

The contemporary issue is clearly not whether early childhood mainstreaming is feasible and should be encouraged, but rather how one can design programs to maximize its effectiveness. (Guralnick, 1990, p. 3)

While the "why" of integrating children with disabilities is quite clear, the "how" is not so evident. (Sainato & Lyon, 1989, p. 305)

The responsibility for providing quality services in integrated settings is not finished with the determination of service delivery. The specific intervention and integration needs that exist must be addressed. (McLean & Hanline, 1990, p. 69)

The curriculum employed and the quality of instruction may have a more powerful effect on developmental outcome and skill acquisition than who is in the class. (Fewell & Oelwein, 1990, p. 115)

These statements indicate that good reasons exist for the practice of mainstreaming, that mainstreaming can be implemented in a variety of ways, that what occurs in mainstreamed placements is of critical importance, and that we have much to learn about how to carry out mainstreaming in the most effective way (Fleming, Wolery, Weinzierl, Venn, & Schroeder, 1991). Recent survey data of early childhood programs, including private-not-for-profit programs, private-for-profit, Head Start, public school prekindergarten programs, and kindergarten programs, indicate that about 75 percent of these programs engage in preschool mainstreaming (Wolery, Fleming, & Venn, 1990). Many of the intervention strategies described in this chapter are used in such mainstreamed programs (Peck, Odom, & Bricker, in press). From that experience it is clear that children with and without disabilities make developmental progress in mainstreamed programs (Odom & McEvoy, 1988), and that much of this progress is in the area of social skills (Buysse & Bailey, 1991). However, over the next few years, considerable research will be needed to ensure that the best intervention practices are used in mainstreamed programs (Wolery, Strain, & Bailey, in press).

Designing Intervention Programs for Families

What major challenges face early childhood special education?

In the last five years, considerable research and information has become available about how to assess family needs, strengths, and resources (Bailey & Simeonsson, 1988a; Dunst et al., 1988). Additionally, we now know some procedures for facilitating a family's adaptation to living with an infant or child with disabilities (Fewell & Vadasy, 1986; Seligman & Darling, 1989). However, three remaining issues continue to challenge the field. The first is how to train individuals to design and implement effective and efficient intervention strategies for families. The early intervention team can no longer be skilled only in working with infants and children; they must also be skilled in working with other adults and in understanding and using a complex service system (Bailey, Palsha, & Simeonsson, 1991). The second major challenge is in meeting the needs of infants and children with disabilities that come from nontraditional families. Examples of such families include mothers who are addicted to cocaine, mothers who have AIDS, and single-parent families with extremely limited resources. Unfortunately, many of our intervention strategies have been developed with more traditional families. Although considerable attention has been given to the possible effects of cocaine and other illegal drugs on children, the current data suggest that the effects of these drugs are varied and interact greatly with other environmental factors such as poverty (Schutter & Brinker, 1992). Nonetheless, when parents are addicted to cocaine, alcohol, and other drugs, intervention is complicated substantially. The third major challenge comes in dealing with culturally and ethnically diverse families (Lynch & Hanson, 1992). The values, beliefs, and practices of various cultures can be quite different from those of the professional. Understanding those differences is critical in developing effective early intervention programs.

Ensuring Adequate Personnel Preparation

As noted throughout this chapter, early childhood special educators and team members from other disciplines must display a variety of competencies. They must be capable of providing services to infants, to toddlers, and to preschoolers who have a wide range of developmental delays and disabilities. In addition, they must be capable of working with families who also vary greatly in their backgrounds, needs, and resources. Further, they must understand complex topics such as child development and intervention program design, implementation, and modification. Unfortunately, with a few exceptions, most individuals across disciplines who

TECHNOLOGY IN ACTION

Lindsey is a 5-year-old who was born with a physical disability that requires her to use a wheelchair to travel from place to place. The team of professionals who evaluated her performance concluded that she has average intellectual ability and should be able to function well in a regular classroom setting. She attends a preschool program sponsored by a hospital that specializes in providing services to children and adults with physical disabilities.

Ms. Anderson, Lindsey's teacher, has the goal of getting Lindsey ready for first grade. She uses a computer with a specially adapted keyboard that has letters of the alphabet arranged in order, not like the keys on a typical keyboard. The keyboard also has some special symbols, such as a stop sign and pictures of the Muppets (puppet characters that appear on the popular children's educational TV program "Sesame Street").

The keyboard comes with computer software that is designed to teach color, letter, and number recognition. Lindsey is currently working on learning her letters. She presses the letter Q and a picture of a queen appears on the computer screen, accompanied by a brief tune. Each letter press produces a picture associated with a word beginning with that letter and an appropriate tune. Ms. Anderson works with Lindsey to ensure that she is able to associate the letters with the keys and the pictures. She maintains records of the letters that Lindsey has learned and provides additional instruction if Lindsey has difficulty with any of them.

Lindsey enjoys the Muppet keyboard and likes to use it independently. Ms. Anderson is pleased with Lindsey's progress and is confident that she is developing the skills that will enable her to be mainstreamed into a regular first grade class with a high probability of being successful.

work in early intervention programs have relatively little training to accomplish these tasks (Bailey, Simeonsson, Yoder, & Huntington, 1990). To complicate matters, few university training programs plan to increase the amount of training they provide in early intervention. Thus, strategies must be developed for ensuring that persons who are hired by early intervention programs receive adequate staff development and training while on the job. The bright side of this coin is that the individual who receives quality preparation in early intervention will be in high demand.

PROBE 4-5   Challenges Faced by Early Intervention Programs

1. Define mainstreaming.
2. T F   Mainstreaming is not a very common practice in the nation's preschool programs.
3. What challenge faces early intervention in terms of the families it serves?
4. T F   There is an excess in the number of personnel trained in early intervention.

SUMMARY

1. Early childhood special education serves infants, toddlers, and preschoolers who have disabilities or developmental delays or who are at risk for developmental delays.
2. Early intervention programs exist in many different agencies and locations; they focus on helping families as well as infants and children.
3. There are early intervention goals for infants and children, for their families, and for society at large; further, providing early intervention services benefits each of these three groups.
4. Qualified research supports the provision of early intervention services to infants and children with disabilities, and the policy of many states is to provide a free appropriate public education to these children.

5. Early intervention is a new field but is sufficiently developed to have several foundational assumptions that guide its operation and practice.
6. Early intervention practices include Child Find and program entry procedures, including screening of children and diagnostic evaluations.
7. In designing interventions, early intervention personnel must assess the needs of the infants or children and their families.
8. Home- and clinic-based intervention programs rely on family members as the primary intervention agents.
9. Center-based programs should use child-directed learning activities, naturalistic teaching strategies, peer-mediated interventions, and direct teaching procedures.
10. Transitions from one program to another should be planned carefully.
11. The field faces many challenges in providing quality intervention to the nation's infants and children with disabilities.

TASK SHEET 4   Field Experiences in Early Childhood Special Education

Select one of the following and complete the assigned task.

Program Visitation

Visit a preschool center that enrolls children with developmental delays and disabilities. Observe the instruction and make a list of the skills being taught and the intervention strategies being used. Also, list your general reactions to the program.

Professional Interview

Arrange an interview with an early childhood special educator or a member from another discipline who works in early intervention. Ask the person about his or her role, how the program includes families, and how the program assesses children. Describe each of these aspects in a two- to three-page report.

Parent Interview

Interview the parents of a young child with developmental delays or disabilities. Ask them what services their child receives, what skills their child is learning, and which professionals work with them. Also, ask them which skills or attitudes of the professionals they find most helpful. Summarize these findings in a two- to three-page report.

Library Study

Select an article from a current issue of each of the following journals. Summarize each article, mentioning its purpose, its major points, and its implications.

Infants and Young Children
Journal of Early Intervention
Topics in Early Childhood Special Education

Design Your Own Field Experience

If you know of a unique experience you can have with young children who have developmental delays or disabilities, discuss this with your instructor and develop a contract for completing the task you agree upon.

Jesus Morales catches the 2:45 P.M. bus after school every day and travels to the University of San Diego where he punches the time clock at 4:00 P.M. In the cafeteria there he prepares desserts and serves the college students. When his shift ends, he catches the 8:25 P.M. bus home.

Jesus is a junior at Morse High School in southeast San Diego, a low-income area with a high unemployment rate. He is 17 years old, and this is his first job. "My teacher in the Job Skills class helped me write a résumé, and the job coach took me to the job interview. When I got the job they both helped me figure out how to get there. I like my job because it's busy, and my supervisor likes me. He gave me a raise last week."

Jesus is one of 25 students who participate in Project WORK, a federally funded demonstration project to provide employ-ability skills and parent support to youth with learning dis-abilities. The Job Skills class, a semester-long elective course, is just one part of the program. Students also receive job development and job support from graduate-student job coaches. In Jesus's case, this means weekly telephone con-tact or on-site visits by the job coach to troubleshoot any on-the-job problems.

When Jesus was first enrolled in the program, a Project WORK family support specialist went to his home to meet his family, explain the program, and obtain signatures. The family support specialist invited Jesus's mother to attend a parent workshop where she could meet parents and learn ways to support her son's transition from school to work. Jesus's mother is grateful that the program is available to her son. "Last year Jesus went around with a bad group, and I worried about him. I worry about what he'll do after high school. Now he goes to work every day. He gets a pay-check, and he's proud."

Plans for adult agency referrals and postsecondary training are overseen by a vocational rehabilitation counselor on the Project WORK staff. Jesus is now an active client of the Department of Rehabilitation and has tentative plans to join the Job Corps to study food service when he graduates next spring.

Project WORK is a collaborative project between the Department of Special Education, College of Education, San Diego State University, and San Diego Unified School District. The project is funded in part by U.S. Department of Education Grant No. 95-6042721. Vignette prepared by Bridget de la Garcia.

5

Transition to Adulthood

Patricia Thomas Cegelka and Gary Greene

Since its enactment in 1975, PL 94-142 has been enormously successful in extending special education services to large numbers of students with disabilities. The quality of special education services also appears to have increased dramatically as a result of this landmark legislation. Still being debated, however, is the ultimate efficacy of special education as determined by the postschool status of special education students. The critical question is the extent to which special education students are being prepared to live productive lives within the community.

What is the range of possible adult adjustment outcomes for students with disabilities?

Individuals with disabilities vary considerably in their abilities to pursue different career options. Some students with learning disabilities, physical disabilities, or sensory impairments will pursue options requiring university-level preparation. Other special education students will select alternative forms of postsecondary specialized training, while still others, such as Jesus Morales (who is described in the vignette on the facing page), will require specialized support and training to be successfully employed in entry-level jobs. Some may be unable to attain employment sufficient to support themselves.

Despite these outcomes, a 1991 Gallup Poll found that public opinion about inclusion of Americans with disabilities in all aspects of life was generally favorable. Ninety-eight percent indicated that everyone should have an equal opportunity to participate in American society, and 90 percent believed that society will benefit economically from such inclusion.

THE RATIONALE FOR TRANSITION PROGRAMS

You should be able to describe typical postschool adjustment outcomes of individuals with disabilities and identify ways in which transition planning may improve these outcomes.

Increasingly, programmatic and research efforts have demonstrated that individuals with disabilities, even severe disabilities, have considerable potential for productive employment in integrated settings (Schalock, 1983; Kiernan & Ciborowski, 1986). Work adjustment, job skill training, and college support services have been developed to facilitate the transition of these individuals into adult environments. Nonetheless, it appears that the employment future for many students with disabilities may not be very bright. Unemployment, underemployment, or dependency on some form of public assistance is frequently the plight of the individual with disabilities.

What employment outcomes have been typical of special education students in the recent past?

In 1986, the Senate Subcommittee on Employment of the Handicapped Report indicated that 67 percent of all Americans with disabilities ages 16–64 were not working. Of those who were working, 75 percent were employed part-time. Of those persons with disabilities who were not working, 67 percent said that they wanted to work (U.S. Senate Subcommittee, 1986). These figures are similar to earlier estimates that between 50 and 80 percent of the special education students exiting the special education system at the end of 1983 would not be employed (U.S. Commission on Civil Rights, 1983). Those who are employed often receive low wages and few benefits, experience a slow rate of employment promotion and advancement, and frequently are segregated from their peers without disabilities.

A study examining postschool outcomes of over a thousand special education students from 1983 to 1986 found that of those students who were working, 80 percent earned less than minimum wage, fewer than 50 percent were living independently, and more than 50 percent were unengaged, that is, not working or not in school (Edgar, 1987). Other postsecondary follow-up studies of special education students have found similar results (Hasazi, Gordon, & Roe, 1985). Further, more than 30 percent of students enrolled in special education drop out of school before completing their education (Edgar, 1988), and approximately two-thirds of students with disabilities who leave school continue, as adults, to live with their parents (Halloran, 1989). Included in these figures are individuals with mild disabling conditions as well as more severe disabilities. This is a particularly disturbing situation considering that dropouts tend to be employed at only about half the rate of those who complete their school programs.

It has become clear that too many individuals with disabilities do not achieve their potential as contributing members of society. The inability of so many special education students to make a successful transition from school to independent community life prompted the U.S. Office of Special Education and Rehabilitation Services in 1984 to establish a national priority on improving the transition from school to adult life for all individuals with disabilities.

Special education, in conjunction with other service providers and programs, is responsible for addressing these transition needs. It can do so by providing training in community living and employability skills that are relevant to the competitive job market, meaningful to lifelong career aspirations, and realistic to students' reaching their fullest potential (Brolin, 1983; Kokaska & Brolin, 1985; Rawlins, 1982). Further, prior to students' completion of high school, their individual transition plans should guarantee referral to appropriate options, including postsecondary training programs as well as other support services. Careful, systematic planning, beginning no later than early high school and ideally much earlier, can help to ensure that individuals with disabilities obtain a high quality of life, characterized by an opportunity to work, a comfortable place to live, and a network of friends (Bellamy, 1987).

Legislative Support

What federal legislation has promoted employment outcomes?

A number of federal laws have been passed to facilitate the transition process. These laws have their roots in general education, where vocational education has long been supported as a part of the regular school program. The Smith-Hughes Act of 1917 endorsed vocational education as an important program option in the secondary schools. In the 1960s and 1970s, federal education legislation began targeting preparation that would lead to "employment and for full participation in society, according to his or her ability" as an education goal for every student.

The 1974 Education Amendments went on to prescribe that the schools should provide "a program of career education to prepare each child for maximum employment and participation in our society according to his or her ability." The Career Education Incentive Act, passed in 1977, was designed "to increase the emphasis placed on career awareness, exploration, decision-making and planning and to do so in a manner which will promote equal opportunity in making career choices through the elimination of bias and stereotyping in such activities, including bias and stereotyping on account of race, sex, economic status and handicap" (U.S. Congress, Career Education Incentive Act, December 13, 1977).

The preparation of individuals with disabilities for employment was also specifically articulated as a programmatic goal in federal legislation. The Education of All Handicapped Children Act of 1975, commonly referred to as PL 94-142 and now amended under the title Individuals with Disabilities Education Act, has mandated *appropriate* education in the least restrictive environment for all students with disabilities. Its regulations specifically refer to vocational education programs that prepare individuals for "paid or unpaid employment or for additional preparation for a career requiring other than a baccalaureate or advanced degree" (Section 121a, 14 [b] [3]). The 1990 reauthorization of PL 94-142 includes a greater emphasis on transition services. Provisions require that a transition component be included in all IEPs. Further, through the provision of special funding, the reauthorization legislation has encouraged the development of exemplary programs and practices involving the use of assistive technology to promote the transition success of students with disabilities.

Beginning with the 1968 amendments to the Vocational Education Act, a portion of the funding flowing to the states for vocational programs and services was earmarked for students with disabilities. Fifteen percent was to be spent on programs for economically disadvantaged students and 10 percent on special services for students with disabilities. Difficulties in allocating these funds in programmatically meaningful ways led to the eventual rescission of this set-aside provision and to an attempt to refocus vocational education programs on services for educationally and economically disadvantaged individuals.

What are the major contributions of vocational rehabilitation legislation?

In the past two decades, vocational rehabilitation legislation has increased incrementally the availability of services to individuals with severe disabilities. Sections 503 and 504 of the 1973 Vocational Rehabilitation Act provided for equity in both training and employment of individuals with disabilities. Subsequent amendments placed increasing emphasis on providing services to individuals with severe disabilities, including the provision of community adjustment assistance to these individuals. The Transition Act, passed in 1983, focused on providing the coordinated services of special education and vocational rehabilitation for individuals with disabilities to promote the transition from school to work.

Finally, the Developmental Disabilities Act of 1990 strengthened the civil rights protection of individuals with disabilities in relation to private-sector employment, all public services, public accommodation, transportation, and telecommunications. Employers with 15 or more employees may not refuse to hire a person because of that person's disability when the individual is qualified to perform the job, given reasonable modifications of the job requirements or structure.

In 1984, amendments to the Developmental Disabilities Act (PL 98-527) required state developmental disabilities councils to adopt employment-related activities, including "supported employment" for persons with developmental disabilities. Supported employment is defined as follows:

What is supported employment?

Paid employment which (i) is for persons with developmental disabilities for whom competitive employment at or above minimum wage is unlikely and who, because of their disabilities, need ongoing support to perform in a work setting; (ii) is conducted in a variety of settings, particularly worksites in which persons without disabilities are employed; and (iii) is supported by any activity needed to sustain paid work by persons with disabilities, including supervision, training, and transportation. (*Federal Register,* 1984)

To summarize, preparation for employment has long been an important priority of education. Federal as well as state legislation has encouraged the development of school-based and community-based programs to prepare individuals to become gainfully employed. Research and programmatic efforts have demonstrated that given appropriate training and support, individuals with disabilities, including severe disabilities, have potential for paid employment that far exceeds earlier estimates. These individuals represent a largely untapped economic resource for the nation. Hence, philosophical, economic, and legislative considerations support the development of vocational training and placement opportunities within the mainstream of society for individuals with disabilities.

PROBE 5-1   The Rationale for Transition Programs

1. Identify the range of productive postsecondary options for individuals with disabilities.
2. T   F   The general public believes that individuals with disabilities can make an economic contribution to society.
3. Describe the postschool status of most individuals with disabilities.
4. T   F   Only recently has legislation supporting a vocational orientation to public education been passed.
5. The 1990 Individuals with Disabilities Education Act (IDEA) requires that a transition component be included in all _____.
6. Supported employment emphasizes which kind of work sites, integrated or segregated?

MODELS TO FACILITATE LIFE ADJUSTMENT

You should be able to identify and describe program models that emphasize the adult adjustment of students with disabilities.

A major purpose of special education is to prepare individuals with disabilities to lead productive, personally satisfying adult lives. For this reason, the adjustment of students with disabilities to eventual employment and community living has always been a primary concern of special educators. Over the years, several different models for facilitating this adjustment have evolved. During the 1960s an innovative approach known as high school work-study programs formalized a focus on work preparation in secondary programs for students with mild and moderate disabilities. These efforts waned in the late 1960s and early 1970s, in large part because the field of special education experienced a shift in emphasis to efforts to prevent the development of cognitive delays through early childhood intervention.

Concurrent with the focus of PL 94-142 on children with severe disabilities, the work of Marc Gold (1975) dramatically demonstrated the potential of individuals with moderate to severe disabilities to perform complex vocational tasks. Gold pioneered efforts to teach these individuals various work tasks, including the assembly of items such as bicycle brakes, thus demonstrating their abilities to work productively in a variety of employment situations.

The career education movement of the 1970s, with its attempt to increase the relevance of education by underscoring the career applications of school learning, provided a much broader picture of the total life adjustment of the individual. It provided a vehicle for articulating many special education goals with these broad career education goals for all of mainstream education.

More recently, the role of vocational rehabilitation services has reemerged as a major contributor to the adult adjustment of special education students, including those with severe impairments. These four program models that have evolved over the decades—work–study, vocational education, career education, and vocational rehabilitation—are described in the following sections.

Work-Study Model

For many years, the work–study programs of the 1950s and 1960s were the primary model for the occupational preparation of secondary students in special education. They continue to be an important curricular option in many self-contained special education programs at the secondary level.

What are the primary features of the work-study model?

As originally conceived, these programs involved cooperative working relationships between special education and rehabilitation services, with vocational rehabilitation counselors working closely with classroom teachers to provide supervised work experiences for students with disabilities. Ideally, students rotated through a series of partial-day job exploration experiences beginning in the sophomore year, with longer-term placements provided during the junior year. As seniors they would participate in paid, supervised occupational placements as a prerequisite to graduation. These culminating experiences were usually either half-day placements for the full academic year or full-day placements for one semester. The integral involvement of the vocational rehabilitation counselor throughout the program meant that job placements appropriate to the skill levels of the individual students could be made. Further, the close supervision of the students by the counselor meant that during the school-based portion of the program, teachers could try to remedy work-related problems noted during on-the-job observations.

What are the advantages and disadvantages of the work-study model?

The cooperative interagency nature of these programs was the basis for their success. They demonstrated that participating students were more likely to become employed after leaving school, and to be employed at higher wages, than similar students who did not participate. They were particularly advantageous for students with mild disabilities, providing them opportunities to practice work behaviors in multiple work environments and giving them both contact with nondisabled persons and locally available work (Bellamy, Rose, Wilson, & Clarke, 1982).

However, the programs focused on the development of work attitudes and basic employee attributes. They prepared students primarily for entry-level jobs that all too frequently were dull, paid low wages, and afforded little opportunity for advancement. In time, studies and analyses demonstrated that the potential of individuals participating in work-study programs was being unnecessarily decreased, and that many of these individuals possessed the capability to hold higher level jobs, given the appropriate training. Attempts were then made to expand the range of occupational options available to them.

Vocational Education Model

Vocational education programs were originally designed to serve general education students at the secondary and postsecondary level. They emphasized the development of the specific skills required for skilled, semiskilled, and unskilled occupations such as auto mechanics, welding, clerical work, data processing, carpentry, horticulture, and electronics. By design, these were seen as rigorous programs geared toward students with average or above-average abilities. As such, they tended to exclude students with disabilities. The 1968 amendments of the Vocational

Education Act attempted to rectify this situation by mandating that 10 percent of programmatic funds allocated to states be spent on providing services for special education students, with another 15 percent going to services for disadvantaged students.

What was the reaction of many vocational educators to legislation that set aside funds for special education students?

Despite these amendments, vocational educators continued to resist serving less capable populations of students. Many objected to "diluting" the sophistication of the preparation programs; others were concerned that they lacked the skills necessary to adapt instruction for students with disabilities. As a result, a large portion of the set-aside funds was not expended on the special education populations, and those funds that were spent frequently supported add-on programs such as segregated classes, instructional resource centers, and inservice staff development efforts. Only infrequently was direct training in regular vocational education classes provided to students with disabilities. Seventy percent of all students with disabilities who received vocational education were enrolled in segregated programs (Olympus Research Corporation, 1974).

The 1976 amendments specified that these students be integrated into existing regular vocational programs, with the facilities and programs being modified to meet their special needs. Nonetheless, continuing problems include the unwillingness and inability of many teachers to adapt their curricula to meet the needs of students with disabilities, and the inflexibility of some programs to accommodate students who cannot master all the relevant job tasks within the courses that are typically offered (Johnson, 1980). A further difficulty has been the lack of access to vocational education by persons with severe disabilities (Rusch, Mithaug, & Flexer, 1986).

In 1990 amendments to the Vocational Education Act rescinded the set-aside funds for students with disabilities and attempted to shift the overall focus of vocational education to special populations. A larger proportion (75 percent) of the money coming to the states has been earmarked for local programs. The allocation of funds to local education agencies is determined by a formula, based 70 percent on the size of the Chapter 1 population (students considered to be economically disadvantaged), 20 percent on the size of its special education population, and 10 percent on the overall size of the local population. At the local level, then, funds are to be allocated to local sites according to each site's concentration of students who are disadvantaged or disabled.

What is the intent of federal vocational education legislation?

The language of this legislation reflects a clear congressional intent that vocational education programs strengthen their efforts to meet the needs of economically disadvantaged and disabled individuals. Recognizing that 85 percent of the new entrants into the work force soon will be either women or minority group individuals, Congress has attempted to shift the focus of vocational education programs to specifically addressing the needs of such special populations as displaced homemakers, foster children, economically disadvantaged students, correctional populations, those with limited English proficiency, and persons with disabilities. Strong program evaluation language is included in the legislation, a further indication of the seriousness of Congress's intent.

To what degree this intent will be realized is unclear. The greater local control of federal funds, coupled with the fact that there are no set-aside funds specifically earmarked for these populations, could mean that the attempt to shift the overall focus of vocational education will be substantially circumvented at the program delivery level. On the other hand, the legislation could prove successful in refocusing the direction of vocational education to meet the labor force realities of the coming years.

Career Education Model

The career education concept combined academic and occupational orientations in an effort to prepare citizens to lead more productive and satisfying lives. By emphasizing the relationship of subject matter to various careers and occupations and by developing needed work skills, career education sought to make education more relevant to the economic and employment realities of the day. Although focused on general education, career education was embraced by special educators as the missing link between academic and vocational preparations and as an integrated approach to addressing the economic and employment needs of students with disabilities.

What is career education?

Career education has been seen as the sum of all experiences through which one learns to live a meaningful, satisfying, productive work life. Within this context, the meaning of "work life" or "productive work" is not restricted to employment, but also encompasses fulfillment through unpaid work and through a variety of societal and personal roles, including such roles as citizen, volunteer, family member, and participant in meaningful leisure time activities. The Council for Exceptional Children Division on Career Development (DCD) has been a particularly strong advocate of this broader view of transition outcomes. Recognizing that "the objectives within transition may differ depending on the needs of a specific individual, the severity of the disability, and other factors," DCD (1987) stated that "the transitional process should include realistic concerns with preparing students for productive work, which may include paid employment" (p. 5).

What are the stages of career education?

Career education has been viewed as a lifelong process, beginning in early elementary school and continuing throughout the school years and beyond. The three distinct stages of career education are outlined in Table 5-1. The first stage, career awareness, begins early in the educational process and helps the students identify various work roles and develop into responsible individuals with good attitudes and values toward work. The second stage, career orientation and exploration, which begins in the middle school years, provides opportunities for students to discover their own career interests, aptitudes, and abilities while exploring

TABLE 5-1   Three Stages of Career Education

Career Awareness. The development of good work habits and realistic attitudes toward occupations and work roles, as well as the development of personal work values, characterize this stage. Children learn to differentiate among occupations by examining the work roles of members of their families, of the school staff, and of others with whom they come in contact. Field trips, such as to a dairy, a zoo, or a factory, expose them to the various occupations involved in the production of goods and/or the maintenance of a facility. Self-awareness, the development of self-confidence, and other attributes of a healthy work personality are stressed. A myriad of success experiences along with exposure to a wide variety of career options and work models are important features of this stage.

Career Exploration. This stage focuses on helping students discover their individual interests, abilities, values, and needs. Students examine a variety of specific occupations and learn to identify the similarities of occupational groupings or clusters as well as the characteristic worker traits for different occupations. They explore occupations through observations and experience with actual jobs, often in simulated work environments. Career guidance becomes increasingly important in organizing exploratory experiences around individual interests and abilities. The effects of various career choices on family life, leisure activities, and other life situations are stressed, as are the relationships between occupations and societal values and beliefs.

Career Preparation. The preparatory stage of career education is designed to ensure that every student either has acquired a salable skill before graduation or has selected an occupation for which advanced training is necessary. Opportunities for in-depth exploration of several jobs of particular interest to the student are provided. Some students participate in work experience programs, some enroll in specific vocational training programs, while others explore postsecondary preparation opportunities such as colleges, universities, technical schools, and other high-level educational programs. Basic academic skills are still emphasized, as is the development of the personal social skills that enhance vocational opportunities. Additionally, attention is paid to the skills needed for family life, avocational pursuits, and citizenship.

various career options available to them after completing their formal education. Beginning about grade 10, career preparation, the third stage of the career education process, emphasizes the development of specific vocational skills, academic competencies, and social interpersonal skills that will prepare students for all aspects of postsecondary education.

Career education was originally conceived as a purposeful sequence of planned educational activities that would systematically coordinate the resources of the school, family, and community to facilitate student development. It was developed as a total educational concept, not as a separate course or program, and it focused on the self-development as well as the career development of the individual (Brolin, 1982).

How do the models of career education differ?

Two basic models of career education have been developed for special education. The Life-Centered Career Education model and curriculum, depicted in Figure 5-1, was published by the Council for Exceptional Children (Brolin, 1978, 1983; 1988). This comprehensive curriculum identifies 22 competencies under three domains of functioning, as displayed in Table 5-2: (1) daily living skills; (2) personal-social skills; and (3) occupational skills. These competency statements are task-analyzed into 102 subcompetencies and over 400 distinct objectives. Instructional activities are suggested for each. The competency statements are stated broadly enough so they can be applied across all levels of instruction (from primary through postsecondary) and incorporated, or infused, into most subject matter areas.

A combined model of the school-based career education and transition education, developed by Clark (1980) and later revised by Clark and Kolstoe (1990), emphasizes the developmental nature of career education from kindergarten through adulthood. As depicted in Figure 5-2 (p. 146), this model encompasses four interrelated domains seen as fundamental

FIGURE 5-1   Life-centered, Competency-based Model for Career Education

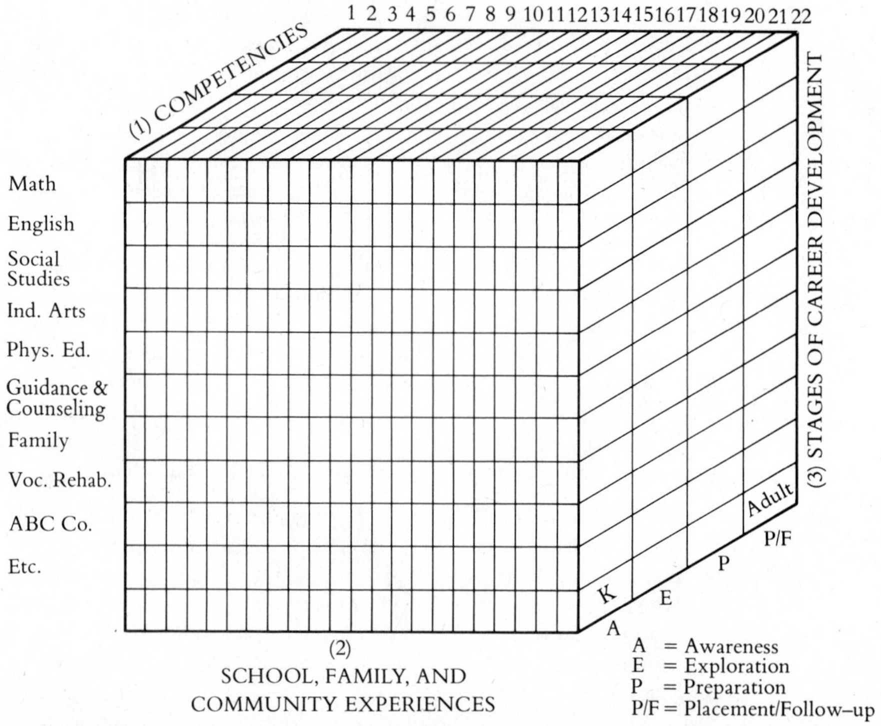

TABLE 5-2   Career Education Competencies

A. Daily Living Skills Curriculum Area	C. Occupational Guidance and Preparation Curriculum Area
1. Managing family finances	15. Making good decisions; problem solving
2. Caring for and repairing home furnishings and equipment	16. Communicating adequately with others
3. Caring for personal needs	17. Knowing and exploring occupational possibilities
4. Raising children; family living	18. Making appropriate occupational decisions
5. Buying and preparing food	19. Exhibiting appropriate work behaviors
6. Buying and making clothing	20. Exhibiting sufficient physical and manual skills
7. Engaging in civic activities	21. Acquiring a specific salable job (Skill is not included because the subcompetencies would be unique to the particular skill being acquired.)
8. Utilizing recreation and leisure	22. Seeking, securing, and maintaining satisfactory employment
9. Mobility in the community	
B. Personal-Social Skills Curriculum Area	
10. Achieving self-awareness	
11. Acquiring self-confidence	
12. Achieving socially responsible behavior	
13. Maintaining good interpersonal relationships	
14. Achieving independence	

to career education: (1) values, attitudes, and habits; (2) human relationships; (3) occupational information; and (4) acquisition of actual jobs and daily living skills. These four domains are viewed as the essential foundations for decision making and individual career achievement.

At the secondary level, the model provides a variety of curriculum tracks as options. Depending on the abilities and preferences of the individual student, the most appropriate option might be college preparation/general education; vocational, technical, or fine arts education; cooperative education or work-study program; or the work evaluation and work adjustment option. These options prepare the student for either initial job entry or for continuing postsecondary preparation. At the postsecondary level, needed assistance in career development and the acquisition of transition knowledge and skills is provided by various adult and continuing education and adult service agencies.

Vocational Rehabilitation

Vocational rehabilitation agencies were established at the state and federal level in 1920 to provide services to injured veterans returning from World War I. Since that time, the range of services and the types of disabilities served have expanded considerably. Financed jointly by state and federal governments, vocational rehabilitation agencies provide services to individuals of employment age, typically ages 16 through 65, who have one or more of the following disabilities: mental retardation, mental illness, limited vision, alcoholism, drug addiction, amputations, epilepsy, cancer, stroke, tuberculosis, congenital deformities, and neurological disabilities—plus, more recently, certain learning disabilities (Brolin, 1982).

A broad array of services is available, ranging from medical, psychological, and vocational evaluations to the purchase of prosthetic devices; support for training costs; living stipends; money for the purchase of tools, equipment, licenses, and supplies; and job placement and follow-up. An individual written rehabilitation plan (IWRP) for each client specifies the goals and types and duration of services to be provided.

Historically, despite such collaborative efforts as the work-study program, vocational rehabilitation services have not been readily available to current and former special education students. A variety of administrative and procedural barriers militated against the provision

What assistance can be provided by vocational rehabilitation services?

FIGURE 5-2   A School-based Career Development and Transition Education Model

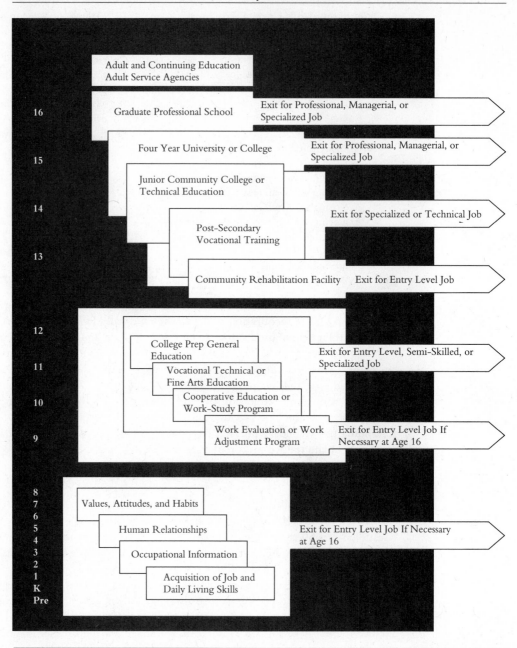

Source: G. M. Clark and O. P. Kolstoe (1990). *Career development and transition education for adolescents with disabilities.* Boston, MA: Allyn and Bacon.

of services to younger and more severely disabled individuals. Primary among these was the stipulation that clients must meet vocational rehabilitation's criteria for a high probability of success in competitive employment in the public or private sector. The language of the 1973 act attempted to rectify this by mandating services for individuals with more severe disabilities.

Five years later, available vocational rehabilitation services were expanded to include independent living services for those individuals so severely disabled that no vocational goal was deemed possible. During this same period, efforts were made to encourage and strengthen collaboration among vocational rehabilitation, vocational education, and special education. A 1977 *Memorandum of Understanding* recognized the overlapping responsibilities of these three agencies and encouraged state agency directors to develop formal written cooperative agreements designed to provide persons with disabilities with comprehensive vocational preparation services (*Federal Register,* 1978).

Since 1980, vocational rehabilitation services have been housed in the Department of Education, in the combined U.S. Office of Special Education and Rehabilitation Services—another attempt to ensure coordination of services. The Transition Act (PL 98-199) of 1983 was yet another attempt to increase the coordination of special education and rehabilitation services.

PROBE 5-2 Models to Facilitate Life Adjustment

1. T F Career education is basically the same as vocational education.
2. What factors have accounted for the restricted access to vocational education programs by students with disabilities?
3. The work-study program model of the 1960s and 1970s had which of the following features? (Select all that apply.)
    a. Vocational rehabilitation counselors working with special education teachers in the placement and evaluation of students during on-the-job training.
    b. A highly integrated, mainstream focus.
    c. A graduated sequence of occupational exploration experiences.
    d. A meshing of classroom instruction and on-the-job training, with the former used to remediate problems identified in the latter.
4. T F The focus of career education has been restricted to paid employment.
5. Vocational rehabilitation services typically serve individuals between the ages of _____ and _____.
6. What has been the primary barrier to the provision of vocational rehabilitation services for individuals with disabilities?

CONCEPTS OF TRANSITION

You should be able to define *transition* and describe two transition models.

In recent years, the term *transition* has been used to encompass those processes and procedures that focus on assisting individuals with disabilities to make the move, or transition, from school life to community life. Transition for persons with exceptionalities implies movement "between the security and structure offered by the school and the opportunities and risks of adult life" (Will, 1984, p. 1).

What is the scope of definitions of transition?

A number of different definitions of transition have been developed. While all have a strong employment focus, some also encompass community living skills. While varying in scope, the definitions are basically similar. One definition, articulated at the federal level by Madeline Will (1984) in her role as head of the Office of Special Education and Rehabilitation Services in the U.S. Department of Education, has a unidimensional focus on employment. It also emphasizes the interagency nature of transition services at both secondary and postsecondary levels.

> The transition from school to working life is an outcome oriented process encompassing a broad array of services and experiences that lead to employment. Transition is a period that includes high school, the point of graduation, additional post-secondary education or adult services, and the initial years of employment. (Will, 1984, p. 1)

A similar definition of transition is offered by Wehman, Kregel, Baraus, and Schalock (1986), as follows:

> [Transition is] a carefully planned process, which may be initiated by school personnel or adult service providers to establish and implement a plan for either employment or additional vocational training of a handicapped student who will graduate or leave school in 3–5 years; such a process must involve special educators, vocational educators, parents and/or the student, an adult service system representative, and possibly an employer. (p. 14)

In contrast to these two interpretations, Halpern (1985) broadened the emphasis of transition to include community adjustment. His research had found that little if any positive correlation exists between the employment status of persons with disabilities and their ability to successfully adjust to various aspects of living in the community (e.g., quality of residential environment and social and interpersonal networks). Halpern believes that competence in social and interpersonal skills and home living is just as important as employment in determining whether individuals with disabilities have made a successful transition to adult life. He noted that "living successfully in one's community should be the primary goal of transition services." Others have endorsed this broad, total life adjustment concept (Edgar, 1987, 1988; Clark & Kolstoe, 1990; Division on Career Development, 1987).

A further broadening of the concept of transition can be seen in the definition provided by the California State Department of Education (1987). Focusing on both "employment and a quality adult life," this definition expands the population of students included in the transition process.

> Transition is a purposeful, organized and outcome-oriented process to help "at risk" students move from school to employment and a quality adult life. . . . "At risk" students are those who experience barriers to successful completion of school including individuals with exceptional needs. (p. 1)

These potentially at-risk students may include those who are limited English proficient, academically disadvantaged, bilingual, chemical dependent, and pregnant minors. According to this definition, transition is seen as beginning early in the school careers of such students and including specific vocational preparation, training in broader employability skills such as grooming and interviewing, and a broad array of other adult living skills.

Models of Transition

Various models of transition have been proposed. Two of the most salient are the Office of Special Education and Rehabilitation Services (OSERS) model of transition and Halpern's (1985) revised model of transition.

THE OSERS MODEL OF TRANSITION. As depicted in Figure 5-3, this model emphasizes employment as the major outcome for high-school-age students with disabilities. It groups the array of services and experiences that can assist persons with disabilities in moving from school to work into three classes or *bridges*. Differentiated in terms of the level of transition assistance required, they include transition with (1) no special services, (2) time-limited services, and (3) ongoing services.

What are the differences among the three levels of transition?

Transition with no special services refers to those employment resources generally available to all citizens, including those with disabilities. Examples include networks of family and friends, contacts gained through work experience programs, or postsecondary vocational training programs (e.g., community college or vocational training schools). Some studies have found that former special education students tend to rely more on their network of family and friends for obtaining jobs than on any other single source (Hasazi et al., 1985).

Transition with time-limited services involves the use of specialized, temporary programs that can lead to potentially permanent employment of the person with disabilities. Vocational rehabilitation is perhaps the best-known of these time-limited services. These federally funded, state-mandated services may offer on-the-job wage subsidies to employers hiring individuals with disabilities, reimburse employers for additional training costs borne by the employer, and provide other supports (e.g., purchase of uniforms and equipment needed to perform a job) needed by the person to enter or reenter the work force. These services are normally terminated after the client obtains employment and remains on the job for a period of up to 60 calendar days. In this way, the services are time-limited.

The third bridge in the OSERS model is ongoing support services. Historically, these services have been nonvocational in nature, offering lifelong custodial care. In contrast, ongoing services in the OSERS transition model encompass whatever ongoing support is necessary to maintain a disabled person's employment. An example of ongoing services is a supported employment program such as a work enclave. Here, a group of people with disabilities is employed in an integrated work setting (meaning nondisabled workers are present) with a supervisor who is paid by state agency resources to provide full-time assistance to these individuals in any and all aspects of their jobs. Supported employment can occur in a

FIGURE 5-3   The OSERS Model of Transition

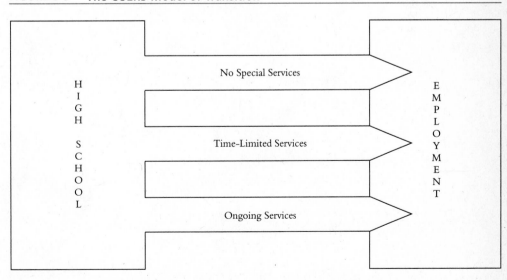

Source: M. Will (1984). *OSERS programming for the transition of youth with disabilities: Bridges from school to working life.* Washington, DC: Office of Special Education and Rehabilitation Services (OSERS), U.S. Department of Education.

variety of settings (e.g., business and industry, community work sites, publicly funded agencies) and can be provided to one or more individuals with disabilities in a given workplace. When the program is successful, full-time employment opportunities—including the full range of employment benefits—can eventually be offered to workers with disabilities who have received supported employment.

What does the Halpern model add to the OSERS view of transition?

THE REVISED TRANSITION MODEL. Developed by Halpern (1985) and depicted in Figure 5-4, this model takes the essential components of the OSERS model and expands them to include community adjustment as the major outcome of transition for persons with disabilities. Based on his research, Halpern has concluded that employment alone does not correlate highly with other important dimensions of successful independent functioning after leaving school. These additional dimensions are the quality and adequacy of the residential environment and social and interpersonal networks of the person with disabilities. These, along with employment, form the essential three pillars of Halpern's revised model of transition. According to Halpern:

> If any of the three pillars are inadequate and do not carry their own weight, then the entire structure is in danger of collapse, and a person's ability to live in the community is threatened. (p. 80)

FIGURE 5-4   Halpern's Model of Transition

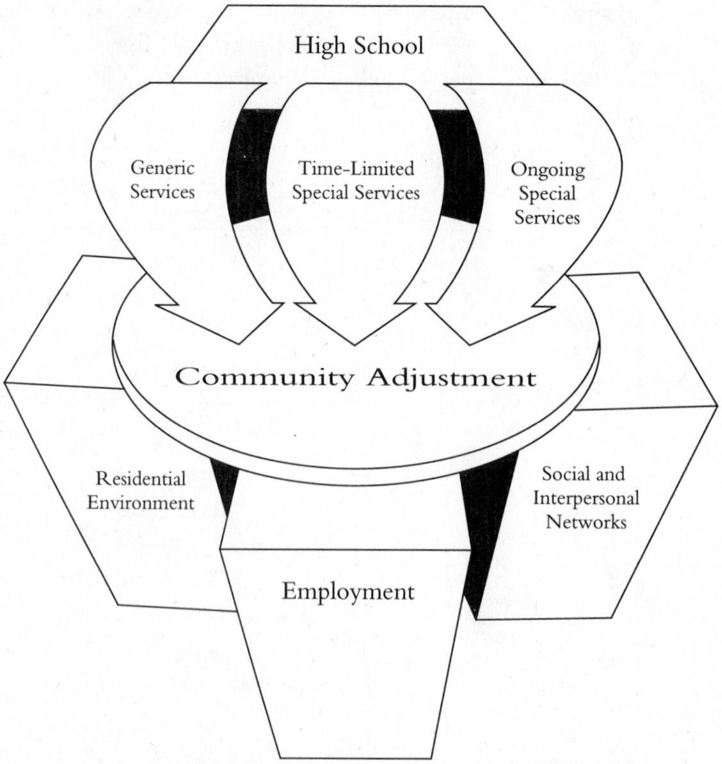

Source: From "Transition: A Look at the Foundations" by A. Halpern, *Exceptional children, 5* (6) 1985, pp. 479–486. Reprinted by permission of The Council for Exceptional Children.

Halpern does not expand on the first pillar of the model, employment, because he feels this dimension of transition is already adequately addressed in the OSERS model. He defines residential environment, the second of the three pillars, as the adequacy of a person's home, the quality and safety of the surrounding neighborhood, and the availability of both community services and recreational activities within reasonable distance of the home. The third pillar, social and interpersonal networks, refers to various aspects of the individual's human relationships, including communication skills, self-esteem, family support, emotional maturity, and intimate relationships. Halpern contends that effective transition programs must address each of these three dimensions and provide specific services in each area, based on the person's needs.

PROBE 5-3   Concepts of Transition

1. The term *transition* has been used to refer to processes and procedures assisting persons with disabilities to make the move from _____ life to _____ life.
2. The various definitions of transition all include a focus on _____ outcomes, while broader definitions also encompass _____ skills.
3. List and describe each of the three bridges identified in the OSERS model of transition.
4. T   F   Research indicates a strong, positive correlation between the postschool employment status of persons with disabilities and the degree of independent functioning.
5. Halpern expanded the OSERS model of transition to include _____ as the major outcome of transition for persons with disabilities.
6. List the three dimensions of successful transition identified in Halpern's revised transition model.

STAGES OF THE TRANSITION PROCESS

You should be able to identify and describe the five stages of the transition process.

Transition is both a product and a process. The outcomes targeted for students when they leave school are the products of transition. These typically encompass employment, independent living, community participation, and a social network of friends and acquaintances, as described in the preceding paragraphs. The process of transition refers to the activities and strategies that lead to the targeted products or outcomes. The transition process can be divided into five distinct stages: (1) input and foundation, (2) vocational assessment, (3) transition planning, (4) transition culmination, and (5) transition follow-up. Each of these stages is depicted in Table 5-3 and described in following sections.

Stage One: Input and Foundation

The transition process can begin well before secondary school. In most instances, however, the foundation for effective transition is established during the high school years. An important foundation for sound transition planning is the assessment of the individual's strengths and weaknesses, aptitudes and interests. This information can guide the decision-making step in the transition process. Assessment strategies are described later in this chapter.

TABLE 5-3   **Five Stages of the Transition Process**

Stage 1: Input and Foundation
  Functional curriculum
  Integrated setting
  Community-based instruction

Stage 2: Vocational Assessment
  Psychological assessments
  Situational assessments
  Curriculum-based vocational assessment

Stage 3: Transition Planning
  Parent and student input
  Interagency cooperation
  ITP development

Stage 4: Transition Culmination
  Sending agency
  Hand-off process
  Receiving environment

Stage 5: Transition Follow-up
  Follow-up survey
  Follow-up study

Bates, Renzaglia, and Wehman (1989) proposed that programs that promote effective transition of youth with disabilities will be characterized by a functional curriculum, an integrated school setting, and community-based instruction. These components can be tailored to the characteristics and needs of individual students, serving as either the major curriculum for students with more severe disabilities or as a means of focusing and extending the general core curriculum experiences of students with milder disabling conditions.

What is a functional curriculum?

A **functional curriculum** contains activities and materials designed to prepare students to live, work, and recreate as independently as possible in an integrated society (Wheeler, 1987). Curricular content can be determined by inventorying various community domains for skills that must be mastered by students with disabilities in order for them to successfully function independently in society. An example of these domains can be found in the competency-based Life-Centered Career Education curriculum published by the Council for Exceptional Children (Brolin, 1978, 1983; 1988). Other functional curricula are published by the Educational Transition Center (1987), and one has been developed by Clark and Greene (1989) for a special education local planning area in California. Similar to the Life-Centered approach, these divide broader goals into more manageable instructional units that can be introduced early in the school experience and expanded upon as students become older.

What does integrated service delivery encompass?

An **integrated service delivery system** is a second major component of the input and foundation stage of the transition process. Wehman et al. (1988) point out that a major weakness of many vocational programs is that students with disabilities are taught separately from their peers. "This arrangement gives rise to a situation where an individual can do the job, but cannot relate to his or her co-workers, most of whom may be nonhandicapped" (p. 10). This is particularly problematic because difficulties with social interactions tend to be the primary reason for job failure among individuals with disabilities. Besides, as noted by Wheeler (1987), "there is nothing that can be taught in a segregated facility that cannot be reasonably taught in an integrated one, particularly if the curriculum is based upon the demands of adult life" (p. 24).

In addition to including students with disabilities and those without disabilities in the same facility, there are several other important integration criteria. The site should be an age-appropriate integrated school setting (e.g., placement of a class for adolescents with severe disabilities on a regular secondary school campus), with ratios of students with and without disabilities approximately equal to those in the population as a whole. Opportunities for interactions among the students during the school day and equal access to all educational facilities within the school should be ensured. A final consideration is the integration of students with disabilities into the normal organization of the school day (e.g., arrival and departure times the same as for all students, passing through the halls and taking breaks and recess in the same manner and at the same time as peers in general education classes).

Why is community-based training important?

Community-based instruction is the third major component of the first stage of the transition process. Providing on-location training and practice at actual community sites is an essential aspect of preparing youths to function as independent adults in society. If the skills and concepts targeted by the transition planning are to be generalized to the real world, then carefully articulated experiences must be planned in the environments where the students will ultimately have to function: the community.

The special educator interested in community-based instruction must meet the challenge of careful planning and implementation. Specific individualized skills must be identified for each student. Classroom activities, tasks, and materials that reinforce those present in the community must be developed. Finally, regular, well-planned trips to community sites with small groups of students must be provided, in preparation for supervised work experiences. The use of transportation systems, the performance of other daily living skills, and the choice of leisure pursuits, as well as actual job training, are all best practiced in the community environments where the students will ultimately have to face them (Wheeler, 1987).

In summary, providing a firm foundation for transition involves the use of a well-researched, longitudinal functional curriculum, integrated learning experiences, and opportunities to develop and practice functional skills in community-based environments.

Stage Two: Vocational Assessment

What is the purpose of vocational assessment?

The purpose of vocational assessment is to determine someone's vocational capability and to predict the degree of success or failure the person may experience in a particular work situation (Stodden & Ianacone, 1981). One early step is a medical evaluation of the individual's physical capacities and limitations. This helps identify factors that might complicate job training and placement, as well as factors that can be corrected (e.g., vision) or for which compensatory measures can be developed (e.g., prosthetic devices). The assessment focus then shifts to vocational variables.

TRADITIONAL PRACTICES. In the past, vocational assessment has focused on measures of prior learning, using formal testing procedures. These procedures probed the vocational potential, abilities, and aptitudes of the individual, as well as his or her interests, skills, and knowledge in different employment areas (Greenan, 1989). Various assessment instruments, procedures, and strategies can be used to obtain this information. By comparing data on the individual's skills, interests, and aptitudes with information on specific job requirements, predictions can be made about the appropriateness of specific jobs or types of jobs for the individual. This database also can provide the basis for identifying and developing vocational curriculum, support services, program modifications, and instructional strategies for special education students (Cobb, 1983, 1985; Cobb & Larkin, 1985).

Why has vocational assessment shifted to the use of real-world environments?

Traditionally, vocational evaluations of individuals with disabilities prior to program placement have been conducted by psychologists and vocational rehabilitation personnel. These evaluators have typically used psychological assessments that provide indirect information about important variables related to the world of work (Stodden & Ianacone, 1981). Examples include measurements of the individual's career interests, values, work personality, ability, achievement, and aptitude. These types of tests have been criticized for their lack of motivational structure and the fact that the results are not easily generalized to real work situations (e.g., they tend to assess performance in single situations that lack the characteristics of real employment settings). Further, the tests seldom have appropriate comparison norms (Brolin, 1983). These characteristics have made them ineffective for evaluating the vocational potential of many individuals with disabilities.

CONTEMPORARY DEVELOPMENTS. In response to these criticisms, the use of work samples and job samples has become relatively popular. This type of assessment offers a more comprehensive approach to vocational assessment in that it involves the direct observation of the individual's work behavior, attitudes, and adjustment in real or mock work situations. Work samples are developed through identification and task analysis of the operations of specific jobs. The vocational evaluator then observes the person performing samples of these operations in a controlled setting.

What are work samples?

Work samples have been defined as "a mock-up, a close simulation of an industrial (actual) operation, not different in its essentials from the kind of work a potential employee would be required to perform on an ordinary job" (Neff, 1966, p. 204). Job samples are models or reproductions of a job or part of a job that exists in an employment setting, and include the use of the tools, standards, and norms associated with that job (Brolin, 1982). Information from both work samples and job samples can be helpful in making vocational decisions, planning vocational training, and communicating with potential employers.

The primary disadvantages of these assessment procedures are that they are time-consuming, can be expensive to set up, may be superficial, and tend to yield subjective results (Brolin, 1982). Some authorities have questioned the extent to which either work samples or psychological measures of "already learned aptitudes, interests, and traits can forecast subsequent learning, performance and adjustment" (Browning & Irvin, 1981, p. 379). Further, neither takes into account that most job failures among individuals with disabilities stem not from deficiencies in manual or job-knowledge skills, but from difficulties in the realms of social interaction and personality as they relate to work behavior.

What are the advantages of situational work assessments?

Situational work assessments were designed to address this shortcoming. They are similar to work or job samples in that they involve real or simulated work settings. In contrast to work or job samples, however, they focus on the general work personality of the individual instead of specific vocational skills. Brolin (1982) identified the following types of vocational behaviors that can be assessed in this manner: ability to get along with co-workers and staff, general interpersonal skills, ability to follow directions and to learn new tasks, accuracy and speed of work, perseverance and on-task behavior, punctuality and attendance, and job interests and attitudes. This comprehensive approach to work evaluation has the advantages of providing meaningful assessment of the person with disabilities in natural, worklike settings that tend to reduce test anxiety and provide opportunities for multiple observation by several staff members.

On the downside, situational assessments can be expensive to set up and time-consuming to administer. Other disadvantages are their dependence on the effectiveness of those who conduct the observations of skills and the restricted range of primarily industrial jobs that can be simulated for this type of evaluation.

Despite the criticisms detailed in the preceding paragraphs, most school-based vocational programs for youth with special needs continue to use one or more of these techniques.

An on-site learning center provides work samples and job samples that can be used to make vocational decisions and conduct vocational training.

Stodden and Ianacone (1981), however, have criticized the continued use of these methods as being random and without consideration or understanding of the educational environment of the school or the individual career development needs of the student.

What is CBVA?   A more informal assessment procedure that has gained increasing attention recently is curriculum-based vocational assessment (CBVA). Characteristics of CBVA include the following:

1. It is an ongoing assessment procedure that gathers information during all phases of the vocational program (e.g., prior to vocational program placement, during the program, and for the duration of transition from school to community).
2. Assessment activity is tied directly to and is an integral part of the student's vocational education program.
3. Personnel directly involved in delivering vocational instruction to the students gather and utilize the assessment data.
4. CBVA uses informal and direct procedures for determining student achievement in local vocational programs (e.g., direct observation, knowledge and performance testing, and interviewing).

ꞏ

Regardless of the type of procedure or strategy selected, vocational assessment is a critical part of the transition process. Information obtained from vocational assessment is needed to successfully complete the next phase of the transition process, transition planning.

Stage Three: Transition Planning

The third stage of the transition process is the planning stage. This involves determining all the necessary services and support needed to facilitate the successful movement of the individual with disabilities from school to employment and community living. Key considerations at this stage are the involvement of the students and their parents, the coordination of the various transition services available within the community, and the development of a formal, individualized transition plan (ITP) for the student.

TECHNOLOGY IN ACTION

In the Fayette County School System of Lexington, Kentucky, vocational interest assessment begins, along with career exploration, in grade 7. During the ninth grade, every student in special education receives a complete vocational assessment for the purpose of identifying career and vocational education goals and objectives for his or her IEP.

This vocational assessment process has two levels: screening and comprehensive assessment. The screening assessment starts during the first few weeks of each school year when special education teachers and school-based teacher consultants administer a six-hour battery of tests that determine vocational interests and attitudes. Psychological and social histories and educational assessments are also obtained, as are medical records.

In each school, screening assessments that focus on aptitudes, independent living skills, and basic work skills are done by a vocational assessment specialist and aides working with groups of three students. These assessments last approximately two hours. Personal interviews with the students also are conducted at this time.

The formal assessment is based upon need as determined by the screening phase. Each student needing intensive vocational evaluation spends approximately five hours at a vocational assessment center that is set up in one of the four high schools in the school district. This comprehensive assessment includes actual hands-on experience with job-related tasks in simulated work settings. Usually it is administered to groups of three students at a time.

After data have been collected from all the assessment instruments, they are entered into a computer that has detailed analyses stored for over 1500 primarily entry-level jobs. The computer matches the abilities of the students with job requirements and identifies clusters of jobs that appear to be appropriate for each student.

Students are then provided with intensive job exploration activities in order to assist them in making decisions about the specific jobs in which they might be interested. Again, the computer is used to develop a more specific match between student and job. This time, the computer selects seven or eight specific jobs that might be appropriate for that student.

Any discrepancies between student characteristics and job requirements are identified at this time. These discrepancies then become the basis for goals and objectives for an individualized vocational plan, which is incorporated into the student's IEP. An internal steering committee evaluates student progress every 12 weeks. Updated matches between students and jobs can be done at any time through a telecommunication system between the secondary schools and the vocational assessment center.

The information generated by this system is also used to make decisions about the length of educational services needed for a particular student. Some students are encouraged to stay in school until age 21 in order to develop and refine their skills further. As students are about to graduate, school personnel work with vocational rehabilitation counselors and local agencies for placement of students into a continuum of community services. For those who need continued development, an interagency cooperative effort is underway to continue the implementation of the individualized vocational plan formulated by the school system.

Parent and student input is critical if the transition plan is to result in successful postschool outcomes. To participate meaningfully, the parents and students must be provided with information about the various options and opportunities for youth with disabilities. Transition awareness education activities should begin by the time the student is in ninth grade or is age 16, whichever comes first. Examples of effective parent and student training activities are individual meetings with school and transition agency personnel, a parent-student transition inservice night, and program visits to local adult service facilities. Wehman et al. (1988) suggest that parent education meetings should orient parents to community agencies that provide postschool services to individuals with disabilities, familiarizing parents with the specific realms of responsibility of special education, vocational education, vocational rehabilitation, and adult service programs. Finally, parent education programs should prepare parents to work with these various agencies in developing transition plans and applying for future services.

In what ways should parental involvement be fostered?

In addition to making parents and students aware of what is involved in planning transition, it is also important to work with parents to determine the transition needs of their child. One approach is to use a parent questionnaire needs assessment instrument that includes questions covering various domains of transition. These domains include academic, vocational, and community adjustment skills of the student. A sample questionnaire is shown in Figure 5-5. Examples of other parent transition questionnaires are offered by Horton, Maddox, and Edgar (1983) and by Wheeler (1987).

The role of parents in the transition process cannot be understated. In addition to exerting a powerful influence on the career attitudes and options of the individual with disabilities (Kernan & Koegel, 1980; Kochany & Keller, 1981), parents and siblings, along with family friends, constitute a key resource in obtaining initial and subsequent jobs (Zetlin & Hosseini, 1989; Hasazi, Gordon, & Roe, 1985). This family-friend network can be the critical variable in the transition to successful adult living.

Interagency cooperation is another key ingredient in transition planning. A variety of services are available for individuals with disabilities after they leave school. Rehabilitation services, adult day programs, and vocational-technical training centers are a few examples. The multiplicity of agencies providing services can create potential problems, however. For example, differences in agency diagnostic terminology and eligibility criteria, duplication of services, political and attitudinal barriers, "turf" wars, and termination of programs can all inhibit interagency cooperation (Johnson, Bruininks, & Thurlow, 1987; Wehman et al., 1988). Coordination among agencies from the earliest stages of transition planning can serve to minimize these problems. This is no small task and must be approached from both state and local levels.

How can barriers to interagency cooperation be resolved?

Tindall and Gugerty (1989) argue that states must assume a central role in structuring interagency cooperation in order to reduce the unnecessary burden on agency personnel at the local level. They call for the development of state-level cooperative agreements among vocational and special education, vocational rehabilitation, and other programs funded by federal dollars for individuals with disabilities. The organization of local core teams at the community level is another approach to facilitating interagency collaboration (Wehman et al., 1988). The primary task of this local core team is as follows:

> Write a local level interagency agreement that establishes the operating and interaction procedures between the agencies for planning and implementing transition services. This plan should include an inter-organizational structure with responsibilities outlined for each participating agency. (p. 101)

Activities that state level teams could use to help implement and maintain local collaborative efforts have been listed by Tindall et al., (1982). They include the following:

FIGURE 5-5   Parent Transition Questionnaire

1. Have educational or other personnel talked with you about the postschool future of your son/daughter?

2. What do you want for your son/daughter during the next year, in 5 years, in 10 years?

   Recreation/Leisure:

   Vocational:

   Community:

   Domestic:

3. What most concerns you about the future of your son/daughter?

4. When your son/daughter made a transition in the past, e.g., from one school to another, what problems were encountered, if any?

5. Are you presently in contact with any agencies that will or may be involved with your son/daughter after graduation?

6. Are you aware of any community agencies that will or might be involved with your son/daughter? Do you plan on making or maintaining contact with them?

7. What do you anticipate to be your level of involvement with your son/daughter upon graduation from high school? Is this acceptable to you?

8. With whom and where would you like your son/daughter to live? Specify the nature of the living situation, e.g., apartment, house, etc.

9. Where would you like your son/daughter to work? Specify the nature of the work.

10. What recreational/leisure facilities has your son/daughter utilized? Which ones would you like him/her to use upon graduation from high school?

Source: From L. Brown et al. (1982). *Educational programs for severely handicapped students. XII.* Madison, WI: University of Wisconsin and Madison Metropolitan School District.

Normalization in Action

Like many children, Marc is a "sleepy-head" in the morning. His parents get him started on a busy day by putting on his leg braces and feeding him breakfast.

Marc has severe developmental disabilities and spends most of his school day in a self-contained special education class in a regular elementary school. However, he participates in a number of activities, such as music classes, with his peers who do not have disabilities. He also receives physical therapy, and his mother has Marc do exercises at home that are prescribed by the physical therapist.

Marc's parents are determined that he participate in as many family activities as possible. In addition to going swimming, he likes to have his brother read to him.

A specially designed table provides support that enables Marc to engage in activities that require him to stand. Similarly, an adapted bicycle lets the entire family go on outings together.

His mother often takes him to the mall in his special wheelchair when she goes shopping. Marc also enjoys a stop at a fast-food restaurant. With all of these activities, it is no wonder that Marc is tired at the end of the day.

As illustrated in this photo essay, it is possible to include children with severe developmental disabilities in many activities that are part of everyday life. Such participation can vastly improve the quality of life for Marc and the other members of his family.

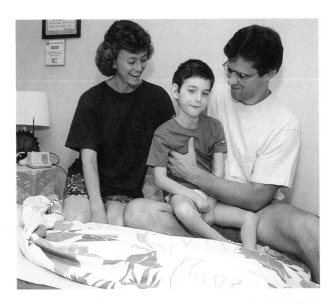

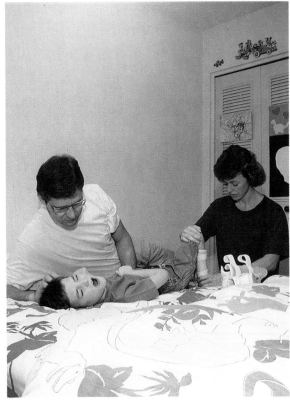

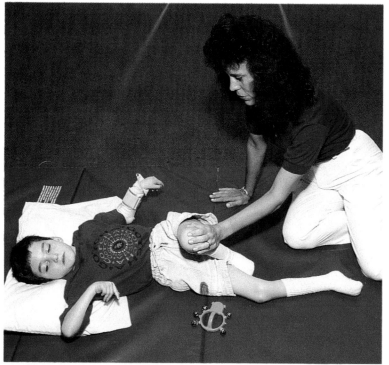

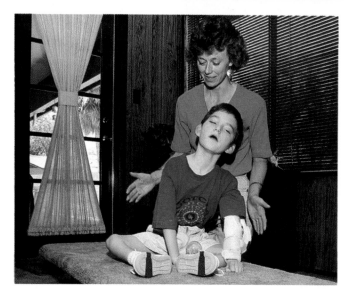

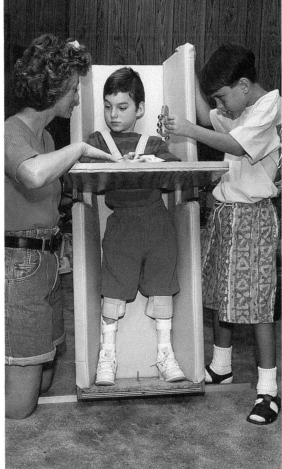

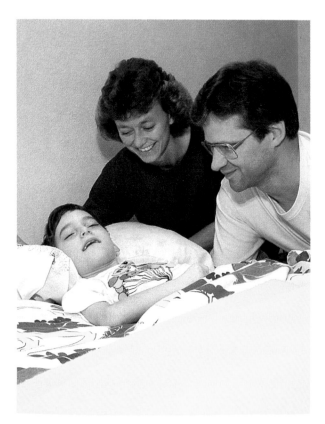

1. Prepare and distribute information on the state-level negotiated agreements to local interagency teams.
2. Design and develop a monitoring and evaluation system to assess process and product outcomes of local linkages.
3. Organize state-level interagency linkage teams to give inservice training and provide technical assistance to local-level personnel.
4. Maintain communication with local-level interagency teams.
5. Periodically review state-level agreements and adjust them as needed.
6. Develop plans designed to increase the number of local interagency agreements and cooperating teams.
7. Evaluate the effectiveness of state and local agreements to ensure that employment and training opportunities of individuals with disabilities are improving.

The **individualized transition plan** (ITP) provides a vehicle for implementing the transition services designed through the transition process. This written document specifies the annual goals and short-term objectives that reflect the skills targeted to function on the job, at home, and in the community. According to Brown et al. (1980), the ITP should be longitudinal in nature and include a comprehensive program of training in domestic, vocational, recreation/leisure, and general community living skills. It should contain transition objectives that functionally relate the training activities, materials, and evaluation strategies to unique subsequent life spaces and involve direct instruction across a wide variety of environments. Finally, it should require the participation of school and adult service personnel, tapping the focused expertise of competent related service personnel.

How does the ITP differ from the IEP?

Wheeler (1987) points out that the ITP can be a separate document or can be incorporated into the student's existing individualized education plan (IEP). She adds that the ITP differs from the IEP in two very important ways: First, it requires active participation and input not only from school personnel and related services (e.g., occupational, physical, and speech therapists) and parents, but from adult service providers as well. Second, the objectives of the ITP should reflect the actual requirements of the specific postschool environments into which the student is expected to pass.

In summary, effective transition planning requires input from both parents and the student in developing transition objectives, their awareness of available postschool service options, and their participation in planning the necessary services. In addition, it requires coordination and cooperation between state and local agencies that provide transition services to youth with disabilities. Finally, it is necessary to formulate a written transition plan specifying how transition for the individual student will best be accomplished. Efficient implementation of this complex planning process requires time, effort, and commitment from all individuals involved.

Stage Four: Transition Culmination

The fourth major stage of the transition process is culmination. This refers to the span of time encompassing

> the last two years of school, the point of separation from school, and two years following separation. During this time, responsibility for transition management shifts from the educational system to the student, the family, and/or the adult service delivery system. (California Department of Education, 1987, p. 1)

What are the
major elements in
the culmination of
transition services?

The three key elements of transition culmination are the sending agencies, the hand-off process and procedures, and the receiving environments (Maddox & Edgar, 1985). The sending agency in most instances is the public school. The hand-off process and procedures involve all the steps required to move the student from one setting to another. Examples of such steps include filling out the necessary paperwork, determining eligibility requirements of the agency or agencies receiving the student, conducting assessments of the student, and obtaining parent or guardian approval for services. The receiving environments are those adult agencies that will assume responsibility for the youth with disabilities after the completion of formal schooling.

It is important to realize that most individuals with disabilities do not make a smooth transition into postschool employment and community adjustment. The years of late adolescence have been referred to as the "floundering years" for all youth, an interim period between formal schooling and acceptance into the employment community (Hamilton, 1986). This is particularly true for individuals with disabilities, who tend to move from one entry-level job to another. One study revealed that former special education students spent an average of ten months in their first jobs, with over half of those with mild disabilities making job changes or requesting some form of intervention during the first year of employment. Therefore, finding the first job should be viewed as one step in the transition process, not the culminating event. Postemployment support services are needed on a continuing basis.

In order for transition culmination to occur in a smooth and efficient manner, decision makers from both the sending and receiving agencies must engage in systematic, formal planning. The formulation of a core transition team can facilitate this planning. The core transition team focuses on developing transition policies and procedures for students with disabilities who are exiting school. Serving on the team would be representatives from public school vocational and special education programs as well as various adult service agencies for the disabled. The team would identify existing community and school resources and services available, conduct follow-up studies of recent graduates from special education to determine transition needs and program development areas, and develop procedures to effectively reduce some of the discrepancies, shortcomings, and inadequacies in the service continuum. For instance, the team might identify the need for writing or revising interagency agreements.

What is the
purpose of the exit
meeting?

The final phase of transition culmination involves an exit meeting for the student. Parents, school personnel, adult service agency representatives, and possibly the student should be present at this meeting. The primary purpose of the meeting is to review the plans and assign responsibilities for implementing the last stage of transition for the student: obtaining meaningful employment and community adjustment (Wehman et al., 1988). Parents need to become fully aware of what postschool services are appropriate and available for their young adult and how to best access these services. This should be discussed during the exit meeting. To facilitate a trouble-free transition process, it is important that, following completion of this exit meeting, communication be maintained between the school, adult service agencies, and the parents.

Stage Five: Transition Follow-up

Evaluation of programs through follow-up studies of the participants is an important feature of a quality transition program. The effectiveness of the entire transition process, including the efficacy of the specific strategies used to move the student from school to work and community life, can be determined by obtaining information from individuals who participated in the transition program. A suggested means for obtaining this information is follow-up surveys sent to special education graduates.

What should be
addressed in a
follow-up study of
graduates?

Follow-up data should be obtained at regular intervals, at least every two or three years, as new groups of students go through the transition process. Wehman et al. (1988) suggest that data gathered from these surveys can assist school and adult personnel determine the following:

1. The number of special education students completing, as opposed to dropping out of, school.
2. The employment status of special education graduates.
3. The behavioral competence of special education students after they have exited school.
4. The effectiveness of the local school program.
5. The degree of coordination among various agencies and their effects on the adjustment of special education graduates.

Another means for obtaining evaluative information on the effectiveness of the transition process is by conducting actual face-to-face follow-up studies. This involves considerably more time and effort, but at the same time provides much deeper and richer information about the transition process and outcomes. Strategies for conducting a follow-up study include the following:

1. Conduct yearly observations of relevant persons in the domestic, vocational, recreation/leisure, and general quality of community life of each graduate.
2. Analyze these observational data to identify the skills necessary to function successfully in the critical environment that is being or will be inhabited by the individual.
3. Make hypotheses as to the reasons for the success or failure of the graduate.
4. Generate reasonable strategies that can be used by the public school and adult service agency personnel and parents or guardians to improve the ITPs.

The core transition team can use the information obtained from follow-up surveys or studies to evaluate the effectiveness of the transition process presently in place. Necessary adjustments can be made in order to increase the likelihood of a more efficient transition for future students with moderate and severe disabilities. Wheeler (1987) recommends joint meetings between adult service providers, school personnel, and parents. In addition, inservice and preservice training activities can prepare responsible parties to evaluate and act upon the results of follow-up studies.

Despite the attention that has been given to laying out systematic, sequential steps for the transition process, the successful transition of individuals with disabilities from school to productive adult lives in the community continues to be problematic. This is because, in large part, "students in transition from school are leaving a somewhat organized provider system and entering a more complex and confusing world, not fully understood by most service professionals and less by parents or consumers" (Will, 1984, p. 1).

PROBE 5-4   Stages of the Transition Process

1. List the five stages of the transition process, in order of their occurrence.
2. T F Regardless of the severity of the disability, all individuals with disabilities require the same type and intensity of transition programming.
3. Describe what is meant by a *functional curriculum.*
4. T F The primary reason why persons with disabilities experience job failure is that they have not been adequately trained to complete the job tasks.
5. Why is community-based instruction essential to preparing youth with disabilities for future employment?

6. The primary purpose of vocational assessment is to determine the _____ of the individual and to predict the _____ that the person may experience in a particular work situation.
7. Contrast the purpose of work sample assessments and situational work assessments.
8. T   F   Curriculum-based vocational assessment (CBVA) is an ongoing assessment procedure that gathers information during all phases of a student's vocational program.
9. List three key components of transition planning.
10. What is the purpose of transition follow-up?

ADDITIONAL TRANSITION CONSIDERATIONS

You should be able to identify aspects of the transition process associated with social skill development, preparation for community living, and employment options.

The planning and implementation of a transition program is more complex than it might appear from a cursory review of the five stages of the transition process. Additional features of the transition process include training procedures and outcomes associated with social skill development, preparation for community living, and the specification of the specific employment outcomes targeted (e.g., supported, sheltered, or competitive). Each of these considerations is discussed in the sections that follow.

Social-Vocational Skills

In addition to specific occupational skills, a variety of social competence skills are necessary for employment success. This is particularly true for those social skills that relate directly to vocational task expectations. The adequacy with which the worker interacts with supervisors and co-workers while performing work tasks is a key component of this social competence.

Evidence suggests that the major reason most individuals with disabilities encounter problems in getting and retaining jobs is the lack of appropriate social skills, not poor job performance (Gold, 1975; Greenspan & Shoultz, 1981; Cheney & Foss, 1984). Individuals with developmental disabilities tend to lose jobs for two main reasons: (1) maladaptive or aggressive behavior (e.g., screaming, destroying property, exhibiting bizarre behaviors, being noncompliant, and being repeatedly late for or absent from work) and (2) social awareness difficulties (e.g., interrupting others, talking about irrelevant and inappropriate topics, being too inquisitive about other people's business, and otherwise showing poor social interaction skills).

How are social skills related to employment success?

Social skills associated with employment success have also been identified. Employers want their workers to be able to verbally communicate at least their basic needs, to be compliant, to be nondisruptive in the work setting, and to follow directions. Chadsey-Rusch (1986) lists social skills that are important to the individual with disabilities in getting and maintaining employment, as follows:

1. Asking supervisors for assistance
2. Responding to criticism
3. Following directions
4. Getting information before a job

5. Offering to help co-workers
6. Using social amenities
7. Extending greetings
8. Giving positive comments (p. 278)

Social behaviors related to work productivity (e.g., listening without interrupting, acknowledging, and expressing appreciation to co-workers) are valued by employers more highly than general personal social behaviors. In jobs carried out in a social context, where workers interact frequently with each other and/or with customers (such as kitchen and food service jobs), social skills are considered more important than in jobs that do not require much social interaction.

Because of the importance of social skills to the perceived social competence of the individual, and the correlation between lack of social skills and unemployment among individuals with disabilities, vocationally related social skills training has become an important component of transition development. The primary goal of social skills training for persons with disabilities is that they be viewed by their employers and co-workers as having adequate social competence (Chadsey-Rusch, 1986). Social competence requires that the individual be able to decode or interpret a social situation correctly and to identify an appropriate response. The individual must then use social performance skills to effectively deliver that response. Skill in monitoring one's own responses in the situation provides an opportunity to modify subsequent responses.

Research has demonstrated that social skills training can effectively decrease inappropriate social behaviors (Rusch, Weither, Menchetti, & Schutz, 1980) as well as develop or increase appropriate social behaviors. Students have been taught job interviewing skills (Kelly, Wildman, & Berler, 1980), to comply with employer directions (Rusch & Menchetti, 1981), to increase the frequency of asking questions during conversation (Chadsey-Rusch, Karlan, Riva, & Rusch, 1984), to handle criticism, to take a joke, and to solicit assistance (Shafer, Brooke, & Wehman, 1985), as well as a sequence of behaviors appropriate for break-times (Breen, Haring, Pitts-Conway, and Gaylord-Ross, 1984). Most of these studies used social skills training packages, although some used a combination of behavioral techniques. Generalization to noninstructional or natural environments appeared to occur in most instances.

Community Living Skills

Although the basic emphasis of transition is on vocational skills and employment, a variety of additional skills are required if the individual is to make a full transition into community living (Halpern, 1985; Clark & Kolstoe, 1990). Areas of potential difficulties in independent living include money management, social networking, home maintenance, food management, conflict over being told what to do versus asking for help, employment, transportation, leisure pursuits, and avoiding or handling problems (Halpern, Close, & Nelson, 1986). Clark and Kolstoe (1990) categorize life skills in terms of accessing/using transportation, health care, financial guidance, legal services, and mental health services. The Life-Centered Career Education program described earlier in this chapter devotes considerable attention to the development of a broad array of adult living skills similar to these, including the use of leisure time.

What are the domains that encompass community living skills?

Dever (1988, 1989) has developed an even more comprehensive taxonomy of community living skills. These skills focus on the requirements of community living and, as such, provide instructional goals for helping individuals with disabilities become functioning members of the community. Dever's taxonomy organizes the goals into five domains, as depicted in Figure 5-6. The three sides of the taxonomy triangle reflect those competencies that must

FIGURE 5-6   Taxonomy of Community Living Skills

The Instructional
Paradigm

Organization of the Taxonomy

```
┌─────────────────┐
│ Establish the Aim │
│  of Instruction   │
└─────────────────┘
         │
         ▼
┌─────────────────┐
│   Set the Goals   │
└─────────────────┘
         │
         ▼
┌─────────────────┐
│ Develop Curricula │
│ Leading to the Goals │
└─────────────────┘
         │
         ▼
┌─────────────────┐
│ Develop Individual │ ◀──┐
│     Programs       │    │
└─────────────────┘    │ REVISE
         │               │
         ▼               │
┌─────────────────┐    │
│      Teach        │    │
└─────────────────┘    │
         │               │
         ▼               │
┌─────────────────┐    │
│    Evaluate       │ ───┘
│  Instruction      │
└─────────────────┘
```

HOMEMAKING AND COMMUNITY LIFE

TRAVEL

PERSONAL
MAINTENANCE
AND
DEVELOPMENT

TRAVEL

VOCATIONAL

LEISURE

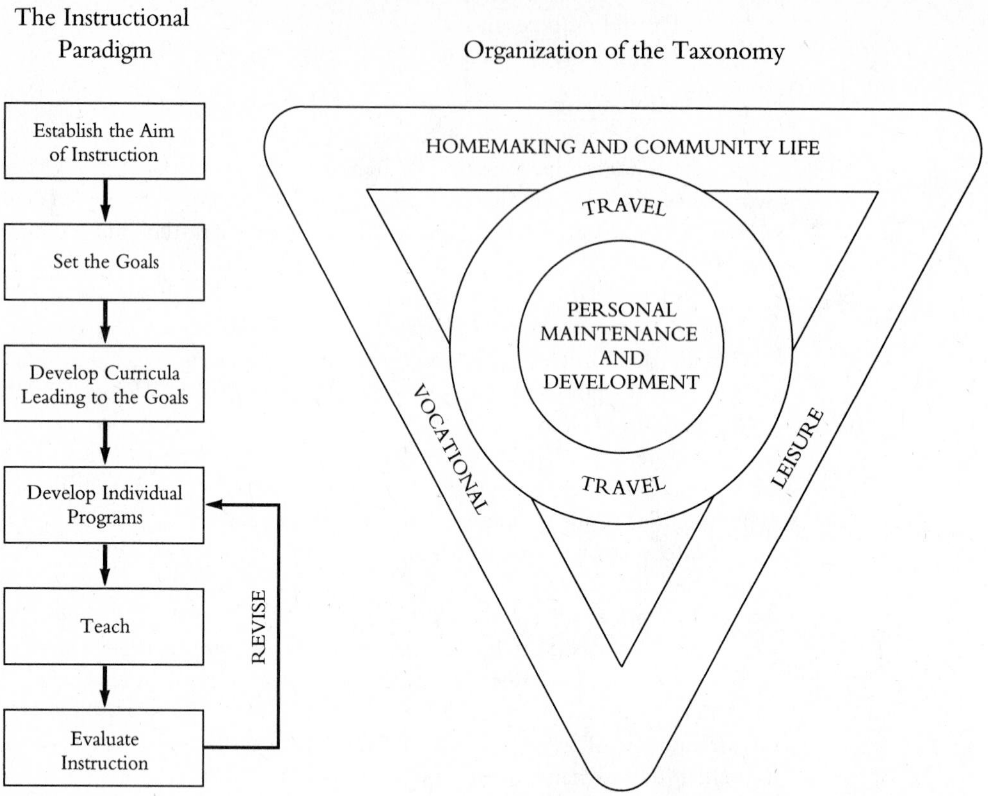

Source: Both figures are from *Community living skills: A taxonomy* by R. B. Dever, 1988. Reprinted by permission of the American Association on Mental Retardation.

be exhibited in community settings (homemaking and community life, vocational adjustment, and leisure pursuits), with the center domain incorporating competencies related to personal maintenance and development. The fifth domain, travel, is represented as a circle that connects the individual with the community. All together, these encompass all the ways in which individuals work, play, and move through the community. The major instructional goals of the taxonomy, outlined in Table 5-4, can be further analyzed into listings of discrete skills that can be individually taught. The development of these skills is consistent with the broader views of transition that include the full range of skills associated with the quality of adult life attained.

Figure 5-7 (p. 167) illustrates another perspective on transition to community living and the work environment, listing some of the ways the environment can be modified to enable people with disabilities to function independently. Note that the modifications involve education, service delivery, interagency collaboration, and public awareness, as well as physical changes to facilities.

Employment Options

A variety of employment alternatives are possible outcomes of the transition process. As discussed earlier in this chapter, some students have disabilities that do not preclude their successful completion of university degree programs at both the undergraduate and graduate

TABLE 5-4   Major Instructional Goals for the Taxonomy of Community Living Skills

Domain P
Personal Maintenance and Development

I. The learner will follow routine body maintenance procedures
   A. Maintain personal cleanliness
   B. Groom self
   C. Dress appropriately
   D. Follow appropriate sleep patterns
   E. Maintain nutrition
   F. Exercise regularly
   G. Maintain substance control
II. The learner will treat illnesses
   A. Use first aid and illness treatment procedures
   B. Obtain medical advice when necessary
   C. Follow required medication schedules

III. The learner will establish and maintain personal relationships
   A. Interact appropriately with family
   B. Make friends
   C. Interact appropriately with friends
   D. Cope with inappropriate conduct of family and friends
   E. Respond to sexual needs
   F. Obtain assistance in maintaining personal relationships
IV. The learner will handle personal "glitches"
   A. Cope with changes in daily schedule
   B. Cope with equipment breakdowns and material depletions

Domain H
Homemaking and Community Life

I. The learner will obtain living quarters
   A. Find appropriate living quarters
   B. Rent/buy living quarters
   C. Set up living quarters
II. The learner will follow community routines
   A. Keep living quarters neat and clean
   B. Keep fabrics neat and clean
   C. Maintain interior of living quarters
   D. Maintain exterior of living quarters
   E. Respond to seasonal changes
   F. Follow home safety procedures
   G. Follow accident/emergency procedures
   H. Maintain foodstock
   I. Prepare and serve meals
   J. Budget money appropriately
   K. Pay bills

III. The learner will co-exist in a neighborhood and community
   A. Interact appropriately with community members
   B. Cope with inappropriate conduct of others
   C. Observe requirements of the law
   D. Carry out civic duties
IV. The learner will handle "glitches" in the home
   A. Cope with equipment breakdowns
   B. Cope with depletions of household supplies
   C. Cope with unexpected depletions of funds
   D. Cope with disruptions in routine
   E. Cope with sudden changes in the weather

Domain V
Vocational

I. The learner will obtain work
   A. Seek employment
   B. Accept employment
   C. Use unemployment services
II. The learner will perform the work routine
   A. Perform the job routine
   B. Follow work-related daily schedule
   C. Maintain work station
   D. Follow employer rules and regulations

   E. Use facilities appropriately
   F. Follow job safety procedures
   G. Follow accident and emergency procedures
III. The learner will co-exist with others on the job
   A. Interact appropriately with others on the job
   B. Cope with inappropriate conduct of others on the job

continued

TABLE 5-4 *(continued)*

Domain V
(continued)

IV. The learner will handle "glitches" on the
    job
    A. Cope with changes in work routine

    B. Cope with work problems
    C. Cope with supply depletions and
       equipment breakdowns

Domain L
Leisure

I. The learner will develop leisure
   activities
   A. Find new leisure activities
   B. Acquire skills for leisure activities
II. The learner will follow leisure activity
    routines
    A. Perform leisure activities
    B. Maintain leisure equipment
    C. Follow leisure safety procedures
    D. Follow accident and emergency
       procedures

III. The learner will co-exist with others
     during leisure
     A. Interact appropriately with others in a
        leisure setting
     B. Respond to the inappropriate
        conduct of others
IV. The learner will handle "glitches" during
    leisure
    A. Cope with changes in leisure routine
    B. Cope with equipment breakdowns
       and material depletions

Domain T
Travel

I. The learner will travel routes in the
   community
   A. Form mental maps of frequented
      buildings
   B. Form mental maps of the community
II. The learner will use conveyances
    A. Follow usage procedures
    B. Make decisions preparatory to travel
    C. Follow travel safety procedures
    D. Follow accident and emergency
       procedures

III. The learner will co-exist with others
     while traveling
     A. Interact appropriately with others
        while traveling
     B. Respond to the inappropriate
        conduct of others while traveling
IV. The learner will handle "glitches"
    A. Cope with changes in travel
       schedule
    B. Cope with equipment breakdowns
    C. Cope with being lost

Source: From *Community living skills: A taxonomy* by R. B. Dever, 1988. Reprinted by permission of the American Association on Mental Retardation.

levels. The employment outcomes targeted for these individuals will likely be professional in nature. Planned transition activities include campus awareness and orientation activities, affective support groups, academic counseling, tutoring and related academic support, strategy training, and study skill development (Dalke & Schmitt, 1987).

For individuals with disabilities that interfere significantly with their abstract thinking processes, the employment alternatives available require various amounts of training and support. The array of vocational alternatives for persons with disabilities include (1) sheltered options, (2) supported employment, and (3) competitive employment.

Sheltered options include adult development centers, special enclaves, businesses and mobile work crews, and sheltered workshops. Adult development centers typically teach clients daily living skills and basic academics, along with providing some work-skill activities and

FIGURE 5-7   A Functional Approach to Exceptionality: Facilitating Transition

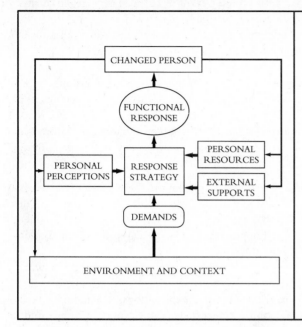

ENVIRONMENTAL MODIFICATION

Following are some ways that modification of the work and community environment can facilitate transition to the community:

- Teach employers about their responsibilities to employ people with disabilities.

- Construct ramps to make facilities and the workplace accessible to those in wheelchairs.

- Mark elevator buttons and office door numbers with braille symbols.

- Develop partnerships between schools and the private sector to train people for jobs.

- Develop public awareness programs for broadcast on radio and TV programs.

- Establish mechanisms for special education, vocational education, and vocational rehabilitation personnel to work together.

recreation opportunities. There are approximately 2000 such centers in the country (Wehman et al., 1988).

Sheltered workshops are more work-centered, providing contract benchwork (e.g., sorting tasks, stuffing bags or boxes) with limited pay that is based on productivity. For decades, sheltered workshops served as the primary option for the individual with moderate to severe disabilities. They provide vocational assessment, general occupational development and work adjustment training, and paid employment opportunities.

With the movement toward normalization, sheltered workshops have been criticized for their failure to move individuals into mainstream employment and living options. Further, the low level of pay available fostered dependence, and the sheltered nature of the workshops contributed to the isolation of individuals with disabilities.

What is the trend in providing sheltered employment options?

Despite severe criticisms, the number of these facilities has increased dramatically in the past two decades, with more than 5000 such workshops available today (Wehman et al., 1988). Many of these facilities are moving toward sponsoring more integrated employment programs, as follows:

1. Mobile work crews go into the community to perform service jobs (e.g., washing cars at an auto dealership, landscape maintenance, highway litter pickup, janitorial services, and so forth) under contracts with government or private agencies or businesses. In addition to serving as an employment option within a sheltered workshop or similar agency, they may operate independently as private, nonprofit corporations. A crew supervisor ensures satisfactory fulfillment of the contract while at the same time providing job training to the crew members. Workers with disabilities are paid from the contractual fee, typically at rates of pay based on the productivity rate (e.g., number of units of work per hour) of other workers performing the same tasks. Their hourly pay tends to be below minimum wage.

2. Sheltered enclaves are composed of six to ten workers with disabilities, working under the supervision of a professional staff person. Located in business and industrial sites as separate units, each enclave has a particular role to play. Workers are paid directly by the employer, typically at pay rates based on productivity, with pay ranging from subminimum to above-minimum rates and including fringe benefits (Clark & Kolstoe, 1990).

3. Specialized sheltered businesses are designed to be competitive in the production of goods and services. Such businesses might specialize in printing, micrographics, and electronic assembly, to name but a few of the options. Some sheltered businesses employ only workers with disabilities, while others employ nondisabled workers as well. Such a facility pays at least minimum wage and may or may not operate under nonprofit organization charters (Clark & Kolstoe, 1990).

Supported employment has been developed as an option for persons with severe disabilities who are considered unable to hold a job without permanent, ongoing support. The Title VII provisions of the 1986 amendments to the Vocational Rehabilitation Act provided money for supported employment as well as for projects to change day programs and adult activity centers to industry-based employment options.

What are the
features of
supported
employment
options?

Supported employment provides job opportunities and training in integrated work settings, supervised by job trainers. Initially the job trainer may be a job coach who provides one-to-one training to develop the skills to meet employer expectations. A paraprofessional, possibly recruited from the ranks of nondisabled co-workers, can then be trained to do maintenance training and supervision as the worker continues in the job (Clark & Kolstoe, 1990).

Regular competitive employment is the most desirable alternative for individuals with disabilities, because it provides for integrated work in community businesses and industry with at least minimum-wage levels of pay. While many individuals with disabilities will locate

This adult with mental retardation is operating a shrink-wrap machine at a sheltered workshop.

The construction foreman is directing a group of workers with mental retardation who are helping to build a house. A job coach at the rear provides ongoing training and supervision.

and succeed in competitive employment with little guidance or support, most do not, as attested to by statistics presented earlier in this chapter.

What services can support competitive employment?

Support services from state vocational rehabilitation agencies can assist in this process, although these agencies typically have insufficient funding to meet the demand for services. A number of employer incentives for hiring individuals with disabilities have evolved out of federal legislation. These include subminimum wage certificates through the Department of Labor, wage subsidies through targeted job tax credits, and JTPA (Job Training Partnership Act) programs.

A recent innovation is the development of the transitional employment support services that provide direct work adjustment and social skills training at the job site. Professional staff assist the workers until they demonstrate job competence, independence, and stability, at which time the support is systematically withdrawn.

PROBE 5-5   Additional Transition Considerations

1. Why is instruction in social competence skills critical to the employment success of individuals with disabilities?
2. T   F   Social skills training is effective in decreasing inappropriate social behaviors, but it has not proved effective in increasing appropriate behaviors.
3. List the five domains of Dever's taxonomy of community living skills.
4. Put these three employment options in order of most to least intensive support: supported employment, sheltered workshops, competitive employment.

This 22-year-old graduate of a special education program holds a clerical job in an office.

TRANSITION ISSUES AND CHALLENGES

You should be able to describe issues that challenge the successful transitions of students with disabilities.

Since the beginning of this century, the major purpose of special education has been to prepare individuals with disabilities to lead productive and personally satisfying adult lives. The transition movement of the past decade, with its emphasis on community-based training and integrated occupational and living opportunities, is a modern reflection of this goal. Adult transition models emphasize employment outcomes while also addressing broader aspects of quality of life. Some models, such as one that provides assistance in the transition from secondary school into colleges and universities, focus on traditional academic curricula as the appropriate alternative. Others provide alternative programs for students for whom traditional school programs do not promote qualitative adult adjustment.

Despite the progress that has been made in articulating, implementing, and documenting these models, a number of societal factors continue to challenge the successful transition of students with disabilities. These include national economic and employment trends, the excellence in education movement, programmatic barriers, parent participation, and personnel preparation.

Economic Trends and Employment Options

What economic trends affect the employment of people with disabilities?

Episodic economic dislocations in the form of energy shortages, factory closings, corporate mergers and bankruptcies, the internationalization of industry, the growing drug culture, and increasing economic polarization of our citizens are evidence that our society is undergoing a dramatic and basic restructuring. There is increasing poverty and a growing underclass in our nation, as evidenced by a 33 percent increase between 1973 and 1988 in the proportion of people living below the poverty level.

The number of manufacturing jobs in this nation declined by 1.7 million in the six years from 1979 to 1985. While there was a dramatic rise in new jobs in retail and service industries, these jobs paid on average only about half the wages of manufacturing jobs, while at the same time requiring higher levels of skill (William T. Grant Foundation, 1988). The overall number of low-skill jobs is declining and may continue to do so as more and more labor-saving devices are created.

As the nation moves out of the industrial age and into the information age, the more-desirable jobs require increasingly complex skills that involve abstract thinking and problem solving. Information management skills (including logic, abstraction, synthesis, and generative thinking behavior) are qualities in which many individuals with disabilities (particularly those with mental retardation) are deficient, a situation that makes their integration into the high-technology society of the future more doubtful (Tawney, 1982). At the same time, the specter of general economic recession reminds us that, historically, during times of economic downturns, those with disabilities have been the most adversely affected.

In light of these trends, particularly the dearth of jobs that pay "livable" wages for youths entering the job market, Edgar (1988) recommended that the mission of general and special education be expanded beyond economic self-sufficiency to one that ensures that

> all of our citizens, disabled and nondisabled, male and female, employed and not
> employed, young and old, have daily food, a place to live, access to basic health care,
> and reasonable hope that their lives, and the lives of their children, will get better.
> This should be an entitlement we provide for all our citizens. (p. 7)

How can the public be made more aware of the vocational capabilities of people with disabilities?

Clearly, articulating transition goals that are realistic in relation to general economic developments is a significant challenge. A related challenge lies in creating public awareness of the capabilities of individuals with disabilities and the responsibilities of employers to hire qualified individuals regardless of disability. Strategies for accomplishing this include (1) hiring and training job developers to find employment for individuals with disabilities; (2) having potential employers observe good employment training programs in the community; (3) developing public awareness programs that inform the general public about the employment potential of persons with disabilities; and (4) arranging for special education students to volunteer their services in exchange for the training opportunity (Wehman et al., 1988).

Educational Excellence Movement

What is the impact of the educational excellence movement?

The excellence in education movement has resulted in increased academic standards and a narrowing of the focus of educational efforts to specific academic skill areas. Increases in the number of "hard" subjects required for graduation, prescribed proficiency standards for both courses of study and the high school diploma, and increased standardization of curricula with fewer options for students who are not college-bound are hallmarks of the current educational reform movement. This trend, coupled with an increasing emphasis on mainstream integration of students with disabilities, has forced special educators to spend even more time and energy on getting students with disabilities through the required academic curricula, and less time on career and vocational experiences. In many secondary schools, vocational education programs have been drastically reduced because students have less time in their class schedules for taking vocational courses.

What is the value of alternative secondary education programs?

It is clear that the transitional life adjustment goals of special education cannot be well served by a single-track, academically focused secondary school curriculum. Many special education leaders believe that current educational theories and program models offer little hope for solving the problems of unemployment among students with disabilities as well as other low-achieving individuals. The development of meaningful alternative secondary education program options has been recommended for youths who are not directly bound for college. One solution would be to develop well-articulated alternative education tracks that, in addition to the general academic track, could lead to the high school diploma. This could be accomplished by determining the correspondence of the skills and components of these alternative programs to the core academic requirements. For example, partial credits for English or math could be awarded when students demonstrate to prescribed criteria specific functional competencies, such as taking phone messages or balancing a checkbook. A curriculum of this nature has been developed by Clark and Greene (1989) and is currently being implemented in 13 school districts in southern California.

Edgar (1987) noted that the "only solution is a radical (no namby-pamby modification or cosmetic addition to existing program) shift in focus of secondary curriculum away from academics to functional, vocational, independent living tasks" (p. 560). The alternative that would result from such a shift should be "socially valued, provide opportunities for youth to engage in activities valued by adult society, focus on problem solving and coping skills, provide opportunities to learn, practice, and demonstrate valued vocational skills, and include ongoing mentor support systems" (Edgar, 1988, p. 6).

Interagency Collaboration

What barriers exist to interagency collaboration?

The extent to which vocational education, special education, and vocational rehabilitation will work together effectively to collaborate in the transition process is another challenge. Historically, vocational rehabilitation has focused on adults with acquired disabilities, not youths with developmental disabilities. Further, the criteria for selecting clients (e.g., high probability of succeeding in competitive employment) precluded many special education students from services. In a similar vein, vocational education carved out its identity as a rigorous alternative to the general education curriculum and has had difficulty identifying with the needs of more challenging students. Further, vocational education teachers have lacked skill in adjusting their curriculum and instruction to students with unique needs.

Special education, on the other hand, typically has had limited real-world expertise to bring to bear on the vocational and life adjustment transition process. Special education teachers tend not to know a great deal about specific job skills or about the training processes related to the acquisition of these skills. While considerable progress has been made, there is still a long way to go in developing optimal partnerships among the three agencies. The extent to which vocational education will be successful in refocusing its overall training efforts on meeting the needs of special populations represents yet another challenge for the future.

A related challenge is the need to develop an interagency core transition team to guide and coordinate the transition process. The more players involved in and committed to the transition process, the greater are the chances of achieving successful postschool outcomes for individuals with disabilities. Administrators from these separate agencies must provide leadership in establishing formal relationships among the agencies, providing intensive staff development for personnel, and working together to address the various issues involved in transition—transportation, liability, and so forth. Determining who is responsible for what services and eliminating territoriality among agencies are key challenges.

Parent Involvement

What concerns do parents have about transition?

Actively involving parents is perhaps the most important factor in the entire transition process. From the early stages of the individualized education planning process, parents must begin to think about what long-term outcomes they want and to select the educational experiences that will lead to these outcomes. They need to recognize that choosing an academic, diploma-bound curriculum may have different outcomes than those associated with more vocational and functional options. Many will have difficulty accepting that their youngster will not be able to go on to college or to attain a professional career. Others will have doubts about the ability of their offspring to become competitively employed. Other concerns include the potential loss of Supplemental Security Income (SSI) payments and other benefits if their child does become employed. Concerns about the independence of the various adult living arrangements will also surface.

Transition personnel must be sensitive to these concerns and attempt to provide information and education to help parents develop realistic expectations that can guide the selection of educational program options. Conveying positive feelings about the student's vocational potential, including vocational objectives on IEPs, and inviting parents to visit local vocational and community living options can contribute to this process.

Personnel Preparation Practices

How can teacher preparation programs better address transition needs?

A final challenge that must be met in order to implement successful transition involves the preparation of personnel who can guide such services. Most secondary special education teachers do not possess adequate training for the work they do (Wheeler, 1987). For example, Halpern (1985) found that nearly 40 percent of high school special education teachers had received their teaching certification at the elementary level. Over two-thirds of the states do not require evidence of special preparation to teach secondary special education students (Beason, 1982). Finally, special education teachers need more training in the areas of vocational preparation and career education, as well as more information related to business and industry (Chadsey-Rusch et al., 1984). At the same time, vocational education teachers require special preparation for working with nontraditional students and in adjusting curriculum and modifying instructional strategies. Vocational education personnel also need preparation for working with younger and more developmentally disabled clients. A few model programs provide specialized interdisciplinary preparation leading to Vocational Transition Specialist Certification for personnel from any of these three programs. The availability of such programs must be greatly increased at the same time that the basic curricula of the separate programs are expanded to encompass this broader array of skills. Transition is a complex undertaking that requires shared responsibility among disciplines, university departments, and public service agencies if the goal of successful adult adjustment is to be realized.

PROBE 5-6   Transition Issues and Challenges

1. T F Recent trends in economic development have resulted in a decline in the number of low-skill jobs available to workers with disabilities.
2. List three strategies special educators can use to increase public awareness of the capabilities of individuals with disabilities and employers' responsibility to hire qualified workers regardless of disability.
3. The excellence in education movement has resulted in an _____ in academic standards and a _____ in emphasis on vocational education programs in many secondary schools.
4. Three key agencies that must collaborate to ensure effective transition programming are special education, _____, and _____.
5. How can transition personnel actively involve parents in the transition process?
6. T F Most secondary special educators do not have sufficient training in vocational preparation and career education, and most vocational educators do not have adequate training in working with special populations.

SUMMARY

1. Too many people with disabilities do not achieve their full potential as contributing members of society.
2. Federal legislation has been developed to provide a greater emphasis on programs to help students with disabilities make the transition from school to community life.
3. The three stages of career education are career awareness, career exploration, and career preparation.
4. Transition programs should focus on the development of a broad array of adult living skills, not just those that deal with employment.
5. Community adjustment is the major goal of transition programs.
6. Residential environment, employment, and social and interpersonal networks are the three pillars that support community adjustment.
7. Foundations for the transition process are a functional curriculum, an integrated setting, and community-based instruction.
8. Curriculum-based vocational assessment (CBVA) is an important part of vocational assessment.
9. The individualized transition plan (ITP) is developed to specify needed transition activities for students.
10. When people with disabilities do not succeed on the job, it is most often because of inappropriate social skills rather than an inability to perform the tasks associated with the job.
11. Types of employment for people with disabilities include sheltered options, supported employment, and regular competitive employment.
12. Personnel from special education, vocational education, and vocational rehabilitation need to work together to provide services to enhance transition.
13. There is a need to increase public awareness about the vocational capability of people with disabilities.

TASK SHEET 5   Field Experiences with Transition Services

Select one of the following and complete the required task.

Workplace Visit

Visit one of the following and write a brief description (two to three pages maximum) about what you observed:

     a. A sheltered workshop
     b. A secondary school transition job placement
     c. A rehabilitation agency
     d. An employment enclave for individuals with disabilities

Interview on Employment

Interview one of the following people and write a three-page paper on the substance of your interview:

     a. A teacher of a secondary school transition program or class
     b. A vocational rehabilitation counselor who works with special education students
     c. A supported employment employee
     d. An employer who hires persons with disabilities

Interview on Work Problems

Interview a person with disabilities about the problems associated with employment and/or community living. Write a three-page paper describing this person's responses.

Program Analysis

Visit a secondary transition class or program. Observe the program and interview the teacher. In a three-page paper, identify the major features of the program and describe its strengths as well as the barriers it encounters in providing transition services.

Transition Planning

Interview a secondary special education teacher to identify the type of transition planning that occurs at a particular school site. Are transition goals incorporated into the IEP or is a separate ITP used? Are specialized classes and experiences available as a part of the transition process? How would the teacher like to see transition services expanded for students at that site?

Library Study

Use the library to locate three recent articles on transition services. Write a one-page abstract of each; conclude with a paragraph about your reactions to the article.

Something was always a little wrong with Christopher in school; sometimes things were a lot wrong. From first grade to fourth, dealings with teachers always were loaded with tension. The average teacher conference started off positive, but my wife and I knew that the bombshell would land before we got safely out of the room.

Bright—but homework not in. Capable—but three-week-old assignments still not begun. Friendly—but peer problems. Willing—but doesn't listen. Pity the 10-year-old who has to face parents after such a meeting.

There are several predictable steps toward finding a solution for a learning problem in a child. The first step comes with recognition; unfortunately, recognition doesn't come until after a good deal of bad blood has developed between parent and child while the parent still believes that the problem is due to lack of motivation, carelessness, laziness, or indifference.

The first step to solution comes with recognition that there is, indeed, a real problem that the child does not have any more control over than do teachers or parents. Once this fact is recognized, then parent and child can begin to work together in a nonblaming way toward finding the diagnosis (the name of the specific problem).

Chris's problem is in auditory sequential memory and, to a lesser extent, in auditory comprehension. Thus, instructions given verbally by teachers went in one ear and out the other. Actually they went in one ear and no further. Chris's difficulty was far less severe than those that plague the majority of children with learning disabilities, but it was profound in the limited area in which he was affected. At 10, his auditory comprehension was at a level lower than is achieved by the average 4-year-old.

I think two new sets of problems arise once the diagnosis has been established. The first problem is obvious and parents of kids with learning disabilities discuss it frequently: to find help to remediate their child's disability. The second set of problems are more personal and consequently harder to talk about. These personal issues usually involve guilt—the parent takes the anger previously turned on the child and turns it back on himself or herself for having mishandled the situation.

Source: Excerpts from "A Father's Struggles with His LD Son: Confessions of a Clinical Psychologist" by Julien Worland. Reprinted by permission of the author.

6

Families of Exceptional Children

James A. McLoughlin

The 1990s will witness families of exceptional children, youth, and adults assuming an ever-greater role in providing appropriate services for their loved ones. As a result of PL 94-142, PL 99-457, and other laws that reflect federal recognition of their basic rights and responsibilities, parents have emerged as a group with a significant role in serving the needs of persons with disabilities; they are increasingly involved in planning and carrying out educational programs. However, in the process, some unrealistic expectations have sometimes been established for parents, given their interests and abilities; there has been a temptation to "professionalize" them, expecting them to take on duties normally performed by various professionals. The current emphasis is a more individualized approach to working with families in a collaborative fashion (Winton & Bailey, 1988).

PL 99-457 has brought a more holistic approach to the role of the family by mandating consideration of family needs in the individualized family service plan that is prepared for infants and preschoolers with disabilities. Greater attention is being given to family and home assessment as a consequence. While families of gifted and talented children and youth are not accorded the same rights and support as families with disabled members (Kitano & Kirby, 1986), they too have similar challenges and needs for which they need understanding and assistance. Thus, when we speak of families of exceptional children in this chapter, we are considering the full spectrum of abilities and include gifted and talented youngsters in our designation.

The increasing involvement of families in providing services for exceptional children requires considerable growth on the part of parents and other family members. In addition to making emotional adjustments to their children's disabilities, as illustrated in the vignette at the beginning of this chapter, parents are learning skills to promote quality programs for their children and to participate in them more fully than ever before. At the same time, the educators of their children are developing both interpersonal and technical skills to facilitate greater family involvement. Educators are relating to parents more as the principal agents of treatment and change than as the principal causative agents (Paul & Porter, 1981). They are also learning to communicate better with parents and involve them more effectively in their children's programs. This progress is evident in the increased number of parenting courses in teacher training programs. Parenting programs are now regarded as essential to the enhancement and implementation of special education programs and go beyond parenting skill development to encompass broader family concerns and advocacy. Educators must apply themselves to involve families of those with disabilities, but the rewards are many.

At the foundation of this effort is a close, trusting relationship between the families and educators. Unless both parents and teachers understand one another and appreciate each other's perspectives, little can be accomplished. The families of these children must wrestle with many emotional aspects of their children's disabilities, which necessarily affect the family dynamics. As we discuss in the following pages, in order to encourage participation, educators must understand and relate to families in the context of needs and concerns that reach far beyond the exceptional condition alone.

RELATING TO FAMILIES

You should be able to describe how to relate effectively to the needs of families of students with disabilities.

Emotional Challenges

Current thinking stresses that the emotional reactions of families of students with disabilities are both *natural* and *unique*. Once parents realize that their child has a disability, it is natural that they experience a series of profound emotional reactions as necessary precursors to accepting the situation. As with any traumatic event, the whole family is affected, and members work together (consciously or unconsciously) to adapt to the situation. The child with disabilities is not only the occasion for this process, but also an integral part of it.

The process is also unique. Families of children with disabilities have to learn to live with more emotional extremes and ultimately at deeper levels than most people (Paul & Porter, 1981). The disabilities of the children place more pervasive, intense, and enduring demands on the family's growth and development. That is why it is important to view emotional reactions to disabilities in a family context. Without understanding and assistance, these families may overprotect the children with disabilities, use them as scapegoats for other family problems, or break up as a family unit (Perosa & Perosa, 1981).

The changes in the modern family also have a strong effect on the family's ability to cope with a child's disability. Birth control, the movement for equal rights for women, alternative living styles (for example, unmarried couples living together), and the high rate of single-parent families are all influential (Lillie, 1981). Medical advances are allowing more premature at-risk infants to survive. Increased use of illegal drugs is resulting in the birth of children with various disabilities. Educators must appreciate how these social realities influence the emotional needs of the families of their students.

Parental Reactions

What factors can influence family reactions to disability?

Parents' reactions to the birth of a child with disabilities vary greatly. Such factors as religion, socioeconomic status, severity and obviousness of the disability, parental knowledge, and order of birth can all affect parental responses. Additionally, efforts to establish a taxonomy of family lifestyles for families of children with severe mental retardation (e.g., cohesive, control-oriented, responsive-to-child, moral-religious oriented, and achievement-oriented) suggest the importance of the overall family dynamics (Mink, Blacher, & Nihira, 1988). A variety of descriptions of the emotional stages parents pass through before they accept their child's disability have been offered, but they are highly speculative (Allen & Affleck, 1985). Most parents, however, appear to experience periods of frustration, fear, guilt, disappointment, and uncertainty. Some parents of youngsters with learning disabilities also report relief after being told of their children's problems, having their suspicions confirmed, and finally having a reason for the difficulties (Faerstein, 1986). Because of the intense feeling of loss felt by many parents, some experience several different stages of response that parallel the adjustment process required by a loved one's death.

What is the initial reaction to learning that one's child is exceptional?

SHOCK. According to Kroth (1985), the initial reaction of parents is shock, even though they frequently suspect that their child has a problem before it is confirmed by professionals. Parents have described this stage by saying:

> "My God, I couldn't believe this was happening to us."

> "I felt like I was in a daze, and the doctor's voice was a thousand miles away."

> "My head spun, I was sick to my stomach, and I fought the urge to faint."

> "My wife turned white and started to shake and sob. I was so shaken, I couldn't do anything for her."

> "I felt my world, my dreams, my plans were crushed. What an enormous disappointment!"

> "I had a hunch about Tommy's problem, but I never anticipated how bad it was."

> "I couldn't speak. I was deaf and dumb."

Educators and other professionals must appreciate the significance of this event for parents and other family members. They may be devastated, immobilized, and very vulnerable. Cold, impersonal, and even cruel factual revelations can add to the blow and often delay the parental action necessary to obtain help.

Unfortunately, professionals who behave improperly are often themselves unhappy and upset about what they have to tell the parents and lack the skills, time, and other resources to do it well. Educators and other professionals have been known to say to parents:

> "Mrs. Jones, I wish I had better news for you, but Billy is permanently blind."

> "I know this may sound like the end of the world, but your baby has a serious problem."

> "There is not time now to get into all of it, but we have a problem."

Among themselves:

> "God, I hate it when I have to tell parents that there is something wrong with their kid."

> "I was so glad the principal was there. I knew that father was going to come after me."

> "Could you believe how those parents reacted? They did not say a damn thing! That poor kid."

Educators should be ready to supply the correct mixture of information, frankness, comfort, and inspiration. They must recognize their own emotional investment in disclosing the disability and channel their feelings constructively.

DENIAL. Next, parents typically go through a period of denial. They may seek other professional opinions during this stage, hoping for a more promising diagnosis. Although parents' lives are often thrown into a state of confusion and turmoil, they may deny that the disability has an emotional effect. Denial may also take the form of unrealistic planning for the child. This state is the result of a number of factors, including cultural pressure for the "ideal" child, the level of success expected by the parent, and parental identification with the exceptional child (that is, regarding the child's problem as a problem in oneself). Another form of denial can be not telling the child about his or her disability (Faerstein, 1986). One of the parents may be suffering more than the other. Some typical denial reactions are these:

"Are you sure? Can you do some more tests?"

"It's too soon to tell how well Johnny hears. Let's wait until he is 5."

"That doctor is always telling people crazy things. Tammie doesn't *look* retarded, does she?"

"Even if there is any truth to what they said, she'll grow out of it. You'll see."

"These days they can do wonders. They'll operate and he'll walk."

"God's good. We'll find a way."

What is the danger in a denial reaction?

Educators should not get annoyed or frustrated with parents at this point. It is easy for the outsider to see the folly in something parents may say and do, but very hard to help them correct their course of action or thinking. The danger is that the child with the disability may not get any services or may receive inappropriate ones. Here are some examples of inappropriate feelings expressed by educators and others when confronted with parental denial:

"Not that charlatan! You wasted your money and time having him test your child."

"Don't you think we are competent to help your child? I am insulted!"

"We are very busy here. If you can't recognize the facts about your child, then you had better go elsewhere."

"You're just shopping around, aren't you? That will not help anybody, especially your child."

The educator can help most by providing accurate assessment information that parents can understand. The implications for treatment and for the future should be explained as clearly as possible. Parents can be given suggestions, including referral to parent support groups, to guide their search for second opinions in order to minimize the possibility of their being victimized by incompetent people. Above all, the reactions of educators and other professionals must be governed by understanding when parents question their judgment and indicate their intention to confirm the diagnosis.

GUILT. After the denial stage, feelings of guilt often appear. Parents may blame themselves, circumstances, other people, or God. The effects of this fault-finding may be felt by physicians, teachers, family members, and other people in the community. Given the parents' emotional state and the pressure on them to act and make decisions (often in the absence of information and guidance), it is natural that they attempt to find some obvious or not-so-obvious reasons for the child's disability. Anger often accompanies these guilt feelings and gets mixed up in emotional outbursts, as the following statements illustrate:

"I can see your crazy brother in so many of Billy's actions. It scares me so!"

"I told you not to smoke grass when you were carrying the baby."

"That period of our life when I was carrying Susan was so traumatic. I never had a moment of peace."

"I will never set foot in that doctor's office again."

"Mrs. Harrison, you are his teacher and you don't teach. It's your fault."

"Why don't you people get your act together? One person tells us one thing, and another tells us something else."

What should teachers do about guilt reactions?

There is some temptation for educators to assume some of the blame for the child's problem, and occasionally it's justified. Generally, though, educators can avoid the blaming game, and particularly avoid even indirectly reinforcing the impression that the disability is the fault of the parents. Some educators who have been caught up in this aspect of the situation have said:

"Look, Mr. Smith, if you weren't so tough on your son, maybe we could reason with him."

"We have the best of medical and educational care here, and your child has not responded. So don't blame us."

"Have you anything in your family background that would explain Mary's behavior?"

Whenever possible, it is helpful to clarify for parents any obvious reasons for their child's disability. Obtaining information for parents and directing them to other resources are also appreciated. When potentially volatile exchanges with parents are anticipated, arranging to have the principal or another colleague present will help everyone involved to maintain composure and perspective.

SORROW. At some point, a deep sense of sorrow and sadness is evident in the families of children with disabilities. Sometimes parents and other family members have a difficult time keeping their spirits up in the face of the effort they must expend to meet the needs of the child with disabilities. Depressed parents may also withdraw into themselves and not seek aid for their child. They may find themselves overprotecting their child and, by so doing, overprotecting themselves. It is a small step for them to imagine that no one really understands or can work with their child as they do. Fear then takes over and adds to the battle parents must wage with themselves. Some have said of these feelings of depression:

"I found myself just hanging around, withdrawing more and more into myself."

"We were so miserable, so lost, that contact with anyone was painful. We even neglected one another."

"I woke up every morning sick to my stomach. I was so sad I couldn't stop crying—for me, for my baby, for everything."

"I just wanted everyone to go away and let my baby and me alone. I felt we could take care of ourselves."

As with parents experiencing guilt and parents who are angry, educators can avoid being drawn into counterproductive exchanges, such as the following:

"I don't know how you do it, Mrs. Thompson. I never could."

"What are you ever going to do when you move next month? I don't know how you will get along without the clinic."

"Those poor parents—my life is so much easier than theirs."

How can parents of children with disabilities help each other?

Besides providing general encouragement and pointing out positive aspects of the situation, educators can best serve parents who have these feelings by putting them in touch with other parents of children with similar disabilities. These parents should be further along in the adjustment process and actively engaged in helping their children. Parents also appreciate an educator who is accessible and who indicates a willingness to talk.

What can result from rejection?

REJECTION. Another possible reaction is rejection of the child with disabilities. Regrettably, some parents abandon their children; others hand them over to someone else to care for. Child abuse is a frequent result of rejection. A review of the current research in child abuse indicates that children with disabilities are at considerable risk for abuse, often because of the greater risk of breakdown of appropriate adult-child interactions (Zirpoli, 1986). Unfortunately, other family members can contribute to devaluing the child with disabilities. The rejection is not always overt, often being disguised with reasonable arguments and concern for other family members or for themselves. The following are some typical expressions of rejection:

"I am earning my place in heaven with this child."

"Johnny, don't bother me now. I have been one hour feeding that child. He'll be the death of me."

"Thank God that Mary is as bright as she is. If we had to help her as we do Lee, it would be impossible."

"Billy takes every ounce of patience we have. Sometimes I want to kill him or myself—anything to end the situation."

"I wonder if we should have put her away. The doctor may be right. What about us and the other kids?"

"Mom, I hate it when Susie and my other friends come for dinner and have to sit at the table with Tommy. He's sickening."

"Elizabeth, you are being a good mother, but you are too young to take the strain of raising a deaf child. I don't mean to meddle, but please see about that special school."

Parents and other family members are not likely to openly disparage the child with disabilities in front of educators. However, educators may witness low expectations for the child and an unwillingness to challenge the child. They must avoid encouraging these attitudes and other forms of rejection by inappropriately saying:

"Yes, I bet she is a handful. How lucky you are to have a normal child as well as her."

"I wish I didn't always have bad reports to give you about Billy."

"I think Mary is going about as fast as she can. Maybe as far, too."

"Now, don't set your goals too high. These children are no Einsteins, you know."

Educators can be sensitive to signs of physical abuse and must report suspected cases as school system or agency policy dictates (Zirpoli, 1986). Stressing the child's positive features and ignoring negative remarks by parents will also help. Professionals should model an upbeat attitude. The child's self-concept is generally affected by these negative attitudes, and educators must counter them by arranging for successful and rewarding experiences. Parents have a hard time rejecting happy, successful children.

What stage of
reaction should be
the goal?

ACCEPTANCE. Finally, most parents reach the stage of acceptance. They admit that the child has a disability but feel no guilt and do not resent society. Some parents reach this stage quickly, some slowly, and some never fully accept the realities of a disabling condition. The parents must face these realities over and over again. As any parent will tell you, they go to bed with them and they wake up with them. However, after the initial struggles and frustration, good information and supportive people can help parents to understand. From their faith and inner strength, they obtain the courage to face the situation. Most of all, their love for the child with disabilities has its way and works wonders. They typically say at this stage:

"I just realized that Judy was my *child,* not my disabled child."

"Once I got some information, calmed down, and got him into a good preschool, I felt better. Things started to flow."

"The parent group has been a big help in understanding what is going on. I see things for what they are now."

"Those first couple of months were hell. But then Sue and I got our heads together and started putting the pieces together."

Educators should seize upon these moments and reinforce parents' positive feelings. Even when they have reached acceptance, parents still need to be reassured and encouraged to have more confidence. Educators must be careful to let parents get their feet on the ground before propelling them into a high level of participation in programs. However, once parents have reached this point, they can benefit their child in a number of ways, both educationally and therapeutically. They can also start giving some advice to other parents struggling with their own children's disabilities.

Parents of gifted and talented children may have some of these feelings and reactions before finally accepting the abilities their children possess. They also may deny that their children are exceptionally bright, have feelings of inadequacy about what to do for them, be frustrated by contradictory professional advice and lack of appropriate services, and so on. These families also make adjustments—and perhaps financial and other self-sacrifices—to provide the best for their children, and they may have to struggle with their child's low self-esteem (Clark, 1988). However, obviously the occurrence of a gifted and talented child in a family is more an occasion for rejoicing than when disabilities occur.

What forms of
interaction should
teachers expect to
have with parents?

In many ways, the point of acceptance is the beginning of establishing a good working relationship with the family. Up to this point parents and educators have been forging the bonds of trust and respect that come from sharing the hard times. Now the real work begins, as parents assume varying degrees of involvement. Educators of today can anticipate a full gamut of emotional exchanges with parents.

Educators should be aware of the emotional impact of children's exceptionalities on their families. Educators also have their own feelings invested in the situation and must monitor them appropriately. If interactions are handled effectively, parents and educators can establish the type of rapport needed to serve the children well.

The Child's Role

Children and youth with exceptionalities obviously have a profound effect on their parents and other family members. There is evidence accumulating that children with disabilities influence how their parents and others interact with them (Paul & Beckman-Bell, 1981).

How can
exceptional
children affect
their parents?

SHAPING PARENT BEHAVIOR. The child's disability may directly shape parental behavior. For example, a child with a severe disability may require constant maternal care because he or she has a contagious disease or a certain feeding schedule. Mothers of blind infants may be slower to initiate self-feeding because of lack of child demand. Videotaped observations of the free-play interactions of mothers and their physically disabled and normal 2-year-olds indicate that parents of children with disabilities are more likely to ignore their children than parents of normal children (Wasserman & Allen, 1985). Maternal ignoring was associated with a significant drop in developmental status among children. However, that does not mean parents of exceptional infants do not respond to them at all. Comparisons of videotaped play sessions of infants with physical disabilities or mental retardation and their mothers with those of infants without disabilities and their parents point out that mothers of infants with disabilities initiate activities more, engage in maintaining attention more, and use touching more—all increasingly so as deficits are more severe (Wasserman, Shilansky, & Hahn, 1986).

In a comparative study of children with and without learning disabilities, mothers of those with learning disabilities tended to exercise considerably more control but be less hostile (Humphries & Bauman, 1980), a finding which suggests that they perceived their children's need for structure. Observations of play activities of normal infants and those with mental retardation and cerebral palsy and their mothers indicate more direction by parents of children with mental retardation and more physical contact in the case of infants with cerebral palsy (Hanzlik & Stevenson, 1986).

Mothers' style of communicating with their children is directly related to the children's own communication (Mahoney, 1988). Videotaped play of mothers and their 1- to 3-year-old children with mental retardation indicates that maternal speech is adjusted to the child's communicative and cognitive competence and that there is considerable variability in mothers' communication styles. Children in this study were more likely to communicate verbally and have higher expressive language scores when their mothers' communication was highly responsive to their verbal and nonverbal communication, when mothers' conversational topics were more child-oriented than mother-oriented, and when mothers requested children to engage in conversation rather than perform actions.

Children also affect parents indirectly. Parental self-confidence and feelings of adequacy can be strained by lack of responsiveness from the child with disabilities. Nonverbal communication deficits, language disorders, and physical limitations can make it more difficult for parent-child interactions to develop well. For example, researchers note that the hyperactivity and language problems associated with most learning disabilities have a heavy impact on families. There is a special stress evident in these family histories (Delamater, Lahey, & Drake, 1981). Such families have a higher incidence of psychiatric disorders, criminal behavior, family hyperactivity (Singer, Stewart, & Pulaski, 1981), and family alcoholism (Idol-Maestas, 1981).

Kitano and Kirby (1986) report various research findings that gifted children can alter family roles because of their adultlike behaviors, and that parents may feel pressured by their children to provide extra experiences and materials (Hackney, 1981). Also, there are budgetary considerations for special lessons and trips. Problems may arise in the neighborhood when the gifted child is not accepted, and with the schools if the gifted child is manipulative. Gifted children may also be the source of sibling jealousy and competition.

How can parents
affect a child's self
concept?

SELF-CONCEPT. If there are some indications of how children with disabilities shape their family's behavior, there is a great deal of evidence indicating that the family forms the child's self-concept and feelings of self-worth. There is no doubt that parental attitudes influence children with disabilities (Klein et al., 1981). When parents have a low regard for school authority, the children get the idea. Another debilitating result occurs when parents do not hold their children responsible for academic or other kinds of progress and deny the seriousness of the learning problems.

Of course, parents who regard their children as intellectually limited can convey that to the children, especially by their lack of interest; similarly, those who know their children are gifted may convey that through excessive attention. Children incorporate that attitude into their self-concepts. Parents of children with learning disabilities have been reported to attribute their children's successes less to ability and more to luck, while attributing their failures more to a lack of ability and less to bad luck (Pearl & Bryan, 1982). These low estimations of their children's academic and social skills are often associated with pessimism about the future (Bryan, Pearl, Zimmerman, & Matthews, 1982).

However, lower parental expectations and negative feelings about children's disabilities may have a positive functional role. Comparisons of observations of parents performing an academic task with primary grade normal students and those with learning disabilities, as well as maternal surveys, indicate that parents of the children with learning disabilities demonstrate more negative nonverbal behaviors when interacting with their children (e.g., frowning) and express lower expectations for performance prior to doing the task than parents of normal learners (Tollison, Palmer, & Stowe, 1987). Parents' lower expectations, however, were associated with higher performance. Additionally, their children's failures were explained as a lack of ability, not effort or luck.

The self-esteem of exceptional youth is influenced by their communication with and feelings about their parents. For example, the self-esteem of adolescents with learning disabilities and emotional disturbance was associated with their positive feelings about their mothers (but not their fathers) and the communication style they had (Omizo, Amerikaner, & Michael, 1985).

Parents of gifted children can also influence their children's achievement and emotional status. Parents who tend to use the term *gifted* to describe their children tend to be more achievement-oriented, are not as likely to encourage family members to express their feelings openly, and regard their children as less well adjusted than do parents who do not use the term (Cornell & Grossberg, 1989).

Terman's (1954) classic follow-up study of gifted males (with IQ's of 140 and above) who had similar elementary school achievement indicated that the more-successful gifted persons had distinctive family backgrounds: college-educated parents, more books at home, and fewer divorces. The more-successful persons also tended to be more persistent, goal-oriented, self-confident, and self-regarding. Kitano and Kirby (1986) conclude that both family practices and personality traits interact.

Parents of highly creative children tend to use more permissive child-rearing practices; stress internal rather than external socially desirable characteristics, especially in friends; and be more independent but less sociable than parents of highly intelligent children (Kitano & Kirby, 1986). Parents of children with special talents begin early to provide their children with materials and emotional support for exploring the talent area. Cultural and economic differences may affect specific child-rearing practices.

Parents also transmit cultural values to children. Parents can overemphasize or de-emphasize academic progress and other forms of achievement, depending on their upbringing and experience. Comparisons of high- and low-achievers who were deaf indicate that parents of deaf academic achievers are more adapted to their children's deafness, more involved in the deaf community, and permissive rather than overprotective in their child-rearing orientation (Bodner-Johnson, 1986). Extreme responses to exceptionalities can hurt the child. However understandable some of these feelings and attitudes might be, parents must monitor their behavior lest they add to the stress that a child is under by increasing the child's confusion, feelings of incompetence, and worry.

The Family's Role

Family members of children with disabilities are greatly influenced by the child and in turn influence the child. There has been a significant shift in research concerning the marital stress associated with having a child with special needs (Turnbull & Turnbull, 1990). In earlier studies, estimates of divorce rates were 75 percent in families with deaf-blind children (Burley, 1977) and nine times higher than normal in families with children who have spina bifida (Tew, Lawrence, Payne, & Townsley, 1977). More recent estimates of marital separations and divorces among parents of children with learning disabilities are 10 to 13 percent, while the child's learning disability seems a factor in one-quarter to one-third of the cases (Association for Children and Adults with Learning Disabilities, 1982). No significant difference in marital satisfaction has been found recently between parents of children with and without spina bifida (Kazak & Marvin, 1984) nor on measures of marriage strength, family strength, and personality characteristics between parents of children with and without exceptionalities (Abbott & Meredith, 1986). In fact, in some of these studies, the exceptional child may serve to strengthen the marital relationship. Turnbull and Turnbull (1990) advise professionals not to jump to conclusions about the negative consequences of having exceptional children.

PARENTS AND RELATIVES. Considerable attention is being given to the needs of single parents of children with disabilities because of the greater incidence of academic and behavioral problems in these families (Werner, 1980). School difficulties are sometimes precipitated or at least exacerbated by the absence of one parent from the home, especially the father. The socioeconomic status of the family and the child's age at the time of the parents' separation make a difference (Roy & Fuqua, 1983).

A survey of parents of gifted children found the same situation. Gifted children, especially males, are more likely to underachieve in school if only one parent is present in the home (Gelbrich & Hare, 1989). They may be overburdened, being treated like adults at home and allowed too much responsibility; as a result, they may have difficulty accepting limits, especially at school.

Certainly single parents need special consideration and understanding in meeting their responsibilities. Educators can support them best by scheduling conferences at convenient times, avoiding criticism of them, and showing regard for the parent's knowledge and experience with the child (Werner, 1980).

How do attitudes of various family members differ?

The fathers of children with disabilities have been receiving special attention lately, even though mothers tend to be the primary caregivers and contact persons for educators. Some fathers may feel worse about the child's problem than mothers do. Fathers of children with language disorders seem to find it more difficult to interact with their children (Kornblum, 1982). Societal mores and social pressure may deprive fathers of the opportunity to deal with their feelings appropriately. Educators should make a special effort to include them.

Grandparents may play a significant role in how a family adjusts to a child's disability. Often, they offer counsel at the difficult time of decision making and otherwise sustain their son or daughter and the family. The attitude they model and how they interact with the child can be a source of inspiration to everyone. As one grandmother remarked, she had to take the time and make the effort to get to know her grandson who had cerebral palsy (McPhee, 1982). As you would expect, grandparents too must cope with their emotions.

SIBLINGS. In large part, siblings adopt the attitudes of their parents toward the child with disabilities. Unless the family is well integrated, the exceptional child may become the scapegoat for the family's problems. Siblings may resent the amount of attention given to such a child if they are neglected in the process. Sibling responses are most favorable when the family members are close and share the same goals. Families with relatively independent children are generally better at accepting the exceptional child. Grossman (1972) found positive reactions among some of the normal siblings he interviewed.

Sibling concerns may include curiosity about the cause of the exceptionality and its effects on them, inability to talk to their parents about the exceptional child in spite of their desire to do so, worry about the reactions of their friends, and worry about whether they will have to care for the exceptional child in the future (McLoughlin & Senn, 1993). But, as an only sister of an autistic child indicated, the whole experience can be worthwhile, even being cast as the "other mother" (Zatlow, 1982). She was prepared for probably being the caregiver for her brother in the future; because of the skills he had and her past experience with him, that posed no threat to her.

Parents, siblings, and other relatives often assume the role of caregivers. A survey of nearly 400 caregivers of people with mental retardation indicated that the extent of their caregiving resources (i.e., financial, time, physical capability) was related to how many and what kinds of services they were using and planned to use in the future (Englehardt, Brubaker, & Lutzer, 1988). A caregiver's sense of competence decreased as the severity of the person's disability increased. The self-confidence of such caregivers seems critical in the delivery of services.

What concerns do children have about their exceptional siblings?

By including their daughter in family activities, these parents are demonstrating their acceptance of her.

Siblings of gifted children may be adversely affected if parents compare their children. The gifted child may enjoy special status in the family and receive more verbal recognition (Cornell & Grossberg, 1989). In such situations, siblings may be less well adapted, especially if parents hold different perceptions of their children (Cornell & Grossberg, 1986).

MINORITY FAMILIES. Since it has been estimated that by the year 2000, nearly one-third of all Americans will be nonwhite (Zeller, 1986), culturally different or minority families of children with disabilities may pose unique challenges to those who serve them. On the positive side, parents of some minority groups may be less overwhelmed than nonminority parents. Feelings of protection and acceptance of children with disabilities may be more common, probably because of the support from their strong extended-family networks, the unique role of religion in their lives, or both. However, other minority groups may find their children's disabilities very difficult to accept, feeling that it reflects badly on them as parents.

In working with Hispanic families of children with visual impairments, Correa (1987) suggests viewing the whole extended family as a support system. Mothers who are the primary caregivers may regard therapists as competitors and misunderstand any advice to "take time for yourself." Hispanic parents may not openly describe or explain their feelings and reactions to nonfamily members, and pride may get in the way of accepting services. These families may expect educators to be more casual and to give advice that fits into their culture and lifestyle.

Hanson and Lynch (1989) caution that families with different cultural and language backgrounds must be approached with special consideration. Language differences aside, some families may be reluctant to acknowledge or discuss children with disabilities, whom they consider a "punishment." Additionally, medical practices may run into conflict with some cultures' belief systems. More passive parental attitudes should not be taken for indifference. Professionals should also be aware of differences in attitude and beliefs between generations within the same minority group.

The problems that occur with minority families seem to arise when the child enters school. Parental concerns center on their negative image of educators, possibly discriminatory testing practices, and suspicion of educators' competence to evaluate their children's ability. These feelings of mistrust may result in angry confrontations with educators or in their refusing to allow their child to participate in the program.

Families of lower socioeconomic status (SES) or different cultural backgrounds pose special challenges in gifted education. For example, the parenting styles in lower SES families generally do not promote the linguistic and cognitive abilities looked for in such programs. Similarly, different cultural values, emphases, and styles may not promote the concepts valued in traditional programs for children who are gifted. Clark (1988) advises special consideration of these factors when involving families in identification of and services for gifted and talented children.

Educators can make special efforts to meet the needs of minority parents (Rodriguez, 1981). Whenever possible, information about their children's rights for services should be shared in appropriate language. Interpreters can be a big help in establishing a culturally appropriate rapport with parents, especially those who view educators as some distant, highly respected authority. Personal contacts are preferable to written messages. It is also recommended to draw educators from the same cultural groups, use existing community support groups to contact families, and use local community newspapers for dissemination. Parents should be made to feel comfortable and welcomed in school for observations and invited to participate in programs informally; professionals should take care not to automatically give advice or take over for them. Given the appropriate support, educators may visit at home those families who cannot come to the schools or who seem to feel threatened, but should remain aware that some cultural groups may respond well to informal styles of communication, others not.

PARENTS WITH MENTAL RETARDATION. It can be anticipated that many more people with mental retardation will be marrying and bearing children in the future as a result of the provisions of PL 94-142, deinstitutionalization, normalization, decrease of involuntary sterilization, and residential alternatives for retarded persons (Lynch & Bakley, 1989). An assessment of twelve 2-year-old children raised by mothers with mental retardation, and of their homes, found that the children were at risk for developmental delays, particularly in language (Feldman, Case, Towns, & Betel, 1985). The inability of the mother to take minimal care of a previous child was a good predictor of future failure in parenting. Appraisals of their homes fell within the average range, except in restrictiveness and punishment; the more restrictive and punishing mothers were also generally more interested in and interactive with their children. There is a consensus that parents with mental retardation are at risk for child abuse and neglect, although not because of any negative intents (Lynch & Bakley, 1989).

However, some adults with mental retardation do become effective parents if they have an appropriate family and agency support system, no additional stress factors (e.g., financial problems, substance abuse), and higher cognitive abilities. Based on their experience with a project to support such parents, Lynch and Bakley (1989) report few success stories—those being instances when extensive family or agency support was present. They recommend considerable community commitment and staff development, as well as early preparation of retarded adolescents for possible parenting roles.

What is the effect of parents with mental retardation?

Special education teachers often conduct home visits to provide support services to parents of exceptional children.

What four crises do families face?

TRANSITIONAL PERIODS. The families of children with disabilities, whatever their makeup and whatever their reactions, go through a variety of adjustments and modifications. Crises seem to occur in four phases: (1) when the parents first become aware of the problem; (2) when the child begins to receive educational services; (3) when the child leaves school; and (4) when aging parents can no longer care for the person with disabilities (MacKeith, 1973). Throughout these phases, educators and other professionals should be prepared to support families in their never-ending process of development as a social unit with a member who has disabilities. Collaborative models are available for providing parental support during transition from infant to preschool programs (Hanline & Knowlton, 1988). Parents are given guidance about the referral process and IEP preparation; they visit classrooms, meet future teachers, and receive follow-up support after their child's placement.

Parents may also need particular assistance when their children reach adolescence. As one mother described it, it was a time of excitement, uncertainty, pleasure, pride, and pain (Barnes, 1982). It is to be hoped that parents of children with disabilities will work for the day when their children attain some measure of independence. Like all parents, they may find their children's movement into adulthood, bonding with peers, sexual awakening, and future planning particularly demanding (Daniels, 1982). Transitions are hard for everyone, but for these families they are especially challenging. An excellent resource for life planning is *Disability and the Family: A Guide to Decisions for Adulthood* by Turnbull et al. (1988).

THE PARENT-EDUCATOR RELATIONSHIP. It should be clear by now that the parents of these students come to educators with a considerable emotional and cultural investment. Although both family and school have the child's best interest at heart, differences in values and experience between parents and educators may hinder the development of a working relationship.

What sometimes happens is that parents and educators each have preconceived notions of the other that hinder communication. Parents may reject educators because they reject most authority figures, especially school-related ones. They may also have different views of the educator's role. Some may see teachers as mere academic instructors and resent any advice in other areas; others may expect educators to serve as lawyers, priests, or in some other capacities.

On the other hand, educators may sometimes see parents as the cause of the child's problem. Some parents seem threatening, and teachers may feel vulnerable to their criticism. Repeated efforts to enroll parental help with the child's program may cause frustration and mistrust. There is also a possibility that teachers will have a different view of the student than the parents do. To arrive at an effective working relationship, it is important to recognize the role of these cultural and value judgments.

Responding to Family Needs

For families to understand and adapt to their child's disability, educators and other professionals must meet their many needs. Families need information on a variety of topics, and they need the skills to obtain quality services for their children. A variety of professional personnel may be involved in working with families of exceptional children, through activities such as those listed in Figure 6-1.

IDENTIFYING NEEDS. A number of studies have investigated the needs of parents and siblings. A group of parents of deaf-blind children listed their needs in this way: legal issues, curriculum and instruction, facts about the disability, behavior management, effective adjustment, family roles and interactions, and health care and maintenance (Kershman, 1982). While

FIGURE 6-1   A Functional Approach to Exceptionality: Family Considerations

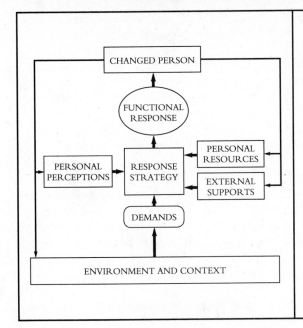

WORKING WITH FAMILIES

Contributions that family members can make to exceptional children fall into the category of *External Supports* in the functional model. Following are some of the ways that professionals can assist families to improve their effectiveness in providing support:

- Provide information to help them understand the nature of the child's problem.

- Advise them about their legal rights and the various services that are available.

- Provide advice and training on child-rearing practices.

- Teach parents how to complement school activities at home.

- Provide advice about how to participate in advocacy activities, including IEP meetings.

- Put family members in touch with support groups.

parents share common needs, regardless of their children's disabilities, there are unique empha-ses that will vary with the nature and extent of the child's problem.

Families' needs may also vary depending on their stage of adjustment, their level of participation, and whether a transition is imminent. In a survey of parents preparing their infants and preschoolers with various exceptional conditions for transition to public school programs, parents indicated that they were most concerned about the lack of information about special education services in the district, a reduction in parental involvement, and lack of confidence in IEP implementation (Hanline, 1988). They most wanted written information and one person in the district to whom they could communicate their needs. Because of the variation, it is clearly advisable to establish parents' priorities for assistance on a regular basis.

What is the first concern of parents?

UNDERSTANDING THE DISABILITY. The first concern of most parents is to understand their child's problem. According to both professionals and parents, most conferences between parents and educators seem to be devoted to the parents' giving and receiving information (Turnbull & Turnbull, 1990).

Families rely heavily on printed material and, more rarely, on nonprint media. While information from various agencies and school systems has improved over the last decade, parents still struggle with the reading level and vocabulary used in much printed matter (McLoughlin, Edge, Petrosko, & Strenecky, 1981). Parents are also at a disadvantage because there is a real lag between the time research is completed and the time it reaches parents (Winton & Turnbull, 1982). Researchers seem to place a low priority on studying topics relevant to these families and reporting results in the lay press. In addition, even when clear, useful information is available through a variety of sources, parents have to know where to get it. Educators can be of great assistance by accumulating copies of information, developing accessible parent libraries, and encouraging agencies to develop appropriate material for parents (McLoughlin, Edge, Petrosko, Strenecky, & Davis, 1983).

Parents must also become familiar with diagnostic procedures. Finding the appropriate specialists can present problems. Once they have been discovered, it is sometimes difficult to get unanimous opinions. A frequent complaint is that diagnostic information has been withheld or that information is presented in professional jargon that is difficult to understand. Physicians are sometimes singled out for criticism (Lynch & Staloch, 1988). The three most common complaints made about physicians are their lack of knowledge about disabilities, their attitude toward and low expectations for children with disabilities, and their lack of skills in sharing information (Wolraich, 1982). Fortunately professionals in every field are improving in this area since they recognize the potential contributions parents can make if they are better informed.

ETIOLOGY. The etiology of the disorder is another area of interest, particularly in the case of genetic disorders such as Down syndrome. Parents may wonder whether exceptionalities such as learning disabilities and emotional disturbance will affect other children they may be planning to have. A knowledge of prenatal, perinatal, and postnatal causes of disabilities will be useful to parents genuinely interested in discovering whether they are responsible for their child's problem. Some exceptionalities, such as emotional disturbance, are influenced by environmental factors. When this is the case, parents may be relieved to discover that they can do something about the problem.

POTENTIAL FOR DEVELOPMENT. An important area of parent concern is the child's potential for development. In a group of low-income mothers of retarded children, the future was reported to be the biggest concern (Eheart & Ciccone, 1982). They wanted parent groups and a program for the children to guarantee successful development. Of course, developmental potential is determined by such factors as the severity of the disability and age of onset.

The parents of young children may be interested in such developmental areas as speech and language. Later concerns may be academic achievement and school behavior. The parents of exceptional adults may have questions about their son's or daughter's employability and what approach to take regarding sexual relations. A recent study of the attitudes of parents with retarded children toward sterilization revealed 71 percent to be for involuntary procedures and 67 percent for voluntary procedures (Wolf & Zarfan, 1982). Parents should be aware of the thinking of other parents on such matters.

As you can see, educators need technical expertise in a variety of areas. In one survey of parents of mentally retarded youths ages 17 and older, the parents thought that work should not be a normal part of their children's lives; their low aspirations were related to their own positive work attitudes, the older age of their children, and the severity of disability (Seyfarth, Hill, Orelove, McMillan, & Wehman, 1987). Whenever possible, educators should put parents in touch with older youngsters or adults who have disabilities like their own child's, to help them develop a realistic perspective on the possibilities for progress.

What questions should teachers anticipate from parents of exceptional children?

AVAILABLE SERVICES. Parents of exceptional children frequently do not know what services are available to them and where to get them. Here are some important questions that are asked about services:

1. *How does one go about finding the specialists appropriate to the child's needs?* Exceptional children may need assistance in several areas, such as language, academic skills, motor skills, vocational training, and social and emotional behavior. Each area has its own specialists.
2. *What medical treatments and adaptive devices would benefit the child?* Parents may have questions about drugs, vitamin therapy, diet control, sterilization, and other medical techniques. They may also be interested in finding out about the maintenance, use,

and repair of braces, wheelchairs, hearing aids, glasses, and other devices. When dealing with specialists, parents must be encouraged to state their child's problem clearly, demand respect, ask questions freely, refuse to be rushed, encourage their child's participation, and be objective about the child (Durio, 1980). Educators can be a big help by being aware of the newest research on important issues.

3. *How much will meeting the needs of the child cost?* Specialists, medication, adaptive devices, and special schools are all expensive. Although PL 94-142 and PL 99-457 guarantee a free and appropriate education to all exceptional children, the cost of additional services can be substantial. One in three parents of exceptional children reports spending an average $1166 per year for supplemental related services (ICD, 1989).

4. *What school programs are available?* Parents should be told of the various options available in the public and private schools and the educational methods and materials used. Some parents will be interested in home-based programs. In consultation with professionals, parents must decide which program is most suitable for their child.

5. *Should the child be placed in a residential facility or kept at home?* This is one of the most difficult decisions parents face. To determine the best course, parents must learn about the facility's procedures, accreditation, program objectives, administrator and teacher qualifications, philosophy and structure, and recreational and social facilities.

Parents should also be aware of what is involved in keeping their child at home, in respite care, or in a community residential facility (German & Maisto, 1982). Respite needs of parents vary. Families who use respite tend to be larger, use more professional support services, and have children who have more severe disabilities and more serious behavior problems (Marc & MacDonald, 1988). Older parents (above age 56) of retarded adults indicated in one survey that they were more interested in out-of-home respite care for 1 to 30 days and had less need than younger parents for parent-cooperative sitting arrangements and for training for family members (Lutzer & Brubaker, 1988). In another study these older caregivers reported that they had a greater need for support services as the severity of the disability worsened (Englehardt, Brubaker, & Lutzer, 1988). Their own assessment of their ability to provide care is related to how many services they use.

Mothers who have not institutionalized their children tend to have a supportive extended family, to have babysitters, not to have another retarded child, and not to have a child with many behavior problems. They are also likely to be married. Educators should have similar facts available to guide parental decision making.

How do parents react to alternative living arrangements?

A national survey of parents of institutionalized persons with mental retardation indicates that their original reasons for institutionalization were medical needs, provision of multiple services, safety, and behavior management; that the institutions were providing appropriate services and they were generally satisfied with them; and that they were strongly opposed to moving their relatives to group homes (Spreat, Tellas, Conroy, Feinstein, & Colombatto, 1987). The return was low in this survey, though, and respondents indicated a poor knowledge about group homes. Nonetheless, this study may indicate a backlash to deinstitutionalization among some parents.

Even so, a follow-up survey of relatives of persons with profound mental retardation who were moved from a large institution to smaller ones closer to their families indicated a significant decrease in stress about the transfer and in dissatisfaction with the concept (Heller, Bond, & Braddock, 1988). The families found that their exceptional relative was not traumatized or harmed by the move and that the resources were better in the new facility. The improved attitudes were related to more frequent visits to their relatives in their new surroundings.

How can support groups help?

SUPPORT GROUPS. Families need support, information, and often inspiration to meet the challenges posed by disabilities. Parent organizations and training groups offer relevant and comfortable environments in which to learn how to adjust and grow. They offer information about transportation, babysitting, camps, and other topics meaningful to family life.

As one group of parents of children with Down syndrome reports, parent groups are particularly relevant when the children are very young, as an emotional support base (Spicker, 1982). They contribute to the accuracy of parental knowledge and to parental willingness to work with their child. It often takes other parents to snap a parent out of self-defeating activity. As one parent of a child with cerebral palsy says, parents must get over feeling guilty, use respite care and babysitters, and get out (Stanzler, 1982). Educators can encourage them in that direction.

PARENT-CHILD INTERACTIONS. A universal area of concern for parents is how to relate to their exceptional children. The parent-child relationship is at the core of the child's successful development and happiness. A danger in programs' emphasizing how parents can give their children skills training is that parents get distracted from simply learning to love and relate to their child.

In one project, family consultants visit the homes of newborns with severe disabilities and adapt suggestions in various areas to the parents' styles and goals (Affleck, McGrade, McQueeney, & Allen, 1982). This service is particularly helpful to mothers with less education, single mothers, and mothers of firstborn infants. Management is an area of particular concern for many parents throughout the lifetime of their children. They are interested in the child's behavior problems at school and want to learn strategies to use in the home. Problems may arise in feeding, toileting, discipline, sexual activity, dating, and other areas. There are a variety of training programs and materials available that educators can provide to help parents handle such situations (Turnbull & Turnbull, 1990).

Parents of gifted children need to establish a close, mutually respectful relationship with their children, become a role model of the behavior they wish to see, and provide an intellectually stimulating, curiosity-provoking atmosphere in their homes (Clark, 1988). They need to be interested in their children's activities at home and school, help them establish time priorities, and guide their interests without setting goals for them.

What is family nurturing?

FAMILY NURTURING. The parents of children with exceptionalities must also tend to the needs of each other and their other children. Educators can do much by reminding parents of each other's needs and encouraging them to make opportunities to be together. While mothers generally get involved in programs more, many projects provide for father meetings and opportunities for father-care activities. At the University of Washington's Model Preschool Center for Handicapped Children, fathers and their infants attend Saturday morning classes together. Discussions and activities encourage awareness of child development and foster contact with the children. Mothers appreciate the respite and the sharing of responsibility for the child. This type of experience fosters better relationships between parents.

Parents must also decide what to tell siblings about the child with disabilities. Their other children may worry about a variety of things, such as frustration at being neglected or having to care for the child. Parents should also clarify how they feel about the normal siblings, since the child with disabilities may require so much attention. Siblings have to be reassured about their responsibility now and in the future for the child. Parent groups can offer advice on this topic. Educators can demonstrate awareness and sensitivity to sibling issues by considering their needs when making requests of parents. Also, children with disabilities can be taught to relate better to their siblings.

ADVOCACY. Parents often need to assert their right to quality programs. For example, parents of children with learning disabilities now struggle with a dearth of services for their children when they get into college (Wallace & McLoughlin, 1988) and as adults (Gray, 1981).

In addition, parents frequently complain that they are not included in decision making, that they are not kept informed about the child's progress, and that they have to maintain constant vigilance to ensure that the child is receiving the necessary services. Professionals should realize that parental anger is partially caused by society's frequent insensitivity and incompetence in meeting the needs of exceptional persons. It should be remembered that the enactment of PL 94-142 and PL 99-457 was largely the result of the activism of concerned parents. Parents today are going beyond asking for information; they want to be involved in deciding such things as what kinds of records are kept on their children, what medical services are needed, and what schools they transfer to (Lusthaus, Lusthaus, & Gibbs, 1981).

How can teachers help advocacy efforts of parents?

Educators and others must be prepared to meet parents' needs and honor their legitimate requests. Some professionals train parents to perform advocate activities by teaching them to use professional terminology, to ask and understand the right questions, to be persistent but diplomatic when the answers they get are less than sufficient, and to recognize quality services and agencies (Muir, Milan, Branston-McLean, & Berger, 1982). Educators have an obligation to make parents aware of their rights and help them realize them.

Some problems are encountered only by the parents of children with a particular kind of disability. Reference works that describe the needs of these parents include the following:

- For children with learning disabilities, Wallace and McLoughlin (1988); Cordoni (1987); and Smith (1980).
- For children with autism, Perske (1973); Goldfarb, Brotherson, Summers, and Turnbull (1986); Akerley (1984); Bristol and Schopler (1983); and Donnellan and Mirenda (1984).
- For children with emotional disturbances, Blechman (1985); Canter and Canter (1982); Clark (1985); and Fleischman, Horne, and Arthur (1983).
- For children with retardation, Featherstone (1980).
- For children with deafness and blindness, Kershman (1982); Bolton and Williamson (1989); Clark, Morgan, and Wilson-Viotman (1983); and Freeman (1985).
- For children with physical disabilities, Batshaw and Perret (1986); Segal (1988); and Tingey-Michaelis (1983).
- For children with blindness, Ferrell (1987) and Webster (1977).
- For children with deafness, Atkins (1987) and Schwartz (1987).
- For children with speech and language impairments, Castle (1983) and Fewell and Vadasy (1983).
- For gifted children, Perino and Perino (1981) and Webb (1982).

Parents Speak Out (Turnbull & Turnbull, 1985) is a collection of essays by parents of individuals with various exceptional conditions.

PROBE 6-1   Relating to Families

1. T F Parents should not discuss their exceptional child with their other children.
2. Name four of the emotional stages the parents of exceptional children typically pass through before they accept their child's condition.
3. What are three problems that the parents of exceptional children may encounter in searching for services?
4. Name six areas about which parents of exceptional children may need to find information.

INVOLVING PARENTS

You should be able to describe ways to involve parents in the education of their exceptional children.

The parents of exceptional children have played an important role in initiating and developing special education programs. They have supported every major effort to develop services. But it was not until after World War II that parents began to organize on behalf of their exceptional children. Groups such as the National Association for Retarded Citizens, the United Cerebral Palsy Association, and the Learning Disabilities Association of America (formerly the Association for Children and Adults with Learning Disabilities) have become very effective in determining policies and establishing programs for exceptional people. They have worked with the executive and legislative branches of government to develop a favorable public climate and to enact laws guaranteeing the rights of exceptional people. When necessary, parent organizations have turned to the courts to obtain the services and support they need (Turnbull, 1981).

Why have some parents been excluded from decisions about their children?

In spite of the many contributions of parents, they have frequently been excluded from crucial aspects of their children's programs. For the most part, education has been left to the professionals. Some educators have been hesitant to involve parents in educational programs for a number of reasons. One reason is that educators are sometimes reluctant to admit that they need help and that they do not have all the answers. Professionals have also claimed that parents are frequently uncaring or overprotective. Some professionals contend that the educational process is too complex for parents to understand, and that contact between the two groups should be limited to parent conferences several times a year. Finally, there have been claims that parents are incompetent in raising their children and that they would add little to educational programs if they became involved in them.

Fortunately, attitudes are changing and more positive approaches to working with parents are emerging, largely because of the enactment of PL 94-142 and PL 99-457, which mandate increased family involvement. As a result, parents are assuming a broader role in the educational process—although many parents question what that role should be, given their qualifications. Educators realize that parents must participate in programs if those programs are to be as effective as possible. Parents are being blamed less for their children's disabilities. Parent and professional organizations are also working together more closely.

What are the legal rights of parents?

The parents of exceptional children have a number of rights specifically guaranteed by law, as follows:

1. The parents of children with disabilities must receive written notice in their native language that the school is considering a change in their children's education program.
2. Parents must give permission for their children to be tested for the purpose of determining whether they should be placed in a special education program.
3. Parents have the right to an independent evaluation if they are dissatisfied with the evaluation performed by school personnel.
4. Parents have the right to be involved actively in the development of the children's individualized education programs (IEPs). In the case of infants' and preschoolers' individualized family service plans (IFSP), there is to be a family needs section in which family strengths and weaknesses are noted and appropriate services are described.
5. Parents must specifically approve the placement of their children.

6. Parents have the right to examine all school records related to their children and to remove inaccurate or misleading data from the children's file.

7. Parents may request an impartial due process hearing if they disagree with procedures or decisions related to the placement of their children. The hearing officer may not be an employee of the school district. The parents have the right to legal counsel, and they may examine witnesses, present evidence, and obtain a written record of the hearing and findings. The hearing must be held no more than 45 days after it is requested.

8. Parents may appeal the results of the due process hearing to the state Department of Education, which must review the appeal within 30 days. Parents can further appeal decisions to the federal courts if they are dissatisfied with the results of their appeal to the state Department of Education. Educators must ensure that proper procedures are established to notify parents about testing, placement, nonbiased assessment, record keeping, and timetables. The information that is collected must be kept confidential.

The last decade has witnessed considerable experimentation in attempts to implement these rights. Parents have been incorporated into their children's programs in a variety of ways. Some are legislated by PL 94-142 and PL 99-457, others merely suggested by those laws and by common sense. In all cases considerable initiative and support are necessary from educators to make the involvement meaningful to parents and themselves.

The sections that follow describe ways to involve parents in the five most common aspects of their children's programs: identification and referral, assessment, planning, implementation, and evaluation (Wallace & McLoughlin, 1988). Careful forethought and planning must go into these efforts. Some parents want and are able to get involved more than others (Kroth, 1985). Individual family circumstances must be considered in planning, and families with less inclination to participate must be encouraged.

It is also important to remember that when children with disabilities start school, this represents a new phase for parents. They may have to acclimate to possibilities of active involvement. For other parents, more sophisticated opportunities may have to be provided (Cervone & O'Leary, 1982). Whatever the case, parent-teacher communication is the key.

Identification and Referral

For reliable early identification of exceptional children, parents must be well informed. State departments of education and other educational agencies provide print material concerning signs of disabilities, available services, and the child's rights to a free and appropriate education (McLoughlin et al., 1981). Much improvement is necessary in this area; for example, such material must be made more accessible and readable. Greater cooperation is needed among educational agencies, parent organizations, and governmental programs to improve the quality and flow of information (McLoughlin et al., 1983).

Other means of conveying information are the mass media, group instruction, and individual conferences. Mass media approaches seem limited to arousing general awareness of disabilities, reinforcing and maintaining parental information and attitudes gained elsewhere, or both (Kurtz, Devaney, Strain, & Sandler, 1982). Group instruction is a better way to impart specific information about early identification, and it encourages follow-up. Efforts to incorporate parents more individually into screening for disabilities are also successful. Parental knowledge of such matters as general development and the child's knowledge of letters and numbers is a good predictor of the child's later successes and failures. In Oregon, parents of at-risk infants complete a set of eight questionnaires when their infants reach 4, 8, 12, 16, 20, 24, 30 and 36 months of age (Bricker & Squires, 1989). Their assessment of their infants' motor, adaptive, communication, and personal skills classifies children similarly to standardized test data from 86 to 91 percent of the time. This system is also relatively inexpensive to maintain and has the advantage over standardized tests of involving parents.

The parents of children referred for special education services should be interviewed to obtain information useful in diagnosing the child's problem. Parents know a great deal about the child that would otherwise be unavailable to the diagnostician, including the child's personal traits, interests, health history, behavior when interacting with adults and other children, and attitudes. Information such as this is necessary for a complete, valid diagnosis.

In seeking information from parents, interviewers must be sensitive to parents' feelings. Only information relevant to the child's disability and the educational program should be solicited. Kroth (1985) has suggested some guidelines for interviewing parents: (1) The interview should be conducted in a quiet, private setting. (2) The interview should be held in a positive atmosphere; at the same time, the interviewer should be prepared for hidden motivations and agendas. (3) Careful attention should be paid to the parents' nonverbal behavior as well as to their verbal responses; by the same token, interviewers should be aware of the nonverbal messages they are sending. (4) In sharing the information obtained, the interviewer should respect the parents' right to privacy. Through improved procedures and technology, educators can be trained to make initial contacts and interviews with parents more productive (McLoughlin & Lewis, 1990). It is critical to future interactions that such sessions go well.

How can teachers conduct effective parent interviews?

Assessment

The diagnostic phase of a child's program is strongly influenced by the degree of cooperation among parents and professionals. The ultimate results are shaped by the status of the referral agent, the degree of agreement between parents and professionals, and parental pressure, as well as the actual data (Bognar & Martin, 1982). It is imperative to involve parents constructively (McLoughlin & Lewis, 1990).

How can parents be involved in assessment?

As discussed above, a verbal interview format and written case history forms are used to profile a child's development history and school background. The use of these approaches is particularly valuable because they acquaint the evaluator with the parents' perceptions of the child's problems and of the available educational opportunities.

More formally, parents are often asked to complete rating forms and other scales. On the *Behavior Rating Profile* (Brown & Hammill, 1983), parents rate their child's behavior at home; the scale is normed, and parental perceptions can be compared to those of teachers and the children. In the adaptive behavior area, the *Vineland Adaptive Scales* (Sparrow, Balla, & Cicchetti, 1984) are frequently completed by interviewers with the child's parents.

Because of the weight placed on such data, educators must be aware of the possible bias in parental views. For example, one group of parents of children with mental retardation tended to rate their children higher than teachers did in adaptive behavior, especially in self-help skills (Mealor & Richmond, 1980). However, more recent comparisons of parental and professional assessments of children with developmental delays indicate moderate to high positive correlations. When parental and professional responses on comparable developmental assessment forms were compared, parents accurately and consistently rated motor and social skills and overestimated self-help and cognitive skills (Schafer, Bell, & Spalding, 1987). After parent training, greater parent-professional agreement was quickly accomplished in the motor domain, but more slowly in the cognitive domain. While parents' experience and greater information in some areas may sometimes justify such results, there is an obvious need to have other independent and objective measures in order to complement parental information.

There are also ways to question parents about a child's basic skills (McLoughlin, 1983). For example, when interested in the student's use of reading and math at home, educators can ask about the use of menus and newspapers or earning and using an allowance. Parents will be familiar with their child's use of these skills and will know what their child is interested in.

Another approach to involving parents in assessment is to have them observe their children at home, in school, or elsewhere. Parents often collect observational data in a systematic fashion as part of the preparation for a program to change some social or academic behavior (Cooper & Edge, 1981). There are a variety of materials available to train parents how to (1) select a specific behavior to observe, (2) design a system to keep track of how often or how much the behavior occurs, and (3) maintain a record of how the child performs over a period of time (Heward, Dardig, & Rossett, 1979).

What is the value of parental observation?

Parents may also gain a better understanding of their child's learning problems and of the instructional program if they observe in the classroom or in other settings. Educators can make such visits more effective and meaningful if they prepare parents in advance by explaining key aspects of the program, telling them where to sit and when to come and go, and suggesting how to behave when the children try to get their attention (Turnbull & Turnbull, 1990). Parents also appreciate the opportunity to discuss what they witness.

Parents who prepare their children for testing or other assessment activities contribute greatly to the success of the effort. Children may feel uneasy about being tested and need to talk about their feelings. Brief explanations of procedures and materials help, as do advance visits to clinics and hospitals. Most of all, parents can avoid letting their own attitudes about the testing (e.g., fear, anger) transfer to the child. After the testing, parents can be encouraged to talk with their children about their feelings and answer their questions. These efforts may guarantee the child's cooperation in similar activities later on.

Parental participation is particularly important in understanding the impact of their child's background and culture on his or her test performances. Multicultural assessments must have a strong parental component. Their experiences and insights are a safeguard against a biased assessment (Rodriguez, 1981).

How can the family be assessed?

Family assessment has become particularly critical with the requirement of PL 99-457 for an individualized family service plan (IFSP), which outlines the support services to be directed at family needs. The main domains for family assessment are child needs and characteristics likely to affect family functioning (such as demands for attention and responsiveness), parent-child interactions, family needs, critical events, and family strengths (Bailey et al., 1988). There are various procedures available to calculate the frequency, nature, and pattern of observed or reported interactions. See Bailey et al. (1988) for a detailed description of assessment techniques in these areas. However, the appropriateness and technical soundness of available instruments are questionable (Hanson & Lynch, 1989).

Of particular usefulness is the family-focused interview to collect information about family variables. The model emphasizes assessment of specific family needs and collaborative goal setting with family members (Winton & Bailey, 1988). It consists of six steps: assessing family needs, generating initial hypotheses regarding family needs, conducting a focused interview, formalizing a plan, providing services, and evaluating effectiveness. Interviewers must have good listening skills, maintain their neutrality, and not take sides in disputes (Hanson & Lynch, 1989). They must be nonjudgmental and regard parents as equals. Professional competence and sincerity are also important.

Conferences

What is the value
of the IEP
conference?

Parents of children with disabilities participate in conferences with educators and others for a variety of reasons: to find out the results of testing, to help design the individualized education program (IEP) or individualized family service plan (IFSP) for preschoolers, to decide how to deliver the needed services, and to help evaluate the child's progress in the program. The law requires that parents be involved in developing their exceptional child's IEP or IFSP. The involvement of parents at this stage serves several purposes. First, it permits parents to understand their child's program better, which may create a more positive attitude at home toward the program. Second, parents are more likely to be interested in a program they are familiar with and helped to develop. Third, parental involvement eliminates the confusion and disagreement that may arise from misinformation and differing priorities. Fourth, parents are encouraged to serve as volunteers; they can provide valuable help and give teachers more time for individual instruction.

PARENTAL ROLES. In spite of a concerted effort over the past decade, parents tend to play a passive role in these conferences (Turnbull & Turnbull, 1990). At IEP conferences a low percentage of parents express opinions or make suggestions; they are more likely to respond to questions directed at them (Vacc et al., 1985). Parents ask few questions, respond little, and yet indicate satisfaction with the conference outcomes and have few questions about the decisions made (Lynch & Stein, 1982; Vaughn, Bos, Harrell, & Lasky, 1988). Their satisfaction seems to be related to whether they (1) are invited to the IEP review, (2) are asked to help prepare the IEP, (3) are informed of their right to appeal, and (4) feel that their child's special education placement is appropriate.

Considerable confusion about what should occur at conferences and who should do what seems to be at the root of the low level of participation. First, many professionals are not attending conferences; meetings usually consist of the child's mother and the special education teacher (Scanlon, Arick, & Phelps, 1981; Vacc et al., 1985). Second, the professionals who do attend such meetings, especially the educators, seem unsure of their goals and the functions they are to perform (Fenton, Yoshida, Maxwell, & Kaufman, 1979). Third, full parent participation is deterred by a variety of factors (Lynch & Stein, 1982). Low-income parents point to logistics (transportation and child care), communication style, lack of understanding of the school system, feelings of inferiority, uncertainty about the child's disability, and concern about how they and the school can help. Special education teachers attribute parents' passivity to apathy; to the parents' lack of time, energy, and understanding; and to devaluation of parent input by school officials. See Turnbull and Turnbull (1990) for suggestions on how to address these issues.

PARENTAL INFLUENCE. Contrary to their legislated rights, parents are not influential at these conferences. Gilliam (1979) reported that meeting participants ranked parents as third in importance before attending meetings; after meetings, however, they ranked parents ninth in actual contribution. The initial estimation may be based on the assumption that parents know their children best, but in fact the main contributors to the conference tend to be members with hard data such as test scores, cumulative records, and diagnostic reports. Psychologists are perceived to be most influential in diagnosis; the special educator, in planning and implementation; the director, in placement; and the supervisor, in due process matters (Gilliam & Coleman, 1981). According to PL 94-142, parents should be highly influential in final placement decisions, but in practice they defer to psychologists and special educators (Knoff, 1983).

There is basis for parent perceptions. In a survey of 145 special education teachers, only half valued parent participation (Gerber, Banbury, Miller, & Griffin, 1986). These teachers were in favor of waiving compulsory parent attendance and viewed the IEP conference as a formality.

PREPARATION. Both parents and educators are responding well to better preparation and training for such conferences, however. Certain strategies increase relevant contributions by parents; for example, sending parents questions prior to the IEP conference and placing a follow-up telephone call, and having the school counselor present as a parent advocate at the conference (Goldstein & Turnbull, 1982). With the group of parents in the Goldstein and Turnbull study, the counselor's support was particularly helpful when he or she introduced the parents, directed questions to them, verbally reinforced their contributions, and summarized the discussion at the end of the conference. Classroom teachers who receive inservice training about their duties at these meetings speak much more than teachers who are not so prepared (Trailor, 1982). Further, 75 percent of their comments are about student performance, behavior, and curriculum; and they are generally directed to the parents.

Parents are also clarifying how they wish to participate in conferences. They seem satisfied with current practices in giving and receiving information about such topics as discipline, proper class placement, evaluation of the child's abilities, grouping for instruction, transportation, and provision of special resources (Lusthaus et al., 1981). They expect a greater part, however, in deciding about such topics as records kept about their children, medical services, and school transfers. A group of parents of retarded children has indicated the desire for greater power in deciding how and when their children's progress is evaluated (Soffer, 1982).

Educators can respond to these indications of interest and desire by encouraging relevant parent participation. Parents and professionals alike need to be educated to the possibilities of parental involvement. This is starting to happen in early childhood education as research related to IFSP development becomes available (Deal, Dunst, & Trivette, 1989; McGonigel & Garland, 1988). Much of the research associated with IEP development is applicable, with the major difference being direct family assessment. Current perceptions and practices may be dysfunctional vestiges of the past rather than the result of considered deliberation.

STRATEGIES. In addition to the conferences held to develop the IEP, meetings should be held at intervals to discuss such factors as the child's progress, school-home cooperative programs, and other issues of concern to parents and teachers. In all professional-parent interactions it is important that professionals communicate candidly and clearly; parents complain that information is sometimes withheld from them and that educators use jargon they cannot understand.

How should teachers interact with parents?

Some rules of professional behavior dictate how educators should speak to parents (Turnbull & Turnbull, 1990). It is important to avoid an authoritarian or judgmental tone. Questioning should be designed to open up discussion rather than limit it. Educators must be considerate of parents' feelings and give parents the same rights and respect they would show to professional colleagues. By following these guidelines, teachers and parents can improve the chances that conferences will be conducted in an atmosphere of cooperation and increase the likelihood of success.

When considering the educational placement of children with disabilities, the advantages and disadvantages of the various service arrangements should be carefully explained to parents. Parental objections to certain kinds of classes or teachers must be taken into account in making the placement decision. It is a good strategy to survey parental attitudes. In one such effort,

Frequent conferences lead to better relationships between parents and teachers. The result is improved education for children enrolled in special education programs.

parents of children ages 2 to 5 years, with and without disabilities, in separate preschool programs, were asked their attitudes about mainstreaming before an integrated program was begun (Reichart et al., 1989). Neither group believed that behavior problems would increase or that children without disabilities would learn immature behaviors from the children with disabilities. They agreed that everyone's needs could be met in the integrated structure. The consequences of diagnostic labels and the possible reactions of others to such labels should also be explained to parents.

School personnel must be as supportive of parents as possible, because parents must give their consent to the placement decision. Parents should be made to feel comfortable in the IEP conference. Their opinions should be solicited, and they should be encouraged to make suggestions about their child's needs. School personnel should express an interest in the child, and ample time should be provided to conduct the meeting. Finally, the staff should realize that the IEP conference can be very trying for parents, and they should be prepared to deal with parents' possible emotional reactions.

How can teachers make parent conferences more effective?

Educators can contribute to the success of conferences by anticipating the needs of parents. Following are some reasonable strategies to use at various phases of the conference process:

1. *Before the conference:*
   - Inform parents of the time, place, and purpose.
   - Deliver oral and written messages in the parents' native language.
   - Send reminders.
   - Gather the necessary reports, material, etc.
   - Choose a private and comfortable setting that allows for full participation by all.
   - Send parents some questions or ideas to consider.
   - Ask parents to bring certain information.
   - Designate someone to serve as advocate or sponsor for the parents at the meeting.
2. *Opening the meeting:*
   - Introduce yourself and others.
   - Establish the purpose of the meeting and any time limitations.
   - Have people explain their roles.
   - Invite parental questions and input.
3. *Interpreting assessment results:*
   - Avoid jargon.
   - Give examples of student test performances and show exhibits of work.
   - Relate the findings to parental experience.
   - Reconcile different findings for parents.
   - Ask parents to confirm or evaluate the results from their experience.
4. *IEP or IFSP development:*
   - Ask about parental goals and priorities.
   - Incorporate goals suggested by parents.
   - Invite parents to help accomplish some school goals.
   - Describe ways parents can assist directly at school.
   - Have parents validate family needs for the IFSP and indicate appropriateness of family services.
   - Explore the possibilities of home-based activities.
   - Demonstrate cooperation among the special and regular teachers responsible for the IEP or IFSP.
   - Make sure all essential IEP or IFSP features are included and meet with parents' approval.
5. *Placement decision:*
   - Explain pros and cons of different settings (e.g., special class, resource room, home-based model, etc.).
   - Clarify how often the child will be with his or her nondisabled peers.
   - Avoid rushing parents to agree to the placement.
   - Invite parents to visit sample programs and placements.
   - Provide the names and phone numbers of other parents with children in the classes who have agreed to talk with parents of incoming children.
   - Explain the parents' right to appeal if they dislike the decision.
   - If applicable, describe how supportive services will be offered in conjunction with the main programs.
6. *Closing the conference:*
   - Summarize the meeting by reviewing major decisions and explaining who will be responsible for follow-through.
   - Offer copies of the IEP, IFSP, and other documents.
   - Explain where the child's records are kept and the rules for confidentiality.
   - Indicate how and when parents will get feedback about the child's progress.

- Ask about parental preferences for format and schedule in receiving progress reports.
- Set a date for at least an annual review of the IEP or IFSP.
- Offer information about parent groups, materials, etc.
7. *After the conference:*
  - Process all documents immediately.
  - Send promised copies and other material.
  - Perform the follow-up activities discussed in the session (Turnbull & Strickland, 1981; Katz, Borten, Brasile, Meisner, & Parker, 1980).

Instruction

Parents of children with exceptionalities can be involved in teaching their children both at home and in the classroom. Many parents begin when their children are infants. Because of the proven effectiveness of early intervention in the case of all disabilities and the paucity of services and professionals at this level, parents often serve as the primary instructors (Wallace & McLoughlin, 1988). Of all possible forms of participation, parents most often assist in educational activities and therapy.

How can parents help teach their children?

PARENT ROLES. Parents of exceptional children become actively involved in instructional programs for a variety of reasons. Besides benefiting from the emotional support such programs provide, the parents who attend these programs seem to be having more trouble engaging their children as well as they would like (Spicker, 1982). This motivation for better parent-child interaction also guarantees greater follow-through with the program.

The lack of profitable communication between parents and children is a prime motivation for many parents to work with their children. While the frequency and length of verbal and nonverbal interactions do not seem to differ between parents of children with and without language disorders, the quality does (Lasky & Klopp, 1982). The more linguistically mature child encourages parents to engage in richer verbal communication (i.e., questioning, providing information, acknowledging the child's statement) and nonverbal behaviors as well. Parents with exceptional children must be taught to communicate well, because their children may not naturally encourage them to do so.

Parents can be trained to teach language and other skills. One group of parents with children who had language disorders was taught to increase their language stimulation skills by such activities as drawing the child's attention to an object, answering appropriately, and directing the child to do something (Lombardino & Mangan, 1983). Their children mastered a large percentage of the material taught.

Parents must also be taught to transfer their newfound skills to play situations and other more informal settings and to encourage the generalization of skills to the home. After a ten-week training period in sign language, one group of parents learned the sign system well, and their children advanced significantly (Williams, Lombardino, MacDonald, & Owens, 1982); but they did not use the system in unstructured settings. Parents of toddlers with Down syndrome learned how to prompt and reinforce speech better (Salzberg & Villani, 1983). After being given feedback through audiotapes and some ideas for adapting their strategies at home, they used the skills more effectively in informal settings. Reese and Serna (1986) recommend the following to facilitate greater generalization and maintenance: attending more to individual family needs, generalizing parental skills across settings, and reinforcing trained skills in the natural setting.

Are parents natural teachers for their children?

PARENT TRAINING. Parents are not necessarily natural teachers, at least of material traditionally taught by educators. When mothers and teachers of children with learning disabilities were observed teaching the same tasks to the same child, the parents differed significantly in teaching style (Steinart, Campbell, & Kiely, 1981). The teachers gave information more useful to performing the task, structured the task more, asked more prompting questions, and requested more independent activities from the children. There is obviously a need to train parents to teach their children effectively. For the child's sake, consistency in style as well as quality should be encouraged.

Observations of mothers and fathers playing with their young children with mental retardation indicated that parents were consistent in their style of interacting across sessions, although mothers changed more (McConachie & Mitchell, 1985). Mothers' and fathers' interactional patterns did not differ greatly, although fathers seemed less successful sometimes.

Even for informal instruction and play, there is a need to shape parents' behavior as effective teachers. Compared to parents of nonretarded preschoolers, one group of parents with developmentally delayed children tended to dominate play sessions (Eheart, 1981). Their children responded less and initiated fewer interactions. Whether the parent or child controls the situation is not of foremost importance here; more important is the fact that parents can and must learn to be more effective, even in playful and casual exchanges.

Observations of the play interactions of mothers and their infants with Down syndrome, ages 1 to 3, further confirm the importance of parents being taught to allow their children to lead the activity and to respond enthusiastically to the children's interest (Mahoney, Finger, & Powell, 1985). This kind of child-oriented maternal behavior was associated with higher developmental skills than parental behavior that was very directive, ignored the children's interests, and was not accepting. Early intervention programs that train parents to be directive need to reconsider that approach, especially in play activities.

Children tend to respond to and attach to parents and teachers differently (Blacher & Bromley, 1987). Case studies of children with severe handicaps indicate that children demonstrate more observable attachment behaviors (e.g., eye contact, reaching, visual tracking) at home in the presence of their mothers than at school in the presence of teachers, and such behaviors were more pronounced with parents than teachers. Also, mothers in this study were more sensitive to their child's needs than teachers, whose sensitivity was more governed by the child's functioning level.

Efforts have been made to identify predictors of successful parental participation in educational activities. Their child-rearing expectations seem to relate to their ability to benefit from participation in language training programs for their children (Strom, Reese, Slaughter, & Wurster, 1980). While socioeconomic status, education, and pretraining experience may affect parents' later retention of the behavior management material they learned, their actual performance during training may be the best predictor of whether they will successfully carry out programs with their children (Clark, Baker, & Heifetz, 1982).

Whether serving as tutors and teacher's aides at home or in the classroom, parents should be given goals that can be met in a short time. If the activity is to be done at home, it should be designed in consideration of the home environment, family schedule, and other demands. Involving parents and siblings in planning the home activity is a wise strategy. Parents should be shown what to do and how to do it and should be given an opportunity to practice the skill under supervision. The criteria for completion should be explained. Parents should, of course, be reinforced for their participation. The activities parents are given to do at home or at school should be clear and contain all the necessary directions. When activities are sent home for completion, the teacher must keep track of what is sent and plan for regular feedback from the families.

TECHNOLOGY IN ACTION

Jill is a preschool child with cerebral palsy. She is having difficulty differentiating between the concepts of big and little. Mrs. Martin, her preschool teacher, believes that extra practice at home can help Jill overcome this problem. Jill's mother was willing to help at home, but she was at a loss about how to proceed.

Mrs. Martin developed a set of systematic procedures for Jill's mother to follow in providing direct instruction to Jill at home. These procedures involved presenting pictures of objects of different size, identifying the relative size of each, encouraging Jill's imitation of the label, reinforcing for correct imitations, and systematic record keeping of the time involved in direct instruction.

Following is the parent activity sheet that Mrs. Martin developed for Jill's mother to use as a guide for home instruction (from Shearer, 1976). You can see from the activity chart that Jill's mother consistently met the goal of providing at least five minutes of daily instruction on the concepts. As it eventually turned out, Jill did learn to differentiate between big and little; and Mrs. Martin is convinced that the efforts of Jill's mother contributed greatly to this accomplishment.

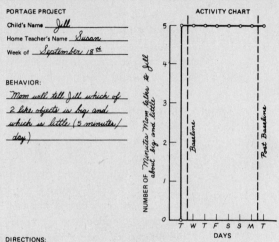

PORTAGE PROJECT

Child's Name _Jill_

Home Teacher's Name _Susan_

Week of _September 18 st_

BEHAVIOR:

Mom will tell Jill which of 2 like objects is big and which is little (5 minutes/day)

DIRECTIONS:

1. Use paired objects or pictures that are the same - except for size.
2. Talk with Jill pointing to and naming the objects that are big and little, and encourage Jill to repeat the size word in imitation of you.
3. Praise her each time she imitates.
4. Use as many different examples of like pictures and objects as possible.
5. Record the number of minutes you spend naming big and little each day.

BEHAVIOR MANAGEMENT. Of all the areas of instruction parents have participated in, behavior management has received the most emphasis. Parents are concerned about their exceptional children's socialization skills and emotional stability. Their interest extends to children's work habits at school, peer relations, and general obedience. Working alone or with educators, parents have learned and used the principles of applied behavioral analysis to modify their children's behavior. They have used the approach to encourage academic progress, speech and language skills, gains in physical therapy, and development in many other areas. Their success at learning and applying the principles is well documented (Cooper & Edge, 1981; Turnbull & Turnbull, 1990). Many materials are available for parents who wish to use this approach (Baker & Brightman, 1989; Klein, VanHasselt, Trafelner, Sandstrom, & Brandt-Snyder, 1988; McElroy, 1987). Behavior-change programs such as these are often developed jointly by parents and educators.

As in all areas of parent participation, however, certain legitimate concerns continue to exist about behavior management programs for parents (Sapon-Shevin, 1982). Since some programs offer parents little guidance in choosing goals and many goals focus on eliminating undesirable behaviors, a potential conflict may arise between the parents' and the child's rights. Also, the selection and evaluation of reinforcers may be weak, and sanctioned use of punishment is a questionable practice. The parent training provided and the professional follow-up and supervision given in parent-directed programs may also be poor.

Behavior management programs are often part of a broader effort by parents and educators to increase communication. A system of daily or weekly report cards or "smiley face" notes helps parents keep abreast of events (Kroth, 1985; Turnbull & Turnbull, 1990). Generally the notes contain an indication of general academic or behavioral achievement for that day or week. Parents sign and return them, sometimes also providing rewards for high performance.

Innovative uses of the phone have enhanced not only parental involvement but also student achievement. When educators called parents to reinforce their tutoring of ten reading words each night and were told of the child's progress, there was an increase in achievement and an improvement in parental attitudes toward the school (Heron & Axelrod, 1976). A telephone answering system has been used with similar efficacy to transmit instructions for parents, requests, and progress notes (Chapman & Heward, 1982).

Parents can serve in a variety of capacities in the school. They can assist in transportation, fund-raising projects, the construction of instructional materials, and classroom activities such as dressing and feeding. Volunteer programs must be well planned and coordinated; volunteers should be trained for specific responsibilities and carefully supervised.

Evaluation

How frequently must parents be involved in evaluating their exceptional child's progress?

Parents are required by law to be involved in at least one review of the child's individualized education program each year. These evaluations are used to determine whether the program has been effective and whether changes in goals, objectives, placement, or procedures are needed.

The effectiveness of parents' involvement in an annual evaluation is determined largely by the extent of communication between teachers and parents during the school year. Educators can communicate with parents in a number of ways. As just discussed, daily or weekly progress reports, graphs of child progress, and report cards that describe the child's skill levels rather than providing grades have all been used effectively (Kroth, 1985; McLoughlin & Lewis, 1990). Most important is that parents and teachers remain in regular contact, whether through phone calls, school conferences, written notes, home visits, casual meetings in the community, or parent groups. Every available opportunity should be used to share constructive comments about the child's behavior.

Including parents in the assessment and programming aspects of exceptional children's programs teaches them what to look for, both in their children's progress and in program quality. Parents belonging to the National Association for Retarded Citizens place a high priority on this aspect of the educational program (Soffer, 1982). They demand a greater say in deciding when their children are evaluated and how they will get feedback. Professionals can help by meeting with parents more often, scheduling more convenient conferences, and using language parents can understand. Parents can also be involved in the evaluation of their child's program by serving on advisory boards and steering committees. In these groups, parent opinions can be solicited about a wide range of matters related to the education of exceptional children and how to encourage productive interactions between professionals and parents.

PROBE 6-2   Involving Parents

1. T F Parents should not be involved in efforts to identify and refer exceptional children.
2. Describe three attitudes you might encounter among teachers opposed to parental involvement in the education of their exceptional children.

3. For each of the following stages of the educational process, describe a way that parents can be of assistance and how a professional could facilitate that particular parental effort:
   a. Identification
   b. Assessment
   c. Conferences
   d. Instruction
   e. Evaluation
4. Give three reasons that parents should be involved in the education of their exceptional children.

SUPPORTING FAMILIES

You should be able to describe ways to support families and train them to perform their various roles and activities.

In addition to participating directly in their children's programs, parents find themselves performing many advocacy and program support roles. They are called upon to challenge inadequate and inappropriate services and to lobby for quality programs. They may need to interact with government officials, school administrators, and others. New programs are often developed and expanded as a result of an impetus created by parents. To them often falls the responsibility of arousing public awareness and creating sensitivity to the issues surrounding their children's needs by serving as speakers at meetings (Blackard & Barsh, 1982). Parents must also continue to provide warm, supportive homes for their exceptional children and their siblings. Of all their possible activities, this one must be paramount. Additionally, parents serve as vital resources to one another, as members of parent organizations or individually.

Professionals can support families in these types of activities in various ways. These include safeguarding the rights of parents and serving as parent advocates.

Fostering Parental Rights

Are the rights of parents of exceptional children being fully observed?

Observance of the parental rights guaranteed by PL 94-142 and PL 99-457 has been mixed. There seems to be an effort to meet the letter of the law, but efforts to meet the spirit of the law are lacking. For example, while prior notices of assessments are generally provided, they often do not mention critical rights—such as the parents' right to an independent evaluation that need not always be at their expense (Yoshida, 1982). Educators need to monitor such notices more closely for content and communication style.

As discussed earlier, the quality of parent participation at IEP conferences also leaves much to be desired. When a group of parents of children with learning disabilities were surveyed about their experience at the IEP conference, 25 percent could not recall the IEP process or confused it with other meetings (McKinney & Hocutt, 1982). While parents claimed that their job or home situation kept them away from such sessions, there was ample evidence that they lacked the knowledge to participate well and comfortably. Educators need to serve as parent educators in regard to these conferences.

In spite of such difficulties, Turnbull and Turnbull (1990) conclude that the implementation of the due process procedures has generally accomplished its purpose: fair treatment, accountability, a new balance of power, and a focus on children's rights and needs. However, there have been a variety of problems related to due process hearings, including the financial expense to parents and school systems, and the emotional trauma and anxiety produced when parents and teachers assume opposing positions (Budoff & Orenstein, 1982).

Strickland's (1982) profile of parental use of due process hearings reflects these mixed results. While often vital to ensure the accountability of schools, due process seems to be a last, drastic recourse for parents who have tried everything else. Parents who seek such hearings have often had numerous contacts, usually negative ones, with the schools about the problem and seem pushed to take a stand against the school's decision. Parents using this option are generally well educated and in the middle to upper socioeconomic levels.

While these parents and the schools both have confidence in the ability of the impartial hearing officer to make a fair decision, many decisions are not implemented for a variety of reasons. Parents often report they would not ask for a due process hearing again, and many conflicts between parents and schools remain unresolved. In fact, relationships between the parties may get worse. There are some positive, though indirect, outcomes of participating in hearings: parents feel they are treated more as equals; they find the hearings to be educational experiences; public awareness of the issues is highlighted; and federal and state policies regarding PL 94-142 are often clarified. All things considered, both parents and schools should consider several factors before requesting a due process hearing, including (1) the limited ability of the hearing officer to resolve the specific question at issue; (2) the required investment of time, energy, and resources as weighed against the probable outcome; and (3) the potential harm to the child and stress on the family. In this area, the saying "an ounce of prevention is worth a pound of cure" is particularly true.

To avoid formal due process hearings or as a prelude to them, some states use a process of mediation in which an intermediary informally helps the two conflicting parties reach a mutually acceptable solution to a problem or part of a problem. Mediation is seen as preferable to the legislative and adversarial atmosphere of the due process hearings (Turnbull & Turnbull, 1990). Since the mediator is chosen by both parties, he or she is in a better position to identify points of agreement and help resolve some issues. Unresolved issues may then be considered in a due process hearing.

Professional Advocacy

What advocacy roles should teachers assume?

There are many avenues for providing support for parents in the effort to sustain their rights. Much of what needs to be done can be considered a form of professional advocacy. There are two kinds of advocacy: external or internal to the school system. External advocacy, or functioning independently outside the system to critique and change services, is untenable for educators since it requires that they be autonomous and engage in activities such as demonstrations, education boycotts, and so on. However, they can be internal advocates, engaged cooperatively as partners in actualizing the rights of the exceptional child to appropriate services. An example of internal advocacy would be the actions of the school counselors in Goldstein and Turnbull's study (1982), who supported parents by introducing them, clarifying jargon, asking questions, reinforcing parental contributions, and summarizing decisions at the end of the conference.

Parents have a crying need to know more about testing, conferences, due process, services for their children, and other aspects of special education. Their lack of knowledge seems to be at the heart of many problems, such as their difficulty in participating at IEP meetings. Parents' lack of knowledge may influence professional perceptions of them and indirectly block fuller roles in decision making (Strickland, 1982).

While a study of all state departments of education indicated a commitment to provide information of this sort to families, the allocation of resources and strategies varied from state to state (McLoughlin, Edge, Strenecky, & Key, 1984). Better cooperative efforts among educational agencies and private parent and professional organizations will improve the quantity and quality of information. State education departments and other groups are stressing common criteria such as visual appeal, legibility, and content; they are correcting problems with readability and gaps in content and are involving parents from different backgrounds to guarantee that the material will be appropriate for a wide parent audience.

Educators and other professionals also have an obligation to research issues relevant to parents (Winton & Turnbull, 1982). They need to become more flexible in deciding where and how they disseminate their research findings so that parents will hear about and understand them. Creative use of the media can also influence parental awareness.

For example, the Parent Education and Resource Center at the University of Louisville developed a set of one-minute audiotapes with suggestions about child-rearing practices in language, social-emotional, and physical development; they were broadcast over radio stations in Kentucky and elsewhere. Recorded telephone messages can also be used to increase parental knowledge as well as help children (Chapman & Heward, 1982).

Educators are also in an excellent position to provide information about two priority items for parents: the child's program and the teacher. Newsletters, handbooks, and parent bulletin boards with information about the school program and the children's activities in it are very well received by parents. Often they are willing to assist in publication efforts.

Another way to develop a trusting relationship with parents is to make home visits (Turnbull & Turnbull, 1990). Educators should have a clear purpose in mind for the visit and communicate it to the family when the appointment is made. Being positive about the child and indicating interest in the family's concerns are important for a successful visit. The family's privacy must be respected. These visits are also a great opportunity to model a good attitude toward the child for the parents—and toward the parents for the child—and to gather a more complete picture of the child's environment and family life.

Educators who have a strong desire to serve as advocates are not deterred by difficult parents. The use of less-structured and less-traditional approaches often works. Being accessible, sharing in their life situations, and approaching them as adults are good beginnings. More specific ideas include being visible in the neighborhood, associating with people the parents trust, sponsoring social events or programs involving their children, communicating clearly and seeking feedback, focusing on real needs, and encouraging parents in meaningful ways. With culturally different families and minorities, educators can be particularly sensitive to possible cultural discrepancies between themselves and the parents. Professionals are urged to consider how the following factors vary, depending on cultural background: the meaning of the disability, attitudes toward professionals and about seeking and receiving help, and family roles and support networks (Turnbull & Turnbull, 1990).

Parental success in participating directly in different aspects of their children's program depends heavily upon professionals' conviction of their importance and efforts to make their role meaningful. When parents request mediation or a due process hearing, educators must remember that it is their duty to advocate the rights of the child in question.

Educators also advocate parental rights by becoming well trained to do so. Training one group of early childhood interventionists in child and family assessments, parent and family interviews, communication, and family goal development had a number of direct impacts on services (Bailey et al., 1988). They learned to rely more on family assessments in writing IFSPs, and increased the number of family goals in plans, thus improving the quality of services.

Parent Programs

Good relations with parents and the successful resolution of problems depend on the educator's confidence in parents' knowledge and decision-making ability. That is why many educators see it as their role to provide enriching and training experiences for parents. The effort also benefits the children. In the long run, such efforts make the educator's job easier.

An important part of the program for the exceptional child should be the development of a parent program. In some cases parents will be involved with the school as part of the regular parent-teacher organization. Generally it is desirable to establish separate groups to deal with the needs of parents of exceptional children or to create formal programs to involve parents in the direct instruction of their children. Regardless of the type of program, the goal is to improve the educational process for everyone involved: teachers, students, and administrators.

What good are parent programs?

CONCEPTUAL BASIS. Parent programs serve many purposes. They are generally designed to give parents social and emotional support. By talking to parents who have similar problems and to professionals who can be of assistance, parents can learn to cope with feelings such as those described at the beginning of the chapter.

Parent programs can also provide a forum for the exchange of information, like the one set up for parents of students with mild handicaps in a resource room program in Iowa (Hallenbeck & Beernik, 1989). Information exchange can involve scheduling guest speakers, maintaining a lending library, or publishing a newsletter.

Parent programs frequently offer parents an opportunity to participate in their child's programs as teacher's aides, volunteers, tutors, data collectors, behavior managers, or field trip monitors. A major goal of all parent programs should be to improve the interactions between parents and their exceptional child. Parent groups can help parents develop appropriate expectations for their children and strategies for better communication.

Several preschool programs have been developed that involve parents intensively in their children's education. In the Portage project, for example, a teacher visits the child's home for $1\frac{1}{2}$ hours a week. During these visits, objectives for the child are developed and teaching strategies are demonstrated. During the rest of the week, the parents give the actual lessons to the child and collect information on performance; this information is reviewed the next time the teacher visits (Shearer & Loftin, 1984). The PEECH project, on the other hand, trains parents to provide assistance in the classroom. Some programs combine both techniques. Parents of older children generally do follow-up work at home.

The 1982–86 Handicapped Children's Early Education Programs have expanded services for new populations and their families in multiple settings, in a mainstreamed format, and with the family as the focus of comprehensive services (Suarez, Hurth, & Prestridge, 1988). Many projects concentrate on parent-child interactions and issues of transition. Interagency cooperation and multicultural community involvement are considered critical features of newer programs. Applications of technology are very evident.

Parent training must be approached carefully. It should be comprehensive and not just develop isolated skills (Bricker & Casuso, 1979). Goals must be based on the family's needs, readiness, and learning style. Educators must recognize the importance of gaining the trust and confidence of parents (Simpson, 1982) or parent education will not yield major gains.

What are appropriate topics for parent programs?

CONTENT. Parent programs can involve a variety of topics and activities, depending on the parents' needs. As Bernstein and Barta (1988) found out in their comparative survey of parents and educators of children with hearing losses, parents were more interested in information and strategies that were child-related (e.g., how to stimulate language and self-concept) than in the anatomy and physiology of the ear. Parents preferred interventions to be discussed over time, rather than once or a few times, to allow thoughtful assimilation. A similar situation was found with parents of children with learning disabilities and behavior disorders (Simpson, 1988). Parents did not have uniform needs, and educators tended to overestimate their needs in some areas.

Sometimes programs are structured around organized, published material. In one program for fathers of deaf children, the topics included the physical causes of deafness as well as linguistic and cognitive development; the fathers also discussed common experiences in the discovery and diagnosis of the problem, and met deaf adults (Crowley, Keane, & Needham, 1982).

Coping with stress is another common topic in parent programs. Zeitlin and Williamson (1988) have parents address the following questions: What is the meaning of this tension-generating event? How does it affect my well-being? And what can I do about it? For answers, they look to internal (belief system) and external (human support) resources. Parents are then assisted in the implementation of a coping strategy and its evaluation.

Adolescent parents of exceptional children are a group requiring special attention (Helm, 1988). Their own developmental needs must be met as they move toward adulthood. Parenting skills must be emphasized because adolescent parent–child interactions are less verbal and positive than they should be, and adolescent parents' expectations for their children are often unrealistic. Parent programs should help them avoid stress by building a solid support system with relatives and peers, meeting their ever-changing need for information, and facilitating life options.

A program designed for siblings of exceptional children can be set up to familiarize them with their brother's or sister's disability and what it means for them (Meyer, Vadasy, & Fewell, 1985). In such a program, siblings have the opportunity to discuss their feelings, to learn games they can play with the exceptional child, and to learn ways to relate better to them. Siblings benefit from sharing experiences among themselves, much as the parents do.

It is wise to cover material not related to school at parent meetings. Parents appreciate discussions about getting babysitters, going shopping or to a restaurant with the exceptional child, or going on vacation. Educators should not shy away from topics such as sex education, marriage, career possibilities, and living arrangements. Specialists should be sought when needed.

Clark (1988) advises that parents of gifted and talented children should be encouraged to help their children make lots of decisions and explain the consequences when they can understand them. They should not confuse the child's IQ with the child and should help the child deal with being different and the pressure that difference creates with peers. Children need assistance in accepting their mistakes and coping with perfectionism and seeing and appreciating individual differences. Parents need to learn to instruct by actions, not only words, and to know when not to push for closure on certain activities. Most of all, they must learn to provide a safe place where children can be themselves.

Many print and nonprint materials are available to facilitate the development of parent programs. See Turnbull and Turnbull (1990) for an annotated list of print and audio-visual materials to use with parents. A national network of Alliance for Technology Access Centers is helping families learn ways to apply technology to their children's lives (Cohn & Green, 1988).

EVALUATION. Parent programs should be evaluated regularly. An initial needs assessment can establish appropriate topics, format, schedule, location, and desirable activities for the parents. When parents are trying to accomplish specific goals with their children, it is essential to provide for feedback so they will not get discouraged or harm the child. It is also helpful to attend to the characteristics and performance of parents in the group. Their socioeconomic status, education, and pretraining experience may dictate certain strategies; these traits were related to one parent group's later knowledge of behavior management techniques (Clark et al., 1982). This research also highlighted the importance of monitoring parents' performance: It seems to affect their follow-through activities.

The benefits to the children should also be examined, both in skill development and effect. Parental satisfaction and attitudes toward the child and school are other important indicators of success. Most of all, parent-child interactions should be examined for improvement. Comparative analysis of different interventions is also important. One early intervention project for language-impaired children compared its home-based approach, in which parents integrated therapy into regular domestic situations, to the center-based therapy sessions (Barnett, Escobar, & Ravsten, 1988). The home-based model proved superior in terms of children's test scores and cost. A media-based program for parents of children with mental retardation proved as effective and satisfying to parents in training self-help skill development as traditional approaches (Kashima, Baker, & Landau, 1988).

TRAINING MODELS. Current thinking about parent training stresses the need to make parents better consumers of educational services and more effective advocates for their children in such situations as evaluation sessions, IEP conferences, problem-solving sessions, and progress report conferences (Simpson, 1982). Training should be directed by a group of parents and educators. Ideally, the format might consist of attitude development activities, content sessions, opportunities for parents to express and share feelings, observations of acceptable role models, simulation activities (e.g., mock conferences), feedback activities, and follow-up arrangements.

In some cases, parents of exceptional children and educators can be trained together (McLoughlin, 1981). This tends to overturn misconceptions and help them build a working relationship more quickly. Suitable topics are program areas over which parents and educators are frequently in communication, such as report cards and grades. Considerable planning is required to accommodate differences in learning style and background.

The traditional series of parent workshops in skills training may not always be the most efficacious. In one study, parents who learned behavior management principles and strategies in a series of workshops were compared to those who had a weekly phone call from a therapist at a mutually agreeable time in addition to reading materials and doing assigned activities (MacDonald & Brazier, 1989). Parents in the phone group acquired as much behavioral knowledge, were as successful at changing their children's problem behaviors, and were as satisfied with what they learned as their counterparts who attended the group workshops.

Individualization is a critical factor. The knowledge of sign language of parents of children with hearing loss was greatly enhanced by viewing videotapes of their preschool children at work and play and by reading an accompanying commentary on the signs used, the context in which they occurred, and strategies to use at home with the children (Seal, 1987). The information was customized to individual family situations and took into account different signing codes.

What organizations exist to assist families?

PARENT ORGANIZATIONS AND RESOURCES. Various national organizations and their state and local affiliates are prepared to provide parents and others with information about exceptional persons and services for them. Some of them, such as the National Association for Retarded Citizens, have state and local branches and offer conferences and informal meetings for parents. Such sessions are a vehicle for parents to keep current with the newest developments in the field, to participate in discussions designed for them, and to share useful strategies with other parents. Often parents are trained for advocacy activities. Some organizations band together to accomplish common goals. PACER, a Minnesota-based coalition of 18 advocacy groups founded in 1979, sponsors a disability awareness program with a puppet show in schools (Binkard, 1985). The puppets portray disabled and nondisabled persons discussing individual differences. The program has since been expanded to the medical and business worlds and to other community groups.

Many organizations also provide regular newsletters, such as *Newsbriefs* from the Learning Disabilities Association of America (formerly the Association for Children and Adults with Learning Disabilities). Siblings for Significant Change is a national group for people with exceptional brothers and sisters. *The Exceptional Parent* is a periodical that specifically addresses parental interests and needs. See Task Sheet 6 for further details about these and other resources.

Such organizations can have a significant role in providing more numerous and more varied social support services for families, identifying both individuals (e.g., physicians) and groups (e.g., day care). A survey of parents of children with a variety of disabilities indicated the positive impact of support networks on personal well-being, attitudes, parent-child play opportunities, and child behavior and development (Dunst, Trivette, & Cross, 1986).

Future Trends

The future in special education will be challenging for families of exceptional persons of all ages. Since the passage of PL 94-142 and PL 99-457, parents have made significant progress toward participation in the development and implementation of services. However, too often the letter of the law has been observed, and not the spirit. The result has been an emphasis on involving the parents in procedural matters. Sometimes the goal of cooperation has been lost in the midst of all the paperwork and meetings.

According to a 1987 national Harris poll of 702 educators, 1000 parents, and 200 youth with disabilities (ICD, 1989), parental knowledge and involvement continues to be a concern. The majority of parents do not know their rights or much about PL 94-142; more than one-third indicate no involvement in IEP development. Only 22 percent belong to parent organizations.

It is important that parents avoid losing ground in this vital area. Their hard-won rights to participate may be overlooked if a backlash of political pressure objects to the necessary commitment of time and personnel to ensure active family involvement. Also, past experience suggests the need to clarify the best ways to have parents participate, since some parents have been unwilling or unable to do so effectively.

Parents can help direct their future involvement by making known how they want to be involved and how their concerns can be best met. There is growing awareness that some parents may have concerns other than those that professionals are aware of, and that they may prefer alternative forms of involvement. We must avoid "professionalizing" parents against their wishes and seeing them as a substitute for professionals performing their responsibilities (Allen & Hudd, 1987); parents should be the initiators in establishing their roles. A broader perspective on family involvement seems more appropriate than a purely "parental rights" approach. This broader perspective would ensure more individualized attention to parental concerns about their children's needs during the preschool years and after they leave formal schooling.

What is the value
of parent
organizations?

Parent organizations must assume a major responsibility for guiding the initiative on behalf of parents of exceptional persons. They must work to counter the indifference of some parents whose children have received services and who are tempted to cease their advocacy activities. Professionals who are committed to the parent movement in special education must be suitably reinforced. The currency and quality of information provided to parents must also be monitored to prevent inappropriate and costly efforts by parents. The gains of the 1980s must be capitalized upon in the 1990s.

PROBE 6-3   Supporting Families

1. Describe three policies you would establish, as a school official, to ensure that the legal rights of parents are protected.
2. Describe four purposes served by parent programs.
3. T   F   Because professionals are familiar with the needs of parents, they should have the major responsibility in developing parent training programs.
4. T   F   Assessment of parental needs is the first step in developing a parent training program.
5. T   F   Parents and educators can never be trained together.

SUMMARY

1. Although reactions vary, the parents of exceptional children may experience periods of shock, denial, guilt, fear, overprotectiveness, and both overt and disguised rejection before reaching the stage of acceptance.
2. The attitudes of parents can improve or adversely affect the behavior of their exceptional children.
3. The siblings of exceptional children generally adopt the attitudes of their parents toward the exceptional child.
4. The parents of exceptional children need a great deal of information about such subjects as diagnosis, treatment, management, and support services.
5. The relationship between parents and professionals concerned with exceptional children is gradually improving. Successful relationships depend on mutual trust and understanding.
6. Parents can assist in the identification, assessment, and programming of their children and in the implementation and evaluation of their children's programs.
7. Parents have the legal right to be involved in all decisions regarding the education of their exceptional children. They also have the protection of due process if they are dissatisfied with the educational program that has been provided.
8. Parent programs should provide emotional support, a forum for the exchange of information, an opportunity to participate in the child's program, and parent-child interaction training.
9. Parent programs must be designed around parental needs and directed toward making them better consumers and advocates.
10. A knowledge of parental needs, awareness of the ways they can get involved, and preparedness to support them are the main dimensions of a parent involvement program.

TASK SHEET 6   Field Experiences with Families of Exceptional Children

Select *one* of the following and complete the required tasks. Write a report of no more than three pages about your activities.

Family Interview

Interview the parents or other family members of a disabled or gifted child. Ask about their reactions when they learned that their child was exceptional. Try to determine what problems the parents encountered in attempting to obtain services. Find out about their home life. If the parents have gone through the due process procedures mandated by PL 94-142, determine how they reacted to that experience.

Observation

Observe the meeting of a placement committee in your local school district. Describe how the professionals interacted with the parents at the meeting, and how the parents participated. Determine whether the parents' rights were correctly observed. What was your reaction to the procedure?

Professional Interview

Interview a professional person about his or her experience with parents of exceptional children. If the professional participates in parental involvement programs, ask him or her to describe them.

Participation

Offer your services to a parent training program or other program in which parents are involved.

Agency Investigation

Request information from three of the following agencies about the services they provide to parents of exceptional children. Write a three-page report summarizing these services and how you might use them if you were a parent of an exceptional child.

American Foundation for the Blind, Inc.
15 West 16th Street
New York, NY 10011

American Speech-Language-Hearing
Association
10801 Rockville Pike
Rockville, MD 20852

Learning Disabilities Association of America
4156 Library Road
Pittsburgh, PA 15234

National Information Center for
Handicapped Children and Youth
Post Office Box 1492
Washington, DC 20013

International Parents' Organization of
the Alexander Graham Bell
Association for the Deaf
1537 35th Street, N.W.
Washington, DC 20007

National Association for Creative
Children and Adults
8080 Springvalley Drive
Cincinnati, OH 45236

National Association for the Deaf-Blind
2703 Forest Oak Circle
Norman, OK 73071

National Association for Retarded Citizens
2709 Avenue E East
Post Office Box 6109
Arlington, TX 76011

National Easter Seal Society for Crippled
Children and Adults
2023 W. Ogden Avenue
Chicago, IL 60612

National Society for Autistic Children
169 Tampa Avenue
Albany, NY 12208

Siblings for Significant Change
823 United Nations Plaza
New York, NY 10017

Library Study

Use the library to locate three articles related to a topic associated with parents of exceptional children. Write a one-page abstract of each. In the last paragraph of your abstract indicate your personal reaction to the article. Possible sources are *The Exceptional Parent* (605 Commonwealth Ave., Boston, MA 02215), newsletters and other publications available from the organizations listed under "Agency Investigation," and the special education journals mentioned elsewhere in this text.

Design Your Own Field Experience

If none of these alternatives appeals to you, or if you have the opportunity to perform some other task with parents of exceptional children, design your own field experience. Check with your instructor to determine its acceptability.

1. Teachers each day will fill lamps, clean chimneys, and trim wicks. Wash windows once each week.

2. Each teacher will bring in a bucket of water and a scuttle of coal for the day's session.

3. Make pen nibs carefully. You may whittle nibs to your individual tastes.

4. Men teachers will be given one evening off each week for courting purposes, or two evenings off a week if they go regularly to church.

5. After ten hours in school, the teacher should spend the remaining time reading the Bible and other good books.

6. All teachers are encouraged to take complete baths with soap at least every week, and change underclothing frequently to avoid offending others.

7. Women teachers who marry or engage in unseemly conduct will be dismissed.

8. Every teacher should lay aside from easy pay a goodly sum of his earnings for his benefit during his declining years so that he will not become a burden on society.

9. Any teacher who smokes Spanish cigars, uses liquor in any form, or frequents pool and public halls or gets shaved in a barber shop, will give good reason to suspect his worth, intentions, integrity, and honesty.

10. The teacher who has performed his labor faithfully and without fault for five years will be given an increase of five cents per day in his pay, providing the Board of Education approves.

7

Continuing Professional Development

A. Edward Blackhurst

The rules for teachers on the facing page are said to have been posted by the principal of a New York school in 1872. They probably reflect the attitudes and expectations of society toward teaching at that point in history. Fortunately, times have changed. Although teachers are still expected to conduct their personal lives in a fashion that is consistent with prevailing community standards, there is now more concern with their professional competence than their personal habits.

The purpose of this text is to serve as an introduction to the terms, definitions, concepts, and ideas needed to understand the field of special education. Some readers may be interested in the text simply to expand their knowledge, but most will use it as a foundation for further study with an eventual goal of assuming a special education teaching career.

If you are among this majority, you should be competent to begin teaching when you complete your formal education. You should realize, however, that you will have to continue to develop your professional skills throughout your career. The field of special education is changing so rapidly that teachers must work diligently to keep up with new information, diagnostic instruments, instructional materials, technology, and teaching methods.

In 1983, the Council for Exceptional Children (CEC) adopted a set of ethical standards to guide professionals who work with exceptional children. One of these guidelines reads as follows:

> Special education professionals systematically advance their knowledge and skills in order to maintain a high level of competence and response to the changing needs of exceptional persons by pursuing a program of continuing education including but not limited to participation in such activities as in-service training, professional conferences/workshops, professional meetings, continuing education courses, and the reading of professional literature. (*Code of Ethics and Standards for Professional Practice,* 1983, p. 208)

In this chapter we discuss professional responsibilities and describe a model and procedures that can be used to design a personal program of professional development. The ideas that follow should be useful to both beginning special education students and practicing professionals. Teachers can use the information to plan for future professional growth, and students can use it to analyze their abilities and the quality of the education that they are receiving.

DESIGNING A PROFESSIONAL DEVELOPMENT PROGRAM

You should be able to design a personal program of professional development in special education.

Much of the professional development of teachers occurs in a rather haphazard fashion. Although almost all special educators are members of professional organizations and attend inservice training programs, they may participate only when it is convenient or when attendance is required by school administrators. Few professionals systematically appraise their needs and develop a plan to meet them. The pressures of work, home, family, and social obligations often relegate professional development to a position of low priority. Although almost everyone has said, "I must learn how to do this" or "I must learn more about that topic," the time and the initiative are frequently lacking.

One reason for this desultory approach is that the subject of professional development is seldom approached systematically. To use time and resources efficiently, it is necessary to design a specific plan and carry out its activities. This process should involve a number of activities, including those illustrated in Figure 7–1.

To use this model to guide professional development activities, you would begin with the task described in the first element of the model, "Develop and maintain your philosophy," and proceed in sequence through the others. The long block at the bottom simply indicates that you must continually evaluate, revise, and refine your program if your approach to professional development is to remain flexible.

In the following pages, we will describe seven steps you can take to develop and implement such a plan. You should note, however, that the success of your plan will depend on three suppositions: (1) that you will apply the principles described in a systematic fashion;

FIGURE 7-1   Professional Development Model

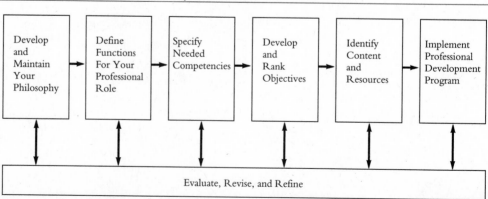

(2) that you will analyze your abilities and needs; and (3) that you will maintain the initiative to conduct the required activities. If you follow these three rules, you should be able to develop a program of professional development that will meet your needs.

Step One: Develop and Maintain Your Philosophy

The first step involves developing a personal philosophy of special education. A *philosophy* can be defined as "an integrated personal view that serves to guide the individual's conduct and thinking" (Good, 1959, p. 395).

Why is a personal philosophy so important?

The development of a philosophy is very important; as the definition implies, it can serve as the conceptual foundation for all professional activities. In most teacher education programs, however, little attention is paid to it. Although many programs expose students to a variety of philosophical viewpoints, and attempts are often made to encourage students to adopt the philosophy held by the program's faculty, usually little emphasis is placed on students' developing their own philosophy.

Rarely are students or professionals asked to articulate their philosophy of special education. As Tymitz (1983) found in her research, the results of such inquiries are not very encouraging. She studied the philosophies of 40 special education teachers. There was general agreement among the teachers that teaching effectiveness is enhanced when one operates with a clearly formulated philosophy; unfortunately, however, most of those interviewed were unable to articulate one. As a result of her study, Tymitz recommended that increased attention be devoted to this important topic in teacher preparation programs.

It is very difficult to design guidelines for the development of a philosophy because so many variables are involved. A person's philosophy is a reflection of his or her values, ethics, logic, aesthetics, and perceptions of knowledge, reality, and truth. There are, however, four criteria that everyone can use in the development of a philosophy, regardless of philosophical orientation:

1. Develop your philosophy to the point that you can articulate it concisely for other professionals. You should also be able to explain it to parents and other people who may not have training in special education.
2. You should be able to defend your philosophy. This entails understanding which aspects of the philosophy can be supported with logic and facts and which aspects are derived from your values.
3. Be flexible. You should be receptive to new information and be willing to modify your philosophy in light of new experiences.
4. Demonstrate your philosophy by applying it in your personal and professional life.

How can a person develop a philosophy of special education?

If you meet these criteria and share with other special educators a commitment to improving the quality of life for exceptional children, your particular philosophical orientation is of no great importance.

In developing your philosophy, the following questions may help you focus on some of the basic issues:

- What are the responsibilities of society in providing for exceptional children?
- What are the responsibilities of the professionals concerned with the welfare of exceptional children?

- What should the relationship be between the special and general educator? How should they interact?
- What are the goals for the group of exceptional children I am working with?
- What theories of learning and instruction do I subscribe to and use in working with exceptional children?
- What is my position on issues such as normalization, human rights, institutionalization, mainstreaming, sterilization, individualized instruction, intelligence testing, genetic counseling, abortion, behavior modification, professional accountability, etiologies, labeling, and other contemporary issues?
- What is my rationale for doing each of my professional activities in one way rather than another?

Many other questions could be posed about the roles of schools and other agencies, about the education profession, and about specific teaching techniques. Many of these are reflected in the questions that appear in the margins of this book. If you cannot answer a question or are dissatisfied with your answer, involve yourself in experiences that will permit you to develop or refine your thoughts about the subject of the question.

Experience shows that the most competent special educators are those who have a well-developed philosophy. They are the most effective teachers, they have the most self-confidence, and they are the most comfortable and secure in their professional activities. The first priority of those who do not have a solid philosophical base should be to develop one. The information in this book should give you a good start in developing your philosophy of special education.

One point deserves to be reemphasized: It is not enough merely to be able to articulate your philosophy; you must be able to demonstrate it in your life as well. It is hypocritical to articulate one philosophical position and act according to the dictates of another; unfortunately some people do just that.

This teacher's philosophy of special education calls for educating children who have disabilities with those who do not have disabilities.

Step Two: Define Functions for Your Professional Role

What roles are generally performed by special education personnel?

The second step in designing a professional development program involves defining the functions for your particular professional role. In a provocative article that examines special education as a profession, Birch and Reynolds (1982) describe special education roles at five different levels. According to these noted authorities, the first level consists of teachers in the regular grades who teach exceptional children integrated into their classes. Second-level personnel are special educators and paraprofessionals who work full-time in individual schools in a variety of settings, including self-contained special classes and resource rooms in which exceptional children spend a portion of their days. These specialists frequently collaborate with the regular class teachers. At the third level are the specialists who perform their roles on a school district-wide or regional basis. These personnel serve as supervisors, administrators, psychologists, educational diagnosticians, parent educators, behavior analysts, consultants on learning problems, teachers of braille, physical therapists, and in many other capacities. Fourth-level personnel work at the college and university level to prepare the personnel at all other levels. Finally, fifth-level personnel are those who engage in research and development activities that generate new knowledge and procedures for the improvement of special education services.

At this point in your education, you may have decided which levels represent your short-term and long-term career goals. Typically, undergraduate students plan to teach children at level one or two. A master's degree student may hope to become a resource teacher or diagnostic-prescriptive specialist at level two or three, while a doctoral candidate might express interest in the roles at level four or five.

Even though students know which role they want to assume when they graduate, they frequently pay too little attention to the specific functions involved in that role. It is not uncommon to hear students who are about to graduate expressing concern about their ability to assume the role they have been preparing for. Part of the reason for their concern, of course, is that they are suddenly faced with reality. Of equal importance, however, is that they never really took the time to analyze the specific tasks or functions that they would be required to perform after they assumed a new position. The student who has made the effort to identify the responsibilities required will not be caught unprepared to assume these responsibilities.

Let us assume that you are interested in becoming a resource teacher for children with mild learning and behavior disorders. One of your most important activities would be to identify the tasks you must be able to perform to do your job successfully. You could do this in a number of ways. You could talk to resource teachers and experts, and observe resource teachers at work. You could research the job in the library. The result might be a list of the tasks the resource teacher must be able to do, like this one (Blackhurst, McLoughlin, & Price, 1977):

- Assess learner behavior.
- Design and implement instructional programs.
- Select and use instructional materials.
- Manage the learning environment.
- Provide for the needs of children with sensory and physical impairments.
- Initiate resource teacher programs.
- Implement due process safeguards.
- Work effectively with parents.
- Maintain student records.
- Demonstrate appropriate professional behavior.

Although this list might not apply to all resource teaching arrangements, it does provide a general guideline for the job's responsibilities. If you were already a resource teacher and planned to stay in that position, you would simply list your job's responsibilities.

Step Three: Specify Needed Competencies

Once the responsibilities of the job are defined, you should ask yourself two questions: (1) Which responsibilities am I completely unprepared for? (2) In which do I need additional experience? The answers would provide the general topic areas for your professional development program.

The next step is to determine what competencies are needed in each of the topic areas. As part of this process, you would also discover more detailed information about the general responsibilities identified in the previous step. This would be accomplished by determining what competencies are involved in each general area of responsibility. To continue with the example begun in the previous section, let's examine some of the competencies associated with each of the functions required of a special educator serving as a resource teacher. A complete list of these competencies can be found elsewhere (Stephens, Blackhurst, & Magliocca, 1988).

What competencies should special education resource teachers have?

ASSESSING LEARNER BEHAVIOR. Special educators must be able to use assessment procedures to identify exceptional children. They must also be able to use in-depth diagnostic procedures to identify the educational strengths and weaknesses of children in each major area of instruction. Because many published tests are inappropriate for exceptional children, special educators must also be skilled in informal assessment and in direct observation of student behavior.

DESIGNING AND IMPLEMENTING INSTRUCTIONAL PROGRAMS. Once the child's educational needs have been assessed, the special education teacher must design the child's instructional program. Objectives must be written, and the instructional tasks to be performed must be analyzed. Instructional methods must be selected and implemented, and student performance must be monitored.

SELECTING AND USING INSTRUCTIONAL MATERIALS. The variety of instructional materials available has grown dramatically in recent years. The quality of these materials varies considerably, however, and the special education teacher must be able to evaluate them and select the most effective. Teachers must know how to use a variety of instructional materials, audiovisual equipment, and other technology.

MANAGING THE LEARNING ENVIRONMENT. A major responsibility of the special educator is to provide individual instruction. To do so, the teacher must be able to manipulate the many variables in the learning environment. The teacher also needs to develop rapport with students and use such management techniques as preventive discipline, behavior modification, active listening, contingency contracting, verbal and nonverbal signals, and precision teaching.

PROVIDING FOR THE NEEDS OF CHILDREN WITH SENSORY AND PHYSICAL IMPAIRMENTS. Special educators frequently work with children who have impairments in vision, hearing, speech, or physical functioning. They must be able to modify their instructional approaches to accommodate the special needs of these children. For example, they need to know how to use special assistive and adaptive equipment, how to safely lift and transfer children with physical disabilities, how to deal with seizures, and how to provide emotional support.

IMPLEMENTING RESOURCE TEACHING PROGRAMS. Because exceptional children are increasingly being educated in the regular classroom, the resource teacher must be able to collaborate with the regular classroom teacher on ways to modify instructional programming to improve the integration of these children into the regular class. The sharing of materials, approaches, equipment, and ideas is required. The ability to coordinate schedules and the services of ancillary personnel is also an important skill.

IMPLEMENTING DUE PROCESS SAFEGUARDS. Special education teachers and school systems are considered legally responsible if the rights of exceptional children or their parents are violated. It is therefore important to have a firm understanding of local, state, and federal laws, regulations, and guidelines that affect special education programs. Great care should be exercised in protecting student and parent rights, and special educators should carry liability insurance to cover them in the event of an inadvertent violation. Such insurance is available through professional organizations such as the Council for Exceptional Children.

WORKING EFFECTIVELY WITH PARENTS. Good parent-teacher interactions are especially important in the education of exceptional children. Children can be educated more efficiently if parents reinforce what happens at school, or they may progress slowly if parents and teachers work at cross-purposes. Therefore, it is necessary to keep communication channels with parents open and maintain a good rapport. Parent conferencing skills are particularly important.

MAINTAINING STUDENT RECORDS. Accurate, up-to-date records are an important tool in the development of the IEP required by federal law. Teachers should be able to collect, organize, and maintain records of academic performance. It is especially important to maintain a system for evaluating student performance using direct measurement and behavior charting. Teachers must also respect the confidentiality of student records.

DEMONSTRATING APPROPRIATE PROFESSIONAL BEHAVIOR. Special educators should be able to develop an educational philosophy and demonstrate it in their professional activities. They should be able to facilitate the activities of others in a sensitive, humanistic fashion. They should also be flexible and receptive to educational change. Furthermore, they should conduct their professional activities in an ethical fashion. These general principles provide the foundation for effective teaching.

Most of the competencies just discussed would be equally applicable to general education teachers. Just as exceptional children resemble other children in more ways than they differ from them, special education teachers resemble general education teachers in many of their responsibilities. Special educators generally have a greater depth of knowledge and more specific skills because they are typically required to take more courses as part of their formal education programs. In addition, they may have responsibilities such as operating resource rooms and providing consultation services, and they have been trained to teach children who present more difficult educational problems.

The development of a competency checklist to analyze your ability to perform various competencies is explained in *Teaching Mainstreamed Students,* a text on integrating children with disabilities into regular classrooms, by Stephens, Blackhurst, and Magliocca (1988). You might find it interesting to set up a competency checklist to keep track of progress during your educational career. Such a checklist could also be used to analyze the extent to which your formal courses and practicum activities are helping develop these competencies. If deficiencies are found, you might be able to design independent studies to rectify them.

Step Four: Develop and Rank Objectives

How can priorities for professional development activities be established?

Once you have determined which competencies you need to work on, you should develop objectives to further guide your professional development efforts. Some competencies will have been stated clearly enough in the previous step that it will not be necessary to make them more specific. For example, a competency involved in working effectively with parents is "Be able to conduct parent conferences." This description alone might be explicit enough to direct activities for some people. For others, however, it may still be too general, in which case it would be necessary to break it down into more specific areas of interest. You might ask questions such as these:

1. How can I establish rapport with parents?
2. Are there general rules for what I should or should not do in conferences?
3. What are some of the common concerns of the parents of exceptional children?
4. How can I make constructive criticisms of parents without being threatening?
5. What should be done when parents obviously disagree with each other about what should be done with their child in a particular situation?

Such questions can be used to develop very specific program objectives. Some people require more specific objectives than others. More experienced persons typically prefer to use relatively general objectives, because they are familiar with the task and with their own professional strengths and weaknesses. What is most important is that the list of objectives be specific enough to provide an orientation for future activities. Once the list is defined, you can then set priorities for accomplishing each.

It also is important not to overlook development in areas for which objectives are difficult to establish, such as affective development or experiential learning. An example of an experiential development activity would be sitting in on another teacher's classes or observing an interdisciplinary meeting to assign staff to a particular student. Activities of this sort might provide insight into personal behavior or into the circumstances that affect an educational situation.

Step Five: Identify Content and Resources

Once you have identified your professional development program's objectives and established priorities, your next step is to identify the materials you will need to attain the objectives.

An obvious source of information is other people, including colleagues, supervisors, people from related professions, university professors, and librarians. Many state and local agencies can provide information, including those concerned with health and mental health, education, rehabilitation, and welfare. Private agencies such as associations for retarded citizens, sheltered workshops, and clinics are also valuable sources. A list of agencies you can contact for information is included at the end of several chapters in this book.

A number of federal agencies can provide valuable information, particularly about the federal resources available to support services to exceptional children. These include such agencies as the President's Committee on Mental Retardation, the President's Committee on Employment of the Handicapped, the Secretary's Committee on Mental Retardation, the National Institutes of Mental Health, the Office of Child Development, and the Office of Special Education Programs in the federal Department of Education.

Another source of information is the reference section of most college libraries. References relevant to working with exceptional children include *Exceptional Child Education Resources; Mental Retardation Abstracts; Deafness, Speech, and Hearing Abstracts; Language and Language Behavior Abstracts; Psychological Abstracts; Education Index; Current Index to Journals in Education;* and *Dissertation Abstracts.*

What is ECER?

Of the above sources, *Exceptional Child Education Resources (ECER)* is probably the best starting place. *ECER* is part of the Educational Resources Information Center (ERIC), which supports a number of information clearinghouses, each dealing with a different educational subject. *ECER* is a journal that contains abstracts of literature on special education. It has a number of interesting features that permit rapid searches for information. By using *ECER* and its abstracts, you can quickly determine which articles contain the information that is of greatest concern to you. Customized searches with a computer can also be performed to rapidly scan the large amount of information in *ECER* to locate literature relevant to a particular inquiry. Most major university libraries store the ERIC documents, and many will conduct computer searches for a nominal fee. More recently, ERIC documents can be retrieved from CD-ROM discs that are accessed by computer.

A number of on-line databases are available by subscription to people who have microcomputers. Users gain access to these databases via telephone lines that are hooked into a computer. Searches on topics ranging from special education literature to evaluations of microcomputer software can be conducted. The reference department at a college or university library should be able to provide information about such services.

Whatever source you use to find information, it is important to know exactly what you are looking for. Librarians and people who work in agencies are best able to deal with specific requests. An important tool in making specific requests is the *Thesaurus of ERIC Descriptors,*

This teacher is using a microfilm machine to read a document located while researching a topic in the ERIC files.

TECHNOLOGY IN ACTION

Linda Lewis is an undergraduate special education major who is taking a course on methods of teaching students with learning disabilities. She has a class assignment to write a term paper on the research that has been done on procedures for using computers to teach spelling to students with learning disabilities.

Linda goes to the College of Education library, where she decides to use the Educational Resources Information Center (ERIC) system to locate articles that relate to her topic. At the reference section of the library, she obtains the *ERIC Thesaurus* and selects several descriptors that she believes will help her conduct a search for the articles she will need for her term paper. The terms she picks are *spelling, research, learning disabilities,* and *computer.*

At the librarian's counter, Linda checks out a compact disc, called a CD-ROM, that contains the database of professional literature contained in the ERIC system. She inserts the disc into the CD-ROM drive that is attached to a computer and starts the ERIC program.

She presses the F4 function key on the computer keyboard and the word FIND: appears on the screen. She types *spelling* and, after a short pause, the computer informs her that there are 1881 articles in the ERIC system on the topic of spelling. She then types *spelling and research;* the computer indicates that there are 964 articles on spelling and research. To further narrow her search, she types *spelling and research and learning disabilities and computer.* The computer then informs her that there are 13 articles containing all of those descriptors.

Linda then presses another key, which displays abstracts of the 13 articles. The abstracts contain the citation for the publication in which the original article appeared. A brief abstract provides information about the article. Linda scrolls through the abstracts and determines that three of the articles don't seem to be appropriate for her term paper. She presses another key and the remaining ten abstracts are printed. She then goes to the section of the library that contains the professional journals and retrieves the articles so that she can do an in-depth analysis of those reports.

In a matter of approximately 15 minutes, Linda was able to locate ten articles specifically related to the topic of her term paper from a vast array of articles on spelling. The CD-ROM and computer technology that she used saved her many hours of performing a manual search of the literature.

which is available in most college libraries. This publication lists and defines many terms, some very broad and some very specific. These terms, or *descriptors,* are used in most organizations and reference works to organize and retrieve information. The use of appropriate descriptors will increase the speed and improve the results of most searches for information.

As an aid to locating information, a list of professional journals dealing with specific special education categories has been provided at the end of many chapters in this book.

Step Six: Implement Professional Development Program

The implementation of your professional development program will depend on your objectives and personal circumstances and will, as a result, be highly subjective. Some general guidelines, however, apply to everyone.

First, professional development activities should be approached systematically. If you have carefully followed the previous steps, you should know what the results of each activity will be. This will be helpful in planning a program of coursework, in selecting inservice or continuing education programs, and in developing independent enrichment or study activities.

Second, you should join the appropriate professional organizations, most of which publish journals, conduct training courses, and provide other benefits. These organizations have been responsible for many of the recent improvements in the education of exceptional children through legislation, litigation, and professional negotiations.

These members of the Council for Exceptional Children are planning a conference at which special education teachers will obtain training to improve their skills.

What is CEC?   Although there are many specialized professional organizations that cater to different special educators, one cuts across all categories: the Council for Exceptional Children (CEC). This organization has more than 54,000 members, of which 9,000 are undergraduate and graduate students preparing for special education careers. Founded in 1922, CEC serves professionals in the United States and Canada who work with exceptional children and adults. CEC has local chapters in every state and province in those countries. Many colleges and universities also sponsor student chapters. Every CEC member receives two major journals. *Exceptional Children* is the official journal of the CEC. It is published six times each year and contains articles, position papers, research reports, and other material related to the state of the art and the future of special education. *Teaching Exceptional Children* is published four times each year and contains articles related to the actual instruction of exceptional children.

CEC provides a number of other services to its members. These include national and special topical conferences and searches of the ERIC database. The group also has a strong voice in the legislative arena on issues facing special education.

Most CEC members join one or more of the eighteen divisions that focus upon specific exceptionalities or a unique aspect of special education. These divisions are identified in the box on page 230. Most of these divisions also publish their own professional journal, newsletter, or both. Student memberships are available at reduced rates. It is a good idea to join CEC and become active in the organization as a student. Not only will you receive the professional journals, you will be eligible to participate in the other benefits of the organization. Student members also receive a copy of *STEPS,* a newsletter only for students, which features tips on student teaching, interviewing for jobs, and legislative updates. Membership in an organization such as CEC also indicates to potential employers that you are actively engaged in professional activities.

DIVISIONS OF THE COUNCIL FOR EXCEPTIONAL CHILDREN

Council of Administrators of Special Education (CASE)
Council for Children with Behavioral Disorders (CCBD)
Division on Career Development (DCD)
Division for Children with Communication Disorders (DCCD)
Division for Early Childhood (DEC)
Council for Educational Diagnostic Services (CEDS)
The Association for the Gifted (TAG)
Division for Learning Disabilities (DLD)
Division on Mental Retardation (CEC-MR)
Division on the Physically Handicapped (DPH)
Division for Research
Pioneer Division
Teacher Education Division (TED)
Division for the Visually Handicapped (DVH)
Technology and Media Division (TAM)
Division for Culturally and Linguistically Diverse Exceptional Learners (DDEL)
Division of International Special Education and Services (DISES)

Another benefit of belonging to a professional organization is related to mental health. Special education teaching is difficult work, and it provides different challenges than teaching in the regular classroom. For example, teachers of children with severe and profound disabilities must often be content with small improvements in their students' skills, and they must have a high tolerance for repetitive teaching and for working with children who may have very limited language skills. What is more, the special education teacher frequently works without interacting with other special education colleagues. As a result of these factors, the teacher often becomes frustrated and depressed. The author knows of many teachers and administrators who have reported feeling "burned out" after a few years of work in this type of situation. Participation in a professional organization can provide you with opportunities to interact with colleagues who may have similar problems; it gives you the chance to share ideas, discuss alternative methods of dealing with situations, and receive support for your efforts.

Step Seven: Evaluate, Revise, and Refine

A program of professional development should be flexible. This means that as a professional, you must continually evaluate your activities and plans and make modifications when necessary. But how do you engage in self-evaluation? Two procedures are suggested. The first involves examining each of the competency statements in this chapter and asking yourself how well you can do the task and whether you should learn how to do it better. Alternatively, you could obtain the forms used to evaluate student teachers or regular school teachers and assess your performance in each of the areas mentioned.

Although the emphasis has been on self-evaluation, you can also benefit by enlisting the assistance of colleagues. CEC Professional Guideline 2.4.2 states: "Professionals participate in the objective and systematic evaluation of themselves, colleagues, services, and programs for the purpose of continuous improvement of professional performance" (*Code of Ethics and Standards for Professional Practice,* 1983, p. 208). Some school systems have successfully implemented a system of peer assistance in planning and evaluating professional development programs. Such a system provides mutual support and fosters greater objectivity in evaluating the elements described in this chapter.

Conclusion

The best special educators engage in an ongoing program of professional development. They become involved in their professional organizations, participate in continuing education programs, and constantly look for ways to improve their professional performance. To begin an effective development program, you must analyze your strengths and weaknesses, locate the necessary resources and information, and efficiently manage time, energy, and personal resources.

Above all, special educators should subscribe to the code of ethics established by the Council for Exceptional Children to govern the professional behavior of its members. The eight points of this Code are listed below.

Is there a code of ethics for special educators?

Special education professionals:
1. Are committed to developing the highest educational and quality of life potential of exceptional individuals.
2. Promote and maintain a high level of competence and integrity in practicing their profession.
3. Engage in professional activities which benefit exceptional individuals, their families, other colleagues, students, or research subjects.

The best special education teachers are those who are continually involved in activities to improve their professional skills. Systematic planning, self-evaluation, and initiative are necessary for a successful professional development program.

4. Exercise objective professional judgment in the practice of their profession.
5. Strive to advance their knowledge and skills regarding the education of exceptional individuals.
6. Work within the standards and policies of their profession.
7. Seek to uphold and improve where necessary the laws, regulations, and policies governing the delivery of special education and related services and the practice of their profession.
8. Do not condone or participate in unethical or illegal acts, nor violate professional standards adopted by the delegate assembly of CEC. (*Code of Ethics and Standards for Professional Practice,* 1983, p. 205)

The seven-step model described in this chapter represents a practical approach to professional development. The use of this model, accompanied by adherence to the CEC ethical standards, will produce highly competent professionals. The ultimate benefit, of course, will be improved services to exceptional children and adults.

PROBE 7-1   Designing a Professional Development Program

1. T F Traditionally, the professional development of special educators has proceeded in a highly systematic fashion.
2. The first step in designing a program of professional development is to develop a _____.
3. List the five levels of roles performed by special education personnel.
4. T F The competencies needed by special education teachers are significantly different from those needed by teachers in regular education.
5. The specification of _____ follows the identification of competencies in the steps for designing a professional development program.
6. The most useful reference journal for special educators is _____.
7. _____ is the most comprehensive professional organization for special education personnel.

SUMMARY

1. Special educators have a responsibility to design educational programs that continue to develop their professional competence after they have completed their formal education.
2. A well-developed philosophy serves as the foundation for success as a special educator.
3. Professional development efforts are most successful if they are approached on a well-planned and systematic basis.
4. The seven steps in designing a professional development program are to develop a philosophy; define functions associated with your professional role; specify competencies needed to perform those functions; develop and rank objectives for meeting the competencies; identify content and resources related to the objectives; implement the program; and evaluate, revise, and refine your efforts.
5. Special educators should become active members of their professional organizations and abide by the standards and ethics of their profession.
6. The major professional organization for special educators is the Council for Exceptional Children.

TASK SHEET 7   Continuing Professional Development

Philosophy of Special Education

This text has been designed to help you begin developing a philosophy of special education. Start a notebook that you can use to jot down ideas about your philosophy as you progress through the book. Be prepared to write your philosophy of special education when you reach the end of the book. Refer to the section on philosophy in this chapter if you need some ideas about how to get started on this assignment.

CEC Membership

Join the Council for Exceptional Children. For a membership application, write to CEC at 1920 Association Drive, Reston, VA 22091. If you are a student, you can join at reduced rates.

Library Study

Locate three articles in the library that might help you develop a philosophy of special education. Write a one-page abstract of each, concluding with a paragraph about your reactions to the article. Here are the names of some journals in which you can find articles about these topics:

Exceptional Children
Journal of Special Education
Journal of Special Education Technology
Remedial and Special Education
Teacher Education and Special Education
Teaching Exceptional Children

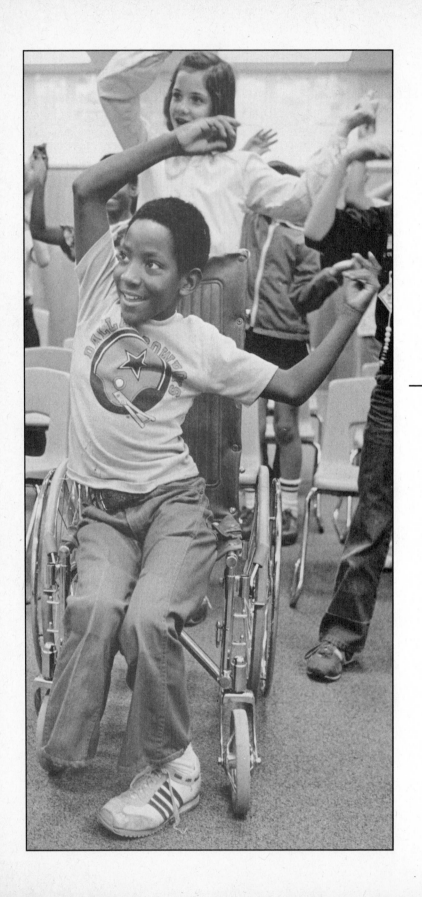

Communication and Sensorimotor Disabilities

An understanding of the principles, issues, and forces that underlie current special education practices serves as a base for studying the various categories of exceptionality. In Part II we consider children who have impairments and disabilities that affect their ability to communicate, hear, see, or move about in their environment. Communication problems are commonly labeled communication disabilities, and problems with hearing, vision, and mobility are jointly referred to as sensorimotor disabilities.

Communication and sensorimotor disabilities are usually easier to identify and can be measured more precisely than learning problems. For example, while a child's visual acuity or hearing loss can be measured accurately, it is far more difficult to assess such internal characteristics as intelligence or learning ability. It does not automatically follow, however, that the needs of children with communication and sensorimotor disabilities are easier to meet. At the same time, these disabilities do not necessarily affect children's intellectual abilities, and the great majority of these children can learn and do school work as well as their peers. We trust you will remember this throughout your professional career.

Although communication and sensorimotor disabilities are presented in separate chapters, you should be aware that children often have more than one type of disability. Determining the nature and intensity of the disability, which is the first step in developing educational and treatment programs, is often difficult. Assessing and educating children

with communication and sensorimotor problems can involve a number of specialists who must be able to work together as a team. The teacher's role is supplemented by the expertise of speech-language pathologists, who evaluate hearing; peripatologists, who offer mobility training to those who are blind; physical therapists, who assist in the rehabilitation of those with physical disabilities; and medical personnel, such as orthopedic surgeons, psychiatrists, and nurses. Special education teachers themselves must also have highly specialized skills. Teachers of students who are deaf, for example, may have to know sign language, and teachers of those who are blind should be able to use braille. Decisions about the education and treatment of a child with cerebral palsy may involve a physician, special education teacher, speech-language pathologist, physical therapist, nurse, principal, and the child's parents.

As these chapters make clear, cooperation among specialists is very important. It has been our experience, however, that some special education teachers, particularly those who are just beginning their careers, occasionally feel intimidated by physicians and other specialists. You should remember that just as physicians are specialists in the treatment of children's physical needs, teachers are specialists in meeting children's educational needs. A professional, well-prepared teacher has no reason to feel intimidated.

In the next four chapters, we take up the study of communication and sensorimotor disabilities.

STUDENTS WITH COMMUNICATION PROBLEMS

More children are potentially affected by communication problems than by any other type of disability. We begin Chapter 8 by defining and differentiating speech and language development. Then, we describe four types of language disorders and three types of speech disorders. We close with a discussion of the roles of the speech-language pathologist and classroom teachers in providing therapeutic services to children with communication problems.

STUDENTS WITH HEARING LOSS

In Chapter 9 we first consider the nature of sound and how we hear. Five conditions that can lead to hearing loss are also explained, and the procedures used by audiologists to measure hearing loss are described. We discuss the effects of hearing loss and examine the treatments and classroom techniques currently in use.

STUDENTS WITH VISUAL IMPAIRMENTS

At the outset of Chapter 10 we describe the characteristics and identification of visual impairments. We analyze six disorders of the visual system and consider their implications for classroom practices. At the end of the chapter, we describe some current educational programs and methods used to teach those with visual impairments, including braille and other aids.

STUDENTS WITH PHYSICAL AND HEALTH-RELATED DISABILITIES

The physical and health-related disabilities that may be encountered by regular and special education teachers are described in Chapter 11. In our discussion of the disabilities that affect children's health, we place particular emphasis on cerebral palsy and epilepsy. The significance of architectural barriers and the ways to eliminate them are also explained.

Brian, 10, has a history of stuttering that began at age 4, with an abnormal number of repetitions of whole words. His parents were told that Brian would outgrow his stuttering and that they should pretend it didn't exist. Brian recalls that even at age 4 he knew there was something wrong, but thought it was so bad that even his parents didn't want to talk about it. For a while there were periods when his speech was normal, but slowly he began to stutter consistently with shorter periods of fluent speech. By the second grade, he knew he was a stutterer. He answered in class, but it got harder to say words. In the third grade he said that he was too embarrassed to ask for help, but wanted to do something about his speech.

At his worst, Brian tended to prolong the initial syllables of words, force his eyes closed and have periods of 2–3 seconds when he was silent after beginning a word. He often repeated the sound "umuh, umuh, umuh" before initiating a sentence. Like many stutterers, however, Brian didn't stutter all the time. He had no difficulty when he sang in his church's children's choir or in unison prayer responses.

Now that he's in a public school, Brian is receiving speech therapy for his stuttering. His speech-language pathologist is working closely with his classroom teacher and parents. The first goal of therapy is for Brian to understand how his speech changes when he stutters. The long-range goal is for Brian to initiate activities that will lead to fluent speech. Precious years have been lost, during which time Brian has been practicing his stuttered speech. However, Brian is beginning to use fluent speech more purposefully and feels less victimized than ever before.

Andrew's mother spent countless hours training him to repeat the letters of the alphabet, name body parts, and identify colors, hoping that he would be able to begin school in a regular kindergarten with other 5-year-olds. Andrew learned his letters and words but repeated them in a parrotlike way. A speech-language pathologist assessed Andrew's language and communication skills and found that Andrew was not using his memorized words appropriately, could not understand simple directions and comments, and did not know the meaning of the words he used. With counseling, Andrew's family was helped to realize that before his language could be meaningful, Andrew had to learn what words meant.

Currently Andrew is in a class for children with developmental disabilities that is providing Andrew with the enriched experiences he needs to learn language. Teachers and parents have been taught to accept Andrew's attempts to communicate, to associate words and phrases with objects and actions, and to teach Andrew words for things that he needs and is interested in. With their focus on teaching words for the things Andrew wants to communicate, Andrew is beginning to use language meaningfully.

8

Students with Communication Problems

Barbara K. Culatta and Richard Culatta

The two children described on the facing page represent success stories in the diagnosis and treatment of speech and language problems. These success stories are examples of how individuals' lives can be enhanced with assistance from trained professionals.

Most of us can speak as easily as we breathe. Our children can tell us quite clearly of the worlds they are discovering as they grow. Although we may have to struggle for words occasionally, and sometimes cannot express ourselves precisely, we can almost always make someone understand what we are trying to say. However, for millions of people in our country, communication is a difficult process. Their communication problems change their lives and hamper their ability to be productive.

This chapter is about the processes of communication and the causes and effects of communication problems. When we are finished, you should know how to tell the difference between speech and language; how speech and language are acquired; how to define a "communication problem"; what the characteristics of some common speech and language disorders are; and what some treatment options are.

It is important to remember that communication problems, like the other disabilities discussed in this book, cannot be considered in isolation. The ability or inability to communicate can have an effect on every other area of development. You should always regard a child's problem in the context of the whole child.

DEFINITIONS AND TERMINOLOGY

You should be able to define language as well as differentiate between speech and language.

What is language? According to the American Speech-Language-Hearing Association (ASHA), language is a complex and dynamic system of conventional symbols that is used for thought and communication. A language system is rule-governed in that a group of people agree on how to let symbols represent or stand for environmental events. Once an individual has knowledge of language rules and shares that knowledge with others, the system can be used to communicate experiences, ideas, and feelings.

A language system consists of several kinds of rules: phonological, grammatical, semantic, and pragmatic. **Phonological** rules specify what speech sounds, or phonemes, can occur in a given language and how these sounds can be combined to form words. In order for words to be differentiated, the phonemes in a language must be distinguishable. *Mat* and *bat* can be used to stand for different things because the phonemes *m* and *b* differ enough not to be confused. While speech sounds mark distinctions between words, they are not meaningful in and of themselves.

Semantic rules refer to the way in which meaning is signaled. Meaning comes from letting one thing symbolically stand for another. Words gain meaning because they stand for real events. The word *dog* refers to certain kinds of furry, four-legged animals that serve as pets. The individual's understanding of the relationship between the word *dog* and a particular group of domestic animals gives the word its meaning.

Grammatical rules refer to the way in which words and parts of words are combined. In English, the sentence "Mary hit John" has a different meaning from "John hit Mary" because our grammar dictates that the actor is stated first in an active sentence. Likewise, we have a rule that states that verbs, such as *walk,* can be changed to past tense by adding *-ed* to the end.

Pragmatic rules are concerned with the way language is used to communicate in various contexts. They deal with mechanisms for achieving needs and desires. For example, a polite *request* of "Could you open the door?" is likely to be more effective than a *command* in achieving assistance in certain situations. Pragmatics also deals with mechanisms for governing conversational exchanges. For example, in most conversational contexts, speakers and listeners follow certain conventions for initiating and relinquishing turns. In certain situations, however, the speaker rarely relinquishes control and the turns are not evenly distributed, for example, in lectures and sermons. The selection of messages to fit desired objectives and contextual demands constitutes pragmatics.

How does speech differ from language?

Speech and language are related, but they are not the same thing. **Speech** is the overt manifestation of oral language. It is the medium by which oral messages are carried or transmitted. Speech includes the making and combining of phonemes and the rhythm and vocal quality with which those sounds are produced.

Language consists of the meaning or intent of a message. Language symbols (words and grammatical rules) acquire meaning only when the speaker or listener knows their relationship to real events. Language symbols do not have to be transmitted through speech. Gestures that have some agreed-upon relation to environmental events—such as American Sign Language gestures used by people who are deaf—can provide an alternative way to transmit messages. Similarly, messages can be transmitted by writing or typing, pointing to words on a display, or selecting symbols pictorially represented on a computer screen. Electronic devices can be used to transform symbol selections into synthetic speech. Pointing to symbols depicted on a computer screen, for example, can activate a voice synthesizer that will generate electronic speech. People who are not capable of acquiring speech can learn to transmit messages by one of these alternative symbol systems. While alternative symbols can be used to transmit messages, it is critical that the people using them know what events they stand for. The transmission of symbols is worthless without an understanding of their meaning (Blackstone, 1986).

A person can have speech without language, language without speech, or a speech problem that doesn't interfere with language. A person who has speech without language can fluently imitate words in a parrotlike manner, and in a pleasant vocal quality, but not know what they mean or be able to use them to communicate. An individual who has language without speech would know the meanings of words but not be able to produce the sounds necessary for their transmission. In this chapter we will discuss both language disorders and speech disorders.

Characteristics of Communication Disorders

There have been many attempts to describe what constitutes a communication disorder. A **communication disorder** exists when an individual is not effective in achieving his or her needs and wants or experiences distress when doing so (Dore, 1986; Fey, 1986; Van Riper, 1978). A person can have a communication disorder for a variety of reasons. People may have defective structures that make it impossible to produce normal speech. They may have neurological damage that makes it impossible to communicate efficiently. Their emotions may affect how they communicate. Some speakers cannot learn the intricacies of communication. For others, their communication problem is the result of some combination of these reasons.

How can you tell when a person has a communication problem?

Perhaps the best way to determine whether a person has a communication problem is to consider the following questions:

1. *Can I understand this person?* This is the simplest judgment you will have to make. If you cannot easily understand what someone is saying, that person may have a communication disorder. It must be kept in mind, however, that very young children should not be expected to make themselves fully understood when communicating to unfamiliar listeners in unfamiliar contexts.

2. *Does this person sound or appear peculiar when speaking?* A 200-pound adult male who sounds like a 9-year-old girl and a person who has a flat, expressionless manner of speaking have communication problems. Likewise, a person who has distracting mannerisms that interfere with the message has a problem. These mannerisms might include unnecessary or unexpected movements of the lips, nostrils, arms, or legs.

3. *Is the communication inappropriate to the situation?* A child who repeatedly asks strangers, "How much money do you have?" or the child who speaks out in class may not be sensitive to the demands of the situation. Likewise, we do not expect a baseball manager to say, "I strenuously object to the judgmental process to which the umpire has subjected me." The point is that we normally select words to fit the demands of a given situation. A speaker unable to do this may have a problem.

4. *Can the person achieve desired intentions?* A child who has an understanding of events but who cannot request the items needed for taking a bath, relate what happened when the dog ran away, formulate questions about changes in a routine, or provide reasons for delaying bedtime may be having difficulty achieving intended effects. Similarly, a school-age child who does not have the ability to comprehend explanations and directions will not be able to meet the demands encountered in class. Communication problems are most readily characterized by how successful the individual is in functioning in the environment.

5. *Is the speaker damaging the speech mechanism?* A cheerleader or rock singer may irritate the tissues of the vocal mechanism by continual screaming or singing too high. Like most other parts of the body, the organs used in speech can be misused. Although diagnosis of physical abuse can be made only by specialists, listeners can often detect signs of strain. Teachers should always refer to professionals any children thought to be injuring their voices. Referral for screening by qualified professionals hurts no one, but overlooking a symptom can have disastrous consequences.

6. *Does the speaker avoid communicating or suffer when attempting to communicate?* Some individuals talk very little or will respond only to direct questions. This may result from limited communication skills or feelings of inadequacy that can make communication even more difficult. Other people are considered normal communicators but suffer emotionally as a result of imagined shortcomings. A listener cannot usually determine how a person feels about efforts to communicate. Communication problems that stem from or contribute to low self-esteem do not always have obvious symptoms and are among the most difficult to treat.

7. *Is the speaker's manner or style of communication noticeably different from others in his or her own community?* In our multicultural society, there are many communication differences from one community to another. For example, in some communities, the verb *be* is often used to signal future events. Different uses of this verb, or any other linguistic feature, would have to be viewed in relation to the individual's own cultural standards (Owens, 1992).

8. *Is the person's communication appropriate to his or her chronological or developmental age?* A 6-year-old child who comprehends language at the 4-year-old level will experience difficulty in school if the language demands are geared toward normally achieving 6-year-olds.

Obviously, as in so many aspects of evaluation, implicit or explicit norms for age and grade level are used to make judgments of adequacy. We will discuss some of the expected norms for communication in this chapter. Like other behaviors, communication skills are developed over time. How old a person is when a judgment is made is often critical information used to help determine what communication skills should be expected.

How many people have communication disorders?

PREVALENCE. More than 24 million people in this country, about 10 percent of the population, have a speech, language, or hearing disorder (ASHA, 1991). This percentage of communication disorders varies by age group, with a preponderance being exhibited among children and elderly populations. It is difficult to isolate the numbers of people with communication disorders since such disorders are frequently intertwined with other handicapping conditions. Autism, mental retardation, hearing loss, and learning disabilities are all correlated with speech-language difficulties.

Development of Communication

At what ages do children develop different language concepts?

Children acquire most language and speech skills between the ages of 12 months and 6 years. There are, however, aspects of language that continue to develop throughout the school years.

Children usually begin to attach meaning to words when they are 8 to 10 months old. At this age the child probably does not know the meanings of individual words, but may associate whole phrases with routine experiences. For example, a child may anticipate going to bed when the phrase "night-night time" is heard. Children at this age also associate words or phrases with specifically taught gestures. For example, a child may begin waving upon hearing "bye-bye" or begin clapping upon hearing "pat-a-cake."

At about 12 months, children begin to comprehend what people say. They may attach meaning to frequently used names of pets, family members, and favorite objects. They may understand simple language that has been frequently associated with everyday routines, such as feeding, bathing, or dressing. They may also understand language that is presented with gestures or that refers to immediately occurring events. For example, a child may respond to the command "Blow" when presented with hot food at dinnertime, or to the command "Be easy" when petting the family cat. At this stage children make additions to their language by relying on knowledge of events and routines to figure out the meanings of words and phrases they hear.

At about the same time, somewhere between 9 and 15 months, children begin to produce their own first words. The first words learned generally refer to familiar people or objects, for example, *mama, bottle,* or *doggie.* The child of this age often fails to generalize words to new situations. For example, a child may produce an approximation of *bottle* to request a baby bottle, but not to refer to bottles that contain juice or are seen in the grocery store. While the child's words are limited at this age, communication is achieved by other means as well, namely, the use of gestures, facial expressions, and vocalizations.

Between 12 and 18 months, the child begins to use words to refer to classes of objects and events instead of just specific events. The word *hot* may refer to a stove, a hot cup of coffee, and freshly popped popcorn. The word *ball* may refer to lots of different balls. By 18 months, children are communicating quite successfully with a large core of single words. This communication is enhanced with gestures, facial expressions, and contextual support.

Until approximately 2 years of age, children typically use single words and may acquire a fairly large single-word vocabulary. Although children use words in lots of different contexts, some words will probably be used inappropriately. For example, they may overgeneralize and call all animals "doggie" or all men "da-da." Overgeneralization indicates that children are trying to figure out the relationship between words and experiences. It also indicates that children know that words stand for classes of events, not just specific events. When children reach this point, they can begin to use words to communicate in any situation.

At about 2 years of age, children begin to learn to combine words. First attempts are simple two-word phrases, in which the words are combined, not at random, but in an organized manner. The child now begins to use word order to signal relationships between people, actions, and objects, with sentences like "Daddy go," "Mommy eat," or "Eat cookie."

At 2½ to 3 years, children begin to use three-word combinations. In this stage, they can specify more than one relationship in a single phrase. The child who says, "Get big cookie," is not only requesting a cookie, but also specifying its size. These children can combine words in all sorts of creative ways. With an increasing vocabulary and knowledge of how to signal relationships among people and objects, a child can even talk about events never before experienced.

Once children have learned to specify most basic meanings in simple word combinations, they begin to include some less common and crucial parts of grammar in their sentences. For example, at about 3 years of age, the child begins to use words such as *is* and *the* in very simple, grammatically correct sentences. The process of adding grammatical parts of speech—such as word endings, pronouns, and helping verbs—continues gradually until the age of 5 or 6.

While acquiring rules for combining words into sentences, children are continuing to develop vocabulary. In fact, vocabulary development is a never-ending process. By 2 years of age, children have learned words that stand for familiar objects, actions, and simple events, such as *car, get, cup, milk, shoe, no, more, all gone, put away, pick up, bear, chair, look,* and *come.* At 3 years of age, they learn words for less common actions; for example, the word *press* or *scatter* might be added to a child's vocabulary. The 3-year-old child also begins to add words that describe particular aspects of experiences, such as *same* or *soft.* Children's word productions sound much like the adult version by age 3 because they are able to produce most speech sounds including /m/, /p/, /h/, /n/, /w/, /k/, /g/, /d/, and /t/.

By the time most children are 6 years old, they produce words with later developing sounds, such as /s/, /r/, /l/, /ch/, /sh/, and /z/, and have mastered language well enough to produce grammatically correct sentences with some adultlike structures. They know the meaning of many spatial and quantity terms, such as *first* and *every;* they can rhyme words; and they can separate words into component syllables, a skill necessary for learning to read. They are also learning to use language to understand explanations, obtain information, and relate experiences. These language skills are necessary for performing successfully in school, because much of what is learned in school is acquired through language. In school a child must understand what is said without reliance on situational or contextual support, because the teacher often talks about things that are not immediately present (Wallach & Miller, 1988).

Language development does not stop in the early school years. Toward the end of the primary grades children gain comprehension of figurative language and metaphors, such as "He's walking on thin ice" (Nippold & Sullivan, 1987). They also develop the ability to reflect on how language works. These children understand that one word can have two meanings, and they can identify sentences that don't make sense. In addition, increased linguistic demands in the classroom require the comprehension of longer passages that express complex interrelated ideas.

It should be emphasized that the ages quoted may vary considerably with a particular child. Some children pass through these stages slower or faster and still develop normal speech and language. The age ranges provided can be considered benchmarks, and any child who develops significantly slower should be closely monitored by trained professionals. There is no penalty for unnecessarily checking the normal developmental process, but ignoring a real problem can have serious consequences.

Language development is a fascinating and complex subject. If you'd like to develop a greater understanding of it, we suggest *Language Development* by Owens (1992), *Normal Language Acquisition* by James (1990), *The Development of Language* by Gleason (1989), and *Language Disorders and Language Development* by Lahey (1988).

PROBE 8-1   Definitions and Terminology

1. _____ percent of the people in the United States have communication disorders.
2. T F   Only people who sound unusual have communication problems.
3. Children can produce words with the /s/ sound by age _____.
4. Match each linguistic event with the approximate age at which it typically occurs.

Linguistic event	*Age*
_____ three-word combinations	a. 10–12 months
_____ use of words	b. 5–6 years
_____ two-word combinations	c. 12–18 months
_____ comprehension of familiar words and sentences	d. 24 months
_____ meaning attached to abstract words *(every, each, last)*	e. 30–36 months

5. T F   Speech and language are basically the same.
6. T F   Speech is part of language.
7. T F   Language is part of speech.
8. T F   Speech is acquired prior to language.
9. T F   Language and speech are developmental processes.
10. T F   By age 6, children should be producing sentences that are grammatically correct.
11. T F   Language develops at the same rate for all children.

LANGUAGE DISORDERS

You should be able to identify some causes of a language disorder.

Of all the communication problems we will discuss, language disorders are the most complex and have the most serious educational effects. Language disorders vary as much as the people who have them. Language disorders can occur in children or adults and are often associated with other disabilities such as mental retardation, autism, and hearing impairment.

Etiology of Language Disorders

Language disorders can result from traumatic brain injury caused by either a blow to the head, as in an automobile accident, or some internal damage, such as bleeding. Language disorders can also result from brain damage that occurred either before or during the birth process. Those language disorders that result from a traumatic insult to the brain are referred to as *aphasia,* while those that are identified as the child develops are referred to as *developmental language disorders.*

What causes aphasia?

APHASIA. Aphasia generally affects individuals who have already mastered language. It can be caused by a traumatic head injury, tumor, or stroke (hereafter termed a cerebral vascular accident, or CVA). A CVA, the most common cause of aphasia, occurs when the flow of blood to the brain is suddenly interrupted by a blocked or burst blood vessel. When the flow of blood is interrupted, brain tissue does not receive oxygen and is very quickly destroyed. If the injury from either a CVA or an insult to the head (e.g., from a fall or gunshot wound) occurs in an area of the brain that deals with communication, a language disorder may result.

What is the difference between receptive and expressive aphasia?

Aphasia is a general term used to describe a variety of problems. It is a breakdown in the ability to formulate, recognize, and retrieve language symbols (Holland, Swindell, & Reinmuth, 1990). Testing may reveal the language difficulty to be either primarily *receptive* or *expressive* in nature. People with receptive aphasia have difficulty understanding what is said to them. They may hear well enough but do not understand the meanings of words. Difficulty understanding spoken language often leads to an inability to talk coherently. The experience of a receptive aphasic is somewhat analogous to communicating in a foreign language that you understand very poorly. This analogy is not completely appropriate, however, because in a foreign language, you would be able to trust your understanding of the words you had learned, whereas someone with aphasia cannot.

People with expressive aphasia have difficulty in using language to send messages. They often do not lack the physical ability to speak but have trouble formulating and editing what they are trying to say. They have difficulty recalling specific words and the grammatical constructions necessary to convey messages. Even though they can recognize words when they hear them, they may not be able to recall or remember them on their own. Their situation is somewhat analogous to yours when you have words you can't recall at the "tip of your tongue," only to a much greater extreme.

DEVELOPMENTAL LANGUAGE DISORDERS. Children who have difficulty acquiring language are said to have a developmental language disorder. Developmental language disorders are believed to stem from neurological damage that occurs before or during birth. It is often difficult to determine the specific site or nature of the injury because brain damage is often subtle and undetectable. It is also difficult to identify a cause because environmental factors can play a role.

While most language problems are believed to have a neurological base, language learning can be impeded by poor language models. To learn language effectively children must be talked to frequently, be given the opportunity to communicate freely, and be exposed to language that is just a little more complex than the language they are already using. It is also important that children be talked to about the events and desires that are most meaningful to them. Parents who are responsive to their child's communicative attempts will facilitate language learning, while unresponsive parents can compound deficits in the language learning process (Hart, 1985).

How can the environment contribute to language disorders?

Nature of Language Learning Deficits

What factors can contribute to language disorders?

Although the cause cannot be identified, each child's unique pattern of language difficulty can be characterized. A child's performance will vary depending on the aspects of language and the language learning process that present difficulty. A child may vary in hearing ability, conceptual knowledge, cognitive processes, knowledge of language, language comprehension, language production, communicative ability, and motor skills. An individual child's language difficulty can be characterized by describing how the child performs in each of these areas.

HEARING. A child who has difficulty hearing will most likely have difficulty acquiring language. This is because a child who cannot hear words will have difficulty attaching meaning to them. A hearing loss may interfere with language learning because, in many cases, the signal the child receives is distorted. A child who cannot distinguish between *top* and *stop*, for example, will have difficulty associating those words with their appropriate meanings. Background noise or a distorted auditory signal would make the process of recognizing words even more difficult for those who have a hearing loss, particularly in the absence of situational or gestural cues. The problems of the person who is deaf or hard-of-hearing will be discussed in much greater detail in Chapter 9.

How can conceptual knowledge affect language development?

CONCEPTUAL KNOWLEDGE. Sometimes children do not have sufficient knowledge of the environment to communicate about events and experiences. Limited conceptual or world knowledge will limit children's ability to communicate because they cannot linguistically symbolize what they do not know. In other words, children who have limited conceptual knowledge will have difficulty representing or symbolizing events (Owens, 1991).

In very young children, conceptual or world knowledge is reflected in how they manipulate or act on objects. Limited knowledge is reflected in such primitive actions as mouthing and banging objects, while more explicit knowledge is reflected in functional object use and the replication of environmental events in play. The more sophisticated a child's play, the greater knowledge of the world the child possesses (Westby, 1988).

For children who have already acquired some language, limited conceptual knowledge may be reflected in difficulty with conveying details about events or conveying how parts of events are related. A child without knowledge of how a grocery store operates will have difficulty describing or conversing about how stores get their merchandise, how the items appear on the shelves, and how workers get paid. Children's discussions will be dependent upon or limited by their world knowledge.

Linguistic expectations are related to a child's level of conceptual knowledge. A 6-year-old child whose knowledge of the world is at the 2-year-old level, for example, should not be expected to exhibit language beyond the 2-year level. More specifically, a child who does not know that socks go with shoes or that lids go with jars will have difficulty learning the meaning of the term *go together*. Since language is used to represent knowledge of events, the expected level of language achievement should be commensurate with that knowledge. This does not mean that children with developmental delays cannot benefit from language teaching; rather it means that expectations should be commensurate with the child's level of world knowledge. Parents of children with developmental delays often correctly believe that their children's other problems would be less handicapping if they could only understand more. They sometimes do not recognize, however, that the child's conceptual delay is limiting the level of language learning (Lund & Duchan, 1988; McLean & Snyder-McLean, 1978).

How can cognitive processes affect language acquisition?

COGNITIVE PROCESSES. The cognitive processes of attention, memory, and perception influence the acquisition of language. Deficits in these processes may be reflected in language learning difficulty.

Attention. Attention is the ability to focus on a stimulus to the exclusion of other stimuli. Attention to language symbols and to the aspects of the environment they stand for is necessary for learning language. Attention is also necessary for comprehending messages and for engaging in relevant conversational exchanges (Brinton & Fujiki, 1989). Any student who daydreams during lectures realizes the need to attend in order to obtain information. Any child with particular difficulty attending will have difficulty learning language, comprehending language, or engaging in meaningful conversations.

Memory. Two types of memory are involved in language learning, long-term memory and short-term memory. Long-term memory refers to the storage of information. Knowledge of language rules is stored in long-term memory. Short-term memory, sometimes referred to as immediate or working memory, is the active holding and processing of information for brief periods of time (Wagner & Torgesen, 1987). Short-term memory is involved when a child hears a word and retains it while searching for its meaning in long-term memory. Short-term memory is also involved in the comprehension of longer messages, such as explanations and directions. The meaning of the first part of the message must be held in short-term memory while the subsequent parts are being processed. Additional information on the relationship between memory and language skills can be obtained from Torgesen (1990), Brady and Schankweiler (1991), and Butler (1984).

Perception. Perception is the ability to recognize regularities in events. To learn language, children must be able to recognize regularities in the environment and associate them with regularities in the language signal (specific words, word endings, and word orderings). Children who cannot notice similarities in environmental events will have difficulty symbolizing them (Kemler, 1983). In order to learn the word *off,* for example, the child would have to be able to notice the regularity that exists in removing burrs from a dog's fur, peeling the sticker off a wall, rubbing a smudge off a window, and pulling off a sock. To learn the word *still,* a child must be able to recognize the word *still* in sentences such as "I *still* hear that music" or "You *still* have a cut," and associate the word with the notion of continuation. Children who associate whole phrases with whole events instead of the isolating aspects of events—as is the case of many children with autism—may have perceptual problems that interfere with language learning (Bernstein & Tiegerman, 1989).

KNOWLEDGE OF LANGUAGE RULES. A child's knowledge of particular words and grammatical rules is stored in long-term memory. Children vary in the number and type of language rules they know (Bernstein & Tiegerman, 1989). Some children demonstrate knowledge of a great many complex rules, while others demonstrate knowledge of only a few basic ones. Knowledge of language is demonstrated when a child can identify or create examples of language rules. For example, a child of 2½ who is able to pick *one* block from a group and place it *under* the table is demonstrating knowledge of the words *one* and *under*. This knowledge is necessary for comprehending the words when they are heard in sentences. Knowledge of word and grammatical rules is also necessary for producing them in a meaningful way. Children cannot be expected to recall or retrieve from memory words that they do not know.

COMPREHENSION OF LANGUAGE. When children hear words in phrases or sentences they search their knowledge of language, stored in long-term memory, for the appropriate meanings. Language comprehension is that ability to attach meaning to linguistic messages (words, sentences, and passages). When a child has difficulty understanding age-appropriate explanations, directions, and statements, a comprehension deficit exists. A comprehension deficit would be evident in a 3-year-old who demonstrates age-level conceptual knowledge but who cannot understand such statements and commands as "Your ball is dirty" and "Find me something you can ride on."

What are some symptoms of a language comprehension problem?

Comprehension problems may be evident in school-age children who have difficulty answering questions and following directions in class. These children might watch or imitate other children's responses for cues. Some of these children can understand words or sentences they hear in isolation but have difficulty processing connected utterances. Such children may not be able to adequately paraphrase passages, retell stories or explanations, or relate new information to their own experiences. Their understanding may also tend to rely on situational and gestural cues to a greater extent than that of other children. Children with comprehension problems will need to have messages presented slowly, clearly, and repeatedly (Lasky, 1991).

PRODUCTION AND RETRIEVAL OF LANGUAGE. While we all understand more language than we can produce, for some children the production of language is particularly difficult (Lahey, 1988). They may not be able to retrieve, recall, or summon words from their memories, or they may produce sentences that are primitive and clumsy. When a child's ability to produce words and sentences is significantly below his or her ability to comprehend those same words and sentences, a deficit in production exists. For example, a child who can comprehend at the 3-year level (i.e., words such as *big, little, chin, socks, hers, heavy, one, all,* and *under;* and simple sentences such as "The baby's not sleeping," or "Mommy is cutting the cake"), but can express only a few words is experiencing specific difficulty in the retrieval or production of language. Children with retrieval problems have trouble selecting appropriate words to use even though they know the meanings of the words they are seeking (Wiig, 1990). Such a child may be unable to recall the word *split* when trying to describe a narrowly cracked pencil but would understand the word *split* when it is spoken.

COMMUNICATIVE FUNCTIONING. Children's communicative functioning can be characterized by the mechanisms they use to convey intentions (obtain desired needs and outcomes) and the effectiveness of their conversational exchanges. Of interest is how the child achieves specific functions and satisfies needs—that is, what the child does to obtain information, comment, request, and express feelings. Also of interest is the child's ability to relate experiences, maintain a topic of conversation, engage in turn taking, and select messages to fit contextual demands (Owens, 1991).

Preschool children vary in the effectiveness with which they communicate. Even children who have limited language abilities may communicate reasonably well nonverbally. Nonverbal communicative behavior consists of gestures, actions, and facial expressions that are produced with the intent of affecting another person's behavior. A child may put an adult's hand on a jar lid to have it opened, for example. The ability to communicate is also reflected in the child's participation in turn-taking games, such as handing a toy back and forth or playing peek-a-boo or pat-a-cake games (Owens, 1992).

School-age children also vary in their ability to follow and participate in conversations. In school, children are expected to maintain exchanges about less familiar topics that are removed in time and space (Nelson, 1984, 1991). They are expected to elaborate and expand on a topic by adding relevant information. The more removed the topic is from immediate or personal experience, the more demanding the task and the less likely it will be for students to relate their own statements to prior remarks. Children who frequently change topics or introduce irrelevant statements may be having difficulty with the conversational process (Damico, 1991).

How do motor skills relate to speech and language?

MOTOR SKILLS. A child must be physically able to send messages to have normal oral language. Even if a child knows words and grammatical rules, verbal communication will not be possible unless the child can physically shape and transmit sounds. As mentioned earlier, children who have motor deficits that preclude oral communication can be given an alternative mode of sending linguistic signals. With an alternative system of communication, the sending of speech sounds is augmented with a device that transmits messages visually (e.g., electronic keyboards, computers, visually displayed symbols) or transforms selections into synthesized voice output.

Figure 8-1 reviews some of the deficiencies in personal resources that can hinder a child's ability to communicate. While the emphasis in this section has been on the identification of elements that influence the development of language, much of the framework is also applicable to the deficits displayed by adults with aphasia. Individuals with aphasia also vary in cognitive

FIGURE 8-1   A Functional Approach to Exceptionality: Factors Influencing Communication

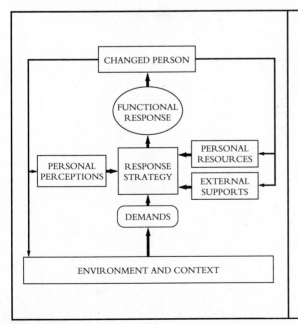

PERSONAL RESOURCES

A child who exhibits a communication disorder may lack certain *personal resources* important to communication. For example:

- A hearing problem may make it difficult for the child to understand good speech models.

- Lack of knowledge about common concepts may impair the child's ability to communicate about those concepts.

- Inability to pay attention may detract from the child's ability to obtain information.

- A memory deficit may interfere with the child's ability to remember language concepts.

- Perception problems may hinder the ability to recognize similarities and differences in concepts.

- Difficulty in comprehending spoken language can delay the production of speech and language.

- Inability to perform the motor activities associated with the production of speech can create communication problems.

processes, knowledge of language, language comprehension, language production, communicative ability, and motor skills.

Identification and Assessment

How can individuals with language disorders be identified?

Children and adults have language problems when they cannot adequately receive and send messages about their world. To thoroughly understand an individual's language disorder, we must assess those aspects of language and the language learning process that were presented in the previous section. Since individual children have problems with different aspects of language, the assessment results must be carefully analyzed before an appropriate strategy of language intervention can be formulated. There is no shortcut to thorough, effective language assessment.

While it is the role of the speech-language pathologist to perform the assessment, there is much that the other team members can contribute. Input is obtained from teachers and parents, and samples of the child's communicative behavior are collected in natural settings. The speech-language pathologist, in collaboration with the teachers, will also determine the influences that language problems are having on classroom performance and the child's response to curriculum demands.

Since the majority of children with speech or language problems are in regular classrooms, teachers can assist in the identification of children who are having difficulty with linguistic demands. To identify children who are exhibiting language deficits, the teacher should use questions such as those listed in Table 8-1, which are designed to guide the detection of academic-related language problems. In order for children to be successful in school, teachers should be alert at all times for language within the curriculum that is too difficult for children to process. The following resources can help you ensure that the language children encounter in the classroom is appropriate: Silliman and Wilkinson (1991); Grunewald and Pollak (1990); Nelson (1991); and Wallach and Miller (1988).

TABLE 8-1   Guidelines for Identifying Language Deficits in the Classroom

1. Does the child have difficulty following complex and novel directions, understanding explanations, or obtaining information?
2. Does the child have difficulty restating explanations?
3. Does the child require demonstrations in order to understand class directions?
4. Does the child dominate or change the topic of conversation or have difficulty participating in a conversation when the topic is not very familiar?
5. Does the child repeatedly relate the same idea or events?
6. Does the child have difficulty telling stories in a sequenced, organized fashion?
7. Does the child have difficulty defining words?
8. Does the child have difficulty connecting pronouns with their nouns?
9. Does the child appropriately use connective words (e.g., *then, so, because, if,* and *therefore*)?
10. Can the child detect errors or misinformation in other people's speech?
11. Does the child attend to verbal directions and explanations?
12. Can the child answer detailed questions about information presented verbally and relate that information to his or her own experiences?
13. Can the child respond to language better when the teacher reduces the rate of speech, repeats, or breaks up information into smaller units?
14. Can the child predict the outcome of stories, or retell novel stories in his or her own words?
15. Can the child retell novel experiences with detail?

Education and Treatment Provisions

In the classroom, language is the primary means of acquiring content; the child must use language to learn the meanings of new words and to gain information. Some children may not be able to perform academic tasks unless vocabulary, directions, and explanations are simplified. In addition, reading and math performance are dependent on adequate language abilities.

Can language
problems affect
academic
achievement?

Children with language deficits often experience difficulty reading. And, many reading problems are believed to be language-based (Velluntino & Shub, 1982; Mann, 1986; Roth & Perfetti, 1980; Catts & Kamhi, 1986). Since reading is a visual representation of oral language, children must have vocabulary and comprehension skills mastered in order to understand what they read. In addition, children must know that words can be segmented into individual sounds in order to decode or "sound out" written words (Velluntino & Shub, 1982; Perfetti & Roth, 1980; Mann, 1986). Phonetic decoding that is particularly slow or laborious may impede comprehension. When the student struggles at the sound or word level, there may be limited cognitive resources available for comprehension (Perfetti, 1985).

Math, as well as reading, is highly dependent on good language skills (Baker & Baker, 1990; Whitin, Mills, & O'Keefe, 1990). Children cannot be expected to solve word problems without having adequate vocabulary and comprehension skills. Students who have language deficits will have difficulty understanding how numbers are verbally manipulated to obtain correct solutions. Try to imagine the handicap students are under if they do not understand such words as *equal, least,* and *more than.* Try also to imagine how difficult it would be to solve a problem without an understanding of the problem situation. Comprehending the problem entails determining "who has what, and who is doing what to whom," or, in other words, understanding the events that are linguistically depicted in the problem statements. To truly function in math, the student must be able to affix values to numerical terms and understand the situation that is described in the problem statements.

SUGGESTIONS FOR FACILITATING LANGUAGE. In this section we will discuss procedures for facilitating the acquisition of language. Although written with children in mind, these procedures are also useful in working with adults with language disorders. The remediation process should incorporate the following principles:

What principles
should be included
in the remediation
process?

1. *Be responsive to the child's spontaneous communicative attempts.* A child learns language by engaging in communicative interactions. If the communication partner is responsive to the child's communicative acts, the language learning process will continue. Being responsive to communicative attempts includes repeating the content, carrying out the child's requests, listening intently, and commenting on the message. Constant and direct correlation of attempts to express ideas can only lead to negative reactions in a child who may already feel communicatively inadequate.
2. *Modify input.* The language trainer should slow speech, pause, repeat, and use gestures as well as intonation to convey meaning. Modified input makes the language signal of more interest to the child. It also permits the child to make associations between words and the aspects of the environment for which they stand.
3. *Provide opportunities for the child to communicate.* A child who communicates a great deal is actively practicing communication skills. As with other aspects of development, practice contributes greatly to skill attainment. There are several mechanisms for increasing the frequency with which the child communicates:
   - *Do not anticipate needs.* A child who is given paper without crayons or who is provided with only a small amount of juice at a time is encountering the need to communicate.

- *Arrange for unusual or novel events to occur.* A child who sees a box of cereal taped to the wall is likely to want to share that event and seek information about it. Language can also be evoked by engaging in such actions as "inadvertently" throwing away toys, wearing clothes that are too big, and trying to eat soup with a fork.
- *Arrange for the child to convey information to others.* In the cafeteria the child may be asked to direct others to their seats, describe the menu, convey the location of utensils, and report the acceptability of the food to the cook. Many opportunities to convey experiences to others can be created throughout the day.
- *Provide the child with choices.* During a snack activity, the child can decide what to drink, where to sit, whether to use a napkin or paper plate, and who should be responsible for cleaning up. Each decision requires communication.

4. *Model or expand the child's language.* Once the child's communicative attempts are accepted, the trainer or parent can expose the child to a slightly better or more complete way of saying the same thing. If the child says, "I want the big, big ball," the trainer can say, "Yes, you want the *very* big ball."

5. *Talk about things of interest to the child.* Provide language input that corresponds with the child's own intentions. Say the same thing that the child is saying, but in slightly different ways. A spilled drink at lunchtime can become a beneficial language learning experience.

6. *Provide many clear examples of language rules.* If children are learning the word *break,* they should be exposed to many repetitions of the word associated with many examples of things that break. For example, they might break cookies and crackers, encounter objects that keep falling apart, break spaghetti in order to glue the pieces on a picture, and break carrot sticks for lunch. Similarly, a child who is ready to learn the word *equal* should be provided with lots of experiences comparing quantities of supplies, snack items, arts and crafts materials, and toys. As training progresses, the contexts are varied and the child is exposed to many naturalistic examples.

7. *Use words the child already knows to teach new words.* For a child who doesn't know the meaning of the word *blend,* the trainer can say, "When we blend, we make things go together smoothly." The trainer can then give examples such as, "When we blend *b* and *e* together, we get *beeee,* not *buh–eee.*" By hearing the meanings of new words explained in simple ways, children easily expand their vocabulary.

8. *Reduce complexity.* Language that is too complex is of little or no benefit to the child. To be optimally effective, the language signal must be only slightly more complex than the child's current level of functioning. Thus, if the child is at the single-word level of language development, communication partners should be speaking in simple two-word combinations.

9. *Tell and retell stories and experiences.* Practice in telling and retelling stories and experiences provides the child with the opportunity to relate events in an organized manner. At first, a child's retelling can be prompted with questions and pictures. Children may need several exposures to a simplified version of a story or event before trying to relate it entirely on their own.

10. *In cases where the child has a profound hearing loss or a motor disability, communicate in the child's mode or form of communication.* Children with hearing losses often need to be exposed to several modes of communication, for example, words paired with gestures or signs. Likewise, a child who is using a picture board to communicate will need to have others acknowledge or incorporate that communication board in interactions that occur in all sorts of natural contexts.

Above all, to facilitate language, we must allow children to communicate. It is also important to expose the children to language models at their level and to provide language training in natural, highly interactive contexts.

PROBE 8-2   Language Disorders

1. T F   The specific cause of a developmental language disorder is often difficult to identify.
2. A language disorder acquired as a result of traumatic brain injury is known as _____.
3. T F   Children who are deaf are likely to have language problems.
4. Name six factors that affect the acquisition of language.
5. Identify the aspects of a child's behavior that must be considered when assessing language.
6. Why is it important to modify and reduce the complexity of language input when speaking to a child who is in the process of learning language?

SPEECH DISORDERS: PROBLEMS WITH ARTICULATION

You should be able to describe different types of articulation disorders.

Speech disorders can disrupt communication as seriously as can language disorders. Of course, speech and language disorders do not necessarily occur in isolation; children often have difficulty with both speech, the transmission of words, and language, the attachment of meaning to words. In this chapter, we discuss three broad kinds of speech disorders: (1) articulation disorders, or problems with speech-sound production, (2) voice disorders, and (3) fluency disorders. This section deals with articulation disorders; voice and fluency disorders will be described in later sections.

Four Types of Articulation Disorders

What are four types of articulation disorders?

Articulation disorders are present when a speaker has difficulty producing the sounds of language. People with articulation problems tend to make four kinds of mistakes when speaking: substitutions, omissions, distortions, and additions. The acronym SODA may help you remember them.

Substitution is the replacement of one sound for another. For example, a person who says "thoup" for *soup* is substituting a /th/ for /s/. Saying "wabbit" for *rabbit* is another example. **Omission** is leaving a sound out altogether; for example, saying "oup" for *soup* or "abbit" for *rabbit*. **Distortion** is the replacement of an acceptable sound with one that does not exist in our language. The slushy Daffy Duck kind of /s/ sound is a good example of distortion. **Addition** is the inclusion of a sound that does not normally occur in a word; for example, saying "warsh" for *wash* or "atpple" for *apple*.

What is the difference between organic and functional articulation disorders?

Articulation disorders can be either organic or functional. Organic problems are caused by a physical or neurological abnormality. Functional problems are not the result of physical problems; they are problems for which an organic cause cannot be determined and may result from improper learning (Newman, Creaghead, & Secord, 1985).

Organic problems can be regarded as having three components. First, there is the symptom—what we hear. With the child who says "toup" for *soup*, we hear /t/ substituted for /s/. Second, there is a physical explanation for the symptom. The child who says "toup" is not directing a stream of air between the tongue tip and the roof of the mouth. Third, there is an underlying neurological or physiological reason for the symptom's physical explanation. In this case, it might be cerebral palsy, resulting in poor muscular control. Functional problems also have symptoms that have physical explanations, but they lack an underlying physiological cause.

The difference between these two kinds of problems affects how we attempt to remediate them. Obviously it would be pointless to ignore a serious organic problem when planning speech therapy.

Etiology of Articulation Disorders

ORGANIC CAUSES. Among the most common organic causes of articulation disorders are **cleft palates** and **cerebral palsy.**

Cleft Palate. Cleft palates can actually be of three types—clefts of the lip only, clefts of the palate only, or clefts of both the lip and the palate. They are caused by the failure of the lip or palate to grow together during the child's fetal development. Doctors are uncertain why this happens. It occurs during the first three months of pregnancy in one of every 750 live births in the United States (McWilliams, Morris, & Shelton, 1984).

As you can see in Figure 8-2, the palate forms the roof of the mouth and the bottom of the nasal cavity. The front two-thirds is called the hard palate, and the back third is called the soft palate. All but three of the sounds in our language (/m/, /n/, and /ng/) require that the soft palate contact the back of the throat, thereby sealing off the nasal cavity. Many children with cleft palates cannot do this; as a result their speech may be excessively nasal, breathy, and difficult to understand.

Lip clefts usually involve only the upper lip. A cleft may appear on either side of the nose or on both sides.

What is the treatment for cleft palates?

Treatment for clefts and the resulting articulation disorders is a long-term, coordinated effort by a team of speech-language pathologists, doctors, and dentists. The repair of physical structures is undertaken by surgeons. Surgery for cleft lip is usually performed when the child

FIGURE 8-2   Different Types of Clefts: (*A*) Cleft of Hard and Soft Palates; (*B*) Unilateral Cleft of Palate and Lip; (*C*) Bilateral Cleft of Palate and Lip

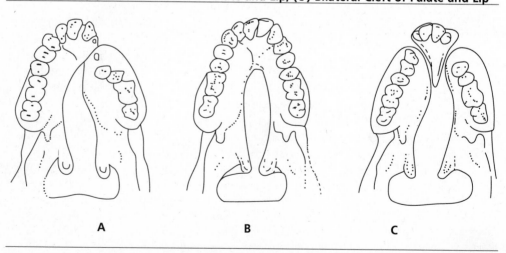

A   B   C

is 1½ to 3 months old. Surgery for cleft palate problems is postponed until the surgeon is certain that it will not alter facial growth. Figure 8-3 shows a patient's surgical result.

Articulation disorders are found much more frequently among those with cleft palates than cleft lips. Unfortunately, surgery alone does not usually lead to normal articulation. In addition to the previously described excessive nasality, those with cleft palates may have trouble making sounds that require the damming up of air pressure, such as /p/, /b/, /t/, /d/, /k/, and /g/. People with clefts need to be taught to take full advantage of the tissue they do have. With effective education some children can be taught to reduce excessive nasality.

Some articulation problems are the result of the soft palate's inability to reach the throat rather than the complete absence of soft palate tissue. When this is the case, the adenoids (tissue located where the back of the throat and the nasal cavity join) are sometimes used to fill the gap. Before the adenoids are removed surgically, it is very important to determine their role in closing off the nasal cavity. Tonsillectomy and adenoidectomy, once the most common operations in pediatric surgery, are now relatively rare as the result of our increased knowledge about the functions of these tissues that were once routinely excised. Careless removal of adenoidal tissue can result in articulation problems that could have been avoided.

Additional information on cleft palates is sometimes available from university and teaching hospitals, many of which maintain cleft palate teams.

Cerebral Palsy. Cerebral palsy, like cleft disorders, is not itself a communication problem; it is, rather, the cause of one. Cerebral palsy is a disorder of muscular activity and coordination that is caused by brain damage. This brain damage impairs the ability to control the articulators (the tongue, lips, soft palate, etc.), which results in an articulation disorder.

FIGURE 8-3   (Left) A Cleft Lip. (Right) Following Corrective Surgery.

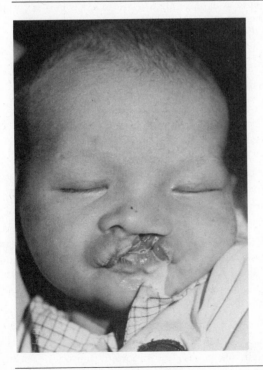 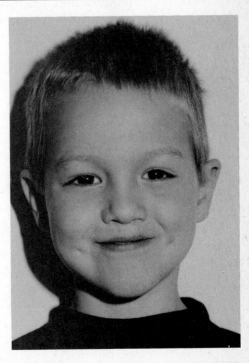

People with cerebral palsy are likely to have slow, labored speech, to articulate words imprecisely, and to slur sounds together or omit them completely. They may also expel air too quickly or not be able to exhale enough air to speak smoothly. One effect is a distortion of the rhythmic patterns we associate with normal speech. Until a listener becomes familiar with these distorted patterns, a person with cerebral palsy may be unintelligible.

People with cerebral palsy speak as they do because they lack the ability to bring together the complex movements necessary for rapid intelligible speech. Normal speakers, on the other hand, make fine rapid adjustments as they combine sounds to formulate words. In fact, we make these adjustments so quickly that we must "cheat" a little to keep up with our thoughts. For example, try saying the sound /p/ as in "pay," and then the sound /p/ as in "play," paying close attention to the different positions of your tongue. You will notice that in saying "play," your tongue anticipates the /l/ sound almost before you finish producing the /p/. Without the ability to make such rapid articulatory movements, the speaker with cerebral palsy may omit the /l/ sound in such words as *play*.

How can people with cerebral palsy compensate for poor articulation?

Although the effects of cerebral palsy cannot be reversed, it is possible to teach a person to compensate for deficits. Most people with cerebral palsy can be helped to become more intelligible, although they may not develop normal articulation. When oral communication is impossible, alternative communication tools, such as the microcomputers and electronic signaling devices referred to earlier, may be the best option. Other aspects of cerebral palsy will be described in Chapter 11.

HEARING DISORDERS. A severe hearing loss will obviously affect a child's ability to learn to articulate correctly. A child who cannot hear an /s/ sound, for example, will have difficulty learning to replicate it.

What causes functional articulation problems?

FUNCTIONAL CAUSES. Functional articulation disorders, as you will remember, are those with no identifiable organic cause. They may be the result of improper learning, short auditory memory span, problems with phonetic discrimination, and many other factors. Research into the causes of functional disorders has not been very fruitful. Unlike many organically caused articulation disorders, functional disorders can often be completely cured. Effective diagnosis and remediation efforts usually result in normal articulation.

Identification and Assessment

An articulation assessment generally entails administering an articulation test, determining stimulability, analyzing a sample of spontaneous speech, and, at times, performing a phonological process analysis.

ARTICULATION TESTING. Most articulation tests require the person being tested to name pictures of objects that contain certain speech sounds. Generally the same sound is tested three times—once at the beginning of a word, once in the middle, and once at the end. Thus, for the sound /s/, a person would name pictures of a saw, a baseball, and a glass while the examiner listened for substitutions, omissions, distortions, and additions.

SPONTANEOUS SPEECH SAMPLE. In addition to using an articulation test, an examiner will listen for errors in spontaneous speech. It is important to listen to a sample of spontaneous speech because sounds are often produced differently in sentences than in isolated words. Some

---

TECHNOLOGY IN ACTION

Art has a severe form of cerebral palsy. The portions of his brain that control many of his voluntary muscles were damaged during a very difficult birth. He is confined to a wheelchair because he cannot walk. His speech is almost impossible to understand, and he has great difficulty controlling the movement of his hands and arms.

There is nothing wrong with Art's intelligence, however. In fact, his teachers believe that he is quite bright. In spite of his difficulties, he learned to read at the same time as other children. Academically, he is at the sixth grade level, which is normal for his age. Art has good receptive language skills; and he understands just about everything that is said to him. Although his expressive language appears to be good, he has a great deal of difficulty communicating because of his poor speech.

Until recently, Art communicated with his teacher by using a specially equipped typewriter. The typewriter had a template over the keyboard with holes in it that corresponded to the positions of the keys. Art hooked his fingers over the holes in the template and pressed the keys. The template kept him from accidentally pressing a wrong key because of the uncontrollable muscle movements in his hands and arms. Although Art was able to type messages this way, it was a difficult and time-consuming process for him. He often typed messages that indicated his frustration with the limitations of this method of communication.

Art's special education resource teacher, Ms. Duke, recently attended a conference on electronic equipment for people with physical disabilities. Upon her return, she persuaded the school to purchase some equipment that was to dramatically improve Art's life.

The school purchased a microcomputer with a disk drive and video monitor, a printer, an Echo speech synthesizer, and a computer software program called the Microcommunicator. A template, similar to the one Art used with the typewriter, was also obtained for the com-

puter. After installation, the Echo software disk was placed in the disk drive and the computer was turned on. A mechanical voice clearly spoke the words, "Hello. I am an Echo speech synthesizer. I can take normal text and turn it into speech."

After presenting a demonstration of its features, the computer asked Art to type in anything and then press the RETURN key. Art slowly typed, "Hello, I am Art and I can talk." He pressed the RETURN key and, amazingly, those words flowed from the speaker.

Art quickly learned that some words had to be typed phonetically in order to be pronounced correctly. Most words, however, only had to be spelled correctly. Any word or sentence that Art could think of could be typed into the computer and "spoken" by the speech synthesizer.

The Microcommunicator program was slightly adapted so that the entries could be "pronounced" by the speech synthesizer. The Microcommunicator permitted Art to store several hundred words, phrases, and sentences that he frequently used. These could be called up and pronounced by a single keystroke, so Art didn't have the laborious job of retyping items that he used frequently. These could also be printed on the printer so that he could compose short messages and notes to his friends. A simple word processor program, called Bank Street Writer, was added to the system so that he could print out his written school assignments.

Art's newly acquired skills have opened immense new vistas for him. Although it takes a little time, he is now able to communicate orally with his teachers and fellow students. His parents have purchased a similar system for use at home. Not surprisingly, Art's grades have improved and his intellectual potential is beginning to be fully realized. When asked about his future, Art recently said (via his speech synthesizer), "I am going to go to college and study computer science. I want to learn how to develop other ways that computers can be used to help people with physical disabilities."

---

people will correctly produce a speech sound when asked to label pictures on an articulation test, but will fail to use that same sound when engaged in conversation.

STIMULABILITY. Once having determined that a person has an articulation problem, the examiner will attempt to determine how readily the individual can produce better sounds with

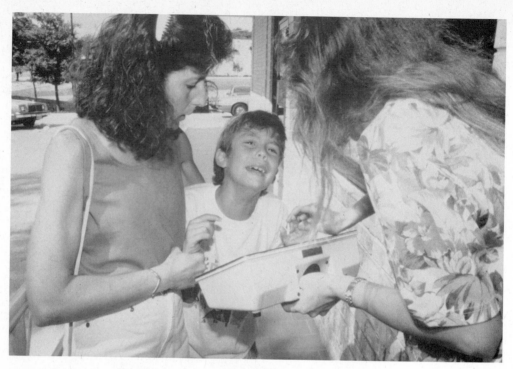

This child is being trained to use an alternate communication device.

imitative support. This is known as stimulability testing. Determining how stimulable an individual is to make a correct sound is often helpful in determining which sound to select as a goal for remediation.

PHONOLOGICAL PROCESS ANALYSIS. A phonological process analysis, often reserved for preschool children who have multiple articulation problems and are difficult to understand, attempts to identify the aspects of sound production that are in error. The underlying theory is that rather than misarticulating individual sounds, children with phonological process errors are using a different rule system. For example, a child may be deleting all final consonants from words rather than deleting only specific final consonants. Perhaps the child is simplifying sound combinations inappropriately, reducing two-syllable words to one syllable, or producing sounds that should be made with the back of the tongue (/k/ and /g/) with the tongue tip instead (/t/ and /d/).

When treating children who have phonological process errors, the goal is to teach the correct rule rather than to teach an individual sound (McReynolds, 1990). Several instruments are available to help analyze children's speech to see if they are using inappropriate phonological rules (Hodson, 1986, Ingram 1981; Kahn & Lewis, 1986).

It is the speech-language pathologist's responsibility to diagnose a child with an articulation problem. Classroom teachers, special educators, parents, and other interested people are helpful in sharing observations with the speech-language pathologist. Correct assessment of articulation errors, however, takes a good deal of skill and practice that comes from specific training.

Education and Treatment Provisions

How does
articulation
therapy aid in the
remediation of
problems?

ARTICULATION THERAPY. Therapy designed to improve speech sound production has traditionally focused on demonstrating the proper positioning of the lips, tongue, and jaw and the direction of the air stream for each error sound. The speech pathologist also models or exemplifies correct production and asks the child or adult to attempt to match or imitate that production. A variety of drill activities are developed to provide opportunities to practice new sounds. The individual practices the sound in isolation, in syllables, in words, in phrases, in sentences, and in conversation, with correct productions being reinforced. The child or adult is then taught to monitor sound production so that the correct sound will be stabilized and transferred to other settings.

When is
augmentative
communication
necessary?

How would motor
capacity and
developmental
level affect
selection of a
communication
system?

AUGMENTATIVE COMMUNICATION. People who have severe speech problems may not have the capacity to produce intelligible words. In such instances, some other form or channel of communication is essential. As previously mentioned, augmentative or alternative communication systems are mechanisms other than speech that assist in the sending of messages. Such mechanisms are not intended to substitute for residual abilities to speak, but rather to be used in conjunction with them (Silverman, 1989). Examples include communication boards with pictures representing objects and actions, computers with synthetic voice output, keyboards for typing out words, and gestures from the American Sign Language.

The selection of a communication system—the symbols used to represent events and the mode used to transmit them—depends on two factors: motor capacity and developmental

This child is receiving therapy from a speech-language pathologist.

level. The motor capacity of the child determines what sort of response requirements can be expected. A child with good manual dexterity may be able to use gestures, to type out words, or to select symbols by pointing. A child with limited use of the hands may have to be provided with a pointing device connected to a switch that is activated by head movements. The developmental level of the child also influences the type of symbols used. Printed words can be used only with children who are able to read. Real photographs rather than abstract line drawings are used with children who have difficulty with symbolism. Pictures of concrete objects and actions (e.g., *eat, drink,* and *shoe*) are used for children who are developmentally young, while symbols for abstract ideas (e.g., *think, guess,* and *know*) are used in systems for children who are higher functioning. The greatest challenge is to select the appropriate system and device, but mechanisms for making such decisions do exist (Shane & Bashir, 1980; Owens & House, 1984; Yorkston & Karlan, 1986).

Additional information on articulation disorders can be found in *Human Communication Disorders* by Shames and Wiig (1990).

PROBE 8-3   Speech Disorders: Problems with Articulation

1. List three characteristics of an organic articulation problem. Put an asterisk next to any characteristic that is also representative of a functional problem.
2. The most common communication problem with speakers who have a cleft palate is _____ .
3. How might cerebral palsy cause an articulation disorder?
4. List the four types of articulation disorders. (Remember SODA.)
5. When would an augmentative communication system be used?

SPEECH DISORDERS: PROBLEMS WITH VOICE

You should be able to identify different types of voice disorders.

Although some voice disorders are the result of changes or abnormalities in the voice mechanism, many problems are caused by abuse of a normal voice. When a normal mechanism is misused, it may show physical signs of abuse. These signs can be seen as the organic result of functional misuse. Men with very high voices and women with very low voices may have organic voice problems that are the result of improper use. Pitch breaks—sudden shifts in pitch that occur primarily in the voices of pubescent males—may have destructive effects if they become chronic. Pitch breaks are associated with growth spurts and rarely last more than six months. Although a period of pitch breaks is normal, a person may develop bad vocal habits in an effort to disguise or avoid them.

How can you determine that a person has a voice disorder?

Psychological or environmental problems can also cause voice disorders. Weak or soft voices may result when people are frequently punished for speaking or drawing attention to themselves. Likewise, a person who speaks in a barely audible voice or in a flat, controlled manner may be attempting to hide powerful emotions. A person who tries to be unobtrusive by rarely speaking or speaking inaudibly may have a serious emotional problem. A person's voice is frequently an accurate indicator of psychological or environmental conditions.

Identification and Assessment

The voice can be evaluated in terms of pitch, loudness, and quality. Unacceptable differences in these areas are considered voice disorders.

How can you determine that a pitch disorder exists?

PITCH DISORDERS. The sound you hear when someone laughs or clears his or her throat is that person's **optimal pitch,** or the sound that can be produced most efficiently with the least effort by the laryngeal mechanism (Reed, 1988). Ideally, optimal pitch is similar to **habitual pitch,** the pitch we use most frequently. When a person's optimal pitch differs significantly from the person's habitual pitch by being too high or too low, a pitch disorder probably exists. Individuals who vary their pitch very little or who speak in very high or low tones may be using a habitual pitch that does not match their optimal pitch. Assessment consists of making comparisons between an individual's optimal and habitual pitch levels.

What are "screamer's nodes"?

LOUDNESS DISORDERS. Inappropriately loud or soft voices are another type of voice disorder. Some loudness problems are caused by the lack of control of the vocal apparatus that results from impaired hearing or cerebral palsy. In some cases, however, excessive loudness may be the result of a family's communication style or involvement in certain activities. Children who have to shout to get attention from their parents or to be heard at a sporting event may learn to speak very loudly at other times. If this continues over a long period, the child may develop "screamer's nodes," growths on the vocal cords that lead to a harsh-sounding voice. It is usually the family, not only the child, that needs treatment in these situations.

How may voice quality vary?

PROBLEMS WITH VOICE QUALITY. Voice quality defects are among the most common and the most difficult to identify and assess. Four of the most common identifiers are excessive or insufficient nasality, breathiness, harshness, and hoarseness.

Nasality problems result from the inability to control the flow of air into the mouth and nasal cavity. As we described in the section on cleft palates, excessive nasality is usually an organic problem and can be measured with instrumentation. Insufficient nasality is the way people sound when they have a cold or allergies. The blockages and swollen tissues associated with those conditions hamper normal resonance and result in a flat-sounding voice. To experience speech produced with insufficient nasality, try saying "Time and tide wait for no man" while holding your nose.

Breathiness is the result of the vocal folds not coming together correctly, which allows air to rush past them without vibrating the folds as it does in normal speakers. The voices of people with breathiness problems have a whisperlike quality because of excessive air flow. This can be the result of callus-like nodes developing on the folds from chronic vocal abuse, or it can be caused by vocal fold paralysis. Breathiness can also result from functional problems and poor vocal habits. This type of disorder can be very distracting to a listener.

Harshness or stridency is usually the result of tension or strain. Some speakers develop harsh voices because they have to strain to be heard at work; others have personality conflicts. The condition can also have organic causes. If eliminating the source of stress does not resolve the problem, a medical examination may be appropriate.

Hoarseness is familiar to everyone. It is usually the result of cheering or shouting too loudly. Another common cause is laryngitis, a swelling of the area around the vocal cords. Hoarseness should never last more than a few days. If it lasts longer, a physician should be consulted; hoarseness is the first symptom of a number of potentially dangerous disorders.

How can a person
who has had a
laryngectomy
produce speech?

PROBLEMS RESULTING FROM LARYNGECTOMY. The final voice disorder we will discuss is that of the person whose larynx, or voice box, has been removed, generally to keep cancer from spreading. When the larynx is removed, the vocal folds are removed as well; as a result, a laryngectomized person can no longer speak with vocal fold vibrations. These people, generally older adults, can be rehabilitated, however. The easiest way for them to produce understandable speech is to use a substitute sound generator, commonly called an *electrolarynx*. This instrument is placed on the neck, and the buzz that it generates can then be altered into speech as the individual forms words with the tongue, lips, and jaw.

Although the electrolarynx device is easy to use, many people find the sound it produces to be highly artificial and unpleasant. A method known as *esophageal speech* is a preferred alternative. The esophageal speaker forces air from the mouth into the throat and a segment of the esophagus vibrates when the air is released. The vibration of this segment of the esophagus is used to shape speech sounds. Esophageal speech takes a relatively long time to learn, but the resulting speech is closer to normal than that produced by the artificial electrolarynx.

The most recent approach to regaining speech in the laryngectomized patient is to surgically implant a prosthesis in the breathing channel (stoma) that was created when the larynx was removed. This device vibrates when the laryngectomized patient directs air through it. The vibrations replace the vibrations originally produced by the vocal folds. The Blom-Singer prosthesis (Blom, Singer, & Hiamaker, 1986) is one of the more popular devices used. This device, when appropriate for the client, can help many laryngectomized people speak very well.

Education and Treatment Provisions

What is an
otorhinolaryn-
gologist?

Because many voice disorders are caused by changing tissue, it is very important that a person with symptoms of a problem get a medical examination before vocal rehabilitation is attempted. An examination by an ear, nose, and throat (ENT) specialist, officially called an otorhinolaryngologist, can determine whether the patient has a serious degenerative disease, a tissue pathology, or a functional problem.

What roles are
played in the team
approach for
treatment of voice
disorders?

Treatment, especially for younger clients, is typically best provided by a team approach. The otorhinolaryngologist is needed to assess tissue change. The speech-language pathologist is needed to facilitate the patient's ability to produce an appropriate voice or to compensate for the inability to speak properly. Teachers and family members are needed to aid the transfer of good habits developed in therapy by reinforcing these habits in the person's real-life situations. The efficiency with which a team operates is often the determining factor in how quickly and how effectively a person overcomes a voice disorder.

PROBE 8-4   Speech Disorders: Problems with Voice

1. How can a functional voice problem become an organic voice problem?
2. People with hay fever may sound _____, whereas a person who is unable to block off the nasal cavity will sound excessively _____.
3. What does ENT stand for?
4. What does an otorhinolaryngologist do?
5. T   F   Occasional pitch breaks in adolescent males should be a cause for concern.
6. List four voice quality defects.

SPEECH DISORDERS: PROBLEMS WITH FLUENCY

You should be able to identify various types of fluency disorders.

What is disfluency? Normal speech is not perfect speech. All speakers pause, hesitate, repeat, and misspeak in a variety of ways that are well within the limits of normal communication. Even the most polished and professional speaker will be disfluent at times. However, when speakers cross the boundary from normal to abnormal disfluencies, they are exposed to the negative evaluations of their listeners. There are at least five different types of disfluent speech. Accurate recognition of which type of disfluency a child may be producing and whether or not it is abnormal is a critical and sometimes challenging task.

Etiology, Identification, and Assessment

Table 8-2 lists the possible types of disfluency. One type, developmental disfluency, is a normal process. The other types are not to be expected in normal speech.

At what age does a child experience developmental disfluency? **DEVELOPMENTAL DISFLUENCY.** As children pass through the developmental stages of language learning, they will be more disfluent at certain stages in development than at others. In mastering our spoken language, we become more fluent as we become more proficient. Normally speaking children usually hit a peak of disfluency between the ages of 2½ and 4 years. These normal developmental disfluencies are characterized by the repetition of whole words and phrases with the occasional interjection of "uh," "er," and "ah" (Yarrii & Lewis, 1984). This is a transitional stage that most children leave behind as they master speech and language. In other words, most children outgrow normal developmental disfluencies. Thus, there is usually no need for therapeutic intervention with these children.

How do you determine that a child is really stuttering? **STUTTERING.** Stuttering is the most commonly recognized type of disfluency. However, for a child to be considered a stutterer, many of the following signs and experiences must be part of the case history. First of all, stuttering is a disorder of childhood. It is developmental in nature and follows a predictable path (Bloodstein, 1987). Initially the disfluency pattern is highly episodic, but it eventually becomes chronic in nature. In addition, despite the folklore that children become stutterers as the result of a traumatic experience, such as being frightened by an animal or falling from a high place, most parents and children cannot point to any

TABLE 8-2   Types of Disfluency

Normal	*Abnormal*
Developmental disfluency	Stuttering
	Neurogenic dysfunction
	Motor speech disfluency
	Neurolinguistic disfluency
	Chemical reaction disfluency
	Psychogenic dysfunction
	Emotionally based disfluency
	Manipulative disfluency
	Language delay

specific circumstances that correlate to the onset of stuttering. True stuttering can be manipulated in a number of ways that distinguish it from other forms of disfluency. Reduction in stuttering usually takes place with the repeated reading of the same passage. Stuttering can also be reduced when distracting noises are introduced while the stutterer is speaking. Having the person talk in time to the beat of a metronome, or in fact introducing any temporary distraction while the person is speaking, will often reduce or eliminate stuttering.

On a more internal level, children who stutter often develop a different belief system about the communication process than do other children. They might identify themselves as being victims of some unknown power that makes it difficult for them to talk. They may develop lifestyles that involve avoiding as many communication situations as possible, which creates the semblance of being withdrawn from their peers.

The observable behaviors of stuttering may include repetitions of sounds, words, or phrases; also the rate and rhythm of stuttered speech can be defective. Stutterers may also display facial grimaces, unusual body gyrations, and many types of struggle behaviors while they are attempting to talk. Yet no stutterer stutters all the time, and these behaviors are absent during the period when speech is normally fluent.

What causes neurogenic disfluency?

NEUROGENIC DISFLUENCY. This type of disfluency is the direct result of an identifiable neuropathology in a child with no history of fluency problems prior to the occurrence of the pathology (Culatta & Leeper, 1987). Motor speech disorders caused by cerebral palsy or conditions that make it difficult for children to plan speech or use their speech mechanisms may lead to a higher-than-expected frequency of disfluent speech. Neurolinguistic disfluencies can appear after seizures or as the result of strokes that affect language formulation. Reactions to some drugs may cause chemically based disfluencies. Helm-Estabrooks (1987), Quader (1977), and McCarthy (1981) all report cases where the onset of disfluent behavior was correlated to the administration of medications.

How can a neurogenic disfluency be identified?

All three types of neurogenically based disfluencies just mentioned can usually be distinguished by the alert clinician or teacher. Onset of the disfluencies is usually abrupt, and the child will not have a history of fluency problems. Initially the child will feel little concern about speaking, as compared to the stutterer who exhibits undue concern. Also, many of the behavioral manipulations that affect stuttering, as previously described, will have little or no effect upon the child manifesting neurogenic disfluencies. Although these guidelines should serve to sensitize the reader, they are not totally inclusive. However, a comparison of the case history profiles of the child who stutters and the child who is neurogenically disfluent should provide enough information to distinguish between the two disfluencies.

What causes psychogenic disfluency?

PSYCHOGENIC DISFLUENCIES. The most striking characteristic of this type of disfluency is its sudden onset and its relationship to an identifiable emotional crisis. The nature and degree of the traumatizing events that can lead to disfluent speech will differ with each person. The case description that follows illustrates how stressful events could lead to a child showing signs of psychogenic disfluency.

The child (Jenna) was 10 years old when the incident occurred. The speech-language pathologist at Jenna's school was contacted several months into the school year by the fourth grade teacher, who reported that Jenna was "suddenly stuttering her head off" in class. The child had been screened by the speech-language pathologist previously and had no history of speech problems. While speaking to Jenna, the speech-language pathologist noted an unusually high disfluency rate that did not change in frequency or form under conditions that usually affect stuttering. That is, stuttering can usually be reduced through repeated readings of a passage, through the presentation of distracting noises, or by having the stutterer talk to the beat of a metronome or talk under other similarly distracting conditions. The failure of these conditions to change Jenna's speech led the speech-language pathologist to think that the child's disfluency was not stuttering. In addition, Jenna seemed both listless and distracted during the tasks. During the session, Jenna revealed that she had overheard her parents discussing the possibility of a divorce. Tearfully, Jenna expressed a fear that she and her sister would be placed in an "orphanage like in the movie *Annie*" and be separated from their friends and family. During a follow-up conference with the school counselor and the child's parents, it was determined that, in fact, a divorce was imminent and had not been discussed with the children. Jenna was informed by both of her parents that they would be separating and that she and her sister would remain with their mother most of the time, visiting with their father on weekends and during school vacations. She was assured that an orphanage was not in her future. Symptoms of disfluency soon disappeared and have not recurred for 48 months (Culatta & Leeper, 1987).

What factors aid in the identification of a psychogenic disfluency?

Jenna's case is typical of many psychogenic disfluencies. The sudden onset, lack of developmental history of stuttering, absence of neurologically significant information, lack of concern about speech, and resistance of the symptoms to modification were clues that the disfluency pattern was not stuttering or neurogenic disfluency.

How can language delays affect fluency?

LANGUAGE DELAY. Language disorders in children can have an impact on their ability to speak fluently. Hall (1977) and Hall, Wray, and Conti (1986) report that the beginning of language therapy with children exhibiting a severe language delay resulted in a marked increase in speech disfluency. Experience seems to indicate that the initial rise in the disfluency patterns of children with language delays is not the result of some newly emerging stuttering problem, but rather the result of the children struggling to learn the new language forms. Learning complex language tasks increases the disfluencies of all children (normal developmental disfluency), and language therapy appears to sometimes have the side effect of increasing the disfluencies of children who have language delays. Fortunately, the preliminary information available about this type of disfluency indicates that maintaining language-based therapy that results in increased communication skills will eventually alleviate the disfluencies that were temporarily created.

Education and Treatment Provisions

What are the treatments for disfluency?

Differentiation of the various types of disfluency has led to the identification of different treatments, each requiring different levels of cooperation among the professionals involved with the disfluent children.

DEVELOPMENTAL DISFLUENCY. If this normal process becomes a concern to parents or other significant people in the child's life, the most effective treatment is providing information about normal speech and language development to the concerned parties. This may be accomplished by the speech-language pathologist, special educator, regular educator, pediatrician, or allied health professional.

STUTTERING. The treatment of stuttering can best be provided by the speech-language pathologist with assistance from other significant people in the child's life. Current therapeutic practices can help children learn to use more effectively the speaking skills they possess. The prognosis with early identification is much more favorable than it is when the problem is allowed to develop untreated. It is critical that children identified as stutterers begin treatment as soon as possible to prevent stuttering from becoming a major factor in their educational and social development.

NEUROGENIC DISFLUENCY. The direct treatment of neurogenic disfluency requires a team approach that usually involves medical, educational, family counseling, and speech-language personnel. The modifications required to help a child attain or approximate normal communication will be the result of the accurate diagnosis of the limitations of the communication mechanisms involved and the attempts of the various service providers to help the children and their families understand the limitations of these mechanisms. Each child will demand different intervention strategies and have different potential for normal communication.

PSYCHOGENIC DISFLUENCIES. Treatment for children showing emotionally based disfluencies can best be provided by counselors, psychiatrists, psychologists, social workers, and other appropriately trained individuals that can aid the child in dealing with the emotional upheaval. Speech-language pathologists, special educators, and regular educators can serve as adjunct members of any team dealing with children who exhibit these disfluencies, but are not usually trained to provide the emotional counseling initially needed by these patients.

LANGUAGE DELAY. Treatment for children who show language delay is the province of the speech-language pathologist. The most effective teams to aid the child in the acquisition of language skills are composed of the speech-language pathologist, the regular education teacher, and the special education teacher, who will interact with the child and interested family members as well as support group members.

PROBE 8-5   Speech Disorders: Problems with Fluency

1. What are the five types of disfluency?
2. Most children pass through a stage called normal developmental disfluency at approximately ____ to ____ years of age.
3. T   F   The speech-language pathologist is the only person who should ever work with a child displaying disfluencies.
4. T   F   Sudden onset of disfluency in a child with no history of fluency failure is usually a sign of stuttering.

PROVISION OF SPEECH-LANGUAGE SERVICES

You should be able to describe implications of the "least restrictive environment" clause of the Individuals with Disabilities Education Act for the education of children with communication disorders.

Classroom-based and Curriculum-based Speech-Language Services

What are some current speech-language service delivery models?

Changes are taking place in the manner and type of speech-language services delivered within educational settings, partly because the Individuals with Disabilities Education Act mandates service provision in the "least restrictive environment." Instead of providing individual pull-

This speech-language pathologist is providing classroom-based intervention.

out therapy, increasing emphasis is being placed on classroom-based and curriculum-based service delivery models. In classroom-based intervention, speech-language services are integrated into classroom settings. The speech-language pathologist works directly in the classroom, consults with teachers and special educators, and participates in team teaching (Hughes, 1989; Ripich, 1989). Together the speech-language pathologist and classroom teacher can model good speech and language, provide opportunities for successful communication, and defuse potential penalties for inadequate communication.

In curriculum-based intervention, clinicians assist teachers in helping their students process the language demands inherent in reading, math, and the content areas (Bashir, 1989; Chabon & Prelock, 1989). The curriculum becomes the context for intervention, with emphasis on teaching the meanings of words encountered, reducing or modifying the complexity of materials, and providing simplified explanations when introducing new topics. The focus is on facilitating the acquisition of related language and academic skills (Nelson, 1989; Miller, 1989; Norris, 1989).

The Speech-Language Professional and ASHA

What are the requirements for preparing to be a speech-language pathologist?

The professionals who work with individuals with communication disorders are called speech-language pathologists. The American Speech-Language-Hearing Association (ASHA) is the national organization that represents speech-language pathologists. The 66 thousand members of ASHA operate with a Code of Ethics, which maintains that a master's degree is the appropriate entry level of training and education to practice the profession. The master's degree plus one year of supervised employment are recognized by the federal government as the minimum level of education and training an individual should have to be considered a "qualified provider" of services.

Once they have completed their training program (typically two years post BA), speech-language pathologists work in hospitals, university clinics, rehabilitation centers, private clinics, and public schools. This is an exciting time to be a speech-language pathologist. Needs for service are at an all-time high; research is pointing the way toward increasingly more efficient service provision; and recognition of the profession is expanding into new and challenging areas. We live in a verbal society that places a greater emphasis on communication than ever before. As members of habilitation and rehabilitation teams, speech-language pathologists are working with regular and special educators as well as parents and healthcare workers to help people achieve their maximum communication potential.

PROBE 8-6   Provision of Speech-Language Services

1. T F The "least restrictive environment" clause of IDEA (Individuals with Disabilities Education Act) has had an impact on the mechanisms used to deliver speech-language services.
2. Speech-language services are integrated into classroom settings in _____-based intervention.
3. The curriculum becomes the context for speech-language intervention in _____-based intervention.
4. The professionals who work with individuals with communication disorders are called _____.
5. The national professional organization for speech-language pathologists is _____.

SUMMARY

1. Communication is disordered when it deviates from accepted norms so much that it calls attention to itself, interferes with the message, or distresses the speaker or listener.
2. Speech results from many parts of the body working cooperatively to produce sound.
3. Speech and language are developmental processes acquired over time.
4. Language disorders are the most complex and most serious of all communication problems.
5. Most speech disorders involve problems with sound production (articulation), voice, or fluency.
6. Speech problems may have an organic cause, or they may be functional problems that do not have an underlying physiological cause.
7. Speech-language pathologists are the professionals trained to deal with communication disorders.
8. The classroom teacher has an important role in the early identification and remediation of communication disorders.
9. Intervention must be conducted in both home and classroom environments for speech therapy to be optimally effective.

TASK SHEET 8   Field Experiences with Communication Problems

Select one of the following alternatives and complete the required activities.

Program Visitation

Arrange to visit a program that provides diagnostic or therapeutic services to children with communication disorders. In no more than three pages, describe the program you visited and what you observed. If you saw children being treated, describe the treatment that was being administered and the condition it was intended to develop, facilitate, or enhance. Describe your general reaction to the program.

Professional Interview

Interview one of the people listed below and determine his or her job responsibilities, the training necessary for the job, the problems encountered, and the rewards of the work. If observation facilities are available, ask to observe the person working with a client.

   a. Speech-language pathologist
   b. Director of a speech clinic at a hospital or private clinic
   c. Member of a cleft palate team at a hospital
   d. An otorhinolaryngologist

Interview with a Person Who Has a Communication Disorder

Using great tact and discretion, either interview or observe a person who has a communication disorder. This may be a stutterer or a person with a cleft palate, cerebral palsy, or an articulation problem. In your interview or observation, pay particular attention to the person's communication. Describe your experience and your reaction to it in no more than three pages.

Speech and Language Analysis

   a. Ask a child of nursery school age ($2^1/_2$ to $3^1/_2$) to tell a story; then ask a child who is two or three years older to tell you a story. Aside from linguistic sophistication, note the difference in the fluency of the speakers. Compare the number of repetitions of words, hesitations, and false starts for the two children. Describe your conclusions and reactions.
   b. Locate two children of different ages, tell them a fairly complex story, then ask them to retell it to you. Describe the differences in sentence length, sentence complexity, detail, vocal inflection, and general storytelling ability. It may be helpful to tape record the stories.

Library Study

Select three articles about communication disorders and write a one-page synopsis of each. Some relevant professional journals, published by the American Speech-Language-Hearing Association, include *Journal of Speech and Hearing Research; Language, Speech, and Hearing Services in Schools;* and *American Journal of Speech-Language Pathology.*

On April 8, 1864, Gallaudet University, the world's only university for the deaf, was founded by Edward Miner Gallaudet. One hundred and twenty-four years later, on March 14, 1988, Dr. I. King Jordan was selected as Gallaudet's first Deaf president.

The events that led up to Dr. Jordan's selection forever changed the manner in which the world would view deaf and hearing impaired individuals. On March 7, 1988, Gallaudet's board of trustees chose as its seventh president Elizabeth Ann Zinser, an outstanding and well-respected university administrator, but one who had no experience with deafness, sign language, or deaf culture. In a protest that drew worldwide attention, students from Gallaudet closed the university and demanded that they have a Deaf president. The demonstration became known as the Deaf President Now movement, and, in the words of Jack Gannon, became "the week the world heard Gallaudet." One week later, Dr. Zinser resigned and Dr. Jordan was selected as the university's first Deaf president.

In his acceptance, Dr. Jordan stated what the world has now come to recognize: "The only thing a deaf person can't do is hear." Moreover, in the words of Edward C. Merrill (Gallaudet's fourth president), "Dr. I. King Jordan's advancement to the Presidency of Gallaudet University was a vindication of Edward Miner Gallaudet's beliefs."

Source: Adapted from Jack R. Gannon (1989). *The week the world heard Gallaudet.* Washington, D.C.: Gallaudet University Press.

9

Students with Hearing Loss

William W. Green and Joseph E. Fischgrund

Helen Keller, renowned author, educator, and advocate for the deaf and hard-of-hearing, succinctly describes the multiple dilemmas of being deaf:

> I am just as deaf as I am blind. The problems of deafness are deeper and more complex;
> if not more important than those of blindness. Deafness is a much worse misfortune. For
> it means the loss of the most vital stimulus—the sound of the voice that brings language,
> sets thoughts astir, and keeps us in the intellectual company of men. (Keller, 1933)

That statement was made by Helen Keller when she was asked to describe the effects of her problems of deafness and blindness. It might surprise you; many of us assume that a loss of vision would have a deeper and more disruptive influence on our daily lives than a loss of hearing. One reason we make that assumption could be that vision problems are relatively easy to imagine—almost everyone has played games that involve being blindfolded or has tried to maneuver in the dark. But how many people have ever tried to function without hearing, even for a little while? Almost no one. We generally take our hearing for granted, and we often remain unaware of the subtle and the not-so-subtle ways we are affected by the sounds that pervade our environment.

By the end of this chapter you should have an increased understanding of the importance of hearing and the education of children with hearing loss.[1]

---

[1]Children with profound and severe hearing losses are often referred to as *deaf* children. While the trend is to move away from applying labels to people with disabilities, it should be noted that cultural identities have evolved around some disability groups. This is the case for many who have severe to profound hearing loss; there is a very active and vibrant culture of individuals who refer to themselves as the Deaf community. In specific references to that cultural group, the word *Deaf* is capitalized.

SOUND AND HUMAN HEARING

You should be able to describe the nature of sound and the different ways we use our hearing.

Unless you are reading in a soundproof room, it is almost impossible for you not to be hearing something. If you stop for a moment, close your eyes, and just listen, you may hear a number of simple and complex sounds: a clock ticking, a bird chirping, the hum of a light or heater, wind rustling through the trees, rain hitting the window, the radio or television, traffic noise, people talking, and so on. Our environment is filled with sounds. We are accustomed to them; they are part of our feeling of well-being or annoyance, of our participation in a world full of life.

The Nature of Sound

Before we discuss hearing and hearing disorders, it is important that you understand what a sound is. Although physicists and acoustic engineers refer to different aspects of sound in many different and often complicated ways, a simple description best serves our purposes. The basic parts of a sound system are identified in Figure 9-1. This configuration is called the TMR system.

How is sound generated, transmitted, and received?

A sound is created by the vibration of an object, a transmitter (T). It may be a string, reed, or column of air, as in a musical instrument, or it may be metal, wood, or some other object. The human vocal folds consist of highly specialized vibrating tissue. Vibration, however, becomes sound only if there is a surrounding medium (M) that can carry it. The most common carrying medium is air, but it is also possible for water, metal, or other substances to carry the vibration. The final link in the sound system is something to receive the sound. This receiver (R) may be electronic in the case of radio or TV, but one of the most sensitive receivers is the ear.

How We Use Our Hearing

The human ear can hear sounds over a remarkable range of frequencies and intensities. Frequency and intensity are two of the measurable physical characteristics of sound. Pitch is

FIGURE 9-1   A Sound System

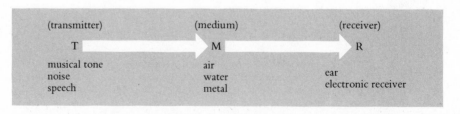

the ears' perception of frequency, and loudness is the ears' perception of intensity. A good way to understand the difference is to regard the lowest and highest keys of a piano keyboard as somewhat representative of the range of frequencies and pitches that the ear can hear, while the intensity and loudness of the sounds are related to how hard the keys are pressed.

What are hertz and decibels?

The frequency of sounds is expressed in a unit called the *hertz* (abbreviated Hz). This is an internationally recognized notation and replaces the use of cycles per second that has predominated in the United States. The human ear can generally hear sounds ranging from 20 to 20,000 Hz, but most sounds in our environment fall between 125 and 8000 Hz. The frequencies of speech sounds fall in the range from 300 to 4000 Hz; it is especially important that the ear be able to hear in this range. Frequencies above 8000 Hz are not crucial to understanding speech, but we do use them to enjoy live and reproduced music.

The intensity of a sound is directly related to the energy or force of the vibration that caused it. Since the human ear is capable of responding to an enormous range of sound energy, a ratio scale is used to describe intensity. The unit of intensity is the *decibel* (dB). Zero dB represents the intensity of the softest sound that the normal young adult ear can hear, and 140 dB represents a level so loud it is painful. The intensity range of the human voice is between 40 dB and 60 dB. Figure 9-2 displays the intensity and frequency ranges for some common environmental and speech sounds.

LEVELS OF HEARING. As we mentioned in the opening paragraphs, most people do not understand how much they depend on their hearing. Ramsdell (1970) describes hearing as having three psychological levels: (1) the *symbolic level,* (2) the *signal* or *warning level,* and (3) the *auditory background* or *primitive level.* An understanding of these three levels will enable us to appreciate the practical implications of hearing loss and its potential effect on educational and psychosocial development.

What is the difference between the symbolic, signal, and auditory background levels of hearing?

The symbolic level of hearing is the level we use to understand spoken words, which are the symbols of objects and concepts, as well as connected oral language that expresses a full range of meaning.

The second level is used as a signal or warning system. We constantly rely on hearing to signal us of changes in our environment and to warn us of approaching danger (e.g., a car horn, a train whistle, or an approaching storm). Our use of this level is generally unconscious, but nevertheless it is important.

Finally, the ear functions on a so-called primitive or background level by constantly monitoring sounds in our environment, thereby keeping us in touch with it. People who have lost the ability to hear background noises often experience almost overwhelming feelings of isolation. These feelings and the frustration that accompanies them can have negative psychological consequences. Many elderly persons with a loss of hearing experience these feelings of isolation and depression.

PROBE 9-1   Sound and Human Hearing

1. What are the three basic components of a sound system?
2. How would you define sound?
3. Two measurable aspects of sound are _____, which is measured in _____, and _____, which is measured in _____.
4. What is the intensity range for average conversational speech?
5. List Ramsdell's three psychological levels of hearing.

FIGURE 9-2   Typical Sound Frequencies and Intensities

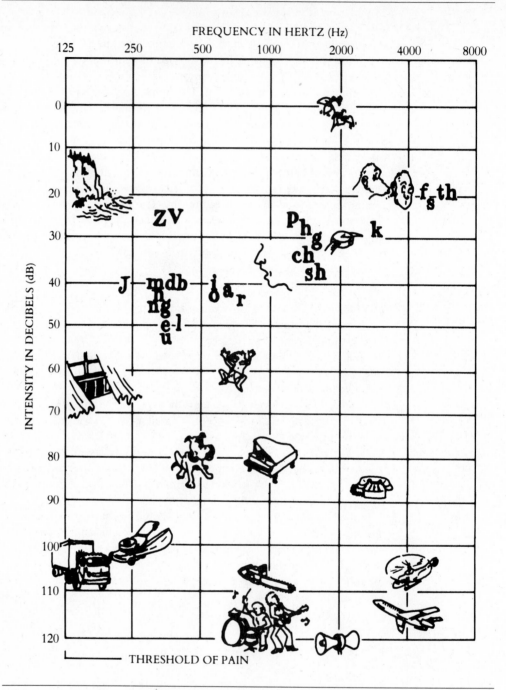

Source: From Jerry L. Northern and Marion P. Downs, *Hearing in Children*, 3rd ed., p. 7. Copyright © 1984 by Williams & Wilkins. Reprinted by permission.

HOW WE HEAR

You should be able to describe how we hear.

Anatomy and Physiology of the Ear

To understand hearing loss, it is necessary to understand the structures and processes involved in normal hearing. It is helpful to consider the ear in three parts, the *outer ear,* the *middle ear,* and the *inner ear.* The parts of the human ear are illustrated in Figure 9-3.

What is the function of the outer ear?

OUTER EAR. The outer ear consists of the **pinna** or **auricle** (the cartilaginous structure on the side of the head) and the external auditory canal. Since the pinna is the only outwardly visible part of the ear, many people think it is more important than it actually is. The function of the pinna is to collect sound waves arriving at the ear and direct them into the auditory

FIGURE 9-3   The Human Ear: Pathways for Sound Waves to Be Transmitted to the Inner Ear Are Shown

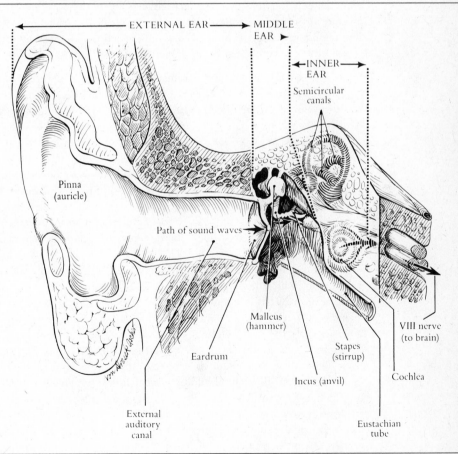

Source: From *Your Health After 60* by Sanders-Brown Research Center on Aging. Copyright © 1979 by the Sanders-Brown Research Center on Aging. Used by permission of the publisher, Dutton, an imprint of New American Library, a division of Penguin Books USA Inc.

canal. If you have a dog or a cat, you have probably noticed that they can move their pinna to improve their hearing. Humans retain only a vestige of this ability. We must turn our entire head to focus the ear on a particular sound.

The **auditory canal** protects the sensitive internal structures in the ear from damage and foreign objects. It is 1 to 2 inches long and has stiff hairs at its outer edge to keep objects from entering. In addition, the skin lining the outer third of the canal secretes a wax called **cerumen** that traps foreign material and keeps the ear canal and eardrum from drying out. Earwax is not dirt, and the process of removing it can sometimes result in irritation and infection. The old adage that you shouldn't put anything smaller than your elbow in your ear is still good advice. A doctor should be consulted if you have a problem with wax buildup.

How do the structures of the middle ear operate?

MIDDLE EAR. The outer and middle ear are separated by the eardrum. The **eardrum** is a membrane that vibrates when it is struck by sound waves; the vibration is then transmitted by a series of three small bones, the **malleus (hammer), incus (anvil),** and **stapes (stirrup).** These bones, which are named for the objects they resemble, carry the vibration across the middle ear cavity to the entrance to the inner ear.

Another important structure generally considered part of the middle ear system is the **eustachian tube,** which extends between the back wall of the throat and the middle ear cavity. This structure opens and closes to equalize the air pressure on the inside of the eardrum with that on the outside. The eustachian tube is the structure that relieves the feeling of pressure or stoppage we have when descending in an airplane or swimming under water. By swallowing, yawning, or using normal muscle action, we cause the tube to open, which allows air to enter the middle ear cavity (Davis & Silverman, 1970; Newby & Popelka, 1985).

INNER EAR. The inner ear is a remarkably intricate structure. The cochlea of the inner ear contains thousands of hair cells (12,000 in the human ear). The two major structures of the inner ear can be differentiated by their function. The vestibular mechanism, consisting of the semicircular canals, is used for balance; the cochlea is used for hearing. Both structures are filled with fluid and are joined by the vestibule, the open area into which sound waves enter from the middle ear.

The **vestibular mechanism** is the structure that enables us to maintain our balance. It consists of three looplike structures, the membranous **semicircular canals.** The angles of the loops correspond to horizontal, vertical, and lateral planes. The canals and two other structures, the utricle and the saccule, relay information about head movement, body movement, and acceleration to the brain, which then adjusts the body to maintain balance (Martin, 1975; Newby & Popelka, 1985).

What is the cochlea?

The **cochlea,** which lies just below the semicircular canals, is important for hearing. This organ, which is shaped like a snail shell, contains the endings of the auditory nerve (Cranial Nerve VIII) in a central channel called the cochlear duct. The movements of the stapes in and out of the opening to the inner ear create waves in the fluid in the cochlea. These waves then stimulate the nerve endings of the auditory nerve, which sends an electrical impulse to the brain (Davis & Silverman, 1970; Martin, 1975; Newby & Popelka, 1985).

These structures are all considered part of the peripheral hearing mechanism, to distinguish them from the central auditory mechanism, which consists of those parts of the brain involved with sound. The peripheral hearing mechanism serves as an extremely efficient sound transmitter. To repeat the steps: a transmission starts with a vibration in air (sound wave), which travels down the auditory canal and causes the eardrum to vibrate. This vibration is then carried across the middle ear cavity mechanically by the three bones of the ossicular chain, to the opening of the inner ear. There the vibration is transferred to a fluid movement that travels through the cochlea. The fluid, vibratory energy is finally changed to electrical energy by the stimulation of the nerve endings of the auditory nerve.

CENTRAL AUDITORY PROCESSING. The operations involved in the central processing of auditory signals are far too complex to discuss in detail in this text. You need only understand that sounds in the form of electrical energy travel along the auditory nerve through several complex lower brainstem areas to the cortex, which is the covering of the brain. One area of the cortex is adapted to manage sound; there the interpretation and perception of sound take place. This area, called the **auditory cortex,** is responsible for the gross and fine discrimination necessary to understand speech and language (Ades, 1959; Northern & Downs, 1984; Lasky & Katz, 1985).

What is the purpose of the auditory cortex?

The function of the auditory cortex and the rest of the central auditory system is roughly comparable to that of a computer. It interprets and analyzes the sounds that are fed into it, organizing them into a pattern that we can understand and use as a language. The analogy is only partially accurate, however—only humans can interpret the emotions, subtleties, and intentions expressed in language.

You may be surprised to learn that a 5-month-old human fetus can hear sounds. At birth, the newborn has been hearing, albeit passively, for four months. After the child is born, he or she begins learning the basic building blocks of oral language. Children gradually refine their cooing, gurgling, and babbling by listening to their own sounds and the sounds of those around them, a process known as an "auditory feedback loop." Children with normal hearing usually produce their first words at about 1 year old, and spoken language develops very quickly thereafter. This process may be delayed in children with hearing loss, and the words these children learn must often be acquired by means other than hearing.

Learning is a complex process that takes place formally and informally throughout our lives. It depends on the senses, particularly vision and hearing. These senses are so basic that problems with any component in their complex arrangement can interfere with learning.

Auditory learning requires an intact peripheral auditory mechanism. The hearing losses that result from problems at this level preclude the processing of raw data (sounds). A partial hearing loss can delay auditory learning, and complete deafness may stop auditory learning altogether and requires a heavy emphasis on visual skills. If the peripheral hearing mechanism functions normally, the central auditory system is the crucial mechanism in auditory learning and the development of speech and oral language.

PROBE 9-2   How We Hear

1. Match each item on the left with the appropriate selection on the right.

____ Incus	a. Cerumen
____ Sense organ of hearing	b. Malleus
____ Outer ear	c. Stapes
____ Ventilation	d. Semicircular canals
____ Balance	e. Anvil
____ Earwax	f. Pinna
____ Transmits sounds to brain	g. Eardrum
____ Hammer	h. Cochlea
	i. Auditory nerve (VIII)
	j. Eustachian tube

2. T   F   Earwax is dirt and should be cleaned from the ears.
3. Trace the pathway of sound through the structures of the ear.
4. The part of the brain most important to hearing is the _____.
5. The human ear begins responding to sound at what age?

HEARING LOSS

You should be able to define hearing loss, describe its prevalence among children, and know its major classifications and causes.

Definition and Classification

Many different systems have been proposed to define and classify hearing loss. Some of these systems are physiologically oriented and focus only on the measurable amount of hearing loss, whereas others focus on the extent to which the hearing loss affects speech and language development, educational achievement, and psychological adjustment (Myklebust, 1964; Newby & Popelka, 1985). Another consideration is the age at which the hearing loss occurred. Very early loss of hearing affects a child's development more than a later loss (Myklebust, 1964). A classification system designed to aid teachers and counselors of those with hearing impairments must take into account all these factors.

An important distinction must be made between the term "deafness" and other more general terms such as "hearing loss," "hearing impairment," and "hard-of-hearing." **Deafness** means a hearing loss so great that hearing cannot be used to develop oral language, whereas the other terms are used to describe any deviation from normal hearing, regardless of its severity. Following are several other definitions:

> **Hearing Impairment:** A generic term indicating a hearing loss that may range in severity from mild to profound. It consists of two groups, those who are *deaf* and those who are *hard-of-hearing*. A *deaf* person is one whose hearing loss precludes successful processing of linguistic information through audition, with or without a hearing aid.
>
> a. The *congenitally deaf:* Those who were born deaf.
> b. The *adventitiously deaf:* Those who were born with normal hearing but in whom the sense of hearing became nonfunctional later through illness or accident.
>
> A person who is **hard-of-hearing** is one who, generally with the use of a hearing aid, has residual hearing sufficient to enable successful processing of linguistic information through audition. (Report of the Ad Hoc Committee to Define Deaf and Hard of Hearing, 1975)

The educator should be very careful not to classify a child as deaf or hearing impaired until his or her hearing has been thoroughly assessed. Even after assessment, professionals should remain flexible about a child's classification. New evidence about a child's ability to hear or speak with proper stimulation, education, or amplification may dictate that he or she be reclassified (Silverman, 1971).

Prevalence

What is the prevalence of hearing impairment?

It is estimated that approximately 8 to 10 percent, or some 20 to 22 million Americans, experience some degree of difficulty hearing or understanding speech (Punch, 1983; National Health Survey, 1988). Table 9-1 provides a further breakdown of hearing impairment by age group and suggests that over one million preschool, elementary, and secondary-age children have hearing loss. Almost 12 million working-age individuals (ages 18–65) suffer hearing loss, while roughly 9 million retired and senior citizens must contend with hearing loss (National Center for Health Statistics, 1988). The 1989–90 Annual Survey of Children and Youth identified over 46,000 students in the United States in educational programs for children who are deaf or have hearing impairments.

TABLE 9-1   Prevalence Rates of Hearing Impairment in the Civilian, Noninstitutionalized Population of the U.S.

Age Group in Years	Number	Prevalence Rate (%)
Under 18 years	1,078,000	4.9%
18 to 44 years	5,021,000	22.9%
45 to 64 years	6,725,000	30.8%
65 to 74 years	4,807,000	22.0%
75 years and over	4,233,000	19.4%
Total	21,864,000	

Note: Rates are based on 1988 interview data.

Causes of Hearing Loss

Up to this point we have considered the nature and process of hearing and its importance in the development of speech and oral language and for auditory learning. Hearing losses can result from a number of conditions and illnesses. There are five major types: conductive, sensorineural, mixed, functional, and central.

CONDUCTIVE HEARING LOSS. A **conductive hearing loss** results from problems with the structures in the outer or middle ear, generally a blockage in the mechanical conduction of sound. Sounds must be amplified to overcome the blockage.

What is otitis media?

The leading cause of conductive hearing loss is middle ear infection, or **otitis media.** This condition usually results from a malfunction of the eustachian tube. If this organ does not allow enough air into the middle ear to equalize the air pressure on the outside of the eardrum, the oxygen in the air trapped in the middle ear is gradually absorbed by the middle ear cavity tissue. This causes a partial vacuum, which pulls the eardrum into the middle ear cavity. Next, the tissues of the middle ear secrete fluid to fill the void created by the absorbed oxygen. This fluid may become infected. If the condition is unchecked, the fluid may build up sufficiently to rupture the eardrum.

Children have smaller, more horizontal eustachian tubes than adults and more frequent colds and allergies, which affect the eustachian tube openings. As a result they have more eustachian tube problems and much more frequent middle ear infections. Teachers should be aware that this is a common problem.

Another cause of conductive loss is the blockage of the auditory canal by excessive earwax or a foreign body. If the ear canal is completely blocked, a mild conductive hearing loss may result. Earwax buildup is not as common a problem as many people think; even a tiny opening through a plug of earwax is sufficient for relatively normal hearing. Often a condition assumed to be caused by earwax has an entirely different cause. Most important, children who complain of ear pain or appear to have trouble listening or discriminating sound should be referred to the school nurse or their family healthcare provider.

What is otosclerosis?

Another cause of conductive hearing loss is a condition called **otosclerosis.** This results from the formation of a spongy-bony growth around the stapes, which progressively impedes its movement and causes gradual deterioration of hearing. This condition can often be overcome by a surgical procedure called a stapedectomy.

Conductive hearing losses are usually temporary, and the amount of hearing loss varies depending on the medical condition that causes it. These losses are seldom severe enough to prevent someone from hearing speech entirely, but they can cause a child to miss sounds and words and delay the development of speech and language. Most conductive hearing loss can be successfully treated with medicine or surgery. Specific treatments will be discussed later in this chapter.

SENSORINEURAL HEARING LOSS. Sensorineural hearing losses result from damage to the cochlea or the auditory nerve. This damage is caused by illness or disease. Sensorineural hearing losses are usually greater than those caused by conductive disorders, and they require extensive treatment.

What are the major causes of sensorineural hearing loss?

Viral diseases are a major cause of hearing loss, particularly in children. These can occur either before or after birth and may cause problems ranging from mild hearing loss to deafness. For example, there is a high probability that pregnant women who contact rubella (German measles) during the first three months of pregnancy will give birth to a child with some sensorineural hearing loss. It is estimated that 10,000 to 20,000 children were born deaf as a result of the rubella epidemics of the early and mid-1960s (Northern & Downs, 1984). The widespread use of vaccinations to prevent rubella has nearly eliminated this phenomenon, although sporadic outbreaks of rubella are still reported. Severe hearing loss or deafness can also result from infectious meningitis, mumps, measles, chicken pox, and influenza. Viral conditions may also result in malformed body parts, retardation, nervous system damage, and congenital heart disease.

Rh incompatibility is the cause of impairment in about 3 percent of the children who have hearing loss (Northern & Downs, 1984). This condition, called *erythroblastosis fetalis,* is the result of the destruction of fetal Rh positive blood cells by maternal antibodies. The condition kills some of the afflicted infants during the first week of life. Of those who survive, 80 percent have partial or complete deafness. Like viral diseases, Rh incompatibility can cause other problems, such as cerebral palsy, mental retardation, epilepsy, aphasia, and behavioral disorders.

Other hearing problems are caused by ototoxic medications, medicines that destroy or damage hair cells in the cochlea. Kanamycin, neomycin, gentamycin, streptomycin, and vancomycin are some of the drugs known to be ototoxic. These drugs can cause partial or complete hearing loss when taken by the child or the pregnant mother. The fetus is particularly susceptible during the first three months of its development, especially the sixth and seventh weeks. The use of drugs by expectant mothers and young children should be carefully controlled.

Hereditary factors can also cause hearing loss. Proctor and Proctor (1967) report that hereditary deafness occurs in one of 2000 to one of 6000 live births. In many cases hearing loss is only one of several symptoms of a genetic problem. A specific group of symptoms may be classified as a syndrome, which may be identified by facial appearance, physical anomalies, mental retardation, sensory deficit, and motor weakness. Alport's syndrome, Treacher-Collins syndrome, and Down syndrome are examples of genetic conditions that may result in hearing loss. The child with a hereditary deficit often presents complex multiple problems that challenge the background and resourcefulness of the special educator.

Can exposure to noise affect hearing?

Although we have emphasized conditions that result in sensorineural hearing loss in children, two other important causes of sensorineural loss should be mentioned—exposure to noise, and aging. The recognition that noise can damage hearing has led to government regulation of acceptable noise levels in industry and the environment. Most of us can expect our hearing to deteriorate as we grow older. Both aging and excessive noise initially affect our ability to hear high-frequency sounds; the loss may gradually progress until we have problems understanding speech.

Unlike conductive hearing losses, sensorineural losses are not medically or surgically treatable. They are usually quite severe and require long-term rehabilitation effort, which will be discussed later in this chapter.

MIXED HEARING LOSS. A mixed hearing loss is one caused by both sensorineural and conductive problems. Such losses can create particularly serious problems for schoolchildren: A physician may focus on the conductive, medically treatable part of the loss and be unaware of the sensorineural component. As a result, children may not receive proper treatment for a problem that affects their classroom performance.

What is a mixed hearing loss?

Most hearing losses are caused by conductive, sensorineural, or mixed problems. However, all three types of problems may affect only one ear or may affect one ear more severely than the other. When this is the case, the child relies on the better ear and may turn that ear toward the speaker; the child also has trouble determining the source of a sound. Generally, however, a child with good hearing in one ear acquires speech and language without major difficulties.

What causes functional hearing loss?

FUNCTIONAL HEARING LOSS. Functional problems are those that are not organic in origin, as you will remember from the last chapter. A **functional hearing loss** is generally affected to compensate for some real or perceived social or psychological difficulties. In some cases, functional hearing loss may be psychosomatic or hysterical in origin, and the person may not be conscious of the assumed loss.

Among children, functional hearing losses occur most frequently between the ages of 9 and 13. The losses are usually discovered in hearing tests given in school. It is not unusual to discover that a child with a functional loss is upset or unhappy. There might, for example, be a new baby in the family who diverts parental attention; there may be a divorce or friction between the child's parents; there may be problems with the child's siblings or peer group; or the child may be receiving poor grades. Any of these conditions could cause the child to assume a hearing loss. Once the loss was assumed, it would be awkward and threatening to admit that it was all a game.

Among adults, functional hearing loss is often consciously intended in order to gain some perceived advantage. Audiologists for the most part can detect losses in adults that are not real. Some functional hearing losses are not intentional, and may result from emotional or psychological problems.

What is a central auditory disorder?

CENTRAL AUDITORY DISORDERS. Central auditory disorders are those in which there is no measurable peripheral hearing loss. Children with this type of disorder may display problems with auditory comprehension and discrimination, auditory learning, and language development. These disorders are the result of lesions or damage to the central nervous system, but specific causes are hard to pinpoint. Children with central auditory disorders have trouble learning and are often considered learning disabled. Interest in children with these disorders is growing as they present serious long-term problems and are difficult to treat effectively.

The Effects of Hearing Loss

A hearing loss is a major sensory deficit, and it can affect many different abilities. Its effects vary depending on a number of factors, including the severity of the loss, the age at which it occurred, and the person's determination to adapt. Those who teach and treat those with hearing impairments must consider the extent of the disability that results from the hearing loss, and whether the disability is exclusively the result of the loss, or of societal expectations and pressures as well.

INFLUENCE OF AGE OF ONSET AND SEVERITY OF HEARING LOSS. Myklebust (1964) stressed the importance of the age of onset and severity of hearing loss on the personality development and emotional adjustment of those with hearing impairments. These factors are also crucial in developing oral language and speech skills, in educational achievement, and in vocational and social development.

ORAL LANGUAGE AND SPEECH DEVELOPMENT. One of the most serious consequences of a hearing loss is the effect it can have on the development of speech and oral language. Language is crucial to personal and societal development. As Northern and Downs (1978) state:

> All the progress that man has made, if one can call a highly technologic society progress, is due to sophistication in the manipulation of language. . . . It follows that language deprivation is the most serious of all deprivation, for it robs us of a measure of our own human-ness. Whether caused by sensory deprivation, by experimental deprivation, or by central disordering, in some degree it keeps one from the complete fulfillment of one's powers. (p. 264)

To understand the effects of a hearing loss, you must understand normal speech and oral language development. The role of hearing in this process was discussed in Chapter 8. For our purposes it is helpful to reiterate the importance of the auditory feedback loop. As you will remember, an auditory feedback loop is a process beginning at birth whereby children monitor their own utterances as well as those of other people and are reinforced as they learn correct speech and language (Northern & Downs, 1984). This process may result in speechlike sounds when a child is 2 months old and the first meaningful words at about 1 year. Although we never stop learning language, the early months and years are especially crucial (Lenneberg, 1967; Menyuk, 1972).

It must also be remembered that a sign language, such as American Sign Language, is a natural language, with its own linguistic structure, visual-spatial syntax, lexicon, and so forth. Thus, many profoundly deaf individuals do have "language," and learn an oral language, such as English, as a second language.

Why does hearing loss have such a negative effect on oral language?

The interruption of this vital auditory feedback loop, or its absence in the case of a child born deaf, can slow speech and oral language development or preclude it altogether. The earlier the onset and the more severe the loss, the greater the difficulty in acquiring oral language. Children with mild to moderate loss will probably develop speech and language skills slowly, but they can usually learn to speak and use oral language effectively with therapy and adequate amplification from a hearing aid (Holm & Kunze, 1969; Quigley, 1970). Children born deaf, on the other hand, generally grow up without acquiring adequate speech or oral language skills (Carhart, 1970).

Those who become deaf after even a brief exposure to speech and language are much more likely to develop oral communication abilities than those who were deaf at birth. According to Lenneberg (1967), "It seems as if even a short exposure to language, a brief moment in which the curtain has been lifted and oral communication established, is sufficient to give a child some foundation on which much later language may be based" (p. 239). Helen Keller, who became deaf and blind from meningitis at age 2, is the classic example. The "lifting of the curtain" for the first two years of her life undoubtedly provided the basis for the excellent communication skills she later developed.

PROBE 9-3   Hearing Loss

1. People who have a hearing loss severe enough that they cannot learn language through hearing are classified as _____.
2. As many as _____ school-age children have some degree of hearing loss.
3. List the five major types of hearing loss.

4. Otitis media is the most common cause of _____ hearing loss. Other possible causes for this condition are _____ and _____.
5. When a "hearing loss" is assumed to explain poor school performance, the "loss" would be termed _____.
6. When there is damage or deterioration of the cochlea or VIII nerve, the hearing loss is termed _____. A major cause of this type of problem is disease. One of these diseases, _____, is a major cause of deafness in children.
7. When a child displays weakness in auditory skills and yet shows no measurable hearing loss, a _____ should be suspected.
8. The most serious effect of hearing loss is on the development of _____ and _____.
9. T   F   Children with normal hearing establish an auditory feedback loop at about 5 months of age.
10. T   F   American Sign Language has the same grammatical rules and syntax as spoken English.

EVALUATING HEARING LOSS

You should be able to discuss how hearing loss is identified and evaluated and be able to read an audiogram.

The hearing problems of children are identified at different ages and by a variety of different people. Children are generally referred first to a physician or **otologist** (a physician who specializes in diseases of the ear), who may in turn refer the child to an audiologist if there is no obvious problem that can be resolved medically or surgically. The audiologist can perform many different types of tests to determine whether a child has a problem, what kind of problem it is, and how it should be remedied.

As is true of other types of disorders, hearing disorders are treated most effectively if they are discovered early. In fact, there is sometimes concern about a child's hearing before birth, if there is a hereditary factor predisposing the child to a hearing problem or if the mother has had an illness, taken ototoxic drugs, had a traumatic accident, or if there is Rh incompatibility. Hearing evaluations are sometimes difficult to perform with very young children, but evaluations must be begun early to give the child every possible advantage.

Hearing problems are often discovered when the child is older, however. Parents may notice that their child does not react to loud sounds, does not turn his or her head when hearing a voice, does not engage in vocal play, or is delayed in speech and language development. Hearing problems may also be identified in hearing screening programs offered through health departments, speech and hearing centers, or school systems. Attentive teachers who notice that a child doesn't pay attention or frequently asks to have things repeated sometimes uncover hearing problems as well. However a problem is discovered, it should be promptly and thoroughly evaluated.

This evaluation is generally medical and audiological. The pediatrician or otologist takes a thorough medical history of the child and does a complete examination of the auditory canal and eardrum with a small light called an otoscope. If the child has an obvious middle ear infection, the doctor may be able to cure the problem. The audiometry may be requested to determine the effects of treatment. If the doctor cannot find the cause of the problem, the parents and child should be referred to an audiologist and/or otolaryngologist (ENT).

Audiometric Evaluation

Special educators should have some knowledge of the means and purposes of audiometric testings and should be able to read an audiogram. A thorough discussion of audiometric testing can be found in Newby and Popelka (1985) and Martin (1975).

Some types of hearing evaluation that yield gross information do not require the use of sophisticated equipment. Observations by parents and doctors provide some information, as do the child's medical history and otoscopic examination. Refined methods of formal audiometric testing, some of which are described in this section, are necessary to determine the precise extent of the hearing problem and the best methods of auditory rehabilitation or educational intervention.

What type of audiometric evaluation is most frequently done in schools?

PURE TONE AUDIOMETRIC SCREENING. Pure tone audiometric screening is usually a child's first encounter with formal hearing testing. Most school systems provide a regular schedule of hearing screening through the school speech-language pathologist or school nurse. Group hearing screening tests (Newby & Popelka, 1985) offer the advantage of testing more than one child at a time, but they are less susceptible to control and less reliable than individual tests.

Pure tone audiometric screening of individual students, often referred to as sweep testing, is performed with a pure tone audiometer (Newby & Popelka, 1985). In this test children are presented with pure tones over the frequency range from 250 Hz through 8000 Hz, and at a set intensity level of 20 to 25 dB. The children are asked to respond if they hear a tone, usually by raising a hand; children who cannot hear sounds at two or more frequencies are referred for more extensive evaluation.

How are the results of air conduction and bone conduction audiometric tests used?

PURE TONE THRESHOLD AUDIOMETRY. Pure tone audiometry is a testing method that requires children to raise a hand or push a button each time they hear a tone. The audiologist presents tones of different frequencies, ranging from 125 Hz to 8000 Hz, and determines the lowest intensity the child can hear—the threshold—at each frequency. This testing is done through earphones (air conduction) or through a vibrator placed on the mastoid bone behind the ear (bone conduction). The **air conduction (AC)** test reveals the presence of hearing loss and shows the amount of loss. **Bone conduction (BC)** testing measures the response of the sensorineural mechanism of the inner ear, bypassing the outer and middle ear systems. A comparison of air conduction and bone conduction thresholds reveals the loss as conductive, sensorineural, or mixed, as follows:

- *Conductive loss* is indicated when AC testing reveals some loss of hearing in the outer or middle ear, but BC testing shows normal hearing because the auditory nerve is functioning properly.
- *Sensorineural loss* is indicated when AC and BC testing show the same amount of loss, which signifies that the outer and middle ear are intact and the inner ear is affected.
- *Mixed loss* is indicated when BC testing shows a loss resulting from a sensorineural problem, and AC testing shows further loss resulting from a middle ear problem.

What is the speech reception threshold?

SPEECH AUDIOMETRY. Speech audiometry is a technique used to determine a child's ability to hear and understand speech. The threshold for speech (that is, the lowest intensity at which words are heard) is called the speech reception threshold, abbreviated SRT. The SRT is discovered by asking children to repeat two-syllable words that they hear, while the audiologist reduces the intensity of the words until they can barely be heard. To determine how well children can understand or discriminate among words heard at a comfortable loudness level, they are presented with a recorded list of one-syllable words and asked to respond. Children are expected to respond to all words whether they understand them or not. The purpose of the test is to determine how many correct responses a child makes in a given word list (usually 25 or 50 words). The number of correct responses is converted to a percentage score, and this is the speech discrimination score. Both the SRT and speech discrimination measures require the use of earphones.

In some cases it is necessary to keep one ear "busy" to test the other ear accurately. This occurs primarily when one ear is better than the other. This technique, called *masking,* involves transmitting a constant hissing noise to the good ear to keep it from hearing a sound being presented to the bad ear.

SPECIAL AUDIOMETRIC TESTS. Pure tone and speech audiometry constitute the standard test battery used to determine what type of hearing loss a child has and how extensive it is. Both tests require that the person being tested understand the test instructions and give a voluntary response, such as pushing a button, raising a hand, or repeating words. Some children cannot be evaluated with these tests, however, because they are too young (under 2 years), have motor or emotional problems, are mentally retarded, or present other difficulties. For these children, special tests and test variations have been devised.

When are special audiometric tests needed?

If a child is too young to understand test instructions or is unwilling to wear earphones, hearing can be evaluated by observing the intensity levels at which the child responds to sounds broadcast through speakers. Using this method, sound field audiometry, the audiologist presents speech, noise, or pure tones, and notes whether the child pays attention to the sounds or consistently turns to determine the sound source. The speech reception threshold of very young children can sometimes be determined by asking them to point to pictures or parts of the body as they are named. The same method can also be used to get an impression of a child's ability to discriminate speech (Northern & Downs, 1984).

Various techniques can be used to entice a frightened or reticent child to participate in testing by setting up a game or challenge (Newby & Popelka, 1985; Northern & Downs, 1984). Play audiometry involves the child in a series of activities that reward the child for responding appropriately to tone or speech. The game might involve putting a block in a bucket, activating a moving toy, turning on a light, or completing a puzzle.

The **impedance audiometer** is used to obtain information about the functioning of the middle ear system to assist the physician in treating otitis media and other middle ear problems. The two major impedance audiometry tests are *tympanometry,* which gives information about the compliance or resistance of the eardrum, and *stapedial reflex testing,* which measures the reflex response of the stapedial muscle to pure tone signals. These tests do not require a behavioral response from the child and are therefore useful with the very young and difficult-to-test children (Northern & Downs, 1984).

The **evoked response technique** requires the use of an electroencephalograph and a computer. It is used to measure the changes in brainwave electrical activity in response to sound. Like impedance audiometry, this type of testing does not require a behavioral response from the child; it can also be performed when the child is asleep or sedated. It is used with infants who are suspected of being deaf and with children who have multiple handicaps (Martin, 1975; Northern & Downs, 1984).

Interpretation of Audiograms

What is an audiogram?

Pure tone conduction and bone conduction results are generally charted on a grid, or **audiogram,** that has the frequencies tested noted at the top and the amount of loss in decibels noted down the side (see Figure 9-4). The type of test and the ear being tested are noted in symbols:

FIGURE 9-4   Extent of Hearing Loss

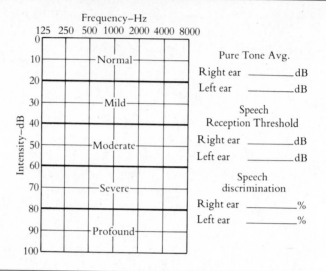

Source: Courtesy of William W. Green.

O — right ear, air conduction (△ when masking is applied to the left ear)
X — left ear, air conduction (□ when masking is applied to the right ear)
< — right ear, bone conduction ([when masking is applied to the left ear)
> — left ear, bone conduction (] when masking is applied to the right ear)

The extent of a hearing loss can be categorized as normal, mild, moderate, severe, or profound (Figure 9-4), based on the average pure tone air conduction loss at 500, 1000, and 2000 Hz (the frequencies on the audiogram most representative of the speech range) for each ear (see "How We Use Our Hearing" earlier in this chapter). The type of loss and its extent determine whether medical treatment or rehabilitation is necessary. Examples of typical audiograms are found in Figure 9-5.

Figure 9-5A shows the test results for a 6-year-old boy who has had a recurrent ear infection. His teacher thinks he doesn't pay attention, and he is having problems in school. This hearing test was requested by his pediatrician. It indicated a mild conductive hearing loss in both ears, which was treated with medication.

Figure 9-5B shows test results for the same 6-year-old boy following his medical treatment. His hearing has returned to normal for both ears. His mother was urged to take her child to a doctor if she suspected a recurrence of the problem. The child's teacher was asked to seat him in the front of the classroom so he would not miss instructions if his problem returned.

Figure 9-5C is the audiogram for a 4-year-old boy who is deaf. His mother had rubella during the first three months of her pregnancy with him. His pediatrician sent him for testing at 3 months of age, and he has had several tests since. He was fitted with a hearing aid when he was 14 months old. He was first enrolled in a preschool program for the deaf and later in a residential school for the deaf.

Figure 9-5D represents the hearing of a 9-year-old girl who was referred for evaluation because a problem with her right ear was discovered in a school screening program. The family doctor found no medically treatable condition and sent her to an audiologist for a complete evaluation. The evaluation indicated that she had normal hearing in her left ear and a profound

FIGURE 9-5   Examples of Typical Audiograms

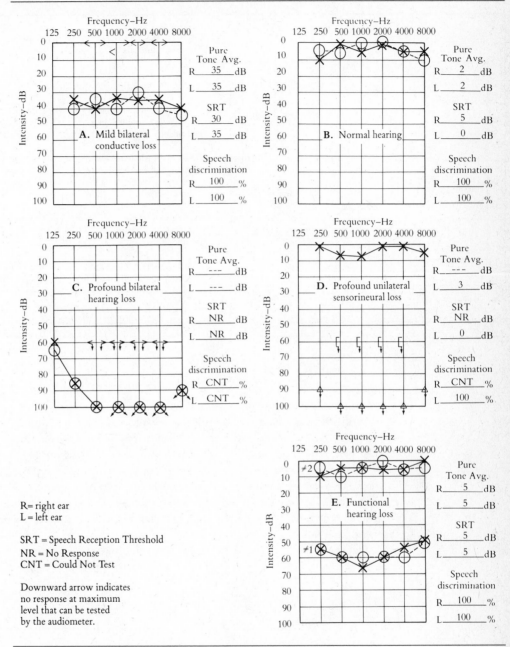

Source: Courtesy of William W. Green.

sensorineural loss in her right ear. Her mother was surprised to learn of the loss, because her daughter had no trouble learning speech and language, got good grades in school, and was an able conversationalist. Her normal hearing in one ear accounts for these abilities. This child did, however, have trouble determining where sounds were coming from, because we rely on differences in the time of arrival of sounds at our two ears to determine their direction of

FIGURE 9-6   A Functional Approach to Exceptionality: The Effects of Hearing Loss

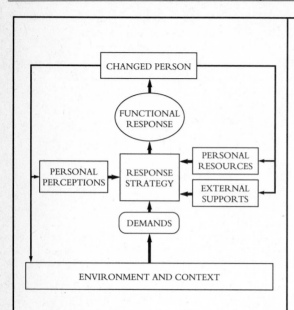

Hearing is a *personal resource* that is important for communication. Following is a summary of some of the effects of hearing loss according to severity:

- 0-20 dB = Normal range: No difficulty in any conversational setting.

- 20-40 dB = Mild loss: Hears in most settings; misses soft or whispered speech; will hear vowels but may miss unvoiced consonants; says, "Huh?"; wants TV turned up loud.

- 40-60 dB = Moderate loss: Hearing is a problem in most conversational settings, groups, or when there is a loss of background noise; hears louder voiced consonants; may need TV and radio up loud and have difficulty using telephone.

- 60-80 dB = Severe loss: Misses all but very loud speech; unable to function in conversation without help; can't use conventional telephone.

- 80 dB or more = Profound loss: Unable to hear speech except loud shout; does not understand spoken language unless good speechreader; can't hear TV or radio; can't use conventional telephone.

origin. Favorable classroom seating was requested for this child. In her case favorable seating was on the front right side of the room so her good left ear was toward the teacher.

Figure 9-5E is the audiogram for a 9-year-old girl whose aunt brought her in for testing. The girl had failed one subject in school and claimed it was because she could not hear the teacher. The pure tone responses labeled #1 are the results of the first attempt to test; they show a functional moderate-to-severe "loss." However, during all the tests, the girl's responses to speech were normal, and she had excellent understanding and discrimination. After considerable counseling, further testing yielded the pattern labeled #2, which shows normal hearing. As with all functional hearing losses affecting children, it was necessary to resolve the problem that prompted this girl to "need" the hearing loss.

Figure 9-6 provides a good perspective of the impact that various levels of hearing loss have on the ability of people to communicate or function within their environment.

PROBE 9-4   Evaluating Hearing Loss

1. What are four signs that might indicate a hearing loss?
2. A graphic portrayal of a person's hearing is called an _____.
3. T   F   An otoscopic examination will determine whether a child has a sensorineural hearing loss.
4. List the different types of audiometric tests.
5. T   F   Children's hearing cannot be tested accurately until they are 6 years of age.
6. The speech frequencies on the audiogram are _____, _____, and _____ Hz.

7. Match the amount of average loss on the right to the descriptive word on the left.

    ____ Mild   a. 0–20 dB
    ____ Profound   b. 20–40 dB
    ____ Moderate c. 40–60 dB
    ____ Normal   d. 60–80 dB
    ____ Severe   e. 80+ dB

8. The audiometric test that measures a person's ability to understand speech is called _____.

INTERVENTIONS FOR HEARING LOSS

You should be able to describe the various types of interventions for hearing loss.

There are many ways to address hearing loss. In some cases the appropriate treatment is medical or surgical; in others, longer-term rehabilitative and educational intervention procedures are required. Although we cannot discuss all types of interventions in detail, we will describe some of the more common ones, emphasizing those that are frequently used with children.

Medical and Surgical Treatment

In most cases conductive hearing loss in children can be overcome by appropriate medical or surgical treatment. The conductive component of a mixed hearing loss may also respond to this type of remedy. Children suffer from more conductive hearing disorders than any other age group. The most common cause is otitis media, or middle ear infection (Davis & Silverman, 1970; Paparella & Juhn, 1979). As you will remember, blockage of the external auditory canal and otosclerosis can also cause conductive loss, but these disorders are relatively uncommon.

What is the treatment of otitis media?

    Otitis media can often be cured with medication (Paradise, 1979). If the condition recurs frequently, the doctor may insert a small tube through the tympanic membranes, to act as a substitute for poorly functioning eustachian tubes, and to help ventilate the middle ear (Paparella, 1979). These tubes tend to work out of the eardrums every few months, and it is sometimes necessary to reinsert them. Physicians can also remove excessive earwax and objects that have become lodged in the auditory canal. Parents should not attempt this operation with cotton-tipped sticks because of the risk of damage to the ear canal.

Can sensorineural problems be cured?

    Sensorineural hearing problems, on the other hand, are not medically or surgically treatable to the extent that hearing can be restored. However, a new treatment option for those individuals with severe to profound sensorineural hearing loss is the cochlear implant. In this procedure, the surgeon implants a sensitive set of electrodes in the cochlea. Environmental sounds and speech are picked up by a receiver and channeled through a speech processor, which codes the information so that the auditory nerve will receive the coded information via the electrodes and send it on to the brain. This procedure is available for both adults and children who have sufficient sensorineural loss that they cannot obtain reasonable benefit from hearing aids. The cochlear implant procedure is not a cure for sensorineural hearing loss, but it does provide an alternative for assisting with communication (McCandless, 1985). This procedure is relatively new and should be approached with great care when suggested for children.

Auditory Rehabilitative Treatment

Sensorineural losses and central auditory disorders are relatively complex and require long-term intensive treatment. Auditory rehabilitation can include the use of hearing aids and assistive listening devices as well as auditory training and speechreading (Davis & Silverman, 1970; Sanders, 1982; Compton, 1989). It is usually a team effort involving an audiologist, a speech pathologist, and a teacher certified to work with those who have hearing impairments, as well as a psychologist and a social worker in many cases.

What is the goal of auditory rehabilitation?

The goal of auditory rehabilitative treatment should be to develop an individual's oral communication skills. This is done most effectively by using a variety of different techniques and approaches.

HEARING AIDS. Hearing aids are electronic devices that make sounds louder to assist in communication (Northern & Downs, 1984; Rubin, 1976; Sanders, 1982; Compton, 1989). The use of a hearing aid does not result in normal hearing, but it often greatly improves communication skills. Hearing aids may be considered for children with mild to severe sensorineural losses. They may even help deaf children by allowing them to detect some environmental sounds.

In recent years technological advances have resulted in smaller, more powerful aids with improved sound quality and fidelity. There are many brands and types on the market. The very young child with a severe or profound hearing loss will probably first use a body hearing aid because it is both powerful and durable. The child may later be able to change to a strong-gain ear-level aid. The aid used most commonly is the over-the-ear or behind-the-ear model. There are also aids that are built into glasses or into an earmold that fits into the external auditory canal.

What should a person with a hearing loss do before purchasing a hearing aid?

Before purchasing a hearing aid, it is important that adults and especially children receive a thorough audiological evaluation and medical clearance. This procedure is required by federal regulations and by many state laws as well. The different considerations in selecting an appropriate aid are too involved to discuss in this chapter; the reader who seeks additional information is directed to Northern and Downs, 1984; Hayes, 1985; and Compton, 1989.

How do hearing aids help their users?

A number of misconceptions about hearing aids prevent people from trying amplification. Sanders (1982), Northern and Downs (1984), and Hayes (1985) discuss several of these issues. One such misconception is that people with sensorineural hearing loss cannot benefit from amplification. This misconception is based on the assumption that damaged nerves cannot be stimulated or regenerated, and amplification is therefore pointless. But most people with sensorineural losses retain the ability to hear some sounds through the parts of the auditory nerve that function correctly, and amplified sound can travel along these structures. In fact, over 95 percent of hearing aid users have sensorineural rather than conductive losses. Those with conductive hearing loss can, of course, benefit from amplification, because their auditory nerves are intact. These individuals can usually be helped medically or surgically, however, and they don't need hearing aids. Everyone with a sensorineural hearing loss should have an opportunity to try amplification.

A second misconception is that a hearing aid will restore hearing to normal. A hearing aid is an amplifying system that makes things louder. It does not heal the ear, and most hearing aid users initially report that the sound through the hearing aid is artificial. Hearing aid technology is improving, however, and with a reasonable effort the hearing aid user will adjust to the artificial quality of the sound.

Some people believe that a hearing aid will result in increased hearing damage. This misconception is derived from the understanding that very loud noise can damage the ear, particularly the sensorineural component that hears high-frequency sounds. It would be possible for damage to result from the use of an aid that was far too powerful. It is doubtful, though, that the hearing aid user would tolerate such overcompensation. The danger is further reduced by relying on the guidance of an audiologist.

Finally, it is believed that hearing aids do not help those with mild or severe losses. No hearing loss is so mild or so severe that hearing aid use should not be attempted. Although people with mild losses do not always find an aid helpful, many like to use them in school, at work, or in social settings. The profoundly deaf can also use aids to help them communicate. Although a hearing aid will not allow them to understand speech, it can be used to supplement their speechreading or to detect environmental sounds.

ASSISTIVE LISTENING DEVICES AND SYSTEMS. There are numerous other listening devices (ALDs) and systems on the market to assist those with hearing loss in classroom and large-group settings. These include large area systems such as loops, infrared, and FM installations to enable individuals with hearing impairments to listen effectively to the teacher or presenter. Alerting and convenience devices for doorbells, intercoms, wake-up signals, and alarms are of great benefit to those with significant hearing losses. Closed captioning on TV has been a significant step forward for people who are deaf and hearing impaired, as are the special phone systems known as TDDs (telecommunication devices for the deaf). Excellent discussions of these devices can be found in Compton (1989) and in a special publication, "Assistive Listening Devices and Systems," published by the American Speech-Language-Hearing Association (1985).

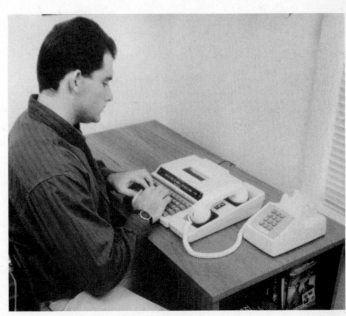

This man is using a TDD (telecommunication device for the deaf). Thanks to the Americans with Disabilities Act, the nation's telephone systems must now provide TDD services on a 24-hour basis.

TECHNOLOGY IN ACTION

In the 1970s several efforts were mounted to superimpose printed captions on television broadcasts so that people who were deaf could understand the programs. Unfortunately, studies found that people who could hear claimed that the captions were distracting and detracted from their viewing pleasure. As a result, this practice was not widely implemented.

A ten-year research and development effort paid off in March 1980, however, At that time a system of "closed captioning" was initiated. Television programs are transmitted so that a series of "lines" are eventually displayed on the screen, which results in the visual images that we see. In 1976, the Federal Communications Commission approved the use of television's line 21 for the purpose of closed captions.

With special encoding equipment, captions can be added to the program video signals in an invisible form that is broadcast to all receivers. With specially equipped TVs or the use of a special device that is available in stores such as Sears, people can decode the signal so that the captions are visible on their TV sets.

You have probably noticed a symbol in your TV viewing guide that looks like a little television screen inside a "cartoon balloon" or have seen that symbol at the beginning of a television program, accompanied by the words, "Closed captioned for the hearing impaired." This means that the program you are watching also can

be enjoyed by people who are deaf or hard of hearing who have the necessary decoding equipment. By having captions available, they can "see" what other people hear.*

The National Captioning Institute has introduced a new device that has the potential of helping thousands of people with hearing loss get more enjoyment from public entertainment. Called AudioLink, it allows the wearer of a specialized headset to control the sound—up to 124 decibels—of an event, film, or play. The system uses invisible infrared light waves to transmit audio from either a television or a public facility's sound system to the headset.

As of early 1992, more than 2000 facilities had the capacity to use AudioLink, including most of New York's Broadway theaters; the John F. Kennedy Center for Performing Arts in Washington, DC; Epcot Center at Disney World; and the Cineplex, Odeon, and Loews movie theaters. With AudioLink, individuals can take their personal headsets into any facility that is appropriately equipped and enjoy clear audio without disturbing those around them.

Contact AudioLink at 1-800-533-9673 (voice) or 1-800-321-8337 (TDD) for more information.

*Source: Adapted from an article by Tracy L. Harris, in Counterpoint, November 1981.

Auditory Training

What are the goals of auditory training programs?

Auditory training is intended to teach those with hearing impairments to use their residual hearing to the greatest extent possible (Sanders, 1982). It is usually provided by an audiologist or speech pathologist in individual or group therapy sessions and reinforced in the regular classroom and at home. In auditory training, the child is taught to use and care for a hearing aid, to use environmental cues in conversation, and to sharpen the ability to discriminate among sounds and words. The goals of an auditory training program may include the following:

1. *To familiarize the child and parents with the nature and extent of the loss.* This involves explaining how the normal ear functions; describing how various types and amounts of hearing loss affect communication, and specifically how the loss will affect the child's communication; and explaining the child's audiogram.
2. *To familiarize the child and parents with hearing aids and hearing aid maintenance.* This involves explaining that hearing aids make things louder, not necessarily clearer; explaining the controls and settings of the hearing aid; and providing the child and parents with information on the care and maintenance of the hearing aid.

3. *To familiarize the child and parents with the methods and goals of the auditory training plan.* This includes developing an awareness of sounds and the basic meanings of sounds; teaching the child to discriminate among sounds; and encouraging the child to make full use of his or her auditory abilities.

4. *To carry out the program designed to meet the individual child's needs.* This requires regularly scheduled therapy sessions with an audiologist or speech pathologist; active involvement of the child's regular classroom or special teacher in reinforcing the auditory training; and active involvement of the parents in reinforcing auditory training in the home and family.

Speechreading

How much speech is visibly displayed by lip movements?

A child who has had a hearing loss naturally becomes more attentive to a speaker's lips and facial movements. Most people with hearing impairments are not even aware that they are doing so. Such lipreading or speechreading can be a valuable skill, but it can be used only to supplement communication, not as a complete communication system. Only 30 to 40 percent of the sounds in our language are produced with visible lip movement, so the speechreader has many gaps to fill in.

Nevertheless, many children with hearing impairments do benefit from formal speechreading training. It is typically provided by the audiologist and speech pathologist in group or individual therapy sessions. These usually take place through speech and hearing clinics or in the school. Speechreading therapy is most effective when it is part of a rehabilitation program that includes auditory training and the use of a hearing aid. Speechreading lessons are most productive when they take advantage of the child's interests and experiences.

Most speechreading programs and materials are designed for adults with hearing impairments and for older students with well-developed language skills, and while the general principles may apply also to young children, the materials often do not. Speechreading correlates higher with language than does any other communication skill; thus it is particularly important that speechreading materials be commensurate with the child's language level. Some people cannot become good speechreaders even with formal training. It requires considerable concentration to speechread successfully.

What can people do to make speechreading easier for a person who is deaf?

Speechreading is usually easier if one is familiar with the speaker. Ideally, the speechreader should be able to see the speaker's entire face from the front. This allows the speechreader to distinguish both lip movements and facial expressions. As much of the speaker's body as possible should be in view of the speechreader, since body gestures are a part of communication. The speaker's lip movements are crucial. A lack of normal movement or exaggerated movement makes speechreading more difficult. Also, the speaker should speak at a normal pace.

The second component in our system is the environment. The distance between the speaker and the speechreader is very important. The greater the distance, the more difficult it is to speechread effectively. To speechread, one must be able to see the speaker's face. Therefore, good lighting is also important. Even when the speaker is clearly seen, however, it is sometimes difficult to speechread if the environment is filled with distractions.

PROBE 9-5   Interventions for Hearing Loss

1. Small tubes may be inserted in the tympanic membrane to _____ the ear.
2. T   F   Hearing aids are electronic devices that make sound clearer.
3. T   F   Medical clearance and an audiological evaluation are required before one can obtain a hearing aid.

4. _____ consists of techniques that help a child with a hearing impairment use residual hearing as much as possible.

5. When a child with a hearing impairment is watching a speaker's lip and facial movement, he or she is _____ .

6. T F From 70 to 80 percent of the sounds in our language are not visible on the speaker's lips.

EDUCATION OF CHILDREN WITH HEARING LOSS

You should be able to describe the educational needs of children who are deaf or hard-of-hearing and describe implications for their education.

Identification

What clues might alert parents to the possibility of a hearing loss in a preschool child?

Many children are identified as having a hearing loss before they enter school, particularly if their loss is severe enough to delay speech and language development. The loss is generally first recognized by a doctor or by the child's parents. A doctor may be especially alert for hearing problems because of (1) a history of hereditary hearing loss; (2) infections or illness of the mother during pregnancy; (3) defects of the child's ears, nose, or throat; (4) low birth weight; (5) prematurity; or (6) infections, diseases, or accidents sustained by the child (Northern & Downs, 1984). Parents may discover a hearing loss by observing that their child does not respond normally to sounds. Children whose hearing problems have been discovered very early have probably undergone audiological evaluation and treatment before they entered school.

What indicators point to possible hearing loss in school children?

Children with hearing losses that have not been discovered when they entered school are frequently identified by their teacher. Signs that may indicate a hearing problem include the following:

- The child does not appear to be paying attention.
- The child complains of frequent earaches or has a discharge from the ears.
- Articulation of speech sounds is poor, or consonant sounds are omitted.
- Easy questions are answered incorrectly.
- The child fails to respond or pay attention when spoken to in a normal manner.
- "Hearing" appears to be better when the child faces the speaker.
- The child often asks the speaker to repeat what was just said.
- When listening to the radio, TV, or other audiovisual equipment, the child turns up the volume to a level that is uncomfortable to those with normal hearing.

Although some of these signs may indicate problems other than hearing loss, any child displaying them should be observed carefully. A child thought to have a hearing loss should be referred to an audiologist.

Most school systems have regularly scheduled hearing screenings. They are usually conducted by the school speech pathologist, audiologist, or nurse, sometimes with the assistance of parent volunteers. In some schools, screening programs make use of university-based audiology training programs. Whoever staffs them, screening programs are an effective method of discovering undetected hearing problems.

Educational Needs

Before planning educational programs for students who have hearing losses, it is important to understand their unique needs. Some of these will be described in this section according to severity of hearing impairment.

CHILDREN WITH MILD TO MODERATE HEARING LOSSES. Students with mild to moderate hearing losses are often referred to as being *hard-of-hearing*. The treatment and educational requirements of such children will depend on the nature and severity of their hearing loss, communication needs, and social-emotional development.

What type of educational placement is most common for children who are hard-of-hearing?

Mild to moderate conductive losses that result from recurrent ear infections often can be successfully treated medically or surgically. Although most children with this type of hearing loss can function in a regular classroom, the teacher should not assume that the child requires no special attention. The child should at least be given favorable seating. Children with mild to moderate sensorineural hearing losses may need a hearing aid, preferential seating in the classroom, speech and language therapy, and possibly speechreading and auditory training therapy. In some cases the child with mild to moderate sensorineural hearing loss may benefit most from being placed in a special class. This is determined by an educational assessment of the child's progress.

Teachers should also be aware that recurrent otitis media may result in delayed speech and language development (Holm & Kunze, 1969; Needleman, 1977). If it does, the child may need speech and language therapy. Children with mild to moderate conductive losses will benefit from the use of a hearing aid only in the uncommon cases that are not curable.

Although most children with mild to moderate sensorineural hearing loss can function fairly well in regular classrooms, many do experience significant problems. Unfortunately, because these children can usually hear and understand conversational speech, their school-related problems are sometimes not thought to be the result of hearing loss.

CHILDREN WITH MODERATE TO SEVERE HEARING LOSSES. A hearing loss in the moderate to severe range has a much greater effect on a child's education than a mild to moderate loss. Most of the more serious losses are caused by irreversible sensorineural problems present at birth or from a very early age. There are some moderate conductive hearing losses, but they are relatively uncommon and can usually be successfully cured.

What types of sound amplification aids are often used with children who have moderate to severe hearing loss?

The child with a moderate to severe sensorineural loss will probably use a hearing aid. These children also may need special therapy, reinforced by classroom drills. If there are several children with hearing loss in a classroom, the teacher may need to use a group auditory training unit, or group listening device such as an FM system. These units enable a teacher to speak to a large number of children through an amplifying device that transmits to a receiving device such as earphones or to the children's hearing aids (Davis & Silverman, 1970; Sanders, 1982; Compton, 1989).

The child with a moderate to severe loss may also need to learn speechreading. As mentioned earlier, most people with hearing impairments speechread to some extent without being aware of it and without having been taught (Berger, 1972). Formal training in speechreading may help the hearing impaired child in general communication, in the class-room, and in maintaining speech.

THE CHALLENGE TO PROFESSIONALS. McDermott (1978) noted that "contributing to the problem of reaching children who are hard-of-hearing is their invisibility. Given inadequate identification systems, they are often found among school failures and labeled as unmotivated, inattentive, or uncooperative. Too often such children are placed in classes for children with learning disabilities, or when their hearing loss frustrates them in education, classes for students who are socially or emotionally disturbed." They are neither—they are children with hearing impairments.

Added to this population are the large numbers of students who suffer from chronic and severe otitis media. A study conducted in the late 1970s found that over one-third of all students in classes for children with learning disabilities had histories of chronic serious otitis media. The failure to understand their hearing loss, and its relationship to language delay—not disorder—is at the crux of this problem.

Diagnosticians, teachers, educational psychologists, and multidisciplinary team members must be aware of the extent to which a mild or moderate hearing loss can affect language development and thus affect educational progress. While proper amplification and preferential seating are two relatively easy-to-manage approaches to helping those with less severe hearing impairments, the fundamental issues have to do with language, language enrichment, and its relationship to educational development.

What can teachers do when they have a child who is hard-of-hearing in their class?

SUGGESTIONS FOR THE CLASSROOM TEACHER. There are many children with mild to moderate hearing loss in regular classrooms. The following suggestions may help the teacher work with them effectively:

1. If the teacher generally teaches from the front of the room, the child who is hard-of-hearing should be seated in the front, preferably slightly off center toward the windows. This allows the child to hear better and read lips more effectively. Light should be directed towards the teacher's face and away from the speechreader's eyes.
2. If the child's hearing impairment involves only one ear, or if the impairment is greater in one ear than the other, the child should be seated in the front corner seat with the better ear toward the teacher.
3. The teacher should pay attention to the posture of the hearing impaired child's head. The habits of extending the head or twisting the neck to hear better can become firmly fixed.
4. The child should be encouraged to watch the face of the teacher whenever the teacher is talking to the child. The teacher should speak at the speechreader's eye level whenever possible.
5. The teacher should try to face the hard-of-hearing child as much as possible when speaking to the class. An effort should be made to give all important instructions from a position close to the child. It's best not to stand between the child and the windows, which may prove distracting.
6. The teacher should not speak loudly or use exaggerated lip movements when speaking to the child who is hard-of-hearing.
7. The child should be encouraged to turn around to watch the faces of children who are reciting.
8. It is easy to overestimate the hearing efficiency of a child. It should be remembered that it takes a greater effort for a child with a hearing impairment to hear than it does for a normal child. As a result, it may be more difficult to hold that child's attention.
9. A hearing loss of long duration can cause a person's voice to become dull and monotonous. It can also result in poor diction. The child with a hearing impairment and the rest of the class should be encouraged to speak clearly and distinctly.
10. Use of an overhead projector allows the teacher to write without having to turn away to write on the blackboard. The overhead projector also helps to illuminate the teacher's face, thus making lipreading easier.

11. Key words, expressions, or phrases should be written on the chalkboard or shown on an overhead projector.

12. Supplementary pictures of diagrams should be used whenever possible.

13. Care should be taken not to talk with one's face either turned downward to read notes or hidden by a book or papers.

14. Since a hearing loss affects all the language processes, the child should be encouraged to compensate by taking a greater interest in reading, grammar, spelling, original writing, and other activities that involve language.

15. The child who is hard-of-hearing should be observed carefully to ensure that he or she doesn't withdraw or suffer emotionally as a direct or indirect result of poor hearing.

16. The child should participate in all activities of the classroom, no matter how language-based they might be.

17. Teachers should watch carefully for illness in children with hearing impairments. Colds, influenza, throat and nose infections, tonsillitis, and other ailments should be treated as soon as possible.

18. The teacher should be able to assist the child who wears a hearing aid in the classroom.

Teaching Children Who Are Deaf

What are the issues involved in the education of children who are deaf?

This section will address the fundamental issues in the education of children with profound and severe hearing losses. The issues are complex, and only the most important will be summarized here: (1) communication, including choice of communication systems; (2) acquisition of language, reading, and writing skills (including English) and language acquisition and speech communication skills; (3) learning environments and educational strategies; (4) cognition and learning; and (5) social and personal issues. Each area itself has a large body of professional literature associated with it; readers seeking further information should consult the list of references for this chapter.

What is the major issue in the education of people who are deaf?

COMMUNICATION. Communication between individuals who are deaf and others in their environment, both hearing and deaf, remains the fundamental issue in the education of the deaf. Powers (1991) noted that the most important principle related to communication is that it is "about hearing impaired people obtaining equity in access to those things that their community holds in common. . . . Unless any method of communication or device can provide hearing impaired people with such community benefits and services as they desire, it cannot be seen as acceptable" (p. 10).

Powers notes that there are two broad categories, with respect to communication, that always seem to exist: "hearing impaired" individuals and "severely and profoundly deaf" individuals. The former group, he notes, "will develop the spoken language of their community . . . use that language in its oral form for communication purposes, and will to a greater or lesser extent function as speaking/hearing persons. They will usually be educated in regular schools alongside hearing children and marry someone who is also speaking/hearing" (p. 11). In reviewing the various educational approaches, sensory aids, and medical advances such as cochlear implants, it is important to remember, according to Powers, that "aids to communication for [those with hearing impairments] must be evaluated in the context of giving them access to that education and family and social life and vocational choice" (p. 11).

The situation and its evaluation, however, for children who are severely and profoundly deaf, is not quite so straightforward. For example, Powers notes that while some educators of the deaf "insist that assimilation into the hearing-speaking community must be the aim of education of the deaf and can occur only if deaf people learn to listen, lipread, and speak, . . . many educators and deaf people themselves have argued that a purely oral existence and education is unnecessarily demanding for severely . . . and profoundly deaf children . . . and is not necessary for a successful and happy existence as a deaf adult" (p. 12). Powers goes on to note that "this latter position has the support of most educators of the deaf in most countries in the latter half of the twentieth century" (p. 12). Powers concludes:

> We should derive our view of what a "good education" communication method for deaf children is from our view of their adult life, not childhood. We have been too often misled by viewing deaf children's education only from their childhood needs, and not from what ensues in their adult lives. (p. 13)

How may communication be taught?

Approaches to Teaching Communication. Following are some of the terms commonly used to define or describe methods, philosophies, and languages related to education of children who are deaf:

1. *Total Communication:* A philosophy that advocates the use of any form or mode of communication that leads to mutual understanding, including (but not limited to) speech, residual hearing, manual codes of English, American Sign Language, speechreading, reading, and writing.
2. *American Sign Language* (ASL): One or more of the varieties of the language of signs commonly used in the Deaf community in America.
3. *Simultaneous Communication* (SimCom): Speaking and signing at the same time, most often with a manual code of English accompanying speech.
4. *Oral-Aural:* An educational method that emphasizes the use of residual hearing and speech as the primary mode of communication and learning for children who are deaf.

What is the controversy over oral vs. manual methods of communication?

Choosing Communication Systems. For many, many years, a fundamental debate about what communication methodology should be used to educate children who are deaf has raged throughout the United States and the world. In 1880, the International Congress of Educators of the Deaf passed the now infamous Milan Decree, which expressed the superiority of speech over sign language. This set the stage for almost a century of exclusively oral education in the United States. In this philosophy or approach, children who were deaf were required to gain an education entirely through the use of residual hearing, speechreading, and print representations. However, sign languages continued to be used for the purposes of communication among the Deaf community throughout the United States.

"How should children who are deaf be taught?" is a topic of international controversy once again, especially in relationship to the form of the language of instruction. Moores (1991) notes, "In a bewilderingly short period of time, in the education of the deaf most countries have gone from oral-only, or predominantly oral-only, to oral-manual." This oral-manual trend, often known as Total Communication, "usually consists of a combination of speech and a sign system designed to be used in conjunction with the spoken language." While Moores (1991) suggests that there is some evidence that the use of Total Communication "contributed to improved academic and linguistic performance in deaf children," their performance, as a group, still lags significantly behind their hearing peers in educational achievement.

AM THINKING ABOUT BOTH THE PAST AND THE

LOOK OVER AT ALL OF MY CLASSMATES AND I F

This student is giving the valedictorian address at her high school graduation. A projector is used to display the words of her speech to classmates and parents in the audience who don't understand sign language.

While the "oral vs. manual" debate continues in some forums, it is less of an issue now than it once was. Programs that espouse the use of Oral-Aural methods are (with a few notable exceptions) less likely to criticize programs that use Total Communication or other manual approaches and simply focus on improving their own approach. Programs that use sign language are now in the majority and are rarely defensive about their use of a sign system. In fact, the major focus among programs using sign language in the instructional process is not whether to, but how to and which sign system to use.

In 1989, sparked by the publication of *Unlocking the Curriculum: Principles for Achieving Access to Deaf Education,* educators began to seriously consider the sign languages used by the Deaf community in the instructional process. For example, in the United States, Johnson, Liddell, and Erting (1989) argue for the use of American Sign Language (ASL) as the language of instruction in American schools for children and youth who are deaf. (ASL is a complex language with its own structure and rules, of which the manual alphabet for fingerspelling words shown in Figure 9-7 is only a very small part.) At the same time, a program mandating the use of Swedish Sign Language as the primary language of instruction in schools for the deaf in Sweden attempted to put this philosophy in practice, as so-called "bilingual" programs were implemented in both Denmark and Sweden (cf. Davies, 1991).

What other considerations are important when considering a communication system?

Much of the debate has focused on *which* language to use, but there unfortunately has been very little discussion about the content and quality of the language used in the instruction of students who are deaf. Choosing the most appropriate language or modality alone does not guarantee full access to curriculum. As important as the form of language we use is *what we talk* about, *how* interactions with children take place, and *what we expect* of language interactions with children. One can still talk about inappropriate, unchallenging, and unstimulating topics with children, even while using a fully appropriate linguistic form. Accessibility to the

FIGURE 9-7   The Manual Alphabet

The manual alphabet as the receiver sees it

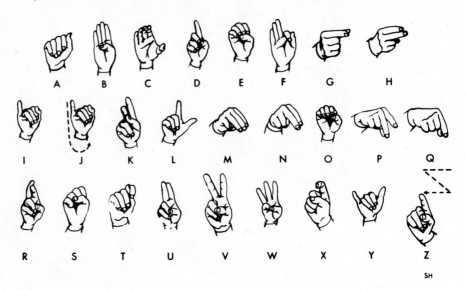

The manual alphabet as the sender sees it

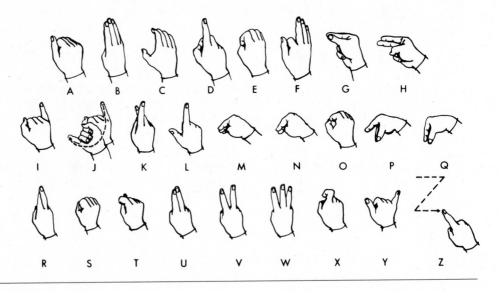

Source: Courtesy of the National Association of the Deaf.

curriculum depends not only on the form, but on the *content and function of language in the classroom*. While the field has chosen to focus on the form issue—perhaps since it is more clearcut—only the more-complex linguistic and communicative issues of how language functions in the classroom can determine whether full accessibility to the curriculum will be achieved.

ACQUISITION OF LANGUAGE, READING, AND WRITING SKILLS. The development of more specific language skills has always been central to the education of school-age children and youth who are deaf. Berruecos (1991) reviewed the history of language education and methodologies and concluded that "since language is a socially maintained functioning institution, it is my preference to approach the topic [of language development] from a sociolinguistic perspective" (p. 3). She goes on to note that teachers of the deaf not only need to know what to teach, what their pupils learn, and how they learn, but "*how they understand and use language functionally*" (p. 3).

Berruecos leans heavily on the work of linguist Michael Halliday (1973) who analyzes language structures and function along three dimensions: the ideational, the interpersonal, and the textual. Applications of this theory in the education of those who are deaf are seen in the United States in the work of Blackwell and his colleagues (1978) and the adaptations of that work in Europe (e.g., Knudsen, 1980; van der Lem & Menke, 1982; Fiksdal & Skallist, 1986).

Use of these more functionally based methodologies is now more widely accepted. As a result, the focus of language teaching has turned toward *how* to utilize this perspective, and away from the debate of so-called structural vs. natural language teaching techniques. In developing or evaluating language teaching methods or approaches for students who are deaf, it is important to know whether or not this more modern, sociolinguistic approach is being used.

English Language Development. Stuckless (1989) writes: "There is a broad agreement that the most critical element in the student's education is the acquisition of English language, both for active participation in society and as a requisite for success in academic content areas. Unfortunately, literacy in English remains beyond the grasp of many, if not most, deaf students" (p. 1).

Quigley and Paul (1989) provide a comprehensive review of research on reading as a secondary English language skill, citing numerous studies using several measures of reading that indicate the pervasive severity of the problem for most students who are deaf. Studies that examined more discrete aspects of reading—for example, the understanding of multiple meanings in vocabulary, or of figurative language such as idioms and metaphors—consistently show students who are deaf being outperformed by hearing students. Quigley et al. (1976), for example, demonstrate that most older adolescent students who are deaf derive less useful information from the syntax of a sentence than do 8-year-old students with hearing.

Quigley and Paul (1989) identify several studies of discourse analysis with students who are deaf, indicating the influence of top-down theories of reading, which emphasize the importance of what the reader brings to the task of reading rather than the reader's linguistic weaknesses. A growing body of knowledge from studies involving both hearing and deaf readers supports an interactive view involving both top-town and bottom-up strategies.

Quigley and Paul (1989) also review the results of research on reader-based variables, beginning with modes of communication used with and by the student who is deaf. They cite two studies in which the use of what is called Simultaneous Communication (SimCom) seemed to lead to higher reading performance than oral approaches alone. Recent research, however (e.g., Geers, Moog, & Schick, 1984), appears to demonstrate just the opposite. In both studies there are great ambiguities in the form of uncontrolled variables.

While there is little or no research directly assessing the effects of American Sign Language (ASL) on English language development, a number of studies conducted in the 1960s compare the English-language performance of deaf children of deaf parents with deaf children of hearing parents. These studies consistently showed the former group of deaf children performing better than the latter. However, factors like parental acceptance could not be controlled, and it may be concluded that manual communication alone, in any form, is not the exclusive determiner of how well the child who is deaf learns to read.

What is the most important academic skill for students who are deaf?

What does research tell us about the use of English language in children who are deaf?

Few studies have been conducted on the effects of oral education where the subjects are profoundly deaf and exposed primarily to an oral approach. Quigley and Paul (1989) find that the demonstrated successes have mostly arisen in conjunction with variables such as a high socioeconomic level environment and call for more well-documented research in this area.

Of interest also are the internal strategies that students who are deaf use for coding print. A phonological or speech-based recording strategy is used by most hearing persons to facilitate the processing of print into meaning. Although numerous studies have shown that most students who are deaf use a non-speech-based code to mediate between print and meaning, some research has shown extensive use of "inner" speech by some, even among those whose speech is rated as unintelligible, and at least two studies have concluded that most good deaf readers use primarily a speech-based code rather than visual or sign codes to mediate print.

There is also a high correlation of variables associated with both reading and writing, with the written language of students who are deaf revealing the same depressed performance level as reading comprehension when compared to that of hearing peers. While citing some evidence that closely links reading and writing at the sequential level, Quigley and Paul (1989) suggest that in many cases the written language problems of students who are deaf might be better handled by examining how sentences relate to one another, as through discourse analysis, rather than focusing on the relationship between the words within a sentence. Too much instructional emphasis may be given to helping students who are deaf understand the structure of a single sentence, and not enough to understanding the sentence within a broader pragmatic context.

What approaches are used for language instruction?

There have been two general approaches taken to language instruction: *natural* and *structured,* but there is no indication that one yields better results than the other. However, many educational programs continue to use some type of symbol system to teach English to students who are deaf, ranging from systems that have students fit words into preset grammatical structures or sentence patterns, to symbols based on transformational grammar, such as the Rhode Island Curriculum (Blackwell et al., 1978).

In summary, little or no change in the mastery of English by students who are deaf has taken place over a 40-year period spanned by measurement. Support for various instructional approaches to reading and writing is more polemic than empirical, and little is really known about the effectiveness of various instructional practices and materials in this critical area. Special educators should be careful to assess language teaching methodologies carefully and with respect to and for the individual child's needs rather than to accept conventional wisdom, which may represent more belief than fact.

Speech Communication. Stuckless (1989) notes: "A relatively small proportion of pre-lingually deaf students acquire what can be considered intelligible speech and probably do not profit as they might from appropriate amplification. Yet there should be no question that the effort to develop the deaf child's potential for oral/aural communication is a legitimate and necessary educational responsibility regardless of prevailing mode of communication or type of school placement" (p. 1).

How can speech communication be developed in students who have hearing impairments?

Levitt (1987) identified the most important first step in improving the speech communication skills of children with hearing impairments: notably, the audibility of the speech signal. For those with severe and profound hearing losses, it is essential to utilize available residual hearing as efficiently as possible, which generally means frequency dependent amplification, by placing the amplification of speech at the most comfortable level for the child at all frequencies.

However, research indicates that children with hearing losses in the 80–100 dB pure tone range are likely to have great difficulty with segmental contrasts in speech. Many of these children are presently enrolled in schools for the deaf. Some research (Levitt, 1987) indicates that among those with this hearing loss who have been successfully mainstreamed, many had

This student is learning how to make sounds that will eventually enable her to communicate with her classmates who can hear.

a fair degree of hearing at the level of 4000 Hz and above, which is generally not taken into account by the usual pure tone average.

What problems are often encountered in auditory training programs?

The speech signal is highly redundant, and a key to success in speech training is identifying these redundancies and putting them to use. There are two limitations to current auditory training programs: first, some are geared to a particular subset of the population, and are not applicable to the broad range of children who may be in the teacher's care; second, teachers are required to develop many of their own materials. In a number of speech training programs, auditory training plays a major part; a common element in these programs is that each systematically trains and tests auditory ability as the child moves along through the curriculum.

What should be included in a speech training program?

Levitt (1987) also described common error patterns in the speech of those with hearing impairments. While major differences exist from child to child in speech intelligibility, there are also major similarities that typify their speech. In order to address these typical error patterns, there must be three basic components in effective speech training programs: a structured curriculum, a curriculum-based evaluation instrument, and teaching materials appropriate to the child's level of language development.

At the same time, Levitt (1987) points out two hazards in teaching speech: (1) too much effort being expended on teaching segmental (actual phonetic) features and not enough on suprasegmental features (e.g., pitch, intonation, word stress); and (2) the tendency to concentrate on those aspects of speech which are easiest to teach, but which may be of only secondary importance to the overall intelligibility. Educators who wish to focus on speech development for children who are deaf must be careful to avoid these pitfalls.

Levitt (1987) describes a series of his longitudinal studies of children with hearing impairments, and indicates some of the more salient findings relative to speech development. Not unexpectedly, speech intelligibility is found to be largely a function of hearing loss. Among the numerous correlates, several other factors stood out. As can be expected, children whose onset of deafness was postlingual have far better speech than those whose deafness is prelingual.

Children with behavioral and/or emotional problems and children whose home language is other than English also fall below the general level. Levitt (1987) and his associates also observed better speech intelligibility among children who had the benefit of early education prior to age 3, and among children with U-shaped audiograms. By and large, mainstreamed children had more intelligible speech than those in schools for the deaf, but most also had considerably more residual hearing.

Levitt (1987) did find a small proportion of children who were profoundly deaf with quite intelligible speech. These children provide convincing evidence that it is indeed possible for some who are profoundly deaf to acquire intelligible speech, pointing to the need to study children such as these—and children at the other end of the speech intelligibility scale—in order to identify factors contributing to success or the lack of it in speech development.

LEARNING ENVIRONMENTS AND EDUCATIONAL POLICIES. Two of the factors that relate to policies for educating children who are deaf and their resulting educational placement are discussed in this section: demographic trends, and the issue of "least restrictive environment."

How are demographics of the deaf population affecting educational practices?

Demographics. Changing demographics are an initial consideration in the education of students who are deaf. First, there is the present decline in the school-age population of children who are deaf, attributed to the fact that victims of the 1959–65 rubella epidemic have now passed through the school system, and to the success of the rubella immunization program, which has now almost eradicated rubella as a cause of childhood deafness.

A more important demographic trend, however, is noted by Silverman (1987), who stated that it was not long ago that "the ratio of students in state residential schools to students in other environments was about 70–30 and that these numbers are now just about reversed." This tremendous swing away from placements in residential and/or day programs is an overriding concern in any discussion of environments and strategies for teaching and learning. Additionally, recent demographic studies (Cohen, Fischgrund, & Redding, 1990) also indicate that approximately 30 percent of all students in programs for deaf and hearing impaired individuals are either of racial, linguistic, or ethnic minority status. These three issues—the departure of the rubella population from school settings, the swing away from residential and center school placements, and the increasing number of minority students who are deaf—are the three most important demographically driven policy issues faced by educators of the deaf today.

What is the least restrictive educational environment for students who are deaf?

Educational Settings. The question of whether children who are deaf should be taught in a special school for the deaf (residential or day) or in a variety of other regular educational classrooms or school programs has been a difficult issue since the passage of PL 94-142. Moores

(1991) notes that "very little is currently known about the relative benefits of different options of the educational placement of deaf children."

Lowenbraun and Thompson (1989) find that research has shed little light on what constitutes "least restrictive environment" (LRE), but do bring together a number of studies on the general topic. One such review of seven studies suggests overall academic advantages to mainstreamed placement and disadvantages relative to social and emotional growth. Other studies conclude that physical integration does not necessarily promote either the use of oral language or social interaction.

It is clear from Lowenbraun and Thompson's (1989) extensive search of the literature and their analysis of the few existing studies that address LRE and the education of children who are deaf, that the investigation of what the concept of LRE means to the child who is profoundly deaf is in great need of exploration. Currently, approaches presenting what is called a continuum (but is really a hierarchy) encourage the perception that special school placements for children who are deaf are inherently more restrictive than regular school placements. There is, however, no objective evidence to support such a view, but only expressions of opinions and belief.

The fundamental principle here is that the choice of an educational placement for children who are deaf should be made on an individual basis for each child and should not be based on prior assumptions about the relative merits of any particular type of setting. As Brownley (1987) notes:

> The placement of a deaf child in a public school does not assure quality. Neither does placement in a special school. . . . Quality happens where committed groups of knowledgeable people working together make individual decisions based on objective evidence for each child's present and future. (p. 341)

COGNITION AND LEARNING. Wood (1991) reviews three dominant historical perspectives on cognition and deafness. Very early perspectives represented the view that people who were deaf, primarily because they did not have oral language, were cognitively deficient. This view, obviously not built upon any data or research, gave way to the view that individuals who were deaf were not necessarily deficient, but instead were cognitively different (cf. Myklebust, 1964). Finally, in the work of Furth (1966), the perspective changed to a recognition that cognitive processes in individuals who are deaf are in fact just like those of hearing individuals.

Do children who are deaf have cognition or learning deficits?

Furth's work also suggested that there was indeed a cognitive delay in children who are deaf. This delay was assigned to experiential deficits and the delay in developing the language of thought. Wood (1991) suggested an entirely different hypothesis: "that deaf children experience developmental and educational delays not because they lack a language of thought, but because hearing people find it more difficult to pass on their knowledge, skill and understanding to them because of problems in communication" (p. 25).

Greenberg and Kusche (1989) review research literature concerning the intelligence of children with hearing impairments and various subgroups within this population and their educational achievement characteristics, but observe a relatively low correlation between the two. They attribute this to the fact that the learning capacity of children with hearing impairments are generally measured nonverbally, whereas most achievement has a high verbal component.

Greenberg and Kusche (1989) also find that "an extensive amount of data suggests that deaf children rely heavily upon visual-spatial processing strategies and show strength in the area of holistic, simultaneous visual processing. Weaknesses, on the other hand, involve areas in which verbal sequential and/or abstract propositional processing are necessary for optimal performance" (pp. 108–109). The dependence on visual-spatial processing may be related to the fact that sign languages are not auditory and linear, but represent meaning in space, often by the use of simultaneous visual markers (e.g., hand shape, location, and orientation are used simultaneously in a single sign).

The demonstrated weakness in "verbal" reasoning on standard psychological instruments is most often not a function of deafness itself, but rather a function of the design of verbal testing tasks, which depend upon oral-language-based questions to test abstract levels of cognitive functioning. It is therefore predictable that children who do not fully hear oral language and depend on vision to acquire it in a written form will perform poorly on these verbal measures. To avoid this problem, it may be necessary to move away from the traditional psychometric paradigm when assessing students who are deaf. More promising approaches, rooted in the work of Feuerstein, are proposed by Keane (1983, 1987) and others; these propose dynamic assessments that use mediated learning experiences and avoid the inherent bias in verbal (oral language) assessments.

As in previous sections of this chapter, the issue of language acquisition and development comes to the forefront in this area as well. Greenberg and Kusche (1989) note: "Overall it appears that language deprivation results in specific experiential deficits, which in turn selectively affects cognitive development and information processing skills and flexibility" (p. 109).

Wood (1991) cites his own research as evidence that the fundamental problem is communication as it relates to the development of cognition; and he links this to an important instructional issue: verbal control of classrooms. According to Wood:

> The short-term effects of high control have been established in some detail. For example, teachers who are high in control, whether their pupils are deaf or hearing, have children who say little, ask few questions, seldom elaborate on their answers to questions, and generally say and contribute little. High adult control results in low child initiative and short child utterances (again whether those utterances are signed, spoken, or both). Teachers who are high in control not only receive short responses but also communicate themselves in short, literal, and concrete utterances. Children with such teachers are seldom exposed to communications which involve speculation, hypothesis formulation, imagination, or negotiation. (p. 25)

Wood also suggests that this situation is not inevitable. In fact, his own studies indicate that "teachers can change their control styles and that, when they do, children, deaf or hearing, reciprocate by showing more initiative in communication." In recommending a future direction for research and practice, Wood suggests that "when we have studied our own contribution to the deaf child's experience we may come to understand his cognitive life more fully and appreciate the role we may have in its formation."

What factors are important in understanding social and emotional adjustment problems of children who are deaf?

SOCIAL AND PERSONAL ISSUES. For hearing people, everyday social and personal interaction takes place primarily through oral conversation. Child development, too, is very dependent on this verbal interaction. Thus, most of the personal and social adjustment problems of children and adults with hearing loss, and especially those who are profoundly deaf, are the result of their having to live in a society that relies heavily on spoken language. This is especially true for children and youth who are deaf, of whom about 95 percent have hearing parents.

Studies of the personal and social development of children and youth who are deaf often indicate disturbing patterns, for which there are a variety of explanations. For example, Keane, Tannenbaum, and Krapf (1992) cite numerous studies that reflect that "as a group, the deaf manifest higher degrees of impulsivity, egocentricity, dependency, lack of reflectivity and rigidity than the population at large." Meadow and Dyssegard (1983) report that teachers of the deaf in the United States and Denmark tended "to see their students (at both young and older age levels) to be lacking in motivation, independence and initiative." Stika (1989), in a survey of parents, found that over half of them felt that their hearing impaired child had more behavioral or emotional problems than hearing children of the same age, and nearly half reported that a teacher or other professional from their child's school had spoken to them about their child's behavior or social or emotional judgment.

It must not, however, be assumed that the above problems are intrinsic to deafness. For example, Vestberg (1989), in a review of literature on personality characteristics in children and adults who are deaf, concludes that "negative personality outcomes were certainly *not* found to be inevitable among deaf children, as has been demonstrated in many studies in which indications of positive personality development were found with great frequency among deaf children reared in deaf families."

Among the factors that may contribute to the apparent high frequency of social and emotional adjustment problems in children and youth who are deaf are parental difficulty with accepting deafness, lack of role models, less mutual communication with parents and teachers, reduction in the transmission of information, and limited school and extra-curricular experiences. Some solutions to these problems are self-evident:

- Parent education and counseling programs.
- Greater involvement of adults who are deaf at all levels of a child's educational setting.
- Increased fluency in sign communication among parents and educators.
- Expanded and enriched educational and social opportunities.

Educators of children and youth who are deaf should carefully examine their programs to ensure that their programs contain these elements.

Conclusion

What trends are emerging in educating children with hearing losses?

The education of children with hearing losses approaches the twenty-first century in a state of ferment, exchange of new ideas, and intense self- and reevaluation. Much of this can be attributed to the Deaf President Now movement at Gallaudet University in 1987. The events of that period had a significant effect on the educational systems of younger children who are deaf as well; they are responsible for the renewed interest in the use of the language of the Deaf community in school and a greater role for Deaf persons in leading and guiding the educational systems for students who are deaf.

This impact was clearly in evidence at the seventeenth International Congress of Educators of the Deaf (ICED), where persons from the Deaf community assumed increasingly significant leadership roles in the planning and implementation of the Congress. This trend toward greater participation by the Deaf community in the decision-making process for the education of children and youth who are deaf signals a deemphasis of the medical/pathological or deficit model of the education of the deaf and an emphasis upon developmental and sociocultural-based approaches that "tap in the wealth of the language and culture of Deaf communities throughout the world to enhance the education of all Deaf children and to give them the pride and confidence they need to become members of the world community" (Hicks & Stuckless, 1991).

McChord (1991) provides a fitting summary and a challenge:

We have challenged the deaf child's right to choose his or her language; we have impeded the opportunities for deaf adult role models to work in his or her school; we have prescribed where and with whom he or she must be educated; we have restricted the opportunities for deaf adults to serve as administrators in educational programs; and inadver-

Members of the Deaf community have become very active in advocating for their rights. This choir is part of a "Disabled but Able" rally.

tently, we have conveyed to that perceptive and tolerant child that he or she does not stand on equal footing with the child who has normal hearing. (p. 55)

McChord challenges educators to reaffirm the "right of every deaf human being to a quality education, and the competence of deaf people to learn, to work, to lead and have premier voice in defining and attaining their individual destinies" (p. 56). This brief introduction to the education of children and youth who are deaf should do no less.

PROBE 9-6   Education of Children with Hearing Loss

1. What are four reasons a physician might suspect a hearing loss in a newborn baby?
2. Name five signs of possible hearing loss that a classroom teacher should watch for.
3. T F Language and speech delay can result from recurrent ear infections.
4. T F Hearing aids are never appropriate for children with conductive hearing loss.
5. Hearing loss has its most significant impact on the development of _____ skills.
6. T F The classroom teacher should use exaggerated lip movement and speak loudly to assist the hearing impaired child.
7. The _____ approach to education stresses the use of residual hearing and speechreading.
8. The use of American Sign Language is considered to be a _____ approach to communication.
9. The _____ _____ approach uses speech, sign language, residual hearing, and other modes to develop communication skills.
10. T F There is a lot of strong research evidence about the way to approach the education of students who are deaf.
11. T F It is virtually impossible for students who are profoundly deaf to develop speech communication skills.
12. Educational settings for children with severe hearing impairments include the _____, _____, and _____.

SUMMARY

1. A person with a substantial hearing loss at the frequencies in the 300–4000 Hz range will be severely handicapped in hearing other people's speech.

2. The intensity, or loudness, of normal conversational speech at a distance of 5 feet is between 40 and 60 decibels.

3. In normal hearing, sound waves are collected by the outer ear and mechanically transferred by the eardrum to the hammer, anvil, and stirrup bones of the middle ear. These bones carry the sound vibration across the middle ear to the inner ear, where fluid motion within the cochlea stimulates the auditory nerve. This nerve transmits electrical impulses to the brain, where they are interpreted.

4. One of the most serious consequences of hearing loss is that it can hamper the development of oral speech and language in young children.

5. Hearing losses are due to conductive, sensorineural, mixed, functional, and central auditory problems. The conductive loss, which is usually caused by middle ear infections, is the easiest to correct.

6. It is estimated that there are 46,000 children in the nation's schools who are deaf or have hearing impairments.

7. The professionals who evaluate hearing by means of audiometry testing are called audiologists.

8. A hearing loss of between 20 and 40 decibels is considered mild. A loss of between 40 and 60 decibels is considered moderate. A 60- to 80-decibel loss is considered severe, and losses of more than 80 decibels are considered profound.

9. Hearing loss can affect speech and language development, as well as educational, vocational, social, and emotional adjustment.

10. Hearing aids make sounds louder. They do not make sounds clearer.

11. For educational purposes, children with hearing losses are classified as either hard-of-hearing or deaf.

12. The philosophy of Total Communication makes use of both oral and manual procedures to teach children who are deaf.

13. Regular class teachers should be able to recognize signs that may indicate hearing losses so that they can refer children for hearing evaluations. Teachers can help children with hearing losses in the regular classroom in many different ways.

14. Children with severe hearing impairments are best educated in a variety of settings, depending on the severity of their problem. These settings include the residential school, day school, special class, and resource room.

15. Special educators for children and youth who are deaf must realize that their future is not bound by their ability to interact with the hearing-speaking community, for most of these individuals will grow up to be fully functioning members of the ASL-Signing Deaf community in America.

TASK SHEET 9   Field Experiences Related to Hearing Loss

Select one of the following and complete the activities that are described. Do a report of no more than three pages on the alternative that you choose.

Professional Interview

Interview a professional who provides hearing services and answer the following:

1. Whom did you interview?
2. What services does this person provide?
3. What questions did you ask?
4. What did you learn from the interview?

Observation of an Audiometric Examination

Observe an audiometric testing of a child or adult and respond to the following:

1. Where did you observe the examination?
2. Describe the person being tested.
3. What did the tester do?
4. What tests were administered?
5. What problem was identified by the tests?
6. What follow-up was recommended?
7. Describe your reaction to the experience.

Observation of a Program for Children with Hearing Loss

Visit an educational program for children who are hard-of-hearing or deaf and respond to the following:

1. Where did you observe?
2. Describe the physical setting.
3. Describe the activities that were being conducted.
4. Interview the teacher about the purposes of the program and what kind of problems are encountered.
5. Describe your reactions to the experience.

Library Study

Use the library to locate three articles related to a topic associated with hearing loss. Write a one-page abstract of each. Here are the names of some journals in which you can find articles:

American Annals of the Deaf
ASHA
Journal of Speech and Hearing Disorders
Journal of Speech and Hearing Research
Language, Speech and Hearing Services in the Schools
Sign Language Studies
Volta Review

Agency Investigation

Request information from three of the following agencies about the services they provide to people with hearing impairments. Write a three-page paper summarizing these services and how you might use them if you were a professional working with children who have hearing problems.

Alexander Graham Bell Association for the Deaf
1537 35th Street, NW
Washington, DC 20007

Deafness Research Foundation
9 East 38th St.
New York, NY 10016

American Speech-Language-Hearing Association
10801 Rockville Pike
Rockville, MD 20852

National Association of the Deaf
814 Thayer Avenue
Silver Spring, MD 20910

National Information Center on Deafness
Gallaudet University
800 Florida Avenue, NE
Washington, DC 20002

National Technical Institute for the Deaf
One Lomb Memorial Drive
Rochester, NY 14623

Design Your Own Field Experience

If you know of a unique experience you can have with hearing disabled persons, discuss your alternative with your instructor and complete the task that you agree on.

A few years after retiring from ABC television, Nan Petnick of Los Angeles bought a Voyager 12-inch closed-circuit television (CCTV). "I learned about it through a friend who helped send a CCTV to Israel," Nan says. The Voyager 12-inch video magnifier enlarges print up to 45 times the original size. And as Nan says, "It's just a matter of turning it on and zooming in on your text. What could be simpler?" She reads her own mail and periodicals. She's also learned to take care of her own checking account.

Just a few months ago, Nan decided she wanted a larger screen and a viewing system that magnifies up to 60 times the original. She chose TeleSensory's Voyager XL. Nan says, "The equipment is a joy." With over 8 percent of the older population likely to experience some degree of functional vision loss, video magnifiers offer help. Reading small print in newspapers and magazines and on medicine bottles, as well as writing checks and letters, can be accomplished with the TeleSensory's family of video magnifiers. (*Focus on Technology,* 1990)

I learned to read three times. Because of visual problems from birth, I attended a visually handicapped program in the Chicago Public School System. I was taught braille and I can remember seeing the dots and reading with my eyes as well as my fingers. When I completed the first grade, my parents moved from the city. Then I attended a school system that did not have a braille classroom but did have a "Sight Saving" class for partially sighted students. I started learning to read again, this time with large print. I was in this classroom for two years when I lost all of my vision and reentered the Chicago Public School system to relearn braille.

Since I learned to read both braille and large print in my early school years, I feel it was beneficial to learn both. I feel that those people with low vision should be encouraged to use the vision they have. I feel low-vision students should be taught large print, but should have the option to learn braille if they so desire. (Vivian Pohlmann, as quoted in Caton, 1991)

10

Students with Visual Impairments

Hilda R. Caton

Most of us who can see take our vision for granted. We watch television, read books and newspapers, use the library, walk from place to place without difficulty, and engage in a host of other activities that depend on our ability to see. But think what your life would be like if you lost your ability to read. The information in newspapers, magazines, textbooks, even letters from your friends would be lost to you. For you the worlds described in poetry and fiction might not exist.

A device such as the video magnifier described on the facing page could have an enormous effect on you if you had low vision. Similarly, if you were totally blind, the use of braille or audiotapes would enable you to obtain the information that is available on the printed page. These technologies, and others that will be explained later in this chapter, would enable you to reduce the handicaps that result from having limited vision. In fact, that is the primary goal of special education for those with visual impairments: to reduce the vision-related handicaps to the greatest extent possible.

In this chapter we describe children with visual impairments and the different degrees of visual impairment. We explain the visual system and some of its common disorders and discuss the developmental characteristics of children with visual impairments, as well as some of their educational alternatives. Finally, we illustrate methods of educational assessment and describe some of the instructional methods and equipment used to reduce the effects of visual impairment.

THE VISUAL SYSTEM

You should be able to identify the parts of the visual system and describe how we see.

The most obvious characteristic of children with visual impairments is that their vision is in some way abnormal. Normal, or unimpaired, vision has four basic components: (1) the object

313

to be viewed; (2) light that reflects from the object; (3) an intact visual organ (the eye); and (4) the occipital lobes of the brain, where visual stimuli are interpreted and "seeing" takes place (Chalkley, 1982; Kirk, 1981).

Parts of the Visual System

The visual system consists of the eye and the parts of the brain responsible for seeing. The eye itself is a complex organ consisting of a number of structures, although each structure is closely related. The eye is illustrated in Figure 10-1. The discussion of the parts of the eye is based on the work of Allen (1963), Chalkley (1982), Vaughn and Ashbury (1989), and Harley and Lawrence (1984).

What parts of the visual system protect the eye?

The bony socket, sclera, eyelids, eyebrows, and conjunctiva all serve as protection for the eye. The bony socket provides a strong outer protection from severe blows, sharp objects, or other wounds. The sclera is the tough outer layer of the eyeball, which holds and protects its contents. The eyelids, eyelashes, and eyebrows trap dust and other particles and keep them from entering the eye, where infection and damage can occur. Further protection from dust and particles is provided by the **conjunctiva,** a thin, transparent layer that lines the eyelids and covers the front of the eye. The tears protect by washing out particles that have entered the eye. They also contain an enzyme that helps prevent infection.

What are the functions of different parts of the eye?

The cornea, aqueous, iris, lens, ciliary body, and vitreous are responsible for making sure that light rays reach the exact point on the retina of the eye that will result in distinct vision. The **cornea, aqueous, lens,** and **vitreous** refract (bend) the light rays that enter the eye and direct them to that point. Part of the function of the **iris,** the colored part of the eye, is to

FIGURE 10-1   Cross-Section of the Human Eye

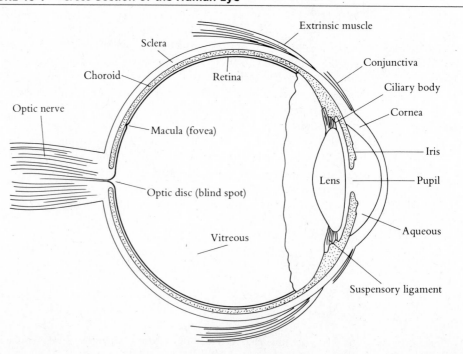

screen out a portion of the entering light rays. The iris is controlled by muscles that contract to allow less light through the pupil or expand to allow more light.

The **ciliary body** has two parts and two functions. One part, the ciliary processes, produces the aqueous fluid. The other part, the ciliary muscle, changes the shape of the lens so that light is focused correctly on the retina.

Where is the light focused when it enters the eye?

The **retina** is the "nerve-layer" of the eye. It consists of a thin layer of tissue and nerves that lines the inside of the eyeball. It is actually an extension of the optic nerve, which enters the back of the eye, coming directly from the brain. For a person to have a clear, distinct vision, the light rays, having been refracted by the structures just described, must strike a small spot on the retina called the macular area. When this occurs, nerve impulses are sent out of the eye through the optic nerve along another nerve system to the occipital area of the brain. There the visual stimuli are interpreted and "seeing" takes place. The retina receives its nourishment from the blood vessels in the choroid, the layer of the eye between the sclera and the retina.

What is strabismus?

The movement of the eye is controlled by extrinsic, or external, muscles. These muscles turn the eyes to enable them to focus simultaneously on specific objects. There are six external muscles, located on each side of the eyeball and above and below it. These muscles move the eye to the left, to the right, upward, and downward. The failure of the muscles to function properly can result in crossed eyes (strabismus) and double vision.

How We See

Seeing is a complex process, with the efficient functioning of one part of the visual system often dependent on the efficient functioning of other parts. The process is illustrated in Figure 10-2. Basically, the process of seeing involves the following sequence of events:

1. Light rays are reflected from an object and enter the eye.
2. The light rays pass through the cornea, which refracts, or bends, them.
3. The light rays, properly refracted, pass through the anterior or aqueous chamber, where they are again slightly refracted.
4. From the anterior chamber, the light rays pass through the pupil. The size of the pupil can be changed by the movement of the iris to allow more or less light as needed.

FIGURE 10-2　The Process of "Seeing"

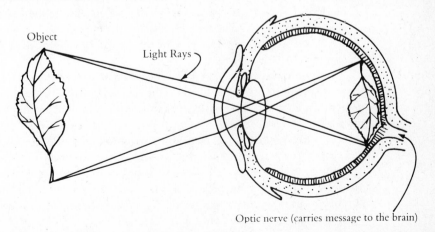

Object

Light Rays

Optic nerve (carries message to the brain)

5. The light rays pass through the lens, the major refracting structure of the eye. The shape of the lens can be changed by the suspensory ligament to focus the light rays on exactly the right place in the eye. This process is called accommodation.

6. The light passes through the vitreous chamber. Its content, the vitreous humor, also has a slightly refractive effect.

7. The light rays are focused on the fovea, a small spot on the macula that produces the clearest, most distinct vision.

8. Light energy is changed to electrical impulses, which are carried by the optic nerve to the occipital lobe of the brain, where "seeing" takes place.

What function does the fovea perform?

PROBE 10-1   The Visual System

1. The two parts of the visual system are the _____ and the _____.

2. Indicate whether each of the following is (a) a protective part of the eye; (b) a refractive part; or (c) a receptive part, by labeling each item with the appropriate letter.

_____ bony socket	_____ optic nerve
_____ retina	_____ tears
_____ cornea	_____ lens
_____ eyelid	_____ vitreous
_____ aqueous	_____ conjunctiva
_____ eyebrow	

3. Describe, in your own words, the process of "seeing."

DISORDERS OF THE VISUAL SYSTEM

You should be able to describe common disorders of the visual system.

Refractive Disorders

Disorders of the refractive structures of the eye are among the most common encountered in children today. The so-called refractive errors are hyperopia (farsightedness), myopia (nearsightedness), and astigmatism. The state of the eyeball in each of these conditions is illustrated in Figure 10-3.

What is the difference between myopia and hyperopia?

Hyperopia, or farsightedness, occurs when the eye is too short and the rays of light from near objects are not focused on the retina. **Myopia,** or nearsightedness, occurs when the eye is too long and the rays of light from distant objects are not focused on the retina. The hyperopic eye can see objects more clearly at a distance, whereas the myopic eye can see them more clearly at close range. **Astigmatism** is "blurred" vision caused by uneven curvature of the cornea or lens. This curvature prevents light rays from focusing correctly on the retina. Except in extreme cases, all of these disorders can be corrected with spectacles or contact lenses, so children with refractive errors are not often placed in special programs. These problems are found very frequently in regular classrooms, however, and can cause serious problems unless they are detected and corrected.

FIGURE 10-3   Refractive Errors of the Eye

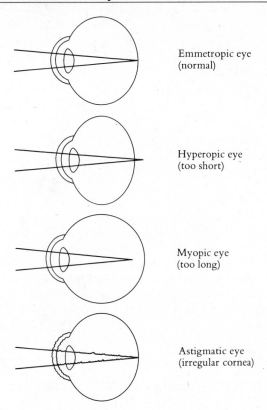

Emmetropic eye
(normal)

Hyperopic eye
(too short)

Myopic eye
(too long)

Astigmatic eye
(irregular cornea)

What are
cataracts?

Cataracts, a common disorder of a refractive structure, often result in the need for special education placement. Cataracts are not, as many believe, growths on the eye. They result, rather, when the semifluid substance in the lens gradually becomes opaque and the vision is obscured. Cataracts can result in severe visual loss. They are an especially serious problem in young children, since the opacity prevents light rays from focusing on the retina. This can result in the retina's failure to develop. Surgical procedures for the treatment of cataracts are quite advanced, however, and visual losses can usually be prevented.

Retinal and Optic Nerve Disorders

Common problems of the receptive parts of the eye include degeneration of the retina and the optic nerve, and detachment of the retina. Although some forms of optic nerve degeneration result from infections, and some forms of retinal degeneration are linked to recessive gene traits, the cause of most cases is unknown. The severity of the visual loss varies widely, since the pace of the structure's degeneration is different for each person affected. Total blindness occurs in many cases, but not in all.

Can degenerative
visual disorders
be treated?

These degenerative conditions are extremely difficult to cope with, both medically and educationally, since little is known about their causes or rate of progress and there is no known treatment for them. Children with these eye conditions are almost always placed in special educational programs.

Retinal detachment is a separation of the retina from the adjacent layers of the eye, the choroid and the sclera. This disorder is sometimes associated with extreme cases of myopia, or nearsightedness, where the eyeball becomes excessively long and pulls the retina away from surrounding tissues. Retinal detachments can also result from retinal degeneration, glaucoma, and other disorders. Although it is now possible to reattach the retina through various surgical techniques, this must be done immediately or extensive visual loss will occur (Chalkley, 1982). Children with retinal detachment are almost always placed in special education programs, because of their visual loss and because they must be protected from sharp blows on the head, falls, and other actions that could cause further detachment.

Muscle Disorders

Disorders of the extrinsic muscles are very common in young children. The are usually the result of the muscles being imbalanced. As noted earlier, such an imbalance creates a condition known as **strabismus,** or crossed eyes. When this occurs, the eyes cannot focus simultaneously on the same object. As a result, the child sees a double image of the object. Normally, the brain reacts by suppressing the image in one eye, and when that eye is not used its vision is lost. **Amblyopia** is a condition of this kind.

How can amblyopia be treated?

Fortunately, amblyopia can be prevented if detected early and properly treated. The treatment sometimes consists of placing a patch over the unaffected eye to bring the affected eye into focus. A simple surgical procedure to straighten the muscles involved can also be used. Because muscle disorders are easily corrected and rarely impair vision severely, children who suffer from them do not often need special education.

Glaucoma

What causes glaucoma?

Glaucoma is a common disorder that is not related to one specific structure of the eye. It is caused by the failure of the aqueous fluid to circulate properly, which results in an elevation of pressure in the eye. This pressure very gradually destroys the optic nerve. The result can be total blindness. Glaucoma can be treated, however, and if the treatment occurs early, visual loss can be prevented. Because their eyes are not fully developed, young children are especially susceptible to harm from glaucoma, and many have severe visual losses. Those who do usually need special education.

Retinopathy of Prematurity

Retinopathy of prematurity (ROP) is a condition in which abnormal blood vessels grow inside the eye of premature infants. In severe cases, it can lead to blindness. This condition was formerly called retrolental fibroplasia, and it primarily affects premature infants who weigh less than three pounds at birth.

In ROP, the blood vessels of the retina do not grow normally. The causes of this abnormal growth are complex and not completely understood. The two most important factors in the development of this disease are (1) degree of prematurity and (2) birth weight. The more premature the baby, and the lower the birth weight, the more likely the development of ROP. It was once thought that the use of high concentrations of oxygen was responsible for all cases of ROP, but newer evidence indicates that this is not true.

In the most severe cases of ROP, the abnormal growth of blood vessels can lead to bleeding and scarring on the surface of the retina. This can damage the retina severely, and such damage to the retina may lead to blindness. Because this problem is in the back of the eye and not visible externally, infants that are at risk to develop ROP must be examined by an ophthalmologist. Babies at risk for ROP are usually examined in the neonatal intensive care unit. These examinations may cause mild discomfort, but they are brief and will not damage the child's eyes in any way. The doctors must watch carefully for signs of abnormal blood vessel growth in the eyes, so that frequent examinations are often necessary.

How can ROP be treated?

If ROP does develop, one of three things can happen:

1. In the vast majority of babies with ROP, the vessels that grew abnormally go away, and the eye heals completely on its own before the baby is 1 year old.
2. In some infants, the abnormal blood vessels leave scarring in the retina when they heal. This can cause the child to develop a lazy eye or to become nearsighted. It is important that an ophthalmologist continue to examine these children regularly, to be sure that they reach school age with the best possible vision.
3. In its most severe stages, scarring from ROP causes retinal detachment. When the retina is detached, it is as though the film in the back of the camera was wrinkled up inside the camera. Retinal detachment means that the child will have poor vision or be completely blind. Fortunately, this happens to only about 5 percent of all babies at risk to develop ROP.

Retinopathy of prematurity is a disease that can last a lifetime. Most children at risk for ROP will have normal vision, but late complications are possible in some patients. Any patient with chances of ROP should see an ophthalmologist at least once a year throughout childhood and into the adult years (Barr, 1990).

Maternal Rubella

What percentage of children whose mothers had rubella have vision problems?

Another disorder related to the visual system is caused by maternal rubella. Women who have **rubella** (German measles) during the first trimester of pregnancy often have babies with severe multiple disabilities. Among these children, visual impairment is very common. McCay, Grieve, and Shaver (1980) have estimated that at least 33 percent of children with congenital rubella syndrome have vision problems.

The last major rubella epidemic in the United States occurred in 1964. It resulted in the establishment of many educational programs and services to children with multiple disabilities, including those who are both deaf and blind. Although much progress has been made in providing services to these children, a great deal remains to be learned about how they function and what services are most appropriate to them.

PROBE 10-2   Disorders of the Visual System

1. If detected early, amblyopia can be corrected by either _____ or _____.
2. T F Cataracts are growths on the eye.
3. Nearsightedness is to _____ as farsightedness is to hyperopia.
4. One disease contracted by the mother during pregnancy that results in large numbers of blind children with multiple disabilities is _____.
5. _____ is the eye disorder that is often found in babies who are born prematurely.

DEFINITIONS OF VISUAL IMPAIRMENT

You should be able to state the definitions of visual impairment and describe the purposes for which each is used.

What is a characteristic common to all children with visual impairments?

Definitions and descriptions of children with visual impairments tend to vary considerably, depending on the purposes for which individuals or groups are being described. Although children identified as visually impaired represent a wide range of visual ability, they share one common characteristic: a visual restriction of sufficient severity that it interferes with normal progress in a regular education program without some modifications (Scholl, 1986). They need specially trained teachers, specially designed or adapted curricular materials, and specially designed educational aids in order to reach their full potential (Ashcroft, 1963).

Different terms are used in the educational literature to describe the children who fall within the broad definition. All these terms are an attempt to differentiate between children who will be visual learners and those who will be tactual learners. The most widely used terms at the present time are *low-vision* children and *blind* children. Two general definitions are accepted for these children, one based on visual acuity, and one based on educational needs.

Some children with visual impairments do not fit neatly into either group described above. In the past, many children classified as "blind" and educated as tactual learners were actually able to use their residual vision for many educational tasks, but were not allowed (or encouraged) to do so. In more recent years, partially because of the work of Barraga (1964, 1980), greater emphasis was placed on the use of residual vision and the efficiency of its use. Although it was not Barraga's intent, the emphasis on the use of residual vision resulted in an inappropriate decrease in the development of braille and tactile skills. The overall result was that many children in this group became functionally illiterate, being unable to communicate in either braille or print. There is now a strong movement nationally to try to overcome this problem by identifying ways in which children can be evaluated and provided with educational programming using the appropriate learning medium, or media, if appropriate. As Spungin (1990) says:

> We need to define what we mean by blind children and braille users and to develop appropriate reliable assessment measures that allow decisions to be made on the use of braille or print or both. Such areas as the working distance from the page, the portability of reading skills, reading rates and accuracy, visual fatigue, and the proper interpretation of the results of assessments all lend themselves to objective measurement and could easily serve as a basis for a uniform assessment tool. CHILDREN WHO DO NOT FIT NEATLY INTO THE CATEGORIES OF BRAILLE OR PRINT USERS DESERVE THE OPTION OF LEARNING BOTH BRAILLE AND PRINT UNTIL THEY CAN MAKE THEIR OWN INFORMED CHOICE. (p. 1)

What are the educational characteristics of students with low vision?

Based on this statement, it is useful to consider the educational definitions by Barraga (1986) in her discussion of the sensory and perceptual development of children with visual impairments, which are summarized in Table 10-1.

Today, most educators of children with visual impairments agree that these terms and their definitions provide more guidance for educational planning than the broader terms *low-vision* and *blind*.

Definitions Based on Visual Acuity

Definitions based on visual acuity are used for legal and economic purposes and for the allocation of federal funds to purchase educational materials. They are called the "legal" definitions of visual impairment.

TABLE 10-1   Educational Characteristics of Students with Low Vision

Levels of Visual Disability	Performance Capability
Moderate visual disability	With use of special aids and lighting, may perform visual tasks almost like students with normal vision.
Severe visual disability	In performance of visual tasks, may require more time, take more energy, and be less accurate, even with aids and other modifications.
Profound visual disability	Performance of even gross visual tasks may be very difficult, and detailed tasks cannot be handled visually at all.

Source: Adapted from A. Colenbrander (1977), Dimensions of visual performance. *Archives of American Academy of Ophthalmology, 83,* p. 335.

What is the legal definition of blindness?

Legally blind children are defined as follows: (1) those whose visual acuity is 20/200 or less in the better eye with the best possible correction; or (2) those whose field of vision is restricted to an angle subtending an arc of 20 degrees or less (American Foundation for the Blind, 1961). Children with low vision are defined as follows: (1) those whose visual acuity is between 20/200 and 20/70 in the better eye with the best possible correction; or (2) those who in the opinion of an eye specialist need either temporary or permanent special education facilities.

Why is the legal definition of blindness not very helpful to teachers?

Although these definitions are useful for the purposes we have mentioned, they do not provide enough information to deliver effective educational services to children with visual impairments. It is important to understand what the definitions can and cannot tell educators about these children.

The first factor to be considered in both definitions is the concept of visual acuity itself. Visual acuity is simply a means of describing the sharpness or clearness of vision. It does not describe the efficiency with which particular individuals use their vision, nor does it take into account the variety of ways in which vision is used in an educational setting.

What is a Snellen Chart?

The visual acuities used in the legal definitions are measures of distance vision. These are almost always obtained through the use of the Snellen Chart, illustrated in Figure 10-4. This chart is designed so that the top letter, when seen from a distance of 200 feet, seems to be the same size as the standard letter when seen from a distance of 20 feet.

The test distance of 20 feet was used because rays of light reflected from objects at that distance are parallel. When light rays entering the eye are parallel, the muscles of the normal eye are at rest, and the visual acuity obtained does not reflect the accommodative power of the eye (the ability of the eye muscles to change the shape of the lens to focus a clear image on the retina). As a result, the visual acuity obtained at 20 feet gives a truer picture of the sharpness and clearness of vision than it would at other distances.

How is an index of visual acuity interpreted?

Visual acuity is expressed as an index, such as 20/20, 20/70, or 20/200. This index does not represent the fraction of remaining vision, as some people think. The top number in the index represents the 20-foot distance between the chart and the person being tested. The bottom number is the distance at which a person with normal vision can distinguish the letters in the line being viewed. For example, if a person being tested can read at 20 feet what the person with normal vision can read at 200 feet, his or her visual acuity is 20/200.

Visual acuity tells educators very little about the child's ability to read or examine educational materials at close range. Barraga (1964) has illustrated that some children with visual acuities as low as 6/300 can learn to use their remaining vision quite efficiently. In educational planning, then, the causes of the visual loss as well as the efficiency with which the child uses remaining vision must be considered. For example, a child with corneal opacities (small opaque areas scattered throughout the cornea) would have an extremely low visual

FIGURE 10-4   Snellen Symbol Chart

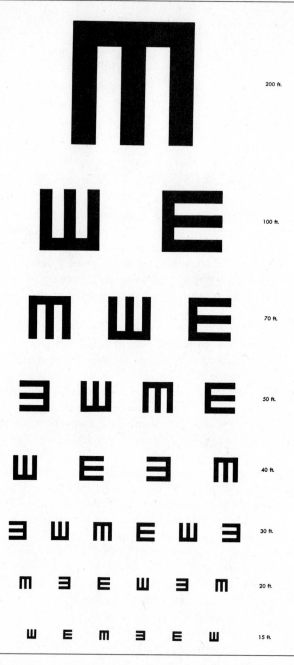

Source: From the National Society to Prevent Blindness, New York, NY. Reprinted by permission.

acuity (around 8/400) as measured by the Snellen Chart, because the child would be unable to see through the opacities when looking directly at the chart. The child might, however, be able to read relatively small print held close to the eyes by turning his or her head to see around the opacities. Many illustrations of this kind could be given. The point is that visual acuity alone is not an adequate measure of a child's ability to function in an educational setting. The limited value to teachers of definitions based on visual acuity should be clear.

How is a person's visual field defined?

The second factor to be considered in these definitions is the visual field, or peripheral vision. Peripheral or "side" vision is measured in degrees of visual arc. The procedure for measurement is to place the individual about 39 inches from a square black chart and ask the person to fix his or her eye on a central point on the chart. A round white object is then moved in from the periphery of the chart in a circular pattern until the individual being tested can see it. The distance at which the stimulus can be seen is then measured. When the widest angle at which the stimulus can be seen is 20 degrees or less in the best eye with the best possible correction, the person is considered to be legally blind. Many educators would also consider the person educationally blind.

What is tunnel vision?

The field of vision is often reported on charts similar to those in Figure 10-5. A separate chart is provided for each eye. The dark lines in the center of the chart represent visual fields, in both eyes, of a person with a visual field loss of 20 degrees. If you examine the fields of vision represented on the charts, you will note that an individual with a field of vision of 20 degrees or less can see little more than what is directly in front of the eye. People with this restricted field of vision are said to have *tunnel vision.*

Tunnel vision causes problems in mobility as well as in reading. The lack of peripheral vision makes it difficult for people to see objects not directly in front of them. This severely limits their knowledge of the area they are traveling through. Reading problems are caused by the inability to see more than one letter at a time or letters too large for the visual field. Even when the visual acuity in the very small visual field is good, the restriction in the field severely impairs the vision.

How do teachers differentiate between children who are blind and those who have low vision?

Definitions for Educational Planning

Although definitions based on visual acuity and field of vision are helpful, definitions that describe children in terms of the type of education they receive are most appropriate for educational planning. This kind of definition, first proposed in 1957 (American Foundation

FIGURE 10-5   Field of Vision Charts (O.S.—Left Eye; O.D.—Right Eye)

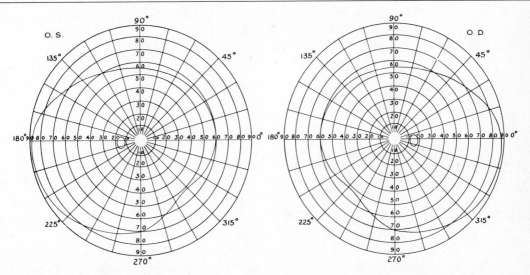

Source: Courtesy of Histacount Corporation.

for the Blind, 1957), is now accepted by educators of children with visual impairments as being useful for planning for most such children. Educationally defined, children who are blind are those whose visual loss indicates that they should be educated chiefly through the use of braille and other tactile and auditory materials. Children with low vision are defined as those who have some remaining useful vision and can use print and other visual materials as part of the educational program.

PROBLEMS WITH DEFINITIONS. Obviously, neither a definition based on visual acuity nor an educational definition should be used as the sole criterion for deciding how and in what programs a child should be educated. The following factors must also be considered: (1) age of student, (2) age of onset of visual impairment, (3) level of achievement, (4) level of intelligence, (5) presence of other disabilities, (6) cause (etiology) of the visual impairment, and (7) emotional stability (Gearhart, 1980).

Why is knowledge of etiology and age of onset of visual impairment important to teachers?

The most important considerations are the etiology and age of onset. The etiology is crucial because some eye conditions require the use of a particular teaching method or set of materials. For example, children affected by atrophy of the optic nerve require a great deal of light and materials with good contrast. They might eventually need to learn braille. Children with visual losses from other causes might require different methods and materials.

The experience a child had before a loss of vision and the age at which the loss occurred also are important. An early visual loss obviously limits what was learned through seeing to a much greater extent than a later visual loss. The knowledge of how much a child knew when the vision became impaired can help a teacher decide what the child needs to learn and how it should be taught.

Intellectual ability and chronological age, though also important in determining how a child should be educated, are not as significant as the factors already discussed. They will be discussed in the section on the developmental characteristics of children with visual impairments.

PROBE 10-3   Definitions of Visual Impairment

1. How would you define children with visual impairments?
2. Children with visual impairments are classified as either _____ or _____.
3. With correction, a child who is legally blind has visual acuity of 20/200. A child with low vision has visual acuity between _____ and _____.
4. T   F   Visual acuity is a term for sharpness and clearness of vision.
5. Explain the meaning of an index of visual acuity that is stated as 20/150.
6. Field of vision is measured in terms of _____.
7. From the perspective of educational definitions, how would you differentiate between a child who is blind and one who has low vision?

IDENTIFICATION AND PREVALENCE

You should be able to describe the procedures used in identifying children who have visual impairments.

To plan for the education of children with visual impairments, the children must first be identified. As was pointed out in the preceding section, a knowledge of visual acuity alone is of limited value. The children who actually need services can only be discovered by careful, systematic identification procedures such as those carried out by school systems. The planner must also know the numbers and types of visual problems to determine how many and what kinds of programs are needed.

Identification

Systematic identification procedures include coordinated preschool and school vision screening programs, as well as national, state, and regional Child Find programs. These programs are team efforts by teachers, doctors, and other people. A good identification program includes the following: (1) comprehensive screenings; (2) referral for complete eye examinations of those who appear to have problems; and (3) follow-ups to ensure that the recommendations resulting from the examination are carried out. The eye specialist, not the people doing the screening, makes the final diagnosis (Harley & Lawrence, 1984). Ideally, every child should have a complete eye examination every year. Unfortunately, most children don't. As a result, preschool and school vision screening programs tend to be the most effective means of identification.

The agency most active in preschool and school vision screening programs is the National Society for the Prevention of Blindness. All across the United States its branches train volunteers, who then conduct the actual screening sessions. Their basic screening program consists of an annual test for distance visual acuity using the Snellen Chart and careful instructions to teachers describing symptoms that may indicate eye disorders (National Society for the Prevention of Blindness, 1990).

The test for visual acuity is used because it has proved to be an effective indicator of children with eye problems, as confirmed in later examinations by ophthalmologists. The society recommends that children be referred for an eye examination if they are unable to read the following lines on the Snellen Chart:

3-year-olds	20/50 or less
4-year-olds through third grade	20/40 or less
Fourth grade and above	20/30 or less

Very strict standards have been set up for the actual testing session. They must be followed exactly in order to obtain valid results. These standards are described in the society's *Handbook for Preschool Vision Screening Team* (Kentucky Society for the Prevention of Blindness, 1990), which is available through the organization's state offices. Standards and procedures for correct screening are also illustrated in a film, *Before We Are Six,* which is available through the national office.

Observations by teachers, parents, and others closely associated with the children are also important in the identification of eye problems. Some symptoms that might suggest an eye problem are as follows:

1. Clumsiness and trouble walking in a new environment.
2. Having to hold one's head in an awkward position, or having to hold material very close to one's eyes, in order to see.
3. "Tuning out" when information is written on the chalkboard or somewhere else a child might have trouble seeing.
4. Constant requests by a child for someone to explain what is going on.
5. Being inordinately affected by glare, or not being able to see things at certain times of the day.
6. A pronounced squint.
7. Excessive rubbing of the eyes.

How does the National Society for the Prevention of Blindness help with vision screening?

How can teachers identify a possible vision problem in a student?

8. Pushing the eyeballs with fingers or knuckles.
9. Obvious physical anomalies such as red and swollen lids, crusts on the eyes, crossed eyes, etc. (Kentucky Society for the Prevention of Blindness, 1990).

Children who exhibit any of the above symptoms should be referred to an eye specialist.

Children with visual impairments are identified through means other than vision screening programs, of course. Doctors discover the problems of many children. In addition, school systems and states now have agencies whose major responsibility is the identification and appropriate referral of people with visual impairments.

What is the difference between an ophthalmologist and an optometrist?

What does an optician do?

Once children have been identified as possibly having eye problems, they are referred to the appropriate eye specialist. Generally this is an ophthalmologist or an optometrist. The **ophthalmologist** is a licensed physician who specializes in eye disorders. The **optometrist** is not a physician, but a professional whose practice is limited to the prescription and fitting of corrective lenses and the treatment of optical defects without drugs or surgery. Other specialists are the **optician,** who grinds lenses or makes glasses, and the **orthoptist,** who provides eye exercises when prescribed by an ophthalmologist.

It is generally best to refer children who have vision problems to ophthalmologists, because they are most familiar with all possible eye defects. All these eye specialists have important roles in eye care, however, and educators should acquaint themselves with the specific services that each provides.

Prevalence

It is very difficult to get an accurate count of the number of children with visual impairments. There are several reasons for this. Definitions of visual impairment vary from state to state, as do the methods of collecting and reporting prevalence data. The accuracy of the data collected varies as a consequence. In addition, a national census of children with visual impairments has never been taken. As a result of these factors, prevalence figures are usually estimates based on a variety of sources.

How many children with visual impairments are there in the United States?

The U.S. prevalence of "severe visual impairment"[1] was estimated in 1987 as almost 2 million (more precisely, 1,980,000) persons. That estimate was based on 1977 age-specific prevalence rates from the National Center for Health Statistics' (NCHS) Health Interview Survey, applied to 1987 general population projections. Age-specific rates range from about one-tenth of 1 percent of the general population under 18 years old, to more than 18 percent of those who are 85 years or older. About four-fifths of the population age 65 years or older have severe visual impairments (Kirchner, Stephen, & Chandu, 1987).

Another source of information on the numbers of children with visual impairments is the annual registration of legally blind children by the American Printing House for the Blind. Although this registration does not tell us what percentage of all children are visually impaired, it does give an accurate count of the legally blind children enrolled in school programs throughout the country. In 1990, a total of 48,071 legally blind children were registered (American Printing House for the Blind, 1990). Of these, approximately 12 percent had to use braille as their reading medium, and approximately 30 percent had sufficient vision to read print. These percentages do not include children with visual acuities better than 20/70 and do not therefore reflect the overall prevalence of children with visual impairments.

---

[1]"Severe visual impairment" was measured in the 1977 Health Interview Survey (HIS) as the self-reported (or proxy-reported) inability to see or read ordinary newsprint, even with glasses (or contact lenses), except for children under 6 years, for whom the mother or other caregiver reported about lack of useful vision. This measure has not been used for the entire national sample in more recent years of HIS.

Even though the accuracy of these estimates is subject to disagreement, it is clear that children with visual impairments make up one of the smallest groups of exceptional children. It should also be noted that more children are classified as having low vision (and thus read print) than being blind (and thus read braille). The most accurate prevalence figure, which states that 0.1 percent of the school-age population has a visual impairment, is the one that should probably be used in planning educational services.

From this discussion it is obvious that a great variety of disorders can affect the vision of children. Unfortunately, there are no recent figures on the relative prevalence of specific eye disorders. The latest available figures are furnished by the United States Department of Health, Education, and Welfare (1976). These figures show that among persons with visual impairments who are not legally blind, the leading causes of impairment are cataract, refractive errors, and glaucoma. Among the legally blind and totally blind, the leading causes of impairment are retinal disorders, glaucoma, and cataract. Most of the children with visual impairments in special education programs have one of these disorders.

PROBE 10-4   Identification and Prevalence

1. Match each profession with its function.

   Profession   *Function*

   _____ Ophthalmologist   a. Provides eye exercises
   _____ Optician   b. Diagnoses eye disorders as licensed physician
   _____ Optometrist   c. Grinds lenses and makes glasses
   _____ Orthoptist   d. Prescribes glasses

2. The name of the most common instrument for screening visual impairments in children is the _____.
3. List five symptoms that may indicate eye problems.
4. The most accurate prevalence figure for visually impaired children is _____.
5. T F Children with visual impairments comprise one of the smallest groups of exceptional children.

DEVELOPMENTAL CHARACTERISTICS

You should be able to describe the physical, learning, and social-emotional characteristics of children with visual impairments.

To plan effectively, persons concerned with the education of children with visual impairments should be familiar with their physical, learning (mental, cognitive, etc.), and social-emotional characteristics.

There is little agreement on the effect of blindness on the physical, mental, and emotional development of children. On one end of the spectrum of opinion are Cutsforth (1951), who states that "no single mental activity of the congenitally blind child is not distorted by the absence of sight" (p. 3), and Carroll (1961), who states that when vision is lost "the sighted man dies" (p. 11). On the other end are Ashcroft (1963), Scholl (1986), and Scott (1982), who state that children with visual impairments are like other children in many more ways than they are different from them.

The latter statement is probably the most accurate. It is worth remembering in educational planning, because it points out that "other" children are not alike; they are individuals, each with their own individual characteristics and developmental patterns. The statement that children with visual impairments are more like children who can see normally than different from them simply means that they are not a homogeneous group who fit easily into a carefully delineated "category." They are just as varied a group as sighted children, and their educational needs vary just as greatly. It is extremely important to keep this in mind during the discussion that follows, since the emphasis on aspects of development unique to these children may appear to set them apart from other children.

Psychomotor Development

Are there any physical differences between children with visual impairments and those who can see normally?

In general, the physical development of children with visual impairments resembles that of children who see normally. They do not tend to be taller, shorter, fatter, or thinner than other children simply because they have a visual impairment. However, visual impairment often does have indirect effects on their physical development (Scholl, 1986a). This is true largely because the physical activity of many children with visual impairments is severely limited.

The visual impairment may of course be related to other disabilities that can retard physical development, such as cerebral palsy, but the visual impairment in and of itself does not retard physical growth and development. In fact, the motor development of the child with simply a visual impairment does not differ markedly from that of any other child during the first few months of life (Warren, 1984). Some indirect influences related to the characteristics of the visual impairment occur later in life and do have an impact on the process; these include (1) the lack of visual stimulation, (2) the inability to make use of imitative learning, and (3) environmental factors (Scholl, 1986a).

The lack of visual stimulation, particularly if the child is blind from birth, can have a severely detrimental effect on physical development because the child is not motivated to move and be active. Additionally, development may be affected by the fact that there is no imitative learning, which is common among children who see. Finally, the environment in which the child lives and is educated can retard physical development if the parents and teachers are overly protective and do not allow the child adequate freedom of movement (Scholl, 1986a).

To overcome these problems, children with visual impairments must be allowed the freedom to move about in their environment and encouraged to participate in the physical activities normal for all children. They can be taught directly many of the physical skills normally learned through visual observation. When they are given this training and a rich, stimulating environment, their physical development will follow the same pattern as that of their seeing peers.

Cognitive Development

Because there is no generally accepted definition of learning, it is difficult to discuss the many factors that influence it. Most experts acknowledge, however, that a child's ability to learn is significantly affected by two factors: intelligence and the ability to develop concepts. Accordingly, our discussion will focus on these two qualities and how and why they affect the child's school achievement.

Does visual
impairment affect
intellectual ability?

INTELLIGENCE. The results of research on the intelligence of people with visual impairments must be viewed with caution, for several reasons. First, the children studied have been enrolled either in segregated residential school programs or in special education programs in public schools. Second, most of the intelligence tests used were originally developed for use by children with normal vision. Third, a child's score on an intelligence test reflects not only intellectual potential, but also the opportunities the child has had to develop that potential. Each of these factors could have an effect on a child's intelligence test score.

Nevertheless, a number of studies of the intelligence of people with visual impairments have been undertaken, but not very recently. Although the evidence is inconclusive, many studies indicate no significant differences between the intelligence of those who are blind and those who see normally. The small differences that are sometimes found are probably attributable to the three factors we have mentioned. Students interested in specific studies are directed to Dauterman, Shapiro, and Swinn (1967); Davis (1970); Goldman (1970); Hammill, Crandell, and Colarusso (1970); Hayes (1941); Parker (1969); Scholl and Schnur (1976); Tillman and Osborne (1969); and Warren (1977, 1984).

Studies of the intelligence of children with low vision are scarce and most are not very recent. However, those conducted have yielded similar results as those for the blind. Livingston (1958), for example, found the average IQ of children characterized as partially seeing to be 98.6, and Pinter, Eisenson, and Stanton (1941) also found intelligence levels in the normal range. Other studies by Bateman (1963) and Birch, Tisdall, Peabody, and Sterrett (1966) came to the same conclusions. It seems likely, then, that the intellectual development of children is not directly affected by visual loss. Intelligence quotients alone, however, are an inadequate measure of a child's ability to learn.

How can visual
impairment affect
concept
development?

CONCEPT DEVELOPMENT. Like intelligence, concept development is affected by the restrictions that result from visual loss, rather than by visual loss itself. A child with a visual impairment has a smaller range and variety of experiences, has trouble moving about freely, and has a more difficult time interacting with the environment (Lowenfeld, 1973). Many children with visual impairments have never visited a farm, a grocery store, a park, and many other places familiar to most of us, and thus have little understanding of spatial relationships, faulty impressions of distance, and little concept of form, size, position, and so on (Nolan, 1978). Those with visual impairments are further handicapped by their inability to learn through imitation of what they see. They must learn through direct experiences—which, as mentioned, they often don't have.

Children with visual impairments do, however, progress through the same sequence of developmental stages as other children, albeit at a much slower pace. This is indicated by a number of studies that compared the performance of children with visual impairments on Piagetian tasks with that of seeing children (Friedman & Pasnak, 1973: Gottesman, 1971, 1973, 1976; Higgins, 1973; Miller, 1969; Simpkins & Stephens, 1974; and Tobin, 1972). Piaget's theory of stages of development is based on the belief that children progress through active interaction with their environment. This argues further that it is the restricted environmental involvement of children with visual impairments that causes their delayed conceptual development, and not the visual impairment itself. It should be noted that the age of onset of the loss of vision will significantly affect the child's concept development.

As Scholl (1986b) states, because concepts grow out of the perceptual process and because visual sensory input is limited or lacking, concept development may also be restricted. The child may never grasp some concepts, such as color; may have difficulty acquiring concepts of distance and time; and may require more direct instruction to compensate for the lack of imitative learning.

Is school achievement affected by visual impairment?

SCHOOL ACHIEVEMENT. As you might expect, children with visual impairments tend to lag behind children with normal vision in school. Children with partial vision are average in their grade placement and somewhat below grade level in academic achievement, according to studies by Bateman (1963) and Birch et al. (1966). The same pattern of achievement is found among blind students who read braille (Caton & Rankin, 1978; Lowenfeld, Abel, & Hatlen, 1969). The children studied in the Caton and Rankin research were from 2 to 4 years over age for grade placement and from $1^1/2$ to 2 years below grade level in reading achievement.

This does not mean that a vision impairment necessarily leads to underachievement in school. Ashcroft (1963) suggests that the academic lag may be the consequence of many factors, including the following:

1. Children with visual impairments usually enter school at a later age than other children.
2. Many children with vision problems are educated in inappropriate programs.
3. Many children miss a great deal of school due to surgery or treatment for eye conditions.
4. All children with severe visual impairments must use braille or large-type editions of books, which retards their ability to gather information.

Therefore, school underachievement, too, is an indirect rather than a direct result of visual impairment.

Though we have considered only a few of the factors that can influence learning, we can draw two general conclusions: (1) visual impairment does not necessarily result in mental retardation; and (2) the delays that are found in the intellectual development of those with visual impairments are the result of inadequate opportunities to explore the environment (Harley, 1973; Scott, 1982). It should be noted that these conclusions do not take into account children with visual impairments who also have other disabilities, such as mental retardation.

Affective Development

What is the primary cause of social problems that children with visual impairments might have?

In general, the social development of children with visual impairments does seem to differ from that of children who can see normally (Warren, 1984). The prevailing opinion is that most of the social and emotional problems of those with visual impairments are caused by the attitudes and reactions of those who can see. Cutsforth (1951), in fact, stated that society's negative attitudes were entirely responsible for their social and emotional problems.

A number of studies (Bauman, 1964; Cowen, Underberg, Verillo, & Benham, 1961; Gowman, 1957; Spivey, 1967) reveal that children with visual impairments either accept the opinions and expectations conveyed to them by society or suffer isolation as a result of rejecting them. In general, children with partial visual impairment tend to be more isolated by their seeing peers than those who are totally blind. This appears to be true because children with less severe disabilities do not elicit the sympathy accorded totally blind children. Harley (1973) suggests that this is at least partially due to the practice of placing children with visual impairments in special schools and classes.

Another factor that causes persons with normal vision to react negatively toward those with visual impairments is the lack of contact between the two groups. This results in misunderstandings by both groups and the formation of unrealistic ideas about the effects of visual impairment on children. For example, a typical attitude of those who can see normally is that all people with visual losses are totally blind and that, as a result, they are basically helpless and dependent. This is, of course, not true. It is this kind of misconception that causes social and emotional problems in children who have visual impairments.

It is possible to improve attitudes, however, as Bateman (1964) found when she studied the attitudes of seeing children who were enrolled in classes with children who had visual impairments. She found that these children had much higher estimations of the abilities of the children with visual impairments than children who had not had direct associations with them. Siperstein and Bak (1980) found similar results when analyzing the results of a study to improve the attitudes of fifth and sixth grade normally sighted students toward their blind peers. This implies that greater integration of children with visual impairments into classes with seeing children, as well as more training for regular classroom teachers about the capabilities of those with visual impairments, would result in improved attitudes toward those students—and more appropriate educational planning and placement, too.

PROBE 10-5   Developmental Characteristics

1. T   F   Although blind children may have delayed physical development due to their inability to do some physical activities, they typically do not differ in physical ability from normally sighted children.
2. List three possible causes of apparent retardation in the intellectual development, school achievement, and concept development of blind children.
3. The most widely accepted reason for social-emotional adjustment problems in blind children is _____. This can be overcome by _____.

INSTRUCTIONAL METHODS AND MATERIALS

You should be able to describe methods and materials used to educate children with visual impairments.

The learning needs of blind and visually impaired children can be divided into three categories: Needs that are met by adapting the curriculum, needs that are met by changes in methodology, and developmental and educational needs that are unique to these children. To fulfill the needs in each category, it is essential that instruction be provided by special teachers of the visually impaired who are knowledgeable of the effects of the loss of vision on learning, trained in effective methods of adaptation and remediation, and sensitized to the emotional needs of this population. (Hatlen & Curry, 1987, p. 7)

Once a child has been placed in the most suitable educational environment, the educator must consider the curriculum that will best meet his or her needs. The term *curriculum* means "the total experiences a learner has under the supervision of the school" (Smith, Krouse, & Atkinson, 1961, p. 969). The curriculum includes the subjects to be taught and the methods and materials used to teach them. The educator must consider the needs that children with visual impairments share with other children, as well as the needs unique to those with visual impairments.

What special skills should be taught to children with visual impairments?

Children with visual impairments are usually taught the same sequence of subjects as children with normal vision, because they need to master the same basic skills. Unlike children with normal vision, however, they will need to be taught additional skills, such as how to orient themselves, how to attain mobility, and how to take care of themselves. Children with visual impairments will also need to be taught certain skills to aid their study of academic subjects—how to read braille, how to use technology that can be used to translate printed materials, and how to use recording equipment, for example. Although the responsibility for implementing the total curriculum plan lies with the regular classroom teacher, the assistance of a specially trained teacher of children with visual impairments will be necessary to teach children the special skills just mentioned.

Many educators believe that the methods of teaching children with visual impairments should not differ from the methods of teaching those with normal vision. Others contend that their instruction requires significantly different strategies (Hatlen, 1980). Both positions have some validity. When adjustments or adaptations are made, they involve changing the media and the manner in which material is presented.

The media through which children with visual impairments obtain information are tactile, visual, and auditory. The selection of the appropriate medium for a particular child was mentioned earlier in this chapter. You will remember that a measurement of visual acuity alone does not provide enough information to decide what medium is best for a child. Some children with extremely low visual acuity can use visual materials quite efficiently, whereas others will need tactile materials, and still others may be able to use both. Decisions about the best medium for a child should be made only after thorough assessment by specially trained professionals. This assessment can be accomplished through various procedures described by Swallow (1981), Genshaft, Dare, and O'Malley (1980), Rabin (1982), and many others; the careful observations of teachers are also helpful. Once the primary medium for learning has been selected, teachers should keep in mind that some children can use both tactile and visual materials, and that all children can and should use auditory materials. In other words, a Total Communication approach for children with visual impairments should be employed.

Special Skills

Children with visual impairments need to learn certain special skills not included in the curriculum of children with normal vision. Broadly defined, the two most important such areas are (1) orientation and mobility, and (2) daily living skills.

Why are orientation and mobility training important?

ORIENTATION AND MOBILITY. The ability of children to move about in their environment and interact with it has important educational and social effects (Lowenfeld, 1971). Educationally, it allows them to develop realistic concepts about their environment and thus enables them to participate more fully in learning experiences with seeing children. Socially, it helps to dispel the notion that persons with visual impairments are helpless and dependent, and fosters the notion they can become fully participating and contributing members of society. Thus, it is very important that schools provide orientation and mobility training for all children who need it (Welsh & Blasch, 1980; Hill, 1986).

Orientation training involves teaching children with visual impairments to understand their environment and to recognize their surroundings and their relationship to them. Mobility training involves teaching the child to move efficiently from place to place in the environment (Welsh & Blasch, 1980). These types of training are generally presented by specially trained instructors, although some preliminary skills can be taught by the regular classroom teacher of those with visual impairments. Orientation and mobility training should not be considered only for the child who is totally blind; many children with partial vision can also benefit from it. The training should begin as early as possible to avoid the formation of unrealistic concepts and attitudes.

How can technology help with mobility?

A number of new and exciting devices to aid in mobility training have recently been developed. Hill (1986) describes the C-5 laser cane, developed by Bionic Instruments, Lynwood, California. This cane works on the principle of infrared light. It is an adapted long cane and is used in the same manner. Wormald International Sensory Aids produces two electronic mobility devices, the Mowat Sensor and the Sonic Guide (Figure 10-6). The Mowat Sensor is a hand-held electronic probe that uses vibration signals to indicate the distance to objects that

FIGURE 10-6   Electronic Mobility Devices. Left: Sonic Guide. Right: Mowat Sensor

fall within its narrow beam (Wormald International Sensory Aids, 1979). The Sonic Guide is an electronic aid in the form of spectacles, which emits sounds to convey spatial information (Wormald International Society Aids, 1979). Other electronic mobility aids continue to be developed. They hold great promise for those with visual impairments.

How do children with visual impairments learn daily living skills?

DAILY LIVING SKILLS. Daily living skills include such things as eating, bathing, toileting, dressing, grooming, and household chores. Most of these skills are acquired by normally sighted children through visual observation alone; none are directly taught in school programs. However, it is usually necessary to teach them directly to children with visual impairments.

Ideally, most of these skills should be acquired at home before the child enters school, but frequently this doesn't occur; thus, the responsibility for teaching the skills falls to the school. In most cases, the special teacher of those with visual impairments provides the training, although regular classroom teachers can also do so with assistance from special teachers (Hatlen & Curry, 1986).

To provide training in a particular daily living task, the task is analyzed and programmed lessons are developed, leading the child through the task in steps, with emphasis on the use of senses other than vision. Welsh and Blasch (1980) provide some guidelines for developing these skills in preschool children, and O'Brien (1976) includes a number of developmental scales in her study of preschool children. The latter are excellent references for planning lessons in daily living skills.

Skills Necessary to Study Academic Subjects

In addition to the skills just described, children with visual impairments need to learn how to use the techniques that have been designed to compensate for their loss of vision. These techniques involve the use of tactile, visual, or auditory media. Children with visual problems acquire information through reading and listening. The two media used for reading are braille and print.

What is braille?

BRAILLE. The primary tactile medium used by people with severe visual impairment is the **braille code,** developed by Louis Braille in 1829 when he was a student at the Paris School for the Blind. The code is based on a braille *cell,* which consists of six raised dots:

1 ● ● 4
2 ● ● 5
3 ● ● 6

Sixty-three combinations of these six dots are possible. With these 63 combinations, four braille codes have been developed—one for presenting literary material, one for mathematics and science, one for music, and one for computer commands. Since the braille cell occupies a great deal of space (each cell takes up a quarter inch), the original code has been altered to make it more compact. For example, many of the single braille units that represent alphabet letters (see Figure 10-7) also represent whole words. Many other words are represented by abbreviations, shortened forms, and nonalphabetic symbols. The total number of meanings assigned to the 63 configurations is 263. All of the duplicate meanings of a single configuration were assigned to conserve space.

The changes in the braille code designed to save space have created problems for children who must use the code to learn how to read. Most materials used to teach reading to those with visual impairments is transcribed directly from material designed to teach print reading. The problems unique to the braille code are not taken into consideration. For example, words sequenced in order of their difficulty for a child who can see may be sequenced inappropriately when transcribed into braille (Caton, 1979; Caton & Bradley, 1978–79). To overcome these problems, the American Printing House for the Blind has now produced a complete basal reading program that is based on the unique characteristics of the braille code and the unique characteristics of visually impaired children (Caton, Pester, & Bradley, 1980).

Because of the problems just discussed, it is absolutely essential that those who teach reading to children who use braille be well trained. When the basic skills of reading and the braille code have been mastered, most braille readers can participate successfully in reading classes with children who read print.

What is the advantage of devices such as the Pocket Braille?

Writing in braille is accomplished in one of three ways: (1) by computers and other technological devices, such as the American Printing House for the Blind's Pocket Braille; (2) the Perkins Brailler illustrated in Figure 10-9; or (3) the slate and stylus illustrated in Figure 10-10.

FIGURE 10-7   The Braille Alphabet

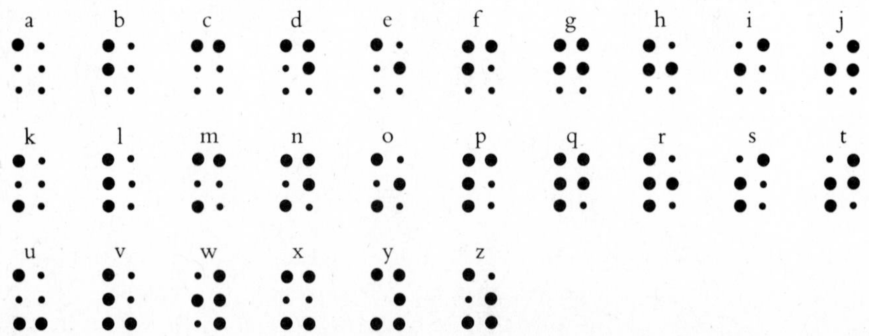

Technology related to braille writing has developed at an extremely rapid rate, thus making it difficult to describe all available materials in a short space. The Pocket Braille is but one of many such devices; others are the Versabraille System produced by TeleSensory Inc., and the Braille 'n Speak (Figure 10-8) produced by Blazie Engineering. The Versabraille System is a complete computer system that includes large type and braille components. The Pocket Braille and the Braille 'n Speak are portable machines that can be used for taking notes, have voice output, and can be attached to braille printers for converting notes into hard-copy braille.

The Perkins Brailler, or braille writer, is a hand-operated machine with six keys, one to correspond to each dot in the braille cell (Figure 10-9). When a key is pressed, a dot is embossed on the paper that is inserted in the back of the machine.

How does one operate the slate and stylus?

There are many different braille slates; the chief variation among them is size. All slates consist of a metal or plastic frame, which is sometimes mounted on a board. A pointed steel stylus is used to hand-punch braille dots (see Figure 10-10, page 337). Each slate has two parts connected by a hinge on the left side. The bottom part has several rows of braille cells indented on its top. The top part has holes that correspond to the indentations. The paper is placed between the two parts, and the stylus is used to punch in the dots from the tip.

The braille writer and the slate have been in use for many years. They are rather slow methods of communicating. However, exciting new technology developments are rapidly solving the problems of slow methods of communication.

Is there an optimal size of type for a child with low vision?

PRINT READING. Children with low vision can read print if it is presented to them appropriately. Such conditions as proper lighting, reduction of glare, print size, spacing, and the use of low-vision aids must be considered to ensure that the child is reading as efficiently as possible.

Print Size. The best print size for a particular child will probably fall between 12 and 24 points, although there is some evidence that normal-sized type is just as efficient if read with the proper optical aid (Peabody & Birch, 1967; Sykes, 1971). The most effective print size will vary with the particular child. Studies have indicated that 18 point type may be the most efficient size for most children with visual impairments (Eakin, Pratt, & McFarland, 1961).

FIGURE 10-8   The Braille 'n Speak

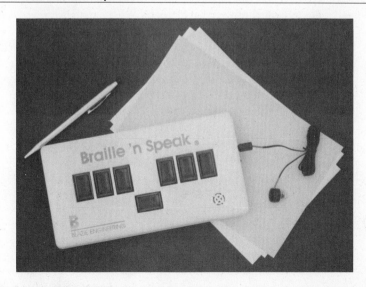

FIGURE 10-9   The Perkins Brailler

Most larger-type books published by the American Printing House for the Blind are printed in this size. Examples of 12, 18, and 24 point type are shown in Figure 10-11 (page 338).

Recently developed technology provides materials on the computer in large type or in color, which can greatly enhance the reading ability of the low-vision child. Many producers of computer software have programs to accomplish this.

What is an optical aid?

Optical Aids. When an optical aid is called for, the user may choose from among several types: (1) magnifiers attached to eyeglass frames, or part of the eyeglass lenses themselves; (2) stand magnifiers, which are mounted on a base to maintain a particular viewing distance; (3) hand-held magnifiers; (4) telescopic aids, which are used like binoculars; (5) television viewers, which magnify print and project it onto a television screen; and (6) computer programs. The type of aid selected will depend on the user's preference and the task for which the device is to be used. The strength of magnification is best determined by a professional in a low-vision clinic, or by a suitably trained teacher (Harley & Lawrence, 1984; Kirk, 1981).

Lighting and Contrast. The child's reading environment is just as important to reading efficiency as print size and the use of optical aids. The chief environmental considerations are the brightness of the lighting and the contrast between the writing itself and its background (Harley & Lawrence, 1984; Kirk, 1981).

The amount of illumination required for comfortable reading will vary considerably from child to child. Generally speaking, the best quality lighting is from fluorescent bulbs evenly distributed throughout the room. Children with optic atrophy will require intense illumination, whereas those with vision problems resulting from albinism will require less illumination. In all cases, care must be taken to avoid glare.

FIGURE 10-10   Slate and Stylus

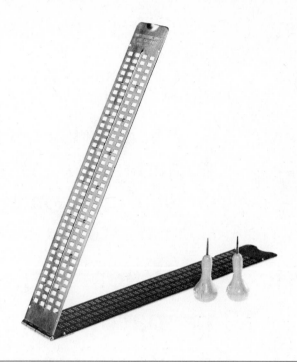

How does contrast affect the readability of material for children with low vision?

Children with low vision are able to read most efficiently when the print they are reading contrasts sharply with the material on which the letters are printed. Most children read dark print on buff-colored paper best, but some prefer dark print on white paper. Buff-colored paper is used because it reduces glare. Contrast is also important when chalkboards are being used. White chalk on a black chalkboard provides the best contrast, but white chalk on a green board is acceptable for some children. In general, contrast is best when the background is clear and uncluttered, and when the shade of the material to be viewed is sufficiently different to stand out clearly.

Variations in Reading Rate. Most children with visual impairments who read print do so at a much slower rate than children who see normally. Those who read large print typically progress at less than half the rate of children with good vision. Those who use optical aids also read relatively slowly. Several factors retard the rate of reading. Some eye disorders permit the reader to see only one or two letters at a time. The reading of large type is slower because it takes longer to pass the eye over larger letters and words. The use of an optical aid reduces the field of vision and requires that the aid be frequently moved or adjusted.

Once the many factors that influence how children with visual impairments read have been considered, the child can be taught to read using normal instructional methods. Children with visual impairments can usually be taught in the regular classroom if the teacher is assisted by a special teacher in setting up an appropriate environment.

What is the Optacon?

READING MACHINES. Two examples of technological alternatives to the reading methods and techniques just discussed are the Optacon (illustrated in Figure 10-12, page 339), and the Kurzweil Reading Machine.

FIGURE 10-11   Samples of Three Type Sizes

12 Point

When darkness fell, the women began preparing a great heap of wood for the circle of ceremonial fires. Then Chanuka slipped into the river and swam silently

18 Point

When darkness fell, the women preparing a great heap of wood circle of ceremonial fires. Then Ch slipped into the river and swam s

24 Point

When darkness fell, th preparing a great heap circle of ceremonial fires slipped into the river an

Source: Courtesy of American Printing House for the Blind.

The **Optacon** (optical-to-tactile converter) "reads" print and reproduces the form of the print letters with a series of small wire rods. The reader fits one hand into an opening in the machine and touches the panel where the letters are formed. With the other hand, the reader scans a page of print with a small camera. The Optacon is especially useful to persons with visual impairments who must read print for their jobs. It has not proved to be useful in the education of children with visual impairments.

The **Kurzweil Reading Machine,** introduced in 1975, converts printed words into synthetic speech. It provides access to a great deal of printed matter that was previously unavailable to those with visual impairments. The machine has been improved significantly since its introduction; it now has greatly improved speech and is both smaller and less expensive than the original version.

LISTENING. There are, of course, means of acquiring information that do not involve reading. Listening is one of the most effective. Accordingly, listening skills have been increasingly emphasized in recent years. A number of guides to developing listening skills have been produced. One of the most valuable is available through the Illinois Instructional Materials Center, where it was developed (Alber, 1978). Most reading programs emphasize the development of listening skills also. Listening is not a solution to all academic problems, but it is effective in such areas as literature and social studies. It is crucial in the education of children who can read neither print nor braille.

Special Education Aids

A number of instructional materials have been designed to meet the needs of children with visual impairments. These include diagrams, charts, and maps available with large print or in tactile form; sets of materials to replace pictures or visual displays in textbooks; mathematics aids such as specially adapted abacuses and tactile graph boards; braille writers; special bold-line paper for writing both braille and print; and many others.

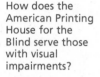

How does the American Printing House for the Blind serve those with visual impairments?

Most of these aids are available from the American Printing House for the Blind in Louisville, Kentucky. Federal funds for purchasing materials produced by the American Printing House for the Blind are available to children who meet the legal definition of blindness given at the beginning of this chapter. These children must be registered at the American Printing House for the Blind by the first Monday in January of each year. Specific information about registration and ordering procedures can be obtained from special education departments in public schools and universities, state departments of education, state residential schools for the blind, or the American Printing House for the Blind.

Organizations other than the American Printing House for the Blind have developed materials to be used in teaching specific subjects to those with visual impairments; among them are the American Foundation for the Blind in New York; Howe Press of the Perkins School for the Blind in Boston; and Mangold Exceptional Teaching Aids in Castro Valley, California.

FIGURE 10-12   Reading with an Optacon

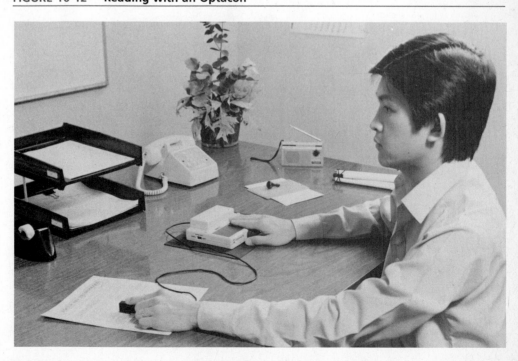

The work of Dr. Natalie Barraga (1964) has had a strong effect on the materials and planning procedures used to educate those with visual impairments. Barraga's work has demonstrated that children with visual impairments can be trained to use their residual vision to a much greater extent than was formerly thought possible, even if the impairment is very severe. A set of materials based on Barraga's work is available through the American Printing House for the Blind. These materials have been revised and are now entitled *Program to Develop Efficiency in Visual Functioning.* They include a diagnostic assessment procedure, a set of lessons, and a vision sourcebook (Barraga, 1980).

The use of special methods and materials alone will not adequately compensate for a child's loss of vision. Regardless of the subject being taught, children must, whenever possible, be given the opportunity to learn through direct experience with their environment. These experiences should be accompanied by thorough verbal explanations from the teacher. In addition, children with visual impairments should be encouraged to interact with sighted members of their environment. A child who is given these opportunities and who makes appropriate use of the methods and materials discussed previously can be regarded as having a completely developed curriculum.

Technology

The use of technology in all areas of education has dramatically increased in recent years. The majority of school-age children have now had some form of computer instruction. Special educators have been aware of this development and have now begun to provide this instruction to many exceptional children.

Children with visual impairments are also beginning to receive instruction in the use of computers. As Ruconich, Ashcroft, and Young (1983) point out, however, the process for these

Special computer software enlarges text so that this student with partial vision can use the computer for his education.

TECHNOLOGY IN ACTION

Blind since shortly after his premature birth, the award-winning singer and composer Stevie Wonder uses technology to create the sounds of the future. Here is what he says on a videotape that illustrates machines that are controlled by computer programs developed by scientists working in the field of artificial intelligence:

Stevie Wonder: OK. Here I am with my new synthesizer. This is great. All these beautiful keys, all these buttons. This is incredible . . . (pointing) . . . but here I have this visual display. Now how do I know what it says? I'd be lost. But because of technology—because of the interfacing of speech synthesizers with these instruments—I can push the button and know . . . by listening to what it says.

The robotic voice of the speech synthesizer: Hit button to start and stop recording. Sequencer activated. Record new sequence.

[*Stevie composes and plays lyrical music on the synthesizer.*]

Narrator: Machines can now read the alphabet as readily as any person. Building on this ability to recognize let-ters, reading machines for the blind can now read those letters aloud as words, sentences, and books.

Stevie Wonder [*demonstrating the use of the Kurzweil reading machine*]: Now with technology I can do things I always wanted to do, immediately, like reading this book. This book is called *Blues from the Delta.*

Robotic voice of the Kurzweil reader: Scanner moving to top of the page. Looking for the first line. . . . No matter how versatile, the solo performer could never match the sound of blues bands which featured several guitars, a harmonica and drums together. . . .

Stevie Wonder: Everyone wants to feel that they can be as independent as possible. Everyone really wants to have the freedom of doing, reading, discovering things on their own. Technology for me has been like a brother, mother, a friend. It has been that very thing that I have not been able to do—it has helped me to see. Without question it has been another one of those sunshines of my life.

Source: The Kurzweil Foundation (1987). *The age of intelligent machines: Machines that think* [Videotape]. Waltham, MA.

---

children has been somewhat slower than for other children. A survey by Young and Ashcroft (1981) indicated that in 1980 only 3 percent of visually impaired students were learning about computers, but one year later, 23 percent of them had received instruction. This survey seems to indicate a trend toward providing instruction in the use of computers to visually impaired children. As Ruconich, Ashcroft, and Young (1983) indicate, this trend has continued as computers have become more accessible to the visually impaired.

What considerations relate to the use of computers by children with visual impairments?

The major consideration when students with visual impairments use computers is that, because of their visual losses, most of these students need additional equipment to translate computer information into a form they can understand. Ruconich, Ashcroft, and Young (1983) provide an excellent description of the types of equipment now being used for this purpose and discuss the advantages and disadvantages of each type. Briefly, the types of equipment they describe are as follows:

1. *Electronic Braille.* This includes both "paperless" braille machines, such as the Pocket Braille, and "paper" braille, which can now be provided by various braille printers. (Subsequent to the Ruconich and Ashcroft article, more braille printers and other paperless braille devices have become available. They are too numerous to mention in this chapter, but information about them can be obtained from the American Printing House for the Blind in Louisville, Kentucky.)
2. *The Optacon.* This device is shown in Figure 10-12 and discussed earlier in the chapter. It allows students to read print by using a small camera.
3. *Synthesized Speech.* Equipment that enables the computer to "talk" sidesteps the need to provide information that those with visual impairments can read.
4. *Enlarged Print.* As with printed reading matter, computer displays in large print are useful to many students with low vision.

Each of these different types of equipment can be extremely valuable in enabling students with visual impairments to use compwuters, and each has its disadvantages. For example, the major advantage of the electronic braille devices is that they can both send and receive information. The disadvantages include the fact that some devices display only one short line at a time, and that some are extremely slow in printing. The Optacon's advantage is that a variety of print material can be read with it, but the reading is very slow for most students with visual impairments. The major advantage of synthesized speech is its speed. The disadvantage is the limited review capabilities of most of the equipment. The advantage of enlarged print is that a large percentage of students with low vision can use it. The disadvantage is that computers that have large print usually have only one size, and this may not be appropriate for all persons; also, the Optacon cannot read all sizes. Finally, a major disadvantage of all these types of equipment has been the cost factor. All are expensive, although costs have been reduced on some (Ruconich, Ashcroft, & Young, 1983).

In spite of the disadvantages just cited, the future of computer use by students who have visual impairments looks bright. A number of exciting research projects are underway and the results look promising. As Ruchonich, Ashcroft, and Young (1983) have stated, the major concern is the development and use of equipment that can provide students with visual impairments access to computers. The equipment exists now. Some of it needs to be refined and some is still too expensive for most users. However, students with visual impairments do appear to be well on the way to becoming successful users of microcomputers.

The majority of information in this section was taken from the unpublished article by Ruconich, Ashcroft, and Young (1983). Others have written on the subject; those interested may want to consult articles by Fullwood (1977), Ryan and Bedi (1978), Pera and Cobb (1978), Schofield (1981), Ashcroft and Bourgeois (1980), and Mack (1990). Figure 10-13 lists examples of the wide variety of aids that can be used by people with visual impairments.

FIGURE 10-13   A Functional Approach to Exceptionality: Visual Impairments

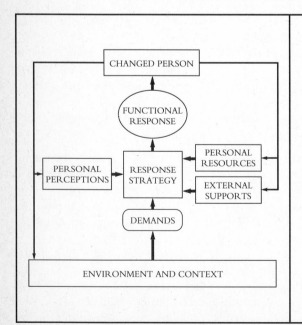

There are numerous *external supports* available to enhance the ability of a person with a visual impairment to function. Included among these are the following:

- Guide dogs to assist in travel.
- Wristwatches with flip-up crystals to give access to braille symbols on the watch face.
- Balls and ring-toss games that emit audible beeps to enable blind children to play.
- "Talking" computers for use in word processing, programming, and other computer operations.
- Special readers that can read printed documents and convert text to speech.
- Braille markings in elevators and on door frames in public buildings.
- People who record books and other printed material on audiotape.
- Specially marked measuring devices to use in cooking and dispensing medicine.
- Oversized playing cards for people with low vision.
- Special education teachers to teach the use of braille and other low-vision aids.

PROBE 10-6   Instructional Methods and Materials

1. T F Children with visual impairments are usually taught the same sequence of subjects as children with normal vision.
2. T F Many instructional procedures that are effective for children who can see normally are also effective for children with visual impairments.
3. List some optical aids that can be used by children with low vision to assist them in reading.
4. The most important skill areas included in the curriculum of those with visual impairments but not in the curriculum of those with normal vision are _____ and _____ .
5. T F Children with low vision who hold their books close to their eyes when reading should be instructed not to hold the materials so close.
6. The media through which children with visual impairments obtain information are _____, _____, and _____.
7. Technological advances have resulted in the development of a number of exciting new devices for those with visual impairments. List three devices related to reading that blind people can use.
8. The major concern in teaching students with visual impairments to use computers is _____.
9. List four types of equipment that can help give students with visual impairments access to computers.
10. T F Students with visual impairments need only one type of access equipment to use computers.
11. T F The question of literacy for children with visual impairments has become a major issue in the educational planning for these children.
12. T F Children with visual impairments need to use only one learning medium in their educational programs.

EDUCATIONAL PROGRAMMING

You should be able to describe the implications of PL 94-142 for educating children with visual impairments in the least restrictive environment.

What are the historical roots for educational practices for children with visual impairments?

To understand current practices in educating children with visual impairments, it is necessary to understand the history and development of educational practices involving such students. The first formal educational program for children with visual impairments was a residential school, primarily for totally blind children, established by Valentin Haüy in Paris in 1784. Haüy was extremely influential in the development of educational programs for those with visual impairments in Europe. Residential schools for people who were blind were eventually established in several European cities.

The first educational programs for children with visual impairments in the United States also were residential schools. These schools were designed for totally blind children, but students with partial vision were eventually enrolled in them as well. The earliest schools, which both opened in 1832, were the Perkins School for the Blind in Boston and the New York Institute for the Blind in New York City. In 1833 the Pennsylvania Institution for the Instruction of the Blind was opened in Philadelphia. This later became the Overbrook School for the Blind. Gradually other residential schools were established in other states.

The first local day school classes for blind children were set up in Chicago in 1900, followed in 1913 by a day school program for those with partial vision in Roxbury, Massachusetts. As you can see, the practice of separating blind and low-vision children in local day school classes was established early. It has continued in some areas until the present. The current trend, however, is to combine programs for children who are blind and for those with low vision. Today there are a variety of types of programs in the United States for children with visual impairments, including the residential school and five types of administrative plans in local day schools.

Residential Schools

How has the role
of residential
schools changed in
recent years?

The residential school has traditionally provided a total educational program for children with visual impairments. This program usually has a complete range of grades from kindergarten through twelfth, and teaches the same curriculum taught in other schools in the state or region. Most residential school students do not attend classes with children with normal vision, although some residential schools have an agreement with the local school system that allows some students with visual impairments to attend regular classes.

The role of the residential school has changed during the past decade. Some residential schools now function as educational source centers for those with visual impairments. They may provide activities that involve such children with sighted children outside the school; some also provide services to local school programs that serve children who have visual impairments. These services can involve storing materials and resources and developing special summer programs to train children in orientation and mobility, daily living skills, and other special skills.

Other residential schools serve as centers for children with visual impairments who have additional disabilities. These schools offer extensive support services, such as physical therapy, occupational therapy, and speech therapy for children with severe disabilities, as well as regular education programs. This reflects the current trend of placing children in local day schools whenever possible, and reserving space in residential programs for those who cannot function successfully in other environments. The effectiveness of such residential programs cannot be assessed until they have been in operation for a longer period of time.

Local Day Schools

What educational
alternatives are
available in day
schools?

Local day schools for children with visual impairments are currently run according to one of five basic administrative plans. These are as follows:

1. *The special class plan:* Students are enrolled in a special class for students with visual impairments and receive most of the instruction in that class. They may participate in some nonacademic activities with sighted children, but they usually do not receive academic instruction outside the special class. This plan is recommended only for children with multiple disabilities who cannot benefit from academic instruction in the regular classroom.
2. *The cooperative class plan:* Students are enrolled in a special class for students with visual impairments in a public school. They do some of their academic work in this room and some in the regular classroom. They also participate in nonacademic activities in the regular classroom. This plan is seldom used today.
3. *The resource room plan:* Students are enrolled in a regular classroom and come to a separate classroom for special help in difficult academic areas. They spend as much time as possible in the regular classroom and leave only when help is necessary.
4. *The itinerant teacher plan:* Students are enrolled in the regular classroom, and a specially trained teacher, who most often serves several different schools, provides them with special instruction and materials.
5. *The teacher-consultant plan:* Students are enrolled in regular classrooms and receive basically the same services as those offered under the itinerant teacher plan. The major difference between the teacher-consultant plan and the itinerant teacher plan is that the teacher-consultant spends a greater part of his or her time working with the

regular classroom teacher or other school personnel to assist them in providing appropriate services (Hatlen, 1980).

All of these plans require a specially trained teacher of children with visual impairments, as well as special equipment and materials for both blind and low-vision children. The major differences among them involve their administrative organization and the instructional duties of the teachers. In the special class plan, for example, the child is enrolled in a special classroom, and the teacher of those with visual impairments is responsible for most of the academic instruction and grading.

In the resource room, itinerant teacher, and teacher-consultant plans, on the other hand, the child is enrolled in the regular classroom, and the regular teacher is responsible for most of the instruction and for grading. Under these plans the teacher of those with visual impairments assists the regular teacher in obtaining materials and provides instruction in subjects in which the child is having difficulty.

The resource room, itinerant teacher, and teacher-consultant plans are preferred today because they permit greater integration of children with visual impairments into regular classrooms. Most special educators believe that the itinerant teacher plan is not appropriate for young visually impaired children; the resource room plan is preferred. In actual practice, many school districts use combinations and adaptations of the plans to suit their needs. This is desirable, of course, since the goal of all educational programming is to provide each child with a program that will meet his or her individual needs. It is very important that program planning remain flexible. The selection of the least restrictive alternative should not be based on existing administrative plans. It must be based on the needs of the individual child.

Selecting the Least Restrictive Environment

PL 94–142 requires that the least restrictive environment for a particular child be selected by an IEP committee. This committee can be regional or local. The committee must be furnished with a variety of evaluation data, including the following: (1) an eye examination report; (2) a medical report; (3) a developmental and social history; (4) reports of behavioral observations by parents and teachers; (5) any other information that might be helpful. The committee reviews the data and then decides what type of educational environment is best suited to the child's needs.

What factors should be considered in selecting an educational program?

The decision to place a child in a particular program should be based on the child's level of independence and the kinds of services the program makes available. Generally speaking, the more independent the child, the less structured the program needs to be. A high school student who can travel independently and succeed academically with only occasional help from the special education teacher may do best in an itinerant teacher program or with the help of a teacher-consultant. Young children who are acquiring basic skills will probably require daily contact with a special education teacher and may be best educated under the resource room plan. Children who have severe impairments or disabilities in addition to blindness will probably function best under the special or cooperative class plans. For some students, residential school placement may be most appropriate.

Because children's needs change as they develop, it is important to remain flexible in determining what program best fulfills a student's needs. A program well-suited to a 6-year-old child may be inappropriate for the same child at age 8. As Taylor (1974) states, "The facility should be selected which fulfills a particular need, at the time of the need, and for only as long as—in light of the total situation—it is fulfilling this need" (pp. 118–120). Children should be educated as much as possible in the classes they would be attending if they were not visually impaired, and they should spend as much time as possible in classes with children who have normal vision.

Several other important factors must be considered in choosing the program best-suited to an individual child's needs. The most important is that the child's parents should be made familiar with all the data on their child and should play an important role in selecting the child's program. Even though the final decision on a child's placement rests with the IEP committee of the local school, parental consent for such placement is required by law. Parents must also consent to the collection of evaluation data (Abeson, Bolick, & Haff, 1976).

It is also very important that placement recommendations be based on all the available information on a child. All too frequently a measurement of the child's visual acuity is used as the primary criterion for placement. Although visual acuity is important, it should be considered in conjunction with other information about the child's level of functioning.

Finally, the availability of appropriate programs should be considered. Unfortunately, there is sometimes a shortage of programs for children with visual impairments, particularly in sparsely populated areas. Federal legislation states, however, that the fact that no program exists in a particular community does not relieve the school district of the responsibility to provide such a program. This means that the recommendations of an IEP committee should be based solely on the needs of the child, and not on the availability of a particular program. In some communities, however, it may be impossible to provide the full range of programs that are available in major population centers.

Planning for Direct Instruction

In addition to selecting the best program for a child, members of the IEP committee are responsible for developing an individualized education program for each child who is referred to them. The IEP is used as the basis for planning direct instruction. To plan effectively, the teacher must be familiar with the characteristics of children who have visual impairments, know what types of assessment tools are available, and know how to interpret their results.

What assessment information is needed for program planning?

CHARACTERISTICS RELEVANT TO EDUCATIONAL PLANNING. Persons involved in assessment should pay particular attention to the effect of visual loss on the formation of concepts. Children whose ability to interact with their environment is restricted by a visual impairment will not perform well on tests that assess concepts usually formed visually. The child's formation of visual concepts is also affected by the age at which the loss of vision occurred, whether the loss occurred gradually or suddenly, and, of course, the severity of the loss. The severity of the loss will influence what reading medium children will use, how efficiently they use their remaining vision, and whether they use optical aids (Scholl & Schnur, 1976).

ASSESSMENT DATA NEEDED. Children with visual impairments vary as much as other children. Thus, the data used to plan their education should be derived from a variety of formal and informal assessment techniques. DeMott (1974) suggests that information in the following areas be included in any educational assessment of students with visual impairments:

1. *Visual efficiency:* the use the child makes of any remaining vision.
2. *Sensory abilities:* the ability to hear, perceive through touch, and use the senses of taste and smell to acquire information.
3. *Other impairments:* the identification of impairments in abilities other than vision that might affect the child's ability to learn.
4. *Motor performance:* the ability to move about to gain information.
5. *Language:* the ability to use speech and listening skills to learn.
6. *Intelligence:* the intellectual ability to learn.
7. *Achievement:* academic progress and ability.

Bauman (1977) suggests that the child's personality, social competency, vocational interests and aptitudes, and readiness to learn be assessed as well. Areas of assessment have also been discussed by Swallow (1981). Hazecamp and Huebner (1989) have developed a detailed plan for assessment and evaluation of educational programs for children with visual impairments, which is very useful for teachers and administrators. It includes discussion of areas to be evaluated as well as checklists to assist in the evaluation.

ASSESSMENT INSTRUMENTS. There are three basic types of assessment instruments available for children with visual impairments:

1. Those developed specifically for those with visual impairments.
2. Those developed for a sighted population, but adapted for use by those with visual impairments.
3. Those developed for a sighted population and used in their original form by those with visual impairments.

The most current discussion of assessment instruments is that by Bradley-Johnson (1986). The American Foundation for the Blind and the American Printing House for the Blind have current lists of instruments and can provide assistance in selecting them.

INTERPRETATION OF ASSESSMENT DATA. Although the interpretation of assessment data is too complicated a topic to cover adequately in this chapter, you should be familiar with two general guidelines:

1. Assessment data should be interpreted only by specially trained persons who are familiar with the characteristics of children with visual impairments.
2. Information about norms (i.e. the population used to establish standards for a test) should be used with caution. If the norm data were based on a sample of children with visual impairments, it is important to know whether the children were enrolled in public schools or in residential school programs. Most of the children in residential schools today have multiple disabilities, and norms based on such children may not be valid for children with visual impairment alone. Norm data based on a sample of children with normal vision will not be valid for those with visual impairments unless they have been modified for an adapted form of the test.

To restate the most important considerations in providing the best education for a particular child: The least restrictive environment consists of the program in which the child can learn best. Generally, this should be the program the child would normally be placed in if he or she were not visually impaired. As much as possible, children with visual impairments should be educated with children who have normal vision. However, they may need to spend part of their day with a certified teacher of those with visual impairments. Ideally, there should be a continuum of services so that a child can be moved from one program to another as needs change. Educators should never regard a child's placement as final; they should, rather, be willing to move the child to a different program if the child's needs change.

PROBE 10-7   Educational Programming

1. The first schools established for children with visual impairments in Europe and the United States were _____ schools.
2. T F The residential school traditionally follows the same curriculum as other schools in the same state or region.
3. How has the role of residential schools changed in recent years?
4. List the five types of local day school programs provided for children with visual impairments.
5. T F The school principal makes the decision about the type of program in which a child with a visual impairment should be placed.
6. List three types of information that are used to make placement decisions for children with visual impairments.

7. T   F   Parents must consent to the collection of evaluation data and to the placement of their child with a visual impairment in a particular program.
8. Persons involved in assessing children with visual impairments should pay particular attention to the effects of the loss of vision on _____ development.
9. DeMott suggests that information about a number of areas be included in the educational assessment of those with visual impairments. List four of these areas.
10. What three types of instruments are used to assess children with visual impairments?
11. T   F   Normative data provided for standardized tests are appropriate for use with children who have visual impairments.

SUMMARY

1. Normal, or unimpaired, vision has four basic components: (a) the object to be viewed; (b) light that reflects from the object; (c) an intact visual organ (the eye); and (d) the occipital lobes of the brain, where visual stimuli are interpreted and "seeing" takes place.
2. The leading causes of visual impairment among those who are not legally blind are cataracts, refractive problems, and glaucoma. Among totally blind persons, the leading causes of blindness are retinal disorders, glaucoma, and cataracts.
3. Definitions of visual impairment based on visual acuity are used primarily for legal and economic purposes, and for the allocation of federal funds for the purchase of educational materials.
4. Educational definitions of visual impairment are based on the media through which the child learns rather than on visual acuity.
5. The incidence of children with visual impairments in the school-age population is generally considered to be one in every 1000.
6. Most children with visual impairments are not totally blind. Approximately two-thirds of all children with visual impairments have some remaining vision.
7. Other than vision, the physical characteristics of children with visual impairments (in the absence of other disabilities) are the same as those of children who are not visually impaired.
8. The intellectual development of children is not directly affected by visual impairment or blindness.
9. Because the loss of vision leads to restrictions in the child's range and variety of experience, ability to get about, and interaction with the environment, the child with visual impairments has problems in concept development.
10. Children with visual impairments tend to lag behind their sighted peers in school achievement.
11. The most widely accepted view is that the social and emotional problems of children with visual impairments are the result of the attitudes and reactions of persons with normal vision, and not the result of the loss of vision itself.
12. The curriculum for programs for those with visual impairments is usually the same as that for the other school programs in a particular state or region.
13. In considering basic instructional methods for children with visual impairments, it is important to remember that many of the techniques and strategies that are effective with seeing children are also appropriate for those who have visual impairments.
14. Children with visual impairments do have some unique instructional needs and will require help from specially trained teachers in some academic areas.

15. In the United States, children with visual impairments are educated in residential schools and a number of different types of programs in local day schools.
16. Those involved in educational planning should remain flexible in their approach to placement.
17. It is important to remember that the most appropriate, least restrictive environment for children with visual impairment is the one in which they learn best. They should be educated to the greatest extent possible with children who can see normally.

TASK SHEET 10   Field Experiences Related to Visual Impairment

Select one of the following and perform the assigned tasks.

Program Visitation

Visit either a residential school, a local day school (self-contained) program, or a resource program for children with visual impairments. In a paper of no more than three pages, describe the program you visited, the curriculum that was being used, the interactions you had with the staff and students, and your general reactions and impressions of the program. How did it differ from programs for normally sighted children?

Professional Interview

Arrange to visit one of the following professionals, and discuss his or her job: ophthalmologist, optometrist, optician, orthoptist, teacher of children with visual impairments, rehabilitation counselor for people with visual impairments, or director of a facility that provides services for people with visual impairments. In a paper of no more than three pages, answer the following questions:

1. Where did you visit?
2. What were the responsibilities of the person you interviewed?
3. What type of training was necessary to enter this profession?
4. What types of problems does the person encounter?
5. What did you learn from this experience, and what was your reaction to it?

Interview with a Person Who Is Visually Impaired

Interview a person who has a visual impairment, or the parents of a person with a visual impairment. Determine the types of problems the person encounters, as well as his or her attitudes toward the disability and toward people with normal vision. Describe your findings and the feelings you had during the interview.

Library Study

Use the library to find three articles related to visual impairment. Write a one-age abstract of each. Here are some journals you might consult:

> *Exceptional Children*
> *Journal of Visual Impairment and Blindness*
> *RE: view*

Design Your Own Field Experience

If you know of a unique experience you can have with someone who has a visual impairment, discuss your alternative with your instructor and complete the task that you agree on.

Five years after an accident left her paralyzed, paraplegic Nan Davis rose from her wheelchair and walked 10 feet to receive her college diploma with a book-size computer telling her numbed legs what to do.

"This is a special day for all of us," she said . . . when she reached the podium at the University of Dayton Arena to receive her bachelor's degree in elementary education from Wright State University.

"The last time she walked in public . . . was in high school, and she wanted to walk in her college graduation," said Dr. Jerrold Petrofsky. He is the developer of the computer system that helped Miss Davis to walk.

Miss Davis, 23, rose from her wheelchair and was accompanied by Petrofsky and colleague Dr. Chandler Phillips. They held her arms as her legs moved to the commands of the computer carried by Petrofsky. . . .

Her first computer-aided walk required a huge stationary computer that selectively activated small electrodes on her skin to make selected leg muscles contract. The computer she used at Saturday's commencement was about 4 inches by 6 inches and less than an inch thick.

Petrofsky's subjects, including Miss Davis, first undergo 6 to 12 months of physical therapy to improve their muscular, bone, and cardiovascular strength. That is necessary, he said, because the bones, muscles, and cardiovascular systems atrophy in paralyzed people, increasing the danger of such things as bone fractures during even mild exertion.

What are the next steps in the research? "We will be looking at further miniaturization of the portable walking system and at implanting the electrodes in the body over the next few years," Petrofsky said. . . . "We will be working on achieving more sophisticated movement with our walking systems, while continuing to run extensive tests on the systems. These are just some of the areas we hope to tackle."

But for Nan Davis, at least one dream has already been realized: She walked up to accept her college diploma on her own two feet.

Source: Adapted from an article by Dale Leach, June 13, 1983, Computer made graduation special, *The Lexington Herald Leader;* and from information provided by Wright State University, Dayton, Ohio.

11

Students with Physical and Health-Related Disabilities

Donald P. Cross

The story about Nan on the facing page illustrates another of several dramatic types of change that have occurred recently in the care of persons with physical disabilities. Recent developments in computer technology have led to an increasing application in areas that yesterday were only imagined in futuristic fiction. The evolution of educational programming has been more subtle, but great progress has been made since the turn of the century, when the following was written:

> Inherited physical deformity means mental deformity, particularly when the former is an affection of the cerebral or sensory nerves, or even of the motor organism. So positively has this been demonstrated that in the treatment of feebleminded and insane children, as well as of adults, physicians attempted to correct physical disorder first. With the normal physical functions restored, mental equilibrium also ordinarily returns. [Taylor, 1898, p. 184]

As this statement indicates, children with visible deformities were perceived at that time as being mentally defective, and it was thought that the mental problem could be cured by correcting the physical problem.

As noted in Chapter 1 of this text, at the beginning of the twentieth century children with physical disabilities either stayed at home or were institutionalized. Gradually, however, educators began to admit children with physical disabilities into the schools, and special schools and hospital classes were developed. Later, programs for individuals with physical disabilities were incorporated into public schools through the establishment of self-contained special classes, but they were frequently housed in substandard facilities, such as church basements or old houses.

Today, educational programs for those with physical disabilities are found in a variety of locations. They may be offered within the public school, or in a segregated day school, residential facility, or hospital setting. Educational programming for those with disabilities may take the form of a class in a segregated facility such as a hospital or day school, or it may occur within a regular school building in the form of a self-contained special class or resource room. Many children with physical disabilities receive no special placement and attend school in the regular classroom. Descriptions of the continuum of special education services are further described in Chapter 2. Each disability area may or may not have specific implications for educational programming. It is not the intent of this chapter to present those educational methods that are relevant to specific disability groups. This information is typically presented in "methods" texts.

Like children with other disorders, those with physical disabilities are typically grouped in categories. Categories are useful in grouping children for education, funding, and research. At the same time, however, children who have been placed in a category for persons with physical disabilities tend to be isolated from other children. The current trend is to eliminate categorical labels that can prevent children with physical disabilities from attending regular education programs.

In this chapter we will discuss children who are grouped according to their abilities to function in a particular area, and children who are grouped according to a medical diagnosis. The functional categories are **ambulation,** which refers to a child's ability to move from place to place, and **vitality,** which refers to the child's health and ability to sustain life. Disabilities that do not fit into either of these categories are discussed in a section labeled *Other Disabilities,* which includes convulsive disorders and traumatic brain injury. The education and treatment of children with physical disabilities is discussed after a brief look at the helping professions that are involved. A discussion of architectural barriers common to those with physical disabilities is presented at the conclusion of the chapter.

DEFINITIONS OF PHYSICAL DISABILITIES

You should be able to define physical disabilities and related terminology.

In this chapter, a child with physical disabilities will be defined as follows: *One whose physical or health problems result in an impairment of normal interaction with society to the extent that specialized services and programs are required.* This does not include persons with visual or hearing impairments or persons who have been labeled severely or profoundly mentally retarded.

The disabilities discussed in this chapter are presented separately, and each of them is described separately in medical literature. This does not mean, however, that children with one type of disability should be separated from children with a different type or from children who have no disability. Children with disabilities resemble one another in more ways than they differ from one another. Particular disorders are discussed separately as an efficient method of presenting the material relevant to each of them.

Terminology Based on Anatomy

Most of the terms used to describe physical disabilities are based on medical usage, which is derived from Greek and Latin. Areas of the body are frequently designated with prefixes, whereas suffixes are used to designate conditions of the body. For example, the prefix *hemi-* refers to one side of the body, whereas the suffix *-plegia* refers to paralysis or the inability to

TABLE 11-1   Common Terms

Term	Body Area Involved
Monoplegia	One limb
Hemiplegia	Both limbs on the same side of the body
Paraplegia	The lower limbs
Diplegia	All four limbs, but the lower limbs more seriously than the upper
Triplegia	Three limbs
Quadriplegia	All four limbs
Double Hemiplegia	Upper limbs more seriously affected than the lower
Anterior	Front
Posterior	Back
Medial	Pertaining to the middle
Lateral	Farther from the midline
Superior	Upper; situated above
Inferior	Lower; situated below

move (Johnston & Magrab, 1976). Thus, the term "hemiplegia" refers to the paralysis of one side of the body.

What are the different -*plegias*?

Some terms commonly used in the discussion of physical disabilities are listed in Table 11-1. Two other terms you should be familiar with are *proximodistal* and *cephalocaudal,* both used to describe the growth of children. The term *proximodistal* is used to describe the sequence of development that begins with the child's gaining control of muscles close to the trunk (proximo) and progresses gradually until the child gains control of muscles located farther away (distal). For example, a child can control shoulder and elbow movements before controlling finger movements. The term *cephalocaudal* refers to the maturation of the nervous system, which begins at the head (cephalo) and progresses down the trunk to the more distant parts of the body to the tail, or anterior end (caudal). Thus, a child can control head movements before arm movements (Johnston & Magrab, 1976).

Other terms and concepts will be explained as they are used. For those who would like further reading, Bleck (1982a, pp. 1–16) is a good source of information on terminology, growth, and anatomical structure. Nealis (1983b; 1983c) also presents basic information on human anatomy and neuroanatomy. The Johnston and Magrab text presents an excellent description of normal motor development and cerebral palsy (Johnston & Magrab, 1976, pp. 15–55), as does the chapter by Capute et al. (1983). The text by Bigge (1991) also provides an excellent overview.

PROBE 11-1   Definitions of Physical Disabilities

1. T F   The term *proximodistal* is used to refer to the process whereby the child gains control of the muscles in the trunk before gaining control of muscles in the fingers.
2. The suffix that means paralysis, or inability to move, is _____.

3. In the illustration below, write the appropriate word in the space next to the part of the figure that it represents.

Anterior	Monoplegia
Cephalad	Paraplegia
Caudal	Posterior
Hemiplegia	Quadriplegia
Inferior	Superior

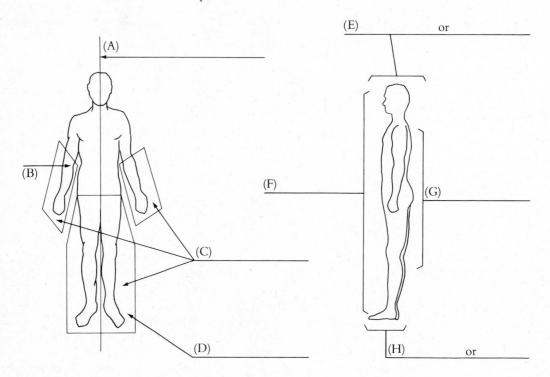

DISABILITIES THAT AFFECT AMBULATION

You should be able to describe disabilities that affect ambulation.

Physical disabilities that prevent a child from entering a building, traveling easily from room to room, using toilet facilities, moving from one floor to another, or traveling in a crowded hallway all cause serious problems. This type of impairment has often restricted children with physical disabilities to special schools and modified self-contained classrooms. As we cannot discuss all the disabilities that affect ambulation, we will restrict ourselves to those most commonly encountered in the classroom. Some ambulatory problems that result from other disabling conditions will be discussed in other parts of this chapter.

Cerebral Palsy

Cerebral palsy is caused by damage to the brain. It is a nonprogressive disorder (that is, it does not become progressively more debilitating) that affects gross and fine motor coordination. It is often associated with convulsions, speech disorders, hearing defects, vision problems, deficits in measured intelligence, or combinations of these problems (McDonald, 1987). Cerebral palsy was originally called Little's Disease, after the English surgeon who first described it. The condition was first called cerebral palsy by Sir William Osler (Wolf, 1969; McDonald, 1987), and the name was brought to common usage by Dr. Winthrop Phelps, a physician who studied cerebral palsy in the 1930s and demonstrated that children with cerebral palsy could be helped.

PREVALENCE. Although the individuals with cerebral palsy have never actually been counted, figures suggest that it affects 1.5 to 2 of every 1000 persons of all ages (Healy, 1984; Cooke, Rosenbloom, & Cooke, 1987). The different types of cerebral palsy are classified according to the motor characteristics, topography, severity of the condition, and associated problems (McDonald, 1987). Bleck's citation of a statement by Phelps is useful in placing cerebral palsy in perspective.

What is the prognosis for children born with cerebral palsy?

Seven children per 100,000 are born with cerebral palsy. Of those seven, one dies the first year. Of the remaining six, two are so severe as to require institutional treatment. Of the four left for treatment, one will receive only home care or day care center treatment. Two are moderately involved and benefit from treatment while the remaining one is so mild that no special treatment is required. (Bleck, 1982b, p. 60)

Today, however, the description would be somewhat different, largely because of advances in medical care, deinstitutionalization, and the current emphasis on services for persons with multiple disabilities. Many of those who would once have been placed in institutions or kept at home are now being educated in public schools, and many children who would once have died are now living to school age. There is some evidence of an upward trend in the prevalence of cerebral palsy among low-birth-weight infants (Cooke, Rosenbloom, and Cooke, 1987). The upward trend was felt to be due to improved survival rather than any actual increase in incidence. Similar increases are seen in Sweden (Stanley, 1987). However, we really do not know whether or not the incidence of cerebral palsy is rising or falling (Nelson, 1986). As you can see, a definitive prevalence rate is difficult to establish.

CLASSIFICATIONS OF CEREBRAL PALSY. Cerebral palsy can be classified and described in several different manners. One way is to describe the limbs that are affected, as discussed in the preceding section. Another classification system is based on motor characteristics and yields seven types of cerebral palsy (McDonald, 1987).

What are the different types of cerebral palsy?

1. **Spasticity.** The spastic type of cerebral palsy is characterized by a "hyperactive stretch reflex." This results in a loss of voluntary motor control. Without this control, the extensor muscles, which are used to extend the arm, and the flexor muscles, which are used to pull the arm toward the body, contract at the same time. This causes movements to be tense, jerky, and poorly contained. The person with spasticity may be easily startled by sudden noises or movements, which can cause rigid extension or flexion of the muscles. As a result, this child may become fixed in a rigid position, which gradually relaxes as the child regains composure. As the child grows, the spastic muscles become shorter, which can cause limb deformities. For this and other reasons it is important that children with spasticity receive physical therapy. Spasticity has been diagnosed in about 63 percent of the cerebral palsy population (McDonald, 1987).

2. **Athetosis.** Athetoid-type cerebral palsy is characterized by involuntary, purposeless movements of the limbs, especially at the extremities. Fluctuating muscle tone affects deliberate muscle exertions, which results in uncontrolled writhing and irregular movements. The throat and diaphragm muscles are also affected, which causes drooling and labored speech. The hands are affected most frequently, followed by the lips and tongue, and then the feet. Excitement

and concentrated efforts to control movement generally result in increased tension and spasticity; by contrast, athetoid movement stops during relaxation or sleep. There are at least two major types of athetosis, tension and nontension. Those with tension athetosis have muscles that are always tense, which tends to reduce the contorted movement of the limb. Those with nontension athetosis have contorted movements without muscle tightness. Athetosis affects approximately 12 percent of the cerebral palsy population (McDonald, 1987). It is not uncommon for spasticity and athetosis to be found in the same individual.

3. **Ataxia.** Ataxia is caused by damage to the cerebellum, which results in balance problems. Persons with ataxic cerebral palsy have poor fine and gross motor movements, poor depth perception, slurred speech, and a staggering gait. They frequently fall. About 5 percent of the population with cerebral palsy are ataxic (McDonald, 1987).

4. **Rigidity.** Rigidity-type cerebral palsy has been described as a severe form of spasticity (Bleck, 1982b). It is characterized by continual, diffuse tension of the flexor and extensor muscles. This "equal pull" of the two muscles renders the limb rigid and hard to bend. The words *lead pipe* are frequently used to describe this type of cerebral palsy. Once a limb is bent, it tends to stay in that position, like a lead pipe. Approximately 7 percent of the population with cerebral palsy are diagnosed as having rigidity (McDonald, 1987).

5. **Tremor.** Tremor-type cerebral palsy is characterized by the shakiness of a limb, which may be evident only when one is attempting a specific movement. This is called *intentional tremor.* The shakiness of the limb is caused by alternating contractions of the flexor and extensor muscles. Tremor cerebral palsy is differentiated from athetosis by the extent of the limb movement: athetoid motor movements are large and changeable, whereas tremor movements are small and rhythmic. McDonald (1987) reports tremor diagnosed in less than 1 percent of the population with cerebral palsy.

6. **Atonia.** This term refers to deficient or absent muscle tone. There is some argument as to whether or not atonia should be classified as a type of cerebral palsy. An individual with atonia is frequently referred to as a "floppy child," due to the lack of muscle tone. Approximately 1 percent of persons with cerebral palsy are diagnosed as having atonia (McDonald, 1987).

7. **Mixed.** Most individuals with cerebral palsy have more than one type of palsy; they are labeled according to the predominant type. A typical combination involves spasticity and athetosis. McDonald (1987) reports 12 percent of the population with cerebral palsy as being mixed.

What causes cerebral palsy?

ETIOLOGY. Cerebral palsy can be caused by a number of disorders, which can arise before birth (prenatal), during birth (perinatal), or after birth (postnatal). Prenatal causes include German measles (rubella), prematurity, Rh incompatibility, lack of oxygen to the brain of the fetus, and metabolic disorders such as maternal diabetes. Perinatal causes include prolonged labor, breech (feet-first) delivery, asphyxia of the fetus, and some obstetric procedures. After birth, cerebral palsy can be caused by infections such as encephalitis, lack of oxygen, and injuries to the head. Postnatal causes are said to be *acquired,* whereas those present at birth are *congenital.* Nelson (1986) questions whether some of the factors thought to be significantly related to causing cerebral palsy are really related. While a newborn may have certain risk factors that are associated with cerebral palsy, ". . . most children with the risk factors do not develop cerebral palsy" (Nelson, 1986, p. 22). Nelson believes that disorders in the formation of the brain are the primary cause of cerebral palsy.

Certain types of cerebral palsy are caused by damage to the pyramidal, extrapyramidal (Capute, 1985), and cerebellar tracts of the brain. Damage to the pyramidal tract, located between the motor and sensory areas of the cortex, affects the nerve cells that initiate motor impulses to the muscles. Damage to the extrapyramidal system, located in the basal ganglia in the midbrain, results in athetosis, rigidity, and tremor in varying degrees. Damage to the cerebellum affects the ability to maintain balance and coordinated movement; it can also cause ataxia. More information on the physiology and anatomy of cerebral palsy is found in Capute (1985, pp. 244–263), Denhoff (1966, pp. 24–77), Jones (1983, pp. 41–58), and McDonald (1987).

ASSOCIATED CONDITIONS. Many people with cerebral palsy have associated disabilities. These include disorders in communication and the sensory systems, intellectual disabilities, and convulsive disorders. The associated disorders can sometimes have effects as serious as the motor limitations of cerebral palsy itself.

Other than the physical disability, what is the most common problem associated with cerebral palsy?

1. *Communication disorders.* Disorders in speech are found in 70 percent of persons with cerebral palsy. Studies indicate that speech defects are found in 88 percent of persons with athetosis, 85 percent of those with ataxia, and 52 percent of those with spasticity. Most of the speech problems are caused by problems controlling the muscles used to make speech sounds (dysarthria). Delayed speech may also be caused by either mental retardation or the cerebral dysfunction. Other communication problems are voice disorders, stuttering, and aphasia.

2. *Sensory disorders.* Jones (1983) states that from 25 to 30 percent of those with cerebral palsy have hearing defects. Hopkins et al. (1954) reported a lower figure, ranging from 7 percent in those with spasticity to 22 percent in those with athetosis. Persons with athetosis were affected more frequently because athetosis was often caused by Rh incompatibility, which also causes hearing disorders. Current medical treatment can reduce the Rh incompatibility problem.

Vision defects in persons with cerebral palsy vary according to the type of disorder. Capute (1985) reports an incidence rate ranging from 30 to 35 percent for strabismus, while Duckman (1987) reports a range of from 15 to 69 percent. Duckman also indicates refractive errors in 40 to 76 percent of the population. Jones (1983) indicates that 50 percent of the population with cerebral palsy have ophthalmological problems. This includes eye muscle incoordination and imbalance. Visual problems are further discussed in Chapter 10.

3. *Intellectual ability.* Studies indicate that 50 to 60 percent of the people with cerebral palsy have cognitive deficits (Capute, 1985). It is important to recognize that accurate measures of the intelligence of those with cerebral palsy are difficult to achieve. Motor and communication problems interfere with the administration of tests, and tests such as the Stanford Binet and the WISC are not standardized on a population that includes those with cerebral palsy. Although it has been reported that adaptations of tests to accommodate a physical disability do not significantly affect test scores (Allen & Jefferson, 1962), the skill with which the test is adapted and the expertise of the examiner may influence the outcome. If a child does better in the classroom than an IQ score leads one to expect, the IQ score should be disregarded in favor of more reliable data about the child's performance. McDonald (1987) indicates that cerebral palsy does not cause mental retardation; rather, the same conditions that caused the cerebral palsy cause the mental retardation.

4. *Convulsive disorders.* Estimates of the percentage of persons who have cerebral palsy and who also have convulsive disorders vary considerably. Healy (1984) estimates 35 to 45 percent, with some studies reporting 60 percent. Capute (1985) estimates 30 to 35 percent of persons with cerebral palsy have convulsive disorders. An older study by Keats (1965) reported that 86 percent of the population with spasticity and 12 percent of the population with athetosis had convulsive disorders.

Cerebral palsy is associated with a wide variety of problems, some very serious, some relatively easy to adapt to. Other associated problems include educational and emotional difficulties. Those who have cerebral palsy can be expected to attend school in regular classrooms, in classes for children with orthopedic disabilities, or in programs designed for children with severe or multiple disabilities. Cross (1983) found that 26 percent of children with cerebral palsy were placed in classes for students with multiple handicaps, and 8 percent were receiving homebound instruction. These children may need physical, occupational, and speech therapy. Some will need minimal extra attention, whereas others will need a great deal of assistance to develop to their full potential.

Muscular Dystrophy

Muscular dystrophy is a disease in which the voluntary muscles progressively weaken and degenerate until they can no longer function. It affects 1 in 3500 males (Kunkel, Beggs, & Hoffman, 1989). The age of onset can vary widely and causes have been identified in people ranging in age from 1 through 80. While there are several types, the *Duchenne* type is the most common. It affects young children and is transmitted to male offspring by the mother, who is the carrier of the condition. Some children are afflicted when there is no family history; this is thought to be caused by gene mutation. The Duchenne type of muscular dystrophy usually appears between the ages of 3 and 6. Growth and development are normal before the initial onset. There is recent evidence ("Scientists Link," 1992) that the genes that cause muscular dystrophy grow bigger each time they are inherited, thereby increasing the severity of the disorder. However, discovery of the gene responsible for this may lead to very accurate diagnosis before birth or before symptoms appear in later life.

PROGRESSION. Muscular dystrophy progresses slowly. In the early stages it is painless and its symptoms are nearly unnoticeable. The first symptoms can include delayed muscle functioning; difficulty in walking and climbing stairs; abnormal gait, in which the trunk sways from side to side; difficulty rising from a sitting position; frequent falling; and difficulty in running (Bender, Schumacher, & Allen, 1976). **Gower's sign** is another symptom. This occurs when the child has been sitting on the floor or a chair and tries to stand. Because the thigh, back, and stomach muscles have been weakened by the disease, the child must place his or her hands on the knees and thighs and literally "walk up" the leg. This process enables the child to straighten the back into a vertical position in order to stand. The child may also grasp something to pull or push the body up into a vertical position; for example, placing the hands on top of the desk in order to push the body up. The child may also walk on tiptoe, a symptom caused by the weakening of the muscle that pulls the feet up to a level position.

In the disease's second stage the child has more difficulty rising from the floor after falling because of muscle degeneration in the calves, front thigh muscles, and the dorsiflexors of the feet. The child will also probably have a swayback and protruding abdomen (lordosis). The calf muscles will appear large and healthy (pseudohypertrophy; false enlargement).

During the third stage the child can no longer walk independently and gradually becomes more and more dependent on a wheelchair for ambulation. Those who have Duchenne muscular dystrophy usually have reached this stage by age 10.

During the final stage, the child is bedridden and totally dependent on others for care. Some children grow obese, which complicates the process of their physical care. In other cases the muscles atrophy and the child becomes very thin. As the muscles weaken, contractures (shortening of the muscles) occur, which can result in disfigurement and the loss of limb functioning. Death is caused most often by heart failure, when the heart muscles become weak, or lung infection due to the weakening of the muscles involved in breathing.

How is muscular
dystrophy treated?

TREATMENT. There is no cure for muscular dystrophy. The primary treatment is physical therapy designed to control contractures. Bleck (1982c) indicates that positioning the joints by weighting them with sandbags or other equipment is more helpful than stretching or exercise. He also describes group games designed to promote good breathing and increase the limbs' range of motion. Bracing can be used to prevent contractures, but it is rarely used after the child becomes dependent on a wheelchair. Surgery can be used to correct deformities in some cases; treatment will vary from child to child. The abnormal gene and missing or defective gene product, dystrophin, have recently been identified (Kingston & Moxley, 1989) and this has led to better genetic mapping, which helps with prevention. Most recently, immature muscle cells have been injected into weakened muscles, resulting in strengthened muscle.

EDUCATIONAL IMPLICATIONS. The goal of a school program for the child with muscular dystrophy should be to keep the child as active as possible and in the regular classroom as long as feasible. When necessary, the child may be moved to a special class or receive homebound instruction. Despite reported IQ scores in the 80s (Bleck, 1982c), and the fact that the child may not live beyond the second decade, the child should be given instruction appropriate to his or her level of functioning. The child, teacher, and the child's family may need counseling about the nature of the illness and the prognosis for improvement. It is important for those working with the child with muscular dystrophy to maintain a positive attitude and, as much as is possible, to have normal expectations of that child.

Spinal Muscular Atrophy

Spinal muscular atrophy affects the spinal cord and may result in progressive degeneration of the motor nerve cells (Koehler, 1982). It may be associated with a number of diseases (see Ford, 1966, pp. 188–312; Goldberg, 1983, pp. 147–156; and Bradford, 1987, pp. 271–301). The degeneration can cause problems ranging from slight weakness to symptoms similar to those of muscular dystrophy. The primary characteristic is the progressive weakening and atrophy of the proximal (trunk) muscles. This may cause delayed motor skills acquisition, and the child may be easily fatigued and appear clumsy. The atrophy of muscles may cause muscle tightening and joint contractures. Bone substance may be lost because of muscle and joint disuse.

What is the cause
of spinal muscular
atrophy?

Spinal muscular atrophy is known to be inherited, and there are three known autosomal recessive forms of the disease: an infantile form, which has a slow progression and early death; a type with later onset (type two Werdnig-Hoffman disease); and a more chronic type that develops between ages 2 and 17 (Bradford, 1987). If both parents are carriers of the defective gene, there is a 25 percent chance that the offspring will have spinal muscular atrophy and a 50 percent chance that the child will be a carrier of the defective gene.

Although there is no cure for spinal muscular atrophy, therapy is used to prevent or reduce joint curvatures and other bone complications. Surgery is frequently used to reduce scoliosis (curvature of the spine). Physical therapy is very important in the prevention of contractures (tightening of the muscles) and maintaining good posture. Respiratory infections and aspiration of food must be carefully avoided.

Children with this disorder have normal intelligence but little or no motor strength. Some children are severely affected, whereas others are affected relatively mildly. In school, tasks that do not require muscular skill or strength should be emphasized. If the child's condition stabilizes, a normal school curriculum may be provided. In some cases vocational training may be required.

Polio

Poliomyelitis (infantile paralysis) is a viral infection that affects or destroys the anterior horn cells in the spinal cord. When these cells are destroyed, the muscles that they serve eventually die or become paralyzed. The paralysis may affect the entire body or just parts of the body. Some persons are kept alive only through the use of a lung machine that helps the person breathe. Many people with polio are bedridden, confined to wheelchairs, or dependent on braces or crutches for ambulation.

What was Jonas Salk's contribution to society?

Polio was once a greatly feared disease that affected thousands of people each year, but the development of the Salk polio vaccine has almost eradicated it. Unfortunately, an increasing number of children are not being vaccinated, and they are extremely vulnerable to the disease. While polio is not currently a major disabling disease today and hence not a serious threat to us, it serves as a good example of what scientific research can do to prevent deadly disorders. It could become a serious threat again if children are not vaccinated.

Spinal Cord Injuries

Spinal cord injuries are most often caused by auto accidents, sports accidents, and accidents at work. In the past most of the victims have been male, but the increasing participation of women in hazardous sports and occupations may increase the number of women with spinal cord injuries. An injury may result in quadriplegia or paraplegia. Depending on the damage that occurs, the injured person may recover completely or not at all.

If a person who has been in an accident complains of neck or back pain or can feel nothing in the legs, he or she should be treated on the assumption that the spinal cord has been injured. The person should be required to lie flat and not be allowed to turn the head or rise to a sitting position. The injured position should be moved without bending or twisting.

How is intelligence affected by spinal cord injury?

Children with injuries of this type will be served in hospital schools and homebound education programs. Some may be able to return to the regular classroom, whereas others will be placed in classes for children with physical disabilities, depending on the extent of the child's recovery. Intelligence is not affected by a spinal cord injury. Further information can be found in Gilgoff (1983).

Computer technology is now being applied to the treatment of spinal cord injuries. The story of Nan, which precedes this chapter, is an example of the work being done by the Wright State University National Center for Rehabilitation Engineering. The solution is not yet found, but a good start has been made.

Spina Bifida

Spina bifida is a congenital defect that results when the bones of a part of the spine fail to grow together. The defect, the cause of which is unknown, occurs during the first 30 days of pregnancy (Bleck, 1982d). The gap in the spine can appear anywhere, but is usually found in the lower part, the lumbar-sacral area, and can cause paraplegia and loss of bowel and bladder control.

What is myelomeningocele?

There are three types of spina bifida. The most severe is called *myelomeningocele* (or *meningomyelocele*). In this type, part of the spinal cord protrudes through the gap in the bones of the spine into a saclike structure that surrounds the gap, causing a neurological problem (see Figure 11-1). If the sac contains cerebrospinal fluid but the spinal cord does not protrude and

These are pictures of Nan Davis, whose remarkable accomplishments were described at the beginning of this chapter. The picture on the left shows her in the experimental laboratory, practicing walking under her own muscle power with computer assistance. Nan was paralyzed from the waist down as the result of an automobile accident on her high school graduation night. The picture on the right shows her getting ready to walk to the podium to receive her bachelor's degree from Wright State University. The computer that controls her movements is contained in the bag under the arms of the system's designer, Dr. Jerrold Petrofsky.

there is no neurological impairment, the condition is called *meningocele.* The least severe form is called *spina bifida occulta.* The only evidence of this form is a growth of hair covering the area of the defect. Myelomeningoceles are four to five times more common than meningoceles (Bleck, 1982d; Williamson, 1987).

Williamson (1987) states that spina bifida is the second most common specific birth defect, following only trisomy 21 (Down syndrome). Its incidence is estimated to be between 0.1 and 4.13 cases per 1000 live births (Bleck, 1982d; Williamson, 1987). The prevalence rate is somewhat lower than the incidence rate because some of the children die shortly after birth. There is evidence that the incidence of spina bifida is decreasing, due in large part to antenatal diagnosis (detection before birth) and subsequent termination of pregnancy (Lorber, 1986; Stone, 1987). However, Lorber (1986) and Stone (1987) also indicate a decrease of spina bifida even where antenatal diagnosis and subsequent termination of pregnancy is not conducted. The reasons for this are not clearly understood. While recent medical advances have decreased the mortality rate, spina bifida is still a dangerous condition frequently accompanied by several other chronic disorders.

FIGURE 11-1   A Myelomeningocele

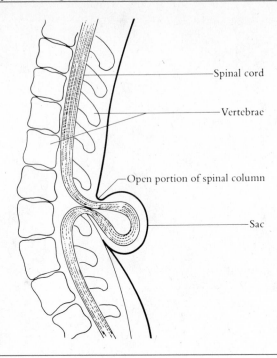

Spinal cord

Vertebrae

Open portion of spinal column

Sac

One of the most common related conditions is *hydrocephalus,* or "water on the brain." This condition occurs when the drainage of cerebrospinal fluid is blocked. The buildup of pressure that results can cause serious brain damage, including mental retardation. Kidney infections caused by poor urinary drainage are another condition associated with spina bifida. If untreated, these infections can lead to kidney failure. Pressure sores are a problem that results when the blood supply to an area of skin is cut off. Persons with normal feeling experience discomfort when this happens and shift their position to allow the blood to circulate normally. Those who are paralyzed, however, do not feel the discomfort. Pressure sores are very difficult to heal and great care should be exercised to prevent them. Other disorders that may accompany spina bifida are dislocation of the hip, clubfoot, and—when the child is older—scoliosis (spinal curvature), kyphosis (humpback), and lordosis (swayback).

TREATMENT. The initial treatment of spina bifida is surgery for the outpouch (sac) and hydrocephalus, if that is a problem. Surgery for hydrocephalus involves placing a shunt to drain excess cerebrospinal fluid to the atria of the heart or to the abdominal cavity. When surgery is successful, there is no brain damage. Surgery for the outpouch frequently takes place during the first week after birth. Sharrard (1968) reports less paralysis and a lower mortality rate among those who receive surgery within 48 hours. Bleck (1982d), however, reports that early surgery does not diminish paralysis.

Most people with spina bifida, particularly those with myelomeningocele, use crutches or wheelchairs as mobility aids. In some cases physical, occupational, and speech therapy will be part of the school program. Most cases require continual medical monitoring. A serious problem is the frequent lack of bowel and bladder control. To assist those with bladder problems, the involved child or teachers can be taught clean intermittent catheterization (CIC) as a procedure to allow the bladder to empty. This procedure is typically done every three or four hours (Taylor, 1990). The CIC procedure can become controversial when children are placed in public school classes, and some teachers have refused to perform it. However, the Supreme Court has held that schools are required to perform CIC, either with a school nurse or a trained lay person (Taylor, 1990; Turnbull, 1990). For a more descriptive statement of the procedures the reader is referred to Taylor (1990). Other useful references regarding this procedure, as well as other related services, are Johnson (1986), Mulligan-Ault, Guess, Struth, and Thompson (1988), and *Handicapped Students and Special Education* (1985).

Osteogenesis Imperfecta

Osteogenesis imperfecta is also known as *brittle bone disease.* The bones of children with this disorder break very easily; the many fractures cause the limbs to be small and bowed. The disorder is inherited and affects both male and female children. The bones of those with osteogenesis imperfecta have been described as being immature, like the bones of a developing fetus. Many children with this disorder are hard of hearing because of defects in the bony structure of the ossicles. Andersen and Hauge (1989) report an incidence of approximately 10 per 100,000 in Denmark.

What is the treatment for osteogenesis imperfecta?

There is no cure for this disorder. Surgery and bracing are used to straighten the legs and aid in ambulation. Many use a wheelchair as well. Since the intelligence of these children is normal, their educational prognosis is good. Great care must be exercised in working with these children, however, because their bones can be broken very easily—even when helping them change position in a wheelchair. The physical activity of these children is often severely restricted.

Multiple Sclerosis

How does multiple sclerosis affect the body?

Multiple sclerosis is a progressive disorder in which portions of the myelin sheath (tissues surrounding the spinal cord) are damaged and replaced by scar tissue, resulting in short-circuiting of nerve impulses to muscles. This demyelination process does not occur in any systematic order. Some persons may experience mild attacks and recover completely. For others, the disease process involves a series of attacks and then periods of remission. With each attack, or active state of the disorder, more damage to the myelin sheath occurs. The initial symptoms may consist of visual disturbances and mild motor incoordination problems. As the disorder progresses, more and more damage occurs, and the person may become blind or severely visually impaired, have a speech disorder, lose bowel and bladder control, and become partially or totally paralyzed in the extremities. At various times during the disorder, the person may need to use a wheelchair for ambulation but later, as remission occurs, may ambulate normally or with the aid of crutches.

There is no known cure for this disorder. However, two promising experimental treatments have been reported (Clark, 1983). Both treatments view the cause of multiple sclerosis as a defect in the body's immune system in which the white blood cells, not bacteria, attack the myelin. The treatment is aimed at periodically suppressing the immune system. McFarland and Dhib-Jaibut (1989) view the cause of multiple sclerosis as being polygenic, and not the effect of a single gene. Environmental influences are also felt to contribute to the disease process. Despite the fact that there is no known cure for this disorder, most persons who have multiple sclerosis live a normal life span. Several medical treatments currently being explored (Yanowitch, 1989) show promise in improvement of the physical condition. Physical therapy is also important in the treatment program. Rehabilitation counselors should help implement other treatment programs and aid in securing transportation.

Juvenile Rheumatoid Arthritis

What are the symptoms of juvenile arthritis?

According to the Arthritis Foundation, there are five common forms of arthritis: rheumatoid, osteoarthritis, ankylosing spondylitis, rheumatic fever, and gout. **Rheumatoid arthritis** is the most common among school-age children. The first signs of the disease are general fatigue, stiffness, and aching of the joints as they swell and become tender. It is a chronic condition, but 60 to 70 percent of those affected are free of the disease after ten years (Miller, 1982). During the active phase, children experience severe pain whenever they move the affected joints. If the condition first appears in childhood, most children recover completely. Those who first acquire the condition as adults have a much smaller chance of a permanent remission.

Arthritis cannot be cured. Recent research has discovered a protein that could halt arthritis ("Scientists Find," 1990). This has not yet been tried on humans, although experiments are ready to begin. Up to this time, aspirin has been used to reduce the pain, and rest and exercise are also important parts of the treatment. The most severe (but infrequent) complication of juvenile rheumatoid arthritis occurs when the heart muscle becomes inflamed (Miller, 1982). Less severe complications are temporary hearing loss, which is caused by taking aspirin, and permanent damage to the joints, which can restrict their mobility. Some types of therapy have proved to have more harmful consequences than the disorder itself. Cortisone, for example, when administered frequently to children, can halt growth, reduce resistance to infection, and cause obesity and brittleness of the bones.

In school, children with arthritis may have difficulty remaining in one position for long periods of time. The child may also need extra time to get from one place to another.

Other Musculoskeletal Disorders

A problem in one part of the body frequently causes problems in another part. Children who have cerebral palsy, spina bifida, muscular disorders, or other disorders frequently have back problems as well. Muscles that pull too hard or that are unequally balanced can cause such disorders as scoliosis, lordosis, and kyphosis. Inadequate muscle tension sometimes results in the complete collapse of the skeletal system.

How do scoliosis, lordosis, and kyphosis differ?

Scoliosis is lateral curvature of the spine. A person with scoliosis will appear to have an S-shaped spinal column when viewed from behind. **Lordosis** is a condition in which the spine is curved inward, resulting in a swayback and protruding abdomen. **Kyphosis** is a condition in which the area surrounding the shoulders is rounded. These disorders are treated with physical therapy, bracing, and in some cases, surgery. If not properly treated they can cause severe physical deformity, threaten breathing and other life-sustaining functions, and may also increase pressure on a number of the body's organs.

A **club foot** is a disorder that can appear by itself or in conjunction with another problem. Children with this disorder are born with one or both feet turned down and in. The condition can be corrected with surgery, bracing, and casts, and children who have clubfeet may learn to walk in the normal fashion. They are indistinguishable from their normal peers by the time they reach school age if successfully treated.

Although a portion of this student's leg was amputated, he is able to fully participate in classroom activities with his peers.

Amputation is another important disability. Amputation can be partial or complete. Most amputations are necessary because of accidents, but some are required because of life-threatening physiological disorders and diseases.

Limbs may also be missing or deformed as the result of disruptions in the early fetal development of the limbs. This sometimes occurs randomly, but it can also be caused by drugs such as **thalidomide,** which was at one time taken by pregnant women as a relaxant. Depending on the time at which it was taken during the first trimester of pregnancy, thalidomide caused a variety of congenital deformities, including extremely short or missing limbs (phocomelia). In this disorder, the hands and feet, which are deformed themselves, are attached directly to the torso and may resemble "seal flippers." Several thousand children with this deformity were born in Germany, where the drug was routinely prescribed in the late 1950s and early 1960s. Once the effects of the drug were established, it was taken off the market. Special schools for thalidomide children were established in Europe. The United States Department of Health did not approve the medication, so the problem in this country was relatively uncommon. Some American women who did obtain thalidomide gave birth to children with birth defects. While drugs such as thalidomide are monitored very carefully in the United States, the tragedy associated with thalidomide underscores the fact that pregnant women must be very careful when taking any kind of medication or drugs, which may harm the fetus.

PROBE 11-2   Disorders That Affect Ambulation

1. T F   Cerebral palsy is caused by brain damage.
2. T F   The incidence of cerebral palsy is increasing.
3. Match each symptom on the left with its associated medical term.

    ____ Tense and jerky movements   a. Athetosis
    ____ Involuntary, writing movements   b. Rigidity
    ____ Staggering gait   c. Spastic
    ____ "Lead pipe" stiffness   d. Tremor
    ____ Shakiness   e. Ataxia

4. _____-natal means before birth, _____-natal means during birth, and _____-natal means after birth.
5. T F   There is a higher incidence of speech disorders, sensory disorders, and mental retardation in the cerebral palsied population than in the "normal" population.
6. T F   Cerebral palsy is rarely accompanied by convulsive disorders.
7. T F   Children with cerebral palsy do not attend public schools.
8. Match each item on the left with the associated disorder on the right.

    ____ Meningocele   a. Polio
    ____ Brittle bones   b. Spina bifida
    ____ Salk vaccine   c. Multiple sclerosis
    ____ Degeneration of the myelin sheath d. Osteogenesis imperfecta
    ____ Curvature of the spine   e. Scoliosis
    ____ Inflammation of joints   f. Muscular dystrophy
    ____ Progressive muscle deterioration g. Juvenile rheumatoid arthritis

9. _____ is a drug that caused numerous congenital deformities of the extremities of children in Europe and elsewhere.
10. T F   Most children with osteogenesis imperfecta have normal intellectual ability.
11. T F   The number of children born with spina bifida is increasing.
12. Which type of supportive service is used to minimize muscular deterioration in children with diseases such as muscular dystrophy, spinal muscular atrophy, and polio?
13. T F   Children with Duchenne muscular dystrophy generally recover.

DISABILITIES THAT AFFECT VITALITY

You should be able to describe disabilities that affect the vitality of children.

Children with disabilities that affect vitality are frequently placed in special classes or programs. Although all of these disorders are life-threatening, some are more dangerous than others. All children with these types of disorders will need special assistance from a primary care worker

Mainstreaming in Action

Linda loves to go to school. Although she has cerebral palsy, she is able to function very well in the regular classroom. While waiting for class to start, she engages in free play activities with a classmate.

Once class begins, she participates fully with the other children in a counting game. She enjoys independent reading but is more comfortable sitting on the floor supported by pillows when engaged in that activity.

The school garden provides a good opportunity for Linda and her classmates to grow plants as part of a science project. She also enjoys the use of the swings during recess.

Following lunch she uses a math game designed by the school's physical therapist that will help to improve her ability to grasp small objects. A special education resource teacher also provides individual assistance in spelling, a subject that is difficult for Linda.

Although Linda is proud of her work, it is clear that her physical disability makes it difficult for her to write quickly and legibly. Consequently, she is being taught to use a computer. As she masters the use of a word processing program, she will be able to produce printed materials that can be easily read.

This photo essay illustrates how many children with physical disabilities can be integrated into the educational mainstream. It is clear that sensitive educators and administrators can work together to bring general education, special education, and related services together in an integrated fashion to serve students with special needs.

or teacher, and special educational, social, and vocational training as well. Table 11-2 relates the modifications and skills required to provide a suitable educational environment for children with a variety of chronic conditions.

Congenital Heart Defects

The symptoms exhibited by persons with congenital heart defect are shortness of breath, cyanosis (blue appearance of the skin), and low tolerance for exercise (Mitchell, 1985). Most congenital heart problems, which are generally recognized at birth or in early childhood, are mechanical in nature (i.e., they do not involve infection or inflammation). They can frequently be repaired surgically. Congenital heart defects are the second most common type of birth defect, occurring in 5 to 8 of each 1000 live births (Bruyere, Kargas, & Levy, 1987).

What should teachers be aware of with children who have heart defects?

Because these children are often restricted physically and have usually spent a lot of time in hospitals, they have not had the opportunity to participate in many of the normal activities of children. Although the intelligence of most of these children is in the normal range, they may not function academically at the level of their peers. The child's classroom activities may be restricted by orders from his or her physician, and the teacher will have to watch the child carefully for signs of overexertion. At the same time, however, the teacher should be aware that the child may try to use the condition as an excuse not to participate in activities that he or she is capable of participating in. The care and education of children with this disorder require careful cooperation among the child's parents, teacher, and physician.

Cystic Fibrosis

Cystic fibrosis (CF) is a chronic genetic disorder that typically affects the pancreas, the lungs, or both. When the lungs are affected, the mucus normally found in the lungs does not drain properly and, when it builds up, blocks the passage of air to and from the affected area. When the pancreas is affected, digestion is impaired and the child may suffer from poor nutrition, even when eating what would normally be an adequate amount of food.

The disease is hereditary and it is estimated that one in every 25 Caucasians carries the defective gene. A series of recent scientific discoveries has identified the gene that causes cystic fibrosis. This has led to the development of a screening test to determine whether one is a carrier. Laboratory studies have led to the discovery of a method to correct the genetic defect ("Gene Therapy," 1990). However, this "gene therapy" has yet to be tried on humans.

Cystic fibrosis has been the most common cause of death from a genetic disorder in the United States (Harvey, 1982b). Today, proper treatment may slow the progress of the disease, which typically has been fatal in childhood. With current medical care, many children with cystic fibrosis will live to adulthood and will require lifelong treatment (Caldwell, Todaro, & Gates, 1989).

Why is percussion used with children who have cystic fibrosis?

In school, the child with cystic fibrosis may cough frequently, have an increased appetite, and have low physical stamina. These children have normal intelligence; they will need special attention only for periods of treatment and restrictions in their physical activities. Treatment typically combines medication with percussion. Percussion is a process designed to dislodge mucus. The child is placed in a position designed to enhance lung drainage while the chest is vigorously clapped and vibrated (Harvey, 1982b). This type of chest physiotherapy and postural drainage should occur two or three times a day (Caldwell, Todary, & Gates, 1989).

TABLE 11-2 Considerations in Treatment of Health-Related Disabilities

Chronic Condition	Potential Modifications	Skills Required
Asthma	Avoidance of allergens Participation in physical activity Administration of medication as needed	CPR Recognition of signs and symptoms of respiratory stress Recognition of medication side effects
Congenital heart disease	Participation in physical activity Administration of medication as needed Diet and/or fluids	CPR Recognition of signs and symptoms of heart failure Recognition of medication side effects
Diabetes	Diet, bathroom frequency, availability of snacks, and source of sugar Balance of exercise and food	Recognition of signs and symptoms of hypoglycemia (rapid onset) Recognition of signs and symptoms of hyperglycemia (slow onset)
Leukemia	Participation in physical activity Environment Administration of medications as needed	Recognition of signs and symptoms of infection Recognition of signs and symptoms of bleeding
Seizure disorder	Participation in physical activity Environment Administration of medications as needed	Seizure management Recognition of signs and symptoms of distress during and after seizure Recognition of medication side effects
Spina bifida	Participation in physical activity Environment to accommodate mobility and movement Diet and/or fluids Movement to prevent pressure sore Bathroom availability	Recognition of signs and symptoms of shunt blockage Recognition of signs and symptoms of urinary infections Recognition of signs and symptoms of skin breakdowns
Sickle cell	Participation in physical activity Fluids	Recognition of signs and symptoms of impending crisis
Juvenile rheumatoid arthritis	Participation in physical activity Environment, i.e., stairs Administration of medication as needed Frequency of movement Classroom activities, i.e., writing, carrying books	Recognition of signs and symptoms of increased inflammation Recognition of broken bones
Hemophilia	Physical activity	Recognition of signs and symptoms of bleeds Management of bleeding, i.e., cuts and scrapes
Cystic fibrosis	Physical activity Administration of medication as needed Diet	Recognition of signs and symptoms of respiratory distress Management of oxygen therapy and respiratory treatments Recognition of medication side effects
Kidney disease	Physical activity Diet and fluids Bathroom privileges Medication administration	Recognition of signs and symptoms of fluid retention Recognition of medication side effects

Note: This table contains general information. Individualized health care plans are recommended.

Source: Adapted from T. Caldwell, A. Todaro, & J. Gates (1989). *Community provider's guide.* New Orleans, LA: Children's Hospital, p. 7.

Diabetes

What should a teacher do if a diabetic child begins to go into insulin shock?

Diabetes is an inherited metabolic disorder. The child with diabetes does not produce enough insulin to absorb the sugar in the bloodstream. The disorder is treated with a special diet and injections of insulin, administered by the diabetic on a prescribed schedule. If properly treated, the condition can be controlled. If too much insulin is taken, however, blood sugar may be consumed too readily, and the diabetic may go into insulin shock. When this occurs, the child must be given some form of concentrated sugar, such as sweet hard candy or sweetened fruit juice, immediately. If the child with diabetes does not have enough insulin, he or she will go into diabetic coma.

Hypoglycemia, a related disorder, is caused when the body produces too much insulin. This may cause a condition similar to insulin shock, although it is usually not as severe.

Children with diabetes or hypoglycemia may need to eat snacks during class time if their blood sugar becomes out of balance. Children with hypoglycemia need to reduce their intake of processed carbohydrates, as well. Cooperation between the teacher and the child's parents in monitoring the child's food intake, exercise, and the administration of insulin is very important in dealing with these disorders effectively.

Asthma

What might precipitate an asthma attack?

Asthma is a chronic condition characterized by wheezing or labored breathing, which is caused by the constriction in the individual's air passages and by excessive secretion in the air tubes of the lungs. The decrease in the size of the air passage makes breathing—particularly exhalation—difficult (Harvey, 1982a). The causes of the condition are not fully understood, but allergic reactions to foods (ingestants) or to particles in the air (inhalants) appear to precipitate it. Excessive emotionality is not considered a primary cause, although it is thought to influence the conditions that may bring on an asthmatic attack.

Asthma tends to run in families. The severity and duration of asthma attacks vary considerably. Harvey reports that it is the fifth most common reason for a child to see a physician in the state of Washington. It is similarly prevalent in other states.

The treatment of asthma involves removing ingestants and inhalants from the child's environment. The child may also be given injections to increase resistance to allergic reaction. Breathing exercises and mechanical drainage of the lungs may also be helpful. During an acute attack, medication can be used to relax the bronchial tree of the lungs. The treatment of asthma is a long-term process. The teacher should find out from the parents whether the child's environment or physical activities need to be controlled and whether the child needs other special attention. Aside from these considerations, the asthmatic child should be treated like any other.

AIDS

Acquired immunodeficiency syndrome (AIDS) has become one of the more recent threats to the health of children, especially those who require frequent blood transfusions or other medical treatment that includes the use of needles or contact with body fluids. This particular disorder seriously impairs the body's immune system, which in turn makes one very susceptible to infectious organisms and cancerous cells (Anderson, Bale, Blackman, & Murph, 1986; Caldwell, Sirvis, Todaro, & Accouloumre, 1991). AIDS is acquired from the **human immunodeficiency virus (HIV),** which is spread through the exchange of body fluids. At the present time, there is no known cure for AIDS. Death from infection or cancer typically follows. Evidence indicates that there are several varieties of this disorder, some of which are more serious than others. AIDS is typically found in certain populations, including homosexual and bisexual men, prostitutes, drug addicts, hemophiliacs, and others receiving blood products. Of those children with AIDS, 19 percent become infected through contaminated blood or needles (HIV/AIDS, 1990), and 30 to 50 percent receive the virus from infected mothers during pregnancy and the birth process (Caldwell, Sirvis, Todaro, & Accouloumre, 1991).

Children who have AIDS should be protected from any type of infection, and every attempt should be made to keep these children alive and as healthy as possible, especially since medical treatment is making advances and positive treatment may soon be available. A major problem for the child and family will be isolation because of the rejection by others (Caldwell, Sirvis, Todaro, & Accouloumre, 1991). Insofar as is possible, a normal environment should be provided that includes opportunities for social, emotional, and developmental growth (Anderson, Bale, Blackman, & Murph, 1986). Schools may have policies that relate to children with AIDS (Stephens, Blackhurst, & Magliocca, 1988), and teachers and others working with the child should be aware of those policies.

When working with children who have AIDS (and children in general), following good hygienic practices is essential. Generally, you should avoid direct skin contact with body fluids. If body contact is necessary, the use of disposable gloves is recommended. If contact is made when the use of gloves is not possible, be sure to wash your hands with soap under a steady stream of water for at least 10–15 seconds. While there is not a direct link between contact with body fluids and AIDS, following the above guideline is recommended in order to minimize the risk of infection (Caldwell, Sirvis, Todaro, & Accouloumre, 1991; Stephens, Blackhurst, & Magliocca, 1988). There is no evidence that the HIV is or has ever been transmitted from one child to another in school, day care, or foster care settings (Caldwell, Sirvis, Todaro, & Accouloumre, 1991; HIV/AIDS, 1990). HIV is very fragile and difficult to acquire except by sexual contact or exchange of blood. Additional information is available from the National AIDS Hotline, which can be reached by dialing 1-800-342-AIDS.

PROBE 11-3 Disorders That Affect Vitality

1. A condition characterized by low tolerance for exercise is _____.
2. Children with asthma typically have difficulty _____.
3. T F Children with cystic fibrosis die during childhood.
4. T F AIDS can be contracted by touching someone infected with AIDS.
5. T F Children with AIDS should be treated like any other child.

OTHER DISABILITIES

You should be able to identify and treat symptoms exhibited by children with convulsive disorders and traumatic brain injury.

Convulsive Disorders

Epilepsy is caused by brain damage that impairs the brain's ability to control its normal electrical activity. This can perhaps best be understood through an analogy: The electrical activity of the brain can be compared to a glass of water filled to just above the brim. The water may bulge slightly over the top of the glass, but it will not spill unless the surface tension is broken by a pin prick, a movement of the glass, or some other disturbance. When the brain has been damaged, the electrical energy that normally flows over the brain becomes disturbed and control of the resultant overload can be lost as a result of a minor disturbance. When control is lost, electrical energy stimulates many different parts of the brain at the same time, and the individual may have a seizure. Prevalence estimates of epilepsy range from 2 percent (Gadow, 1986) to 5 percent (Haslam, 1985).

Epilepsy has been a recognized disorder for thousands of years. Hippocrates was the first to suggest that seizures were caused by brain malfunctions. The term **seizure** itself, which is used to describe the active motor states of epilepsy, is derived from Greek and Latin and means "seized by the gods." The Romans called epilepsy "the sacred disease."

Today, epilepsy and seizures are categorized under the general heading of **convulsive disorders.** Epilepsy can occur in anyone at any age. Young children may have convulsions during high fever, but these are considered febrile seizures rather than epilepsy. Prolonged high fever can cause brain damage that results in epilepsy, however. Epilepsy can also be caused by injuries when the child is being born, or later by head injuries. Epilepsy that has no apparent cause is called *cryptogenic* or *idiopathic* (Berg, 1982).

Types of Epilepsy

There are many types of epilepsy. Three types will be discussed in this section: generalized seizures, absence seizures, and partial seizures. An excellent discussion of epilepsy is presented in Gadow (1986). Additional information can be found in Menkes (1990) and obtained from the Epilepsy Foundation of America (1989).

How do generalized, absence, and partial seizures differ?

GENERALIZED SEIZURES. Generalized seizures were previously called *grand mal* and may also be referred to as *tonic-clonic* seizures (Graff, Ault, Guess, Taylor, & Thompson, 1990; Gadow, 1986). They are very conspicuous; this is the type of seizure referred to by the lay person as a fit, spell, attack, or convulsion. The person may fall to the ground, become stiff and rigid (tonic stage), begin to jerk or thrash (clonic stage), and cry out or make noises. People in generalized seizures may hurt themselves by falling, biting the tongue, or hitting objects when thrashing on the floor. They may also lose bowel and bladder control momentarily. As the seizure progresses, the movements gradually slow and finally cease. When consciousness is regained, the person will not remember the seizure or anything that happened during it. The individual may also be confused and very tired, particularly if the seizure was a severe one. In some cases, however, the individual simply gets up and continues activities.

Generalized seizures may be precluded by a warning, or aura, of some kind. An aura can be a sensation, a sound, a light perception, or some other indication. If someone is aware that he or she is about to have a seizure, the person should be quickly taken to as safe a place as possible. Generalized seizures may last from two to five minutes (Bigge, 1991). They may occur rarely or several times a day. Wolraich (1984) indicates that generalized seizures account for 60 percent of all convulsive disorders.

ABSENCE SEIZURES. This type of seizure was previously called *petit mal.* It is technically classified as part of a generalized seizure (Berg, 1982). The absence seizure frequently goes unnoticed. It lasts five to ten seconds, and its only visible symptoms may consist of lip smacking, staring, momentary suspension of activity, a "frozen" posture, or perhaps a fluttering of the eyelids. The individual may appear to be daydreaming or going to sleep. Absence seizures may happen as often as 10 to 15 times a minute or only occasionally. Untreated, they may occur several times a day (Graff et al., 1990). Wolraich states that approximately one-third to one-half of persons with absence seizures (petit mal) will have or eventually develop generalized seizures (Wolraich, 1984).

The main effect of an absence seizure is a momentary lapse of consciousness. It can be compared to a radio that has a short in its system so that only parts of a broadcast can be heard. Hence, a child may miss portions of classroom instructions. Even when teachers notice the child is behaving oddly, they may not realize what is happening. It is important that parents and teachers collect accurate data on the seizures to aid the doctor in prescribing treatment.

PARTIAL SEIZURES. This type of seizure has been previously referred to as a *psychomotor seizure* (complex partial seizure). It is characterized by automatic, stereotyped movements, which may be purposeless, inappropriate, or both. This type of seizure progresses through the following stages: suspension of activity, repetitions, automatic movements, incoherent or irrelevant speech, possibly followed by a fit of rage or anger. Persons who have this type of seizure are often identified as emotionally disturbed or as having a temper tantrum. When the seizure is over, the individual will be confused and will probably not remember what has happened. This type of seizure activity may also spread to become a generalized seizure (Graff et al., 1990).

FACTORS THAT CAN PRECIPITATE SEIZURES. Seizures are most likely to occur one to two hours after a person falls asleep or one to two hours before awakening. Physicians use this knowledge to help diagnose epilepsy by comparing the results of electroencephalogram (EEG) testing, which is used to record brain wave activity, with observed abnormal motor activity.

What can precipitate seizures?

Seizures can also be caused by *emotional disturbances* and *stress.* They are more common among women during the menstrual period. Drug withdrawal, hyperventilation, fever, photic stimulation (such as sunlight glittering through leaves or on water), television, and fluorescent lights have also been known to precipitate seizures. If an individual's seizures tend to be precipitated by a certain kind of environmental event, the seizures can sometimes be controlled by avoiding the events that precipitate them.

The newspaper article (see box on page 373) illustrates some of the misconceptions held by the general public about epilepsy and the consequences of these misconceptions for the person with epilepsy.

Treatment of Epilepsy

What is the primary treatment for epilepsy?

Epilepsy is treated primarily with chemotherapy, which refers to the administration of drugs. The drugs are used to prevent seizures or to reduce their frequency. Many drugs have serious side effects that vary with the child and the medication being taken. Dilantin, for example, causes a condition known as gingival hyperplasia, in which the gums become swollen and tender and grow over the teeth. The gums bleed easily and are susceptible to infection. Other side effects of concern to the classroom teacher are hyperactivity, irritability, lethargy, and restlessness. The reader is referred to Gadow for a more extensive discussion of treatment, especially with medication (Gadow, 1986).

Another part of the treatment program involves classroom adjustment and efforts to ensure that the child with epilepsy is accepted by the teacher and the child's peers. Children are much more likely to accept the child with epilepsy if seizures have been explained to them. The teacher may also have to control classroom activities that regularly precipitate generalized seizures. If, for example, the child regularly has a seizure after heated classroom discussion, the

A young man wakes up from his epileptic seizure to find a woman bystander dancing over him, trying to exorcise what she believes is a devil that has possessed him. . . .

Quoting from a national survey about charitable causes to which the public is most likely to contribute, the board president of the financially ailing Epilepsy Foundation of Kentucky says: "We're right down at the bottom, just one notch above venereal disease."

Welcome to the uncertain, somewhat secret world of the epileptic.

They are suffering—or have suffered sometime—seizures ranging from dramatic convulsions to brief lapses of consciousness. More than that, they have suffered from public ignorance and uneasiness over the ailment. . . .

"The average citizen is not hostile to epilepsy. It's just they don't know very much about it, and sometimes they're scared of it," said E. Wayne Lee, a 27-year-old epileptic. . . .

Greater understanding in the schools can prevent some of the embarrassment and ridicule faced by students who suffer from epilepsy.

This embarrassment sometimes prompts teen-age epileptics not to take their seizure-preventing drugs in an attempt to prove they are really like everyone else.

Source: From R. L. Peirce (March 6, 1978). Epileptics share a world of uncertainty and secrecy because of public's ignorance. Louisville, KY, *Courier-Journal.*

discussion may have to be lessened, or the child may have to be occupied with another activity. Persons working with children with epilepsy should also know how drugs affect schoolwork.

HOW TO DEAL WITH SEIZURES. Although seizures can generally be controlled with medication, a teacher may occasionally have to manage seizures in the classroom or elsewhere. Absence seizures are more difficult to control with medication than generalized seizures. The teacher of children who experience absence seizures may have to repeat instructions several times to be certain they are clearly understood. The teacher, and others who work with the individual, should also realize that the child is not merely daydreaming.

The child who experiences an aura or warning that precedes a generalized seizure should be taken immediately to as safe a place as possible. If the child falls to the floor, these instructions should be followed:

1. Give the child room to thrash. The immediate area should be cleared of children or objects on which the child could be hurt.
2. Allow the child to remain on the floor. The child should not be moved, restrained, or held during the seizure.
3. Protect the child's head by cradling it in your hands. Do not restrain head movement, however. Move with the child.
4. When possible, turn the child's head to one side. This allows saliva to drain. If it flows back into the throat, the child may choke. Turning the head to one side also keeps the child from choking on the tongue, which may be caused by gravity forcing the tongue to the back of the throat if the child is lying face-upward.
5. Don't put your fingers in the child's mouth. The child could bite and seriously injure them. Tremendous strength is exerted during a seizure. Do not force anything between the teeth.
6. Don't lay the child on his or her stomach; to do so will impair breathing. When possible, the child should be turned to one side.
7. Loosen tight clothing.

8. Get on the floor with the child. Do not stand up and look down at the child.
9. Allow the child to remain lying down for a while after regaining consciousness.
10. Talk to the child in a calm voice. Acknowledge the seizure but don't make a major issue of it.
11. When the child is ready, help the child to stand.
12. Allow the child to lie down or sit at a desk with the head down. The child should be permitted to go to sleep.
13. Unless otherwise instructed, you need not call the physician. You should report the seizure to the parents and principal and note its severity and duration in the anecdotal seizure record.
14. Children near the child should be assigned the task of moving tables, chairs, and other objects away from the child, because they are closer than the teacher. Other children should be instructed to go on with their work.
15. Children in the classroom should be prepared for the event. Discuss the appropriate procedures for dealing with seizures with the child's parents and obtain parental and school permission to discuss seizures with the class. A discussion can perhaps be related to health instruction. After the child has regained consciousness, appropriate reactions (do not stare, do not avoid the child) should be discussed with the class.
16. Above all, try to remain calm.

Partial seizures should generally be treated in the same way as generalized seizures. It is important to recognize the emotional component and when necessary clear the room or take an individual from the room. The individual may resist attempts to be moved, however; if this occurs, the child should be allowed to remain.

What is status epilepticus?

If the child is still convulsing after five minutes, or seems to go from one seizure into another, the child's parents and the physician (or school nurse if one is available) should be consulted immediately. This condition, called status epilepticus, can cause death if allowed to continue. This condition requires treatment by a physician (Nealis, 1983a). Cell damage can result from seizures lasting longer than 30 minutes (Menkes, 1990). Any seizure lasting more than five minutes is cause for concern, and medical help should be sought.

Educational Implications of Epilepsy

Children with epilepsy will be found in the regular classroom and in the special class. Epilepsy alone is not sufficient to place a child in a special class or program, but it is often found in conjunction with other disabilities, such as mental retardation and cerebral palsy. The teacher must watch for the side effects of medication and adjust the classroom to reduce the effects of the seizure on both the child and other students. The teacher should collect data on side effects and the incidence, duration, and severity of seizures, which should be reported to the child's physician to aid in monitoring the child's disorder. Epilepsy is not a progressive disorder, nor does it cause mental retardation. It is not contagious. As noted, the child will require some adaptations and adjustment but otherwise should be treated as normally as possible.

Traumatic Brain Injury

The Individuals with Disabilities Education Act (PL 101-476, 1990), in the definition of children with disabilities, has designated traumatic brain injury as a separate disability category. The proposed definition of **traumatic brain injury** refers to ". . . an injury to the brain caused by an external physical force or by an internal occurrence such as stroke or aneurysm, resulting in total or partial functional disability or psychosocial maladjustment that adversely affects educational performance. The term includes open or closed head injuries resulting in mild, moderate, or severe impairments in one or more areas, including cognition; language; memory; attention; reasoning; abstract thinking; judgment; problem-solving; sensory, perceptual and motor abilities; psychosocial behavior; physical functions; information processing; and speech. The term does not include brain injuries that are congenital or degenerative, or brain injuries induced by birth trauma" (Department of Education, 1991, p. 41271).

Bigge (1991) reports an occurrence rate of traumatic brain injury of 23 per 10,000. Traumatic brain injury is typically caused by a variety of factors including car accidents, falls, child abuse, gunshot wounds, or other severe blows to the head. A frequent result of traumatic brain injury is coma. Bigge (1991) states that a child who has a coma experiences a much higher mortality rate (ten times higher in children than in adults). People who are in recovery from a coma are frequently agitated or will have physical, cognitive, and behavioral deficits. They may experience associated problems of attention span, self-control, and poor judgment. The educational program will need to consider behavior management, social skills, poor memory, and activities of daily living. More detailed information about the topic can be found in Bigge (1991, pp. 67–70), Accouloumre and Caldwell (1991), and Mira, Tucker, and Tyler (1992).

PROBE 11-4   Other Disabilities

1. A temper tantrum may sometimes be confused with what type of seizure?
2. A child who falls to the ground, thrashes around, and loses bowel and bladder control may be suffering from a _____ seizure.
3. The type of seizure that often goes unnoticed is called an _____ seizure.
4. T   F   Epilepsy is treated primarily through chemotherapy.
5. T   F   In treating a person having a generalized seizure, you should place your fingers between the teeth to prevent swallowing of the tongue.
6. When is it necessary to call in professional help for a child having a generalized seizure?
7. Differentiate between a child with traumatic brain injury and a child with cerebral palsy.

EDUCATION AND TREATMENT OF CHILDREN WITH PHYSICAL DISABILITIES

You should be able to describe educational and treatment procedures for children with physical disabilities.

Many different educational and treatment procedures are used with children who have physical disabilities. A number of these will be addressed in this section of the chapter. We will begin with a discussion of the contributions that professionals from different disciplines can make to this endeavor.

Related Services

Teachers who work with individuals with disabilities do not work alone. Many professionals, paraprofessionals, and school personnel are involved in providing appropriate educational experiences to help children with physical disabilities function to their maximum potential. In fact, these related services are mandated by federal legislation, namely PL 94-142, as amended by PL 101-476 in 1990. However, what is and what is not a "related service" cannot always be easily determined, and in some instances the courts have had to decide whether or not a specific service was mandated by law. For example, the issue of whether clean intermittent catheterization (CIC) as a related service was the responsibility of a school district was reviewed by the U.S. Supreme Court (*Irving Independent School District v. Tatro,* 1984), who decided it was the responsibility of a school to provide such services (see the earlier section on spina bifida for further information). Consequently, classroom teachers can be required to perform CIC on children as a necessary related service.

Other aspects of related service may involve transportation, speech therapy, physical therapy, occupational therapy, audiological services, assessment, counseling, psychological services, recreation, school health services, social work services in school, and early identification and assessment (Turnbull, 1990). Any service that "directly benefits a child to be educated or even placed in a school building or regular school program . . . is apt to be a related service" (Turnbull, 1990, p. 138).

What are related services and who provides them?

For purposes of discussion, the following descriptions of related services personnel should serve to clarify relevant terms and concepts. The more typical related services of speech therapy, physical therapy, occupational therapy, adaptive physical education, and school nurses are briefly described. However, the list of related services could also include such professionals as music teachers or therapists, media specialists, art teachers or therapists, vocational education teachers, reading teachers, guidance counselors, social workers, school psychologists, assistive technology specialists, and others that provide service to those with a physical disability. Westling and Koorland (1988) provide additional descriptive information about some of these other related services.

SPEECH-LANGUAGE THERAPY. Speech and language therapy services are provided by speech-language pathologists, professional who have undergone extensive training. They have at least a master's degree and are certified by the American Speech-Language Hearing Association. They are able to evaluate the speech, language, and communication deficits of individuals and implement the necessary remedial services. More recently, they are becoming increasingly adept at evaluating persons for the use of various kinds of adaptive and assistive equipment aimed at enhancing communication. This includes the use of computers and adapted switches that enable the person with a disability to open access to such devices. These professionals are typically employed by a school, hospital, or private agency.

PHYSICAL THERAPY. Physical therapists are trained at the bachelor's or master's degree level to work with individuals who have physical or motor impairments or severe multiple disabling conditions. They provide exercises designed to reduce or minimize the physical disability. In many instances, the exercises help maintain or enhance the range of motion of the involved body parts or modify how the individual sits (positioning), which, in turn, helps the person to perform other motor tasks.

Physical therapists may be employed full-time by a school, but frequently provide services to a school through a contractual arrangement. Most hospital schools will have the full-time services of a physical therapist. Teachers and parents may be called upon to implement many of the exercises in the classroom or at home. In the classroom, the scheduling of services may become an issue and requires the cooperation of all concerned.

OCCUPATIONAL THERAPY. Occupational therapists are prepared to provide services designed to enhance self-care activities, including feeding, dressing, toileting, and other activities that require fine motor coordination. They may be directly involved in training children how to button clothes, put on shoes, sweaters, and pants, and how to hold a spoon or fork, or cut with a knife. They may also be involved in training individuals how to use various types of adaptive equipment designed to enhance a needed body function. Occupational therapists are also concerned about the social, psychological, and cognitive development of individuals.

ASSISTIVE TECHNOLOGY SERVICES. With the rapid increase of assistive technologies (as described in detail in Chapter 3), a new professional role is emerging. Assistive technology specialists are those who can perform assessments to determine the needs for assistive and adaptive devices and services. Often, these individuals are particularly skilled in making determinations about the selection and development of switches that people with physical disabilities can use to operate equipment, and the selection and programming of alternative keyboards for computer operation. Often, an assistive technology specialist serves as the chairperson for a team of other related services personnel who make recommendations about the selection and use of devices and services for students with a variety of disabilities.

SCHOOL NURSING SERVICES. Many schools employ a full-time nurse. If the school is large enough, the nurse will be there throughout the day. However, smaller school districts will have a nurse schedule visits to each school at selected times during the week. Nurses can be important resources when dealing with children with physical disabilities or chronic health impairments. Graff, Mulligan-Ault, Guess, Taylor, and Thompson (1990) provide an excellent resource for dealing with the health care of individuals with disabilities. They discuss such things as seizure monitoring, teeth and gum care, medication administration, skin care, bowel care, nutrition monitoring and supplementation, therapeutic management, cast care, glucose monitoring for a student with diabetes, colostomy or ileostomy care, nasogastric and gastrostomy tube feeding, clean intermittent catheterization, and tracheostomy care. All these

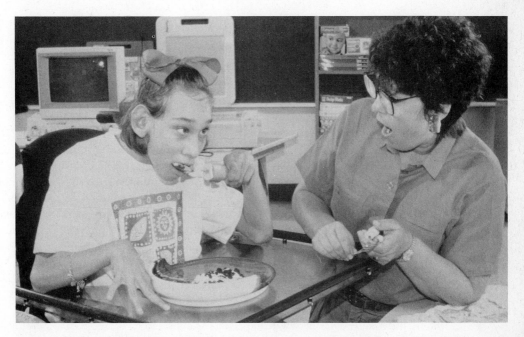

An occupational therapist is teaching this student to use adapted utensils to feed herself independently.

activities may be the school's responsibility. The nurse is especially useful when dealing with such things during school hours.

ADAPTIVE PHYSICAL EDUCATION. Adaptive physical education personnel are in charge of programs designed to improve a child's general physical development, muscle development, and coordination. The programs are typically therapeutic, and the teachers have been trained to use specialized techniques. Such programs are integrated into the regular physical education activities of the school.

TRANSPORTATION SERVICES. Transportation is a related service typically provided to all children, but especially to those with physical disabilities. Transportation is important in helping those with a physical disability gain access to special education services. The successful provision of this related service requires the cooperation of the parents, principals, teachers, director of special education, and bus driver. Persons who need this service frequently have physical disabilities that impair their movement (wheelchair, crutch, braces, poor motor coordination, etc.) and need special help in getting on and off the bus. Once on the bus, special care may be required to ensure their safety while traveling. Bluth (1985) provides an excellent resource that reviews the legal requirements of a school district and provides guidelines regarding transportation safety, personnel training, length of ride, pickup and drop-off location, and disciplinary and suspension procedures.

All of the above professionals, plus others who represent very specialized areas, may be involved in decision making about the educational and treatment program for a particular child. Often these individuals are called upon to participate in the development of a child's IEP. At other times, they are involved in providing direct services. On still other occasions, they may consult with the special education teacher or the general education teacher to advise them about ways to work with the child.

Child Abuse and Neglect

It is important for all teachers to be able to identify symptoms of child abuse and neglect. This is particularly true for teachers working with children who have physical disabilities, since some of these children are particularly subject to abuse and neglect from parents or guardians who can become frustrated with the children's inability to perform many tasks. Extreme frustration may lead to abuse or neglect.

To complicate the issue, some physical disabilities may result in symptoms that are similar to those exhibited by victims of child abuse or neglect. For example, a child who is on large doses of seizure medication may exhibit a condition known as "Dilantin gums," which causes the gums to swell and bleed. This condition may parallel a situation in which a child's dental hygiene is being neglected. It is important for teachers to be aware of such factors and recognize that there may be different causes for the physical conditions they observe in children.

How can teachers identify abused or neglected children?

In Section 3 of the Child Abuse Prevention and Treatment Act (PL 93-247) child abuse and neglect are defined as "the physical or mental injury, sexual abuse, negligent treatment, or maltreatment of a child's welfare under circumstances which indicate that the child's health or welfare is harmed or threatened thereby." Some symptoms that might indicate abuse or neglect have been described by Kline (1977) and are shown in Table 11-3.

Zirpoli (1990) presents a list of factors associated with physical child abuse organized according to caregiver characteristics (e.g., caregiver was a victim of child abuse and spouse

TABLE 11-3   Symptoms of Abuse and Neglect

Symptoms of Abuse	*Symptoms of Neglect*
Evidence of repeated injury	Clothing inappropriate for weather
New injuries before previous ones have healed	Torn, tattered, unwashed clothing
Frequent complaints of abdominal pain	Poor skin hygiene
Evidence of bruises	Rejection by other children because of body odor
Bruises of different ages, welts	
Wounds, cuts, or punctures	Need for glasses, dental work, hearing aid, or other health services
Scalding liquid burns with well-defined parameters	Lack of proper nourishment
Caustic burns	Consistent tiredness or sleepiness in class
Frostbite	Consistent, very early school arrival
Cigarette burns	Frequent absenteeism or chronic tardiness
	Tendency to hang around school after dismissal

abuse), environmental influences (e.g., general condition of poverty and family disorganization or dysfunction), sociocultural factors (e.g., social acceptance of physical punishment), and victim characteristics (e.g., prematurity and dysmaturity, difficult temperament, irritability). It is important to note that only nonaccidental or deliberate injuries are considered abusive.

In 1990, over 2 million children were reported as being abused or neglected (Zirpoli, 1990). More than 400,000 of these involved sexual abuse; one in four girls and one in eight boys under age 18 were or had been sexually molested (NASDSE, 1991). The NASDSE (National Association of State Directors of Special Education) report also notes that 89 percent of some 22,000 school teachers surveyed report abused or neglected children to be a problem in their school. This report further estimates that 16 percent of all children under the age of 3 are involved in child abuse and neglect (NASDSE, 1991).

The causes of child abuse are hard to determine. Child abusers come from all income levels, geographic areas, family settings, religious backgrounds, ethnic groups, and residential environments. They do not necessarily use drugs or alcohol. There is one factor that seems related to child abuse: Many child abusers were themselves abused as children. And, although a cause-effect sequence has not been demonstrated, Kline (1977) reported a clear relationship between child abuse and handicapping conditions. His research found that, of children judged to be abused or neglected, 27 percent were subsequently enrolled in special education classes. Many of these children had symptoms resembling those of behavior disorders. Benedict, White, Wulff, and Hall (1990) report data that tends to support this. They found that more severely disabled children were less at risk for abuse than were marginally functioning children, or children who were able to perform some tasks but not others.

PL 94-142 (as amended by PL 101-476) programs designed to locate children with disabilities will probably identify a number of children who have been abused or neglected. Zirpoli (1990) cites evidence that children with disabilities are at greater risk for physical abuse if appropriate family support services are not implemented. However, he also indicates that "having a disability alone does not place a child at greater risk for abuse treatment" (Zirpoli, 1990, p. 10). Caregivers must be given appropriate support in order to prevent abuse. Cohen and Warren (1987) report survey results that indicate a high incidence of abuse among children who have disabilities and who are in preschool programs, but less abuse among children with disabilities who are in respite care programs.

Cases of child abuse should be identified and reported as soon as possible to treat existing injuries and to ensure that the child is protected from further injury. Teachers have not only humane and professional responsibilities to report possible cases of abuse, in at least 36 states, they also have a legal responsibility to do so. In other states, persons and institutions providing social services have similar reporting obligations. Failure to report a suspected case is a misdemeanor in nearly half the states (Kline, 1977). Providing proof of abuse is *not* the responsibility of the teacher; this is done by the agency that receives the report. In fact, every state except Oklahoma provides immunity from civil or criminal liability to those who report cases in good faith (Kline, 1977).

The careful professional will be aware that the effects of some disabilities may be confused with child abuse. For example, a child with osteogenesis imperfecta (brittle bones disease) will frequently and easily break bones. One who is alert to child abuse but not aware of the physical disorder could make a mistake. The person working with children with physical disabilities should be alert to potential child abuse, yet be aware that many children with physical disabilities will show conditions that resemble physical abuse.

Educational Considerations

What should teachers be aware of when teaching a child with physical disabilities?

Children with physical disabilities can frequently be educated in the regular classroom with the help of some of the devices mentioned in Chapter 3. Depending on the severity of the child's disability and the extent to which he or she requires special attention, the child might be placed in any of the environments described in Chapter 2. The information in Table 11-2 (presented earlier in this chapter) lists general information about potential modifications to the classroom and the skills required of those working with the child. However, the need for an individualized health care plan is still important and should be initiated. Procedures for IEP development for the child with physical disabilities or special health needs are presented by Caldwell, Todaro, and Gates (1989) and are also thoroughly discussed in Chapter 2.

If a child with a physical disability or a health problem is assigned to your school program, you and members of the child's IEP team should review the child's records, contact the child's parents and those who have worked with the child in the past, and, in conjunction with other related service personnel (nurses, speech therapists, physical therapists, occupational therapists, adaptive physical educators, etc.), obtain answers to the questions in the areas listed on the following checklist, and others as they arise.

A Beginning Checklist for IEP Development

This checklist can be used to initiate thinking about an individualized education program for a child with physical disabilities or special health problems.

MEDICAL CONCERNS. (The parents, nurse, and child's physician should be consulted in regard to medical concerns.)

_____ In addition to the child's primary disorder, does the child have additional problems, such as seizures or diabetes? Does the child have any sensory disorders?

_____ Does the child take medication? How frequently, and in what amounts?

_____ If medication is taken, is the school authorized to administer the medication during school hours?

_____ What are the expected side effects of the medication? What are the other possible side effects?

_____ What procedures should be followed in the event of a seizure, insulin shock, diabetic coma, or other problem, with regard to contacting the child's parents or medical personnel?

_____ Should the child's activities be restricted in any way?

TRAVEL. (The child's parents and school officials must be consulted about travel.)

_____ How will the child be transported to school?

_____ Will the child arrive at the usual time?

_____ Will someone need to meet the child at the entrance to the school to provide assistance in getting the child on and off the vehicle?

_____ Will the child need special accommodations to travel within the school building or the classroom?

TRANSFER AND LIFTING. (The physical therapist and parents should be consulted for these activities.)

_____ What methods are used to get the child on and off the school bus?

_____ What is the preferred way to lift and transfer the child out of a wheelchair and onto a chair or to the floor?

_____ What cautions or limitations are there regarding transfer and lifting?

_____ How much help does the child need with movement and transfer?

COMMUNICATION. (The teacher of a child with a communication problem should consult the speech-language pathologist and the child's parents.)

_____ If the child does not communicate verbally, what particular or unique means of communication does the child use?

_____ Does the child have a speech or language problem?

_____ Does the child use gestures? If so, what are they? Is a pointer used? Does the child use the same signal consistently for _yes, no,_ or other common words?

_____ Can the child write? Type? How?

_____ Is an electronic communication aid used? If so, are there any special instructions necessary for the child to use it or for the teacher to understand and maintain it? Are fresh batteries or a charger needed?

_____ Can the child make his or her needs known to the teacher? How?

SELF-CARE. (The school nurse and occupational therapist should be in contact with the parents about these activities.)

_____ What types of help does the child need with self-care activities such as feeding, dressing, toileting, and so forth?

_____ What equipment, such as a special feeding tray, does the child need?

POSITIONING. (The physical therapist should be involved in conversations with parents about this area of concern.)

_____ What positioning aids or devices (braces, pillows, wedges, etc.) does the child use?

_____ What particular positions are the most useful for specific academic activities? What positions for resting?

_____ What positions are best for toileting, feeding, dressing, and other activities?

_____ Are there any other special aids or devices that I should know about?

EDUCATIONAL NEEDS. (The school psychologist, educational diagnostician, previous teachers, and other personnel associated with the child should be consulted. The following represent only a few of the considerations.)

—— What is the child's current level of achievement, and of developmental and vocational functioning?
—— What are the child's academic strengths and weaknesses?
—— To what extent is achievement in school affected by physical disabilities?
—— What medical considerations must be taken into account (that is, to what extent is the child able to participate in classroom activities?)
—— What physical modifications to the classroom need to be made?
—— What special equipment must be acquired?
—— What related services will be needed?

Psychosocial Needs

Individuals with disabilities have needs similar to nondisabled persons. The impact of a disability frequently interferes with the attainment of these needs. Best, Carpignano, Sirvis, and Bigge (1991) discuss the psychosocial aspects of a physical disability and present numerous suggestions about helping individuals to achieve psychological adjustment. The concepts of acceptance, appropriate expectations, attempts at independence, appropriate discipline, and awareness of self-concept development are critical to successful adjustment by the individual with a disability. The reader is referred to Best, Carpignano, Sirvis, and Bigge (1991) and to Wright (1983) for a more detailed discussion of the psychosocial aspects of a disability.

Assistive Technology

As noted in Chapter 3, there are many devices now available to help children with physical disabilities overcome problems of everyday living. The story of Nan at the beginning of this chapter is an example of one of the more dramatic applications of modern technology. Medical science has been using technology for a number of years: pacemakers to enable the heart to beat at a given pace; dialysis to assist kidney function; devices that will deliver insulin to people with diabetes; cochlear implants for some people who have damaged auditory nerves; and, most dramatically, artificial hearts. Modern technology has enabled the nonspeaking to speak, the nonhearing to hear, and the nonseeing to see. One has only to attend a convention for professionals who work with those who have disabilities to recognize the dramatic increase in the application of modern technology to adaptive-assistive devices and techniques.

In the realm of communications, many technological devices are used extensively. Some devices enable people to communicate with only a sip or puff on a strawlike device. Voice synthesizers attached to microcomputers enable persons who could not speak to have a voice. People who cannot normally open a door, turn on a radio or TV set, or flip on a light switch can now do so with vocal commands such as "Open the door." In these instances, a microcomputer is programmed to recognize the person's voice (and only that person's voice) and to activate a motor connected to a door or a light switch when it hears the right command. The motor then performs the desired function.

Computers can also be used in the classroom to introduce, practice, maintain, and generalize academic skills and concepts. Math, reading, writing, science, and social studies are just a few of the curricular areas in which microcomputers are being used. Access to the standard computer keyboard may be impossible for persons with physical disabilities. However, adapted keyboards, alternative keyboards, keyboard emulators, switches, infrared light, and the human voice can all be used to activate the computer. A person with limited movement of the limbs and good head control might use a head- or chin-activated switch or an infrared light attached to a headband to work the computer. Someone with limited range of motion may use a hand-activated switch or miniature keyboard. Oversized keyboards with programmable keys of various sizes may be suitable for persons with unrefined hand movement. Chapter 3 provides additional information about the use of assistive technologies.

What is the difference between an orthosis and a prosthesis?

There are also many less highly technical devices used by persons with physical disabilities to overcome problems of everyday living. *Prosthetic* devices such as artificial arms and legs are used to replace missing body parts. *Orthotic* devices are attachments, such as a leg brace or a splint, that assist a body function. Other types of adaptive equipment, such as wheelchairs, machines that turn pages, and long forceps used to reach objects that would otherwise be out of reach, are also available.

In a survey of public school special classes that contained children with physical disabilities, Cross (1983) found that providing for communication disorders was the most common adaptation to enable the child to function in the classroom. Adaptations for self-care activities such as feeding, toileting, and dressing were frequently reported, as were devices relating to travel. Surprisingly, instructional adaptations were not among the most frequently reported provisions for children with physical disabilities.

TECHNOLOGY IN ACTION

In April 1992, the Alliance for Technology Access (ATA) celebrated its fifth birthday. Since its inception, the original group of 11 technology access centers in 10 states grew into a national organization of 45 resource centers in 34 states. Each center is an autonomous, nonprofit, community-based organization directed by a collaborative group of parents of children with disabilities, adults with disabilities, professional service providers, and others in the community with an interest in issues related to disability and technology.

Depending on their size and the resources available, ATA centers offer an array of services. ATA centers may do any of the following:

- Respond to requests for information about how technology can be used to enhance the potential of people with disabilities.
- Provide information about how technology can enhance learning in the school environment.
- Provide demonstrations and training on the whole range of assistive technology.
- Help consumers find technology solutions to improve their independence.

- Loan assistive technologies and adapted toys for short-term use and trials prior to making purchase decisions.
- Provide consultations and referrals to other agencies that may be able to provide assistance, such as technology assessments and funding for technology devices.
- Operate walk-in facilities to enable people to try out technology hardware and software.

During 1991, staff members and volunteers associated with the 45 ATA centers provided services to more than 72,000 people. They conducted nearly 23,000 individual consultations and more than 2700 training and information workshops.

Centers associated with the Alliance for Technology Access are valuable community resources, particularly to those with disabilities and their families. For information about the availability of an ATA center near you, contact the Foundation for Technology Access, 1128 Solano Avenue, Albany, CA 94706 or call (510) 528-0747.

Source: Impact report: Alliance for Technology Access 1990–1991. Albany, CA: Foundation for Technology Access.

The Alliance for Technology Access: Parent-run resource centers. *Exceptional Parent,* November/December 1990, pp. 16–19.

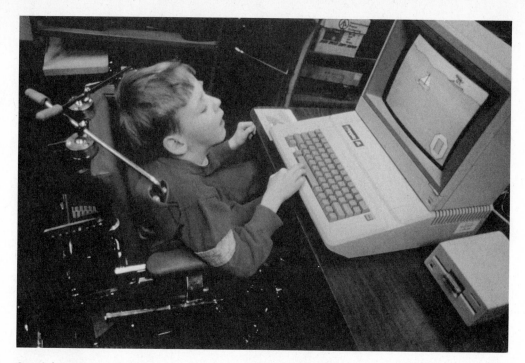

Special seating and positioning supports were designed to enable this student to use the computer.

Although assistive technologies may be beneficial to those with physical disabilities, they should not be recommended without a careful examination of their potential effect. In some cases, modifications of positioning, movement, or communication may lead to a dependency that adversely affects independent functioning. Those who do not use adaptive aids may become more independent and thereby prevent or slow the loss of function and in some cases, enhance function. Some prosthetic devices actually hinder body functioning or motor movement and tasks may be accomplished more efficiently without them. Careful evaluation of body positioning and support by the appropriate specialist must be made before adaptive techniques are implemented. Questions about the use of a particular device or modifications of positioning or movement should be referred to the appropriate medical specialists or to the communication, physical, or occupational therapists available.

Figure 11-2 lists some of the assistive technology devices and services that can be used to facilitate the functioning of people with physical disabilities.

PROBE 11-5   Education and Treatment of Children with Physical Disabilities

1. Is CIC a related service that the school district is required to provide?
2. Describe what the following professionals do in their roles as related service personnel:
    a. Physical therapist
    b. Occupational therapist
    c. Speech therapist
    d. Assistive technology specialist
    e. Adaptive physical educator
    f. Transportation specialist
    g. School nurse
3. List three symptoms of child abuse.

FIGURE 11-2   A Functional Approach to Exceptionality: Reducing the Effects of Physical Disabilities

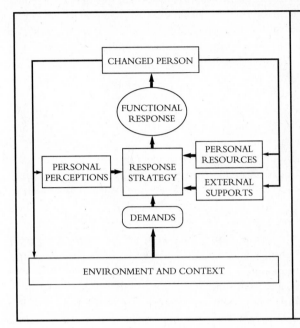

Numerous *external supports*, in the form of assistive technologies and related services, can reduce the handicapping effects of physical disabilities. Following are some examples:

- Devices called augmentative communication aids enable those who cannot talk to communicate with others.

- Switches operated by the smallest muscle movements permit people with limited movement to control appliances.

- Electric wheelchairs and van lifts can enhance the mobility of those with mobility restrictions.

- Modified keyboards can be used by those with limited finger control to operate computers.

- Hand-operated controls can permit those with limited leg control to drive motor vehicles.

- Activities of daily living can be facilitated through a variety of devices to assist with eating, grooming, personal hygiene, and housekeeping.

- Related service personnel can provide advice and training in the use of the above devices.

4. List three symptoms of child neglect.
5. Describe the conditions under which you would recommend that children with physical disabilities be placed in the regular classroom for their education.
6. What criteria would you propose for selecting children with physical disabilities for placement in a self-contained special class?
7. List one question you should ask the parents of a child with physical disabilities in each of the following areas to help develop procedures for caring for the child:
   a. Medicine
   b. Travel
   c. Transfer
   d. Communication
   e. Self-care
   f. Positioning
8. Differentiate between a prosthesis and an orthosis.
9. When would it be inappropriate to recommend an assistive or adaptive device for use by a person with physical disabilities?

ARCHITECTURAL BARRIERS

You should be able to describe the current standards for making facilities accessible to persons with physical disabilities.

What provisions are being made to reduce architectural barriers in America?

People with physical disabilities are frequently faced with architectural barriers that prevent them from using facilities easily accessible to people without disabilities. Several important laws have been passed by Congress, however, that are designed to reduce or eliminate architectural barriers. The Americans with Disabilities Act (PL 101-336, 1990) provides protection for persons with disabilities in all aspects of daily living and ensures that all persons with a disability will be treated the same as those with no disabilities. The Americans with Disabilities Act ensures that all new buildings and buildings undergoing renovation, all public transportation, and all public facilities be accessible to persons with disabilities. This legislation was designed to prevent and eliminate discrimination against individuals with disabilities and to provide enforceable standards. The intent was to involve the federal government in this enforcement through congressional authority.

The Architectural and Transportation Compliance Board, and the Equal Employment Opportunity Commission in cooperation with the U.S. Department of Justice (EEOC and DOJ), have published guidelines specifying the requirements of the Americans with Disabilities Act concerning the following: accessibility guidelines for buildings and facilities; accommodations in commercial facilities; nondiscrimination on the basis of disability in state and local government services; accessibility guidelines for transportation vehicles; and amendments to the final guidelines (*Federal Register,* 1991e; EEOC and DOJ, 1991). These guidelines were developed by the American National Standards Institute (ANSI). They are used by planners and builders for specifications of numerous building features, including accessible elements and spaces, accessible routes, protruding objects, ground and floor surfaces, parking, curb cutouts, ramps, stairs, elevators, platform lifts, windows, doors, entrances, drinking fountains and water coolers, water closets, toilet stalls, urinals, lavatories, sinks and mirrors, bathtubs, shower stalls, toilet facilities, storage, grab bars, controls and operating mechanisms, alarms, detectable warnings, signage, telephones, seating, auditorium and assembly areas, and dwelling units (ANSI, 1986). These standards were modified slightly by the Americans with Disabilities Act (*Federal Register,* 1991e, pp. 45519, 45644) and should prove to be a valuable resource for planning facilities for persons with disabilities.

What are the ANSI standards?

Within these guidelines, the definition of the term *physical disabilities* becomes very important to those individuals affected. According to the Americans with Disabilities Act (PL 101-336, 1990) a person with a disability is defined as follows:

> (1) a person with a physical or mental impairment that substantially limits that person in some major life activity (such as walking, talking, breathing, or working); (2) a person with a record of such a physical or mental impairment (such as a person with a history of mental illness or heart disease who no longer has the disease, but who is discriminated against because of [his or her] record of an impairment); or (3) a person who is regarded as having such an impairment (such as a person who has a significant burn on his/her face which does not limit him/her in any major life activity but who is discriminated against). (PRECIS, 1990)

Who must comply with the provisions of ADA?

All government agencies and private employers of 15 or more persons cannot refuse to hire or promote persons with a disability because of that disability when a person with a disability is qualified to perform the job. The Americans with Disabilities Act (ADA) ensures that employers make modifications to accommodate persons with disabilities if such accommodations will enable the person to perform those tasks necessary for the successful completion of the job. With regard to transportation, the act requires new vehicles purchased by public transit authorities to be accessible to persons with disabilities. "Paratransit" or an alternative service is required for persons who cannot use the mainline system. Trains must provide one car per train that is accessible, and all new and existing rail stations must be made accessible.

Additionally, all public accommodations must be accessible. This includes such facilities as hotels, restaurants, dry cleaners, grocery stores, schools, and parks. New buildings must be made accessible, and existing buildings must remove existing barriers if this is "readily

This wheelchair lift enables this person to use the public transit system.

achievable" (PRECIS, 1990). All telephone companies must offer appropriate services to those who require telecommunication devices (such as those who are deaf) or similar devices. State and local governments may not discriminate against individuals with disabilities. All government facilities, services, and communications must be accessible and consistent with Section 504 of the rehabilitation Act (PRECIS, 1990).

Access to the Community

Most of us can do everyday things like open doors, climb stairs, answer the phone, and use a lavatory without giving them a thought. But consider the problems you would face in these situations:

- You are blind and must find a certain office or house number.
- You are in a wheelchair and must get into a building that has only stairs and revolving doors, or you are in a wheelchair and cannot reach the elevator button for the floor you want.
- You are on crutches and can't carry your groceries or push a grocery cart.

As you can see, tasks most of us accomplish easily can present impenetrable barriers to persons with disabilities. Some obstacles cause just a minor inconvenience—being late for an appointment, perhaps. Others can have grave consequences. What if you are deaf and can't hear the fire alarm in your apartment building? With the implementation of the Americans with Disabilities Act, beginning January 1992, all buildings undergoing renovation must be made accessible to people with disabilities, and beginning January 1993, all *new* buildings must be made accessible as well. Colleges and universities, too, are prohibited from discriminating against persons with disabilities; many are renovating their physical plants to give access to previously inaccessible facilities.

What must be accessible to people with disabilities? .

For those involved in school programs, it is important to remember that *all parts* of all buildings need not be accessible; rather, all *programs* must be accessible. Thus, access to a second-floor science classroom need not be provided to a student in a wheelchair. The science class may, however, have to be moved to the first floor to make the science program accessible to all.

Heightened sensitivity to the needs of those with disabilities is also reflected in the use of the international symbol of access for persons with disabilities (Figure 11-3A). You've probably seen it along highways, where it is used to indicate the availability of restrooms equipped for persons with physical disabilities. You may also have seen the signs in Figure 11-3B and C, which indicate the route a person with physical disabilities should take to enter or leave a building. The signs in Figure 11-4A through D call attention to public facilities specifically designed to accommodate persons with disabilities.

The Americans with Disabilities Act of 1990 will have significant impact on the lives of those with disabilities as well as those without disabilities and should ensure that those with disabilities are afforded an equal opportunity to share in the American way of life. PL 101-336 indicates that some 43 million Americans have one or more physical or mental disabilities. Although few people would argue that access for individuals with disabilities is undesirable, it has been controversial because it is so expensive. The Lexington, Kentucky, Transit Authority (1992) estimated that it costs $16–20,000 to outfit a bus with a lift and a ramp. The National Council of Mayors has stated a preference for alternative services, such as dial-a-van. Some

FIGURE 11-3   International Access Symbols: (*A*) General Access for Persons with Disabilities; (*B*) Go Straight Ahead for Access Route; (*C*) Turn Right for Access Route

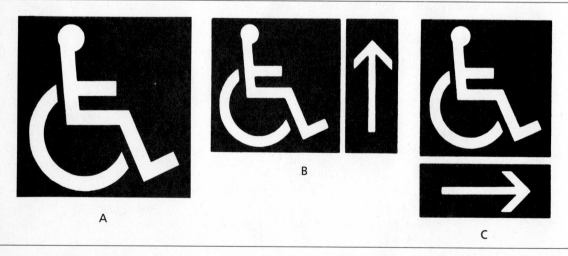

**FIGURE 11-4   More International Access Symbols: (*A*) Ramp; (*B*) Telephone;
(*C*) Parking; (*D*) Elevator**

A

B

C

D

groups of persons with disabilities have gone to court to force full access to buses. With the Americans with Disabilities Act of 1990, such actions should no longer be necessary.

The following narrative describes some of the barriers you might encounter on a trip to the dentist if you were in a wheelchair. Also discussed are the standards that should be met to overcome these barriers as, under the Americans with Disabilities Act of 1990, we work to ensure that buildings are made completely accessible to those with physical disabilities.

As can be seen from the examples in the narrative, a building designed to be accessible for those with disabilities is significantly different from a traditional building in a number of respects. It is not necessary, however, to renovate *every* building constructed prior to the enactment of access legislation. Section 504 as amended by PL 101-336 requires only that all *programs* be accessible. For example, every dormitory on a college campus does not have to be accessible, but some dormitories must be. Similarly, the entire building housing a math department need not be free of barriers, but the math program must be available to students with disabilities. The expense of making accessible all buildings constructed before the mid-1970s would be enormous. However, when alterations are made, PL 101-336 requires that the modifications being made comply with the requirements for new facilities, unless technically unfeasible (Federal Register, 1991e, p. 45654).

A Trip to the Dentist

Walkways

You will need to travel on sidewalks in order to get to the building. A walkway is defined as a predetermined, prepared surface that leads to or from a building and is on the same level as the adjacent ground. Walks should be at least 36 inches wide (32 inches at open doors) and should have a continuous surface that is not interrupted by steps or abrupt changes of more than 1/4 inch. Vertical changes larger than this may obstruct the small wheels on wheelchairs and trip people who have trouble walking.

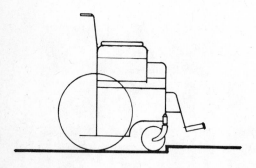

Ramps

You must get from the walk up the stairs to the entrance of the building. To do so, you must use a ramp. A ramp is a sloping walkway that enables a person to move from one floor elevation to another without encountering any obstruction. Ramps should be at least 4 feet wide and should have a slope of not more than 1:12, which is a drop (or rise) of 1 inch in every 12 inches. The maximum rise for any run must not exceed 30 inches.

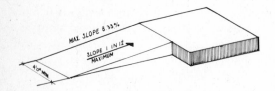

Doormats and Grates

After wheeling up the ramp, you encounter a grate that has been installed in front of the doorway to trap snow and sand. The width of the grid openings in the grate should be no more than 1/2 inch in one direction. Larger openings will create hazards for those who use canes and will make wheelchair travel difficult.

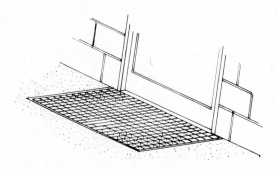

After you have traveled across the grate, you come to a doormat. Thick, bristly doormats of hemp or plastic bunch up under the small wheels of chairs and make the wheelchair difficult to push. Doormats must not be more than 1/2 inch thick. The edges must be beveled. If possible, thin mats of woven rubber should be used.

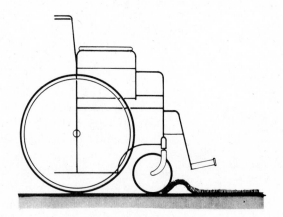

(continued)

A Trip to the Dentist *(continued)*

Entrances

You are successful in maneuvering over the grate and doormat and are now ready to open the door to the building. Revolving doors and turnstiles should have accessible doorways placed immediately beside them. The threshold of an exterior door should be beveled and have a maximum edge height of 1/2 inch so that you can get your chair over it without difficulty. You should be able to open the door with one hand, and the passageway with the door open should be at least 32 inches wide. An adult wheelchair is approximately 27 inches wide, so a 32-inch doorway allows 2 1/2 inches on each side for the hands as they are used to turn the wheels.

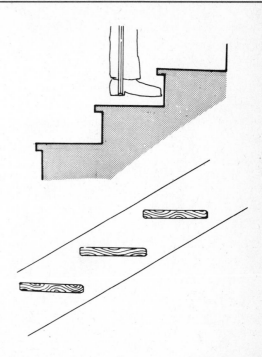

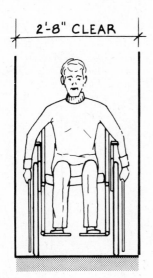

Acceptable stairs have either vertical or slanted risers. They can be used by people who have to lift their legs straight up or drop them straight down without any risk of catching their toes on the top of each step. Two acceptable types are shown below.

Stairways

Now you are in the building. Ideally, there would be an elevator to take you to the second floor where the dentist's office is located. If there were no elevator and you could ambulate with crutches or leg braces, you would have to use the stairs. Open riser stairs are attractive, but they are hazardous and are no longer permitted. People who wear braces also have a difficult time climbing stairs that have abrupt or square lips that stick out over the stair riser. The following two side views are examples of unacceptable stairs.

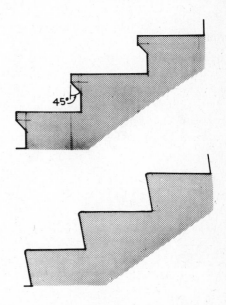

(continued)

A Trip to the Dentist *(continued)*

The handrails of stairways should also be modified to make it easier for someone with limited grasping power to hold on to them.

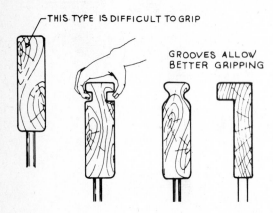

After arriving at the dentist's office, you must move from the wheelchair to the dental chair. You have chosen for your dentist a man who has been trained in lifting and transfer techniques. He straddles one of your knees, places his wrists under your arms, and bending his knees, leans you forward. Then, using his legs for lifting, the dentist pivots you 90 degrees so that you are seated in the chair. The same procedure is used to get you back in the wheelchair after the dentist informs you that you have no cavities.

Restrooms

If you need to go to the restroom after your visit to the dentist, you may encounter obstacles there as well. Many restrooms have self-closing doors that can make toilet facilities inaccessible. Time-delay door closers and automatic, power-operated doors that slide or pivot should be used for restrooms (as well as other entrances and doorways).

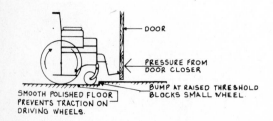

After you have gotten through the door, you must still gain access to the stall. Standards now require one toilet for men and one for women be accessible to persons with disabilities in each restroom. There are three basic techniques for transferring from a wheelchair to a toilet in a stall. The first two methods, used in ordinary stalls, are difficult or impossible for many people who have not had extensive training. You have probably seen the grab rails that have been installed in some stalls to assist those with physical disabilities with their toileting.

Method 1

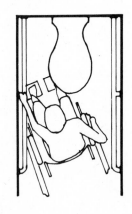 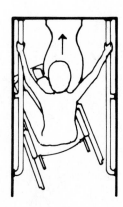

1. (Left) Enters stall, turns at an angle, placing footrests and feet to one side of the toilet.

2. (Right) Leans forward, placing hands on rails near wall, and pulls torso forward, sliding onto seat in sideways position.

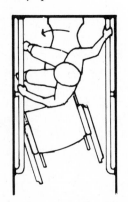 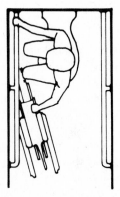

(continued)

A Trip to the Dentist *(continued)*

3. (Left) Switches right hand from right rail to left, arriving in side seated position.

4. (Right) Maintains balance with right hand while using left to fold chair or push it back.

5. With chair folded or pushed back, swings legs around to front, switching left hand to opposite rail.

Method 2

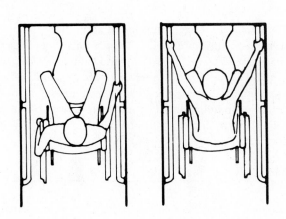

1. (Left) Enters stall straight in and pulls chair up to seat, placing legs to each side of toilet.

2. (Right) Leans forward, placing hands on bars near walls. Pulls torso forward, sliding onto seat.

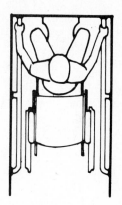

3. Remains in "backward" position facing wall.

Method 3

This side-approach method can be used by most people in wheelchairs. Stalls that allow space for this method are preferred.

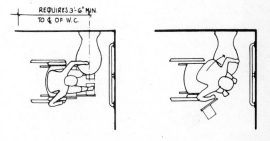

1. (Left) Approaches toilet from side.

2. (Right) Removes arm rests and swings foot rest to side. Places one hand on seat or grab bar and other on chair.

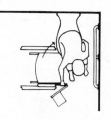

(continued)

A Trip to the Dentist *(continued)*

3. (Left) With a lifting and sliding motion, shifts torso onto seat.

4. (Right) Maintains balance by using grab bar and wheelchair.

To complete your use of the restroom, you will need to wash and dry your hands. Each restroom should have a sink no more than 34 inches from the floor. There

should be a space of at least 29 inches between the floor and the bottom of the sink so that a wheelchair can be pushed close to it. The temperature of the water should not exceed 120 degrees Fahrenheit. Exposed hot water pipes should be insulated to avoid burning people who have no feeling in their legs.

If the restroom contains mirrors and shelves, one of each should be placed above the sink for people with disabilities. The shelf and bottom of the mirror should be no more than 40 inches from the floor. The operating mechanisms (cranks, coin slots, buttons) of towel racks, dispensers, disposal units, vending machines, and other appliances should be within 40 inches of the floor as well.

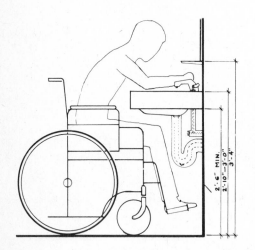

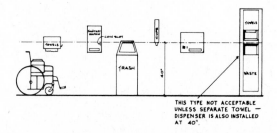

More recent sources of information about providing architectural accessibility include guidelines from the American National Standards Institute (1986), the training manual *Conducting an Architectural Access Audit, Access Surveyor Training,* by Ferrero and Fleming (1992), and the *Americans with Disabilities Handbook* (EEOC & DOJ, October 1991). Seeger and Bailes (1990) provide information about building design for young people with disabilities. Information about prosthetic and orthotic devices can be found in the Adaptive Device Locator System (1990), HyperABLEDATA (1992), and other sources listed in Chapter 3.

PROBE 11-6   Architectural Barriers

1. Standards for elimination of architectural barriers have been developed by an organization called _____.
2. Doorways should be at least _____ inches wide to accommodate wheelchairs.
3. Ramps should be at least _____ feet wide.
4. T F A lavatory stall can be made accessible to all persons in wheelchairs by placing grab bars at convenient heights.
5. T F Thick doormats should be used in front of doors to give wheelchair travelers better traction on wet days.
6. T F Open-riser stairs are particularly well suited for persons who are wearing braces.

7. Restroom towel dispensers and other appliances should be mounted no more than _____ inches above the floor.

8. Abrupt rises on walkways should not be more than _____ high or they may cause travel problems.

9. T   F   Although there may be architectural barriers in a given school, all programs must be accessible to those with disabilities.

SUMMARY

1. The text defines children with physical disabilities as those whose physical or health problems result in an impairment of normal interaction with society to the extent that specialized services and programs are required for them.

2. PL 101-336 defines a person with a physical disability as "(1) a person with a physical or mental impairment that substantially limits that person in some major life activity (such as walking, talking, breathing, or working); (2) a person with a record of such a physical or mental impairment (such as a person with a history of mental illness or heart disease who no longer has the disease, but who is discriminated against because of [his or her] record of an impairment); or (3) a person who is regarded as having such an impairment (such as a person who has a significant burn on his/her face which does not limit him/her in any major life activity but who is discriminated against)" (PRECIS, 1990).

3. Cerebral palsy is caused by damage to the brain. It is characterized by impaired motor coordination. There are several types of cerebral palsy, including spasticity, athetosis, ataxia, rigidity, tremor, and mixed.

4. Muscular dystrophy is a progressive weakening and degeneration of the voluntary muscles.

5. Other disorders that affect ambulation are spinal muscular atrophy, poliomyelitis, multiple sclerosis, arthritis, osteogenesis imperfecta, and spinal cord injuries.

6. Spina bifida is a congenital defect caused by the failure of the bones of the spine to grow together completely.

7. Thalidomide, a drug once taken by pregnant mothers, caused a large number of children to be born with physical defects in the late 1950s and early 1960s.

8. Some of the disabilities that can affect the vitality of children are congenital heart defects, cystic fibrosis, diabetes, asthma, and AIDS.

9. Epilepsy is caused by uncontrolled electrical discharges in the brain. The three primary types of seizures that result from epilepsy are generalized, absence, and partial seizures. Epilepsy can usually be controlled with medication.

10. Traumatic brain injury is a disability recently recognized by the federal government.

11. There are many abused and neglected children in special education programs. Teachers need to be particularly alert for signs of child abuse and neglect.

12. The great majority of children with physical disabilities can be educated in regular classrooms with the use of assistive equipment and special teaching aids.

13. Modern technology holds great promise in aiding people who have physical disabilities with communication, travel, and daily existence.

14. Standards have been developed to aid in the elimination of the architectural barriers encountered by persons with physical disabilities. Federal law now requires that all buildings, transportation, and public services be barrier-free.

TASK SHEET 11   Field Experiences with Persons with Physical Disabilities

Complete *one* of the following alternatives:

Building Accessibility Survey

Acquire a copy of the Accessibility Compliance Checklist included in the Ferrero and Fleming (1992) workbook, another appropriate checklist, or develop your own. Select a public building in your area and survey it for accessibility. Try to select a building that has been constructed relatively recently, since buildings constructed prior to the mid-1970s are less likely to be in compliance with accessibility standards. If you find areas out of compliance, try to talk to the building owner or supervisor. What was his or her reaction, and what problems did you encounter in your survey?

Program Visit

Arrange to visit an education program for children with physical disabilities. Describe the type of program that you visited, the physical setting, the assistive and adaptive equipment that was being used, the modifications that were made in the physical environment to adapt to the needs of the children, the type of lesson that you observed, and your general reaction to the program. If possible, interview the teacher and ask what types of problems he or she encounters in teaching children with physical disabilities. Describe what you learned and how you felt about the experience.

Professional Interview

Interview one of the following professionals: physical therapist; orthotist; director of a facility serving individuals with physical disabilities; affirmative action officer or person responsible for supervising accessibility at the public school, university, or hospital; anyone else who works with people who have physical disabilities. Describe whom you interviewed, the person's responsibilities, the problems the person encounters in performing the job, the type of training needed, what you learned from the interview, and how you felt about it.

Interaction with a Person with a Physical Disability

Arrange to help a person with a physical disability with a routine daily task such as traveling or shopping. Describe whom you helped, the activities you helped with, where you went, the problems you encountered, the adaptations that had to be made, and what you learned from the experience.

Agency Investigation

Write to three of the following agencies, inquiring about the services that they provide to people with physical or health-related disabilities. Write a three-page paper describing what you learned and how you as a professional might use their services.

Allergy Foundation of America
801 Second Ave.
New York, NY 10017

American Academy for Cerebral Palsy and
Developmental Medicine
1910 Byrd Avenue, Suite 110
Richmond, VA 23230

American Heart Association
7320 Greenville Ave.
Dallas, TX 75231

American Occupational Therapy
Association
1383 Piccard Dr.
Rockville, MD 20850

Architectural and Transportation
Compliance Board
1111 18th Street NW, Suite 501
Washington, DC 20036

Arthritis Foundation
1212 Avenue of the Americas
New York, NY 10036

Epilepsy Foundation of America
4351 Garden City Drive, Suite 406
Landover, MD 20785

Juvenile Diabetes Foundation
60 Madison Ave.
New York, NY 10010

March of Dimes Birth Defect Foundation
1275 Mamaroneck Ave.
White Plains, NY 10605

Muscular Dystrophy Association of America
3561 E. Sunrise Dr.
Tucson, AZ 85718

National Cystic Fibrosis Foundation
6931 Arlington Rd.
Bethesda, MD 20814

National Easter Seal Society
70 East Lake St.
Chicago, IL 60601

National Head Injury Foundation, Inc.
1140 Connecticut Ave., NW, Suite 812
Washington, DC 20036

National Rehabilitation Information Center
 (NARIC)
8455 Colesville Rd., Suite 935
Silver Spring, MD 20910-3319

Osteogenesis Imperfecta Foundation
P.O. Box 24776
Tampa, FL 33623

United Cerebral Palsy Association, Inc.
7 Penn Plaza, Suite 804
New York, NY 10001

Library Study

Select three articles concerning children with physical or health-related disabilities and write a one-page abstract of each, concluding with your personal impressions about the value of the article. Here are some journals in which you can find articles.

American Journal of Physical Medicine
American Journal of Nursing
American Journal of Occupational Therapy
Archives of Physical Medicine Rehabilitation
Assistive Technology
DPH Journal
Electronics
Engineer
Exceptional Children
Human Factors
Physical Therapy

Design Your Own Field Experience

If you prefer, design your own field experience and, after discussing it with your instructor, perform the designated tasks.

Individual Differences in Learning and Behavior

In the preceding section on communication and sensorimotor disabilities, many of the characteristics we described were shown to have educational implications. For example, a child who is legally blind and cannot read print will probably use braille, and a child with a profound hearing loss may use sign language. Among the disabilities discussed in this section, however, the disability category in which children are placed does not automatically have implications for their education. More important than the label is how the child performs in an educational setting. Children who cannot differentiate among initial consonants, for example, will often be taught with the same techniques, whether those children are labeled educable mentally retarded, learning disabled, or mildly behaviorally disordered. In fact, many children with sensorimotor disabilities will respond to regular teaching techniques, once their impairments and disabilities have been corrected to the greatest extent possible.

Despite such educational commonalities across the various disabilities, there are three reasons for dividing our coverage into separate categorical chapters. First, classification is a process scientists go through to organize and systematize information, permitting them to make useful statements about the phenomenon being classified. Thus, we have chosen to follow the common practice by presenting the material in these categories. We do try, however, to limit the use of certain terms frequently heard in special education circles, such as *neurotic, psychotic, dyslexic, minimal brain dysfunction, developmental retardation,* and so on.

Second, most public school programs use categories in their special education programs. For example, there are often separate classes for those with mild mental retardation,

learning disabilities, and behavioral disabilities. Also, we find that categorization is used at both state and local levels because it is traditional ("We've always done it this way"); because of funding ("You have to label the kids to get the money"); and because of certification practices ("I'm certified to teach the emotionally disturbed"). Fortunately, the categories for placing children in public schools are becoming more flexible. The current trend in state funding is to permit groupings based on educational variables. In addition, some states have moved to teacher certification that is noncategorical, or generic.

Third, many colleges and universities are still training teachers in categorical areas. Consequently, we must include chapters on the various categories if we hope to have special education departments adopt this text for use in their program.

Throughout the chapters you are about to read, we have tried to focus on specific behavior and learning characteristics that have relevance for education. While the material has been organized into categories, you will notice considerable overlap among the characteristics of children who have been categorized as mentally retarded, behavior disordered, learning disabled, or severely developmentally disabled. We believe this repetition will reinforce some of the major concepts.

A BEHAVIORAL ORIENTATION

The authors of the chapters in this section subscribe to the behavioral approach to instructing children with exceptionalities. The word *approach* is difficult to define, but it involves a way of thinking about a phenomenon, as well as the kind of theory used and the techniques or methods employed when teaching or providing other services. Although there is wide support for the behavioral approach, other paradigms are espoused and used by researchers and special education teachers. Many teachers draw on different parts of several approaches, depending on the demands of the task they are trying to accomplish. They do this in part because there are few data to support the contention that one approach is conclusively better than another. There is evidence that each of these approaches can be applied successfully, especially when used by devoted and resourceful teachers. A brief description of five approaches found in special education follows.

THE HUMANISTIC APPROACH. Advocates of this approach believe that children's problems are caused by psychological or emotional conflicts that interfere with the ways in which they try to understand or cope with their feelings and emotions. Many humanists also assert that children so affected cannot learn in traditional school settings and recommend that alternative school environments be developed. The school environment should be "open," with many opportunities for self-directed activity. Humanists believe that the teacher should be a friend to the students and should serve as a facilitator for the students' self-directed activities. More information on this approach is available in the classic work of Peter Knoblock (1973).

THE PSYCHODYNAMIC APPROACH. The psychodynamic approach is based primarily on the work of Sigmund Freud. Adherents to this philosophy believe that a person's actions are governed by unconscious impulses that were formed by the emotional atmosphere in which the person was reared. Problems that arise are considered the result of conflicts the individual went through during a previous stage of development. Psychodynamically oriented teachers would create a permissive environment in which children could act out their impulses. Accordingly, teachers would not try to change the behavior of children directly; rather, they would attempt to uncover the symbolic meaning of the behavior and help the children work through their conflicts. Bruno Bettelheim (1950, 1967) provides additional information on the psychodynamic approach.

THE PSYCHOEDUCATIONAL APPROACH. This approach is an outgrowth of the psychodynamic model. Proponents of both approaches search for the cause of behavior, but advocates of the psychoeducational model strive for a balance between psychiatric and educational concerns. Teachers who subscribe to psychoeducational thinking focus attention on the cognitive processes involved in learning and use diagnostic and educational techniques designed to evaluate and change these processes. Moreover, they favor structure in academics and set up highly individualized instructional programs. Carl Fenichel (1966) has written on how the psychoeducational approach can be applied in classrooms.

THE ECOLOGICAL APPROACH. Ecologists are concerned with how organisms interact with their environment. They contend that children with learning or behavior problems are out of balance with their ecosystem, and they believe that an imbalance in one part of the system affects all the other parts. The design of education or treatment programs must reflect, therefore, conditions in the family, school, community, and all other systems of which the child is a part, as well as the child's classroom. As will be seen in chapters in this section, the ecological approach can be combined with other approaches to education. More information about the ecological approach is available in the work of Nicholas Hobbs (1966, 1974).

THE BEHAVIORAL APPROACH. The behavioral approach is based on the work of B. F. Skinner. Behaviorists believe that all behavior is learned and that searching for the psychological causes of behavior is futile; instead, they focus their attention on behaviors that can be observed, measured, and recorded. Educational programs developed by behaviorists emphasize the modification of children's behavior by the manipulation of their environment, especially through altering the effects of particular behaviors. Because in recent years the influence of behaviorism on special education has perhaps been greater than that of any other approach, it is useful at this point to explore a bit further the salient principles of behaviorism. You can find additional information in books by Hewett (1968), Haring and Schiefelbusch (1976), Alberto and Troutman (1990), and Wolery, Ault, and Doyle (1992), all of whom provide good examples of the application of the behavioral approach in special education.

PRINCIPLES ASSOCIATED WITH THE BEHAVIORAL APPROACH

In describing the field of applied behavior analysis, Kerr and Nelson (1989) have listed several principles that are basic to its understanding and application. Principle number one is that behavior is controlled by its consequences. Some consequences increase or decrease the frequency of behavior while others maintain behavior. The other principles are as follows: behavior is strengthened by either positive or negative reinforcement; behavior is weakened by punishment and by removing consequences that have been associated with it; consequences must be applied consistently and immediately following the behaviors they are meant to influence; and modeling can strengthen, weaken, or maintain behavior.

Using behaviorism in special education is generally accomplished through intervention, therapy, or instruction—often collectively referred to as behavior modification or applied behavior analysis. There are many behavior modification procedures, and O'Leary and O'Leary recommend that they be considered in two groups: those intended to increase performance or behavior, and those intended to decrease performance or behavior (1972, p. 26). This dichotomy is somewhat arbitrary, but it does bring to the array of available procedures an order that allows the teacher to find an appropriate procedure quickly. Ready access to a proven procedure can be very important to teachers of children with severe behavior problems.

PROCEDURES USED TO "INCREASE" BEHAVIORS

Let us look at the procedures identified by O'Leary and O'Leary that are used to *increase* behavior (1972, pp. 26–31).

PRAISE AND APPROVAL. A positive response by the teacher to desired student behavior can increase the frequency of the behavior. The response could be verbal praise, gestures, giving the student a star, or some other expression of approval.

MODELING. Showing or demonstrating the desired behavior and then having the student repeat the behavior is an effective teaching technique. The results of modeling can be enhanced by using praise and other expressions of approval. Modeling can be done either by the teacher or by another student.

SHAPING. A teacher using a shaping procedure rewards successive approximations of the desired behavior, rather than waiting for the student to make a completely correct response. By rewarding successive approximation, the teacher helps ensure repeated success and keeps learners aimed in the right direction.

PASSIVE SHAPING. A passive shaping procedure is often used with children who cannot or will not imitate or model behavior. The teacher demonstrates the desired behavior and then actively helps the student imitate the behavior.

TOKEN REINFORCEMENT. This process involves the systematic use of either tangible reinforcers, such as food, tokens, or grades, or intangible reinforcers, such as a smile or praise from the teacher, to reinforce behaviors. Generally, a token reinforcement system, or "economy," involves (1) rules specifying which behaviors will be rewarded and which will not; (2) a system for issuing the token that does not disrupt the activity that is occurring; (3) a system for exchanging the tokens for tangible items, like prizes, or for special privileges.

SELF-SPECIFICATION OF CONTINGENCIES. Allowing children to participate in the selection of backup reinforcers in a token economy can significantly improve the economy's effectiveness. This procedure can also help the teacher determine what a particular child enjoys doing, and the teacher can often use this knowledge to encourage the child to do something he or she does not enjoy. For example, if reading is a low preference for a child but listening to records with earphones is a high preference, the teacher can make listening to records contingent on the child's reading appropriately. This is called contingency contracting.

PROGRAMMED INSTRUCTION. Several discrete steps are involved in this practice. The student is presented with relatively brief segments of content, is required to respond actively, and is given immediate feedback about performance on each step. The steps are progressively sequenced from lesser to greater difficulty, and the feedback information can be used in a task at the next level. Techniques using programmed instruction and task analysis have revolutionized some types of special education.

SELF-REINFORCEMENT. As the student becomes familiar with the token economy and the effects of appropriate behavior, behavior will gradually become influenced more by self-reward than by rewards from others. In addition, the student often begins to model the behavior exhibited by authority figures. If those figures have clearly defined high standards of performance, the student will often adopt similar standards. Although self-reinforcement is often thought of as the end result of successful behavioral programming, it does require specific attention from the teacher.

ESTABLISHING CLEAR RULES AND DIRECTIONS. In all the behavior modification procedures just described, it is important that rules and directions be stated clearly. The relationship between expectations and conditions for reward must be understood by both teachers and students. Developing contracts between teachers and students is common in many special education settings, because contracts permit classroom rules and directions to be altered to meet individual children's needs. Contracts can also be made with the entire class to help establish an effective learning environment.

PROCEDURES USED TO "DECREASE" BEHAVIORS

Now we examine some procedures for *decreasing* behavior, described by O'Leary and O'Leary (1973, pp. 32–38).

EXTINCTION. The extinction procedure involves selectively ignoring inappropriate behavior. Extinction has been used effectively in a wide variety of settings; it is especially effective when coupled with the reinforcement of appropriate behavior. However, some inappropriate behaviors (self-mutilation, aggressive acts) cannot be safely ignored.

REINFORCING BEHAVIOR INCOMPATIBLE WITH UNDESIRABLE BEHAVIOR. Reinforcement is often used with extinction. Basically, it involves analyzing the undesirable behavior to determine what behaviors would decrease the probability that the undesirable behavior would occur. For example, children being out of their seats without permission is undesirable. The teacher can generally decrease the frequency with which they leave their seats by (1) reinforcing the children when they remain seated, and (2) ignoring the children when they are out of their seats.

SOFT REPRIMANDS. Often, teachers use unobtrusive reprimands in conjunction with extinction. By keeping the reprimand between the teacher and the child, the teacher reduces the chances that the child will be reinforced by increased class attention.

TIME-OUT. This technique involves removing students to a position in which they cannot be reinforced in any way for a specified period of time. Time-out procedures may involve removing the child to an isolation room, changing the child's seat to a remote area of the classroom, or seating the child in a carrel or cubicle. The specific technique used is often determined by school policy and the availability of resources.

RELAXATION. Children who are easily frustrated, agitated, or angered often benefit from being taught how to relax. A relaxed child will often exhibit fewer symptoms of emotional or behavioral disorders than one who is not relaxed.

GRADUAL PRESENTATION OF FEARFUL STIMULI *IN VIVO.* A gradual process is frequently used to decrease or eliminate unrealistic fears or phobias. For example, a child who has a fear of school might first be placed in real-life *(in vivo)* situations that don't resemble school, then systematically brought into increasingly comparable situations and reinforced for appropriate behavior at each step along the way.

DESENSITIZATION. This procedure consists of completely relaxing individuals and then asking them to talk about situations that arouse anxiety. It has been found that after repeated sessions, clients are able to control anxiety or fears and maintain their relaxed state. The desensitization procedure is not commonly used with young children, but it has been used with considerable success with young adults and older individuals.

RESPONSE PROMPTING STRATEGIES. These procedures involve provisions for both giving and fading teacher assistance (i.e., prompts) to students to increase the probability that a targeted behavior will occur under the planned stimulus conditions, thereby allowing reinforcement of the targeted behavior or student response.

RESPONSE COST. Commonly used in contingency management or token economy programs, the response cost procedure involves establishing rules for removing or deducting tokens or rewards for inappropriate behavior. This type of system helps the children understand that a behavior can have either a positive or a negative consequence. Students quickly learn the effects of a particular behavior and begin to control ensuing acts.

This list of applied behavior analysis methods does not include all the procedures currently in use, but it does feature those most important in special education. These procedures, along with increased use of educational technology, have had a great impact on special education as it is practiced today.

Applied behavior analysis is a powerful tool for teachers. Because it is easy to misuse these techniques, all teachers should be sure they understand the principles and implications of behavioral methods. Applied behavior analysis is not used solely to eliminate undesirable behavior, as many people seem to believe. Rather, these techniques can be used quite effectively to help improve academic and social skills.

OVERVIEW

STUDENTS WITH MENTAL RETARDATION. In Chapter 12 we look at the nature of mental retardation, genetic and environmental causes, and major methods of prevention and treatment. New information on etiology and genetic counseling reflects current research. We also examine the learning characteristics of persons with intellectual disabilities and describe contemporary educational and service programs.

STUDENTS WITH SEVERE DEVELOPMENTAL DISABILITIES. Placing children with severe developmental disabilities in public schools is a relatively recent phenomenon that was brought about largely by federal and state litigation and legislation. In Chapter 13, we begin with a discussion of the diversity of characteristics of persons with severe developmental disabilities. The major issue of their educability is analyzed, and we devote attention to the process of educational assessment. We conclude the chapter with a look at contemporary service delivery options.

STUDENTS WITH LEARNING DISABILITIES. Children with learning disabilities are the largest group currently receiving special education services. We begin Chapter 14 with an introduction to the controversy surrounding the definition of learning disabilities and to the process of identifying children with learning disabilities. More detailed attention is then given to research findings about both effective and ineffective educational and treatment practices. We conclude with a look at implications for mainstreaming students with learning disabilities.

STUDENTS WITH BEHAVIORAL DISABILITIES. As with learning disabilities, controversy surrounds the definition and labeling of children with behavioral disabilities. After examining their characteristics, we go on to describe the classification and diagnosis of children with behavioral disabilities. Causes of behavioral disabilities are examined from both the biophysical and environmental perspectives. Educational and treatment options are our final topics.

STUDENTS WITH UNIQUE GIFTS AND TALENTS. The education of students who are gifted and talented has long been neglected. The reasons for this neglect and many of the misconceptions about this group of students serve as a basis for our discussion. Our look at characteristics and identification procedures of students who are gifted leads to a comprehensive description of educational provisions, trends in gifted education, and barriers to achievement. Of particular interest to special education teachers is the discussion of gifted children with disabilities.

COATESVILLE, Pa.—Joan Boundonna's death settled an argument. It was an argument other people were having about her life.

Boundonna, 47, who was mentally retarded, lived at Embreeville Center in Coatesville in southeastern Pennsylvania. She died July 16 after a hospital declined to give her the kidney dialysis deemed necessary to keep her alive.

A second hospital was considering accepting her but ultimately decided not to do so.

Doctors at both hospitals were against administering a very difficult treatment to a very difficult patient. Embreeville was fighting to keep her alive.

They could not ask Boundonna. She would not know what to tell them. She was mentally incapable of consenting to her own medical treatment.

"It was in the process of being debated," said Ronald Werrin, one of the physicians who treated Boundonna at Chester County Hospital.

The dilemma—how to treat people who cannot consent to their own medical care—is one of the tragic questions that haunt a place like Embreeville, a state institution for the mentally retarded.

The fact that she died has distressed the state Department of Public Welfare and advocates for the mentally retarded. State officials say they are investigating.

This story has emerged:

On July 2, Boundonna was given a routine medical checkup and found to be disturbingly anemic.

She was taken to nearby Chester County Hospital, where doctors discovered her kidneys did not function, Werrin said. The treatment was dialysis, which involves hooking up catheters connected to a machine for several hours.

The closest relative able to decide was an uncle who had not seen her in years. He did not approve, doctors and officials said.

On July 12, Embreeville successfully petitioned in court to become Boundonna's legal guardian. Eric Bost, Embreeville's interim director, then authorized the dialysis.

But doctors at Chester County resisted because Boundonna had some extreme behavior problems.

Werrin said she would have ripped out the catheters.

Embreeville then contacted officials at Hershey Medical Center and asked them to take Boundonna.

"First they said they'd take her, but not until July 15 because they didn't have a bed available," Bost said. "Then, on the morning of July 15, they called and said they couldn't take her and they didn't give us any reason."

But Mary Waybill, a physician at Hershey, said, "We said we would consider it, and ultimately it did not seem that we would be able to offer her anything that she could not get at Chester County Hospital."

Source: "Woman too retarded to approve treatment for kidneys dies" from the *Lexington Herald-Leader,* July 28, 1991. Knight-Ridder/Tribune News Service. Reprinted by permission.

12

Students with Mental Retardation

William H. Berdine

The vignette that opens this chapter may shock many. However, for those with any history of involvement in the field of mental retardation, whether as a layperson, a professional, or a person with mental retardation, this is not an unfamiliar set of circumstances—extreme in nature, perhaps, but certainly not a new phenomenon. What the vignette portrays is a continuation of the problem that service delivery agencies and individuals with mental retardation have had for decades, that problem being a shocking inability to achieve a level of effective communication in which a person with an intellectual disability is treated as an individual, not a *label* or *statistic*.

The fact that this type of circumstance occurs less frequently than a generation ago, and that federal and state legislation has been created to protect the civil liberties of persons with disabilities, does not ease the pain for individuals who may find themselves experiencing similar circumstances or events. That the events surrounding Ms. Boundonna's death are considered newsworthy by major news services is heartening. Perhaps with continued public exposure, more individuals will take interest and become advocates for equal rights for all persons, regardless of disability, disease, or the existence of handicapping conditions.

The opening vignette also reflects the need for new advocacy efforts by both laypersons and professionals working with persons exhibiting mental retardation. The new advocacy places considerable emphasis on community-based services. This position, which has evolved slowly over the past 20 years, reflects a shift in the emphasis of educational programs and services; early services focused exclusively on persons with mild retardation, whereas now the focus is on persons with severe and profound retardation who typically have multiple handicapping conditions. The process has not necessarily been an easy one for anyone involved. Out of this process, it is to be hoped, persons with mental retardation, regardless of educational classification, have gained a broader, more normalized, humane, and effective continuum of services.

What impact has advocacy had on legislation?

The shift of advocacy emphasis and prioritization of services to community-based programs and services is, to a large extent, due to the emergence of a nationwide lobby for persons classified as severely and profoundly retarded in their intellectual development. This

405

special education population entered the civil rights scene in the late 1970s through federal legislation such as Section 504 of the Vocational Rehabilitation Act of 1973 (PL 93-112) and the original Education for All Handicapped Children Act (PL 94-142) in 1975. These laws, and others described in Chapter 1, thrust the issues of equal protection of due process rights and access to public school education for all persons, *regardless of handicapping conditions,* into the public's awareness. Legislative support for change was found outside of special education. For example, the preface to the Vocational Rehabilitation Act of 1973 (PL 93-112) states that there should be a "special emphasis on services to those with the most severe handicaps." The highest priorities of PL 94-142 are on *serving unserved* children and on *serving the most severely handicapped who are underserved.* Later in the same decade, the Comprehensive Rehabilitation Services Amendments of 1978 (PL 95-178) stipulated that "Comprehensive services should be provided to handicapped persons who may not be ready for vocational rehabilitation" (Haywood, 1979, p. 430).

In the 1980s, significant landmark legislation was passed by the United States Congress, including the 1983 Rehabilitation Act and its 1988 Amendments, the 1983 (PL 98-199) and 1986 (PL 99-457) revisions of PL 94-142, and the 1984 Carl D. Perkins Vocational Education Act. The real significance of all this legislation is the clear direction of public policy: It has provided both fiscal resources and a legal mandate to provide public support services beyond the traditional school years, with emphasis on total habilitation across the entire life span of persons with mental retardation.

INTELLECTUAL FUNCTIONING AND MENTAL RETARDATION

You should be able to discuss intellectual assessment as it relates to the identification of children who are mentally retarded.

What considerations are important to educators in defining intelligence?

Knowledge of the current research on intelligence and its measurement provides a necessary perspective on understanding persons with intellectual disabilities or mental retardation. Within the twentieth century, several definitions of intelligence have been suggested (e.g., Bruner, 1964; Cattel, 1971; Guilford, 1956; Hebb, 1942; Piaget, 1950). These definitions have ranged from the simplistic "intelligence is what is measured by intelligence tests" to the complex conceptualizations of Guilford (1956), who proposed a structure that describes 120 types of intelligence; to Sternberg and Spear's (1985) triarchic theory of intelligence; and to Gardner and Hatch's (1990) concept of multiple intelligences.

For the special educator, it seems appropriate to define intelligence in terms of students' history of interactions with their environment, particularly those interactions that require or stress intellectual ability. Thus, intellectual capacity reflects how well they meet the demands made on them by their school, family, community, and other social institutions. A student who is consistently unable to meet those demands without some form of special assistance is likely to be considered intellectually disabled, incompetent, or, most commonly, mentally retarded. To be classified as mentally retarded, children must be unable to demonstrate behavior based on intellectual functioning that is appropriate for their age or social situation (Salvia, 1978).

How is intellectual incompetence different from other developmental impairments or behavioral deviance?

It is important to distinguish between intellectual incompetence and other forms of behavioral incompetence. For example, children who are blind may be incapable of performing some academic or motor tasks at the age considered normal for children with sight, but this is because they have a visual impairment, not an intellectual defect. The concept of incompetence is also important in distinguishing students who exhibit mental retardation from those with other forms of deviant interpersonal behavior. For example, children with mental retardation may be *willing* to perform tasks appropriate for their age but be *unable* to perform the tasks. At that particular time, they do not have the competence to perform the task. Other children may be *able* to perform the same task but be *unwilling* to do so as an act of social defiance or disobedience. In this case, the requisite competence is there, but the motivation is absent.

Identification and Assessment of Mental Retardation

For educational purposes, mental retardation is generally considered a person's inadequacy in performing certain behaviors that society values and that are appropriate for the individual's age group. Intelligence tests are used to assess the intellectual ability that theoretically determines whether a person can perform specified educational tasks. The forms of intelligence tests vary widely, but the majority are standardized (see Chapter 2 for a discussion of standardized tests). The test items are designed to determine the person's level for certain aspects of intellectual functioning. If a particular culture believes that the test measures qualities that are important for that culture, the tests become a generally accepted means of measuring intellectual functioning in that culture.

The most frequently used intelligence tests yield two types of scores, an intelligence quotient (IQ) and a mental age (MA). Most of the commonly used IQ tests are designed such that the average IQ is 100. In theory, this means that if a test such as the Wechsler Intelligence Scale for Children–Revised (WISC-R) (Wechsler, 1974) was administered to a large number of children, the test scores would range from very low to very high, but the average (or mean) score would be 100. If the scores were plotted on a graph, the result would be a bell-shaped curve, called a Gaussian or normal curve (see Figure 12-1).

A statistical computation yields a figure known as the standard deviation (SD), which can be used to determine where a person's score falls in relation to others in the population. For example, the standard deviation for the WISC-R is 15. If you look at Figure 12-1, you will see that one SD below the mean is 85. A person who receives a score of 100 on the

FIGURE 12-1   The Normal Curve

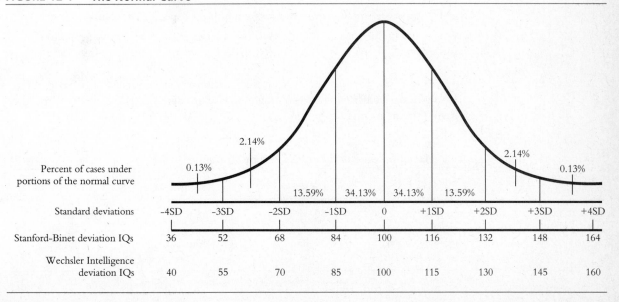

	-4SD	-3SD	-2SD	-1SD	0	+1SD	+2SD	+3SD	+4SD
Percent of cases under portions of the normal curve	0.13%	2.14%	13.59%	34.13%	34.13%	13.59%	2.14%	0.13%	
Standard deviations	-4SD	-3SD	-2SD	-1SD	0	+1SD	+2SD	+3SD	+4SD
Stanford-Binet deviation IQs	36	52	68	84	100	116	132	148	164
Wechsler Intelligence deviation IQs	40	55	70	85	100	115	130	145	160

WISC-R is average; about 50 percent of the population scored below that average and 50 percent scored above it. Between each pair of SD cutoff points is written the percentage of the population that falls between them. By starting at the left of the normal curve, an estimation of the number of people who fall below a particular score can be calculated by adding the percentages. Thus, the child who scored 85 would have a score that was higher than about 16 percent of the population and lower than about 84 percent. Conversely, a person who scored 115 would have a score that was higher than about 84 percent of the general population and lower than approximately 16 percent.

The scores shown in Figure 12-1 represent plus or minus 4 standard deviations from the mean (100). In theory, however, the scores could go into infinity, because intelligence does not have absolute limits. Intelligence is viewed by most developers of intelligence tests as a continuum of abilities, not as a discrete or finite entity.

SOCIAL ISSUES RELATED TO CUTOFF SCORES. The determination of a score below which children are considered mentally retarded is an issue of great social, political, and educational concern. Intellectual ability is generally considered socially valuable as long as it meets the standards of the majority or predominant cultural group. Similarly, the same cultural influence typically determines what will be considered normal intelligence. In special education, the IQ score of 70 adopted by the American Association on Mental Retardation (AAMR) is generally considered the score below which individuals are described as exhibiting mental retardation (Grossman, 1983).

Some variation in cutoff scores is found among different intelligence tests. For example, the standard deviation for the revised Wechsler Intelligence Scale for Children (WISC-R) is 15, and the cutoff for retardation is any score below 70 (Wechsler, 1974); whereas the revised Stanford-Binet (fourth revision, or S-B IV) has a standard deviation of 16, and the cutoff for mental retardation is any score below 68. Table 12-1 illustrates the cutoff scores established by the AAMR for different levels of mental retardation. Notice that the scores are different because of variations in the respective tests' standard deviations.

Problems with Using IQ Scores

The use of IQ test scores in education presents a number of specific problems:

1. To provide useful scores, a test must include a large enough normative group to reflect the cultural, social, and economic variables that affect the children in a given classroom.
2. The items in a particular test may measure a relatively small variety of behaviors. The IQ score derived from such a test should be considered in the context of the test items and the normative group.

TABLE 12-1   Level of Retardation Indicated by IQ Range

Level of Retardation	IQ Range	Stanford-Binet	Wechsler
Mild mental retardation	50–55 to 70	52 to 68	55 to 70
Moderate mental retardation	35–40 to 50–55	52 to 36	55 to 40
Severe mental retardation	20–25 to 35–40	36 to 20	40 to 25
Profound mental retardation	Below 20 or 25	Below 20 or 25	Below 20 or 25

Source: Adapted from H. Grossman (1983). *Manual on terminology and classification in mental retardation.* Washington, DC: AAMD, p. 13.

3. A test score may be inaccurate and may not reflect a person's actual level of intellectual functioning.

4. An IQ score should be considered only in conjunction with information about the child's chronological age and home life, the child's school and other environmental variables.

5. An IQ score is not very useful for planning the education of a particular child. The knowledge that one pupil has an IQ score of 69 and another has an IQ score of 75 does not help a teacher develop appropriate instruction.

How are the IQ scores of children with mental retardation used?

Educators should not overemphasize the importance of IQ scores. The major reason for assessing the IQs of children with mental retardation is related to determining their eligibility for special education services. In spite of the limitations in their use, intelligence test scores are one of the most reliable types of data on problem-solving abilities and intellectual functioning, and they will probably continue to be used in the diagnosis and assessment of mental retardation. Today, however, classification of mental retardation and determination of eligibility for special education services requires that IQ test scores be corroborated with assessment information on adaptive behavior functioning.

Measuring Adaptive Behavior

What is adaptive behavior?

The AAMR defines **adaptive behavior** as "the effectiveness or degree with which individuals meet the standards of personal independence and social responsibility expected for age and cultural group" (Grossman, 1983, p.1). The AAMR qualifies its definition by stating that "the quality of general adaptation is mediated by the level of intelligence." (Grossman, 1983, p. 42). This qualification clearly indicates that the two terms, adaptive behavior and intelligence, have a functional relationship. When the two terms are used by educators, it should always be kept in mind that the term *adaptive behavior* "refers to what people do to take care of themselves and to relate to others in daily living rather than the abstract potential implied by intelligence" (Grossman, 1983, p. 42). Few researchers question that intelligence and adaptive behavior are related. However, the relationship is not very well understood. Nevertheless, all diagnoses of mental retardation should take into careful account both current intellectual functioning and adaptive behavior.

What are the four levels of impairment in adaptive behavior?

The AAMR has historically recognized four levels of adaptive behavior impairment: mild, moderate, severe, and profound. Note that these degrees of impairment are described with the same terms used to describe levels of intelligence (as in Table 12-1). Adaptive behavior impairment is generally considered to be the result of problems in maturation, learning capacity, and social adjustment. Most assessment scales examine areas that special educators are familiar with, such as self-help (e.g., dressing), language and communication skills (e.g. writing a letter), self-direction and responsibility (e.g., doing a chore reliably), and relationships with others (e.g., playing with other children) (Helton, Workman, & Matuszek, 1982).

What are the problems in assessing adaptive behavior?

INSTRUMENT PROBLEMS. While the use of adaptive behavior assessment scales has become fairly routine for educational classification and placement purposes, their use is the subject of considerable debate. For example, one of the most widely used adaptive behavior assessment scales is the American Association on Mental Deficiency's Adaptive Behavior Scale–School Edition (ABS-SE) (Lambert & Windmiller, 1981). The ABS-SE has been questioned for its reliability, its validity, and the representativeness of its norm population (Helton, Workman, & Matuszek, 1982; Salvia & Ysseldyke, 1981). The 1981 version of ABS-SE does include wider norm population representation (from both California and Florida). However, the issues of reliability and validity have not been addressed and are still questioned. The criticisms leveled at the ABS-SE are representative of criticisms of most of the other adaptive behavior scales.

The major components of the AAMD's ABS-SE are outlined in Table 12-2. Design inadequacies in adaptive behavior scales have been a chronic problem over several decades for professionals responsible for diagnosis, identification, service planning, and classification in the various fields of mental retardation (Adams, 1973; Frankenberger, 1984; Patrick & Reschly, 1982; Robinson, 1980; Smith & Polloway, 1979; Zigler, Balla, & Hodapp, 1984). In spite of the design problems, the current ABS-SE is generally considered a major improvement over its 1975 predecessor, the ABS–Public School Version (Lambert, Windmiller, Cole, & Figueroa, 1975), and it is being widely used for both program placement and instructional planning.

CULTURAL PROBLEMS WITH ADAPTIVE BEHAVIOR MEASUREMENT. The issues of defining and agreeing on the composite of behaviors that are representative of a culture's adaptive behavior are particularly noteworthy. This is a problem shared by both intelligence tests and adaptive behavior assessment instruments. In both cases, a fundamental design concern is whether the normative populations are adequately representative of the general population, especially of smaller subcultural and cultural groups.

Reschly (1981) noted that when the two standard deviation cutoffs for both IQ and adaptive behavior are used, the prevalence of mental retardation for both African Americans and Native Americans dropped significantly. This evidence is not cited to advocate a change in the definition's dual requirements, but rather to note the continued need for research in finding valid ways to better correlate the two for diagnostic and classification purposes.

Probably the best example of an attempt to deal with cultural and pluralistic issues in the assessment of mental retardation can be found in the System of Multicultural and Pluralistic Assessment (SOMPA) (Mercer, 1979). While the SOMPA instrumentation is generally not used today, its accompanying Adaptive Behavior Scale for Children (ABIC) may still be of some value to special educators programming in a pluralistic and multicultural setting.

ABIC attempts to provide a nondiscriminatory assessment of public school-age children (ages 5–11 years) by collecting information in three different dimensions: children's medical circumstances, their social system, and their "pluralistic" abilities. The medical dimension is concerned with data relevant to pathology, disease, or any other body system dysfunction that might account for the person's behavior during the data collection. The social system dimension is concerned with the extent to which the person is currently meeting the expectations of the social system of which he or she is a member. The pluralistic dimension is essentially a measure of the person's ability to solve problems within that social system; it is intended to determine a person's potential for learning or current level of intelligence.

Altogether, ABIC includes 242 items covering the following six subscale areas: (1) family role performance; (2) community role performance; (3) peer group role performance; (4) nonacademic school role performance; (5) earner-consumer role performance; and (6) self-maintenance role performance. Data for ABIC are gathered through interviews with primary care givers (i.e., parents or legal guardians). Keeping Reschly's (1981) criticism in mind, the ABIC component of SOMPA may still be of interest to special educators working with Hispanics, African Americans, and Caucasians, who were represented in the SOMPA normative population.

PROBLEMS DUE TO LEGISLATIVE REGULATION. With the legal mandate to provide data on adaptive behavior as well as intelligence for classification purposes in the area of mental retardation, better assessment scales are needed. The 1983 revision of the Vineland Social Maturity Scale (VSMS) appears to have better reliability and validity as well as improved provisions for a representative norm population (Helton et al., 1982). However, for the

TABLE 12-2   Components of the AAMD Adaptive Behavior Scale–School Edition (ABS-SE)

Part One Domains	*Part Two Domains*

Domain 1
Independent functioning
    Eating
    Toilet use
    Cleanliness
    Appearance
    Care of clothing
    Dressing and undressing
    Travel
    Other independent functioning
	Domain 10
	Aggressiveness

Domain 2
Physical development
    Sensory development
    Motor development
	Domain 11
	Antisocial vs. social behavior

Domain 3
Economic activity
    Money activity
    Money handling and budgeting
    Shopping skills
	Domain 12
	Rebelliousness
	
	Domain 13
	Trustworthiness

Domain 4
Language development
    Expression
    Comprehension
    Social language development
	Domain 14
	Withdrawal vs. involvement
	
	Domain 15
	Mannerisms

Domain 5 Number and time	**Domain 16** Appropriateness of interpersonal manners
Domain 6 Prevocational activity	**Domain 17** Acceptability of vocal habits

Domain 7
Self-direction
    Initiative
    Perseverance
    Leisure times
	Domain 18
	Acceptability of habits
	
	Domain 19
	Activity level
	
	Domain 20
	Symptomatic behavior

Domain 8 Responsibility	**Domain 21** Use of medications
Domain 9 Socialization	

Source: N. M. Lambert and M. B. Windmiller (1981). *ABS-SE manual.* Monterey, CA: Publishers Test Service.

immediate future, a very real legal problem may exist. With the passage of PL 98-149, currently Part B of PL 94-142, the requirement that the condition of mental retardation be evidenced across *all settings* in which the person lives means that many persons now classified as mentally retarded would not meet the full criteria for such classification.

The most obvious example of this dilemma is found in the single largest classification of mental retardation, those diagnosed as mildly mentally retarded (conservatively comprising anywhere from 60 to 75 percent of the total population of persons classified as mentally retarded). This is the school population that the President's Committee on Mental Retardation (1970) referred to as the "six-hour retarded child," with reference to the time they typically spend in school. It was noted by that committee that these children, classified as mildly mentally retarded, are only classified as such because of their functioning in school and its academic environment. Once out of school, this population tends to disappear since there is typically no significant adaptive behavioral skill deficit.

More recently, MacMillan (1988) termed this same population the "stepchildren of special education," who continue to be underserved even though they are an established population within the context of special education services. Recently, concern has been voiced that the school-age population of students with mild mental retardation is reemerging as the "new educable mentally retarded" (Forness, 1985; Polloway & Epstein, 1985). Additional information is provided later in this chapter, under "The 'New' Population of Educable Mentally Retarded."

USING ADAPTIVE BEHAVIOR IN DEFINING MENTAL RETARDATION: A SUMMARY.
Strong cases for and against the use of adaptive behavior assessment (ABA) data to define mental retardation can be found in the current literature (Grossman, 1983; Reschly, 1981, 1988a; Zigler et al., 1984; Zucker & Polloway, 1987). One of the better balanced perspectives on the issues is provided by Patton, Beirne-Smith, and Payne (1990). They state: "Instead of being a criterion, ABA should play a supporting role in (a) justifying eligibility for individuals with IQs above 70; (b) questioning the certification of an individual with an IQ below 70 but with acceptable adaptive behavior skills; and (c) influencing placement and curricular decisions" (p. 62). This appears to be a workable compromise for the role of adaptive behavior assessment in defining and classifying persons with mental retardation. It offers practitioners options that will ensure that available services to the population of individuals traditionally identified as being mentally retarded will not be reduced.

PROBE 12-1   Intellectual Functioning and Mental Retardation

1. T F A diagnosis of mental retardation should never be made solely on the basis of an intelligence test.
2. The popularly used tests of intelligence generally report a summary of performance in the form of an _____ score.
3. The AAMR requires that a child's _____ be considered in diagnosing mental retardation.
4. What is the range of IQ scores for each of the following levels of retardation, according to the AAMR? (Do not use a particular IQ test as a referent.)
   a. Mild retardation
   b. Moderate retardation
   c. Severe retardation
   d. Profound retardation
5. T F The AAMR's Adaptive Behavior Scale (ABS) is the only adaptive behavior instrument that research has documented as being both reliable and valid for use with persons exhibiting mental retardation.
6. T F All IQ tests have a mean score of 100 and a standard deviation of 16.
7. List four problems related to the use and interpretation of IQ tests.
8. T F Special education teachers could not teach if they did not have the IQ scores of the children exhibiting mental retardation in class.
9. Define adaptive behavior.
10. SOMPA is a good example of what aspect of assessment for educational purposes?

MENTAL RETARDATION: DEFINITIONS, TERMINOLOGY, AND ISSUES

You should be able to define mental retardation.

What are acceptable components for a definition of mental retardation?

This chapter views mental retardation as representing one facet of a continuum of measurable intellectual behavior (i.e., an instance of the concept of human intelligence). Understanding the characteristics of the concept of mental retardation is essential for all who work with, provide services for, or care for persons with significant intellectual disabilities.

According to MacMillan (1982), a definition of mental retardation should meet three criteria: (1) all conditions that must be met for classification as mentally retarded must be specifically stated; (2) every person with retardation must share the elements described in the definition; and (3) those who are not classified as mentally retarded must fail to exhibit at least one element of the definition.

Contemporary Definitions of Mental Retardation

The development in the early 1900s of a standardized test of intelligence by Alfred Binet and Theodore Simon heralded a move away from a reliance on medical models to account for retardation and toward the measurement of human intellectual functioning. One of these movements is referred to as the *psychometric approach,* which evolved out of the work of Binet and Simon. This approach focuses on innate intelligence and problem-solving ability. The second approach, less well known by the lay public, is the *cognitive-developmental approach,* much of which is based on the theoretical works of Piaget, Vygotsky, and Werner. This approach focuses on innate human growth and development milestones. While the two approaches differ considerably in their theoretical underpinnings, Zigler, Balla, and Hodapp (1984) point out that both attempt to assess the same phenomena, namely, the formal cognitive structure and its information-processing features.

THE AMERICAN ASSOCIATION ON MENTAL DEFICIENCY (AAMD) 1983 DEFINITION.[1] Currently only one definition, developed by the American Association on Mental Retardation (AAMR), has fairly uniform acceptance among the educational, psychological, legal, and medical professions.[1] The AAMR definition has been revised frequently over the past four decades (Grossman, 1973, 1977, 1983; Heber, 1959, 1961). In its 1983 form, it represented a compromise between the interests of those who require statistical objectivity, such as IQ test scores, and those who require environmental performance data, such as adaptive behavior assessment. The 1983 AAMR definition of **mental retardation** is as follows:

> Mental retardation refers to significantly subaverage general intellectual functioning resulting in or associated with concurrent impairments in adaptive behavior and manifested during the development period. (Grossman, 1983, p. 1)

What are the key terms of the 1983 AAMR definition of mental retardation?

The key terms in the 1983 AAMR definition are defined by Grossman (1983) as follows:

- General intellectual functioning is operationally defined as the results obtained by assessment with one or more of the individually administered standardized general intelligence tests developed for that purpose.
- Significantly subaverage is defined as an IQ of 70 or below on standardized measures of intelligence. The adoption of a 2 standard deviation (SD) from the norm on a standardized test of intelligence from the historic 1 SD has had significant direct impact on school

[1]The American Association on Mental Deficiency (AAMD) adopted the revised title of the American Association on Mental Retardation (AAMR) in 1984. The acronyms AAMD and AAMR are used interchangeably throughout this text, depending on the particular date of the citation in question.

services. The new upper limit of 70 is intended as a guideline and could be extended upward depending on the reliability of the test used.

- Impairments in adaptive behavior are defined as significant limitations in an individual's effectiveness in meeting the standards of maturation, learning, personal independence, and/or social responsibilities that are expected for his or her age level and cultural group as determined by standardized clinical assessment scales.
- Developmental period is defined as the period between conception and the eighteenth birthday. Developmental deficits may be manifested by slow, arrested, or incomplete development resulting from brain damage, degenerative processes in the central nervous system, or regression from previously normal states due to psychosocial factors. (p. 1)

THE AMERICAN ASSOCIATION ON MENTAL RETARDATION (AAMR) 1992 DEFINITION. During the Future Issues and Challenges in Mental Retardation/Developmental Disabilities Conference held January 14, 1992, Polloway (1992) discussed the most recent revision to the AAMR definition of mental retardation. Polloway noted that the AAMR's Terminology and Classification Committee met over a period of approximately four years, investigating the need for a revision of the 1983 definition of mental retardation. The committee was composed of eight members representing the fields of special education, psychology, clinical psychology, rehabilitation, adult services, community adjustment, medicine, and law. As a result of their deliberations the following definition was adopted during 1992 by the AAMR's membership:

> Mental retardation refers to substantial limitations in certain personal capabilities. It is manifested as significantly subaverage intellectual functioning, existing concurrently with related disabilities in two or more of the following applicable adaptive skill areas: communication, self-care, home living, social skills, community use, self-direction, health and safety, functional academics, leisure, and work. Mental retardation begins before age 18. (Polloway, 1992, p. 8)

Polloway (1992) cautions that anyone using the definition must keep in mind that the 1992 definition continues the AAMR's movement away from the relative equity given to measurement of intellectual abilities and the measurement of adaptive behavior and skills. The AAMR's Terminology and Classification Committee recommends a flexible cutoff for mental retardation in the IQ 70–75 range. Additionally, the 1992 *Manual on Terminology and Classification* stresses the importance of "functionality" and particularly the importance of functioning across targeted adaptive behavior skill areas. Previous AAMR definitions did not target specific aspects of adaptive behavior as being critical for a classification of mental retardation. The 1992 definition targets the adaptive behavior skill areas of communication, self-care, functional academics, leisure, and work as they apply across a person's life span. Explicit in the 1992 definition of mental retardation are the following three key assumptions underlying application of the new definition:

- Specific adaptive disabilities often coexist with strengths in other adaptive skills or other personal capabilities.
- The existence of disabilities in adaptive skills occurs within the context of community environments typical of the individual's age peers and is indexed to the person's individualized needs for support.
- With appropriate supports over a sustained period, the life functioning of the person with mental retardation will generally improve.

Polloway (1992) additionally notes that the 1992 AAMR *Manual on Terminology and Classification* recommends that IQ scores *not be used for classificatory purposes* in designating four levels of mental retardation (i.e., mild, moderate, severe, profound). The 1992 manual recommends instead that adaptive behavior skills or functioning be used to differentiate between two

What is the 1992 AAMR definition of mental retardation?

classification levels, mild and severe, rather than the traditional four levels of mental retardation just mentioned.

How does the 1992 AAMR definition differ from the 1983 definition of mental retardation?

The key differences between the 1983 and the 1992 AAMR definitions are as follows:

- *Diagnosis.* The 1992 definition places greater emphasis on measuring the individual's adaptive behavior functioning in his or her community. The 1983 definition based eligibility on a minimum IQ score at least two standard deviations below the mean on a standardized test of intelligence.
- *Classification.* The 1983 definition stressed the use of adaptive behavior skills for the designation of functioning levels such as mild, moderate, severe, and profound mental retardation. The 1983 definition relied on the use of IQ scores and their respective standard deviation parameters. The 1992 definition calls for two levels of mental retardation, mild and severe. The two classifications are specifically linked to adaptive behavior functioning and not the four traditional levels based upon intellectual functioning or ability. Additionally, the bilevel classification system is based exclusively on adaptive skill disabilities and is not equated with educational placement or services.
- *Adaptive Behavior Measurement.* With regard to both diagnosis and classification, the 1992 definition targets specific aspects of adaptive behavior functioning for measurement (i.e., communication, self-care, home living, social skills, community use, self-direction, health and safety, functional academics, leisure, and work). In addition to exhibiting significantly subaverage intellectual abilities, an individual additionally must concurrently exhibit disabilities in two or more of these targeted adaptive behavior areas. The 1983 definition required that an individual classified as mentally retarded, in addition to meeting the minimum IQ criteria, exhibit concurrent impairments in adaptive behavior. The 1983 definition did not, however, identify critical areas of adaptive behavior.

The 1992 AAMR definition of mental retardation will certainly have a significant impact on the field of special education. The adoption of the 1992 proposed definition will further advance the attempts made in the field of mental retardation over the past several decades to move toward a more equitable involvement in community-based services and quality of life for persons with intellectual disabilities.

Alternative Definitions of Mental Retardation

What are two alternative definitions of mental retardation?

DEVELOPMENTAL RETARDATION. MacMillan (1988) notes that the term *developmental retardation* has emerged from research on early intervention with children at risk for school failure because of environmental factors; the term is a result of the influence of applied behavioral analyses of human growth and development. **Developmental retardation** describes the negative effects of certain environmental factors on normal human growth and development. This term found wide use in the research on the positive value of early intervention with children from environments that historically have resulted in children with measured decreases in expected cognitive and/or social skills (Ramey & MacPhee, 1986). Developmental retardation is frequently used as a synonym for mental retardation by professionals and laypersons wishing to avoid the use of what is perceived to be a more negative term.

BEHAVIORAL DEFINITION. Another approach to defining mental retardation has been referred to as *behavioristic, behavioral, naturalistic,* or *behavior analytical.* While not widely used, it is consistent with the theoretical underpinnings of this text with regard to effective methodology for changing behavior in a positive, predictable, and systematic manner.

The articulation of the first widely accepted behavioral definition is generally attributed to Bijou in the early 1960s. This approach shuns the use of terminology, methodology, or measurement of unseen and theoretical mental constructs. The behavioral definition of mental retardation as originally postulated by Bijou (1966) states: "a retarded individual is one who has a limited repertory of behavior shaped by events that constitute [his or her] history" (p. 2).

The essence of this definition is that the person's repertoire of behavior (i.e., responses available for interaction with others) is limited by historical factors or other events that have had an effect on the development of that repertoire. Thus, the person is not *inherently* mentally retarded. Implicit in the behavioral definition is the idea that the retarded repertoire is a learned phenomenon and therefore changeable. The behavioral approach is largely responsible for the notion that persons with developmental or mental retardation exhibit behavior that can be changed or modified through education and training.

The IQ Controversy Continues

Why do we continue to use IQ scores in education?

The emphasis in the AAMR's 1992 definition on the importance of adaptive behavior measurement, as well as its more liberal interpretation of an upper IQ limit (i.e., 70–75) for a classification of mental retardation, is significant for educators. Classification within the two proposed levels of mental retardation based upon the individual's adaptive behavior functioning will, for all intents and purposes, significantly limit the continued use of IQ testing and scores in educational decision making. Educators must develop procedures to ensure that this new flexibility of interpretation is not used to inappropriately place students into special education instead of more appropriate regular class services.

PROBE 12-2   Mental Retardation: Definitions, Terminology, and Issues

1. Paraphrase the 1983 definition of mental retardation used by the American Association on Mental Deficiency.
2. Paraphrase the 1992 definition of mental retardation proposed by the American Association on Mental Retardation.
3. The most widely accepted definition of mental retardation is that of the _____.

   a. APA   d. CEC
   b. AAMR   e. ABS
   c. AMA

4. What is Bijou's behavioral definition of mental retardation? For the special educator, what is the principle value of a behavioral definition of mental retardation?

PREVALENCE OF MENTAL RETARDATION

You should be able to identify the major factors and issues involved in determining the number of persons that are classified as mentally retarded.

The prevalence of individuals with mental retardation in society is difficult to determine accurately. An actual census would be prohibitively expensive. The process of obtaining accurate figures is complicated by differing definitions, public apathy, and the reluctance to label a child as mentally retarded. As a result of these problems, estimates are based on studies of various communities with the results extrapolated to cover the entire population. Many geographical, cultural, and social factors influence estimates. For example, MacMillan (1988) reports on a 1985–86 school-year survey of all 50 state and the District of Columbia covering children (birth–20) served in programs for persons with mental retardation under Chapter 1 (a federally funded remedial reading and language arts program). This survey found variation in prevalence of mental retardation ranging from a *high of 4.7 percent* in Alabama to a *low of .65 percent* in Alaska, California, and Nevada. The variation found in this survey further highlights the degree of variability in prevalence that is found across classifications of mental retardation among school-age children and youth.

METHODOLOGICAL FACTORS AFFECTING PREVALENCE. Substantive methodological problems in the collection and calculation of prevalence data have been documented (Patton, Beirne-Smith, & Payne, 1990; Westling, 1986). Four factors, all relating to the way assessment data are collected about individual subject differences, have been consistently found to affect prevalence data. The four factors are summarized in Table 12-3.

What data sources should be used in determining mental retardation?

BEST PRACTICE IN DETERMINING ELIGIBILITY FOR SPECIAL EDUCATION SERVICES. It is clear that neither an intelligence test score nor an adaptive behavior assessment score is comprehensive enough to be used as a sole criterion for determining that a child is mentally retarded. Not only would the use of a single measure be professionally unwise, but it is illegal under the provisions of PL 94-142. The best procedure is to use data from a variety of sources, including assessments of intelligence and adaptive behavior, anecdotal records from teachers, an analysis of the home and family situation, direct observation of the child's group and individual behavior in the classroom, and measures of school achievement.

Current Estimate of Mental Retardation

Although the actual number of individuals with mental retardation in the population is not known, the current consensus is that the "identifiable prevalence" is 1 percent whereas the "true prevalence" may be as high as 3 percent. In special education, the 3 percent prevalence figure is often attributed to the work of Mercer (1973), who noted that a one-dimensional definition of mental retardation (e.g., IQ scores only) might yield a prevalence rate approaching 3 percent. The use of a two-dimensional definition that includes both IQ and adaptive behavior, however, yields a prevalence rate of roughly 1 percent. This prevalence estimate is

TABLE 12-3   Major Factors Affecting Prevalence Determination

Methodological differences: Variations due to differences in how data are collected through traditional collecting procedures (i.e., census versus survey, case management, personal interview)

Gender differences: Variations due to gender differences associated with X chromosome biological or body systems defects as reflected prenatally or as birth defects (more male expression of X chromosome anomalies); societal/cultural expectations and differences for males and females.

Age differences: Variations due to school-age versus post-school-age (adulthood) differences; societal/cultural expectations, and impact of federal legislation.

Socioeconomic differences: Variations due to ethnic/cultural differences; impact of federal legislation and related sociopolitical activity; relative ability of communities to provide services with existing resources.

based on the work of Tarjan, Wright, Eyman, and Keeran (1973). The 1 percent prevalence figure means that about 1000 people in a city of 100,000 are mentally retarded. This figure has been corroborated in studies conducted by Birch, Richardson, Baird, Horobin, and Illsley (1970); Heber (1970); and Mercer (1973), who actually conducted a census of a city with a population over 100,000 people.

As noted earlier, determining prevalence figures for persons with mental retardation can be both complex and difficult. The U.S. Department of Education (1989) reported a mental retardation prevalence figure of 1.21 percent of the school-age population between 6 and 17 years of age. This figure of 1.2 percent is considerably lower than the 2.27 percent figure that department consistently used in the past. In this same 1989 report to Congress, the U.S. Department of Education estimated that 15 percent of all the school-age children classified as handicapped were individuals with mental retardation. McLaren and Bryson (1987) provided a review of epidemiological research in this area and report the prevalence of mental retardation according to IQ (see Table 12-4). The reader is cautioned that these estimates are subject to variability based on the dates in which the prevalence data were collected, as well as the factors just outlined regarding problems in determining prevalence.

IMPACT OF ETHNICITY AND RACIAL MINORITY GROUP OVERREPRESENTATION. The problem of overrepresentation of ethnic or racial minority groups in the mild mental retardation classification has been documented by Reschly (1988b). Where overrepresentation of a recognized minority group is found, Reschly (1988b) cautions that concerned individuals first examine the statistics documenting the overrepresentation, and second, examine the school system's referral, assessment, and placement processes.

In looking at the statistics documenting overrepresentation, three indices need to be identified: percentage of program by ethnic group, percentage of total student population by ethnic group, and percentage of ethnic group in the program. Reschly (1988b) notes that in the landmark litigation of *Larry P. v. Riles* (1972) (through which it was established that no African American student may be placed in a class for children with mild mental retardation solely on the basis of an IQ test), the school program for students classified as mild mentally retarded (MMR) was 25 percent African American. However, only 10 percent of the total student population was African American. Furthermore, Reschly notes that at the time of the trial, only 1 percent of the MMR population under investigation was African American. While African Americans were overrepresented in the *Larry P.* case, their actual numbers were relatively small.

To avoid such ethnic overrepresentation, careful attention must be paid to the concept of *equal treatment*. Equal treatment refers to the notion that given the same behaviors, diagnosis, assessment data, or disabilities, the same decisions are made at the referral, assessment, and placement steps, regardless of race or ethnicity of the student (Lerner, 1981; Reschly, 1988c).

TABLE 12-4   Prevalence of Mental Retardation According to IQ

Mild mental retardation: (IQ = 55–69): 3.7 to 5.9 per 1000
(Fishbach & Hull, 1982)

Moderate mental retardation: (IQ = 40–54): 2.0 per 1000
(Fishbach & Hull, 1982; McQueen, Spence, Garner, Pereira, & Winsor, 1987)

Severe mental retardation: (IQ = 25–39): 1.3 per 1000
(Fishbach & Hull, 1982; McQueen, Spence, et al., 1987)

Profound mental retardation: (IQ = less than 25): 0.4 per 1000
(Baird & Sadovnick, 1985; McQueen et al., 1987).

IMPACT OF FEDERAL LEGISLATION AND AAMR POLICY CHANGES. Considerable variability and change in estimates of prevalence can be expected because of the legislative mandates that have affected the process of identifying and serving individuals with developmental disabilities and handicapping conditions (e.g., PL 94-142) and that have enhanced their visibility by expanding the age ranges for those services (PL 99-457 and PL 89-313). Not only do these legislative acts mandate additional special education services for all individuals with disabilities, they support—and in many respects call specifically for—the use of adaptive behavior functioning and its measurement as an integral part of determining eligibility. The 1992 AAMR definition of mental retardation specifically relies on the use of adaptive behavior measurement for classification purposes. It can be expected that this strengthened mandate to use adaptive behavior measurement data will make estimating the prevalence of mental retardation somewhat more difficult. The reader is referred to our earlier discussion of adaptive behavior and problems with its reliable and valid measurement.

PROBE 12-3   Prevalence of Mental Retardation

1. Which of the following may negatively affect attempts to accurately estimate prevalence of mental retardation?

   a. Geography
   b. Cultural background
   c. Social status
   d. All of the above
   e. None of the above

2. List three methodological factors that may affect prevalence estimates of mental retardation.
3. The identifiable prevalence of mental retardation is estimated to be _____.

   a. 5%   d. 3%
   b. 1%   e. 10%
   c. 2.9%

4. The true prevalence of mental retardation is estimated to be _____.

   a. 5%   d. 3%
   b. 1%   e. 10%
   c. 2.9%

5. T   F   Recent legislative and AAMR emphasis on using adaptive behavior data for diagnosis and classification in mental retardation poses no problems for estimating mental retardation.

CLASSIFICATION SYSTEMS FOR PERSONS WITH MENTAL RETARDATION

> You should be able to describe the current classification systems used in the field of mental retardation and the major educational and developmental differences within each.

Issues in Classification Systems

Over the years a number of systems have been used to classify school-age children with mental retardation. It is generally believed that classification is both a necessary and useful practice because persons with mental retardation are such a heterogeneous group. For one thing, classifying those with common characteristics within categories makes communication among professionals more productive. Also, classification should facilitate placement in appropriate, and therefore the most effective, treatment and educational programs. However finding agreement on how to accomplish these tasks is not easy.

Over the past century, three primary systems of classification of mental retardation have emerged—systems based on *etiology,* on *clinical type,* and on *severity of symptoms.*

Classification According to Etiology

Professionals in the field of mental retardation have long argued over determining causes and their role in classification. Much of this discussion stems from the so-called *Nature-Nurture* debate that has been waged for decades, over the relative impact of genetic endowment (Nature) as compared to, or contrasted with, that of an individual's environment (Nurture).

It is generally believed that an individual's genetic endowment (genotype), as provided by the parents, accounts for anywhere from 50 to 80 percent of the variation found in IQs (Thiessen, 1972; Willerman, 1979; Zigler et al., 1984). This variation in IQ is most often manifested in individuals with IQs in the 50s and above. For those individuals with IQs in the 50s and below, it is more typical to find evidence of some form of maternal problem, such as maternal toxicity during pregnancy, or organic dysfunction of the individual in question, such as tuberous sclerosis, that appears to account for the failure of the individual's genetic inheritance to be fully or positively expressed.

While variation in IQ in the lower classifications may not be as widely found, the reasons for this are not well documented. Some of the reduced variation may be due to relatively fewer numbers of persons with IQs below 50. Additionally, inadequacies of current standardized tests of intelligence for use with persons with atypical or dysfunctional communication may account for less variation in IQ in the classifications of mental retardation below the IQ of 50.

At different periods it has been fashionable to classify children with mental retardation according to the etiology (or cause) of their retardation. A number of etiological classification systems have simply divided the children into two groups: those for whom a cause of the retardation could be identified, and those for whom a cause could not be identified. Some of the terms used during the past 50 years to classify known and unknown etiologies are given in Table 12-5. The language and terminology provide some insight into relative progress with regard to the adoption of negative labels in classification systems for persons with mental retardation.

These early etiological classification systems were of little value for educational purposes and were often considered offensive by parents. Imagine being told that your child had "garden-variety mental retardation," or that his or her retardation is due to a family genetic inadequacy or problem.

The *cultural-familial* classification, while not widely used by educators, is still used by some psychologists and social workers who believe that mental retardation is often caused by a combination of environmental and hereditary factors. The term *psychosocial disadvantaged* has become more commonly used by special educators and professionals working in the field of mental retardation. Regardless of terminology or vocabulary used, this view of mental retardation derives from a concept called the *interaction hypothesis.* The interaction hypothesis is based on the assumption that mental retardation of unknown origin is caused by a combination of biological weaknesses and environmental deprivation.

What role does etiology play in classification systems?

What is the interaction hypothesis?

TABLE 12-5   Known and Unknown Etiology of Mental Retardation

Known Etiology		Unknown Etiology	
Extrinsic	Tredgold, 1936	Intrinsic	Tredgold, 1937
Pathological	Lewis, 1933	Subcultural	Lewis, 1933
Exogenous	Strauss & Lehtinen, 1947	Endogenous	Strauss & Lehtinen, 1947
		Garden Variety	Sarason, 1953
		Cultural-familial	Zigler, 1967

Source: Donald L. MacMillan (1982). *Mental retardation in school and society* (2nd ed.). Tab. 2-2. Copyright © 1982, Donald L. MacMillan.

Almost all cases of cultural-familial mental retardation are found in severely economically depressed communities, and many professionals attribute them to the effects of malnutrition and other dietary problems in combination with the psychological effects of poverty. The results of research into the effects of sociocultural factors on intellectual performance are inconclusive. However, the data show that environmental factors such as poverty can seriously affect the intellectual development of children, and there is some evidence that heredity sometimes limits intellectual development. The child's environment clearly influences whether he or she achieves maximum hereditary potential, a fact that has significant implications for early childhood and parent education.

It is still most common for professionals working with persons classified as mentally retarded to use classification systems based almost exclusively on IQ (Smith & Polloway, 1979; Zigler et al., 1984). Until recently, individuals were still classified as being mentally retarded according to etiology by major national professional service and advocacy organizations, such as the American Association on Mental Retardation. The 1983 AAMD *Manual on Terminology and Classification in Mental Retardation* listed ten medical classifications, including those based on the following causes: infections and intoxicants, trauma (injury), metabolism or nutrition, brain disease, conditions due to unknown prenatal influence, chromosomal abnormality, gestational disorders, psychiatric disorders, environmental influences, and others. The last category, "other," reflects the continued inability of the medical sciences to determine the cause of all possible dysfunctions.

The study of causes of mental retardation has historically revolved around debates over single versus multiple etiological factors and how they result in persons with various levels of mental retardation. Debate continues, but some significant changes are occurring. For instance, historically, many professionals have expressed the belief that the more severe mental retardation classifications could typically be accounted for by a single pathological event or cause. However, McLaren and Bryson (1987) note that when attempting to identify persons with mental retardation classified in the moderate to severe range (IQ below 50), only 60 to 75 percent of the population demonstrate an identifiable pathological etiology. This leaves a rather large proportion of this classification (25 to 40 percent) with either no known cause or multiple causes, rather than a single causative factor.

Furthermore, in the mild mental retardation classification (IQ between 50 and 69), where multiple organic (including environmentally induced) causes have long been thought to be the major etiological factors, the data are beginning to note single causative or etiological factors. McLaren and Bryson (1987) report that 25 to 40 percent of all individuals classified in the mild mental retardation range have an identifiable etiology or cause for their disabilities.

Classification According to Clinical Type

Individuals with mental retardation may also be classified according to the clinical type of their retardation. In this classification system an attempt is made to separate the symptoms of the retardation from its causes. Like etiological classifications, clinical type classification systems are used primarily by physicians.

The cause of a particular clinical type of retardation may or may not be known. What is more, it is possible that within a given clinical classification, the causes of some children's retardation will be known and the causes of the retardation of others unknown. For example, some types of cretinism (a thyroid deficiency) are caused by genetic problems, and other types are caused by a chronic lack of iodine in the diet. Children with both types exhibit similar symptoms, making the identification of the cause difficult.

What is a syndrome?

A *syndrome* is a cluster or constellation of symptoms. Perhaps the most common involving mental retardation is Down syndrome, which is discussed in the section on genetic irregularities.

Systems that classify children according to clinical type are generally of little use to educators. Most children for whom this classification system is appropriate have distinct physical symptoms that are readily observable by the physician or diagnostician.

Classification According to Severity of Symptoms

What is the most widely used classification system for individuals with mental retardation?

The 1987 survey data by Utley, Lowitzer, and Baumeister (1987) indicate that no one system of classification has a clear edge on use across the various professional fields that provide services to persons with mental retardation. The 1983 four-level classification system of the AAMR is probably the system most widely used by diagnosticians, research organizations, the courts, and legislators, although terminology varies. For example, the term *handicapped* is frequently substituted for the term *retarded*. *Mildy retarded* is frequently interchanged with *educable mentally retarded* or *handicapped*. The terms *moderately retarded* and *trainable mentally retarded* (or handicapped) are also frequently used interchangeably. Many organizations combine the *severely* and *profoundly mentally retarded* (or handicapped) classifications into one—severely/profoundly mentally retarded (or handicapped), or S/PR (S/PH)—and use a three-level classification system of EMR, TMR, and S/PR.

This text delineates severe/profound intellectual disabilities as a component of the field of mental retardation. Persons with severe/profound multiple disabling conditions, which may or may not include mental retardation, are dealt with separately in Chapter 13. Table 12-6 outlines some of the major demographic and observational differences in the classifications of mental retardation most widely used in the United States.

The "New" Population of Educable Mentally Retarded

Are there new classifications of mental retardation?

As noted earlier, a "new" educable mentally retarded (EMR) population may have been created. Members of the so-called new EMR population are different from their historical namesakes in prevalence, in their primary learning problems, in the type of school services

TABLE 12-6   Major Demographic and Observational Differences of Mental Retardation

Level of Retardation	Communication Skills	Physical Dimensions	Social Adjustment	Independent Functioning	Occupational/ Vocational Level	Academic Performance
Mild	Ability to listen and speak effectively Can carry on an involved conversation May have difficulty understanding some concepts and vocabulary Restricted expressive vocabulary	No major problems	Interactions with others are reasonably acceptable Some social skill deficiencies	Self-supporting	Good potential for competitive employment	Can achieve academic competence and literacy
Moderate	Can carry on simple conversations Problems in listening and speaking are likely	Some motor and health problems	Can interact with others but may be awkward Friendships possible	Can master self-help skills Typically live in supported settings May require financial support	Can gain employment in competitive or supported settings	Survival and functional skills can be learned
Severe	Can understand very simple communication Limited verbal skills May use nonverbal techniques (e.g., gestures, sign language)	Typically have significant motor and health problems	Social interactions may be limited	Need certain amount of assistance with daily activities	Employment possible for some Typically found in sheltered settings but can perform in support settings	Focus on functional needs Can acquire requisite self-help skills
Profound	Communication skills are very limited, if they exist at all Often communication is through nonverbal sounds No effective speech	Few useful motor skills May be medically fragile	May be nonexistent	Totally dependent	Employment or training not likely	Focus on basic skills such as attending, positioning

Source: From *Manual on Terminology and Classification in Mental Retardation* by H. Grossman, 1983. Reprinted by permission of the American Association on Mental Retardation.

they need, and perhaps in their cultural and racial makeup. Forness (1985) examined available federal school census data for the school years 1976–77 through 1981–82 and found a 17 percent reduction in the number of children classified as mentally retarded at all levels. During this same period, Forness found a 104 percent increase in the school population identified as learning disabled (LD). Similar significant reductions in the numbers of students classified as mildly mentally retarded were found by Polloway and Smith (1983), with a decrease of 12.9 percent between 1976–77 and 1980–81.

The new population of EMR also appears to present a different learner's "portrait" than historical counterparts. First, the new students present more significant behavioral problems, such as attentional deficits (Polloway, Epstein, & Cullinan, 1985). MacMillan and Borthwick (1980) describe the new EMR population as being "a more patently disabled group" (p. 155) than was served in EMR programs prior to major landmark litigation (i.e., *Diana v. State Board of Education* [1970] and *Larry P. v. Riles* [1972]) that severely curtailed the sole use of standardized tests of intelligence for special education placement.

As early as 1980, MacMillan and Borthwick noted that, because of the new population of EMR's "lower functioning level," they were "unmainstreamable." Similarly, Polloway, Epstein, Patton, Cullinan, and Luebke (1986) found that few students with the new EMR classification would spend more than 50 percent of their school day in a mainstream class setting. While the research data are not overwhelmingly clear, it appears that the new EMR population is mostly comprised of individuals in the lower end of the mild mental retardation range (IQ from 55 to 69) (Gottlieb, 1981). Polloway, Epstein, and Cullinan (1985) describe this group as being more likely to exhibit serious behavior disorders such as attention deficits, thereby compounding their problems in any learning environment.

An additional significant difference between the new EMR population and the same special education classification one or two generations earlier is found in their racial and cultural makeup. In 1982, one year before the AAMD changed to a 2 SD below the mean criterion for mental retardation, Heller, Holtzman, and Messick (1982) confirmed that while Hispanic populations were becoming less disproportionately represented in special education, African Americans were becoming increasingly overrepresented. Brady, Manni, and Winikur (1983) reconfirmed these findings of disproportionate overrepresentation of African Americans in special education programs. Also, African American children tend to test in a lower IQ range than their Caucasian counterparts referred for special education (Flynn, 1984). Speculation as to why this disparity occurs abounds among both professional and laypersons. MacMillan (1988) noted that the reasons for the disparity in representation may lie in the reluctance many teachers may have to refer African American children for special education services, so that those who *are* referred tend to be those with the more obvious learning disabilities and educational handicapping conditions.

It is critical that decisions about the classification of children as being mentally retarded be made cautiously. Children should be classified only when that classification leads to the development of an appropriate educational program that will meet their needs.

PROBE 12-4   Classification Systems for Persons with Mental Retardation

1. List the three major systems used to classify children as being mentally retarded.
2. Match the acronyms to the traditionally used classification terms.

_____ Severely/profoundly retarded   a. EMR
_____ Moderately retarded   b. TMR
_____ Mildly retarded   c. S/PR

3. Cite two problems in the use of classification systems for children with mental retardation.
4. Define *syndrome* as used in genetic research.
5. T F Children exhibiting mental retardation should be classified only when classification leads to the development of an appropriate educational program.

CAUSES AND PREVENTION OF MENTAL RETARDATION

You should be able to describe the major causes of mental retardation.

While the cause of mental retardation has little relevance in planning an educational program, teachers do encounter medical terms and diagnostic labels in diagnostic reports and should be able to answer the questions of parents and other laypeople. Knowledge of causes makes a teacher a better-rounded professional, even if the information is not directly applicable to teaching.

More than 250 causes of mental retardation have been identified. It's hard to believe, but these account for only about 10 percent of the cases of mental retardation, with the remaining 90 percent having unknown causes (Maloney & Ward, 1979).

Genetic Irregularities

What are the basic functions of genes?

Genes are the basic units of heredity. They direct and control the processes of growth and development that occur in each of the body's cells. A defect in a gene can interrupt the biochemical processes that occur in the cells, which can in turn affect certain physical and mental characteristics.

The **genes** are located in **chromosomes,** of which every body cell has 46. At the moment of conception, 23 chromosomes from the male sperm and 23 from the female ova are combined to form a new cell of 46 chromosomes, which then begins to divide and ultimately forms a new human being.

What is the difference between dominant and recessive genes?

The genes are arranged along the chromosomes almost like matched strings of beads. When the chromosomes pair up at conception, the genes from both parents that relate to eye color, hair color, and so forth are matched up with one another. A **dominant gene** generally determines a characteristic, regardless of the gene that it is matched up with on its paired chromosome. A **recessive gene** determines a characteristic only when it is matched up with a similar recessive gene on its paired chromosome. If two recessive genes do not match up, the offspring will not exhibit the trait that they are responsible for; in that case, however, the offspring will be a carrier of the trait and may pass it on to future offspring if the recessive gene does match up with a recessive mate.

DOMINANT GENE DEFECTS. Fortunately, mental retardation caused by single defective dominant genes is quite rare. Conditions such as tuberous sclerosis and neurofibromatosis are caused by dominant genes and typically result in severe mental retardation. However, these conditions are rare because the parents have the disorder themselves, and they frequently cannot pass on the traits because of sterility or lack of opportunity (Telford & Sawrey, 1977).

What are some of the problems that can be caused by recessive genes?

RECESSIVE GENE DEFECTS. Sometimes children with mental retardation are born to seemingly normal parents. This is often the result of the inheritance of matching recessive genes from the child's parents. Recessive genes can cause problems in metabolism, endocrine disturbances, and cranial anomalies, any of which can result in retardation. These conditions are, however, relatively rare, and actual incidence figures are probably not available.

Phenylketonuria (PKU) is a recessive gene disorder that affects the metabolism of proteins. PKU can be identified in infants by a simple blood test that should be routinely administered shortly after birth. The probability that the disorder will result in retardation can be reduced through a diet low in phenylalanine, one of the amino acids. There are several conditions that affect the metabolism of proteins, but discussion of these is beyond the scope of a survey chapter; for more information, the reader is referred to the extensive treatment by Koch et al. (1988).

Another recessive gene disorder is **galactosemia,** a condition that affects the metabolism of carbohydrates. If this disease is detected before brain damage has occurred, retardation can be prevented with a milk-free diet. Several other disorders of carbohydrate metabolism can also cause retardation (Telford & Sawrey, 1977).

Tay-Sachs disease affects the metabolism of fats; it is most prevalent in Jewish families but also occurs in other populations. This disease can cause paralysis, blindness, and convulsions; it usually causes death by the time the child is 3 years old (Robinson & Robinson, 1976).

Cretinism, a disorder of the endocrine system, is characterized by lack of the thyroid hormone. Although this condition is sometimes caused by recessive genes, it can also be caused by a diet that is chronically deficient in iodine. Early treatment with thyroxin can prevent some of the physical symptoms associated with cretinism, but persons with this disorder are almost always mentally retarded (Robinson & Robinson, 1976).

Microcephaly is one of several cranial disorders that can be caused by recessive genes. Children with microcephaly are generally short and have small skulls, curved spines, and rather severe retardation. This condition can also be caused by nongenetic factors, such as the exposure of the mother to excessive dosages of x-rays during pregnancy (MacMillan, 1982).

What are the most common conditions involving chromosomal aberrations?

What is Down syndrome?

CHROMOSOMAL ABERRATIONS. Some cases of mental retardation are associated with conditions that result from chromosomal irregularities. Two of these conditions, Down syndrome and Fragile-X syndrome are discussed in this section.

Down Syndrome. Mental retardation is occasionally caused by improper cell division, which can result in an anomaly—cells that have an abnormal structure. The most common condition involving such an anomaly is **Down syndrome.** The term *syndrome* means a constellation or cluster of symptoms. Down syndrome used to be called *mongolism,* primarily because children with this symptom have almond-shaped eyes that slightly resemble those of the Mongol race.

Etiology of Down Syndrome. Children with Down syndrome have three number 21 chromosomes (called trisomy-21). These children constitute about 10 percent of the moderately-severely retarded population. The risk of having a child with Down syndrome is generally believed to be related to the age of the mother. For example, between the ages of 20 and 30, the statistical probability or risk is 1 in 1500, and at age 45, around 1 in 30. There is some evidence that in approximately 25 percent of the cases of Down syndrome, the father contributes the extra chromosome (Abroms & Bennet, 1980). The paternal contribution, however, has not been widely documented or accepted by medical or genetic research (Carlson, 1984). In all instances, Down syndrome is identifiable during the first 12 to 15 weeks of pregnancy by either amniocentesis or chorionic villus sampling (CVS). However, in those instances where undiagnosed twins exist, Tucker (1978) notes that amniocentesis will only detect Down syndrome in one twin. Both amniocentesis and CVS are discussed later under "Early Detection of Chromosomal Irregularities."

  Behavioral and Learning Characteristics of Persons with Down Syndrome. Until recently, it was a fairly commonly held assumption among medical and educational professionals that persons with Down syndrome would almost always test in an IQ range indicative of moderate to severe mental retardation. Rynders and Horrobin (1990) report databases that now challenge the assumption that school-age persons with Down syndrome are "always trainable and never educable." These authors cite the growing body of early intervention longitudinal research efforts, with findings that have only recently been reported in professional journals. Specifically, Rynders and Horrobin describe the results of four early intervention studies involving young children with Down syndrome that have implications for special education classification. The four longitudinal studies are Buckley and Wood (1983, as cited in Buckley, 1987); DuVergeas (1984, as cited in Dmitriev, 1988); Pieterese and Treloar (1981, as cited in Lane & Stratford, 1987); and Rynders and Horrobin (1990). All four studies investigated the impact of a variety of early intervention methodologies (e.g., behavior modification, structured play, integrated programming with regular education, home-based programs with parent teachers) on reading, language, and preacademic or academic skill development.

  According to Rynders and Horrobin (1990), the data from the four studies support other research that has indicated that children with Down syndrome who experience early education intervention frequently score in the educable range on any of several well-documented IQ tests (e.g., Stanford-Binet, Wechsler, Griffiths' Developmental Scale). However, Rynders and Horrobin further note that the studies also support earlier findings (Carr, 1987) that as the chronological age of children with Down syndrome increases, there is a concomitant annual decrease in IQ score.

  The implications of these apparently contradictory findings are significant for parents concerned about appropriate early school placement of their child with Down syndrome. Rynders and Horrobin (1990) suggest that an IQ in the educable range may be sufficient data to request placement in a classroom with other students classified as educable mentally retarded; however, the fact that the IQ of children with Down syndrome often decreases with age exposes the problem with making such a decision solely on the basis of IQ.

  Rynders and Horrobin (1990) recommend that *early education* (not necessarily just *special education*) class placements be determined using IQ scores in conjunction with educationally relevant performance indices. These would include adaptive behavior assessment results (including assessment of expressive and receptive language repertory, conceptualization abilities, and socialization skills relevant to instructional settings) and a parent interview regarding school-relevant skills, such as reading, and special interests their child may have. Rynders and Horrobin report that there are data to support the notion that many persons with Down syndrome will benefit from an array of regular, age-appropriate class placements ranging from partial to full-time participation. The key to making good placement decisions is to use a broad set of data that document the child's relevant school skills.

  Physical Characteristics Correlated with Down Syndrome. A fairly well documented array of physical characteristics are typically found in persons exhibiting Down syndrome. Typically, all or most of the following are evidenced:

- Short height compared to that of siblings or general population age-mates.
- Flat, broad-appearing face with ears and nose small for head size.
- Eyes that appear to be upward slanting at the outside corners (Asiatic in appearance) with excessive epicanthic folds at the inside corners.
- Hands that appear to be short with fingers curving inward.

Many students with Down syndrome can be integrated into age-appropriate school activities.

- Mouth that appears to be smaller, including oral cavity, often resulting in protrusion of tongue—which may in turn negatively effect speech articulation.
- Single crease or fissure across both palms.
- Reduced muscle tone (i.e., hypotonia) as well as hyperflexibility of joints, permitting unusually large ranges of rotation and movement.
- Coronary and/or circulatory defects in approximately one-third of the population.
- Increased susceptibility to upper respiratory infections.
- Delayed puberty and/or incomplete sexual development.

What is fragile-X syndrome?

Fragile-X Syndrome. While persons with Down syndrome may account for 5 to 6 percent of those individuals identified as exhibiting mental retardation (Patton et al., 1990), there is growing evidence that another genetic anomaly, Fragile-X, may account for an even larger percentage of the population than was initially suspected when it was first identified in the late 1970s. **Fragile-X syndrome, or fra(X),** has been diagnosed as a cause of mental retardation for nearly two decades; it has also been identified as Martin-Bell syndrome (Bishop, 1982; Giraud, Aymes, Mattei, & Mattei, 1976; Harvey, Judge, & Wiener, 1977; Richards, Sylvester, & Brookes, 1981; Turner et al., 1986).

Incidence of Fragile-X. Fra(X) is the most frequently encountered form of inherited mental retardation, accounting for an estimated *incidence* of 1 in 1350 males and 1 in 2033 females (Sudhalter, Cohen, Silverman, & Wolf-Schein, 1990). Among school-age individuals, Webb, Bundley, Thake, and Todd (1986) indicate probable incidence rates in males to be 0.73

per 1000, and in females 0.48 per 1000. Webb et al. report an overall *prevalence* of 0.61 per 1000. The larger incidence of males than females follows the typical inheritance pattern of dominant sex cell anomalies, in that males have only one X chromosome (XY) and females have two (XX). Prenatal diagnosis is possible with amniocentesis or chorionic villus sampling and will be discussed later. Sudhalter et al. (1990) caution that diagnosis of fra(X) is often complicated because an as-yet-to-be determined number of males suspected of being carriers do not exhibit any of the known physical or genotypic characteristics.

Behavioral and Learning Characteristics of Persons with Fragile-X. Research on fra(X) is relatively new, especially as it relates to special education. Behaviorally, fra(X) typically results in moderate to severe mental retardation (Lachiewicz, Gullion, Spiridigliozzi, & Aylsworth, 1987). However, Hagerman, McBogg, and Hagerman (1983) note that current research literature suggests that children with fra(X) may range in intelligence from average to severely retarded. These authors also note that adults with fra(X) appear to test more often in the moderate to severe range of mental retardation. Hagerman et al. (1985) caution that parents of children with fra(X) be warned that a decline in measured intellectual performance (IQ) may occur over the childhood period—similar to the declines noted in persons diagnosed with Down syndrome.

Considerable recent research (Paul et al., 1987; Wolf-Schein et al., 1987) indicates that significant speech and language problems are characteristic of individuals with fra(X). Wolf-Schein et al. (1987) report that the speech and language of persons with fra(X) (nonautistic) may often be characterized by the following:

- Unusual voice qualities or effects.
- Dysrhythmia (voice quality with irregular rhythm).
- Difficult to understand or poor intelligibility (e.g., excessive use of jargon, not matching answers to questions).
- High rate of sound repetitions.
- Perseveration (inappropriate delay in responding to a changing topic of discussion).
- Inappropriateness (e.g., talking to themselves).
- Echolalia (inappropriate repetition of sounds or words).[2]

Recent research also indicates that fra(X) appears to be a common biomedical cause of autism, affecting perhaps 10 to 12 percent of the population diagnosed with *infantile autism* (Brown, Jenkins et al., 1986; Fisch, Cohen, Jenkins, & Brown, 1988). (See Chapter 15 for a discussion of autism.) Among males currently in schools for persons with autism, Brown, Jenkins et al. (1986) estimate that as many as 15.7 percent manifest fra(X). Across all male fra(X) carriers, these same authors report prevalence rates that vary from 5 to 46 percent. Other behavioral manifestations include atypical social gaze, social avoidance, and repetitive behaviors (Cohen et al., 1988). Sudhalter et al. (1990) speculate that the interaction of social-linguistic variables may account for the deviant repetitive language behavior noted by Cohen et al. (1988). However, educational behavioral research in the area of fra(X) began in earnest only during the 1980s, and much remains to be learned.

Physical Characteristics Associated with Fragile-X. Rogers and Simensen (1987) indicate that affected males have no strikingly abnormal physical characteristics except for long narrow faces with a prominent jaw, large ears and hands in proportion to the skull or body trunk, prominent foreheads, and large skull in proportion to body trunk. Adult males often have abnormally large testicles (macro-orchidism). A full understanding of fra(X) remains in the

---

[2]An important distinction is that these speech and language problems were identified in person diagnosed as exhibiting fra(X), but who were not simultaneously classified as autistic.

future, but the initial breakthrough linking it to persons with mental retardation is significant and has direct implications for those concerned with the prevention of mental retardation.

EARLY DETECTION OF CHROMOSOMAL IRREGULARITIES. As noted earlier, **amniocentesis** can determine whether a pregnant woman is carrying a child with Down syndrome or other chromosomal aberrations. In this test, a small portion of the amniotic fluid that surrounds the fetus is withdrawn by syringe through the abdominal and uterine walls and examined. As with any intrusion into the womb, some danger of causing a spontaneous abortion is present with amniocentesis. Tucker (1978) places the risk factor to both the mother and fetus at 1 percent. The procedure is considered medically safe when used between the fourteenth and sixteenth weeks of gestation.

What is chorionic villus sampling?

Another genetic defect diagnostic procedure that has great significance is **chorionic villus sampling (CVS).** Unlike amniocentesis, which is typically performed after the sixteenth week of pregnancy, chorionic villus sampling can be performed optimally any time between the eighth and tenth weeks of pregnancy (Cowart, 1983). The procedure also differs from amniocentesis in that it does not require puncturing the abdominal wall and womb. CVS involves collecting a sample of approximately 30 milligrams of amniotic fluid from the chorionic tissue surrounding the developing fetal placenta. The sample is obtained by passing a "16 cm plastic catheter with a 1.5 mm flexible aluminum obturator through the vagina into the uterus and up to the chorionic villi under ultrasound guidance" (Cowart, 1983, p. 1249).

RECENT ADVANCES IN DETECTING DOWN SYNDROME AND FRAGILE-X. Elias (1991) reported that for the first time, researchers have diagnosed genetic disorders such as Down syndrome through maternal blood tests. While the blood-testing techniques require additional research, the technique reported by Elias may offer an early reliable diagnostic procedure that is even less intrusive than that offered by amniocentesis or CVS and not at all dangerous to the developing fetus. The cost of this type of blood test is anticipated to be less than the cost of either amniocentesis or CVS, thereby making it more readily available to all pregnant women.

As for fra(X), Pieretti et al. (1991) report that the gene that causes fragile-X syndrome has been identified. The discovery of the exact gene and the location on its X chromosome should greatly facilitate early and reliable diagnosis of fra(X), which is now believed to be the single largest genetic cause of mental retardation. The rapid advances in medical technology related to early detection has heightened the need for special education professionals to be more aware of the availability of genetic counseling for parents, families, and especially pregnant women.

Genetic Counseling. It is estimated that existing prenatal genetic analysis procedures can reliably detect at least 1600 genetic disorders (McKusick, 1982). Once these modern medical techniques become generally available to persons from all segments of society, it will be easier to provide all would-be parents with accurate genetic counseling.

What should be the function of genetic counseling?

The function of genetic counseling should be twofold: (1) to inform interested persons of their genetic makeup as individuals and as parents; (2) if pregnancy occurs, to offer parents, in a nondirective manner, information about the probable genetic predisposition of their unborn child. In most segments of American society, this form of genetic counseling is generally available only for those known to be at risk.

In addition to counseling about education and preparation-for-life skills, most families with children exhibiting mental retardation will benefit from the experience of knowing that they are not alone; that there are research-validated approaches to education and training; and that there are many local, regional, and national service options available. For those families in which a genetic factor is directly correlated with their child's mental retardation, counseling may also help them address future family-planning options. The complexity of such family-planning counseling, along with the moral, ethical, and legal issues involved, is beyond the scope of this chapter. The reader is referred to the work of Orelove and Sobsey (1984) and Turnbull and Turnbull (1990) for additional information. In 1988, the Council for Exceptional Children's Division on Mental Retardation published a position statement on the "right of children with mental retardation to life sustaining medical care and treatment" (Smith, 1988). The CEC-MR Division's position statement (see box, next page) serves as an apt conclusion to this discussion, as well as a timely juxtaposition to this chapter's opening vignette.

Problems During Pregnancy

When can prenatal factors have the most serious consequences?

Prenatal factors have the most serious consequences during the first three months of pregnancy, although some factors can endanger the fetus at any point during gestation. Maternal disease, such as serious kidney disease or *diabetes mellitus,* can cause complications during pregnancy (Berlin, 1978). Certain drugs, exposure to large doses of radiation, and poor maternal nutrition can also harm the fetus.

Infections during pregnancy are also a major cause of retardation. Rubella, or German measles, in the first trimester of pregnancy can have disastrous consequences. Rubella can now be prevented with vaccinations. Syphilis is another infectious disease that can injure the fetus.

What is Rh incompatibility?

A woman with Rh-negative blood who is impregnated by an Rh-positive male has a chance of producing a fetus with Rh-positive blood. When this occurs, the mother's body produces antibodies that attack the fetus as they would attack a foreign substance that has entered the body. **Rh incompatibility** rarely affects a first-born child, and a vaccine called RhoGam has been developed that prevents Rh-factor problems in later pregnancies. In some cases, it is necessary to give the child a blood transfusion to eliminate antibodies that are damaging to the child's tissues.

There is also some evidence that LSD, heroin, and cigarette smoking can negatively affect the fetus (MacMillan, 1982). Pregnant women should limit their use of tobacco and over-the-counter drugs such as aspirin, taking only those drugs that are recommended or prescribed by a physician.

What impact can alcohol have on a developing fetus?

The effect of alcohol on the developing fetus has been the subject of much concern and research. There is a definite link between **fetal alcohol syndrome (FAS)** and mental retardation. Research by Ouellette et al. (1976, 1977) indicates that FAS may be the third most common cause of mental retardation. Additionally, exposure to alcohol can cause significant problems in the development of oral communication skills, as documented by Becker, Warr-Leeper, and Leeper (1990).

Alcohol is probably the most popular controlled drug in the United States. It is certainly, next to caffeine, the most readily available. Its effects on the developing fetus are only now beginning to be understood. In addition to what is known about learning processes and individuals with FAS, research is beginning to document other deleterious effects on skeletal and cranial growth, as well as heart defects. Furey (1982), citing past research, suggests that an average daily consumption of 89 ml (approximately 3 ounces) or more of absolute alcohol (the equivalent of three hard drinks) per day presents high risks to the fetus. Scientists studying FAS are not certain about the amount of alcohol consumption acceptable without risk to the fetus, but the following observations seem to reflect a consensus on daily consumption of absolute alcohol:

Up to 1 ounce	Little risk
1 to 2 ounces	Moderate risk
2 ounces or more	Significant risk

A POSITION STATEMENT ON THE RIGHT OF CHILDREN WITH MENTAL RETARDATION TO LIFE SUSTAINING MEDICAL CARE AND TREATMENT

Position Statement

The Board of Directors of the Division on Mental Retardation of the Council for Exceptional Children resolves that the fact that a person is born with mental retardation or acquires mental retardation during development is not a justifiable reason, in and of itself, for terminating the life of that person. Mental retardation alone is not a nullification of quality or worth in an individual's life and should not be used as a rationale for the termination of life through direct means nor the withholding of nourishment or life sustaining processes.

Background

The issue of pediatric euthanasia is complex and troubling to professionals in the field of mental retardation. A most basic question posed by this dilemma is that of who is to make the decision to deny treatment or nourishment to a child who has mental retardation. Most often involved in this decision are parents, physicians, and, in most cases which become public, the courts. Arguments have been made for and against the role of each of these parties in making such a decision.

Support for parents as decision makers derives from the concept that children are the property of their parents and that they have the final voice in any crucial matter concerning their offspring. Critics of this view believe that parents are often emotionally distraught and lack adequate information on which to base their decision when faced with such a dilemma. Their decision may be unduly influenced by fears concerning raising the child or of institutional placement.

Physicians often feel that they are in the best position to make an objective decision. It has been observed, however, that they often are motivated by their perception of what will prevent suffering in the family. It is argued that physicians should not be the decision makers because their duty is to preserve life, not to judge which lives deserve preservation.

Parents of newborns and physicians have rarely had the opportunity to experience living or working with individuals having mental retardation across the course of their lives. As special educators serving children with disabilities from infancy through adulthood, the Board of Directors of CEC-MR observes that mental retardation alone does not necessarily cause a life of pain, suffering or absence of life quality for the affected persons, and that it should not imply a justification for the termination of life. Research and experience with persons having mental retardation demonstrate that all people can learn, all can participate (at least partially) in the wide range of human experiences and most become productive citizens and are valued as human beings by persons who truly know them. It is with these factors in mind that CEC-MR takes a public position on this issue.

Source: "A Position Statement on the Right of Children with Mental Retardation to Life Sustaining Medical Care and Treatment," Division on Mental Retardation of the Council for Exceptional Children. Reprinted by permission.

Until the effects of alcohol on the developing fetus are specified, it would seem appropriate to warn all women not to drink any alcohol during pregnancy. Additionally, the early identification of children with FAS and determination of their educational needs should become a national priority with special educators. As Umbreit and Ostrow (1980) note, there is little longitudinal research on the child with FAS; such research must be undertaken if adequate educational services are to be provided. Unfortunately, as Baumeister and Hamlett (1986) report with the results of a survey of the United States, neither longitudinal research nor nationwide commitment to either diagnosis or prevention of FAS has occurred. The significance of this failure to act decisively is increased when we consider that the probable third leading cause of mental retardation is preventable.

Problems at Birth

What is asphyxia?

A number of problems that can result in retardation sometimes occur during labor and delivery. Although there is no direct cause-effect relationship between prematurity and retardation, premature babies are more susceptible to disease and more fragile than full-term babies, and are as a result more susceptible to retardation (MacMillan, 1982). Brain damage can be caused by prolonged or difficult labor, by difficult forceps manipulation, and by problems related to a mother's small pelvis. **Asphyxia** (also referred to as **anoxia**), or the deprivation of oxygen, may be caused by compression of the umbilical cord or other problems (MacMillan, 1982). This is probably the major cause of cerebral palsy.

Treatment for some genetic disorders must begin shortly after birth to be effective. Children born to mothers with Rh antigens must be monitored to ensure that high levels of bilirubin do not result in brain damage. The blood sugar levels of infants born to diabetic mothers should be monitored to determine whether the child needs treatment. PKU and galactosemia tests should also be conducted, and treatment should be initiated if it is warranted. Surgery may be necessary in cases of spina bifida, as mentioned in Chapter 11. Hydrocephaly, a related condition, can also be identified shortly after birth. This condition is characterized by the buildup of cerebrospinal fluid in the skull. If untreated, the head will expand, resulting in severe brain damage. Surgical procedures have been developed that involve inserting a shunt to drain the fluid into the general circulatory system.

Problems After Birth

What are some of the causes of mental retardation after birth?

Mental retardation can also be caused by problems occurring after the child is born, including head injuries, brain tumors, infectious diseases such as meningitis and encephalitis, hunger and malnutrition, and some food additives. Lead and mercury poisoning can also cause retardation, as can complications arising from childhood diseases such as whooping cough, chicken pox, and measles. Lead poisoning from house paints and lead water pipes—thought by many to be a thing of the past, as lead-based paint and lead water pipes are no longer permitted in the United States—is still very much a threat to young developing children. As early as 1976, the President's Committee on Mental Retardation warned that in high-risk areas with impoverished housing and in economically distressed areas, up to 50 percent of all children have elevated levels of lead in their blood. In 1978, the U.S. Consumer Product Safety Commission lowered the legal maximum lead content in most kinds of paint to 0.06 percent (a trace amount). Lead poisoning is particularly a factor in areas of poverty, either urban or rural, and in some rural settings where prolonged exposure to older dwellings that are painted with lead-based paints and have water supplied by lead piping is still quite common. Currently, a blood lead level of 25 micrograms per deciliter is considered evidence of lead poisoning (U.S. Consumer Product Safety Commission, 1990).

Psychosocial Factors

What causes the many cases of relatively mild intellectual retardation?

The President's Committee on Mental Retardation (1976) concluded that 75 percent of children with mental retardation come from urban and rural poverty areas. Professionals can only speculate on why so many children diagnosed as being mildly retarded come from impoverished environments. While considerable research has been completed since 1976, there is little empirical evidence to document the causes of mental retardation that do not have a known or clearly manifested genetic origin. The evidence that has emerged tends to indicate that the developing child's physical, social, and psychological environment play an important role in the etiology of the behavioral phenomenon referred to as mild mental retardation.

What are the psychosocial factors relating to mental retardation?

It seems reasonable to assume that malnutrition, inadequate medical and prenatal care, disease-producing conditions, and other health hazards associated with poverty all contribute to lowered intellectual functioning. In addition, it appears that several other less readily observable factors help produce mental retardation. These are related to child-rearing practices, the home environment, family structure, and the like, and are known as *psychosocial* factors.

The AAMR's 1983 *Manual on Classification in Mental Retardation* identifies four elements that must be present if an individual's mental retardation is to be attributed to psychosocial factors, as follows:

1. Intelligence and adaptive behavior are at retarded levels of functioning.
2. There is retarded intellectual functioning in the immediate family and usually the larger family circle as well.
3. There is no clear evidence of brain damage in the child.
4. In most instances, the home environment is impoverished.

Mild retardation caused by psychosocial factors is almost always difficult to identify in young children. Most of the youngsters in this category appear to develop fairly normally; they are generally only slightly slower than their peers without mental retardation. Thus, most of these children are not identified until they reach school age, when it is discovered that they have difficulty with educational tasks.

Most authorities on mental retardation do not believe that intelligence and other characteristics of the personality are caused exclusively by either genetic or environmental factors. The current belief is that these traits result from the interaction of genetic and environmental variables. Children who have the genetic potential to be only mildly retarded may have a much lower level of intelligence if they are raised in a very poor environment. Thus, it is important that children be raised in an environment that is as nurturing and stimulating as possible.

Prevention of Mental Retardation

As research further identifies the causes of mental retardation, our knowledge of ways to prevent its occurrence improves. Known preventive measures include the following:

- Vaccination against rubella.
- Surgical procedures to correct hydrocephaly.
- Amniocentesis or CVS to detect chromosomal aberrations in the fetus.
- Use of drugs to control the effects of childhood illnesses.
- Blood transfusions of Rh-factor babies and vaccination of Rh-sensitized mothers.

- Laws that prohibit the use of lead-based paint on baby toys and furniture, and urban renewal standards that remove both lead-based paints and lead water pipes from older homes.
- Dietary treatment of PKU and galactosemia.
- Improved maternal nutrition and prenatal health care.
- Sustained public information campaigns about alcohol and other drugs and their impact on the developing fetus.
- Genetic counseling for persons who are carriers of potential genetic defects.
- Enrichment of impoverished environments, both urban and rural.

Educating the public about the causes of mental retardation and the methods of preventing it is one of the major challenges facing the special educator today.

PROBE 12-5   Causes and Prevention of Mental Retardation

1. T F   A knowledge of the causes of retardation can be very helpful to a teacher in the actual instruction of children with mental retardation.
2. T F   The causes of most cases of mental retardation cannot be clearly identified.
3. T F   Down syndrome produces a high number of individuals classified as mentally retarded.
4. T F   All persons diagnosed as exhibiting Down Syndrome are intellectually disabled.
5. T F   Fragile-X syndrome is most frequently identified with females classified as exhibiting mild intellectual disabilities.
6. T F   Significant and chronic psychosocial disadvantage may result in mental retardation at any of the current AAMR classifications of mental retardation.
7. Match each item on the left with the associated condition on the right.

   _____ Dominant gene defect   a. Down syndrome
   _____ Preventable with diet   b. Cretinism
   _____ Treated by blood transfusion c. Cerebral palsy
   _____ Thyroid deficiency   d. Rh incompatibility
   _____ Trisomy-21   e. Tuberous sclerosis
   _____ Small skull   f. Hydrocephalus
   _____ Correctable with surgery   g. PKU
   _____ Asphyxia a major cause   h. Microcephaly

8. List five methods of preventing mental retardation.

EDUCATING INDIVIDUALS WITH MENTAL RETARDATION

You should be able to describe the major learning characteristics of individuals with mental retardation and considerations for their education.

Individuals with mental retardation "learn" no differently than individuals with normal development. Differences are more likely to be found in their rate of skill acquisition, ability to attend to relevant tasks, memory, generalization and transfer of recently acquired skills, and language development.

Learning Characteristics

One characteristic that is essential for efficient learning, mastery of new skills, and use of learned content or skills is the ability to attend to relevant stimuli in the learning environment. Efficient learning requires the ability to discriminate among various available stimuli, as well as to attend to a task long enough to acquire a skill, practice its proper usage, and place it into one's repertoire of available responses, or memory. Persons with mental retardation, when compared to their normally developing age-mates, typically exhibit inefficient learning without direct instruction.

How may discrimination problems be reduced?

ATTENTION. Many individuals with mental retardation have trouble attending to relevant cues while performing tasks. They do not appear to differentiate the more significant aspects of the situation from those that are less useful (Zeaman & House, 1963, 1979). Learners with mental retardation also have a tendency to focus on specific cues, perseverating rather than shifting attention to new cues (Lovaas, Schreibman, Koegel, & Rehm, 1971). They may also have a narrower breadth of attention. They do not simultaneously attend to as many dimensions of a given task as individuals with normal development, typically requiring more frequent and lengthier opportunities to practice a task before they demonstrate mastery.

Once a task is mastered, however, persons with mental retardation often can perform it at a rate similar to that of persons without mental retardation. Zeaman and House (1979) suggest that discrimination problems can be reduced through (1) using three-dimensional objects; (2) sequencing tasks from the easiest to the more difficult; (3) emphasizing the relevant aspects of tasks; (4) increasing the novelty of the negative and positive stimuli; (5) avoiding failure; and (6) establishing a "set" to attend to relevant dimensions.

What is meant by limited memory?

MEMORY. Individuals exhibiting mental retardation often perform poorly on nonserial short-term memory tasks such as memorizing numbers out of rote order. This problem occurs because their use of strategies is limited. For example, they may lack spontaneous rehearsal techniques and therefore will not practice unless they are specifically directed to do so (Belmont & Butterfield, 1977; Butterfield, Wambold, & Belmont, 1973). Given lists of words or pictures to recall, individuals with mental retardation do not appear to cluster items according to recognizable categories (Jensen & Fredrickson, 1973). The clustering that does occur is most often idiosyncratic. Many individuals classified as mentally retarded have trouble recognizing recurring patterns or redundancy in stimuli (Spitz, 1973).

Marcell, Harvey, and Cothran (1988) and Varnhagen, Das, and Varnhagen (1987) note that in auditory and visual memory skills, individuals with Down syndrome tend to perform more poorly than individuals classified as TMR (with mixed etiologies other than Down syndrome). Specifically, Varnhagen et al. (1987) indicate that persons with Down syndrome tend to have particular difficulty with learning tasks that require long-term memory access for stimulus identification (as when matching to a sample such as lists of different letters), and similarly with short-term storage and processing of auditory information (as when discriminating between similar-sounding words).

It has been demonstrated that persons with mental retardation retain less information in sensory storage and iconic memory (memory involving symbolic images that have inherent meaning, such as ↑ for *up* and ↓ for *down* (Pennington & Luszcz, 1975). Research seems to indicate that individuals with mental retardation are slower to transfer information from sensory to short-term memory. This deficit increases as the amount of information increases (Baumeister, 1979). Many of these memory deficits respond to training and educational intervention strategies.

What is generalization and transfer training?

GENERALIZATION AND TRANSFER. The ability to generalize or transfer recently learned skills to new situations is another problem area for persons with mental retardation, and training in this area is an important part of their educational programs. In programs for individuals with moderate and severe mental retardation, it is not unusual to require the pupil to demonstrate mastery of a skill (1) in reaction to, or in the presence of, at least three different persons; (2) in at least three different natural settings; (3) in response to at least three different sets of instructional materials; and (4) in response to at least three different appropriate language cues (Brown, Nietupski, & Hamre-Nietupski, 1976).

In what areas do children exhibiting mental retardation manifest language delays?

LANGUAGE. Language learning is closely tied to cognitive development. A language deficit is very often a criterion for the definition of mental retardation. Most researchers suggest that children with mental retardation develop language at a slower rate but in a similar manner to children who are developing normally (Evans & Hampson, 1968; Lackner, 1968; Ryan, 1975). Children with mental retardation are often delayed in such areas as sentence length, sentence complexity, speech sound discrimination, and percentage of nouns in the vocabulary (Spreen, 1965). Delays may be caused in part by delayed development of the prerequisite cognitive structures required for meaningful communication (Bowerman, 1976).

A higher incidence of voice and articulation defects is found among individuals with mental retardation than their age peers, in part because of delays in motor development (Dunn, 1973; Edwards & Edwards, 1970; MacMillan, 1982; MacMillan & Borthwick, 1980). Differences in language development problems also appear across the mild and moderate classifications of mental retardation. Evidence exists to document that speech and language problems are the most frequent secondary handicapping conditions identified within the classification of mild mental retardation (Epstein, Polloway, Patton, & Foley, 1989).

Speech and language problems are also probably the most common secondary handicapping conditions found within the classification of moderate retardation. In either classification, persons with Down syndrome tend to have concomitant oral cavity disabilities, such as enlarged or protruding tongue, which cause both breathing and articulation problems. Surgery to reduce tongue size and protrusion has had mixed success, depending on the criteria used to determine success (Parsons, Iacone, & Rozner, 1987). However, when parental opinion on speech and language improvement is part of the criteria for success, the data tend to indicate that surgery is a positive factor (Lemperle, 1985; Olbrisch, 1982). When criteria included number of articulation or speech errors compared to presurgery rates, the data do not tend to support the notion that surgery alone makes a significant difference.

The delayed development of language and its crucial role in social and cognitive development make this a major area of concern for those working with pupils exhibiting mental retardation. The real value of research in this area of learning is its utility in the development of curricula and behavior change or teaching strategies.

Implications for the Educational Curriculum

What impact do community-based services have on curricula for students with mental retardation?

The curricula designed for the three most commonly used educational classifications of mental retardation (educable mentally retarded, trainable mentally retarded, and severely/profoundly mentally retarded) differ in both the complexity of skills taught and the actual skills or subjects covered. The educational needs of pupils with mental retardation vary so greatly that it is not feasible to utilize just one curricular approach for even a single educational classification.

The use of teacher aides has enabled more students with severe retardation to be integrated into public schools.

The recent emphasis on community-based services and program delivery options means that parents and educators need to give more emphasis to the development of skills that will help integrate persons with mental retardation into the community. Such skills as using public transportation, purchasing from store clerks, using pay telephones, and attending to traffic signals are curricular areas that institutional or residential programs often ignore, since these are not "functionally relevant" to institutional life. Today's emphasis on community-based programs cannot leave these and myriad other *functional skills* out of the educational and training options for individuals with mental retardation.

How are curricula for children with mental retardation similar to those used with children who are developing normally?

The past three decades have witnessed considerable controversy over curriculum development, implementation, and evaluation. The deinstitutionalization movement of the 1960s and 1970s has resulted in a host of community-based curricula designed to facilitate the movement of persons with mental retardation from large congregate settings to smaller facilities and to settings located within local communities. While great variation can be found across curricula of this kind, the principles of normalization and applied behavior analysis, both discussed earlier, seem to represent a common theme.

Instructional techniques and rates of progress for students with mental retardation may differ from those for individuals not exhibiting retardation, but learning sequences, skill hierarchies, and other aspects of human growth and development are similar for all students when matched for mental age. The major curricular efforts in the preschool and early childhood education of children with mental retardation closely approximate those offered in regular preschool education programs. The emphasis in curricula for very young children with mental retardation is on early intervention, including infant stimulation and program implementation in the child's home as much as possible. See Chapter 4 for a detailed examination of special education programming for preschoolers with disabilities.

More obvious curricular differences are found in secondary special education programs. A useful model for developing secondary curricula has been suggested by Brown et al. (1979) for use by teachers of students with severe handicaps. The model could readily be applied by any teacher working with students exhibiting mental retardation. In this model, the educator follows six steps in establishing a curriculum. These are the steps:

1. Organize the curriculum into four performance or skill domains:
    a. Daily living
    b. Leisure/recreational
    c. Community functioning
    d. Vocational
2. With a specific student in mind, identify the natural environments in which the individual currently functions (e.g., natural home, school) and may eventually function.
3. Further divide the student's natural environments into specific sub-environments (i.e., natural home subdivided into bathroom, dining room; school subdivided into classroom, lavatory, gymnasium).
4. Make an inventory of the typical activities that occur in the sub-environments in which the student may be a participant.
5. Identify the skills needed to participate successfully in the activities identified in #4.
6. Write goals and objectives for instructional programs that teach the skills identified in #5.

This approach to curriculum development is often referred to as a top-down approach because it starts with where the pupil is expected to be when formal instructional activities are completed. The more traditional approach is often referred to as *developmental* or bottom-up approach, in which prerequisite skills are identified and taught first and then followed by successive approximations that eventually achieve some form of criterion or standard for completion.

Essentially, in a top-down approach, the person(s) responsible for changing specific behavior, regardless of type, must first decide what the criterion performance for the task or skill should be (e.g., rate, quality, duration) and under what stimulus conditions it should occur. These considerations may be based on individual learner needs or those of groups of individuals with approximately similar abilities, history of experiences relevant to the criterion performance, and age—in other words, a normative group. Prerequisite skills are not attended to unless the learner's ability level clearly indicates that the skill is not functional and is needed for the individual to meet the targeted criterion. Once the criterion has been identified, the steps or sequences that lead up to it can be determined by assessing the learner's abilities and the resources available that will facilitate acquisition of the targeted performance, and then task-analyzing the actual performance approximations, from beginning to finish, that result in the targeted criterion performance.

A good example of this type of curriculum is *The Syracuse Community-Referenced Curriculum (SCRC) Guide for Students with Moderate and Severe Disabilities* (Ford, Schnorr, Meyer, Davern, Black, & Dempsey, 1989). The SCRC embraces the concept that a curriculum guide should not present a "cookbook" or "prescription" of procedures, but rather provide users with a decision-making system to be applied on a student-by-student bases, on the basis of their individual educational needs or plans. The content covered in the SCRC places great emphasis on skill development in four domain areas: *self-management/home living; vocational; recreation/leisure;* and *general community functioning.* An additional section on *functional academic skills* is included, but these too are aimed at achieving skills needed to function in community-based settings. The philosophy underpinning the SCRC embodies the principles of normalization and full inclusion of persons with disabilities and handicapping conditions in their community's public services. These principles include the following:

- When necessary, schooling should include direct preparation for the activities of daily life. Some members of a student body may need direct instruction in areas pertaining to community living in order to become active participants in everyday life.
- Social integration is an essential element of an appropriate education. Becoming a part of school life is viewed as an essential step toward becoming a part of community life.
- Home-school collaboration is vital to the success of an educational program. Sincere effort to establish strong partnerships with parents must take place.
- Instructional decision making must be individualized. Decisions should reflect unique learner characteristics, chronological age, student and parent input, and so forth.
- Interdependence and partial participation are valid educational goals. Students should not be excluded from an activity because they will not be able to do it independently.

Additional features of the SCRC are an instructional framework that provides for individualizing the curriculum, documentation where instruction fits into a larger instructional scope and sequence, and suggestions for possible sites or situations where instruction

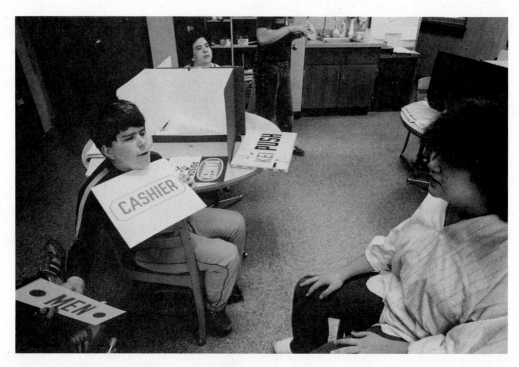

As part of their community-based curriculum, these students are learning to read signs they will encounter outside of school.

could occur. Table 12-7 illustrates the suggested scope and sequence for reading and writing in the functional academic skills domain area, as well as suggested sites for implementing instruction within a school setting. Within each domain's scope and sequence, a series of recommended steps for implementation are provided. The steps are stated in language readily understood by professionals and laypersons and typically range from one to five in number.

Included within the steps are implied questions intended to focus the user on the student's existing performance abilities. For the functional academic area of reading and writing outlined in Table 12-7, the following five implementation procedures are recommended as part of Step 1:

Step 1: Gain an understanding of the student's existing repertoire in reading and writing.

1. How would you describe the student's present reading performance in terms of word identification?
2. What types of materials does the student read and what is the highest level of difficulty in which the text can be written?
3. What is the student's comprehension ability for written materials?
4. What are the student's reading interests, and how fluent is his or her reading ability?
5. What are the student's writing abilities?
   a. Mechanics?
   b. Conveying messages and ideas? (Ford et al., 1989, p. 99)

TECHNOLOGY IN ACTION

Carol teaches children with mild mental retardation. She is interested in conducting research to determine the effectiveness of a new computer program that is designed to teach math facts. She knows that she will have to use a single subject research design to conduct her research because she does not have enough students in her class to do group research. However, she is unsure about which of the 15 single subject research designs she should use.

She decides to consult a computer program called the Single Subject Research Advisor. This is a type of computer program known as an expert system. Expert systems are an outgrowth of research and development activities in the field of artificial intelligence. They combine the computer's capacity for storing specialized knowledge and rules that replicate the decision-making process of a human expert.

The program presents a series of questions to Carol about her proposed research. Questions such as "Do you want to determine the effectiveness of a single treatment or do you want to compare different treatments?" and "Can you collect baseline data?" (Baseline data are the math facts that students know before they use the computer math program.) Carol responds to these questions by selecting from a list of possible answers displayed on the computer screen.

Options are available for Carol to obtain information, called "Decision Aids," to help her decide how to respond to each question. The computer also keeps track of the questions that were asked and Carol's responses.

Eventually, the computer reaches a conclusion based on the information Carol provides and recommends a particular single subject research methodology, called the *multiple probe across subjects* design. Carol is then presented with a database that enables her to obtain a description of the design, and additional information about applications, advantages, limitations, validity, procedures, and ways to troubleshoot the use of the design. She can also retrieve abstracts of studies in which that design was used in special education research projects.

The Single Subject Research Advisor is a valuable tool for Carol and others who are interested in single subject research. Not only can they obtain advice about which research designs to use, they can also obtain information that can help them interpret studies using single subject methodologies that appear in the research literature.

Source: A. E. Blackhurst and J. W. Schuster. *Development of an expert system to teach special educators about single subject research designs.* Lexington, KY: University of Kentucky, Department of Special Education.

TABLE 12-7   Scope and Sequence for Reading and Writing

Approach		Age-Level Goals			Outcome Upon Graduation (by age 21)
		Elementary School		Middle and High School (by age 18)	
		Primary (by age 8)	Intermediate (by age 12)		
Regular The teacher uses the scope and sequence that is outlined in the reading/writing program adopted by the school district.	R E A D I N G	• Word identification: Has strong sight-word vocabulary; uses phonics, contextual cues, and structural analysis to decode new words at approximately the 2nd-grade mastery level. • Materials: Reading series or program adopted by the school district, magazines and books; also language experience stories, personal journal, and functional reading activities • Comprehension: Develops comprehension skills outlined in reading series or program. • Reading interest and fluency: Develops reading interest and fluency in accordance with the guidelines in the reading series or program.	• Word identification: Has strong sight-word vocabulary; uses phonics, contextual cues, and structural analysis to decode new words at least at the 4th-grade mastery level.	• Word identification: Has strong sight-word vocabulary; uses phonics, contextual analysis to decode new words beyond a 5th-grade mastery level.	• Uses a 5th–12th+ grade reading ability to comprehend printed material for the purpose of gaining new information from literature for pleasure and for functional use in everyday life.
	W R I T I N G	• Writes words, phrases, sentences, and passages in accordance with the guidelines in the writing program; spells from memory.			• Writes papers, reports, letters, and other products for school/work, pleasure, and everyday use.
Regular-adapted The teacher modifies the reading/writing program by placing greater emphasis on essential skills/concepts and ensuring simultaneous application to everyday life.	R E A D I N G	• Word identification: Sight reads 50+ words; uses basic phonics, contextual cues, and structural analysis to decode new words. • Materials: Reading program that has been adapted or streamlined to ensure steady progress in essential skills, or high-interest/low-vocabulary reading program; also, language experience stories, personal journal, and functional reading events. • Comprehension: Forms mental pictures or acts out situations described, recalls facts or details, relates key points or main ideas, understands basic relationships between ideas (e.g., cause and effect, sequential happenings), summarizes content, thinks creatively beyond passage. • Reading interest and fluency: Enjoys being read to, expresses preferences for favorite reading materials, applies reading skills to novel situations, reads phrases and sentences with appropriate intonation patterns and pacing.	• Word identification: Has growing sight-word vocabulary (150+); uses phonics, contextual cues, and structural analysis to decode new words at the 1st-grade mastery level.	• Word identification: Has strong sight-word vocabulary; uses phonics, contextual cues, and structural analysis to decode new words at the 2nd-grade (at least) mastery level. • Materials: High-interest/low-vocabulary reading program, magazines, and books; also, language experience stories, personal journal, and functional reading events	• Uses at least a 2nd-grade reading ability to read books and magazines (e.g., *People* magazine) and interprets words, sentences, and passages encountered across settings in everyday life.
	W R I T I N G	• Writes words, phrases, and sentences that are connected with a language experience story, personal journal, and functional writing events.	• Writes words, phrases, sentences, and passages that are connected with the structured writing program, language experience story, personal journal, and functional writing events.		• Writes letters, journal/diary, and other passages for pleasure, and writes key words and sentences as needed in everyday life.

TABLE 12-7   (continued)

Functional-language experience The teacher uses the experiences of the student, his or her interests, and language repertoire to create printed materials and develop basic reading skills.	R E A D I N G	• Word identification: Reads set of key words and pictures. • Materials: Experience stories written by teachers (5–6 sentences), information charts, messages, signs and labels, selected books, names, cards, lists. • Comprehension: Forms mental pictures or acts out situations described, recalls facts or details, relates key points or main ideas, understands basic relationships between ideas (e.g., cause and effect, sequential happenings), summarizes content, thinks creatively beyond passage. • Reading interest and fluency: Enjoys being read to, expresses preferences for favorite books and other reading materials, applies reading skills to novel situations, reads phrases and sentences.	• Word identification: Reads 100+ words; uses basic phonics, contextual cues, and structural analysis to decode new words. • Materials: Collection of experience stories written by student or teacher (of varying length), information notices, messages, signs and labels, lists, journal/diary, letters/cards, phrases in magazines and books.	• Reads phrases in magazines and selected books, looks at pictures, and enjoys being read to; uses an expansive sight-word vocabulary and basic decoding skills to interpret words, phrases, and passages in everyday life (e.g., reads key words/symbols on recipes, menus, lists).
	W R I T I N G	• Traces, copies, and writes words that are connected with a language experience story, personal journal, and/or functional writing event.	• Writes phrases and sentences that are connected with a language experience story, personal journal, and/or functional writing event.	• Writes key words and phrases in journal/diary and letters as they are needed in daily routines (e.g., name on belongings, messages, calendar reminders, lists).
Functional-embedded symbol usage The teacher identifies ways for a student to interpret and use graphic symbols as they occur within daily routines.	R E A D I N G	• Interprets increasing numbers of pictures, line drawings, and objects within naturally occurring events (may also interpret some words). • Listens to and enjoys story that is being read; looks at pictures in magazines.		• Looks at pictures in magazines and books, and enjoys being read to; interprets key symbols (words, pictures, line drawings, objects) within naturally occurring events.
	W R I T I N G	• Uses an identifiable stroke (or rubber stamp) for writing name, or actually writes out name and other key words needed in daily routines.		• Uses a controlled stroke (or rubber stamp) for writing name, or actually writes out name and other key words needed in daily routines.

The implementation and evaluation of curricula is typically a long and expensive process, and to date, not much empirical evidence exists to document one curricular approach as being more effective than another. Curricula, like the SCRC, with a systematic scope and sequence that meets the demands of normalization and is functional and community-based, seem to offer the best alternative to traditional developmental approaches, in which persons with mental retardation are compelled to demonstrate skill acquisition and mastery out of context with their daily lives and the reality of their community's resources. The process of making a successful transition out of the public school service sector and into the community in which they live is dependent on an effective, well-coordinated, and functional school-based education and training program.

ISSUES OF TRANSITION. The role of public schools in producing individuals capable of entry into their community as contributing and valued members has become a major area of focus for educators directly responsible for students with mental retardation. Beyond the considerations of providing for least restrictive and normalized school and community environments, one of the most difficult curriculum issues related to persons with mental retardation, regardless of classification, is their transition across school programs (horizontal transition), and their transition to their community's services and the so-called world of work (vertical transition).

CURRICULUM AND TRANSITION FOR PERSONS WITH MILD MENTAL RETARDATION. Recent research, although not national in scope, has indicated that high school graduates of special education programs for students classified as educable mentally retarded have not been notably successful in preparing individuals for independent, community-based living (Affleck, Edgar, Levin, & Kortering, 1990; Edgar, 1987, 1988, 1991). For example, the U.S. Department of Education's Office of Special Education and Rehabilitative Services (OSERS) reported that, based on their five-year (1982–87) National Transition Longitudinal Study of 8000 students, only 50 percent of all persons classified as mentally retarded exited secondary schooling by way of graduation. This is in comparison to a little over 60 percent of persons with learning disabilities and 56 percent of all persons with disabilities combined (OSERS, 1990). Affleck et al. (1990) compared the postsecondary transition status for three school populations (nonhandicapped, learning disabled, and mild mentally retarded) who had either graduated from or "aged out" of secondary education programs. The following data for percentage of persons in "Paid Employment" and "Independent Living" are of particular interest, demonstrating the relative effectiveness of secondary school curricula in providing the necessary skills for independent living in community-based settings.

Percentage in Paid Employment

	6 months	18 months	30 months
Nonhandicapped	73%	79%	67%
Learning disabled	65%	71%	68%
Mild mentally retarded	41%	50%	47%

With respect to employment, the data for those without disabilities and those with learning disabilities appears to be fairly comparable, their respective members having secured and maintained paid employment with similar declining percentages or rates across the three time periods. The data for those with mild mental retardation, while also relatively stable, indicate that these individuals were typically employed at a much lower rate over all three time periods.

Percentage in Independent Living

	6 months	18 months	30 months
Nonhandicapped	32%	49%	57%
Learning disabled	22%	34%	39%
Mild mentally retarded	8%	18%	21%

As for independent living, substantive gains are noted across all three comparison groups. Again the nonhandicapped and learning disabled groups show marked increases over time, as compared to the mild mentally retarded group. Comparable percentages show the mild mentally retarded group performing well below either the nonhandicapped or learning disabled group in the comparison areas of "Current Status" and "Postsecondary Education." Clearly, if the foregoing data can be even cautiously generalized to young adults with mild mental retardation, then current preparation for transition into their community as independent and employable members is not effective.

Polloway, Patton, Smith and Roderique (1991) address the problems of designing transition-oriented curriculum for elementary- and middle-school age students with mild mental retardation; those problems have direct bearing on curricular issues for all the population. Polloway et al. note that because educators have students for only a finite period of time, there is a need to better focus curricular attention on the subsequent environments that these individuals must pass through as they age. The notion of curriculum development based on the subsequent environments that school-age children will pass through is not new. However, adopting the notion of subsequent environments as an *attitude* or a professional position—one that commits curriculum to the long-term development of realistic adult outcomes for every student, with concomitant considerations for the achievement of maximum levels of functioning—is, if not new, not yet widely found in either regular or special education.

VERTICAL TRANSITION. It is not unusual to find elementary curricula that build their instructional programs around a set of skills and competencies needed for success in middle or junior high school, and similarly from that level on, to the skills and competencies needed for success in high school. Secondary programs in turn develop and implement curricula that teach the skills and competencies needed for leading an independent and productive life in a community-based setting. This process, termed *vertical transition,* typically focuses across the life span on three developmental and age-appropriate variables: academic content, life skills preparation, and integrated curriculum (Polloway et al., 1991).

Academic Content. Academic instruction has relevance for students with mild mental retardation in the following goals:

- It will assist in successful mainstreaming, since certain levels of academic performance are requisite to success in regular education.
- It will have positive implications for adult outcomes and have functional value, particularly to the degree that students progress and acquire skills that are useful in everyday living.
- It will achieve the related goal of increased self-esteem, as students make progress in academic skills.

What is vertical transition?

• It will transform traditionally poor scholastic expectations associated with students with mental retardation.[3] (Adapted from Polloway et al., 1991, pp. 145–146)

With consistent attention to these four goals of academic instruction, vertical transition to mastery of life skills has a greater probability of success.

Life Skills Preparation. As used here, career education (see Chapter 5) and life skills are essentially synonymous. Including life skills instruction in a curriculum without a significant diminution of basic academic skills instruction poses several problems; one major problem is the issue of best use of available time. Patton (1986, as cited in Polloway et al., 1991) suggests that the problems of balancing academic instruction and life skills preparation in vertical transition may be alleviated through *augmentation* and *infusion* of career education content into the existing curricular offerings.

Augmentation refers to the use of career education content as a supplement to the existing curriculum. *Infusion* refers to retaining all the existing curriculum, but infusing it with specific relevant career education features as a part of regular lesson presentations. Patton (1986) additionally addresses a third process for incorporating life skill preparation into curricula: the use of an *integrated curriculum.*

Integrated Curriculum. Developing an integrated curriculum involves drawing together or linking a variety of instructional objectives or curricular topics and providing instruction as a whole, or as a unit. Life preparation skills can be readily built into instruction in other skill areas. For example, the academic skills of mathematics can be linked to such life preparation skills as *using money* (fiscal responsibility) while purchasing goods needed for *meal preparation* (home economics). Polloway et al. (1991) report that the use of an integrated curriculum has notable advantages, in that it promotes the generalization of skills acquired through direct instruction.

What is horizontal transition?

HORIZONTAL TRANSITION. While vertical transition within a school setting is closely linked to sequencing the curriculum across the life span, horizontal transition focuses on broadening the curriculum. Horizontal transition is typically a part of the normalization process that educators use to provide students with learning problems, disabilities, and handicapping conditions access to mainstream school curricular offerings. Horizontal transition, to be effective, requires careful planning on the part of all educators. It must be systematic in nature and not categorically designated to a minority group, such as special educators within a given school building or district.

The data currently available on the effectiveness of mainstreaming efforts do not support the notion that they have been uniformly successful. In fact, Polloway, et al. (1991) note that from the data available from the annual reports by the U.S. Department of Education to Congress regarding compliance with the mandate of PL 94-142 for mainstreaming of students with mental retardation, "one could conclude that these students cannot be successfully integrated or, more likely, that they simply have not been integrated" (p. 147).

In addition to problems directly related to inadequate planning, the declining prevalence of the classification *mild mentally retarded* may also be influencing the current data about problems with mainstreaming. Current prevalence figures for mental retardation declined rather dramatically—about 3% annually—through the 1980s, as indicated by the annual reports to Congress (U.S. Department of Education, 1989). Polloway et al. (1991) speculate that a portion of the prevalence decline may be accounted for by the trend in many school districts

---

[3]With this fourth point, the reader should be reminded of our earlier discussion of the educability of persons with Down syndrome.

not to classify students as educable mentally retarded if they are able to adapt to mainstream settings, or can fit into local or state guidelines for the classification of learning disabilities. These students may also account for the rather remarkable increase during the 1980s in the population classified as learning disabled. The students who are not able to adequately manage with mainstreaming continue to be classified as educable mentally retarded, and they present very definite learning and behavior intervention needs. Both groups of students, those "de-classified" and mainstreamed and those remaining in the mildly retarded classification, need educational programs that incorporate horizontal transition concepts, systematically dealing with curricular social integration and adaptation.

What is curricular social integration?

Social Integration. Wolfensberger (1983) suggests that the term *social role valorization* may prove to be a suitable substitute for the term *normalization*. Polloway et al. (1991) note that "ultimately, the goal of integration is not simply school integration but rather community or 'life' integration" (p. 148). Finding a balance between building the functional academic skill repertoires needed for independent functioning in the community and simultaneously building the social-interpersonal skills that facilitate social integration and the development of positive self-esteem is critical for educators to achieve. Not achieving this balance between vertical transition, life-span needs and horizontal transition, social-integration needs may be one of several critical factors accounting for the demonstrated failure of mainstreaming to be effective in our schools.

Similar transition and curricular issues are found with students exhibiting severe/profound intellectual disabilities; these are discussed in Chapter 13.

The multitude of variables, persons, places, logistics, supplies, evaluation, and monitoring make the process of curriculum design for subsequent environments a fairly daunting task. The available research indicates that the process of curriculum design must start when formal schooling begins and continue through adulthood. In designing school curriculum, it is clear that the notion of subsequent environments as a prime feature of instructional delivery must become an "attitude," embedded in school policy and practice (Brown et al., 1991).

To conclude, two final statements from Brown et al. seem appropriate: "We now have the ability to teach any student much more than time allows. . . . We now have the luxury of deciding which of many possibilities to teach. That luxury also requires the responsibilities of deciding what will not be taught" (p. 45).

Total Habilitation of Persons with Mental Retardation

What is total habilitation?

Over the past three decades we have witnessed rapid growth, probably unprecedented, in the documentation of successful intervention strategies, programs, methodologies, and technologies for persons with mental retardation. For the most part, this documentation has dealt with intervention programs that had as their focus behavioral or skill "amelioration, remediation, rehabilitation, normalization, or acceleration of developmental gains" (Drash, Raver, & Murrin, 1987). Most contemporary intervention efforts have, according to Drash et al., been narrowly focusing on increasing skill repertoires—that is, on amelioration—and not on the complete restoration of a person with mental retardation to a level of "normal," independent functioning, or total habilitation.

The widespread use by professionals of terms such as *remediation, normalization,* and *rehabilitation* may not discriminate effectively and therefore may unintentionally restrict further advances in program research and development. Drash et al. (1987) argue that professionals need to use terminology that functionally discriminates the specific type of change that is being documented. They postulate that wider use of the term *total habilitation* will increase awareness and acceptance of the concept as an achievable and realistic goal of both research and development efforts in the field of mental retardation. Historically, several noteworthy examples of total and permanent recovery from mental retardation buttress the argument for total habilitation as an achievable goal of intervention efforts (Begab, 1974; Bijou, 1981; Drash, 1972; Lovass, 1985; Shearer & Shearer, 1976; and Skeels, 1966).

TOTAL HABILITATION DEFINED. Wolfensberger (1987), in response to Drash et al. (1987), outlines some of the "classical" (Baller, 1936, 1939; Charles, 1953) as well as more recent research citations (Baller, Charles, & Miller, 1966; Skeels, 1966) that provide longitudinal data to support the argument that mental retardation, as a behavioral skill deficit condition, can be totally habilitated, to the extent that independent living is feasible for persons so classified. Wolfensberger's response is also a reminder that perhaps total habilitation is not a new concept in the field—nor does it owe its current status to contemporary intervention efforts, but rather to longitudinal intervention research and its subsequent documentation.

Wolfensberger (1987) notes that in addition to important current research efforts, early and longitudinal studies regarding intervention and its relative effectiveness with persons exhibiting mental retardation should be reviewed. Further, Wolfensberger observes the need for greater clarity in the use of the term *total habilitation*. He argues that individuals working with persons with mental retardation need to remember that discrepancies can exist between social adaptation and intellectual skills, as well as between adaptation and environmental skill demonstration or mastery. With this in mind, Wolfensberger provides a definition of **total habilitation,** as follows:

> a person being able to hold a job and earn enough income for economic independence, to cope adequately with the challenges of daily living, and not to get into social difficulties that society finds intolerable. (p. 68)

PREREQUISITES TO TOTAL HABILITATION. The chief prerequisite to the total habilitation of persons with mental retardation is the structuring of their lives in a way that "embeds them into a matrix of valid, powerful, coherent, and holistic pedagogies, that does so intensively (meaning for the predominant portion of their time), and does so from a very early age" (p. 68). Providing a community-based curriculum in special education programs for individuals with mental retardation can facilitate their total habilitation. Figure 12-2 lists some of the features of the community environment that should be considered in developing and implementing a community-based curriculum.

Wolfensberger provides a caveat about societally based obstacles to achieving total habilitation, speaking generally for further development of all the fields that provide services for persons with mental retardation. When we take into consideration that these obstacles and their description are provided by the very person generally considered to be responsible for initially promulgating the North American concept of normalization (see earlier discussion of normalization in this chapter), the following passages provide a sobering and challenging closing to the chapter.

What are the major obstacles to total habilitation?

OBSTACLES TO TOTAL HABILITATION. According to Wolfensberger (1987), the obstacles to effecting an intervention program that would result in total habilitation are as follows:

FIGURE 12-2   A Functional Approach to Exceptionality: Community-based Curriculum

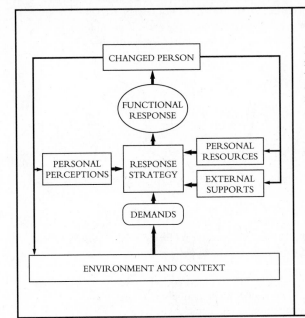

It is important to design a community-based curriculum for students with mental retardation in order to provide them with the functional skills that will enable them to respond to the *demands* placed on them by the *environment* and its various *contexts*. Some of the things teachers need to know about the community include the following:

- The nature of the neighborhoods where the students live.
- Social activities in which the students are involved.
- Student membership in groups and clubs.
- Types of stores the students may use.
- Community and social services that are available to students and graduates.
- The way students spend their leisure time.
- Public transportation that is available.
- The kinds of jobs graduates may eventually hold.
- Recreational opportunities that are available.
- Expectations of parents and family members.

Assessment of the demands placed on students in the above contexts can significantly influence the curriculum that is planned for them.

1. There prevails in our society a tremendous amount of (largely irrational) opposition to intensive early pedagogic structuring of the lives of children in general, and this opposition can be expected to generalize to children with mental retardation.

2. As a result of certain orientations in our larger society, there prevails in our contemporary human services an overemphasis on highly specific, narrow, particularistic, disjointed technologies, which neither add up to a true global pedagogy nor take into account the totality of individuals. In today's human service climate, a verbalized commitment to "total habilitation" is apt to express itself in yet more of this mindless hypertechnologization uncoupled from the rest of reality. . . .

3. There is a dearth of clinical mastery. What human service workers nowadays practice consists largely of an incoherent conglomerate of isolated mini-technologies that they very often poorly understand and poorly master. Even among people with the highest professional credentials, clinical mastery is rare. . . .

4. Attitudes toward mental retardation are so primitive and deeply embedded that persons who come with a pessimistic or even nihilistic developmental stance (i.e., expecting little or nothing—as many practitioners still do) might very well see children develop from a retarded stage to a technically nonretarded or even intellectually normal one and yet deny what actually happened and what they witnessed. . . .

5. Our human service structures are now largely under the control of high-order societal dynamics that prevent and prohibit a reduction of our impaired and dependent population. This means that some individuals may sporadically benefit from the aggregate of societal services that they receive, but on the whole and over the long run, as many or more people are being "manufactured" to be impaired and/or dependent—in large part by the very service system that is interpreted to be educative,

curative, and habilitational. No amount of clinical busybodying can defeat these systemic realities. The vast majority of human service workers who live out a commitment to societally devalued people will be seduced, co-opted, persecuted, extruded, or destroyed. Those who make the valid commitment that is called for will end up in a bad way if they are not aware of, and prepared for, this reality. (pp. 68–69)

PROBE 12-6   Educating Individuals with Mental Retardation

1. T F There is higher incidence of voice and articulation defects among individuals with mental retardation.
2. List six ways that the learning characteristics of individuals with mental retardation differ from those of children developing normally or without intellectual disabilities.
3. List three attending problems often exhibited by individuals with mental retardation.
4. Generalization and transfer training students with mental retardation, to be considered successfully acquired, requires responses across what four performance domains?
5. T F Many sensory and symbolic memory deficits of persons with mental retardation will not respond to training.
6. List two ways that curricula designed for students classified as educable mentally retarded, trainable mentally retarded, and severely/profoundly retarded often differ.
7. T F Individuals with mental retardation often demonstrate educational characteristics similar to normal children.
8. T F Language deficit is often included when defining mental retardation.
9. T F Total habilitation is essentially a new concept and owes its existence to legislation of the 1980s and 1990s.
10. T F A prerequisite to total habilitation is the involvement of persons with mental retardation at a very early age in a valid, coherent, structured, supportive environment.
11. T F A major obstacle to total habilitation for persons with mental retardation is the continued existence in our society of attitudes opposing early educational intervention.

SUMMARY

1. To be diagnosed as mentally retarded, a person must be significantly subaverage in both intelligence and adaptive behavior.
2. Mental retardation refers to substantial limitations in certain personal capabilities. It is manifested as significantly subaverage intellectual functioning, existing concurrently with related disabilities in two or more of the following applicable adaptive skill areas: communication, self-care, home living, social skills, community use, self-direction, health and safety, functional academics, leisure, and work. Mental retardation begins before age 18.
3. IQ scores are crucial in the 1983 AAMD classification of mental retardation; however, they are of little use in the educational programming for students with retardation.
4. The 1992 AAMR definition of mental retardation focuses greater attention on an individual's functioning in key adaptive behavior domains and less on the use of individual tests of intelligence.

5. The 1992 AAMR definition of mental retardation proposes two classification levels of mental retardation, mild and severe, rather than the traditional four levels of mild, moderate, severe, and profound.

6. Level of adaptive behavior is determined by comparing a child's performance to the standards of independence and social responsibility expected for his or her age and cultural background. Adaptive behavior is very difficult to assess.

7. Classification systems based on etiology or clinical type have little value in education. The most widely used is an adaptation of the AAMR's 1983 system, which categorizes persons as educable mentally retarded, trainable mentally retarded, or severely/profoundly retarded.

8. The identifiable prevalence—those presently identified and served by an agency—of mental retardation is 1 percent, whereas the true prevalence—those who meet the criteria for inclusion in a category but who are not yet served—may be as high as 3 percent. Identifiable prevalence figures are most often reported.

9. Accurately determining the prevalence of mental retardation is compounded by methodological problems, social and cultural factors, and problems related to the current professional emphasis on using adaptive behavior measurement rather than standardized tests of individual intelligence.

10. Genetic irregularities, problems during pregnancy, problems at birth, problems after birth, and psychosocial factors account for mental retardation in about 10 percent of the cases; in the other 90 percent, the cause is unknown.

11. In many cases, mental retardation can be prevented through proper prenatal and postnatal care.

12. Individuals with mental retardation often demonstrate intellectual characteristics similar to those of children developing normally, although they may differ in the rate of skill acquisition, ability to attend to task, memory, generalization and transfer, and language development.

13. Students classified as educable mentally retarded with good adaptive behavior skills can often be successfully integrated into regular classes with few special or supportive services.

14. Children classified as trainable mentally retarded or severely/profoundly retarded are usually educated in special classes. Students in such a classroom should be allowed opportunities to participate with their nondisabled schoolmates in social and non-academic situations.

15. The recent emphasis on community-based services has necessitated a greater emphasis on functional living skills in programs for persons with mental retardation.

16. Recent federal legislation and litigation has caused a new emphasis on providing services to persons with severe and profound mental retardation.

17. A new era of advocacy is stressing a transition of services throughout the life span of the person with mental retardation.

18. Total habilitation is defined as "a person being able to hold a job and earn enough income for economic independence, to cope adequately with the challenges of daily living, and not to get into social difficulties that society finds intolerable" (Wolfensberger, 1987, p. 68).

19. A prerequisite to total habilitation is being able to structure the life of the person with retardation so that he or she is immersed into the matrix of society for much of the day from a very early age. Unfortunately, society has raised obstacles that prevent the achievement of total habilitation.

TASK SHEET 12 Field Experiences in Mental Retardation

Select any one of the following alternatives and complete the assigned tasks.

Program Visitation

Visit a program that serves individuals with intellectual disabilities, such as a public school, group home, any form of ALU, community-based services, or rehabilitation center, and respond to the following:

1. Where did you visit?
2. Describe the physical setting.
3. Describe the activities you observed.
4. Interview one of the professionals at the facility about the program and some of the problems typically encountered in that setting.
5. Describe your reactions to the experience.

Professional Interview

Interview a professional who provides services to person with intellectual disabilities. Describe whom you interviewed, the services this person provides, the questions you asked, the person's responses, and what you learned from this experience. (If you prefer and can make the necessary arrangements, interview a parent of a child diagnosed as having an intellectual disability.)

Reading

Read *Christmas in Purgatory* (Blatt & Kaplan, 1966) and write a 150-word report on your reactions to the book and its photo essay.

Agency Investigation

Write to and request information from one of the following agencies about the services they provide in the area of mental retardation. Write a three-page, double-spaced paper, summarizing these services and how you might use them if you were a professional working with persons with mental retardation.

American Association on Mental Retardation
1719 Kalorama Drive
Washington, DC 20009

National Association for Retarded Citizens
2709 Avenue E, East
Arlington, TX 76011

The Council for Exceptional Children
1920 Association Drive
Reston, VA 22091

Library Study

Select three articles concerning mental retardation or intellectual disabilities and write a one-page synopsis of each. Conclude by writing your personal reaction to each article. You can find articles about mental retardation in the following journals:

American Journal on Mental Retardation
Exceptional Citizen
Education and Training of the Mentally Retarded
Mental Retardation
Teaching Exceptional Children
Exceptional Parent

Design Your Own Field Experience

If you know of a unique experience you can have with children or adults with mental retardation, discuss your alternative with your instructor and complete the task that you agree upon.

Kristie is a 17-year-old who is enrolled in a self-contained classroom for students with severe disabilities, located in a regular public high school. For Kristie the school day begins at 7:00 A.M. when an instructional assistant from the school arrives at her home to teach her how to turn off her alarm clock, get up, take a shower, get dressed, and eat breakfast. At 8:10 A.M., Kristie boards the regular education school bus and sits with her peers without disabilities, one of whom is a peer tutor.

Throughout the day, Kristie learns skills that will make her more independent as an adult. Since Kristie does not talk, she is learning to use pictures placed on a ring to make requests. A speech-language therapist has helped Kristie's teacher develop the picture communication system. When her teacher takes her to a fast-food restaurant during the school day, Kristie shows the counterperson a picture of a hamburger, french fries, and soda. After lunch, if Kristie has to use the bathroom, she shows her teacher a picture of the word *women*. Kristie then locates the restroom, and by matching the word on her card with the word on the bathroom door, she enters the correct restroom.

Two afternoons a week, Kristie goes with a job coach to the local library and receives job training. Her job is to stamp books with the appropriate date when people check out books. After her job at the library, Kristie usually likes to take a break in the staff lounge. Though Kristie has not learned to count coins, she has a card on her ring that has a picture of a soda and two quarters. She then opens her change purse, matches the two quarters on the card, puts them in the machine, and makes her selection.

Kristie is learning many skills throughout the school day, including using a picture grocery list to select groceries from the shelf, using the microwave to make simple snacks, and using a variety of pictures to communicate her wants and needs. In addition, with the assistance of a recreational therapist, Kristie is learning numerous leisure skills, such as operating a portable tape player and radio.

Kristie does not spend all her instructional time in the classroom. Instead, she may be found learning to dust the main office, empty the trash cans in the cafeteria, or collect the attendance sheets from all the teachers in the high school. Now that Kristie is closer to adulthood, she has been spending more time in the community during the school day, learning skills that will help her function in everyday life, including how to make purchases at stores, and how to use community recreational facilities such as the bowling alley and the video arcade in the mall.

Kristie's educational team believes that by teaching her only chronologically age-appropriate, functional skills, in a variety of training environments, Kristie will learn the skills she needs to become as independent as possible.

13

Students with Severe Developmental Disabilities

David L. Gast and John W. Schuster

Great strides have been made in the education of students with severe disabilities since the passage of the Education for All Handicapped Children Act (PL 94-142) in 1975. These gains are paralleled by an increased availability of appropriate residential, medical, and recreational services in the community. In the not-too-distant past, children who exhibited severe developmental disabilities lived their lives in large state residential institutions, specifically designed to serve people with mental retardation. Although those who directed and worked in these facilities were well-intentioned, there was little opportunity for residents to have a quality life. These facilities were basically self-contained, making minimal use of community services and resources. There was, for example, minimal use of the public school system, recreation programs, or local businesses. This was particularly true for those with the most severe mental, physical, or behavioral disabilities. These students were for the most part excluded from the normal routines of daily life.

Because community-based services were not available to persons with severe disabilities, many parents had no alternative but to institutionalize their son or daughter. With the passage of PL 94-142, however, local school districts were required to provide all students, regardless of the severity or type of disability, a free and appropriate education. For this and many other reasons, institutional populations decreased by 17 percent between 1984 and 1988, and this trend has continued for many years (Braddock, Fujuri, Hemp, Mitchell, & Bachelder, 1991). In conjunction with this decline, Braddock et al. (1991) note that the closing of entire institutions for persons with mental retardation continued to occur throughout the past decade. Parents now have an alternative to residential placement; they can keep the family intact, knowing that a day educational program is available.

The mandate securing children with severe and multiple disabilities a right to community-based public education has presented a number of challenges for local school districts. First, most districts were initially unable to hire special education teachers who had the skills to assess and teach children with severe developmental disabilities. Second, few school districts had money for the adaptive equipment and materials needed to provide an age-appropriate

What challenges have schools faced in providing services to children with severe disabilities?

curriculum for children with multiple disabilities. Third, some educational agencies objected to spending their limited resources on a population of students they believed would never be self-sufficient or productive citizens in the community. Fourth, many did not have the physical facilities accessible to students with such extensive disabilities. In short, most local education agencies were not prepared to address the needs of this most challenging population of students when PL 94-142 was passed.

During the period since the passage of PL94-142, some school districts and community service agencies have met the challenges; others have not. In most communities considerable progress has been made in serving these students and their families. The gains are primarily a result of the coordinated advocacy efforts of parents, professionals, and concerned citizens. Much has been accomplished in recent years to ensure that children with severe disabilities have a brighter future. There is, however, much more that can be done.

This chapter addresses current practices in the education of students with severe disabilities. More specifically, it describes the strategies for deciding what to teach, where to teach, when to teach, and how to teach. As you read the chapter, you should realize that many of the concepts presented are new and evolving. Changes will undoubtedly be made as new information becomes available about how to best meet these students' needs. Through continuing research and development, more effective instructional methodologies, curricula, and service delivery systems will be implemented. It is imperative that those who plan to work in this area of special education keep abreast of recent advances by attending professional conferences and reading the relevant professional literature.

CHARACTERISTICS OF PERSONS WITH SEVERE DEVELOPMENTAL DISABILITIES

You should be able to describe the characteristics of individuals with severe developmental disabilities.

This chapter focuses on children who have been identified as exhibiting severe learning and behavioral disabilities. These students have typically been referred to as children with severe developmental delays, severe or profound mental retardation, severe/profound disabilities, severe multiple handicaps, or severe/profound handicaps. Regardless of the specific label, these children are characterized by severe functional retardation, multiple disabilities, and a need for more services than children with mild and moderate disabilities require.

How diverse is the population of children with severe developmental disabilities?

Children with severe developmental disabilities are an extremely heterogeneous population. Their developmental delays may have been caused by a genetic irregularity, prenatal hazard, birth injury, or postnatal trauma as discussed in Chapter 12. For many, the cause of their developmental delay has gone unidentified. They also differ in their sensory, motor, social, and cognitive abilities. Some are deaf, others are blind, some are deaf and blind. Some are ambulatory, others are nonambulatory. Some engage in self-stimulatory behaviors, others engage in appropriate social interactions. All require highly structured educational programs to acquire new skills. A visitor to a classroom serving students with severe and profound disabilities would quickly conclude that this is a most diverse population.

Some people still consider children with severe and multiple disabilities to be ineducable, despite overwhelming evidence to the contrary. Such an attitude is based on a restricted definition of education and a lack of familiarity with, or understanding of, the educational research literature. With few exceptions, children with severe disabilities were denied access to public education programs prior to 1975. Because of the reauthorization of that federal mandate in the form of PL 101-476, the Individuals with Disabilities Education Act (IDEA), society remains committed to educating all persons. The federal mandate will continue to encourage expansion of services and knowledge regarding the education of persons with disabilities. Efforts to maximize these children's learning capabilities are being furthered through the coordinated efforts of local education agencies, state departments of education, university personnel preparation and research programs, and organizations such as The Association for Persons with Severe Handicaps (TASH), the American Association on Mental Retardation (AAMR), the National Association for Retarded Citizens (NARC), the Association for Behavior Analysis (ABA), and the Council for Exceptional Children (CEC).

Toward a Definition

Although there is general agreement among professionals about the behaviors that characterize persons with severe disabilities, there is as yet no universally accepted definition of this population. Before 1977, the most common approach to defining students with severe and profound disabilities was to list the medical and behavioral conditions professionals thought characterized the group (Sontag, Burke, & York, 1973). As you might imagine, using such an approach proved to be nearly impossible because of the heterogeneity of the population. In the years since students with severe disabilities gained the attention of special educators, several definitions have been presented, some based on general behavioral descriptors and service needs, and others on service needs alone.

What are the common elements of definitions of this population?

At least two common threads are either directly stated or implied in all definitions of children with severe disabilities. First, students with severe developmental disabilities require instruction in basic adaptive behavior skills. Second, students with severe disabilities require more services than those with moderate disabilities to attain their maximum level of functioning. A currently well-accepted definition of this population has been formulated by The Association for Persons with Severe Handicaps (TASH). TASH describes persons with severe disabilities as follows:

> . . . [people] who have traditionally been labelled as severely intellectually disabled. These people include individuals of all ages who require extensive ongoing support in more than one major life activity in order to participate in integrated community settings and to enjoy a quality of life that is available to citizens with fewer or no disabilities. Support may be required for life activities such as mobility, communication, self-care, and learning, as necessary for independent living, employment, self-sufficiency. (*TASH Newsletter,* July 1988)

According to this definition, an individual with severe disabilities is described on the basis of his or her current level of functioning. The definition is educationally oriented in that it recognizes the need for additional services and support for these individuals. The definition also implies that instruction will focus on basic skills (self-feeding, expressive communication, personal hygiene) and skills that will be immediately useful to the learner once acquired and that will help the individual participate more fully in society.

Why is a definition so important?

Much effort has been devoted to defining the population, but why is having a definition so important? Quite simply, an agreed-upon definition has a far-reaching influence on efforts to provide students appropriate support services. Categorical labels are used by schools to establish classes for students, determine placement criteria, and recruit and hire qualified teachers. State departments of education determine competencies needed by teachers of students with severe disabilities and set certification requirements. Universities develop teacher education programs and address teacher competencies based on a categorical system. All three must use the categorical definition adopted by the U.S. Office of Special Education to report prevalence data and to apply for supplemental funds. Although many educators argue against adopting a category of special education named *severe disabilities,* the fact remains that a categorical system is in place. Geiger and Justen (1983) found that 70 percent of all states have a definition of the term *severely handicapped.* In addition, this categorical label is used by 21 states to offer teacher certification and/or endorsement in "severely handicapped." If students with severe developmental disabilities are to receive their fair share of funds and receive appropriate educational services, educational agencies must agree upon a definition of what constitutes a severe developmental disability.

Prevalence

What percentage of the school-age population is labeled severely disabled?

The number of persons with severe and profound disabilities in the general population is difficult to establish. It is estimated that 0.13 percent of the population have severe mental retardation while 0.04 percent of the population may be profoundly retarded (McQueen, Spence, Garner, Pereira, & Winsor, 1988). It should be noted that these figures include only persons with cognitive deficits; they do not include persons with severe speech, orthopedic, auditory, or visual impairments, or students labeled multihandicapped, autistic, or deaf-blind.

Behavioral Characteristics

It is important to understand that the problems experienced by individuals with severe and profound disabilities differ in degree, not in kind, from the problems of other child populations. That is, the *extent* of the disability is what results in the child's classification, not the *type* of disability. Many children have visual, auditory, motor, or neurological impairments. Adaptive equipment such as glasses, hearing aids, or braces can correct some children's disabilities. But children whose disabilities are so severe that they cannot be corrected with adaptive or prosthetic equipment may be rendered **functionally retarded.**

What is functional retardation?

The concept of functional retardation differs from the concept of mental retardation. Grossman (1983, p. 11) defined mental retardation as "significantly subaverage general intellectual functioning resulting in or associated with concurrent impairments in adaptive behavior and manifested during the developmental period." This definition, which is similar to the definition of "psychological retardation" discussed and criticized by Bijou (1981), implies defective mental functioning based on some biological abnormality that adversely affects adaptive behavior regardless of the environment in which the behavior occurs. In contrast, the concept of functional retardation emphasizes the importance of environmental events in shaping and maintaining adaptive behavior. Some environments in which people interact are deficient, providing insufficient support or structure for persons to attain their maximum potential. The result is "retarded" behavior. On the other hand, some environments provide maximum levels of support that minimize a disability's effects on an individual's ability to learn new skills and function more independently. Such an environment might provide students with adaptive devices (hearing aids, communication boards, wheelchairs), prosthetic equipment (artificial limbs), barrier-free access to activities (ramps, curb cut-outs, automatic doors), and consistent consequences for acquiring and using functional skills (differential reinforcement). With this distinction in mind, we can say that students with severe disabilities are those for whom maximum environmental support has been provided and who, in spite of this support, continue to manifest functional retardation in adaptive behavior. Within this population, we find the following types of children:

> Those who are not toilet trained; aggress toward others; do not attend to even the most pronounced social stimuli; self-mutilate; ruminate; self-stimulate; do not walk, speak, hear, or see; manifest durable and intense temper tantrums; are not under even the most rudimentary forms of verbal control; do not imitate; manifest minimally controlled seizures; and/or have extremely brittle medical existences. (Sontag et al., 1973, p. 21)

An elaboration of some of the characteristics in this list will illustrate the wide variety of behaviors that a teacher of children with severe and profound disabilities *may* encounter. The meaning of some of the characteristics is clear. The others can be described as follows:

- *Aggression toward others* refers to behaviors that can inflict bodily harm on other persons, such as biting, kicking, hitting, hair pulling, and throwing things.
- *No attention to even the most pronounced social stimuli* means that the child does not make eye contact with adults and other children, does not look at instructional materials, and does not respond to simple verbal instructions.
- *Self-mutilation* refers to behaviors such as head banging, biting oneself, eye gouging, and hitting oneself on the head. This class of behaviors is commonly referred to as SIB, or self-injurious behavior.
- *Self-stimulation* refers to purposeless, repetitive behaviors such as body rocking, hand flapping, and finger twirling; these may also be called stereotypic behavior.
- *Imitation* is the ability to mimic or repeat a behavior immediately after someone (referred to as the "model") demonstrates it; it is a primary mechanism for learning that is frequently absent in children with severe learning disabilities.
- *Extremely brittle medical existence* refers to the presence of life-threatening conditions, such as heart failure, respiratory difficulties, central nervous system disorders, digestive system malfunctions, and behaviors that threaten the life or safety of the individual. Often these students require tube feeding, catheterization, and oxygen supplementation.

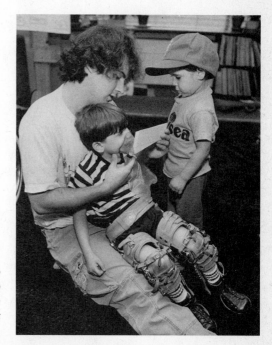

Some students with severe developmental disabilities have medical problems that need attention during the day. This student requires periodic administration of oxygen.

Note that not all children with severe disabilities exhibit all of the above characteristics. Children with severe developmental disabilities present a variety of disabling conditions. Although these children have been assigned a common categorical label, they by no means represent a homogeneous group. What all these students do share, however, is a need for systematic instruction and environmental adaptation in order to acquire and maintain basic adaptive or life-sustaining skills. They are children who are dependent on others for their care and who manifest functional retardation. These students, as individuals, present a challenge to special educators. Remember that until fairly recently, the vast majority of these children were placed in residential state institutions for their entire lives. Not until the 1970s was it recognized that children with severe disabilities can and do benefit from placement in public school educational programs and life in the community.

PROBE 13-1   Characteristics of Persons with Severe Developmental Disabilities

1. What are the three primary components of the definition of persons with severe disabilities presented in this chapter?
2. List five uses for definitions and categorical labels of the population with severe and multiple disabilities.
3. What is the prevalence of persons with severe and profound disabilities in the general population?
4. What is meant by the statement, "The problems of children with severe and profound disabilities differ in degree, not in kind"?
5. Describe how the concept of functional retardation differs from the concept of mental retardation.
6. Describe four characteristics commonly found in children enrolled in classrooms serving students with severe and profound disabilities

EDUCABILITY OF STUDENTS WITH SEVERE DEVELOPMENTAL DISABILITIES

You should be able to discuss the arguments of opponents and proponents of the view that all students with severe and multiple disabilities are educable.

Can all children, regardless of the severity of their disability, benefit from an education? This question about the educability of persons with severe and profound disabilities is being asked by laypersons and professionals alike. That the question has been raised implies doubt on the part of some. Note that our question is not whether all children have the *right* to an education (that right has been guaranteed by PL 94-142 and PL 101-476), but whether all children can *benefit* from an education. The answer to this question is not as clear as one might think, particularly in the light of the differences among the children who carry the label of severely disabled.

Undoubtedly there are students who have benefited considerably from their enrollment in public education programs. Children who had no means of communication prior to entry have learned to communicate through the use of nonspeech augmentative communication systems, such as manual signs, communication boards, or computer-aided devices. Other students who entered the public school system with a history of maladaptive or aberrant behaviors, such as hand flapping, eye gouging, or biting others, have learned to suppress these behaviors through systematic behavior management programs, communication training, and the provision of a functional curriculum in more natural settings and arrangements. Still other children, considered unlikely to learn to walk because of their physical disabilities, now walk as a result of motor programs that inhibited their abnormal reflexes and facilitated the use of normal motor patterns. Few would argue the notion that these children and others like them have benefited from their participation in educational programs. But what about those children whose development our educational system has not been able to enhance significantly? These children are the ones often cited as being "ineducable," and thus the question of educability must revolve around them.

Definition of Education

What is the definition of education for persons with severe disabilities?

The question of who is educable depends on how we define education. Some think of education as learning to read, write, and do arithmetic, but by today's standards, this definition is very restrictive. *Webster's New World Dictionary* (1988, p.432) defines education as "the process of training and developing knowledge, skill, mind, character, etc., esp. by formal schooling; teaching; training." Numerous court cases involving the right to education and the right to treatment, most of which addressed the rights of persons with severe developmental disabilities, have defined education without regard to the level of instruction. To quote Noonan, Brown, Mulligan, and Rettig (1982):

> The judgment in *Maryland Association for Retarded Children v. Maryland* (1974) defined education as a plan "to help individuals achieve their full potential" with no distinction made between "training" and "education." *Mills v. D.C. Board of Education* (1972) stated that education must be suited to individual needs. *Pennsylvania Association for Retarded Children v. Commonwealth of Pennsylvania* (1971) similarly defined special education as appropriate to a student's learning capabilities; and *Armstrong v. Kline* (1979) ruled that education allows a child "within the limits of his or her handicap, to become self-sufficient." (p. 4)

From these definitions of education, it would be difficult to conclude that there is a class of children who could not benefit from education. Such a conclusion would have to be based on evidence that there are children who are incapable of learning *any* skill or behavior under optimal instructional conditions. For additional information on court decisions regarding the issue of education for students with severe disabilities, see Brady, McDougall, and Dennis (1989).

Educability: Both Sides of the Issue

Why do some oppose education for children with severe disabilities?

A comprehensive discussion of the educability of persons with severe and multiple disabilities appears in a special issue of *Analysis and Intervention in Developmental Disabilities*. In this issue, respected special educators and behavioral psychologists present numerous arguments on both sides of the issue. Three primary arguments have been forwarded by those who believe that not all children are educable. First, there is the argument that some children are not amenable to instruction because of severe physical disabilities, a damaged central nervous system, and profound mental retardation (Bailey, 1981). Second, some believe that if, after extensive training by highly qualified professionals, a child fails to acquire a "meaningful skill," that child can be presumed to be ineducable (Kauffman & Krouse, 1981). And third, for some children with certain disabilities, an adequate technology is lacking to improve significantly their functioning capabilities. Bailey's position (1981) is typical of many who argue against the educability of all persons with disabilities:

> The normalization movement has led us to believe that all clients can benefit from training, but the data do not support such a conclusion. I do not believe that the multiply physically handicapped, profoundly retarded, who have been unresponsive over an extended period to consistent efforts to train them, ought to be subjected to further harassment. Our enthusiasm to train greatly exceeds our expertise, and that at this point we need to recognize the place of "stimulation programming" with the unresponsive profound individual. Lack of a functioning central nervous system is a limiting condition of habilitation, and our resources to provide such training are also severely limited. It is time to recognize these limiting conditions and to adjust our expectations accordingly. Stimulation programming, as opposed to teaching programming is, I believe, most appropriate with these clients, and this shift in emphasis represents an advance in our understanding of the right-to-treatment model. Such a shift in no way implies that our efforts to train the mildly, moderately, or severely retarded should be in any way reduced. Indeed, if the suggestion here is followed, we should have more success with them, since trainers will be freed as the new adjustments are made. (p. 51)

Why do some support education for children with severe and profound disabilities?

Proponents of the position that all children can benefit from an education base their argument on the belief that education, like development, is an ongoing process and that ineducability cannot be proven. As Baer (1981) states:

> A child cannot be declared unteachable in fact until teaching has been tried and has failed; teaching is too large a set of procedures (even in its own world) to have been tried and to have failed in its entirety, within the lifetimes of the child and the child's teachers. This point can also be stated in more mundane terms: The cost of truthfully affirming a child to be unteachable is no less than the cost of continuing to attempt teaching the child.
>
> Thus there is no way to affirm at the level of fact that some children cannot be taught effectively; and there is no way to affirm at the level of fact that all children can be taught effectively. Any issue that hinges on either of these principles is automatically an eternally fruitless issue, if a factual answer is desired. . . . Extremely difficult-to-teach children constitute a challenge to their society and to the behavioral science of their society. I submit that it will enrich the society and the society's behavioral science to adopt, not as fact but as policy, the assumption that all children can be taught effectively. (pp. 96–97)

For fear of not providing educational services to a child who has been arbitrarily declared ineducable and who might have benefited from education had services been provided, proponents of educability have adopted the position that all children can be taught effectively. In so doing they assure all children, regardless of the multiplicity and severity of their disabilities, a fair chance to achieve their full potential. Can a responsible profession deny children services that might improve their ability to function more independently in their community, home, or classroom? No. Society must constantly keep in mind that educability is a relative term, and that one's ability to be educated depends on advances in educational technology. As more effective educational methods, adaptive equipment, and prosthetic devices are developed and used with students with severe developmental disabilities, who can predict what level of independent functioning these students might attain? Rather than relaxing our efforts to educate all children, it seems prudent that our efforts be intensified.

PROBE 13-2   **Educability of Students with Severe Developmental Disabilities**

1. T   F   Children with severe developmental disabilities are ineducable according to current definitions of education.
2. What are three arguments forwarded by persons who believe that children with severe and profound disabilities are *not* educable?
3. What is the primary argument forwarded by persons who believe that all children, regardless of the severity of their disability, can benefit from an education?

CURRICULUM CONSIDERATIONS

You should be able to discuss current best practices in determining what to teach students with severe developmental disabilities.

Teachers of students with severe and multiple disabilities must make numerous decisions that will affect the quality of the education a child receives. As part of the assessment process, the educational team must decide what to teach, where to teach, when to teach, and how to teach. Decisions about *what* to teach involve curriculum issues, while those about *how* to teach involve instructional methods. As will be discussed, teams have several options for what and how to teach. There is no "cookbook" curriculum; nor is there a single instructional strategy that works for all students. Individualization of instruction is critical to the success of students

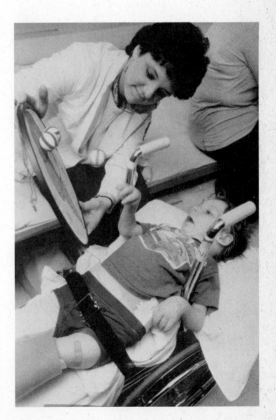

Special education teachers constantly search for ways to provide education to students with severe developmental disabilities.

with disabilities in attaining their maximum level of functioning, particularly those with severe and multiple disabilities. Decisions about where and when to teach a particular skill were once thought to be relatively unimportant. Generally, skills were taught in the classroom, out of context, and at times convenient to faculty and staff. Special educators today better appreciate the importance of where and when a skill is taught, and how these decisions influence the effectiveness and efficiency of instruction.

The Transdisciplinary Model

What is the transdisciplinary team approach?

Deciding what skills to teach is not solely a teacher's decision; rather it is a decision made by a student's educational team, which includes a student's parents. Table 13-1 lists some of the potential professional team members and a brief description of the type of information and

TABLE 13-1   Transdisciplinary Team Members and Their Contributions

Team Member	Contribution
Special education teacher	Assess cognitive and sensory motor skills; assist in the design of programs to facilitate cognitive development; maintain continuity in the children's programs as they move from infant to preschool to public school programs.
Physical therapist	Assess gross motor skills; assist in the design of programs to facilitate normal motor development; teach care providers how to physically handle, position, and move a child; identify appropriate prosthetic and adaptive equipment.
Occupational therapist	Assess fine and gross motor skills; assist in the design of appropriate feeding programs; recommend exercises to facilitate fine and gross motor skills.
Speech-language pathologist	Assess communication and language skills; design programs to facilitate vocal and nonvocal communication skills; assess oral-muscular mechanism; assist in the design of feeding programs.
Psychologist	Assess cognitive skills; design programs to prevent or manage behavioral problems (self-stimulatory behaviors, self-injurious behaviors).
Pediatric nurse	Assist in monitoring and managing medical and health problems.
Nutritionist	Prescribe special feeding programs and diets.
Ophthalmologist	Assess for suspected visual problems and prescribe treatment.
Neurologist	Assess for seizures; prescribe medication for seizure control; monitor central nervous system activity.
Audiologist	Assess for suspected hearing problems.
Social worker	Assist families in locating support services (e.g., family counseling, financial assistance).
Dentist	Monitor oral hygiene, including teeth and gum problems.
Orthopedist	Assess musculature and prescribe treatment to enhance physical development.

Source: W. Sailor and D. Guess (1983). *Severely handicapped students: An instructional design.* Boston: Houghton Mifflin. Used by permission.

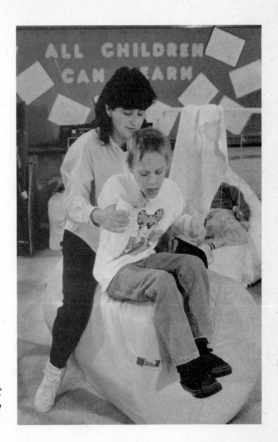

Physical therapy is an important service for students with severe developmental disabilities.

service each can contribute. Related services (e.g., recreational therapy, physical therapy) are a very important part of the student's total education. Typically one team member is designated the "case manager," which simply means that one person has the responsibility of coordinating assessment activities, chairing meetings, ensuring that appropriate due process procedures are followed, and developing an individualized education plan (IEP) that reflects the input and priorities of team members. This team decision approach is referred to as the transdisciplinary education model (Downing & Eichinger, 1990; Orelove & Sobsey, 1987). Sailor and Guess (1983) describe the model as follows:

> The transdisciplinary (TD) approach is an education/treatment model that effectively integrates program goals and objectives from various disciplines and professions. The integration begins in the assessment process and extends through direct programming efforts. In this approach, each team member is responsible for sharing information and skills so that multiple interventions with the child can occur simultaneously. (p. 207)

Who serves on a transdisciplinary team?

The transdisciplinary model shown in Figure 13-1 is the approach most commonly used in the development of IEPs for students with severe disabilities. It is important to remember that parents or legal guardians have an equal voice with professional team members and, in fact, should be listened to most closely because of the vested interest they have in their child's level of independence. The role of families in a student's education is more fully described in Chapter 6. Depending on a student's needs and characteristics, additional team members may be necessary and could include a job coach, a transition specialist, and a recreational therapist.

The team member from each related service will bring a particular approach or philosophy of education to the IEP conference. The education plan that the team develops will reflect the orientation of team members, and thus the type of skills that will be targeted for

FIGURE 13-1   Transdisciplinary Model for Providing Services to Infants with Severe Disabilities in the Home, Using Parents for Primary Intervention

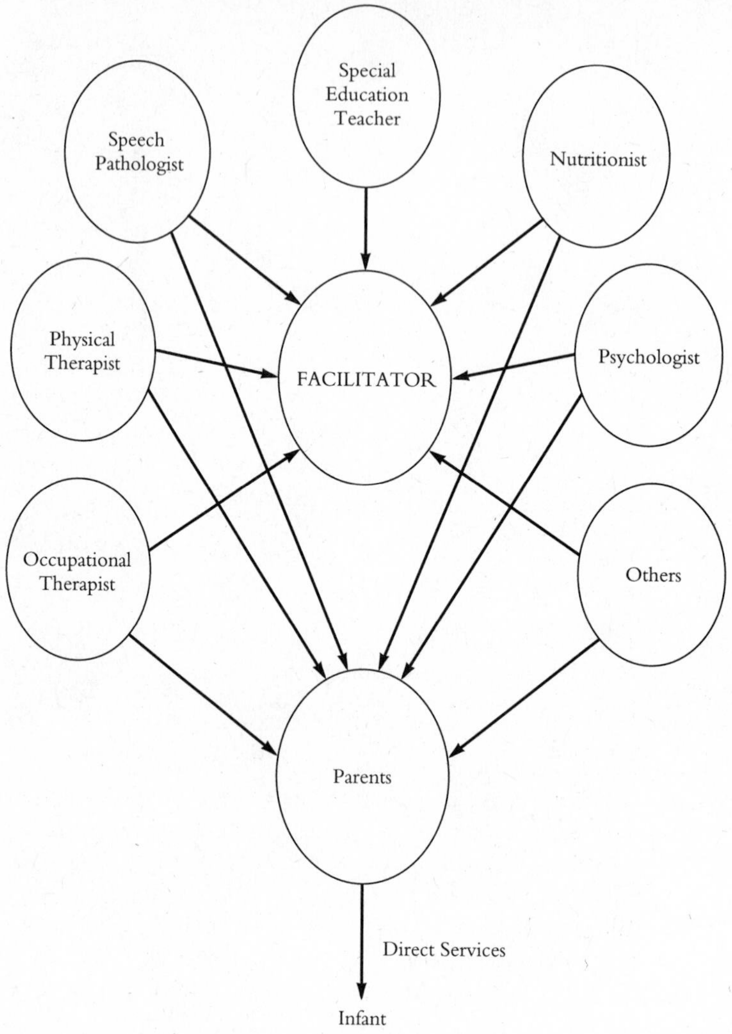

Note: It should be noted that a TD approach applied to a particular child may not have either the specific disciplines presented in this figure or as many.

Source: W. Sailor and D. Guess (1983). *Severely handicapped students: An instructional design.* Boston: Houghton Mifflin, p. 211. Used by permission.

instruction. Two curriculum and development approaches predominate: the developmental domains approach and the functional skills approach.

THE DEVELOPMENTAL CURRICULUM APPROACH. The *developmental curriculum approach* is based on the developmental milestones assessment model (Gesell, 1928, 1938, 1940) and developmental theory (Piaget, 1963), both of which hold that children develop skills and abilities in a predetermined, invariant sequence. These skills and abilities, which are associated with a given age, are referred to as developmental milestones. For those who subscribe to this curriculum approach, emphasis is placed on teaching skills that are not in the student's repertoire in the sequence in which a normally functioning child would acquire them, regardless of the chronological age of the child and the immediate usefulness of the skill. Skills are, for the most part, clustered in one of seven domains: self-care, receptive language, expressive language, gross motor, fine motor, social, and cognitive skills. Within each domain a student must master a lower-level skill before being instructed on a higher-level skill. A more in-depth description and discussion of the developmental curriculum approach, as well as the developmental assessment model, are presented in Chapter 4. The developmental curriculum approach continues to be used with young children (infant, toddler, preschool, and early elementary) with developmental disabilities; however, it has for the most part been replaced by the functional or life skills curriculum approach with older children and teenage students (Browder, 1987; Brown et al., 1979; Falvey, 1986; Ford et al., 1989; Neel & Billingsley, 1989; Wehman, Renzgalia, & Bates, 1985).

What is the functional curriculum approach?

THE FUNCTIONAL CURRICULUM APPROACH. The *functional curriculum approach* is very different from the developmental milestone approach. In the functional model, emphasis is placed on teaching skills that are chronologically age-appropriate and immediately useful to the learner. The primary purpose of the approach is to increase students' influence over their environment and thus increase their independence (Neel & Billingsley, 1989). Even though a 16-year-old student may be functioning in the severe range of mental retardation (IQ 20–35) and at a developmental age of 2½ years, the student would be taught skills appropriate for a 16-year-old without disabilities, such as grocery shopping, ordering in a restaurant, dancing, doing yard work, or riding the city bus. These skills, though not developmentally age-appropriate, are chronologically age-appropriate. That is, you would not expect a 2½-year-old to perform these skills independently, but you would expect independent performance by a 16-year-old.

What is the criterion of ultimate functioning?

The functional approach, which is based on what Brown, Neitupski, and Hamre-Nietupski (1976) describe as the criterion of ultimate functioning, has very high expectations for students with disabilities. Its success in enhancing the independence of students with severe disabilities is well known among special educators and is therefore considered current best practice. Not to adopt a functional curriculum approach with older children, teenage students, and adults with moderate to profound disabilities demands explanation and justification.

Identifying What to Teach

What is an ecological inventory?

AN ECOLOGICAL INVENTORY. The identification of functional and chronologically age-appropriate skills is accomplished by an ecological inventory (Browder, 1987; Brown et al., 1979). The ecological (or environmental) inventory strategy individualizes instruction by identifying specific skills each student needs to function more independently in his or her current and probable future environments. Brown et al. (1979) identify six steps for conducting an ecological inventory, as described in the following paragraphs.

1. *Identify curriculum domains.* The most commonly identified curriculum domains are domestic living, vocational skills, community living, and recreation/leisure. These domains contrast greatly with the more traditional developmental curriculum domains (self-care, gross and fine motor skills, receptive and expressive language, etc.). These four domains represent major life skill areas in which specific instructional objectives are written. The exclusion of language-communication, motor, and social skills domains does not mean that these skill areas are not addressed in the functional curriculum. Rather, they are included and embedded throughout all activities and in all domains. The teaching of skills in the context in which they are used is fundamental to the functional curriculum approach.

2. *Identify current and future environments.* Through interviews, surveys, and direct observation, the teacher identifies those environments or settings in which a student lives, works, and plays. Common environments include home, school, neighborhood, and workplace. Identifying current settings in which a student spends time is not particularly difficult, but it can be time-consuming. Identifying probable future environments requires some speculation on the part of the teacher, particularly when working with high-school-age students. When working with teenagers with severe disabilities, it is important to develop a transition plan that reflects the parents' plans and priorities as to where their son or daughter is likely to live and work upon graduation. These plans are of course discussed with other team members. Wilcox and Bellamy (1982) describe the process for developing transition plans for secondary students with severe disabilities.

3. *Identify subenvironments within each environment.* A subenvironment is an area within the larger identified setting. For example, the kitchen, bathroom, and bedroom are three subenvironments of a home; the work floor, break area, and restroom are three subenvironments of a workplace; and the sidewalk, park, and grocery store are subenvironments of a neighborhood. The goal of the teacher and team is to identify those areas frequented by the student and assess the environmental characteristics (lighting, noise level, crowding) and demands (stairs or ramps, height of furniture, door handles). Such information is helpful when deciding how to teach a skill and determining whether an environmental adaptation or modification is needed.

4. *Identify those activities or routines that are performed in each of the subenvironments.* Examples of activities include making lunch, bathing, dancing, and grocery shopping. Each of these activities can be broken down into discrete skills or behaviors which, when performed in some sequence, result in the completion of that activity. Grocery shopping, for example, entails making a grocery list, getting to the store, locating items on the list, placing them in the cart, paying for the items, returning home, and putting the groceries away. As you can see, grocery shopping involves a complex series of skills; instruction will need to include cognitive skills (matching the picture of the item on the grocery list to the actual item on the shelf), fine motor skills (manipulating the money to pay for the groceries), gross motor skills (maneuvering the cart through the aisles), and social and communication skills (eye contact and communication with the cashier), to name only a few. For this reason, the functional curriculum model is sometimes referred to as an activity model for deciding what, where, when and how to teach.

5. *Identify those skills that are needed to function independently when performing the activities.* The process for identifying skills to be taught is called *task analysis*. Task analyzing an activity entails performing the activity oneself (or watching someone proficient at the activity perform it) and writing down, in sequence, all those skills involved. The grocery shopping activity just discussed exemplifies one level of task analysis in which a series of skills are identified for completing the activity. A much finer breakdown of skills is possible and desirable when teaching a student with severe disabilities. Ford et al. (1989) and Wilcox and Bellamy (1982) provide excellent task analyses of activities appropriate for teenage students and adults. The critical point here is that the activity be divided into teachable units.

6. *Design instructional programs to teach each skill.* In this step the teacher must decide where, when, and how to teach each targeted skill, so as to increase the likelihood that once a skill is learned, the student will have greater control over his or her environment. More on this step will be discussed later.

What is a
community
catalog?

A COMMUNITY CATALOG. It should be obvious that using an ecological inventory to develop a curriculum for students with severe disabilities is very different from focusing on developmental milestones. Taking an ecological inventory is both complex and time-consuming.

An alternative strategy known as the *community catalog* has been developed by Wilcox and Bellamy (1982). A **community catalog** is typically developed by a group of teachers in the same four domains used in the ecological inventory (community living, domestic living, vocational skills, and recreation/leisure). The purpose of a community catalog is to identify common environments and subenvironments frequented by similar students and to assess what types of activities are performed in those settings. This information helps teachers put together a "master" list of settings, activities, and skills for students of a similar age, thus precluding the need to repeatedly survey the same environment for each student. Using a community catalog does not preclude individualizing either the activities to be taught or the instructional strategies to be used. It is understood that targeted activities and skills may require modification based on each student's particular environment and abilities. Individualization is the key to developing a functional curriculum for students with severe and multiple disabilities.

STUDENT ASSESSMENT. Once an ecological inventory has been conducted, or a community catalog developed, the team must assess students to determine their competence in performing activities. Since it is not practical to assess students on all activities in all environments, some system for prioritizing instructional activities must be in place. Snell and Grigg (1987) provide a concise guideline for prioritizing: "The main guide for prioritizing skills is to select for immediate instruction those skills the student requires most often to function more independently in least restrictive settings" (p. 71). This guideline emphasizes the importance of skill frequency and skill usefulness. If a skill appears more than once in the ecological inventory, it likely should be given higher priority than a skill that appears only once. The exception would be a skill that is required to enter a future environment or a skill that is critical for safety reasons (street crossing, handling knives, avoiding poisons). All skills, of course, should be chronologically age-appropriate and be designated by a team member as important for the student's development or independence. Priorities of parents and family members should be given special consideration since acquisition of a particular skill may give the parents greater freedom (e.g., self-feeding, self-dressing, operating a cassette recorder) or permit the child's inclusion in family activities (playing a game, sitting appropriately at a theater, using tools). The teacher's and team's responsiveness to the parents' instructional priorities is particularly important in obtaining parental cooperation and establishing a good home-school working relationship. Remember, the parents and family members have the most at stake in the student's achieving maximum independence.

After prioritizing activities, team members pinpoint those skills that must be taught in order for the student to participate in the activity. Browder (1991) provides an excellent in-depth discussion of the assessment process for individuals with severe and multiple disabilities. The primary assessment strategy for identifying such a student's instructional needs is a *discrepancy analysis*. Discrepancy analysis entails observing the student perform the skills necessary to participate in an activity while recording whether the student can perform each skill independently and fluently. If the student cannot independently perform the skill, a number of things are recorded by the teacher: (1) the type of assistance needed to complete the step, such as verbal, gestural, model, or physical help or prompting; (2) the level of assistance (partial or full); (3) possible material, response, or sequence adaptations; and (4) any other type of procedural modification (a change in an attention cue, task direction, consequent event, pace). Ideally, an activity will be assessed in the natural environment over three or more days to ensure a truer measure of what the student can and cannot do. Because of the complexity of this type of task-analytic or criterion-referenced assessment, the assessment process is ongoing, with high-priority activities assessed first and lower-priority activities assessed as time in the teaching schedule permits. It is also a good idea to videotape these assessment activities to

How are instructional goals selected?

What is the discrepancy analysis assessment strategy?

ensure an accurate appraisal of the student's performance. The discrepancy analysis assessment strategy yields vital information on what to teach, as well as insight on how to teach.

What is the difference between form and function?

ADAPTING INSTRUCTIONAL OBJECTIVES. In deciding what to teach, it is important to remember that activities and skills can be adapted in ways that make them achievable by students with the most severe disabilities. White (1980) suggests that when writing instructional objectives, emphasis should be placed on the critical *function* (effect or result) of the skill rather than the *form* (specific behaviors) used to perform the skill. For any skill, a variety of forms can be used; the form is less important than the fact that the function is accomplished. For example, asking for help is an important skill for students with severe developmental disabilities. The critical function (effect) is that the help is received. The form (topography of the behavior) used to ask for help may vary and is less important than the fact that help is requested. Examples of forms would be saying "help," manually signing "help," making a gesture and pointing to the situation for which one needs help, or activating a switch that would signal caregivers that help is needed. Locomotion is another good example. The critical function (effect) is getting from one place to another. The possible forms (behaviors) used in locomotion may be walking, walking with crutches or a walker, crawling, using a wheelchair, or asking someone for transport to the desired location.

What is the principle of partial participation?

The notion of critical functions and adapted performance objectives was expanded by Baumgart et al. (1982) in their description of the principle of partial participation. The principle affirms that individuals with severe disabilities should participate in chronological and functional activities in a variety of school and nonschool environments. In these settings, students should receive direct and systematic instruction to ensure that their level of participation is increased. To accomplish a maximum level of participation by adulthood and to have others perceive the student as a valuable and contributing member of the community, instruction should begin at an early age.

Baumgart et al. (1982) discuss five types of adaptations that can maximize a person's participation:

1. Commercially available adaptive or prosthetic devices (wheelchairs, hearing aids, communication boards) can be used to maximize functioning. In addition, certain items may be substituted for more complex materials, such as substituting a lunch voucher or bus pass for money, when they seem more suitable for a particular student.

2. People who interact with the student can be taught to provide assistance in ways that enhance the student's level of participation. This could entail instructing parents, siblings, and friends on when and how to deliver verbal, gestural, or physical prompts and assistance.

3. Skill sequences can be altered to facilitate maximum participation when performing a functional activity. For example, a person with poor balance may need to be seated while performing dressing skills (putting on a shirt, pants, belt, socks, and shoes). While this may not be the typical position for completing each of the skills, this minor modification may permit the student to participate. For a student with poor equilibrium, someone may need to provide physical support for the process of pulling pants up from the thighs to the waist. Such minor adaptations are important to consider when task analyzing a skill for assessment and instruction.

4. Rules that govern behavior in a particular setting, or that govern play in an activity or game, may need to be modified. For example, students with poor locomotion skills may need more time to walk from one classroom to another and, therefore, may need to leave 5 minutes before the bell; students with motor disabilities may need more than 25 minutes to eat lunch; and children with lower extremity involvement may

need someone to run for them after hitting the baseball during the physical education period. Such minor adaptations in rules could make the difference in whether or not a student participates in some activities.

5. Finally, we need to make adaptations in how we behave toward persons with disabilities. More specifically, we should teach peers and others not to allow students with severe mental retardation to jump in line or grab something that doesn't belong to them. Those without disabilities must adapt the way they think about people with disabilities and increase their expectations. Letting a student with a disability get away with some socially unacceptable behavior serves only to increase the likelihood that the student will engage in that behavior again. It is far more appropriate to use the episode as a teaching opportunity, whereby the student is taught by the peer (or teacher) the appropriate behavior—for example, go to the end of the line, or ask if you want to see something.

Before deciding upon an adaptation, the teacher should consider its effectiveness; its efficiency; its generalizability across persons, activities and settings; the level of independence it gives to students; possible interference with later development; and its appearance in natural settings (White, 1980).

Figure 13-2 summarizes the primary features of the functional curriculum for students with severe developmental disabilities.

PROBE 13-3   Curriculum Considerations

1. A transdisciplinary team approach is suggested for students with severe and multiple disabilities. Describe this approach and list potential members of the transdisciplinary team and their responsibilities.

FIGURE 13-2   A Functional Approach to Exceptionality: Severe Disabilities

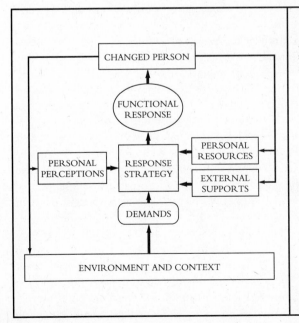

FUNCTIONAL CURRICULUM

A functional curriculum is a primary *external support* for children with severe disabilities. Following are several principles for the development and implementation of such a curriculum:

- Focus on teaching skills that are chronologically age-appropriate and immediately useful to the learner.

- Use ecological inventories and compile a community catalog of current and future environments that are important for students.

- Define goals based on the prior step.

- Prioritize goals based on their potential for enhancing independence.

- Task analyze the skills needed to perform successfully.

- Conduct a discrepancy analysis to determine what the student can and cannot do.

- Use principles of applied behavior analysis when teaching.

- Provide instruction in integrated and community settings.

2. T   F   A developmental curriculum approach should always be used with students with severe and multiple disabilities.
3. Describe the differences between a *developmental* and a *functional* curriculum approach.
4. What is an ecological inventory and how is it conducted?
5. What is a discrepancy analysis and why is it important to use when deciding what to teach to students with severe and multiple disabilities?
6. What is the primary difference between an ecological inventory and a community catalog?
7. What is the principle of partial participation? List five adaptations that can help students participate more fully.

INSTRUCTIONAL SETTINGS

You should be able to discuss where and when instruction should occur for students with severe developmental disabilities.

In order to teach students with severe and multiple disabilities functional, chronologically age-appropriate skills, instruction should occur in a variety of integrated settings both in and out of the school building. This will enable these students to experience the broad range of activities that are necessary to function in the everyday world.

Where to Teach: Integrated Settings

Why are integrated settings important?

Integrated settings, where students with severe and multiple disabilities can fully interact with students without disabilities, provide many educational opportunities that are not available in segregated environments. Brown et al. (1983) have cited the many advantages of integrated instructional settings to students with severe and profound disabilities, as follows: (1) Integrated settings allow friendships to be established between students with and without disabilities; (2) they provide more opportunities for extracurricular activities; (3) they allow maximal participation in "normalized" activities; (4) they are less costly than segregated settings; (5) they have better psychological and social effects for the personnel who teach students with disabilities; and (6) they allow for related services to be delivered more conveniently.

Integrated settings are more appropriate than segregated settings because they allow persons with and without disabilities the opportunity to interact. Such interactions are thought to be useful to both groups; students with disabilities can learn through imitation of appropriate peer models, and children without disabilities learn more accurate views of persons with disabilities and thus become more tolerant and understanding. Instruction in integrated settings also is more apt to focus on the development of functional or adaptive behaviors than is instruction in segregated settings. Further, integrated settings are more likely than segregated ones to provide longitudinal curricular activities to establish age-appropriate functional skills that will be useful in the environment (Brown et al., 1979).

Although some professionals feel that integrated settings are not always in the best interests of the student or teacher (Link, 1991), research has shown that integrated education improves the social and communication skills of students with severe disabilities (Jenkins, Speltz, & Odom, 1985), improves interactions between students with and without disabilities (Brinker, 1985; Gaylord-Ross, Stremel-Campbell, & Storey, 1986), and improves future adjustment to community life as adults (Hasazi, Gordon, & Roe, 1985). Educating students with severe and multiple disabilities in integrated settings is beneficial to persons without disabilities as well (Peck, Donaldson, & Pezzoli, 1990). Regardless of a student's age, integrated education opportunities provide the most functional curriculum possible.

Determining the amount of time that a student with severe disabilities should spend in integrated environments (e.g., regular education classrooms and other nonschool environments) is not easy. Brown et al. (1991) recommend that professionals base this decision on nine considerations, including a student's chronological age, necessary or required related services, the number of environments in which a student functions, the personnel and staff involved and their qualities, the effects that the integration will have on social relationships, the parents' or guardians' and student's preferences, the probability of acquiring skills in those environments, the functional nature of those environments, and the preparation for postschool life that the student will receive in those environments. As Brown and his colleagues (1991, p. 45) suggest, determining the number and type of integrated opportunities in both regular education classrooms and in other non–special education environments will require sacrifices, trade-offs, and compromises.

Benefits of Both School and Community Settings

Why are a variety of instructional settings necessary?

Skill generalization refers to performing a skill in numerous settings once it has been learned in one setting. Students with severe and multiple disabilities have difficulty in generalizing skills that they learn. For example, a student with severe disabilities may learn to use the soda machine in the school lounge, but later may not be able to purchase a soft drink from the vending machine at the bowling alley. A student may be able to reach and grasp a spoon at lunch in the cafeteria while eating; however, that student may not be able to reach and grasp a toothbrush in the home bathroom or reach and grasp a hanger from the closet. Therefore, an important aspect of teaching students with severe and multiple disabilities is the use of numerous instructional settings and materials located within the school and in other places where the student will be expected to function (e.g., malls, libraries, post offices, banks, grocery stores).

Where should instruction occur?

When teaching specific skills to students with severe and multiple disabilities, teachers have a number of choices as to where instruction can occur. Instruction can occur in the classroom, elsewhere in the school, and out in the community. Many variables influence the selection of the instructional location, including such practical issues as costs, liability insurance, student-teacher ratio, transportation, location of the school, and school board policy. In addition, when selecting the best location, teachers must also consider the age of the student, the acceptance of community agencies and businesses in allowing instruction to occur during business hours, and the type and frequency of aberrant behavior that may be displayed by students.

There are several advantages to using schools or classrooms as the only instructional setting for students with severe and multiple disabilities. As Brown et al. (1983) suggest, schools and classrooms are convenient from an administrative, staff, and instructional perspective. Special arrangements for transportation, scheduling, liability, and other logistical matters need not be addressed when instruction occurs in the classroom. Teachers do not have to secure community training sites and teach in natural settings that may present distractions and interruptions not found in the school setting. In addition, the classroom setting allows for multiple opportunities for teaching the same skill. For example, when teaching students how to make a purchase, trials can be conducted repeatedly within the classroom setting. Nonetheless, the classroom alone is not the ideal setting for teaching students with severe and multiple disabilities. A classroom setting usually shares very few characteristics with the natural environment. If only school settings are used, students will not be able to perform all the skills required in nonschool environments.

Natural settings, where the targeted skills will be required (i.e., community settings), are the preferred instructional sites for students with severe disabilities. Community-based instruction does not mean taking students on field trips; it means giving direct and systematic instruction on functional skills in community settings. This approach allows students with severe and multiple disabilities to learn and practice the necessary skills in the locations where they will later be expected to perform. However, community-based training sites result in fewer opportunities to perform or practice a skill in comparison to classroom instruction. Community-based training also requires school districts to develop policies regarding logistical matters, such as transportation and insurance. Scheduling concerns, appropriate student-teacher ratios, and working with persons in the community will add to a teacher's responsibilities when community-based instruction is used.

Although natural community settings are most appropriate for students with severe and multiple disabilities, it is unlikely that all instruction can occur in those sites. In order to take advantage of the benefits of both school and community sites, teachers should develop a concurrent training model. A concurrent training model emphasizes the importance of both school and nonschool training sites. Using this model, a teacher would teach some functional skills in the school setting, others in nonschool settings. Teachers could also use community training sites for probing or testing skills that are being directly trained in the classroom. Teachers might decide to teach skills in the classroom on a daily basis, using community training sites once a week. Once students have demonstrated the targeted skills in the community setting, classroom instruction in those skills could be ended.

When selecting instructional sites, teachers should be aware that the closer the teaching setting resembles the natural setting in which the skill is to be performed, and the more opportunities the student has to perform the skill, the greater the likelihood that the skill will be generalized and maintained. Therefore, teachers should work to make the classroom or school setting closely resemble the natural setting.

How can classrooms become simulated training environments?

In providing classroom training sites that are comparable to the natural environment where skills are to be performed, teachers need to simulate the characteristics of the natural environment to the greatest degree possible. The goal is to ensure that *community-referenced instruction* will occur within the classroom setting. Community-referenced instruction entails teaching those skills needed by students with severe and multiple disabilities across a broad range of settings and activities in both current and future environments. Once a community-referenced instructional approach is in place, teachers can then begin to simulate the relevant settings within the classroom or school environment. When simulation is used, generalization to the natural environment is affected by the authenticity of the simulation. That is, the more the simulated training environment "looks" like the natural environment, the more generalization will occur (Neef, Lensbower, Hockersmith, DePalma, & Gray, 1990).

While instruction under simulation conditions in the school should never replace community instruction, Nietupski, Hamre-Nietupski, Clancy, and Veerhusen (1986) have provided guidelines for making simulation an effective adjunct to instruction in community settings, as described in the following paragraph.

1. *Inventory the community to determine the range of variations required.* This involves determining the physical layouts of the community environments, delineating the critical steps involved in each activity within a community environment, developing task analyses of the required activities, and assessing the variety of natural cues that will signal the students to perform the necessary behaviors. For example, each grocery store will most likely have a different physical layout in terms of where the doors, office, cashiers, and groceries are located. Because of these differences, the behaviors required to perform independently will vary from store to store, and individual task analyses need to be developed. In addition, the signals that cue students to respond will also vary both across and within each grocery store. When students

have completed their shopping and are required to pay for their purchases, the signal or cue may be the cashier saying, "That will be 4 dollars, 39 cents," or simply "Four-thirty-nine please"; or the signal might be the amount shown on the cash register. The information gathered from this inventory can then be used to make simulated training settings more comparable to the natural environment.

2. *Provide variety within the simulated training environment to cover the range of situations found in the natural environment.* Instead of setting up the classroom to look like one particular convenience market, teachers should systematically vary the physical layout, materials, cues, and persons so that students can learn to respond to the variety of convenience markets they may encounter in the natural environment. For example, when teaching the making of purchases, teachers should require students to respond appropriately to all types of verbal requests typically heard in the natural environment. Thus, students should learn to give the appropriate amount of money when they see the price on the cash register ($4.39), or when they hear "Four-thirty-nine," "Four dollars and 39 cents," or any similar cue. With this approach, teachers will encourage the transfer of skills from simulated to community instructional settings.

3. *Modify the simulated settings in response to student performance in community settings.* Teachers should analyze student errors during community-based instruction and then modify the simulated setting so that students can be better prepared to perform under diverse circumstances. For example, one teacher instructed students in the classroom how to order food from the deli at a grocery store (verbally stating their order when asked). When the students went to the grocery store and attempted to order something from the deli, no store employee was there. Students were unable to order because they had not been taught how to ring the bell to gain the employee's attention. The teacher consequently modified the simulated classroom training environment so that students had the opportunity to learn how to perform in the absence of a store employee.

4. *Use simulated instructional settings for intensified practice of skills.* In community settings, it is often difficult to correct student errors. For example, if a student makes an error using the vending machine at the bowling alley, a teacher may not be able to adequately correct the error because other patrons may be waiting in line to use the machine. Therefore, simulated environments should be used for providing repeated practice on those steps that the student performs incorrectly within the natural setting.

5. *Provide teaching opportunities in both simulated and natural instructional settings.* In line with the concurrent training model, it is imperative that both types of settings be used on a regular basis. Precisely how much instruction should occur in each type of setting cannot be established. Students with severe and multiple disabilities will require intensive training efforts to acquire skills. The more time spent in systematic, direct instruction, regardless of the setting, the more skills these students will acquire. As a general guideline, as students get older, the time spent in natural, community-based instructional settings should increase. Sailor et al. (1986) suggest that elementary students spend 25 percent of their instructional day in the community and 75 percent of their time in the school and classroom setting, while students ranging in age from 12 to 16 should spend 25 percent of their time in school and classroom settings and 75 percent of their instructional day in community settings.

When to Teach

When should instruction occur?

As discussed in previous sections, students with severe and multiple disabilities learn most effectively when taught functional, chronologically age-appropriate skills in a variety of school and nonschool settings using natural cues, materials, and environments. In deciding *when* to teach these students, the teacher should also capitalize on naturally occurring events and activities. As a general rule, skill instruction should occur frequently throughout the day at naturally occurring times and as part of natural routines. For example, if a student is learning how to put on and take off a coat, it is best to teach this upon arrival at school, before leaving for community-based activities, before and after recess, and before going home. Similarly, rather than teaching a student to set the table each afternoon, instruction on this skill should occur before lunch and snack time.

Skills should also be grouped in skill clusters. Students will have numerous skills targeted for instruction on their IEPs. Washing hands, setting the table, identifying objects, and the use of a fork may all be part of a student's IEP. Rather than teaching each of these skills separately throughout the day, a skill cluster approach can be used. Thus, the teacher would first instruct the student in hand washing, immediately followed by a lesson in setting the table. A snack preparation activity can then be conducted, in which the student is taught to identify specific objects. Once the snack is prepared and served, instruction in the appropriate use of a fork naturally follows. In addition, the student would be taught to wash hands at other naturally occurring times throughout the day (after using the bathroom, before eating, and after activities in which hands normally become dirty). Teaching object identification would occur wherever and whenever naturally appropriate (seeing the objects in the grocery store, walking past them in the hallway, etc.). Students would learn to use a fork at all meals, whenever a fork is necessary.

This approach, in which skills are embedded in functional activities and routines throughout the day, is called a *distributed trial format*. It helps students with severe disabilities learn the relationship between skills currently taught and those previously learned. In addition, this approach provides students with a rationale for learning the skills and helps them understand the effects of their behavior on the environment.

It may not always be possible to teach students in skill clusters or at naturally occurring times throughout the day. For example, if bed making is included on a student's IEP, no naturally occurring time for this skill arises during the school day. In such a case, teachers will have to teach the skill in isolation in the school setting and encourage parents to follow through each morning at home. Another problem with teaching at naturally occurring times is that the school day may provide only a limited number of opportunities in which to teach a skill. Reading the words *men, women, push, pull, enter,* and *exit* may be targeted for instruction, yet there may be infrequent opportunities during the school day to teach these words (when going to the bathroom, when entering and leaving school, when entering and leaving the cafeteria, etc.). Therefore, teachers may want to supplement the distributed trial format described above with *massed trial instruction*. During massed trial instruction, the teacher would conduct multiple, repeated trials on a specific skill. Massed trial instruction should serve as a supplement to, not a replacement for, teaching skills at naturally occurring times as part of naturally occurring routines.

PROBE 13-4   Instructional Settings

1. Why is using a variety of school and nonschool training sites important in the education of students with severe and multiple disabilities?
2. What is community-based instruction, and why is it important to students with severe developmental disabilities?
3. What does it mean to teach at naturally occurring times in naturally occurring routines?
4. How can skill clusters be used to help students meet their IEP objectives?

5. What are the differences between distributed and massed trial instruction? Which type is preferred, and why?
6. T   F   The use of simulated settings is sufficient for students to learn how to perform in a variety of natural environments.

INSTRUCTIONAL METHODS

You should be able to describe the four phases of learning and the empirically verified procedures for teaching students with severe and multiple disabilities.

Goals of Instruction

The goal of all instruction, regardless of the student's age or level of functioning, is to teach skills that maximize independent functioning. To accomplish this goal, special educators individualize instruction by identifying and teaching skills that are both age-appropriate and functional for students. You will recall that age-appropriate skills are those performed by persons of a similar chronological age who do not have disabilities; functional skills are those that permit students more control over their own lives as soon as the skills are learned. The learning process occurs in four phases: skill acquisition, fluency, generalization, and maintenance.

SKILL ACQUISITION. In the first phase, skill acquisition, students are taught skills not previously in their repertoires. Initially, a very specific set of instructional conditions may be necessary to teach a new skill. A teacher might begin by using one set of materials, controlling the pace at which materials are presented, adding cues or prompts to the task to reduce the number of errors a student makes, and delivering reinforcers with every correct response.

SKILL FLUENCY. Once a skill has been acquired, students begin learning skill fluency, that is, performing the skill more proficiently and at more acceptable rates. For example, after a student has been taught the body mechanics of using a walker (acquisition phase) to facilitate independent mobility, the next instructional objective would be to teach proficient use of the walker, reducing the amount of time it takes the student to walk a specified distance. A later objective might be to teach the student to walk for longer periods of time and for longer distances.

How do teachers provide training in skill generalization?

SKILL GENERALIZATION. The third phase of learning is skill generalization. Unlike many regular education teachers, special educators do not assume that a skill taught in the classroom will generalize to the community environment; they specifically program for skill generalization. Students must be able to perform skills in a variety of settings (classroom, lunchroom, home), with several persons (teacher, teacher's aide, therapist, parent), and under natural environmental conditions. To accomplish this, special education personnel systematically vary the conditions under which a skill is performed. They teach students to use natural cues and prompts by moving instruction to a student's home, neighborhood, and other sites where the student will find the skill useful. The cooperation of parents and the school district is essential for this part of the learning process. This phase is extremely important for teachers of students with severe disabilities.

SKILL MAINTENANCE. During the fourth and final phase of the learning process, skill maintenance, students must learn to maintain a skill without the assistance of instructional supports such as artificial cues, prompts, and reinforcers. To facilitate skill maintenance, teachers attempt from the outset to make the instructional conditions similar to the conditions found in the student's natural environment. They use familiar and age-appropriate materials, teach functional skills, and utilize natural cues, prompts, and reinforcers as much as possible. Only when these natural cues and prompts are inadequate should teachers use less natural cues and more intrusive prompts.

Similarly, when natural consequences fail to result in skill acquisition, it may be necessary to supply artificial consequences contingent upon each correct response. Although added or exaggerated cues and prompts and unnatural positive reinforcers are often necessary for skill acquisition, they interfere with skill generalization and maintenance if they are not systematically removed. During the skill generalization phase of learning, instructional cues and prompts are faded out and control is transferred to more natural cues and prompts. In the skill maintenance phase, natural reinforcers replace artificial reinforcers, and the schedule of delivering these reinforcers is systematically thinned—a process termed *reinforcement schedule thinning*. During this process, rather than reinforcing students every time they make a correct response (continuous reinforcement schedule), the teacher delivers a reinforcer after every two correct responses (fixed ratio 2 reinforcement schedule), and then on the average of every third correct response (variable ratio 3 reinforcement schedule), and so on. Such reinforcement schedule thinning enhances the durability of a behavior over time and under natural environmental conditions (Stokes & Osnes, 1988).

Various instructional methods are available to teachers who must program for skill acquisition, fluency, generalization, and maintenance. The approach most commonly used by those who teach children with special needs, particularly students with moderate, severe, profound, and multiple disabilities, is **applied behavior analysis** (Wolery, Bailey, & Sugai, 1988). This methodology systematizes instruction and permits continuous evaluation of the student's performance toward his or her individualized instructional objectives.

The Behavioral Model of Teaching

The behavioral model of teaching is an instructional approach that places responsibility for a student's progress squarely on the shoulders of the teacher. If a student acquires a skill, then the teacher is credited with designing and implementing an effective instructional program. If a student fails to acquire, generalize, or maintain a skill, the teacher must take responsibility for the student's lack of progress.

BASIC ASSUMPTIONS. There are several basic assumptions associated with applied behavior analysis and the behavioral model of teaching. First, regardless of a student's etiology and whether the deficiencies are cognitive, sensory, or motor, the child's problems are viewed as behavioral. Teachers who subscribe to the behavioral approach believe their responsibility as teachers is to identify those optimal instructional conditions. In the educability debate presented earlier, the position espoused by Baer (1981) best reflects the behavioral model.

A second assumption of the behavioral model is that students learn best when teachers systematically order tasks in a sequence from easy to hard, beginning where the student is on a task and differentially reinforcing correct and incorrect responses. Through the systematic sequencing of tasks, cues, and prompts and the differential reinforcement of student responses, students can be taught complex functional skills with a minimum number of errors. It is differential reinforcement that causes the child to learn; the sequencing of tasks, cues, and

Transition in Action

A recent graduate of a special education program for students with moderate mental retardation, Tim begins his day at the group home by tending to his personal hygiene and grooming needs. After breakfast, he catches the bus to the public library, where he is receiving training to perform a variety of jobs, including assisting with book checkouts.

After work, Tim stops by the grocery store to buy some produce needed for dinner. On returning home, he does a load of laundry and then plays a game of "one-on-one" with the counselor who supervises the residents of the group home and who provides training that enables them to function appropriately in the community.

Tim's dinner responsibilities include making the salad. After dinner, he sharpens his pool game.

On the weekend, Tim and his roommate go to a movie. They end their day with a "bull" session.

The activities in this photo essay illustrate the results that are possible with good transition programs. Community-based training provided in special education programs, coupled with vocational rehabilitation, alternative living arrangements, and related social services, enables Tim, and many people like him, to live with a high degree of independence.

prompts determines how efficiently a skill is learned (e.g., number of errors to criterion, number of trials to criterion, amount of direct instructional time to criterion).

What is "zero degree inference strategy"?

A third assumption of educators who adopt the behavioral approach to teaching is what Brown, Nietupski, and Hamre-Nietupski (1976) have referred to as "zero degree inference strategy." According to this strategy, "no inferences are made that training to a criterion on any task in one situation will result in criterion performance in similar but different situations requiring similar or slightly different actions. Each time a situation changes for a student, it will be necessary to verify empirically that he or she can perform the skill required by that new situation" (p. 6). This strategy suggests that teachers need to design instructional programs that facilitate skill generalization and maintenance.

The fourth assumption subscribed to by behaviorally oriented educators is that instructional programs fail, not students. This assumption has led special educators to define teaching in functional terms. Teaching is defined as the arrangement of instructional conditions (pace, materials, cues, prompts, and consequences) in such a way that a positive change in student behavior results. Such changes must be of practical value to students, permitting them greater independence and control over their environment. The responsibility and credit for positive behavior change rests with the student's teachers.

Given these four assumptions, it is not surprising that special educators who have adopted this model of teaching individualize instruction, systematically present cues, prompts, and reinforcers, and frequently evaluate the effectiveness of their instructional programs, modifying them based on the data.

How do pretask, task, and posttask components differ?

TASK COMPONENTS. Simply described, the behavioral model of teaching breaks down any instructional task into three components: (1) pretask, (2) task, and (3) posttask (Becker, Engelman, & Thomas, 1975). The pretask component requires that a teacher have the attention of students before presenting task materials and directions. Teachers can ensure student attention by requiring eye contact or having students make some other attentional response, such as saying "ready" or placing their hands in their laps or on the desk top.

Once the students are paying attention, the teacher can proceed to the task component. In the task component, the teacher presents the materials (fork and spoon), directions ("Pick up the spoon"), cues (teacher holds up identical spoon), and response prompts (teacher assists student in grasping and scooping with the spoon). In this component, teachers tell students what to do and arrange cues and prompts to help them make the correct response with the least amount of assistance.

In the posttask component, teachers differentially reinforce correct and incorrect responses. This process may entail providing descriptive verbal praise ("Good, you picked up the spoon") and a desirable object (such as a spoonful of preferred food) for each correct response, or initiating a correction procedure following an incorrect response (saying "Wrong—pick up the spoon" as the teacher physically guides the student through the correct response without delivering the preferred food). It is important that each of these three components be addressed when designing instructional programs for students with severe disabilities.

The behavioral model of teaching provides a framework within which to approach instruction. For teachers to teach, they must secure students' attention, consistently present directions, cues, and prompts that are appropriate for each student's level of functioning, and differentially reinforce students' responses. As previously described, many students with severe disabilities do not attend to even the most pronounced auditory and visual stimuli, do not imitate, and frequently engage in stereotypic behaviors. For these pupils, instructional programs must be designed that teach (1) attention to task, (2) motor imitation, and (3) suppression of inappropriate and interfering behaviors. Teachers of children with severe developmental delays give priority to such behaviors because they are viewed as prerequisites to learning. However, as with other skills, these behaviors are not taught in isolation; they are embedded in and taught throughout all instructional activities and routines.

Decreasing Inappropriate Behaviors

How frequent is self-injurious behavior?

Teachers of children with severe or profound mental retardation soon discover that many students engage in inappropriate behaviors that interfere with their learning functional skills. For example, these children commonly engage in repetitive behaviors that have no apparent purpose, such as body rocking, hand flapping, or finger twirling. This class of behaviors is called stereotypic or self-stimulatory behavior. Although these behaviors frequently interfere with teaching, they seldom threaten the health or physical well-being of the student. Self-injurious behaviors, on the other hand, can be life-threatening—as are rumination, pica (craving unnatural foods or nonfoods), or head banging—or at least physically harmful—as are eye gouging, face slapping, or self-biting. In a publication of the American Association on Mental Deficiency, Hollis and Meyers (1982) present a detailed analysis and comprehensive review of life-threatening behavior observed in persons with mental retardation. Because of the relatively high prevalence of self-injurious behavior (8 to 14 percent) among persons with severe mental retardation, special educators must be skilled at designing and implementing behavior management programs to suppress severe behavior problems (Maurice & Trudel, 1982). As Spradlin and Spradlin (1976) have pointed out, meaningful instruction can occur only after self-stimulatory, self-injurious, and other severe behavior problems are eliminated or reduced to acceptable levels.

Not all behavior problems confronted by special educators working with students with severe disabilities are as potentially devastating to a student's development and well-being as self-stimulatory and self-injurious behaviors. Some students may engage in behaviors that are simply embarrassing and annoying to teachers, parents, and school administrators (e.g., stealing food). Teachers should be able to control these behaviors through positive behavior management techniques as well. They should be familiar with such procedures as differential reinforcement of appropriate behaviors incompatible with the inappropriate behavior, systematic ignoring, time out from positive reinforcement, and overcorrection.

The past decade has seen a growth in the knowledge base regarding the treatment and elimination of inappropriate behavior, with emphasis placed on a technology of nonaversive behavioral support (Horner et al., 1990). Research has indicated that the type of curriculum, daily schedule, the environment, or the context in which the behavior occurs can play a role in the exhibition of inappropriate behavior (Berkman & Meyer, 1988; Brown, 1991; Haring & Kennedy, 1990), in addition to such variables as student choice, the type of task, and the amount of task variation (Parsons, Reid, Reynolds, & Bumgarner, 1990; Winterling, Dunlap & O'Neill, 1987). In addition, many professionals believe that inappropriate behavior is attributed to various communicative or pragmatic intents (Carr & Durand, 1985; Donnellan, Mirenda, Mesaros, & Fassbender, 1984). These and other behavior management procedures have been reviewed in detail by Gast and Wolery (1987), Alberto and Troutman (1990), Evans and Meyer (1985), and Kerr and Nelson (1989), and many offer decision models to guide practitioners when intervening in problematic behavior.

Teaching New Skills

What is "putting through"?

PHYSICAL PROMPTING AND FADING. Several instructional procedures have been used successfully to teach new skills to students with severe learning and physical disabilities. The procedure used most frequently to teach complex skills has been *physical prompting and fading,* sometimes referred to as physical guidance or "putting through." This procedure involves breaking down a skill into several component behaviors through task analysis.

Figure 13-3 is an example of how the self-care skill of putting on pants can be task analyzed into ten smaller steps or behaviors for instructional purposes. To teach this skill, the teacher would begin by physically guiding the student through all ten steps. If the student does not resist teacher assistance during the first instructional session, the student is physically guided through steps 10 through 2 during the next session, leaving the last step (step 1) for the student to do. With each new session, if the student meets the criterion level on all steps to be performed independently, the teacher provides less assistance and requires the student to perform more steps independently.

It is important that students receive positive reinforcement each time they complete the sequence of steps. This increases the probability that they will continue to work on learning the skill. The procedure described here is an example of physical prompting and fading using *backward chaining,* in which teacher assistance is systematically faded out beginning with the

FIGURE 13-3   Terminal Objective: Student Unfolds Pants and Independently Puts Them On

Step Component Behaviors

1. Pulls pants up from thighs to waist	10	10	10	10	10	10	10	10	10	10	10	10	10	10	10	10	10	10	10	10
2. Pulls pants up from knees to thighs	9	9	9	9	9	9	9	9	9	9	9	9	9	9	9	9	9	9	9	9
3. Pulls pants up from ankles to knees	8	8	8	8	8	8	8	8	8	8	8	8	8	8	8	8	8	8	8	8
4. Stands up	7	7	7	7	7	7	7	7	7	7	7	7	7	7	7	7	7	7	7	7
5. Puts on pants with one foot in and other started in the legs	6	6	6	6	6	6	6	6	6	6	6	6	6	6	6	6	6	6	6	6
6. Puts on pants with one foot started in just past crotch	5	5	5	5	5	5	5	5	5	5	5	5	5	5	5	5	5	5	5	5
7. Puts on pants when placed in front in correct position	4	4	4	4	4	4	4	4	4	4	4	4	4	4	4	4	4	4	4	4
8. Positions pants in lap, front facing up	3	3	3	3	3	3	3	3	3	3	3	3	3	3	3	3	3	3	3	3
9. Unfolds pants and puts them on	2	2	2	2	2	2	2	2	2	2	2	2	2	2	2	2	2	2	2	2
10. Positions self correctly (sitting) and puts on pants	1	1	1	1	1	1	1	1	1	1	1	1	1	1	1	1	1	1	1	1
Sessions	1	2	3	4	5	6	7	8	9	10	11	12	13	14	15	16	17	18	19	20
Dates																				

Sessions/Dates

Source: Adapted from H.D. Fredericks et al. (1980). *The teaching research curriculum for moderately and severely handicapped: Self-help and cognitive.* Springfield, IL: Charles C. Thomas, p. 86.

last step of the task analysis. With some skills it is preferable to fade out assistance on the first step of the task analysis, as in assembly tasks; this sequence of fading is called *forward chaining*. Physical prompting and fading have been used to teach a variety of self-care, motor, and vocational skills to students with severe and multiple disabilities (Snell, 1987). It is therefore imperative that special educators be thoroughly familiar with the design, implementation, and evaluation of this type of program.

How does a teacher use the "time delay procedure"?

Other instructional procedures that have been successful with students who have severe developmental disabilities include the system of least prompts (Doyle, Wolery, Ault, & Gast, 1988), stimulus shaping, stimulus fading, time delay (Wolery, Ault, Doyle, & Gast, 1986), and behavior chain interruption strategies (Romer & Schoenberg, 1991). It is beyond the scope of this chapter to describe each of these instructional procedures, but the time delay procedure deserves some discussion in light of its relatively recent introduction into special education classrooms.

TIME DELAY. The time delay procedure has proved to be an effective, efficient way to teach a range of skills to learners with severe disabilities, including eye contact, object recognition, meal preparation, manual sign reading, bed making, instruction following, self-feeding, and the initiation of verbal requests. Quite simply, the time delay procedure entails systematically increasing the amount of time between the moment a teacher asks a student to make a response ("Show me the sign for *more*") and the time the teacher prompts the correct response (the teacher models the manual sign for *more* for the student to imitate). Initially, the task direction and the prompt are paired. Over successive trials or blocks of trials, the teacher waits longer and longer (e.g., 1 second, 2 seconds, 3 seconds, and so on) before presenting the prompt. This allows the student more time over successive trials to perform the correct response independently. If the student is unsure of the correct response, he or she can wait, and the teacher will provide the prompt. Regardless of whether the student responds correctly before or after the prompt, the student will be reinforced. Only if he or she makes an incorrect response is the reinforcer withheld and a correction procedure employed. Students with severe disabilities have typically anticipated the correct response 100 percent of the time before the 7-second delay period; that is, they have achieved independent performance. Figure 13-4 is a diagram of the time delay procedure for a coin identification task. For more information on the time delay procedure, see Wolery, Ault, and Doyle (1992), Gast, Wolery, Doyle, Ault, and Alig (1988), and Schuster and Griffen (1990).

What is a behavior chain interruption strategy?

BEHAVIOR CHAIN INTERRUPTION STRATEGIES. Another instructional procedure for use with students with severe and profound disabilities, the behavior chain interruption strategy, has received recent attention in the research literature (Goetz, Gee, & Sailor, 1985; Hunt, Goetz, Alwell, & Sailor, 1986; Romer & Schoenberg, 1991). The procedure has been effective in teaching students a variety of communicative behaviors. A behavior chain interruption strategy is used while a student is engaged in some type of chained task, such as bed making. During the task, the trainer interrupts the student and a "communicative response is then required in order to gain access to subsequent steps in the activity" (Romer & Schoenberg, 1991, p. 70). In addition, the student can be interrupted without direct intervention from the teacher. Materials can be missing from the task, which would require the student to make a communicative response requesting the materials. Although the research on behavior chain interruption strategies is limited, the current data are promising.

What role does the environment play in the teaching and learning process?

OTHER INSTRUCTIONAL ISSUES. Effective instructional procedures are helpful and necessary when teaching functional skills to students with severe disabilities. However, other instructional issues are also important to consider while teaching these students. One such issue is the instructional environment. Environments can enhance or impede skill development,

FIGURE 13-4   Progressive Time Delay Teaching Model

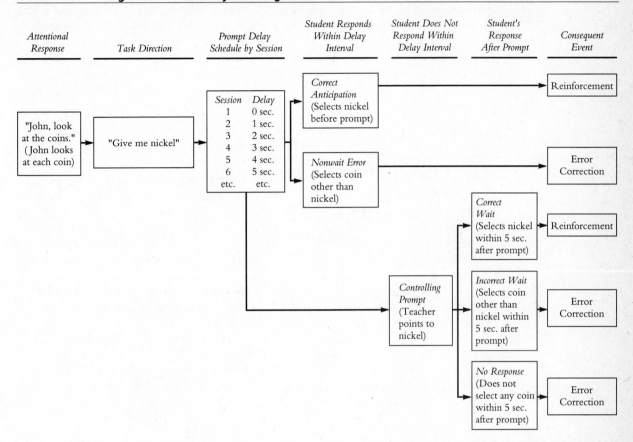

especially in the area of communication. For example, the development of communication skills can be affected by (1) other people in environments where persons with severe disabilities interact (Bryen & McGinley, 1991), and (2) the arrangement of the environment through teaching procedures (Haring, Neetz, Lovinger, Peck, & Semmell, 1987). The environment can provide cues for students to engage in communication skills. Ostrosky and Kaiser (1991) describe seven strategies for arranging the instructional environment in order to promote communication. Some of the strategies include providing interesting materials; placing some wanted materials and objects out of reach so that students will make requests for those objects; delivering inadequate portions of material or not all of the materials necessary to complete a task, so that students will need to ask for more; giving students choices; and creating situations in which students need assistance so that they may request help.

Another issue to consider is the type of instructional arrangement. Students with severe disabilities can be taught in both individual and group arrangements. Recent research has shown not only that students with severe disabilities *can* learn in group instructional arrangements, but that they often learn skills taught to other students during the same group lesson (i.e., observational learning), as well as information presented incidentally (Collins, Gast, Ault, & Wolery, 1991; Farmer, Gast, Wolery, & Winterling, 1991; Gast, Doyle, Wolery, Ault, & Farmer, 1991).

A third issue is the finding that giving students choices throughout the day can affect their skill development (Ostrosky & Kaiser, 1991), on-task behavior (Parsons et al., 1990), and the exhibition of appropriate behavior (Winterling et al., 1987). Teaching students with severe disabilities to make choices has become a growing area of concern for service providers (Parsons & Reid, 1990), especially since most caregivers and teachers of students with severe disabilities cannot adequately predict the choices these students would make (Green et al., 1988; Parsons & Reid, 1990).

It should also be remembered that each student is unique and will require differing amounts and types of instruction. For some students with sensory impairments, enhancing visual and auditory stimuli as well as using tactile teaching strategies will be important (Downing & Eichinger, 1990).

How does technology relate to the education of students with severe disabilities?

TECHNOLOGY. The role of technology for individuals with severe and multiple disabilities cannot be overstated. Chapter 3 covers the wide range of technology available for students with varying disabilities. Although the field of assistive and adaptive devices and other technology is new, it appears that students with severe and multiple disabilities will be primary consumers of this technology. Communication devices, interactive video systems, environmental control instruments, improved prosthetics, and other technological advances have a major role in the education of students with severe disabilities (Lahm, 1989). The use of technology will also "play a critical role in facilitating optimal participation" of these individuals in all areas of society (Parette, 1991). Technology allows students with severe disabilities to perform a wide range of behaviors, including learning new skills (e.g., Horn, Jones, & Hamlett, 1991); controlling the environment (e.g., Brown & Cavalier, as cited in Lahm, 1989); showing preferences (Dattilo & Mirenda, 1987); and communicating through many different types of technologically related devices (Mirenda, Iacono, & Williams, 1990).

Many instructional procedures have been effective in teaching functional skills to students once thought to be unteachable. Although optimal instructional methods have yet to be identified for some students, research continues, and for the vast majority of persons with severe learning disabilities, an instructional technology is available. Although the database of "how to teach" is continually expanding, teachers still face the challenge of discovering new and more efficient procedures for teaching students with severe and developmental disabilities.

PROBE 13-5   Instructional Methods

1. Explain what is meant by a "functional chronologically age-appropriate skill" for an adolescent with a severe developmental disability.
2. List the four phases of learning and the instructional purpose of each.
3. List two basic assumptions about learning that are associated with the behavioral model of teaching (applied behavior analysis).
4. How do behaviors classified as self-injurious differ from those classified as self-stimulatory? Describe two behaviors in each category.
5. Describe the method of physical prompting and fading frequently used to teach students with severe disabilities gross motor skills (e.g., dressing, bathing, throwing a ball, opening a can).

TRANSITION

You should be able to describe the basic components of a transition plan for students with severe disabilities, tell why transition plans are needed, and discuss how they should be developed.

Most students without disabilities usually have very few problems when making the many transitions required throughout their educational experiences. That is, students without disabilities seem to adapt relatively well when going from preschool to elementary school, from

TECHNOLOGY IN ACTION

Anita is a nonverbal 5-year-old child enrolled in a classroom that serves children with severe multiple disabilities. She seldom makes eye contact with adults when her name is called and does not imitate movements that are being presented by her teacher. A meeting with her parents and a communication specialist was called by Mr. Tsao, her teacher, to discuss this problem.

All parties at the meeting agreed that Anita must be taught to make eye contact with adults. The reason that this is so important is that eye contact is a prerequisite for learning other skills. For example, if eye contact can be established on command and maintained, then Anita can observe and learn things from others who share her environment. There was agreement at the meeting that Anita should be taught to make eye contact within five seconds of her name being called, and that eye contact should be maintained for a minimum of ten seconds.

Before starting the eye contact training program, Mr. Tsao identified four items that Anita liked, which could be used as reinforcers for correct responses. He then developed two objectives, one for each phase of the eye contact program. His Phase 1 objective was "Anita will turn her head in the direction of the teacher within five seconds of her name being called 90 percent of the time over three consecutive days without teacher prompts." The Phase 2 objective was "Anita will turn her head in the direction of the teacher, make eye contact within five seconds of her name being called, and maintain eye contact for ten seconds 90 percent of the time over three consecutive days without teacher prompts."

Mr. Tsao taught the objective for Phase 1 (head orientation) through a progressive time delay procedure. For the first instructional session, he said, "Anita (pause), look at me" and immediately (zero-second delay) physically guided Anita's head so it was facing forward. He verbally praised Anita while holding her head in place and presenting her with a small spoonful of applesauce, which was one of the reinforcers that had been identified earlier. This zero-second delay procedure continued for all ten trials of the first training session.

In the second session, Mr. Tsao conducted trials exactly as in the first session, except that he waited one second before physically guiding Anita's head forward. With each subsequent session, he waited an additional second before prompting Anita to turn her head. By the sixth session (five-second delay interval), Anita met the criterion for Phase 1; but she was not making eye contact with Mr. Tsao.

In the seventh training session, Mr. Tsao initiated Phase 2 training. To teach Anita to make and maintain eye contact, he said, "Anita (pause), look at me," which resulted in Anita's turning her head forward. Once her head was in this position, Mr. Tsao moved a strawberry (one of the other reinforcers) into her line of vision and slowly moved it to his eye level, making sure Anita was visually fixating on it the entire distance. When Anita was looking at the strawberry positioned at Mr. Tsao's eye level, he covered it with his hand, said "Good looking," and then immediately gave her the strawberry.

With each subsequent training session, Mr. Tsao made two subtle changes, provided that Anita met the preceding eye contact duration criterion. First, he required Anita to raise her head more each session (approximately 3 inches) in order for the reinforcer to be in her direct line of vision. Second, he covered the reinforcer with his hand for longer periods of time (session two for one second; session three for two seconds, etc.), while continuing to require Anita to maintain eye contact before delivering the reinforcer.

By systematically requiring Anita to perform more of the behavior independently and maintain eye contact for longer periods of time before receiving the reinforcer, Anita was taught an important basic skill in nearly errorless fashion. Mr. Tsao gradually eliminated the use of tangible reinforcers and found that Anita would respond appropriately for a social reinforcer—praise.

Through this carefully designed instructional program, which used task analysis, a response prompting procedure (progressive time delay), behavioral shaping, and differential reinforcement, Anita was able to begin working on her next educational objective, which was motor imitation. Although some people may not see Anita's learning to establish and maintain eye contact on command as a significant achievement, it served as a basic first step on the road to greater independence.

elementary to middle school, from middle school to high school programs, and from high school to postschool environments, whether work or college. However, students with severe disabilities will most likely encounter difficulties when going through transition unless systematic instruction occurs (Brown et al., 1981).

What is an ITP?

To ensure that students with severe and multiple disabilities get the most out of their education, it is important for teachers to develop plans, in advance, to help these students make the transition from one setting to the next, whether from one school to another, or from school to postschool placements, such as supported or competitive employment (Hasazi & Clark, 1988; Moon, Inge, Wehman, Brooke, & Barcus, 1990; Wehman, Moon, Everson, Wood, & Barcus, 1988). According to Brown et al. (1981), when a student's educational environment changes, it "cannot be assumed that he or she will adjust, adapt, function appropriately, generalize skills, or transfer training, to the extent that performance in the new environments will be as independent and as productive as possible" (p. 628). Planning must occur if transition is to be successful, especially from school to the workplace (Powell et al., 1991). An individualized transition plan (ITP) will help alleviate the difficulties that students with severe disabilities experience during transition. Transition issues are covered in depth in Chapter 5.

Each individualized plan is based on information from a variety of sources about the requirements of current and future environments where the student must function. In addition, the transition plan outlines the services that will be provided to ensure a smooth transition. Brown et al. (1981) outline seven basic components of an individualized transition plan:

1. An individualized transition plan must be comprehensive in nature. Plans must represent skills from all curricular domains and activities that the student is expected to perform.
2. An individualized transition plan must be truly individualized for each student. Like individualized education, each student will have unique needs and requirements.
3. An individualized transition plan must have the involvement of parents or guardians. Research has shown that many parents were not aware of the transition plan for their child even though most all parents wanted some involvement in their child's transition to postschool life (McNair & Rusch, 1991).
4. An individualized transition plan requires the actual participation of both sending and receiving personnel. If a student is moving from a preschool to an elementary setting, staff from both educational settings must be involved in developing the transition plan.
5. An individualized transition plan should include the focused experience of competent related service personnel. In addition to the student's former and future teachers, it is important that other members of the student's current and future transdisciplinary teams be included in the development of the transition plan.
6. An individualized transition plan requires direct instruction in a variety of actual subsequent environments. Prior to transition, students with severe disabilities should be instructed within numerous settings of the environment in which they will be subsequently placed.
7. An individualized transition plan should be longitudinal in nature. The transition plan should be developed for a student long before the transition is to occur. For example, Brown et al. (1981) suggest that the plan for a high school student's transition to postschool environments be started no later than age 15. (pp. 628–630)

PROBE 13-6   Transition

1. Why are transition plans necessary for students with severe disabilities?
2. List the transitions that students proceed through that require transition plans.
3. Describe the basic components of a transition plan.

SERVICE DELIVERY

> **You should be able to describe the advantages of an integrative service delivery model and the types of services necessary to maintain persons with severe developmental disabilities in the community.**

Philosophical, ethical, legal, and practical forces have shaped current service delivery systems for students with severe developmental disabilities. The roles of some of these forces are briefly described below.

Normalization

As discussed in Chapter 2, the principle of normalization suggests that persons with disabilities should have the opportunity to live as much like persons without disabilities as possible, and that this goal can be met by exposing them to the living conditions common to their culture (Wolfensberger, 1972). This philosophy provided the impetus for the deinstitutionalization of persons with severe developmental disabilities. It was hoped that the social interactions and demands of the community environment would result in adaptive behavior. This view is, of course, oversimplified. If students with severe developmental disabilities are to adapt to the community environment, then medical, educational, and other social services must be available. It is essential that these services be coordinated.

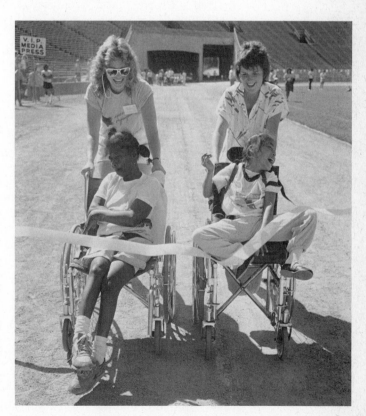

Activities such as Special Olympics provide normalization opportunities for people with severe developmental disabilities.

Access to Educational Services

LITIGATION. As students moved out of residential institutions and as parents began to keep their children in the community rather than institutionalize them, parents began to seek educational services. However, students were frequently refused such services because of their disabilities. Parents sought help from the courts. One of the earliest and most important cases that addressed the educational rights of students with disabilities was *Pennsylvania Association for Retarded Children v. the Commonwealth of Pennsylvania* (1971). This landmark case successfully secured the right to a free, appropriate, public education for all children with mental retardation (see Chapter 1 for a description of the provisions of this case). In another landmark case, *Mills v. The Board of Education of the District of Columbia* (1972), the educational rights of students with mental retardation, secured in the *Pennsylvania* case, were extended to all children with disabilities, regardless of type (mental retardation, physical handicaps, or emotional disturbances). These two cases, in conjunction with court cases addressing the right to treatment and rehabilitation of persons with mental illness residing in state institutions (*Wyatt v. Anderholt,* 1970; *Wyatt v. Stickney,* 1972), set in motion a movement on behalf of all persons with disabilities that changed the direction and model for service delivery.

LEGISLATION. Advances were also made in Congress. Section 504 of the Rehabilitation Act of 1973 stated that persons with disabilities could not be discriminated against by any program receiving federal financial assistance. As a result of these successes and considerable cooperation between parent and professional groups, Public Law 94–142 (Education for All Handicapped Children Act) was written and passed. The provisions of this law, as well as PL 101-476, are described in Chapter 1. It is mentioned again here to emphasize that the provisions do apply to students with severe developmental disabilities. One of the provisions of the law is that "to the maximum extent appropriate," students with disabilities are to be educated with students without disabilities.

Community-based Services

The exodus of students from residential state institutions to the community and the provision of appropriate services for students in the community involve more than the educational system. Many families have shown that they can care for and provide stimulating environments for children with severe developmental disabilities. Not all families, however, have the desire or capability to do so. Further, as parents grow older and as they attempt to establish more independent behaviors in their young adult with disabilities, alternative living arrangements are needed. Beyond foster family or natural family living, Sailor and Guess (1983) have discussed a continuum of possibilities ranging from group homes to independent living. Options between the two extremes include cluster apartments and room-and-board facilities. One of the most common options is group homes—facilities in which a small group of persons (usually six to ten) live together under supervision. For information on the cost-effectiveness of group homes as well as other residential options, see Templeton, Gage, and Fredericks (1982); Gage, Fredericks, Johnson-Dorn, and Lindley-Southard (1982); and Ashbaugh and Nerney (1990).

When is respite care needed?

Besides living arrangements, other family and student support services are needed. These include specialized medical care, dental care, recreation programs, arrangements for participation in religious services, transportation, and work centers (Kenowitz, Gallaher, & Edgar, 1977). Families will probably need *respite care* (Salisbury & Intagliata, 1986). Respite care involves someone other than a family member caring for the person with disabilities while the parents or family are away. The period of respite may range from a few hours to several days.

The last decade has seen a proliferation in employment programs for students with severe disabilities, including both supported and competitive options. Gone are the days when the only option for students was a sheltered workshop. The literature documents many successes in providing the training and support needed for persons with severe disabilities to obtain and maintain employment (e.g., Conley, Rusch, McCaughrin, & Tines, 1989; Kregel, Wehman, & Banks, 1989; McDonnell, Nofs, Hardman, & Chambliss, 1989; Shafer, Banks, & Kregel, 1991; Shafer, Wehman, Kregel, & West, 1990). Although the data are very encouraging, professionals will continue to be challenged by the multitude of vocational needs exhibited by these students.

Finally, it is unlikely that students with severe developmental disabilities will be maintained in the community without group and individual advocacy. Traditionally, groups of parents and professionals such as the National Association for Retarded Citizens, National Society for Autistic Children, United Cerebral Palsy Association, and others have served important functions. They have started new services, stimulated communities to start services, monitored services, initiated court cases, and helped develop and pass legislation. Professional groups such as The Association for Persons with Severe Handicaps (TASH) and the Council for Exceptional Children (CEC) have clarified issues, assisted in court cases, helped develop legislation, prompted research, and disseminated information. These activities are needed and must continue. However, a need also exists for persons in local communities to serve as advocates for individual students (Sailor & Guess, 1983). Such persons ensure that students receive appropriate education and related services.

As Sailor and Guess (1983) indicate, the entry and maintenance of students with severe developmental disabilities into the educational system and community is an exciting yet demanding process. Although considerable gains have been made, there remains a need for innovative service delivery systems and applied research.

PROBE 13-7   Service Delivery

1. Describe the concept of normalization as it relates to providing services to persons with developmental disabilities.
2. Name two court cases that helped establish the current level of services to students with severe developmental disabilities.
3. List four types of services that must be available if students with severe developmental disabilities are to be successfully integrated into the community.

SUMMARY

1. Students with severe developmental disabilities are a heterogeneous population. They are characterized by low cognitive abilities and are likely to exhibit additional behavioral, physical, and sensory handicaps.
2. Research has shown that students with severe and multiple disabilities are educable and can benefit from instruction if it is systematic and data-based.
3. To maximize independent functioning, instruction focuses on the acquisition, fluency, generalization, and maintenance of functional skills.

4. Assessment of students with severe and multiple disabilities requires input from professionals in a variety of disciplines. The transdisciplinary approach facilitates the design of educational program plans that address individual student needs across the curriculum areas.

5. Students with severe and profound disabilities, to function as independently as possible, should be taught chronologically age-appropriate, functional skills in a variety of school and nonschool environments.

6. Instruction for students with severe and multiple disabilities should take place at naturally occurring times and as part of naturally occurring routines and skill clusters.

7. Teachers of students with severe disabilities must be able to design, implement, evaluate, and modify instructional programs in accordance with applied behavior analysis principles and procedures. They must be able to handle severe behavior problems and to understand and manage a wide range of medical and physical problems.

8. Teachers of students with severe behavior problems must learn to change inappropriate behaviors through the use of nonaversive procedures.

9. Like other children with developmental disabilities, students with severe disabilities are entitled to be educated in the least restrictive environment appropriate.

10. Students with severe disabilities require individualized transition plans for the smooth transition from school to postschool programs.

TASK SHEET 13   Field Experiences with Students with Severe Developmental Disabilities

Select one or more of the following alternatives and complete the required tasks. Write a report of no more than three pages about your activities.

Parent Interview

Interview the parents of a student with severe disabilities. Try to determine some of the problems the parents have encountered or will encounter in raising their child and placing him or her in educational programs. Try to find out what services the parents have found helpful or not helpful, as well as additional services that they need.

Observation

Visit an educational program that includes students with severe disabilities and talk with administrators, teachers, peer tutors, related service personnel, parents, teaching assistants, and/or other staff members. Describe the physical setting, the type of program, and the activities that you observed. In your report, answer the following questions about the provision of the "least restrictive opportunity" (items 1 and 2); also include a student description (item 3) and your assessment of the program (item 4).

1. *Facility*
   • Is the facility placed near the center of the community agency?
   • To what extent does the facility isolate children from other students with and without disabilities?
   • What related services do the individuals with severe disabilities receive, and how are the services delivered?
   • What architectural barriers did you observe?

2. *Opportunities for Normal Integration*
   - What opportunities are the students given to practice in the community those skills that they learned in the classroom?
   - What opportunities are there for students to interact with students without disabilities? How frequently are these opportunities offered?
3. *Students*
   Write a brief description of one of the students with severe disabilities that you observed. What skills are targeted for instruction for this student? What related services does this student receive? What are the student's likes and dislikes? How is the student similar to you?
4. *Appropriate Educational Programming*
   Use your observations to comment on the training of the staff, the staff expectations for student performance, assessment procedures, the goals established for the students, the adequacy of instruction, and evaluation procedures.

Participation

Volunteer your services at a school or agency serving persons with severe disabilities and record your activities, impressions, and questions. Describe the areas in which you think individuals with severe disabilities would require intensive training before they could function in the community.

Community Resources

Develop a list of the community agencies and their services that are available to persons with severe disabilities and their families. Write a three-page summary that synthesizes your findings, including how you might use the services if you were a professional working in the field of severe disabilities.

Library Study

Use the library to identify at least three articles related to the education of children with severe and multiple disabilities. Write a one-page abstract of each, concluding with a paragraph about your reactions to the article. Here are the names of some journals in which you can find articles:

> *Education and Training in Mental Retardation*
> *Exceptional Children*
> *Exceptionality*
> *Journal of Applied Behavior Analysis*
> *Journal of Behavioral Education*
> *Journal of the Association for Persons with Severe Handicaps*
> *Mental Retardation*
> *Research in Developmental Disabilities*
> *Teaching Exceptional Children*

Design Your Own Field Experience

If none of these alternatives appeals to you or you have an opportunity to perform some other task with students with severe disabilities, design your own field experience. Check with your instructor to determine its acceptability.

Tony was a 10-year-old boy with bright eyes and a beautiful smile. Until he started school, his parents never imagined that he had a learning disability. He could carry on an adult-level conversation and loved to listen to stories, although he showed little interest in looking at books.

Yes, his mother said, it was hard for him to learn to ride a bike and to zip his coat, and he did wear her out with all of that activity—he was touching, poking, tapping something all the time and never wanted to take a nap.

In kindergarten and first grade he scribbled on the color sheets, wouldn't copy lines or circles, refused to try to print his name. He wouldn't sit still while others looked at little books in reading circle, and at the end of the year, he still couldn't recognize any of the words the other children knew.

When Tony was tested, the psychologist said his vision and hearing were normal, his intelligence was above average, but that he had something called a "learning disability."

14

Students with Learning Disabilities

Deborah Bott Slaton and Catherine V. Morsink

Learning disabilities is a label for problems in learning that are not the direct result of disadvantaged background, mental retardation, sensory impairments, or behavioral disorders. As can be seen from the case on the facing page, an individual with learning disabilities can be easily misunderstood by teachers and parents. These disabilities are extremely varied and complex; they include specific difficulties in learning to read, write, calculate, and solve problems. The potential impact of a learning disability is not limited to academic skills; individuals may also find it unusually difficult to use a map, start conversations, or manage money. Learning disabilities may impede academic, social, and vocational performance; therefore, they can affect the degree to which individuals attain success and independence across home, school, work, and community environments. More students are identified as eligible for special education services for learning disabilities than for any other disability. The next section defines learning disabilities and describes a variety of terms associated with this category of disability.

TERMS AND DEFINITIONS FOR LEARNING DISABILITIES

> **You should be able to name alternative terms for *learning disability* and to paraphrase the elements found in the federal and professional organizations' definitions.**

Only since the 1960s have people used the term *learning disabilities.* This probably does not mean that learning disabilities are a modern phenomenon. Just as in sciences such as physics or biology, identifying a condition marks the beginning of inquiry and understanding, not necessarily the beginning of the phenomenon. Interpretations of historical evidence have led some scholars to conclude that Thomas Edison, Woodrow Wilson, Hans Christian Andersen, and Leonardo da Vinci had symptoms of learning disabilities (Aaron, Phillips, & Larsen, 1988). It is likely that there have always been individuals with these difficulties.

Creation of the Term *Learning Disability*

Who coined the term *learning disability*?

The term *learning disability* was created in the early 1960s by one of the pioneers in this field, Dr. Samuel Kirk. The term appeared in the professional literature when Kirk used it in his 1962 textbook, *Educating Exceptional Children.* The first organization to adopt the term was the Association for Children with Learning Disabilities (ACLD), which was organized under that name in 1963. Kirk advised that the term *learning disability* might be preferable to other terms prevalent at that time (e.g., *cerebral dysfunction* or *brain-injured*), since it was more related to teaching and learning.

The term *learning disability* was popularized in response to social and political influences (McGrady, 1987). For example, the ACLD was an influential organization created by parents who were concerned that their children were not learning in school and yet were not eligible for special services. Advocates emphasized that individuals with learning disabilities represented a group of students who were not being adequately served in most public schools. In 1969, passage of the Children with Specific Learning Disabilities Act (PL 91-230) represented the first official use of the term by the United States government. This act provided funding for teacher training and led to learning disabilities being included as an area of exceptionality within PL 94-142 when it was passed in 1975.

Alternative Terms for *Learning Disability*

What other terms are used when referring to learning disabilities?

Labels attached to learning disabilities have changed over time. Before we had the term *learning disability,* individuals who had difficulty learning were described using many different terms. Even though the term *learning disabilities* is widely recognized today, people still use a variety of terminology to describe all or part of the population that has them.

The identification and study of individuals with learning problems distinct from mental retardation began during the 1930s. Early research in the field was conducted by physicians, psychologists, and neuropsychiatrists, so the vocabulary they used to describe learning problems had a medical orientation. Many terms used during the 1940s, 50s, and 60s reflected an emphasis on the suspected cause of the disabilities, which was brain injury. Examples of terms reflecting the medical model include *brain-injured* (Strauss & Werner, 1942), *minimal brain dysfunction* (Clements, 1966), and *psychoneurological learning disorder* (Myklebust, 1964). Terms such as these refer to unseen and frequently unsubstantiated damage to the brain or central nervous system.

Some labels avoid implications of brain injury and emphasize a cognitive process as the basis of the learning problem. Phrases such as *perceptual disability* (Cruickshank, 1976) or *specific language disabled* (Slingerland, 1976) indicate a belief that the learning problem is closely related to an impaired process such as auditory discrimination or receptive language.

Other terms used to identify learning problems are limited to describing disabilities in specific areas of the curriculum. There is a whole family of these terms: *dyslexia,* meaning difficulty with reading; *dyscalculia,* meaning difficulty with mathematics; *dysgraphia,* meaning difficulty with handwriting or written expression, and so forth. The term **dyslexia** is sometimes applied casually when referring to a person with learning problems, but educators and researchers most often use it to describe a severe impairment in reading. When used alone, these terms may not describe the range and complexity of an individual's difficulties with learning. Some educators avoid these terms because of the narrow scope of each term, the possibility for misinterpretation, and the "medical sound" of the labels.

Unfortunately, other descriptors of individuals with learning problems have been used by teachers, parents, and possibly the individuals themselves. Persons with learning disabilities report being called *lazy* or *uncooperative* by people who had no other explanation for why an intelligent person who did not have a visible disability or disadvantage failed to learn as efficiently as his or her peers.

In the United States, federal, state, and local government regulations include learning disabled as a category of disability. Children, youth, and adults who qualify as learning disabled are eligible for government-supported special education services from schools and agencies. The phrase *learning disabilities* is also used outside the context of government regulation and public services where eligibility criteria are applied. Only a portion of all people with learning disabilities are designated as such within schools. Some people with learning disabilities are adults who were in school before the label was widely used or services were available. Other people experience a learning disability that is less severe than that required to be eligible for special services, and still others may not be detected by the schools' assessment process, which is sometimes imperfect.

Definitions of Learning Disabilities

People adopted the term *learning disabilities* (LD) with little difficulty. Developing a definition that everyone agrees on has been a much different story. Formal definitions of learning disabilities have been and continue to be controversial. Keogh (1987) suggests that this debate results from the mistaken belief that there is one true definition of learning disabilities. She advocates a "multidefinitional approach to LD" (p. 6) in which definitions are designed to fit specific purposes. Parents, individuals with learning disabilities, researchers, teachers, school administrators, and representatives of government agencies all have different purposes for defining the category. These purposes are not always compatible. For example, public schools with limited resources may define learning disabilities in narrow terms to limit the number of students eligible for services to those with severe learning problems. On the other hand, parents who wish to arrange extra help for their children may prefer a broader definition that includes students with milder learning problems. The definitions provided below are from a government agency and a coalition of professional organizations, so they are designed for purposes of identification, provision of services, and advocacy.

What definition is used by the federal government?

FEDERAL DEFINITION. The primary purpose for governmental definitions of learning disabilities is to describe those individuals who will receive special services supported by public funds. The inclusion of learning disabilities as a category of exceptionality in PL 94-142 meant that the federal government needed a definition of the category. The definition adopted by the U.S. federal government in December 1977 is the same one contained in current federal regulations. This definition appears in Table 14-1.

During 1978, guidelines accompanying this definition were widely discussed, expanded, and modified. The original guidelines and definition were so controversial that changes were required. Final guidelines for the learning disabilities definition in PL 94-142 were not agreed on until January 1979, although the law was passed in 1975. The federal definition and guidelines are not totally operational; that is, they are not sufficient for identifying students with learning disabilities. It is left to state education agencies to develop further guidelines for identifying students whose learning disability makes them eligible for special education services. The controversy surrounding the federal definition is reflected by the fact that only

---

TABLE 14-1   Two Prominent Definitions of Learning Disabilities

---

The United States Office of Education Definition

"Specific learning disability" means a disorder in one or more of the basic psychological processes involved in understanding or in using language, spoken or written, which may manifest itself in an imperfect ability to listen, think, speak, read, write, spell, or to do mathematical calculations. The term includes such conditions as perceptual handicaps, brain injury, minimal brain dysfunction, dyslexia, and developmental aphasia. The term does not include children who have learning problems which are primarily the result of visual, hearing, or motor handicaps, or mental retardation, or of environmental, cultural, or economic disadvantage. (*Federal Register,* December 29, 1977, p. 65083)

The National Joint Committee on Learning Disabilities (1988) Definition

Learning disabilities is a general term that refers to a heterogeneous group of disorders manifested by significant difficulties in the acquisition and use of listening, speaking, reading, writing, reasoning, or mathematical abilities. These disorders are intrinsic to the individual, presumed to be due to central nervous system dysfunction, and may occur across the life span. Problems in self-regulatory behaviors, social perceptions, and social interaction may exist with learning disabilities but do not by themselves constitute a learning disability. Although learning disabilities may occur concomitantly with other handicapping conditions (for example, sensory impairment, mental retardation, serious emotional disturbance) or with extrinsic influences (such as cultural differences, insufficient or inappropriate instruction), they are not the result of those conditions or influences. (NJCLD, 1988, p. 1)

---

22 states use the exact wording of the federal definition in their special education regulations (Mercer, Hughes, & Mercer, 1985).

What are criticisms of the federal definition?

PROFESSIONAL ORGANIZATIONS DEFINE LEARNING DISABILITIES. Controversy over defining learning disabilities persisted after the federal definition was adopted in 1979. According to Hammill, Leigh, McNutt, and Larsen (1981), the major areas of dissatisfaction with the federal definition included the following:

- The word *children* is too limited; it misleads readers to believe that learning disabilities do not occur in older students or adults.
- The list of labels, such as *perceptual handicap* and *developmental aphasia,* is confusing and controversial.
- The "exclusion" clause leads to the misconception that learning disabilities can't be present in persons who also have other kinds of disabilities.

Many experts and professional organizations have devised formal definitions for the term *learning disabilities.* In an effort to build a consensus, representatives of six professional and advocacy organizations formed the National Joint Committee for Learning Disabilities (NJCLD). This group met in 1981 to consider an alternative definition, and five members of the coalition supported a position paper in which an alternative definition appeared. The 1981 definition has recently been revised, and this definition also appears in Table 14-1. The 1988 NJCLD wording has emerged as the most comprehensive and widely accepted definition available to date (Hammill, 1990).

What elements are common to most definitions of learning disability?

There are many other definitions of learning disabilities in addition to those just described. Hammill (1990) systematically analyzed 11 of the most prominent definitions and found the NJCLD definition to contain the elements appearing most frequently among the others. He also reported the following elements as common to the current popular definitions:

1. *Underachievement.* There is a difference between what the individual should be able to do, given his or her level of intelligence or skills in other areas, and what the person is actually doing.
2. *Potential for specific problems in spoken language, academics, and reasoning.* There are specific learned tasks that the individual is unable to master after exposure to conditions under which most peers are successful at performing the task. Individual problems will vary considerably, but there is potential for problems in areas such as speaking, listening, reading, writing, mathematics, and problem solving.
3. *Disruption of the learning process.* The individual has unusual difficulty learning and performing some skills, and the problem is thought to be centered on one or more of the basic psychological processes involved in learning. Examples of "basic psychological processes" include attention, memory, and perception. There are many different theories describing possible learning processes and the disruptions experienced by people with learning disabilities.
4. *Known or suspected central nervous system dysfunction.* Because learning takes place in the brain, learning disabilities are likely related to the **central nervous system** (CNS). In some individual cases, there is medical evidence for CNS dysfunction or damage, but in other cases there is no evidence, only a suspicion.
5. *Potential for multiple disabilities.* While learning disabilities are not the direct result of poor vision or hearing, disadvantage, behavior disorder, or mental retardation, it is possible for these conditions to coexist with a learning disability. These dimensions are reflected in the wide range of terms used to describe learning disabilities and in current definitions.

PROBE 14-1   Terms and Definitions for Learning Disabilities

1. List three alternative terms for learning disabilities. How do these terms influence the way one thinks about the category? What are some limitations of these terms?
2. Federal guidelines indicate that a learning disability means a disorder in _____ _____ , spoken or written, which may manifest itself in imperfect ability to _____ . It excludes children whose learning problems are primarily the result of _____ .
3. Describe each of the following five elements common to the most prevalent LD definitions: underachievement, specific problems in academics and reasoning, disruption of the learning process, central nervous system dysfunction, and potential for multiple disabilities.
4. Reread the chapter vignette. Describe how each of the five elements listed in item 3 may or may not apply to Tony.

CHARACTERISTICS AND PREVALENCE

You should be able to recognize some characteristics of learning disabilities and to distinguish them from simple learning difficulties.

The study of characteristics of learning disabilities is wide-ranging and reflective of many different theories and orientations. This discussion of characteristics is organized using three major features: chronicity, impact, and heterogeneity. That is: (1) learning disabilities are chronic; (2) the impact and severity of learning disabilities falls along a continuum; and (3) many different specific characteristics may be found among people with learning disabilities.

This section also addresses the distinction between learning disabilities and situation-specific difficulties that do not represent a disability. Following the discussion of characteristics, prevalence rates for learning disabilities are described.

Chronicity

Are learning disabilities a temporary condition?

The first major feature of learning disabilities is that they are long-lasting. Because most learning disabilities are detected during elementary grades when academic tasks are first presented to children (Cone, Wilson, Bradley, & Reese, 1985), a great deal of the research and intervention literature emphasizes elementary-age children. This should not lead to the conclusion that learning disabilities are found only in elementary schools. A learning disability is a condition that persists throughout life. In the words of McKinney and Feagans, "learning disabilities do not disappear with time, but constitute a real and lasting handicap" (1984, p. 263).

Demographic studies of adolescents and young adults with learning disabilities revealed that the effects of a learning disability may stay with an individual (Alley, Deshler, Clark, Schumaker, & Warner, 1983). These researchers documented that individuals with learning disabilities were present in secondary schools, vocational schools, the military, and colleges and universities. In a review of research dealing with the long-term effects of learning disabilities, Kavale (1988) concluded that in many instances, deficits detected during childhood could also be detected in later years. Specific and serious disorders such as severe reading problems and attention deficits appear to have a more significant impact on an adult's functioning than do general and mild learning problems.

Viewing learning disabilities as a chronic disability logically leads to the possibility that children of preschool age may exhibit characteristics that predict difficulties in mastering academic skills. Because of the academic emphasis, many children's learning disabilities are detected after they enter school and fail to learn basic skills at an expected rate. However, there is increasing emphasis on preschool screening for learning problems. Esterly and Griffin (1987) identify some key issues in the early education of children with learning disabilities, including the desirability of labeling very young children as being learning disabled, the need for improved assessment and identification criteria, and the lack of consensus on effective prevention or intervention strategies. In much of the early childhood literature, the label *learning disabled* is not used; young children are more typically called *developmentally disabled, developmentally delayed,* or *attention deficit disordered.*

The fact that learning disabilities are chronic means it is important to teach people who have one how to minimize the impact of their disability. We have no evidence of a cure for learning disabilities, but there is evidence that people with learning disabilities can succeed in academic, social, and vocational environments.

Continuum of Impact

How does the concept of a continuum relate to the impact of learning disabilities?

A second feature of learning disabilities is that they may range from mild to severe in how they influence the individual. In most American schools, special education services are a limited and precious resource. Because of funding constraints, it is necessary to sort out who is most in need of services and establish cutoffs for eligibility. Students with the most pronounced and troublesome disabilities are typically those who are referred by classroom teachers and labeled by the school system. Individuals labeled learning disabled are not equally affected by their disability. There is a continuum of severity among such students that indicates the need for a range of educational services.

It is important to separate the school-based process of labeling from the existence of the condition called learning disabilities. It is possible for an individual to have a learning disability that interferes with efficient learning but is not considered severe enough to meet eligibility criteria for special education. For example, a high school student may find that he cannot complete his homework in the same amount of time as his friends. He must read a chapter two and three times in order to complete the study guide, yet his study partner usually only has to read the chapter once to find answers to all the questions. This young man may have mild reading problems that affect how quickly he is able to read and understand his textbooks. His reading problem is not so severe as to qualify him for special services, but it does require him to devote more time and effort to his studies than his peers.

Ellis (1985) suggests that a proper analogy for learning disabilities is not a condition such as the measles—you have it or you don't—but rather a condition such as obesity that occurs along a continuum. A person who is a few pounds overweight will experience few negative consequences. But as the degree of obesity becomes more serious, so do the negative consequences, including both health complications and social stigma. When the obesity analogy is applied to learning disabilities, it is reasonable to assume that mild learning disabilities will have minimal impact on a person's ability to succeed in academic, social, and vocational settings. Learning disabilities that are in the middle or toward the severe end of the continuum will have a more significant impact on the individual and call for more intensive interventions.

Recent research evidence supports the continuum concept. Stanovich (1988) presented evidence that reading problems are not discrete, and he described factors that promote or inhibit good reading as being "continuously arrayed in multidimensional space" (p. 599). A longitudinal study that followed a group of children from first through sixth grades (Shaywitz, Escobar, Shaywitz, Fletcher, & Makuch, 1992) demonstrated that reading problems among the children fell along a continuum, and that there was not a distinct subgroup of children with "dyslexia." This view challenges us to consider the full range of learning disabilities and the possibility that they do not constitute a unitary phenomenon with clear boundaries.

Heterogeneity

What specific characteristics may be found among the population with learning disabilities?

A third major feature of learning disabilities is heterogeneity. Researchers and practitioners have not identified any one specific behavior or symptom that distinguishes all individuals with learning disabilities (Kavale & Nye, 1985; Keogh, 1988). The idea of heterogeneity—diversity within a group—implies that if we are to understand what characterizes learning disabilities, we must have knowledge about a wide range of behaviors and attributes. Researchers have identified a variety of characteristics that occur within the population, but any individual with learning disabilities will likely exhibit a unique combination of those characteristics.

In what four domains do the characteristics of people with learning disabilities fall?

Keep the concepts of chronicity and continuum of impact in mind as you read the descriptions of characteristics. For people with learning disabilities, the qualities described in the following section persist across time and vary in intensity. This description of characteristics is organized by the four domains that Kavale and Nye (1985) used in their systematic review of experimental research on learning disabilities: linguistic, achievement, neuropsychological, and social behavior domains. Table 14-2 summarizes these four categories. Even though the domains are discussed separately, the characteristics interact. For example, many achievement deficits are probably related to both linguistic and neuropsychological factors. Some research-

TABLE 14-2   **Characteristics That May Be Found Among People with Learning Disabilities**

Linguistic Deficits

Receptive language: listening, interpreting
Expressive language: speaking, writing

Academic Deficits

Reading: decoding, comprehension
Writing: spelling, mechanics, structure, style
Mathematics: calculation, problem solving
Problem solving

Neuropsychological Deficits

Self-concept
Attribution of successes and failures
Attention to appropriate stimuli; sustained attention
Perception of auditory and visual stimuli
Motor skills: fine motor (handwriting); gross motor
Memory

Social Behavior Deficits

Interpersonal skills
Task-related and independence skills

ers are trying to identify patterns of characteristics that recur as specific subtypes of learning disabilities, and this research is also described.

What role does language play in learning disabilities?

LINGUISTIC DEFICITS. Some researchers suggest that learning disabilities are related to overall language facility (Kavale & Nye, 1985; Wiig & Semel, 1984). A frequent observation is that learners with disabilities continue to use language incorrectly long after it has been mastered by age-mates with comparable education and background. Linguistic deficits can involve both receptive and expressive abilities. For example, Knight-Arest (1984) found that preadolescent boys with learning disabilities were less effective giving an oral description of how to play checkers than were normally achieving boys in a comparison group. Specifically, the boys with learning disabilities used more words to relay less information, relied more on physical gesturing and demonstration, and often did not adapt their message to meet the needs of the listener. Magee and Newcomer (1978) investigated the relationship between oral language and academic achievement in children with learning disabilities. They indicated that (1) correct grammar and understanding words and sentences are more closely related to academic achievement than are articulation and speech discrimination skills; (2) math proficiency is related to language ability; and (3) language skill seems to enhance children's ability to acquire general information about their environment. Because communication is such a pervasive human activity, problems in language can affect an individual in complex and serious ways.

ACHIEVEMENT DEFICITS. Persons with learning disabilities are characterized most often by their difficulties in learning academic skills. A great deal of research on learning disabilities has focused on characteristics in basic skill areas such as reading, mathematics, and writing.

Some researchers are also examining higher-order thinking skills such as problem solving and strategy application.

In what academic areas do individuals with learning disabilities have difficulty?

Reading. Reading problems characterize the majority of individuals labeled learning disabled (Cone et al., 1985), and there is evidence that severe difficulties in reading may be detected as early as the end of first grade (Felton & Wood, 1989). At present, several researchers are focusing on phonological processing as the basis for specific reading disabilities (Felton & Wood, 1989; Stanovich, 1988; Torgesen, 1988). The phonological process required for reading involves learning, remembering, and rapidly retrieving the sound-symbol matches that comprise the system of written language used in English or any other written language. The extreme difficulty some persons have in learning and using phonological skills may be an example of a specific cognitive deficit that distinguishes people with learning disabilities from others who experience reading problems due to general mental disabilities or disadvantaged background. Difficulty with phonological skills results in poor word identification and spelling skills.

Certainly poor decoding makes comprehension of printed material difficult. However, Englert and Thomas (1987) found evidence that some students' difficulties with comprehension may represent deficits that are distinct from decoding problems. They found that students with learning disabilities were less sensitive to the structural cues in text that successful readers use to help comprehend the meaning of written material. For example, text that is written in a sequential structure describes first-to-last temporal relationships among events. Students with learning disabilities were often not able to identify sentences that would fit within a sequential paragraph and those that were not compatible with the text structure. Disabled readers are not all alike. Some have extreme difficulty in figuring out new words (decoding) but are able to understand very well when someone reads the information to them. Others can recognize words but have extreme difficulty comprehending meaning or analyzing and applying information. The nature and source of reading disabilities is an active area of research.

Written Expression. Like reading, written expression is highly influenced by an individual's understanding and use of language structures. People with learning disabilities who have difficulties with language are likely to experience difficulties in the complex task of producing written language. In a report to the U.S. Congress, the Interagency Committee on Learning Disabilities (1987) cited studies suggesting that the majority of people with learning disabilities have difficulty with some aspect of written expression (e.g., spelling, handwriting, and composition), but that not every individual will have difficulty with the same component. These findings suggest that a general underlying problem with language frequently extends to difficulty in written communication.

Mathematics. Johnson and Mycklebust (1967) were among the first to study the mathematical disorders of students with learning disabilities. They hypothesized that there were two main types of disorders: those related to difficulty in processing auditory or visual information, and those characterized by an inability to perform arithmetic calculations. More recently, several other factors have been described as contributing to some individuals' difficulties with mathematics, including language problems, memory deficits, conceptual difficulties, and use of strategies that are inadequate or inefficient (Interagency Committee on Learning Disabilities, 1987).

What are metacognitive skills?

Problem-solving Deficits. Recent research has gone beyond basic skills to examine problem-solving skills of individuals with learning disabilities. A term often used within this literature is *metacognition,* which means "thinking about thinking." You are using metacognitive skills when you consider the best way to use your time during an objective test or use a memory trick to remember a list of items. There is evidence that many students with learning disabilities do not spontaneously generate and apply effective problem-solving strategies (Deshler et al., 1982; Palincsar & Brown, 1987; Stone & Forman, 1988). Researchers working

TECHNOLOGY IN ACTION

Libby Holmes is a resource teacher for students with learning disabilities in a middle school. She has a computer in her classroom, which she uses for a variety of tasks that support her teaching.

One of her students, Edna, is having difficulty adding numbers with carrying. Ms. Holmes knows that Edna can add with carrying. She suspects that Edna has forgotten some of her adding skills and that a review would be all that is needed to rectify the problem.

She selects a computer program that enables her to generate four different sets of 44 addition problems that require carrying. The first is to be used as a diagnostic test, the second as a worksheet following instruction on the concepts that Edna has forgotten, the third is to be used as a homework assignment, and the fourth as a test to check whether she has mastered the concepts.

To use the program, Ms. Holmes simply follows the instructions that appear on the screen. She is asked to indicate the type of problems that she wants. After selecting *addition* from the menu, she is asked for the number of digits, whether carrying is wanted, and the number of problems. Following her answers, the computer prompts her to turn on the printer and the worksheets are printed, complete with a second set of problems that contain the answers, which will help her quickly evaluate Edna's responses. No two pages are identical.

Five of the students who come to Ms. Holmes' room are learning how to type. They are using a computer program that is designed to improve their speed and accuracy. Ms. Holmes loads that program into her computer, enters her password, and is shown a record of each student's performance during the previous week. She then makes a decision about which students need additional work.

A program that generates crossword puzzles is used to develop a puzzle for Scotty, who is studying internal combustion engines in his science class. Ms. Holmes enters 20 scientific words into the computer, each followed by a brief definition. The computer generates a crossword puzzle and puts the definitions at the bottom of the page. Again, an answer sheet is printed for teacher reference.

Ms. Holmes then stores the grades from the papers she has corrected over the weekend onto a computer disk that is used with a grade book program. She keeps all her student records on the computer.

This teacher also turns to the computer for help in reviewing a new English textbook that the school is considering purchasing for her use. Using another computer program, she types in three 100-word passages; the computer then analyzes the reading level. She determines that the reading level is too high for most of her students.

Finally, using a word processor, she writes a brief note to the parents of one of her students. She had previously recorded several paragraphs related to items of classroom business that occur on a frequent basis. She calls several of these paragraphs up for use in the letter. She then adds information that is unique to that piece of correspondence. This procedure has enabled her to communicate more frequently with the parents of her students, who have reported that they appreciate the extra contact.

Ms. Holmes completes her work in a little more than two hours. Previously, if she had attempted to do all these things by hand, it would have taken her most of the day. She is convinced that the availability of the microcomputer is helping her to become a more efficient teacher.

in this area have established that some persons with learning disabilities differ from normal learners in their abilities to develop, execute, and evaluate approaches for complex tasks. Much of this evidence is based on the study of adolescents who, because of their age, would normally be expected to have developed strategic approaches to complex tasks. The fact that many individuals with learning disabilities do not appear to be actively applying successful problem-solving strategies led Torgesen (1982) to identify the phenomenon of the "inactive learner." The inactive learner idea is very closely related to self-concept and attribution, which are discussed in the following section.

NEUROPSYCHOLOGICAL DEFICITS. Neuropsychological processes are associated with behavior, cognition, and the central nervous system. Because each of these factors is related to learning, neuropsychological deficits can be characteristic of persons with learning disabilities.

Specific areas within neuropsychological deficits are self-concept and attribution, attention, perceptual and motor skills, and memory.

Self-Concept and Attribution. Self-concept refers to the way in which individuals view themselves. People who experience repeated failure in learning skills valued by society might logically react to these failures in ways that negatively affect their self-concept. Indeed, there is evidence that persons with learning disabilities sometimes have lower academic self-concepts and lower expectations for success than do their peers without disabilities (Hiebert, Wong, & Hunter, 1982). But it is not correct to automatically assume that a learning disability leads to a generally negative self-concept. A two-year longitudinal study by Kistner and Osborne (1987) that involved students with school-identified learning disabilities indicated that while the children did report more negative perceptions of their academic abilities, many of them felt positive about some nonacademic abilities and generally exhibited positive self-esteem. These findings may only apply to individuals labeled learning disabled in schools. As Kistner and Osborne emphasized, the formal identification process may allow individuals to attribute academic failure to a specific cause not within their control, to experience greater academic success within special classrooms, and to adopt a peer comparison group of other students with learning disabilities.

Related to the idea of self-concept is the term *attribution,* which refers to people's beliefs about how success or failure may be related to their efforts and abilities. Most people attribute success to ability and effort. Pearl, Bryan, and Donahue (1980) found that students in their samples who had learning disabilities did not believe their achievement was under their control. Other researchers found that, although a group of adolescents with learning disabilities verbalized a desire to do well, they failed to expend greater effort and also predicted that they would score lower on subsequent tasks of equal difficulty (Tollefson, Tracy, Johnsen, Buenning, Farmer, & Barke, 1982). Negative expectations paired with reduced effort may put some individuals with learning disabilities into a cycle of failure in which the learner doesn't expect to succeed, doesn't expend sufficient effort to succeed, and is reinforced for this viewpoint by not succeeding (Rogers & Saklofske, 1985).

Attention Disorders. Early work in the field of learning disabilities suggested that some children with serious learning difficulties found it hard to focus their attention on a teacher giving a lesson, on a written assignment, or on a selected sound, word, number, or line of print (Cruikshank, Bentzen, Ratzeburg, & Tannhauser, 1961; Strauss & Lehtinen, 1947). Some professionals refer to difficulties such as these as *attention deficit–hyperactivity disorder* (ADHD) (American Psychiatric Association, 1987) and the broader term, **attention deficit disorder** (ADD). Attention deficits are well established as factors that can inhibit learning.

During 1990 and 1991, the U.S. Department of Education requested comments from citizens regarding special education and children with ADD. After receiving over 2000 written comments and conducting a careful review, department personnel issued a memorandum in which they clarified that children with ADD may be served in special education if their disorder affects their school performance to such a degree that they meet eligibility requirements for any of the following disability categories: learning disabilities, seriously emotionally disturbed, and other health impaired. Approximately 5 to 20 percent of individuals with learning disabilities also have attention disorders (Interagency Committee on Learning Disabilities, 1987).

Individuals with ADD are described as overactive, restless, impulsive, inattentive, distractible, easily frustrated, aggressive, and unpredictable. Pihl and Niaura (1982) suggested that the ability of some children with learning disabilities to sustain task attention deteriorates over time (most markedly after ten trials) rather than as a function of task complexity. In addition to the problem of sustaining attention is the ability to selectively attend to relevant information. Another possible consequence of an attention problem is that students may focus on the

In what ways are self-concept and learning disabilities related?

What is an attention disorder?

irrelevant details while missing the central issue (Hallahan, Gajar, Cohen & Tarver, 1978). Another possible problem is that individuals may guess at answers impulsively, without looking at the word, listening to the question, or thinking through their response. Even though there may be improvements in attention due to any combination of natural development, behavioral interventions, or medication, there is evidence that ADD characteristics can continue into adulthood (Kavale, 1988).

What are
perceptual
disorders?

Perceptual and Motor Skill Deficits. Early researchers in the learning disabilities field emphasized perceptual disorders, or apparent difficulties in organizing, interpreting, and using sensory input. Learners with disabilities were observed to have difficulty recalling the orientation and sequence of letters, a phenomenon that the neurologist Orton (1937) termed *strephosymbolia,* or twisted symbols. Reversals of letters and words are behaviors that many people continue to closely associate with learning disabilities, although some individuals with learning disabilities do not seem to have difficulty with reversals. Strauss and Lehtinen (1947) noted that children they called neurologically impaired tended to perceive fragmented parts rather than integrated wholes, that they were distracted by extraneous details, and that they did not perceive figures as distinct from their backgrounds. Strauss and Lehtinen also discussed these students' difficulty in relating sound patterns to letters in words. They suggested that some individuals had a tendency to perseverate (repeat the same response over and over again) or to respond impulsively. Reports of perceptual deficits have persisted in the literature on learning disabilities, especially as auditory and visual perception relate to reading (Chall, 1987; Stanovich, 1986). Although most definitions of learning disabilities do not include motor disorders, poor motor skills have long been associated with these learning problems. Motor incoordination, which ranges from general awkwardness to poor handwriting, may be observed in individuals who have other characteristics of learning disabilities.

Memory Deficits. Many students with learning disabilities and their teachers find it frustrating when the student appears to know information one day and forgets it the next. Memory deficits have been reported as characteristic of learning disabilities for many years, and there is evidence that affected students do not perform well on memory tasks when

*This student is receiving individual
attention from the teacher.*

compared to average and low-achieving students (Swanson, Cochran, & Ewers, 1990). Swanson (1982) theorized that memory deficits represent an important "structural limitation" (p. 27) that differentiates persons with learning disabilities from normal learners. Torgesen (1979) proposed that memory deficits result from the individual's failure to use effective mnemonic strategies that facilitate remembering. Memory strategies include rehearsing important material, categorizing similar items, and grouping large numbers of items into smaller clusters. In his more recent work, Torgesen (1988) links memory deficits to "inefficiency in coding, or representing, the phonological features of language" (p. 605).

SOCIAL SKILL DEFICITS. Social behavior is a complex area of learning, and it should not be surprising that many persons who have difficulty learning academic subjects also experience problems learning appropriate social behavior. Although a learning disability is primarily defined as an academic problem, researchers and educators are increasingly concerned about the inappropriate or inadequate social behavior demonstrated by many persons with learning disabilities. Schumaker and Hazel (1984) found that some adolescents with learning disabilities demonstrated social behaviors that were less acceptable than those of their peers without disabilities and resembled those of juvenile delinquents. A large-scale review of research literature in this area (Gresham, 1988) revealed that students with learning disabilities were no different from their peers without disabilities in terms of frequency of social interactions, but the quality of these interactions tended to be more negative and inappropriate. In addition to interpersonal behavior, there is evidence that some students with learning disabilities demonstrate serious deficits in the area of task-related behavior, which includes such skills as being on-task, completing tasks, following directions, and working independently (Gresham & Reschly, 1986).

Because social behavior requires interactions among people, perceptions of others become an important factor when studying social skills. These perceptions are described by sociometric studies in which other people (e.g., teachers, parents, and classmates) were asked about the social status of individuals with learning disabilities. Overall, sociometric research indicates that people with learning disabilities are often rejected or ignored by others (Gresham, 1988). Dudley-Marling and Edmiaston (1985) also reviewed sociometric research and caution us not to generalize that having learning disabilities always leads to social rejection. These authors point out that some students with learning disabilities were actually found to be popular, and it is more accurate to consider them as "at risk" for difficulties with social interactions. A sociometric study (Stone & La Greca, 1990) in which students with and without learning disabilities were differentiated as popular, rejected, neglected, average, and controversial found that 75 percent of the children with learning disabilities and 45 percent of the children without such disabilities were placed in the low-status groups of "rejected" and "neglected." The rejected children were more likely to be aggressive and disruptive. The neglected children, who were typically ignored by others, were more likely to be quiet and withdrawn.

SUBTYPE THEORIES. Some researchers have not been satisfied to say that learning disabilities represent a heterogeneous collection of characteristics, and they have tried to analyze the heterogeneity in ways that might reveal certain subtypes. These researchers look for subgroups within the population of those with learning disabilities that share distinctly similar characteristics. The purpose of this line of research is to eventually develop interventions that are differentially effective for members of each subgroup. One distinction some people make is distinguishing learners on the basis of preferred modality. It is not uncommon to hear people refer to individuals as "auditory" or "visual" learners, but the research evidence for this distinction and its utility for instruction is very weak (Arter & Jenkins, 1977; Kavale & Forness, 1987; Larrivee, 1981; Tarver & Dawson, 1978).

Can social learning also be affected by a learning disability?

How do other people react to individuals with learning disabilities?

Does everyone agree on subtypes of learning disabilities?

Recent subtypes research has relied on sophisticated statistical techniques called *cluster analysis*. Lyon (1985) studied children identified as having reading disabilities and eventually distinguished two groups, one for whom synthetic phonics instruction was superior, and one for whom whole-word instruction plus analytic phonics instruction was superior. Other researchers (McKinney, Short, & Feagans, 1985) arrived at a different subtype schema based on a complex classification battery; they identified three groups of children with learning disabilities who were found to have abnormal and distinct profiles in terms of their strengths and weaknesses across language and perceptual skills.

The concept of subtypes is not accepted by all. For example, Stanovich (1988) rejected the concept for reading disabilities and cited evidence indicating that subtypes are the result of "arbitrarily imposed partitioning" (p. 600). To date, subtypes research has not produced results that are easily translated into practice.

Distinguishing Learning Disabilities from Common Learning Problems

How can learning disabilities be distinguished from common learning problems that do not represent a chronic disability?

When reading the descriptions of characteristics of learning disabilities, the reader may say, "I have that problem," or "That's just the way my nephew acts—I wonder if he has a learning disability." Everyone experiences difficulties in learning certain things under particular conditions, but these common learning problems are not related to learning disabilities. They are temporary and normal reactions to confusing stimuli, fatigue, or lack of background and experience. Following are some examples of common learning problems experienced by many of us:

1. We all occasionally have problems focusing our attention. We may be distracted by other thoughts, or we may not know where to focus our attention. Can you read Figure 14-1A? If you focused on the words hidden behind the lines, you read, "Are you paying attention?" The question, "Can you read Figure 14-1A?" may have given you a clue to look for words. Materials that present distractions—as this one did—are particularly difficult for people with learning disabilities. But difficulty in attending to the relevant stimuli in a distracting background is common to everyone.

2. You can understand part of the mystery of perception by reflecting on your experiences with visual illusions like the one in Figure 14-1B. If you stare at the cube for about ten seconds, it seems to flip over. Your perception of its orientation changes. In a similar manner, some individuals with learning disabilities seem to be unstable in their perception of images, especially printed words. Everyone has that difficulty sometimes, but it isn't a learning disability unless it's pervasive and persistent.

3. What kinds of things are hardest for you to remember? Try this experiment. Look at Figure 14-1C for five seconds. Write what you saw. Now try Figure 14-1D. Look at it for five seconds. Write what you saw. Now check yourself. Why was BRIOGANTRY easier? Probably because it looked more like a word, and the letters could be placed in chunks, or clusters of two or more letters, to simplify learning them. Some people with learning disabilities don't seem to know how to group things into meaningful parts to help them recall. Many people try to remember things one fragment at a time, just as you may have with XTMSLFKBQH. They need help to understand how parts are meaningful and can be grouped. They also need lots of interesting practice and continued reinforcement to achieve mastery. It is difficult for anyone to remember unrelated facts or abstract figures that don't make sense.

4. Some people with learning disabilities have difficulty with cognitive skills. Try this example to see how you respond to problems that require careful thinking (Whimby, 1977, p. 255):

What follows the day before yesterday if two days from now will be Sunday?

FIGURE 14-1   **Examples of Perceptual Problems**

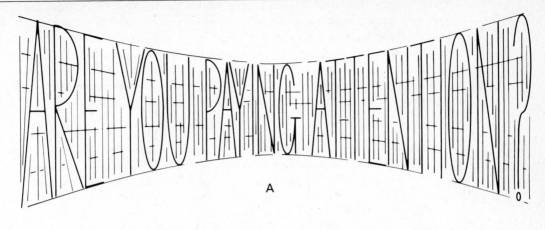

A

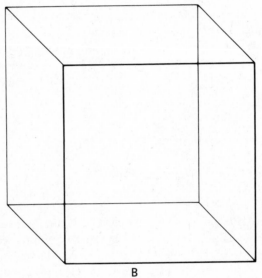

B

BRIOGANTRY

C

XTMSLFKBQH

D

Can you answer the question quickly? What did you try to do when you read this problem? If you're a systematic problem solver, you tried to take it apart and solve it one step at a time. On the other hand, you may have been tempted to be a one-shot thinker, as some people with learning disabilities are, and just guess at the answer. Of course, you'd find this problem harder to solve if it was read to you out loud and you had to hold the details in mind while solving each step. Certain circumstances can turn anyone into an impulsive learner, but unless the behavior occurs frequently and interferes with learning, it's not a characteristic of learning disabilities.

5. Language problems related to multiple meanings illustrate a common learning problem. When you were little, did you think shoetrees were trees that grew shoes? Actor Fred Gwynne has written a delightful children's book called *A Chocolate Moose for Dinner* (Gwynne, 1976). It illustrates children's simpler ideas of words that adults know have multiple meanings. It shows, for example, a picture of how "lions *pray* (prey) on other animals." (Picture that in your mind's eye!) Such difficulties with language are understandable, because our language is filled with abstraction and multiple meanings. This behavior isn't a characteristic of learning disabilities unless it continues long after language abilities have matured and the individual has received appropriate vocabulary instruction.

All these examples were, of course, vastly oversimplified for the purpose of illustration. They were intended to show that all of us have some of the problems often attributed to people with learning disabilities. It is important to remember that they may just be common problems and not symptoms of a disability.

Incidence and Prevalence in School Population

How many individuals have learning disabilities?

Estimates on the number of individuals who meet the criteria for learning disabilities vary according to what definition or purpose is applied. When learning disabled was first included as a category of disability within special education, the school-age incidence was predicted to be 2 percent. A 1987 report by the Interagency Committee on Learning Disabilities stated that good prevalence data are not available, but members of the committee estimated that 5 to 10 percent of people in the United States are affected by learning disabilities. Learning disabled is by far the most frequently used category within special education programs for school-age students; during the 1989–90 school year, 49 percent of the students in special education programs for students ages 6 to 21 were labeled learning disabled (United States Department of Education, 1991). The number of students identified as having learning disabilities in public schools rose by 140 percent between 1977 and 1988 (Gerber & Levine-Donnerstein, 1989). (See the later section on identification and assessment for a discussion of this trend.) Chalfant (1987) estimates that between 20 and 30 percent of the school-age population have learning problems; however, estimates of prevalence depend on how one defines learning disabilities or learning problems. For example, Chalfant includes all learning problems resulting from "social isolation, dependence, poverty, family difficulty, or other causes" (p. 240).

PROBE 14-2   Characteristics and Prevalence

1. What evidence do we have that learning disabilities are a chronic disability?
2. Is the school-identified population the entire population of people with learning disabilities? Explain your answer.
3. How might the conditions of obesity and learning disabilities be analogous?
4. Define *heterogeneity* and describe why this is an important concept when considering characteristics of learning disabilities.

5. List ten characteristics associated with learning disabilities.
6. According to the most recent report from the federal government, what percentage of the school-age population is identified as having learning disabilities?

ETIOLOGIES: CAUSES OF LEARNING DISABILITIES

You should be able to identify both physiological and environmental causes of learning disabilities; you should also be able to describe why it may or may not be important to identify the origins of a learning disability.

Establishing cause, or causes, of an individual's learning disability is often difficult. Just as learning disabilities have many characteristics and symptoms, they probably have many causes. The search for the etiology of a learning disability is often complicated and imprecise because it can be extremely difficult to make a direct cause-effect link between possible causes and observed symptoms. There are parallels between the multiple definitions for learning disabilities, the multiple estimates of their prevalence, and the multiple theories about their etiologies. An individual's viewpoint about the definition of learning disabilities is closely related to what range of causes that person will accept.

Are the causes physiological, environmental, or both?

Before examining specific etiologies, think about this question: *Under what conditions does efficient and effective learning take place?* There are two essential components to productive learning: the learner and the environment. The learner must be able to attend to, process, understand, and use information present in the environment. In order to do this, the physical, emotional, and cognitive conditions of the learner must be conducive to learning. The other essential component to learning is the environment. If learning is to take place, the environment must contain information that is useful, appropriate, and intelligible. Further, the environment must, at the very least, not inhibit the learner's access to available information. At best, the environment will facilitate the learning process. When searching for causes of learning disabilities, it makes sense to consider both the learner and the environment.

People argue and disagree about the origins of learning disabilities. One point of view emphasizes abnormality within the individual, usually neurologically based dysfunction. An alternative viewpoint focuses on the environment. People emphasize environment either because knowing physiological etiology is not particularly helpful in improving learning, or because an environmental influence is the source of the problem. Another viewpoint accepts both physical and environmental origins as playing an interactive role in the etiology of learning disabilities. The following descriptions of suspected causes illustrate the complexities involved in establishing cause. Because no single theory of etiology is sufficient to explain all cases of learning disabilities, it is important to be aware of the wide range of suspected causes. A discussion of the utility of establishing the origins of learning disabilities is also provided.

Etiologies That Focus on the Learner

Theories about within-the-learner causes for learning disabilities primarily involve an assumption of physical damage or abnormality within the brain and central nervous system (CNS). Among students served in LD programs, about 20 percent are thought to have had a prior brain injury (Bigler, 1987), which means that most people with learning disabilities do not have a clear diagnosis of brain injury. To further complicate the picture, abnormalities in CNS functions are also documented for a part of the population of learners without learning disabilities (Kavale & Forness, 1985). The Venn diagram in Figure 14-2 illustrates these relationships. However, learning is a brain-based function, and it is important to understand that current evidence about neurological functioning is limited to current diagnostic technologies.

Linking learning disabilities to CNS dysfunction leads to questions about what caused the damage. Researchers have nominated many different possibilities as causes of CNS dysfunction, including hereditary and genetic conditions, biochemical imbalances, malnutrition, oxygen deprivation, toxins including harmful drugs, weakened immune system, and head injury (Smith, 1991). Exposure to these factors may occur before, during, or after birth. One example of a postbirth factor is exposure to lead-based paint or water from old lead pipes, which is known to cause permanent brain damage. A study of young adults who were exposed to lead as children indicated that these people were six times more likely than their peers to be identified as having learning disabilities (Needleman, Schell, Bellinger, & Leviton, 1990). Another example of a physical etiology for learning disabilities is the evidence that attention deficit disorder can result from biochemical imbalance (Silver, 1987). Even for individuals with diagnosed CNS dysfunction, identifying the specific cause can be impossible. Neurologists may not have physical evidence that reveals cause, and if the injury or exposure was in the distant past, it may not have been recorded or remembered by anyone.

Etiologies That Focus on the Environment

Theories that point to the environment as contributing to learning disabilities primarily focus on the school environment. It is plausible that poor teaching causes many children to fail to make progress in school (Felton & Wood, 1989). While poor teaching alone may not cause learning disabilities, the student who has a learning disability may be more susceptible to teaching that is disorganized or inappropriate. Related to the issue of poor teaching is the idea that while teaching may not be of inferior quality, it may still be a mismatch for the learner's needs. An example of this relationship between the child and the environment is early entry into school. Maddux, Green, and Horner (1986) found that children who entered first grade between the ages of 6 years, 0 months and 6 years, 5 months—categorized as early-entering—

FIGURE 14-2   Venn Diagram

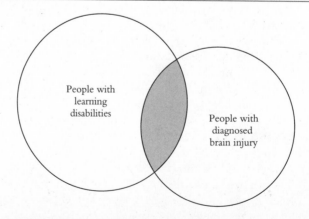

were found to have learning disabilities more frequently than were children categorized as late-entering. The researchers concluded that many of the young children in their study were not in a school environment that met their needs, and they subsequently failed to learn at a rate commensurate with their abilities.

There is also evidence that traditional school environments are a mismatch for some students who are members of minority cultures or students who are from disadvantaged backgrounds. As an example, the percentage of African American students placed in classes for those with learning disabilities more than doubled during the six-year period from 1978 to 1984 (Wyche, 1989). The relatively high numbers of students from minority cultures identified as having learning disabilities could mean that being culturally different places students at a disadvantage in some classrooms, and they are subsequently identified as having learning disabilities (Gerber & Levine-Donnerstein, 1989). These examples raise the possibility that there is not a problem within the learner; there is a problem within the environment. Certainly factors in the environment beyond school may also influence how efficiently an individual learns. Disadvantaged backgrounds frequently do not provide individuals with the conditions necessary for effective learning, such as motivation, nutrition, safety, and consistency.

While according to the current U.S. federal definition, learning disabilities may not be caused by environmental, cultural, or economic disadvantages, determining the impact of these differences and deprivations as opposed to any other cause of a learning disability is often beyond the expertise of the school personnel and parents who are making placement decisions.

Utility of Establishing Etiologies

Why be concerned with etiology for learning disabilities?

There are two primary goals in establishing the causes for learning disabilities. The first is the possibility that knowledge about origins of the disorder can lead to interventions. That is, based on etiology, perhaps steps may be taken to correct, cure, or alleviate the cause, thus lessening the severity of the disability. Ethics require professionals and parents to seek treatment for any correctable physiological or environmental problem related to learning disabilities. It is important to note, however, that in many individual cases, etiology is never clearly established; yet educational interventions can still be effective in improving academic achievement and social competence. A second goal for establishing etiologies is the possibility that learning disabilities could be prevented in the future. Identifying physiological and/or environmental factors that cause learning disabilities is an area of research that can indicate preventive measures. For example, the findings about exposure to lead toxins as an etiology for some cases points to preventive action. There are educational parallels to this concept. If inferior or inappropriate teaching causes some cases, then it is necessary to change that classroom teaching in order to prevent other cases.

Some professionals want to use etiology as the single determining factor between those who have "true" learning disabilities and those who experience simple learning problems. The single factor most frequently raised in this discussion is *CNS dysfunction* (Adelman, 1989). This is an interesting state of affairs, because at present we can only "presume" CNS dysfunction in most cases; so calling for this distinction appears to go beyond what medical and educational diagnostics are able to deliver. Before CNS dysfunction becomes the litmus test for learning disabilities, there will need to be much stronger evidence about the reliability, validity, and function of assessment procedures designed to detect CNS dysfunction. At present, etiology plays a very minor role in identifying learning disabilities (Chalfant, 1985); this is probably because etiology has not emerged as a functional concept for either identification for special education or design of educational programs.

PROBE 14-3   Etiologies: Causes of Learning Disabilities

1. Why is central nervous system dysfunction a suspected cause of learning disabilities?
2. List six possible causes of CNS dysfunction.
3. Describe two environmental factors that could be related to learning disabilities.
4. To what extent is knowledge of etiology helpful when working with individuals who have learning disabilities?

IDENTIFICATION AND ASSESSMENT

You should be able to describe and critique assessment procedures used with individuals suspected of having a learning disability.

What are two purposes of assessment?

Just as the definitions, characteristics, and etiologies of learning disabilities are controversial and varied, so are identification and assessment techniques. These techniques are used for the purposes of designating individuals as eligible for special services and for providing educators with information necessary to design and evaluate interventions. The two purposes of eligibility decisions and monitoring students' progress are discussed separately.

Assessment for Determining Eligibility for Special Services

Federal guidelines for PL 94-142 give individual states responsibility for defining specific guidelines to apply when designating which individuals to label as learning disabled and serve in special education. This results in many different criteria and procedures used to determine eligibility. In summarizing a National Task Force Report on identifying students with learning disabilities, Chalfant (1985) reported that many school districts find the task of identifying students with learning disabilities to be quite difficult. As a result, some individuals are said to have a learning disability when they probably do not, and others who have a learning disability go undetected.

Why is the identification of learning disabilities often controversial and imprecise?

Chalfant summarized the factors that contribute to misidentification, as follows: (1) heterogeneity of characteristics; (2) lack of a precise definition; (3) difficulty in establishing cutoffs for when a learning problem becomes a disability; (4) lack of services for students with other learning problems (e.g., mild mental disabilities, disadvantaged backgrounds, and conduct disorders); (5) use of tests that are not valid or reliable; (6) multidisciplinary teams that are not prepared to work effectively as a group; (7) parental pressure to use the term *learning disabilities* rather than *mental retardation* or *emotional disturbance*; and (8) poorly defined procedures for dismissing students from special education or for serving students with learning disabilities in mainstream settings. In a comprehensive study of students classified as having learning disabilities in Colorado, Shepard and Smith (1983) concluded that 57 percent of the sample did not meet the legal criteria for such a classification; they also found that approximately half of the funds available for services for those with learning disabilities were spent on identification and placement.

Each time the federal government has conducted a count of the number of students with disabilities served under PL 94-142, the number of students with learning disabilities has increased. According to Graham and Harris (1989), "overidentification of learning disabilities is a socioeconomic political event" (p. 503). Identification of students as having learning disabilities is done within a context of school systems operating with limited resources in the face of increasing numbers of students at risk for school failure. One way to get students extra help is to say they have a learning disability and send them to special education. It is easy to see how school-identification of learning disabilities may not be a technically accurate and consistent identification process, but rather a means to an end—the end being extra help with academic learning.

Why is aptitude-achievement discrepancy difficult to determine?

One example of how the identification process may be manipulated to serve larger or smaller numbers of students is the **aptitude-achievement discrepancy** component found in many state regulations. The discrepancy between what an individual is capable of doing (aptitude or intelligence) and how he or she is performing (achievement) is a measure frequently used in determining eligibility for services for learning disabilities. For example, if a sixth grade student has an IQ of 105 (which is within the average range), and the student's standard score on a reading achievement test is 55 (well below the average score of 100), then this student exhibits a discrepancy between aptitude and reading achievement. There is a discrepancy because we would expect that an individual with average intelligence would be reading at a level that matched age and intelligence. That is not the case for this student. An aptitude-achievement discrepancy tells us that the individual is underachieving, and a learning disability is only one explanation for underachievement. Students may not achieve up to their potential for a variety of factors, including chronic absences, poor instruction, transient history, and so forth. While aptitude-achievement discrepancy is an important part of some eligibility requirements, it alone is not sufficient evidence to determine the presence of a learning disability.

Aptitude-achievement discrepancy is widely described as a key concept for the identification of learning disabilities, but there is no consensus on how to determine such a discrepancy. Sometimes the discrepancy is determined by examining the differences between standard scores from IQ and achievement tests, and sometimes complex statistical formulas are applied. Algozzine and Ysseldyke (1987) question the scientific basis of the discrepancy concept and the way in which it is used to make decisions about eligibility for special services. It is possible to manipulate the number of students who will qualify for LD services by setting relatively strict or permissive standards for discrepancy. There is no one "true" discrepancy level that indicates a learning disability, and as Algozzine and Ysseldyke describe it, decisions about criteria for discrepancy are really entitlement decisions that are made to select out who will receive special services.

What criteria are used for identifying individuals with learning disabilities?

CRITERIA FOR IDENTIFICATION. Because of the problem of misidentification, some states are changing the criteria for classifying a student as having a learning disability. Often, reasons for changes are the classification of too many students as having learning disabilities and the inconsistent application of identification procedures among local districts. Mercer, Hughes, and Mercer (1985) surveyed all 50 state departments of education and documented how state guidelines in effect during the mid-1980s directed practitioners to go about identifying learning disabilities. In terms of specific criteria for identification, the following factors were included: academic difficulties (96 percent of the states); exclusion of other sources of difficulty (92 percent); process disorders (86 percent); language disorders (84 percent); discrepancy between intelligence and academic achievement (84 percent); thinking deficits (68 percent); neurological impairment (62 percent); miscellaneous factors such as attention deficits (16 percent); and intraindividual differences (6 percent). These authors found variability across state definitions and guidelines, which leads to the possibility that a student could be classified as having a learning disability in one state, move with his or her family to another state, and not meet eligibility criteria in the new location.

THE IDENTIFICATION PROCESS. Given the variation in how states go about identifying students with learning disabilities, the following description of the identification process is intended to be generic and not a detailed description of any single agency's guidelines for formal testing.

Prereferral or Child Study Activities. Some state and local guidelines require that prior to any formal testing for learning disabilities, activities take place to assist the classroom teacher in meeting the needs of any children with learning problems. Examples of prereferral activities, also called child study, include the use of alternative instructional techniques and curriculum, assistance from a consultant to a classroom teacher, and teams of teachers doing cooperative problem solving about individual children (Chalfant, 1985). The hope is that these types of activities can support classroom teachers in maintaining more students in the regular classroom environment, and that fewer students will be referred to and placed in special education.

Formal Testing Procedures. After a student is referred to special education within due process procedures, formal testing begins. Tests given to a student suspected to have a learning disability are designed to do the following: (1) provide data on the student's overall intelligence level and academic strengths and weaknesses; (2) summarize the student's approach to the learning process; and (3) rule out other factors (visual, hearing, or motor disorders; low intelligence; environmental disadvantage) as primary causes of the problem.

Academic strengths and weaknesses are typically determined by achievement tests. Although the scores on group tests might be used for screening, they are not adequate for identification of learning disabilities. The achievement tests should be those specifically designed to be individually administered by a qualified professional. They might be norm-referenced tests, which provide scores comparing the student's performance to others at a particular age or grade level. Or they might be criterion-referenced tests, which indicate which of a set of sequential skills the student has mastered. The academic areas of reading, mathematics, and spelling are almost always evaluated. When necessary, the other areas in which the disorders may be manifested—listening, thinking, talking, writing—are also tested. The examiner tries to discover whether the student's academic achievement is significantly below the level of expectation for students of similar ability, age, and grade level, and also whether the student has a pattern of academic strengths as well as weaknesses.

For some learning disability eligibility regulations, it is also important that the examiner try to determine whether the referred student shows any signs of disorder in the "psychological processes" involved in understanding or using spoken or written language. An individually administered IQ test is used to determine whether the student's level of intelligence is significantly higher than his or her academic performance. Often, other tests may be given to assess psychological and language processes such as auditory-visual association and verbal expression. There is a great deal of controversy over the meanings of these mysterious "psychological processes"; yet there is some agreement that unless a learning disability can be related to such a basic disorder, every student whose performance is below average could be said to have a learning disability. Since there is so much question about the use of standardized tests to document a "process disorder," most examiners also include data collected through classroom observations and work samples for the documentation of any process disorder.

The examiner also tries to rule out other factors as primary causes of the learning problem, as specified in the definition's "exclusion" clause. For example, there should be evidence that visual and auditory acuity are within normal range in order to rule out poor vision or hearing as causes of inadequate performance. If intelligence testing indicates an overall low level of cognitive functioning and achievement commensurate with potential, the

(margin notes)

What steps are typically followed in a formal evaluation for learning disabilities?

What type of academic testing is necessary?

How are intelligence tests used?

How are exclusions addressed during testing?

category mental retardation would probably be more appropriate than learning disability. The area of behavioral and emotional disorders can be especially problematic when applying the exclusion concept, as many students exhibit both learning and behavior problems. Establishing the "primary" cause of the disability often challenges the diagnostic skills of the multidisciplinary team.

Are there alternatives to formal testing?

Curriculum-based Assessment. The formal assessment process is complex and lengthy, involving the judgment of many professionals as well as careful documentation of the evidence. Even so, the assessment of learning disabilities is controversial and imperfect. Shinn and Marston (1985) describe **curriculum-based assessment** (CBA) as an alternative to the expensive and sometimes imprecise testing procedure described in the preceding paragraphs. In their study, elementary-age students were given brief, informal tests that measured how accurately and quickly they read passages, spelled words, and computed arithmetic problems. On the basis of these relatively simple measures, the researchers were able to distinguish students who were placed in special education from those who were low-achieving and normally achieving. Using CBA did not distinguish among categories of mild disabilities. Shinn and Marston suggest that school districts adopt an "explicit percentage model" (p. 36) in which professionals determine the number of students for whom resources are available in special education, and then use CBA to select those most in need of special services. They suggest that this process would be much less expensive than formal testing procedures currently used for identification. Marston and Magnusson (1985) demonstrated the feasibility of using curriculum-based measurement in a large, urban school district for purposes of screening, identification, program planning, and monitoring.

CBA may be used to identify those students performing academic tasks at a level significantly below that of their age-mates. The fact that CBA may be less expensive and more closely tied to instruction than are norm-referenced testing procedures lends additional appeal to the use of CBA for identification. However, under current federal regulations, students must be identified as belonging to a category of disability, such as learning disabilities, and CBA procedures do not reliably distinguish among learning disabilities, behavior disorders, and mild mental retardation. Issues of assessment challenge professionals to consider the value of using a system of distinct categories for funding decisions and service delivery.

Assessment for Designing Interventions

What type of assessment can help teachers decide what and how to teach?

If the data collected for determining eligibility rely on standardized and formal testing, those data will probably not be helpful when designing intervention. For example, knowing that a student scored in the 42nd percentile on a standardized reading test and scored 114 on an IQ test may all be necessary for determining eligibility for special services, but that information is of limited use to the classroom teacher who needs to make decisions about instructional objectives, materials, and teaching approaches. Assessment for designing interventions typically relies on curriculum-based assessment (CBA), that is, criterion-referenced measures based on the curricula used in the student's program and direct observation of the learner in classroom settings. CBA is an ongoing process, and collecting data on a student's progress within the curriculum is necessary for determining when to continue with an intervention that appears effective, when to change an ineffective intervention, and when to go on to a new instructional objective. There is strong evidence that including CBA as part of the instructional program for students with mild disabilities results in improved academic achievement (Fuchs & Fuchs, 1986).

PROBE 14-4   **Identification and Assessment**

1. List six factors that contribute to the misidentification of learning disabilities.
2. Why is it possible for an individual to be classified as having learning disabilities in one state and not in another?
3. Summarize the process used during formal testing.
4. What is an alternative to formal testing?

EDUCATION AND TREATMENT PROVISIONS

You should be able to describe effective educational and medical interventions and identify those interventions that have limited research-based support.

Are there "cures" for learning disabilities?

Professionals and parents have tried many different education and treatment provisions for individuals with learning disabilities. An optimal treatment would be fast, inexpensive, and result in a cure; this has not happened. There are, however, educational interventions that have been demonstrated effective across large numbers of people. Other interventions are effective with only limited numbers of people, and some are not sufficiently effective to warrant their use at all. Anyone involved in education, counseling, or medical treatment of individuals with learning disabilities has an ethical responsibility to select interventions on the basis of their proven effectiveness. This evidence can come either from the existing research literature or from ongoing assessment of the individual for whom the intervention is selected.

Educational Interventions

Education is by far the predominant intervention approach for learning disabilities. Silver (1987) said that "the best intervention for learning disabilities is special education" (p. 498). Special education can be defined in many ways, and it is important to examine the specific characteristics of special education services that are effective with students with learning disabilities.

What educational techniques are most effective for persons with learning disabilities?

EDUCATIONAL INTERVENTIONS SUPPORTED BY RESEARCH. Educational interventions supported by research and found to be most effective for students with learning disabilities are those in which the academic difficulty is addressed directly (Lloyd, 1988). Direct interventions include those techniques that involve a structured, teacher-directed approach to teaching clearly defined skills, content, or strategies. Some research on direct interventions has not been specific to learning disabilities or special education (Brophy & Good, 1986; Rosenshine & Stevens, 1986), but the positive effects of direct interventions have been replicated with students identified as having learning disabilities and placed in special education (Carnine, Silbert, & Kameenui, 1990; Englert, 1983; White, 1987). Table 14-3 provides a list of features associated with direct interventions.

What are features of direct instruction?

Direct Instruction. One specific example of direct intervention is a comprehensive model known as **Direct Instruction** (DI), developed by Engelmann and his colleagues. As described by Gersten, Woodward, and Darch (1986), the distinctive characteristics of DI are not only teaching procedures—including demonstration, guided practice, and feedback—but also carefully constructed materials in which the content is carefully analyzed and presented

TABLE 14-3   Features of Direct Interventions for Academic and Social Skills

Classroom Organization

Adequate amounts of time scheduled for priority learning activities.
Materials arranged for efficient, easy access by teacher and students.
High levels of engaged time in which students are actively involved.

Design of Instruction

Instructional objectives with a focus on specific academic or social skills.
Instructional objectives based on task analysis, sequenced easy to difficult.
Explicit instruction on skill, concept, or strategy.
Sufficient amounts of practice and repetitions for students to reach mastery.
Students placed in curricula based on pretests.
Continuous assessment of students' progress through curricula.
Frequent review and delayed testing to ensure retention.
Instructional decisions based on student performance data.

Teacher Behaviors

Goals and performance expectations made clear to students.
Modeling (demonstration) of skills, concepts, and strategies.
Clear, precise language during lessons.
Lively pace to lessons.
Unison responses controlled by gestures that signal when to respond.
Frequent questioning and monitoring of individuals' performance.
Feedback and error correction contingent on students' responses.
Reinforcement for correct responding and academic growth.

to the learner in formats that enhance understanding and retention. Students are given frequent and multiple opportunities for practice and feedback, and skills are taught to mastery.

DI is a clearly defined model with distinctive characteristics, but many other examples of direct instruction (not capitalized) are found in the research literature relating to effective instruction for students with learning disabilities. One interesting aspect of this literature is that many of the same teaching procedures are successfully applied across different skills and content areas. For example, modeling the desired behavior—giving the learner a clear demonstration before he or she is asked to perform the behavior—has been used to teach arithmetic skills (Sugai & Smith, 1986), social skills (Schumaker & Hazel, 1984), and memory strategies (Mastropieri, Scruggs & Levin, 1985) to students with learning disabilities. In addition, direct instruction features are not limited to teacher-directed lessons, but may also be found in computer-assisted lessons (Woodward, Carnine, Gersten, Gleason, Johnson, & Collins, 1986). Teachers selecting software and other materials for students with learning disabilities should carefully screen materials for features of direct and effective instruction.

Metacognitive Strategies. Recently, researchers have found that many persons with learning disabilities are deficient in generating and using successful metacognitive strategies for learning (Deshler, Schumaker, & Lenz, 1984; Palinscar & Brown, 1987; Wong, 1987). When learners use successful metacognitive strategies, they assess the demands of the situation, plan how to approach the learning task, and continuously evaluate and monitor the success of their strategy. Expanding the concept of learning beyond basic skills and content information has extended the concept of curriculum for students with learning disabilities to include metacognitive strategies.

A typical resource room for students with learning disabilities.

Can people with
learning disabilities
be taught to be
strategic?

A good deal of research and curriculum development in the area of metacognitive strategies comes from the Institute for Research in Learning Disabilities at the University of Kansas (KU–IRLD), which was funded by the federal government in 1978 and given the mission of studying adolescents and young adults. The Strategies Instructional Model (Deshler & Schumaker, 1986) developed at KU–IRLD applies direct instruction teaching methodology to a curriculum focused on metacognitive strategies. The goal of teaching metacognitive strategies is to enable individuals to function independently in situations that call for academic skills and problem solving. One example of a learning strategy developed at KU–IRLD is the word identification strategy, DISSECT, which was effective for adolescents with reading problems (Lenz & Hughes, 1990). Wong (1987) emphasizes that situations calling for strategic behavior do not just occur in school, and that the real potential of instruction in metacognitive strategies will be realized when educators adopt a life-span view of instruction that prepares students to generalize learned strategies to applications in everyday living.

What do effective
interventions look
like?

Features of Effective Interventions. On the basis of his review of intervention research in learning disabilities, Lloyd (1988) identified common features among effective intervention techniques and predicted that these features will be applied in future techniques developed for students with learning disabilities. These features are the following:

1. *Structured.* They will be characterized by a great deal of teacher direction in the initial stages. However, in the later stages they will probably emphasize increasing self-direction.
2. *Goal-oriented.* They will closely correspond to terminal objectives.
3. *Practice-loaded.* They will provide adequate repetitions of actions to ensure that pupils acquire and maintain skills. This practice will take a massed form early in teaching and a distributed form later in teaching.
4. *Strategy-laden.* They will teach students processes or algorithms for performing academic tasks.
5. *Independence-oriented.* Successful interventions will teach students how to perform academic tasks on their own.

6. *Detailed and comprehensive.* Effective interventions will cover all the bases (e.g., include training about how to apply skills in atypical situations or to exceptional cases). (pp. 359–360)

In summary, direct interventions have proved successful in improving the performance of students with learning disabilities across all age levels and areas of instruction. Thus far, knowing the etiology of an individual's learning disability has not been essential for designing a successful direct intervention. Systematic and direct instruction represents a powerful teaching approach with which the environment may be structured to provide optimal learning experiences for persons who have a history of problems with learning. Figure 14-3 illustrates how appropriate, high-quality instruction can enhance the personal resources available to an individual as he or she reacts successfully to an environmental demand.

EDUCATIONAL INTERVENTIONS WITH MIXED OR LIMITED RESEARCH SUPPORT. Many instructional techniques used with students who have learning disabilities have resulted in limited success. Interventions described in this section have not been found to be consistently effective in addressing the needs of people with learning disabilities. They are described here to provide background information, especially because some people continue to value and apply these techniques. Any professional using the techniques described in the following paragraphs should collect extensive, ongoing data regarding effects of the intervention on the performance of each individual exposed to it. If the data do not indicate improvement in academic or social learning, then the intervention should be modified or discontinued.

What are some educational techniques about which educators should be cautious?

Perceptual and Process Training. Although the presence of perceptual problems among those with learning disabilities has been documented, there is little evidence to suggest that these problems are responsive to existing "treatment" programs. Early work in the field of learning disabilities emphasized perceptual and process disorders, and this work logically led

FIGURE 14-3   A Functional Approach to Exceptionality: Developing Personal Resources

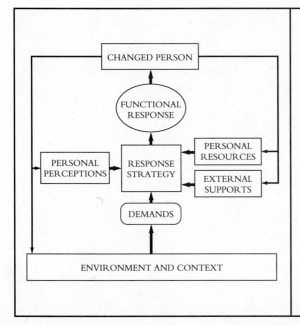

GOOD TEACHING

Personal resources can be enhanced through good instruction. Practices that have been found to be effective in developing and improving personal resources of children with learning disabilities include:

- Curriculum-based assessment to design instruction and determine when to change it.

- Systematic, direct instruction on clearly defined skills and content.

- Development of highly structured classroom environments.

- Modeling of desired responses for students.

- Many opportunities to practice desired responses.

- Liberal use of feedback to students about the accuracy and appropriateness of responses.

- Teaching metacognitive strategies to enhance independent problem solving.

- Use of good teaching strategies that are based on research findings.

to interventions in which the process thought to cause learning problems was the target of training. For example, Frostig felt that impaired visual perception was the key to learning disabilities, and she developed tests and training programs designed to assess and train this aspect of perception (Frostig & Horne, 1964). Students using these materials completed worksheets consisting of simple or complex mazes through which they drew lines. Although students' skills at drawing lines through mazes may have improved, this approach did not result in students improving their abilities to read, write, or do mathematics. Hammill and Larsen (1978) analyzed research on psycholinguistic training programs, one example of process training, and concluded that the evidence does not justify their use. Other attempts to train processes rather than skills, content, or strategies are also controversial and appear to be of limited applicability. These include optometric training and attention training.

Multisensory Training. Another approach to instruction involves using several senses, or modalities, during instruction; this approach is called *multisensory.* These instructional techniques for reading and language involve combined use of auditory, visual, tactile, and kinesthetic stimuli and responses. Research on multisensory methods does not provide compelling evidence in favor of their use, and when positive results were found, it was often unclear as to what aspect of the instructional package—multisensory or some other variable—was related to any improvements in learning (Lloyd, 1988). Possibilities for these "other" variables include high numbers of repetitions of models and responses, breaking complex skills into smaller steps, and a phonetic approach to reading instruction. It may be that multisensory training used in isolation is insufficient to improve learning. When used in combination with features of direct and effective instruction, it is a good teaching approach to provide active practice in which students actually perform functional and appropriate skills for sufficient repetitions to master them.

Modality Matching. In contrast to multisensory approaches that involve using all modalities during learning activities, *modality matching* involves classifying learners as having strengths in one mode of perception and then matching instruction to the preferred modality. Thus, visual learners would prefer to receive information through reading or observation, while auditory learners would prefer listening. This idea was very popular as services for learning disabilities were first being developed in schools, and it continues to be mentioned in lay and professional literature. However, researchers have examined the evidence and found no support for modality matching as an effective part of instruction for individuals with learning disabilities (Arter & Jenkins, 1977; Kavale & Forness, 1987; Larrivee, 1981; Tarver & Dawson, 1978).

It appears that those interventions that take an indirect approach to teaching academic skills do not result in efficient academic or social learning. The educational interventions supported by research as effective are those in which a comprehensive, systematic, and direct approach is applied.

Medical Treatments

Physicians, especially pediatricians, are sometimes involved in the treatment of individuals with learning disabilities. As was mentioned earlier, if a correctable physical condition is found to be interfering with learning, treatment steps should be taken. As is the case for educational interventions, people have tried many different medical interventions designed to alleviate or correct conditions associated with learning disabilities. To date, there is only one effective medical treatment, and it is useful with a limited number of individuals with learning disabilities

MEDICAL TREATMENT SUPPORTED BY RESEARCH. The only generally accepted medical intervention for learning disabilities is the use of psychostimulant medications for the treatment of some individuals with attention deficit disorder (ADD). Silver (1987) cautions that even though medications such as Ritalin, Dexedrine, and Cylert can improve an individual's ability to concentrate, they are not a direct treatment for the learning disability. In

Is it a good idea to provide a visual presentation for a visual learner?

What is the one medical treatment for learning disabilities that is supported by research?

Silver's words, these medications can "make the student more available for learning" (p. 498). Professionals typically consider psychostimulant drugs as one part of an intervention package that also involves educational techniques and behavior modification. This means that teachers, parents, counselors, and physicians should collaborate when working with an individual who experiences both a learning disability and ADD. It is important to remember that among those who have learning disabilities, only 5 to 20 percent will also have ADD (Interagency Committee on Learning Disabilities, 1987).

MEDICAL TREATMENTS NOT SUPPORTED BY RESEARCH. Physicians continue to search for medical interventions that play a role in reducing the negative effects of learning disabilities. In addition, individuals other than physicians "prescribe" interventions that are akin to medical interventions. One example of this is the as yet unsubstantiated practice of prescribing colored lenses to correct reading problems in some individuals. (For more information, see the special series of articles in the December 1990 issue of *Journal of Learning Disabilities.)* The pursuit of medical treatments for learning disabilities led to the conclusion that drug therapy for attention disorders can be effective for some individuals; the pursuit has also identified some interventions that in most cases are ineffective.

People have tried several dietary approaches to correct or diminish learning disabilities, including use of megadoses of vitamins (Cott, 1972), eliminating artificial colors and flavors from the diet (Feingold, 1975), and the popular idea that eliminating refined sugars from the diet will decrease hyperactivity. Levinson (1980) proposed treating dyslexia with medication for motion sickness because he suspected that inner-ear functions were related to learning disabilities. Some chiropractors (Ferreri, 1983) claim to have a cure based on a theory that learning disabilities are caused by damage to cranial bones. Research data to support these ideas are limited, and controlled studies indicate that these ideas are of little value in the treatment of learning disabilities (Silver, 1987).

Parents, individuals with a learning disability, and professionals should use extreme caution when considering medical treatments. Any physician or other professional suggesting a medical treatment for learning disabilities should be able to provide documentation of effectiveness. If an individual is involved in a controlled experiment in which an unproven medical intervention is being studied, participants and their guardians should carefully consider all possible side effects before consenting to participate in such a study and understand that it is possible to withdraw from a study at any time.

PROBE 14-5   **Education and Treatment Provisions**

1. List five features of direct instruction.
2. What is a metacognitive strategy?
3. List three educational interventions that have limited support in the research literature.
4. What is the only medical intervention for learning disabilities that has credible research and clinical support?

IMPLICATIONS FOR MAINSTREAMING

You should be able to describe the features of effective mainstreaming for students with learning disabilities.

The majority of students receiving special services for learning disabilities spend a portion of the school day in mainstream settings (U.S. Department of Education, 1988). Classroom teachers work with some students identified as having learning disabilities who never lose contact with the mainstream, either because they remain in the regular classroom and the special services come to them, or they leave for part of the day and go to resource rooms. Other students reenter the mainstream from more restrictive settings such as all-day special classes or special schools.

Features of Successful Mainstreaming

Will the use of successful mainstreaming techniques have any adverse effects for students who have no disabilities?

Classroom teachers will find that many features of successful mainstreaming are not exclusive to students with learning disabilities. Factors that promote mainstreaming can potentially have a positive effect on overall classroom management and the academic and social learning of all students.

EFFECTIVE INSTRUCTION. There are no boundaries placed on where effective teaching techniques may be applied, and teaching approaches described as effective for students with learning disabilities may be used in both regular and special education classrooms. Most competent teachers already know a great deal about what is necessary for effective mainstreaming. Teachers can be successful at mainstreaming if they do the following: (1) develop an awareness of the needs of students who are mainstreamed; (2) use curriculum-based assessment and adjust instruction as necessary; (3) implement direct instruction techniques; (4) create a structured classroom management system; (5) apply metacognitive approaches; and (6) use peer tutoring and cooperative learning techniques when grouping students (Campbell & Clevenger, 1987; Franklin, Little, & Teska, 1987; Lawrence, 1988). Other teaching behaviors that result in positive outcomes for mainstreamed students are listed in Table 14-4. Classroom teachers who apply principles of effective instruction increase the likelihood that they will successfully meet the instructional needs of students identified as having learning disabilities, as well as those students experiencing learning difficulties but not identified for special education.

TABLE 14-4   Teacher Behaviors Resulting in Desired Outcomes for Mainstreamed Students Identified as Having Learning Disabilities

1. Frequent positive feedback to students.
2. Provision of sustaining feedback to students responding incorrectly to questions.
3. Supportive, encouraging response to students in general.
4. Supportive response to low-ability students in particular.
5. Supportive response to problem behaviors indicative of a learning problem (as distinguished from conduct problems).
6. The asking of questions students answer correctly.
7. Provision of learning tasks students can accomplish with a high rate of success.
8. Efficient use of classroom time.
9. Low incidence of teacher intervention.
10. Infrequent need to discipline students.
11. Limited use of punitive interventions.
12. Minimal punitive response to students.
13. Rare criticism of student responses.
14. Little student transition or noninstructional time.
15. Low rate of student off-task time.

Source: B. Larivee (1986). Effective teaching for mainstreamed students is effective teaching for all students. *Teacher Education and Special Education, 9*(4), p. 175.

Why is social
integration of
concern to
teachers?

SOCIAL INTEGRATION. Apparently, just placing students in regular classroom settings is not sufficient for the development of appropriate social skills by students identified as having learning disabilities (Gresham, 1982), and social integration may be the most difficult aspect of mainstreaming. Pullis (1985) surveyed teachers' reactions to students with learning disabilities and found that inappropriate social behavior was viewed as being a more significant barrier to mainstreaming than were the students' academic deficits. If students served in the regular classroom do not have the necessary social skills to achieve integration on their own, then adults must take deliberate steps to promote involvement in classroom activities and acceptance by others. Certainly this issue applies not only to students officially identified as having learning disabilities, but all students who are rejected or neglected by their peers. Two broad categories of interventions offer promise in helping teachers accomplish social integration among all their students; these include direct instruction in social skills and cooperative grouping arrangements.

How can teachers
help students learn
appropriate social
interactions?

Many commercial curricula are available to help teachers at all grade levels implement social skills instruction with their students (see Carter & Sugai, 1989, for a review of available materials). Social skills curricula include objectives for behaviors such as accepting criticism, starting and maintaining conversations, and resisting peer pressure. Students other than those with learning disabilities are likely to benefit from learning more appropriate social skills, so forming integrated social skills groups should be feasible in most classrooms. Improved social skills among students should make classroom management easier for the teacher and promote a more positive classroom atmosphere.

Cooperative grouping includes peer tutoring and team arrangements in which students of different abilities work together to accomplish an academic goal. Peer tutoring in which students from regular classes were paired with students identified as having learning disabilities was found to promote positive changes in social attitudes among students with and without disabilities, especially when students with disabilities were tutors (Eiserman, 1988). Use of cooperative learning with groups of heterogeneous abilities has been found to promote social acceptance of students with academic difficulties (Anderson, 1985; Johnson & Johnson, 1980; Madden & Slavin, 1983).

COLLABORATION AMONG EDUCATORS. Productive interactions among teachers and other professionals can be as essential to successful mainstreaming as are interactions between teachers and their students (Morsink, Thomas, & Correa, 1991). Collaboration, or professionals working together to serve students, is receiving increased attention as a critical component of successful mainstreaming. Factors that can expedite successful collaborations include the following: (1) sufficient time allotted to collaboration activities; (2) administrative support; (3) teacher attitudes and values in support of collaboration; (4) behaviors that actively promote collaboration; and (5) development of collaboration skills among all persons involved (Idol & West, 1987). These factors are not category-specific to learning disabilities, but relate broadly to all professionals involved in serving students with special needs.

What are some
adaptations that
may help students
with learning
disabilities succeed
in the mainstream
classroom?

REASONABLE ADAPTATIONS. Some students with learning disabilities can participate in mainstream classroom activities if they are provided with adapted materials. A frequently mentioned adaptation is using audiotapes in place of or in addition to reading material. The research results are mixed on this adaptation, but one study indicated that a conversational presentation of the content was superior to verbatim reading of the text (Wiseman, Hartwell, & Hannifin, 1980). Other material adaptations to consider are graphic organizers (Horton, Lovitt, & Bergerud, 1990), study guides (Horton & Lovitt, in press), advance organizers (Lenz, Alley & Schumaker, 1987), and the use of simplified texts containing information parallel to grade-level textbooks (Beech, 1983). Fagen, Graves, and Tessier-Switlick (1984) compiled an

Collaborative consultation is a valuable strategy for teaching students with learning disabilities. This special education teacher is providing assistance with a science lesson in a regular classroom.

extensive list of adaptations nominated as reasonable by classroom teachers, and some of these suggestions are listed in Table 14-5. Finding adaptations that are realistic and effective calls for ingenuity and systematic evaluation using curriculum-based assessments. Some individuals with learning disabilities may find that they can gradually become less reliant on adaptations, and others may find adaptations that are necessary and helpful for the long term.

The Regular Education Initiative and Learning Disabilities

The Regular Education Initiative (REI) described in the introductory chapters of this text is especially germane to the field of learning disabilities. REI has raised a great deal of controversy over where to best serve students with learning disabilities—in special classes or in mainstream classes. In some areas, pull-out programs have been drastically reduced, and students identified as having learning disabilities are served in classrooms using full-time mainstreaming models, such as the Adapted Learning Environments Model (ALEM) (Wang & Birch, 1984). While integration of students with and without disabilities is desirable, full-time mainstreaming may not be appropriate for all students with learning disabilities (Bryan, Bay, & Donahue, 1988; Carnine & Kameenui, 1990; Schumaker & Deshler, 1988). The resource or self-contained special education classroom can provide intensity, structure, and alternative curricula that may be difficult to provide in mainstream classrooms. Silver (1991) expressed concern that REI could be used to decrease rather than improve services for students with learning disabilities. Before definitive statements may be made on what is the preferred location for such students to receive their education, a great deal more research is needed. It may be that the "where" of instruction is not as critical as the "what" and "how." At present, professionals and parents making decisions about instructional programs for individual students should select options that allow for the best balance between a least-restrictive environment and a successful school experience.

TABLE 14-5   Selected Classroom Accommodations for Students with Learning Disabilities Recommended by Teachers

Written Materials: Tests, Worksheets, Textbooks, and Blackboard

Provide copies that are clear and uncluttered.
Seat students close to blackboard.
Provide a verbal description of printed materials, especially directions and other key points.
Directly teach students how to use textbook format.

Lectures (Any Subject)

Begin lecture with a review of previous content.
Pause periodically for questions and allow time for notes to be completed.
Close with a review of key points; involve students.
Assist students in detecting key points with tone of voice, gestures.
Allow a peer to use carbon paper to create an extra set of notes for a student who has difficulty taking complete notes.
Use meaningful, informative visual aids.

Reading

Systematically introduce new vocabulary.
State a purpose for any independent reading.
Use colored highlighting pens to emphasize key information.
Allow students to work in pairs or cooperative groups.

Spelling and Written Expression

Maintain a posted list of correct spellings for commonly misspelled words.
Teach students to maintain a personal notebook with correct spellings of words that are troublesome.

Mathematics

Give verbal descriptions of each part of a multistep process or algorithm.
Encourage students to verbalize steps as they work problems.
Highlight operation signs in practice activities involving a mix of operations.
Provide a model problem and solution at top of practice worksheet.

Source: S. A. Fagen, D. L. Graves, and D. Tessier-Switlick (1984). *Promoting successful mainstreaming: Reasonable classroom accommodations for learning disabled students.* Rockville, MD: Montgomery County Public Schools.

PROBE 14-6   Implications for Mainstreaming

1. Will techniques that help classroom teachers work with students identified as having learning disabilities be detrimental to students not so identified? Why or why not?
2. List at least five teacher behaviors or classroom accommodations that classroom teachers can use to promote successful mainstreaming.
3. How can classroom teachers promote social integration among students?
4. What conditions are necessary for successful collaboration among educators?
5. Describe at least four material adaptations that some students with learning disabilities may find helpful.

SUMMARY

1. *Learning disabilities* is a relatively new term created to describe individuals who experience significant difficulties in learning that cannot be attributed to intellectual disabilities, disadvantaged background, cultural differences, sensory impairments, or behavior disorders.
2. A multidefinitional approach is probably preferable to the idea that there is one true definition of learning disabilities.
3. Learning disabilities may affect preschoolers, school-age children and youth, and adults. Learning disabilities are a chronic rather than a temporary condition.
4. Individual cases of learning disabilities may fall anywhere along a continuum ranging from mild to severe.
5. While many linguistic, achievement, neuropsychological, and social characteristics are associated with learning disabilities, there is no single, specific characteristic that distinguishes all individuals with learning disabilities.
6. Current estimates of prevalence indicate that between 5 and 10 percent of the population in the United States is affected by learning disabilities.
7. Origins of learning disabilities are varied, complex, and probably involve a combination of factors within the individual and within the environment.
8. Current identification procedures do not result in errorless identification of individuals with learning disabilities, and curriculum-based assessment may offer an alternative to formal testing procedures.
9. Education is by far the prevalent treatment for learning disabilities, and direct interventions have proved to be most successful.
10. Effective mainstreaming techniques are not uniquely beneficial for students with learning disabilities, but can result in improved classroom atmosphere and learning for many other students as well.

TASK SHEET 14   Field Experiences in Learning Disabilities

Select *one* of the following and complete the assigned tasks:

Program Visitation

Visit an educational program for children with learning disabilities. Talk with teachers, administrators, or other relevant staff. Describe the facility you visited, the activities conducted, and any successes and any problems described by the staff. Summarize your reactions to this experience.

Program Comparison

Visit a program for children who have been diagnosed as having learning disabilities. Then visit either a regular elementary school program or a class for children who have been diagnosed as mentally retarded. Describe each visit and your general impressions of the students and the instructional programs. How were the groups and programs alike and how were they different?

Parent Interview

Interview the parent (or other family member) of a child who has been diagnosed as having a learning disability. Find out what the reactions were when the learning disability was first discovered. Describe the actions taken by the parents in obtaining educational services for the child. Determine the extent of satisfaction with the services that the child is receiving. Describe the problems that have been encountered by the parents.

Definitions

Ask two educators (teachers, principals, college professors, fellow teacher education students, etc.) to define what a learning disability is. Record their definitions. Analyze each of the definitions according to the dimensions of learning disabilities described in this chapter.

Library Study

Read three articles related to the topic of learning disabilities and write a one-page abstract of each. You can find articles in the following journals:

> *Academic Therapy*
> *Journal of Learning Disabilities*
> *Learning Disabilities Quarterly*
> *Learning Disabilities Research and Practice*

Agency Investigation

Write to these agencies and inquire about services they provide to children with learning disabilities. Write a three-page paper describing these services and how you might use them as a professional.

Council for Learning Disabilities
P.O. Box 40303
Overland Park, KS 66204

Division for Learning Disabilities,
    Council for Exceptional Children
1920 Association Drive
Reston, VA 22091

Foundation for Children with Learning
    Disabilities
99 Park Avenue, 6th Floor
New York, NY 11016

Learning Disabilities Association
4156 Library Road
Pittsburgh, PA 15234

Design Your Own Field Experience

If none of the above learning activities fits your needs or circumstances, design one of your own after discussing the idea with your instructor.

Peter

His voice is usually high-pitched, rapid, sing-song: "What color is your house do you have a dog what's his name what's your dog's name does he have spots on his face where's your house do you have a dog what's his name what's your dog's name what's the color of your house do you have a dog my dog's name is Choo-Choo she has spots on her face what's your name your name is Laurie my name is Peter Lee Eaton Peter Lee Eaton that's my name you don't have a house you don't have a dog my dog's name is Choo-Choo my house is white what's your dog's name your name is Laurie. . . ."

Sally

Sally is at her desk coloring. She begins to whistle a tune.

Teacher: "Please, please, if everyone did that we wouldn't get our work done."
Sally: Stops a few seconds, then begins whistling again.
Teacher: "Sally, stop it. What did I just tell you?"
Sally: Continues whistling but at a lower volume.
Teacher: "Cut it out RIGHT NOW. . . . Do you want to go to the office?"
Sally: Begins laughing and loud singing.
Teacher: "STOP IT. . . . ALL RIGHT, IF YOU WANT TO GO TO THE OFFICE THE REST OF THE DAY, THAT'S WHAT YOU'LL DO. *RIGHT NOW.* . . . LET'S GO."
Sally: Gets up and runs across the room.
Teacher: Grabs Sally's arm and takes her back to her seat.
Sally: Sings loudly.
Teacher: Puts her hand over Sally's mouth and whispers in her ear.
Sally: Resumes coloring quietly while the teacher has her arm around her.

Source: "Peter" is from L. P. Van Veelan, Cheer Soap Opera, unpublished manuscript, University of Kentucky, 1975, p. 1. "Sally" is from B. Ray, Emotionally Disturbed, or "Sit Down, Shut Up and You'll Stay Out of Trouble," unpublished manuscript, University of Kentucky, 1978, p. 6. Reprinted by permission.

15

Students with Behavioral Disabilities

C. Michael Nelson

The two children described on the facing page are behaving very differently from one another. Peter seems completely out of touch with reality, whereas Sally appears to be willfully misbehaving. Yet they have something in common: Both have been identified and labeled by their school systems as exhibiting emotional or behavioral disabilities.[1]

Have you ever seen children like Peter and Sally in school? If so, how were they different from other students? How did their teachers respond to them?

Almost everybody would agree that something is wrong with the children in these situations—that they are different, strange, and don't fit in with other children or conform to our conception of "normal" behavior. But what exactly is wrong with them? Why are Peter and Sally different? How did they get that way? What can schools do to help such children? These questions are not easily answered. Children with behavioral disabilities pose serious challenges to schools and educators, just as they do to their parents and peers. The problems of many such pupils have not been successfully resolved by the time they complete their public school education.

One reason that schools have not helped many students exhibiting behavioral disabilities is that, because of the lack of appropriately trained educators and appropriate special education programs, this student population is chronically underidentified and underserved in the public schools (Nelson, Rutherford, Center, & Walker, 1991). However, they are abundantly present in our society. Whether you work in the schools, a mental or social service agency, for the juvenile justice system, or for a community-based or institutional program, you are sure to encounter children with behavioral problems. If you are an educator, whether you teach in a regular or a special classroom for any disability group, you will be involved with students who exhibit varying degrees of behavioral disabilities.

According to Smith, Wood, and Grimes (1988), 20 percent or more of children and youth may have serious psychological problems. Although the proportion of students whose emotional or behavioral problems interfere with their educational performance to such an extent

[1]In this chapter, the terms *behavioral disabilities, emotional disturbance, seriously emotionally disturbed,* and their variations (e.g., *behaviorally impaired, emotionally handicapped, emotionally and behaviorally disordered*) are considered synonymous. The term *behavioral disabilities* will be used to refer to all.

that they require special education is much smaller, it is likely that one or more students in any class of 30 will be difficult to manage in the classroom. Few regular classroom teachers have the skill or desire to deal with students like Peter or Sally. Even special educators, unless they have received training in managing severely deviant behavior, find students with behavioral disabilities extremely challenging.

Are regular education classrooms able to meet the needs of students with behavioral disabilities?

Another reason that schools are not successful with many students who exhibit behavioral disabilities is that their problems are difficult and complex. Increasingly, it is being recognized that the needs of these students and their families extend well beyond the services that schools are presently able to offer (Nelson & Pearson, 1991). The Individuals with Disabilities Education Act has mandated that schools provide appropriate special education and related services to children who are identified as having disabilities. To date, no other human service system has been given such a mandate.[2] Therefore, public school districts face the awkward dilemma of whether to identify a group of students who may require very expensive and labor-intensive services (such as individual psychotherapy), or not to identify them and attempt to deal with their problems in regular classrooms. The latter strategy seldom is effective, resulting in a small but significant proportion of the student population who are eventually excluded from the public schools through suspension, expulsion, or being shunted off to other systems, such as psychiatric hospitals or juvenile correctional programs.

Who would bother you more as a teacher, Peter or Sally? Why?

In this chapter we explore the puzzling nature of children like Peter and Sally and discuss what schools can do to help them. We also examine some of the controversies involved in providing educational services to children and youth with behavioral disabilities.

DEFINITIONS AND TERMINOLOGY

You should be able to define terms related to behavioral disabilities.

How behavioral disabilities are identified or diagnosed, and ultimately what kinds of interventions are applied, are influenced by the words used to describe this phenomenon and how these words are defined. Underpinning the terminology used to define and describe behavioral disabilities is the manner in which such problems are characterized. There are several divergent concepts about the nature of behavioral disabilities, and some understanding of these will provide a context for defining the condition, the terminology used in discussing it, and the variety of methods used to deal with it.

Conceptual Models of Behavioral Disabilities

In the psychodynamic model, finding the cause of the behavioral disability is very important. Why?

The study of children's behavioral disabilities has been heavily influenced by Freudian psychology, which views mental disorders as disease processes that are essentially the same as physical diseases. According to this **psychodynamic model,** the disease produces symptoms, which are regarded as behavioral manifestations of the underlying disorder. To cure the disorder, one must diagnose and treat the disease process that caused it.

[2]In 1986, Title V of PL 99-660, entitled "State Comprehensive Mental Health Service Plans," required that states develop a balanced system of care that encompasses a full range of community-based service options for adults with mental illness. The most recent amendments of PL 99-660, in PL 101-639 of 1991, mandate state plans for children with severe emotional disturbances as well.

According to this view, the elimination of symptoms alone will result only in the appearance of new symptoms. And, in fact, it has been widely believed for many years that mental disorders should be treated medically. This **medical model** dominated the field from the turn of the twentieth century until the late 1950s and early 1960s, and medical treatment is still advocated by professionals who subscribe to a psychodynamic or a biophysical model of deviant behavior.

The **biophysical model** seeks to explain disordered behavior in terms of biochemical, neurological, or genetic causes, whereas the psychodynamic model focuses more on past psychological experiences, especially those created by parental attitudes and behaviors. Both may be classified as medical models, in that both emphasize medically oriented treatments, such as psychoanalysis or psychoactive drugs.

How are the biophysical and psychodynamic models different? Why are both considered medical models?

Are behavioral disabilities analogous to physical diseases?

Szasz (1960) challenged the medical model, arguing that an analogy to physical disease is inappropriate when applied to social problems (i.e., those that involve living and getting along with other people). Problems in living cannot be readily traced back to neurological or other biochemical defects; moreover, labeling a behavior as a "symptom" of mental illness involves a subjective social judgment, not an objective physical diagnosis. Szasz also criticized the assumption that social relationships are naturally harmonious, since every person occasionally has problems in his or her social environment.

Ullmann and Krasner (1965) also criticized the medical model, offering as an alternative the psychological or **behavioral model,** which derives from learning theory. Rather than concentrating on an underlying psychological pathology that is not directly observable, they emphasized the specification and direct treatment of overt behavior; that is, the treatment of symptoms themselves. This model explains behavior in terms of the environmental variables that influence it, particularly those that immediately precede or follow behavior. Over the past two decades, the behavioral model has had a major impact on the field of behavioral disabilities. Interventions based on this model have been successful in ameliorating very challenging behavioral disorders exhibited by both children and adults (see Nelson & Rutherford, 1988).

As a teacher, would you be more comfortable with a medical model of behavioral disabilities or a behavioral model?

An important distinction between medical and behavioral models of deviant behavior concerns the different assumptions each model holds about the sources and nature of the child's problems. These assumptions influence the methods used in providing treatment. Persons advocating a psychodynamic or a biophysical model are more likely to apply treatment to underlying personality problems or to prescribe **psychoactive drugs** such as tranquilizers, stimulants, or antipsychotic or antidepressant medications. The purpose of such treatment is to address the underlying problem (e.g., personality disturbance, neurological dysfunction) assumed to produce the behavioral symptoms, although psychoactive medications frequently are prescribed simply to control behaviors that interfere with the child's responsiveness to educational or psychological interventions. Professionals with a behavioral orientation, on the other hand, believe that replacing the child's inappropriate behavior with more adaptive behavior patterns constitutes effective treatment.

How do you feel about the use of psychoactive drugs to treat children's behavioral disabilities?

These two approaches are by no means incompatible, and in recent years behavioral interventions have been used to augment or support the improvements achieved through psychoactive drugs. Through behavioral interventions, families and teachers have learned more effective ways of dealing with children with behavioral disabilities, so that a regime of psychoactive medication can be systematically withdrawn.

Like behaviorists, those who follow the **ecological model** tend not to attribute behavior to internal states. Rather, they view behavioral disabilities as the product of interactions between the child and others in the immediate environment. Whereas behaviorists traditionally focus on teaching the child appropriate behaviors while decreasing undesired behaviors, ecological practitioners also concentrate on changing the expectations, reactions,

How do medical, behavioral, and ecological models differ with respect to who is responsible for a child's behavioral disability?

and behavior patterns of other persons in the settings in which problematic interactions occur, as these factors are viewed as contributing significantly to the problem.

Two other models have influenced those who work with behavioral disabilities. The **sociological model** emphasizes conditions in the child's larger social environment (cultures and subcultures) that foster and maintain deviant behavior. Treatment is usually directed toward ameliorating these conditions or increasing the child's resistance to them. Finally, the **counter theory model** rejects theories that attempt to reduce disordered behavior to a limited set of theoretical assumptions. It focuses instead on advocacy for the deviant child and the delivery of effective services. The goal of intervention is often to change the broad social values and expectations that contribute to narrow views of behavior as "deviant" or "normal." The ultimate goal of counter theorists is to change the educational system and society itself to encourage broader acceptance and understanding of individual differences.

Of the models that have been described, which is the most appealing to you? Why?

Each of these models has contributed to the understanding and treatment of children's behavioral disabilities, and the trend today is to recognize the contribution of many different individual and environmental factors. Rizzo and Zabel (1988) offer more detailed explanations of these models.

Definitions Related to Behavioral Disabilities

Why are definitions of educational disabilities important?

Those who plan and deliver educational programs must be able to define the population of students to be served. Each category of educational disability includes a population definition that establishes a central concept around which information about the population can be organized and school practices can be guided. It is also necessary in most states for schools to identify and label students in order to qualify for federal funds to support special education programs. The Education of the Handicapped Act (renamed the Individuals with Disabilities Education Act by PL 101-436) defines *seriously emotionally disturbed* as follows:

(i). A condition in which are exhibited one or more of the following characteristics over a long period of time and to a marked degree, which adversely affects educational performance:
  a. An inability to learn which cannot be explained by intellectual, sensory, or health factors;
  b. An inability to build or maintain satisfactory interpersonal relationships with peers or teachers;
  c. Inappropriate types of behavior or feelings under normal circumstances;
  d. A general pervasive mood of unhappiness or depression; or
  e. A tendency to develop physical symptoms or fears associated with personal or school problems.

(ii). The term includes children who are schizophrenic or autistic.[3] The term does not include children who are socially maladjusted, unless it is determined that they are seriously disturbed. (Department of Health, Education, and Welfare, 1977, p. 42478)

As a teacher, would you find the federal definition useful?

The federal definition has been criticized by many authorities and professional groups in the field because of its ambiguity, redundancy, and arbitrary exclusion of pupils exhibiting social maladjustments (Bower, 1982; Council for Children with Behavioral Disorders, 1987; Kauffman, 1987; Nelson & Rutherford, 1990). The definition's basic weakness lies in its failure

---

[3]The National Society for Autistic Citizens successfully lobbied to have autism removed from the federal definition of seriously emotionally disturbed. Until recently, it was included as a condition in the Other Health Impaired category. However, Public Law 101-476 authorized the creation of autism as a separate category of disability.

to provide clear guidelines for separating children with behavioral disabilities from those who do not have behavioral disabilities. For instance, what constitutes a "marked degree"? What is "a long period of time"? How are practitioners to determine what constitutes "an inability to learn" or to build "satisfying relationships"? The subjectivity of these statements makes it difficult to decide to whom the label should be applied and when treatment is necessary. Such ambiguity leaves a great deal to the discretion of the person making the judgment.

Schizophrenia refers to a psychotic disorder characterized by distorted thinking, abnormal perceptions, and bizarre behavior and emotions. The term **psychotic** is applied to behavior disorders that involve major departures from normal patterns of thinking, feeling, and acting (Kauffman, 1989). **Autism,** a psychotic condition characterized by bizarre behavior, extreme social isolation, and delayed development, which first appears before the age of 3, was excluded from the federal definition in a subsequent amendment of the Education of the Handicapped Act because of the belief that it is caused by biological factors (Coleman, 1992).

Social maladjustment has no widely accepted definition, but it is used in reference to children and youth whose behavior, although in violation of established social mores and standards, is not deviant with reference to the individual's peer group. This term attempts to identify youths who have been socialized in a deviant peer culture (e.g., a delinquent gang). The exclusion of this group from the federal definition has been attacked as meaningless and impossible, given that pupils displaying the characteristics of serious emotional disturbance are by definition socially maladjusted in school (Bower, 1982), and given that no instruments or procedures have been found that accurately discriminate between these groups (Nelson et al., 1991).

The Individuals with Disabilities Education Act permits individual states to adopt their own definitions of the population of seriously emotionally disturbed students, as long as these definitions identify a group of pupils similar to those identified under the federal definition. However, state definitions are so varied that whether students are identified as having behavioral disabilities for purposes of receiving special education services depends, to some extent, upon the state in which they reside (Council for Children with Behavioral Disorders, 1987). The Council for Children with Behavioral Disorders has recommended that the federal definition be revised and, specifically, that the clause excluding socially maladjusted pupils be removed.

In 1991, the Delegate Assembly of the Council for Exceptional Children (CEC) approved a revised definition and label for the population currently labeled seriously emotionally disturbed (see Table 15-1). This definition was proposed by the Definition Task Force of the Mental Health and Special Education Coalition and was modified by the CEC Advocacy and Governmental Relations Committee. Although the proposed definition includes some redundant phrasing (i.e., inclusion of schizophrenia, affective disorders, anxiety disorders, or other sustained disturbances of conduct, attention, or adjustment), it does not contain a clause that excludes socially maladjusted pupils. However, until this new label and definition is passed into law by the Congress, the population of students with behavioral disabilities will continue to be labeled and defined as seriously emotionally disturbed.

Refer back to the vignettes at the beginning of this chapter. Do any of these labels seem appropriate to either Peter or Sally?

Is the proposed definition better than the existing one? Why or why not?

PROBE 15-1   Definitions and Terminology

1. You are a special education consultant, and a girl who displays aggressive behavior has been referred to you. Briefly describe the questions you would ask to assess the problem. (Hint: Think in terms of various school settings, the persons in these settings, and the kinds of information you would collect.)

TABLE 15-1   **Proposed New U.S. Federal Label and Definition**

Emotional or behavioral disorder (EBD) refers to a condition in which behavioral or emotional responses of an individual in school are so different from his/her generally accepted, age-appropriate, ethnic, or cultural norms that they adversely affect educational performance in such areas as self-care, social relationships, personal adjustment, academic progress, classroom behavior, or work adjustment.

- EBD is more than a transient, expected response to stressors in the child's or youth's environment and would persist even with individualized interventions, such as feedback to the individual, consultation with parents or families, and/or modifications of the educational environment.
- The eligibility decision must be based on multiple sources of data about the individual's behavioral or emotional functioning. EBD must be exhibited in at least two different settings, at least one of which is school-related.
- EBD can co-exist with other handicapping conditions, as defined elsewhere in the law.
- This category may include children or youth with schizophrenia, affective disorders, anxiety disorders, or with other sustained disturbances of conduct, attention, or adjustment.

Source: Delegate Assembly of the Council for Exceptional Children, April 1991.

CHARACTERISTICS AND PREVALENCE

You should be able to describe factors associated with the characteristics and prevalence of behavioral disabilities.

Characteristics of Behavioral Disabilities

What is the significance of the subjectivity inherent in deciding that a student has a behavioral disability?

What is an ecological setting?

As the descriptions of Peter and Sally that begin the chapter illustrate, behavioral disabilities encompass a wide range of problems. Moreover, students who exhibit other disabling conditions also may display behavioral problems. As we shall see later, the identification of a student as having a behavioral disability is based on discrepancies between expected and observed behavior. The standards upon which these expectations are based, as well as the degree to which the student's behavior departs from these, are specific to each ecological setting in which the student finds him- or herself.

The school ecology actually is comprised of many different settings (i.e., classrooms, gym, cafeteria, halls, playground, buses), each of which has somewhat different standards for behavior, according to the person or persons supervising each setting. Furthermore, until very recently, there have been no instruments or procedures for objectively assessing behavioral standards or the degree to which a child's behavior deviates from these. Thus, the determination that a behavior pattern is disordered is individualistic and subjective; one teacher may be extremely tolerant of behavior that another teacher considers unacceptably disruptive. For example, the teacher interacting with Sally in the introductory vignette may consider her to have a behavioral disability, but another teacher may view her behavior as only mildly disruptive. The way in which different persons interact with the student also influences whether that student is seen as deviant in that setting. For example, Sally's teacher appears to be forcing a power struggle that increases the probability of future conflict.

Should teachers be more concerned with externalizing or internalizing behavioral disabilities? Why?

Walker and Fabré (1987) have pointed out that behavioral disabilities exist on two broad dimensions. The externalizing dimension is characterized by acting-out, disruptive, non-compliant, or aggressive behavior patterns. On the other hand, the internalizing dimension includes socially withdrawn and depressed behavior patterns. Students exhibiting externalizing behavior patterns are referred for special education placement much more frequently than those with internalizing behavior patterns because pupils who act out are more obvious and more bothersome to school staff.

In addition to the dimensions of acting-out or withdrawal, behavioral disabilities are characterized according to their severity. In terms of severity, behavior disabilities range from those that are annoying to those that are bizarre or even life-threatening (e.g., some forms of self-injurious behavior). Children with mild and moderate behavioral disabilities can be managed by their teachers and parents with relatively short-term consultation by a specialist (Hallahan & Kauffman, 1988). Children with severe and profound behavioral disabilities, on the other hand, are more likely to require intense and prolonged intervention. These students are more likely to be placed in a segregated setting.

Consistent with the emphasis given in this chapter to an ecological approach to understanding behavioral disabilities, behaviors will be grouped according to whether they are disturbing (i.e., they threaten classroom order and discipline, or cause individuals in the classroom—including both peers and the disruptive child—to be concerned or unhappy, but in either case tend to be specific to just one setting) or disturbed (i.e., they occur with excessive intensity, frequency, or both, across several settings).

In terms of internalizing or externalizing and mild/moderate or severe/profound, how would you characterize Sally and Peter?

DISTURBING BEHAVIORS. Two general types of behavior are "disturbing" to classroom teachers: behaviors that cause management or discipline problems, and behaviors that affect the social climate of the classroom. The first group includes children who talk excessively, leave their seats, don't do their work, don't follow directions, or are generally disruptive. The children are frequently labeled hyperactive.[4] This label may be appropriate when children are consistently overactive in many different settings, but it often is applied to children who present problems only in a particular classroom. This label is so widely misused, and it has such undesirable ramifications, that in most cases it is preferable to describe the specific behaviors of concern instead.

Behaviors that threaten the teacher's authority and control also create management problems. Defiance and aggression toward authority figures are especially likely to alarm teachers and other school officials. Such behavior should be evaluated in the context of the demands and expectations of the adults in authority. Unless these behaviors extend to all authority figures or are extremely intense, as when a child strikes a teacher or threatens the safety of other pupils, it is best to provide intervention where the problem occurs rather than moving the child to a segregated environment.

Internalizing behavior patterns also may be confined to a limited number of settings. For example, a student may react to a teacher's authoritarian style by withdrawing. However, students who exhibit internalizing behavior that is sufficiently intense to be considered a *condition* under the federal definition are more likely to do so across settings. This is not to suggest, however, that withdrawn behavior should be ignored if the child does not display it in more than one setting. As with acting-out behavior confined to a single setting, intervention for internalizing problems should take place where these problems occur and should address factors in the setting that may cause the social withdrawal, as well as the child's reaction.

Behaviors affecting the classroom social climate are also disturbing because the teacher must take time from normal teaching functions to arbitrate disputes and encourage appropriate interaction with other children. The child who fails to play with or talk to peers or who does not join group games or class discussions needs help to participate fully in the social life of the classroom. The child whose bullying or clowning causes classmates to react with rejection or

---

[4]*Attention deficit–hyperactivity disorder* (ADHD) is the term currently used to describe children who exhibit hyperactive, distractible, and impulsive behavioral disorders (American Psychiatric Association, 1987).

What is the relationship between disturbing behavior and ecological settings?

ridicule also needs help. Teachers often have trouble dealing with such behaviors because the variables controlling them (e.g., peer reactions) are not under their control.

An important characteristic of disturbing behavior is that it tends to occur in some situations and not in others. A child who is a severe management problem in one teacher's classroom may be no problem at all in another's. Similarly, a child's behavior may be disturbing to some persons but not to others. During assessment an effort is made to determine in which situations the child is perceived as causing problems, and the differences between these situations and those in which the child is not perceived as a problem. Intervention is applied only in those settings where the disturbing behavior occurs. Other settings may contribute resources for the intervention plan, but there is no need to intervene in situations where no problems exist. Disturbing behaviors are clearly the result of reciprocal interactions between the child and others in his or her environment.

The belief that children exhibiting disturbing behavior should receive intervention in the regular classroom is based on the assumption that the classroom teacher will be able to manage the child with special education consultation. However, the concept that behavioral disabilities may be the result of interactions between the child and persons in the environment is unpopular with many teachers and school administrators, who sometimes use special education programs as dumping grounds for problems with which they are unwilling to deal.

DISTURBED BEHAVIORS. As defined here, "disturbed" behaviors are more deviant and intense (e.g., extreme aggression, psychosis, or social withdrawal), and occur in diverse settings, that is, in the presence of different people and in various locations. The child exhibits undesired or maladaptive behaviors in most interactions, across all or many different settings. But it

Children with "disturbed" behavior exhibit it in many settings; "disturbing behavior" occurs with specific environments or persons. In either case it is most productive to focus on the interactions between the children and those in their environment.

TECHNOLOGY IN ACTION

Andrew was a hyperactive, disruptive student in his regular third-grade class. He had become such a management problem that he was referred for special education placement by his teacher. After an assessment and a conference with Andrew's parents, teacher, the principal, and the school special education consulting teacher, it was agreed that special services should be provided for Andrew in his regular classroom because: (1) he needed to learn appropriate student behaviors for "survival" in the regular classroom; (2) a special class environment would be too much unlike the regular classroom to facilitate adjustment to the latter; and (3) his academic performance and general social maturity were on a par with his age-mates. His IEP goals were to reduce hyperactive and disruptive behaviors (calling out in class, getting out of his seat, interrupting the teacher and other students, making noises, and throwing things) and increase appropriate student behaviors (remaining in seat, completing assignments, obtaining permission to speak or leave seat).

The program the IEP team developed for Andrew involved the use of a kitchen timer and a behavior management strategy called the "hero procedure" (Kerr & Nelson, 1989). The consulting teacher divided the first one-hour period of the day into brief, variable time intervals averaging five minutes in length. For several days she sat in the classroom to observe and record Andrew's behavior. He engaged in disruptive behavior an average of 67 percent of each one-hour observation over five school days.

Following this "baseline" assessment, Andrew's teacher presented him with a set of special rules: (1) remain in your seat unless you have permission to leave; (2) do not talk out without first getting the teacher's permission; and (3) keep your eyes and hands on your own work. The teacher then explained that Andrew and his classmates would play a "timer game" (Wolf, Hanley, King, Lachowicz, & Giles, 1970). She would set the kitchen timer (according to a prearranged schedule) at her desk. If Andrew was following his rules when the timer rang, he would earn a point that could be exchanged at the end of the hour for an equivalent amount of free time for the entire class. (This technique is called the hero procedure because Andrew's good behavior could earn a reward desired by the whole group of students.)

The timer game and hero procedure quickly reduced Andrew's disruptive behavior. One week later, the average amount of time Andrew spent engaging in disruptive behavior during the first hour was 12 percent, according to the consulting teacher's observations. The other children, who previously had avoided contact with Andrew, encouraged him to earn more points and praised him for his good behavior.

Over the next several weeks, the length of the timer intervals was gradually extended to an average of 20 minutes, and the game was expanded to encompass the entire school day. Earned free time was given at the end of the day instead of after each hour. Eventually the timer itself was phased out, and Andrew earned points for the group when the teacher periodically "caught him being good." Andrew's disruptive behavior remained at less than 10 percent per day (which was about the same as that of the other pupils in the class) for the remainder of the school year.

should never be assumed that a child who has been labeled as "disturbed" meets this criterion. As we have seen, the label used in the federal definition suggests a serious disturbance, but children do not have to exhibit grossly deviant behavior to need or qualify for special education services under this label.

How would you go about conducting a behavioral-ecological assessment?

The conclusion that a child's serious behavior problems exist across many different settings can be reached only after the behavior has been assessed in all ecological settings; and even then, the most useful view for intervention is that the disturbance is a reciprocal phenomenon between the child and the social environment. A complete behavioral-ecological assessment (Polsgrove, 1987) identifies environmental as well as personal variables that should be incorporated into a comprehensive individualized education plan (IEP). Interventions for disturbed behavior tend to involve intensive and prolonged treatment and removal of the child from the regular classroom. In addition, ancillary related services, such as psychotherapy or medical evaluation to assess the need for control by psychoactive drugs, are more likely to be included in these students' IEPs.

A great variety of behaviors may be characterized as disturbed. The behaviors previously described as disturbing could be included if they occur across several ecological settings. The child who defies *all* authority figures, or the child who withdraws from *all* social contacts, presents a treatment problem different from that of the child who acts these ways only in some situations. Peter and Sally both may say inappropriate things, but Sally's performances tend to take place only in the classroom, whereas Peter appears to babble meaninglessly in all situations.

Why do you think some behaviors are called self-stimulatory?

Behaviors that do not appear to be controlled by specific environmental stimuli may also be considered disturbed. For example, such **self-stimulatory behaviors** as rocking, hand flapping, and self-mouthing may occur without environmental provocation or reinforcement. Or, the child may not respond appropriately to verbal requests or directions. For example, when told "Stop," the child continues the same behavior without interruption.

In cases where children consistently fail to recognize or respond appropriately to verbal instructions, gestures, or prompts, the problem is characterized as a lack of appropriate stimulus control (Kerr & Nelson, 1989). For example, verbal commands may not affect the student's behavior because the words don't have stimulus value for that child. To respond appropriately to the command "Stop," the student must understand what the word means; in other words, the child must respond differently to the word *stop* than to another word, such as *go.* Verbal deficits of this sort are severe and occur across different social settings.

Autism is often characterized as a verbal or language disorder, because children with this condition often have no functional language, in addition to exhibiting grossly inappropriate social behavior and deficient self-help skills. Once again, only a complete behavioral-ecological assessment will reveal whether the failure to respond appropriately to verbal and nonverbal stimuli is generalized or occurs only in specific ecological settings.

Deficits in self-help or daily living skills also qualify as disturbed behavior. Children who do not feed or dress themselves or look after their own toilet needs require intensive educational efforts that extend beyond the school setting. **Enuresis** (bladder incontinence) and **encopresis** (lack of appropriate bowel control) are two problems that can keep the child from entering the regular class. It is important to know whether the child is incontinent just before or during school or at other times as well. The appropriate intervention for a child who regularly wets his or her pants just before reading group, for example, would be very different from that for a child who has never acquired any bladder control.

In terms of disturbing or disturbed, how would you classify Peter and Sally?

PSYCHOTIC BEHAVIOR. The intense, chronic, and pervasive behavior displayed by Peter is an example of a disturbed behavior pattern that could be labeled psychotic. Such children frequently are described as remote and unreachable, or out of touch with reality, and they often function like children with severe cognitive impairments (Kauffman, 1989). While psychotic children can be differentiated rather easily from children whose behavior is less disordered (i.e., their behavior is both qualitatively and quantitatively different), it is much more difficult to separate them into meaningful subcategories. A variety of diagnostic labels have been applied to children exhibiting psychotic behavior, including autism, schizophrenia, and pervasive developmental disorder.

Autism, or autistic disorder, is a rare syndrome characterized by several specific factors. The American Psychiatric Association (1987) describes autism this way:

A. Qualitative impairment in reciprocal social interaction as manifested by the following:
   (1) marked lack of awareness of the existence of feelings of others (e.g., treats a person as if he or she were a piece of furniture; does not notice another person's distress; apparently has no concept of the need of others for privacy)

(2) no or abnormal seeking of comfort at times of distress (e.g., does not come for comfort even when ill, hurt, or tired; seeks comfort in a stereotyped way, e.g., says "cheese, cheese, cheese" whenever hurt)

(3) no or impaired imitation (e.g., does not wave bye-bye; does not copy mother's domestic activities; mechanical imitations of others' actions out of context)

(4) no or abnormal social play (e.g., does not actively participate in simple games; prefers solitary play activities; involves other children in play only as "mechanical aides")

(5) gross impairment in ability to make peer friendships (e.g., no interest in making peer friendships; despite interest in making friends, lack of understanding of conventions of social interaction, for example, reads phone book to uninterested peer)

B. Qualitative impairment in verbal and nonverbal communication, and in imaginative activity, as manifested by the following:

(1) no mode of communication, such as communicative babbling, facial expression, gesture, mime, or spoken language

(2) markedly abnormal nonverbal communication, as in the use of eye-to-eye gaze, facial expression, body posture, or gestures to initiate or modulate social interaction (e.g., does not anticipate being held, stiffens when held, does not look at the person or smile when making a social approach, does not greet parents or visitors, has a fixed stare in social situations)

(3) absence of imaginative activity, such as playacting of adult roles, fantasy characters, or animals; lack of interest in stories about imaginary events

(4) marked abnormalities in production of speech, including volume, pitch, stress, rate, rhythm, and intonation (e.g., monotonous tone, question-like melody, or high pitch)

(5) marked abnormalities in the form or content of speech, including stereotyped and repetitive use of speech (e.g., immediate echolalia or mechanical repetition of television commercial); use of "you" when "I" is meant (e.g., using "You want cookie?" to mean "I want a cookie"); idiosyncratic use of words or phrases (e.g., "Go on green riding" to mean "I want to go on the swing"); or frequent irrelevant remarks (e.g., starts talking about train schedules during a conversation about sports)

(6) marked impairment in the ability to initiate or sustain a conversation with others, despite adequate speech (e.g., indulging in lengthy monologues on one subject regardless of interjections from others)

C. Markedly restricted repertoire of activities and interests, as manifested by the following:

(1) stereotyped body movements (e.g., hand flicking or twisting, spinning, head banging, complex whole-body movements)

(2) persistent preoccupation with parts of objects (e.g., sniffing or smelling objects, repetitive feeling of texture of materials, spinning wheels of toy cars) or attachment to unusual objects (e.g., insists on carrying around a piece of string)

(3) marked distress over changes in trivial aspects of environment (e.g., when a vase is moved from usual position)

(4) unreasonable insistence on following routines to precise detail (e.g., insisting that exactly the same route always be followed when shopping)

(5) markedly restricted range of interests and a preoccupation with one narrow interest (e.g., interested only in lining up objects, in amassing facts about meteorology, or in pretending to be a fantasy character)

D. Onset during infancy or childhood

Source: American Psychiatric Association, 1987. *The diagnostic and statistical manual of mental disorders: III-revised.* Washington, DC: APA, pp. 38–39.

Some students with autism can be taught to communicate via sign language.

Parents of autistic children often report first suspecting that something is wrong with their child when the infant fails to make anticipatory responses to being picked up—that is, fails to hold out arms to accept the parents reach (Rimland, 1964). While some autistic children display normal intelligence, most function in the retarded range, although some display amazing skill in isolated areas (e.g., memorizing TV commercials or song lyrics). In addition, many display intense temper tantrums or aggressive behavior when thwarted, self-stimulatory behaviors such as rocking or twirling objects, or self-injurious behaviors such as head banging or self-biting. They may have few self-help skills. It should be noted that while the syndrome of autism is quite rare, many children with severe developmental delays and even some with mild-to-moderate disabilities display some behaviors characteristic of autism. To avoid applying a label as potentially damaging as *autistic* to children, use of the term *autistic-like* is preferred (Strain, 1983).

The causes of autism are unknown. The failure to find close relatives of autistic children who also exhibit the syndrome suggests that genetic factors are not involved. Neurological dysfunction plays a role in most theories about etiology (see Kauffman, 1989).

Schizophrenia is rarely diagnosed in children, emerging instead during adolescence or young adulthood. For diagnostic purposes, the classification **pervasive developmental disorder** has replaced *childhood schizophrenia*. It is characterized by marked and chronic impairment of social relationships, communication skills, and imaginative activity; a restricted repertoire of activities and interests; and one or more associated features, including abnormalities in cognitive development, posture, or motor behavior; odd responses to sensory input; abnormalities in eating, drinking, or sleeping; abnormalities in mood; or self-injurious behavior. In contrast to autistic disorder, symptoms of pervasive developmental disorder are more difficult to detect in infancy (American Psychiatric Association, 1987).

As you can see, many of the characteristics of pervasive developmental disorder also apply to autism. In fact, age of onset is the most common way to differentially diagnose these subgroups (Kauffman, 1987). Like autistic children, youngsters manifesting pervasive developmental disorders tend to function as persons with retardation, although their retardation

In your opinion, how can the public schools best serve children with autism?

How might pervasive developmental disorder be confused with autism or severe cognitive disabilities?

appears not to be as severe as that of most autistic children. Adding to the diagnostic confusion is the fact that many "psychotic" behaviors are observed in children with severe cognitive disabilities.

The prognosis for improvement in children with severe and profound behavioral disabilities tends to be very poor. However, some autistic children have been successfully mainstreamed into regular classrooms, provided they have the intellectual and academic ability and their autistic behaviors have been controlled (Strain, 1989).

Prevalence of Behavioral Disabilities

Why are accurate prevalence data on behavioral disabilities difficult to establish?

We stated earlier that up to 20 percent of children and youth may have psychological problems. However, the federal government set the prevalence estimate for those with serious emotional disturbance at 2 percent, then later reduced this figure to 1.2 percent of the school population. As you have learned, many subjective factors (such as personal judgments about what constitutes normal behavior, or tolerance for deviant behavior) may go into identifying and labeling a child as having a behavioral disability. The federal prevalence estimate is used as a basis for allocating federal support of research, teacher training, and direct educational services.

Estimates of the percentage of students needing special services for serious behavior problems vary considerably, but most prevalence figures are above 2 percent. Authorities consider 3 to 6 percent to be a more realistic estimate of the prevalence of behavioral disorders among the school-age population (Institute of Medicine, 1989). Most of these students would be considered to have mild or moderate behavioral disabilities.

Kauffman (1989) observes that an accurate estimate of the prevalence of childhood psychosis cannot be made, as psychotic behavior and a clinical diagnosis of psychosis are not synonymous. Because psychotic behavior may be exhibited by children who are not labeled psychotic (e.g., children with severe/profound developmental disabilities), Kauffman suggests that 2 percent is a reasonable guess for the prevalence of children and youth who exhibit psychotic behavior.

Juvenile delinquency is a category of behavioral disability defined by the legal system. The population of children identified as delinquent overlaps the population identified as having behavioral disabilities. That is, children who exhibit behavior problems in school may or may not get into trouble with the law; adjudicated delinquents may or may not have been labeled behaviorally disabled by the school system. Because much delinquency is unreported, and many youths who commit delinquent acts are not apprehended, accurate prevalence data are not available. However, according to Arnold and Brunghardt (1983), about 20 percent of all youth are "officially" delinquent at some time, and approximately 3 percent are adjudicated in any given year.

In your opinion, should children and youth who have been adjudicated as delinquent be entitled to special education and related services if they demonstrate educational disabilities?

A large proportion of youth who have been adjudicated and placed in juvenile correctional programs because of their delinquent behavior have been found to have educational disabilities, including those involving behavior (Rutherford, Nelson, & Wolford, 1985). Estimates of the prevalence of disabilities among the incarcerated delinquent population vary from state to state and from one disability to another. These estimates, for all disabilities, range from 30 to 60 percent (Nelson, 1987). The prevalence of behavioral disabilities among the incarcerated juvenile population is even more varied, because of differences in state definitions and identification criteria for this category. For example, Morgan's (1979) survey of state juvenile correctional programs revealed prevalence estimates ranging from 0 to 80 percent with an average of 16.23 percent.

Some states and individuals have interpreted the exclusion of the socially maladjusted from the PL 94-142 definition of seriously emotionally disturbed to mean that pupils labeled **conduct disordered** belong in the former category and therefore are not eligible for services under the federal definition of seriously emotionally disturbed (e.g., Kelly, 1990; Slenkovitch, 1984). Such conclusions defy logic and appropriate practices, since the majority of students with behavior disabilities exhibit externalizing behavior, such as acting-out and aggressive, disruptive, or antisocial behavior patterns (Walker & Fabré, 1987).

Behavioral disabilities are not evenly distributed across all ages, genders, or socioeconomic levels. Although studies are not consistent in finding more boys than girls with behavior problems, boys tend to be overrepresented in school programs for students with behavioral disabilities by as much as ten to one (Rich, 1977). Schools have a particularly low tolerance for acting-out (aggressive) behavior, which is more often displayed by boys, members of minority groups (Rich, 1977), and children from lower socioeconomic levels (Kauffman, 1989). As girls grow older, they have a greater tendency to develop personality problems, whereas older boys develop conduct problems or exhibit immaturity (Clarizio & McCoy, 1976).

Although the federal prevalence estimate is regarded as grossly underestimating the number of children needing special education and related services for their behavioral disabilities, the number of students actually served in this category is less than 1 percent (U.S. Department of Education, 1991), making pupils with behavioral disabilities one of the most underserved special education populations in the United States. In 1990, only 9 percent of all children placed in special education programs were identified as seriously emotionally disturbed (U.S. Department of Education, 1991). The reasons for this failure to identify and serve these students include the lack of qualified educators, the reluctance of school officials to deal with student behavior that is offensive and/or challenging, interpretations of the socially maladjusted exclusionary clause, and the disincentive to identify students disabled by their behavior unintentionally promoted by the U.S. Supreme Court's *Honig v. Doe* (1988) decision. In this decision, the Court ruled that a student with a disability may not be suspended for long periods of time (i.e., over ten school days) or expelled for behaviors that are related to his or her disability.

It would be difficult to prove that such behaviors as aggression, defiance of authority, or school vandalism, when exhibited by students labeled as behaviorally disabled, is not related to their condition. On the other hand, if these students are not identified as disabled, the school may employ traditional disciplinary measures (e.g., suspension and expulsion) for such behaviors. Many schools would prefer not to deal with students whose behavior is repugnant and who do not respond to normal in-school disciplinary practices (e.g., reprimands, notes home, in-school detention, paddlings), and, lacking adequately trained staff, find that the easiest strategy for handling difficult behavior problems is to exclude the students who exhibit them.

How does the *Honig v. Doe* decision affect the education of students with behavioral disabilities?

PROBE 15-2   Characteristics and Prevalence

1. A teacher in your school complains about a "behaviorally disordered" child in her class. If you were using an ecological approach to the identification of behavior disabilities, would you agree with her use of this term? Why or why not?
2. Describe the behavior patterns that might characterize a child who exhibits externalizing behavior problems. How do these differ from internalizing behavior problems?
3. What is autism? How is this condition distinguished from childhood-onset pervasive developmental disorders?
4. Why is the prevalence of students with severe and profound behavioral disabilities difficult to estimate accurately?

5. Why do you think more boys than girls are identified as having behavior problems?
6. A reasonable estimate of the number of school-age children with behavioral disabilities is
_____ .

   a. 2 percent
   b. 1 percent
   c. 3–6 percent
   d. 10 percent

ETIOLOGY: BIOPHYSICAL AND ENVIRONMENTAL CORRELATES

You should be able to describe the biophysical and environmental correlates of behavioral disabilities.

Why is it so difficult to establish the causes of behavioral disabilities?

The hypothesis that behavioral disabilities have specific causes is derived from the medical model; the term *etiology* itself refers to the study of the causes of diseases. For the physician, finding the cause of a disease may be helpful in curing it, but that is not the case in the behavioral sciences. In the first place, the causes of disordered behavior may have occurred in the child's remote past, which makes them difficult to discover and impossible to treat. Second, it is usually not necessary to know the cause of a behavioral disability to provide effective intervention (Nelson & Polsgrove, 1981). In addition, behavior is the result of the interaction of multiple "causes." As Ross (1980) puts it, "Any specific behavior, taking place at any one time, represents the end point of the interaction of genetic-constitutional factors, the current physiological state of the person, current environmental conditions and past learning, which in turn was a function of similar interaction" (p. 4).

Nevertheless, behavioral scientists have been trying to understand causality for many years. There are many studies with much discussion of the subject, but most have yielded little valuable information. This is true largely because of limitations in the ways causal agents can be studied. Whereas medical researchers can isolate a suspected causal agent (a virus or bacterium, for example), inject it into a laboratory animal, and observe its effects while keeping all environmental variables constant, the behavioral scientist has to rely on less precise strategies.

Many years ago Watson and Rayner (1920) developed a generalized conditioned fear response in the infant Albert, thereby establishing a direct cause-effect relationship. However, the ethics of this kind of research would be severely criticized today and the research halted. Another insurmountable problem is the control of environmental variables, which could be accomplished only by raising experimental subjects in a laboratory.

As a result of these factors, investigations of the causes of children's behavioral disabilities have usually involved retrospective examination of the case histories of children who have been given similar diagnostic labels. (The assumption that children having the same label are a homogeneous population is false, of course.) These studies identify factors that are associated, or correlated, with behavioral disabilities. Statistical correlation techniques demonstrate how factors vary together, but it is very important to understand that they do not establish that one factor causes another. Behavioral disabilities have been correlated with poor home environments, inadequate parental discipline, low socioeconomic status, learning problems in school, and other influences, but it would be a mistake to reason that these factors inevitably cause behavioral disabilities.

The relatively high correlation between a variable such as low socioeconomic status and behavioral disabilities does suggest that the former contributes to the problem, but there is also a possibility that a mutual relationship between these two conditions and a third, perhaps unknown, variable could account for the correlation. Many variables are associated with low socioeconomic status, such as the absence of a father in the home and the presence of deviant peer models (see Nelson & Polsgrove, 1981). Correlational studies that fail to take into account the simultaneous influence of such variables may reach the inaccurate conclusion that a single cause-effect relationship exists.

Inferences about causes must be made very carefully, even when a behavioral disability is consistently related to a biophysical causal agent. For example, **Lesch–Nyhan syndrome** is a disorder of the nervous system that results in cerebral palsy, mental retardation, and—apparently without exception—self-mutilating behavior, such as severe biting of the lips and fingers (Slater & Cowie, 1971). The consistent relationship of self-mutilation to this syndrome could lead one to conclude that Lesch-Nyhan syndrome causes self-mutilation (or more precisely, that the biochemical defect responsible for the syndrome produces all of its symptoms, one of which is self-mutilation).

Anderson and Herrmann (1975) studied the effects of punishment, time-out from positive reinforcement, and positive reinforcement of behavior other than self-mutilation on five boys with Lesch-Nyhan. They found that these behavioral techniques quickly eliminated self-mutilation. The authors observed different rates of one subject's self-injurious behavior in the presence of his grandfather, grandmother, and mother. In a 15-minute session with another subject, following self-mutilation with social attention caused the behavior's rate of occurrence to triple. Furthermore, they observed that in all subjects the behavior occurred only in the presence of parents. These observations led Anderson and Herrmann to conclude that environmental factors play a role in the maintenance, if not the development, of the disability.

One cannot assume, however, that because a particular behavior responds to a specific environmental event, the event caused the behavior in the first place. Specifically, that Anderson and Herrman's subjects responded to adult attention does not mean that adult attention was the cause of the behavior's appearance. It does suggest, however, that a particular biochemical condition alone may not be sufficient to produce a behavioral disability.

If behavioral disabilities were shown to have a high positive correlation to birth order, what would be wrong with stating that birth order is a cause of behavioral disability?

What are the implications of this for the behavioral scientist? All factors (biophysical and environmental) that may contribute to a behavioral disability must be investigated. "To assume that any one alone will provide a necessary and sufficient explanation is to ignore the complexity of the phenomenon that is human behavior" (Ross, 1980, p. 4). These factors cannot be identified very accurately outside the laboratory.

Speculations about etiological factors have been classified into three groups. *Predisposing* causes set the stage for a potential behavior disorder; *precipitating* causes may trigger a behavioral reaction; and *contributing* factors are events that are consistently associated with behavioral disabilities and that may influence them (Hallahan & Kauffman, 1991). Thus, Lesch-Nyhan may predispose a child to develop self-injurious behavior, the presence of certain adults may precipitate it, and social attention may inadvertently contribute to its development and maintenance. These factors and conditions are not causes, but rather etiological correlates. These can be divided into two groups: biophysical and environmental.

Biophysical Correlates

Biophysical factors include genetic, neurological, or biochemical conditions. Although the evidence is inconclusive, studies indicate that severe and profound behavioral disabilities more frequently are of biological origin than are milder disabilities (Kauffman, 1989). Biophysical agents have been linked to a variety of behavioral disabilities, including autism and hyperactivity. For example, Rimland (1964) suggested that autism is a defect in relating new stimuli to former experience, caused by lesions in the brain. Because autism tends to occur in children born prematurely, and such children were until recently exposed to pure oxygen, Rimland hypothesized that the cause of the neurological defect was hypersensitivity to oxygen. However, Rimland's theory regarding this causal factor has not been supported by subsequent research.

A more direct approach to the question of etiology of behavioral disabilities was taken by Chess, Thomas, and Birch (1967), who monitored 136 children over a ten-year period. Thirty-nine children in their original sample developed behavioral disabilities of various types and degrees of severity. From extensive interviews with the mothers of these children, the authors developed patterns of reactivity that could be used to characterize three basic temperaments in the children in their sample. The "easy" children were biologically regular, approached new stimuli, adapted quickly and easily to change, and showed a predominantly positive mood. The "slow to warm up" children responded negatively to new stimuli and adapted slowly to new situations. The willingness of parents and teachers to let such children adapt at their own pace was important to their adjustment. The "difficult" children resisted interference and efforts to divert them from an activity. Arbitrary or forceful adult interference could cause adjustment problems for these children.

Can you identify biophysical factors that seem to be related to your behavior?

Chess et al. (1967) found that behavior problems were most likely to develop in children whose biological functions were irregular, who tended to withdraw when faced with new stimuli, who adapted slowly or not at all to new situations, whose moods were frequently negative, and who tended to react intensely. Whether children with these temperamental patterns acquired behavioral disabilities depended on the way they were handled by their parents. The authors cautioned against concluding that the parents have a major role in the development of behavior problems, however. They found no evidence that the parents of difficult infants were different from the other parents studied. It can be concluded that the reciprocal influence of the infant's temperament on the parents and the parents' reaction to the child's temperament are more important in the etiology of disordered behavior than either innate behavioral tendencies or parental practices that are independent of the child's temperament.

Environmental Correlates

Because children spend most of their time in school and at home, the possible contributions of these environments to behavior disorders have been widely discussed.

HOME FACTORS. Ever since the popularization of Freudian theory, parents of children with behavioral disabilities have been accused of contributing to the problems of their children. Freud implicated parental discipline and toilet-training techniques, and others have blamed broken homes, maternal deprivation, parental reinforcement patterns, and faulty child-rearing practices. Research, however, has not led to discovery of the origins of behavioral disabilities in family relationships. It is therefore inappropriate to hold parents solely responsible for the behavioral disabilities of their children.

Patterson and his colleagues (Patterson, Reid, Jones, & Conger 1975; Patterson, 1986) have studied interactions in families of aggressive children compared to those in families of nonaggressive children. The interactions of the families of aggressive children tend to be hostile, whereas interactions in the families of nonaggressive children tend to be more positive. Studies such as this do *not* show whether the interaction pattern caused the behavioral disability or whether the behavioral disability was responsible for the disturbing interactions.

It is likely that these factors affect each other reciprocally or that aggressive behavior is the result of other factors altogether.

SCHOOL FACTORS. As Kauffman (1989) observes, the fact that many children develop behavior problems only after they enter school implies that schools may contribute to the appearance of behavioral disabilities. Studies of children exhibiting behavioral disabilities in school indicate that, as a group, they do relatively poorly on tests of intelligence and achievement (Coleman, 1992). This could lead one to assume that school failure may be a cause of behavior problems, but it is also possible that behavioral disabilities cause school failure. Research on this topic has been inconclusive.

Some authorities have argued that schools themselves have become maladaptive social institutions, working in the service of the cultural values of conformity and mediocrity. Although such criticism may be unjustifiably harsh, it is clear that schools tend to enforce conformity and punish children who violate standards of order and discipline, or who don't fit the pattern expected of the average child. In the vignette, Sally's teacher may not have caused her behavior problems, but she hasn't helped her overcome them, either.

That schools sometimes contribute to behavior problems is also indicated by the observation that behavioral disabilities are more common among boys than girls in school, whereas parents report fewer problems with them at home. Ross (1980) cited evidence suggesting that this may be because boys have more learning difficulties than girls and may as a result find school more difficult. They may respond with behaviors that school personnel regard as hyperactive, aggressive, or antisocial.

PEER FACTORS. The peer group may also influence the development of behavioral disabilities in school or other settings. Children influence each other's behavior in many ways (i.e., through modeling, reinforcement, and punishment). If the peer group has adopted deviant standards and values for behavior, they can exert strong pressure on members to conform to these standards and values. This influence may exceed that of parents and other adult models, especially among older children.

Some peer groups (e.g., delinquent gangs) may uphold standards and expectations for behavior that violate the norms of the adult culture. Although some authorities (e.g., Kelly, 1990) maintain that youths whose behavior conforms to the standards of a deviant peer reference group should not be considered to have behavioral disabilities, their behavior does violate the standards of the mainstream culture. Furthermore, no instruments are available that can accurately separate students whose deviant behavior is due to conformity to a deviant peer group from those whose behavior is due to individual pathology (Nelson & Rutherford, 1990).

What are some environmental factors that may have influenced your behavior patterns?

A succinct summation of our understanding of the etiology of behavioral disorders has been provided by Kauffman (1989, p. 140): "In all but extremely rare cases, we are not able to answer the question 'Why?' with much confidence." This is true whether we are considering the case of a child with severe disorders like Peter, or a child like Sally, who presents classroom management problems. Behavioral disabilities may be associated with predisposing, precipitating, or contributing factors. Research on the subject does little to increase our understanding because it must rely on correlational methods and because influential variables are almost impossible to control.

As research into the causes of behavioral disabilities continues, additional correlates may be found. For example, the influence of viewing televised violence on children's aggressive behavior has been well documented (Bandura, 1973; Comstock & Strasburger, 1990;

Lefkowitz, Eron, Walder, & Huesmann, 1977). Although it would be helpful to identify specific causes of behavioral disabilities in order to control their influence, fortunately, effective intervention can be provided without identifying specific etiologies.

Later Adjustment of Children with Behavioral Disabilities

Related to the question of what causes behavioral disabilities is the question of the effects such problems have on the future status of afflicted children and youth. The great diversity of behavioral disabilities, in terms of severity and type, makes a simple answer to this question impossible; however, research has demonstrated that both externalizing and internalizing behavioral disabilities bode ill for future adjustment. For example, longitudinal studies of a group of middle school boys identified as having antisocial behavior patterns (Shinn, Ramsey, Walker, Stieber, & O'Neill, 1987; Walker, Shinn, O'Neill, & Ramsey, 1987; Walker, Stieber, & O'Neill, 1990) revealed that these boys exhibited significantly less academic engaged time in instructional settings, initiated and were involved in significantly more negative peer interactions, were rated by teachers as substantially less socially competent and adjusted, and had much greater exposure to special education services and placements than subjects in at-risk control groups. These differences persisted across grades 5, 6, and 7, which suggests that these behavior patterns become quite durable by the middle school years.

Looking even further ahead, Robins (1966) investigated the adult adjustment of deviant children and found that juvenile antisocial behavior was the single most powerful predictor of adult psychiatric status. Wagner (1989) followed up students who had been identified as behaviorally disabled in school and learned that nearly 50 percent had been arrested within two years of leaving school.

Students with internalizing behavioral disabilities appear to fare no better in adult life. For example, Luftig (1988) reports that socially withdrawn children have significantly increased risk of later adjustment problems, including dropping out of school, delinquency, and suicide. Although intervention technology for students with severe disabilities has improved dramatically, the prognosis for children with severe and profound behavioral disabilities is generally poor (Coleman, 1992).

What role do schools play in attempting to change such debilitating and persistent behavior patterns? The remainder of this chapter examines the efforts of schools to serve students with behavioral disabilities.

What do you think could be done to improve the long-term adjustment of students with behavioral disabilities?

PROBE 15-3   Etiology: Biophysical and Environmental Correlates

1. A noted psychiatrist, addressing a professional group of which you are a member, states that all severe mental illnesses are caused in part by genetic factors. You clear your throat, raise your hand, and rise to speak. All eyes turn toward you. What will you say?
2. Environmental correlates that may influence a child to exhibit behavior problems are (choose one):
   a. Peers
   b. Home
   c. School
   d. All of the above
   e. *b* and *c* only
3. What would you say to a mother who was worried that she had caused her child's behavior problem?

IDENTIFICATION AND ASSESSMENT

> You should be able to describe identification and assessment practices in mental health clinics and schools.

Several considerations are involved in identifying a student as having a behavioral disability: (1) the perception that the child's behavior departs from acceptable standards; (2) the degree to which his or her behavior deviates from these standards; and (3) the length of time the behavior pattern has continued.

Behavior That Departs from Acceptable Standards

Refer to the earlier discussion of teacher tolerance. How may this play a major role in identification?

In defining behavioral disabilities by referring to standards for behavior, we must ask, what is normal behavior, and who decides what is normal or abnormal? The answer to the first question is difficult to determine. Behaviors that are considered to be indications of psychological disorders (e.g., severe temper tantrums, tics, enuresis, behaviors suggestive of physical tension) have been observed by parents and teachers of many normal children—those who have not been referred by their parents or teachers for help because of behavior problems (Ross, 1980).

The behavior of children considered disordered or disturbed differs in degree, and not in kind, from that of those children considered "normal." That is, the majority of children with behavioral disabilities display higher rates of problem behaviors, rather than exhibiting entirely different behavior patterns, than their peers without disabilities. In answer to the second question, the judgment of whether a child's behavior is aberrant is made by an adult—a parent or teacher. Peers also make judgments and place labels on children, but these judgments rarely result in official action, such as a referral to a child guidance clinic or a special education program.

Implicit in an adult's judgment that a child is behaviorally deviant is the assumption that the child's actions violate the standards of the culture or subculture. Social standards may be based on such factors as age, sex role, and setting. For example, thumb sucking is considered normal in 2-year-olds, but in an 11-year-old the same behavior would be considered deviant. A 10-year-old boy who wears dresses and makeup would qualify for a deviant label in the American culture. Running and screaming are considered normal behaviors on a playground, but they are cause for alarm if they occur in church. Since it is adults who interpret these standards and apply them to children's behavior, whether or not a child is labeled deviant is largely a function of adult expectations (Kauffman, 1989).

The tolerance of adults for behavior, as well as their expectations, affects which children are identified as deviant. Thus, an extremely active child might not attract undue attention in teacher A's classroom; but teacher B, who values quiet and order, might find the same behavior intolerable. Teachers have found that it is relatively easy to get their judgments confirmed by mental health professionals. They are thus reinforced for identifying "problem" children by getting them moved from their classrooms into special education programs.

Teachers and other adults who work with children must be sensitive to cultural differences that may account for the behaviors that adults find repugnant. Failure to take into consideration students' cultural backgrounds may cause teachers to judge behavior as "deviant" because it differs from that exhibited by children in the majority culture. Although such behaviors as aggression and sustained disruptiveness cannot and should not be tolerated, the failure to recognize and understand cultural differences, reflected in children's language, values, and social behaviors, may lead to the inappropriate identification of a student as potentially having a behavioral disability (Morsink, Thomas, & Correa, 1991).

Degree of Deviation from Acceptable Standards

What are acceptable standards for behavior in school?

A second element involved in identifying a student as having a behavioral disability is the judgment that the child' behavior is extreme. Sally is out of her seat too often. Too much of Peter's verbal behavior is repetitive and bizarre. Behavior can also vary to the opposite extreme, as in the case of children who are excessively isolated and withdrawn or grossly deficient in their ability to use language. Extremely high or low rates of behavior call attention to children and are likely to result in their being labeled and assigned to a "deviant" category. Remember, it is the degree or amount of behavior more than the particular type of behavior that distinguishes deviant from other children. In addition, extremely intense behavior—such as violent tantrums—can result in a child's being labeled deviant even if such behavior is infrequent.

Duration of the Behavior Pattern

What period of time would be considered long enough for a behavior problem to be identified as a behavioral disability?

The federal definition of serious emotional disturbance assumes that the student's problems are chronic rather than transient. Peter has been strange since he was old enough to walk and talk. Sally's reputation as a behavior problem has extended through several years of school. Everyone is capable of behaving abnormally during periods of stress. The death of a loved one, failure in a marriage or career, or leaving home for the first time can all result in transient disturbances. Only when such behavior patterns persist long after the stressful situation has passed is an individual considered disabled.

Intense behavior problems of short duration occur rather frequently in children (Clarizio & McCoy, 1976). While such transient behavior disorders may require professional help, at this point it is better to label the *behavior* as "disordered" rather than the child as "disturbed" or "disabled" (Kerr & Nelson, 1989). However, as mentioned previously, agreement about what constitutes "a long period of time" in defining behavioral disabilities has not been reached. Six months tends to be regarded as a sufficient time period to establish that disordered behavior represents a condition, as opposed to a transient problem, except in the case of behavior that is dangerous to the student or to others (e.g., suicidal tendencies or extreme aggression).

In summary, then, a child's behavior may be judged disordered under the following conditions: (1) if it deviates from the range of behaviors for the child's age, gender, and cultural reference group that significant adults perceive as normal; (2) if it occurs very frequently or too intensely; or (3) if it occurs over an extended period of time.

Identification and Assessment Procedures

What are the advantages of systematic screening for behavioral disabilities in the schools?

The formal identification of students as behaviorally disabled for special education purposes occurs in three stages: (1) screening to identify students at risk for behavioral disabilities; (2) assessment to determine which students actually have behavioral disabilities; and (3) certification of the assessment decision by a special education IEP committee, which also determines the nature and extent of the services to be provided (Kerr & Nelson, 1989).

Until recently, screening and assessment procedures were largely haphazard and unsystematic, leading to IEP certification decisions based on inadequate and subjective documentation. Both the standards used to evaluate a student's behavior as well as the degree to which his or her behavior departs from these standards were left to the subjective judgment of the person or persons identifying the student.

The absence of objective identification criteria or procedures led to a reliance on teacher referral as the basis for screening and identifying students for special education programs and related services. This practice has resulted in both the underidentification of students needing special education for their behavioral problems as well as the overrepresentation of pupils with externalizing as opposed to internalizing behavioral disabilities in special education programs.

SCREENING. These subjective and unsystematic practices fortunately are giving way to comprehensive and sound empirical screening and assessment procedures (McConaughy & Achenbach, 1989; Walker, Severson, Stiller, Williams, Haring, Shinn, & Todis, 1988). Systematic screening procedures are available to identify both students at risk for behavioral disabilities (who would benefit from early intervention designed to prevent the development of more intractable problems) and those who exhibit disordered behavior of such an extent and nature that special education is necessary.

These procedures involve assessing students in a sequence of progressively more precise and elaborate steps. Initially, the teacher ranks the students in his or her class according to their risk for externalizing or internalizing behavioral disabilities, using specific criteria for each

Teachers need to be alert for students who appear to withdraw from contact with others. Not all students with behavior disabilities engage in aggressive or disruptive behaviors.

dimension. Students ranked near the top of these lists are then evaluated by the teacher on behavior rating instruments. Those children whose rating scale scores exceed local norms are advanced to the next step, which involves systematic observations of their behavior in several school settings. The frequency, or rate of occurrence, of their behavior problems is compared to that of peers who are not considered at risk for behavioral disabilities.

Pupils who emerge from this screening process at risk for behavioral disabilities are provided with intervention services designed to ameliorate their behavior problems before referral for special education evaluation is considered. Only students whose problems are not mitigated by such interventions, or who display behavior that is dangerous to themselves or to others, are referred for formal evaluation.

ASSESSMENT. Formal evaluation involves a series of assessments that are used as a basis for determining the student's eligibility for special education services. Many school districts do not have the personnel to conduct comprehensive assessments of students with behavioral problems. These school districts must rely on other agencies or professionals to conduct such evaluations. Mental health practitioners are often used to conduct such external evaluations. The assessment procedures used by many such professionals are based on the medical mode, which, as we have seen, assumes underlying personality or disease processes which produce behavioral symptoms. Diagnostic labels are applied to these processes.

The major tool used in arriving at a diagnostic label is the *Diagnostic and Statistical Manual for Mental Disorders, Third Edition–Revised,* or DSM III–R (American Psychiatric Association, 1987).[5] DSM III–R classifies psychological disorders along five axes or dimensions. Most children's diagnoses involve only an Axis I diagnosis, consisting of the major pattern of symptoms, or *clinical syndrome.* The Axis I and II diagnostic categories for behavioral disorders of children and adolescents are grouped into the following broad classes:

     I. Developmental Disorders
    II. Disruptive Behavior Disorders
   III. Anxiety Disorders of Childhood or Adolescence
   IV. Eating Disorders
    V. Gender Identity Disorders
   VI. Tic Disorders
  VII. Elimination Disorders
 VIII. Speech Disorders Not Elsewhere Classified
   IX. Other Disorders of Infancy, Childhood, or Adolescence

Although the educational relevance of DSM III-R diagnoses has been criticized (Kerr & Nelson, 1989; Rizzo & Zabel, 1988), the lack of qualified assessment personnel in many schools forces a reliance on external mental health professionals to conduct formal evaluations. Thus, DSM III-R labels are applied to many students receiving special education services in the public schools.

What procedures are used to assess behavioral disabilities in your state?

School-based assessment procedures are a more functional approach to assessment of students suspected of needing special education for their behavior problems. Although the process of assessing students for behavioral disabilities historically has been unsystematic and haphazard, more comprehensive and accurate procedures are now available (Emotional/Behavioral Disabilities Committee, 1992; Wood, Smith, & Grimes, 1985). Table 15-2 summarizes the assessment process.

[5]A new edition of the *Diagnostic and Statistical Manual* is being developed. It will be referred to as DSM-IV.

TABLE 15-2   Pupil Identification Assessment Process

I. *Compilation of Screening and Pre-Referral Data*
    Documentation that student's problem behaviors occur more frequently and/or more intensely than non-referred peers, have occurred for a long period of time, and have not been solved through systematic management in the regular education setting
    Acceptable procedures:
    - Standard behavior ratings completed by 2 or more teachers, or teachers and parents
    - Direct observation data (including data on non-deviant peer)
    - Evidence that problems have occurred for prolonged time period
    - Evidence that problems are not due to temporary stress, or to curriculum or cultural factors
    - Evidence that interventions in regular programs have been systematically implemented and have not been effective
    - Verification by school personnel that behavior is dangerous to student or to others

II. *Intellectual Assessment*
    Documentation that behavior is not due to impaired cognitive functioning, or, if cognitive deficits are present, that appropriate programming has not solved behavior problems
    Acceptable procedures:
    - Acceptable individual measure of intelligence or aptitude, administered by qualified examiner

III. *Academic Assessment*
    Documentation that academic performance/progress has not been satisfactory for a period of time
    Acceptable procedures:
    - Individually administered norm-referenced measures of academic achievement
    - Group administered achievement tests, *and* written analysis of classroom products and documentation of classroom academic progress
    - Curriculum-based/criterion-referenced assessments documenting progress across curriculum
    - Direct observation of academic time on task
    - Samples of classroom work across time and tasks

IV. *Social Competence Assessment*
    Documentation that student is deficient in social skills or that social status is seriously affected
    Acceptable procedures:
    - Administration of approved standardized social skills inventories/checklists
    - Administration of adaptive behavior scales
    - Administration of sociometric scales/procedures
    - Direct observation in unstructured social setting (include peer comparison data)

V. *Social/Developmental and School History*
    Documentation that problem is not due to any previously undiscovered factors
    Acceptable procedures:
    - Interviews with parents/guardians, referring teacher, other teachers, student
    - Review of student's cumulative school records

VI. *Medical Evaluation*
    Documentation that problem is not due to health factors
    Acceptable procedures:
    - Medical screening by physician, school nurse, or physician's assistant
    - Comprehensive medical evaluation if student fails to pass screening

Source: Reprinted with the permission of Merrill Publishing Company an imprint of Macmillan Publishing Company, Inc., from *Strategies for Managing Behavior Problems in the Classroom,* Second Edition, edited by Mary Margaret Kerr and C. Michael Nelson. Copyright © 1989, 1983 by Merrill Publishing Company.

In reviewing these evaluation procedures, you will note that assessment of intellectual, academic, and social domains includes information from a variety of sources. Moreover, the process includes a thorough analysis of screening and prereferral intervention data, as well as medical evaluation to rule out contributing health factors. Comprehensive assessment practices such as these are not in wide use at the present time, but recent advances in evaluation technology and schools' obligation to thoroughly and competently evaluate students considered for special education services have encouraged their adoption.

CERTIFICATION. It is the responsibility of the IEP committee to evaluate the assessment data and then to decide whether the student should be certified as eligible for special education services for behavioral disabilities. In making such decisions, it is important that primary consideration be given to the student's needs (what services are necessary to accomplish educational and treatment goals that the IEP committee agrees upon). After these needs are established, the next step is to consider placement (the setting or settings where the student's needs can best be met).

It also is important that the committee considers how and when the pupil's educational program will be evaluated, and to set criteria for decertification of the student as behaviorally disabled. These steps are needed to ensure that students receive appropriate and effective services, and that they are not identified as behaviorally disabled beyond the point where they no longer require special education.

PROBE 15-4   Identification and Assessment

1. Explain the three considerations involved in identifying students as having behavioral disabilities.
2. The purpose of screening for behavioral disabilities is to (choose one):
   a. Identify students who have behavioral disabilities
   b. Identify students at risk for developing behavioral disabilities
   c. Identify pupils who should be in self-contained classrooms for students with behavioral disabilities
   d. All of the above
   e. *a* and *b.*
3. What are the components of assessment of behavioral disabilities?
4. What decisions are made by an IEP committee regarding students with behavioral disabilities?

EDUCATION AND TREATMENT PROVISIONS

You should be able to describe the options for educating children with behavioral disabilities in the least restrictive environment.

The educator of children with behavioral disabilities is able to draw on a continually expanding array of service delivery options. The current emphasis on providing all school-related services in the least restrictive environment possible has added considerably to the educator's repertoire of intervention strategies. The continuum of services available to children with behavioral disabilities and their families is vastly different today from what was available even a decade or two ago.

Special education for children with serious behavior problems scarcely existed before the middle of the twentieth century. Early school programs were heavily influenced by psychoanalytic theory. They also were affected by the work of Alfred Strauss and Laura Lehtinen, who pioneered a highly structured approach for children with learning and behavioral disorders (Strauss & Lehtinen, 1947).

Strauss and Lehtinen's approach was based on the assumption that children exhibiting hyperactive, impulsive, or distractible behavior are brain-injured. Brain damage was assumed to cause disorders in perception and attention as well, which was thought to account for significant learning problems in the same children. This constellation of symptoms and behaviors was termed the *Strauss syndrome*. The methods developed by Strauss and Lehtinen were later extended by Cruickshank (Cruickshank, Bentzen, Ratzeburg, & Tannhauser, 1961) and were applied by Haring and Phillips (1962) to children with emotional disturbance.

During the 1960s and early 1970s, school programs for children exhibiting behavioral disabilities expanded. Most of these programs emphasized the use of self-contained classrooms, the efficiency of which was questioned in the light of follow-up studies of children returned to the regular classroom (e.g., Vacc, 1972). Critics of the widespread practice of assigning children with disabilities to self-contained special classes welcomed the passage of PL 94-142 and its mandate for education in the least restrictive environment.

The following continuum of services are potentially available to children who are at risk for or who are identified as having behavioral disabilities. Although the continuum is described in terms of settings, primary consideration should be given to the services the student needs. The setting in which these services can best be provided should be determined next, with emphasis placed on maintaining the student in the least restrictive environment possible.

1. *Regular classroom.* Most children with behavior problems are educated in this setting. Prereferral and other types of preventive services are applied in these mainstream settings with the goal of avoiding the need for special education labeling and placement. Increasingly, schools are developing procedures for offering supportive educational assistance to children and their teachers in regular classrooms. These services may be in the form of special problem-solving consultation with the classroom teacher. Consultation may be offered by special education consultants, school psychologists, or other qualified staff.

Another approach to consultation is to train teacher assistance teams (Chalfant, Pysh, & Moultrie, 1979; Phillips, McCullough, Nelson, & Walker, in press), composed of staff within the school who are available to help the regular classroom teacher develop and implement interventions to assist students who are at risk for the development of behavioral disabilities.

As pointed out in the preceding section, efforts to remediate behavior problems in least restrictive settings now are required in many states before referrals for formal special education evaluation may be initiated. Consultation also may be provided to assist teachers working with certified behaviorally disabled children who are mainstreamed in their regular classrooms.

2. *Resource rooms* are available on a part-time basis for children requiring more intensive help with learning or behavior problems than the regular classroom teacher can provide. Some resource teachers also offer both consultation to regular teachers and direct services to the child. In resource rooms, students with behavioral disabilities may receive help with their academic problems (which frequently accompany disordered behavior), with social skills deficits, with specific behavior problems, or any combination of these.

3. *Self-contained classrooms* accommodate children whose behaviors limit their access to the mainstream to such an extent that they need a highly structured, special environment for most of the school day. Because such classrooms are located within the school building, systematic efforts to mainstream students can be accomplished in gradual steps during the school year. The priority placed by the Individuals with Disabilities Education Act and its

amendments on serving students with severe disabilities has prompted the development of public school programs for children with severe and profound behavioral disabilities.

The lower intellectual functioning of these children, their lack of adequate language and self-care skills, and the relatively high frequency with which they exhibit bizarre and inappropriate behavior often dictate placement in a self-contained special class or a special school, the next step in the continuum of services. It should not, however, be assumed that a child labeled autistic, for example, cannot function at all in the mainstream. It is better to locate programs for such children in public schools than in segregated settings, where the opportunities to model and learn more normalized behavior patterns are severely limited (see Koegel, Rincover, & Egel, 1982).

4. *Special day schools* are a fairly restrictive option for providing special education services. These may be public or private, and may serve one or several categories of children with disabilities. The child's access to the mainstream is severely restricted by physical removal from the public school building. Unfortunately, segregated programs for students with behavioral disabilities often serve the needs of school staff at the expense of the students' needs. That is, removal of students with challenging behaviors relieves educators of the obligation for dealing with them. At the same time, this option limits students' exposure to more appropriate behavioral models than may be available in segregated school settings.

5. *Re-education schools* are a special type of residential school program found throughout the United States. Founded by Nicholas Hobbs (1966), "Re-ED" is based on the ecological model. For this program, children are removed from the normal school environment only because they require such extensive intervention. Contact is maintained with each student's natural ecology through intensive liaison work and through the child's home visits, which typically occur every weekend. Furthermore, any child's stay in the residential program is intentionally brief, averaging about six months. Re-ED support is provided from the time children leave the residential program until they and others in their natural school and living settings (e.g., teachers, parents) can function without it.

6. *Residential treatment programs* provide comprehensive intervention, which may include psychotherapy, chemotherapy, or other medical therapies in addition to education. A child's stay in such programs is generally relatively long (one or two years), and contact with the natural ecology is more severely limited. The trend today is away from such custodial facilities.

7. *Correctional programs* represent the most restrictive placement option for children and youth (Rutherford et al., 1985). Youths are placed in a correctional program because of their persistent norm-violating behavior rather than because of their educational needs. As we have seen, the prevalence of youths with disabilities in correctional programs is higher than that in the public schools. The Individuals with Disabilities Education Act requires that identified offenders with disabilities under the age of 22 who have not completed their public education must receive appropriate special education and related services, just as in the public schools.

In this continuum of services, fewer children and more severe behavior problems will be found each step away from the least restrictive environment. In theory, children should be moved toward more restrictive environments one step at a time, and they should be returned to less restrictive settings as soon as feasible. In practice, however, the philosophy of "out of sight, out of mind" prevails; and except for programs like Re-ED, which provide support systems for transitions from one level to another, there is little evidence that program placement is as flexible as it should be.

At any point in this continuum, students may be afforded related services to help them benefit from their educational experiences. The Individuals with Disabilities Education Act defines related services as "transportation, and such developmental, corrective, and supportive services as may be required to assist a handicapped child to benefit from special education" (*Federal Register,* 1977, p. 42479). Related services include speech pathology, audiology, psycho-

Some authorities have argued that all students, regardless of their disabilities, should be educated in regular classrooms with their nondisabled peers. How do you feel about this with regard to students with behavioral disabilities?

logical services, physical therapy, occupational therapy, recreation, early identification and assessment of disabilities, counseling, medical services (for diagnostic and evaluation purposes), and parent counseling and training (Rosenfield, 1980). The most recent amendments (PL 101-476 of 1990) added rehabilitation counseling and social work services to this list. Unfortunately, schools often have to pay for the related services that IEP committees identify as needed by students exhibiting behavioral disabilities. Therefore, many IEP committees are not encouraged to recommend related services that cannot be provided in the local school district. School-based services to the families of students with behavioral disabilities are especially lacking.

Recent innovations in educational and community-based strategies are helping to overcome such problems, however. For example, special education programs that emphasize the development of skills needed to advance to less restrictive educational placements have paved the way for students exhibiting severe behavioral disabilities to progress from segregated environments to settings where they are integrated with their peers without disabilities. These innovations include such important additions to the curriculum as social skills and school survival skills (see Kerr & Nelson, 1989).

In addition, procedures for assessing the specific expectations and needs for assistance of mainstream educators makes it possible to teach special education students relevant and useful skills prior to their placement in regular classrooms, and to ensure that appropriate technical assistance will be available to regular classroom teachers who accept students with behavioral disabilities into their classes (Walker, 1986). Greater emphasis also has been given to transition planning and services to facilitate the successful movement of students with behavioral disabilities to less restrictive school settings and to postschool working and living environments (Kerr, Nelson, & Lambert, 1987).

Finally, many states have initiated interagency planning and collaboration agreements to break down the barriers between agencies and professional disciplines serving children and families affected by behavioral disabilities (Huntze, 1988; Nelson & Pearson, 1991). At the federal level, the National Special Education and Mental Health Coalition (Forness, 1988) is identifying shared responsibilities and forging working relationships among disciplines serving children who are disabled by their behavior. These developments are paving the way for programs that achieve a merger of school- and community-based services for both children and their families. Because most children with behavioral disabilities are disabled not only in the school setting, but also beyond, such integrated programming is more likely to address the range of children's and families' needs.

PROBE 15-5   Education and Treatment Provisions

1. List the seven levels of educational services generally available to the child with behavioral disabilities. Identify each level's distinguishing characteristics.
2. You are a member of several IEP committees that recommend educational placements and services for children with disabilities. For each of the children described, indicate at which of the seven levels of the educational continuum you would recommend that services be provided and briefly explain your reasons.
   a. *Peter:* A 10-year-old with "psychotic" behaviors. He has good speech and language but no academic skills. He has violent outbursts and behaves aggressively in many situations without apparent provocation.
   b. *Sally:* An 8-year-old third grader who has been a discipline problem all year. She is about one year behind her grade level in arithmetic and functions at the readiness level in reading and language arts. Her teacher complains that she does not do assignments without constant supervision and disrupts the class with "silly" behavior.

    c. *Tim:* A 14-year-old who spends most of his time in Spanish class sleeping or daydreaming. Although he has better than average intellectual potential, his teacher complains that he hasn't learned a thing.

    d. *James:* A 12-year-old who has been expelled from school for aggressive attacks on a teacher and for vandalism. He already belongs to a street gang, and his parents are unable to control him.

    e. *Alice:* A 17-year-old who is taking algebra (a required college-prep course) for the second time and still failing. Her work in other classes is average or slightly above average. Both Alice and her parents express a desire for her to attend college.

IMPLICATIONS FOR MAINSTREAMING

You should be able to list factors that may increase the likelihood that students with behavioral disabilities will be integrated successfully into regular education and community settings.

The integration of students with disabilities into educational settings with their peers without disabilities is a laudable goal, and it has numerous advocates in the special education profession. Some special educators have proposed a complete merger of special and regular education, including the abandonment of all programs that remove students with disabilities from the regular classroom (Gartner & Lipsky, 1987; Pugach, 1987; Stainback & Stainback, 1984). You will recall from Chapter 2 that this radical restructuring of educational programming has become known as the Regular Education Initiative (REI). Its advocates base their arguments on the observations that segregated special class programs are stigmatizing and ineffective, that a two-track educational system (regular and special) is inefficient, and that students both with and without disabilities benefit from integrated placement. They also claim that regular education teachers, with appropriate support services, can effectively deal with children who are difficult to teach.

    On a philosophical level, these arguments are incontrovertible. However, the feasibility of providing all the appropriate educational services to effectively meet the needs of children with behavioral disabilities in regular classroom settings has been questioned (Braaten, Kauffman, Braaten, Polsgrove, & Nelson, 1988; Council for Children with Behavioral Disorders, 1989). Children with behavioral disabilities, particularly those with externalizing behaviors, can be extremely challenging under the best of circumstances (i.e., small, highly structured classrooms with specially trained teachers and aides). The number of students in regular classrooms, teachers' lack of sophisticated training in classroom management procedures, and the unavailability of adequate technical assistance to classroom teachers make the total mainstreaming of many students with behavioral disabilities implausible.

    To compound these problems, most children with serious behavioral problems do not interact well with their peers, nor are they accepted by them (Nelson, 1988). Moreover, the regular class curriculum often falls short of meeting the needs of students who are behind their age-mates, both academically and socially. Many students with mild disabilities (those who are closest to their peers without disabilities in terms of functional levels), especially those with behavioral disabilities, drop out or are "elbowed out" of school by the time they reach adolescence (Edgar, 1987).

    This dilemma—whether to redouble efforts to integrate these students into nonfunctional academic programs or to educate them in segregated environments, in which they miss many of the curricular and extracurricular opportunities available in the mainstream, and in which they are likely to remain throughout their public school years—has no ready solution. The most promising approach may be to continue improving and expanding the range of educational and related services across the entire continuum of educational and community settings in which children and youth with behavior problems are found. This entails the following elements:

1. Systematic screening of all students should be conducted, particularly during the early school years, to identify those who are at risk for the development of behavioral disabilities.

2. Supportive educational assistance should be available to at-risk students through such strategies as teacher assistance teams and collaborative consultation, which provide technical assistance to students and teachers in least restrictive educational environments.

3. Comprehensive assessments should be done for students referred for special education evaluation because of their behavior problems. Assessment procedures should address all relevant ecological settings and the perception of all significant persons, including those outside the school. Assessments of the standards and expectations of the settings in which the child currently functions should also be conducted.

4. Decisions to place students with behavioral disabilities in special education programs should involve careful consideration of discrepancies between students' current behavior and the standards and expectations of less restrictive environments, as well as between their behavior and that of peers without disabilities. IEP committees (which include staff from the regular education program who will participate in the development and implementation of students' IEPs) then develop IEP objectives that are based on these discrepancies. The IEP committees should set criteria that, when met, result in students' decertification as behaviorally disabled and their full return to the regular education system.

5. The functional IEPs developed for students identified as having behavioral disabilities should include objectives and strategies addressing academic, social, school survival, vocational (if appropriate), and recreational skills. IEPs should also include specific goals and strategies for mainstream educational placements, rather than simply indicating that the student will be physically integrated into regular education settings.

6. Skills developed in special education programs should be functional (appropriate and useful) in less restrictive educational settings, as well as in noneducational environments.

7. Successful participation in mainstream educational settings should be facilitated by careful transition planning and collaboration between regular and special education personnel, appropriate technical assistance to mainstream staff, and programming to ensure the maintenance and generalization of academic and behavioral gains.

8. Students whose behavioral disabilities are so severe that they must receive special education services throughout their school careers should also receive supported and carefully supervised mainstream experiences, which include teaching peers without disabilities strategies for achieving more effective and appropriate social interactions with them. Supportive educational programs for these students should extend to transition services that facilitate their adjustment to adult life.

9. Coordinated interagency services should be provided, especially for children and youth with severe behavioral disabilities. These services must extend the scope and impact of interventions to home and community settings, and provide support and advocacy for families as well as the children involved.

Figure 15-1 provides guidelines for identifying the services needed by children and their families and matching these to resources in schools and communities.

FIGURE 15-1   A Functional Approach to Exceptionality: Integrating Services for Students with Behavioral Disabilities

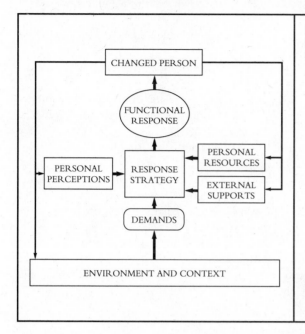

In addition to schools, many other agencies provide *external supports* for children with behavioral disabilities. Teachers can facilitate interagency coordination through strategies such as the following:

- Learn about students' needs in other settings: neighborhood, peer groups, clubs, church, job.

- Develop a list of agencies, private practitioners, and programs offering services of potential value to students and their families, including names, addresses, and phone numbers of contact people.

- From families, find out what services students are receiving in the community and secure family permission to talk with appropriate professionals about programs and needs, and how these can be coordinated.

- Participate with professionals from other disciplines in planning strategies for integrating services.

- Develop a list of the continuum of services available for children with behavioral disabilities in the community and state.

- Advocate for integrated professional services at meetings, conferences, and in everyday work.

What advances in school and community services for children and youth with behavioral disabilities have been made in your state and community?

The components of effective planning and service delivery are not easy to implement. The large number of students with behavioral disabilities who fail to succeed in the mainstream of society as adolescents and adults (Edgar, 1987; Neel, Meadows, Levine, & Edgar, 1988), as well as the overrepresentation of students with disabilities in correctional programs (Murphy, 1986; Rutherford et al., 1985) testify to the failure of current approaches. However, in recent years, progress in the development of services such as those just alluded to, and in the technologies for delivering and evaluating these services, has been dramatic. The new decade promises many exciting challenges and accomplishments.

PROBE 15-6   Implications for Mainstreaming

1. What is the Regular Education Initiative? What are its implications for students with behavioral disabilities?

SUMMARY

1. Defining behavioral disabilities is complicated by the variety and range of behavior problems exhibited by students, by differences in the standards and expectations of persons in the ecological settings in which students are found, by the number of conceptual approaches to studying disordered behavior, and by subjective factors inherent in judgments made about behavior.

2. Rather than discuss the "characteristics" of students with behavioral disabilities, teachers should differentiate "disturbing" behaviors, which tend to be specific to one setting, and "disturbed" behaviors, which occur with excessive intensity and/or frequency across several settings.

3. Factors such as age, gender, and socioeconomic variables interact with prevalence estimates of behavior disabilities.

4. The ecological approach to the diagnosis and classification of behavioral disabilities has found wide acceptance by special educators.

5. Examination of the biophysical and environmental correlates of behavioral disabilities is more productive for intervention than traditional investigations of etiological factors.

6. Screening and assessment practices for identifying and evaluating behavioral disabilities are becoming more systematic, comprehensive, and functional.

7. The scope and sophistication of educational services to students with behavioral disabilities have increased in recent years. Services to students identified as at risk for the development of behavioral disabilities are particularly noteworthy, given the shortage of special education programs for students with behavioral disabilities in the public schools.

8. The provision of services to students with behavioral disabilities in the least restrictive environment requires that a broad array of services be available to the individual, the family, and the professionals involved.

TASK SHEET 15   Field Experiences in Behavioral Disabilities

Thought Experiments

A thought experiment is a way of thinking about a reality you may not have experienced. In thought experiments, you simply put yourself in the situation or scenario described and think about how you might act, think, or feel. Try the thought experiments suggested below and answer the questions about each experience. Spend at least ten minutes thinking about each situation.

Thought Experiment 1. Imagine that you are a person with a behavioral disability. Place yourself in several different environments and imagine how you would act, feel, and how others would respond to you.

Write a brief response to each of the following questions about this thought experiment:

1. How did you act during your "thought trip"? Were you acting-out and aggressive, or were you withdrawn and passive? What does this say, if anything, about how we view people with behavioral disabilities?

2. Specifically, what were some of your behaviors? Were they of the "disturbing" or the "disturbed" type? Were they stereotyped?

3. Did you act the same way in different environments? Is this the case with people exhibiting behavioral disabilities?

Thought Experiment 2. Imagine that you are a top network television producer. The network has asked you to develop a new drama series. You are aware that television is beginning to include people with certain disabilities in its programs. You also realize that people with behavioral disabilities are rarely depicted in television programs, and if they are, it is generally in a very stereotyped fashion. You decide to produce a half-hour pilot program that realistically deals with an adolescent who exhibits behavioral disabilities. Think about what the program would be like.

Write a brief response to the following:

1. What is your main character like? Is the character a male or a female? What does he or she look like? What are some of his or her demographic characteristics (e.g., how old, rich or poor, living at home or somewhere else)? Is he or she in school? If so, in what kind of program? If not, is he or she working, in vocational training, hospitalized, or doing something else? What are his or her personality characteristics? What behavior problems does he or she exhibit? What are his or her strengths?
2. Briefly describe the premise or point of the program. What is it trying to illustrate about persons exhibiting behavioral disabilities?

Thought Experiment 3. Imagine that you are an adult with a behavioral disability and with antisocial tendencies. As you pull into a handicapped parking space outside your favorite shopping mall, a police officer comes over to you and asks to see your handicapped parking permit. What will you say to the officer?

Write a brief response to the following questions:

1. How did you react to the officer's request? Were you belligerent or quiet? Did you say that you were disabled?
2. Did you insist that you should be able to park in a handicapped space? If so, why?

Real Life Experience

If, in your life experiences, you have been in contact with a person who might be considered to have behavioral disabilities, briefly describe that person. What was the person like? Why do you feel he or she had behavioral disabilities? How was that person viewed by others? By you? What was he or she like to be around? What, if any, treatment was the person receiving?

Group Project

With three or four other students, conduct a survey of the programs and services for persons in your community who exhibit behavioral or emotional disabilities. Include services for adults as well as children, and look at school, group living, vocational, and psychiatric hospital programs. Write a brief description of each service and program. Did you find any gaps in the services available? Share the results of your survey with your class.

Lydia Patton seems older than she is. The 15-year-old is confident, focused and polite. She's also a high school graduate.

Has accelerating school and devoting summers to her dreams of being a ballerina robbed her of a childhood? She doesn't think so.

"It's sort of like the old thing that youth is wasted on the young," Patton said. "I don't think I'll look back and regret anything. I love ballet and being in ballet class. Before ballet, I was pretty shy. It sort of gave me more confidence."

She explained that in ballet you have to practice in front of a mirror and critique yourself. Part of the critique involves finding something positive in your reflection each day. That helped build her self-esteem, she said.

"I probably wouldn't have had much of a childhood without ballet. I have fun doing it or I wouldn't do it," she said. "I get to do things kids my age don't do without as many restrictions. It's kind of neat. I get to go away from home and still get away with some things that an 18-year-old wouldn't."

Patton graduated recently from Huntington East High School at the age of 14. She barely had time to celebrate her 15th birthday Sunday, with all the preparations for leaving Saturday for summer dance classes at Point Park College in Pittsburgh, where she'll begin college this fall.

Her parents, Paul and Gail Patton of Huntington, aren't any more worried about her going off to college at a young age than they would be if she were 18. It's sort of the same philosophy the Pattons had when they decided to let Lydia advance two grades in elementary school.

"Academically, she's always been very eager and ahead of most of the kids her age," Gail Patton said. "She was going to stick out no matter where she was."

The only tough transitional time for Lydia was junior high school, which is hard on most students.

"I really started getting nervous in junior high school," she said. "It's such a heavy scene for anyone. It was just more stress on an already stressful situation. The age difference wasn't that much of a problem. We got past it. People started looking at me as a person instead of a 10-year-old seventh-grader." . . .

A long-term ballet goal for Lydia, who is also a National Merit Scholar Finalist, is to get into "the best company I can find that will take me."

Then her dad joked, "If all else fails, she can audition at Six Flags Over Texas."

"Or Las Vegas," her mom said.

"Or Dollywood . . . Opryland. . . Kings Island. . . ."

Source: John Gillespie, "At 15, She'll Be Waltzing into College," Herald-Dispatch (Huntington, WV). June 18, 1992, p. B-1.

16

Students with Unique Gifts and Talents

Edwina D. Pendarvis

It may seem strange that Lydia and children like her need the services of special education. They have the ability to succeed at virtually any intellectual task they undertake. But ability is not the only factor in success; there are many factors that influence a child's development and performance. The purpose of this chapter is to help you gain a basic understanding of giftedness and the educational provisions that are best suited to students who are gifted.

DEFINITIONS AND NEED FOR PROGRAMS

You should be able to define giftedness and explain why children who are gifted should be provided with special education.

Misconceptions About Persons Who Are Gifted

Recognition of the importance of modifying instruction for children who are gifted is increasing, but students who are exceptionally bright still spend much of their time in school practicing what they already know, reading books that are too easy for them, and answering questions that require little mental effort. Difficulty in bringing about changes in the educational programs of children who are gifted stems, in large part, from opposition based on the belief that gifted programs are (1) unnecessary and (2) elitist.

CHILDREN WHO ARE GIFTED WILL SUCCEED WITHOUT SPECIAL PROGRAMS. Despite a large body of literature to the contrary, many educators think that gifted programs are unnecessary because children who are gifted will succeed without them. There are two flaws in this argument against special education for students who are gifted. One is that about

What leads people to have a negative view of special education for students who are gifted?

half the students who could qualify for gifted education are not recognized as gifted by their teachers (Gear, 1978). We cannot know that gifted children succeed if we do not know who they are. Another flaw in the argument that children who are gifted will excel without special programs is that research shows that many children identified as gifted are unsuccessful both in their academic efforts and in their careers (Whitmore, 1980).

It is true that history offers many examples of persons whose talents went unrecognized during their school years, but who later became eminent. Clark (1977) notes that almost as soon as Thomas Edison began school, he was dubbed a failure. His teachers described him as "addled." However, his family might not have been upset about it if they had realized that he was in good company. Leonardo da Vinci, Hans Christian Andersen, Niels Bohr, Isaac Newton, Sir Humphrey Davys, and Albert Einstein all share the distinction of having been considered stupid by their teachers.

These gifted people did succeed without special education, at least as a part of their formal education; but many persons who are equally gifted have failed. Research indicates that over half the students who are gifted in school are achieving far below their capabilities (Marland, 1972); many even drop out of school early (French, 1975). Students such as these are far less likely to excel today than in Edison's era because success in most fields now requires many years of formal education.

Why are gifted programs sometimes considered elitist?

GIFTED PROGRAMS ARE ELITIST. Belief that gifted programs are elitist presents another barrier to special provisions for children who are talented. Contributing to the elitist argument is the incontrovertible fact that minority groups are underrepresented in gifted programs (Perrone & Male, 1981). Until a greater proportion of children from ethnic, racial, economic, and other minorities is included in gifted programs, the elitist label will not be eradicated. Although educators are becoming more sensitive to the need to employ equitable identification criteria in order to locate and serve gifted members of minority groups, gifted education is still far from "culture-fair" (Van Tassel-Baska, Patton, & Prillaman, 1989). Until programs have a more representational mix of majority and minority groups, advocates of gifted education can only document improvements and point out, as has Shirley Chisholm (Education of the Handicapped, 1979), that special programs benefit the large number of children from minority groups who are identified as gifted.

A less serious charge, that special education encourages snobbery in students identified as gifted, has been countered by the suggestion that undue feelings of superiority are promoted, not by gifted programs, but by the lack of them. In the regular classroom, students who are gifted can often, with little effort, outperform most other students. It is not elitist to give children appropriately difficult work and to allow them to discover that there are other children as talented as they.

Why do children who are gifted need special education?

Effective education depends on matching the level and pace of instruction with the students' level and rate of achievement (Bloom, 1976; Robinson, Roedell, & Jackson, 1979). The advanced conceptual level and rapid learning rate of students who are gifted make most regular classroom instruction unsuited to their educational needs (Parke, 1989). Special education for students who are gifted provides instruction commensurate with their exceptional ability.

Definitions of Giftedness

What purposes does a definition of giftedness serve?

Many people equate giftedness with a high IQ score, but giftedness can be defined in many ways. How giftedness is defined is critical for two reasons: (1) the definition communicates to educators, as well as to the public, precisely whom gifted education is intended to serve; and

(2) it guides the development of identification procedures and educational programs. If the definition is too narrow, children who need special education may go unserved because they are ineligible for the gifted program. If the definition is too broad, children who are gifted may be inadequately served because identification procedures and educational provisions are diluted in an effort to address too great a diversity of levels and types of ability. Both pragmatic and theoretical considerations enter into the task of developing a definition of giftedness.

How do pragmatic considerations affect definitions of giftedness?

PRAGMATIC CONSIDERATIONS IN DEFINING GIFTEDNESS. There are two major pragmatic considerations for school systems or other agencies serving children identified as gifted: (1) priorities regarding the type or types of ability the system is most concerned with developing; and (2) budgetary constraints, or limits on funds that can be allocated to gifted education. These considerations determine both the content of the definition and the eligibility criteria that establish the level of ability required for inclusion in the gifted program.

One school system may define giftedness as exceptional academic ability and require scores in the 95th percentile or above on standardized, individually administered achievement or aptitude tests. Another system, with different educational priorities, may define giftedness as exceptional ability in any of several areas: academics, performing arts, and visual arts, for example. Given the same proportion of funds to spend on gifted education, the school district with the broader definition could limit its population of students identified as gifted by establishing a higher criterion level in each area.

If it seems strange that the condition of the economy can determine whether or not a child is gifted, you should recognize that budgetary allocations are, in effect, an expression of the public's educational priorities. In any society, the type of abilities that are cultivated and the level of effort directed to their development reflect the values of the culture.

THEORETICAL CONSIDERATIONS. The concept of superior ability, particularly intellectual ability, is the critical attribute of most definitions of **giftedness.** Differences in definition that do not arise for pragmatic reasons may arise because the originators of the definitions subscribe to different theories about the nature of intelligence.

Who first applied statistical concepts to the study of intelligence?

Although interest in intelligence and its measurement has a long history, Francis Galton, whose *Hereditary Genius* was published in 1869, is often credited with laying the groundwork for quantitative investigation of ability by applying the concept of deviation from the mean to intellectual performance. Galton's conception of giftedness was broad, and he included in his studies several types of eminent persons: writers, government leaders, rowers, and wrestlers. Based on his investigation, Galton concluded that there are three elements necessary for outstanding achievement in any field: the *capacity,* the *zeal,* and the *power* to do laborious work.

In the early 1900s, influenced by Galton's work, Alfred Binet developed the prototype of intelligence tests in use today. Binet, who was interested in predicting children's scholastic performance, took a commonsense approach and assembled a variety of practical tasks, such as counting money (Gould, 1981). Based on the child's performance on the different tasks, Binet estimated how much special help the child would need to succeed in school.

Binet's approach was relatively atheoretical, but Galton's work influenced theories of intelligence as well as its measurement. Among the most famous theories is that of Charles Spearman (1914), a contemporary of Binet. Spearman based his model of intelligence on factor analyses of children's performance on tests like Binet's (Gould, 1981). He hypothesized that performance on any intellectual task is determined by a general intellectual factor and by one or more specific factors relevant to the task at hand. Success in spelling, for example, is, according to this theory, determined by the speller's general intellectual ability level and by the level of those specific factors needed in spelling as opposed to some other task, such as solving mathematical problems.

Who first defined giftedness in terms of IQ?

Spearman's theory provides the basis for the practice of representing cognitive ability by an IQ score, which indexes a general ability level. Thus, his theory forms the basis for definitions of giftedness such as that used by Lewis Terman, who revised a version of Binet's test to develop the Stanford-Binet Intelligence Scale and used it in the identification of approximately 1500 students as gifted (Terman et al., 1925). Because of the magnitude of Terman's longitudinal study of gifted students and its impact on education, defining giftedness in terms of an IQ score in the 98th or 99th percentile has been common practice since the 1920s.

In contrast to definitions based on Spearman's two-factor model are definitions based on multifactor models. Most famous of these are Guilford's (1967) "structure of intellect" model with 120 independent cognitive factors, and Howard Gardner's (1983) seven "frames of mind." Although Guilford's model has been used in both research and practice, it is not very useful in defining giftedness because it breaks abilities into such specialized skills. Gardner's model may prove more effective because it is inclusive enough to encompass the abilities that most people in our society value, and it is specific enough to give guidance to efforts to identify children as gifted. Gardner hypothesized seven types of intelligence: (1) linguistic, (2) logical-mathematical, (3) spatial, (4) musical, (5) kinesthetic, (6) interpersonal, and (7) intrapersonal. These last two categories refer to social and emotional intelligence. The former refers to the ability to recognize and respond to other people's social and emotional behavior. The latter refers to the ability to understand one's own feelings.

Perhaps the most recent theoretical perspective on intelligence is Sternberg's (1985) hierarchical, componential view. Based on an information-processing approach to intelligence, Sternberg proposes that there are three different types of cognitive processes: (1) metacomponents are the higher-order control processes that carry out executive planning and decision making; (2) performance components carry out the comparisons, inferences, and other problem-solving activities scheduled by the metacomponents; and (3) acquisition, retention, and transfer components allow the recall and use of new information. Sternberg believes that his definition of intelligence, if used as a basis for a definition of giftedness, would be more likely than other definitions to locate those children with the greatest potential for attaining success in their chosen careers.

A multifactor perspective is reflected in the federal definition of giftedness in Public Law 100-297, the Jacob K. Javits Gifted and Talented Children's Education Act of 1988. The Javits Act retains the broad definitions of two earlier gifted education laws. These acts define giftedness in terms of demonstrated ability or potential in such areas as the intellect, creativity, specific academic achievement, leadership, and the performing or visual arts. It has been estimated that, in applying a broad definition of giftedness (such as this federal definition), at least 3 to 5 percent of the total school-age population would be considered gifted (Marland, 1972). This percentage includes talented children who might be excluded under a definition that is based only on general intellectual ability.

CURRENT DEFINITIONS OF GIFTEDNESS. Some states have adopted a definition of giftedness similar to the federal definition. However, most states have adopted definitions that focus on intellectual ability (Seaberg & Stafford, 1991). Although the general trend is toward broadening definitions, it is, because of funding difficulties, a gradual trend. Gradual expansion allows state or local school systems with limited funds an opportunity to conduct needs assessments, document the benefits of established gifted programs, and build support for larger funding allocations.

Do any definitions of giftedness include motivation as a criterion?

Taking into consideration the large body of research that shows that achievement is not solely a function of high ability, Renzulli (1978) defines giftedness as a combination of above-average ability, task commitment, and creativity. This definition includes children who may not have extremely high IQ scores but who are talented in areas not measured by IQ tests. On the other hand, it excludes children who have high IQ scores but who are not identified as exceptionally creative or committed to a field of interest.

One of the major considerations in acceptance of Renzulli's definition is whether task commitment is viewed as a given or as a quality that develops as students become expert in subjects in which they are interested and capable. Advocates of a definition that includes task commitment, or motivation to achieve, point out that some children who are gifted never fulfill their potential and that talent alone does not determine success. On the other hand, advocates of a definition that requires only evidence of superior ability subscribe to the view that if an appropriate education is provided, students' task commitment will develop. There is research that supports this view as well, demonstrating that motivation improves as mastery over a discipline increases (Bloom, 1976). Although multifactor definitions seem to be the most valid definitions of giftedness (Sternberg, 1990), many advocates of programs for gifted underachievers object to the requirement that students exhibit motivation to achieve in order to qualify for special instruction.

The theoretical perspectives and pragmatic considerations important to the person or agency defining giftedness determine whether Terman's definition, the federal definition, Renzulli's definition, or another is adopted; but, as mentioned earlier, the issue is important because the definition determines who will receive special education. Each of the definitions discussed in this section describes overlapping but somewhat distinct populations of children. The characteristics of those populations suggest the types of identification procedures, programs, and instruction that will be most effective with the students included in that definition.

PROBE 16-1   Definitions and Need for Programs

1. T F   Children who are gifted seldom drop out of school.
2. T F   Most children who are both gifted and disadvantaged are identified by using traditional assessment methods.
3. T F   Children who are gifted consistently excel in school whether they receive special provisions or not.
4. List three different theories about human intelligence.
5. Following the work of Lewis Terman in the 1920s, giftedness was often determined solely on the basis of _____ .
6. T F   Some educators believe that high motivation is a necessary element in defining giftedness.

CHARACTERISTICS OF CHILDREN WHO ARE GIFTED

You should be able to describe the distinctive characteristics of children who are gifted.

No two children are alike, and there is great diversity among children identified as gifted. Nevertheless, there are some traits that many of these children share; knowledge of these traits enables educators to identify students as gifted, place them in the most appropriate programs, and modify their instruction.

Kam Hunter as a twelve-year-old sophomore in the Honors College of Michigan State University. Obviously too young to play football, he participated as a student manager.

As you read this section, keep in mind that most of the studies designed to discover characteristics of children who are gifted have been based on samples composed of largely white, middle- or upper-class children who are high achievers. The characteristics of these children are not necessarily descriptive of gifted children who are underachievers, especially those who are economically disadvantaged or members of a minority group.

Intellectual Ability

What are the characteristics of children identified as intellectually gifted?

Children who are intellectually gifted have many abilities that make them likely to succeed academically. They can memorize rapidly and retain what they have learned; they read with superior comprehension and often begin reading at an early age. They see relationships among ideas and have an advanced vocabulary (Ehrlich, 1982; Terman & Oden, 1947). These abilities enable them to master the basic school curriculum more quickly than other children. In fact, an early researcher in the field of gifted education (Hollingsworth, 1942) estimated that children with IQ scores of 140 and above could master the 12 years of school in one-half to one-quarter of that time.

A large body of research documents that there is indeed a large discrepancy between the rate at which children who are gifted learn and the pace at which material is presented to them (Daurio, 1979; Kulik & Kulik, 1984). The lockstep nature of public instruction, in effect, tends to "normalize" students with intellectual gifts by instructing them at a level two or more years below the level at which they could learn comfortably. The needs of children with such exceptional learning ability cannot be met without significant advancement of their educational program.

LEARNING PREFERENCES. Personality characteristics attributed to students who are gifted also suggest changes that should be made in their educational program. One of the most commonly cited qualities is an almost insatiable curiosity about a variety of subjects (Ehrlich, 1982; Terman & Oden, 1947). Because of their inquisitiveness, these children welcome instruction on topics such as geometry, astronomy, foreign languages, and others that may not be included in the regular school program at their grade level. The high levels of independence (Lucito, 1964) and motivation (Ehrlich, 1982) of many students identified as gifted suggest that they are capable of planning and carrying out special interest projects without much supervision, and that they should be given opportunities for independent study. Their interest in abstract ideas (Tidwell, 1980) can cause children with intellectual gifts to object to rote memory assignments and drill at least as strenuously as other children object to them, if not more so (McNeill, 1988; Whitmore, 1980). These children excel in classes that offer opportunity for analysis, argument, and debate.

Are children with intellectual gifts misfits?

ADAPTIVE BEHAVIOR. The social and emotional development of children who are intellectually gifted generally equals or exceeds that of other children their age (Gallagher, 1985). Research on gifted students who are high achievers shows that they are self-sufficient, resourceful, participate in many extracurricular activities, and tend to be well liked by other children, at least at the elementary school level (Gallagher, 1985; Terman & Oden, 1947).

These positive traits should not lead you to believe that these children are "super-children," however. They have many problems in common with other children and some distinct problems that result from feelings of being different. A teacher of children identified as gifted reports, "They often get pressure because they're bright or different. They are not the elitists they're criticized for being. They're struggling for their own identities" (Maunder, 1977, p. 8). Pressure to conform and outright hostility may threaten the child's social and emotional adjustment and result in the bitterness and frustration evident in this remark by a highly gifted student: "If I offend people just by existing that is not my fault" (Nevin, 1977, p. 81).

Children who are gifted sometimes contribute to their own alienation by being harshly critical of others. In contrast, many children who are gifted are too critical of themselves (Whitmore, 1980). These children need help in accepting failure as a valuable part of learning because it signals the need for renewed effort and suggests direction for the new effort to take. In short, children with intellectual gifts need the same understanding and encouragement that all children need.

Creativity

Are creativity and intelligence related?

The nature and processes of creativity have been studied in a variety of ways by psychologists interested in defining and developing human capacities for original thought. In spite of extensive research on the subject, however, many issues are still unresolved. Researchers have found a positive correlation between intelligence as measured by IQ tests and creativity as measured by original work in science (Roe, 1953), creative writing (Gallagher, 1985), and performance on tests of divergent thinking (Torrance, 1974). Above-average intelligence appears to be important in creative endeavors. However, special skills, certain personality traits, or a combination of both contribute an element of creative performance not explained by above-average intelligence.

MEASURING CREATIVITY. The requirements for creative accomplishment vary across disciplines (Gardner, 1982); different skills are needed for creativity in drama than are needed for creativity in physics or music, for example. However, the possibility that some cognitive or affective traits are common to creativity across all disciplines has formed a basic assumption in efforts to identify creative potential in young children. This assumption is, in part, a function of the desire to predict superior creativity rather than to judge creative accomplishment. Because children are not often highly skilled in a particular discipline, educators who are interested in early identification and development of creativity use instruments based on traits associated with creative products, processes, or persons (Callahan, 1978). The most commonly used cognitive tests of creativity measure **divergent thinking** ability, which is characterized by original responses to questions or problems (Torrance, 1974).

What is divergent thinking?

Divergent thinking contrasts with convergent thinking, which seeks "correct" responses to questions or problems. High scorers on tests of divergent thinking, such as Torrance's (1966) *Tests of Creative Thinking,* produce many unusual answers to questions that require imagination and knowledge. "List some ways to change textbooks to make them more interesting," or "List inventions that could be made by combining a video recorder and a typewriter," are examples of divergent thinking tasks similar to those used on both standardized and teacher-made tests of creativity.

How do children superior in divergent thinking differ from other children?

LEARNING PREFERENCES. Studies show that children who earn high scores on divergent thinking tests share certain characteristics. They are intellectually playful, have a reputation for wild ideas, and respond to assignments in a novel way (Torrance, 1962). These children generally prefer loosely structured, open-ended learning activities that allow them to develop and express their own ideas (Torrance, 1974). Moreover, Strom and Torrance (1973) found that students who were good at divergent thinking not only expressed a strong dislike for programmed instruction, which is highly structured, they also learned less from that type of instruction than did other children. Not surprisingly, creative children sometimes become impatient with the routine in the regular classroom. As one highly creative child put it, "It's amazing how difficult a subject becomes if you study it slowly enough" (Aschner & Bish, 1965, p. 233).

Studies of creative adults have found certain personality traits to be common to the group. Although these traits are not necessarily found in creative children, they have been used with some success as a basis for identifying children as being creative. Among the most often-cited characteristics are the following: energetic, self-confident, solitary, playful, reflective, and interested in artistic and intellectual activities (Davis & Rimm, 1989).

Special Talents

What is *talent*?

Although the terms *giftedness* and *talent* are used interchangeably throughout most of this chapter, **talent** is used here to refer to specialized ability. Any discussion of talent used in that sense raises the issue of general intellectual ability versus special abilities. That children with musical gifts, children with mathematical gifts, and other children with exceptional aptitude in a particular field are likely to score above average on an IQ test has been determined by many research studies (Tannenbaum, 1983). It has also been found that children identified as gifted according to intelligence test scores tend to score above average on tests of special ability (Gallagher, 1985). However, many children would qualify as gifted on the basis of their IQ scores and not on the basis of a special aptitude test, and vice versa. Some children, of course, would qualify as gifted under either criterion (Stanley, 1977; Tannenbaum, 1983). Since most studies of children with special talents include many children with IQ scores in the highest percentiles, you should not be surprised to find that the characteristics of children identified as gifted in a specific field are similar to those discussed under intellectual ability. In addition, the characteristics attributed to one group of children with special abilities are also often attributed to children with other kinds of special ability.

ACADEMIC TALENT. The children who are talented in academic areas are most likely to share skills common to those children who score high on IQ tests. Stanley (1976) reported: "It would be rare, indeed, for a person to have excellent mathematical reasoning ability and yet be inferior to average thinkers in verbal reasoning ability . . . Though its [Study of Mathematically Precocious Youth] participants are not chosen explicitly for high IQ, virtually none of them have average or below-average IQs" (p. 81).

Bloom (1982) found that mathematicians who enjoy an international reputation for their ability were, as children, characterized by the abundance of questions they began asking at a very early age; a great deal of time spent in solitary play; and a proclivity for independent learning through books and observation of others. These characteristics, particularly a preference for reading as a way to spend leisure time (see, e.g., Van Tassel-Baska, 1983), recur throughout the literature, not only in regard to children with mathematical talents but to children with verbal ability and children who excel in science.

Although boys and girls who are mathematically gifted value theoretical pursuits and are less likely to seek as much social stimulation as more extroverted children seem to desire, they are as socially adroit and comfortable as most other children (Haier & Denham, 1976). Children who are identified on the basis of exceptional verbal ability also seem to value abstract ideas more than do other children their age (Fox, 1976). Although both groups are self-confident, girls who are identified as gifted on the basis of their mathematical ability tend to be much more unconventional than other girls of high ability (Haier & Denham, 1976).

ARTISTIC TALENT. Students who are artistically talented share with students who are academically talented a preference for theoretical and aesthetic pursuits (Getzels, 1979). Ability to work alone and a preference for solitude may be important to outstanding achievement in both scholarly and artistic pursuits (Getzels, 1977).

The artistic disciplines that have received the most attention in the research literature on children who are gifted are music and the visual arts. Although children with artistic gifts may be less likely to exhibit traits common to children with high IQs than are academically gifted children, there is still considerable overlap between the groups. This seems to be particularly true in music, which is a special interest of students who are mathematically and verbally gifted (Van Tassel-Baska, 1983).

The characteristics that the parents of extremely talented musicians report as distinguishing their children are a natural feeling for music and a great sensitivity and emotional responsiveness to it. At a young age, these musicians were able to play by ear, and some displayed perfect pitch (Bloom, 1982). Specific attributes that may contribute to the general traits are an *acute auditory sense,* which allows discrimination of fine differences in tonal pitch, loudness, and timbre; and *tonal memory,* which allows retention for comparative and reproductive purposes (Capurso, 1961).

The student who is gifted in the visual arts possesses traits analogous to those of the student who is gifted in music. Acute powers of observation, a vivid visual memory, a keen sense of color, and enjoyment of artwork are characteristics ascribed to promising artists (Tannenbaum, 1983). In addition, children with talent in the visual arts show more control over artistic media than other children do. Skill in drawing, for example, is considered to be especially important (Clark & Zimmerman, 1984).

Students with musical talents are often identified at a very young age.

Whatever the field, an ability to learn new techniques, ideas, and processes rapidly seems to be critical to the development of a high level of talent (Bloom, 1982). Researchers who have studied prodigies' specialized ability emphasize the role that early and increasingly advanced instruction seems to play in developing talent (Bloom, 1982; Feldman, 1979; Pressey, 1955). Bloom (1982) reported that the young world-class musicians, athletes, mathematicians, and scientists he studied had spent at least ten years of their life developing their talent.

Ability in the two other major arts, drama and dance, has received less attention in the literature on gifted education than has ability in music and the visual arts. We know less about the characteristics of children who are talented in these areas than about children who are academically gifted, children who are musically gifted, and children who are gifted in the visual arts. However, we do know that dancers, like musicians, usually begin to study their art very early (Kirstein, 1983). Some of the characteristics attributed to these groups are summarized in Table 16-1.

What is leadership ability?

LEADERSHIP. The federal definition of giftedness mentions another group that has received relatively little attention in schools' efforts to identify talented students; children with leadership ability. Identification of gifted leaders is problematic because leadership, apart from a situation in which to lead, seems to have little meaning. Because leaders usually represent the dominant values of their group, children who are leaders in most classrooms are likely to be high-achieving, articulate, compliant, enthusiastic, and well dressed. Other traits may be more important for adult leadership positions in groups such as trade unions, academic societies, and research teams.

Within groups, leadership is sometimes simply accorded to whoever is willing to assume responsibility. Stodgill (1974) points out that different situations require different types of leaders. Transactional leaders, for example, whose job is to carry out specified actions within well-accepted and fairly narrow limits, tend to be spontaneous, tolerant of different ideas, and accepting. Transformational leaders, whose role is to make major changes, do not usually derive their power from being likeable. In fact, many great transformational leaders have been tactless and overbearing (Pendarvis, Howley, & Howley, 1990).

Interpersonal skills are perhaps more relevant for leaders in situations in which the stakes are low; however, many situational variables determine the personality traits that are important for leadership, for example, the degree of structure in the task or tasks to be accomplished, the nature of the task, and the cooperativeness of the group (Bavelas, 1984). The number and complexity of the factors determining effective leadership make it so difficult to identify students who are likely to be leaders in their adult lives that many schools have abandoned any systematic effort to identify and develop leadership potential.

PSYCHOMOTOR ABILITY. Although psychomotor ability is not mentioned in the definition of giftedness under PL 100–297, it was specified as an area of giftedness as defined in a United States Office of Education report to Congress (Marland, 1972). Because psychomotor skill is important in many disciplines, traits associated with superior psychomotor ability are included in Table 16-1.

Perhaps the most salient feature that children who are gifted bring to their responses to school tasks is their ability to excel in academics, the arts, or sports. Figure 16-1 provides examples of the wide range of unique personal resources found in this population. These personal resources are often augmented by strong external support. Their parents typically value achievement, and they provide considerable emotional and material support to promote development of their child's ability.

TABLE 16-1   Characteristics of Children with Special Talents

Talent Area	Abilities	Personality Attributes
Mathematics	Ability to manipulate symbolic material more effectively and more rapidly than classmates	Highly independent Enjoy theoretical and investigative pursuits Talented girls less conforming than other girls
Science	Ability to see relationships among ideas, events, and objects Elegance in explanation; the ability to formulate the simplest hypothesis that can account for the observed facts	Highly independent, "loners" Prefer intellectually rather than socially challenging situations Reject group pressures Methodical, precise, exact Avid readers
Language Arts	Capability of manipulating abstract concepts, but sometimes inferior to the high general achiever in working with mathematical material Imagination and originality	Highly independent Social and aesthetic values (girls) Theoretical and political values (boys) Avid readers
Leadership	Ability to effect change Good decision-making ability Proficiency in some area, such as athletics or academics Ability to communicate	Empathic Sensitive Charisma—can transform the group through their enthusiasm and energy Superior communication skills
Psychomotor Ability	Gross motor strength, agility, flexibility, coordination, and speed Excellence in athletics, gymnastics, or dance Fine motor control, deftness, precision, flexibility, and speed Excellence in crafts—jewelry making, model building, mechanics, working with electronic equipment, etc. Ability to use complicated equipment with little or no training	Enjoy and seem to need considerable exercise Competitive Interested in mechanics, electronics, or crafts. Have hobbies such as model building, origami, pottery Early participation in sports
Visual or Performing Arts	Ability to disregard traditional methods in favor of their own original ones Resourcefulness in use of materials Ability to express their feelings through an art form Attention to detail in their own and others' artwork Responsive to music, sculpture, etc.	Self-confident Competitive Prefer working alone Sensitive to their environment Gain satisfaction through expressing their feelings artistically

Sources: Bloom, 1982; Ellison, Abe, Fox, Corey, and Taylor, 1976; Kalinowski, 1985; Kough and DeHaan, 1958; Kranz, n.d.; Lindsay, 1977; Passow and Goldberg, 1962; Renzulli and Hartman, 1971; Roe, 1953; Stanley, George, and Solano, 1977.

FIGURE 16-1   A Functional Approach to Exceptionality: Unique Gifts and Talents

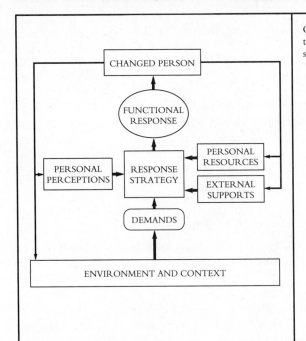

Children who are gifted and talented have unique *personal resources* that enable them to make special contributions to society. Examples of some of those are as follows:

- Intellectual abilities that enable them to excel at problem solving.

- Creativity that encourages the generation of original ideas, inventions, and new knowledge.

- Academic talents that can result in excellence in scholarly activities.

- Artistic talent that can produce new visual arts such as painting and sculpture.

- Musical talents that can generate new musical compositions and exceptional performance on musical instruments.

- Special talents in dance that can lead to new choreography and innovative dance performances.

- Exceptional dramatic abilities that can enrich dramatic performances.

- Special talents for leadership that can enhance governmental, business, and social enterprises.

- Psychomotor talents that can result in spectacular feats in sports.

PROBE 16-2   Characteristics of Children Who Are Gifted

1. T F   Most children who are intellectually gifted are less emotionally and socially mature than other children their age.
2. The personality trait shared by children with high mathematical ability, science aptitude, and language arts ability (see Table 16-1) is that they tend to _____ .
3. Which of the following requires divergent thinking?
    a. As president of the United States, what would you do to solve the energy shortage problem?
    b. What were Mercutio's final lines in his famous death scene in *Romeo and Juliet?*
    c. What were the major causes of the Great Depression?
4. Describe the relationship between intelligence test scores and performance on measures of special ability.
5. Identify which kind of giftedness each of the following statements typifies:
    a. Among her activities were membership in the debate society, the National Honor Society, and the band; still, her favorite pastime is reading.
    b. When asked what procedure should be followed, she had well-organized, goal-oriented suggestions to offer.
    c. Classmates are often critical of her original, sometimes bizarre ideas and behavior.
6. T F   Instruction plays only a minor role in the development of outstanding talent.
7. The type of ability omitted from the current federal definition of giftedness is _____ .
    a. Creative ability
    b. Leadership ability
    c. Artistic ability
    d. Psychomotor ability

IDENTIFYING CHILDREN AS GIFTED

> You should be able to describe methods of identifying children as gifted.

Identification Procedures

What are three stages in the identification process?

The definition of giftedness and characteristics of the student population subsumed by the definition guide the selection and development of identification methods. In general, the more kinds of ability included in the definition, the more complex the procedures needed to identify children who qualify for gifted education. No matter what definition is used, however, there are three overlapping but distinguishable stages in the identification process: (1) referral, (2) screening, and (3) evaluation.

REFERRAL. The initial step in the identification process is the referral stage. At this stage, the names of children who may need special education are submitted to personnel responsible for screening and evaluation. Referral is usually based on observation of performance in the classroom; review of students' records of past performance, such as standardized achievement test scores, awards, grades, and anecdotal reports; and completion of behavior checklists or rating scales by teachers, parents, peers, or the students under consideration for placement.

Is it easy to recognize which children should be referred for possible placement?

Unfortunately, many children who could qualify for gifted education are never referred because teachers have difficulty recognizing some students' exceptional ability. This difficulty is due, in part, to the fact that the level of the classroom curriculum is often too low to elicit the advanced skills possessed by gifted children (Stanley, 1976). It also results from the influence of extraneous factors on teachers' judgment of children's intellectual ability. For example, teachers tend to perceive children who participate readily in new learning activities as brighter than children who are more reluctant to participate (Roedell, Robinson, & Jackson, 1980); and they tend to give attractive children higher ratings on intellectual ability than unattractive children (Ysseldyke & Algozzine, 1982). Another difficulty stems from the fact that some children who are gifted achieve far below their ability level.

For reasons such as these, parents appear to be better at identifying superior ability in their children than are the children's teachers, at least in kindergarten and the early grades (Jacobs, 1971; Roedell, Jackson, & Robinson, 1980). Soliciting referrals from parents, as well as teachers and students, increases the possibility of locating talent at every grade level.

How can the effectiveness and efficiency of referrals be improved?

Questionnaires or behavior checklists are sometimes used to guide the observation of persons who are making the referral (Gear, 1978). Whether in the form of checklists, questionnaires, or rating scales, descriptions of characteristic behaviors or traits must be specific and must distinguish children who are gifted from other children. Specific items such as "Does your child comment on words that have two or more meanings?" (Roedell, Robinson, & Jackson, 1980, p. 58), offer more guidance to the person rating the child than general descriptions such as "Has a good memory." Items that are too general are not reliable indicators of giftedness because they can be interpreted in several ways.

Specificity alone is not sufficient to offer guidance to observers; the items must also correlate positively with superior performance on the measures used for screening and evaluation. To the extent that the behaviors on the checklist fail to correlate with those measures, they fail to identify children as gifted and result in the referral of children who do not qualify for placement.

Since no referral procedures allow perfect correlation with performance on screening and evaluation instruments, testing all students at certain grade levels to identify children who may be gifted is an established practice in many school systems. Another practice used to increase the number of referrals that result in placement is the provision of inservice training workshops to inform teachers and parents of the characteristics of children who are gifted and the procedures for referring children for screening or evaluation (Gear, 1978).

What are some strategies used to screen referrals?

SCREENING. Screening consists of the collection and review of easily obtainable information to determine the likelihood that the referred student will qualify according to evaluation criteria. This intermediate stage is sometimes combined with the referral process when, for example, teachers are asked to refer only children with test scores above a certain level. Common screening strategies are as follows: (1) the administration of aptitude, intelligence, or achievement tests that do not require a psychologist to administer and interpret; (2) review, by a gifted education teacher or subject matter specialist, of work samples such as poems, essays, or musical compositions written by the referred student; and (3) review of checklists, rating scales, or questionnaires to determine eligibility for further evaluation.

Screening is required when evaluation measures are too time-consuming and costly to administer to all children referred to the program. This is often the case when specialized or noninstructional personnel such as psychologists, educational diagnosticians, or professional artists are needed for a comprehensive, in-depth evaluation.

As in referral, the screening process seeks maximum effectiveness and efficiency by including measures that identify as many children as possible who will qualify for placement while identifying as few children as possible who will not qualify. Selection or development of appropriate screening instruments and evaluation of the instruments' usefulness are essential elements of procedures to identify children as gifted.

Evaluation

The final stage in the identification process consists of collecting and analyzing information to determine referred children's eligibility for gifted education programs. Evaluation often consists of a comprehensive measure of ability and a committee review of relevant referral and screening information. Common evaluation strategies are as follows: (1) individual administration of a comprehensive intelligence test (Howley, Howley, & Pendarvis, 1986); (2) auditions or review of student portfolios or projects (Mills & Ridlon, 1980); (3) administration of high-level achievement tests (George & Solano, 1976); and (4) analysis of case studies of children referred for placement (Renzulli & Smith, 1977; Richert, 1987). A summary of commonly used methods of evaluation is shown in Table 16-2.

What are the results of using "breadth" as opposed to "depth" approaches to determine placement eligibility?

Placement criteria usually represent either a multitalent approach to determining eligibility, or an approach that seeks to locate the highest level of performance on a single measure of talent. The former places greater emphasis on breadth or on high—but not necessarily outstanding—performance on a number of measures. The latter focuses on outstanding level of ability, or depth (Dirks & Quarfoth, 1981). If a **breadth model** is used, students must qualify on more than one measure. They might, for example, qualify on the basis of superior scores on three out of five measures: grades, intelligence test, creativity test, achievement test, rating scale. This approach tends to identify students who are well-rounded achievers and to exclude children who are underachievers (Dirks & Quarforth, 1981).

The **depth model** may use a single-criterion approach, which requires a high level of performance on a particular measure, such as an IQ test; or it may offer alternative placement criteria. In the latter instance, students must score in the highest range on any one of several measures, such as IQ tests, aptitude tests, or rating scales, in order to qualify for special education. The depth model allows the inclusion of children who score very high on one measure regardless of their performance on other measures. State or local educational priorities

TABLE 16-2   Summary of Commonly Used Methods of Evaluation

Method	Strengths	Limitations	Comments
Teacher evaluation via behavior checklists or questionnaires	Familiar with student's work Familiar with "normal" performance for grade level.	Teacher perceptions may be influenced by irrelevant factors such as appearance, willingness to conform, and attitudes toward classwork.	Teachers may fail to recognize as many as half the gifted students. Teacher nomination may be improved through inservice training on the characteristics of gifted children.
Peer evaluation via behavior checklists or questionnaires	Familiar with student's work. May be aware of interests or abilities of which the teacher is unaware.	Students' perceptions may be influenced by whether they like or dislike their classmate and whether or not the teacher appears to like their classmate.	Little research has been done on the effectiveness of peer evaluation.
Parent evaluation via behavior checklists or questionnaires	Familiar with child's development, interests, and abilities.	Parents may not know how their child's behavior compares with that of other children of the same age.	In kindergarten and at the primary level, parents may be better than teachers at identifying gifted children.
Grades	Information is readily available.	Review of grades fails to identify underachievers and children who are gifted in nonacademic areas.	Referral of children with an average of "B" or better results in the inclusion of most gifted children, but many nongifted children are referred as well.
Work samples	Can be collected in all talent areas, including the visual or performing arts.	Requires availability of experts such as music teachers and art teachers to judge the work sample.	Work samples reflect both the student's ability and commitment.
Interest inventories	Seem to be more "culture-fair" than IQ or achievement tests.	Ability level may not be as high as interest level.	One of the few measures that reflect commitment to an area of art or science.

usually determine whether a breadth or depth model is used in the evaluation of children as being gifted.

Considerations for Selecting Identification Instruments

Regardless of the evaluation model employed in determining eligibility for placement, the referral, screening, and evaluation instruments are the key factors in efforts to identify students as gifted.

TABLE 16-2   (continued)

Method	Strengths	Limitations	Comments
Achievement tests	Indicate academic aptitude in particular subject areas. Test scores are usually on record in children's cumulative folders. They are a readily available source of information.	May fail to identify underachievers, especially children from culturally different environments and gifted children with disabilities.	Success on most achievement tests requires superior verbal comprehension.
Group intelligence tests	Can indicate aptitude even when achievement is low. Test scores are often on record in children's cumulative folders.	If high cutoff points (e.g., 130 IQ or above) are used, as many as half the gifted children may be overlooked. Fails to differentiate the highly gifted from the moderately gifted.	For screening purposes, a relatively low cutoff point such as 115 IQ can reduce the number of gifted children missed.
Creativity tests	Usually considered more "culture-fair" than IQ or achievement tests.	Administration and interpretation often require special personnel. May be difficult to distinguish "original" but relevant responses from "bizarre" and irrelevant responses.	The relationship between ability to do well on a creativity test and consistent, outstanding creative performance hasn't been established.
Individual intelligence tests	Is most reliable single indicator of intellectual giftedness in middle- and upper-class socioeconomic levels. Many individual tests measure both verbal and nonverbal ability.	Require special personnel for administration and interpretation. Can be biased against minority groups and gifted children with disabilities. Fail to assess important abilities such as specific artistic or academic aptitude.	Interpretation of the quality and character of responses by a competent tester can provide considerable insight into a child's ability.

What are some limitations of the usefulness of IQ tests?

For many years, virtually the only way students could gain entrance into most gifted programs was by getting a high score on an IQ test. Although IQ scores are still considered important by most educators involved in the identification of exceptionally able students, the use of the IQ score as the single determining factor in identification has been harshly criticized. One of the most compelling criticisms is that the tests are biased against children who are not from white middle- or upper-class homes. Another is that IQ tests (particularly group IQ tests) often lack a sufficient number of questions difficult enough to distinguish the relatively few children who are gifted from other children who are above average in ability, but not so significantly advanced as to require a highly differentiated program of instruction.

Are IQ tests
diagnostic
instruments?

TEST BIAS AGAINST MINORITIES. IQ tests do not tap an innate dimension psychologically distinct from that reflected by achievement test scores (Mercer, 1981). Rather, they are distinguished primarily in that they draw from a broader domain of experience than do tests that are limited to particular subject areas. Individually administered intelligence tests are useful prognostic devices because they predict scholastic performance with moderate reliability; but they do not provide a fair estimate of the ability of children from minority groups (Mercer, 1981).

Are nonverbal tests
culture-fair?

The solution to the problem of test bias is not through development of culture-fair tests; in fact, it is clear that no test can be culture-fair (Mercer, 1981). Some educators advocate the use of nonverbal tests on the grounds that they are less culturally biased (e.g., Ortiz & Volkoff, 1987). Their use in identification of children as gifted is not a completely satisfactory solution, however. In some instances, students from minority groups score lower on nonverbal tests, relative to majority norms, than on verbal IQ tests (Martinson, 1974; Sternberg, 1982).

Although some creativity tests offer the advantage that they do not penalize children from minority groups to as great a degree as IQ tests (Torrance, 1971), it is not clear that scores on creativity tests predict outstanding creative accomplishment. Moreover, compared to their scores on the WISC-R, one group of bright minority students scored lower on a creativity test (Ortiz & Volkoff, 1987). Certainly, creativity test scores should not be a primary determiner of eligibility for placement in a gifted program.

Establishment of separate norms for large minority groups or for economically disadvantaged schools is a promising solution to the problem of test bias. Using this approach, the highest-scoring 2 to 5 percent (for example) of the students from minority groups might be identified as gifted, even though their test scores are not in the highest percentiles according to the majority population on which the test was originally standardized. Limiting comparison to children with similar backgrounds is a strategy successfully used in projects designed to identify disadvantaged children as gifted (e.g., Maker, Morris, & James, 1981).

Do all IQ tests
adequately reflect
children's
intellectual
strengths?

LOW TEST CEILINGS. Most tests do not have enough difficult questions to distinguish the most brilliant children from other bright children. The result is that two children with very different abilities may earn the same score on a test. A score of 124 IQ on a particular test, for example, may be reported for many children the same age, each having missed approximately the same number of questions on the test. However, the instrument tested the limits of some students' knowledge, while others might have been able to answer much more advanced questions. Since there were no higher-level questions on the test, both groups received the same score; yet, because of differences in their ability, the students would need quite different educational programs.

What is a solution
to the problem of
low test ceilings?

This problem applies to all standardized measures; achievement, aptitude, and IQ tests; but it can be avoided where higher-level tests are available, even though the tests may have been designed for older students. The study of Mathematically Precocious Youth (Stanley & Benbow, 1982) relies on off-level testing to identify children as gifted. Using the mathematical section of the College Entrance Examination Board's *Scholastic Aptitude Test* (SAT-M), the project identifies elementary and junior high school students with extraordinary mathematical ability. According to Julian Stanley (1976), who initiated the project, "The harder tests spread out the top 2 percent over a wide range from good through excellent to superb. . . . Teachers may be able to identify the upper 1 percent or 2 percent by observation and with the aid of in-grade tests, but they can hardly be expected to find the top 1 in 200 or 500 or 10,000 without special assistance" (p. 313).

Identification of children as gifted is one of the most important tasks facing educators who are interested in talent development. If children who are exceptionally able are not identified as gifted, it is unlikely that they will be provided an education that develops their abilities. Unfortunately, identification is as difficult as it is important. No single test can be relied on to identify giftedness. Educators responsible for identification determine which combination of assessment methods is most appropriate for the population defined as gifted in their schools and for the individual child who may qualify according to that definition. Factors such as the age, socioeconomic status, personality, and type of ability of the child must be weighed against the advantages and disadvantages of different instruments.

What factors must be considered in selecting the best test or combination of tests for a particular child?

There are three important considerations in selecting and developing procedures and instruments that can be combined in the identification of children as gifted: (1) the validity and reliability of the tests and checklists proposed for use in the referral, screening, and evaluation process; (2) alternative procedures, such as separate norms, for students who are ethnic or racial minorities, who are economically disadvantaged, and who have disabilities; and (3) high test ceilings to assure adequate measurement of the referred students' mastery of advanced concepts.

PROBE 16-3   Identifying Children as Gifted

1. What are three steps in the identification process?
2. Give an example of an activity that might occur at each of the steps in the identification process.
3. For very young children, _____ is often more effective than teacher nomination in identifying children as gifted.
4. T   F   Teacher referrals may miss many of the students who are gifted.
5. Give an example of a poor item that might appear on a gifted behavior checklist and tell why it is poor.
6. Write a better item for a gifted behavior checklist.
7. T   F   The multitalent approach to identification may miss children who are highly gifted but are not well-rounded in their interests.
8. T   F   In general, children who are disadvantaged perform better on nonverbal tests of intelligence.
9. Using tests designed for older students to identify young students as gifted is an attempt to offset the problem of a _____ on tests designed for children the same age as the children to be identified.
10. T   F   Creativity tests are clearly superior to other measures in identifying children with the potential to make original contributions in the arts and sciences.

EDUCATIONAL PROVISIONS FOR CHILDREN WHO ARE GIFTED

You should be able to describe the educational practices that are appropriate for children who are gifted.

Barriers to Achievement

What are some reasons for underachievement in students who are gifted?

Because instruction tends to be directed to the average achievement level for each grade in a school, meeting the educational needs of the most talented students requires modification of their program. For many of these students, underachievement is simply an effect of an instructional level that is too easy and instructional pace that is too slow. For some students, however, there are additional barriers to achievement. Debilitating family circumstances, social stereotypes, or physical impairments render these students more vulnerable to the effects of inappropriate instruction. Special education includes strategies that recognize and address the major factors that place these students at risk for academic failure.

INCONSISTENT OR INAPPROPRIATE EXPECTATIONS. Damon is in the sixth grade. His unusual intellectual capacity is reflected by his IQ score, 130 on the Stanford-Binet Intelligence Scale, and by his ready grasp of abstract ideas, reasoning ability, and insight into relationships between facts. However, Damon does C or D work in most of his subjects; since the second grade, his work has fallen far short of his intellectual capability.

Damon's written work is messy and almost always incomplete. He resents having to redo his papers and uses any excuse to get out of going to school. His parents and teachers have tried punishing, encouraging, coaxing, and lecturing to get him to try harder. When asked why he does not do well in class, Damon usually responds that classwork is boring, the teacher does not like him, and that he is not all that smart anyway.

Damon is typical of a group of students who are gifted underachievers—a group that has been the subject of a great deal of research. Most of the research on bright, middle-class underachievers was conducted during the period from the 1940s to the mid-1960s, when definitions of giftedness were based largely on intelligence test scores. Because the children studied had IQ scores in the 90th percentile and above, researchers looked for factors that affected the children's motivation. Among the factors investigated were personality traits, parent-child interactions, and attitudes toward school. There is evidence now that in addition to those factors, specific learning disabilities often contribute to the underachievement of students with high IQs (Fox, Brody, & Tobin, 1983; Redding, 1990; Whitmore, 1980).

Although most of Terman's subjects (Terman & Oden, 1947) grew up to be outstandingly productive adults, some of his subjects had a history of underachievement that began in the primary grades and continued throughout their lives. These students could be differentiated from students who were gifted achievers by four qualities: (1) inability or unwillingness to persist to achieve goals; (2) lack of integration of goals and a tendency toward purposelessness; (3) lack of self-confidence; and (4) feelings of inferiority (Terman & Oden, 1947).

Other studies have confirmed Terman's results. For example, in a study reported in *Able Misfits* (Pringle, 1970), lack of confidence was found to be the personality trait most frequently associated with children who are gifted underachievers. Some other personality traits associated with underachievement are immaturity, irresponsibility, and rigidity (Pringle, 1970; Whitmore, 1980). A study of highly intelligent dropouts, however, found the male dropouts more assertive and more independent, if more rebellious, than equally bright boys who stayed in school (French, 1975).

Poor study habits and inconsistent work characterize the school performance of students who are gifted underachievers (Rimm, 1984). One explanation for their negative attitude toward school is that, for various reasons, some children who are gifted have not learned that effort makes a difference in their academic performance. According to Rimm (1984), "Underachieving children don't believe that they could achieve even if they made appropriate efforts" (p. 2).

The reasons for underachievers' negative attitude toward school have not been established, but poor parent-child relationships appear to be a contributing factor. One study (Rimm & Lowe, 1988) found that parents of students who are gifted underachievers tend to provide inconsistent discipline and fail to model satisfaction with their own intellectual achievements.

Counseling underachievers and their parents, however, has not consistently resulted in improved performance (Gallagher, 1985). Educational modifications seem to have been more successful. Perhaps this is because the classroom as well as the home environment contributes to underachievement. Primary grade students displaying underachievement report that several

What are some strategies for improving underachievers' performance?

characteristics of the classroom have a debilitating effect on their performance; these factors include pressure to conform, a competitive climate, and the judgmental attitude of their teachers (Whitmore, 1980). Low teacher expectations and presentation of academic material below their conceptual level also contribute to underachievement in students who are gifted. Greater emphasis on academics can improve gifted students' underachievement so that they make nearly as much progress during the school year as students who are gifted achievers (Fearn, 1982).

The best way to remove the barriers to achievement may be to use a combination of methods. The Cupertino School District in California combined remediation, behavior modification, techniques of self-control, and a stimulating curriculum in a supportive setting to create a program that met with unusual success (Whitmore, 1980). The results of this program and others have implications for teachers:

- Don't give the students lectures or "pep talks" to get them to try harder. This has been shown to have detrimental effects on achievement.
- Show support and respect for the students' efforts.
- Establish appropriate standards and provide the instruction, guidance, and support to help students meet them.
- Encourage cooperation, rather than competition, in the classroom.
- Reward small gains in achievement and do not expect quick success.

What are some identified strengths of children who are culturally different?

INADEQUATE EXPOSURE TO THE CULTURAL "MAINSTREAM." Because of cultural biases in testing and instruction, many children who are gifted but are not from the white majority are never identified and never receive instruction that could develop their talents (Richert, Alvino, & McDonnel, 1982). Ruiz (1989) suggests that children from minority groups should not be expected to exhibit the same strengths as children from white, middle- or upper-class backgrounds; we should instead seek strengths that reflect their experiences. These strengths may include the ability to improvise with commonplace materials, responsiveness to concrete materials, and expressiveness in speech (Torrance, 1977). An example of the creative expressiveness of a young Appalachian student in a program for children who are both culturally different and gifted is provided in Hauck and Freehill's *The Gifted—Case Studies* (1972, p. 99):

The Worst Punishment for a Man

by Junior _____

Sitting here at my desk, it seems the day will never end. It's just now 3:30 P.M. and I have a conference with the Secretary of State at 4:00 P.M., at 5:00 P.M. a conference with Mike Mansfield and Senator Long. Oh God, I am tired. I'm not as young as I once was. The pages of history may contain but a paragraph about my life or my work, but at least I sure's hell have won the paragraph. "More critics than any U.S. President ever"— that's what the papers say. It seems nobody's satisfied with what I do. Viet Nam is really a hellava mess—and guess who gets all the blame for everything—me: Damn it! When will those demonstrators with the long hair and low morals and the intellectuals with no common sense learn that if we leave that little nation we are breaking our word, breaking our commitments, giving the communists another base of strength? Oh damn it! Nobody listens to me . . . and this election coming up—McCarthy, Wallace, and all the other S.O.B.'s who disapprove of the Great Society and how I try to run it. God help them though. Let one of 'em win—please. That's the worst punishment I can think of for a man—to be President of the United States.

The ability to see things from an unusual perspective, the concern for social issues, and the intellectual playfulness apparent in this composition illustrate the creativity sometimes found among children who come from environments not conducive to success in school.

584 PART III Individual Differences in Learning and Behavior

Special efforts must be made to counteract factors that can inhibit the performance of these children. These factors include the following: (1) inexperience with the concepts and vocabulary of middle-class society; (2) the low expectations educators have for children who are culturally different; (3) the children's expectations of failure (Baldwin, Gear, & Lucito, 1978); and (4) the fact that achievement in school may conflict with peer loyalty (Hauck & Freehill, 1972).

The deficits exhibited by children who are culturally different are sometimes created by teachers' low expectations for them (Good & Brophy, 1987). These children's achievement may be improved by making teachers aware of the damaging effects that suppressed, but still prevalent, stereotypes and prejudice have on the performance of children who are culturally different (Thunberg, 1981).

The achievement of children from culturally different or economically disadvantaged environments can be dramatically improved by providing intensive, compensatory programs (Smilansky & Nevo, 1979) and by recognizing and developing the children's cognitive strengths (Maker, Morris & James, 1981). Placement in a gifted program can greatly reduce the dropout rate among minority students (Smith, LeRose, & Clasen, 1991). Educators should also look at the unusual success of some cultural minorities, such as Chinese students (Stanley, 1989), to determine what factors contribute to their high achievement. American educators might benefit all of their students, especially students from minority groups, by adopting the attitude that differences in experiences, rather than differences in ability, usually explain differences in achievement. Because they emphasize effort rather than innate ability, Asian parents and educators encourage their children to maximize their achievement. Programs that motivate students to make greater efforts toward academic achievement and that teach students how to make their efforts effective are likely to make a significant difference in the students' achievement.

GIFTED STUDENTS WITH DISABILITIES. Children can be gifted and have disabilities at the same time. Thomas Edison was deaf; Aldous Huxley was blind; Elizabeth Barrett Browning suffered from spinal injuries; and, according to some researchers, Einstein had learning disabilities. There is no disabling condition that precludes giftedness. Talent has been found in every group, including persons with retardation. One discovery of giftedness among persons with disabilities was that of Yoshihiko Yamamoto, a Japanese boy with a reported IQ of 40 (see Figure 16-2), who won international acclaim for his artwork (Morishima, 1974). Using a broad definition of giftedness, June Maker, author of *Providing Programs for the Gifted Handicapped* (1977), suggests that the incidence of giftedness among persons with disabilities is 3 to 5 percent, about the same as it is among people without disabilities.

Language and speech problems, associated with many disabling conditions, are probably the major obstacle to identification of gifted students with disabilities. Even relatively minor problems, such as poor spelling, can affect teachers' perceptions of students' intellectual ability and, consequently, their willingness to refer them for evaluation. Yet, performance on measures of spelling skill, for example, has little correlation with performance on measures of general intelligence and creativity. Students with language problems can be highly gifted, but teachers may need to look for strengths rather than weaknesses in order to recognize these students' ability. A teacher who is distracted by spelling and punctuation errors might overlook the liveliness, imagination, and descriptive language in compositions such as the following scene, written by a sixth grader who is gifted and yet also has learning disabilities:

The Drogen
Eat your hart out said the dragen as it rose to full hight and with one swop it killed the last man in my party except me. I drew my steel speer adn therw it strate at his stomic. but the dragon cot it and threw it at me. I jumpet of the rock I was standing on just in

Margin notes:

What are some strategies for improving the academic performance of children who are culturally different?

Do some students have both gifts and disabilities?

FIGURE 16-2   Nagoya Castle, Produced by Yamamoto in the Ninth Grade

Source: Courtesy of Akira Morishima.

time to see the speer split the rock. I trid to run but it was to late the drogon grabd me I drew my sord in time to stick it in his pom. He squremd in pain. I toke this chans to drive my wood spear into his stomic.

Children who are gifted and have disabilities are often unusually difficult to identify, because a disabling condition can mask unusual potential. For example, Krippner (1967) described the case of a boy who was deaf and also in a school for persons with mental retardation until he was 17, when he was discovered to be gifted—but only by accident. An employee of the institution happened to leave a transistor radio kit on a work table, and the youngster assembled it with ease.

The low expectations of many educators contribute to this failure to recognize giftedness in students with disabilities. Low expectations not only prevent recognition of talent, they can destroy students' faith in their abilities. The low self-esteem that can result seems to be caused in part by the discrepancy between the extremely high goals the students set for themselves and the low expectations of others. Gifted adults with disabilities suggest that if educators want to improve the performance of children with disabilities who are gifted, they must expect more than mediocre performance from them (Maker, 1977).

Students who are gifted and also have learning disabilities have received more attention in the literature than gifted students with other disabilities. This may be due to the relatively specific effect of learning disabilities on academic achievement. Although students with learning disabilities are often hard to identify as gifted, other students with disabilities may be even more difficult to identify. Conditions such as hearing impairments may have a more subtle effect, depressing achievement over all academic areas (Yewchuk & Bibby, 1989). To identify children with disabilities as gifted, a combination of methods is needed. These include the following: (1) using tests that are normed on populations of persons with particular disabilities, such as children with hearing or vision impairments; (2) adapting test procedures so they accommodate the student's condition (e.g., using an interpreter to sign the questions for a student who is deaf); and (3) supplementing standardized test information with informal observation and work samples.

Students with disabilities who are gifted, perhaps even more than students with talents alone or those with disabilities alone, need individualized education programs. These individualized programs should be sure to address the students' strengths as well as their weaknesses (Silverman, 1989). There is a tendency to pay much more attention to the academic deficits of students with disabilities who are gifted than to their academic and intellectual accomplishments.

How do boys and girls compare in school achievement?

SEX-ROLE STEREOTYPES. Research has yet to establish consistent differences in the intellectual ability of girls and boys, but there are significant differences in their achievement. Until puberty, when both boys and girls become more conscious of sex-role expectations, girls make better grades than boys (Wentzel, 1988). Then, at the junior high school and high school level, boys begin to outperform girls on achievement tests in mathematics and science (Hallinan & Sorensen, 1987). In math, the gap in achievement continues to widen with age (Keating, 1976).

As girls grow up they yield progressively more to boys in achievement and competitiveness. Many researchers feel that social stereotypes and expectations are responsible for women's failure to pursue advanced study and careers commensurate with their ability. Despite the feminist movement, girls are still expected to be more conforming and less assertive than boys.

What are strategies for improving girls' achievement in traditionally masculine fields?

Girls who are gifted tend to be less self-confident than boys who are gifted. Surprisingly, research has found IQ to be inversely correlated with expectations of success among girls (Crandall, Katkovsky & Preston, 1972; Walberg, 1969). In other words, the brighter a girl is, the less well she expects to do. This lack of self-confidence may result from a conflict between characteristics of giftedness and society's perceptions of how a girl should behave. A research study on teacher and pupil stereotypes of boys and girls who are gifted (Solano, 1976) showed that although gifted boys are viewed favorably, gifted girls are viewed quite unfavorably. Disapproval by peers and teachers may undermine the confidence of bright girls.

Since teachers tend to reward passivity in girls (Sadker & Sadker, 1985), special efforts should be made to promote the achievement motivation of girls who are gifted. Especially important to the achievement of girls who are gifted are the following: (1) early entry into intellectually challenging programs; (2) provision of models that contradict sex-role stereotypes; and (3) provision of information about scholastic requirements for career alternatives in nonstereotypical disciplines (Callahan, 1979). In addition, Silverman (1986) recommends that high schools combine several programmatic features to promote the development of gifted girls' intellectual ability. Among her recommendations are the recruitment of girls in Advanced Placement mathematics and science courses; the establishment of mentorships and internships so that girls can work with women who are experts in their fields; the revision of the curriculum to include a more representational proportion of women's accomplishments in literary, artistic, political, scientific, and mathematical fields; and the selection of nonsexist textbooks.

Programs for Children Who Are Gifted

Although there are many kinds of programs for children who are gifted, most of them have similar goals. Whether children identified as gifted are placed in special schools, sent to resource rooms for part of the day, or given special assignments in the regular classroom, educational modifications are designed to do the following:

- Quicken the pace of learning by moving the students through activities faster than would be appropriate for children of average ability.
- Broaden the range of experiences and knowledge of children who are gifted by teaching subjects not offered in the regular curriculum at the children's grade level.
- Develop skills of analysis and expression in academic or artistic disciplines.
- Provide opportunity for concentrated, in-depth study of areas in which the students are especially interested or able.

As you will see from descriptions of some of the most common types of programs in Table 16-3, some programs emphasize one goal more than others. Some focus on broadening the student's knowledge base, while others increase the pace of instruction or allow students to study more advanced subjects than in the regular program. Development of expressive and analytic skills is generally an important element of all gifted programs. Because no single program can meet the diverse needs of all the children in a school system, who have unique gifts and talents, every system needs a variety of program options (Feldhusen, 1982).

TABLE 16-3   Programs for Children Who Are Gifted

Advanced Placement (AP)

Prepares high school students for AP examinations, which earn credit at many colleges and universities. AP courses provide college-level instruction on the high school campus. The course curricula include Latin, physics, music, European history, studio art, PASCAL, and a number of other subjects.

Mentorships

Usually are provided off-campus in business and professional offices. Mentorships, or internships, allow students to learn firsthand about different careers, such as veterinary medicine, law, and architecture. The size of the community has an effect on the variety of experiences that can be offered through a mentorship program.

Seminars

Offer students an opportunity to learn through a series of discussions on topics not usually considered in-depth in the regular curriculum.

Acceleration

Offers students the opportunity to move through their school career at the pace that is most suitable to their rate of learning. This may involve skipping several grades, early entrance to kindergarten, and early entrance to college. Advanced classes and honors programs are often considered forms of acceleration.

Independent Study

Allows students to delve into areas of particular interest. The teacher assists the students in locating resources and helps them define their goals and outline strategies for reaching them.

Tutorials

Match tutors with students who are interested and talented in a subject that the teacher may lack time or expertise to offer. Tutors may be peers, older students, or adult volunteers.

School programs for gifted students should provide opportunities for exploration and independent study of topics of interest.

PROGRAM OPTIONS. The goals of gifted education are accomplished through a combination of (1) grouping arrangements; (2) developmental placement based on consideration of individual students' achievement level and conceptual, physical, and social development (Christopherson, 1981); and (3) special activities in the regular classroom. Within each of these three classes of alternatives, there are a number of program options (see Table 16-4). Research offers stronger support for the first two approaches than for the third. Grouping children who are bright in homogeneous classes has a significant, positive impact on their academic progress (Kulik & Kulik, 1982). The research in support of advancing students to placements more suited to their cognitive development is "both massive and impressive" (Tannenbaum, 1983, p. 201), with advantages reported by parents and children (Alexander & Skinner, 1980).

What are some methods for accomplishing the goals of gifted education?

The practice of providing special instruction in the classroom for children who are gifted is not as well researched as grouping and acceleration options. Since the size of most regular classrooms prohibits significant modifications in instruction to accommodate individual needs (Sizer, 1983), that option is probably best considered supplemental and not sufficiently differentiated to meet fully the educational needs of most students identified as gifted. However, independent study and programs such as Junior Great Books and Philosophy for Children can enrich the classroom curriculum for gifted students as well as others (Parke, 1989).

How can IEPs be used in educating children identified as gifted?

IEPs FOR CHILDREN IDENTIFIED AS GIFTED. Several states have mandated individualized education programs (IEPs) for gifted students, even though these students are not included under PL 94-142 (Seaberg & Stafford, 1991). IEPs are an effective means of designing and implementing the combination of alternatives that is most suitable for each student. Based on assessment that identifies the individual student's strengths and weaknesses, IEPs for children

---

TABLE 16-4   Programs Options for Gifted Education

Grouping
  Cluster grouping (placing several students who are gifted in the same regular classroom).
  Resource center (on or off campus).
  Special class (seminars, honors, Advanced Placement).
  Self-contained classroom (all subjects taught by gifted education teacher).
  Special schools.

Developmental Placement
  Early admission to kindergarten or first grade.
  Grade skipping.
  Cross-grade placement (acceleration in one or two subjects).
  Fast-paced classes (cover two years of material in one school year, for example).
  Credit by examination (students "test out" of units, courses, or grades).
  Early admission to college.

Classroom Activities
  Independent study with advanced-level textbooks.
  Independent and small-group projects/activities.
  Autoinstructional materials.
  Schoolwide enrichment programs or workshops.
  Special interest clubs or classes.
  Computer-assisted instruction.

---

identified as gifted ensure that they are not simply placed in an enrichment center for one day a week, or in an honors class, or some other option that constitutes the "gifted program." Instead, each child has an individualized program that combines a number of educational options in accordance with the child's assessed learning needs.

Depending on the children's level and type of ability, some may be best served in full-time programs, such as a specialized arts school or a self-contained classroom. Some may need to enroll in college courses, and some may be adequately served through a combination of developmental placement and a resource room program. A range of options is needed at every grade level, but developmental factors influence the relative importance of different alternatives at the preschool and primary grade level, the intermediate and middle school level, and the high school and the postsecondary level of education.

How do preschool and primary grade programs accommodate the needs of young children who are gifted?

PRESCHOOL AND PRIMARY GRADES. At the preschool level and in the primary grades, one of the major considerations in modifying instruction is the discrepancy between the conceptual development of children who are gifted and their motor development. Although it is sometimes hard for teachers to accept that some 5-year-olds who cannot write their name can read and understand books written for fifth- or sixth-graders, they need to plan and provide academic tasks appropriate to children's conceptual level and motor tasks appropriate to their physical development.

The University of Washington Child Development Preschool program provides preschoolers who are highly gifted with individual instruction using first- through seventh-grade workbooks and other instructional materials adapted to the young children's motor skill level (Roedell, Jackson, & Robinson, 1980). The University of Illinois primary school for gifted 3- to 5-year-olds emphasizes family involvement in school programs (Karnes & Johnson, 1987).

Because of the large discrepancy between the academic skills of children who are highly gifted and their physical development, self-contained classrooms with a small enough enrollment to allow individualization offer the most viable alternative for meeting their needs. Provisions for early admission to school, cross-grade placement, and grade skipping are also important at this age level.

INTERMEDIATE AND MIDDLE SCHOOL. In the fourth through eighth grades, grouping for special instruction is a primary means of meeting the educational needs of children who are gifted (Sicola, 1990). Resource rooms, resource centers, and advanced classes are common at this level. Emphasis on grouping is based partly on the belief that children at this preadolescent and early adolescent stage need peers who share their interests and concerns. Otherwise, desire for acceptance by their classmates may have a negative effect on development, and the incidence of underachievement tends to increase.

> Why is grouping important at the intermediate level?

Despite its continued popularity, grouping at the middle school level is controversial. Because middle school philosophy emphasizes normative social goals over academic goals, many of its advocates caution against special classes for bright children (Sicola, 1990). Slavin (1990), for example, regards heterogeneous groups, especially cooperative learning teams, as the fairest and most effective means of educating all middle school students. Many advocates for children who are gifted question the validity of this view, since there is a substantial body of research demonstrating academic gains made by students enrolled in advanced, enriched, or accelerated classes (Robinson, 1990).

A major consideration at this level of school is the need to counter the effects of sex-role stereotyping on the cognitive development of students who are gifted. Girls in particular are likely to begin underachieving during this period (Sadker, Sadker, & Steindan, 1989). As a consequence of their perception of science and mathematics as "masculine subjects," they may lose interest in them and begin a pattern of opting out of high-level science and mathematics classes (Becker, 1989).

During the middle school or junior high school years, concerns about acceptance and interest in social interactions cause girls who are gifted to resist alternatives that separate them from long-time classmates or put them in highly competitive situations with boys. Early admission to high school or early entry into a challenging program may help educators interest such girls in accelerated mathematics courses (Callahan, 1979; Fox, 1976). Casserly (1979) suggests that high school girls who are interested in science and mathematics could serve as role models for younger girls by giving science demonstrations and discussing the relevance of science or mathematics to various careers.

HIGH SCHOOL AND POSTSECONDARY LEVEL. The diversity of student interests and abilities within the gifted group is greater at the high school and the postsecondary school level than at any earlier point in the students' career. By high school, students who are gifted often surpass their teachers in some subjects (Renzulli, 1982). Because of this diversity and the high level of student ability, making adequate provision for high school students who are gifted requires a variety of advanced materials as well as subject matter experts. Cooperative high school and college programs such as Advanced Placement courses, dual enrollment in high school and college, college correspondence courses, and early admission to college are important alternatives for students at this level.

> Are there special schools for students who are gifted?

In some large cities, specialized schools provide high school students who are gifted access to full-time comprehensive programs in academic or artistic disciplines. The Bronx High School of Science and other specialized schools are available to talented students in New York. The North Carolina School for the Performing Arts, one of the most recently established specialized schools, is innovative because it provides both high school and college programs (Cox & Daniel, 1983). Because of the limited number of such schools, the majority of high school and postsecondary school students who are gifted are served through acceleration, special classes, and the cooperative high school and college programs mentioned earlier (Cox, Daniel, & Boston, 1985).

Instruction

Most educators of students who are gifted subscribe to a humanistic philosophy of education. Inherent in this philosophy are a concern for the rights of the individual student and respect for individual differences. The qualities considered important for humanistic teaching include tolerance for diverse opinions, willingness to admit mistakes, and empathy with children (Maker, 1975).

Must teachers of children who are gifted be gifted themselves?

TEACHER QUALIFICATION. Whether teachers of students who are gifted should be gifted themselves is a matter of some controversy. Some educators argue that it is sufficient for the teachers to be gifted at teaching. Others contend that the teachers should be gifted themselves if they are to empathize with the problems of children identified as gifted, provide sufficiently challenging instruction, and even to keep up with them as they learn. Following are some compromise positions: (1) teachers should be above-average in intelligence but not necessarily gifted; (2) teachers of elementary children who are gifted need not be gifted themselves, but teachers of high school students who are gifted should be; and (3) teachers, whether gifted or not, should be familiar with many subjects and expert in at least one.

Lack of resolution of this issue is due, in part, to teacher educators' reluctance to use procedures that might exclude persons capable of becoming excellent teachers of students who are gifted. A more pragmatic approach is to define the abilities and skills that the teacher of students who are gifted should have and base teacher preparation on these. Listed among such skills needed by gifted education teachers are expertise in the subject or subjects they teach (Gallagher, 1985), knowledge and skills needed to assist in planning for individualization of the students' programs (Reynolds & Birch, 1977), and knowledge and skills needed to help students identify and expand their interests (Renzulli, 1977).

What constitutes enrichment for children who are gifted?

ENRICHMENT IN GIFTED PROGRAMS. Because of the humanistic orientation of gifted programs and because the students are usually advanced in several subject areas and have mastered the basic skills taught at their grade level, the content of enrichment programs is often based primarily on students' academic interests. Enrichment based on student interest alone, however, does not constitute a meaningful education for students identified as gifted. Enrichment must be more than interesting; it must be educationally relevant and challenging (Stanley, 1977). Popular enrichment program activities—such as field trips, creativity exercises, and educational games comprising a series of loosely related lessons—are not defensible as differentiated instruction (Renzulli, 1977).

The content and the learning environment of gifted programs should reflect the primary purpose of special instruction for talented students, that is, the development of academic or artistic skills. A substantial and stimulating curriculum and a psychologically safe environment are crucial to high achievement. In this environment, the teacher acknowledges different levels of accomplishment but teaches students to persist in their efforts to master difficult concepts and skills.

What are some
uses and limitations
of the Enrichment
Triad Model?

Much of the instruction designed for children who are gifted is intended to improve skills that are requisite for making original contributions to the arts, humanities, and sciences. The Enrichment Triad Model (Renzulli, 1977) suggests a possible approach to teaching these skills. One component of the model, *exploration,* assists students in identifying topics of interest to them. The second component, *skill building,* teaches research and communication skills related to various disciplines. The third component, *investigation of real problems,* encourages students to assume the role of a "professional" and develop an original product.

Although there is little research documenting its effectiveness, the Enrichment Triad Model is a widely used approach to differentiated instruction for students who are gifted (Maker, 1982). The model offers a coherent approach to independent study in students' areas of genuine interest; however, it must be used in combination with other educational alternatives. Alone, it addresses only the needs of students who are highly motivated to pursue independent work in an area of interest. Like most program models, the Enrichment Triad Model is but one of several alternatives to be considered when developing an IEP for a child identified as gifted.

A program model that provides a continuum of alternatives is the Pyramid Project (Cox, Daniel, & Boston, 1985), which has been established in several Texas schools. Based on the premise that students should move ahead as they master content and skills, project schools move bright students to higher grade levels or bring advanced material to students who stay in the grade associated with their age. Special classes and special schools are provided for the relatively small number of students who are exceptionally gifted or who have specialized talents.

EVALUATION OF INSTRUCTION. Evaluation of the gifted education program is an important, but often neglected, activity. Evaluation not only documents the benefits of the program, it also identifies ways in which the program can be improved (Callahan, 1983). Evaluative input—based on student progress measures, program records, and questionnaires completed by students, parents, and other involved persons—helps educators determine which elements of the program are effective and which need to be modified, strengthened, or eliminated.

What are some
important
principles in
evaluating
programs for
children who
are gifted?

Some principles of evaluation are particularly relevant to the evaluation of the effectiveness of gifted programs. First, progress tests must measure what was taught in the program. This basic principle is sometimes overlooked, and inappropriate tests are selected for evaluation. Because the tests fail to measure what the students learned, the program's benefits are not demonstrated (Howley, Howley, & Pendarvis, 1986). Second, tests used to evaluate student progress must have many difficult questions so that gains made by students who are gifted can be measured. Otherwise, if a pretest-posttest design is used to evaluate the program, and the students score very high on the pretest, they may score lower on the posttest simply because of carelessness or a statistical artifact, regression toward the mean. Thus, it could look as though students forgot what they knew before instruction began. Finally, evaluation of student academic progress must include achievement tests. Surveys of students' opinions about their progress are insufficient to document gains. Although the surveys provide valuable information and can form a part of the evaluation effort, they provide less compelling evidence than measures of skill or knowledge.

New Trends in Gifted Programs

The predominant method of providing enrichment is the pull-out program, which is too heavily relied on throughout the United States (Cox, Daniel, & Boston, 1985). Pull-out programs are usually resource room or itinerant teacher programs in which students identified as gifted receive special instruction for one or two days a week—sometimes, for only one or two hours of those days. The amount of special instruction depends on factors such as the size of the resource teacher's caseload, the number of schools the teacher serves, and how far apart the schools are.

The major problem with this model is that it does not offer much continuity or depth of learning. In many districts, it is the only special option for students who are gifted in spite of the fact that these students need special instruction every day, not just a few hours a week (Belcastro, 1987). Part-time programs, by themselves, cannot achieve all of the needed modifications in the education of students identified as gifted. Recognition of the limitations of this type of program has led educators to draw increasingly more on other options, such as acceleration and computer-assisted instruction.

Is acceleration effective?

ANOTHER LOOK AT ACCELERATION. In the past, acceleration has been viewed with distrust by many educators, but the work of Julian Stanley and his co-workers in their study of Mathematically Precocious Youth has compelled educators to take a new look at this method. Stanley has shown that unusually capable children who are eager to move ahead can meet the demands of college courses without suffering the social and emotional maladjustment predicted by opponents of acceleration (Stanley, 1977, 1991). Their findings confirm what many years of research have shown: The academic achievement of students who are accelerated is generally superior to that of students of similar ability who are not accelerated, and their social acceptance is equal to that of peers who are not accelerated (Daurio, 1979).

It is important to bear in mind, however, that acceleration should be contingent not on ability alone but on the desire to move ahead in school as well. Seven of the children accelerated in Stanley's programs, interviewed for an article in *Smithsonian* magazine, were all eager to get on with their studies, and they all placed a high value on intellectual pursuits. One of the youths, Michael Kotschenreuther, "burns to discover something 'that hasn't been known before' " (Nevin, 1977, p. 81).

How is computer instruction in gifted programs different from that in regular education programs?

COMPUTER EDUCATION. Computers in gifted education are used in much the same way as in other types of educational programs, but the emphases are different. Whereas the use of computers as purveyors of drill and practice programs is predominant in the regular education program (Tucker, 1983), in gifted education, computers are often used to teach computer programming and other computer skills. The early introduction of programming skills distinguishes computer education in gifted programs from computer education in regular classrooms. Instruction in computer programming begins at the first grade level in many gifted programs (Doorly, 1981) and is not limited to simplified languages such as LOGO, but teaches more difficult languages, such as BASIC (Nazarro, 1981). The argument about whether knowledge of programming skills is a component of computer literacy, still debated in regular education, seems to have been decided in the affirmative by educators of children who are gifted.

An introductory computer science course for high school students who plan to major in computer science or in another field that requires knowledge of computers and programming has been developed by the College Entrance Examination Board (1983) as part of its Advanced Placement program. The course curriculum requires the students to learn PASCAL, a programming language that teaches widely applicable programming skills. Other goals of the course curriculum include learning how to design programs that solve different types of problems and learning the basic components and functions of computer hardware and software. Like other Advanced Placement courses, this course allows students to demonstrate mastery of the material by completing an examination. Many colleges and universities grant college credit for passing grades on Advanced Placement examinations. Thus, this option allows students who are gifted and interested in computers an opportunity to earn both high school and college credit.

Individualized instruction, both accelerated and for enrichment, is provided in a limited fashion through computer programs that teach concepts not usually presented at the chronological-age grade level of the students who are gifted. Despite limits in the quality, quantity, and comprehensiveness of educational software, students can work through programs of basic skills in highly structured subjects (e.g., mathematics, spelling, or grammar) at a faster rate than through traditional instruction (Suppes, 1980). They can also be introduced to subjects that are not included in the curriculum at the elementary school level, such as chemistry, algebra, or physics (Parke, 1989). The enrichment provided by computer instruction in less-structured subjects, including literature and social studies, is not so well documented as in convergent subjects (Kulik, Bangert, & Williams, 1983). However, enrichment through computer simulations—for example, a simulation of weather conditions during an ocean crossing used to teach meteorological concepts (Barstow, 1981)—are popular with students who are gifted and their teachers.

The use of the computer as a tool for solving problems is also emphasized in gifted education. Students at the North Carolina School of Science and Mathematics, for example, use computers to store and analyze data for their experiments (Davis & Frothingham, 1981). The word processing capabilities of computers lend themselves to students' efforts to compose original reports, essays, and stories (Papert, 1981). The capability to use computers and computer software to access information, process data, and improve verbal and graphic products is viewed by some educators as the most vital outcome of computer education (Tucker, 1983).

Many young students have learned more about programming at home than at school. Children with access to home computers quite commonly develop skills that are far more advanced than those of adults who are responsible for computer instruction in the schools. Although these children almost always have a knowledgeable adult or older child they can go to for assistance, talented young programmers are primarily self-taught.

In a sense, computer programming is a "self-correcting" instructional activity, and it lends itself to sequential skill development. Because mistakes in programming are usually immediately apparent when the program is run, the novice programmer is forced to ask questions and try different approaches until a solution is found. As the student's skills develop, more complex tasks are attempted. A computer and informational resources—other programmers, books, and magazines—seem to be sufficient for students who are highly motivated to learn how to program and who have unlimited access to the computer.

Feature articles, such as the one quoted in the Technology in Action box, both reflect public interest in children who are talented programmers and typify a young programmer's history and attitudes.

Implications for Mainstreaming Children Who Are Gifted

Is the goal of normalization appropriate for the education of children who are gifted?

The principle of education in the least restrictive environment is based on the belief that segregated settings impair the progress of children with disabilities, in part because of the absence of children without disabilities to serve as models from whom they can learn appropriate behavior. In other words, educators hope to normalize the behavior of children with disabilities. Awareness of this principle has caused some people to question whether children who are gifted should spend even part of the day away from the regular classroom. It is as important for students who are gifted to be educated in the least restrictive environment as it is for students with disabilities—but what is the least restrictive environment for children

TECHNOLOGY IN ACTION

The game is called "Snake Byte," and for lack of a better description, it could be called an arcade game, one of those electronic quarter-eaters you see from coast to coast these days. The inventor of the game is a 21-year-old Huntington native who stands to earn at least $25,000 from the invention in the next 12 months. (Peyton, 1982, p. 9)

Like many 13-year-olds, Chuck Sommerville, inventor of Snake Byte, was fascinated by computers. When his teacher in the gifted program announced an upcoming class on computers, he was eager to participate. Unlike the other students, whose interest was satisfied with that one computer class, Chuck asked for and received permission to learn how to program on a computer in the science department of a nearby university.

Through a combination of trial and error and innumerable questions asked of the computer center staff,

Chuck learned how to program in BASIC. Soon he was spending so much time at the computer center that to keep him home more often, his father bought and assembled a computer terminal kit so that Chuck could use the university computer from his home. This arrangement worked well until the public account was closed. About that time, the first Apple microcomputers became available by mail order. By working at a local grocery store to help pay for it, Chuck was able to purchase his own microcomputer. Shutting himself in his room for all-night programming sessions, he quickly became a proficient programmer. By the time he was 15, he was earning money writing original programs.

Asked what appeal computers hold for him, Chuck responds that their primary appeal is their limitless potential and complexity. The computer, he says, is like an infinite puzzle with new features appearing all the time.

who are gifted? Do we want the behavior of these children to be like that of other students? Full-time placement in the regular classroom may meet the goal of normalization, but in the case of children who are gifted, that goal is not appropriate. Many children who are gifted are already "normalizing" themselves in regular classrooms by hiding their abilities so that they will be accepted by teachers and classmates.

Do some children who are gifted require totally differentiated programs?

Gifted children's potential for outstanding performance demands a different goal, one of denormalization. The learning characteristics of these children are different from those of other children, but these differences should be nurtured. For the realization of learning potential, the regular classroom can be the "*most* restrictive environment" for children who are gifted.

COORDINATION OF RESOURCES. It takes flexibility, hard work, and cooperation, but teachers can provide challenging, relevant instruction to children who are gifted. Probably the most common obstacle to such instruction is that teachers tend to underestimate the ability of their students. Once teachers realize that most children who are gifted are capable of working one or more grade levels above the grade level for their chronological age, they are better able to meet these children's educational needs. In many cases, they can do so even with relatively few material resources. Cathleen's schooling (described in the box) illustrates this point.

COOPERATION BETWEEN CLASSROOM AND SPECIAL EDUCATION TEACHER. For the many children who are instructed in both the regular classroom and in a special class, the classroom teacher and the teacher of gifted classes share the responsibility of providing effective instruction. The classroom teacher is in a position to observe the gifted child's work in all subjects. In some subjects, the child who is gifted may be at the same level as the other children or may even need remedial work. In other subjects, the teacher may find that the child has already mastered the material at that grade level. The gifted teacher can assist in these subjects by planning activities and finding methods and materials for advancement. Together, the

Cathleen attended a rural school in West Virginia, a state that has limited resources but a strong legislative mandate for gifted education. Like many children who are gifted, she could read a little when she started school. Recognizing Cathleen's high achievement and need for special instruction, her first grade teacher referred her for testing. Since the law requires that gifted students be provided education at a level commensurate with their ability, once Cathleen was identified as gifted, her parents and teachers had legal support for individualizing her education.

Because school systems can be inflexible, this support was essential. For example, it allowed Cathleen to be accelerated even though local policy discouraged acceleration. By the end of the first grade, Cathleen had mastered both first and second grade skills, so she was placed in the third grade. She did well in the third and fourth grade, and by the time she was in the fifth grade, she was reading at an adult level—as are many gifted 10- and 11-year-olds. Her fifth grade teacher provided an individualized reading and composition program for her, helping her select several books that suited her comprehension level and her interests. Among the novels she read that year were *Pride and Prejudice, All Creatures Great and Small,* and *The Return of the Native.* After reading each novel, Cathleen wrote an essay on some element of the book. Rather than having Cathleen complete fifth grade grammar exercises, the teacher taught her only the grammar that she seemed to need, based on her compositions and on her results on ACT practice tests. In the sixth-grade Cathleen took a fast-paced math class that combined sixth and seventh grade math into one school year. In the seventh grade, she took algebra.

Cathleen's love of learning and her rapid progress suggested that early entry to college would be a good option for her, and that turned out to be true. She thoroughly enjoyed college life. She was popular with other students, had several close friends, was liked and respected by her professors, and played an active role in a number of campus organizations. Had her parents failed to take advantage of the state law ensuring an appropriate education to gifted students, and had teachers been unwilling to modify instruction for her, Cathleen would have lost several years to busywork in the classroom. Like many students, she might have become bored and dissatisfied, she might have become a behavior problem, or, as happens most commonly, she might have adjusted her study habits and goals to match the undemanding routine and become a "normal" student, making good grades with little effort.

teachers can plan learning experiences involving such modifications as independent study, cross-grade placement, directed readings, and computer-assisted instruction.

Alternatives such as these can be used to provide individual instruction to all children, not just children identified as gifted. In fact, the teacher may find that these learning experiences result in the discovery of previously unrecognized talent. As mentioned earlier, giftedness may be overlooked if learning activities are not difficult enough to allow children to display their exceptional ability. By providing advanced work, the teacher may find that some students are capable of accomplishing much more than was expected.

The regular classroom teacher plays an important role in the social and emotional development of children who are gifted. It is a difficult role, and the responsibilities involved will be met more readily when the teacher has a strong conviction of the unique worth of every child in the classroom. The climate of support and recognition for individual differences that is based on such a conviction will forestall resentment of children who are gifted by their classmates and intellectual arrogance among children who are gifted.

What is the least restrictive environment for children who are gifted?

In summary, the least restrictive environment for children who are gifted is that which provides instruction commensurate with ability and which includes consideration of the children's social and emotional development. The variety of social, emotional, and instructional needs of children identified as gifted requires a continuum of alternative settings, ranging from support in the regular classroom to full-time placement in a special school or college. The key to finding and providing the least restrictive environment for each child is commitment to the idea of shared responsibility. Through the combined efforts of both general and gifted education personnel, we can identify talented children and provide them an education that promotes their development.

PROBE 16-4   Educational Provisions for Children Who Are Gifted

1. Reread the case study of Damon at the beginning of this section. Identify four characteristics that are typical of classic underachievers or that contribute to underachievement.
2. Suggest some strategies that could be used to improve Damon's academic performance.
3. T   F   Educational modifications have been more successful than counseling in improving the performance of students who are gifted underachievers.
4. T   F   A major difficulty in providing special programs for children from minority groups who are gifted is in finding procedures that offset bias in testing instruments.
5. Identify two factors that contribute to underachievement among children who are gifted and also have disabilities.
6. T   F   Adolescent girls who are gifted usually respond favorably to accelerated mathematics classes.
7. Check your knowledge of gifted programs by matching the descriptions on the left with the appropriate labels:

    _____   A broad term for programs that expand students'   a. Seminars
              experience or knowledge base   b. Tutorial/mentorships
    _____   A program usually offered to children in   c. AP
              kindergarten through third grade.   d. Exploration
    _____   Programs that match gifted students with   e. Independent study
              volunteers who are skilled in the student's ability   f. Acceleration
              or interest area.
    _____   Grade skipping
    _____   A learning program that permits a student to study
              in depth an area of special interest.

8. T   F   Research on acceleration has found no serious negative effect on social or emotional development of bright children.
9. T   F   Computer instruction for children who are gifted consists primarily of the use of individualized software for drill and practice in basic academic skills.
10. Why may education in a regular classroom not be the least restrictive environment for children who are gifted?
11. T   F   Providing challenging instruction in the classroom may lead to identification of students as gifted.
12. T   F   Most needs of students who are gifted may be adequately addressed in the regular classroom.
13. Describe at least three ways that the classroom teacher can improve the education of children who are gifted in the regular classroom.

SUMMARY

1. Common arguments against special provision for students who are gifted are based on the beliefs that gifted programs are unnecessary and elitist.
2. The concept of giftedness includes many kinds of ability, including intellectual ability, creativity, leadership, academic talent, and artistic talent.

3. Characteristics common to children who are gifted suggest the need for special educational programs; among these characteristics are advanced academic skills, rapid comprehension and learning, and knowledge about a wide range of subjects.

4. The identification of children as gifted is best accomplished through the combined use of a variety of evaluative methods, such as standardized testing, work sampling, and classroom observation.

5. Gifted programs typically seek to accelerate learning, broaden experience, develop academic skills, and provide opportunity for in-depth study.

6. A humanistic, student-centered approach is characteristic of gifted programs.

7. Acceleration is a desirable alternative for most students identified as gifted.

8. IEPs for children who are gifted differ from IEPs for children who have disabilities in several respects; the chief difference is their emphasis on academic strengths of the individual student.

9. Poor parent-child interaction patterns, social stereotypes, and learning, behavior, physical, or sensory disabilities inhibit the achievement of many students who are gifted.

10. Full-time placement in the regular classroom may be the most restrictive environment for many children who are gifted.

TASK SHEET 16   Field Experiences with Children Who Have Unique Gifts and Talents

Select *one* of the following and complete the assigned tasks:

Definitions

Ask five people to define *giftedness*. Record their answers and respond to the following questions:

1. What did the definitions have in common?
2. What was the narrowest definition?
3. What was the broadest definition?
4. How many definitions fell into each of the following categories?
   • Very restrictive—few abilities would be included.
   • Moderate—several or many abilities would be included.
   • Broad—most or all abilities would be included.
5. Write your own definition of giftedness.

Interview on Acceleration

Interview an educational administrator, a teacher, and a parent about their views on acceleration. Ask each to give at least two reasons supporting his or her views. Record the views and reasons given by each, and respond to the following:

1. Were the majority for or against acceleration?
2. Were some of the reasons given similar? If so, what were they?
3. On the basis of your reading and interviews, summarize and defend your position on acceleration.

Program Visitation

Visit a program for gifted children in a public or private school. Report on your visit, answering the following questions:

1. Where did you visit?
2. When were you there and for how long?
3. What activities did you observe?
4. What types of programming were used?
5. In what ways, if any, did the instruction and materials seem more suitable for gifted students than for other students?

Observation

If you know a parent of a gifted child, ask to observe one of the child's IEP meetings (about one-quarter of the states require IEPs for gifted students). Report on your observation of the IEP development process. Include a discussion of the committee's responses to various members of the IEP committee. Tell whose opinion seemed to carry the most weight, and whose seemed to matter the least. Speculate about why particular members had more or less influence and describe the effect of the child's educational plan.

Agency Investigation

Request information from the following agencies about the services they provide in the area of gifted education. Write a three-page paper summarizing these services and how you might use them if you were a professional working with children who are gifted.

Gifted Child Society
Suite 6
190 Rock Road
Glen Rock, NJ 07452

The Association for the Gifted (TAG)
The Council for Exceptional Children
1920 Association Drive
Reston, Virginia, 22091

National Association for Gifted Children
1155 15th St. NW, #1002
Washington, DC 20005

World Council for Gifted and Talented
  Children
Lamar University
P.O. Box 10034
Beaumont, Texas 77710

Library Study

Read three articles related to children who are gifted and write a one-page abstract of each. You can find articles about gifted children in these journals:

> *Gifted Child Quarterly*
> *G/C/T (Gifted Child Today)*
> *The Journal for the Education of the Gifted*
> *Roeper Review*

Alternatively, read a biography of a gifted person. Describe the characteristics of that person which are typical of people who are gifted. List any atypical characteristics. If you were the person's teacher, what modifications in educational programming would you have suggested? Why?

Design Your Own Field Experience

If you know of a unique experience you can have with people who are gifted or talented, discuss your idea with your instructor and complete the tasks that you agree on.

PHOTO CREDITS

PART I

Part I Opener (facing page 1): Alan Carey/The Image Works. **Chapter 1:** page 11, David Young-Wolff/Photo Edit; page 19, Alan Carey/The Image Works; page 21, author provided; page 25, Bob Daemmrich/Stock Boston. **Chapter 2:** page 42, Alan Carey/The Image Works; page 47, Oscar Palmquist/Lightwave; page 54, Alan Carey/The Image Works; page 72, Paul D. Mazell/Stock Boston. **Chapter 3:** page 79, Elaine Rebman; page 85, Joel Gordon Photography; page 95, Bob Daemmrich/The Image Works. **Chapter 4:** page 111, Elaine Rebman; page 119, Elaine Rebman; page 125, Alan Carey/The Image Works; page 130, Laimute E. Druskis/Stock Boston. **Chapter 5:** page 155, Claudia Lewis; page 168, M. Siluk/The Image Works; page 169, Harriet Gans/The Image Works; page 170, Paul Conklin. **Chapter 6:** page 187, Paul Conklin; page 189, Elaine Rebman; page 202, Claudia Lewis. **Chapter 7:** page 222, Alan Carey/The Image Works; page 227, Claudia Lewis; page 229, Fredrik D. Bodin/Stock Boston; page 231, Alan Carey/The Image Works.

PART II

Chapter 8: page 234, Bob Daemmrich/Stock Boston; page 258, Bob Daemmrich/Stock Boston; page 259, Bob Daemmrich/Stock Boston; page 267, Robert Finken. **Chapter 10:** page 336, Bob Daemmrich; page 339, Telesensory Systems, Inc.; page 341, Billy E. Barnes/Stock Boston. **Chapter 11:** page 377, Bob Daemmrich/The Image Works; page 384, Stott/The Image Works; page 387, Joel Gordon Photography.

PART III

Part III Opener (page 398): Sports Information, University Relations, Michigan State University. **Chapter 12:** page 428, Elaine Rebman. **Chapter 13:** page 459, David H. Wells/The Image Works; page 463, Nik Kleinberg/Stock Boston; page 465, Bob Daemmrich/Stock Boston; page 487, Nita Winter/The Image Works. **Photo Essay (following page 478):** Robert Finken. **Chapter 14:** page 504, Bob Daemmrich/Stock Boston; page 518, Alan Carey/The Image Works; page 524, Joel Gordon Photography. **Chapter 15:** page 536, Jack Prelutsky/Stock Boston; page 540, Alan Carey/The Image Works; page 550, Bob Daemmrich/Stock Boston. **Chapter 16:** page 568, Sports Information, University Relations, Michigan State University; page 572, Elizabeth Zuckerman/Photo Edit; page 588, Richard Hutchings/Info Edit.

Glossary

Academic disciplines: The branches of knowledge and inquiry traditionally associated with scholarship in Western society, e.g., music, literature, history, physics.

Acceleration: Any of a number of educational provisions used to move students through the curriculum more rapidly than usual, e.g., early school admission, grade skipping, accelerated classes.

Acquired immunodeficiency syndrome (AIDS): A disorder that impairs the body's immune system, making one susceptible to infectious organisms and cancerous cells. The disorder is spread through the direct exchange of body fluids. At present there is no known cure.

Adaptive behavior: The effectiveness or degree with which an individual meets the standards of personal independence and social responsibility expected for age and cultural group.

Addition: Articulation disorder wherein the speaker adds a sound or sounds not normally occurring in words.

Adventitiously deaf: Condition of those who were born with normal hearing but whose sense of hearing became nonfunctional through illness or accident.

Advocacy (and consumerism): A trend in which parents and professionals are working in an assertive fashion to gain better services for people with disabilities.

Agnosia: Inability to attach meaning to sounds, words, or visual experiences.

Air conduction test: A pure tone hearing test using earphones.

Alchemy: A pseudoscience that alleges to create gold from other chemical compounds.

Alternative living unit: Any form of residential setting other than a person's natural family residence. Included are such settings as foster family homes, supervised apartment living, group homes, and residential care facilities.

Amblyopia (lazy eye): A condition in which the brain will not tolerate double vision and suppresses the image being transmitted by the weaker eye.

Ambulation: Ability to move from place to place.

American Sign Language (ASL): One or more of the varieties of the language of signs commonly used in the Deaf community in America.

Amniocentesis: A test that may be done during pregnancy to identify certain genetic disorders in the fetus. It consists of extracting a small amount of amniotic fluid, which surrounds the fetus in the womb, for examination.

Anoxia: Also referred to as asphyxia. The deprivation of oxygen in the blood to the extent that normal tissue functioning is not possible. Tissues of the brain or central nervous system are particularly susceptible to damage from asphyxia.

Anterior: Toward the front of the body.

Anvil (incus): One of the bones of the middle ear that carry vibrations across the middle ear cavity.

Aphasia: Acquired language impairment caused by brain damage.

Applied behavior analysis: A structured approach to teaching and behavior management that employs observation and charting of student behavior, task analysis, systematic application of sequenced teaching procedures, reinforcement, and monitoring of student performance.

Apraxia: Difficulty with voluntary or purposeful muscular movement with no evidence of motor impairment.

Aptitude-achievement discrepancy: Difference between a student's achievement performance and potential as measured by standardized tests.

Aqueous humor: Watery substance between the cornea and the lens of the eye.

Architectural barrier: Any condition of the physical environment that can inhibit or prevent people with disabilities from using facilities or moving about.

Arthritis: Condition affecting the joints and muscles, causing pain, stiffness, and inflammation.

Arthrogryphosis: A congenital disease in which the muscles may be poorly developed with crooking or contraction of the joints.

Articulation: The movements of the vocal system that result in the production of speech sounds and words.

Articulation disorder: A communication disorder associated with substitutions, omissions, distortions, and/or additions of speech sounds.

Assistive technology: Devices and services that can help people with disabilities improve their ability to function within their environment. The continuum of devices ranges from low-tech to high-tech.

Asthma: Chronic condition characterized by wheezing or labored breathing caused by a constriction of the air passages in the bronchial tubes and by increased amounts of thick secretions in the air tubes of the lungs.

Astigmatism: Blurred vision caused by uneven curvature of the cornea or lens.

Ataxia: A type of cerebral palsy in which lack of muscle coordination results in loss of coordinated movements, especially those relating to balance and position.

Athetosis: A form of cerebral palsy characterized by involuntary, jerky, purposeless, repetitive movements of the extremities, head, and tongue.

Atonia: Deficient or absent muscle tone.

Atrophy: The degeneration or death of tissue.

Attention deficit disorder (ADD); attention deficit–hyperactivity disorder (ADHD): Chronic difficulty with any aspect of attention including alertness, selection, and effort. The disorder may also involve problems with impulse control.

Audiogram: A graphic portrayal of the results of a hearing test.

Audiologist: A specialist in evaluation and remediation of auditory disorders.

Audiology: A science concerned with hearing losses, including their detection and remediation.

Auditory analysis: Ability to isolate components of an auditory message.

Auditory canal: *See* External auditory canal.

Auditory cortex: The portion of the brain covering that is associated with the sense of hearing.

Auditory discrimination: Ability to detect the differences between sounds.

Auditory figure-ground perception: Ability to isolate a particular sound or a word from other sounds or words occurring simultaneously.

Auditory integration: Ability to associate a sound or sound combinations (words and sentences) with other experiences.

Auditory nerve: Cranial nerve VIII that carries auditory impulses from the cochlea to the brain.

Auditory processing: Use of the auditory channel to identify and attach meaning to specific recurring linguistic units that are heard.

Auditory training: Training designed to teach a person with hearing loss to make the best of residual hearing.

Auditory-visual integration: Ability to combine sound with symbol in the understanding of, for example, phonetic symbols.

Augmentative communication: Techniques that are used to supplement speech for communication (pointing to pictures or symbols, writing, gestures, etc.).

Aura: A condition that occurs in some individuals with epilepsy just before a seizure. The person may see unusual colors, hear ringing sounds, smell peculiar odors, or experience other phenomena during this time.

Auricle (pinna): The externally visible part of the ear, consisting of a flaplike, cartilaginous structure on the side of the head.

Autism: A behavioral disorder characterized by extreme withdrawal and self-stimulation, requiring intense and prolonged intervention.

Behavior checklist: A list of traits or behaviors that research has shown to be characteristic of a group of children. Such checklists are often used to rate children to determine whether they should be referred for special services.

Behavior disorder: Disorder in which behavior deviates from a normal range, occurs over an extended period of time, and is extreme in terms of intensity and frequency.

Behavior modification: See introduction to Part III for list of concepts and their definitions.

Behavioral excesses: Behaviors that are excessive in terms of frequency, intensity, duration, or occurrence under conditions when their socially sanctioned frequency is close to zero.

Behavioral model: Assumptions that behavior disorders are primarily a result of inappropriate learning and that the most effective preventive actions and therapeutic interventions will involve controlling the child's environment in order to teach appropriate behaviors.

Biophysical model: Assumptions that behavior disorders are primarily a result of dysfunction of the central nervous system due to brain lesions, neurochemical irregularities, or genetic defects, and that the most effective preventive actions and therapeutic interventions will involve prevention or correction of such biological defects.

Blind: Condition of those whose visual acuity is 20/200 or less in the better eye with the best possible correction, or those who have a restriction in the field of vision to an angle subtending an arc of 20 degrees or less. Those who are blind must use braille and/or tactile and auditory materials in their education.

Bone conduction test: A hearing test that measures the response of the sensorineural mechanism in the inner ear, bypassing the outer and middle ear system.

Bottom-up approach to curriculum development: The process of identifying those skills or behaviors that represent the most basic or entry level of a curriculum area or strand and then identifying subsequent critical skills or behaviors.

Braille code: A reading code for the blind that is based on a braille cell, which consists of six raised (embossed) dots. Four braille codes which use combinations of these dots have been developed.

Breadth model: A model of identification of gifted children that requires performance in the superior range on more than one measure (e.g., an achievement test and an IQ test).

Breathiness: Speech sound caused by air rushing past the vocal folds without vibrating them; a whisperlike quality of speech.

Buckley amendment: Guarantees parental control of the school records of their children.

Career: The totality of work one does in his or her lifetime.

Career awareness: Program emphasized during elementary years that examines the relationship of work to the total life process and emphasizes basic work values.

Career education: The totality of experiences through which one learns about and prepares to engage in work as part of his or her way of living.

Case finding: Activities designed to make initial contact with the target populations.

Cataract: Clouding of the lens of the eye that obstructs the passage of light and occurs when the semifluid substance in the lens gradually becomes opaque.

Caudal: Toward the tail-end or hind part of the body.

Central auditory disorder: Disorder of auditory comprehension, perception, and discrimination where there is no disorder or damage to the peripheral hearing mechanism.

Central nervous system (CNS): The part of the nervous system to which the sensory impulses are transmitted and from which motor impulses develop.

Cephalad: Toward the head or anterior end of the body.

Cephalocaudal: A process of maturation that begins at the head (cephalo) and progresses to the lower parts of the body (caudal).

Cerebellum: An area of the brain, damage to which results in an inability to maintain balance and coordinated movement, or ataxia-type cerebral palsy.

Cerebral palsy: An abnormal alteration of human movement or motor functioning arising from a defect, injury, or disease of the tissues of the central nervous system.

Cerumen: Waxlike material secreted by glands in the skin lining along the outer two-thirds of the auditory canal.

Chemotherapy: Administration of drugs to control or cure a problem.

Child Find: A concerted effort by state and local educational agencies to identify all children with disabilities who are in need of special education services.

Chorionic villus sampling: A prenatal diagnostic procedure accomplished by collecting a 30-mg sample from the chorion tissues surrounding the developing fetal placenta. The sample is collected by a catheter inserted through the uterus by way of the vagina, so the process does not invade or break the wall of the patient's womb as is the case with amniocentesis. Can be safely used as early as the first eight to twelve weeks of pregnancy.

Choroid: Layer of the eye between the sclera and retina that contains blood vessels that provide nourishment to the retina.

Chromosomes: Human matter which contains genes and controls heredity. Humans have 46 chromosomes acquired at conception, 23 from the mother and 23 from the father.

Ciliary body: Part of the eye that produces aqueous fluid and controls the focus of the eye.

Cinefluoroscopy: X-ray motion pictures.

Classroom performance: Academic behavior in the classroom. As indexed by grades, classroom performance is a common measure of achievement, but not always a valid one because of confounding influences on grades, such as teacher expectations.

Cleft palate: Cleft in the lip and/or palate caused by failure of the lip or palate to grow together during fetal development.

Club foot: A congenital abnormality in which the foot is turned downward and inward at the ankle.

Cochlea: Snail-shell shaped auditory part of the inner ear. The sense organ of hearing.

Cognition: Awareness of understanding of information.

Collaborative consultation: The process whereby regular classroom teachers work with special education resource teachers and other specialists to solve the problems of special education students who are integrated into their classes.

Communication disorder: Inability of a person to express his or her needs or wants; person may experience distress when doing so.

Community catalog: An assessment strategy that is typically developed by a group of teachers across four curriculum domains (community, domestic, vocational, recreational and leisure) to identify the settings where students with severe disabilities participate and the activities and skills required in those settings.

Community-based instruction: The teaching of functional skills to students on location at actual sites in the community.

Community-referenced instruction: The teaching of those skills needed and used across a broad range of settings and activities in both current and future environments.

Competency-based teacher education (CBTE): A systematic method of preparing teachers based on the competencies that are required for them to be effective. Many of the features associated with CBTE are incorporated into the design of this book.

Competitive employment: Integrated work setting with at least minimum-wage levels of pay.

Computer skills: Ability to make informed use of computers and major types of computer software programs, such as word processing, file storage, and data analysis programs. Computer skills may also include programming in popular computer languages, such as BASIC or PASCAL.

Concept: Thought, opinion, or mental image.

Conduct disorder: A behavioral disorder characterized by a pattern including both verbal and physical aggressive behavior of antisocial nature.

Conductive hearing loss: Hearing disorder caused by blockage or damage to the structures of the outer or middle ear.

Congenital condition: Condition present at birth.

Congenitally deaf: Condition of those who are born deaf.

Conjugate eye movement: The movement of both eyes together in a coordinated manner.

Conjunctiva: Thin transparent layer that lines the eyelids and covers the front of the eye and prevents dust or other particles from entering.

Continuum (or cascade) of services: A hierarchy of educational service alternatives for children with disabilities, ranging from the least restrictive regular classroom to the highly restrictive hospital or institutional setting.

Convergent thinking: Thinking that is intended to arrive at a "correct" answer, such as a solution to a math problem or a definition of a vocabulary word. (*Compare* Divergent thinking.)

Core Home: A cluster of community-based residential living options available to persons with mental retardation or other developmental disabilities. A client can move from one to another based on need, ability, and the availability of those options.

Cornea: Transparent cover in front of the iris and pupil that refracts light rays.

Counter theory model: A model that rejects theoretical assumptions of disordered behavior. The focus is on advocacy for the deviant child and the delivery of effective services. The goal of intervention is to change the broad social values and expectations that contribute to narrow views of behavior as either *deviant* or *normal.*

Creativity: Production of original or imaginative work. Creativity is one of the five performance areas included in the federal definition of giftedness.

Cretinism: Congenital thyroid deficiency that can stunt physical growth and cause mental retardation.

Criterion-referenced test: A test of academic achievement in which a student's performance is compared to a pre-established level. Criteria are often in the form of specific numbers or percentages of items correct.

Cultural bias: Partiality of educational practices in favor of the majority culture.

Curriculum-based assessment: A system of assessment that analyzes the ability of students to perform the skills they need to master the curriculum that has been designed for them.

Cyanosis: A blue discoloration of the skin caused by a lack of oxygen in the blood.

Cystic fibrosis: A chronic genetic disorder affecting the pancreas, lungs, or both. When the lungs are affected, the individual is prevented from proper exchange of oxygen. When the pancreas is affected, digestion is impaired and the person may suffer from poor nutrition.

Deaf: Condition of those whose hearing loss precludes successful processing of linguistic information through audition, with or without a hearing aid, and who, culturally, may be part of the Deaf community.

Decibel: A dimensionless unit expressing the logarithmic ratio of two amounts of pressure, power, or intensity; the measure of loudness of a particular sound. Abbreviated dB.

Deinstitutionalization: Term used to describe the movement away from placing persons with disabilities in large residential institutional facilities.

Depth model: A model of identification of gifted children that requires performance in the superior range on one of several measures of aptitude or achievement. This model is generally considered to be more effective than the breadth model, to which it is contrasted.

Developmental delay: Indication that a child's progress in cognitive, communication, social, physical, and self-care areas is less than expected for the particular chronological age level. Decisions about developmental delays are frequently made by comparing the child's performance to norms for human development.

Developmental model: A model based on milestones of normal human development.

Developmental placement: Placing individual students into the grade level commensurate with their academic, social, and physical developmental level, rather than placing them on the basis of chronological age.

Developmental retardation: Retardation in development that is attributed to psychosocial factors, such as poverty, malnutrition, or other external environmental variables.

Diabetes: A metabolic disorder in which the body is not able to properly utilize carbohydrates in the diet because of a failure of the pancreas to secrete an adequate supply of insulin.

Diabetic coma: A condition in which not enough insulin is available to help the body convert the intake of glucose.

Digital grasp: Grasping an object with the fingers (digits) rather than the whole hand.

Diphthong: Speech sound made with voicing that is a combination of two vowels coming together in the same syllable.

Direct instruction: A systematic teaching method, one feature of which is a model-lead-test format for teacher-delivered lessons.

Disability: A condition due to the reduction of function or absence of a particular body part or organ (e.g., paraplegic, amputee); synonymous with *disorder* or *dysfunction.*

Discrepancy analysis: An assessment procedure, used after targeted activities have been identified, which entails observing a student perform the skills necessary to participate in an activity while recording whether the student can perform each skill independently and fluently.

Discriminative stimulus: A stimulus that is consistently paired with reinforcement.

Disfluency: Speech marked by repetition, hesitation, prolongations, and, in general, a lack of flow which calls attention to itself; referred to by some as stuttering.

Distal: Away from the body or trunk.

Distortion: Articulation disorder wherein an acceptable sound is replaced by a sound that doesn't exist in a given language.

Divergent thinking: A type of thinking characterized by a response that is original or imaginative. Divergent thinking is usually contrasted with convergent thinking, which seeks responses that are "correct." Assignments requiring divergent thinking might ask a student to compose a story or a musical score, whereas a question requiring convergent thinking might ask a student to match the names of chemical elements with their symbols.

Dominant genes: Genes that override the effect of recessive genes and determine the expression of certain traits. When one parent has a dominant gene for a particular trait, there is a 50 percent chance that all offspring will exhibit that trait.

Down syndrome: A chromosomal aberration (usually to chromosome 23) caused by improper cell division, which results in incorrect cell structure. Originally referred to as Mongolism, a term that is not accepted today. The syndrome is characterized by mild to moderate mental retardation, epicanthic folds of the eyelids (hence the approximation of an oriental or Mongol appearance), large fissured tongue, broad and flat bridge of the nose, and typically poor muscle tone. It may account for the single largest number of persons manifesting mental retardation with a known cause. Can be detected prior to birth through either amniocentesis or chorionic villus sampling.

Dynamic assessment: A method that combines the assessment of a student's readiness to learn with immediate instruction about the learning task. This variation of the test-teach-test model has been particularly advocated for children from culturally diverse backgrounds.

Dysarthria: Term referring to any speech disorder that has as its base an impairment of the central or peripheral nervous system.

Dyslexia: A severe disability in learning to read.

Eardrum (tympanic membrane): The semitransparent membrane that separates the outer and middle ear.

Early childhood special education: *See* Early intervention.

Early intervention: Services provided to promote the development and well-being of infants and young children and their families when those infants and young children are at risk for, or display, developmental delays and/or disabilities.

Echolalia: Imitation of the sounds of others.

Ecological inventory: A strategy that individualizes instruction by identifying specific skills needed by each student to function more independently in current and probable future environments.

Ecological model: Assumptions that behavior disabilities are the product of interactions between the child and others in the immediate environment.

Educable mentally retarded (EMR): A term commonly used to classify students with mild mental retardation. These students can typically profit from education and training in fundamental academic skills, including reading, arithmetic, and science. Vocational training in both skilled and unskilled areas is typically feasible, and as adults, this group comprises highly dependable employees. Unsupervised living through adulthood is typically achieved by persons in this educational classification. The IQ parameters for this group are usually in the 50–55 to 70 range.

Educational lockstep: The practice of placing all students of the same chronological age into one grade level and ignoring other relevant criteria for grade placement.

Educational synthesizer: A teacher who incorporates available resources such as physical therapists into daily educational programs.

Electroencephalogram: Graphic record of the electrical output of brain waves.

Eligibility determination: The decision as to whether a student meets the criteria for placement in a program, such as a gifted education program.

Elitism: Partiality or favored treatment to a group on the basis of its supposed superiority.

Emmetropic eye: The normal eye; one that is perfectly focused for distance so that the image of an object focuses directly on the retina.

Encephalitis: A condition causing inflammation of the brain, which may result in brain damage.

Encopresis: Lack of bowel control.

Enrichment: Educational experiences not usually included in the curriculum, such as opportunities to study archeology, filmmaking, etc.

Enuresis: Lack of bladder control.

Epilepsy (seizure, convulsive disorder): A disorder caused by damage to the brain, which impairs the brain's ability to control its normal electrical activity. This may result in abnormal motor discharges or convulsive movements. Can often be controlled with medication.

Etiology: The causes or origins of a disease or condition.

Eustachian tube: Tubelike structure connecting the middle ear and the nasopharynx.

Evoked response technique: A special electrophysiological test of hearing using a computerized electroencephalogram (EEG) technique.

Exceptional children: Those who have physical, mental, behavioral, or sensory characteristics that differ from the majority of children to such an extent that they require special education and related services in order to develop to their maximum capacity.

Expressive language: Ability to produce language in oral, written, or signed form.

Extensor muscles: Muscles used to extend the arm, such as in reaching.

External auditory canal: An irregularly shaped, tubelike passage extending from the inside of the head to the middle ear, approximately 1 inch long in adults.

Fading: During instruction, the gradual removal of additional stimuli such as prompts.

Fetal alcohol syndrome (FAS): A clinical type of mental retardation caused by maternal ingestion of alcohol during pregnancy. The amount of daily alcohol consumption and risk to the fetus has not been definitively determined, but it is believed that anything more than 89 ml (equivalent to 3 ounces) presents high risk for the fetus. Pregnant women should probably abstain from consuming alcohol.

Fine motor skills: Use of small muscles for reaching, grasping, and the manipulation of objects such as puzzles, cubes, and drawing materials.

Flexor muscles: Muscles used to pull the arm toward the body, as if flexing the muscles.

Fragile-X or fra(X) syndrome: A chromosomal aberration that may rival Down syndrome for causing mental retardation. A recessive genetic trait that can be detected prior to birth through either amniocentesis or chorionic villus sampling.

Frequency: The number of vibrations that occur at the same rate over a period of time in a sound wave. Measured in Hertz (Hz).

Function: An action that a person takes in response to a demand to meet some need. Human functions include existence, communication, body alignment, travel, environmental adaptation, learning, sports, leisure, and recreation.

Functional curriculum: A program of studies in which emphasis is placed on teaching skills that are chronologically age-appropriate and immediately useful to the student.

Functional hearing loss: Hearing loss which has a psychological, as opposed to organic, cause.

Functional learning handicap: Handicap in learning that develops as a result of difficulties in functioning in the environment.

Functional retardation: Mental retardation that appears to be the result of environmental events that have shaped—and are maintaining—retarded adaptive behavior.

Galactosemia: An inherited metabolic disorder in which certain types of naturally occurring sugars cannot be metabolized into useful glucose.

Generalization: Process of a skill being performed in different environments with different persons, different instructional materials, different language cues, and under different stimulus conditions.

Genes: The basic units of heredity. Genes direct and control the process of human growth and development.

Gifted: A term used to refer to children with outstanding ability or potential. The term is usually applied to children who perform in the top 3 to 5 percent on measures of aptitude or achievement in such areas as general intellectual ability, specific academic aptitude, creativity, leadership, or artistic ability.

Glaucoma: Severe disorder that occurs when the aqueous fluid does not circulate properly and results in an elevation of pressure in the eyes. The pressure gradually destroys the optic nerve. The condition is treatable if identified at an early stage of development.

Global retardation: Profound, inclusive difficulty in learning, as opposed to specific difficulty in a single area such as reading or math.

Gower's sign: A symptom of Duchenne-type muscular dystrophy in which the child is seen "walking up" the lower limbs with the hands.

Grammatical rules: The way in which words and groups of words are combined in language. The rules govern such items as placement of nouns and verbs and rules for tense.

Grand mal seizure: A severe type of disorder involving loss of consciousness and extreme convulsions. This term is no longer used in the professional literature, but may still appear in common usage.

Gross motor skills: Use of large muscles for walking, running, and other whole-body movements.

Grouping: Placing students of similar academic aptitude or achievement together for instruction; for example, high mathematics achievers grouped together for an advanced algebra class.

Habilitation: The training of skills and attitudes that are not part of an individual's past experiences.

Habitual pitch: Pitch used most frequently.

Halfway house: A small residential facility established to bridge the gap from institution to community.

Handicap: One of the problems that people with impairments or disabilities have in interactions with their environment (e.g., the inability of a person in a wheelchair to use a revolving door).

Hard-of-hearing: Condition of those who, with the use of a hearing aid, have residual hearing sufficient to enable successful processing of linguistic information through audition.

Harshness: Strident speech quality.

Hoarseness: Coarse, rough speech quality.

Hearing aid: Wearable electronic device that amplifies sound to assist in communication.

Hearing impairment: A generic term indicating a hearing loss that may range in severity from mild to profound. It includes two conditions, *deaf* and *hard-of-hearing*.

Hemiplegia: Paralysis of the extremities on one side of the body.

Human immunodeficiency virus (HIV): Virus that causes acquired immunodeficiency syndrome (AIDS).

Hydrocephalus: A condition in which blockage causes an abnormal accumulation of cerebrospinal fluid in the head, which in turn causes the head to enlarge. Pressure causes damage to the brain, resulting in mental retardation. A shunt can be surgically implanted to drain off excess fluid.

Hyperactivity: Excessive physical or muscular activity characterized by excessive restlessness and mobility; sometimes associated with learning disabilities. Hyperactivity may be one symptom of attention deficit disorder.

Hyperopia (farsightedness): A condition that occurs when the eye is too short and the rays of light from near objects are not focused on the retina.

Hypertonicity: A heightened state of excessive tension in which muscles are tight and tense.

Hypotonicity: Flaccid muscle tone or the inability to maintain tension or resistance to stretch.

Impairment: A condition resulting from diseased or defective tissue (e.g., cerebral palsy, birthmark, nearsightedness).

Impedance audiometer: A testing device for measuring the compliance/resistance of the middle ear system and the presence or absence of the stapedial reflex.

Incidence: Estimates of the numbers of individuals in the population who may exhibit a particular characteristic at some time during their lifetime.

Incus (anvil): The second or middle bone in the chain of bones in the middle ear joining the malleus and stapes; anvil-shaped.

Individualized education program or plan (IEP): A component of Public Law 94-142 that requires a written plan of instruction for each child receiving special services; the IEP must include a statement of the child's present levels of educational performance, annual goals, short-term objectives, specific services needed by the child, dates when these services will begin and be in effect, and when the child should be reevaluated.

Individualized family service plan (IFSP): A component of Public Law 99-457 that requires a written plan of intervention for each infant and toddler receiving special services; the IFSP must include a statement of (a) the infant's or toddler's present level of development; (b) the family's resources, priorities, and concerns; (c) the major outcomes and criteria; and (d) specific early intervention services necessary, including the dates of initiation and expected duration of services, name of the case manager, steps taken to plan transition to other services, and the extent to which services will occur in natural environments.

Individualized transition plan (ITP): A written document specifying the annual goals and short-term objectives that reflect skills the student with disabilities needs to function on the job, at home, and in the community. It also specifies the long-term training components required to meet those goals and objectives.

Infusion approach: Stresses that career education should not be approached as a separate content area, but infused into the existing curriculum.

Instructional technology: The hardware, software, and systematically designed content that can be used for instructional purposes. (See the first section of Chapter 3 for a discussion that provides alternative definitions.)

Insulin: A protein hormone produced by the pancreas and secreted into the blood where it regulates carbohydrate metabolism.

Integrated service delivery system: School programs that include people with disabilities and those without disabilities of the same chronological ages. Activities follow the normal operation of the school day.

Integrated settings: Environments that typically contain persons with and without disabilities.

Intellectual ability: A broad cluster of cognitive skills, including memory, comprehension, and reasoning.

Intelligence quotient (IQ): Score on a test designed to measure intellectual abilities, such as memory, comprehension, and reasoning. The average score for the general population is usually 100.

Interindividual differences: The differences between students.

Intermediate Care Facility/Mental Retardation/Developmental Disabilities (ICF/MR/DD): A residential facility for persons with mental retardation or other developmental disabilities. Typically provides care and training throughout a client's life span.

Intervention assistance: Educational intervention that is attempted prior to referring a student for special education services.

Intraindividual differences: The differences within students.

Iris: Colored part of the eye that expands or contracts depending upon the amount of light passing through the eye.

Juvenile delinquency: A category of behavior disability identified by the legal system.

Juvenile rheumatoid arthritis: A chronic condition common to school-age children beginning with general fatigue, stiffness, and aching of the joints.

Kinesthetic approach: An instructional technique that utilizes sensations derived from the student's muscles or movement sensations.

Kurzweil Reading Machine: A machine that converts printed words to synthetic speech.

Kyphosis: A condition in which the back around the shoulder area is rounded.

Labeling: The process of assigning a child to a diagnostic category as a result of assessment. For example, a child may be labeled as "mentally retarded" after undergoing a psychological evaluation. Although useful for obtaining services, labeling may have negative psychological consequences.

Language: System of symbols communities use to represent their environment, thoughts, and emotions.

Laryngectomy: Removal of all or part of the larynx.

Learning disability: Disorder in one or more of the basic psychological processes involved in understanding or in using language, spoken or written, which may manifest itself in an imperfect ability to listen, think, speak, read, write, spell, or do mathematical calculations.

Least restrictive environment: The educational environment that is the closest approximation to that of children without disabilities in which appropriate educational services can be delivered to children with disabilities. There is a continuum of environments ranging from the regular classroom to resource rooms, to self-contained classes, to residential facilities.

Lens: Structure of the eye that refines and changes the light rays passing through the eye.

Lesch-Nyhan syndrome: A disorder of the nervous system that results in cerebral palsy, mental retardation, and self-mutilating behavior.

Linguistic functioning: Ability to use language to communicate.

Lipreading: *See* Speechreading.

Local norms: A distribution of test scores established for a particular school, community, or region. Local norms allow comparison of individual students with other students in a similar environment.

Lordosis: A condition in which the spine is curved inward, resulting in a swayback and/or protruding abdomen.

Mainstreaming: The placement of the child in the least restrictive educational setting. Commonly used to refer to the integration of students with disabilities into classrooms for those without disabilities.

Malleus (hammer): The first of a chain of three small bones in the middle ear extending from the eardrum to the incus; hammer-shaped.

Manual communication: Communication through a natural or invented sign system.

Masking: The stimulation of one ear of a subject by controlled noise to prevent the hearing with that ear of the tone or speech being presented to the opposite ear.

Medical model: An assumption that to cure a disorder, one must diagnose and treat the disease process that caused it.

Meningitis: Inflammation of the membranes that surround the brain and spinal cord.

Meningocele: A saclike pouch that protrudes through an opening in the skull or spinal column.

Mental retardation: Significantly subaverage general intellectual functioning existing concurrently with deficits in adaptive behavior and manifested during the developmental period. (See page 414 for an expanded definition.)

Metacognition: Cognitive processes by which individuals are aware of their own thinking and control aspects of thinking such as planning, self-evaluation, and strategies.

Microcephaly: A cranial disorder characterized by the development of small head with a sloping forehead; retardation results from lack of space for brain development.

Minimal brain dysfunction: A term some people apply to children of average or above-average intelligence who have learning disabilities associated with problems of the central nervous system. The term is considered inappropriate for educational purposes since a confirming diagnosis of brain dysfunction is extremely difficult to obtain.

Mixed hearing loss: Hearing disorder that involves a combination of conductive and sensorineural loss.

Monoplegia: Paralysis of one limb.

Multiple sclerosis: A progressive disorder in which portions of the myelin sheath (tissues surrounding the spinal cord) are damaged (demyelination) and replaced by scar tissue, resulting in impairment of the transmission of nerve impulses to the muscles. The progression may be steady and rapid or may be slow, interspersed with periods of remission. May be fatal.

Multiple-factor theories of intelligence: Theories proposing that human intelligence is composed of a number of independent abilities which cannot be adequately indexed by a single score, such as an IQ score.

Muscular dystrophy: A hereditary disorder that causes a loss of vitality and progressive deterioration of the body as a result of the death of muscle tissue.

Myopia (nearsightedness): Occurs when the eye is too long and the rays of light from distant objects are not focused on the retina.

Nasal sound: A sound produced by the blocking of the oral cavity, the opening of the soft palate, and the emission of air through the nasal cavity.

Nasality: Problem in making speech sounds resulting from inability to control the flow of air into the mouth and nasal cavity.

Neurologically impaired: Having problems in the functioning of the central nervous system.

Normalization: The concept that all people with disabilities should be provided with the opportunity to live according to the patterns and conditions of everyday life that are as close as possible to the norms and patterns of the mainstream of society.

Norm-referenced test: Shows student performance in comparison to the group of people on which the test was standardized.

Occipital lobe: A portion of the brain where visual stimuli are interpreted and "seeing" takes place.

Omission: Articulation disorder wherein a sound or sounds are omitted from words.

Operant conditioning: Changing behavior by altering its consequences; altering the future probability of the occurrence of a response by providing reinforcement or punishment as a consequence.

Ophthalmologist: A licensed physician who specializes in eye disorders.

Optacon: An optical-to-tactile converter which reproduces the form of print letters with a series of small, vibrating wire rods. The raised images of letters are "read" with the fingers.

Optic nerve: The nerve that sends impulses to the occipital area of the brain where visual stimuli are interpreted.

Optician: A specialist trained to grind lenses to prescription.

Optimal pitch: Sound that can be produced most efficiently with the least amount of effort by the laryngeal mechanism.

Optometrist: A professional in eye care who is not a physician and whose practice is limited to the prescription and fitting of corrective lenses and treatment of optical defects without drugs or surgery.

Oral-Aural: An educational method that emphasizes the use of residual hearing and speech as the primary mode of communication and learning for children who are deaf.

Organic disability: A disability that is inherent, inborn, or of constitutional origin.

Orthopedic disability: A disabling condition caused by physical impairments, especially those related to the bones, joints, and muscles.

Orthoptist: A specialist who provides eye exercises when prescribed by an ophthalmologist.

Ossicles: Three small bones of the ear that transfer sound waves from the eardrum.

Osteogenesis imperfecta (brittle bone disease): An inherited disorder that affects the structure of the bones, causing them to break very easily. Fractures of the bones may occur prior to birth. Frequently accompanied by hearing impairments.

Otitis media: Infection of the middle ear.

Otolaryngologist: A physician who specializes in diseases of the ear and throat.

Otologist: A physician who specializes in diseases of the ear.

Otosclerosis: Condition of the middle ear wherein a bony growth develops around the base of the stapes, impeding its development.

Otoscope: Small light used to examine the auditory canal and eardrum.

Paraplegia: Paralysis of the lower half of the body, including both legs.

Parent surrogate: A person who represents the child with a disability when the parent or guardian is unavailable or unwilling to advocate for the child during IEP development and other negotiations with school personnel.

Partially seeing: Condition of those whose visual acuity is between 20/200 and 20/70 in the better eye with the best possible correction, or who, in the opinion of an eye specialist, need either temporary or permanent special education facilities. People who are partially seeing can use ink print in their education.

Perceptual skills: Ability to select, organize, and interpret the stimuli that surround us.

Perinatal: During birth.

Pervasive developmental disorder: A diagnostic classification that has replaced the term *childhood schizophrenia*. It is characterized by marked and chronic impairment of social relationships and communication skills, a restricted repertoire of activities and interests, or one or more associated features such as odd responses to sensory input.

Petit mal seizure: A mild form of convulsive disorder characterized by dizziness and momentary lapse of consciousness. This term is no longer used in the professional literature, but may still appear in common usage.

Phenylketonuria (PKU): A genetic disorder which, if undetected, may cause mental retardation. May be detected at birth and can be controlled by diet if discovered early enough.

Phocomelia: A type of congenital deformity in which the hands and/or feet are directly attached to the torso and may resemble "seal flippers." Commonly found in children whose mothers took thalidomide to control morning sickness during pregnancy.

Phonological process disorder: Deficit in the sound system or rules for producing speech sounds. Patterns in error productions are isolated for treatment rather than training isolated speech sounds.

Phonological rules: Specification of speech sounds that can occur in a given language and how these are combined to form words.

Physical prompting/fading: An instructional method that involves manually manipulating a student to perform a behavior and then systematically fading the manual assistance over time.

Pinna: *See* Auricle.

Pitch: The psychological attribute of auditory sensation by which people perceive the highness or lowness of sound.

-plegia: Suffix referring to paralysis or inability to move (e.g., paraplegia).

Poliomyelitis (polio or infantile paralysis): An acute disease that inflames nerve cells of the spinal cord or brain stem and leaves a residual paralysis or muscular atrophy; preventable through vaccination.

Postnatal: After birth.

Pragmatics: Rules that specify how language is used in contexts to achieve a specific function.

Prehension: Grasping skills in fine motor development.

Prenatal: Occurring or existing before birth.

Prereferral intervention: A process whereby students who are at risk for school failure are provided with systematic experiences to determine the extent to which the regular curriculum can meet, or be adapted to meet, their needs.

Prevalence: The number of individuals in the population who currently exhibit a particular characteristic.

Proximal: Close to the body or trunk.

Proximodistal: The sequence of development beginning with the child first gaining control of muscles close to the trunk (proximo) and progressing until the child attains control of muscles located farther away (distal).

Psychoactive drugs: Tranquilizers, stimulants, or antipsychotic or antidepressant medications frequently prescribed to control behaviors that interfere with the child's responsiveness to educational or psychological interventions.

Psychodynamic modeling: A conceptualization in which the behaviors are regarded as symptoms of underlying disorders.

Psychomotor: A term used to describe operations that combine cognitive and physical processes, such as playing a violin, playing tennis, handwriting, etc.

Psychomotor seizure: A seizure characterized by many automatic, stereotyped movements. This term is no longer used in the professional literature, but may still appear in common usage.

Psychotic: A term used to describe a severe behavior disorder that involves major departures from normal patterns of thinking, feeling, and acting.

Pupil: The contractive opening in the middle of the iris.

Pure tone air conduction test: An audiometric test using pure tones of varying frequencies which are presented through earphones.

Pure tone audiometric screening: A brief hearing test using pure tone signals to identify possible hearing loss that would require more complete audiometric testing.

Pure tone bone conduction test: An audiometric test using pure tones of varying frequencies which are presented through a vibrator that transmits sound through the bones of the head.

Pyramidal tract: Area of the brain located between the motor and sensory areas of the cortex. Damage in this area results in spastic cerebral palsy.

Quadriplegia: Paralysis involving all four of the body extremities.

Receptive language: Ability to receive and understand transmitted language.

Recessive genetic traits: Traits that are expressed only when both parents carry the gene. Children of parents who both carry a recessive trait gene have a 25 percent probability of exhibiting the trait, a 25 percent probability of not inheriting that gene trait nor exhibiting it, and a 50 percent probability of inheriting one gene from one parent and becoming a carrier of the recessive gene trait.

Refraction: The bending of light rays.

Regular Education Initiative (REI): A movement to maintain students in need of special education in regular classrooms. The REI has been the subject of considerable controversy among professional educators.

Rehabilitation: The retraining or reorganizing of skill patterns in individuals.

Related services: Services provided by specialists to support the education of exceptional children. Such services are provided by professionals such as speech-language pathologists, physical and occupational therapists, audiologists, psychologists, medical personnel, and others.

Reliability: The consistency with which a test measures a particular trait.

Retina: Back portion of the eye, containing nerve fibers connected to the optic nerve.

Retinopathy of prematurity (ROP): A condition in which abnormal blood vessels grow inside the eyes of premature infants. It primarily affects infants who weigh less than 3 pounds at birth.

Retrolental fibroplasia: Eye disorder caused by too much oxygen in the incubators of premature babies. This condition is now subsumed under the more general cluster of conditions known as retinopathy of prematurity.

Rh incompatibility: A condition in which the fetus has Rh-positive blood and the mother has Rh-negative blood. The mother consequently builds up antibodies that attack the fetus, resulting in birth defects.

Rheumatic fever: Disease usually following a streptococcal infection that is characterized by acute inflammation of the joints, fever, chorea, skin rash, nosebleeds, and abdominal pain. It often damages the heart by scarring its tissues and valves.

Rheumatoid arthritis: A chronic condition in which the joints become severely inflamed, causing general fatigue, stiffness, and aching of the joints as they swell and become tender. This may result in deformities.

Rigidity cerebral palsy: A type of cerebral palsy in which hypertension of the muscles creates stiffness.

Rubella (German measles): A communicable disease transmitted by a virus; infection of a woman during the early stages of pregnancy produces a high probability of severe disabilities in her infant, the most common of which is visual impairment.

Schizophrenia: A psychotic disorder characterized by abnormal perceptions, bizarre behavior and emotions, and distorted thought processes.

School phobia: Intense fear of a teacher, a classroom, peers, or any other aspect of the school. When it is time to go to school, the child develops psychosomatic symptoms.

Sclera: Tough outer layer of eyeball which protects the contents as well as holding contents in place.

Scoliosis: Muscle weakness allowing a serious abnormal curvature of the spine, which may be corrected through surgery or the use of a brace.

Screening: The process of testing a large number of people with a relatively fast, easy, and inexpensive procedure in order to identify those who may need further in-depth evaluation to determine whether they have a problem in need of treatment.

Seizure: An impairment of consciousness which may or may not be accompanied by active disruption of the motor state.

Self-stimulatory behaviors: Bizarre behaviors that do not appear to be controlled by environmental stimuli; may include rocking, hand flapping, self-mouthing; may persist in response to requests to stop.

Semantic rules: The way meaning is conveyed in a language; rules that assign meaning to words and phrases.

Semicircular canals: Three canals within the inner ear that function to maintain balance.

Sensorineural hearing loss: Hearing disorder caused by damage to, or dysfunction of, the cochlea or the auditory nerve.

Severely emotionally disturbed: A condition characterized by serious primary disabilities that are cognitive and/or behavioral, and by the high probability of additional physical and/or sensory disabilities. An individual who is severely emotionally disturbed requires significantly more resources than are provided for those in special programs with mild and moderate disabilities.

Severely/profoundly retarded (S/PR): A term commonly used to classify students with severe to profound mental retardation. These students can typically profit from training in basic self-help skills, ambulation, and functional life skills. Because of multiple handicapping conditions, individuals so classified typically need intensive direct support throughout their lives.

Sex-role stereotyping: Approval or disapproval of behavior based on preconceptions of what is masculine or feminine. Sex-role stereotyping inhibits students' endeavors in nontraditional roles, e.g., female mathematician.

Shaping: Reinforcement of successive approximations to a target response.

Snellen chart: A white background with black letters or symbols of graded size used to test distant field visual acuity.

Social maladjustment: Term used to refer to children and youth whose behavior, although in violation of established social mores and standards, is not deviant with reference to their peer group.

Sociological model: Assumptions that the social cultures and subcultures in the child's environment foster and maintain deviant behavior.

Spasticity: A type of cerebral palsy characterized by muscular incoordination resulting from muscle spasms, opposing contractions of muscles, and paralytic effects.

Special education: Instruction designed for children who have needs that cannot be met by the standard school curriculum.

Speech: The physical process involved in producing the sound and sound combinations of a language.

Speech reception threshold (SRT): The lowest intensity at which a person can repeat two-syllable words at least 50 percent of the time.

Speechreading: Interpreting the movements of the lips, face, head, and gestures as an aid to communication; also called lipreading.

Spina bifida: A congenital defect that results when the bones of a part of the spine fail to grow together, which may or may not allow the spinal cord (meninges) to protrude into a saclike structure on the back.

Spinal muscular atrophy: Disease that affects the spinal cord and results in progressive degeneration of motor nerve cells.

Stages of learning: Phases that students go through during the learning process. The five stages are acquisition, proficiency, generalization, maintenance, and application.

Standardized tests: Tests that have been administered to a large number of people under identical conditions. All tests have been scored the same way and typically are published with norms that enable a person's score to be compared with those in the norm group. Commercially produced achievement tests administered in schools typically are standardized.

Stanford-Binet Intelligence Scale: An individually administered, comprehensive test of intellectual ability. The Stanford-Binet is often used to identify gifted students because it predicts scholastic success with fair reliability.

Stapes (stirrup): The last or innermost bone in the chain of bones in the middle ear extending from the incus to the oval window; stirrup-shaped.

Stereotypic or self-stimulatory behavior: Repetitive, bizarre behaviors that serve no observable function (e.g., body rocking, finger flipping, head banging).

Stoma: Opening at the base of the neck created to allow air to pass to the lungs of a laryngectomized person.

Strabismus: A condition in which the two eyes fail to move in a coordinated fashion, resulting in what appears to be crossed eyes. Caused by an imbalance of the extrinsic muscles of the eye.

Stroke, or CVA (cerebral vascular accident): Sudden interruption of blood flow to the brain.

Stuttering: *See* Disfluency.

Substitution: Articulation disorder wherein one sound of a language is replaced by another sound of that language.

Supported employment: Provides job training and work opportunities in integrated settings to people with disabilities. Support is provided by job trainers and/or job coaches.

Symbolization: The representation of perceptions in memory, comprehension, and communication. Symbols used to represent perceptions may be iconic, linguistic, musical, etc.

Syndrome: A cluster or constellation of symptoms.

Syntax: The part of a grammar system that deals with the arrangement of word forms to show their mutual relations in the sentence.

Talented: A term often used synonymously with *gifted,* or to refer to superior ability in a specific area (e.g., talented musically, artistically).

Task analysis: The process of breaking a skill down into smaller component behaviors so that teaching is made easier.

Task commitment: One of three criteria suggested by J. S. Renzulli to define giftedness. Task commitment is evidenced by the voluntary assumption of difficult and lengthy work in a particular field, such as mathematics.

Tay-Sachs syndrome: A genetically transmitted recessive gene condition typically found in persons with northeastern European Jewish family backgrounds. Characterized by progressive paralysis, blindness, and usually death in early childhood (3 years of age).

Technology dependent: Term used to describe students who require devices, such as respirators and dialysis machines, to sustain life.

Technology of teaching: Highly systematic approaches to instruction, including procedures such as direct instruction, applied behavior analysis, and competency-based instruction.

Test ceiling: The upper limits of a test's usefulness as an estimate of achievement or aptitude. For example, a test designed for children 5 to 10 years of age often does not adequately assess the knowledge and skills of bright children within that age range who take the test.

Thalidomide: A drug used as a relaxant that can cause congenital deformities when taken by pregnant women.

Threshold of hearing: The minimal value of sound wave pressure that will produce the sensation of sound; the point at which a person just begins to hear a sound.

Time delay procedure: Procedure used during acquisition of a response in which the presentation of a prompt is systematically delayed.

Top-down approach to curriculum development: The process of identifying those skills or behaviors that are found at the exit or completion of a curriculum area or strand, and then identifying antecedent critical skills or behaviors which become the content for a curriculum.

Total Communication: A philosophy that advocates the use of any form or mode of communication that leads to mutual understanding, including (but not limited to) speech, residual hearing, manual codes of English, American Sign Language, speechreading, reading and writing.

Total habilitation: Occurs when a person with a disability is living in an environment comparable to the one he or she would have been in if never classified as having a disability.

Trainable mentally retarded (TMR): A term commonly used to classify students with moderate mental retardation. These students can typically profit from education and training in basic academic and self-help skills as well as unskilled vocational activities. Some form of supervision

can typically be expected for this group through adulthood. The IQ parameters for this group are usually in the 20–25 to 50–55 range.

Transdisciplinary approach: Planning and delivery of services by teams of individuals representing various disciplines.

Traumatic brain injury: An injury to the brain caused by an external physical force or by an internal occurrence such as stroke or aneurysm, resulting in impairment of cognitive abilities, physical functioning, and/or behavioral or emotional functioning.

Tremor: A type of cerebral palsy characterized by the shakiness of a limb. Often only noticed when the person is attempting a specific movement.

Triplegia: Paralysis of three of the body's limbs.

Tuberculosis: An infectious disease characterized by the formation of small nodules in the tissue of the lungs.

Underachiever: Any child whose scholastic performance is below that suggested by performance on IQ tests or other indicators of aptitude.

Validity: The extent to which a test actually measures what it purports to measure.

Vestibular mechanism: The balance mechanism located in the inner ear.

Visual acuity: Sharpness or clearness of vision.

Visual field (peripheral vision): Side vision, measured in terms of degrees of visual arc.

Vitality: A person's health and ability to sustain life.

Vitreous humor: A jelly-like clear substance in the center of the eyeball which helps hold the shape of the eye and has slight refractive power.

Vocation: Primary work role in which one is engaged at any particular time.

Voice disorder: Occurs when an individual's voice does not present an appropriate and consistent sound as a result of misuse of the voice structures or tissue change in the vocal tract.

Voiced sounds: All sounds that use vocal fold vibration.

Work: Conscious effort aimed at producing benefits for oneself and/or others.

Probe Answers

PROBE 1-1 Definitions and Related Concepts (p. 16)

1. Components of the definition should include the following:
   - instruction that is part of the regular education program
   - instruction that is individually designed to meet the needs of exceptional children
   - designed for children whose needs cannot be met by the regular school curriculum
   - may call for supportive services
2. False
3. *Disability* refers to reduction of function or absence of a particular body part or organ; *handicap* refers to problems a person with a disability may have when interacting with the environment.
4. *child with a disability:* this term focuses on the child first. The disability is secondary. The other terms are viewed as being demeaning.
5. function
6. Any three of the following: existence; communication; body support, alignment, and positioning; travel and mobility; environmental adaptation; learning, education, and rehabilitation; sports, leisure, and recreation. See text for examples of special education and related services in each category.
7. g; f; d; e; c; a; b
8. Helps explain how people function; factors affecting human function and how they interact; can help with referral, assessment, and instructional planning; can provide implications for IEPs.

PROBE 1-2 Prevalence (p. 19)

1. Between 6.6 and 9.5 million
2. There are different definitions; categories often overlap; all who need services have not yet been identified.
3. Poverty; social class; attitudes toward disabilities; quality of health care; inappropriate diagnosis—particularly of children from diverse cultures, the inner city, or sparsely populated areas.
4. True
5. Any three of the following:
   - increase of 26.4 percent in special education since 1976
   - increase from 8.2 to 9.9 percent of those needing special education
   - early identification will improve success rate

- greater drug and alcohol use in pregnant women will increase rate
- learning disability numbers have increased; mental retardation has decreased
- speech and language disorders greater at early age
- emotional disturbance higher in teen years

   Trends are due to greater precision in identification; attitudes about disabilities and the effect of services; changing behavior patterns of parents; greater realization of potential impact of special education and related services.
6. Affect teacher preparation; planning for services; teacher supply and demand; public education programs; provision of preventive programs; facility planning.

PROBE 1-3 Historical Developments (p. 27)

1. c; e; a; b; d; h; g
2. Any four of the following:
   - education for all exceptional children
   - education, not institutionalization, should be provided
   - early identification
   - individualization of instruction
   - stimulating educational activities; progress from easy to difficult
   - reinforce correct responses and behavior
   - prepare for gainful employment and social adjustment
3. False
4. False
5. National Association for Retarded Citizens (originally Children)
6. PARC verified that children with mental retardation were entitled to a publicly supported education; Mills extended this right to all exceptional children.

PROBE 1-4 Legislative Implications (p. 34)

1. A *law* is made by elected representatives and generally represents broad policy. A *regulation* is written by appointed officials and specifies the procedures to be followed in the implementation of a law.
2. a. 504; b. 94-142; c. 100-407; d. 101-336; e. 94-142; f. 101-336; g. 504; h. 100-407; i. 100-407; j. 94-142; k. 504; l. 101-336; m. 94-142
3. True
4. b

PROBE 2-1   Student Identification (p. 44)

1. False
2. False
3. *Informal assessment:* observation, teacher-constructed tests; interviews. *Formal assessment:* standardized achievement test, IQ test, interest inventory.
4. validity
5. reliability
6. *Norm-referenced tests* compare the student's performance to those of the group on which the test was standardized; *criterion-referenced tests* compare the student's performance to a specific standard of mastery for a particular domain of content.
7. assessment for (a) identification, (b) teaching, and (c) program evaluation
8. Skills needed to master the curriculum are identified and teachers then test, teach, and test again to determine if students are mastering the skills.
9. Any three of the following: labels are applied imprecisely; labeled children are stigmatized; labels don't contribute to intervention; tends to be deviance-oriented; classification systems are vague and insensitive to changes that take place in children; labeling can cause one to disregard other important information about the person.
10. Any of the following: to qualify for funding for programs; to focus public attention and legislation on a particular area; to organize information about a particular category.

PROBE 2-2   Normalization (p. 58)

1. deinstitutionalization and education in the least restrictive environment (or mainstreaming)
2. Any four of the following: foster family homes; supervised apartment living; small group settings; residential care facilities; nursing/geriatric care facilities.
3. True
4. 7; 2; 10; 1; 8; 4; 6; 3; 9; 5
5. The placement of a special education student in regular class for at least part of the school day.
6. False
7. Being able to maintain the student in the regular classroom or providing useful information to specialists who will be conducting assessments to determine potential placement in a special education program.
8. They provide an option for parents who desire their children to be educated in such facilities; provide concentrated services for students with similar characteristics; provide an option for students who are unsuccessful in regular schools.
9. Makes specialists available to provide suggestions for the teacher; provides support services to teachers; assists with problem solving.

10. *Pros:* maintains students in regular class; reduces barriers posed by pull-out programs; includes students who may not meet eligibility requirements for special education; good for prevention of disabilities; research supports it. *Cons:* regular teachers are not prepared for integration; support services are often not available; reluctance on the part of some teachers to participate; curriculum is often not appropriate; research doesn't support it.

PROBE 2-3   Individualized Instruction (p. 64)

1. True
2. Present level of performance; annual student goals; short-term objectives; special education and related services to be provided; extent of participation in regular class; date for initiating services; duration of services; objective evaluation procedures.
3. True
4. False
5. True

PROBE 2-4   Cultural Diversity (p. 68)

1. True
2. dynamic assessment
3. They are a minority, with disabilities, and poor.
4. b
5. True
6. language

PROBE 2-5   Students at Risk (p. 73)

1. False
2. 1 million
3. to report suspected cases of child abuse
4. False
5. Focus on prevention, referral, and reentry; learn about the local drug culture; learn how to discuss the problem with parents; refer students to treatment programs.
6. culturally and linguistically different exceptional
7. Any two of the following: use noneducation personnel; establish rapport with community leaders; use technology.

PROBE 3-1   The Technology of Teaching (p. 81)

1. False
2. model-lead-test
3. True
4. reinforcement
5. competency-based teacher education
6. Any three of the following: identification of competencies; specify objectives and evaluation criteria; alternative learning activities; time variable and achievement constant; shared accountability.

PROBE 3-2   Instructional Technology (p. 89)

1. False
2. equipment; materials; messages
3. False
4. tutorial
5. True
6. gifted
7. Acquisition—learning; proficiency—practicing and developing speed; maintenance—remembering; generalization—demonstrating mastery in a different context; application—using the learning in some other context.
8. *Multimedia:* combination of media that uses terms such as text, graphics, sound, animation; *hypermedia:* same as multimedia, but computer operated, and interaction is under control of the user.
9. SpecialNet
10. Applications will be based on theory and results of additional research.

PROBE 3-3   Assistive Technology (p. 98)

1. Devices and services used to enhance functional capabilities of people with disabilities.
2. True
3. Any four of these: existence; communication; body support and positioning; travel; environmental adaptation; learning, education, and rehabilitation; sports, leisure, and recreation.
4. High-tech; medium-tech; low-tech; no-tech
5. body support and positioning
6. They help a person adapt to the environment. Thus, they are in the adaptation category.
7. Don't need to know the names of devices or vendors; based on functional categories.
8. HyperABLEDATA
9. To help avoid errors; to get advice about selection and proper use of devices.
10. Any three of these: voice recognition; robotics; computer-controlled prostheses; virtual reality; additional employment opportunities.
11. True

PROBE 3-4   Technology Competencies (p. 102)

1. Any four of the items that are in boldface in Figure 3-8.
2. TAM

PROBE 4-1   Introduction to Early Childhood Special Education (p. 112)

1. False
2. True

3. Realization that the environment influences development and the fact that many children from economically disadvantaged families were failing in school.
4. See Table 4-2 (p. 110).
5. These services may allow secondary disabilities to be identified and treated; may prevent the occurrence of some secondary disabilities; may be cheaper in the long run as families will be helped, and children will ultimately be more advanced and independent.

PROBE 4-2   Effectiveness of and Current Policy on Early Intervention (p. 115)

1. True
2. See Table 4-3 (p. 113).
3. False
4. Head Start
5. For infants and toddlers, at-risk children can be served, and an IFSP is required.

PROBE 4-3   Practices in Early Intervention (p. 119)

1. False
2. True
3. The teachers must design the environment and activities to assist infants and children in learning.
4. The first level consists of individuals and agencies with whom the family interacts on a regular basis. These constitute the primary support system for the family, and the actions and beliefs of these individuals and agencies influence the functioning of the family.
5. False
6. The intervention team must monitor the changes and adjust the intervention accordingly.
7. May vary from child to child and from program to program; the team often includes an early childhood special educator, speech-language pathologist, physical therapist, occupational therapist, and social worker.

PROBE 4-4   Components of Early Intervention Practice (p. 132)

1. Screening; referral by individuals who have regular contact with them.
2. *Cognitive:* sensorimotor skills, concept development, preacademic skills; *communication:* semantic functions and relationships, pragmatic functions, syntactical and morphological development, lexical development, phonological development; *social:* parent-infant or parent-child interactions, child-child interactions and social play, toy play, social skills; *self-care:* eating and feeding, dressing and undressing, toileting; *motor:* gross and fine motor skills.

3. Their strengths, resources, goals, and critical events that influence their functioning.

4. They are to be participants in its development.

5. Assisting families in promoting their child's development through instruction; assisting families in interacting with their infant or child.

6. child-directed activities

7. *Naturalistic strategies:* incidental teaching, mand-model procedure, naturalistic time delay; *direct teaching strategies:* system of least prompts, most-to-least prompts, time delay.

8. From hospital program to community program; from infant-toddler program to preschool program; from preschool program to school-age program; from segregated program to mainstreamed program.

PROBE 4-5 Challenges Faced by Early Intervention Programs (p. 134)

1. Enrollment of children with disabilities in programs for children without disabilities, and attention to the needs of both groups of children.

2. False

3. Preparing personnel to work with families as well as infants and children; meeting the needs of infants and children from nontraditional families; working with culturally and ethnically diverse families.

4. False

PROBE 5-1 The Rationale for Transition Programs (p. 140)

1. Higher education to postsecondary vocational or technical training, to full-time competitive employment, to supported, enclave, or sheltered employment.

2. False

3. Unemployed or partially employed at low-paying jobs with few benefits or opportunities and frequently segregated from the mainstream.

4. False

5. IEPs

6. integrated

PROBE 5-2 Models to Facilitate Life Adjustment (p. 147)

1. False

2. Rigorous program design focused on specific skill development; lack of teacher skills or confidence for adapting the curriculum and the instructional approaches; segregated programming.

3. a; c; d

4. False

5. 16 and 65

6. The statutory requirement that individuals served be likely to obtain private-sector, competitive employment.

PROBE 5-3 Concepts of Transition (p. 151)

1. school; community/adult

2. employment; community living/adult life

3. a. transition with no special services refers to services available to all citizens; b. transition with time-limited services involves the use of specialized, temporary programs that can lead to potentially permanent employment of a person with a disability; c. ongoing support services include ongoing support needed to maintain employment.

4. False

5. community adjustment; employment, residential environment, social and interpersonal network

PROBE 5-4 Stages of the Transition Process (p. 161)

1. Stage 1: Input and foundation
   Stage 2: Vocational assessment
   Stage 3: Transition planning
   Stage 4: Transition culmination
   Stage 5: Transition follow-up

2. False

3. A functional curriculum contains activities and materials designed to prepare students to live, work, and recreate as independently as possible in an integrated society.

4. False

5. Actual on-location training helps students to generalize skills and concepts to the real world.

6. vocational capabilities; degree of success or failure

7. *Work samples* assess the individual's ability to do specific vocational tasks, while *situational work assessments* focus on the general work personality of the individual.

8. True

9. Parent and student input; interagency cooperation, and the individualized transition plan.

10. To determine the effectiveness of the entire transition process, including the efficacy of the specific strategies used.

PROBE 5-5 Additional Transition Considerations (p. 169)

1. Evidence suggests that the major reason that most individuals with disabilities experience difficulties getting and keeping jobs is a lack of appropriate social skills.

2. False

3. homemaking and community life; vocational adjustment; leisure pursuits; personal maintenance and development; travel

4. sheltered workshops; supported employment; competitive employment

PROBE 5-6 Transition Issues and Challenges (p. 174)

1. False

2. Hire and train job developers to obtain employment opportunities for individuals with disabilities; have potential employers observe good employment programs in the community; arrange for special education students to volunteer their services in exchange for the training opportunity.
3. increase; decrease
4. vocational education; vocational rehabilitation
5. Sensitively address parents' concerns; provide information and education to assist them in developing realistic expectations; convey positive feelings about the student's vocational potential.
6. True

PROBE 6-1 Relating to Families (p. 195)

1. False
2. Any four of the following: shock; guilt; denial; sorrow; rejection.
3. See pp. 190–195.
4. See pp. 190–195.

PROBE 6-2 Involving Parents (p. 207)

1. False
2. Authoritarian; inconsiderate of feelings; not respectful of legal rights.
3. a. Identification and referral: see p. 197.
   b. Assessment: see p. 198.
   c. Conferences: see p. 200.
   d. Instruction: see pp. 204 (strategies) to 206.
   e. Evaluation: see p. 207.
4. Instruction; parent training; evaluation

PROBE 6-3 Supporting Families (p. 215)

1. See Professional Advocacy, p. 209.
2. See Conceptual Basis, p. 219.
3. False
4. True
5. False

PROBE 7-1 Designing a Professional Development Program (p. 232)

1. False
2. philosophy
3. (1) regular class teachers; (2) special education teachers; (3) specialists, such as administrators, diagnosticians, and other related service personnel; (4) special education college faculty; (5) researchers
4. False
5. objectives
6. Exceptional Child Education Resources (ECER)
7. Council for Exceptional Children

PROBE 8-1 Definitions and Terminology (p. 244)

1. ten
2. False
3. 5–6
4. e; c; d; a; b
5. False
6. True
7. False
8. False
9. True
10. True
11. False

PROBE 8-2 Language Disorders (p. 253)

1. True
2. aphasia
3. True
4. hearing acuity; conceptual knowledge; environmental input; perceptual abilities; retrieval skills; motor skills
5. Conceptual knowledge, communicative behavior, knowledge of language rules, comprehension of language, production of language, and communicative functioning.
6. Input that is reduced in complexity makes it easier for the child to attach meaning to the individual language rules.

PROBE 8-3 Speech Disorders: Problems with Articulation (p. 260)

1. symptoms*; physical explanation*; underlying neurological or physiological cause
2. excess nasality
3. Lack of motor coordination may prohibit rapid enough movement of the articulators.
4. substitution; omission; distortion; addition
5. When the child with a severe speech problem is not capable of producing intelligible words.

PROBE 8-4 Speech Disorders: Problems with Voice (p. 262)

1. If a normal voice mechanism is misused, it may break down and show the results of physical damage, which may be interpreted as an organic problem.
2. denasal; nasal
3. ear, nose, and throat specialist
4. Specializes in the treatment of problems of the ear, nose, and throat.
5. False (unless they last longer than 6 months)
6. excess or deficient nasality; breathiness; harshness; hoarseness

PROBE 8-5 Speech Disorders: Problems with Fluency (p. 266)

1. developmental; stuttering; neurogenic; psychogenic; language delay
2. 2½; 4
3. False
4. False

PROBE 8-6 Provision of Speech-Language Services (p. 268)

1. True
2. classroom
3. curriculum
4. speech-language pathologists
5. ASHA (American Speech-Language-Hearing Association)

PROBE 9-1 Sound and Human Hearing (p. 273)

1. transmitter; medium; receiver
2. Sound is created by the vibration of some object. This vibration is carried across some medium and can be heard by the ear.
3. frequency; Hz; intensity; dB
4. 40–60 dB
5. symbolic level; signal level; primitive or background level

PROBE 9-2 How We Hear (p. 277)

1. e; h; f; j; d; a; i; b
2. False
3. See p. 276: "A transmission starts . . . the auditory nerve."
4. cortex
5. fifth month

PROBE 9-3 Hearing Loss (p. 282)

1. deaf
2. 46,000
3. conductive; sensorineural; mixed functional; central
4. conductive; blocked auditory canal; otosclerosis
5. functional
6. sensorineural; rubella
7. central auditory disorder
8. speech; oral language
9. False
10. False

PROBE 9-4 Evaluating Hearing Loss (p. 288)

1. Any four of the following:
   • illness or disease of the mother during pregnancy
   • child does not react to loud sounds
   • child does not engage in normal amount of vocal play
   • child is delayed in speech and language development
   • child does not pay attention in class
2. audiogram
3. False
4. Pure tone audiometric screening; pure tone threshold audiometry; speech audiometry; sound field audiometry; behavioral play audiometry; impedance audiometer; evoked response technique
5. False
6. 500; 1000; 2000
7. b; e; c; a; d
8. speech discrimination score from speech audiometry technique

PROBE 9-5 Interventions for Hearing Loss (p. 293)

1. ventilate
2. False
3. True
4. auditory training
5. lipreading or speechreading
6. False

PROBE 9-6 Education of Children with Hearing Loss (p. 308)

1. Any four of the following:
   • history of hereditary hearing loss
   • infections or illness of mother during pregnancy
   • defects of child's ear, nose, or throat
   • low birth weight
   • prematurity
   • infections, diseases, or accidents sustained by the child
2. Any five of the following:
   • frequent earaches or ear discharge
   • poor articulation of speech sounds, or consonant sounds omitted
   • incorrect answers to easy questions
   • child doesn't respond when spoken to in a normal manner
   • hearing appears to be better when child faces speaker
   • child often asks for things to be repeated
   • child turns up TV or radio too loud
3. True
4. False
5. language
6. False
7. oral
8. manual
9. Total Communication
10. False
11. False
12. residential setting; day school, special class; resource room

PROBE 10-1   The Visual System (p. 316)

1. eye; brain
2. a; c; b; a; b; a; c; a; b; b; a
3. The process of seeing begins when light is reflected from an object and enters the eye. As the light rays pass through the cornea, aqueous, lens, and vitreous, they are bent, or refracted, so that they will strike the retina in the macular area. From there, nerve impulses relay the impressions of visual stimuli to the brain, where "seeing" takes place.

PROBE 10-2   Disorders of the Visual System (p. 319)

1. placing a patch over the unaffected eye; surgery to straighten the eye muscles
2. False
3. myopia
4. maternal rubella
5. Retinopathy of prematurity or ROP

PROBE 10-3   Definitions of Visual Impairment (p. 324)

1. Children with visual impairments are those who have a visual restriction severe enough that it interferes with normal progress in a regular education setting. They need specially trained teachers, specially designed or adapted curricular materials, and specially designed educational aids, so that they can realize their full potential.
2. blind; partially seeing
3. 20/200; 20/70
4. True
5. The index of 20/150 means that an object which can be seen clearly from a distance of 150 feet by a person who sees normally must be 20 feet from the person with visual impairments to be seen clearly.
6. visual arc
7. Children who are blind are those whose visual loss indicates that they must use braille and other tactile and auditory materials to learn. Children with low vision have some useful vision; they can use print and other visual materials in their educational programs.

PROBE 10-4   Identification and Prevalence (p. 327)

1. b; c; d; a
2. Snellen chart
3. Any five of the following:
   - child appears clumsy in a new situation and has trouble walking
   - child holds head in awkward position or holds material close to eyes
   - child "tunes out" when information is on chalkboard or in books he or she cannot read
   - child constantly asks someone to explain what is going on
   - child is inordinately affected by glare from sun and not able to see things at certain times of day
   - child has a pronounced squint
   - child rubs eyes excessively
   - child pushes eyeball with finger or knuckle
   - child has obvious physiological anomalies or signs of eye disease, such as red swollen lids, crusts on lids, or crossed eyes
4. 0.1 percent
5. True

PROBE 10-5   Developmental Characteristics (p. 331)

1. True
2. Restrictions in the range and variety of experiences they have had; restrictions in the ability to move about in the environment and observe people and objects around them; restrictions in their integration into all aspects of their environment.
3. the negative attitudes of those who can see; the integration of blind children with seeing peers and inservice training for teachers

PROBE 10-6   Instructional Methods and Materials (p. 343)

1. True
2. True
3. eyeglass magnifiers; stand magnifiers; hand-held magnifiers; telescope aids; television viewers
4. orientation; mobility
5. False
6. tactile; visual; auditory
7. Any three of the following: braille; paperless brailler; Optacon (optical-to-tactile converter); Kurzweil Reading Machine.
8. the use of access equipment
9. electronic braille; Optacon; synthesized speech; enlarged print
10. False
11. True
12. False

PROBE 10-7   Educational Programming (p. 347)

1. residential
2. True
3. In recent years some residential schools have functioned as educational centers for children with visual impairments and have provided activities and experiences for their students that involve interaction with sighted children outside their school. Residential schools have also

provided consultative services to local school programs. In addition, some residential schools are functioning as centers for children with visual impairments who also have multiple disabilities.

4. special class plan; cooperative class plan; resource room; itinerant teacher plan; teacher consultant plan
5. False
6. Any three of the following: eye examination report; medical report; educational assessments; reports of behavioral observations by parent and teachers; any assessment information that might be helpful in placement.
7. True
8. concept
9. Any four of the following: visual efficiency; sensory abilities; other impairments; motor performance; language; intelligence; achievement.
10. Instruments developed especially for people with visual impairments; those adapted for use with people who have visual impairments; those developed for use with the seeing population and used as is for people with visual impairments.
11. False

PROBE 11-1 Definitions of Physical Disabilities (p. 353)

1. True
2. -plegia
3. A. hemiplegia; B. monoplegia; C. quadriplegia; D. paraplegia; E. cephalad or superior; F. anterior; G. posterior; H. caudal or inferior.

PROBE 11-2 Disabilities That Affect Ambulation (p. 366)

1. True
2. False
3. c; a; e; b; d
4. prenatal; perinatal; postnatal
5. True
6. False
7. False
8. b; d; a; c; e; g; f
9. thalidomide
10. True
11. False
12. physical therapy
13. False

PROBE 11-3 Disabilities That Affect Vitality (p. 370)

1. a congenital heart defect

2. breathing
3. False (current treatment prolongs life to adulthood for many)
4. False
5. True

PROBE 11-4 Other Disabilities (p. 375)

1. partial seizure
2. generalized
3. absence
4. True
5. False
6. When seizure activity continues for more than 5 minutes, or when it appears that the person is going into repeated generalized seizures.
7. Both may have a motor component. TBI is not congenital; cerebral palsy may be. Cerebral palsy may be caused by birth trauma; TBI is not.

PROBE 11-5 Education and Treatment of Children with Physical Disabilities (p. 384)

1. Yes; determined by Supreme Court decision.
2. See pp. 376–378 for descriptions.
3. Any three symptoms of child abuse (see p. 379).
4. Any three symptoms of child neglect (see p. 379).
5. Improved physical problems to the extent that the child no longer requires special education.
6. Physical impairment to the extent that a child no longer has the ability to interact in the regular classroom.
7. a. Does the child take medication?
   b. How will the child be transported to school?
   c. What methods are used to get the child on and off the school bus?
   d. Can the child write? Type? By what means?
   e. What equipment, such as a special feeding tray, does the child need?
   f. What positions does the child assume for resting?
8. An *orthosis* supports or assists a body function and a *prosthesis* replaces a missing body part.
9. When a careful evaluation of the potential effect of the device has not been conducted.

PROBE 11-6 Architectural Barriers (p. 394)

1. American National Standards Institute (ANSI)
2. 32
3. 4
4. False
5. False
6. False

7. 40
8. $\frac{1}{2}$ inch
9. True

PROBE 12-1   Intellectual Functioning and Mental Retardation (p. 412)

1. True
2. IQ
3. adaptive behavior
4. a. 69 to 55; b. 54 to 40; c. 39 to 25; d. below 25.
5. False
6. False
7. Adequacy of normative population's size; limitations due to numbers of test items; errors in administration or scoring; IQ score by itself is of little educational value.
8. False
9. Adaptive behavior is the effectiveness or degree with which individuals meet standards of personal independence and social responsibility expected for their age and cultural group.
10. Attempting to account for cultural and ethnic diversity.

PROBE 12-2   Mental Retardation: Definitions, Terminology, and Issues (p. 416)

1. Mental retardation refers to significantly subaverage general intellectual functioning resulting in or associated with concurrent impairments in adaptive behavior and manifested during the developmental period.
2. Mental retardation refers to substantial limitations in certain personal capabilities. It is manifested as significantly subaverage intellectual functioning, existing concurrently with related disabilities in two or more of the following applicable adaptive skills areas: communication, self-care, home living, social skills, community use, self-direction, health and safety, functional academics, leisure, and work. Mental retardation begins before age 18.
3. b
4. Mental retardation refers to a limited repertory of behavior shaped by events that constitute an individual's history. It focuses on observed behavior exhibited by an individual, rather than relying on internal characteristics that are difficult to measure, such as IQ.

PROBE 12-3   Prevalence of Mental Retardation (p. 419)

1. d
2. methodological differences; gender differences; age differences; socioeconomic differences
3. b. 1 percent

4. d. 3 percent
5. False

PROBE 12-4   Classification Systems for Persons with Mental Retardation (p. 424)

1. Classification systems based on etiology, clinical type, and severity of symptoms.
2. c; b; a
3. Etiology in moderate and severe/profound typically clearer than in mild mental retardation; inadequacies of standardized tests for persons with moderate, severe, and profound intellectual disabilities; symptoms of the various classifications are often used interchangeably across types or levels, depending on the purposes for which the classification is being used (i.e., educational versus medical).
4. A cluster or constellation of symptoms.
5. True

PROBE 12-5   Causes and Prevention of Mental Retardation (p. 435)

1. False
2. True
3. False
4. False
5. False
6. True
7. e; g; d; b; a; h; f; c
8. Any five of the following: vaccination against rubella; surgical procedures to correct hydrocephaly; amniocentesis to detect chromosomal anomalies; stricter laws concerning lead in household products; dietary supplements for newborns identified as PKU; enrichment of impoverished environments in both rural and urban settings; sustained information for the public concerning alcohol and other drug use, particularly for pregnant women.

PROBE 12-6   Educating Individuals with Mental Retardation (p. 450)

1. True
2. Differences are likely to be found in rate of skill acquisition; ability to attend to relevant tasks; memory; generalization; transfer of recently acquired skills; and language.
3. Tendency to focus on specific cues in the environment; perseverating rather than shifting attention to new relevant cues; generally, a narrower breadth of attention.
4. In reaction to, or in the presence of, at least three different persons; in at least three different natural settings; in response to at least three different sets of instructional ma-

terials; in response to at least three different appropriate language cues.
5. False
6. Complexity of skills taught; actual skills or subjects taught.
7. True
8. True
9. False
10. True
11. True

PROBE 13-1 Characteristics of Persons with Severe Developmental Disabilities (p. 460)

1. Serious primary disabilities that are cognitive; high probability of additional physical or sensory disabilities; requiring significantly more resources than are provided for the population with mild and moderate disabilities.
2. to establish classes; to determine placement criteria; to recruit and hire qualified teachers; to set certification requirements; to report prevalence data
3. It is estimated that 0.13 percent of the population have severe mental retardation while 0.04 percent of the population are labeled profoundly retarded.
4. It is the *extent* or intensiveness of children's disabilities that serves to have them classified as severely disabled, not the *type* of disabilities.
5. Mental retardation is "significantly subaverage general intellectual functioning resulting in or associated with concurrent impairments in adaptive behavior and manifested during the developmental period." The concept of functional retardation emphasizes the importance of environmental events in shaping and mainstreaming adaptive behavior.
6. Any four of the following: aggression toward others; no attention to even the most pronounced social stimuli; self-mutilation; self-stimulation; absence of imitation; extremely brittle medical existence.

PROBE 13-2 Educability of Students with Severe Developmental Disabilities (p. 463)

1. False
2. Some children are not amenable to instruction due to severe physical disabilities, damaged central nervous systems, and profound mental retardation; if a child fails to acquire a meaningful skill after extensive training, then the student is presumed ineducable; an adequate technology is lacking to improve significantly the functioning capabilities for some children with certain disabilities.
3. Education, like development, is an ongoing process, and ineducability cannot be proven.

PROBE 13-3 Curriculum Considerations (p. 471)

1. This approach integrates goals and objectives from various disciplines and professions. Typically, one member is assigned the role of case manager. Members may include a special education teacher (who assesses cognitive and sensory skills, develops educational programs, etc.), a physical therapist (who assesses gross motor skills and develops programs to teach normal motor development, etc.), an occupational therapist (who assesses fine motor skills and assists in developing appropriate feeding programs, etc.), a speech/language pathologist (who assists in assessing and developing programs for communication and language skills, etc.), a psychologist (who assesses cognitive skills and designs programs to manage behavior problems, etc.). Other members may include a nurse, nutritionist, job coach, recreational therapist, etc.
2. False
3. In the functional model, emphasis is placed on teaching skills that are chronologically age-appropriate and immediately useful to the learner. When a developmental approach is used, emphasis is placed on teaching skills that are not in the student's repertoire in the sequence in which a normally functioning child would require them, regardless of the chronological age of the child and the immediate usefulness of the skill.
4. The ecological inventory is a strategy of individualizing instruction by identifying skills needed by each student to function more independently in his or her current and probable future environments. It is accomplished through the following six steps:
   • Identify curriculum domains.
   • Identify current and future environments.
   • Identify subenvironments within each environment.
   • Identify activities or routines in each subenvironment.
   • Identify skills needed to perform those activities and routines.
   • Design instructional programs to teach each of those skills.
5. The primary assessment strategy for identifying a student's instructional needs is a discrepancy analysis, which entails observing the student perform the skills necessary to participate in an activity while recording whether the student can perform each skill independently and fluently. It yields vital information on *what* to teach, as well as insight on *how* to teach.
6. An ecological inventory is both complex and time-consuming to create. A community catalog is typically developed by a group of teachers in the same four domains, but results in a master list of settings, activities, and skills for all students of a similar age, thus precluding the need to repeatedly survey the same environment for each student.
7. The principle of partial participation affirms that each student should participate in chronological and functional

activities in a variety of school and nonschool settings, although the student may not be able to perform the entire skill. Five possible adaptations are as follows: use of adaptive or prosthetic devices; providing assistance; altering skill sequences; changing rules; changing attitudes and behaviors of persons without disabilities.

PROBE 13-4 Instructional Settings (p. 476)

1. To achieve generalization of skills.
2. Community-based instruction is teaching students in natural settings, where the targeted skills will be required; it does not mean taking students on field trips. It is important for generalization.
3. This means to teach at times when the targeted behavior naturally occurs and as part of the natural routine. For example, teaching a student to put on or take off a coat should be done when the student is coming in from outside or going outside, not at other times throughout the day.
4. Rather than teaching each skill separately, a skill cluster approach can be used. For example, if a student has *setting a table, washing hands, identifying utensils,* and *use of a napkin* on his or her IEP, these skills can be clustered through a snack or cooking activity and be taught together.
5. Distributed trial instruction (performing and teaching targeted skills across time, embedded into functional routines, etc.) is preferred over massed trial instruction (teaching a skill repeatedly in succession) because the skill will be performed at naturally occurring times and as part of naturally occurring routines.
6. False

PROBE 13-5 Instructional Methods (p. 484)

1. A functional age-appropriate skill for an adolescent would be a skill that same-age peers are expected to perform. A functional skill is frequently used, results in more independence, and prepares a student for less restrictive environments.
2. The four phases and their purposes are as follows:
   • *Acquisition:* to teach a student to perform a new skill.
   • *Fluency:* to teach a student to be proficient at performing the skill.
   • *Generalization:* to teach a student to use the skill across all settings, environments, materials, persons, etc., that are necessary.
   • *Maintenance:* to teach a student to continue to use the skill even after training has stopped.
3. Any two of the following: all problems are viewed as behavioral; all children can learn under appropriate instructional conditions; students learn best when teachers systematically order tasks in sequence from easy to hard.

4. Self-injurious behaviors cause harm to the person, such as hitting oneself or head banging. Self-stimulatory behaviors do not necessarily cause physical harm to the individual; these include such behaviors as hand flapping or rocking.
5. This procedure involves breaking down a skill through a task analysis. The teacher begins by physically guiding a student through all steps of the task analysis. Over training sessions, the teacher systematically provides less physical assistance until the student can perform the behavior independently.

PROBE 13-6 Transition (p. 486)

1. Transition plans are necessary because these students will most likely encounter difficulties when going through transitional periods unless systematic instruction occurs.
2. Home to preschool services; preschool to elementary school; elementary to middle or junior high school; middle or junior high school to high school; high school to next environment (e.g., work).
3. Components of a transition plan include the following:
   • The plan must be comprehensive in nature.
   • It must be individualized.
   • It must have the involvement of parents or guardians.
   • It must have participation from sending and receiving agencies.
   • It should include focused experience of related service personnel.
   • It requires direct instruction in a variety of actual subsequent environments.
   • It should be longitudinal in nature.

PROBE 13-7 Service Delivery (p. 489)

1. The principle of normalization suggests that persons with disabilities should have the opportunity to live as much like persons without disabilities as possible, and that this goal can be met by exposing them to the living conditions common to their culture.
2. *PARC v. Commonwealth of Pennsylvania; Mills v. Board of Education of the District of Columbia*
3. vocational services; residential services; transportation services; advocacy services

PROBE 14-1 Terms and Definitions for Learning Disabilities (p. 497)

1. Any three of the following terms: minimal brain dysfunction; psychoneurological learning disorder; perceptual disability; specific language disabled; dyslexia; dyscalculia; dysgraphia. Terms may reflect a medical orientation to learning disabilities that implies brain damage or a belief

that the disability is the result of impaired processes within the individual. Limitations include implying the presence of brain damage or central nervous system damage when there is no evidence of such damage. The *dys-* family of terms describes problems in narrow curricular areas and fails to convey that learning disabilities may be part of a complex disorder that influences more than the individual's ability to read or write or compute.

2. using language; listen, think, speak, read, write, spell, or do mathematical calculations; visual, hearing or motor disabilities, or mental retardation, or environmental, cultural, or economic disadvantage

3. The five common elements are as follows:
   - *Underachievement:* There is a difference between what the individual should be able to do, given his or her level of intelligence or skills in other areas, and what the person is actually doing.
   - *Potential for specific problems in spoken language, academics, and reasoning:* There are specific learned tasks that the individual is unable to master after exposure to conditions under which most peers are successful at performing the task. Individual problems will vary considerably, but there is potential for problems in areas such as speaking, listening, reading, writing, mathematics, and problem solving.
   - *Disruption of the learning process:* The individual has unusual difficulty learning and performing some skills, and the problem is thought to be centered on one or more of the basic psychological processes involved in learning. There are many different theories describing possible learning processes and the disruptions experienced by people with learning disabilities, but we have relatively little hard information on these processes at this time.
   - *Known or suspected central nervous system dysfunction:* Because learning takes place in the brain, learning disabilities are likely related to the central nervous system (CNS). In some individual cases, there is medical evidence for CNS dysfunction or damage, but in other cases there is no evidence, only a suspicion.
   - *Potential for multiple disabilities:* While learning disabilities are not the direct result of poor vision or hearing, disadvantage, behavior disorder, or mental retardation, it is possible for these conditions to coexist with a learning disability.

4. Tony appears to demonstrate underachievement, potential for specific problems in academics, and disruption of the learning process. We don't know if there is CNS dysfunction. He does not appear to have multiple disabilities.

PROBE 14-2 Characteristics and Prevalence (p. 508)

1. Demographic studies of adolescents and young adults show that learning disabilities can persist past childhood.

2. No. Schools identify those students with the most severe problems; the scarcity of resources for special education services means that individuals with milder learning problems will not be labeled as learning disabled. In other cases, the identification process may be imperfect and may not detect a learning disability. Finally, adults with learning disabilities who were in school before PL 94-142 mandated services for individuals with learning disabilities may not have been identified and served.

3. Obesity can range from mild to severe, and the same is true for learning disabilities. Being slightly overweight does not significantly impair an individual's ability to function; the same is true for a mild learning disability. Extreme obesity is a serious problem that calls for intense intervention; the same is true for a severe learning disability.

4. Heterogeneity means that there is diversity within a group. Individuals with learning disabilities are similar in that they all have difficulty learning, but the individual characteristics vary.

5. Ten characteristics include the following: linguistic deficits; achievement deficits in reading, written expression, mathematics, or problem solving; neuropsychological deficits, including poor self-concept, attention disorders, perceptual disorders, and memory deficits; social skill deficits.

6. The committee estimated that 5 to 10 percent of people living in the United States are affected by learning disabilities.

PROBE 14-3 Causes of Learning Disabilities (p. 512)

1. CNS dysfunction is suspected because learning is a brain-based activity.

2. Any six of the following: heredity and genetic conditions; biochemical imbalances; malnutrition; oxygen deprivation; toxins including harmful drugs, lead, etc.; weakened immune system; head injury.

3. poor teaching; education that is a mismatch for learners' needs, based on developmental age, cultural background, etc.

4. Etiology may be helpful if knowing the basis of the disorder can lead to specific interventions, but this is rarely the case today. The second goal of finding etiology is prevention of other cases of learning disabilities in the future.

PROBE 14-4 Identification and Assessment (p. 516)

1. Any six of the following:
   - heterogeneity of characteristics of learning disabilities
   - lack of a precise definition of learning disabilities
   - difficulty in establishing cutoffs for when a learning problem becomes a disability
   - lack of services for students with other learning problems
   - use of tests that are not valid or reliable

- multidisciplinary teams that are not prepared for working effectively as a group
- parental pressure to use the "learning disabilities" label rather than "mental retardation" or "emotional disturbance"
- poorly defined procedures for dismissing students from special education or serving students with learning disabilities in mainstream settings.

2. The federal guidelines and definition do not provide specific eligibility criteria, and the states all have different eligibility requirements for services for those with learning disabilities.

3. The formal testing process is designed to do the following: provide data on the student's overall intelligence level and academic strengths and weaknesses; summarize the student's approach to the learning process; and rule out other factors (visual, hearing, or motor disorders; low intelligence; environmental disadvantage) as primary causes of the problem.

4. Curriculum-based assessment may be an alternative to formal testing, but CBA methods cannot distinguish among categories of disability.

PROBE 14-5 Education and Treatment Provisions (p. 521)

1. Any five of the following: demonstration; guided practice; feedback; carefully constructed materials with formats that enhance acquisition and retention; multiple opportunities for practice; skills taught to mastery.

2. A metacognitive strategy helps learners assess the demands of a situation, plan how to approach the learning task, and continuously evaluate and monitor their success.

3. perceptual and process training; multisensory training; modality matching

4. The only medical intervention consistently supported by research findings is the use of psychostimulant medications for the treatment of some individuals with attention deficit disorders who also have a learning disability.

PROBE 14-6 Implications for Mainstreaming (p. 525)

1. No. Many students who are not eligible for special education will benefit from their teachers' use of teaching procedures effective for students with learning disabilities.

2. Any five of the following: develop awareness of the needs of students with learning disabilities; curriculum-based assessment; direct instruction; positive and instructive classroom management; metacognitive strategies instruction; peer tutoring; cooperative learning.

3. Teachers may directly teach social skills that improve interactions among classmates. Cooperative grouping arrangements, including peer tutoring and teams, can promote social integration.

4. Factors that can expedite successful collaborations include the following: sufficient time allotted to collaboration activities; administrative support; teacher attitudes and values in support of collaboration; behaviors that actively promote collaboration; and development of collaboration skills among all persons involved.

5. Any four of the following: audiotapes of reading materials; graphic organizers; study guides; advance organizers; simplified texts that contain information parallel to that in grade-level texts.

PROBE 15-1 Definitions and Terminology (p. 533)

1. Where is she aggressive: in specific classes, in halls, restrooms, the cafeteria, on the bus, at school functions? In which settings is she *not* aggressive? Are there any differences between the settings in these two groups (e.g., in persons present, expectations, activities, physical characteristics, etc.)? Talk with peers and adults in these settings, talk with the girl herself about her perceptions, perhaps interview parents, etc. Gather information through interviews, behavior rating scales, direct observation of behavior.

PROBE 15-2 Characteristics and Prevalence (p. 542)

1. No. It is inappropriate to conclude that the student "owns" a behavioral disability. According to the ecological perspective, a behavioral disorder is defined in terms of interactions between persons. The teacher's (or other students') responses to the identified child may be part of the disorder.

2. *Externalizing* behavior problems consist of acting-out behavior; general examples are aggression, noncompliance, excessive activity, antisocial behavior. Specific examples may include fighting, refusing to comply with adult requests, disruptive behavior in the classroom, or stealing. *Internalizing* behavior problems are characterized by social withdrawal, and may be manifested through anxiety, shyness, fears, worries, and physical problems. It is important to recognize that in either case, these problems are extreme when compared to peers in the same age and cultural-reference groups.

3. Autism is a severe developmental disability that is presumed to be of neurological origin. It is characterized by impairments in social skills, cognitive functioning, and communication. It is differentiated from childhood onset pervasive developmental disorders chiefly on the basis of age of onset, which in the case of autism appears to be at birth or in infancy.

4. Students with severe and profound behavioral disabilities are like those with severe and profound developmental disabilities in their extremely limited repertoires of social, academic, cognitive, and communicative functioning. Also, students with developmental disabilities often display behavioral disorders that may appear "psychotic."

5. Parents, teachers, and other adults tend to have less toler-ance for aggressive, acting-out behavior, which is more characteristic of young male behavior patterns. Particularly in school, students are expected to be docile, compliant, and studious. Girls tend to have more experience learning through listening, reading, and following directions, and therefore exhibit more desirable "student" behaviors.

6. c

PROBE 15-3 Etiology: Biophysical and Environmental Correlates (p. 547)

1. While genetic factors *may* be involved in severe mental illnesses, research evidence suggests that the causes of such disorders are multiple and interacting. Environmental and health factors, for example, also seem to play a part. If genetic factors were the *only* cause, how can we explain why psychotic disorders have been identified in one iden-tical twin but not the other?

2. d

3. It is very unlikely that one person or factor is the only cause of a behavior problem. Such problems are better conceptualized as interactions between persons than as conditions that exist in a single person. Therefore, it is likely that many factors contributed to your child's behav-ior patterns, both good and bad. If you have these con-cerns, perhaps it would help to discuss them with a professional.

PROBE 15-4 Identification and Assessment (p. 553)

1. (1) Does the behavior deviate from acceptable standards in the settings in which the student functions daily? Before identifying a student as behaviorally disabled, it should be shown that the standards for behavior in the child's settings are reasonable, that the problems extend across settings, and that the student is being evaluated fairly against these standards. The adults who set the standard for each setting should be interviewed to determine their expectations. (2) How much does the behavior depart from these standards? Students whose behavior deviates from standards to only a small degree should not be identified and labeled. While adults can provide some information regarding the degree of deviancy, the best approach is to compare the behavior of the student in question with that of peers who are identified as behaviorally "normal" by the teacher. This can be done through behavior rating scales or direct observa-tion. (3) How long has the behavior pattern continued? Children normally exhibit transient behavioral difficulties at various stages of their development. Situational factors (e.g., divorce of the parents, death of a relative) also may create short-term behavioral disorders. Except in the case of extreme behavioral problems (e.g., behavior that is dan-gerous to oneself or to others), it should be established that the problems have existed for a period of time. If situa-tional factors are identified, these should be addressed, regardless of whether the student is identified as behavior-ally disabled.

2. e

3. (1) Screening and prereferral intervention data should be collected and evaluated to determine the extent and nature of the student's problems, and to identify existing evalua-tive data. (2) Individual intellectual assessment should be conducted to establish that the behavior problems are not due to cognitive impairment. If cognitive deficits exist, it should be documented that behavior problems persist after these deficits have been addressed. (3) Academic perfor-mance should be assessed to determine whether progress has been affected by the behavior problems. (4) Social competence should be evaluated to document that the student's social skills are deficient or that the behavior problems have affected social status. (5) A medical screen-ing or evaluation should be performed to rule out health factors that may cause or contribute to behavior problems.

4. The first decision is whether the student is eligible for special education services for behavioral disabilities. This decision is based on the student's needs, as identified in the assessment process. The identification of needs and the determination of eligibility lead to the development of goals to be accomplished by the educational program (in-cluding special education, regular education, and related services). After setting goals and determining what services will meet the student's needs, the next decision is in what educational settings (i.e., placements) these needs can best be met. Finally, the IEP committee should set criteria for determining when the student will no longer be in need of special education.

PROBE 15-5 Education and Treatment Provisions (p. 556)

1. Currently available options include the following:
   - *Regular classroom:* Standard educational program available to all students; preventative interventions carried out by regular education personnel with possible consultation by others.
   - *Resource room:* Specific academic remediation and social skill instruction.
   - *Self-contained classroom:* Highly structured program offer-ing full- or partial-day programming in academic, social, vocational, and self-help skill areas. Located in the school building, these classrooms offer the opportunity to provide mainstreaming experiences.
   - *Special day school:* Physically segregated setting in which students with disabilities are educated together. The availability of a team of professionals in such schools must be balanced against the extremely limited oppor-tunities for mainstreaming students.

- *Re-education school:* A special residential school in which students spend five days a week, returning home on weekends. Staff work with the parents, teachers in the child's community school, and other elements of the community, as well as the child.
- *Residential treatment program:* A comprehensive, multidisciplinary residential program in which the child receives around-the-clock supervision and services.
- *Correctional program:* The most restrictive placement in the juvenile justice system, for youths who have been adjudicated as delinquent and placed in a correctional facility. The nature of correctional programs varies tremendously from region to region, but in general, educational needs are secondary to security considerations. As a result, youths leave these programs with no more functional (i.e., personally useful or marketable) skills than they had when they entered, with the possible exception of gains in criminal skills and antisocial attitudes.

2. Placement recommendations should be similar to the following:
   a. Peter exhibits his problem behaviors across settings and to a marked extent. His behavior problems probably would not be tolerated in regular classroom settings; therefore the least restrictive placement is likely to be a self-contained special classroom.
   b. Sally is exhibiting behavior that her teacher considers intolerable. Because she is working far below grade level and exhibits disruptive behavior, she probably would benefit from instruction in a resource room for part of the day.
   c. Tim is having a problem in his Spanish class. Unless he is having similar difficulties in other classes, he and his Spanish teacher probably would benefit from intervention in that setting. Consultative assistance through a school specialist or a teacher assistance team is likely to be helpful.
   d. James's antisocial behavior involves both the school and the community. Intervention in only one setting is unlikely to be successful. Perhaps a program can be developed that meets his multiple needs through collaboration among such agencies as the school, juvenile court, child welfare, and mental health. Another alternative would be short-term residential placement, such as in a Re-ED school, which provides a therapeutic milieu in addition to close liaison with the home and community.
   e. Alice appears to be having serious problems in one academic subject. Although her motivation may be faltering, she apparently is not exhibiting problems sufficient to label her behaviorally disabled. She should receive assistance through the regular education program. Perhaps a teacher assistance team can help her algebra teacher design an effective remedial plan.

PROBE 15-6 Implications for Mainstreaming (p. 559)

1. The Regular Education Initiative is a set of proposals for restructuring the educational system to integrate all students with disabilities into the mainstream of American education. Implementation of the REI would mean that regular classroom teachers would have the primary responsibility for the education and classroom management of students with behavioral disabilities. Although the initiative is well-intentioned, the educational system, as presently structured and supported, is poorly prepared to cope with the challenges these students present to the educational mainstream. Extensive reform is needed to provide the supports required by these students and their teachers in order for both to profit from mainstream education. Until this is accomplished, the best approach seems to involve efforts to provide "best practice" services for these students. The optimal strategy at this point seems to involve integrated services that span all the relevant settings in which these children and youth are found.

PROBE 16-1 Definitions and Need for Programs (p. 567)

1. False
2. False
3. False
4. Any three of these: Spearman's theory of a general intellectual factor and specific factors; Guilford's Structure of Intellect model; Gardner's seven "frames of mind"; Sternberg's componential theory.
5. IQ score
6. True

PROBE 16-2 Characteristics of Children Who Are Gifted (p. 575)

1. False
2. Be highly independent (and/or enjoy intellectual pursuits)
3. Although you could make a case for *c,* the clearest example of a divergent-thinking problem is *a.*
4. Intelligence test scores and scores on measures of special ability tend to be positively correlated. *Within* the gifted range, however, because you are considering a restricted range of scores, the correlation tends to lessen.
5. a. general intellectual or verbal ability; b. leadership; c. creativity
6. False
7. d

PROBE 16-3 Identifying Children as Gifted (p. 581)

1. referral; screening; evaluation

2. *Referral:* observation of classroom performance; review of students' records, including test scores, awards, grades, anecdotal reports; completion of behavior checklists or rating scales.

   Screening (sometimes combined with the referral process): collection and review of easily obtainable information, e.g., by administering short screening tests; review of work samples; review of checklists, rating scales, or questionnaires.

   Evaluation: administration of a comprehensive measure of ability; auditions or review of portfolios or projects; administration of high-level achievement tests; analysis of case studies.

3. parent nomination

4. True

5. A poor item would be so general that it doesn't exclude many children, for example: "Is curious," or "Likes to read." It would be a poor item to identify gifted children because (1) it would tend to include more children than those likely to be identified as gifted; and (2) it would tend to reflect teacher's subjective impressions—some teachers might regard half their students as "curious," some might regard only one or two as "curious."

6. A better item would be highly specific and reflect a characteristic of giftedness, for example: "When given free time, the student chooses to read most of the time."

7. True

8. False

9. low test ceiling

10. False

PROBE 16-4 Educational Provisions for Children Who Are Gifted (p. 597)

1. unwillingness to persist to achieve goals; tendency toward purposelessness; lack of self-confidence; feelings of inferiority

2. Show support and respect for him. Ask his opinions and let him give input into his educational program. Encourage cooperation, not competition in the classroom. Praise him for even small improvements in academic performance.

3. True

4. True

5. society's lowered expectations for persons with disabilities; society's failure to recognize and make provisions for superior ability in the population that has disabilities

6. False

7. c; d; b; f; e

8. True

9. False

10. Education of gifted children in the regular classroom may meet the goal of normalization, but this goal is not appropriate for gifted children. They have a tendency to hide their abilities from peers and teachers so that they will be accepted.

11. True

12. False

13. Any three of the following: planning activities and finding methods and materials for advancement; independent study; cross-grade placement; directed readings; learning centers.

About the Editors and Contributors

WILLIAM H. BERDINE

William H. Berdine is an Associate Professor, Chairperson, and Director of Graduate Studies in the Department of Special Education at the University of Kentucky. He also coordinates the certification program for teachers of students classified with low incidence intellectual disabilities. He has taught classes for students with mental retardation in both elementary and secondary settings. Current areas of interest are the design and implementation of community-based education programs for those with moderate to severe intellectual disabilities.

A. EDWARD BLACKHURST

A. Edward Blackhurst is a Professor in the Department of Special Education at the University of Kentucky. He has taught students with mild mental retardation and was principal of a school for students with mental retardation. He is past president of the Association for Special Education Technology and the Teacher Education Division of the Council for Exceptional Children. He is the recipient of the latter organization's highest honor, the TED/Merrill Award for Excellence in Teacher Education. He was also instrumental in developing *Teaching Exceptional Children*, a journal for special education teachers. His current professional interests focus on applications of technology in special education.

HILDA R. CATON

Hilda R. Caton is a Professor in the Vision Impairment Program at the University of Louisville and Director of Braille Projects at the American Printing House for the Blind. She has also worked as a resource and itinerant teacher of students with visual impairments in elementary and secondary day school programs, as a special teacher of reading in a residential school for students with visual impairments, and as a vision consultant in a State Department of Education. Her current areas of interest are research and curriculum development for people who are blind and development of assessment instruments for those with visual impairments.

PATRICIA THOMAS CEGELKA

Patricia Thomas Cegelka is a Professor and past Chairperson of the Department of Special Education at San Diego State University and has been involved in the preparation of special education personnel for over two decades. Prior to that, she was a teacher of secondary special education, a methods and materials consultant for children with learning disabilities, and a school psychologist. Her areas of professional interest, in addition to transition programs, include career and vocational education, bilingual and multicultural special education, secondary special education, personnel development, mental retardation, and learning disabilities.

BARBARA K. CULATTA

Barbara K. Culatta is a Professor at the University of Rhode Island. She has developed several language intervention programs. Her primary research interest is the relationship between perceptual and linguistic deficits in children with language impairments.

RICHARD CULATTA

Richard Culatta is a Professor of Communication Disorders in the Department of Language, Reading, and Exceptionalities at Appalachian State University. Current areas of interest are disfluency in children and adults and clinical supervision. He has worked as a speech-language pathologist in public schools, hospitals, rehabilitation centers, and university clinics.

DONALD P. CROSS

Donald P. Cross is an Associate Professor in the Department of Special Education at the University of Kentucky and Director of the Educational Assessment Clinic operated by the Department of Special Education at the University of Kentucky. He is a member of the Division for Physically Handicapped, the Division for Learning Disabilities, the Technology and Media Division, and the Teacher Education Division of the Council for Exceptional Children. He is also past president of the Kentucky Federation of the Council for Exceptional Children.

JOSEPH E. FISCHGRUND

Joseph E. Fischgrund is Headmaster of the Pennsylvania School for the Deaf in Philadelphia, Pennsylvania, a school widely recognized for its innovative and progressive educational practices. His special areas of interest are linguistics and language acquisition and the education of children from multicultural environments who are deaf.

DAVID L. GAST

David L. Gast is a Professor in the Department of Special Education and Coordinator of Graduate Studies in Special Education at the University of Georgia. Current areas of interest include designing databased instructional programs and studying instructional methods for students with severe developmental disabilities.

WILLIAM W. GREEN

William W. Green is a Professor of Otolaryngology, Neurology, and Special Education, and is also Director of the Communicative Disorders Program at the University of Kentucky Medical Center. Current areas of interest include audiological evaluation of infants, vestibular and balance disorders, cochlear implants, noise induced hearing loss, and environmental hearing conservation.

GARY GREENE

Gary Greene is a lecturer in special education in the College of Education at California State University–Long Beach. He is the coordinator of the Special Education Department and the graduate transition services training program in the Occupational Studies Department in the College of Health and Human Services. His background includes ten years of special education teaching experience in the public schools, where he worked as a resource specialist. His research interests are in the area of vocational special needs mnemonic instruction of students with disabilities, and mathematics education.

JAMES A. McLOUGHLIN

James A. McLoughlin is a Professor in the Department of Exceptional and Remedial Education at the University of Louisville. He is a board member for a variety of parent organizations and is an author of many articles on the topic of families of children with disabilities.

CATHERINE V. MORSINK

Catherine V. Morsink is Dean of the College of Education at Slippery Rock University of Pennsylvania. Her professional experience includes teaching special classes for children with learning and mental disabilities and a regular class in which students with learning disabilities were mainstreamed.

C. MICHAEL NELSON

C. Michael Nelson is a Professor and Coordinator of the Special Education Leadership Training Program at the University of Kentucky. He is past president of the Council for Children with Behavior Disorders and has written extensively on interventions with children's behavioral disabilities. His current interests include juvenile offenders with disabilities and interagency services for children and youth with emotional and behavioral disabilities.

EDWINA D. PENDARVIS

Edwina D. Pendarvis is a Professor and Coordinator of the certification program for teachers of gifted children at Marshall University in Huntington, West Virginia. She has teaching experience in regular elementary and secondary classrooms and in a resource room serving gifted children in kindergarten through junior high school.

JOHN W. SCHUSTER

John W. Schuster is an Associate Professor in the Department of Special Education and Coordinator of Programs in Severe and Profound Disabilities at the University of Kentucky. Current areas of interest include single subject research, instructional effectiveness and efficiency, and personnel preparation. He has teaching experience with secondary students and adults with moderate to profound intellectual disabilities.

DEBORAH BOTT SLATON

Deborah Bott Slaton is an Associate Professor in the Department of Special Education at the University of Kentucky, where she coordinates the program to certify teachers in the area of Learning and Behavior Disorders. Her professional experience includes teaching special classes for children and adolescents with learning disabilities.

MARK WOLERY

Mark Wolery is a Senior Research Scientist in the Early Childhood Intervention Program of Allegheny-Singer Research Institute and a Professor of Psychiatry at the Medical College of Pennsylvania. He has been a teacher and teacher supervisor in programs serving infants, toddlers, and preschoolers with disabilities. He is currently the editor of *Topics in Early Childhood Special Education*. His current research interests are instruction of young children with disabilities and preschool mainstreaming.

References

AARON, P. G., PHILLIPS, S., & LARSEN, S. (1988). Specific reading disability in historically famous persons. *Journal of Learning Disabilities*, *21*(9), 523–538.

ABBOTT, D. A., & MEREDITH, W. H. (1986). Strengths of parents with retarded children. *Family Relations*, *35*, 371–375.

ABESON, A., & BALLARD, J. (1976). State and federal policy for exceptional children. In F. J. Weintraub, A. Abeson, J. Ballard, & M. L. Lavor (Eds.), *Public policy and the education of exceptional children* (pp. 83–85). Reston, VA: Council for Exceptional Children.

ABESON, A., BOLICK, N., & HAFF, J. (1976). *A primer on due process: Education decisions for handicapped children*. Reston, VA: Council for Exceptional Children.

ABROMS, K. K., & BENNETT, J. W. (1980). Current genetic and demographic findings in Down syndrome: How are they presented in college textbooks on exceptionality? *Mental Retardation*, *18*, 101–107.

ACCOULOUMRE, D., & CALDWELL, T. (1991). Neurological conditions: Traumatic brain injury. In T. Caldwell, B. Sirvis, A. Todaro, & D. Accouloumre (Eds.), *Special health care in the school* (pp. 5–13). Reston, VA: Council for Exceptional Children.

ACTIVISION (1988). The manhole [Computer game on CD-ROM]. Menlo Park, CA: Author.

ACTIVISION (1989). Cosmic osmo [Computer game on CD-ROM]. Menlo Park, CA: Author.

ADAMS, J. (1973). Adaptive behavior and measured intelligence in the classification of mental retardation. *American Journal of Mental Deficiency*, *78*, 77–81.

Adaptive Device Locator System (1992). User's manual. Lexington, KY: Academic Software, Inc.

ADELMAN, H. S. (1989). Beyond the learning mystique: An interactional perspective on learning disabilities. *Journal of Learning Disabilities*, *22*(5), 301–304, 328.

ADES, H. W. (1959). Central auditory mechanisms. In J. Field, H. W. Magoun, & V. E. Hall (Eds.), *Handbook of physiology* (Vol. 1). Washington, DC: American Psychology Society.

AFFLECK, J. Q., EDGAR, E., LEVINE, P., & KORTERING, L. (1990). Postschool status of students classified as mildly mentally retarded, learning disabled, or nonhandicapped: Does it get better with time? *Education and Training in Mental Retardation*, *25*(4), 315–324.

AFFLECK, G., McGRADE, B. J., McQUEENEY, M., & ALLEN, D. (1982). Relationship-focused early intervention in development disabilities. *Exceptional Children*, *49*, 259–260.

AKERLEY, M. (1984). Developmental changes in families with autistic children. In E. Schopler & G. B. Mesibov (Eds.), *The effects of autism on the family*. New York: Plenum.

ALBER, M. B. (Ed.) (1978). *Listening: A curriculum guide for teachers of visually impaired students*. Springfield, IL: Specialized Educational Services Department, Materials Development and Dissemination Section, State Board of Education.

ALBERTO, P. A., & TROUTMAN, A. C. (1990). *Applied behavior analysis for teachers* (3rd ed.). Columbus, OH: Merrill.

ALEXANDER, P., & SKINNER, M. (1980). The effects of early entrance on subsequent social and academic development: A follow-up study. *Journal for the Education of the Gifted*, *3*(3), 147–150.

ALGOZZINE, B., & YSSELDYKE, J. E. (1987). Questioning discrepancies: Retaking the first step 20 years later. *Learning Disability Quarterly*, *10*(4), 301–312.

ALIG-CYBRIWSKY, C. A., WOLERY, M., & GAST, D. L. (1990). Use of a constant time delay procedure in teaching preschoolers in a group format. *Journal of Early Intervention*, *14*, 99–116.

ALLEN, D. A., & AFFLECK, G. (1985). Are we stereotyping parents? A postscript to Blancher. *Mental Retardation*, *23*(4), 200–202.

ALLEN, D. A., & HUDD, S. S. (1987). Are we professionalizing parents? Weighing the benefits and pitfalls. *Mental Retardation*, *25*(3), 133–139.

ALLEN, J. H. (1963). *May's diseases of the eye* (23rd ed.). Baltimore: Williams & Wilkins.

ALLEN, R. M., & JEFFERSON, T. W. (1962). *Psychological evaluation of the cerebral palsied person: Intellectual, personal and vocational applications*. Springfield, IL: Thomas.

ALLEY, G. R., DESHLER, D. D., CLARK, F. L., SCHUMAKER, J. D., & WARNER, M. M. (1983). Learning disabilities in adolescent and adult populations: Research implications (Part II). *Focus on Exceptional Children*, *15* (9), 1–14.

ALPERN, G., BOLL, T., & SHEARER, M. (1980). *The developmental profile II*. Aspen, CO: Psychological Development Publications.

America 2000: An educational strategy. (1991). Washington, DC: U.S. Government Printing Office.

AMERICAN FOUNDATION FOR THE BLIND (1957). *Itinerant teaching services for blind children*. New York: Author.

AMERICAN FOUNDATION FOR THE BLIND (1961). *A teacher education for those who serve blind children and youth*. New York: Author.

AMERICAN NATIONAL STANDARDS INSTITUTE (1986). *American national standards for buildings and facilities: Providing accessibility and usability for physically handicapped people* (ANSI A117.l-1986). New York: Author.

AMERICAN PRINTING HOUSE FOR THE BLIND (1981). *English braille American edition, 1959*. Louisville, KY: Author.

AMERICAN PRINTING HOUSE FOR THE BLIND (1990). *Distribution of federal quota based on the January 1, 1990 registration of eligible students*. Louisville, KY: Author.

AMERICAN PSYCHIATRIC ASSOCIATION (1987). *Diagnostic and statistical manual of mental disorders: III-Revised*. Washington, DC: Author.

AMERICAN SPEECH-LANGUAGE-HEARING ASSOCIATION (ASHA) (1985). *Assistive Listening Devices and Systems*. Rockville, MD: Author.

AMERICAN SPEECH-LANGUAGE-HEARING ASSOCIATION (ASHA) (1991). Fact sheet on communications disorders. Rockville, MD: Author.

ANDEREGG, M. L., & VERGASON, G. A. (1989). An analysis of one of the cornerstones of the Regular Education Initiative. *Focus on Exceptional Children*. *20*(8), 1–7.

ANDERSEN, P. E., & HAUGE, M. (1989). Osteogenesis imperfecta: A genetic, radiological, and epidemiological study. *Clinical Genetics*, *36*(4), 250–255.

ANDERSEN, R. D., BALE, J. F., JR., BLACKMAN, J. A., & MURPH, J. R. (1986). *Infections in children: A source book for educators and child care providers*. Rockville, MD: Aspen.

ANDERSON, L. T., & HERMANN, L. (1975, December). *Lesch-Nyhan disease: A specific learning disability*. Paper presented at the ninth annual convention of the Association for the Advancement of Behavior Therapy, San Francisco.

ANDERSON, M. A. (1985). Cooperative group tasks and their relationship to peer acceptance and cooperation. *Journal of Learning Disabilities, 18,* 83–86.

APPLE COMPUTER, INC. (1990). *Apple computer resources in special education and rehabilitation.* Allen, TX: DLM Teaching Resources.

APPLE COMPUTER, INC. (1990). *Solutions* [Computer program]. Cupertino, CA: Author.

APPLE COMPUTER, INC. (1990). *Visual almanac: An interactive multimedia kit.* San Francisco: Apple Multimedia Lab.

ARMSTRONG v. KLINE, 476 F. Supp. 590–92, 600 (1979).

ARNOLD, W. R., & BRUNGARDT, T. M. (1983). *Juvenile misconduct and delinquency.* Boston: Houghton Mifflin.

ARTER, A., & JENKINS, J. R. (1977). Examining the benefits and prevalence of modality considerations in special education. *Journal of Special Education, 11,* 281–298.

ASCHNER, M. J., & BISH, C. E. (Eds.) (1965). *Productive thinking in education.* Washington, DC: National Education Association.

ASHBAUGH, J., & NERNEY, T. (1990). Costs of providing residential and related support services to individuals with mental retardation. *Mental Retardation, 28,* 269–273.

ASHCROFT, S. C. (1963). Blind and partially seeing children. In L. M. Dunn (Ed.), *Exceptional children in the schools.* New York: Holt, Rinehart & Winston.

ASHCROFT, S. C., & BOURGEOIS, M. S. (1980). Recent technological developments for the visually impaired: State of the art. *Journal of Special Education Technology, 3*(2), 5–10.

ASSOCIATION FOR CHILDREN AND ADULTS WITH LEARNING DISABILITIES (ACLD) (1982). Vocational committee survey. *ACLD Newsbriefs, 145,* 21.

ATKINS, D. (Ed.) (1987). Families and their hearing impaired children. *Volta Review, 89*(5).

BACA, L. (September, 1990). *Theory and practice in bilingual/cross-cultural special education: Major issues and implications for research, practice, and policy.* Washington, DC: U.S. Government Printing Office.

BACA, L., & ALMANZA, E. (1991). *Language minority students with disabilities.* Reston, VA: Council for Exceptional Children.

BACA, L., & CERVANTES, H. (1989). *The bilingual special education interface.* Columbus, OH: Merrill.

BACA, L., & CHINN, P. C. (1982). Coming to grips with cultural diversity. *Exceptional Education Quarterly, 2*(4), 33–45.

BAER, D. M. (1981). A hung jury and a Scottish verdict: "Not proven." *Analysis and Intervention in Developmental Disabilities, 1*(1), 91–97.

BAGNATO, S. J., NEISWORTH, J. T., & MUNSON, S. M. (1989). *Linking developmental assessment and early intervention: Curriculum-based prescriptions.* Rockville, MD: Aspen.

BAILEY, D. B. (1988a). Assessing family stress and needs. In D. B. Bailey & R. J. Simeonsson (Eds.), *Family assessment in early intervention* (pp. 95–118). Columbus, OH: Merrill.

BAILEY, D. B. (1988b). Assessing critical events. In D. B. Bailey & R. J. Simeonsson (Eds.), *Family assessment in early intervention* (pp. 119–138). Columbus, OH: Merrill.

BAILEY D. B., & McWILLIAM, R. A. (1990). Normalizing early intervention. *Topics in Early Childhood Special Education, 10*(2), 33–47.

BAILEY, D. B., PALSHA, S. A., & SIMEONSSON, R. J. (1991). Professional skills, concerns, and perceived importance of work with families in early intervention. *Exceptional Children, 58,* 156–165.

BAILEY, D. B., & SIMEONSSON, R. J. (Eds.) (1988a). *Family assessment in early intervention.* Columbus, OH: Merrill.

BAILEY, D. B., & SIMEONSSON, R. J. (1988b). Home-based early intervention. In S. L. Odom & M. B. Karnes (Eds.), *Early intervention for infants and children with handicaps: An empirical base* (pp. 199–215). Baltimore: Paul H. Brookes.

BAILEY, D. B., SIMEONSSON, R. J., ISBELL, P., HUNTINGTON, G. S., WINTON, P. J., COMFORT, M., & HELM, J. (1988). Inservice training in family assessment and goal-setting for early interventionists:

Outcomes and issues. *Journal of the Division for Early Childhood, 12*(2), 126–137.

BAILEY, D. B., SIMEONSSON, R. J., YODER, D. E., & HUNTINGTON, G. S. (1990). Preparing professionals to serve infants and toddlers with handicaps and their families: An integrative analysis across eight disciplines. *Exceptional Children, 57,* 26–35.

BAILEY, D. B., & WOLERY, M. (1984). *Teaching infants and preschoolers with handicaps.* Columbus, OH: Merrill.

BAILEY, D. B., & WOLERY, M. (1989). *Assessing infants and preschoolers with handicaps.* Columbus, OH: Merrill.

BAILEY, D. B., & WOLERY, M. (1992). *Teaching infants and preschoolers with disabilities* (2nd ed.). New York: Macmillan.

BAILEY, J. S. (1981). Wanted: A rational search for the limiting conditions of habilitation in the retarded. *Analysis and Intervention in Developmental Disabilities, 1*(1), 45–52.

BAIRD, P. A., & SADOVNICK, A. D. (1985). Mental retardation in over half a million consecutive livebirths: An epidemiological study. *American Journal of Mental Deficiency, 89,* 323–330.

BAKER, A., & BAKER, J. (1990). *Mathematics in process.* Portsmouth, NH: Heinemann.

BAKER, B. L., & BRIGHTMAN, A. J. (1989). *Steps to independence* (2nd Ed.). Baltimore: Paul H. Brookes.

BALDWIN, A. Y., GEAR, G. H., & LUCITO, L. J. (Eds.) (1978). *Educational planning for the gifted overcoming cultural, geographic, and socioeconomic barriers.* Reston, VA: Council for Exceptional Children.

BALLER, W. R. (1936). A study of the present social status of a group of adults, who, when they were in elementary school, were classified as mentally deficient. *Genetic Psychology Monographs, 18,* 165–244.

BALLER, W. R. (1939). A study of the behavior records of adults, who, when they were in school, were judged to be dull in mental ability. *Journal of Genetic Psychology, 55,* 365–379.

BALLER, W. R., CHARLES, D. C., & MILLER, E. L. (1966). *Mid-life attainment of the mentally retarded: A longitudinal study.* Lincoln, NE: University of Nebraska.

BANDURA, A. (1973). *Aggression: A social learning analysis.* Englewood Cliffs, NJ: Prentice-Hall.

BARBER, P. A., TURNBULL, A. P., BEHR, S. K., & KERNS, G. M. (1988). A family systems perspective on early childhood special education. In S. L. Odom & M. B. Karnes (Eds.), *Early intervention for infants and children with handicaps: An empirical base* (pp. 179–198). Baltimore: Paul H. Brookes.

BARNARD, K. E., & KELLY, J. F. (1990). Assessment of parent-child interaction. In S. J. Meisels & J. P. Shonkoff (Eds.), *Handbook of early childhood intervention* (pp. 278–302). Cambridge, U.K.: Cambridge University Press.

BARNES, K. (1982). Life with our charming teenagers. *Exceptional Parent, 12,* 37–39.

BARNETT, W. S., ESCOBAR, C. M., & RAVSTEN, M. T. (1988). Parent and clinic early intervention for children with language handicaps: A cost-effectiveness analysis. *Journal of the Division for Early Childhood, 12*(4), 290–298.

BARR, C. C. (1990). Retinopathy of prematurity. *VIPS Newsletter, 6*(2), 6–7.

BARRAGA, N. C. (1964). *Increased visual behavior in low vision children.* New York: American Foundation for the Blind.

BARRAGA, N. C. (1980). *Program to develop efficiency in visual functioning.* Louisville, KY: American Printing House for the Blind.

BARRAGA, N. C. (1986). Sensory perceptual development. In G. T. Scholl (Ed.), *Foundations of education for blind and visually handicapped children and youth: Theory and practice* (pp. 83–98). New York: American Foundation for the Blind.

BARSTOW, D. (1981). The Talcott Mountain Science Center. In J. N. Nazzaro (Ed.), *Computer connections for gifted children and youth.* Reston, VA: Clearinghouse on Handicapped and Gifted Children.

BASHIR, A. (1989). Language intervention and the curriculum. *Seminars in Speech and Language, 3,* 181–191.

BATEMAN, B. (1963). *Reading and psycholinguistic processes of partially seeing children.* (CEC Research Monograph, Series A, No. 5.) Arlington, VA: Council for Exceptional Children.

BATEMAN, B. (1964). The modifiability of sighted adults' perceptions of blind children's abilities. *New Outlook for the Blind, 13,* 101–106.

BATES, P., RENZAGLIA, A., & WEHMAN, P. (1989). Characteristics of an appropriate education for severely handicapped students. *Education and Training of the Mental Retarded, 16,* 142–159.

BATSHAW, M. L., & PERRET, Y. M. (1986). *Children with handicaps: A medical primer.* Baltimore: Paul H. Brookes.

BAUMAN, M. K. (1977). Group differences disclosed by inventory items. *International Journal for the Education of the Blind, 13,* 101–106.

BAUMEISTER, A. A. (1979). *Processing of information in iconic memory: Differences between normal and retarded subjects.* Unpublished manuscript, George Peabody College of Vanderbilt University, Nashville, TN.

BAUMEISTER, A. A., & HAMLETT, C. L. (1986). A national survey of state-sponsored programs to prevent fetal alcohol syndrome. *Mental Retardation, 24,* 169–173.

BAUMGART, D., BROWN, L., PUMPIAN, I., NISBET, J., FORD, A., SWEET, M., MESSINA, R., & SCROEDER, J. (1982). Principle of partial participation and individualized adaptations in educational programs for severely handicapped students. *Journal of the Association for the Severely Handicapped, 7*(2), 17–27.

BAVELAS, A. (1984). Leadership: Man and function. In W. E. Rosenbach & R. L. Taylor (Eds.), *Contemporary issues in leadership* (pp. 117–123). Boulder, CO: Westview Press.

BAYLEY, N. (1969). *Bayley scales of infant development:* New York: Psychological Corporation.

BEASON, E. (1982). *Vocational education for the handicapped: Perspectives on certification.* Personnel Development Series: Document 3. ERIC Document Reproduction Services No. ED 224952.

BECKER, B. J. (1989). Sex equity intervention programs which work. *School Science and Mathematics, 87*(3), 223–232.

BECKER, M., WARR-LEEPER, G.A., & LEEPER, H.A. (1990). Fetal alcohol syndrome: A description of oral motor, articulatory, short-term memory, grammatical, and semantic abilities. *Journal of Communication Disorders, 23,* 97–124.

BECKER, W. C. (1986). *Applied psychology for teachers* (rev. ed.). Chicago: Science Research Associates.

BECKER, W. C., & CARNINE, D. W. (1980). Direct instruction: An effective approach to educational intervention with disadvantaged and low performers. In B. B. Lahey & A. E. Kazdin (Eds.), *Advances in clinical child psychology* (Vol. 3). New York: Plenum.

BECKER, W. C., & CARNINE, D. W. (1981). Direct instruction: A behavior theory model for comprehensive educational intervention with the disadvantaged. In S. W. Bijou & R. Ruiz (Eds.), *Behavior modification: Contributions to education.* Hillsdale, NJ: Lawrence Erlbaum Associates.

BECKER, W. C., ENGLEMANN, S., & THOMAS, D. R. (1975). *Teaching 2: Cognitive learning and instruction.* Chicago: Science Research Associates.

BEECH, M. C. (1983). Simplifying text for mainstreamed students. *Journal of Learning Disabilities, 16,* 400–402.

BEGAB, M. J. (1974). The major dilemma of mental retardation: Shall we prevent it? (Some implications of research in mental retardation). *American Journal of Mental Deficiency, 78,* 519–529.

BEHRMANN, M. M. (1984a). Babies and robots: Technology to assist learning of young multiply disabled children. *Rehabilitation Literature, 45*(7), 194–201.

BEHRMANN, M. M. (1984b). *Microcomputers in special education.* Boston: College-Hill.

BELCASTRO, F. P. (1987). Elementary pull-out program for the intellectually gifted—boon or bane? *Roper Review, 9*(4), 22–32.

BELLAMY, G. T., ROSE, H., WILSON, D. J., & CLARKE, J. Y. (1982). Strategies for vocational preparation. In B. Wilcox & G. T. Bellamy (Eds.), *Design of high school programs for severely handicapped students* (pp. 139–152). Baltimore: Paul H. Brookes.

BELLAMY, T. (1987, April). Office of Special Education Programs and long-range plans: Least restrictive environment, early childhood, transition. Paper presented at the convention of the International Council for Exceptional Children, Chicago.

BELMONT, J. M., & BUTTERFIELD, E. C. (1971). Learning strategies as determinants of memory deficiencies. *Cognitive Psychology, 2,* 411–420.

BENDER, E., SCHUMACHER, B., & ALLEN, H. H. (1976). *A resource manual for medical aspects of disabilities.* Carbondale, IL: Rehabilitation Counselor Training Program, Rehabilitation Institute, Southern Illinois University.

BENEDICT, M. I., WHITE, R. B., WULFF, L. M., & HALL, B. J. (1990). Reported maltreatment in children with multiple disabilities. *Child Abuse and Neglect: The International Journal, 14*(2), 207–217.

BENNETT, R. E. (1987). *Planning and evaluating computer education programs.* Columbus, OH: Merrill.

BERDINE, W. H., & MEYER, S. A. (1987). *Assessment in special education.* Boston: Little Brown.

BERG, B. O. (1982). Convulsive disorders. In E. E. Bleck & D. A. Nagel (Eds.), *Physically handicapped children: A medical atlas for teachers* (pp. 171–181). New York: Grune & Stratton.

BERGEN, A. F., PRESPERIN, J., & TALLMAN, T. (1990). *Positioning for function: Wheelchairs and other assistive technologies.* Valhalla, NY: Valhalla Rehabilitation Publications.

BERGER, K. W. (1972). *Speechreading: Principles and methods.* Baltimore: National Education Press.

BERKMAN, K. A., & MEYER, L. H. (1988). Alternative strategies and multiple outcomes in the remediation of severe self-injury: Going "all out" nonaversively. *Journal of the Association for Persons with Severe Handicaps, 13,* 76–86.

BERLIN, C. M., JR. (1978). Biology and retardation. In J. T. Neisworth & R. M. Smith (Eds.), *Retardation: Issues assessment and intervention* (pp. 117–137). New York: McGraw-Hill.

BERNSTEIN, D., & TIEGERMAN, E. (1989). *Language and communication disorders in children.* Columbus, OH: Merrill.

BERNSTEIN, M. E., & BARTA, L. (1988). What do parents want in parent education? *American Annals of the Deaf, 133,* 235–246.

BERRUECOS, M. P. (1991). The development of language skills. In D. Hicks & E. Stuckless (Eds.), *1990 International Congress of Education of the Deaf: Proceedings II: Topical addresses.* Rochester, NY: National Technical Institute for the Deaf, Rochester Institute of Technology.

BESSANT-BYRD, H. (1981). Competencies for educating culturally different exceptional children. In J. N. Nazzaro (Ed.), *Culturally different exceptional children in school.* Reston, VA: ERIC Clearinghouse on Handicapped and Gifted Children.

BEST, S., CARPIGNANO, J., SIRVIS, B., & BIGGE, J. (1991). Psychosocial aspects of physical disability. In J. L. Bigge (Ed.), *Teaching individuals with physical and multiple disabilities* (3rd Ed.). New York: Macmillan.

BETTELHEIM, B. (1950). *Love is not enough.* New York: Macmillan.

BETTELHEIM, B. (1967). *The empty fortress.* New York: Free Press.

BICKEL, W. E., & BICKEL D. (1986). Effective schools, classrooms, and instruction: Implications for special education. *Exceptional Children 52*(6), 489–500.

BIGGE, J. L. (1991). *Teaching individuals with physical and multiple disabilities* (3rd ed.). New York: Macmillan.

BIGLER, E. D. (1987). Acquired cerebral trauma: An introduction to the special series. *Journal of Learning Disabilities, 20*(8), 454–457.

BIJOU, S. W. (1966). A functional analysis of retarded development. In N. R. Ellis (Ed.), *International review of research in mental retardation,* (Vol. 1, pp. 1–19). New York: Academic Press.

BIJOU, S. W. (1981). The prevention of retarded development in disadvantaged children. In M. S. Begab, H. C. Haywood, & H. L. Garber

(Eds.), *Psychosocial influences on retarded performance*. Baltimore: University Park Press.

BIJOU, S. W., & BAER, D. M. (1961). *Child development: A systematic and empirical theory* (Vol 1). Englewood Cliffs, NJ: Prentice-Hall.

BIJOU, S. W., & BAER, D. M. (1965). *Child development: Universal stage of infancy* (Vol. 2). Englewood Cliffs, NJ: Prentice-Hall.

BIJOU, S. W., & BAER, D. M. (1978). *Behavior analysis of child development*. Englewood Cliffs, NJ: Prentice-Hall.

BINKARD, B. (1985, Fall). A successful handicap awareness program—Run by special parents. *Teaching Exceptional Children, 18,* 12–16.

BIRCH, H., RICHARDSON, S., BAIRD, D., HOROBIN, G., & ILLSLEY, R. (1970). *Mental subnormality in the community: A clinical and epidemiological study*. Baltimore: Williams & Wilkins.

BIRCH, J. W. (1974). *Mainstreaming: Educable mentally retarded children in regular classes*. Reston, VA: Council for Exceptional Children.

BIRCH, J. W., & REYNOLDS, M. C. (1982). Special education as a profession. *Exceptional Education Quarterly, 2*(4), 1–13.

BIRCH, J. W., TISDALL, W., PEABODY, R., & STERRETT, R. (1966). *School achievement and effect of type size on reading in visually handicapped children* (Cooperative Research Project No. 1766. Contract No. OEC-3-10-028). Pittsburgh: University of Pittsburgh.

BISHOP, J. E. (1982, January 29). Gene defect linked to retarded males may solve mysteries. Does fragile X chromosome account for many cases of hereditary condition? *Wall Street Journal*, pp. 18, 19.

BLACHER, J., & BROMLEY, B. (1987). Attachment and responsibility in children with severe handicaps: Mother and teacher comparison. *Child Study Journal, 17*(2), 121–131.

BLACKARD, M., & BARSH, E. (1982). Changing community attitudes. *Exceptional Parent, 12,* 43–46.

BLACKHURST, A. E. (1977). Competency-based special education personnel preparation. In R. D. Kneedler & S. G. Tarver (Eds.), *Changing perspectives in special education*. Columbus, OH: Merrill.

BLACKHURST, A. E., & MacARTHUR, C. A. (1986). Microcomputer use in special education personnel preparation programs. *Teacher Education and Special Education, 9,* 27–36.

BLACKHURST, A. E., MacARTHUR, C. A., & BYROM, E. (1988). Microcomputing comptencies for special education professors. *Teacher Education and Special Education, 10,* 153–160.

BLACKHURST, A. E., McLOUGHLIN, J. A., & PRICE, L. M. (1977). Issues in the development of programs to prepare teachers of children with learning and behavior disorders. *Behavior Disorders, 2,* 157–168.

BLACKSHEAR, P. B., SULLIVAN, A. R., EWELL, Y., & ROGERS, K. (1980). *Black and gifted children*. Reston, VA: ERIC Clearinghouse on Handicapped and Gifted Children.

BLACKSTONE, S. W. (Ed.) (1986). *Augmentative communication: An introduction*. Rockville, MD: American Speech-Language-Hearing Association.

BLACKWELL, P., ENGEN, E., FISCHGRUND, J. E., & ZARCA-DOOLAS, C. (1978). *Sentences and other systems: A language and learning curriculum for hearing impaired learners*. Washington, DC: A. G. Bell Association of the Deaf.

BLATT, B., & KAPLAN, F. (1966). *Christmas in purgatory*. Boston: Allyn & Bacon.

BLATT, B., OZOLINS, A. & McNALLY, J. (1979). *The family papers: A return to purgatory*. New York: Longman.

BLECHMAN, E. A. (1985). *Solving child behavior problems at home and at school*. Champaign, IL: Research Press.

BLECK, E. E. (1982a). Anatomy—Basic parts and terms of the nervous and musculo-skeletal systems. In E. E. Bleck & D. A. Nagel (Eds.), *Physically handicapped children: A medical atlas for teachers* (pp. 1–16). New York: Grune & Stratton.

BLECK, E. E. (1982b). Cerebral palsy. In E. E. Bleck & D. A. Nagel (Eds.), *Physically handicapped children: A medical atlas for teachers* (pp. 59–132). New York: Grune & Stratton.

BLECK, E. E. (1982c). Myelomeningocele, meningocele, spina bifida. In E. E. Bleck & D. A. Nagel (Eds.), *Physically handicapped children: A medical atlas for teachers* (pp. 345–362). New York: Grune & Stratton.

BLECK, E. E. (1982d). Nonoral communication. In E. E. Bleck & D. A. Nagel (Eds.), *Physically handicapped children: A medical atlas for teachers* (pp. 145–169). New York: Grune & Stratton.

BLOM, E. P., SINGER, M. I., & HIAMAKER, R. C. (1986). A prospective study of tracheoesophageal speech. *Archives of Otolaryngology, Head & Neck Surgery, 112,* 440–447.

BLOODSTEIN, O. (1987). *A handbook on stuttering*. Chicago: National Easter Seal Society.

BLOOM, B. S. (1976). *Human characteristics and social learning*. New York: McGraw-Hill.

BLOOM, B. S. (1982). The role of gifts and markers in the development of talent. *Exceptional Children, 48*(6), 510–522.

BLUTH, L. F. (1985). *Transporting handicapped students: A resource manual and recommended guidelines for school transportation and special education personnel*. Washington, DC: National Association of State Directors of Special Education, Inc.

BODNER-JOHNSON, B. (1986). Family environment and achievement of deaf students. *Exceptional Children, 52,* 443–449.

BOGNAR, C. J., & MARTIN, B. W. (1982). A sociological perspective on diagnosing learning difficulties. *Journal of Learning Disabilities, 15,* 347–351.

BOLTON, S., & WILLIAMSON, K. S. (1989). *One step at a time: A manual for families of children with hearing and vision impairments*. Monmouth, OR: TASH Technical Assistance Project.

BOURLAND, B., & HARBIN, G. (1987). *START resource packet: Child Find* (U.S. Department of Education, Grant No. G00-84C-3515). Chapel Hill, NC: Frank Porter Graham Child Development Center, University of North Carolina.

BOWER, E. M. (1982). Defining emotional disturbance: Public policy and research. *Psychology in the Schools, 19,* 55–60.

BOWERMAN, M. (1976). Semantic factors in the acquisition of rules for word use and sentence construction. In D. Morehead & A. Morehead (Eds.), *Directions in normal and deficient child language*. Baltimore: University Park Press.

BRAATEN, S. R., KAUFFMAN, J. M., BRAATEN, B., POLSGROVE, L., & NELSON, C. M. (1988). The Regular Education Initiative: Patent medicine for behavioral disorders. *Exceptional Children 55,* 21–27.

BRADDOCK, D., FUJIURI, G., HEMP, R., MITCHELL, D., & BACHELDER, L. (1991). Current and future trends in state-operated mental retardation institutions in the United States.

BRADFORD, D. S. (1987). Neuromuscular spinal deformity. In D. S. Bradford, J. E. Lonstein, J. H. Moe, J. W. Ogilvie, & R. B. Winter (Eds.), *Moe's textbook of scoliosis and other spinal deformities* (2nd ed.). Philadelphia: Saunders.

BRADLEY-JOHNSON, S. (1986). *Psychoeducational assessment of visually impaired and blind students: Infancy through high school*. Austin, TX: Pro-Ed.

BRADY, M. P., McDOUGALL, D., & DENNIS, H. F. (1989). The schools, the courts, and the integration of students with severe handicaps. *Journal of Special Education, 23,* 43–58.

BRADY, P. M., MANNI, J. L., & WINIKUR, D. W. (1983). Implications of ethnic disproportion in programs for the educable mentally retarded. *The Journal of Special Education, 17,* 295–302.

BRADY, S., & SHANKWEILER, D. (Eds.) (1991). *Phonological processes in literacy: A tribute to Isabelle Y. Liberman*. Hillsdale, NJ: Lawrence Erlbaum Associates.

BREDEKAMP, S. (Ed.) (1987). *Developmentally appropriate practice in early childhood programs serving children from birth through age 8*. Washington, DC: National Association for the Education of Young Children.

BREEN, C., HARING, T., PITTS-CONWAY, V., & GAYLORD-ROSS, R. (1984). The training and generalization of social interaction during breaktime at two job sites in the natural environment. In R. Gaylord-Ross, T. Haring, C. Breen, M. Lee, V. Pitts-Conway, & D.

Roger (Eds.), *The social development of handicapped students*. San Francisco: San Francisco State University.

BRICKER, D., BAILEY, E., GUMMERLOCK, S., BUHL, M., & SLENTZ, K. (1986). *Evaluation and programming system for infants and young children*. Eugene, OR: University of Oregon.

BRICKER, D., & CASUSO, V. (1979). Family involvement: A critical component of early intervention. *Exceptional Children, 46*, 108–117.

BRICKER, D., & CRIPE, J. J. W. (1992). *An activity-based approach to early intervention*. Baltimore: Paul H. Brookes.

BRICKER, D., & SQUIRES, J. (1989). Low cost system using parents to monitor the development of at-risk infants. *Journal of Early Intervention, 13*(1), 50–60.

BRICKER, D., & VELTMAN, M. (1990). Early intervention programs: Child focused approaches. In S. J. Meisels & J. P. Shonkoff (Eds.), *Handbook of early childhood intervention* (pp. 373–399). Cambridge, U.K.: Cambridge University Press.

BRIGANCE, A. H. (1978). *Inventory of early development*. North Billerica, MA: Curriculum Associates.

BRINCKERHOFF, J. L., & VINCENT, L. J. (1986). Increasing parental decision making at the individualized educational program meeting. *Journal of the Division for Early Childhood, 11*(1), 46–58.

BRINKER, R. (1985). Interaction between severely retarded students and other students in integrated and segregated public school settings. *American Journal on Mental Deficiency, 89*, 587–594.

BRINTON, B., & FUJIKI, M. (1989). *Conversational management with language-impaired children*. Rockville, MD: Aspen.

BRISTOL, M. M., & SCHOPLER, E. (1983). Stress and coping in families of autistic adolescents. In E. Schopler & G. B. Mesibov (Eds.), *Autism in adolescents and adults*. New York: Plenum.

BROLIN, D. E. (1973). Career education needs of secondary educable students. *Exceptional Children, 39*, 619–624.

BROLIN, D. E. (1978, 1983, 1988). *Life-centered approach to career education: A competency-based approach*. Reston, VA: Council for Exceptional Children.

BROLIN, D. E. (1982). *Vocational preparation of persons with handicaps* (2nd ed.). Columbus, OH: Merrill.

BRONFENBRENNER, U. (1979). *The ecology of human development*. Cambridge, MA: Harvard University Press.

BROPHY, J. E., & GOOD, T. L. (1986). Teacher behavior and student achievement. In M. C. Wittrock (Ed.), *Handbook of research on teaching* (3rd ed.) (pp. 328–375). New York: Macmillan.

BROWDER, D. (1991). *Assessment of individuals with severe handicaps*. Baltimore: Paul H. Brookes.

BROWN, F. (1991). Creative daily scheduling: A nonintrusive approach to challenging behaviors in community residences. *Journal of the Association for Persons with Severe Handicaps, 16*, 75–84.

BROWN, L., & HAMMILL, D. (1983). *Behavior rating profile*. Austin, TX: Pro-Ed.

BROWN, L., BRANSTON, M. B., HAMRE-NIETUPSKI, S., PUMPIAN, I., CERTO, N., & GRUENEWALD, L. (1979). A strategy for developing chronological age-appropriate and functional curricular content for severely handicapped adolescents and young adults. *Journal of Special Education, 13*, 81–90.

BROWN, L., FALVEY, M., PUMPIAN, I., BAUMGART, D., NISBET, J., FORD, A., SCHROEDER, J., & LOOMIS, R. (1980). *Curricular strategies for teaching severely handicapped functional skills in school and non-school environments*. Madison, WI: University of Wisconsin–Madison and Madison Metropolitan School District.

BROWN, L., FORD, A., NISBET, J., SWEET, M., DONNELLAN, A., & GRUENEWALD, L. (1983). Opportunities available when severely handicapped students attend chronological age-appropriate regular classrooms. *Journal of the Association for Persons with Severe Handicaps, 8*, 16–24.

BROWN, L., NIETUPSKI, J., & HAMRE-NIETUPSKI, S. (1976). The criterion of ultimate functioning and public school services for se-

verely handicapped children. In M. A. Thomas (Ed.), *Hey, don't forget about me!* Reston, VA: Council for Exceptional Children.

BROWN, L., NISBET, J., FORD, A., SWEET, M., SHIRAGA, B., YORK, J., & LOOMIS, R. (1983). The critical need for nonschool instruction in educational programs for severely handicapped students. *Journal of the Association for Persons with Severe Handicaps, 8*(3), 71–77.

BROWN, L., PUMPIAN, I., BAUMGART, D., VANDEVENTER, P., FORD, A., NISBET, J., SCHROEDER, J., & GRUNEWALD, L. (1981). Longitudinal transition plans in programs for severely handicapped students. *Exceptional Children, 47*, 624–630.

BROWN, L., SCHWARZ, P., UDVARI-SOLNER, A., KAMPSCHROER, E. F., JOHNSON, F., JORGENSEN, J., & GRUENEWALD, L. (1991). How much time should students with severe intellectual disabilities spend in regular education classrooms and elsewhere? *Journal of the Association for Persons with Severe Handicaps, 16*(1), 39–47.

BROWN, S., & DONOVAN, C. M. (1985). *Developmental programming for infants and young children*. Ann Arbor, MI: University of Michigan Press.

BROWN, V. B., RIDGELY, M. S., PEPPER, B., LEVINE, I. S., & RYGLEWICZ, H. (1989). The dual crisis: Mental illness and substance abuse. *American Psychologist, 44*, 565–569.

BROWN, W. T., JENKINS, E. C., COHEN, I. L., FISCH, G. S., WOLF-SCHEIN, E. G., GROSS, A., WATERHOUSE, L., FEIN, D., MASON-BROTHERS, A., RITVO, E., RUTTENBERG, B. A., BENTLEY, W., & CASTELLS, S. (1986). Fragile X and autism: A multicenter study. *American Journal of Medical Genetics, 23*, 341–352.

BROWN v. TOPEKA BOARD OF EDUCATION, 347 U.S. 483 (1954).

BROWNLEY, J. (1987). Quality education for all deaf children: An achievable goal. *American Annals of the Deaf, 135*(5), 340–343.

BROWNING, P., & IRVIN, L. K. (1981). Vocational evaluation, training and placement of mentally retarded persons. *Rehabilitation Counseling Bulletin, 25*, 374–409.

BROWNING, P., & WHITE, W. A. T. (1986). Teaching life enhancement skills with interactive video-based curricula. *Education and Training of the Mentally Retarded, 21*(4), 236–244.

BRUNER, J. S. (1964). The course of cognitive growth. *American Psychologist, 19*, 1–15.

BRUNKEN, P. (1984). Independence for the visually impaired through technology. *Education of the Visually Handicapped, 15*(4), 127–133.

BRUYERE, H. J., KARGAS, S. A., & LEVY, J. M. (1987). The causes and underlying developmental mechanism of congenital cardiovascular malformations: A critical review. *American Journal of Medical Genetics—Supplement, 3*, 411–431.

BRYAN, T., PEARL, R., ZIMMERMAN, D., AND MATTHEWS, F. (1982). Mothers' evaluations of their learning disabled children. *Journal of Special Education, 16*, 149–160.

BRYAN, T., BAY, M., & DONAHUE, M. (1988). Implications of the learning disabilities definition for the regular education initiative. *Journal of Learning Disabilities, 21*(1), 23–28.

BRYEN, D. N, & McGINLEY, N. (1991). Sign language input to community residents with mental retardation. *Education and Training in Mental Retardation, 26*, 207–213.

BUCKLEY, S. (1987). Attaining basic educational skills: Reading, writing, and numbers. In D. Lane & B. Statford (Eds.), *Current approaches to Down's syndrome* (pp. 315–343). East Sussex, Great Britain: Holt, Rinehart & Winston.

BUDOFF, M., & ORENSTEIN, A. (1982). *Due process in special education: On going to a hearing*. Cambridge, MA: Ware Press.

BURGDORF, R. L. (1980). *The legal rights of handicapped persons: Cases, materials and text*. Baltimore: Paul H. Brookes.

BURGDORF, R. L., & SPICER, P. P. (1983). *The legal rights of handicapped persons; Cases, materials and text* (1983 Supplement). Baltimore: Paul H. Brookes.

BURKETT, G., YASIN, S., & PALOW, D. (1990). Perinatal implication of cocaine exposure. *Journal of Reproductive Medicine, 35*(1), 35–42.

BURLEY, M. (1977). A parent's perspective of the future. In G. Kranz & P. Varian (Eds.), *The needs of multiple handicapped individuals: Proceedings of the Annual Spring Conference.* Columbus, OH: Madison Co. Board of Education.

BUTLER, K. (1984). Language processing: Halfway up the down staircase. In G. Wallach & K. Butler (Eds.), *Language learning disabilities in school-age children.* Baltimore: Williams & Wilkins.

BUTTERFIELD, E. C., WAMBOLD, C., & BELMONT, J. M. (1973). On the theory and practice of improving short-term memory. *American Journal on Mental Deficiency, 77*, 654–669.

BUYSSE, V., & BAILEY, D. B. (1991). *Mainstreaming versus specialized settings: Behavioral and developmental effects on young children with handicaps.* Manuscript submitted for publication.

CALDWELL, T., SIRVIS, B., TODARO, A., & ACCOULOUMRE, D. (1991). Pediatric HIV, AIDS and AIDS-related complex.. In T. Caldwell, B. Sirvis, A. Todaro, & D. Accouloumre (Eds.), *Special health care in the school* (pp. 14–21). Reston, VA: Council for Exceptional Children.

CALDWELL, T., TODARO, A., & GATES, A. (1989). *Community provider's guide: An information outline for working with children with special health needs.* New Orleans: Children's Hospital.

CALIFORNIA STATE DEPARTMENT OF EDUCATION (1987). *Definition of transition.* Sacramento: Author.

CALLAHAN, C. M. (1978). *Developing creativity in the gifted and talented.* Reston, VA: Council for Exceptional Children.

CALLAHAN, C. M. (1979). The gifted and talented woman. In A. H. Passow (Ed.), *The gifted and the talented: Their education and development.* The Seventy-eighth Yearbook of the National Society for the Study of Education, Part 1 (pp. 401–423). Chicago: University of Chicago Press.

CALLAHAN, C. M. (1983). Issues in evaluating programs for the gifted. *Gifted Child Quarterly, 27*(1), 3–7.

CAMPBELL, C., & CLEVENGER, B. (1987). Effective teaching for mildly handicapped learners. *Focus on Exceptional Children, 20*(2), 11–12.

CAMPBELL, P. H. (1987a). Physical management and handling procedures with students with motor dysfunction. In M. E. Snell (Ed.), *Systematic instruction of persons with severe handicaps* (pp. 174–187). Columbus, OH: Merrill.

CAMPBELL, P. H. (1987b). Programming for students with dysfunction in posture and movement. In M. E. Snell (Ed.), *Systematic instruction of persons with severe handicaps* (pp. 188–211). Columbus, OH: Merrill.

CANTER, L., & CANTER, M. (1982). *Assertive discipline for parents.* Santa Monica, CA: Canter & Associates.

CAPURSO, A. (1961). Music. In L. A. Fliegler (Ed.), *Curriculum planning for the gifted.* Englewood Cliffs, NJ: Prentice-Hall.

CAPUTE, A. (1985). Cerebral palsy and associated dysfunctions. In R. H. Haslam & P. J. Valletutti (Eds.), *Medical problems in the classroom* (pp. 243–263). Austin TX: Pro-Ed.

CAPUTE, A., WACHTEL, R., SHAPIRO, B., PALMER, F., & ALLEN, M. (1983). Normal motor and reflex development. In J. Umbreit (Ed.), *Physical disabilities and health impairments: An introduction* (pp. 29–38). Columbus, OH: Merrill.

CARHART, R. (1970). Development and conservation of speech. In H. Davis & S. R. Silverman (Eds.), *Hearing and Deafness.* New York: Holt, Rinehart & Winston.

CARLSON, E. (1984). *Human genetics.* Lexington, MA: Heath.

CARNINE, D. W., & KAMEENUI, E. J. (1990). The general education initiative and children with special needs: A false dilemma in the face of true problems. *Journal of Learning Disabilities, 23*(3), 141–148.

CARNINE, D. W., SILBERT, J., & KAMEENUI, E. J. (1990). *Direct instruction reading* (2nd ed.). Columbus, OH: Merrill.

CARR, E. G., & DURAND, V. M. (1985). Reducing behavior problems through functional communication training. *Journal of Applied Behavior Analysis, 18*, 111–126.

CARR, J. (1987). The development of intelligence. In D. Lane & B. Statford (Eds.), *Current approaches to Down syndrome* (pp. 167–186). East Sussex, Great Britain: Holt, Rinehart & Winston.

CARRASQUILLO, A. L. (1991). Teaching the bilingual special education student. In A. L. Carrasquillo & R. E. Baecher (Eds.), *Bilingual special education: The important connection* (pp. 4–24). Norwood, NJ: Ablex.

CARRASQUILLO, A. L., & BAECHER, R. E. (Eds.) (1991). *Bilingual special education: The important connection.* Norwood, NJ: Ablex.

CARROLL, T. J. (1961). *Blindness: What it is, what it does, and how to live with it.* Boston: Little, Brown.

CARTER, J., & SUGAI, G. (1989). Social skills curriculum analysis. *Teaching Exceptional Children, 22*(1), 36–39.

CASSERLY, P. L. (1979). Helping able young women take math and science seriously in school. In N. Colangelo & R. Zaffrann (Eds.), *New voices in counseling the gifted* (pp. 346–369). Dubuque, IA: Kendall/Hunt.

CASTLE, K. (1983). *The infant and toddler handbook.* Atlanta: Humanics Limited.

CASTO, G. (1988). Research and program evaluation in early childhood special education. In S. L. Odom & M. B. Karnes (Eds.), *Early intervention for infants and children with handicaps: An empirical base* (pp. 51–62). Baltimore: Paul H. Brookes.

CASTO, G., & MASTROPIERI, M. A. (1986a). The efficacy of early intervention programs: A meta-analysis. *Exceptional Children, 52*, 417–424.

CASTO, G., & MASTROPIERI, M. A. (1986b). Strain and Smith do protest too much: A response. *Exceptional Children, 53*, 266–268.

CASTO, G., & MASTROPIERI, M. A. (1986c). Much ado about nothing: A reply to Dunst and Snyder. *Exceptional Children, 53*, 277–279.

CATON, H. (1979). A primary reading program for beginning braille readers. *Journal of Visual Impairment and Blindness, 73*, 309–313.

CATON, H. (Ed.) (1991). *Print and braille literacy: Selecting appropriate learning media.* Louisville, KY: American Printing House for the Blind.

CATON, H., & BRADLEY, E. L. (1978–1979). A new approach to beginning braille readings. *Education of the Visually Handicapped, 10*, 66–87.

CATON, H., PESTER, E., & BRADLEY, E. J. (1980–1983). *Patterns: The primary braille reading program.* Louisville, KY: American Printing House for the Blind.

CATON, H., & RANKIN, E. (1978). Variability in age and experience among blind students using basal reading materials. *Journal of Visual Impairment and Blindness, 74*, 147–149.

CATTEL, R. B. (1971). *Abilities: Their structure, growth, and action.* Boston: Houghton Mifflin.

CATTS, H. W., & KAMHI, A. G. (1986). The linguistic basis of reading disorders: Implications for the speech-language pathologist. *Language, Speech and Hearing Services in the Schools, 17*, 329–341.

CENTER ON HUMAN POLICY (1979). *The community imperative: A refutation of all arguments in support of institutionalizing anybody because of mental retardation.* Center on Human Policy, Syracuse University.

CERVONE, B. F., & O'LEARY, K. (1982). A conceptual framework for parent involvement. *Educational Leadership, 40*, 48–49.

CHABON, S. S., & PRELOCK, P. A. (1989). Strategies of a different stripe: Our response to a zebra question about language and its relevance to the school curriculum. *Seminars in Speech and Language, 3*, 241–251.

CHADSEY-RUSCH, J. (Ed.) (1984). *Enhancing transition from school to the workplace for handicapped youth: Personnel preparation implications.* ERIC Document Reproduction Service No. ED 280231.

CHADSEY-RUSCH, J. (1986). Identifying and teaching valued social skills. In F. R. Rusch (Ed.), *Competitive employment issues and strategies.* Baltimore: Paul H. Brookes.

CHADSEY-RUSCH, J., KARLAN, G. R., RIVA, M., & RUSCH, F. R. (1984). Competitive employment: Teaching conversation skills to adults who are mentally retarded. *Mental Retardation 22*, 218–222.

CHALFANT, J. D. (1985). Identifying learning disabled students: A summary of the national task force report. *Learning Disabilities Focus, 1,* 9–20.

CHALFANT, J. D. (1987). Providing services to all students with learning problems: Implications for policy and programs. In S. Vaughn & C. S. Bos (Eds.), *Research in learning disabilities: Issues and future directions* (pp. 239–251). Boston: College-Hill.

CHALFANT, J. C., PYSH, M., & MOULTRIE, R. (1979). Teacher assistance teams: Findings of an introspective study. *Learning Disability Quarterly, 6,* 321–331.

CHALKLEY, T. (1982). *Your eyes: A book for paramedical personnel and the lay reader* (2nd ed.). Springfield, IL: Thomas.

CHALL, J. S. (1987). The importance of instruction in reading methods for all teachers. In E. Ellis (Ed.), *Intimacy with language* (pp. 15–23). Baltimore: Orton Dyslexia Society.

CHAPMAN, J. E., & HEWARD, W. L. (1982). Improving parent-teacher communication through recorded telephone messages. *Exceptional Children, 49,* 79–81.

CHARLES, D. C. (1953). Ability and accomplishment of persons earlier judged mentally deficient. *Genetic Psychology Monographs, 47,* 3–71.

CHARLOP, M. H., & WALSH, M. E. (1986). Increasing autistic children's spontaneous verbalizations of affection: An assessment of time delay and peer modeling procedures. *Journal of Applied Behavior Analysis, 19,* 307–314.

CHENEY, D., & FOSS, G. (1984). An examination of the social behavior of mentally retarded workers. *Education and Training of the Mentally Retarded, 19,* 216–221.

CHESS, S., THOMAS., A., & BIRCH, H. G. (1967). Behavior problems revisited: Findings of an anterospective study. *Journal of the American Academy of Child Psychiatry, 6,* 321–331.

CHINN, P. C., & HUGHES, S. (1987). Representation of minority students in special education classes. *Remedial and special education, 8*(4), 41–46.

CHRISTOPHERSON, S. L. (1981). Developing placement in the regular school program. *G/C/T, 19,* 40–41.

CHURCH, G., & GLENNEN, S. (1992). *The handbook of assistive technology.* San Diego, CA: Singular Publishing Group.

CICIRELLI, V., et al. (1969). *The impact of Head Start: An evaluation of the effects of Head Start on children's cognitive and affective development.* Report of the U.S. Office of Economic Opportunity by Westinghouse Learning Corporation and Ohio University. Washington, DC: U.S. Government Printing Office.

CLARIZIO, H. F., & McCOY E. F. (1976). *Behavior disorders in children* (2nd ed.). New York: Thomas Y. Crowell.

CLARK, B. (1988). *Growing up gifted: Developing the potential of children at home and at school* (3rd ed.). Columbus, OH: Merrill.

CLARK, D., BAKER, B. & HEIFETZ, L. (1982). Behavioral training for parents of mentally retarded children: Prediction of outcome. *American Journal of Mental Deficiency , 87,* 14–19.

CLARK, D., & GREENE, G. (1989). *Southwest SELPA transition curriculum and planning.* South Bay Union High School District, Redondo Beach, CA.

CLARK, G., & ZIMMERMAN, E. (1984). Identifying artistically talented students. *School Arts, 83*(3), 26–31.

CLARK, G. M. (1980). Career education: A concept. In G. M. Clark & W. J. White (Eds.), *Career education for the handicapped: Current perspectives for teachers.* Boothwyn, PA: Educational Resources Center.

CLARK, G. M., & KOLSTOE, O. P. (1990). *Career development and transition education for adolescents with disabilities.* Boston: Allyn & Bacon.

CLARK, L. (1985). *SOS: Help for parents: A practical guide for handling common everyday behavior problems.* Bowling Green, KY: Parents Press.

CLARK, M. (1983, February 7). A promising therapy for MS. *Newsweek,* p. 62.

CLARK, R. W. (1977). *The man who made the future.* New York: Putnam.

CLARK, T. C., MORGAN, E. C., & WILSON-VIOTMAN, A. L. (1983). *The INSITE model: A parent centered, in-home, sensory interventive, training and educational program.* Ogden, UT: Project INSITE.

CLEMENTS, S. D. (1966). *Minimal brain dysfunction in children.* (NINDS Monograph No. 3, U.S. Public Health Service Publication No. 1415). Washington, DC: U.S. Government Printing Office.

Closing the Gap (1991, February/March). *Resource directory.*

COBB, R. B. (1983). Curriculum-based vocational assessment. *Teaching Exceptional Children, 15,* 216–219.

COBB, R. B. (1985). *Vocational assessment of the special needs learner: A special education perspective.* Paper presented at the American Vocational Association Convention, Atlanta, GA.

COBB, R. B., & LARKIN, D. (1985). Assessment and placement of handicapped pupils into secondary vocational education programs. *Focus on Exceptional Children, 17*(7). 1–14.

CODE OF ETHICS AND STANDARDS FOR PROFESSIONAL PRACTICE (1983). *Exceptional Children 50,* 205–209.

COGGINS, T., & CARPENTER, R. (1979). Introduction to the area of language development. In M. Cohen & P. Gross (Eds.), *The developmental resource; Behavioral sequences for assessment and program planning.* New York: Grune & Stratton.

COGGINS, T., & SANDALL, S. (1983). The communicative handicapped infant: Application of normal language and communication development. In S. G. Garwood & R. R. Fewell (Eds.), *Educating handicapped infants: Issues in development and intervention* (pp. 165–214). Rockville, MD: Aspen.

COHEN, I. L., FISCH, G. S., SUDHALTER, V., WOLF-SCHEIN, E. G., HANSON, D., HAGERMAN, R., JENKINS, E. C., & BROWN, W. T. (1988). Social gaze, social avoidance, and repetitive behavior in fragile X males: A controlled study. *American Journal on Mental Deficiency, 92*(5), 436–446.

COHEN, O., FISCHGRUND, J., & REDDING, R. (1990). Deaf children from ethnic, linguistic and racial minority backgrounds. *American Annals of the Deaf, 135*(2), 67–73.

COHEN, S., & WARREN, R. D. (1987). Preliminary survey of family abuse of children served by United Cerebral Palsy centers. *Developmental Medicine and Child Neurology, 29,* 12–18.

COHN, L., & GREEN, P. (1988). No longer "just a parent": The role of parents in the NSEA. *Exceptional Parent, 18*(7), 52–53.

COLEMAN, M. C. (1992). *Behavior disorders: Theory and practice* (2nd ed.). Boston: Allyn & Bacon.

COLLEGE ENTRANCE EXAMINATION BOARD (1983). *Advanced placement course description: Computer science.* Princeton, NJ: Author.

COLLINS, B. C., GAST, D. L., AULT, M. J., & WOLERY, M. (1991). Small group instruction: Guidelines for teachers of students with moderate to severe handicaps. *Education and Training in Mental Retardation, 26,* 18–32.

COMFORT, M. (1988). Assessing parent-child interaction. In D. B. Bailey & R. J. Simeonsson (Eds.), *Family assessment in early intervention* (pp. 65–94). Columbus, OH: Merrill.

COMMISSION ON INSTRUCTIONAL TECHNOLOGY (1970). *To improve learning: A report to the President and the Congress of the United States.* Washington, DC: U.S. Government Printing Office.

COMPTON, C. L. (Ed.) (1989). Assistive devices. *Seminars in Hearing, 10*(1), 1–118.

COMSTOCK, G., & STRASBURGER, V. C. (1990). Deceptive appearances: Television violence and aggressive behavior. *Journal of Adolescent Health Care, 11,* 31–44.

CONE, T. E., WILSON, L. R., BRADLEY, C. M., & REESE, J. H. (1985). Characteristics of LD students in Iowa: An empirical investigation. *Learning Disability Quarterly, 8,* 211–220.

CONLEY, R. W. (1979). Economics and mental retardation. In E. LaFramboise & G. Provencal (Eds.), *Where do we want to be in five years? A report of the American Association on Mental Deficiency's 1979 Annual Conference.*

CONLEY, R. W., RUSCH, F. R., McCAUGHRIN, W. B., & TINES, J. (1989). Benefits and costs of supported employment: An analysis of the Illinois supported employment program. *Journal of Applied Behavior Analysis, 22,* 441–448.

CONOLEY, J. C. (1987). "Consultation in special education: II. Training and practice": Comment. *Journal of Learning Disabilities, 20*(8), 497.

CONSORTIUM ON ADAPTIVE PERFORMANCE (CAPE) (1980). *Adaptive performance instrument.* Moscow, ID: Department of Special Education, University of Idaho.

COOKE, P. T., ROSENBLOOM, I., & COOKE, R. W. (1987). Trends in birth prevalence of cerebral palsy. *Archives of Disease in Childhood, 62,* 379–384.

COOPER, J. V., & EDGE, D. (1981). *Parenting: Strategies and educational methods.* Louisville, KY: Eston Corp.

CORDONI, B. (1987). *Living with a learning disability.* Carbondale, IL: Southern Illinois University Press.

COREY, S. M. (1967). The nature of instruction. In P. C. Lange (Ed.), *Programmed Instruction: The Sixty-sixth Yearbook of the National Society for the Study of Education (Part III).* Chicago: University of Chicago Press.

CORNELL, D. G., & GROSSBERG, I. N. (1986). Siblings of children in gifted programs. *Journal for the Education of the Gifted, 9,* 253–264.

CORNELL, D. G., & GROSSBERG, I. N. (1989). Parent use of the term "gifted": Correlates with family environment and child adjustment. *Journal for the Education of the Gifted, 12*(3), 218–230.

CORREA, V. I. (1987). Working with Hispanic parents of visually impaired children: Cultural implications. *Journal of Visual Impairments & Blindness, 81,* 260–264.

COTT, A. (1972). Megavitamins: The orthomolecular approach to behavioral disorders and learning disabilities. *Academic Therapy, 7,* 245–256.

COUNCIL FOR CHILDREN WITH BEHAVIORAL DISORDERS (1987). Position paper on definition and identification of students with behavioral disorders. *Behavioral Disorders, 13,* 9–19.

COUNCIL FOR CHILDREN WITH BEHAVIORAL DISORDERS (1989). Position statement on the regular education initiative. *Behavioral Disorders, 14,* 201–207.

COWART, V. (1983, September 9). First-trimester prenatal diagnostic method becoming available in U.S. [Medical News]. *Journal of the American Medical Association, 250*(10), 1249–1250.

COWEN, E. L., UNDERBERG, R., VERRILLO, R. T., & BENHAM, F. G. (1961). *Adjustment of visual disability in adolescence.* New York: American Foundation for the Blind.

COX, J., & DANIEL, N. (1983). Specialized schools for high ability students. *G/C/T, 28,* 2–9.

COX, J., DANIEL, N., & BOSTON, B. (1985). *Educating able learners: Programs and promising practices.* Austin, TX: University of Texas Press.

CRANDALL, V. J., KATKOVSKY, W., & PRESTON, A. (1972). Motivational and ability determinants of young children's intellectual achievement behaviors. *Child Development, 33,* 643–661.

CROSS, D. P. (1983). *Survey of classes for the physically disabled.* Unpublished manuscript, University of Kentucky, Lexington.

CROWLEY, M., KEANE, K., & NEEDHAM, C. (1982). Fathers: The forgotten parents. *American Annals of the Deaf, 127,* 38–40.

CRUICKSHANK, W. M. (1976). In J. M. Kauffman & D. P. Hallahan (Eds.), *Teaching children with learning disabilities: Personal perspectives* (pp. 94–127). Columbus, OH: Merrill.

CRUICKSHANK, W. M., BENTZEN, F., RATZEBURG, F., & TANNHAUSER, M. (1961). *A teaching method for brain-injured and hyperactive children.* Syracuse, NY: Syracuse University Press.

CRUICKSHANK, W. M., & JOHNSON, G. O. (Eds.) (1975). *Education of exceptional children and youth* (3rd ed.). Englewood Cliffs, NJ: Prentice-Hall.

CULATTA, R., & LEEPER, L. (1987). Dysfluency in childhood: It's not always stuttering. *Journal of Childhood Communications Disorders, 210,* 95–106.

CUTSFORTH, T. D. (1951). *The blind in school and society: A psychological study.* New York: American Foundation for the Blind.

DALKE, C., & SCHMITT, S. (1987). Meeting the transition needs of college-bound students with learning disabilities. *Journal of Learning Disabilities, 20*(3), 176–180.

DAMICO, J. (1991). Clinical discourse analysis: A functional approach to language assessment. In C. Simon (Ed.), *Communication skills and classroom success.* Eau Claire, WI: Thinking Publications, A Division of McKinley Co., Inc.

DANIELS, S. M. (1982). From parent-advocacy to self-advocacy: A problem of transition. *Exceptional Education Quarterly, 3,* 25–32.

DATTILO, J., & MIRENDA, P. (1987). An application of a leisure preference assessment protocol for persons with severe handicaps. *Journal of the Association for Persons with Severe Handicaps, 12,* 306–311.

DAURIO, S. (1979). Educational enrichment versus acceleration: A review of the literature. In W. George, S. Cohn, & J. Stanley (Eds.), *Educating the gifted: Acceleration and enrichment.* Baltimore: Johns Hopkins University Press.

DAUTERMAN, W. L., SHAPIRO, B., & SWINN, R. M. (1967). Performance of intelligence for blind reviewed. *International Journal for the Education of the Blind, 17,* 8–16.

DAVIES, S. N. (1991). *The transition toward bilingual education of deaf children in Sweden and Denmark: Perspectives of language.* Washington, DC: Gallaudet University, Gallaudet Research Institute, Occasional Paper 91-1.

DAVIS, C. J. (1970). *New developments in intelligence testing of blind children.* Proceedings of the conference on new approaches to the evaluation of blind persons. New York: American Foundation of the Blind.

DAVIS, G., & RIMM, S. (1989). *Education of the gifted and talented* (2nd ed.). Englewood Cliffs, NJ: Prentice-Hall.

DAVIS, H., & SILVERMAN, S. R. (1970). *Hearing and deafness* (3rd ed.). New York: Holt, Rinehart and Winston.

DAVIS, S., & FROTHINGHAM, P. S. (1981). Computing at a new public high school for gifted students. In J. N. Nazzaro (Ed.), *Computer connections for gifted children and youth.* Reston, VA: Clearinghouse on Handicapped and Gifted Children.

DEAL, A. G., DUNST, C. J., & TRIVETTE, C. M. (1989). A flexible and functional approach to developing individualized family support plans. *Infants and Young Children, 1*(4), 32–43.

DEKLYEN, M., & ODOM, S. L. (1989). Activity structure and social interactions with peers in developmentally integrated play groups. *Journal of Early Intervention, 13,* 342–352.

DELAMATER, A., LAHEY, B., & DRAKE, L. (1982). Toward an empirical subclassification of "learning disabilities": A psychological comparison of "hyperactive" and "nonhyperactive" subgroups. *Journal of Abnormal Child Psychology, 9,* 65–77.

DeMOTT, R. (1974). Visually impaired. In N. G. Haring (Ed.), *Behavior of exceptional children: An introduction to special education* (pp. 529–563). Columbus, OH: Merrill.

DENHOFF, E. (1966). Cerebral palsy: Medical aspects. In W. M. Cruickshank (Ed.), *Cerebral palsy: Its individual and community problems* (2nd ed.) (pp. 24–100). Syracuse, NY: Syracuse University Press.

DENO, E. (1973). *Instructional alternatives for exceptional children.* Reston, VA: Council for Exceptional Children.

DENO, S. L., MARUYAMA, G., ESPIN, C., & COHEN, C. (1990). Educating students with mild disabilities in general education classrooms: Minnesota alternatives. [Special issue: Enhancing the education of difficult-to-teach students in the mainstream: Federally-sponsored research]. *Exceptional Children, 57*(2), 150–161.

DESHLER, D. D., & SCHUMAKER, J. B. (1986). Learning strategies: An instructional alternative for low-achieving adolescents. *Exceptional Children, 52*(6), 583–590.

DESHLER, D. D., SCHUMAKER, J. B., ALLEY, G. R., WARNER, M. M. & CLARK, F. L. (1982). Learning disabilities in adolescent and young adult populations: Research implications. *Focus on Exceptional Children, 15*(1), 1–12.

DESHLER, D. D., SCHUMAKER, J. B., & LENZ, B. K. (1984). Academic and cognitive intervention for learning-disabled adolescents, Part I. *Journal of Learning Disabilities, 17*, 108–117.

DEVER, R. B. (1988). *Community living skills: A taxonomy* (Monograph). Washington, DC: American Association on Mental Retardation.

DEVER, R. B. (1989). A taxonomy of community living skills. *Exceptional Children, 55*(5), 395–404.

DIANA v. STATE BOARD OF EDUCATION, C-70-37 R. F. P. (N. D. California, Jan. 7, 1970, and June 18, 1972).

DIRKS, J., & QUARFOTH, J. (1981). Selecting children for gifted classes: Choosing for breadth vs. choosing for depth. *Psychology in the Schools, 18*, 437–449.

DIVISION ON CAREER DEVELOPMENT (DCD) (1987). *The transition of youth with disabilities to adult life: A position statement.* Reston, VA: Council for Exceptional Children.

DMITRIEV, V. (1988, January 6–11). Cognition and the acceleration and maintenance of developmental gains among children with Down syndrome: Longitudinal data. Down syndrome, Papers and Abstracts for Professionals.

DOLL, E. (1962). A historical survey of research and management of mental retardation in the United States. In E. P. Trapp & P. Himmelstein (Eds.), *Readings on the exceptional children.* New York: Appleton-Century-Crofts.

DONALDSON, J., & MARTINSON, M. C. (1977). Modifying attitudes toward physically disabled persons. *Exceptional Children, 43*, 337–341.

DONNELLAN, A. M., & MIRENDA, P. (1984). Issues related to professional involvement with families of individuals with autism and other severe handicaps. *Journal of the Association for Persons with Severe Handicaps, 9,* 16–25.

DONNELLAN, A. M., MIRENDA, P. L., MESAROS, R. A., & FASSBENDER, L. L. (1984). Analyzing the communicative functions of aberrant behavior. *Journal of the Association for Persons with Severe Handicaps, 9,* 201–212.

DOORLY, A. (1981). Microcomputers for gifted microtots. In J. N. Nazzaro (Ed.), *Computer connections for gifted children and youth.* Reston, VA: Clearinghouse on Handicapped and Gifted Children.

DORE, J. (1986). The development of conversational competence. In R. Schiefelbusch (Ed.), *Language competence: Assessment and intervention.* Boston: College-Hill.

DOWNING, J., & EICHINGER, J. (1990). Instructional strategies for learners with dual sensory impairments in integrated settings. *Journal of the Association for Persons with Severe Handicaps, 15,* 98–105.

DOYLE, P., WOLERY, M., AULT, M., & GAST, D. (1988). System of least prompts: A review of procedural parameters. *Journal of the Association for Persons with Severe Handicaps, 13*(1), 28–40.

DRASH, P. W. (1972). Habilitation of the retarded child: A remedial program. *Journal of Special Education, 6,* 149–159.

DRASH, P. W., RAVER, S. A., & MURRIN, M. R. (1987). Symposium: Issues in total habilitation. *Mental Retardation, 25,* 67–69.

DUCKMAN, R. H. (1987). Visual problems. In E. T. McDonald (Ed.), *Treating cerebral palsy* (pp. 105–132). Austin, TX: Pro-Ed.

DUDLEY-MARLING, C. C., & EDMIASTON, R. (1985). Social status of learning disabled children and adolescents: A review. *Learning Disability Quarterly, 8,* 189–204.

DUNLAP, G., JOHNSON. L. F., & ROBBINS, F. R. (1990). Preventing serious behavior problems through skill development and early interventions. In A. C. Repp & N. N. Singh (Eds.), *Perspectives on the use of nonaversive and aversive interventions for persons with developmental disabilities* (pp. 273–286). Sycamore, IL: Sycamore Publishing.

DUNN, L. M. (1973). Children with moderate and severe general learning disabilities. In L. M. Dunn (Ed.), *Exceptional children in schools* (2nd ed.). New York: Holt, Rinehart & Winston.

DUNST, C. J. (1981). *Infant learning: A cognitive-linguistic intervention strategy.* Hingham, MA: Teaching Resources.

DUNST, C. J., LESKO, A. E., HOLBERT, K. A., WILSON, L. L., SHARPE, K. L., & LILES, R. F. (1987). A systematic approach to infant intervention. *Topics in Early Childhood Special Education, 7,* 19–37.

DUNST, C. J., & SNYDER, S. W. (1986). A critique of the Utah State University early intervention meta-analysis research. *Exceptional Children, 53,* 269–276.

DUNST, C. J., TRIVETTE, C. M., & CROSS, A. H. (1986). Mediating influences of social support: Personal, family, and child outcomes. *American Journal of Mental Deficiency, 90*(4), 403–417.

DUNST, C. J., SNYDER, S. W., & MANKINEN, M. (1989). Efficacy of early interventions. In M. C. Wang, M. C. Reynolds, & H. J. Walberg (Eds.), *Handbook of special education: Research and practice: Vol. 3. Low incidence conditions* (pp. 259–294). New York: Pergamon Press.

DUNST, C. J., TRIVETTE, C. M., & DEAL, A. (1988). *Enabling and empowering families: Principles and guidelines for practice.* Cambridge, MA: Brookline Books.

DURAN, R. (1989). Assessment and instruction of at-risk Hispanic students. *Exceptional Children, 56,* 154–159.

DURIO, H. F. (1980). Talking with your child's physician. *Pointer, 25,* 12–14.

DuVERGAS, G. (1984). *A comparative follow-up study of Down syndrome children who attended the Model Preschool Program.* Unpublished doctoral dissertation, University of Washington, Seattle.

EAKIN, W. M., PRATT, R. J., & McFARLAND, T. L. (1961). *Type size research for the partially seeing child.* Pittsburgh: Stanwix House.

EDELMAN, M. W. (1989). Economic issues related to child care and early childhood education. *Teachers College Record, 90,* 342–351.

EDGAR, E. (1987). Secondary programs in special programs in special education: Are many of them justifiable? *Exceptional Children, 53,* 555–561.

EDGAR, E. (1988). Employment as an outcome for mildly handicapped students: Current status and future directions. *Focus on Exceptional Children, 21,* 1–8.

EDGAR, E. (1991). Providing ongoing support and making appropriate placements: An alternative to transition planning for mildly handicapped students. *Preventing School Failure, 35*(2), 36–39.

EDGAR, E. Education's role in improving our quality of life: Is it time to change our view of the world? *Beyond Behavior, 1*(1), 9–13.

Education of the handicapped: The independent biweekly news service on federal legislation, programs and funding for special education (1979). Washington, DC: Capitol Publications, Inc., *4*(11), 4–5.

EDUCATION TRANSITION CENTER (1987). *Synthesis of individual transition plans: Format and process.* Sacramento, CA: California Department of Education.

EDWARDS, J. S., & EDWARDS, D. (1970). Rate of behavior development: Direct and continuous measurement. *Perceptual & Motor Skills, 31,* 633–634.

EEOC and DOJ (Equal Employment Opportunity Commission and the U.S. Department of Justice) (1991). *Americans with disabilities act handbook* (EEOC-BK-19). Washington, DC: U.S. Government Printing Office.

EHEART, B. K. (1982). Mother-child interactions with nonretarded and mentally retarded preschoolers. *American Journal of Mental Deficiency, 87,* 20–25.

EHEART, B., & CICCONE, J. (1982). Special needs of low-income mothers of developmentally delayed children. *American Journal of Mental Deficiency, 87,* 26–33.

EHRLICH, V. Z. (1982). *Gifted children: A guide for parents and teachers.* Englewood Cliffs, NJ: Prentice-Hall.

EISERMAN, W. D. (1988). Three types of peer tutoring: Effects on the attitudes of students with learning disabilities and their regular class peers. *Journal of Learning Disabilities, 21*(4), 249–252.

ELIAS, S. (1991, May 30). *Mother's blood used to detect fetal disorders* [Interview with Sherman Elias, University of Tennessee in Memphis]. Washington, DC: Associated Press.

ELLIS, A. W. (1985). The cognitive neuropsychology of developmental (and acquired) dyslexia: A critical survey. *Cognitive Neuropsychology, 2* (2), 169–205.

ELLISON, R., ABE, C., FOX, D., COREY, K., & TAYLOR, C. (1976, Winter). Using biographical information in identifying artistic talent. *Gifted Child Quarterly, 20* (4), 402–413.

EMOTIONAL/BEHAVIORAL DISABILITIES COMMITTEE (1992). *Emotional/behavioral disabilities technical assistance manual.* Frankfort, KY: Kentucky Department of Education.

ENDERS, A., & HALL, M. (Eds.) (1990). *Assistive technology sourcebook.* Washington, DC: RESNA Press.

ENELL, N. C., & BARRICK, S. W. (1983). *An examination of the relative efficiency and usefulness of computer-assisted individualized education programs.* San Juan Unified School District, Carmichael, CA.

ENGLEMANN, S., & BRUNER, E. C. (1973). *DISTAR Reading 1.* Chicago: Science Research Associates.

ENGLEMANN, S., & CARNINE, D. W. (1982). *Theory of instruction: Principles and applications.* New York: Irvington.

ENGELHARDT, J. L., BRUBAKER, T. H., & LUTZER, V. D. (1988). Older caregivers of adults with mental retardation: Service utilization. *Mental Retardation, 26* (4), 191–195.

ENGLERT, C. S. (1983). Measuring special education teacher effectiveness. *Exceptional Children, 50* (3), 247–254.

ENGLERT, C. S., & THOMAS, C. C. (1987). Sensitivity to text structure in reading and writing: A comparison between learning disabled and non-learning disabled students. *Learning Disability Quarterly, 10,* 93–105.

EPILEPSY FOUNDATION OF AMERICA (1989). *Questions and answers about epilepsy.* Landover, MD: Author.

EPSTEIN, M. H., POLLOWAY, E. A., PATTON, J. R., & FOLEY, R. (1989). Mild retardation: Student characteristics and services. *Education & Training of the Mentally Retarded, 24,* 7–16.

ESTERLY, D. L., & GRIFFIN, H. D. (1987). Preschool programs for children with learning disabilities. *Journal of Learning Disabilities, 20* (9), 571–573.

EVANS, D., & HAMPSON, M. (1968). The language of mongols. *British Journal of Disorders of Communication, 3,* 171–181.

EVANS, I. M., & MEYER, L. H. (1985). *An educative approach to behavior problems: A practical decision model for interventions with severely handicapped learners.* Baltimore: Paul H. Brookes.

FAERSTEIN, L. M. (1986). Coping and defense mechanisms of mothers of learning disabled children. *Journal of Learning Disabilities, 19* (1), 8–11.

FAGEN, S. A., GRAVES, D. L., & TESSIER-SWITLICK, D. (1984). *Promoting successful mainstreaming: Reasonable classroom accommodations for learning disabled students.* Rockville, MD: Montgomery County Public Schools.

FALVEY, M. A. (1986). *Community-based curriculum: Instructional strategies for students with severe handicaps.* Baltimore: Paul H. Brookes.

FARMER, J. A., GAST, D. L., WOLERY, M., & WINTERLING, V. (1991). Small group instruction for students with severe handicaps: A study of observational learning. *Education and Training in Mental Retardation, 26,* 190–201.

FEARN, L. (1982). Underachievement and rate of acceleration. *Gifted Child Quarterly, 26,* 121–125.

FEATHERSTONE, H. (1980). *Difference in the family.* New York: Basic Books.

Federal Register (1984, September 25). Developmental Disabilities Act of 1984. Report 98-1074, Section 102 (11) (F).

Federal Register (1991a, January 22). Architectural and Transportation Barriers Compliance Board—Part V. *Americans with disabilities act (ADA) accessibility guidelines for buildings and facilities: Proposed rule (36 CFR Part 1191), 56* (14), 2296–2395.

Federal Register (1991b, February 22). Department of Justice—Part II, *Nondiscrimination on the basis of disability by public accommodations and in commercial facilities: Proposed rule and hearing (28 CFR Part 36), 56* (36), 7452–7495.

Federal Register (1991c, February 28). Department of Justice—Part IV, *Nondiscrimination on the basis of disability in state and local government services: Proposed rule and hearing (28 CFR Part 35), 56* (40), 8538–8557.

Federal Register (1991d, March 20). Architectural and Transportation Barriers Compliance Board—Part II. *Americans with disabilities act (ADA) accessibility guidelines for transportation vehicles: Proposed rule (36 CFR Part 1192), 56* (54), 11824–11883.

Federal Register (1991e, September 6). Architectural and Transportation Barriers Compliance Board—Part II–IV. *Americans with disabilities act (ADA) accessibility guidelines for buildings and facilities: Amendment to final guidelines. 56* (173), 45550–45778.

FEINGOLD, B. F. (1975). *Why your child is hyperactive.* New York: Random House.

FELDHUSEN, J. (1982). Myth: Gifted education means having a program! Meeting the needs of gifted students through differentiated programming. *Gifted Child Quarterly, 26* (1), 37–41.

FELDMAN, D. (1979). The mysterious case of extreme giftedness. In A. H. Passow (Ed.), *The gifted and the talented: Their education and development* (pp. 335–351). The seventy-eighth yearbook of the National Society for the Study of Education, Part 1. Chicago: University of Chicago Press.

FELDMAN, M. A., CASE, L., TOWNS, F., & BETEL, J. (1985). Parent education project: Development and nurturance of children of mentally retarded parents. *American Journal of Mental Deficiency, 90* (3), 253–258.

FELTON, R. H., & WOOD, F. B. (1989). Cognitive deficits in reading disability and attention deficit disorder. *Journal of Learning Disabilities, 22* (1), 3–13, 22.

FENICHEL, C. (1966). Psychoeducational approaches for seriously emotionally disturbed children in the classroom. In P. Knoblock (Ed.), *Intervention approaches in education for emotionally disturbed children.* Syracuse, NY: Syracuse University Press.

FENTON, K. S., YOSHIDA, R. K., MAXWELL, J. P., & KAUFFMAN, J. J. (1979). Recognition of team goals: An essential step toward rational decision making. *Exceptional Children, 43,* 638–644.

FERRELL, K. A. (1987). *Reach out and teach—Parent handbook.* New York: American Foundation for the Blind.

FERRERI, C. A. (1983). Dyslexia and learning disabilities cured. *The Digest of Chiropractic Economics, 25,* 74.

FERRERO, R., & FLEMING, B. (1992). *Conducting an architectural access audit, access surveyor training.* Lexington, KY: FireStarr Publications.

FEUERSTEIN, R. (1979). *The dynamic assessment of retarded performers: The learning potential assessment device. Theory, instruments and techniques.* Baltimore: University Park Press.

FEWELL, R. R., & OELWEIN, P. L. (1990). The relationship between time in integrated environments and developmental gain in young children with special needs. *Topics in Early Childhood Special Education, 10,* 104–116.

FEWELL, R. R., & SANDALL, S. (1987). *Seattle early learning inventory.* Seattle: Specialty Software.

FEWELL, R. R., & VADASY, P. (1986). *Families of handicapped children: Needs and supports across the life span.* Austin, TX: Pro-Ed.

FEY, M. (1986). *Language intervention with young children.* Boston: College-Hill.

FIGUEROA, R. (1989). Psychological testing of linguistic-minority students: Knowledge gaps and regulations. *Exceptional Children, 56,* 145–153.

FIKSDAL, B., & SKALLIST, L. (1986). *Undervisningsplan: Norsk berbeiding av Rhone Island-Planen.* Grunnskoleradet, Oslo.

FISCH, G. S., COHEN, I. L., JENKINS, E. C., & BROWN, W. T. (1988). Screening developmentally disabled male populations for fragile X: The effect of sample size. *American Journal of Medical Genetics, 30,* 655–663.

FISHBACH, M., & HULL, J. T. (1982). Mental retardation in the province of Manitoba. *Canada's Mental Health, 30,* 16–19.

FLEISCHMAN, M., HORNE, A., & ARTHUR, J. L. (1983). *Troubled families: A treatment program.* Champaign, IL: Research Press.

FLEMING, L. A., WOLERY, M., WEINZIERL, C., VENN, M., & SCHROEDER, C. (1991). A model for assessing and adapting teachers' roles in mainstreamed preschool settings. *Topics in Early Childhood Special Education, 11*(1), 85–98.

FLORIDA DEPARTMENT OF EDUCATION (1987). *Parent/professional task force report: Involving minority and isolated parents of exceptional children.* Tallahassee, FL: Division of Public Schools, Bureau of Education for Exceptional Students.

FLYNN, T. M. (1984). IQ tests and placement. *Integrated Education, 21,* 124–126.

Focus on Technology (Fall, 1990). Mountain View, CA: TeleSensory (No. 12).

FORD, A., SCHNORR, R., MEYER, L., DAVERN, L., BLACK, J., & DEMPSEY, P. (1989). *The Syracuse community-referenced curriculum guide for students with moderate and severe disabilities.* Baltimore: Paul H. Brookes.

FORD, F. R. (1966). *Diseases of the nervous system: In infancy, childhood and adolescence* (5th ed.). Springfield, IL: Thomas.

FORNESS, S. R. (1985). Effects of public policy at the state level: California's impact on MR, LD, and ED categories. *Remedial and Special Education, 6*(3), 36–43.

FORNESS, S. R. (1988). Planning for the needs of children with serious emotional disturbance: The National Special Education and Mental Health Coalition. *Behavioral Disorders, 13,* 127–132.

FOSTER, M., BERGER, M., McLEAN, M. (1981). Rethinking a good idea: A reassessment of parent involvement. *Topics in Early Childhood Special Education, 1,* 55–65.

FOWLER, S. A., SCHWARTZ, I., & ATWATER, J. (1991). Perspectives on the transition from preschool to kindergarten for children with disabilities and their families. *Exceptional Children, 58,* 136–145.

FOX, C. L., & FORBING, S. E. (1991). Overlapping symptoms of substance abuse and learning handicaps: Implications for educators, *24* (1), 24–39.

FOX, L. (1976). Sex differences in mathematical precocity: Bridging the gap. In D. P. Keating (Ed.), *Intellectual talent research and development.* Baltimore: Johns Hopkins University Press.

FOX, L., BRODY, L., & TOBIN, D. (Eds.). (1983). *Learning disabled/gifted children.* Baltimore: University Park Press.

FRANKENBERGER, W. (1984). A survey of state guidelines for identification of mental retardation. *Mental Retardation, 22,* 17–20.

FRANKENBERGER, W. K., DODDS, J. B., & FANDAL, A. W. (1975). *Denver Developmental Screening Test.* Denver: LADOCA Project and Publishing Foundation.

FRANKLIN, M. E., LITTLE, E., & TESKA, J. A. (1987). Effective teaching strategies used with the mildly handicapped in the mainstream. *Focus on Exceptional Children, 20*(3), 7–11.

FREDERICKS, H. D., et al. (1980). *The teaching research curriculum for moderately and severely handicapped.* Springfield, IL: Thomas.

FREEMAN, P. (1985). *The deaf/blind baby book.* London: William Heinemann Medical Books.

FRENCH, J. L. (1975). The highly intelligent dropout. In W. B. Barbe & J. R. Renzulli (Eds.), *Psychology and education of the gifted* (2nd ed.). New York: Irvington.

FRIEDMAN, J., & PASNAK, R. (1973). Attainment of classification and seriation concepts by blind and sighted subjects. *Education of the Visually Handicapped, 5,* 55–62.

FRIEND, M. (1984). Consultation skills for resource teachers. *Learning Disability Quarterly, 7*(3), 246–250.

FRIEND, M., & COOK, L. (1992). *Interactions: Collaboration skills for school professionals.* New York: Longman.

FROSTIG, M., & HORNE, D. (1964). *The Frostig program for the development of visual perception: Teacher's guide.* Chicago: Follett.

FUCHS, L. S., DENO, S. L., & MIRKIN, P. K. (1984). Effects of frequent curriculum-based measurement and evaluation on pedagogy, student achievement, and student awareness of learning. *American Educational Research Journal, 21,* 449–460.

FUCHS, L. S., & FUCHS, D. (1986). Effects of systematic formative evaluation: A meta-analysis. *Exceptional Children, 53*(3), 199–208.

FULLWOOD, N. N. (Ed.) (1977). *Technology and the handicapped: Telecommunications services in the rehabilitation of the blind.* Raleigh, NC: North Carolina State University, School of Education.

FUREY, E. M. (1982). The effects of alcohol on the fetus. *Exceptional Children, 49*(1), 30–32.

FURONO, S., O'REILY, K., HOSKA, C. M., INSTAUKA, T., ALLMAN, T. L., & ZEISLOFT, B. (1985). *Hawaii early learning profile.* Palo Alto, CA: VORT.

FURTH, H. G. (1966). *Thinking without language: Psychological implication of deafness.* New York: Free Press.

GADOW, K. D. (1986). *Children on medications: Volume II: Epilepsy, emotional disturbance, and adolescent disorders.* Boston: College-Hill.

GAGE, M. A., FREDERICKS, H. D., JOHNSON-DORN, N., & LINDLEY-SOUTHARD, B. (1982). Inservice training for staffs of group homes and work activity centers serving developmentally disabled adults. *Journal of the Association for the Severely Handicapped, 7*(4), 60–70.

GALLAGHER, J. J. (1985). *Teaching the gifted child* (3rd ed.). Boston: Allyn & Bacon.

GALLAGHER, J. J., & BRISTOL, M. (1989). Families of young handicapped children. In M. C. Wang, M. C. Reynolds, & H. J. Walberg (Eds.), *Handbook of special education: Research and practice: Vol. 3. Low incidence conditions* (pp. 295–317). New York: Pergamon Press.

GALLAGHER, J. J., TROHANIS, P. L., & CLIFFORD, R. M. (1989). *Policy implementation and PL 99-457: Planning for young children with special needs.* Baltimore: Paul H. Brookes.

GARBARINO, J. (1987). The abuse and neglect of special children: An introduction to the issues. In J. Garbarino, P. E. Brookhouser, & K. J. Authier (Eds.), *Special children special risks: The maltreatment of children with disabilities.* Hawthorne, NY: Aldinede Gruyter.

GARDNER, H. (1982). *Art, mind, and brain.* New York: Basic Books.

GARDNER, H. (1983). *Frames of mind: The theory of multiple intelligences.* New York: Basic Books.

GARDNER, H., & HATCH, T. (1990). Multiple intelligences go to school: Educational implications of the theory of multiple intelligences. Technical Report 4.

GARTNER, A., & LIPSKY, D. K. (1987). Beyond special education: Toward a quality system for all students. *Harvard Educational Review, 57,* 367–395.

GARWOOD, S. G., & SHEEHAN, R. (1989). *Designing a comprehensive early intervention system: The challenge of PL 99-457.* Austin, TX: Pro-Ed.

GAST, D. L., DOYLE, P. M., WOLERY, M., AULT, M. J., & FARMER, J. A. (1991). Assessing the acquisition of incidental information by secondary-aged students with mental retardation: Comparison of response prompting strategies. *American Journal on Mental Deficiency, 96,* 63–80.

GAST, D., & WOLERY, M. (1987). Severe maladaptive behaviors. In M. Snell (Ed.), *Systematic instruction of persons with severe handicaps.* Columbus, OH: Merrill.

GAST, D., WOLERY, M., DOYLE, P., AULT, M., & ALIG, C. (1988). *How to use time delay.* Lexington, KY: University of Kentucky, Department of Special Education, Comparison of Instructional Strategies Project.

GAYLORD-ROSS, R., STREMEL-CAMPBELL, K., & STOREY, K. (1986). Social skill training in natural contexts. In R. Horner, L. Meyer, & H. Fredericks (Eds.), *Education of learners with severe handicaps: Exemplary service strategies* (pp. 161–188). Baltimore: Paul H. Brookes.

GEAR, G. (1978). Effects of training on teacher's accuracy in the identification of gifted children. *Gifted Child Quarterly, 22*(1), 90–97.

GEARHART, B. R. (1974). *Organizations and administration of educational programs for exceptional programs.* Springfield, IL: Thomas.

GEARHART, B. R. (1980). *Special education for the '80s*. St. Louis, MO: C. V. Mosby.

GEERS, A., MOOG, J., & SCHICK, B. (1984). Acquisition of spoken and signed English by profoundly deaf children. *Journal of Speech and Hearing Disorders, 49*, 378–388.

GEIGER, W. L., & JUSTEN, J. W. (1983). Definitions of severely handicapped and requirements for teacher certification: A survey of state departments of education. *Journal of the Association for Persons with Severe Handicaps, 8*, 25–29.

GELBRICH, J. A., & HARE, E. K. (1989). The effects of single parenthood on school achievement in a gifted population. *Gifted Child Quarterly, 33*(3), 115–117.

Gene therapy may hold cure for cystic fibrosis (1990). *Counterpoint, 2*(1), 3.

GENSHAFT, J. L., DARE, N. L., & O'MALLEY, P. (1980). Assessing the visually impaired child: A school psychology view. *Journal of Visual Impairment and Blindness, 74*(9), 344–349.

GENTRY, C. G. (1991). Educational technology: A question of meaning. In G. J. Anglin (Ed.), *Instructional technology: Past, present, and future* (pp. 1–10). Englewood, CO: Libraries Unlimited.

GEORGE, W. C., & SOLANO, C. H. (1976). Identifying mathematical talent on a statewide basis. In D. P. Keating (Ed.), *Intellectual talent research and development* (pp. 55–89). Baltimore: Johns Hopkins University Press.

GERBER, M. (1990). Effectiveness of computerized drill and practice games in teaching basic math facts. *Exceptionality, 1*(3), 149–165.

GERBER, M. M., & LEVINE-DONNERSTEIN, D. (1989). Educating all children: Ten years later. *Exceptional Children, 56*(1), 17–27.

GERBER, P. J., BANBURY, M. M., MILLER, J. H., & GRIFFIN, H. P. (1986). Special educators' perceptions of parental participation in the individual education plan process. *Psychology in the Schools, 23*, 158–163.

GERMAN, M., & MAISTO, A. (1982). The relationship of a perceived family support system to the institutional placement of mentally retarded children. *Education and Training of the Mentally Retarded, 17*, 17–23.

GERSTEN, R., WOODWARD, J., & DARCH, C. (1986). Direct instruction: A research-based approach to curriculum design and teaching. *Exceptional Children, 56*(1), 17–27.

GESELL, A. (1928). *Infancy and human growth*. New York: Macmillan.

GESELL, A. (1938). *The psychology of early growth*. New York: Macmillan.

GESELL, A. (1940). *The first five years of life: A guide to the study of the preschool child*. New York: Harper.

GESELL, A., HALVERSON, H. M., THOMPSON, H., ILG, F. L., CASTNER, B. M., AMES, L. B., AMATRUDA, C. S. (1940). *The first five years of life: The preschool years*. New York: Harper & Row.

GETZELS, J. W. (1979). From art student to fine artist: Potential, problem finding, and performance. In A. H. Passow (Ed.), *The gifted and the talented: Their education and development* (pp. 372–387). The seventy-eighth yearbook of the National Society for the Study of Education, Part 1. Chicago: University of Chicago Press.

GILGOFF, I. S. (1983). Spinal cord injury. In J. Umbriet (Ed.), *Physical disabilities and health impairment: An introduction* (pp. 132–146). Columbus, OH: Merrill.

GILLIAM, J. (1979). Contributions and status rankings of educational planning committee participants. *Exceptional Children, 45*, 466–467.

GILLIAM, J. E., & COLEMAN, M. C. (1981). Who influences IEP committee decisions? *Exceptional Children, 47*, 642–644.

GILLUNG, T. B., & RUCKER, C. H. (1977). Labels and teacher expectations. *Exceptional Children, 43*, 464–465.

GIRAUD, F., AYMES, S., MATTEI, J. F., & MATTEI, M. G. (1976). Constitutional chromosome breakage. *Human Genetics, 34*, 125–136.

GLEASON, J. B. (Ed.) (1989). The development of language (2nd ed.). Columbus, OH: Merrill.

GLOECKLER, T., & SIMPSON, C. (1988). *Exceptional students in regular classrooms: Challenges, services, and methods*. Mountain View, CA: Mayfield.

GLOVER, M. E., PREMINGER, J. L., & SANFORD, A. R. (1978). *Early learning accomplishment profile*. Winston-Salem, NC: Kaplan.

GOETZ, L., GEE, K., & SAILOR, W. (1985). Using a behavior chain interruption strategy to teach communication skills to students with severe handicaps. *Journal of the Association for Persons with Severe Handicaps, 10*, 21–38.

GOLD, M. (1975). Vocational training. In J. Wortis (Ed.), *Mental retardation and developmental disabilities: An Annual Review* (Vol. 7) (pp. 254–264). New York: Brunner/Mazel.

GOLDBERG, M. J. (1983). Spinal muscular dystrophy. In J. Umbriet (Ed.), *Physical disabilities and health impairment: An introduction* (pp. 147–156). Columbus, OH: Merrill.

GOLDFARB, L. A., BROTHERSON, M. J., SUMMERS, J. A., & TURNBULL, A. P. (1986). *Meeting the challenge of disability or chronic illness: A family guide*. Baltimore: Paul H. Brookes.

GOLDMAN, H. (1970). Psychological testing of blind children. *Research Bulletin, American Foundation for the Blind, 21*, 77–90.

GOLDSTEIN, S., & TURNBULL, A. P. (1982). Strategies to increase parent participation in IEP conferences. *Exceptional Children, 48*, 360–361.

GOLLNICK, D. M., & CHINN, P. C. (1990). *Multicultural education in a pluralistic society* (3rd ed.). Columbus, OH: Merrill.

GOOD, C. V. (Ed.) (1959). *Dictionary of education* (2nd ed.). New York: McGraw-Hill.

GOOD, T., & BROPHY, J. (1987). *Looking in classrooms* (4th ed.). New York: Harper & Row.

GOTTESMAN, M. A. (1971). A comparative study of Piaget's developmental schema of sighted children with that of a group of blind children. *Child Development, 42*, 573–589.

GOTTESMAN, M. A. (1973). Conservation development in blind children. *Child Development, 44*, 824–827.

GOTTESMAN, M. A. (1976). Stage development of blind children: A Piagetian view. *New Outlook for the Blind, 70*, 94–100.

GOTTLIEB, J. (1981). Mainstreaming: Fulfilling the promise? *American Journal of Mental Deficiency, 86*, 115–126.

GOULD, S. J. (1981). *The mismeasure of man*. New York: Norton.

GOWMAN, A. G. (1957). *The war blind in American social structure*. New York: American Foundation for the Blind.

GRADEN, J. L. (1989). Redefining "prereferral" intervention as intervention assistance: Collaboration between general and special education. *Exceptional Children, 56*, 227–231.

GRAFF, C. J., AULT, M. M., GUESS, D., TAYLOR, M., & THOMPSON, B. (1990). *Health care for students with disabilities*. Baltimore: Paul H. Brookes.

GRAHAM, S., & HARRIS, K. R. (1989). The relevance of IQ in the determination of learning disabilities: Abandoning scores as decision makers. *Journal of Learning Disabilities, 22*(8), 500–503.

GRAHAM, M. A., & SCOTT, K. G. (1988). The impact of definitions of high risk on services to infants and toddlers. *Topics in Early Childhood Special Education, 10*, 1–17.

GRAY, R. (1981). Services for the LD adult: A working paper. *Learning Disability Quarterly, 4*, 426–434.

GREEN, C. W., REID, D. H., WHITE, L. K., HALFORD, R. C., BRITTAIN, D. P., & GARDNER, S. M. (1988). Identifying reinforcers for persons with profound handicaps: Staff opinion versus systematic assessment of preferences. *Journal of Applied Behavior Analysis, 21*, 31–43.

GREENAN, J. (1989). Identification, assessment, and placement of persons needing transition assistance. In D. E. Berkell & J. M. Brown (Eds.), *Transition from school to work for persons with disabilities*. New York: Longman.

GREENBERG, M., & KUSCHE, C. (1989). Cognitive, personal and social development of deaf children and adolescents. In M. C. Wang,

M. C. Reynolds, & H. J. Walberg (Eds.), *Handbook of special education: Research and practice. Vol. 3. Low incidence conditions.* New York: Pergamon Press.

GREENSPAN, S., & SHOULTZ, B. (1981). Why mentally retarded adults lose their jobs: Social incompetence as a factor in work adjustment. *Applied Research in Mental Retardation, 2,* 23–38.

GRESHAM, F. M. (1982). Misguided mainstreaming: The case for social skills training with handicapped children. *Exceptional Children, 48,* 420–433.

GRESHAM, F. M. (1988). Social competence and motivational characteristics of learning disabled students. In M. C. Wang, M. C. Reynolds, & H. J.. Walberg (Eds.), *Handbook of special education: Research and practice* (Vol. 2) (pp. 283–302). New York: Pergamon Press.

GRESHAM, F. M., & RESCHLY, D. J. (1986). Social skill deficits and low peer acceptance of mainstreamed learning disabled children. *Learning Disability Quarterly, 9* (1), 23–32.

GROSSMAN, F. K. (1972). *Brothers and sisters of retarded children.* Syracuse, NY: Syracuse University Press.

GROSSMAN, H. (1973, 1977, 1983). *A manual on terminology and classification in mental retardation* (rev. ed.). Washington, DC: American Association on Mental Deficiency.

GRUENEWALD, L., & POLLACK, S. (1990). *Language interaction in curriculum and instruction.* Austin, TX: Pro-Ed.

GUETZLOE, E. C. (1991). *Depression and suicide: Special education students at risk.* Reston, VA: Council for Exceptional Children.

GUILFORD, J. P. (1956). The structure of intellect. *Psychological Bulletin, 53,* 267–293.

GUILFORD, J. P. (1967). *The nature of human intelligence.* New York: McGraw-Hill.

GURALNICK, M. J. (1990). Major accomplishments and future directions in early childhood mainstreaming.. *Topics in Early Childhood Special Education, 10,* 1–17.

GWYNNE, F. (1976). *A chocolate moose for dinner.* New York: Windmill Books.

HACKNEY (1981). The gifted child, family, and the school. *Gifted Child Quarterly, 25,* 51–54.

HAGERMAN, R. J., McBOGG, P. M., & HAGERMAN, P. J. (1983). The fragile X syndrome: History, diagnosis, and treatment. *Journal of Developmental and Behavioral Pediatrics, 4,* 122–130.

HAIER, R. J., & DENHAM, S. A. (1976). A summary profile of the nonintellectual correlates of mathematical precocity in boys and girls. In D. P. Keating (Ed.), *Intellectual talent research and development* (pp. 225–241). Baltimore: Johns Hopkins University Press.

HALL, D. E., WRAY, D. F., CONTI, D. M. (1986). The language-disfluency relationship: A case study. *Hearing,* Fall, 110–113.

HALL, P. K. (1977). The occurrence of disfluencies in language-disordered preschool children. *Journal of Speech and Hearing Disorders, 42,* 364–369.

HALLAHAN, D. P., GAJAR, A., COHEN, S., & TARVER, S. (1978). Selective attention and focus of control in learning disabled and normal children. *Journal of Learning Disabilities, 11* (4), 47–52.

HALLAHAN, D. P., & KAUFFMAN, J. M. (1988). *Exceptional children: An introduction to special education* (4th ed.). Englewood Cliffs, NJ: Prentice-Hall.

HALLAHAN, D. P., & KAUFFMAN, J. M. (1991). *Exceptional children: Introduction to special education* (5th ed.). Englewood Cliffs, NJ: Prentice-Hall.

HALLAHAN, D. P., KELLER, C. E., McKINNEY, J. D., LLOYD, J. W., & BRYAN, T. (1988). Examining the research base of the Regular Education Initiative: Efficacy Studies and the Adaptive Learning Environments Model. *Journal of Learning Disabilities, 21,* 29–35.

HALLE, J. W., BAER, D. M., & SPRADLIN, J. E. (1981). Teachers' generalized use of delay as a stimulus control procedure to increase language use in handicapped children. *Journal of Applied Behavior Analysis, 14,* 389–409.

HALLENBECK, M., & BEERNINK, M. (1989). A support program for parents of students with mild handicaps. *Teaching Exceptional Children, 21* (3), 44–47.

HALLIDAY, M. A. K. (1973). *Explorations in the functions of language.* London: E. Arnold.

HALLINAN, M. T., & SORENSEN, A. B. (1987). Ability grouping and sex difference in mathematics achievement. *Sociology of Education, 60,* 64–72.

HALLORAN, W. J. (1989). Preface in D. E. Berkell and J. M. Brown (Eds.), *Transition from school to work for persons with disabilities.* New York: Longman.

HALPERN, A. (1985). Transition: A look at the foundations. *Exceptional Children, 5* (16), 479–486.

HALPERN, A. A., CLOSE, D. W., & NELSON, D. J. (1986). *On my own: The impact of semi-independent living programs for adults with mental retardation.* Baltimore: Paul H. Brookes.

HAMILTON, S. F. (1986). Excellence and the transition from school to work. *Phi Delta Kappan, 68* (4), 239–242.

HAMMILL, D. D. (1990). On defining learning disabilities: An emerging consensus. *Journal of Learning Disabilities, 23* (2), 74–84.

HAMMILL, D. D., & LARSEN, S. C. (1978). The effectiveness of psycholinguistic training: A reaffirmation of position. *Exceptional Children, 44,* 402–414.

HAMMILL, D. D., LEIGH, J. E., McNUTT, G., & LARSEN, S. C. (1981). A new definition of learning disabilities. *Learning Disability Quarterly, 4,* 336–342.

HAMMILL, P., CRANDELL, J. M., & COLARUSSO, R. (1970). The Slossen Intelligence Test adapted for visually limited children. *Exceptional Children, 36,* 535–536.

Handicapped students and special education (2nd Ed.) (1985). Rosemount, MN: Data Research, Inc.

HANLINE, M. F. (1988). Making the transition to preschool: Identification of parent needs. *Journal of the Division for Early Childhood, 12* (2), 98–108.

HANLINE, M. R., & KNOWLTON, A. (1988). A collaborative model for providing support to parents during their child's transition from infant intervention to preschool special education public school programs. *Journal of the Division for Early Childhood, 12* (2), 116–126.

HANSON, M. J. (1987). *Teaching the infant with Down syndrome: A guide for parents and professionals.* Austin, TX: Pro-Ed.

HANSON, M. J., & LYNCH, E. W. (1989). *Early intervention: Implementing child and family services for infants and toddlers who are at-risk or disabled.* Austin, TX: Pro-Ed.

HANZLIK, J. R., & STEVENSON, M. B. (1986). Interaction of mothers with their infants who are mentally retarded, retarded with cerebral palsy, or nonretarded. *American Journal of Mental Deficiency, 90* (5), 513–520.

HARING, N. G. (1970). The new curriculum design in special education. *Educational Technology, 10,* 24–31.

HARING, N. G., & PHILLIPS, E. L. (1962). *Educating emotionally disturbed children.* New York: McGraw-Hill.

HARING, N. G., & SCHIEFELBUSCH, R. L. (Eds.) (1976). *Teaching special children.* New York: McGraw-Hill.

HARING, N. G., WHITE, O. R., EDGAR, E. B., AFFLECK, J. Q., HAYDEN, A. H., MUNSON, M. G., & BENDERSKY, M. (Eds.) (1981). *Uniform performance assessment system.* Columbus, OH: Merrill.

HARING, T. G., & KENNEDY, C. H. (1990). Contextual control of problem behavior in students with severe disabilities. *Journal of Applied Behavior Analysis, 23,* 235–243.

HARING T. G., NEETZ, J. A., LOVINGER, L., PECK, C., & SEMMELL, M. I. (1987). Effects of four modified incidental teaching procedures to create opportunities for communication. *Journal of the Association for Persons with Severe Handicaps, 12,* 218–226.

HARLEY, R. K. (1973). Children with visual disabilities. In L. M. Dunn (Ed.), *Exceptional children in the schools* (2nd ed.). New York: Holt, Rinehart & Winston.

HARLEY, R. K., & LAWRENCE, G. A. (1984). *Visual impairment in the schools* (2nd ed.). Springfield, IL: Thomas.

HARPER-BARDACH, P. (1986). Education of the deaf. In C. W. Cummings (Ed.), *Otolaryngology: Head and neck Surgery* (Vol. 4) (pp. 3279–3291). St. Louis: C. V. Mosby.

HART, B. (1985). Naturalistic language training techniques. In S. Warren & A. Rogers-Waren (Eds.), *Teaching functional language*. Baltimore: University Park Press.

HARVEY, B. (1982a). Asthma. In E. E. Bleck and D. A. Nagel (Eds.), *Physically handicapped children: A medical atlas for teachers* (pp. 31–42). New York: Grune & Stratton.

HARVEY, B. (1982b). Cystic fibrosis. In E. E. Bleck and D. A. Nagel (Eds.), *Physically handicapped children: A medical atlas for teachers* (pp. 255–264). New York: Grune & Stratton.

HARVEY, J., JUDGE, C., & WIENER, S. (1977). Familial X-linked mental retardation with an X chromosome abnormality. *Journal of Human Genetics, 14,* 46–50.

HASAZI, S. B., & CLARK, G. M. (1988). Vocational programming for high school students labeled mentally retarded: Employment as a graduation goal. *Mental Retardation, 26,* 343–349.

HASAZI, S. B., GORDON, L. R., & ROE, C. A. (1985). Factors associated with the employment status of handicapped youth exiting high school from 1979–1983. *Exceptional Children,* 51 (6), 455–469.

HASKINS, R. (1989). Beyond metaphor: The efficacy of early childhood education. *American Psychologist, 44,* 274–282.

HASLAM, R. H. (1985). Common neurological disorders in children. In R. H. Haslam & P. J. Valletutti (Eds.), *Medical problems in the classroom: The teacher's role in diagnosis and management*. Austin TX: Pro-Ed.

HASSELBRING, T. S. (1990). Improving education through technology: Barriers and recommendations. *Preventing School Failure, 35*(3), 33–37.

HASSELBRING, T. S., & HAMLETT, C. L. (1984). Planning and managing instruction: Computer-based decision making. *Teaching Exceptional Children 16,* 248–252.

HATLEN, P. H. (1980). *Important concerns in the education of visually impaired children: MAVIS sourcebook 5*. Boulder, CO: Social Science Education Consortium.

HATLEN, P. H., & CURRY, S. A. (1987). In support of specialized programs for blind and visually impaired children: The impact of vision loss on learning. *Journal of Visual Impairment and Blindness, 81*(1), 7–13.

HAUCK, B. B., & FREEHILL, M. F. (1972). *The gifted: Case studies*. Dubuque, IA: William C. Brown.

HAYES, D. (1985). Amplification for hearing-impaired children. *Seminars in Hearing, 6*(3), pp. 223–321.

HAYES, S. P. (1941). *Contributions to a psychology of blindness*. New York: American Foundation for the Blind.

HAYWOOD, H. C. (1979). What happened to mild and moderate mental retardation? *American Journal of Mental Deficiency, 83,* 427–431.

HAZECAMP, J., & HUEBNER, K. (1989). *Program planning and evaluation for blind and visually impaired students: National guidelines for excellence*. New York: American Foundation for the Blind.

HEALY, A. (1984). Cerebral palsy. In J. A. Blackman (Ed.), *Medical aspects of developmental disabilities in children birth to three* (pp. 31–38). Rockville, MD: Aspen.

HEBB, D. O. (1942). The effect of early and late brain injury upon test scores, and the nature of adult intelligence. *Proceedings of the American Philosophical Society, 85,* 275–292.

HEBER, R. F. (1959, 1961). *A manual on terminology and classification in mental retardation*. Washington, DC: American Association on Mental Deficiency.

HEBER, R. F. (1970). *Epidemiology of mental retardation*. Springfield, IL: Thomas.

HEFLIN, L., & RUDY, K. (1991). *Homeless and in need of special education*. Reston, VA: Council for Exceptional Children.

HEINEMANN, A. W., DOLL, M., & SCHNOLL, S. (1989). Treatment of alcohol abuse in persons with recent spinal cord injuries. *Alcohol, Health, and Research World, 13,* 110–117.

HELGE, D. (1990). *A national study regarding at-risk students*. Bellingham, WA: National Rural Development Institute.

HELGE, D. (1991). *Rural, exceptional, at risk*. Reston, VA: Council for Exceptional Children.

HELLER, K. A., HOLTZMAN, W. H., & MESSICK, S. (Eds.) (1982). *Placing children in special education: A strategy for equity*. Washington, DC: National Academy Press.

HELLER, T., BOND, M. A., & BRADDOCK, D. (1988). Family reactions to institutional closure. *American Journal on Mental Retardation, 92*(4), 336–343.

HELLER, H. W., & SCHILIT, J. The Regular Education Initiative: A concerned response. *Focus on Exceptional Children, 20, 1–6.*

HELM, J. M. (1988). Adolescent mothers of handicapped children: A challenge for interventionists. *Journal of the Division for Early Childhood, 12*(4), 311–319.

HELM-ESTABROOKS, N. (1987). Diagnosis and management of neurogenic stuttering in adults. In K. O. St. Louis (Ed.), *The atypical stutterer: Principles and practices of rehabilitation* (pp. 193–217). San Diego: Academic Press.

HELTON, G. B., WORKMAN, E. A., & MATUSZEK, P. A. (1982). *Psychoeducational assessment: Integrating concepts and techniques*. New York: Grune & Stratton.

HERON, T. E., & AXELROD, S. (1976). Effectiveness of feedback to mothers concerning their children's word recognition performance. *Reading Improvement, 13,* 74–81.

HERSHEY, M. (1977). Telephone instruction: An alternative educational delivery system for teacher in-service. *Gifted Child Quarterly, 21,* 213–217.

HEWARD, W. L., DARDIG, J. C., & ROSSETT, A. (1979). *Working with parents of handicapped children*. Columbus, OH: Merrill.

HEWETT, F. M. (1968). *The emotionally disturbed child in the classroom*. Boston: Allyn & Bacon.

HICKS, D., & STUCKLESS, E. (Eds.) (1991). *1990 International Congress of Education of the Deaf: Proceedings II: Topical addresses*. Rochester, New York: National Technical Institute for the Deaf, Rochester Institute of Technology.

HIEBERT, B., WONG, B., & HUNTER, M. (1982). Affective influences on learning disabled adolescents. *Learning Disability Quarterly, 5,* 334–343.

HILL, E. W. (1986). Orientation and mobility. In G. T. School (Ed.), *Foundations of education for blind visually handicapped children and youth: Theory and practice* (pp. 315–340). New York: American Foundation for the Blind.

HIV/AIDS (1990). Excerpt from *HIV/AIDS Education: Resources for Special Educators*, a joint publication of the Council for Exceptional Children and the Association for the Advancement of Health Education. Reston, VA: Council for Exceptional Children.

HOBBS, N. (1966). Helping the disturbed child: Psychological and ecological strategies. *American Psychologist, 21,* 1105–1115.

HOBBS, N. (1975) *The future of children*. San Francisco: Jossey-Bass.

HODSON, B. W. (1986). *The assessment of phonological process—Revised*. Austin, TX: Pro-Ed.

HOFMEISTER, A., & FERRERA, J. M. (1986). Expert systems and special education. *Exceptional Children, 53*(3), 235–239.

HOLLAND, A., SWINDELL, C., & REINMUTH, O. (1990). Aphasia and related adult disorders. In G. Shames and E. Wiig (Eds.), *Human communication disorders*. Columbus, OH: Merrill.

HOLLINGWORTH, L. (1942). *Children above 180 IQ*. New York: Harcourt Brace Jovanovich.

HOLLIS, J. H., & MEYERS, E. (Eds.) (1982). *Life-threatening behavior: Analysis and intervention*. Washington, DC: American Association on Mental Deficiency.

HOLM, V. A., & KUNZE, L. H. (1969). Effect of chronic otitis media on language and speech development. *Pediatrics, 43,* 833.

HONIG v. DOE, 56 S. Ct. 27 (1988).

HOPKINS, T. W., BICE, H. V., & COLTON, K. C. (1954). *Evaluation and education of the cerebral palsied child.* Arlington, VA: International Council for Exceptional Children.

HORN, E., JONES, H. A., & HAMLETT, C. (1991). An investigation of the feasibility of a video game system for developing scanning and selection skills. *Journal of the Association for Persons with Severe Handicaps, 16,* 108–115.

HORNER, R. H., DUNLAP, G., KOEGEL, R. L., CARR, E. G., SAILOR, W., ANDERSON, J., ALBIN, R. W., & O'NEILL, R. E. (1990). Toward a technology of "nonaversive" behavioral support. *Journal of the Association for Persons with Severe Handicaps, 15,* 125–132.

HORTON, S. V., & LOVITT, T. C. (in press). Using study guides with three classifications of secondary students. *Journal of Special Education.*

HORTON, S. V., & LOVITT, T. C., & BERGERUD, D. (1990). The effectiveness of graphic organizers for three classifications of secondary students in content area classes. *Journal of Learning Disabilities 23*(1), 12–22, 29.

HORTON, S. V., MADDOX, M., & EDGAR, E. (1983). *The adult transition model: Planning or post school services.* Seattle: University of Washington.

HOWELL, K. W., & MOREHEAD, M. K. (1987). *Curriculum-based evaluation in special and remedial education.* Columbus, OH: Merrill.

HOWELL, R. (1988). The ethics of technological intervention with disabled learners. Symposium: Technological equity: Issues in ethics and theory. Proceedings of selected research papers presented at the Annual Meeting of the Association for Educational Communications and Technology, New Orleans.

HOWLEY, A., HOWLEY, C., & PENDARVIS, E. (1986). *Teaching gifted children: Principles and strategies.* Boston: Little, Brown.

HOYSON, M., JAMIESON, B., & STRAIN, P. S. (1984). Individualized group instruction of normally developing and autistic-like children: The LEAP curriculum model. *Journal of the Division for Early Childhood, 8,* 157–172.

HUGHES, D. (1989). Generalization from language therapy to classroom academics. *Seminars in Speech and Language. 10*(3), 218–230.

HUMPHRIES, T. W., & BAUMAN, E. (1980). Maternal child rearing attitudes associated with learning disabilities. *Journal of Learning Disabilities, 13,* 459–462.

HUNT, J. McV. (1961). *Intelligence and experience.* New York: Ronald.

HUNT, P., GOETZ, L., ALWELL, M., & SAILOR, W. (1986). Using an interrupted behavior chain strategy to teach generalized communication responses to students with severe disabilities. *Journal of the Association for Persons with Severe Handicaps, 11,* 196–204.

HUNTZE, S. L. (1988). Cooperative interface of schools and other child care systems for behaviorally disordered students. In M. C. Wang, M. C. Reynolds, & H. J. Walberg (Eds.), *Handbook of special education: Research and practice* (Vol. 2) (pp. 125–153). New York: Pergamon Press.

HyperABLEDATA (1992). Madison, WI: Trace Research and Development Center, University of Wisconsin [CD-ROM disk].

IDOL, L., PAOLUCCI-WHITCOMB, P., & NEVIN, A. (1986). *Collaborative consultation.* Austin, TX: Pro-Ed.

IDOL, L., & WEST, J. F. (1987). Consultation in special education (Part II): Training and practice. *Journal of Learning Disabilities, 20,* 474–494.

IDOL-MAESTAS, L. (1981). Behavior patterns in families of boys with learning and behavior problems. *Journal of Learning Disabilities, 14,* 347–349.

INGRAM, D. (1981). *Procedures for the phonological analysis of children's language.* Baltimore: University Park Press.

INSTITUTE OF MEDICINE (1989). *Research on children and adolescents with mental, behavioral, and developmental disorders.* Washington, DC: National Academy Press.

INTERAGENCY COMMITTEE ON LEARNING DISABILITIES (1987). *Learning disabilities: A report to the U.S. Congress.* Washington, DC: U.S. Department of Health and Human Services.

IRETON, H., & THWING, E. (1974). *Manual of the Minnesota Child Development Inventory.* Minneapolis: Behavior Science Systems.

IRVING INDEPENDENT SCHOOL DISTRICT v. TATRO, 468 U.S. 833, 104 S. Ct. 3371, 82 L. Ed. 2d 664 (1984).

ITARD, J. M. (1932). *The wild boy of Aveyron* (G. Humphrey & M. Humphrey, Trans.). New York: Appleton-Century-Crofts. (Originally published 1894.)

JACOBS, J. C. (1971). Effectiveness of teacher and parent identification of gifted children as a function of school level. *Psychology in the Schools, 8,* 140–142.

JAMES, S. (1990). *Normal language acquisition.* Boston: College-Hill.

JENKINS, J., SPELTZ, M., & ODOM, S. (1985). Integrating normal and handicapped preschoolers: Effects on child development and social interaction. *Exceptional Children, 52,* 7–17.

JENKINS, M. W. (1987). Effect of a computerized individual education program (IEP) writer on time savings and quality. *Journal of Special Education Technology, 8*(3), 55–66.

JENSEN, A. R., & FREDERICKSON, J. (1973). Free recall of categorized and uncategorized lists: A test of the Jensen hypothesis. *Journal of Educational Psychology, 3,* 304–314.

JOHNSON, C. M. (1980). *Preparing handicapped students for work: Alternative secondary programming.* Reston, VA: Council for Exceptional Children.

JOHNSON, D., & MYKLEBUST, H. (1967). *Learning disabilities: Educational principles and practices.* New York: Grune & Stratton.

JOHNSON, D. R., BRUNINKS, R. H., & THURLOW, M. L. (1987). Meeting the challenge of transition service planning through improved interagency cooperation. *Exceptional Children, 53,* 522–530.

JOHNSON, D. W., & JOHNSON, R. T. (1980). Integrating handicapped students into the mainstream. *Exceptional Children, 47,* 90–98.

JOHNSON, J. L. (1988). The challenge of substance abuse. *Teaching Exceptional Children, 20*(4), 29–31.

JOHNSON, P. T. (1986). *The principal's guide to the educational rights of handicapped students.* Reston, VA: National Association of Secondary School Principals.

JOHNSON, R. E., LIDDELL, S. K., & ERTING, C. J. (1989). *Unlocking the curriculum: Principles for achieving access in deaf education.* Washington, DC: Gallaudet University, Gallaudet Research Institute Working Paper 89-93.

JOHNSON-MARTIN, N., ATTERMEIER, S. M., & HACKER, B. (1990). *The Carolina curriculum for preschoolers with special needs.* Baltimore: Paul H. Brookes.

JOHNSON-MARTIN, N., JENS, K. G., & ATTERMEIER, S. M. (1986). *The Carolina curriculum for handicapped infants and infants at risk.* Baltimore: Paul H. Brookes.

JOHNSTON, L. K., O'MALLEY, P. M., & BACHMAN, J. G. (1988). *Illicit drug use, smoking, and drinking by America's high school students, college students, and young adults, 1975–1987.* Rockville, MD: National Institute on Drug Abuse.

JOHNSTON, R. B., & MAGRAB, P. R. (Eds.) (1976). *Developmental disorders: Assessment, treatment, education.* Baltimore: University Park Press.

JONES, G. A. (1989). Alcohol abuse and traumatic brain injury. *Alcohol, Health, and Research World, 13,* 104–109.

JONES, M. H. (1983). Cerebral palsy. In J. Umbriet (Ed.), *Physical disabilities and health impairment: An introduction* (pp. 41–58). Columbus, OH: Merrill.

KAHN, L., & LEWIS, N. (1986). *Kahn-Lewis phonological analysis.* Circle Pines, MN: American Guidance Service.

KAISER, A. P., ALPERT, C. L., & WARREN, S. F. (1987). Teaching functional language: Strategies for language intervention. In M. E. Snell (Ed.), *Systematic instruction of persons with severe handicaps* (3rd ed.). Columbus, OH: Merrill.

KAISER, A. P., YODER, P. J., KEETZ, A. (1992). Evaluating milieu teaching. In S. F. Warren & J. Reichle (Eds.). *Causes and effects of communication and language intervention* (pp. 9–47). Baltimore: Paul H. Brookes.

KALINOWSKI, A. G. (1985). The development of Olympic swimmers. In B. S. Bloom (Ed.), *Developing talent in young people* (pp. 139–192). New York: Ballantine Books.

KAMEENUI, E. J., & SIMMONS, D. C. (1990 *Designing instructional strategies: The prevention of academic learning problems.* Columbus, OH: Merrill.

KANNER, L. (1964). *A history of the care and study of the mentally retarded.* Springfield, IL: Thomas.

KARNES, M. B., & JOHNSON, L. J. (1987). An imperative: Programming for the young gifted/talented. *Journal for the Education of the Gifted, 10*(3), 195–214.

KASHIMA, K. J., BAKER, B. L., & LANDAU, S. J. (1980). Media based versus professionally led training for parents of mentally retarded children. *American Journal of Mental Retardation, 93*(2), 209–217.

KATZ, S., BORTEN, J., BRASILE, D., MEISNER, M., & PARKER, C. (1980). The IEP process. *Pointer, 25*, 35–45.

KAUFMAN, A. S., & KAUFMAN, N. L. (1983). *The Kaufman Assessment Battery for children.* Circle Pines, MN: American Guidance Services.

KAUFFMAN, J. M. (1987). Social policy issues in special education and related services for emotionally disturbed children and youth. In N. G. Haring (Ed.), *Measuring and managing behavior disorders* (pp. x–xx). Seattle: University of Washington Press.

KAUFFMAN, J. M. (1989). *Characteristics of behavior disorders of children and youth* (4th ed.). Columbus, OH: Merrill.

KAUFFMAN, J. M., GERBER, M. M., & SEMMEL, M. I. (1988). Arguable assumptions underlying the Regular Education Initiative. *Journal of Learning Disabilities, 21*, 6–11.

KAUFFMAN, J. M., & KROUSE, J. (1981). The cult of educability: Searching for the substance of things hoped for; the evidence of things not seen. *Analysis and Intervention in Developmental Disabilities, 1*(1), 53–60.

KAVALE, K. A. (1988). The long-term consequences of learning disabilities. In M. C. Wang, M. C. Reynolds, & H. J. Walberg (Eds.), *Handbook of special education: Research and practice* (Vol. 2) (pp. 303–344). New York: Pergamon Press.

KAVALE, K. A., & FORNESS, S. R. (1985). Learning disability and the history of science: Paradigm or paradox? *Remedial and Special Education, (6)*4, 12–23.

KAVALE, K. A., & FORNESS, S. R. (1987). Substance over style: Assessing the efficacy of modality testing and teaching. *Exceptional Children, 54*(3), 228–239.

KAVALE, K. A., & NYE, C. (1985). Parameters of learning disabilities in achievement, linguistic, neuropsychological, and social/behavioral domains. *Journal of Special Education, 19*(4), 443–458.

KAZAK, A. E., & MARVIN, R. S. (1984). Differences, difficulties, and adaptation: Stress and social networks in families with a handicapped child. *Family Relations, 33*, 67–77.

KEANE, D. (1987). Assessing deaf children. In C. S. Lidz (Ed.), *Dynamic assessment* (pp. 360–376). New York: Guilford.

KEANE, K. (1983). *Application of mediated learning theory to a deaf population: A study in cognitive modifiability.* Unpublished doctoral dissertation, Columbia University, New York.

KEANE, K., TANNENBAUM, A., & KRAPF, G. (1992). Cognitive competence: Reality and potential in the deaf. In H. C. Haywood & D. Tzuriel (Eds.), *Interactive Assessment.* New York: Springer-Verlag.

KEATING, D. P. (1976). Creative potential of mathematically precocious boys. In D. P. Keating (Ed.), *Intellectual talent research and development* (pp. 262–272). Baltimore: Johns Hopkins University Press.

KEATS, S. (1965). *Cerebral palsy.* Springfield, IL: Thomas.

KELLER, H. (1933). Helen Keller in Scotland. London: McThuen & Co.

KELLY, E. J. (1990). *The differential test of conduct and emotional problems.* Aurora, IL: Slossen.

KELLY, J. A., WILDMAN, B. G., & BERLER, E. S. (1980). Small group behavioral training to improve the job interview skills repertoire of mildly retarded adolescents. *Journal of Applied Behavioral Analysis, 13*, 461–471.

KEMLER, D. G. (1983). Wholistic and analytic modes of perceptual and cognitive development. In T. J. Tighe & B. E. Shepp (Eds.), *Interactions: Perception, cognition, and development.* Hillsdale, NJ: Lawrence Erlbaum Associates.

KENOWITZ, L. A., GALLAGHER, J., & EDGAR, E. B. (1977). Generic services for the severely handicapped and their families: What's available? In E. Sontag (Ed.), *Educational programming for the severely and profoundly handicapped.* Reston, VA: Council for Exceptional Children, Division on Mental Retardation.

KENTUCKY ASSOCIATION FOR RETARDED CHILDREN ET AL. v. KENTUCKY STATE BOARD OF EDUCATION ET AL., Civil Action No 435 (E. D. KY, filed September 12, 1973).

KENTUCKY SOCIETY FOR THE PREVENTION OF BLINDNESS (1990). *Handbook for preschool vision screening.* Louisville, KY: Author.

KEOGH, B. K. (1987). A shared attribute model of learning disabilities. In S. Vaughn & C. S. Bos (Eds.), *Research in learning disabilities* (pp. 3–12). Boston: College-Hill.

KEOGH, B. K. (1988). Learning disability: Diversity in search of order. In M. C. Wang, M. C. Reynolds, & H. J. Walberg (Eds.), *Handbook of special education: Research and practice* (Vol. 2) (pp. 225–251). New York: Pergamon Press.

KERNAN, K., & KOEGEL, R. (1980). *Employment experiences of community-based mildly retarded adults.* Working paper No. 14, Socio-Behavioral Group, Mental Retardation Research Center, School of Medicine, University of California, Los Angeles.

KERR, M. M., & NELSON, C. M. (1989). *Strategies for managing behavior problems in the classroom* (2nd ed.). Columbus, OH: Merrill.

KERR, M. M., NELSON, C. M., & LAMBERT, D. L. (1987). *Helping adolescents with learning and behavior problems.* Columbus, OH: Merrill.

KERSHMAN, S. (1982). The training needs of parents of deaf-blind-multihandicapped children. *Education of the Visually Handicapped, 13*, 98–108.

KESSALBRENNER v. ANONYMOUS, 33 N. Y. 2d 161, 305N. E. 2d 903, 350 N. Y. S. 889 (1973).

KIERNAN, W. E., & CIBOROWSKI, J. (1986). Survey of employment for adults with developmental disabilities. *Remedial and Special Education, 7*(6), 25–30.

KINDRED, M., COHEN, J., PENROD, D., & SHAFFER, T. (1975). *The mentally retarded citizen and the law.* New York: Free Press.

KINGSTON, W. J., & MOXLEY, R. T. (1989). Treatment of muscular dystrophies. *General Pharmacology, 20*(3), 263–268.

KIRCHNER, C., STEPHEN, G., & CHANDU, F. (1987). Statistics on blindness and visual impairment. *Yearbook of the Association for Education and Rehabilitation of the Blind and Visually Impaired, 5*, 121.

KIRK, E. C. (1981). *Vision pathology in education.* Springfield, IL: Thomas.

KIRK, S. A. (1962). *Educating exceptional children.* Boston: Houghton Mifflin.

KIRK, S. A., & GALLACHER, L. T. (1979). Children with visual impairments. In *Educating exceptional children* (3rd ed.) (pp. 237–239). Boston: Houghton Mifflin.

KIRSTEIN, L. (1983). Classic ballet: Aria of the aerial. In R. Copeland and M. Cohen (Eds.), *What is dance? Readings in theory and criticism* (pp. 238–243). Oxford: Oxford University Press.

KISTNER, J., & OSBORNE, M. (1987). A longitudinal study of LD children's self-evaluations. *Learning Disability Quarterly*, 258–266.

KITANO, M. K., & KIRBY, D. F. (1986). *Gifted education: A comprehensive view.* Toronto: Little, Brown.

KLEIN, B., VanHASSELT, V. B., TREFELNER, M., SANDSTROM, D. J., & BRANDT-SNYDER, P. (1988). The parent and toddler training project for visually impaired and blind multihandicapped children. *Journal of Visual Impairment and Blindness, 82*(2), 59–64.

KLEIN, R. S., ALTMAN, S. D., DREIZEN, K., FRIEDMAN, R., & POWERS, L. (1981). Restructuring dysfunctional parental attitudes toward children's learning and behavior in school. *Journal of Learning Disabilities, 14,* 99–101.

KLINE, D. F. (1977). *Child abuse and neglect: A primer for school personnel.* Reston, VA: Council for Exceptional Children.

KNIGHT-AREST, I. (1984). Communicative effectiveness of learning disabled and normally achieving 10-to-13-year-old boys. *Learning Disability Quarterly, 7,* 237–245.

KNOBLOCK, P. (1973). Open education for emotionally disturbed children. *Exceptional Children, 39,* 358–365.

KNOFF, H. M. (1983). Investigating disproportionate influence and status in multidisciplinary child study teams. *Exceptional Children, 49,* 367–369.

KNUDSEN, G. (1980). "Om 'Rhode Island Curriculum,'" in *Nordisk Tidskrift for Dovundervisningen.*

KOCH, R., FRIEDMAN, E. C., AZEN, C., WENZ, E., PARTON, P., LEDUE, X., & FISHLER, K. (1988). Inborn errors of metabolism and the prevention of mental retardation. In F. J. Menolascino & J. A. Stark (Eds.), *Preventive and curative intervention in mental retardation* (pp. 61–90). Baltimore: Paul H. Brookes.

KOCHANY, L., & KELLER, J. (1981). An analysis and evaluation of the failures of severely disabled individuals in competitive employment. In P. Wehman (Ed.), *Competitive employment: New horizons for severely disabled individuals* (pp. 181–198). Baltimore: Paul H. Brookes.

KOEGEL, R. L., RINCOVER, A., & EGEL, A. L. (1982). *Educating and understanding autistic children.* Boston: College-Hill.

KOEHLER, J. (1982). Spinal muscular atrophy of childhood. In E. E. Bleck and D. A. Nagel (Eds.), *Physically handicapped children: A medical atlas for teachers* (pp. 477–481). New York: Grune & Stratton.

KOHLER, F. W., & STRAIN, P. S. (1990). Peer-assisted interventions: Early promises, notable achievements, and future aspirations. *Clinical Psychology Review, 10,* 441–452.

KOKASKA, C. J., & BROLIN, D. E. (1985). *Career education for handicapped individuals* (2nd ed.). Columbus, OH: Merrill.

KORNBLUM, H. (1982). A social worker's role with mothers' language disordered preschool children. *Journal of Learning Disabilities, 13,* 406–408.

KOUGH, L., & DeHAAN, R. (1958). *Teachers' guidance handbook* (Vol. 1, Elementary Edition). Chicago: Science Research Associates.

KRANZ, B. (1978). *Multidimensional screening device for the identification of gifted talented children* (3rd ed.). Fairfax, VA: Fairfax County Public Schools.

KREGEL, J., WEHMAN, P., & BANKS, P. D. (1989). The effects of consumer characteristics and types of employment model on individuals' outcomes in supported employment. *Journal of Applied Behavior Analysis, 22,* 407–416.

KRIPPNER, S. (1967). *Characteristics of gifted and talented youth.* Paper presented at a workshop sponsored by Science Research Associates. Washington, DC: U.S. Department of Health, Education, and Welfare, Office of Education.

KRIVACSKA, J. J. (1987). *Computerized IEP management systems.* Paper presented at the Annual Meeting of the National Assocation of School Psychologists in New Orleans.

KROTH, R. L. (1985). *Communicating with parents of exceptional children* (2nd ed.). Denver: Love.

KULIK, C. C., & KULIK, J. A. (1982). Research synthesis on ability grouping. *Educational Leadership, 39*(8), 619–621.

KULIK, J., & KULIK, C. (1984). Effects of accelerated instruction on students. *Review of Educational Research, 54*(3), 409–425.

KULIK, J. A., BANGERT, R. L., & WILLIAMS, G. W. (1983). Effects of computer-based teaching on secondary school students. *Journal of Educational Psychology, 75,* 19–26.

KUNKEL, L. M., BEGGS, A. H., & HOFFMAN, E. P. (1989). Molecular genetics of Duchenne and Becker muscular dystrophy: Emphasis on improved diagnosis. *Clinical Chemistry, 35* (7 supplemental), 21–24.

KURTZ, P. D., DEVANEY, B., STRAIN, P., & SANDLER, H. (1982). Effects of mass-media and group instruction on increasing parent awareness of early identification. *Journal of Special Education, 16,* 329–340.

KURZWEIL, R. (1990). A machine that reads. *Reading Teacher, 43,* 512–513.

LaMAR, K., & ROSENBERG, B. (1988). *Synthesis of individual transition plans: Format and process.* Sacramento: Education Transition Center Program, Curriculum, and Training Unit, Special Education Division, California State Department of Education.

LACHIEWICZ, A. M., GULLION, C. M., SPIRIDIGLIOZZI, G. A., & AYLSWORTH, A. S. (1987). Declining IQs of young males with the fragile X syndrome. *American Journal of Mental Deficiency, 92,* 272–278.

LACKNER, J. (1968). A developmental study of language behavior in retarded children. *Neuropsychologia, 6,* 301–320.

LAHEY, M. (1988). *Language disorders and language development.* New York: Macmillan.

LAHM, E. A. (Ed.) (1989). *Technology with low incidence populations: Promoting access to education and learning.* Reston, VA: Council for Exceptional Children.

LAMBERT, N., & WINDMILLER, M. B. (1981). *AAMD adaptive behavior scale—School edition.* Monterey, CA: Publishers Test Service.

LAMBERT, N., WINDMILLER, M., COLE, L., & FIGUEROA, R. (1975). *Manual for American Association on Mental Deficiency adaptive behavior scale public school version* (1974 revision). Washington, DC: American Association on Mental Deficiency.

LANE, D., & STRATFORD, D. (1987). Current approaches to Down's syndrome. East Sussex, Great Britain: Holt, Rinehart & Winston.

LANE, H. (1976). *The wild boy of Aveyron.* New York: Bantam Books.

LANGLEY, M. B. (1989). Assessing infant cognitive development. In D. B. Bailey & M. Wolery (Eds.). *Assessing infants and preschoolers with handicaps* (pp. 249–274). Columbus, OH: Merrill.

LARIVEE, B. (1981). Modality preference as a model for differentiating beginning reading instruction: A review of the issues. *Learning Disability Quarterly, 4*(2), 180–188.

LARIVEE, B. (1986). Effective teaching for mainstreamed students is effective teaching for all students. *Teacher Education and Special Education, 9*(4), 174–179.

LARRY P. v. RILES, C-71-2270 (RFD, District Court for Northern California 1972).

LASKY, E. (1991). Comprehending and processing of information in clinic and classroom. In C. S. Simon (Ed.), *Communication skills and classroom success.* Eau Claire, WI: Thinking Publications, A Division of McKinley Companies, Inc.

LASKY, E. Z., & KATZ, J. (1985). *Central auditory processing disorders.* Baltimore: University Park Press.

LASKY, E., & KLOPP, K. (1982). Parent-child interactions in normal and language disordered children. *Journal of Speech and Hearing Disorders, 47,* 7–18.

LAU v. NICHOLS, 94 S. Ct. 786 (1974).

LAWRENCE, P. A. (1988). Basic strategies for mainstream integration. *Academic Therapy, 23*(4), 349–355.

LeBLANC, J. M., HOKO, J. A., AANGEENBRUG, M. H., & ETZEL, B. C. (1985). Microcomputers and stimulus control: From the laboratory to the classroom. *Journal of Special Education Technology, 7*(1), 23–31.

LEFEBVRE, D., & STRAIN, P. S. (1989). Effects of a group contingency on the frequency of special interactions among autistic and nonhandicapped preschool children: Making LRE efficacious. *Journal of Early Intervention, 13,* 329–341.

LEFKOWITZ, M. M., ERON, L. D., WALDER, L. O., & HUESMANN, L. R. (1977). *Growing up to be violent.* Elmsford, New York: Pergamon Press.

LeMAY, D. W., GRIFFIN, P. M., & SANFORD, A. R. (1978). *Learning accomplishment profile—Diagnostic.* Chapel Hill, NC: Chapel Hill Training and Outreach Project.

LEMPERLE, G. (1985). Plastic surgery. In D. Lane & B. Stratford (Eds.), *Current approaches to Down's syndrome* (pp. 131–145). Sydney: Holt, Rinehart & Winston.

LENNEBERG, E. H. (1967). *Biological foundations of language.* New York: Wiley.

LENZ, B. K., ALLEY, G. R., & SCHUMAKER, J. B. (1987). Activating the inactive learner: Advance organizers in the secondary content classroom. *Learning Disability Quarterly, 10,* 53–67.

LENZ, B. K., & HUGHES, C. A. (1990). A word identification strategy for adolescents with learning disabilities. *Journal of Learning Disabilities, 23*(3), 149–163.

LEONE, P. E. (1991). *Alcohol and other drugs: Use, abuse and disabilities.* Reston, VA: Council for Exceptional Children.

LERNER, J. (1988). *Learning disabilities: Theories, diagnosis, and teaching strategies.* (3rd ed.). Boston: Houghton Mifflin.

LESSARD v. SCHMIDT, Civil No. 71-C-602 (E. D. Wisc. 1972).

LEVINSON, H. N. (1980). *A solution to the riddle of dyslexia.* New York: Springer.

LEVITT, H. (1989). Speech and hearing in communication. In M. C. Wang, M. C. Reynolds, & H. J. Walberg (Eds.), *Handbook of special education: Research and practice: Vol. 3. Low incidence conditions.* New York: Pergamon Press.

LEWIS, E. D. (1933). Types of mental deficiency and their social significance. *Journal of Mental Science, 79,* 298–304.

LEWIS, R. B., & DOORLANG, D. H. (1983). *Teaching special students in the mainstream.* Columbus, OH: Merrill.

LIDZ, C. S. (1987). *Dynamic assessment: An interactional approach to evaluate learning potential.* New York: Guilford.

LILLIE, D. (1981). Educational and psychological strategies for working with parents. In J. L. Paul (Ed.), *Understanding and working with parents of children with special needs* (pp. 89–118). New York: Holt, Rinehart & Winston.

LILLIE, D. L. (1983). *Comparison of microcomputer-generated IEPs and teacher written IEPs: A pilot study.* Paper presented at the Annual Convention of the Association for Children and Adults with Learning Disabilities in Washington, DC.

LILLY, S. M. (1988). The regular education initiative: A force for change in general and special education. *Education and Training in Mental Retardation, 23*(4), 253–260.

LINDSAY, B. (1977). Leadership giftedness: Developing a profile. *Journal for the Education of the Gifted, 11*(1), 63–69.

LINDSEY, J. D. (1987). *Computers and exceptional individuals.* Columbus, OH: Merrill.

LINK, M. P. (1991). Is integration really the least restrictive environment? *Teaching Exceptional Children, 23*(4), 63–66.

LIVINGSTON, J. S. (1958). Evaluation of enlarged test forms used with partially seeing. *Sight Saving Review, 28,* 37–39.

LLOYD, J. W. (1988). Direct academic interventions in learning disabilities. In M. C. Wang, M. C. Reynolds, & H. J. Walberg (Eds.), *Handbook of special education: Research and practice: Vol. 2. Mildly handicapped conditions* (pp. 345–366). New York: Pergamon Press.

LOMBARDINO, L., & MANGAN, N. (1983). Parents as language trainers: Language programming with developmentally delayed children. *Exceptional Children, 49,* 358–361.

LORBER, J. (1990). Where have all the spina bifida gone? *Midwife Health Visitor & Community Nurse, 22,* 94–95.

LOUIS HARRIS AND ASSOCIATES, INC. (1989). *The ICD survey III: A report card on special education.* New York: International Center for the Disabled.

LOVAAS, O. I., SCHREIBMAN, L., KOEGEL, R., & REHM, R. (1971). Selective responding by autistic children to multiple sensory input. *Journal of Abnormal Psychology, 77,* 211–222.

LOVAAS, I. (1985, September). *Behavioral treatment and recovery in young autistic children.* Paper presented at the annual meeting of the Florida Association for Behavior Analysis, Tampa.

LOWENBRAUN, S., & THOMPSON, M. (1989). Environments and strategies for learning and teaching. In M. C. Wang, M. C. Reynolds, & H. J. Walberg, (Eds.), *Handbook of special education: Research and practice: Vol. 3. Low incidence conditions.* New York: Pergamon Press.

LOWENFELD, B. (1971). *Our blind children: Growing and learning with them* (3rd ed.). Springfield, IL: Thomas.

LOWENFELD, B. (1973). History of the education of visually handicapped children. *The visually handicapped child in school.* New York: John Day.

LOWENFELD, B. (1975). *The changing status of the blind: From separation to integration.* Springfield, IL: Thomas.

LOWENFELD, B., ABEL, G., & HATLEN, P. (1969). *Blind children learn to read.* Springfield, IL: Thomas.

LUBS, H. A. (1969). A marker X chromosome. *American Journal of Human Genetics, 21,* 231–244.

LUCITO, L. (1964). Independence-conformity behavior as a function of intellect: Bright and dull children. *Exceptional Children, 31*(1), 5–13.

LUFTIG, R. L. (1988). Assessment of the perceived school loneliness and isolation of mentally retarded and nonretarded students. *American Journal of Mental Deficiency, 92,* 472–475.

LUND, N. J., & DUNCHAN, J. F. (1988). Assessing children's language in naturalistic contexts. Englewood Cliffs, NJ: Prentice-Hall.

LUSTHAUS, C. S., LUSTHAUS, E. W., & GIBBS, H. (1981). Parents' role in the decision process. *Exceptional Children, 48,* 256–257.

LUTZER, V. D., & BRUBAKER, T. H. (1988). Differential respite needs of aging parents of individuals with mental retardation. *Mental Retardation, 26*(1), 13–15.

LYNCH, E. C., & STALOCH, N. H. (1988). Parental perceptions of physicians' communication in the informing process. *Mental Retardation, 26*(2), 77–81.

LYNCH, E. W., & BAKLEY, S. (1989). Serving young children whose parents are mentally retarded. *Infants and Young Children, 1*(3), 26–38.

LYNCH, E. W., & HANSON, M. J. (1992). *Developing cross-cultural competence: A guide for working with young children and their families.* Baltimore: Paul H. Brookes.

LYNCH, E. W., & STEIN, R. (1982). Perspectives on parent participation in special education. *Exceptional Education Quarterly, 3*(2), 56–63.

LYON, G. R. (1985). Identification and remediation of learning disability subtypes: Preliminary findings. *Learning Disabilities Focus, 1*(1), 21–35.

MacDONALD, L., & BRAZIER, B. (1989). Behavioral parent training by telephone. *Journal of Practical Approaches to Developmental Handicaps, 13*(1), 14–19.

MacKEITH, R. (1973). The feelings and behavior of parents of handicapped children. *Developmental Medicine and Child Neurology, 15,* 524–527.

MACK, C. G., KOENIG, A. J., & ASHCROFT, S. C. (1990). Microcomputers and access technology in programs for teachers of visually impaired students. *Journal of Visual Impairment and Blindness, 84*(10), 526–530.

MacMILLAN, D. L. (1982). *Mental retardation in school and society* (2nd ed.). Boston: Little, Brown.

MacMILLAN, D. L. (1988). Issues in mental retardation. *Education and Training in Mental Retardation, 23*(4), 273–284.

MacMILLAN, D. L. (1991). *Hidden youth: Dropouts from special education.* Reston, VA: Council for Exceptional Children.

MacMILLAN, D. L., & BORTHWICK, S. (1980). The new educable mentally retarded population: Can they be mainstreamed? *Mental Retardation, 18,* 155–158.

MADDEN, N. A., & SLAVIN, R. E. (1983). Effects of cooperative learning on the social acceptance of mainstreamed academically handicapped students. *Journal of Special Education, 17,* 171–182.

MADDOX, M., & EDGAR, E. (1985). Maneuvering through the maze: Transition planning for human service agency clients. In J. Chadsey-Rusch (Ed.), *Enhancing transition from school to the workplace for handicapped youth* (pp. 58–69). Urbana-Champaign, IL: National Network for Professional Development in Vocational Special Education, University of Illinois.

MADDUX, C. D., GREEN, C., & HORNER, C. M. (1986). School entry age among children labeled learning disabled, mentally retarded, and emotionally disturbed. *Learning Disabilities Focus, 2*(1), 7–12.

MAGEE, P. A., & NEWCOMER, P. L. (1978). The relationship between oral language skills and academic achievement of LD children. *Learning Disabilities, 1,* 63–67.

MAGER, R. F. (1962). *Preparing instructional objectives.* Belmont, CA: David S. Lake.

MAHONEY, G. (1988). Maternal communication style with mentally retarded children. *American Journal on Mental Retardation, 92*(4), 352–359.

MAHONEY, G., FINGER, I., & POWELL, A. (1985). Relationship of maternal behavioral style to the development of organically impaired mentally retarded infants. *American Journal of Mental Deficiency, 90*(3), 296–302.

MAHONEY, G., & POWELL, A. (1986). *Transactional intervention program teacher's guide.* Farmington, CT: Pediatric Research and Training Center.

MAHONEY, G., & POWELL, A. (1988). Modifying parent-child interaction: Enhancing the development of handicapped children. *Journal of Special Education, 22,* 82–96.

MAKER, C. J. (1975). *Training teachers for the gifted and talented: A comparison of models.* Reston, VA: Council for Exceptional Children.

MAKER, C. J. (1977). *Providing programs for the gifted handicapped.* Reston, VA: Council for Exceptional Children.

MAKER, C. J. (1982). *Teaching models in education of the gifted.* Rockville, MD: Aspen.

MAKER, C. J., MORRIS, E., & JAMES, J. (1981). The Eugene field project: A program for potentially gifted young children. In National/State Leadership Training on the Gifted, *Balancing the scale for the disadvantaged gifted.* Ventura, CA: Office of the Ventura County Superintendent of Schools.

MALE, M. (1988). *Special magic: Computers, classroom strategies, and exceptional students.* Mountain View, CA: Mayfield.

MALONEY, M., & WARD, M. P. (1979). *Mental retardation and modern society.* New York: Oxford University Press.

MANN, J. (1986). Why some children encounter reading problems: The contribution of difficulties with language processing and phonological sophistication to early reading disability. In J. Torgeson & B. Wong (Eds.), *Psychological and educational perspectives on learning disabilities.* Orlando, FL: Academic Press.

MARC, D. L., & MacDONALD, L. (1988). Respite care—who uses it? *Mental Retardation, 26*(2), 93–96.

MARCELL, M. M., HARVEY, C. F., & COTHRAN, L. P. (1988). An attempt to improve auditory short-term memory in Down syndrome individuals through reducing distractions. *Research in Developmental Disabilities, 9,* 405–417.

MARDELL-CZUDNOWSKI, C. D., & GOLDENBERG, D. (1983). *DIAL (developmental indicators for the assessment of learning)—revised.* Edison, NJ: Childcraft Educational Corp.

MARGOLIS, L. H., & MEISELS, S. J. (1987). Barriers to the effectiveness of EPSDT for children with moderate and severe developmental disabilities. *American Journal of Orthopsychiatry, 57,* 424–430.

MARLAND, S. (1972). *Education of the gifted and talented.* Report to the Congress of the United States by the U.S. Commissioner of Education. Washington, DC: U.S. Government Printing Office.

MARSTON, D., & MAGNUSSON, D. (1985). Implementing curriculum-based measurement in special and regular education settings. *Exceptional Children, 52,*(3), 266–276.

MARTIN, F. N. (1975). *Introduction to audiology.* Englewood Cliffs, NJ: Prentice-Hall.

MARTINSON, R. A. (1974). *The identification of the gifted and talented.* Ventura, CA: Office of the Ventura County Superintendent of Schools.

MARYLAND ASSOCIATION FOR RETARDED CHILDREN v. STATE OF MARYLAND, Equity No. 100-182-77676 (Cir. Ct., Baltimore, MD, 1974).

MASTROPIERI, M. A., SCRUGGS, T. E., & LEVIN, J. R. (1985). Memory strategy instruction with learning disabled adolescents. *Journal of Learning Disabilities, 18,* 94–100.

MAUNDER, J. (1997, August 28). Using one's gifts. *The Floridian* (pp. 6–11). St Petersburg, FL: The Times Publishing Company.

MAURICE, P., & TRUDEL, G. (1982). Self-injurious behavior prevalence and relationships to environmental events. In J. H. Hollis & E. Meyers (Eds.), *Life threatening behavior: Analysis and intervention.* Washington, DC: American Association on Mental Deficiency.

McCANDLESS, G. A. (1985). Cochlea implants. *Seminars in Hearing, 6*(1), pp. 1–94.

McCARTHY, D. (1972). *Manual for the McCarthy scales of children's abilities.* New York: Psychological Corporation.

McCARTHY, M. M. (1981). Speech effects of theophylline (Letter to the editors). *Pediatrics, 68,* 5.

McCAY, V., GRIEVE, B., & SHAVER, K. (1980). Handicapping conditions associated with the congenital rubella syndrome. *American Annals of the Deaf, 125*(8), 993–997.

McCHORD, W. (1991). Organization and administration of schools. In D. Hicks & E. Stuckless (Eds.), *1990 International Congress of Education of the Deaf: Proceedings II: Topical addresses.* Rochester, New York: National Technical Institute for the Deaf, Rochester Institute of Technology.

McCOLLUM, J. A., & HUGHES, M. (1988). Staffing patterns and team models in infancy programs. In J. B. Jordan, J. J. Gallagher, P. L. Hutinger, & M. B. Karnes (Eds.), *Early childhood special education: Birth to three* (pp. 129–146). Reston, VA: Council for Exceptional Children.

McCONACHIE, H., & MITCHELL, D. R. (1985). Parents teaching their young mentally handicapped children. *Journal of Child Psychology and Psychiatry and Allied Disciplines, 26*(3), 389–405.

McCONAUGHY, S. M., & ACHENBACH, T. M. (1989). Empirically based assessment of serious emotional disturbance. *Journal of School Psychology, 27,* 91–117.

McCORMICK, D., BALLA, D. A., & ZIGLER, E. (1975). Resident care practices in institutions for retarded persons. *American Journal of Mental Deficiency, 80,* 1–17.

McCOY, K. M., & PREHM, H. J. (1987). *Teaching mainstreamed students: Methods and techniques.* Denver: Love.

McDERMOTT, L. (1976). Serving hard-of-hearing pupils: Alternative strategies for personnel preparation. In *Papers presented at the Summary Conference.* Washington, DC: Bureau of Education for the Handicapped, U.S. Office of Education.

McDONALD, E. T. (1987). Cerebral palsy: Its nature, pathogenesis, and management. In E. T. McDonald (Ed.), *Treating cerebral palsy* (pp. 1–20). Austin, TX: Pro-Ed.

McDONNELL, J., NOFS, D., HARDMAN, M., & CHAMBLISS, C. (1989). An analysis of the procedural components of supported employment programs associated with employment outcomes. *Journal of Applied Behavior Analysis, 22,* 417–428.

McELROY, E. (1987). *Children and adolescents with mental illness: A parents guide.* Kensington, MD: Woodbrine House.

McEVOY, M. A., NORDQUIST, V. M, TWARDOSZ, S., HECKMAN, K. A., WEHBY, J. H., & DENNY, R. K. (1988). Promoting autistic children's peer interaction in an integrated early childhood setting using affection activities. *Journal of Applied Behavior Analysis, 21,* 193–200.

McEVOY, M. A., TWARDOSZ, S., & BISHOP, N. (1990). Affection activities: Procedures for encouraging young children with handicaps to interact with their peers. *Education and Treatment of Children, 13,* 159–167.

McFARLAND, H. F., & DHIB-JAIBUT, S. (1989). Multiple sclerosis: Possible immunological mechanisms. *Clinical Immunology and Immunopathology, 50,* 96–105.

McGONIGEL, M. J., & GARLAND, C. W. (1988). The individualized family service plan and the early intervention team: Team and family issues and recommended practices. *Information of Young Children, 1*(1), 10–21.

McGONIGEL, M. J., KAUFMANN, R. K., & JOHNSON, B. H. (1991). *Guidelines and recommended practices for the individualized family service plan* (2nd ed.). Bethesda, MD: Association for the Care of Children's Health.

McGRADY, H. J. (1987). Eligibility: Back to basics. In S. Vaughn & C. C. Bos (Eds.), *Research in learning disabilities: Issues and future directions* (pp. 105–115). Boston: College-Hill.

McKINNEY, J. D., & FEAGANS, L. (1984). Academic and behavioral characteristics of learning-disabled children and average achievers: Longitudinal studies. *Learning Disability Quarterly, 7,* 251–265.

McKINNEY, J. D., & HOCUTT, A. M. (1982). Public school involvement of parents of learning-disabled and average achievers. *Exceptional Education Quarterly, 3,* 64–73.

McKINNEY, J. D., SHORT, E. J., & FEAGANS, L. (1985). Academic consequences of perceptual-linguistic subtypes of learning disabled children. *Learning Disabilities Research, 1*(1), 6–17.

McKUSICK, V. A. (1982). *Mendelian inheritance in man: Catalogs of autosomal dominant, autosomal recessive, and X-linked phenotypes.* Baltimore: Johns Hopkins University Press.

McLAREN, J., & BRYSON, S. E. (1987). Review of recent epidemiological studies of mental retardation: Prevalence, associated disorders, and etiology. *American Journal of Mental Retardation, 92*(3), 243–254.

McLEAN, J. E., & SNYDER-McLEAN, L. K. (1978). *A transactional approach to early language training.* Columbus, OH: Merrill.

McLEAN, M., & HANLINE, M. F. (1990). Providing early intervention services in integrated environments: Challenges and opportunities for the future. *Topics in Early Childhood Special Education, 10,* 62–77.

McLOUGHLIN, J. A. (1981). Training together to work together: A parent/teacher education model. *Teacher Education and Special Education, 4,* 45–54.

McLOUGHLIN, J. A. (1983). Assessing secondary school students: Dilemmas and challenges. *Pointer, 27,* 42–46.

McLOUGHLIN, J. A., EDGE, D., PETROSKO, J., & STRENECKY, B. (1981). PL 94-142 and information dissemination: A step forward. *Journal of Special Education Technology, 4,* 50–58.

McLOUGHLIN, J. A., EDGE, D., PETROSKO, J., STRENECKY, B., & DAVIS, C. (1983). Interagency cooperation to disseminate materials concerning exceptional people's needs. *Journal of Special Education Technology, 6,* 40–47.

McLOUGHLIN, J. A., EDGE, D., PETROSKO, J., STRENECKY, B., & KEY, P. (1984). Information about the handicapped: A nation's effort. *Parenting Studies, 1,* 33–37.

McLOUGHLIN, J. A., & LEWIS, R. B. (1990). *Assessing special students* (3rd ed.). Columbus, OH: Merrill.

McLOUGHLIN, J. A., & SENN, C. (1993). Siblings of exceptional children. In S. Alper, P. Schloss, & Schloss (Eds.), *Families of persons with disabilities: Consultation and advocacy.* Englewood, NJ: Prentice-Hall.

McNAIR, J., & RUSCH, F. R. (1991). Parent involvement in transition programs. *Mental Retardation, 29,* 93–101.

McNEIL, J. D. (1988). Elements to include in the language arts curriculum for gifted students. *Journal for the Education of the Gifted, 11*(2), 62–78.

McPHEE, N. (1982). A very special magic: A grandparent's delight. *Exceptional Parent, 12,* 13–16.

McQUEEN, P. C., SPENCE, M. W., GARNER, J. B., PEREIRA, L., & WINSOR, E. J. (1987). Prevalence of major mental retardation and associated disabilities in the Canadian Maritime Provinces. *American Journal of Mental Deficiency, 91,* 460–466.

McREYNOLDS, L. V. (1990). Articulation and phonological disorders. In G. H. Shames & E. Wiig (Eds.), *Human communication disorders: An introduction.* Columbus, OH: Merrill.

McWILLIAM, R. A. (1991). Targeting teaching at children's use of time: Perspectives on preschoolers' engagement. *Teaching Exceptional Children, 23*(4), 42–43.

McWILLIAM, R. A., & BAILEY, D. B. (1992). Promoting engagement and mastery. In D. B. Bailey & M. Wolery (Eds.), *Teaching infants and preschoolers with disabilities* (2nd ed.) (pp. 229–255). New York: Macmillan.

McWILLIAMS, B. J., MORRIS, H. L., & SHELTON, R. L. (1984). *Cleft palate speech.* Toronto: B. C. Decker, Inc.

MEADOW, K., & DYSSEGARD, B. (1983). Social-emotional judgements of deaf children: Teachers' rating of deaf children. An American-Danish comparison. *International Journal of Rehabilitation Research, 6*(3) 345–348.

MEALOR, D. J., & RICHMOND, B. O. (1980). Adaptive behavior: Teachers and parents disagree. *Exceptional Children, 46,* 386–393.

MEISELS, S. J., & SHONKOFF, J. P. (1990). *Handbook of Early Childhood Intervention.* Cambridge, U.K.: Cambridge University Press.

MEISELS, S. J., & WISKE, M. S. (1983). *The early screening inventory.* New York: Teachers College Press.

MELICHAR, J. F., & BLACKHURST, A. E. (1992). *Introduction to a functional approach to assistive technology* [Training Module]. Lexington, KY: Department of Special Education, University of Kentucky.

MENKES, J. H. (1990). *Textbook of child neurology* (4th ed.) (pp. 602–665). Philadelphia: Lea & Febiger.

MENYUK, P. (1972). *The development of speech.* Indianapolis: Bobbs-Merrill.

MERCER, C. D. (1987). *Students with learning disabilities* (3rd ed.). Columbus, OH: Merrill.

MERCER, C. D., HUGHES, C., & MERCER, A. R. (1985). Learning disabilities definitions used by state education departments. *Learning Disability Quarterly, 8,* 45–55.

MERCER, J. R. (1973). The myth of the 3 percent prevalence. In R. K. Eyman, C. E. Meyers, & G. Tarian (Eds.), *Sociobehavioral studies in mental retardation: Papers in honor of Harry F. Dingman.* Monographs of the American Association on Mental Deficiency, *1,* 1–18.

MERCER, J. R. (1979). *System of multicultural and pluralistic assessment (SOMPA): Technical manual.* New York: Psychological Corporation.

MERCER, J. R. (1981). The system of multicultural pluralistic assessment: SOMPA. In National/State Leadership Training on the Gifted, *Balancing the scale for the disadvantaged gifted.* Ventura, CA: Office of the Ventura County Superintendent of Schools.

MEYER, D. J., VADASY, P. F., & FEWELL, R. R. (1985). *Living with a brother or sister with special needs: A book for sibs.* Seattle: University of Washington Press.

MILLER, C. K. (1969). Conservation in blind children. *Education of the Visually Handicapped, 12,* 101–105.

MILLER, J. J. (1982). Juvenile rheumatoid arthritis. In E. E. Bleck and D. A. Nagel (Eds.), *Physically handicapped children: A medical atlas for teachers* (pp. 423–430). New York: Grune & Stratton.

MILLER, J., & ALLAIRE, J. (1987). Augmentative communication. In M. E. Snell (Ed.), *Systematic instruction of persons with severe handicaps* (pp. 273–297). Columbus, OH: Merrill.

MILLER, L. (1989). Classroom-based language intervention. *Language Speech and Hearing Services in the Schools, 2,* 153–168.

MILLS, E. A., & RIDLON, J. A. (1980). A conversation about the NY State Summer School of the Visual Arts. *School Arts, 79*(9), 62–68.

MILLS v. BOARD OF EDUCATION OF THE DISTRICT OF COLUMBIA, 348 Supp. 866 (D.D.C., 1972).

MINK, I. T., BLACHER, J., & NIHIRA, K. (1988). Taxonomy of family life styles: III. Replication with families with severely mentally retarded children. *American Journal of Mental Retardation, 93*(3), 250–264.

MIRA, M. P., TUCKER, B. F., & TYLER, J. S. (1992). *Traumatic brain injury in children and adolescents: A sourcebook for teachers and school personnel.* Austin, TX: Pro-Ed.

MIRENDA, P., IACONO, Z. T., & WILLIAMS R. (1990). Communication options for persons with severe and profound disabilities: State of the art and future directions. *Journal of the Association for Persons with Severe Handicaps, 15,* 3–21.

MOON, M. S., INGE, K. J., WEHMAN, P., BROOKE, V., & BARCUS, J. M. (1990). *Helping persons with severe mental retardation get and keep employment.* Baltimore: Paul H. Brookes.

MOORE, D., & POLSGROVE, L. (1991). Disabilities, developmental handicaps, and substance misuse: A review. *International Journal of the Addictions, 26,* 65–90.

MOORES, D. (1991). Educational policies and services. In D. Hicks & E. Stuckless (Eds.), *1990 International Congress of Education of the Deaf: Proceedings II: Topical addresses.* Rochester, New York: National Technical Institute for the Deaf, Rochester Institute of Technology.

MORGAN, D. J. (1979). Prevalence and types of handicapping conditions found in juvenile correctional institutions. A national survey. *Journal of Special Education, 13,* 283–295.

MORISHIMA, A. (1974). Another Van Gogh of Japan: The superior artwork of a retarded boy. *Exceptional Children, 41,* 92–96.

MORRIS, S. E., & KLEIN, M. D. (1987). *Prefeeding skills: A comprehensive resource for feeding development.* Tucson, AZ: Therapy Skill Builders.

MORSINK, C. V. (1984). *Teaching special needs students in regular classrooms.* Boston: Little, Brown.

MORSINK, C. V., THOMAS, C. C., & CORREA, V. I. (1991). *Interactive teaming: Consultation and collaboration in special programs.* New York: Macmillan.

MUCCIGROSSO, L., SCAVARDA, M., SIMPSON-BROWN, R., & THALACKER, B. E. (1991). *Double jeopardy: Pregnant and parenting youth in special education.* Reston, VA: Council for Exceptional Children.

MUIR, K., MILAN, M., BRANSTON-McLEAN, M., & BERGER, M. (1982). Advocacy training for parents of handicapped children: A staff responsibility. *Young Children, 37,* 41–46.

MULLIGAN-AULT, M., GUESS, D., STRUTH, L., & THOMPSON, B. (1988). The implementation of health-related procedures in classrooms for students with severe multiple impairments. *Journal of the Association for Persons with Severe Handicaps* (JASH), *13*(2), 100–109.

MURPHY, D. M. (1986). The prevalence of handicapping conditions among juvenile delinquents. *Remedial and Special Education, 7*(3), 7–17.

MUSSLEWHITE, C. R. (1986). *Adaptive play for special needs children: Strategies to enhance communication and learning.* Boston: College-Hill.

MYKLEBUST, H. R. (1964a). Learning disorders: Psychoneurological disturbances in childhood. *Rehabilitation Literature, 25,* 354–359.

MYKLEBUST, H. R. (1964b). *The psychology of deafness* (2nd ed.). New York: Grune & Stratton.

NATIONAL ASSOCIATION OF STATE DIRECTORS OF SPECIAL EDUCATION (NASDSE) (1991). *Reference notes for speechmaking for understanding the forces at work which are driving social policy.* Washington, DC: Author.

NATIONAL CENTER ON CHILD ABUSE AND NEGLECT (1988). *Study findings: Study of national incidence and prevalence of child abuse and neglect: 1988.* Washington, DC: U.S. Department of Human Services, Office of Human Develoment Services, Administration for Children, Youth and Families, Children's Bureau.

NATIONAL CENTER FOR HEALTH STATISTICS (1988). Unpublished data from the 1985 National Health Survey.

NATIONAL JOINT COMMITTEE ON LEARNING DISABILITIES (1988). [Letter to NJCLD member organizations.]

NATIONAL SOCIETY FOR THE PREVENTION OF BLINDNESS (1990). *Vision screening in schools.* New York: Author.

NAZZARO, J. N. (1977). *Exceptional timetables: Historic events affecting the handicapped and gifted.* Reston, VA: Council for Exceptional Children.

NAZZARO, J. N. (Ed.) 1981. *Computer connections for gifted children and youth.* Reston, VA: Clearinghouse on Handicapped and Gifted Children.

NEALIS, J. T. (1983a). Epilepsy. In J. Umbriet (Ed.), *Physical disabilities and health impairment: An introduction* (pp. 74–85). Columbus, OH: Merrill.

NEALIS, J. T. (1983b). Human anatomy. In J. Umbriet (Ed.), *Physical disabilities and health impairment: An introduction* (pp. 3–15). Columbus, OH: Merrill.

NEALIS, J. T. (1983c) Neuroanatomy. In J. Umbriet (Ed.), *Physical disabilities and health impairment: An introduction* (pp. 16–28). Columbus, OH: Merrill.

NEEDLEMAN, H. L. (1977). Effects of hearing loss from recurrent otitis media on speech and language development. In B. F. Jaffe (Ed.), *Hearing Loss in Children.* Baltimore: University Park Press.

NEEDLEMAN, H. L., SCHELL, A., BELLINGER, D., & LEVITON, A. (1990). The long-term effects of exposure to low doses of lead in childhood: An 11-year follow-up report. *New England Journal of Medicine, 322,*(2), 83–88.

NEEF, N. A., LENSBOWER, J., HOCKERSMITH, I., DePALMA, V., & GRAY, K. (1990). In vivo versus simulation training: An interactional analysis of range and type of training exemplars. *Journal of Applied Behavior Analysis, 23,* 447–458.

NEEL, R. S., & BILLINGSLEY, F. F. (1989). *IMPACT: A functional curriculum handbook for students with moderate to severe handicaps.* Baltimore: Paul H. Brookes.

NEEL, R. S., MEADOWS, N., LEVINE, P., & EDGAR, E. B. (1988). What happens after special education: A statewide follow-up study of secondary students who have behavioral disorders. *Behavioral Disorders, 13,* 209–216.

NEFF, W. S. (1966). Problems of work evaluation. *Personal and Guidance Journal, 24,* 682–688.

NELSON, C. M. (1987). Handicapped offenders in the criminal justice system. In C. M. Nelson, R. B. Rutherford, & B. I. Wolford (Eds.), *Special education in the criminal justice system* (pp. 2–17). Columbus, OH: Merrill.

NELSON, C. M. (1988). Social skills training for handicapped students. *Teaching Exceptional Children, 20*(4), 19–23.

NELSON, C. M., & PEARSON, C. A. (1991). *Integrating services for children and youth with emotional/behavioral disabilities.* Reston, VA: Council for Exceptional Children.

NELSON, C. M., & POLSGROVE, L. (1981). The etiology of adolescent behavior disorders. In G. B. Brown, R. L. McDowell, & J. Smith (Eds.), *Educating adolescents with behavior disorders.* Boston: Little, Brown.

NELSON, C. M., & RUTHERFORD, R. B. (1988). Behavioral interventions with behaviorally disordered students. In M. C. Wang, M. C. Reynolds, & H. J. Walberg (Eds.), *Handbook of special education: Research and practice* (Vol. 2) (pp. 125–153). New York: Pergamon Press.

NELSON, C. M., & RUTHERFORD, R. B. (1990). Troubled youth in the public schools: Emotionally disturbed or socially maladjusted? In P. E. Leone (Ed.), *Understanding troubled and troubling youth* (pp. 38–60). Newbury Park, CA: Sage.

NELSON, C. M., RUTHERFORD, R. B., CENTER, D. B., & WALKER, H. M. (1991). Do public schools have an obligation to serve troubled youth? *Exceptional Children, 57,* 406–415.

NELSON, C. M., RUTHERFORD, R. B., Jr., & WOLFORD, B. I. (1987). *Special education in the criminal justice system.* Columbus, OH: Merrill.

NELSON, K. B. (1986). Cerebral palsy: What is known regarding cause? *Annals of the New York Academy of Sciences, 477,* 22–26.

NELSON, N. W. (1984). Beyond information processing: The language of teachers and textbooks. In G. Wallach & K. Butler (Eds.), *Language learning disabilities in school-age children.* Baltimore: Waverly Press.

NELSON, N. W. (1989). Curriculum-based language assessment and intervention. *Language Speech and Hearing Services in the Schools, 2*, 170–184.

NELSON, N. W. (1991). Teacher talk and child listening: Fostering a better match. In C. Simon (Ed.), *Communication skills and classroom success*. Eau Claire, WI: Thinking Publications, A Division of McKinley Co., Inc.

NEVIN, D. (1977, October). Young prodigies take off under special program. *Smithsonian*, 76–82.

NEWBORG, J., STOCK, J. R., WNEK, L., GUIDUBALDI, J., & SVINICKI, J. (1984). *Battelle developmental inventory*, Allen, TX: DLM Teaching Resources.

NEWBY, H. A., & POPELKA, G. A. (1985). *Audiology*. Englewood Cliffs, NJ: Prentice-Hall.

NEWMAN, P., CREAGHEAD, N., & SECORD, W. (Eds.) (1985). *Assessment and remediation of articulatory and phonological disorders*. Columbus, OH: Merrill.

NIETUPSKI, J., HAMRE-NIETUPSKI, S., CLANCY, P., & VEERHUSEN, K. (1986). Guidelines for making simulation an effective adjunct to in vivo community instruction. *Journal of the Association for Persons with Severe Handicaps, 11*, 12–18.

NIPPOLD, M., & SULLIVAN, M. (1987). Verbal and perceptual analogical reasoning and proportional metaphor comprehension in young children. *Journal of Speech and Hearing Research, 30*, 367–376.

NIRJE, B. (1969). The normalization principle and its human management implications. In R. B. Kugel & W. Wolfensberger (Eds.), *Changing patterns in residential services for the mentally retarded* (pp. 231–240). Washington, DC: U.S. Government Printing Office.

NOLAN, C. Y. (1978). The visually impaired. In E. Meyen (Ed.), *Exceptional children and youth: An introduction*. Denver: Love.

NOONAN, M. J., BROWN, F., MULLIGAN, M., & RETTIG, M. A. (1982). Educability of severely handicapped persons: Both sides of the issue. *Journal of the Association for the Severely Handicapped, 7*(1), 3–12.

NORRIS, J. A. (1989). Providing language remediation in the classroom: An integrated language to reading intervention method. *Language Speech and Hearing Services in the Schools, 2*, 205–218.

NORTHERN, J. L., & DOWNS, M. P. (1984). *Hearing in children*. Baltimore: Williams & Wilkins.

OAKLAND, T. (1980). Predictive validity of the WISC-R IQs and estimated learning potential. Paper presented at the Annual Meeting of the American Psychological Association (Montreal, September 1980).

O'BRIEN, R. (1976). *Alive . . . aware . . . a person: A development model for early childhood services with special definition for visually impaired children and their parents*. Rockville, MD: Montgomery County Public Schools.

ODOM, S. L., HOYSON, M., JAMIESON, B., & STRAIN, P. S. (1985). Increasing handicapped preschoolers' peer social interactions: Cross-setting and component analysis. *Journal of Applied Behavior Analysis, 18*, 3–16.

ODOM, S. L., & KARNES, M. B. (Eds.) (1988). *Early intervention for infants and children with handicaps: An empirical base*. Baltimore: Paul H. Brookes.

ODOM, S. L., & McCONNELL, S. R. (1989). Assessing social interaction skills. In D. B. Bailey & M. Wolery (Eds.), *Assessing infants and preschoolers with handicaps* (pp. 390–427). Columbus, OH: Merrill.

ODOM, S. L., & McEVOY, M. A. (1988). Integration of young children with handicaps and normally developing children. In S. L. Odom & M. B. Karnes (Eds.), *Early intervention for infants and children with handicaps: An empirical base* (pp. 241–267). Baltimore: Paul H. Brookes.

OFFICE OF CIVIL RIGHTS (1987). *1986 elementary and secondary school civil rights survey*. Washington, DC: U.S. Department of Education.

OFFICE OF SPECIAL EDUCATION AND REHABILITATIVE SERVICES (OSERS) (1990). Community integration: The next step. *OSERS News In Print, 2*(2), 11–13.

OLBRISCH, R. R. (1982). Plastic surgical management of children with Down syndrome: Indications and results. *British Journal of Plastic Surgery, 35*, 195–200.

O'LEARY, K. D., & O'LEARY, S. G. (1972). *Classroom management: The successful use of behavior modification*. New York: Pergamon Press.

OLYMPUS RESEARCH CORPORATION (1974). *An assessment of vocational education programs for the handicapped under Part B amendments of the Vocational Education Act*. Salt Lake City: Author.

OMARK, D. R., & ERICKSON, J. G. (Eds) (1983). *The bilingual exceptional child*. Boston: College-Hill.

OMIZO, M. M., AMERIKANER, J. J., & MICHAEL, W. B. (1985). The Coopersmith self-esteem inventory as a predictor of feelings and communication satisfaction toward parents among learning disabled, emotionally disturbed, and normal adolescents. *Educational and Psychological Measurement, 45*, 389–395.

O'NEIL, J. (1988, September). How "special" should the special ed curriculum be? Experts debate merits of academics, "life skills." *Curriculum Update*.

ORELOVE, F. P., & SOBSEY, D. (1984). *Educating children with multiple disabilities*. Baltimore: Paul H. Brookes.

ORELOVE, F. P., & SOBSEY, D. (1987). *Educating children with multiple disabilities: A transdisciplinary approach*. Baltimore: Paul H. Brookes.

ORTIZ, V., & VOLKOFF, W. (1987). Identification of gifted and accelerated Hispanic students. *Journal for the Education of the Gifted, 11* (1), 45–55.

ORTON, S. (1937). *Reading, writing, and speech problems in children*. New York: Norton.

OSTROSKY, M. M., & KAISER, A. P. (1991). Preschool classroom environments that promote communication. *Teaching Exceptional Children, 23*(4), 6–10.

OUELLETTE, E. M., & ROSETTE, H. L. (1976). A pilot prospective study of the fetal alcohol syndrome at the Boston City Hospital. Part II, The infants. *Annals of New York Academy of Sciences, 273*, 123–129.

OUELLETTE, E. M., ROSETTE, H. L., ROSMAN, N. P., & WEINER, L. (1977). Adverse affects on offspring of maternal alcohol abuse during pregnancy. *New England Journal of Medicine, 297*, 528–530.

OWENS, R. E. (1991). *Language disorders: A functional approach to assessment and intervention*. New York: Macmillan.

OWENS, R. E. (1992). *Language development: An introduction*. New York: Macmillan.

OWENS, R. E., & HOUSE, L. (1984). Decision-making processes in augmentative communication. *Journal of Speech and Hearing Disorders, 49*, 18–25.

PALINSCAR, A. S., & BROWN, D. A. (1987). Enhancing instructional time through attention to metacognition. *Journal of Learning Disabilities, 20*, 66–75.

PAPARELLA, M. (1979). Use and abuse of tympanostomy tubes. *Otitis Media*, 86–89. Publication of the Second National Conference on Otitis Media. Columbus, OH: Ross Laboratories.

PAPARELLA, M., & JUHN, S. R. (1979). Otitis media: Definition and terminology. *Otitis Media*, 2–8. Publication of the Second National Conference on Otitis Media. Columbus, OH: Ross Laboratories.

PAPERT, S. (1981). Computers and computer cultures. In J. N. Nazzaro (Ed.), *Computer connections for gifted children and youth*. Reston, VA: Clearinghouse on Handicapped and Gifted Children.

PARADISE, J. L. (1979). Medical treatment of acute otitis media: A critical essay. *Otitis Media*, 79–84. Publication of the Second National Conference on Otitis Media. Columbus, OH: Ross Laboratories.

PARETTE, H. P. (1991). The importance of technology in the education and training of persons with mental retardation. *Education and Training in Mental Retardation, 26*, 165–178.

PARKE, B. N. (1989). *Gifted students in regular classrooms*. Boston: Allyn & Bacon.

PARKER, J. (1969). Adapting school psychological evaluation of the blind child. *New Outlook for the Blind, 63*, 305–311.

PARKER, L. A. (1977). Teleconferencing as an educational medium: A ten year perspective from the University of Wisconsin–Extension. In M. Monson, L. Parker, & B. Riccomini (Eds.), *A design for interactive audio*. Madison, WI: University of Wisconsin–Extension.

PARSONS, C. L., IACONE, T. A., & ROZNER, L. (1987). Effect of tongue reduction on articulation in children with Down's syndrome. *American Journal of Mental Deficiency, 91*, 328–332.

PARSONS, M. B., & REID, D. H. (1990). Assessing food preferences among persons with profound mental retardation: Providing opportunities to make choices. *Journal of Applied Behavior Analysis, 23*, 183–195.

PARSONS, M. B., REID, D. H., REYNOLDS, J., & BUMGARNER, M. (1990). Effects of chosen versus assigned jobs on the work performance of persons with severe handicaps. *Journal of Applied Behavior Analysis, 23*, 253–258.

PASE v. HANNON, 506 F. Supp. 831 (N.D. Ill. 1980).

PASSOW, A. H., & GOLDBERG, M. L. (1962). *The gifted: Digests of major studies*. Manuscript prepared for the Council on Exceptional Children, NEA (ERIC document ED 001303).

PATTERSON, G. R. (1986). Performance models for antisocial boys. *American Psychologist, 41*, 432–444.

PATTERSON, G. R., REID, J. B., JONES, R. R., & CONGER, R. E. (1975). *A social learning approach to family intervention: Vol. 1. Families with aggressive children*. Eugene, OR: Castalia.

PATTON, J. R. (1986). *Transition: Curricular implications*. Honolulu: Project Ho-ho-ko, University of Hawaii.

PATTON, J. R., BEIRNE-SMITH, M., & PAYNE, J. S. (1990). *Mental retardation* (3rd ed.). Columbus, OH: Merrill.

PATRICK, J. L., & RESCHLY, D. J. (1982). Relationship of state educational criteria and demographic variables to school-system prevalence of mental retardation. *American Journal of Mental Deficiency, 86*, 351–360.

PAUL, J. J., & PORTER, P. B. (1981). Parents of handicapped children. In J. L. Paul (Ed.), *Understanding and working with parents of children with special needs* (pp. 1–22). New York: Holt, Rinehart & Winston.

PAUL, R., DYKENS, E., LECKMAN, J. F., WATSON, M., BREG, W. R., & COHEN, D. (1987). A comparison of language characteristics of mentally retarded adults with fragile X syndrome and those with nonspecific mental retardation and autism. *Journal of Autism and Developmental Disorders, 17*, 457–468.

PAYNE, J. S., KAUFFMAN, J. H., PATTON, J. R., BROWN, G. B., & DeMOTT, R. H. (1979). *Exceptional children in focus*. Columbus, OH: Merrill.

PEABODY, R. L., & BIRCH, J. W. (1967). Educational implications of partial vision: New findings from a national study. *Sight Saving Review, 37*, 92–96.

PEARL, R., & BRYAN, T. (1982). Mothers' attributions for their learning disabled child's successes and failures. *Learning Disability Quarterly, 5*, 53–57.

PEARL, R., BRYAN, T., & DONAHUE, M. (1980). Learning disabled children's attributions for success and failure. *Learning Disability Quarterly, 3*, 3–9.

PECK, C. A., DONALDSON, J., & PEZZOLI, M. (1990). Some benefits nonhandicapped adolescents perceive for themselves from their social relationships with peers who have severe handicaps. *Journal of the Association for Persons with Severe Handicaps, 15*, 241–249.

PECK, C. A., ODOM, S. L., & BRICKER, D. (Eds.) (in press). *Integrating young children with disabilities into community programs: From research to implementation*. Baltimore: Paul H. Brookes.

PEIRCE, R. L. (1979, March 6). Epileptics share a world of uncertainty and secrecy because of public's ignorance. *The Courier-Journal*, Louisville, KY.

PENDARVIS, E., HOWLEY, A., & HOWLEY, C. (1990). *The abilities of gifted children*. Englewood Cliffs, NJ: Prentice-Hall.

PENNINGTON, F. M., & LUSZCZ, M. A. (1975). Some functional properties of iconic storage in retarded and nonretarded subjects. *Memory & Cognition, 3*, 295–301.

PENNSTAR (1987). [Computer program]. Harrisburg, PA: Bureau of Special Education, Pennsylvania Department of Education.

PENNSYLVANIA ASSOCIATION FOR RETARDED CHILDREN v. COMMONWEALTH OF PENNSYLVANIA, 334 F. Supp. 1257 (E.D.Pa., 1971).

PENNSYLVANIA ASSOCIATION FOR RETARDED CHILDREN v. COMMONWEALTH OF PENNSYLVANIA, 343 F. Supp. 279 (E.D.Pa., 1972). Consent Agreement.

PERA, T. B., & COBB, E. S. (1978). A microcomputer-based learning analysis system for optimizing PSI instructional materials for the visually handicapped. *Behavior Research Methods and Instrumentation, 10*, 231–237.

PERFETTI, C. A. (1985). *Reading ability*. New York: Oxford University Press.

PERFETTI, C. A., & ROTH, S. F. (1980). A framework for reading, language comprehension, and language disability. *Topics in Learning and Learning Disabilities, 2*, 15–27.

PERINO, J., & PERINO, S. C. (1981). *Parenting the gifted child: Developing the promise*. New York: R. R. Bowker.

PEROSA, L., & PEROSA, S. (1981). The school counselor's use of structural family therapy with learning-disabled students. *The School Counselor, 29*, 152–155.

PERRONE, P. A., & MALE, R. A. (1981). *The developmental education and guidance of talented learners*. Rockville, MD: Aspen.

PERSKE, R. (1973). *Hope for the families*. Nashville, TN: Abingdon Press.

PERSKE, R. (1988). *Circle of friends*. Nashville, TN: Abingdon Press.

PETERSON, P. L. (1979). Direct instruction: Effective for what and for whom? *Educational Leadership, 37*, 46–48.

PEYTON, D. (1982, August 10). Snakebyte. *The Huntington* (WV) *Herald Dispatch*, p. 4.

PHELPS, M. S., & PROCK, G. A. (1991). Equality of educational opportunity in rural America. In A. DeYoung (Ed.), *Rural education issues and practice* (pp. 269–312). New York: Garland.

PHILLIPS, V., McCULLOUGH, L., NELSON, C. M., & WALKER, H. M. (in press). Teamwork among teachers: Promoting a statewide agenda for students at risk for school failure. *Special Services in the Schools*.

PIAGET, J. (1950). *The psychology of intelligence*. New York: Harcourt Brace Jovanovich.

PIAGET, J. (1952). *The origins of intelligence in children*. New York: Norton.

PIAGET, J. (1963). *The origins of intelligence of children*. New York: Norton.

PIERETTI, M., ZHANG, F. B., FU, Y. H., WARREN, S. T., OOSTRA, B. A., CASKEY, C. T., & NELSON, D. L. (1991). Absence of expression of the FMR-1 gene in fragile-X syndrome. *Cell, 66*(4), 817–822.

PIHL, R. O., & NIAURA, R. (1982). Learning disability: An inability to sustain attention. *Journal of Clinical Psychology, 38*, 632–634.

PINTER, R. J., EISENSON, J., & STANTON, M. (1941). *The psychology of the physically handicapped*. New York: F. S. Crofts.

PL 99-457 (1986). Education of the handicapped act amendments of 1986, part H, Section 677 (d) S 2294–6.

PL 101-336 (1990). Americans with disabilities act of 1990. *Public Law 101-336, 104 Stat. 327*. Washington, DC: 101st Congress, July 26, 1990.

PL 101-476 (1990). Individuals with disabilities education act. *Public Law 101-476*, Washington, DC: 101st Congress, October 30, 1990.

POLLOWAY, E. A. (1992). AAMR proposed definition: Helping to define our future. *MR Express, 2*(3) [February]. Reston, VA: Council for Exceptional Children, Division on Mental Retardation.

POLLOWAY, E. A., EPSTEIN, M. H. (1985). Current research issues in mild mental retardation: A survey of the field. *Education and Training of the Mentally Retarded, 20*, 171–174.

POLLOWAY, E. A., EPSTEIN, M. H., & CULLINAN, D. (1985). Prevalence of behavior problems among educable mentally retarded students. *Education and Training of the Mentally Retarded, 20*, 3–13.

POLLOWAY, E. A., EPSTEIN, M. H., PATTON, J. R., CULLINAN, D., & LUEBKE, J. (1986). Demographic, social, and behavioral characteristics of students with educable mental retardation. *Education and Training of the Mentally Retarded, 21,* 27–34.

POLLOWAY, E. A., PATTON, J. R., SMITH, J. D., & RODERIQUE, T. W. (1991). Issues in program design for elementary students with mild retardation: Emphasis on curriculum development. *Education and Training in Mental Retardation, 26*(2), 142–150.

POLLOWAY, E. A., & SMITH, J. D. (1983). Changes in mild mental retardation: Population, programs, and perspectives. *Exceptional Children, 50,* 149–159.

POLSGROVE, L. (1987). Assessment of children's social and behavioral problems. In W. H. Berdine & S. M. Meyer (Eds.), *Assessment in special education* (pp. 141–180). Boston: Little, Brown.

POLSGROVE, L., & REITH, H. (1985). Microcomputer application to students with learning and behavior disorders. Unpublished manuscript. Lexington, KY: Department of Special Education, University of Kentucky.

POWELL, T. H., PANCSOFAR, E. L., STEERE, D. E., BUTTERWORTH, J., ITZKOWITZ, J. S., & RAINFORTH, B. (1991). *Supported employment: Providing integrated employment opportunities for persons with disabilities.* New York: Longman.

POWERS, D. (1991). Communication. In D. Hicks & E. Stuckless (Eds.), *1990 International Congress of Education of the Deaf: Proceedings II: Topical addresses.* Rochester, New York: National Technical Institute for the Deaf, Rochester Institute of Technology.

PRECIS (1990). Americans with Disabilities Act of 1990: What should you know? Supplement to *Exceptional Children, 57*(2).

PRESIDENT'S COMMITTEE ON MENTAL RETARDATION (1970). *The six hour retarded child.* Washington, DC: U.S. Government Printing Office.

PRESSEY, S. L. (1955). Concerning the nature and nurture of genius. *Scientific Monthly, 81,* 123–129.

PRINGLE, M. L. (1970). *Able misfits.* London: Longman.

PROCTOR, C. A., & PROCTOR, B. (1967). Understanding hereditary nerve deafness. *Archive of Otolaryngology, 85,* 23–40.

PUGACH, M. (1987). The national education reports and special education: Implications for teacher preparation. *Exceptional Children, 53,* 308–314.

PUGACH, M. C., & JOHNSON, L. J. (1989). Prereferral interventions: Progress, problems, and challenges. *Exceptional Children, 56,* 217–226.

PULLIS, M. (1985). LD students' temperament characteristics and their impact on decisions by resource and mainstream teachers. *Learning Disability Quarterly, 8,* 109–122.

PUNCH, J. (1983). The prevalence of hearing impairment. *ASHA, 25,* 27.

QUADER, S. E. (1977). Dysarthria: An unusual side-effect of tricycle antidepressants. *British Medical Journal, 9,* 97.

QUIGLEY, S. P. (1970). *Some effects of impairment upon school performance.* Manuscript prepared for the Division of Special Education Services, Office of the Superintendent of Public Instruction for the State of Illinois.

QUIGLEY, S., & PAUL, P. (1989). English language development. In M. C. Wang, M. C. Reynolds, & H. J. Walberg (Eds.), *Handbook of special education: Research and practice, Vol. 3. Low incidence conditions.* New York: Pergamon Press.

QUIGLEY, S., WILBUR, R., POWER, D., MONTANELLI, D., & STEINKAMP, M. (1976). *Syntactic structures in the language of deaf children.* Urbana, IL: University of Illinois, Institute for Child Behavior and Development.

RABIN, A. T. (1982). Does vision screening tell the whole story? *Reading Teacher, 35*(5), 524–527.

RAMEY, C. T., & MacPHEE, D. (1986). Developmental retardation: A systems theory perspective on risk and preventive intervention. In

D. C. Farran & J. D. McKinney (Eds.), *Risk in intellectual and psychosocial development* (pp. 61–81). Orlando, FL: Academic Press.

RAMSDELL, D. A. (1970). The psychology of the hard-of-hearing and the deafened adult (pp. 435–446). In H. Davis & S. Silverman (Eds.), *Hearing and deafness.* New York: Holt, Rinehart & Winston.

RAWLINS, L. (1982). LD's—What happens when they are no longer children? *Academic Therapy, 20,* 133–148.

REDDING, R. E. (1990). Learning preferences and skill patterns among underachieving gifted adolescents. *Gifted Child Quarterly, 34*(2), 72–75.

REED, C. G. (1988). Voice disorders in the adult. In N. S. Lass, L. V. McReynolds, J. L. Northern, & D. R. Yoder (Eds.), *Handbook of speech-language pathology.* Toronto: B. C. Decker.

REESE, R. M., & SERNA, L. (1986). Planning for generalization and maintenance in parent training: Parents need I.E.P.s too. *Mental Retardation, 24*(2), 87–92.

REICHART, D. C., LYNCH, E. C., ANDERSON, B. C., SVOBODNY, L. A., DICOLA, J. M., & MERCURY, M. G. (1989). Parental perspectives on integrated preschool opportunities for children with handicaps and children without handicaps. *Journal of Early Intervention, 13*(1), 6–13.

RENZULLI, J. S. (1977). *The enrichment triad model: A guide for developing defensible programs for the gifted and talented.* Wethersfield, CT: Creative Learning Press.

RENZULLI, J. S. (1978). What makes giftedness? *Phi Delta Kappan, 60*(3), 180–184, 261.

RENZULLI, J. S. (1982). What makes a problem real: Stalking the illusive meaning of qualitative differences in gifted education. *Gifted Child Quarterly, 26*(4), 156–167.

RENZULLI, J. S., & HARTMAN, R. K. (1971). Scale for rating the behavioral characteristics of superior students. *Exceptional Children, 38,* 243–248.

RENZULLI, J. S., & SMITH, L. H. (1977). Two approaches to identification of gifted children. *Exceptional Children, 43*(8), 512–518.

Report of the Ad Hoc Committee to Define Deaf and Hard of Hearing (1975). *American Annals of the Deaf, 120,* 509–512.

RESCHLY, D. J. (1981). Evaluation of the effects of SOMPA measures on classification of students as mentally retarded. *American Journal of Mental Deficiency, 86,* 16–20.

RESCHLY, D. J. (1988a). Assessment issues, placement litigation, and the future of mild mental retardation classification and programming. *Education and Training of the Mentally Retarded, 23*(4), 285–301.

RESCHLY, D. J. (1988b). Incorporating adaptive behavior deficits into instructional programs. In G. A. Robinson, J. R. Patton, E. A. Polloway, & L. R. Sargent (Eds.), *Best practices in mental disabilities* (Vol. 2). Des Moines: Iowa Department of Education.

RESCHLY, D. J. (1988c). Minority MMR overrepresentation and special education reform. *Exceptional Children, 54,* 316–323.

REYNOLDS, M. C., & BIRCH, J. W. (1982). *Teaching exceptional children in all America's schools* (2nd ed.). Reston, VA: Council for Exceptional Children.

REYNOLDS, M. C., WANG, M. C., & WALBERG, H. J. (1987). The necessary restructuring of special and regular education. *Exceptional Children, 53,* 391–398.

RICH, H. L. (1977). Behavior disorders and school: A case of sexism and racial bias. *Behavioral Disorders, 2,* 201–204.

RICHARDS, B. W., SYLVESTER, R. E., & BROOKES, C. (1981). Fragile-X-linked mental retardation: The Martin-Bell syndrome. *Journal of Mental Deficiency Research, 25,* 253–258.

RICHERT, E. S. (1987). Rampant problems and promising practices in the identification of disadvantaged gifted students. *Gifted Child Quarterly, 32*(4), 149–154.

RICHERT, E. S., ALVINO, J. J., & McDONNEL, R. C. (1982). *National report on identification: Assessment and recommendations for comprehensive identification of gifted and talented youth.* Sewell, NJ: Educational Improvement Center–South.

RIMLAND, B. (1964). *Infantile autism.* New York: Meredith.

RIMM, S. (1984, January-February). Under achievement . . . or if God had meant gifted children to run our homes, she would have created them bigger. *G/C/T*, 27–29.

RIMM, S., & LOWE, B. (1988). Family environments of under-achieving gifted students. *Gifted Child Quarterly, 32*(4), 353–358.

RIPICH, D. N. (1989). Building classroom communication competence: A case for multi-perspective approach. *Seminars in Speech and Language,* 3, 231–239.

RIZZO, J. V., & ZABEL, R. H. (1988). *Educating children and adolescents with behavioral disorders: An integrative approach.* Boston: Allyn & Bacon.

ROBERTS, J. E., & CRAIS, E. R. (1989). Assessing communication skills. In D. B. Bailey & M. Wolery (Eds.), *Assessing infants and preschoolers with handicaps* (pp. 339–389). Columbus, OH: Merrill.

ROBINS, L. N. (1966). *Deviant children grown up.* Baltimore: Williams & Wilkins.

ROBINSON, A. (1990). Cooperation or exploitation? The argument against cooperative learning for talented students. *Journal for the Education of the Gifted, 14*(1), 9–27.

ROBINSON, H. B., ROEDELL, W. C., & JACKSON, N. (1979). Early identification and intervention. In A. H. Passow (Ed.), *The gifted and the talented: Their education and development.* The seventy-eighth yearbook of the National Society for the Study of Education, Part 1. Chicago: University of Chicago Press.

ROBINSON, N. (1980). Editor's note: Terminology, classification, and description in mental retardation research. *American Journal of Mental Deficiency, 85,* 99–107.

ROBINSON, N. M., & ROBINSON, H. B. (1976). *The mentally retarded child: A psychological approach* (2nd ed.). New York: McGraw-Hill.

RODRIGUEZ, R. F. (1981). The involvement of minority group parents in school. *Teacher Education and Special Education,* 4, 40–44.

ROE, A. (1953). *The making of a scientist.* New York: Dodd, Mead.

ROEDELL, W. C., JACKSON, N. E., & ROBINSON, H. B. (1980). *Gifted young children.* New York: McGraw-Hill.

ROGERS, H., & SAKLOFSKE, D. H. (1985). Self-concepts, locus of control and performance expectations of learning disabled children. *Journal of Learning Disabilities, 18,* 273–278.

ROGERS, R. C., & SIMENSEN, R. J. (1987). Fragile X syndrome: A common etiology of mental retardation. *American Journal of Mental Deficiency, 91,* 445–449.

ROMER, L. T., & SCHOENBERG, B. (1991). Requests made by people with developmental disabilities through the use of behavior interruption strategies. *Education and Training in Mental Retardation, 26,* 70–78.

ROSENBERG, S. A., & ROBINSON, C. C. (1988). Interactions of parents with their young handicapped children. In S. L. Odom & M. B. Karnes (Eds.), *Early intervention for infants and children with handicaps: An empirical base* (pp. 159–177). Baltimore: Paul H. Brookes.

ROSENFIELD, S. J. (1980, January–February). Advocates and educators lock horn over "related services." *Amicus, 6*–7, 48.

ROSENSHINE, B., & STEVENS, R. (1986). Teaching functions. In M. C. Wittrock (Ed.), *Handbook of research on teaching* (3rd ed.) (pp. 376–391). New York: Macmillan.

ROSS, A. O. (1980). *Psychological aspects of learning disabilities and reading disorders.* New York: McGraw-Hill.

ROTHSTEIN, L. F. (1990). *Special education law.* New York: Longman.

ROY, C., & FUQUA, D. (1983). Social support systems and academic performance of single-parent students. *The School Counselor, 30,* 183–192.

RUBIN, M. (1976). *Hearing aids: Current developments and concepts.* Baltimore: University Park Press.

RUCONICH, S. K., ASHCROFT, S. C., & YOUNG, M. F. (1983). *Making microcomputers accessible to blind persons.* Unpublished manuscript, George Peabody College of Vanderbilt University.

RUIZ, R. (1989). Considerations in the education of gifted Hispanic students. In C. J. Maker & S. W. Schiever (Eds.), *Critical issues in gifted education: Defensible programs for cultural and ethnic minorities.* Austin, TX: Pro-Ed.

RUSCH, F. R., & MENCHETTI, B. M. (1981). Increasing compliant work behavior in a non-sheltered work setting. *Mental Retardation, 19* (3), 187–194.

RUSCH, F. R., MITHAUG, D. E., & FLEXER, R. W. (1986). Obstacles to competitive employment and traditional program options for overcoming them. In F. R. Rusch (Ed.), *Competitive employment issues and strategies.* Baltimore: Paul H. Brookes.

RUSCH, F. R., WEITHERS, J. A., MENCHETTI, B., & SHUTZ, R. P. (1980). Social validation of a program to reduce repetition in a non-sheltered setting. *Education and Training in Mental Retardation, 15*(3) 187–194.

RUTHERFORD, R. B., NELSON, C. M., & WOLFORD, B. I. (1985). Special education in the most restrictive environment: Correctional special education. *Journal of Special Education, 19,* 59–71.

RYAN, J. (1975). Mental subnormality and language development. In E. Lenneberg & E. Lenneberg (Eds.), *Foundations of language development* (Vol. 2). New York: Academic Press.

RYAN, L. B., & RUCKER, C. N. (1986). Computerized vs. non-computerized individualized education programs: Teachers' attitudes, time, and cost. *Journal of Special Education Technology, 8*(1), 5–12.

RYAN, S. G., & BEDI, D. N. (1978). Toward computer literacy for visually impaired students. *Journal of Visual Impairment and Blindness, 72* (8), 302–306.

RYNDERS, E. J., & HORROBIN, J. M. (1990). Always trainable? Never educable? Updating educational expectations concerning children with Down syndrome. *American Journal of Mental Deficiency, 95*(1), 77–83.

SACHS, J. (1988). Teacher preparation, teacher self-efficacy, and the Regular Education Initiative. *Education and Training in Mental Retardation, 23*(4), 327–332.

SADKER, M., & SADKER, D. (1985). Sexism in the schools. *Psychology Today,* 55–57.

SADKER, M., SADKER, D., & STEINDAN, S. (1989, March). Gender equity and educational reform. *Educational Leadership,* 44–48.

SAFFORD, P. L. (1989). *Integrated teaching in early childhood: Starting in the mainstream.* White Plains, NY: Longman.

SAFRAN, J. S., & SAFRAN, S. P. (1987). Teachers' judgments of problem behaviors. *Exceptional Children, 54*(3), 240–244.

SAILOR, W., & GUESS, D. (1983). *Severely handicapped students: An instructional design.* Boston: Houghton-Mifflin.

SAILOR, W., HALVORSEN, A., ANDERSON, J., GOETZ, L., GEE, K., DOERING, K., & HUNT, P. (1986). Community intensive instruction. In R. Horner, L. Meyer, & H. D. Fredericks (Eds.), *Education of learners with severe handicaps: Exemplary service strategies.* Baltimore: Paul H. Brookes.

SAINATO, D. M., & LYON, S. R. (1989). Promoting successful mainstreaming transitions for handicapped preschool children. *Journal of Early Intervention, 13,* 305–314.

SALISBURY, C. L. (1991). Mainstreaming during the early childhood years. *Exceptional Children, 58,* 156–155.

SALISBURY, C. L., & INTAGLIATA, J. (1986). *Respite care: Support for persons with developmental disabilities and their families.* Baltimore: Paul H. Brookes.

SALISBURY, C. L., & VINCENT, L. J. (1990). Criterion of the next environment and best practices: Mainstreaming and integration 10 years later. *Topics in Early Childhood Special Education, 10,* 78–89.

SALVIA, J. (1978). Perspectives on the nature of retardation. In J. T. Neisworth & R. M. Smith (Eds.), *Retardation: Issues, assessment, and intervention* (pp. 27–47). New York: McGraw-Hill.

SALVIA, J., & HUGHES, C. (1990). *Curriculum-based assessment: Testing what is taught.* New York: Macmillan.

SALVIA, J., & YSSELDYKE, J. E. (1991). *Assessment in special and remedial education* (5th ed.). Boston: Houghton Mifflin.

SALZBERG, C., & VILLANI, T. (1983). Speech training by parents of Down Syndrome toddlers: Generalization across settings and instructional contexts. *American Journal of Mental Deficiency, 87,* 403–413.

SANDERS, D. A. (1982). *Aural rehabilitation management model* (2nd ed.). Englewood Cliffs, NJ: Prentice-Hall.

SAPON-SHEVIN, M. (1982). Ethical issues in parent training programs. *Journal of Special Education, 16,* 341–358.

SARASON, S. B. (1953). *Psychological problems in mental deficiency* (2nd ed.). New York: Harper & Row.

SATCHELL, M. (May 6, 1979). Ladies, start your engines. *Parade Magazine.*

SCANLON, C., ARICK, I., & PHELPS, N. (1981). Participation in the development of the IEP: Parents' perspective. *Exceptional Children, 47,* 373–376.

SCHAFER, D. S., BELL, A. P., & SPALDING, J. B. (1987). Parental vs. professional assessment of developmentally delayed children after periods of parent training. *Journal of the Division for Early Childhood, 12* (1), 47–55.

SCHALOCK, R. L. (1983). *Services for developmentally disabled adults.* Austin, TX: Pro-Ed.

SCHAPIRO, J., & EIGERDORF, V. (1975). Options in living arrangements, workshop report F. In J. C. Hamilton & R. M. Segal (Eds.), *Proceeding—A consultation conference on the gerontological aspects of mental retardation.* Ann Arbor: University of Michigan, Institute of Gerontology.

SCHLATER, A. (1987). *Seattle inventory of early learning software.* Seattle: Specialty Software.

SCHOFIELD, J. (1981). Computer-based aids for the blind. *Inter-Regional Review, 69,* 4–9.

SCHOLL, G. T. (1986a). Growth and development. In G. T. Scholl (Ed.), *Foundations of education for blind and visually handicapped children and youth: Theory and practice* (pp. 65–81). New York: American Foundation for the Blind.

SCHOLL, G. T. (1986b). What does it mean to be blind? In G. T. Scholl (Ed.), *Foundations of education for blind and visually handicapped children and youth: Theory and practice* (pp. 23–33). New York: American Foundation for the Blind.

SCHOLL, G., & SCHNUR, R. (1976). *Measures of psychological, vocational, and educational functioning in the blind and visually handicapped.* New York: American Foundation for the Blind.

SCHUBERT, M. A., & GLICK, H. M. (1981). Least restrictive environment programs: Why are some so successful? *Education Unlimited, 3* (2), 11–13.

SCHUMAKER, J. B., & DESHLER, D. D. (1988). Implementing the regular education initiative in secondary schools: A different ball game. *Journal of Learning Disabilities, 21*(1), 36–42.

SCHUMAKER, J. B., & HAZEL, J. S. (1984). Social skills assessment and training for the learning disabled: Who's on first and what's on second? Part II. *Journal of Learning Disabilities, 17,* 492–499.

SCHUSTER, J., GAST, D., WOLERY, M., & GUILTINAN, S. (1988). The effectiveness of a constant time delay procedure to teach chained responses to adolescents with mental retardation. *Journal of Applied Behavior Analysis, 21*(2), 169–178.

SCHUSTER, J., & GRIFFEN, A. K. (1990). Using time delay with task analyses. *Teaching Exceptional Children, 22*(4), 49–54.

SCHUTTER, L. S., & BRINKER, R. P. (1992). Conjuring a new category of disability from prenatal cocaine casualties? *Topics in Early Childhood Special Education, 11*(4), 84–111.

SCHWARTZ, S. (Ed.) (1987). *Choices in deafness: A parent's guide.* Kensington, MD: Woodbine House.

Scientists find protein that could halt arthritis (1990, February 1). *Herald Leader,* Lexington, KY, p. 26.

Scientists link gene to cause of dystrophy (1992, February 6). *Herald Leader,* Lexington, KY, p. A3.

SCOTT, E. P. (1982). *Your visually impaired student: A guide for teachers.* Baltimore: University Park Press.

SCOTT, K. G., & CARRAN, D. T. (1989). Identifications and referral of handicapped infants. In M. C. Wang, M. C. Reynolds, & H. J. Walberg (Eds.), *Handbook of special education: Research and practice: Vol. 3. Low incidence conditions* (pp. 227–241). New York: Pergamon Press.

SEABERG, V. T., & STAFFORD, P. B. (1991). Council of State Directors of Programs for the Gifted—Nationwide trends in gifted education: The state of the states. Presentation to the Council for Exceptional Children International Convention, Atlanta, April 4.

SEAL, B. C. (1987). Working parents' dream: Instructional videotapes for their signing deaf child. *American Annals of the Deaf, 132,* 386–387.

SEEGER, B., & BAILS, J. (1990). Ergonomic building design for physically disabled young people. *Assistive Technology, 2*(3), 79–92.

SEGAL, M. (1988). *In time and with love: Caring for the special needs baby.* New York: Newmarket Press.

SEITZ, V., & PROVENCE, S. (1990). Caregiver-focused models of early intervention. In S. J. Meisels & J. P. Shonkoff (Eds.), *Handbook of early childhood intervention* (pp. 400–427). Cambridge, U.K.: Cambridge University Press.

SELIGMAN, M., & DARLING, R. B. (1989). *Ordinary families, special children: A systems approach to childhood disability.* New York: Guilford Press.

SEYFORTH, J., HILL, J. W., ORELOVE, F., McMILLAN, J., & WEHMAN, P. (1987). Factors influencing parents' vocational aspirations for their children with mental retardation. *Mental Retardation, 25*(6), 357–362.

SHAFER, M. S., BANKS, P. D., & KREGEL, J. (1991). Employment retention and career movement among individuals with mental retardation working in supported employment. *Mental Retardation, 29,* 103–110.

SHAFER, M. S., BROOKE, V., & WEHMAN, P. (1985). Developing appropriate social-interpersonal skills in a mentally retarded worker. In P. Wehman & J. W. Hill (Eds.), *Competitive employment for persons with mental retardation: From research to practice* (Vol. 1, pp. 358–375). Richmond, VA: Virginia Commonwealth University, Rehabilitation Research and Training Center.

SHAFER, M. S., WEHMAN, P., KREGEL, J., & WEST, M. (1990). National supported employment initiative: A preliminary analysis. *American Journal on Mental Retardation, 95,* 316–327.

SHAMES, G. H. (1990). Disorders of fluency. In G. H. Shames & E. H. Wiig (Eds.), *Human communication disorders.* Columbus, OH: Merrill.

SHANE, H. H., & BASHIR, A. (1980). Election criteria for the adoption of an augmentative communication system: Preliminary considerations. *Journal of Speech and Hearing Disorders, 45,* 408–414.

SHARRARD, W. J. W. (1968). Spina bifida and its sequelae. *South African Medical Journal* (1968), *42,* 915–918. In D. D. Peterson (Ed.), *The physically handicapped* (pp. 207–210). [A book of readings]. New York: MSS Educational.

SHAYWITZ, S. E., ESCOBAR, M. D., SHAYWITZ, B. A., FLETCHER, J. M., & MAKUCH, R. (1992). Evidence that dyslexia may represent the lower tail of a normal distribution of reading ability. *The New England Journal of Medicine, 326*(3), 145–150.

SHEARER, D. E., & LOFTIN, C. R. (1984). The Portage project: Teaching parents to teach their preschool children at home. In R. F. Dangel & R. A. Polster (Eds.), *Parent training* (pp. 93–126). New York: Guilford Press.

SHEARER, D. E., & SHEARER, M. S. (1976). The Portage project: A model for early childhood intervention. In T. D. Tjossem (Ed.), *Intervention strategies for high risk infants and young children* (pp. 335–350). Baltimore: University Park Press.

SHEPARD, L. A., & SMITH, M. L. (1983). An evaluation of learning disabled students in Colorado. *Learning Disability Quarterly, 6*(2), 115–127.

SHINN, M., & MARSTON, D. (1985). Differentiating mildly handicapped, low-achieving, and regular education students: A curriculum-based approach. *Remedial and Special Education, 6*, 31–38.

SHINN, M. R., RAMSEY, E., WALKER, H. M., STIEBER, S., & O'NEILL, R. (1987). Antisocial behavior in school settings: Initial differences in an at-risk and normal population. *Journal of Special Education, 21*, 69–84.

SHONKOFF, J. P., & MEISELS, S. J. (1990). Early childhood intervention: The evolution of a concept. In S. J. Meisels & J. P. Shonkoff (Eds.), *Handbook of early childhood intervention* (pp. 3–31). Cambridge, U.K.: Cambridge University Press.

SICOLA, P. K. (1990). Where do gifted students fit? An examination of middle school philosophy as it relates to ability grouping and the gifted learner. *Journal for the Education of the Gifted, 14*(1), 37–49.

SILLIMAN, E., & WILKINSON, L. (1991). *Communication for learning: Classroom observation and collaboration.* Rockville, MD: Aspen.

SILVER, L. B. (1987). The "magic cure": A review of the current controversial approaches for treating learning disabilities. *Journal of Learning Disabilities, 20*(8), 498–512.

SILVER, L. B. (1991). The Regular Education Initiative: A deja vu remembered with sadness and concern. *Journal of Learning Disabilities, 24*(7), 389–390.

SILVERMAN, F. (1989). *Communication for the speechless* (2nd ed.). Englewood Cliffs, NJ: Prentice-Hall.

SILVERMAN, L. K. (1986). What happens to the gifted girl? In C. J. Maker (Ed.), *Critical issues in gifted education: Defensible programs for the gifted.* (pp. 43–89). Austin, TX: Pro-Ed.

SILVERMAN, L. K. (1989). Invisible gifts, invisible handicaps. *Roeper Review, 12*(1), 37–42.

SILVERMAN, R. (1987). Laying the groundwork for the future of deaf education. *American Annals of the Deaf, 132*(5), 351–353.

SILVERMAN, S. R. (1971). The education of deaf children. In L. E. Travis (Ed.), *Handbook of speech pathology and audiology.* Englewood Cliffs, NJ: Prentice-Hall.

SIMEONSSON, R. J., & BAILEY, D. B. (1990). Family dimensions in early intervention. In S. J. Meisels & J. P. Shonkoff (Eds.), *Handbook of early childhood intervention* (pp. 428–444). Cambridge, U.K.: Cambridge University Press.

SIMPKINS, K., & STEPHENS, B. (1974). Cognitive development of blind subjects. *Proceedings of the 52nd Biennial Conference of the Association for the Education of the Visually Handicapped,* 26–28.

SIMPSON, R. L. (1982). Future training issues. *Exceptional Children Quarterly, 3*, 91–88.

SIMPSON, R. L. (1988). Needs of parents and families whose children have learning and behavior problems. *Behavioral Disorders, 14*(1), 40–47.

SIMPSON, R. L., MILES, B. S., WALKER, B. L., ORMSBEE, C. K., & DOWNING, J. A. (1991). *Programming for aggressive and violent students.* Reston, VA: Council for Exceptional Children

SINGER, S., STEWART, M., & PULASKI, L. (1981). Minimal brain dysfunction: Differences in cognitive organization in two groups of index cases and their relatives. *Journal of Learning Disabilities, 14,* 470–473.

SINGLETON, R. (1981, December). *Applying the normalization principle in the United Kingdom: Barnardo's Skelmersdale Project.* Paper presented to the International Seminar on Planning for Integration of the Mentally Handicapped, Delft University, The Netherlands.

SIPERSTEIN, G. N., & BAK, J. T. (1980). Improving children's attitudes toward blind peers. *Journal of Visual Impairment and Blindness, 74*(4), 132–135.

SITKA, K. (1989). *Empathy and its enhancement in hearing impaired children.* Unpublished doctoral dissertation, Syracuse University.

SIZER, T. R. (1983). High school reform: The need for engineering. *Phi Delta Kappan, 64*(10), 679–683.

SKARNULIS, E. (1980). *Key concepts: Core and cluster.* Public information brochure. Division for Community Services for Mental Retardation. Bureau for Health Services. Department of Human Resources, Frankfort, KY.

SKEELS, H. M. (1966). Adult status of children with contrasting early life experiences: A follow-up study. *Monographs of the Society for Research in Child Development, 31*(39) (Serial No. 105).

SLATER, E., & COWIE, V. (1971). *The genetics of mental disorders.* London: Oxford University Press.

SLAVIN, R. (1990). Ability grouping, cooperative learning, and the gifted. *Journal for the Education of the Gifted, 14*(1), 9–27.

SLENKOVITCH, J. E. (1984). *Understanding special education law* (Vol. 1). Cupertino, CA: Kinghorn Press.

SLINGERLAND, B. (1976). *A multisensory program for language arts for specific language disability children: A guide for primary teachers.* Cambridge, MA: Educator's Publishing Service.

SMILANSKY, M., & NEVO, D. (1979). *The gifted disadvantaged: A ten year longitudinal study of compensatory education in Israel.* New York: Gordon & Breach.

SMITH, B. J. (1988). Early intervention public policy: Past, present, and future. In J. B Jordan, J. J. Gallagher, P. L. Hutinger, & M. B. Karnes (Eds.), *Early childhood special education: Birth to three* (pp. 213–228). Reston, VA: Council for Exceptional Children.

SMITH, C. (1991). *Learning disabilities.* Boston: Allyn & Bacon.

SMITH, C. R., WOOD, F. H., & GRIMES, J. (1988). Issues in the identification and placement of behaviorally disordered students. In M. C. Wang, M. C. Reynolds, & H. J. Walberg (Eds.), *Handbook of special education: Research and practice* (Vol. 2) (pp. 95–123). New York: Pergamon Press.

SMITH, E. W., KROUSE, S. W., & ATKINSON, M. M. (1961). *Educators encyclopedia.* Englewood Cliffs, NJ: Prentice-Hall.

SMITH, J., LeROSE, B., & CLASEN, R. E. (1991). Underrepresentation of minority students in gifted programs: Yes! It matters! *Gifted Child Quarterly, 35*(2), 81–83.

SMITH, J. D. (September, 1988). CEC-MR position statement on the right of children with mental retardation to life sustaining medical care and treatment. *CEC-MR Report.*

SMITH, J. D., & POLLOWAY, E. A. (1979). The dimension of adaptive behavior in mental retardation research: An analysis of recent practices. *American Journal of Mental Deficiency, 84,* 203–206.

SMITH, M. S., & BISSELL, J.S. (1970). Report analysis: The impact of head start. *Harvard Educational Review, 40,* 51–104.

SMITH, P. D. (1989). Assessing motor skills. In D. B. Bailey & M. Wolery (Eds.), *Assessing infants and preschoolers with handicaps* (pp. 301–328). Columbus, OH: Merrill.

SMITH, S. (1980). *No easy answers.* New York: Bantam Books.

SNELL, M. E. (Ed.) (1987). *Systematic instruction of persons with severe handicaps* (3rd ed.). Columbus, OH: Merrill.

SNELL, M. E., & GAST, D. L. (1981). Applying time delay procedure to the instruction of the severely handicapped. *The Journal of the Association for the Severely Handicapped, 6*(3), 3–14.

SNELL, M. E., & GRIGG, N. C. (1987). Instructional assessment and curriculum development. In M. E. Snell (Ed.), *Systematic instruction of persons with severe handicaps* (3rd ed.). Columbus, OH: Merrill.

SNELL, M. E., & RENZAGLIA, A. M. (1986). Moderate, severe, and profound handicaps. In N. G. Haring & L. McCormick (Eds.), *Exceptional children and youth.* Columbus, OH: Merrill.

SOFFER, R. (1982). IEP decisions in which parents desire greater participation. *Education and Training of the Mentally Retarded, 17,* 67–70.

SOLANO, C. H. (1976, September 3–7). *Teacher and pupil stereotypes of gifted boys and girls.* Paper presented at the 84th annual conference of the American Psychological Association. Washington, DC.

SONTAG, E., BURKE, P., & YORK, R. (1973). Considerations for serving the severely handicapped. *Education and Training of the Mentally Retarded, 8,* 20–26.

SOUDER v. BRENNAN, Civil Action No. 482-73 (U.S. District Court for the District of Columbia, 1973).

SOUTHEASTERN COMMUNITY COLLEGE v. DAVIS (1979). In (Vol. 99 S. Ct. 2361, 442 US 397).

SOUTHEASTERN REGIONAL COALITION (1979). Issues in certification for teachers of the severely handicapped. In National Association of State Directors of Special Education, *Special education programs for severely and profoundly handicapped individuals: A directory of state education agency services* (pp. 32–50). Washington, DC: NASDSE.

SPARROW, S. S., BALLA, D. A., & CICCHETTI, D. V. (1984). *Vineland Adaptive Behavior Scales.* Circle Pines, MN: American Guidance Service.

SPEARMAN, C. (1914). The hereditary of abilities. *Eugenics Review, 6,* 219–237.

SPICKER, D. (1982). Parental involvement in early intervention activities with their children with Down syndrome. *Education and Training of the Mentally Retarded, 17,* 24–29.

SPITZ, H. H. (1973). Consolidating facts into the schematized learning and memory system of educable retardates. In N. R. Ellis (Ed.), *International review of research in mental retardation* (Vol. 6). New York: Academic Press.

SPIVEY, S. A. (1967). *The social position of selected children with a visual loss in regular classes in the public schools of Atlanta, Georgia.* Specialist in education thesis. George Peabody College for Teachers, Nashville, TN.

SPRADLIN, J. E., & SPRADLIN, R. R. (1976). Developing necessary entry skills for entry into classroom teaching arrangements. In N. G. Haring & R. L. Schiefelbusch (Eds.), *Teaching special children.* New York: McGraw-Hill.

SPREAT, S., TELLES, J. L., CONROY, J. W., FEINSTEIN, C., & COLMBATTO, J. J. (1987). Attitudes toward deinstitutionalization: National survey of families of institutionalized persons with mental retardation. *Mental Retardation, 25*(5), 267–274.

SPREEN, O. (1965). Language functions in mental retardation: A review. *American Journal of Mental Deficiency, 69,* 482–494.

SPUNGIN, S. J. (1990). *Braille literacy: Issues for blind persons, families, professionals, and producers of braille.* New York: American Foundation for the Blind.

STAINBACK, W., & STAINBACK, S. (1984). A rationale for the merger of special and regular education. *Exceptional Children, 51,* 102–111.

STANLEY, F. J. (1987). The changing face of cerebral palsy? *Developmental Medicine and Child Neurology, 29,* 258–270.

STANLEY, J. C. (1977). Rationale of the study of mathematical precocious youth (SMPY) during its first five years of promoting educational acceleration. In J. C. Stanley, W. C. George, & C. H. Solano (Eds.), *The gifted and the creative: A fifty-year perspective* (pp. 75–112). Baltimore: Johns Hopkins University Press.

STANLEY, J. C. (1989). How greatly do Chinese students eclipse ours? *Journal for the Education of the Gifted, 12*(4), 306–309.

STANLEY, J. C. (1991). Critique of "Socioemotional Adjustment of Adolescent Girls Enrolled in a Residential Acceleration Program," *Gifted Child Quarterly, 35*(2), 67–70.

STANLEY, J. C., & BENBOW, C. P. (1982). Using the SAT to find intellectually talented seventh graders. *The College Review Board, 122,* 3–7, 26.

STANLEY, J. C., GEORGE, W. C., & SOLANO, C. H. (Eds.) (1973). *The gifted and the creative: A fifty-year perspective.* Baltimore: Johns Hopkins University Press.

STANLEY, J. S. (1976). The case for extreme educational acceleration in intellectually brilliant youths. *Gifted Child Quarterly, 20*(1), 66–75.

STANOVICH, K. E. (1986). Cognitive processes and the reading problems of learning-disabled children: Evaluating the assumption of specificity. In. J. Torgesen & B. Wong (Eds.), *Psychological and educational perspectives on learning disabilities* (pp. 87–132). New York: Academic Press.

STANOVICH, K. E. (1988). Explaining the differences between the dyslexic and the garden-variety poor reader: The phonological-core variable-difference model. *Journal of Learning Disabilities, 21,* 590–604.

STANZLER, M. (1982). Taking the guilt out of parenting. *Exceptional Parent, 12,* 51–53.

State of the States: Gifted and talented educated, 1986–1987 (1988). Helena, MT: Council of State Directors of Programs for the Gifted.

STEINART, Y. E., CAMPBELL, S. B., & KIELY, M. C. (1981). A comparison of maternal and remedial teacher teaching styles with good and poor readers. *Journal of Learning Disabilities, 14,* 38–42.

STEPHENS, T. M., BLACKHURST, A. E., & MAGLIOCCA, L. A. (1988). *Teaching mainstreamed students* (2nd ed.). New York: Pergamon Press.

STERNBERG, R. (1982). Nonentrenchment in the assessment of intellectual giftedness. *Gifted Children Quarterly, 26*(2), 63–67.

STERNBERG, R. (1985). *Beyond IQ: A triarchic theory of human intelligence.* Cambridge, U.K.: Cambridge University Press.

STERNBERG, R. (1990). What constitutes a good definition of giftedness? *Journal for the Education of the Gifted, 14*(1), 96–100.

STERNBERG, R. J., & SPEAR, L. C. (1985). A triarchic theory of mental retardation. *International Review of Research in Mental Retardation, 13,* 301–326.

STEVENS, G. (1962). *Taxonomy in special education for children with body disorders: The problem and a proposal.* Pittsburgh: University of Pittsburgh.

STEVENS, K. B., & BLACKHURST, A. E. (1992). The Waiting to Learn Series [Computer Programs]. Lexington, KY: Department of Special Education, University of Kentucky.

STEVENS, K. B., BLACKHURST, A. E., & SLATON, D. B. (1992). Teaching memorized spelling with a microcomputer: Time delay and computer-assisted instruction. *Journal of Applied Behavior Analysis.*

STEVENS, K. B., & SCHUSTER, J. W. (1988). Time delay: Systematic instruction for academic tasks. *Remedial and Special Education, 9*(5), 16–21.

STODDEN, R. A., & IANACONE, R. N. (1981). Career/vocational assessment of the special needs individual: A conceptual model. *Exceptional Children, 47*(8), 601–608.

STODGILL, R. (1974). *Handbook of leadership: A survey of theory and research.* New York: Free Press.

STOKES, T. F., & OSNES, P. G. (1988). The developing applied technology of generalization and maintenance. In R. H. Horner, G. Dunlap, & R. L. Koegel (Eds.), *Generalization and maintenance: Life-style changes in applied settings* (pp. 5–20). Baltimore: Paul H. Brookes.

STONE, C. A., & FORMAN, E. A. (1988). Differential patterns of approach to a complex problem-solving task among learning disabled adolescents. *Journal of Special Education, 22*(2), 167–185.

STONE, D. H. (1987). The declining prevalence of anencephalus and spina bifida: Its nature, causes and implications. *Developmental Medicine and Child Neurology, 29,* 541–549.

STONE, W. C., & LaGRECA, A. M. (1990). The social status of children with learning disabilities: A reexamination. *Journal of Learning Disabilities, 23*(1), 32–37.

STRAIN, P. S. (1983). Generalization of autistic children's social behavior change: Effects of developmentally integrated and segregated settings. *Analysis and Intervention in Developmental Disabilities, 3,* 23–34.

STRAIN, P. S. (1985). Social and nonsocial determinants of handicapped preschool children's social competence. *Topics in Early Childhood Special Education, 4*(4), 47–58.

STRAIN, P. S. (1989, April). Behavioral recovery in young autistic children. William J. Tisdall Distinguished Lecture in Special Education, University of Kentucky.

STRAIN, P. S., & ODOM, S. L. (1986). Peer social initiations: Effective intervention for social skills development of exceptional children. *Exceptional Children, 52,* 543–551.

STRAIN, P. S., & SMITH, B. J. (1986). A counter-interpretation of early intervention effects: A response to Casto and Mastropieri. *Exceptional Children, 53,* 260–265.

STRAUSS, A. A., & LEHTINEN, L. E. (1947). *Psychopathology and education of the brain injured child.* New York: Grune & Stratton.

STRAUSS, A. A., & WERNER, H. (1942). Disorders of conceptual thinking in the brain-injured child. *Journal of Nervous and Mental Diseases, 96,* 153–172.

STREISSGUTH, A., SAMPSON, P., & BARR, H. (1989). Neurobehavioral dose-response effects of prenatal alcohol exposure in humans from infancy to adulthood. In D. Hutchings (Eds.), *Prenatal abuse of licit and illicit drugs* (p. 562). Annals of the New York Academy of Sciences.

STRICKLAND, B. (1982). Parental participation, school accountability, and due process. *Exceptional Education Quarterly, 3,* 41–49.

STROM, R., REES, R., SLAUGHTER, H., & WURSTER, S. (1980). Role expectations of parents of intellectually handicapped children. *Exceptional Children, 47,* 144–148.

STROM, R. D., & TORRANCE, E. P. (1973). *Education for effective achievement.* Chicago: Rand McNally.

STUCKLESS, E. R. (1989). Education of deaf children and youth: An introduction. In M. C. Wang, M. C. Reynolds, & H. J. Walberg (Eds.), *Handbook of special education: Research and practice: Vol. 3. Low incidence conditions.* New York: Pergamon Press.

SUAREZ, T. M., HURTH, J. L., & PRESTRIDGE, S. (1988). Innovation in services for young children with handicaps and their families: An analysis of the handicapped children's early education program projects funded from 1982 to 1986. *Journal of the Division for Early Childhood, 12*(3), 224–238.

SUDHALTER, V., COHEN, I. L., SILVERMAN, W., & WOLF-SCHEIN, E. G. (1990). *American Association on Mental Deficiency, 94*(4), 431–441.

SUGAI, G., & SMITH, P. (1986). The equal additions method of subtraction taught with a modeling technique. *Remedial and Special Education, 7*(1), 40–48.

SUPPES, P. (1980). Impact of computers on curriculum in the schools and universities. In R. P. Taylor (Ed.), *The computer in the school: Tutor, tool, tutee* (pp. 236–247). New York: Teachers College Press.

SWALLOW, R. M. (1981). Fifty assessment procedures commonly used with blind and partially seeing individuals. *Journal of Visual Impairment and Blindness, 75*(2), 65–72.

SWANSON, H. L., COCHRAN, K. F., & EWERS, C. A. (1990). Can learning disabilities be determined from working memory performance? *Journal of Learning Disabilities, 23,* 59–67.

SWANSON, L. (1982). Verbal short-term memory encoding of learning disabled, deaf, and normal readers. *Learning Disability Quarterly, 5,* 21–28.

SYKES, K. S. (1971). A comparison of the effectiveness of standard print and large print in facilitating the reading skills of visually impaired students. *Education of the Visually Handicapped, 3,* 97–106.

SZASZ, T. S. (1960). The myth of mental illness. *American Psychologist, 15,* 113–118.

TANNENBAUM, A. J. (1983). *Gifted children.* New York: Macmillan.

TARJAN, G., WRIGHT, S., EYMAN, R., & KEERAN, C. (1973). Natural history of mental retardation: Some aspects of epidemiology. *American Journal of Mental Deficiency, 77,* 369–379.

TARVER, S. G., & DAWSON, M. M. (1978). Modality preference and the teaching of reading: A review. *Journal of Learning Disabilities, 11,* 5–17.

TASH definition (1988, July). *The Association for Persons with Severe Handicaps Newsletter.*

TAWNEY, J. W. (1977). Educating severely handicapped children and their parents through telecommunications. In N. G. Haring & L. J. Brown (Eds.), *Teaching the severely handicapped* (Vol. 2). New York: Grune & Stratton.

TAWNEY, J. W. (1982). The future. In P. T. Cegelka & H. J. Prehm (Eds.), *Mental Retardation.* Columbus, OH: Merrill.

TAYLOR, A. R. (1898). *The study of the child.* New York: D. Appleton.

TAYLOR, J. L. (1974). Selecting facilities to meet educational needs. In B. Lowenfeld (Ed.), *The blind preschool child.* New York: American Foundation for the Blind.

TAYLOR, M. (1990). Clean intermittent catheterization. In C. J. Graff, M. M. Ault, D. Guess, M. Taylor, & B. Thompson (Eds.), *Health care for students with disabilities* (pp. 241–252). Baltimore: Paul H. Brookes.

TAYLOR, O. (1973). Language, cultural contrasts and the black American. In L. A. Bransford, L. Baca, & K. Lane (Eds.). *Cultural diversity and the exceptional child* (pp. 34–41). Reston, VA: Council for Exceptional Children.

TELFORD, C. W., & SAWREY, J. M. (1977). *The exceptional individual* (3rd ed.). Englewood Cliffs, NJ: Prentice-Hall.

TEMPLETON, D., GAGE, M. A., & FREDERICKS, H. D. (1982). Cost-effectiveness of the group home. *Journal of the Association for the Severely Handicapped, 6*(4), 11–16.

TERMAN, L. M. (1954). The discovery and encouragement of exceptional talent. *American Psychologist, 9,* 221–230.

TERMAN, L. M., et al. (1925). *Genetic studies of genius: Vol 1. The mental and physical traits of a thousand gifted children.* Stanford, CA: Stanford University Press.

TERMAN, L. M., & ODEN, M. H. (1947). *Genetic studies of genius. Vol. 4. The gifted child grows up.* Stanford, CA: Stanford University Press.

TEW, B. F., LAWRENCE, K. M., PAYNE, H., & TOWNSLEY, K. (1977). Marital stability following the birth of a child with spina bifida. *British Journal of Psychiatry, 131,* 77–82.

THIESSEN, D. (1972). *Gene organization and behavior.* New York: Random House.

THORKILDSEN, R., BECKEL, W. K., & WILLIAMS, J. G. (1979). Microcomputer/videodisc CAI package to teach the retarded. *Education and Industrial Television, 11*(5), 40–42.

THORP, D. K., & McCOLLUM, J. A. (1988). Defining the infancy specialization in early childhood special education. In J. B. Jordan, J. J. Gallagher, P. L. Hutinger, & M. B. Karnes (Eds.), *Early childhood special education: Birth to three* (pp. 147–161). Reston, VA: Council for Exceptional Children.

THUNBERG, U. (1981). The gifted in minority groups. In B. S. Miller & M. Price (Eds.), *The gifted, the family, and the community.* New York: Walker.

THURLOW, M. L., & YSSELDYKE, J. E. (1979). Current assessment and decision-making practices in model programs for the learning disabled. *Learning Disability Quarterly 2,* 15–24.

TIDWELL, R. (1980). A psycho-educational profile of 1,593 gifted high school students. *Gifted Child Quarterly, 24* (2), 63–68.

TILLMAN, M. H., & OSBORNE, R. T. (1969). The performance of blind and sighted children on the Wechsler Intelligence Scale for Children: Interaction effects. *Education of the Visually Handicapped, 1,* 1–4.

TINDALL, L. W., & GUGERTY, J. J. (1989). Collaboration among clients, families, and service providers. In D. E. Berkell & J. M. Brown (Eds.), *Transition from school to work for persons with disabilities.* New York: Longman.

TINDALL, L. W., GUGERTY, J., et al. (1982). *Vocational education models for linking agencies serving the handicapped: Handbook on developing effective linking strategies.* Madison, WI: University of Wisconsin, Vocational Studies Center.

TINGEY-MICHAELIS, C. (1983). *Handicapped infants & children: A handbook for parents & professionals.* Austin, TX: Pro. Ed.

TOBIN, J. J. (1972). Conservation of substance in the blind and sighted. *British Journal of Educational Psychology, 42*(2), 192–197.

TOLLEFSON, N., TRACY, D. B., JOHNSEN, E. P., BUENNING, M., FARMER, A., & BARKE, C. R. (1982). Attribution patterns of learning disabled adolescents. *Learning Disability Quarterly, 5*(1), 14–20.

TOLLISON, P., PALMER, D. J., & STOWE, M. L. (1987). Mothers' expectations, interactions, and achievements attributions for their learning disabled or normally achieving sons. *Journal of Special Education, 21*(3), 83–93.

TORGESEN, J. K. (1979). Factors related to poor performance on memory tasks in reading disabled children. *Learning Disability Quarterly, 2,* 17–23.

TORGESEN, J. K. (1982). The learning-disabled child as an inactive learner: Educational implications. *Topics in Learning and Learning Disabilities, 2,* 45–52.

TORGESEN, J. K. (1988). Studies of children with learning disabilities who perform poorly on memory span tasks. *Journal of Learning Disabilities, 21*(10), 605–612.

TORGESEN, J. K. (Ed.) (1990). *Cognitive and behavioral characteristics of children with learning disabilities.* Austin, TX: Pro-Ed.

TORRANCE, E. P. (1962). *Guiding creative talent.* Englewood Cliffs, NJ: Prentice-Hall.

TORRANCE, E. P. (1966). *Tests of creative thinking.* Princeton, NJ: Personnel Press.

TORRANCE, E. P. (1971). Are the Torrance tests of creative thinking biased against or in favor of disadvantaged children? *Gifted Child Quarterly, 15,* 75–80.

TORRANCE, E. P. (1974). *Norm-technical manual: Torrance tests of creative thinking.* Lexington, MA: Ginn.

TORRANCE, E. P. (1977). *What research says to the teacher: Creativity in the classroom.* Washington, DC: National Education Association.

TRAILOR, C. B. (1982). Role clarification and participation in child study teams. *Exceptional Children, 48,* 529–530.

TREDGOLD, A. F. (1937). *A textbook of mental deficiency* (6th ed.). Baltimore: William Wood.

TUCKER, M. (1983). Computers alone can't save education or protect us in the world economy. *American School Board Journal, 170*(3), 31–32.

TUCKER, S. M. (1978). *Fetal monitoring and fetal assessment in high-risk pregnancy.* St. Louis: C. V. Mosby.

TURNBULL, A. P., & STRICKLAND, B. (1981). Parents and the educational system. In J. L. Paul (Ed.), *Understanding and working with parents of children with special needs* (pp. 231–263). New York: Holt, Rinehart & Winston.

TURNBULL, A. P., & TURNBULL, H. R. (1985). *Parents speak out.* Columbus, OH: Merrill.

TURNBULL, A. P., & TURNBULL, H. R. (1990a). A tale about lifestyle changes: Comments on "toward a technology of nonaversive behavioral support." *Journal of the Association for Persons with Severe Handicaps, 15,* 142–144.

TURNBULL, A. P., & TURNBULL, H. R. (1990b). *Families, professionals & exceptionality: A special partnership* (2nd ed.). Columbus, OH: Merrill.

TURNBULL, H. R. (1981). Parents and the law. In J. L. Paul (Ed.), *Understanding and working with parents of children with special needs* (pp. 205–230). New York: Holt, Rinehart & Winston.

TURNBULL, H. R. (1990). *Free appropriate public education: The law and children with disabilities* (3rd ed.). Denver: Love.

TURNBULL, H. R., & TURNBULL, A. P. (1978). *Free appropriate public education: Law and implementation.* Denver: Love.

TURNBULL, H. R. III, TURNBULL, A., BUZZ BRONICKI, G. J., SUMMERS, J. A., & GORDON, C. R. (1988). Disability and the family: A guide to decisions for adulthood. *Exceptional Parent, 18*(8), 47–50.

TURNER, G., OPITZ, J. M., BROWN, W. T., DAVIES, K. E., JACOBS, P. A., JENKINS, F. C., MIKKELSEN, M., PARTINGTON, M. W., & SUTHERLAND, G. R. (1986). Conference report: Second International Workshop on the Fragile X and on X-Linked Mental Retardation. *American Journal of Medical Genetics, 23,* 573–580.

TYMITZ, B. L. (1980). When legislation precedes the state of the art in teacher training: Problems and implications. *International Journal of Rehabilitation Research, 3*(4), 485–495.

TYMITZ, B. L. (1983). Do teachers need a philosophy of education: An exploratory study. *Journal of Special Education, 19,* 1–10.

TYMITZ-WOLF, B. (1982, March). Guidelines for assessing IEP goals and objectives. *Teaching Exceptional Children,* 198–201.

ULLMANN, L. P., & KRASNER, L. (Eds.) (1965). *Case studies in behavior modification.* New York: Holt, Rinehart & Winston.

UMBREIT, J., & OSTROW, L. S. (1980). The fetal alcohol syndrome. *Mental Retardation, 18,* 109–111.

U.S. CONSUMER PRODUCT SAFETY COMMISSION (1990, September). What you should know about lead-based paint in your home. *Consumer Product Safety Alert.*

U.S. DEPARTMENT OF EDUCATION (1989). To assure the free appropriate public education of all handicapped children. *Eleventh annual report to Congress on the implementation of the Education of the Handicapped Act.* Washington, DC: U.S. Government Printing Office.

U.S. DEPARTMENT OF EDUCATION (1991a). Assistance to states for education of handicapped children: Notice of proposed rulemaking. *Federal Register, 56*(180), 41266–41275.

U.S. DEPARTMENT OF EDUCATION (1991b). *Thirteenth annual report to Congress on the implementation of the Individuals with Disabilities Act.* Washington, DC: U.S. Government Printing Office.

U.S. DEPARTMENT OF HEALTH, EDUCATION, AND WELFARE, OFFICE OF EDUCATION (1977; Tuesday, 23 August). Education of handicapped children: Implementation of Part B of the Education of the Handicapped Act. *Federal Register, 42*(163).

U.S. DEPARTMENT OF HEALTH, EDUCATION AND WELFARE, PUBLIC HEALTH SERVICES, NATIONAL INSTITUTES OF HEALTH (1976). *Interim Report of the National Advisory Eye Council 1976.* (DHEW Publication No. 76-1098).

U.S. GOVERNMENT PRINTING OFFICE (1983). *Physical disabilities and health impairments: An introduction.* Columbus, OH: Merrill.

UTLEY, C. A., LOWITZER, A. C., & BAUMEISTER, A. A. (1987). A comparison of the AAMD's definition, eligibility criteria, and classification schemes with state departments of education guidelines. *Education and Training of the Mentally Retarded, 22,* 35–43.

VACC, N. A. (1972). Long-term effects of special class intervention for emotionally disturbed children. *Exceptional Children, 39,* 15–22.

VACC, N. A., VALLECORSA, A. L., PARKER, A., BONNER, S., LESTER, C., RICHARDSON, S., & YATES, C. (1985). Parents' and educators' participation in IEP conferences. *Education and Treatment of Children, 8*(2), 153–162.

van der LEM, T., & MENKE, R. (1982). *Verslag van de workshop Blackwell* [Report of the Blackwell Workshop]. Nederlandse Stichting voor he Dove en Slechthorande Kind, Amsterdam.

VAN RIPER, C. (1978). *Speech correction: Principles and methods* (6th ed.). Englewood Cliffs, NJ: Prentice-Hall.

VAN TASSEL-BASKA, J. (1983). Profiles of precocity: The 1982 midwest talent search finalists. *Gifted Child Quarterly, 27*(3), 139–144.

VAN TASSEL-BASKA, J., PATTON, J., & PRILLAMAN, D. (1989). Disadvantaged gifted learners: At risk for educational attention. *Focus on Exceptional Children, 22*(3), 1–15.

VARNHAGEN, C. K., DAS, J. P., & VARNHAGEN, S. (1987). Auditory and visual memory span: Cognitive processing by TMR individuals with Down syndrome or other etiologies. *American Association on Mental Deficiency, 91*(4), 398–405.

VAUGHN, D., & ASHBURY, T. (1989). *General ophthalmology* (10th ed.). Los Altos, CA: Lange Medical.

VAUGHN, S., BOS, C. S., HARRELL, J. E., & LASKY, B. A. (1988). Parent participation in the initial placement/IEP conference ten years after mandated involvement. *Journal of Learning Disabilities, 21*(2), 82–89.

VELLUTINO, F., & SHUB, M. (1982). Assessment of disorders in formal school language: Disorders in reading. *Topics in Language Disorders, 2,* Rockville, MD: Aspen.

VESTBERG, P. (1989). *Beyond stereotypes: Perspectives on the personality characteristices of deaf people.* Gallaudet Research Institute Working Paper 89-2. Washington, DC: Gallaudet University.

VINCENT, L. J., POULSEN, M. K., COLE, C. K., WOODRUFF, G., & GRIFFITH, D. R. (1991). *Born substance exposed, educationally vulnerable.* Reston, VA: Council for Exceptional Children.

Vital and Health Statistics (1988). National Health Interview Survey. U.S. Department of Health and Human Services, DHHS Pub. No. (PHS) 89-1501.

WACHS, T. D., & SHEEHAN, R. (Eds.) (1988). *Assessment of young developmentally disabled children.* New York: Plenum.

WAGNER, M. (1989). *The national longitudinal transition study.* Palo Alto, CA: Stanford Research Institute.

WAGNER, R., & TORGESEN, J. K. (1987). The nature of phonological processing and its causal role in the acquistion of reading skills. *Psychological Bulletin, 101,* 192–212.

WALBERG, H. J. (1969). Physics, femininity, and creativity. *Developmental Psychology, 1,* 47–54.

WALKER, H. M. (1970). *Walker problem behavior identification checklist.* Los Angeles: Western Psychological Services.

WALKER, H. M. (1986). The assessment for integration into mainstream settings (AIMS) assessment system: Rationale, instruments, procedures, and outcomes. *Journal of Clinical Child Psychology, 15,* 55–63.

WALKER, H. M., & FABRÉ, T. R. (1987). Assessment of behavior disorders in the school setting: Issues, problems and strategies revisited. In N. G. Haring (Ed.). *Measuring and managing behavior disorders* (pp. 198–243). Seattle: University of Washington Press.

WALKER, H. M., SEVERSON, H., STILLER, B., WILLIAMS, G., HARING, N. G., SHILL, M. R., & TODIS, B. (1988). Systematic screening of pupils in the elementary age range at risk for behavior disorders: Development and trial testing of a multiple gating model. *Remedial and Special Education, 9*(3), 8–14.

WALKER, H. M., SHINN, M. R., O'NEILL, R. E., & RAMSEY, E. (1987). A longitudinal assessment of the development of antisocial behavior in boys: Rationale, methodology, and first year results. *Remedial and Special Education, 8*(4), 7–16.

WALKER, H. M., STIEBER, S., & O'NEILL, R. E. (1990). Middle school behavioral profiles of antisocial and at risk control boys: Descriptive and predictive outcomes. *Exceptionality, 1,* 61–77.

WALLACE, G., & McLOUGHLIN, J. A. (1988). *Learning disabilities: Concepts and characteristics* (3rd ed.). Columbus, OH: Merrill.

WALLACH, G., & MILLER, L. (1988). *Language intervention and academic success.* Boston: College-Hill.

WANG, M. C., & BIRCH, J. W. (1984). Effective special education in regular classes. *Exceptional Children, 50*(5), 391–398.

WANG, M. C., REYNOLDS, M. C., & WALBERG, H. J. (1986). Rethinking special education. *Educational Leadership, 44*(1), 26–31.

WARGER, C. L., TEWEY, S., & MEGIVERN, M. (1991). *Abuse and neglect of exceptional children.* Reston, VA: Council for Exceptional Children.

WARREN, D. H. (1984). *Blindness and early childhood development* (2nd ed. rev.). New York: American Foundation for the Blind.

WARREN, S. F., & GAZDAG, G. (1990). Facilitating early language development with milieu procedures. *Journal of Early Intervention, 14,* 62–83.

WARREN, S. F., & KAISER, A. P. (1988) Research in early language intervention. In S. L. Odom & M. B. Karnes (Eds.), *Early intervention for infants and children with handicaps: An empirical base* (pp. 89–108). Baltimore: Paul H. Brookes.

WASSERMAN, G. A., & ALLEN, R. (1985). Maternal withdrawal from handicapped toddlers. *Journal of Child Psychology and Psychiatry and Allied Disciplines, 26*(3), 381–387.

WASSERMAN, G. A., SHILANSKY, M., & HAHN, H. (1986). A matter of degree: Maternal interaction with infants of varying levels of retardation. *Child Study Journal, 16*(4), 241–253.

WATSON, J. B., & RAYNER, R. (1920). Conditioned emotional reactions. *Journal of Experimental Psychology, 3,* 1–14.

WEBB, J. T. (1982). *Guiding the gifted child: A practical source for parents and teachers.* Columbus, OH: Ohio Psychological Publishing.

WEBB, T. P., BUNDLEY, S. E., TAHKE, A. I., & TODD, J. (1986). Population incidence and segregation ratios in the Martin-Bell syndrome. *American Journal of Medical Genetics, 23,* 573–580.

WEBSTER, R. (1977). *The road to freedom: A parents' guide to preparing the blind child to travel independently.* Jacksonville, IL: Katan.

Webster's New World Dictionary (1988). New York: Simon & Schuster.

WECHSLER, D. (1974). *Wechsler intelligence scale for children: A manual.* New York: Psychological Corporation.

WEHMAN, P. H., KREGEL, J., BARCUS, J. M., & SCHALOCK, R. L. (1986). Vocational transition for students with developmental disabilities. In W. E. Kiernan & J. A. Stark (Eds.), *Pathways to employment for adults with developmental disabilities.* Baltimore: Paul H. Brookes.

WEHMAN, P., MOON, M. S., EVERSON, J. M., WOOD, W., & BARCUS, J. M. (1988). *Transitions from school to work: New challenges for youth with disabilities.* Baltimore: Paul H. Brookes.

WEHMAN, P., RENZAGLIA, A., & BATES, P. (1985). *Functional living skills for moderately and severely handicapped individuals.* Austin, TX: Pro-Ed.

WEINTRAUB, F. J., & ABESON, A. (1976). New education policies for the handicapped: The quiet revolution. In F. J. Weintraub, A. Abeson, J. Ballard, & M. L. LaVor (Eds.), *Public policy and the education of exceptional children* (pp. 7–13). Reston, VA: Council for Exceptional Children.

WEINTRAUB, F. J., ABESON, A., BALLARD, J., & LAVOR, M. L. (Eds.) (1976). *Public policy and the education of exceptional children.* Reston, VA: Council for Exceptional Children.

WELSH, R. L., & BLASCH, B. B. (1980). *Foundations of orientation and mobility.* New York: American Foundation for the Blind.

WENTZEL, K. R. (1988). Gender differences in math and English achievement: A longitudinal study. *Sex Roles, 18*(11/12), 691–699.

WERNER, M. S. (1980). Single parents and adolescent school crisis: Alienation or alliance. *The Pointer, 25,* 46–51.

WEST, M., LECONTE, J., & CAHN, K. (1988). Child abuse and developmental disabilities. In *Special Issues.* Seattle: National Resources Institute on Children and Youth with Handicaps.

WESTBY, C. (1988). Children's play: Reflections of social competence. *Seminars in Speech and Language, 9,* 1–14.

WESTLING, D. L. (1986). *Introduction to mental retardation.* Englewood Cliffs, NJ: Prentice-Hall.

WESTLING, D. L., & KOORLAND, M. (1988). *The special educator's handbook.* Boston: Allyn & Bacon.

WHEELER, J. (1987) *Transitioning persons with moderate and severe disabilities from school to adulthood: What makes it work.* Menomonie, WI: University of Wisconsin, Materials Development Center.

WHIMBY, A. (1977). Teaching sequential thought: A cognitive-skills approach. *Phi Delta Kappan, 59,* 255.

WHITE, O. R. (1980). Adaptive performance objectives: Form versus function. In W. Sailor, B. Wilcox, L. Brown (Eds.), *Methods of instruction for severely handicapped students.* Baltimore: Paul H. Brookes.

WHITE, W. A. T. (1987). A DI meta-analysis. *Direct Instruction News, 6*(3), 1, 5, 7, 8, 15, 18.

WHITIN, D., MILLS, H., & O'KEEFE, T. (1990). *Living and learning mathematics.* Portsmouth, NH: Heinemann.

WHITMORE, J. (1980). *Giftedness, conflict, and underachievement.* Boston: Allyn & Bacon.

WIDERSTROM, A. H., MOWDER, B. A., & SANDALL, S. R. (1991). *At-risk and handicapped newborns and infants: Development, assessment, and intervention.* Englewood Cliffs, NJ: Prentice-Hall.

WIECK, P. R. (1979, March 1). Van meets handicapped regulations for now. *Albuquerque Journal.*

WIIG, E. (1990). Language disabilities in school-age children and youth. In G. H. Shames & E. H. Wiig (Eds.), *Human communication disorders.* Columbus, OH: Merrill.

WIIG, E., & SEMEL, E. M. (1984). *Language assessment and intervention for the learning disabled.* Columbus, OH: Merrill.

WILCOX, B., & BELLAMY, G. T. (1982). Curriculum content. In B. Wilcox and G. T. Bellamy (Eds.), *Design of high school programs for severely handicapped students.* Baltimore: Paul H. Brookes.

WILL, M. C. (1984). *OSERS programming for the transition of youth with disabilities: Bridges from school to working life.* Washington, DC: Office of Special Education and Rehabilitative Services (OSERS), U.S. Department of Education.

WILL, M. C. (1986). Educating children with learning problems: A shared responsibility. *Exceptional Children, 52,* 411–415.

WILLERMAN, L. (1979). *The psychology of individual and group differences.* San Francisco: Freeman.

WILLIAM T. GRANT FOUNDATION COMMISSION ON WORK, FAMILY, AND CITIZENSHIP (1988). The forgotten half: Non-college bound youth in America. *Phi Delta Kappan,* February, 409–414.

WILLIAMS, L., LOMBARDINO, J., MacDONALD, J., & OWENS, R. (1982). Total communication: Clinical report on a parent-based language training program. *Education and Training of the Mentally Retarded, 17,* 293–298.

WILLIAMSON, G. G. (1987). Children with spina bifida and their families. In G. G. Williamson (Ed.), *Children with Spina Bifida* (pp. 1–10). Baltimore: Paul H. Brookes.

WILLOUGHBY-HERB, S. J., & NEISWORTH, J. T. (1980). *The HICOMP curriculum.* San Antonio, TX: Psychological Corporation.

WINTERLING, V., DUNLAP, G., & O'NEILL, R. (1987). The effects of task variation on the aberrant behavior of students with autism. *Education and Treatment of Children, 10,* 105–119.

WINTON, P., & TURNBULL, A. (1982). Dissemination of research to parents. *Exceptional Parent, 12,* 32–36.

WINTON, P. J., & BAILEY, D. B., Jr. (1988). The family-focused interview: A collaborative mechanism for family assessment and goal-setting. *Journal of the Division for Early Childhood, 12*(3), 195–207.

WISEMAN, D. E., HARTWELL, L. K., & HANNAFIN, M. J. (1980). Exploring the reading and listening skills of secondary mildly handicapped students. *Learning Disability Quarterly, 3,* 56–61.

WOLERY, M. (1989a). Child find and screening issues. In D. B. Bailey & M. Wolery (Eds.), *Assessing infants and preschoolers with handicaps* (pp. 119–143). Columbus, OH: Merrill.

WOLERY, M. (1989b). Transitions in early childhood special education: Issues and procedures. *Focus on Exceptional Children, 22*(2), 1–16.

WOLERY, M., AULT, M. J., & DOYLE, P. M. (1992). *Teaching students with moderate and severe disabilities: Use of response prompting procedures.* White Plains, NY: Longman.

WOLERY, M., AULT, M., DOYLE, P., & GAST, D. (1986). *Comparison of instructional strategies.* Lexington, KY: University of Kentucky, Department of Special Education, Comparison of Instructional Strategies Project.

WOLERY, M., & BAILEY, D. B. (1984). Alternatives to impact evaluations: Suggestions for program evaluation in early intervention. *Journal of the Division for Early Childhood, 9,* 27–37.

WOLERY, M., & BAILEY, D. B (1989). Assessing play skills. In D. B. Bailey & M. Wolery (Ed.), *Assessing infants and preschoolers with handicaps* (pp. 428–446). Columbus, OH: Merrill.

WOLERY, M., BAILEY, D. B., & SUGAI, G. M. (1988). *Effective teaching: Principles and procedures of applied behavior analysis with exceptional students.* Boston: Allyn & Bacon.

WOLERY, M., & BROOKFIELD-NORMAN, J. (1988). (Pre) academic instruction for handicapped preschool children. In S. L. Odom & M. B. Karnes (Eds.), *Early intervention for infants and children with handicaps: An empirical base* (pp. 108–128). Baltimore: Paul H. Brookes.

WOLERY, M., & FLEMING, L. (in press). Implementing individualized curriculum in integrated settings. In C. A. Peck, S. L. Odom, & D. Bricker (Eds.), *Integrating young children with disabilities into community programs: From research to implementation.* Baltimore: Paul H. Brookes.

WOLERY, M., FLEMING, L., & VENN, M. (1990). *Year 01 report: Curriculum modification component of the research institute on preschool mainstreaming* (Grant No. Ho24K900002). Allegheny Singer Research Institute, Pittsburgh, PA.

WOLERY, M., & GAST, D. L. (1984). Effective and efficient procedures for the transfer of stimulus control. *Topics in Early Childhood Special Education, 4*(3), 52–77.

WOLERY, M., STRAIN, P. S., & BAILEY, D. B. (in press). Applying the developmentally appropriate practice to children with special needs. In S. Bredekamp & T. Rosegrant (Ed.), *Reaching potentials: Appropriate curriculum and assessment for young children.* Washington, DC: National Association for the Education of Young Children.

WOLERY, M., & WOLERY, R. A. (1992). Promoting functional cognitive skills. In D. B. Bailey & M. Wolery (Eds.), *Teaching infants and preschoolers with disabilities* (2nd ed.) (pp. 521–572). New York: Macmillan.

WOLF, J. M. (1969). Historical perspective of cerebral palsy. In J. M. Wolf (Ed.), *The results of treatment in cerebral palsy* (pp. 5–44). Springfield, IL: Thomas.

WOLF, L., & ZARFAN, D. (1982). Parents' attitudes toward sterilization of their mentally retarded children. *American Journal of Mental Deficiency, 87,* 122–129.

WOLF, M. M., HANLEY, F. L., KING, L. A., LACHOWICZ, J., & GILES, D. K. (1970). The times gone: A variable interval contingency for the management of out-of-seat behavior. *Exceptional Children, 37,* 113–117.

WOLF v. LEGISLATURE OF UTAH, Civ. No. 182464 (3rd Dist., Salt Lake City, Jan 8, 1969).

WOLFENSBERGER, W. (1971). Will there always be an institution? II: The impact of new service models. *Mental Retardation, 9*(6), 31–38.

WOLFENSBERGER, W. (1972). *The principle of normalization in human services.* Toronto: National Institute on Mental Retardation.

WOLFENSBERGER, W. (1976). The origin and nature of our institutional models. In R. B. Kugel & A. Shearer (Eds.), *Changing patterns in residential services for the mentally retarded* (rev. ed.). Washington, DC: President's Committee on Mental Retardation.

WOLFENSBERGER, W. (1983). Social role valorization: A proposed new term for the principle of normalization. *Mental Retardation, 21,* 234–239.

WOLFENSBERGER, W. (1987). Response to Drash, Raver, and Murrin: Total habilitation—A meritorious concept requiring judicious application. *Mental Retardation, 25,* 79–81.

WOLF-SCHEIN, E. G., SUDHALTER, V., COHEN, I. L., FISCH, G. S., HANSON, D., PFADT, A. G., HAGERMAN, R., JENKINS, E. C., & BROWN, W. T. (1987). Speech-language and the fragile X syndrome: Initial findings. *Journal of the American Speech and Hearing Association, 29,* 35–38.

WOLMAN, C., THURLOW, M. L., & BRUININKS, R. H. (1989). Stability of categorical designation for special education students: A longitudinal study. *Journal of Special Education, 23,* 213–222.

WOLRAICH, M.L., (1982) Communication between physicians and parents of handicapped children. *Exceptional Children, 48,* 324–331.

WOLRAICH, M. L. (1984). Seizure disorders. In J. A. Blackman (Ed.), *Medical aspects of developmental disabilities in children birth to three* (rev. ed.). Rockville, MD: Aspen.

WONG, B. (1987). How do the results of metacognitive research impact the learning-disabled individual? *Learning Disability Quarterly, 10*(3), 189–194.

WOOD, D. J. (1991). Cognition and learning. In D. Hicks & E. Stuckless (Eds.), *1990 International Congress of Education of the Deaf: Proceedings II: Topical addresses.* Rochester, New York: National Technical Institute for the Deaf, Rochester Institute of Technology.

WOOD, F. H., SMITH, C. R., & GRIMES, J. (Eds.) (1985). *The Iowa assessment model in behavioral disorders: A training manual.* Des Moines, IA: Department of Public Instruction.

WOODWARD, J., CARNINE, D., GERSTEN, R., GLEASON, M., JOHNSON, G., & COLLINS, M. (1986). Applying instructional design principles to CAI for mildly handicapped students: Four recently conducted studies. *Journal of Special Education Technology, 8,* 13–26.

WORLAND, J. (1990). A father's struggle with an LD son: Confessions of a clinical psychologist.

WORMALD INTERNATIONAL SENSORY AIDS (1979). *Electronic travel aids.* Bensenville, IL.

WRIGHT, B. A. (1983). *Physical disability: A psychosocial approach.* New York: Harper & Row.

WYATT v. ANDERHOLT, Vol. 503 2d, 1305 (1970).

WYATT v. STICKNEY, 325 F. Supp. 781, 784 (M. D. Ala., 1972).

WYCHE, L. G. (1989). The tenth annual report to Congress: Taking a significant step in the right direction. *Exceptional Children, 56*(1), 14–16.

YANOWITCH, N. (1989, Spring). Stalking MS: The clues are mounting. *Spinal Network,* 18–19.

YARRII, E., & LEWIS, B. (1984). Dysfluencies at the onset of stuttering. *Journal of Speech and Hearing Research, 27,* 154–159.

YEWCHUK, C. R., & BIBBY, M. A. (1989). Identification of giftedness in severely and profoundly hearing impaired students. *Roeper Review, 12*(1), 42–48.

YORKSTON, K., & KARLAN, G. (1986). Assessment procedures. In S. Blackstone (Ed.), *Augmentative communication: An introduction* (pp. 163–196).

YOSHIDA, R. K. (1982). Research agenda: Finding ways to create more options for parent involvement. *Exceptional Education Quarterly, 3,* 74–80.

YOUNG, M., & ASHCROFT, S. C. (1980 & 1981). Survey of microcomputer access in programs serving the visually impaired. Unpublished manuscript (available from M. Young and S. C. Ashcroft, Peabody College of Vanderbilt University, Nashville, Tennessee 37203).

YSSELDKYE, J. E., & ALGOZZINE, B. (1982). *Critical issues in special and remedial education.* Boston: Houghton Mifflin.

ZATLOW, G. (1982). A sister's lament. *Exceptional Parent, 12,* 50–51.

ZEAMAN, D., & HOUSE, B. J. (1963). The role of attention in retardate discriminative learning. In N. R. Ellis (Ed.), *Handbook of mental deficiency.* New York: McGraw-Hill.

ZELLER, D. (1986). Real numbers: Real changes. *Proceedings of Reaching Out: A Special Education Symposium on Cultural Differences and Parent Programs,* 5–33.

ZEITLIN, S., & WILLIAMSON, G. G. (1988). Developing family resources for adaptive coping. *Journal of the Division for Early Childhood, 12*(2), 137–147.

ZETLIN, A. G., & HOSSEINI, A. (1989). Six postschool case studies of mildly learning handicapped young adults. *Exceptional Children, 55* (5), 405–511.

ZIGLER, E. (1967). Familial mental retardation: A continuing dilemma. *Science, 155,* 292–298.

ZIGLER, E., BALLA, D., & HODAPP, R. (1984). On the definition and classification of mental retardation. *American Journal of Mental Deficiency, 89,* 215–230.

ZIGMOND, N., VALLECORSA, A., & SILVERMAN, R. (1983). *Assessment for instructional planning in special education.* Englewood Cliffs, NJ: Prentice-Hall.

ZIRPOLI, T. J. (1986). Child abuse and children with handicaps. *Remedial and Special Education, 7*(2), 39–48.

ZIRPOLI, T. J. (1990). Physical abuse: Are children with disabilities at greater risk? *Intervention In School and Clinic, 26,* 6–11.

ZUCKER, S. H., & POLLOWAY, E. A. (1987). Issues in identification and assessment in mental retardation. *Education and Training of the Mentally Retarded, 22,* 69–76.

Name Index

O'Keefe, T., 251
Olbrisch, R. R., 437
O'Leary, K., 197
O'Malley, P., 332
O'Malley, P. M., 70
Omark, D. R., 68
Omizo, M. M., 185
O'Neil, J., 56
O'Neil, Kitty, 8–9
O'Neill, R., 480, 483, 547
O'Neill, R. E., 480
Oostra, B. A., 430
Opitz, J. M., 428
O'Reily, K., 122
Orelove, F., 192
Orelove, F. P., 124, 431, 465
Orenstein, A., 209
Ormsbee, C. K., 73
Ortiz, V., 580
Orton, S., 504
Osborne, M., 503
Osborne, R. T., 329
Osler, William, 355
Osnes, P. G., 478
Ostrosky, M. M., 483
Ostrow, L. S., 432
Ouellette, E. M., 431
Owens, R., 204
Owens, R. E., 242, 244, 246, 248, 249, 260
Ozolins, A., 24, 45

Palinscar, A. S., 501, 517
Palmer, D. J., 185
Palmer, F., 353
Palow, D., 71
Palsha, S. A., 133
Pancsofar, E. L., 486
Paolucci-Whitcomb, P., 56
Paperella, M., 289
Papert, S., 594
Paradise, J. L., 289
Parette, H. P., 484
Parke, B. N., 564, 588, 594
Parker, A., 200
Parker, C., 204
Parker, J., 329
Parker, L. A., 87
Parsons, C. L., 437
Parsons, M. B., 480, 483, 484
Partington, M. W., 428
Parton, P., 426
Pasnak, R., 329
Passow, A. H., 574
Patrick, J. L., 410
Patterson, G. R., 545
Patton, J., 564
Patton, J. R., 20, 412, 417, 423, 424, 428, 437, 445, 446, 447
Patton, Lydia, 562

Paul, J. J., 177, 178
Paul, J. L., 183
Paul, P., 301, 302
Paul, R., 429
Payne, H., 186
Payne, J. S., 20, 412, 417, 423, 428
Peabody, R., 329, 330
Peabody, R. L., 335
Pearl, R., 185, 503
Pearson, C. A., 530, 556
Peck, C., 483
Peck, C. A., 119, 133, 473
Peirce, R. L., 373
Pendarvis, E., 573, 577, 592
Pennington, F. M., 436
Penrod, D., 26
Pepper, B., 70
Pera, T. B., 342
Pereira, L., 418, 458
Perfetti, C. A., 251
Perino, J., 195
Perino, S. C., 195
Perosa, L., 178
Perosa, S., 178
Perret, Y. M., 195
Perrone, P. A., 564
Perske, R., 55, 195
Pester, E., 334
Peterson, P. L., 79
Petnick, Nan, 312
Petrofsky, Jerrold, 97, 350, 361
Petrosko, J., 191, 197, 210
Peyton, D., 595
Pezzoli, M., 473
Pfadt, A. G., 429
Phelps, M. S., 71
Phelps, N., 200
Phelps, Winthrop, 355
Phillips, Chandler, 350
Phillips, E. L., 554
Phillips, S., 494
Phillips, V., 554
Piaget, J., 108, 121, 329, 406, 413, 466
Pieretti, M., 430
Pihl, R. O., 503
Pinter, R. J., 329
Pitts-Conway, V., 163
Pohlmann, Vivian, 312
Pollak, S. A., 250
Polloway, E. A., 410, 412, 414, 421, 424, 437, 445, 446, 447
Polsgrove, L., 44, 57, 70, 86, 537, 543, 544, 557
Popelka, G. A., 276, 278, 284, 285
Porter, P. B., 177, 178
Poulsen, M. K., 70
Powell, A., 107, 123, 125, 205
Powell, T. H., 486
Power, D., 301
Powers, D., 297–298

Powers, L., 184
Pratt, R. J., 335
Prehm, H. J., 58
Prelock, P. A., 267
Preminger, J. L., 122
Presperin, J., 96
Pressey, S. L., 573
Preston, A., 586
Prestridge, S., 211
Price, L. M., 223
Prillaman, D., 564
Pringle, M. L., 582
Prock, G. A., 71
Proctor, B., 280
Proctor, C. A., 280
Provence, S., 107
Pugach, M., 557
Pugach, M. C., 52, 56
Pulaski, L., 184
Pullis, M., 523
Pumpian, I., 159, 439, 467, 470, 472, 485, 486
Punch, J., 278
Pysh, M., 554

Quader, S. E., 264
Quaforth, J., 577
Quigley, S., 301, 302
Quigley, S. P., 282

Rabin, A. T., 332
Rainforth, B., 486
Ramey, C. T., 415
Ramsdell, D. A., 273
Ramsey, E., 547
Rankin, E., 330
Ratzeburg, F., 503, 554
Raver, S. A., 447, 448
Ravsten, M. T., 213
Rawlins, L., 138
Ray, B., 528
Rayner, R., 543
Redding, R., 304
Redding, R. E., 582
Reed, C. G., 261
Reese, J. H., 498, 501
Reese, R., 205
Reese, R. M., 204
Rehm, R., 436
Reichart, D. C., 202
Reid, D. H., 480, 483, 484
Reid, J. B., 545
Reinmuth, O., 245
Reith, H., 86
Renzaglia, A., 152, 467
Renzaglia, A. M., 54
Renzulli, J. S., 566–567, 574, 577, 590, 591, 592
Reschly, D. J., 410, 412, 418, 505
Rettig, M. A., 461

Subject Index